Oxford
Mini Thesaurus

OXFORD
UNIVERSITY PRESS

OXFORD
UNIVERSITY PRESS

Great Clarendon Street, Oxford OX2 6DP

Oxford University Press is a department of the University of Oxford.
It furthers the University's objective of excellence in research, scholarship,
and education by publishing worldwide in

Oxford New York

Auckland Bangkok Buenos Aires Cape Town Chennai
Dar es Salaam Delhi Hong Kong Istanbul Karachi Kolkata
Kuala Lumpur Madrid Melbourne Mexico City Mumbai
Nairobi São Paulo Shanghai Taipei Tokyo Toronto

Oxford is a registered trade mark of Oxford University Press
in the UK and in certain other countries

Published in the United States
by Oxford University Press Inc., New York

British Library Cataloguing in Publication Data

Data available

Library of Congress Cataloging in Publication Data

Data available

ISBN 0-19-8607113

10 9 8 7 6 5 4 3 2 1

Typeset in Swift and Arial
by Kolam Information Services, India
Printed in Great Britain
by Charles Letts & Co Ltd

Contents

Note on trademarks and proprietary status

Guide to the thesaurus

Entries are divided into numbered sections according to sense. The first synonym in each section is the most useful and helps to identify its sense.

Most of the synonyms given are part of standard English, but some have restricted use. These are placed at the end of each group and have the following labels in front of them:

informal, e.g. *swig*: normally only used in speech or informal writing.

formal, e.g. *thereupon*: normally only used in writing, such as official documents.

technical, e.g. *admixture*. Words used in specific fields are labelled *Medicine*, *Nautical*, etc.

poetic/literary, e.g. *plenteous*.

dated, e.g. *rotter*.

historical, e.g. *serfdom*: only used today to refer to things that are no longer part of modern life.

humorous, e.g. *posterior*.

archaic, e.g. *aliment*: not in use today except for old-fashioned effect.

Synonyms are also labelled if they are exclusively or mainly British, Scottish, North American, Australian, or New Zealand expressions.

Abbreviations

adj	adjective	**prep**	preposition	**Austral.**	Australian
adv	adverb	**pron**	pronoun	**Brit.**	British
n	noun	**v**	verb	**N. Amer.**	North American
pl	plural			**NZ**	New Zealand

abandon v **❶** DESERT, leave, forsake, depart from, leave behind, cast aside, jilt; *informal* run out on. **❷** GIVE UP, renounce, relinquish, dispense with, forgo, desist from; *formal* forswear. **❸** YIELD, surrender, give up, cede, relinquish, abdicate, deliver up, resign.
– OPPOSITES keep.
▶ LACK OF RESTRAINT / INHIBITION, wildness, impulse, impetuosity, immoderation, wantonness.
– OPPOSITES self-control.

abandoned adj **❶** DESERTED, forsaken, cast aside. **❷** RECK-LESS, unrestrained, uninhibited, impetuous, wild, careless, wanton.

abashed adj EMBARRASSED, ashamed, shamefaced, mortified, humiliated, taken aback, disconcerted, nonplussed, discomfited, discomposed, perturbed, confounded, dismayed, dumbfounded, confused, put out of countenance, discountenanced.

abbreviate v SHORTEN, reduce, cut, cut short/down, contract, condense, compress, abridge, truncate, crop, shrink, constrict, summarize, abstract, precis, synopsize, digest.
– OPPOSITES expand.

abdicate v **❶** RESIGN, stand down, retire; *informal* quit.

❷ GIVE UP, renounce, relinquish, abjure, repudiate, reject, disown, waive, yield, forgo, refuse, abandon, surrender, cast aside.

abduct v KIDNAP, carry off, run away/off with, make off with, seize, hold as hostage, hold to ransom; *informal* snatch.

aberration n DEVIATION, anomaly, abnormality, irregularity, variation, freak.

abhorrent adj DETESTABLE, loathsome, hateful, hated, abominable, repellent, repugnant, repulsive, revolting, disgusting, distasteful, vile, horrible, horrid, heinous, obnoxious, odious, offensive, execrable; *informal* yucky.
– OPPOSITES delightful, admirable.

abide v STAND, tolerate, bear, put up with, endure, accept, stomach; *formal* brook; *archaic* suffer.
■ **abide by** KEEP TO, comply with, observe, follow, obey, agree to, hold to, conform to, adhere to, stick to, stand by.

ability n **❶** TALENT, competence, competency, proficiency, skill, expertise, expertness, adeptness, aptitude, dexterity, adroitness, qualification, cleverness, flair, gift, knack, savoir faire; *informal*

know-how. ❷ CAPACITY, capability, potential, potentiality, power, facility, faculty, propensity.
– OPPOSITES inability.

ablaze adj ❶ ON FIRE, burning, blazing, alight, flaming, aflame; *poetic/literary* afire. ❷ LIT UP, gleaming, glowing, aglow, illuminated, brilliant, radiant, shimmering, sparkling, flashing, incandescent.

able adj COMPETENT, capable, talented, skilful, skilled, clever, intelligent, accomplished, gifted, proficient, fit, expert, adept, efficient, effective, qualified, adroit.
– OPPOSITES incompetent.

abnormal adj UNUSUAL, strange, odd, peculiar, uncommon, curious, queer, eccentric, extraordinary, unexpected, exceptional, irregular, weird, unnatural, erratic, singular, atypical, anomalous, deviant, deviating, divergent, aberrant; *informal* oddball, off the wall, wacko.
– OPPOSITES normal.

abolish v DO AWAY WITH, put an end to, end, stop, terminate, axe, eliminate, eradicate, exterminate, destroy, annihilate, stamp out, obliterate, wipe out, extinguish, quash, expunge, extirpate, annul, cancel, invalidate, nullify, void, rescind, repeal, revoke, abrogate.
– OPPOSITES retain.

abominable adj HATEFUL, loathsome, detestable, odious, obnoxious, base, despicable, contemptible, damnable, cursed, disgusting, revolting, repellent, repulsive, offensive, repugnant, abhorrent, foul, vile, wretched, horrible, nasty, disagreeable, unpleasant, execrable; *informal* yucky, god-awful.
– OPPOSITES good, admirable.

aboriginal adj INDIGENOUS, native, original, earliest, first, ancient, primitive, primeval, primordial, autochthonous.
– OPPOSITES immigrant.

abortive adj FAILED, unsuccessful, non-successful, vain, futile, useless, worthless, ineffective, ineffectual, fruitless, unproductive, unavailing.
– OPPOSITES successful.

abound v BE PLENTIFUL, proliferate, teem, overflow, swarm, thrive, flourish; *informal* be two/ten a penny.

abrasive adj ❶ EROSIVE, eroding, corrosive, chafing, rubbing, coarse, harsh. ❷ CAUSTIC, cutting, grating, biting, rough, harsh, irritating, sharp, nasty.
– OPPOSITES smooth, kind, gentle.

abridge v SHORTEN, cut down, summarize, condense, precis, abstract, epitomize, synopsize, digest, contract, compress, abbreviate, reduce, decrease, diminish, curtail, truncate, lessen, trim.
– OPPOSITES expand.

abridgement n ❶ SUMMARY, synopsis, precis, abstract,

outline, résumé, digest, cut-down version. ❷ SHORTENING, cutting, condensation, contraction, reduction, summarization.
– OPPOSITES expansion.

abrupt adj ❶ SUDDEN, quick, hurried, hasty, swift, rapid, precipitate, headlong, instantaneous, surprising, unexpected, unanticipated, unforeseen. ❷ CURT, blunt, brusque, short, terse, brisk, crisp, gruff, unceremonious, rough, rude; *informal* snappish.
– OPPOSITES gradual, gentle.

abscond v RUN AWAY, bolt, clear out, flee, make off, escape, take flight, fly, decamp, slip/steal/sneak away, take to one's heels, run for it, make a quick getaway, beat a hasty retreat; *informal* show a clean pair of heels, skedaddle, skip; *Brit. informal* do a bunk, do a runner.

absent adj ❶ AWAY, off, out, gone, missing, truant. ❷ ABSENT-MINDED, distracted, preoccupied, daydreaming, dreaming, dreamy, faraway, blank, empty, vacant, inattentive, vague, absorbed, abstracted, musing, unheeding.
– OPPOSITES present, attentive.

absent-minded adj DISTRACTED, preoccupied, absorbed, abstracted, vague, inattentive, forgetful, oblivious, in a brown study, distrait; *informal* scatterbrained.
– OPPOSITES alert.

absolute adj ❶ COMPLETE, total, utter, out-and-out, outright, perfect, entire, undivided, unqualified, unadulterated, unalloyed, downright, undiluted, solid, consummate, unmitigated. ❷ FIXED, independent, non-relative, non-variable, rigid, established, set, definite. ❸ UNLIMITED, unrestricted, unrestrained, unbounded, boundless, infinite, ultimate, total, supreme, unconditional, full, utter, sovereign, omnipotent.
– OPPOSITES qualified.

absolve v FORGIVE, pardon, excuse, reprieve, give amnesty to, give dispensation/indulgence to, clear, set free, vindicate.

absorb v ❶ SOAK UP, suck up, draw up/in, take up/in, blot up, mop, sponge up, sop up. ❷ TAKE IN, incorporate, assimilate, appropriate, co-opt. ❸ OCCUPY, engage, preoccupy, captivate, engross, spellbind, rivet.

absorbent adj SPONGY, sponge-like, porous, permeable, pervious, penetrable, absorptive, assimilative, receptive.
– OPPOSITES impervious.

absorbing adj FASCINATING, gripping, interesting, captivating, engrossing, riveting, spellbinding, intriguing.
– OPPOSITES boring.

abstain v REFRAIN, decline, forbear, desist, hold back, keep from, refuse, renounce, avoid, shun, eschew.

abstemious adj MODERATE, temperate, abstinent, self-denying, austere, sober, self-restrained, ascetic, puritanical.
– OPPOSITES self-indulgent.

abstract adj ❶ THEORETICAL, conceptual, notional, intellectual, metaphysical, philosophical. ❷ NON-REPRESENTATIONAL, non-realistic, unrealistic.
– OPPOSITES actual, concrete
▶ v EXTRACT, remove, take out/ away, separate, detach, draw away, isolate.
▶ n SUMMARY, synopsis, precis, résumé, outline, abridgement, condensation, digest.

abstruse adj OBSCURE, deep, profound, complex, hidden, esoteric, mysterious, incomprehensible, unfathomable, inscrutable, enigmatic, perplexing, puzzling, recondite, arcane, nebulous.
– OPPOSITES comprehensible.

absurd adj RIDICULOUS, foolish, silly, idiotic, stupid, nonsensical, senseless, inane, crazy, ludicrous, funny, laughable, comical, preposterous, farcical, hare-brained, asinine; Brit. informal daft.
– OPPOSITES sensible.

abundance n PLENTY, plentifulness, profusion, copiousness, amplitude, affluence, lavishness, bountifulness; informal heaps, bags, stacks, loads, tons, oodles.
– OPPOSITES scarcity.

abundant adj PLENTIFUL, large, great, huge, ample, well

supplied, well provided, profuse, copious, lavish, bountiful, teeming, overflowing, galore.
– OPPOSITES scarce.

abuse v ❶ MISUSE, misapply, misemploy, mishandle, exploit. ❷ MISTREAT, maltreat, ill-use, illtreat, manhandle, injure, hurt, harm, beat, damage, wrong, oppress, torture. ❸ INSULT, swear at, curse, scold, rebuke, upbraid, reprove, inveigh against, revile, vilify, slander; formal castigate; archaic vituperate against.
▶ n ❶ MISUSE, misapplication, misemployment, mishandling, exploitation. ❷ MISTREATMENT, maltreatment, ill-use, illtreatment, manhandling, injury, hurt, harm, wronging, oppression, torture. ❸ SWEARING, cursing, scolding, rebuke, upbraiding, reproval, invective, revilement, vilification, vituperation, defamation, slander, insults, curses, expletives, swear words; formal castigation.

abusive adj INSULTING, rude, offensive, disparaging, denigratory, derogatory, defamatory, derisive, scornful, vituperative, opprobrious, slanderous, libellous; formal castigating, calumniating.

abysmal adj VERY BAD, dreadful, awful, terrible, frightful, atrocious, deplorable, lamentable; informal rotten, appalling, pathetic, pitiful, woeful, lousy, dire; Brit. informal chronic.
– OPPOSITES excellent.

abyss n CHASM, gorge, ravine, canyon, crevasse, cavity, void, pit, bottomless pit, hole, gulf, depth.

academic adj ❶ EDUCATIONAL, scholastic, instructional, pedagogical. ❷ SCHOLARLY, studious, literary, well read, intellectual, erudite, highbrow, learned, cultured, bookish, pedantic, donnish, cerebral; *informal* brainy. ❸ THEORETICAL, hypothetical, abstract, conjectural, notional, impractical, unrealistic, speculative.
▶ n SCHOLAR, lecturer, don, teacher, tutor, professor, fellow.

accede
■ **accede to** AGREE TO, consent to, accept, assent to, acquiesce in, endorse, comply with, go along with, concur, grant, yield to.

accelerate v SPEED UP, go faster, pick up speed, hasten, hurry, quicken.
– OPPOSITES decelerate.

accent n ❶ PRONUNCIATION, intonation, enunciation, articulation, inflection, tone, modulation, utterance. ❷ STRESS, emphasis, accentuation, force, beat, prominence. ❸ EMPHASIS, stress, prominence, importance, accentuation, priority, underlining, underscoring.

accentuate v EMPHASIZE, stress, highlight, underline, draw attention to, give prominence to, heighten, point up, underscore, accent.

accept v ❶ RECEIVE, take, get, gain, obtain, acquire. ❷ ACCEDE TO, agree to, consent to, acquiesce in, concur with, endorse, comply with, go along with, defer to, put up with, recognize, acknowledge, cooperate with, adopt, admit. ❸ BELIEVE, trust, credit, be convinced of, have faith in, count/rely on.
– OPPOSITES reject.

acceptable adj ❶ WELCOME, agreeable, delightful, pleasing, desirable, satisfying, gratifying. ❷ SATISFACTORY, good enough, adequate, passable, admissible, tolerable.
– OPPOSITES unacceptable.

accepted adj ❶ APPROVED, recognized, sanctioned, authorized, received, allowable, acceptable. ❷ USUAL, customary, normal, expected, standard, conventional, recognized, acknowledged, established, traditional.

access n ENTRY, entrance, way in, means of entry/entrance, admittance, admission, approachability, accessibility, approach, means of approach.

accessible adj ❶ ATTAINABLE, reachable, available, approachable, obtainable, achievable; *informal* get-at-able. ❷ APPROACHABLE, available, easy-going, informal, friendly, pleasant, agreeable, obliging, congenial, affable, cordial.
– OPPOSITES inaccessible.

accessory n ❶ ATTACHMENT, fitment, extra, addition, adjunct, appendage, supplement.

❷ ACCOMPLICE, associate, confederate, abetter, helper, assistant, partner.

▶ adj ADDITIONAL, extra, supplementary, contributory, subsidiary, ancillary, auxiliary, secondary.

accident n **❶** MISHAP, misfortune, misadventure, injury, disaster, tragedy, blow, catastrophe, calamity. **❷** CRASH, smash, collision; informal pileup; Brit. informal shunt. **❸** CHANCE, mere chance, fluke, fate, twist of fate, fortune, good fortune, luck, good luck, fortuity, hazard.

accidental adj CHANCE, unintentional, unintended, inadvertent, unexpected, unforeseen, unlooked for, fortuitous, unanticipated, unplanned, uncalculated, unpremeditated, unwitting, adventitious.
– OPPOSITES intentional.

acclaim v APPLAUD, cheer, celebrate, salute, welcome, approve, honour, praise, commend, hail, extol, eulogize, exalt; formal laud.

▶ n APPLAUSE, ovation, praise, commendation, approval, approbation, homage, tribute, extolment, cheers, congratulations, plaudits, bouquets, salutes, eulogies; formal laudation.

acclimatize v ADJUST, adapt, accustom, get used, accommodate, become seasoned, familiarize oneself, become inured.

accommodate v **❶** PUT UP, house, cater for, board, lodge, shelter, give someone a roof over their head, harbour, billet. **❷** HELP, assist, aid, oblige, meet the needs/wants of, cater for, fit in with, satisfy.

accommodating adj OBLIGING, cooperative, helpful, considerate, amenable, unselfish, willing, polite, kindly, hospitable, kind, friendly, agreeable.

accommodation n HOUSING, lodging, board, shelter, place of residence, house, billet, lodgings, quarters; informal digs, pad.

accompany v **❶** ESCORT, go with, go along with, keep someone company, attend, usher, show, see, conduct, squire, chaperone, convoy. **❷** OCCUR WITH, go with, go together with, go hand in hand with, coexist with, supplement.

accomplice n PARTNER IN CRIME, associate, accessory, confederate, collaborator, abetter, henchman, fellow conspirator; informal sidekick.

accomplish v ACHIEVE, carry out, fulfil, perform, attain, realize, succeed in, bring off, bring about, effect, execute; formal effectuate.
– OPPOSITES fail in.

accomplished adj SKILLED, skilful, expert, gifted, talented, proficient, adept, masterly, polished, practised, capable, able, competent, experienced,

professional, deft, consummate.
– OPPOSITES incompetent.

accomplishment n
TALENT, ability, skill, gift, attainment, achievement, capability, proficiency.

accord v AGREE, concur, fit, correspond, tally, match, conform, harmonize, suit, be in tune.
– OPPOSITES disagree, differ.
▶ n AGREEMENT, consensus, unanimity, harmony, rapport, unison, amity; *formal* concord.
– OPPOSITES disagreement.

account n ❶ DESCRIPTION, report, statement, record, narration, narrative, story, recital, explanation, tale, chronicle, history, relation, version. ❷ FINANCIAL RECORD, ledger, balance sheet, financial statement, books. ❸ BILL, invoice, reckoning, tally, charges, debts. ❹ IMPORTANCE, consequence, significance.

accumulate v ❶ GATHER, pile up, build up, collect, amass, increase, augment, cumulate, accrue. ❷ AMASS, gather, collect, stockpile, pile up, heap up, store, hoard.

accumulation n PILE, heap, build-up, mass, collection, store, supply, stockpile, hoard, stock, conglomeration, gathering, growth.

accurate adj CORRECT, right, true, exact, precise, authentic, factual, truthful, faultless, reliable, scrupulous, faithful, meticulous, careful, sound, sure,

certain, strict; *Brit. informal* spot on, bang on; *formal* veracious.
– OPPOSITES inaccurate.

accusation n CHARGE, allegation, indictment, complaint, summons, arraignment, citation, denunciation, imputation; *N. Amer.* impeachment.

accuse v ❶ CHARGE, indict, bring/prefer charges against, make allegations against, arraign, prosecute, summons, cite; *N. Amer.* impeach. ❷ BLAME, hold responsible, denounce, censure, condemn, incriminate, tax; *informal* point the finger at.
– OPPOSITES defend.

accustomed adj ❶ USUAL, customary, habitual, regular, established, normal, conventional, expected, routine, familiar, common, fixed, traditional, ordinary, set, prevailing; *poetic/literary* wonted. ❷ USED TO, familiar with, habituated, adapted.
■ **become/get accustomed** see ADAPT.

ache n PAIN, soreness, discomfort, hurt, distress, throbbing, twinge, pang, suffering, anguish, smart.
▶ v HURT, be sore, be painful, smart, sting, pound, throb, suffer.

achieve v ❶ SUCCEED IN, accomplish, manage, do successfully, carry out, complete, attain, bring off, effect, perform, conclude, finish, discharge, fulfil, execute, engineer, consummate. ❷ GAIN, obtain, get, acquire, earn, reach, win, score, procure.

acid adj ❶ SHARP, tart, sour, vinegary, tangy, stinging. ❷ CAUSTIC, acerbic, sharp, sardonic, scathing, trenchant, vitriolic.
– OPPOSITES sweet, pleasant.

acknowledge v ❶ ADMIT, concede, accept, agree, confirm, allow, confess, grant, own, affirm, profess. ❷ GREET, salute, address, hail, say hello to. ❸ ANSWER, reply to, respond to, react to, return.
– OPPOSITES deny, ignore.

acquaint v FAMILIARIZE, make familiar, make aware of, inform of, advise of, notify of, apprise of, let know, get up to date, brief, prime; *informal* fill in on.

acquaintance n ❶ CONTACT, associate, colleague. ❷ ASSOCIATION, relationship, contact. ❸ FAMILIARITY, awareness, knowledge, experience, understanding, grasp.

acquire v GET, obtain, buy, purchase, procure, come by, pick up, receive, earn, secure, appropriate; *informal* get hold of, get one's hands on.
– OPPOSITES lose.

acquisition n POSSESSION, gain, purchase, property, prize, addition, accession; *informal* buy.
– OPPOSITES loss.

acquit v CLEAR, find innocent, declare innocent, absolve, set free, free, release, liberate, discharge, reprieve, vindicate, exonerate; *informal* let off; *formal* exculpate.
– OPPOSITES condemn.
■ **acquit oneself** *See* BEHAVE (1).

acrid adj PUNGENT, sharp, bitter, harsh, acid, caustic.

acrimonious adj BITTER, angry, rancorous, caustic, acerbic, scathing, sarcastic, acid, harsh, sharp, cutting, virulent, spiteful, vicious, vitriolic, hostile, venomous, bad-tempered, ill-natured, malicious, waspish.
– OPPOSITES good-natured.

act v ❶ DO SOMETHING, take action, move, react, take steps. ❷ BEHAVE, carry on, conduct oneself; *formal* comport oneself. ❸ PERFORM, play, appear as, enact, portray, represent, assume the character of, overact; *informal* tread the boards. *See also* PRETEND (1). ❹ FUNCTION, work, operate, have an effect, take effect, serve.
▶ n ❶ DEED, action, feat, exploit, undertaking, effort, enterprise, achievement, step, move, operation, proceeding. ❷ LAW, statute, bill, decree, order, enactment, edict. ❸ PERFORMANCE, routine, number, turn, item, sketch.

acting adj TEMPORARY, provisional, interim, stopgap, substitute, stand-in, fill-in, surrogate, deputy, pro tem.
– OPPOSITES permanent.

action n ❶ DEED, act, feat, exploit, undertaking, process, enterprise, measure, step, effort, endeavour, proceeding, performance, work. ❷ ACTIVITY, movement, motion, exertion, drama, liveliness, excitement, vigour, energy, vitality, initiative, exercise, enterprise. ❸ STORY, events, incidents, happenings. ❹ MECHANISM, works, operation, functioning, working.

activate V SET OFF, set in motion, operate, start, trigger, initiate, actuate, energize, trip.

active adj ❶ ENERGETIC, lively, sprightly, spry, mobile, vigorous, vital, dynamic, sporty, busy, occupied; *informal* on the go, full of beans. ❷ HARD-WORKING, busy, industrious, diligent, tireless, effective, enterprising, involved, enthusiastic, keen, committed, devoted, zealous. ❸ OPERATIVE, working, functioning, functional, operating, operational, in action, in operation, live; *informal* up and running.
– OPPOSITES inactive.

activity n ❶ MOVEMENT, action, bustle, motion, excitement, liveliness, commotion, energy, industry, hurly-burly, animation, life, hustle, stir. ❷ HOBBY, pastime, interest, task, job, venture, project, occupation, undertaking, scheme, pursuit. *See also* WORK n.

actual adj REAL, authentic, genuine, true, factual, verified, realistic, bona fide, definite, existing, current, legitimate, indisputable, unquestionable, tangible, certain, truthful, in existence, living, confirmed, corporeal.
– OPPOSITES imaginary.

acute adj ❶ SERIOUS, urgent, pressing, grave, critical, crucial, precarious. ❷ SEVERE, critical, intense. ❸ SHARP, piercing, intense, severe, extreme, fierce, excruciating, cutting, sudden, violent, shooting, keen, exquisite, racking. ❹ INTELLIGENT, shrewd, sharp, quick, penetrating. *See also* CLEVER (1).
– OPPOSITES mild, chronic, dull.

adapt V ❶ GET USED, adjust, get accustomed, habituate oneself, acclimatize, reconcile oneself, attune, accommodate, become hardened, become inured. ❷ ALTER, change, modify, adjust, convert, remodel, transform, rebuild, remake, refashion, reshape, reconstruct, tailor.

add V ATTACH, append, put on, affix, tack on, include, combine.
– OPPOSITES subtract.
■ **add up** TOTAL, count, reckon, tot up. **add to** *see* INCREASE V (2).

addict n ABUSER, user; *informal* junkie, druggy, — freak, —head.

addiction n DEPENDENCY, craving, habit, compulsion, obsession, enslavement, dedication, devotion.

addition n ❶ INCREASE, enlargement, expansion, supplement, extension, increment, augmentation, gain, adjunct, accessory, addendum,

appendage, development, additive, appendix, postscript, afterthought, attachment, annex, amplification, accession; *technical* admixture. **❷** ADDING UP, counting, totalling, calculation, reckoning, computation; *informal* totting up.
– OPPOSITES reduction, subtraction.

additional adj EXTRA, more, further, added, supplementary, other, new, fresh, increased, spare, supplemental.

address n **❶** LOCATION, whereabouts, place, home, house, residence, situation; *formal* dwelling, abode, domicile. **❷** SPEECH, talk, lecture, oration, sermon, homily, diatribe, discourse, disquisition, harangue; *poetic/literary* philippic.
▶ v **❶** SPEAK TO, talk to, lecture, give a speech to, declaim to, harangue, preach to. **❷** GREET, speak to, talk to, engage in conversation, approach, accost, hail, salute; *informal* buttonhole. **❸** DIRECT, label, inscribe, superscribe.
■ **address oneself to** *see* TACKLE v (1).

adept adj EXPERT, proficient, clever, accomplished, talented, gifted, practised, masterly. *See also* SKILFUL.
– OPPOSITES inept.

adequate adj **❶** TOLERABLE, passable, all right, average, satisfactory, competent, unexceptional, acceptable, unexceptionable, mediocre, good enough; *informal* OK, so-so.

❷ COMPETENT, up to, capable, able, qualified.
– OPPOSITES inadequate.

adhere v STICK, cling, bond, attach, bind, fuse.

adherent n SUPPORTER, follower, devotee, disciple, advocate, fan, upholder, defender, stalwart, partisan.

adjacent adj NEIGHBOURING, adjoining, bordering, next, close, next door, touching, attached, abutting, contiguous.

adjourn v BREAK OFF, interrupt, discontinue, postpone, put off, delay, defer, shelve, suspend, prorogue.

adjournment n INTERRUPTION, break, breaking off, postponement, pause, delay, deferral, deferment, recess, suspension, prorogation.

adjust adj **❶** GET USED TO, become accustomed to, adapt, reconcile oneself, accommodate, acclimatize, habituate oneself, conform. **❷** MODIFY, alter, adapt, fix, repair, regulate, put right, put in working order, rectify, change, arrange, amend, set to rights, tune, rearrange, tailor, balance, vary, position, set, refashion, remake, remodel, reorganize.

administer v **❶** MANAGE, direct, run, administrate, control, organize, supervise, oversee, preside over, superintend, regulate, govern, conduct, rule, command. **❷** GIVE, dispense, issue, provide, supply, treat with, hand out, deal out, distribute, measure out, dole out. ❸ DISPENSE, provide, implement, carry out, mete out, distribute, disburse, execute.

admirable adj COMMENDABLE, worthy, praiseworthy, laudable, good, excellent, fine, exemplary, wonderful, great, marvellous, enjoyable, respectable, creditable, pleasing, meritorious, first-rate, first-class, masterly, awe-inspiring, deserving, estimable.
– OPPOSITES deplorable.

admiration n APPROVAL, regard, respect, praise, appreciation, commendation, approbation, esteem, awe, veneration, honour.
– OPPOSITES contempt.

admire v APPROVE OF, like, respect, appreciate, praise, have a high opinion of, look up to, think highly of, applaud, wonder at, esteem, value, commend, sing someone's praises, love, honour, idolize, revere, venerate, hero-worship, marvel at, be delighted by; formal laud. See also LOVE V (1).
– OPPOSITES hate.

admissible adj ALLOWABLE, allowed, accepted, permitted, permissible, tolerable, justifiable.

admission n ❶ ADMITTANCE, entry, entrance, access, entrée, ingress. ❷ ACKNOWLEDGEMENT, acceptance, confession, declaration, disclosure, profession,

divulgence, utterance, avowal, revelation, affirmation.
– OPPOSITES denial.

admit v ❶ ALLOW IN, let in, permit entry to, grant access to. ❷ ACKNOWLEDGE, confess, reveal, concede, own up to, declare, make known, accept, disclose, agree, profess, recognize, allow.
– OPPOSITES exclude, deny.

admonish v see REPRIMAND V.

adolescent adj TEENAGE, youthful, pubescent, immature, childish, juvenile, puerile, girlish, boyish.
▶ n TEENAGER, youth, youngster, young person, juvenile.

adopt v ❶ TAKE IN, foster, take care of, take under one's wing. ❷ ACCEPT, endorse, approve, support, back, sanction, ratify. ❸ EMBRACE, assume, take on, espouse, appropriate, affect.

adore v LOVE, worship, dote on, cherish, idolize, adulate, revere, venerate, honour, glorify. See also ADMIRE.
– OPPOSITES hate.

adorn v DECORATE, embellish, ornament, enhance, beautify, grace, emblazon, bedeck, trim.

adrift adj ❶ DRIFTING, unmoored, unanchored, floating. ❷ UNFASTENED, untied, loose, detached. ❸ WRONG, amiss, astray, awry, off course.

adult adj FULLY GROWN, grown up, mature, fully developed, of age, nubile.
– OPPOSITES immature.

adulterate v CONTAMINATE, make impure, taint, pollute, debase, degrade, doctor, corrupt, alloy, defile, dilute, thin, water down, weaken.

advance v ❶ MOVE FORWARD, move ahead, go forward, proceed, forge ahead, gain ground, make headway, approach, push forward, press on, press ahead, push on, bear down, make strides. ❷ PROGRESS, move forward, go ahead, improve, flourish, thrive, prosper. ❸ SPEED UP, bring forward, accelerate, step up, expedite, forward, hurry, hasten. ❹ PUT FORWARD, suggest, present, propose, introduce, offer, proffer, adduce, furnish. ❺ LEND, pay in advance, loan, provide, supply, proffer.
– OPPOSITES retreat.
▶ n DEVELOPMENT, breakthrough, discovery, finding, progress, improvement, invention.

advanced adj ❶ SOPHISTICATED, modern, latest, up to date. ❷ PROGRESSIVE, innovative, original, new, forward-looking, inventive, contemporary, revolutionary, experimental, novel, avant-garde, pioneering, trend-setting, ahead of the times; *informal* way-out. ❸ HIGHER-LEVEL, complex, complicated, difficult, hard. ❹ MATURE, grown up, precocious, sophisticated, well developed.
– OPPOSITES backward.

advantage n ❶ BENEFIT, good point, asset, gain, convenience, profit, use, boon, blessing.
❷ SUPERIORITY, dominance, edge, upper hand, whip hand, trump card.
– OPPOSITES disadvantage.
■ **take advantage of** see EXPLOIT v (2).

advantageous adj ❶ BENEFICIAL, helpful, useful, of benefit, profitable, valuable, worthwhile. ❷ FAVOURABLE, dominant, superior, powerful.

adventure n ❶ EXPLOIT, deed, feat, experience, incident, escapade, venture, undertaking, operation. ❷ EXCITEMENT, danger, hazard, risk, peril, precariousness.

adventurous adj ❶ DARING, brave, bold, courageous, heroic, enterprising, intrepid, daredevil, valiant, venturesome, reckless, rash. ❷ RISKY, dangerous, exciting, hazardous, challenging, perilous, precarious.
– OPPOSITES cautious, boring, uneventful.

adverse adj ❶ UNFAVOURABLE, unfortunate, harmful, disadvantageous, inauspicious, unlucky, detrimental, untoward, prejudicial, unpropitious, uncongenial, deleterious, contrary. ❷ HOSTILE, unfriendly, antagonistic, negative, disapproving, derogatory, attacking, uncomplimentary, opposing, unkind, unsympathetic, hurtful, unfavourable, censorious, inimical.
– OPPOSITES favourable.

adversity n MISFORTUNE, bad luck, trouble, disaster, sorrow, misery, hard times, tribulation, woe, affliction.

advertise v PUBLICIZE, promote, market, display, tout, make known, call attention to, merchandise, flaunt, show off, announce, promulgate, proclaim; *informal* push, puff, plug, hype.

advertisement n COMMERCIAL, promotion, display, publicity, announcement, notice, circular, handout, small ad, leaflet, placard; *informal* ad, plug, puff, blurb; *Brit. informal* advert.

advice n GUIDANCE, help, counsel, suggestions, recommendations, hints, pointers, tips, ideas, views, warnings, caution, admonition.

advisable adj PRUDENT, recommended, sensible, appropriate, expedient, judicious, politic. *See also* WISE (2).
– OPPOSITES inadvisable.

advise v GIVE GUIDANCE, guide, counsel, enjoin, offer suggestions, caution, instruct, urge, exhort, advocate, warn, encourage, commend, admonish.
■ **advise someone of** *see* INFORM (1).

advocacy n SUPPORT, backing, promotion, argument for, advising, recommendation.

advocate n SUPPORTER, proponent, backer, spokesman, exponent, apologist.
▶ v ADVISE, recommend, support, back, argue for, urge, favour, endorse, champion.

aesthetic adj ARTISTIC, tasteful, beautiful, sensitive, in good taste, cultivated.

affable adj FRIENDLY, agreeable, pleasant, amiable, good-natured, civil, courteous.
– OPPOSITES unfriendly.

affair n ❶ EVENT, occurrence, episode, incident, happening, circumstance, case, proceeding, occasion, matter, issue, subject, topic. ❷ BUSINESS, concern, activity, responsibility, province, preserve, problem, worry; *Brit. informal* lookout. ❸ RELATIONSHIP, love affair, romance, involvement, liaison, intrigue, amour, attachment; *Brit. informal* carry-on.

affect[1] v ❶ HAVE AN EFFECT ON, influence, act on, change, have an impact on, modify, shape, transform. ❷ MOVE, touch, upset, trouble, disturb, concern, perturb, stir, agitate, hit, grieve.

affect[2] v ADOPT, assume, feign, sham, simulate; *informal* put on. *See also* PRETEND (1).

affectation n PRETENCE, affectedness, pretentiousness, pretension, posturing, artificiality. *See also* PRETENCE (3).

affected adj UNNATURAL, contrived, put on, artificial, mannered, insincere, studied. *See also* PRETENTIOUS.
– OPPOSITES natural.

affecting adj MOVING, touching, heart-rending, poignant, upsetting, pathetic.

affection n FONDNESS, liking, love, warmth, devotion, attachment, tenderness, friendship,

partiality, amity, warm feelings; *informal* soft spot. *See also* LOVE n (1).
– OPPOSITES dislike, hatred.

affectionate adj FOND, loving, caring, devoted, tender, doting, warm, friendly. *See also* LOVING.
– OPPOSITES cold.

affinity n ❶ LIKING, fondness, closeness, relationship, kinship, like-mindedness, rapport, empathy, understanding; *informal* chemistry. ❷ LIKENESS, closeness, similarity, resemblance, correspondence, similitude.

affirm v STATE, assert, declare, maintain, attest, avow, swear, pronounce, proclaim; *formal* aver.
– OPPOSITES deny.

affirmation n STATEMENT, assertion, declaration, confirmation, proclamation, pronouncement, oath, attestation; *formal* averment.
– OPPOSITES denial.

affirmative adj ASSENTING, agreeing, concurring, consenting, positive, approving.
– OPPOSITES negative.

afflict v TROUBLE, burden, distress, affect, try, worry, bother, harm, oppress, pain, hurt, torture, plague, rack, torment, beset, harass, wound, bedevil, grieve, pester, annoy, vex.

affluence n WEALTH, prosperity, riches, fortune, substance, resources.
– OPPOSITES poverty.

affluent adj RICH, wealthy,

prosperous, well off, well-to-do, moneyed, opulent, comfortable; *informal* well heeled, loaded.
– OPPOSITES poor.

afford v ❶ PAY FOR, find enough for, have the means for, spare the price of, meet the expense of, run to, stretch to, spare. ❷ *See* PROVIDE (2).

afraid adj ❶ FRIGHTENED, scared, terrified, fearful, apprehensive, terror-stricken, timid, intimidated, nervous, alarmed, anxious, trembling, cowardly, panicky, panic-stricken, uneasy, agitated, pusillanimous, faint-hearted, reluctant, craven, diffident, daunted, cowed, timorous; *informal* chicken, yellow, jittery; *Brit. informal* windy. ❷ SORRY, apologetic, regretful, unhappy.
– OPPOSITES brave, confident.

aftermath n AFTER-EFFECTS, consequences, repercussions, results, outcome, end result, upshot.

afterwards adv LATER, subsequently, then, next, after; *formal* thereupon.
– OPPOSITES beforehand.

age n ❶ MATURITY, old age, advancing years, seniority, elderliness; *Biology* senescence. ❷ ERA, epoch, period, time, generation. ❸ A LONG TIME, an eternity, aeons, hours, days, months, years; *Brit. informal* yonks.
▶ v GROW OLD, mature, grow up, ripen, develop, mellow, wither, fade.

aged adj OLD, elderly, ancient, long in the tooth, superannuated; Biology senescent; informal getting on, over the hill.
– OPPOSITES young, youthful.

agent n REPRESENTATIVE, middleman, go-between, broker, negotiator, intermediary, mediator, emissary, envoy, proxy, factor, trustee, delegate, spokesperson, spokesman, spokeswoman, executor.

aggravate v ❶ MAKE WORSE, worsen, exacerbate, intensify, inflame, exaggerate, make more serious, compound, increase, heighten, magnify, add to. ❷ See ANNOY.
– OPPOSITES alleviate, improve.

aggressive adj ❶ HOSTILE, violent, belligerent, combative, attacking, destructive, quarrelsome, warlike, antagonistic, provocative, pugnacious, bellicose, bullying, contentious, jingoistic, militant. ❷ ASSERTIVE, forceful, pushy, insistent, vigorous, dynamic, bold, enterprising, energetic, zealous, pushing; informal go-ahead.
– OPPOSITES peaceable, retiring.

aggrieved adj RESENTFUL, affronted, indignant, angry, distressed, piqued, disturbed; informal peeved.

agile adj NIMBLE, lithe, fit, supple, sprightly, graceful, acrobatic, lively, spry, adroit, deft, quick-moving, limber, in good condition; informal nippy.
– OPPOSITES clumsy, stiff.

agitate v ❶ UPSET, worry, fluster, perturb, disturb, disconcert, trouble, alarm, work up, ruffle, disquiet, unsettle, unnerve, rouse, excite, discomfit, confuse, shake up; informal rattle. ❷ STIR, whisk, beat, shake, toss, work, churn, froth up, ruffle, ferment.
– OPPOSITES calm.

agitator n TROUBLEMAKER, rabble-rouser, agent provocateur, instigator, firebrand, fomenter, revolutionary, demagogue.

agonizing adj EXCRUCIATING, painful, acute, harrowing, searing, unendurable, torturous.

agony n SUFFERING, anguish, hurt, torment, torture, distress. See also PAIN.

agree v ❶ CONCUR, be of the same mind, comply, see eye to eye. ❷ MATCH, correspond, accord, conform, coincide, fit, tally. ❸ CONSENT TO, accept, assent to, approve, allow, admit, acquiesce in.
– OPPOSITES disagree.

agreeable adj PLEASING, enjoyable, nice, delightful, acceptable, likable, to one's liking, pleasurable. See also PLEASANT.
– OPPOSITES disagreeable.

agreement n ❶ ACCORD, concurrence, harmony, accordance, unity, assent; formal concord. ❷ CONTRACT, deal, compact, settlement, pact, bargain, treaty, covenant, concordat. ❸ CORRESPONDENCE,

similarity, conformity, match, harmony, accordance, coincidence.
– OPPOSITES disagreement.

agricultural adj ❶ FARMING, farm, agrarian, pastoral, rural. ❷ FARMED, cultivated, planted, productive, tilled.
– OPPOSITES urban.

agriculture n FARMING, cultivation, tillage, husbandry, agronomy, agronomics, agribusiness; *Brit.* crofting.

aground adv & adj GROUNDED, beached, ashore, shipwrecked, on the bottom, stranded, stuck, high and dry.
– OPPOSITES afloat.

aid n ❶ HELP, assistance, support, succour, encouragement, a helping hand, cooperation. ❷ CONTRIBUTION, gift, donation, subsidy, loan, debt remission, relief, sponsorship, backing, grant; *historical* alms.
– OPPOSITES hindrance.
▶ v ❶ HELP, assist, support, succour, lend a hand, sustain, second. ❷ FACILITATE, speed up, hasten, help, encourage, expedite, promote, contribute to, sustain.
– OPPOSITES hinder.

ailing adj UNWELL, sick, poorly, sickly, indisposed, infirm; *informal* under the weather. *See also* ILL adj (1).
– OPPOSITES healthy.

ailment n ILLNESS, disease, sickness, disorder, complaint, malady, infirmity, affliction. *See also* ILLNESS.

aim v ❶ POINT, direct, take aim, train, sight, focus, address, zero in on. ❷ INTEND, mean, resolve, wish, aspire, want, plan, propose, seek, try, strive, endeavour.
▶ n AMBITION, objective, object, end, goal, purpose, intention, intent, plan, target, hope, aspiration, desire, wish, design, direction, focus, dream, destination.

aimless adj ❶ POINTLESS, purposeless, futile, undirected, goalless, objectless. ❷ PURPOSELESS, drifting, wandering, undirected, unambitious, undisciplined, wayward.
– OPPOSITES purposeful.

air n ❶ SKY, atmosphere, airspace; *poetic/literary* heavens, ether. ❷ OXYGEN, breath of air, breeze, draught, puff of wind; *poetic/literary* zephyr. ❸ APPEARANCE, impression, look, mood, atmosphere, quality, feeling, ambience, character, flavour, demeanour, effect, manner, bearing, tone, aspect, mien. ❹ AFFECTATIONS, pretension, pretentiousness, affectedness, airs and graces, posing, posturing. ❺ MELODY, tune, song, theme, strain.
▶ v ❶ EXPRESS, make known, voice, publicize, broadcast, give vent to, publish, communicate, reveal, proclaim, divulge, circulate, disseminate, vent, disclose. ❷ VENTILATE, aerate, freshen, refresh.

airless adj STUFFY, close, stifling, suffocating, muggy, unventilated, oppressive, sultry.
– OPPOSITES airy.

airy adj ❶ WELL VENTILATED, fresh, spacious, uncluttered, light, bright. ❷ NONCHALANT, casual, light-hearted, breezy, cheerful, jaunty, flippant, blithe, insouciant; *dated* gay.
– OPPOSITES stuffy, studied.

aisle n PASSAGE, passageway, gangway, walkway, corridor, lane, alley.

akin adj RELATED TO, allied with, connected with, corresponding to, similar to.
– OPPOSITES unrelated, different.

alacrity n READINESS, promptness, eagerness, enthusiasm, willingness, haste, swiftness.
– OPPOSITES reluctance, sluggishness.

alarm n ❶ FEAR, apprehension, anxiety, uneasiness, distress, consternation, panic, fright, trepidation, disquiet. *See also* FEAR n (1). ❷ WARNING SOUND, siren, alert, alarm bell/signal, danger/distress signal; *archaic* tocsin.
▶ v FRIGHTEN, scare, panic, terrify, unnerve, agitate, distress, disturb, startle, shock, upset, worry; *Brit. informal* put the wind up.
– OPPOSITES reassure.

alcohol n DRINK, liquor, spirits; *informal* booze, hard stuff, the demon drink, the bottle, grog, tipple; *Brit. informal* bevvy.

alcoholic adj INTOXICATING, strong, inebriating, hard; *formal* spirituous.
– OPPOSITES soft.

▶ n DRUNKARD, drunk, hard/heavy drinker, dipsomaniac, problem drinker, inebriate, tippler, sot, imbiber; *informal* boozer, lush, dipso, wino, alky.
– OPPOSITES teetotaller.

alert adj ❶ AWARE, alive to, watchful, vigilant, observant, wary, wide awake, on one's guard, attentive, on the alert, sharp-eyed, heedful, circumspect, on the lookout, on one's toes. ❷ SHARP, quick, bright, perceptive, keen, lively, wide awake; *informal* on the ball, quick off the mark.
– OPPOSITES inattentive, slow, absent-minded.
▶ v WARN, make aware, caution, advise, forewarn, inform, apprise, notify; *informal* tip off.

alibi n EXCUSE, defence, justification, explanation, pretext, plea, vindication.

alien adj FOREIGN, strange, unfamiliar, outlandish, remote, exotic, extraterrestrial.
– OPPOSITES familiar.
▶ n FOREIGNER, stranger, outsider, newcomer, extraterrestrial.
– OPPOSITES native.

alight¹ v GET OFF, come down, get down, dismount, disembark, come to rest, land, descend, touch down, settle, perch.

alight² adj ❶ ON FIRE, burning, ablaze, blazing, lighted, lit, aflame. ❷ LIT UP, shining, bright, illuminated, brilliant.

align v ❶ LINE UP, arrange in

line, put in order, straighten, rank, range. ❷ ALLY, associate, affiliate, cooperate, side, join, unite, combine, join forces.

alike adj SIMILAR, like, resembling, indistinguishable, identical, interchangeable, corresponding, matching, the same, twin, uniform.
– OPPOSITES differently.
▶ adv SIMILARLY, just the same, identically, in a like manner, in the same way.
– OPPOSITES differently.

alive adj ❶ LIVING, breathing, live, animate; *informal* alive and kicking, in the land of the living; *archaic* quick. ❷ *see* ALERT.
– OPPOSITES dead.

allay v LESSEN, diminish, reduce, alleviate, calm, assuage, ease, quell, relieve, appease, moderate, mitigate, check, lull, subdue, soothe.
– OPPOSITES increase, stimulate.

allegation n CHARGE, accusation, claim, assertion, statement, declaration, testimony, deposition, avowal.

allege v CLAIM, declare, state, profess, assert, maintain, affirm, avow, attest, contend, lay a charge; *formal* aver.

alleged adj SUPPOSED, claimed, declared, so-called, professed, stated.

allegiance n LOYALTY, faithfulness, adherence, fidelity, devotion, duty, obedience; *historical* fealty.

allergic adj ❶ HYPERSENSITIVE, sensitive, sensitized, suscep-

tible. ❷ AVERSE, opposed, antagonistic, disinclined, hostile, antipathetic, loath.

alleviate v REDUCE, lessen, diminish, relieve, ease, allay, mitigate, assuage, abate, palliate, lighten, soothe, subdue, temper, ameliorate, check, quell, soften, make lighter.
– OPPOSITES aggravate.

alliance n ASSOCIATION, union, coalition, partnership, affiliation, agreement, league, confederation, federation, relationship, connection, pact, bond, understanding, treaty, marriage, compact, concordat, syndicate, cartel, consortium, bloc, combination, covenant, entente.

allot v ALLOCATE, assign, apportion, distribute, give out, share out, award, dispense, deal out, ration, divide up, mete out, dole out, dish out.

allow v ❶ PERMIT, let, give permission to, authorize, consent to, sanction, approve, license, enable; *informal* give the go-ahead to, give the green light to. ❷ ADMIT, acknowledge, concede, recognize, grant, confess.
– OPPOSITES forbid, deny.

allowance n ❶ QUOTA, allocation, ration, portion, share. ❷ PAYMENT, subsidy, remittance, grant, contribution. ❸ REBATE, discount, deduction, concession, reduction.
■ **make allowances** ❶ TAKE INTO ACCOUNT, bear in mind, have regard to. ❷ EXCUSE, make excuses, forgive, pardon.

alloy n MIXTURE, blend, amalgam, combination, compound, composite; *technical* admixture.

allude
■ **allude to** REFER TO, mention, speak of, touch on, make an allusion to, cite, suggest, hint at; *formal* advert to.

allure v ATTRACT, fascinate, charm, seduce, captivate, enchant, bewitch, beguile, tempt, magnetize, lure, entice, cajole, draw, inveigle.

allusion n REFERENCE, mention, suggestion, citation, hint, intimation.

ally n ASSOCIATE, colleague, partner, friend, supporter, collaborator, confederate, accomplice, abetter, accessory.
– OPPOSITES enemy, opponent.
▶ v JOIN, unite, join forces, combine, merge, go into partnership, band together, form an alliance, team up, link up, affiliate, be in league, cooperate, collaborate, side.

almighty adj ❶ ALL-POWERFUL, supreme, most high, omnipotent. ❷ *see* HUGE, LOUD (3).

almost adv NEARLY, just about, close to, not quite, practically, virtually, as good as, approaching, not far from, verging on, well-nigh.

alone adj & adv BY ONESELF, on one's own, solitary, apart, unaccompanied, isolated, single, separate, unassisted, solo, lonely, friendless, forlorn, deserted, desolate, lonesome.
– OPPOSITES accompanied.

aloof adj DISTANT, unapproachable, remote, stand-offish, unfriendly, unsociable, reserved, unresponsive, reticent, supercilious, cold, chilly, haughty, formal, inaccessible, detached, undemonstrative, unsympathetic, unforthcoming.
– OPPOSITES familiar, friendly.

aloud adv OUT LOUD, clearly, audibly, distinctly, plainly, intelligibly.
– OPPOSITES silently.

already adv ❶ BY NOW, by this time, previously, before, before now. ❷ AS SOON AS THIS, as early as this, so soon, so early.

also adv IN ADDITION, additionally, moreover, besides, too, to boot, on top of that.

alter v CHANGE, make different, adjust, adapt, modify, convert, reshape, remodel, remake, vary, amend, revise, transform, emend, edit.

alteration n CHANGE, adjustment, modification, adaptation, revision, amendment, transformation, conversion, metamorphosis, reorganization, transfiguration.

alternate v TAKE TURNS, follow each other, rotate, interchange, substitute for each other, replace each other, oscillate, seesaw.

alternative n ❶ CHOICE, option, preference. ❷ SUBSTITUTE, back-up, replacement.

alternatively adv ON THE OTHER HAND, as an alternative, instead, otherwise, if not, or.

although conjunction THOUGH, even though, even if, despite the fact that, whilst, albeit.

altogether adv COMPLETELY, totally, entirely, thoroughly, fully, utterly, absolutely, perfectly, quite, wholly.

always adv ❶ EVERY TIME, on every occasion, invariably, consistently, repeatedly, unfailingly. ❷ CONTINUALLY, constantly, repeatedly, forever, perpetually, incessantly, eternally. ❸ FOREVER, forever and ever, evermore, endlessly, everlastingly, eternally.
– OPPOSITES never.

amalgamate v COMBINE, merge, unite, join, blend, integrate, mingle, intermingle, mix, intermix, incorporate, fuse, come together, join forces, coalesce, associate, compound, link up.
– OPPOSITES split.

amass v COLLECT, gather, accumulate, pile up, assemble, store up, hoard.

amateur n NON-PROFESSIONAL, layman, dabbler, dilettante, enthusiast.
▶ adj UNPAID, inexperienced, lay, unqualified.
– OPPOSITES professional, expert.

amateurish adj UNPROFESSIONAL, unskilful, untrained, unskilled, incompetent, inexpert, clumsy, crude, bungling, shoddy, unpolished, inept, second-rate, rough and ready.
– OPPOSITES skilled.

amaze v ASTONISH, surprise, astound, startle, dumbfound, rock, shock, stagger, stun, bewilder, stupefy, daze, disconcert, confound, awe; informal flabbergast, bowl over.

amazement n ASTONISHMENT, surprise, bewilderment, shock, wonder, stupefaction.

amazing adj ASTONISHING, astounding, stunning, staggering, surprising, breathtaking, extraordinary, incredible, remarkable, sensational, phenomenal, prodigious, stupendous, exceptional; informal mind-boggling.

ambassador n ENVOY, consul, diplomat, emissary, representative, plenipotentiary; archaic legate.

ambiguous adj ❶ AMBIVALENT, equivocal, double-edged. ❷ OBSCURE, cryptic, vague, unclear, uncertain, indefinite, woolly, indeterminate, confusing, puzzling, perplexing, enigmatic.

ambition n ❶ DRIVE, enterprise, desire, initiative, eagerness, thrust, push, zeal, pushiness, striving, yearning, hankering; informal get-up-and-go, oomph. ❷ GOAL, aim, objective, desire, object, intent, purpose, design, target, wish, aspiration, dream, hope, ideal.

ambitious adj ❶ FORCEFUL, enterprising, purposeful, assertive, pushy, aspiring, zealous, enthusiastic, committed, eager, energetic; informal

go-ahead, on the make. ❷ CHALLENGING, formidable, demanding, difficult, exacting, bold, unrealistic.
– OPPOSITES aimless, apathetic, easy.

ambivalent adj EQUIVOCAL, ambiguous, uncertain, doubtful, inconclusive, unclear, unresolved, unsettled, confusing, mixed, conflicting, clashing, opposing, vacillating, two-faced.
– OPPOSITES unequivocal.

ambush n TRAP, snare, surprise attack, pitfall, lure; *archaic* ambuscade.
▶ V LIE IN WAIT FOR, lay a trap for, pounce on, entrap, ensnare, intercept, surprise, waylay, swoop on, decoy; *archaic* ambuscade.

amenable adj AGREEABLE, accommodating, persuadable, cooperative, tractable, compliant, responsive, willing, acquiescent, adaptable, open-minded, biddable, complaisant, submissive, deferential.
– OPPOSITES uncooperative.

amend v ❶ ALTER, change, revise, correct, modify, adjust, emend, reorganize, reshape, transform. ❷ IMPROVE, remedy, fix, set right, repair, enhance, better, ameliorate, mend.

amenity n FACILITY, service, convenience, resource, advantage.

amiable adj FRIENDLY, agreeable, pleasant, charming, likeable, sociable, genial, amicable, congenial, good-natured, well disposed.
– OPPOSITES unfriendly, disagreeable.

amnesty n PARDON, general pardon, reprieve, forgiveness, absolution, dispensation, indulgence.

amorous adj LOVING, passionate, sexual, sexy, erotic, carnal, lustful, affectionate, ardent, fond, enamoured, impassioned; *Brit. informal* randy.
– OPPOSITES unloving, cold.

amorphous adj FORMLESS, shapeless, structureless, unstructured, unformed, nebulous, vague, ill-organized, indeterminate.
– OPPOSITES shaped, definite.

amount n QUANTITY, number, total, aggregate, sum, volume, mass, weight, measure, bulk, extent, expanse.
■ **amount to** ADD UP TO, total, come to, equal, make, correspond to, approximate to.

ample adj ENOUGH, sufficient, plenty, more than enough, enough and to spare, abundant, considerable, copious, lavish, substantial, bountiful, profuse, liberal, generous, munificent, unstinting; *poetic/literary* plenteous.
– OPPOSITES insufficient.

amplify v ❶ BOOST, increase, intensify, augment, heighten, magnify, supplement. ❷ EXPAND, enlarge on, add to, expound on, go into detail about, elaborate on, fill out, make longer, flesh out, develop, extend, lengthen, broaden, explicate, expatiate on, dilate on, supplement.

amputate v **❶** CUT OFF, sever, chop off, saw off, remove, lop off, excise, dismember, truncate, dock, poll.

amuse v **❶** ENTERTAIN, delight, enliven, gladden, cheer, make laugh, please, divert, beguile, regale with, raise a smile in. **❷** OCCUPY, entertain, divert, interest, absorb, engross.

amusement n **❶** LAUGHTER, mirth, hilarity, fun, gaiety, pleasure, delight, enjoyment, merriment. **❷** ENTERTAINMENT, interest, diversion, recreation, pastime, hobby, sport, game, pleasure.

amusing adj see FUNNY (1), ENJOYABLE.

anaemic adj PALE, colourless, pallid, ashen, sickly, unhealthy, wan, bloodless, weak, feeble, powerless, ineffective, ineffectual, impotent, vigourless.
– OPPOSITES healthy, rosy, vigorous.

analogous adj SIMILAR, comparable, parallel, corresponding, related, matching, equivalent, like, kindred, homologous.

analyse v **❶** BREAK DOWN, dissect, separate out, anatomize, fractionate, test, assay. **❷** STUDY, examine, investigate, review, evaluate, interpret, scrutinize, enquire into, dissect.

analysis n **❶** BREAKDOWN, dissection, anatomization, frac-

tionation, assay. **❷** STUDY, examination, investigation, enquiry, review, evaluation, interpretation.

analytical, analytic adj INVESTIGATIVE, inquisitive, critical, diagnostic, interpretative, enquiring, searching, systematic, questioning, rational, methodical, in depth.

anarchy n **❶** ABSENCE OF GOVERNMENT, lawlessness, nihilism, misrule, misgovernment, mobocracy, revolution. **❷** DISORDER, riot, chaos, pandemonium, tumult, mayhem, rebellion, insurrection, mutiny.
– OPPOSITES order, law.

ancestor n FOREBEAR, forerunner, forefather, progenitor, predecessor, precursor, antecedent.
– OPPOSITES descendant, successor.

ancestry n **❶** LINEAGE, descent, parentage, extraction, origin, genealogy, stock, blood, pedigree, derivation. **❷** ANTECEDENTS, forebears, forefathers, progenitors, family tree.

anchor n MAINSTAY, cornerstone, linchpin, bulwark, support.
▶ v **❶** MOOR, berth, make fast, tie up. **❷** SECURE, fasten, attach, connect, bind.

ancient adj **❶** EARLY, earliest, prehistoric, primeval, primordial, immemorial, bygone. **❷** VERY OLD, time-worn, age-old, antique, long-lived, venerable, elderly. **❸** OLD-FASHIONED, antiquated, out of date, out-moded, obsolete, archaic, superannuated, antediluvian, atavistic.

ancillary adj SECONDARY, auxiliary, subsidiary, supplementary, additional, subordinate, extra.

angelic adj ❶ HEAVENLY, seraphic, cherubic, ethereal, beatific, holy, divine, blessed. ❷ INNOCENT, pure, virtuous, saintly, beautiful, adorable. *See also* GOOD adj (1).

anger n RAGE, fury, wrath, rancour, temper, annoyance, irritability, antagonism, vexation, exasperation, outrage, indignation, spleen, pique, passion, hostility, tantrum; *poetic/literary* ire, choler.
▶ v MAKE ANGRY, infuriate, enrage, madden, incense, outrage, irritate, annoy, exasperate, provoke, antagonize, rile, vex, inflame, aggravate; *informal* make someone's blood boil, needle, bug, drive crazy.
– OPPOSITES pacify, placate.

angle n ❶ BEND, corner, fork, nook, niche, recess, elbow. ❷ POINT OF VIEW, approach, viewpoint, standpoint, opinion, position, slant.
▶ v ❶ TILT, slant, slope, turn, bend. ❷ SLANT, distort, skew.

angry adj FURIOUS, irate, enraged, incensed, maddened, outraged, wrathful, seething, raging, annoyed, irritated, exasperated, fuming, indignant, bitter, irascible, vexed, heated,

provoked, raving, wild, fiery, apoplectic, hot-tempered, ill-humoured; *informal* hot under the collar, mad, up in arms; *Brit. informal* aerated.
– OPPOSITES calm, pleased.

anguish n AGONY, suffering, pain, distress, torment, torture, misery, sorrow, grief, woe, heartache, tribulation.
– OPPOSITES pleasure, happiness.

angular adj ❶ BENT, crooked, jagged, zigzag, pointed, V-shaped, Y-shaped, forked, bifurcate. ❷ BONY, gaunt, spare, scrawny, skinny, lean.
– OPPOSITES rounded.

animal n ❶ CREATURE, beast, brute, organism, being. ❷ BRUTE, beast, savage, fiend, barbarian, monster; *informal* swine.
▶ adj SENSUAL, carnal, physical, bodily, fleshly, brutish, bestial.

animate v ENLIVEN, give life to, liven up, cheer up, gladden, brighten up, make lively, revitalize, perk up, inspire, excite, exhilarate, rouse, stir, stimulate, invigorate, fire, move, energize, rejuvenate, revive, encourage, galvanize, urge, arouse, activate, spark, kindle, incite; *informal* buck up, pep up.
▶ adj LIVING, alive, live, breathing, conscious, sentient.
– OPPOSITES inanimate.

animated adj LIVELY, energetic, excited, enthusiastic, spirited, exuberant, vivacious, bubbling, vibrant, cheerful, bright, ebullient, dynamic,

eager, zestful, busy, brisk, active, alive, sprightly, passionate, vigorous, quick.
– OPPOSITES lethargic, lifeless.

animation n LIVELINESS, energy, excitement, enthusiasm, passion, dynamism, vitality, vivacity, eagerness, ebullience, exhilaration, zest, exuberance, life, spirit, high spirits, verve, buoyancy, forcefulness, sparkle, briskness, activity, vigour, sprightliness; *informal* pep, zing.
– OPPOSITES apathy, lethargy.

animosity n DISLIKE, enmity, unfriendliness, hostility, resentment, antagonism, hate, hatred, loathing, antipathy, bitterness, spite, bad blood, rancour, venom, ill will, acrimony, vindictiveness, malice, animus, asperity, sourness, malignancy, malignity, odium, acerbity, virulence, sharpness.
– OPPOSITES goodwill, friendliness.

annex v SEIZE, take over, conquer, appropriate, acquire, occupy, usurp.

annihilate v DESTROY, wipe out, exterminate, obliterate, eliminate, eradicate, extirpate, erase, liquidate, raze, extinguish, slaughter, kill off, finish off.

annotate v COMMENT ON, gloss, add notes to, explain, interpret, elucidate, explicate.

annotation n NOTE, comment, gloss, footnote, commentary, explanation,

interpretation, elucidation, observation.

announce v ❶ MAKE KNOWN, make public, publish, put out, report, state, give out, reveal, declare, disclose, divulge, broadcast, proclaim, advertise, notify of, promulgate, propound, blazon, intimate. ❷ INTRODUCE, present, give someone's name, name, usher in, herald.
– OPPOSITES suppress.

announcement n ❶ DECLARATION, reporting, proclamation, disclosure, publication, statement, promulgation, notification, advertisement, intimation, revelation. ❷ STATEMENT, report, bulletin, message, communiqué.

announcer n PRESENTER, newsreader, broadcaster, newscaster, reporter, commentator, anchorman, anchor, herald, master of ceremonies, compère, MC.

annoy v ❶ IRRITATE, exasperate, displease, infuriate, anger, madden, vex, provoke, upset, put out, try someone's patience, drive mad, antagonize, irk, gall, nettle, make cross, pique, jar; *Brit.* rub up the wrong way; *informal* get on someone's nerves, aggravate, bug, peeve, get to. ❷ BOTHER, disturb, pester, harass, trouble, fret, worry, plague, harry, badger, molest; *informal* bug.

annoyance n ❶ IRRITATION, exasperation, anger, displeasure, vexation, chagrin, pique;

poetic/literary ire. ❷ NUISANCE, pest, bother, irritant, trial, offence, provocation; *informal* pain, hassle, pain in the neck, bind, bore.

annoyed adj IRRITATED, exasperated, cross, displeased, upset, vexed, riled, put out; *informal* miffed, peeved, huffy, in a huff; *Brit. informal* shirty; *N. Amer. informal* sore.
– OPPOSITES pleased.

annoying adj IRRITATING, infuriating, exasperating, maddening, upsetting, trying, galling, tiresome, grating, troublesome, worrying, vexing, irksome, bothersome, vexatious, wearisome; *informal* aggravating, pestilential.

annul v NULLIFY, cancel, declare null and void, invalidate, rescind, revoke, repeal, quash, void, negate, abrogate.

anoint v ❶ OIL, apply ointment to, spread over, rub, smear, lubricate, grease. ❷ CONSECRATE, bless, sanctify, ordain, hallow.

anomalous adj ABNORMAL, irregular, atypical, aberrant, deviant, exceptional, unusual, odd, eccentric, bizarre, peculiar.

anonymous adj ❶ UNNAMED, unidentified, nameless, unknown, unspecified, incognito, uncredited, unattributed, unsigned. ❷ CHARACTERLESS, unremarkable, impersonal, nondescript, boring, dull, uninteresting.
– OPPOSITES named, known.

answer n ❶ REPLY, response, acknowledgement, rejoinder, retort, riposte; *informal* comeback. ❷ SOLUTION, explanation, resolution. ❸ DEFENCE, plea, refutation, rebuttal, vindication.
▶ v ❶ REPLY TO, respond to, acknowledge, react to, come back, retort, riposte, make a rejoinder, rejoin. ❷ SOLVE, explain, resolve. ❸ MEET, satisfy, fulfil, suit, measure up to, serve. ❹ FIT, match, correspond to, be similar to, conform to, correlate to.
■ **answer back** TALK BACK, argue with, be cheeky, contradict, be impertinent. **answer for** ❶ PAY FOR, suffer for, be punished for, make amends for, atone for. ❷ VOUCH FOR, be accountable for, be responsible for, be liable for.

answerable adj RESPONSIBLE, accountable, liable.

antagonism n ANIMOSITY, hostility, enmity, antipathy, rancour, opposition, rivalry, friction, conflict, dissension.
– OPPOSITES friendship.

antagonize v ANNOY, anger, irritate, alienate, offend, provoke, put out, upset, make an enemy of, arouse hostility in.
– OPPOSITES pacify.

anthem n HYMN, psalm, song of praise, chorale, chant, canticle, paean.

anthology n COLLECTION, compilation, miscellany, selection, treasury, compendium, digest.

anticipate v ❶ EXPECT, predict, forecast, foresee, await, prepare for, reckon on, look for, look forward to. ❷ PREVENT, intercept, forestall, pre-empt; *informal* beat to it, beat to the draw.

anticipation n ❶ EXPECTATION, prediction, preparation, contemplation. ❷ EXPECTANCY, hopefulness, hope.

anticlimax n DISAPPOINTMENT, let-down, disillusionment, comedown, bathos; *Brit.* damp squib.

antics pl n PRANKS, capers, escapades, tricks, romps, frolics, clowning, horseplay, skylarking; *informal* larking about.

antidote n COUNTERMEASURE, antitoxin, neutralizing agent, cure, remedy, corrective.

antipathy n DISLIKE, hostility, enmity, opposition, hatred, animosity, antagonism, loathing, repugnance, animus.
– OPPOSITES liking, affinity.

antiquated adj OLD-FASHIONED, out of date, outmoded, old, dated, outdated, ancient, aged, archaic, antique, obsolete, antediluvian, outworn, passé, medieval, primitive, primeval, quaint; *informal* prehistoric, past it, superannuated.

antique adj ❶ ANTIQUARIAN, collectable, vintage, historic, traditional, veteran. ❷ *See* ANTIQUATED.
▶ n COLLECTOR'S ITEM, heirloom, collectable, curiosity, curio, objet d'art, rarity, relic.

antiquity n CLASSICAL TIMES, former times, bygone age, the past, days gone by, olden days.

antiseptic adj ❶ DISINFECTED, disinfectant, sterile, sterilized, sterilizing, hygienic, sanitized, germ-free, medicated, germicidal, bactericidal. ❷ CLINICAL, characterless, anonymous, unexciting, undistinguished.

antisocial adj ❶ UNSOCIABLE, unfriendly, uncommunicative, reserved, withdrawn, retiring, misanthropic, alienated. ❷ DISRUPTIVE, disorderly, rude, unruly, undisciplined, offensive, obnoxious, rebellious, lawless, asocial.
– OPPOSITES sociable.

antithesis n OPPOSITE, reverse, converse, inverse, other extreme.

anxiety n ❶ WORRY, concern, apprehension, disquiet, uneasiness, nervousness, dread, stress, tension, tenseness, strain, misgiving, foreboding, fear, uncertainty, fretfulness, distress, angst. ❷ DESIRE, eagerness, longing, keenness, enthusiasm, avidity.
– OPPOSITES serenity.

anxious adj ❶ WORRIED, concerned, apprehensive, fearful, nervous, nervy, uneasy, disturbed, afraid, perturbed, agitated, alarmed, edgy, troubled, upset, tense, distraught, fraught, overwrought, fretful; *informal* jittery, on edge. ❷ EAGER, keen, longing, desperate, yearning, impatient, intent,

avid, desirous; *informal* dying, itching.
– OPPOSITES unconcerned, nonchalant.

anyhow adv ❶ IN ANY CASE, in any event, no matter what, at all events. ❷ HAPHAZARDLY, carelessly, heedlessly, negligently; *informal* all over the place.

apathetic adj UNINTERESTED, indifferent, unenthusiastic, unconcerned, unmotivated, impassive, half-hearted, uncommitted, uninvolved, unresponsive, casual, cool, dispassionate, unfeeling, unemotional, emotionless, phlegmatic, unambitious.
– OPPOSITES enthusiastic.

apathy n INDIFFERENCE, lack of interest, lack of enthusiasm, unconcern, impassivity, unresponsiveness.
– OPPOSITES enthusiasm, passion.

aperture n OPENING, gap, hole, crack, slit, window, orifice, fissure, breach, eye.

apex n ❶ TOP, peak, summit, tip, head, crest, crown, pinnacle, vertex. ❷ HIGH POINT, height, zenith, climax, culmination, apogee, acme.
– OPPOSITES nadir.

apocryphal adj UNVERIFIED, unsubstantiated, debatable, questionable, dubious, spurious, mythical, fictitious, untrue, false; *informal* phoney.
– OPPOSITES authentic.

apologetic adj REGRETFUL, sorry, remorseful, contrite, re-pentant, penitent, conscience-stricken, ashamed, rueful.
– OPPOSITES unrepentant, impenitent.

apologize v SAY SORRY, make an apology, express regret, ask forgiveness, ask for pardon, beg pardon, eat humble pie.

apology n ❶ REGRETS, expression of regret. ❷ MOCKERY, travesty, caricature, substitute, poor excuse.

apostle n EVANGELIST, missionary, spreader of the word, preacher, crusader, teacher, supporter, advocate, propagandist.

appal v SHOCK, dismay, horrify, sicken, disgust, outrage, astound, alarm, nauseate, revolt.

appalling adj SHOCKING, horrifying, disgusting, dreadful, awful, frightful, ghastly, dire, hideous, harrowing. *See also* BAD.

apparatus n DEVICE, equipment, instrument, contraption, mechanism, appliance, machine, machinery, tackle, gadget, tool, plant; *informal* gear.

apparel n CLOTHING, clothes, dress, garments, garb, attire, costume; *informal* gear.

apparent adj ❶ OBVIOUS, clear, plain, evident, recognizable, noticeable, perceptible, manifest, discernible, visible, unmistakable, patent, perceivable. ❷ SEEMING, ostensible, superficial, outward.
– OPPOSITES hidden.

apparition n GHOST, phantom, spirit, presence,

spectre, manifestation, vision, wraith, shade, chimera; *informal* spook; *poetic/literary* phantasm.

appeal n ❶ REQUEST, plea, call, application, entreaty, petition, prayer, solicitation, cri de cœur, supplication. ❷ ATTRACTION, interest, allure, charm, temptation, fascination, seductiveness.

▶ v ❶ ASK, request, beg, plead, implore, entreat, solicit, call, petition; *poetic/literary* beseech. ❷ INTEREST, tempt, fascinate, charm, engage, entice, enchant, beguile.

appear v ❶ TURN UP, come into view, come out, emerge, materialize, loom up, arrive, enter, surface, bob up; *informal* show up. ❷ OCCUR, materialize, be revealed, be seen, arise, develop, originate, crop up, spring up. ❸ SEEM, look, give the impression of, have the appearance of. ❹ PERFORM, act, take part, play, come on.
– OPPOSITES disappear.

appearance n ❶ COMING INTO VIEW, emergence, arrival, advent, materialization, surfacing. ❷ LOOK, impression, air, manner, bearing, demeanour, aspect, expression, mien. ❸ IMAGE, impression, semblance, guise, pretence.
– OPPOSITES disappearance.

appease v ❶ PLACATE, pacify, conciliate, mollify, soothe, propitiate. ❷ SATISFY, assuage, relieve, blunt, diminish, take the edge off.
– OPPOSITES provoke.

appendage n ❶ ADDITION, attachment, addendum, adjunct, appurtenance, affix. ❷ LIMB, extremity, projection, protuberance.

appendix n SUPPLEMENT, addition, addendum, postscript, adjunct, codicil, rider, epilogue, extension.

appetite n ❶ HUNGER, taste, relish, desire, palate, stomach. ❷ KEENNESS, eagerness, passion, desire, lust, hunger, thirst, yearning, longing, craving, zest, gusto, relish, zeal, hankering, yen, predilection.

appetizing adj ❶ DELICIOUS, mouth-watering, tasty, succulent, palatable. ❷ INVITING, tempting, appealing, enticing, alluring.
– OPPOSITES unappetizing.

applaud v ❶ CLAP, cheer, give a standing ovation to; *informal* put one's hands together for, give someone a big hand, bring the house down. ❷ PRAISE, admire, express approval of, commend, compliment on, congratulate, salute, acclaim, hail, extol.
– OPPOSITES condemn, criticize.

applause n ❶ CLAPPING, ovation, cheering, bravos, encores, curtain calls. ❷ PRAISE, acclaim, admiration, approval, commendation, approbation, accolades, plaudits.

appliance n DEVICE, gadget, instrument, apparatus, machine, mechanism, tool, implement, contraption.

applicable adj RELEVANT, appropriate, pertinent, apposite, apropos.
– OPPOSITES inapplicable.

applicant n CANDIDATE, interviewee, competitor, claimant, enquirer, petitioner, supplicant, suitor, postulant.

apply v ❶ USE, employ, exercise, bring to bear, utilize, put into practice, bring into effect. ❷ PUT ON, rub on/in, cover with, spread, smear, administer. ❸ BE RELEVANT, relate, have a bearing on, be germane, appertain. ❹ ENQUIRE AFTER, put in for, request, try for, seek, appeal.
■ **apply oneself** MAKE AN EFFORT, be industrious, commit oneself, devote oneself, persevere, persist.

appoint v ❶ SET, fix, arrange, decide on, establish, settle on, determine, ordain, designate. ❷ SELECT, name, choose, designate, settle on, plump for, elect, assign, delegate, install as, vote for, co-opt.

appointment n ❶ MEETING, engagement, date, arrangement, interview, rendezvous, assignation, fixture; poetic/literary tryst. ❷ SELECTION, choice, naming, nomination, commissioning, election. ❸ JOB, post, position, office, situation, place.

appreciable adj CONSIDERABLE, substantial, sizeable, significant, goodly.

appreciate v ❶ BE GRATEFUL FOR, be thankful for, be appreciative of, be indebted for. ❷ RATE HIGHLY, prize, value, enjoy, admire, approve of, respect, treasure, hold in high regard, think much of, esteem. ❸ RECOGNIZE, realize, acknowledge, see, know, be aware of, understand, comprehend, perceive. ❹ INCREASE, rise, grow, go up, gain, mount, soar, escalate.
– OPPOSITES disparage, ignore, depreciate.

appreciative adj GRATEFUL, thankful, obliged, indebted, beholden.
– OPPOSITES ungrateful.

apprehensive adj WORRIED, uneasy, nervous, frightened, afraid, alarmed, fearful, mistrustful, concerned, troubled; informal on edge, jittery.
– OPPOSITES fearless, unconcerned.

apprentice n TRAINEE, learner, pupil, student, beginner, novice, probationer, neophyte, cub, tyro; informal rookie; N. Amer. informal greenhorn.

approach v ❶ REACH, come/draw near, come/draw close, near, move/advance towards, bear down on. ❷ APPEAL TO, make overtures to, proposition, solicit, sound out. ❸ SET ABOUT, tackle, begin, start, make a start on, embark on, commence, undertake. ❹ COME NEAR / CLOSE TO, compare with, be comparable with, approximate to.
– OPPOSITES leave.
▶ n ❶ METHOD, procedure, way, style, attitude, manner, technique, means, mode, modus

operandi. ❷ APPEAL, application, proposal, overture, proposition. ❸ COMING NEAR, advance, arrival, advent. ❹ DRIVE, driveway, avenue, access road.

approachable adj FRIENDLY, open, affable, relaxed, accessible, sympathetic, well disposed.
– OPPOSITES aloof.

appropriate adj SUITABLE, fitting, right, apt, timely, applicable, seemly, proper, becoming, correct, well judged, relevant, germane, well suited, pertinent, apposite, opportune, apropos.
– OPPOSITES inappropriate.
▶ v ❶ TAKE OVER, take possession of, seize, confiscate, requisition, commandeer, annex, expropriate, arrogate. ❷ STEAL, embezzle, misappropriate, pilfer, purloin, pocket; *informal* filch, swipe; *Brit. informal* nick, pinch.

approval n ❶ ADMIRATION, acceptance, praise, liking, support, favour, appreciation, respect, esteem, commendation, approbation. ❷ ACCEPTANCE, agreement, endorsement, authorization, confirmation, assent, consent, ratification, sanction, blessing, permission, mandate, concurrence, acquiescence, licence, seal, validation, imprimatur; *informal* OK, thumbs up, go-ahead, green light.
– OPPOSITES disapproval, rejection, refusal.

approve v ❶ BE PLEASED WITH, think well of, like, look on with favour, give one's blessing to, hold in regard/esteem, admire, respect, praise. ❷ AGREE TO, accept, consent to, permit, pass, allow, sanction, authorize, bless, support, back, uphold, endorse, ratify, validate, accede to, countenance; *informal* go along with, rubberstamp.
– OPPOSITES disapprove, condemn, refuse, veto.

approximate adj ROUGH, estimated, near, close, inexact, imprecise, loose.
– OPPOSITES exact.
■ **approximate** v BE CLOSE/NEAR TO, come near to, approach, border on, verge on, resemble, be similar to, roughly equal.

approximately adv ROUGHLY, about, round about, around, just about, circa, more or less, nearly, close to, near to, in the region/neighbourhood of, approaching, almost, not far off.
– OPPOSITES precisely.

apt adj ❶ SUITABLE, appropriate, fitting, applicable, apposite, felicitous. ❷ LIKELY, inclined, prone, liable, given, disposed.
– OPPOSITES inappropriate, unlikely.

aptitude n TALENT, ability, gift, skill, flair, knack, bent, capability, capacity, faculty.

arbiter n JUDGE, authority, determiner, controller, director, governor, expert, master, pundit.

arbitrary adj ❶ CAPRICIOUS,

unreasonable, whimsical, irrational, illogical, personal, subjective, random, chance, erratic, wilful, unreasoned, inconsistent, unpredictable, unplanned, unjustified. ❷ DICTATORIAL, despotic, autocratic, absolute, tyrannical, imperious, domineering, high-handed.
– OPPOSITES rational, reasoned.

arbitrate V ADJUDICATE, judge, referee, sit in judgement, mediate, umpire, settle, decide, determine, decide the outcome of.

arbitration n ADJUDICATION, judgement, settlement, decision, determination, mediation, negotiation, good offices.

arbitrator n ADJUDICATOR, judge, referee, umpire, arbiter, ombudsman, mediator, negotiator, intermediary, go-between, peacemaker.

arc n CURVE, bend, bow, crescent, semicircle, half-moon, arch, curvature.

arch[1] n ARCHWAY, vault, span, bridge.
▶ v CURVE, bend, bow, arc.

arch[2] adj PLAYFUL, mischievous, roguish, artful, sly, knowing.

archetype n PROTOTYPE, example, pattern, model, original, standard, ideal, paradigm, precursor.

architect n ❶ DESIGNER, planner, building consultant, draughtsman. ❷ CREATOR, author, engineer, originator, planner, deviser, instigator, founder, prime mover.

ardent adj PASSIONATE, fervent, impassioned, eager, enthusiastic, intense, keen, zealous, vehement, fierce.
– OPPOSITES apathetic.

arduous adj HARD, difficult, demanding, exhausting, laborious, strenuous, tiring, gruelling, punishing, tough, onerous, heavy, rigorous, backbreaking, taxing, Herculean.
– OPPOSITES easy, effortless.

area n ❶ REGION, district, environment, vicinity, locality, zone, territory, neighbourhood, environs, terrain, sector, quarter, province, precinct, realm, domain. ❷ FIELD, subject, sphere, discipline, sector, realm. ❸ SIZE, extent, expanse, measurement, space, compass, range, square footage, acreage, dimensions.

argue v ❶ CLAIM, maintain, hold, reason, insist, contend, declare, assert, demonstrate, make a case, plead, suggest. ❷ QUARREL, differ, disagree, fall out, have an argument, bicker, have words, bandy words, fight, squabble, debate, dispute, answer back, object, take exception, wrangle, feud, remonstrate; *informal* row. ❸ DISPUTE, debate, discuss.

argument n ❶ DISAGREEMENT, quarrel, fight, squabble, dispute, difference of opinion, falling-out, altercation, wrangle, conflict, clash, feud, controversy, remonstration; *informal* row, tiff, set-to, dust-up. ❷ CASE, reasoning, reasons, line of reasoning, grounds, logic, evidence, polemic, argumentation. ❸ SUBJECT MATTER, theme, topic, gist, outline, storyline, summary, synopsis, abstract, precis.

argumentative adj QUARRELSOME, contentious, combative, belligerent, disputatious, litigious.

arid adj ❶ DRY, dried up, waterless, parched, moistureless, scorched, desiccated, barren, infertile, desert, lifeless, sterile. ❷ DULL, tedious, dreary, dry, boring, uninteresting, monotonous, flat, vapid, lifeless. – OPPOSITES wet, fertile, interesting.

arise v ❶ COME TO LIGHT, turn/crop up, emerge, occur, begin, come into being. *See also* APPEAR. ❷ RESULT, be caused, originate, follow, proceed, emanate, ensue.

aristocracy n NOBILITY, peerage, upper class, gentry, high society, elite, ruling class, patriciate; *informal* upper crust.

aristocratic adj ❶ NOBLE, titled, high-born, blue-blooded, upper-class, patrician. ❷ WELL BRED, dignified, refined, courtly, elegant, gracious, haughty, proud.

arm¹ n ❶ INLET, creek, cove, fjord, bay, estuary, firth, sound. ❷ BRANCH, department, section, wing, division, sector, offshoot, extension.

arm² v EQUIP, supply, provide, issue, furnish.

armaments pl n WEAPONS, guns, arms, firearms, weaponry, munitions, ordnance.

armistice n CEASEFIRE, truce, peace, treaty, agreement, suspension of hostilities.

armoury n ARSENAL, arms depot, ammunition dump, magazine, ordnance depot.

army n ❶ ARMED FORCE, troops, soldiers, infantry, land force, soldiery. ❷ CROWD, horde, throng, swarm, pack, host, multitude, mob.

aroma n SMELL, scent, odour, fragrance, perfume, bouquet, savour; *poetic/literary* redolence.

arouse v ❶ INDUCE, prompt, trigger, kindle, provoke, engender, stir up, spark off. ❷ WAKE, wake up, awaken, rouse. – OPPOSITES allay.

arrange v ❶ PUT IN ORDER, set out, sort, lay out, organize, position, group, sift, align, tidy, file, rank, classify, categorize, array, systematize. ❷ FIX, settle on, set up, agree, determine, plan, organize, schedule, bring about, coordinate, make preparations for. ❸ SCORE, adapt, set, orchestrate, harmonize. – OPPOSITES disturb, cancel.

arrangement n ❶ ORDER, ordering, organization, positioning, grouping, distribution, disposition, system, alignment, filing, marshalling, ranging, spacing, tabulation. ❷ AGREEMENT, plan, deal, contract, compact, bargain, pact, understanding, settlement, terms, preparations, provisions. ❸ SCORE, orchestration, adaptation, instrumentation, setting, harmonization.

array n ❶ ARRANGEMENT, collection, line-up, formation, presentation, display, exhibition, show, parade, assemblage, muster. ❷ DRESS, attire, clothing, garments, garb, finery; *formal* apparel.
▶ v ❶ *See* ARRANGE (1). ❷ CLOTHE, dress, fit out, adorn, garb, rig out, deck, robe, accoutre.

arrest v ❶ TAKE INTO CUSTODY, apprehend, take prisoner, capture, detain, seize, catch, lay hold of; *informal* pick up, pinch, collar, haul in, nab, bust, run in; *Brit. informal* nick. ❷ STOP, halt, block, end, prevent, obstruct, hinder, impede, interrupt, delay, slow down, bring to a standstill, check, restrain, stem, retard, nip in the bud.
– OPPOSITES release, start.
▶ n APPREHENSION, capture, detention, seizure, taking into custody.
– OPPOSITES release.

arresting adj STRIKING, remarkable, extraordinary, impressive, outstanding, unusual, stunning, conspicuous, noticeable.
– OPPOSITES inconspicuous.

arrival n ❶ COMING, appearance, approach, advent, entrance, entry, occurrence. ❷ VISITOR, incomer, guest, immigrant, newcomer, caller.
– OPPOSITES departure, leaver.

arrive v ❶ COME, appear, enter, get here/there, turn up,

get in, put in/make an appearance, drop by/in; *informal* show up, roll in/up, blow in. ❷ *See* SUCCEED (1).
– OPPOSITES leave, depart.

arrogant adj HAUGHTY, proud, conceited, self-important, pompous, overbearing, patronizing, superior, high-handed, egotistical, condescending, snobbish, disdainful, imperious, lordly, swaggering, presumptuous, cocky, boastful, supercilious, overweening, blustering, insolent; *informal* stuck up, high and mighty, snooty, uppity.
– OPPOSITES modest, diffident.

art n ❶ PAINTING, drawing, fine art, design, visual art. ❷ SKILL, craft, talent, flair, aptitude, gift, knack, facility, technique, proficiency, expertise, ingenuity, skilfulness, mastery, dexterity, virtuosity, adroitness.

artful adj CUNNING, sly, wily, clever, shrewd, canny, crafty, devious, tricky, subtle, ingenious, astute, scheming, designing; *informal* smart, foxy; *Brit. informal* fly.
– OPPOSITES ingenuous.

article n ❶ THING, object, item, commodity. ❷ STORY, piece, item, account, report, feature, column.

articulate adj FLUENT, eloquent, lucid, expressive, clear, comprehensible, coherent, intelligible, understandable, glib, silver-tongued.
– OPPOSITES inarticulate.
▶ v ENUNCIATE, say, utter,

express, pronounce, vocalize, voice.

articulated adj HINGED, jointed, segmented, flexible, bendy.

artifice n TRICKERY, cunning, deceit, deception, craftiness, artfulness, slyness, duplicity, guile, chicanery.

artificial adj ❶ MANUFACTURED, man-made, fabricated, synthetic, imitation, simulated, ersatz. ❷ FALSE, affected, fake, unnatural, insincere, forced, sham, contrived, pretended, assumed, put on, mock, unreal, feigned, bogus, pseudo, laboured, hollow, spurious, meretricious; *informal* phoney.
– OPPOSITES natural, genuine.

artist n ❶ PAINTER, drawer, sculptor, old master. ❷ CRAFTSMAN, craftswoman, expert, master, past master, genius, adept. ❸ See PERFORMER.

artistic adj ❶ CREATIVE, imaginative, talented, gifted, accomplished, sensitive, cultured, cultivated. ❷ ATTRACTIVE, tasteful, decorative, beautiful, stylish, elegant, graceful, aesthetic, ornamental, exquisite.
– OPPOSITES ugly.

artistry n SKILL, art, talent, ability, flair, gift, expertise, creativity, proficiency, craftsmanship, workmanship, brilliance.

ascend v CLIMB, go/move up, rise, mount, soar, take off, lift off, fly up, levitate, scale.
– OPPOSITES descend.

ascendancy n DOMINATION, dominance, control, authority, power, rule, command, supremacy, sway, mastery, sovereignty, the upper hand.

ascent n CLIMB, rise, hill, slope, ascension, gradient, ramp.
– OPPOSITES descent.

ascertain v FIND OUT, establish, discover, learn, determine, decide, identify, confirm, make certain, get to know, verify, make sure/certain, settle, pin down.

ascribe v ATTRIBUTE, put down, assign, impute, credit, accredit, chalk up, lay on, blame, charge with.

ashamed adj ❶ EMBARRASSED, shamefaced, sorry, apologetic, sheepish, red-faced, blushing, humiliated, conscience-stricken, remorseful, mortified, crestfallen, discomfited, bashful, contrite, penitent, repentant, rueful, chagrined; *informal* with one's tail between one's legs. ❷ RELUCTANT, loath, unwilling, indisposed.
– OPPOSITES proud, shameless.

asinine adj IDIOTIC, stupid, foolish, nonsensical, ridiculous, half-witted, imbecilic, fatuous, moronic; *informal* batty, nutty, dumb, gormless; *Brit. informal* daft.
– OPPOSITES intelligent, sensible.

ask v ❶ QUESTION, inquire, query, quiz, put a question to, interrogate, cross-examine, give the third degree to; *informal* grill, pump. ❷ REQUEST, demand, appeal to, apply to, beg, solicit, implore, plead, seek, supplicate; *poetic/literary* beseech. ❸ INVITE, summon, bid. – OPPOSITES answer.

asleep adj ❶ SLEEPING, fast/ sound asleep, in a deep sleep, dozing, resting, slumbering, snoozing, napping, catnapping, reposing, comatose, unconscious, sedated, dormant; *informal* out like a light, dead to the world; *Brit. informal* kipping; *humorous* in the land of Nod. ❷ NUMB, without feeling, deadened. – OPPOSITES awake.

aspect n ❶ FEATURE, viewpoint, facet, side, circumstance, angle, characteristic, element, light, standpoint, slant, attribute. ❷ APPEARANCE, look, expression, features, air, manner, demeanour, bearing, countenance, mien, visage. ❸ DIRECTION, outlook, prospect, orientation, view, exposure, situation, location, position.

asphyxiate v SUFFOCATE, choke, smother, stifle, strangle, throttle, strangulate.

aspiration n AIM, desire, objective, ambition, goal, wish, hope, dream, longing, yearning, craving, eagerness, enthusiasm.

aspire v DESIRE, hope to/for, long for/to, wish to/for, dream of, yearn for/to, seek, pursue, crave, hunger for.

aspiring adj WOULD-BE, potential, hopeful, expectant, ambi-

tious, optimistic, wishful, striving.

assail v ATTACK, assault, set on/ upon, fall on, rush, storm; *informal* lay into, tear into, pitch into.

assassin n MURDERER, killer, executioner, contract killer, liquidator; *informal* hit man; *poetic/ literary* slayer.

assassinate v MURDER, kill, execute, eliminate, liquidate; *informal* hit; *poetic/literary* slay.

assault v ❶ ATTACK, charge, storm, rush at, set about/on, strike at. ❷ STRIKE, hit, attack, beat up, aim blows at; *informal* lay into, pitch into, wade into, do over. ❸ MOLEST, rape, sexually assault, interfere with.

assemble v ❶ COME TOGETHER, collect, gather, congregate, meet, convene, join up, flock together, converge, rally round, throng around. ❷ BRING/ PUT TOGETHER, collect, gather, round up, summon, muster, mobilize, accumulate, marshal, rally, amass; *formal* convoke. ❸ CONSTRUCT, build, erect, put together, set up, piece together, fit together, fabricate, manufacture, connect, join. – OPPOSITES disperse, dismantle.

assembly n GATHERING, meeting, crowd, group, congregation, throng, rally, convention, conference, congress, conclave, synod; *informal* get-together. *See also* CROWD.

assent n AGREEMENT, consent, acceptance, approval,

permission, sanction, acquiescence, compliance, accord, accordance, approbation.
– OPPOSITES dissent.
▶ ▼ AGREE, accept, consent, be willing, comply, approve, acquiesce, concede, concur, give one's permission, submit, yield, accede.
– OPPOSITES refuse.

assert v ❶ DECLARE, state, maintain, proclaim, pronounce, emphasize, insist on, profess, claim, swear to, stress, affirm, avow; *formal* aver. ❷ UPHOLD, insist on, stand up for, defend, press/push for, vindicate.
■ **assert oneself** BEHAVE CONFIDENTLY, make one's presence felt, stand up for oneself, exert one's influence.

assertive adj CONFIDENT, self-assured, assured, forceful, pushy, strong-willed, positive, authoritative, dominant, domineering, strong, aggressive, decisive, firm, definite, emphatic, uncompromising, stubborn, opinionated; *informal* bossy.

assess v JUDGE, evaluate, estimate, gauge, appraise, weigh up, rate, determine, reckon, work out, assay, compute, calculate, fix; *informal* size up.

asset n ADVANTAGE, benefit, strength, strong point, help, aid, resource, support, blessing, boon, godsend.
■ **assets** WEALTH, money, resources, capital, means, property, possessions, belongings,

holdings, goods, valuables, reserves, securities, estate, effects, chattels.

assiduous adj DILIGENT, industrious, hard-working, persistent, indefatigable, zealous, persevering, sedulous.

assign v ❶ ALLOCATE, allot, distribute, share out, give out, dispense, apportion, consign. ❷ APPOINT, select for, nominate, designate, name, install, delegate, commission. ❸ ASCRIBE, put down, attribute, accredit, credit, chalk up. ❹ TRANSFER, make over, convey.

assignation n RENDEZVOUS, date, meeting, appointment; *poetic/literary* tryst.

assignment n ❶ TASK, job, duty, mission, responsibility, obligation, charge, commission. ❷ ALLOCATION, distribution, allotment, apportionment, dispensation, consignment. ❸ TRANSFER, making over, handing down, consignment.

assimilate v ❶ ABSORB, take in, incorporate, ingest, digest. ❷ ADAPT, adjust, accustom, become like, acclimatize, blend in, homogenize.

assist v ❶ HELP, help out, aid, support, lend a hand, rally round, cooperate with, collaborate with, work with, play a part, abet, succour. ❷ FACILITATE, make easier, boost, further, promote, expedite.
– OPPOSITES impede, hinder.

assistance n HELP, aid, support, cooperation, collabor-

ation, succour, a (helping) hand, encouragement, patronage, sponsorship, subsidy, contribution.
– OPPOSITES hindrance, impedance.

assistant n ❶ DEPUTY, subordinate, second-in-command, auxiliary, right-hand man/woman, man/girl Friday, henchman, minion. ❷ HELPER, collaborator, associate, partner, colleague, mainstay, accessory, abetter. ❸ SHOP / SALES ASSISTANT, salesperson, salesman, saleswoman, checkout operator, server; N. Amer. clerk.

associate v ❶ LINK, connect, identify, equate, bracket, relate. ❷ MIX, socialize, keep company, mingle, fraternize; informal hobnob, run/go around, hang out. ❸ AFFILIATE, connect, combine, join, attach, band together, team up, ally, incorporate, syndicate.
– OPPOSITES dissociate.

association n FEDERATION, affiliation, alliance, partnership, union, confederation, syndicate, coalition, combination, league, fellowship, merger, cartel, consortium, club.

assorted adj MIXED, varied, various, diverse, miscellaneous, sundry, multifarious, manifold, motley, heterogeneous, variegated; poetic/literary divers.

assortment n MIXTURE, selection, variety, collection, range, jumble, miscellany, medley, diversity, melange,

farrago, pot-pourri, mishmash, hotchpotch.

assume v ❶ SUPPOSE, presume, think, presuppose, take for granted, believe, suspect, understand, expect, imagine, guess, gather, surmise, fancy. ❷ TAKE ON, adopt, take up, acquire, put on, affect, come to have, don. ❸ UNDERTAKE, accept, take upon oneself, shoulder, embark on, enter upon. ❹ SEIZE, take over, appropriate, commandeer, usurp, pre-empt.

assumption n SUPPOSITION, presumption, belief, hypothesis, presupposition, theory, suspicion, guess, expectation, conjecture, surmise, premise.

assurance n ❶ SELF-CONFIDENCE, confidence, self-assurance, poise, nerve. ❷ GUARANTEE, commitment, word, promise, undertaking, oath, pledge, affirmation.

assure v ❶ DECLARE, give one's word, affirm, guarantee, promise, swear, pledge, certify, vow, attest. ❷ ENSURE, make sure/certain, guarantee, confirm, secure, clinch, seal.

assured adj CONFIDENT, self-confident, self-assured, self-reliant, poised, positive.

astonish v AMAZE, astound, stagger, stun, surprise, dumbfound, leave speechless, take someone's breath away, take aback, startle, stupefy, daze, bewilder, dazzle; informal flabbergast, floor, wow.

astonishing adj AMAZING, astounding, staggering, surprising, breathtaking, striking, stunning, bewildering, impressive.
– OPPOSITES unremarkable.

astound v SEE ASTONISH.

astray adv & adj ❶ OFF COURSE, lost, off the right track, adrift. ❷ WRONG, into sin, into wrongdoing, into error; informal off the rails.

astute adj SHREWD, clever, quick, quick-witted, acute, cunning, intelligent, sly, artful, knowing, canny, ingenious, perceptive, observant, crafty, wily, calculating, perspicacious, sagacious; informal foxy; Brit. informal fly.
– OPPOSITES stupid, dull.

asylum n ❶ REFUGE, sanctuary, shelter, safety, protection, safe keeping, haven, retreat, harbour, port in a storm. ❷ MENTAL HOSPITAL, psychiatric hospital, institution; informal loony bin, madhouse, funny farm.

asymmetrical adj UNEVEN, irregular, crooked, distorted, lopsided, unbalanced, misshapen, malformed.
– OPPOSITES symmetrical.

atheist n UNBELIEVER, disbeliever, non-believer, sceptic, freethinker, heretic, heathen, pagan, infidel.
– OPPOSITES believer.

athletic adj ❶ MUSCULAR, strong, well built, powerful, fit, active, energetic, sturdy, robust, strapping, wiry, hardy, vigorous, brawny. ❷ SPORTING, sports, gymnastics.
– OPPOSITES puny.

atmosphere n ❶ AIR, sky, aerospace, stratosphere; poetic/literary heavens, ether. ❷ ENVIRONMENT, climate, mood, feeling, spirit, ambience, surroundings, setting, milieu, character, tone, quality, flavour, vibrations, aura, tenor; informal vibes.

atom n BIT, particle, scrap, shred, speck, spot, fragment, jot, trace, iota, dot, crumb, grain, morsel; informal smidgen.

atone v MAKE AMENDS, compensate, pay for, be punished, do penance, answer, pay the penalty/price, make reparations, redeem oneself, redress, expiate.

atrocious adj ❶ WICKED, vicious, brutal, barbaric, evil, dreadful, horrific, horrifying, sickening, abominable, savage, cruel, murderous, frightful, revolting, villainous, heinous, ruthless, monstrous, inhuman, gruesome, hideous, fiendish, diabolical, outrageous, vile. ❷ VERY BAD, terrible, appalling, dreadful.
– OPPOSITES commendable, excellent.

atrocity n OUTRAGE, crime, offence, horror, abomination, monstrosity, violation, evil.

atrophy v WASTE AWAY, wither, shrivel, decay, wilt, deteriorate, decline, degenerate.

attach v ❶ FASTEN, stick, affix, join, connect, link, tie, couple, pin, hitch, bond, add, append,

annex. ❷ PLACE, put, ascribe, assign, attribute, lay, impute, invest with. ❸ ASSIGN, appoint, second, allocate, detail.
– OPPOSITES detach.

attached adj ❶ MARRIED, engaged, spoken for, having a partner. ❷ FOND OF, devoted to, having a regard for.

attack v ❶ ASSAULT, set on/upon, beat up, strike, strike at, rush, storm, charge, pounce upon, beset, besiege, beleaguer; *informal* lay/wade into, let someone have it, do over. ❷ CRITICIZE, berate, reprove, censure, rebuke, find fault with, denounce, revile, blame, harangue, vilify, snipe at, fulminate against, impugn, malign, inveigh against, traduce. ❸ BEGIN, set about, get/go to work on, get started on, embark on, undertake.
– OPPOSITES defend, praise.
▶ n ❶ ASSAULT, offensive, raid, ambush, sortie, onslaught, charge, strike, invasion, rush, foray, incursion, battery, bombardment. ❷ CRITICISM, abuse, censure, outburst, tirade, rebuke, reproval, vilification, diatribe, impugnment, invective. ❸ FIT, seizure, bout, spasm, convulsion, paroxysm, stroke.

attacker n ASSAILANT, aggressor, assaulter, mugger, opponent, raider, critic, detractor, persecutor, slanderer.

attain v ACHIEVE, accomplish, gain, obtain, get, win, earn, acquire, reach, realize, arrive at,

fulfil, succeed in, bring off, grasp, secure, procure.

attempt v TRY, strive, endeavour, tackle, seek, set out to, venture, aim, undertake, make an effort, bid; *informal* have a go/shot at, give something a whirl, have a crack at.
▶ n TRY, effort, endeavour, venture, undertaking; *informal* go, shot, crack.

attend v ❶ BE PRESENT, be at, be there/here, appear, put in an appearance, turn up, visit, show, frequent, haunt; *informal* show up. ❷ PAY ATTENTION, listen, concentrate, follow, heed, pay heed, take note, notice, mark, watch. ❸ LOOK AFTER, take care of, care for, nurse, tend, see to, mind, minister to. ❹ ESCORT, accompany, guard, follow, chaperone, squire, usher, convoy.

attendant n ❶ STEWARD, waiter, waitress, porter, servant. ❷ ESCORT, companion, retainer, aide, lady in waiting, equerry, chaperone.
▶ adj RELATED, accompanying, consequent, resulting, concomitant, accessory.

attention n ❶ CONCENTRATION, attentiveness, notice, observation, scrutiny, heed, regard, diligence, thought, thinking, studying. ❷ NOTICE, awareness, recognition, regard, consciousness. ❸ CARE, treatment, therapy, ministration. ❹ OVERTURES, approaches, suit, wooing, compliments, flattery; *dated* courting.

attentive adj ❶ ALERT, aware, watchful, awake, observant, wide awake, vigilant, intent, mindful, on guard, heedful. ❷ CONSIDERATE, thoughtful, conscientious, polite, kind, obliging, accommodating, gallant. – OPPOSITES inattentive.

attire n CLOTHING, dress, clothes, garments, garb, costume, outfit, wear, ensemble, accoutrements; *informal* gear, togs, glad rags, rig; *formal* apparel; *archaic* habit.
▶ v *see* DRESS V (1).

attitude n ❶ VIEW, point of view, opinion, viewpoint, outlook, belief, standpoint, frame of mind, position, approach, perspective, reaction, stance, thoughts, ideas. ❷ POSITION, pose, stance, bearing, carriage; *Brit.* deportment.

attract v ❶ APPEAL TO, interest, fascinate, charm, entice, captivate, tempt, engage, bewitch, seduce, beguile, lure, allure, inveigle; *informal* turn on. ❷ CAUSE, generate, encourage, provoke, incite, stir up. ❸ DRAW, pull, magnetize. – OPPOSITES repel.

attractive adj ❶ GOOD-LOOKING, beautiful, handsome, pretty, lovely, stunning, striking, gorgeous, irresistible, glamorous, desirable, appealing, captivating, fascinating, charming, adorable, enchanting, alluring, enticing, seductive, bewitching, fetching, prepossessing, winsome; *informal* tasty; *N. Amer. informal* cute; *archaic* comely. ❷ APPEALING, agreeable, interesting, tempting, pleasing, inviting. – OPPOSITES ugly, uninviting.

attribute n QUALITY, feature, characteristic, property, mark, sign, trait, indicator, distinction, idiosyncrasy.
▶ v ASCRIBE, assign, put down, accredit, credit, impute, chalk up, lay at the door of.

attrition n ❶ WEAKENING, wearing down, debilitation, sapping, enfeebling. ❷ ABRASION, friction, rubbing, corroding, corroding, erosion, wearing/eating away, grinding, scraping, excoriation.

attune v ACCUSTOM, adjust, familiarize, adapt, acclimatize.

audacious adj BOLD, daring, fearless, brave, courageous, adventurous, intrepid, valiant, plucky, reckless, brazen, daredevil; *informal* gutsy. – OPPOSITES timid.

audacity n ❶ BOLDNESS, daring, fearlessness, bravery, courage, valour, pluck; *Brit. informal* guts. *See also* COURAGE. ❷ EFFRONTERY, cheek, impudence, brazenness, impertinence, shamelessness, presumption; *informal* sauce. – OPPOSITES timidity.

audible adj DISCERNIBLE, perceptible, clear, distinct, recognizable, hearable, detectable. – OPPOSITES inaudible, faint.

audience n ❶ SPECTATORS, LISTENERS, viewers, onlookers, crowd, gathering, assembly, house, turnout, congregation, gallery. ❷ INTERVIEW, meeting, hearing, consultation, discussion, reception.

audit n INSPECTION, examination, investigation, scrutiny, review, check.
▶ v INSPECT, examine, review, check, scrutinize, investigate, go over/through.

augment v INCREASE, enlarge, make larger/greater, add to, expand, multiply, grow, extend, boost, enhance, raise, inflate, heighten, strengthen, intensify, amplify, swell, supplement, magnify.
– OPPOSITES decrease, diminish.

augur v BE A SIGN OF, bode, foretell, predict, herald, prophesy, foreshadow, harbinger, portend, forecast, presage.

august adj DIGNIFIED, solemn, stately, majestic, noble, imposing, impressive, exalted, grand, illustrious.
– OPPOSITES obscure, insignificant.

auspicious adj FAVOURABLE, promising, hopeful, encouraging, bright, fortunate, propitious, timely, felicitous.
– OPPOSITES inauspicious.

austere adj ❶ PLAIN, severe, simple, unadorned, unornamented, stark, subdued, sombre, unembellished. ❷ STERN, formal, serious, solemn, severe, cold, distant, aloof, stiff, forbidding, unsmiling, unbending, unyielding, harsh, rigorous, stringent, un-

relenting. ❸ STRICT, abstemious, disciplined, puritanical, spartan, frugal, ascetic, self-denying, restrained, chaste, celibate, abstinent.
– OPPOSITES elaborate, genial, immoderate.

authentic adj ❶ GENUINE, real, true, bona fide, actual, legitimate, valid, legitimate; informal the real McCoy. ❷ TRUE, accurate, honest, credible, reliable, dependable; informal straight from the horse's mouth.
– OPPOSITES fake, unreliable.

authenticate v VERIFY, validate, confirm, substantiate, certify, guarantee, endorse, ratify.

author n ❶ WRITER, composer, novelist, dramatist, playwright, poet, screenwriter, essayist, journalist, reporter, columnist. ❷ CREATOR, originator, producer, designer, architect, planner, cause, prime mover, maker, initiator, inventor; poetic/literary begetter.

authoritarian adj DICTATORIAL, tyrannical, strict, domineering, despotic, autocratic, imperious, harsh, Draconian, disciplinarian, dogmatic; informal bossy.
– OPPOSITES democratic, liberal.

authoritative adj ❶ RELIABLE, accurate, authentic, sound, dependable, factual, definitive, valid, certified. ❷ CONFIDENT, self-assured, assertive, commanding, masterful,

imposing, arrogant, overbearing, imperious.
– OPPOSITES unreliable, timid.

authority n ❶ RIGHT, power, jurisdiction, authorization, influence, might, prerogative, rule, command, charge, dominion, sovereignty, supremacy, ascendancy; *informal* say-so. ❷ PERMISSION, authorization, consent, sanction, licence, mandate, warrant. ❸ GOVERNMENT, administration, officialdom, management, establishment, bureaucracy; *informal* powers that be. ❹ EXPERT, specialist, master, scholar, pundit, adept.

authorize v PERMIT, allow, agree to, give permission, consent to, approve, sanction, endorse, back, license, ratify, legalize, certify, countenance, give leave to, warrant, commission; *informal* give the go-ahead for, give the green light to.

authorized adj *see* OFFICIAL.

automatic adj ❶ AUTOMATED, mechanical, mechanized, electronic, self-regulating, self-activating, push-button, programmable, robotic. ❷ INSTINCTIVE, spontaneous, involuntary, unconscious, reflex, habitual, natural, unintentional, unthinking, mechanical, conditioned. ❸ INEVITABLE, routine, certain, assured.
– OPPOSITES manual, deliberate.

autonomous adj INDEPENDENT, free, self-governing, sovereign.

autonomy n INDEPENDENCE, self-determination, self-sufficiency, individualism, autarchy.

auxiliary adj SECONDARY, subsidiary, subordinate, ancillary, supporting, additional, extra, reserve, back-up, spare, supplementary, substitute.

available adj FREE, untaken, obtainable, to hand, handy, procurable, unoccupied, vacant, usable, ready, convenient, accessible, employable.
– OPPOSITES unavailable, inaccessible.

avarice n GREED, acquisitiveness, covetousness, materialism, meanness, miserliness.
– OPPOSITES generosity.

avaricious adj GREEDY, grasping, covetous, acquisitive, miserly, parsimonious; *informal* tight-fisted, stingy.
– OPPOSITES generous.

average adj ❶ NORMAL, typical, ordinary, common, regular, usual, commonplace, everyday, widespread, unexceptional, medium, middling, moderate; *informal* run-of-the-mill. ❷ MEDIOCRE, unexceptional, moderate, second-rate, pedestrian, banal.
– OPPOSITES exceptional, outstanding.
▶ n MEAN, midpoint, median, centre, norm, standard, rule, yardstick.
▶ v EVEN OUT, equalize, normalize, standardize.

averse adj OPPOSED, hostile, antagonistic, unwilling, disinclined, reluctant, resistant, loath, ill-disposed.

aversion n DISLIKE, distaste, hatred, repugnance, antipathy, reluctance, unwillingness, evasion, avoidance, shunning.
– OPPOSITES liking, inclination.

avid adj KEEN, eager, enthusiastic, fervent, dedicated, ardent, fanatical, zealous, passionate.
– OPPOSITES apathetic, indifferent.

avoid v ❶ EVADE, elude, hide from, keep away from, keep clear of, shun, ignore, dodge, steer clear of, give a wide berth to, shirk, eschew; *informal* duck. ❷ ABSTAIN FROM, circumvent, refrain from, bypass; *Brit. informal* skive off.
– OPPOSITES face, seek.

await v ❶ ANTICIPATE, expect, wait for, hope for, look out for. ❷ BE IN STORE FOR, wait for, be ready for, lie ahead for, lie in wait for, be round the corner.

awake adj ❶ WAKEFUL, sleepless, wide awake, insomniac, open-eyed, restless, tossing and turning. ❷ AWARE, alert, conscious, attentive, vigilant.
– OPPOSITES asleep, unaware.

awaken v ❶ WAKE, wake up, awake, waken, rouse, call, alert. ❷ KINDLE, arouse, stimulate, call forth, stir up, excite, revive.

award n ❶ PRIZE, reward, trophy, honour, decoration, medal, badge, cup, grant, scholarship. ❷ GIFT, grant, conferment, bestowal, presentation.
▶ v CONFER, present, give, grant, accord, allot, assign, bestow, endow.

aware adj CONSCIOUS, alive to, informed, knowledgeable, familiar, acquainted, mindful, heedful, sensitive, responsive, observant, attentive, sensible, conversant, cognizant, versed in.
– OPPOSITES ignorant, insensitive.

awareness n CONSCIOUSNESS, perception, realization, knowledge, sense, feeling, understanding, sensitivity, perceptiveness.
– OPPOSITES ignorance, insensitivity.

awe n WONDER, amazement, admiration, reverence, veneration, respect, dread, fear.

awesome adj BREATHTAKING, awe-inspiring, magnificent, stupendous, overwhelming, sublime, majestic, solemn, imposing, dramatic, grand, formidable, marvellous, amazing, staggering, stunning, fearful, impressive; *informal* mind-blowing; *poetic/literary* wondrous. *See also* WONDERFUL.
– OPPOSITES unimpressive.

awful adj ❶ *see* BAD. ❷ *See* AWESOME.

awfully adv ❶ VERY, extremely, intensely, deeply, exceedingly; *informal* terribly, dreadfully; *Brit. informal* ever so; *informal, dated* frightfully.

❷ TERRIBLY, badly, dreadfully, appallingly, atrociously, disgracefully, frightfully.

awkward adj ❶ UNWIELDY, cumbersome, unmanageable, inconvenient, bulky. ❷ INCONVENIENT, difficult, troublesome, problematic, unhelpful, unsuitable. ❸ TRICKY, difficult, perplexing, taxing, puzzling, thorny, troublesome, trying, vexed. ❹ UNCOOPERATIVE, unhelpful, disobliging, contrary, obstructive, perverse, troublesome, trying, exasperating, obstinate, stubborn, refractory, intractable; *Brit. informal* bloody-minded, bolshie; *N. Amer.* ornery. ❺ CLUMSY, blundering, bungling, ungainly, uncoordinated, inelegant, inexpert, clownish, inept, unskilled, maladroit, gawky, gauche, wooden; *informal* ham-fisted. ❻ UNCOMFORTABLE, uneasy, strained, embarrassing, unnatural; *informal* edgy.
– OPPOSITES convenient, handy, cooperative, graceful, skilful, relaxed.

Bb

babble v CHATTER, prattle, burble, gabble, jabber, gibber, murmur, mutter; *informal* waffle; *Brit. informal* rabbit.
▶ n CHATTER, chat, gabble, prattling, murmur, clamour.

baby n INFANT, newborn, child; *poetic/literary* babe; *technical* neonate.
▶ adj TINY, miniature, mini, little, dwarf, diminutive, minute.
▶ v COSSET, pamper, spoil, indulge, coddle, mollycoddle, pet.

babyish adj CHILDISH, infantile, immature, juvenile, puerile, silly, inane.
– OPPOSITES mature.

back n ❶ REAR, rear end, stern, tail end, hindquarters, posterior, end. ❷ REVERSE, reverse side, other side.
– OPPOSITES front.
▶ adj ❶ REAR, hind, end, hindmost, last. ❷ DORSAL, spinal.
– OPPOSITES front.
▶ v ❶ See SUPPORT v (5), UPHOLD. ❷ REVERSE, go backwards, move back, back away, back off, retreat, retire, recede, recoil, withdraw, backtrack.
■ **back down** see WITHDRAW (4).

backer n SUPPORTER, sponsor, promoter, patron, advocate, benefactor, champion, seconder; *informal* angel.

background n ❶ BACKDROP, setting, surroundings, context, circumstances, conditions, framework, environment. ❷ FAMILY, origins, ancestry,

upbringing, education, milieu, culture, training, tradition, experience, qualifications, credentials, history.
– OPPOSITES foreground.

backing n ❶ SUPPORT, encouragement, approval, endorsement, promotion, recommendation, assent, agreement, assistance, help, aid, sponsorship, funding, patronage, subsidy, funds, grant, loan. ❷ ACCOMPANIMENT, obbligato.

backlash n REACTION, recoil, rebound, response, retaliation, counterblast, repercussion, reversal.

backward adj ❶ REVERSE, retreating, rearward, retrograde, regressive, retrogressive. ❷ SLOW, late-starting, behind, behindhand, retarded, undeveloped, unprogressive, underdeveloped, disadvantaged, handicapped; dated subnormal. ❸ SHY, bashful, timid, diffident, hesitant, self-effacing, reticent, unforthcoming, reserved, unassertive, modest, coy, inhibited.
– OPPOSITES forward, advanced, precocious, confident.

bad adj ❶ POOR, inadequate, unsatisfactory, substandard, inferior, imperfect, defective, deficient, faulty, incompetent, inefficient, incorrect, unsound, useless, worthless, shoddy, abysmal, awful, appalling, disgraceful, atrocious, dreadful, frightful, hopeless, abominable; informal lousy, rotten, diabolical; Brit. informal grotty, ropy. ❷ UNSUITABLE, unpropitious, unfavourable, inappropriate, adverse, unhelpful, inconvenient, unlucky, dangerous, harmful, deleterious, detrimental, damaging, unhealthy, risky, injurious, hurtful, destructive. ❸ UNPLEASANT, disagreeable, nasty, horrid, horrible, harsh, unwelcome, gloomy, distressing, dreadful, awful, frightful, terrible, foul, appalling, atrocious. ❹ SERIOUS, severe, grave, dangerous, disastrous, calamitous, terrible, awful, dreadful, frightful, critical, acute, dire, hideous. ❺ IMMORAL, wicked, evil, wrong, corrupt, sinful, vicious, criminal, depraved, villainous, vile, rotten, delinquent, guilty, blameworthy, reprehensible, dishonest, dishonourable, ignoble, base, reprobate. ❻ NAUGHTY, mischievous, unruly, wayward, disobedient, disorderly. ❼ ROTTEN, decayed, mouldy, off, rancid, tainted, spoiled, sour, decomposing, putrid, contaminated, foul, polluted, mildewed, diseased. ❽ see ILL adj (1). ❾ REMORSEFUL, regretful, ashamed, guilty, sorry, unhappy, contrite, apologetic, penitent.
– OPPOSITES good, favourable, fine, fresh.

badge n EMBLEM, pin, crest, insignia, medal, token, sign, mark, symbol, logo, device, characteristic, trademark; N. Amer. button.

bad-tempered adj IRRITABLE,

short-tempered, quick-tempered, peevish, touchy, prickly, crotchety, irascible, cross, angry, ill-humoured, testy, quarrelsome, truculent, grumpy, acrimonious, querulous, petulant, gruff, sullen, moody, sulky, disgruntled, grumbling, scowling, churlish, cantankerous, dyspeptic, bilious, crabbed, shrewish; *informal* snappy; *Brit. informal* shirty.
– OPPOSITES good-humoured, affable.

baffle v ❶ BEWILDER, bemuse, mystify, perplex, puzzle, confuse, confound, nonplus, floor; *informal* flummox, bamboozle, stump. ❷ THWART, foil, frustrate, defeat, prevent, check, hinder, block, obstruct.

bag n HANDBAG, carrier bag, shoulder bag, case, grip, satchel, sack, holdall, rucksack, haversack, reticule.
▶ v ❶ CATCH, capture, shoot, kill, trap, snare, land. ❷ GET, gain, acquire, obtain, reserve, secure, get hold of.

baggage n LUGGAGE, bags, cases, belongings, things, equipment, accoutrements, paraphernalia, impedimenta; *informal* gear.

bait n LURE, attraction, enticement, temptation, incentive, inducement, bribe, decoy, carrot.
▶ v TEASE, provoke, goad, pester, annoy, harass, plague, torment, persecute, taunt; *informal* needle; *Brit. informal* wind up.

balance n ❶ STABILITY, poise, steadiness, equilibrium. ❷ CORRESPONDENCE, equivalence, symmetry, equality, parity, equipoise, evenness, proportion. ❸ REMAINDER, rest, difference, surplus, excess, residue. ❹ SCALES, weighing machine.
– OPPOSITES imbalance, instability.
▶ v ❶ KEEP BALANCED, poise, steady, stabilize, support. ❷ OFFSET, cancel out, counterbalance, match, compensate for, even up, level, equalize, parallel, counterpoise, counteract, neutralize.

bald adj ❶ HAIRLESS, bare, smooth, bald-headed; *informal* thin on top. ❷ BLUNT, frank, plain, straightforward, forthright, direct, not beating about the bush, stark, uncompromising, downright, simple, unadorned, unembellished.
– OPPOSITES hairy.

ball n SPHERE, globe, orb, globule, spheroid.

ballot n VOTE, poll, election, referendum, plebiscite.

ban v PROHIBIT, forbid, veto, outlaw, put a ban on, proscribe, suppress, disallow, interdict, bar, debar, prevent, restrict, exclude, banish, ostracize.
– OPPOSITES authorize, permit, sanction.
▶ n PROHIBITION, veto, embargo, boycott, bar, interdict, interdiction, proscription, restriction, taboo, suppression.

banal adj TRITE, clichéd, hackneyed, commonplace, unori-

ginal, cliché-ridden, unimaginative, uninspired, stale, boring, dull, everyday, stock, stereotyped, platitudinous, obvious, predictable, tired, pedestrian, humdrum, prosaic, vapid, fatuous; *informal* corny, old hat.
– OPPOSITES interesting, original.

band[1] n ❶ STRIPE, strip, line, belt, bar, streak, border, swathe. ❷ BRAID, belt, fillet, sash, tie, ribbon, cord, loop, girdle.

band[2] n ❶ GROUP, troop, crowd, crew, gang, company, body, pack, mob, horde, flock, bunch, gathering, party, throng, society, club, clique, set, association. ❷ ENSEMBLE, group, orchestra; *informal* combo.

bandit n BRIGAND, outlaw, robber, highwayman, footpad, marauder, desperado, gangster, gunman, pirate, buccaneer, hijacker, plunderer, thief.

bandy[1] adj BOWED, crooked, curved, bent, bow-legged, misshapen.

bandy[2] v ❶ EXCHANGE, swap, trade, pass, reciprocate. *See also* ARGUE. ❷ SPREAD, circulate, pass on, disseminate.

bang n ❶ BOOM, crash, thud, slam, knock, clash, clap, report, explosion. ❷ BLOW, bump, hit, knock, slap, punch, stroke, cuff, smack, rap; *informal* whack.
▶ adv ❶ WITH A BANG, crash, thump, thud, noisily, violently. ❷ EXACTLY, precisely, absolutely, right; *informal* slap bang.

banish v ❶ EXILE, expel, exclude, deport, expatriate, ostracize, transport, eject, evict, outlaw, oust, throw out, proscribe. ❷ DISMISS, drive away, dispel, shut out, eliminate, get rid of, dislodge, remove, bar, ban, suppress.

bank[1] n ❶ SLOPE, mound, embankment, hillock, incline, ridge, rise, rampart, ramp, dyke, pile, mass. ❷ EDGE, shore, brink, side, margin, embankment. ❸ ROW, array, collection, display, panel, rank, tier.
▶ v TILT, lean, slope, slant, list, tip, incline.

bank[2] n STORE, reserve, supply, fund, stock, hoard, repository, pool, reservoir.
▶ v DEPOSIT, save, put by, save up, keep, store, hoard.
– OPPOSITES withdraw.
■ **bank on** See RELY ON.

bankrupt adj ❶ INSOLVENT, ruined, failed, in liquidation, destitute, penniless; *informal* broke, bust. ❷ MORALLY BANKRUPT, deficient, lacking, poor, impoverished, worthless.
– OPPOSITES solvent.

banner n FLAG, standard, pennant, pennon, colours, ensign, banderole, streamer.

banquet n FEAST, repast, dinner, meal, party; *informal* binge, blowout, spread.

banter n REPARTEE, joking, badinage, persiflage, pleasantry, jesting, wordplay.

bar n ❶ BEAM, rod, pole, shaft, stake, stick, spar, rail, batten, girder, crosspiece. ❷ BARRIER, obstacle, obstruction, impediment, hindrance, check, deterrent, drawback, prohibition, prevention, problem, difficulty. ❸ BAND, stripe, belt, strip, streak, line. ❹ CAKE, slab, chunk, block, piece, wedge, lump, hunk, nugget, ingot. ❺ HOSTELRY, inn, tavern; *Brit. pub.* public house; *Brit. informal* local, boozer.

▶ v ❶ EXCLUDE, ban, banish, keep out, prohibit, forbid, preclude, outlaw, ostracize, proscribe. ❷ BLOCK, check, impede, obstruct, prevent, hinder, stop, halt, deter, restrain, arrest, thwart.

barbarian n SAVAGE, vandal, boor, yahoo, churl, brute, ruffian, hooligan, heathen, pagan, philistine, ignoramus; *Brit. informal* yob, yobbo.

▶ adj *see* BARBARIC.

barbaric adj ❶ UNCIVILIZED, primitive, wild, savage, barbarian, uneducated, unsophisticated, crude, brutish. ❷ CRUEL, brutal, savage, bestial, barbarous, vicious, ferocious, inhuman. *See also* CRUEL.
– OPPOSITES civilized.

bare adj ❶ NAKED, nude, undressed, unclad, uncovered, stripped, unclothed, exposed, denuded; *informal* in the buff, butt naked; *Brit. informal* starkers; *N. Amer. informal* buck naked. ❷ EMPTY, unfurnished, undecorated, plain, austere, unadorned, vacant. ❸ BLEAK, barren, featureless, treeless, unsheltered, desolate, open. ❹ PLAIN, simple, unadorned, unvarnished, un-

embellished, uncompromising, basic, essential, literal, straightforward, bald, stark, direct, uninterpreted, unelaborated. ❺ MERE, basic, essential, minimum, minimal, least, smallest, meagre, scanty, inadequate.

▶ v REVEAL, uncover, expose, lay bare, undress, unmask, unveil, show, disclose, make known, publish, betray.
– OPPOSITES conceal.

barely adv HARDLY, scarcely, just, only just, by the skin of one's teeth, with difficulty.

bargain n ❶ AGREEMENT, deal, pact, contract, arrangement, settlement, treaty, transaction, understanding, promise, pledge, compact, covenant, concordat, engagement, negotiation. ❷ GOOD BUY, good deal, special offer, discount, reduction; *informal* snip, giveaway.

▶ v NEGOTIATE, haggle, barter, argue, discuss, deal, trade, traffic, compromise, agree, settle, promise, pledge, engage.

■ **bargain for** EXPECT, allow for, anticipate, be prepared for, take into account. **into the bargain** *see* MOREOVER.

barrage n ❶ BROADSIDE, gunfire, bombardment, fusillade, salvo, volley, battery, shelling, cannonade. ❷ ONSLAUGHT, deluge, torrent, stream, hail, storm, flood, mass, avalanche, abundance, plethora. ❸ *See* BARRIER (1).

barrel n CASK, keg, vat, butt, tub, tank, firkin, hogshead.

barren adj ❶ INFERTILE, unproductive, unfruitful, waste, desert, arid, bare, bleak, desolate, lifeless, empty. ❷ STERILE, infertile, childless; *technical* infecund.
– OPPOSITES fertile.

barricade n *see* BARRIER (1).
▶ v BLOCK OFF, blockade, bar, obstruct, close up, fortify, defend.

barrier n ❶ BAR, fence, railing, barricade, obstruction, blockade, barrage, roadblock, rampart, palisade, bulwark, dam, stockade. ❷ OBSTACLE, hindrance, impediment, handicap, difficulty, problem, restriction, check, bar, limitation, drawback, stumbling block.

barter v BARGAIN, trade, traffic, exchange, swap, deal, haggle.

base¹ n ❶ FOUNDATION, bed, foot, bottom, basis, support, stand, rest, pedestal, prop, plinth, substructure. ❷ BASIS, core, fundamentals, essence, essentials, root, heart, source, origin, mainspring. ❸ HEADQUARTERS, centre, camp, station, post, starting point, settlement, site.
▶ v ❶ FOUND, build, settle, support, ground, rest, derive from, construct, establish. ❷ LOCATE, station, centre, post, situate, place, install.

base² adj IGNOBLE, mean, low, sordid, contemptible, shameful, vulgar, shabby, despicable, unworthy, inferior, corrupt, depraved, vile, dishonourable, disreputable, unprincipled, immoral, evil, wicked, sinful, detestable, degrading.
– OPPOSITES noble.

bashful adj SHY, diffident, timid, shrinking, backward, modest, self-effacing, retiring, nervous, self-conscious, reserved, inhibited, reticent, unforthcoming, hesitant, coy, demure, shamefaced, abashed, sheepish, embarrassed, blushing, uneasy.
– OPPOSITES confident.

basic adj ❶ FUNDAMENTAL, essential, intrinsic, underlying, primary, elementary, central, key, indispensable, vital, main, principal, chief, crucial, rudimentary. ❷ PLAIN, simple, austere, spartan, unadorned, stark, minimal.
– OPPOSITES luxurious.

basin n BOWL, dish, pan, vessel, container, receptacle.

basis n ❶ FOUNDATION, base, grounding, support, rest, stand, stay, infrastructure, bottom. ❷ STARTING POINT, source, origin, core, essence, beginning, impetus, impulse, material, ingredients, stimulus.

bask v ❶ LIE, laze, relax, sunbathe, lounge, loll. ❷ REVEL, wallow, exult, delight, take pleasure, luxuriate, glory, rejoice, enjoy, relish, savour.

bastard n ❶ ILLEGITIMATE CHILD; *dated* love child; *archaic* natural child. ❷ SCOUNDREL, villain, brute, rogue; *informal* beast; *dated* cad, blackguard.

batch n SET, group, lot, cluster, bunch, quantity, collection, accumulation, assemblage, pack, crowd, aggregate, conglomeration.

bathe v ❶ WASH, clean, cleanse, rinse, soak, steep, moisten, wet, immerse. ❷ SWIM, go swimming, take a dip. ❸ SUFFUSE, envelop, cover, soak.

baton n STICK, wand, rod, bar, cane, staff, club, truncheon, mace.

batter v ❶ BEAT, hit, strike, bludgeon, assault, belabour; informal bash. See also HIT (1). ❷ DAMAGE, injure, hurt, harm, crush, shatter, exhaust, ruin, destroy, buffet, wear down, wear out, impair, squash, mar, spoil, demolish.

battle n CONFLICT, fight, fighting, clash, engagement, skirmish, struggle, confrontation, combat, encounter, collision, campaign, war, tussle, scuffle, melee, action, strife, hostilities, fray, crusade; informal scrap.
▶ v STRUGGLE, fight, contend, compete, contest, combat, feud, quarrel, wrangle, argue, war, cross swords.

battlefield n BATTLEGROUND, front, battle lines, combat zone, theatre of war, arena.

bawdy adj RIBALD, lewd, indecent, salacious, earthy, broad, suggestive, indelicate, naughty, racy, risqué, off colour, obscene, dirty, filthy, smutty, erotic, prurient, pornographic, gross, coarse, titillating, licentious, lascivious, unseemly, vulgar,

Rabelaisian; informal blue, raunchy.
– OPPOSITES decent, proper.

bawl v ❶ SHOUT, cry, yell, roar, bellow, thunder, clamour, vociferate; informal holler. ❷ SOB, wail, cry, roar, howl, weep, blubber, squall, snivel, grizzle.

bay¹ n COVE, inlet, gulf, basin, harbour, indentation, sound, arm, bight, creek, firth, fjord, estuary.

bay² n ALCOVE, recess, niche, opening, nook, booth.

bazaar n ❶ MARKET, mart, souk, exchange. ❷ FÊTE, fair, sale; Brit. jumble sale, bring-and-buy (sale); N. Amer. rummage sale.

be v ❶ EXIST, live, be alive, breathe. ❷ BE SITUATED, be located, be positioned, stay, remain, continue, dwell, live, inhabit, be present, attend, persist, survive, endure, last. ❸ TAKE PLACE, occur, be due, be planned for, happen, come about, arise, transpire; poetic/literary come to pass, befall.

beach n SHORE, seashore, sands, sand, seaside, coast, coastline, littoral, margin, foreshore, water's edge, waterfront; poetic/literary strand.

beached adj STRANDED, aground, grounded, ashore, high and dry, stuck, cast up, marooned, wrecked, abandoned.

bead n BALL, pellet, pill, drop, globule.

beaker n CUP, mug, glass, goblet, tumbler, tankard.

beam n ❶ BAR, spar, rafter, girder, support, boom, plank, board, joist, timber, stanchion, scantling. ❷ RAY, shaft, bar, stream, streak, pencil, gleam, glimmer, glow, glint.
▶ v ❶ EMIT, radiate, shine, broadcast, transmit, direct, aim. ❷ SMILE, grin, laugh, be radiant.
– OPPOSITES frown.

bear v ❶ HOLD, support, carry, uphold, sustain, prop up, shoulder, take. ❷ BRING, carry, transport, convey, fetch, deliver, move, take, transfer; *informal* tote. ❸ BE MARKED WITH, display, exhibit, show, present. ❹ ENDURE, tolerate, abide, accept, stand, put up with, submit to, suffer, sustain, cope with, live with, stomach, admit, allow, resign oneself to; *formal* brook. ❺ PRODUCE, yield, give, give forth, supply, provide. ❻ GIVE BIRTH TO, produce, breed, generate; *archaic* bring forth.
■ **bear out** *see* CONFIRM (1), SUPPORT v (4). **bear up** COPE, survive, endure, manage, keep on, hold out, keep going. **bear with** BE PATIENT WITH, be tolerant towards, make allowances for, tolerate, suffer, indulge.

bearable adj ENDURABLE, tolerable, supportable, sustainable, sufferable, acceptable, admissible, manageable.
– OPPOSITES intolerable, unbearable.

bearing n ❶ CARRIAGE, posture, gait, demeanour, air, aspect, behaviour, manner, attitude, mien, composure, stance, style; *Brit.* deportment; *formal* comportment. ❷ COURSE, direction. ❸ RELEVANCE, pertinence, connection, implication, significance, relation, relationship, application, effect, consequence.

beast n ❶ ANIMAL, creature, brute. ❷ BRUTE, savage, monster, fiend, devil, sadist, barbarian, wretch; *archaic* blackguard.

beat v ❶ HIT, strike, batter, thrash, slap, whip, lash, cuff, cudgel, buffet, cane, scourge, smack, thwack, thump, pound, drub, hammer, flog, chastise; *informal* bash, whack, clout, wallop, lay into, rough up, knock about, tan, biff. ❷ PULSATE, throb, pound, pulse, palpitate, thump, vibrate. ❸ DEFEAT, outdo, conquer, surpass, trounce, vanquish, overcome, excel, subdue, master, best, outclass, outdistance, outpace, outwit, quash, worst; *informal* thrash, lick. ❹ WHISK, whip, stir, agitate, blend, mix. ❺ FLAP, flutter, quiver, vibrate, tremble.
▶ n ❶ PULSE, vibration, throb, throbbing, pounding, palpitation. ❷ RHYTHM, stress, accent, pulse, tempo, metre, measure, time. ❸ ROUND, rounds, route, circuit, path, track, course, way, itinerary.

beautiful adj LOVELY, attractive, pretty, gorgeous, ravishing, stunning, handsome, good-looking, elegant, exquisite,

charming, delightful, pleasing, picturesque, decorative, scenic, spectacular, superb, fine, glamorous, graceful; *poetic/literary* beauteous, pulchritudinous; *archaic* fair, comely; *Scottish & N. English* bonny.
– OPPOSITES ugly.

beautify v ADORN, embellish, decorate, ornament, bedeck, enhance, improve, prettify, glamorize, smarten, gild; *informal* do up, doll up, titivate.
– OPPOSITES spoil.

beauty n ATTRACTIVENESS, loveliness, prettiness, handsomeness, good looks, allure, appeal, charm, picturesqueness, glamour, elegance, grace, magnificence, radiance, splendour, artistry; *poetic/literary* pulchritude.
– OPPOSITES ugliness.

because conjunction SINCE, as, for the reason that, in that, seeing that.
■ **because of** ON ACCOUNT OF, owing to, due to, as a result of, in view of, by reason of, by virtue of, thanks to.

beckon v ❶ GESTURE, signal, motion, gesticulate, call, summon, bid, invite, encourage. ❷ ATTRACT, tempt, pull, draw, allure, entice.

become v ❶ TURN INTO, turn out to be, change into, grow into, develop into, be transformed into, evolve into, metamorphose into. ❷ SUIT, flatter, look good on, sit well on, set off, enhance, go well with, grace.

becoming adj FLATTERING, pretty, attractive, elegant, stylish, chic.
– OPPOSITES unflattering.

bed n ❶ COUCH, cot, berth; *informal* the sack, the hay; *Brit. informal* one's pit. ❷ BASE, foundation, bottom, basis, support, substratum, substructure, layer.

bedraggled adj DISHEVELLED, untidy, unkempt, disordered, muddy, wet, soiled, drenched, soaked, stained, soaking, sodden, soggy, messy, dirty, muddied.
– OPPOSITES neat, clean.

beef n BRAWN, muscle, strength, sinew, physique, bulk, burliness, robustness, muscularity.

befall v HAPPEN, occur, happen to, take place, come about, chance, arise, ensue, follow, transpire; *poetic/literary* come to pass, betide.

before prep ❶ PRIOR TO, ahead of, earlier than, sooner than. ❷ IN FRONT OF, in the presence of, in the sight of.
– OPPOSITES after.
▶ adv EARLIER, previously, beforehand, in advance, formerly, ahead.

befriend v ❶ MAKE FRIENDS WITH. ❷ TAKE UNDER ONE'S PROTECTION, protect, look after, take under one's wing, support, assist, succour.

beg v ❶ ASK FOR MONEY, solicit; *informal* scrounge, cadge. ❷ PLEAD, entreat, ask, request, seek, crave, importune, implore, pray, supplicate, petition, cajole, wheedle; *poetic/literary* beseech.

beggar n VAGRANT, tramp, down-and-out, derelict, vagabond, mendicant; *informal* scrounger, sponger, cadger.

begin v ➊ START, commence, set about, start on, set in motion, set going, activate, spark off, embark on, initiate, establish, institute, inaugurate, originate, found, pioneer, open, launch, give rise to, cause, instigate, be the source of. ➋ COME INTO BEING, start, commence, arise, emerge, appear, occur, happen, originate, materialize, dawn, spring up.
– OPPOSITES finish, disappear.

beginner n NOVICE, learner, trainee, apprentice, student, recruit, tyro, fledgling, neophyte, novitiate; *N. Amer.* tenderfoot; *informal* rookie; *N. Amer. informal* greenhorn.
– OPPOSITES expert, veteran.

beginning n ➊ START, origin, opening, commencement, outset, dawn, birth, inception, starting point, source, emergence, onset, genesis, conception, germ, root, spring. ➋ ESTABLISHMENT, foundation, institution, inauguration, opening, creation, introduction. ➌ PRELUDE, introduction, preface, opening.
– OPPOSITES end, conclusion.

begrudge v GRUDGE, resent, give unwillingly, be jealous of, object to, envy, mind, be dissatisfied with.

beguile v ➊ CHARM, attract, delight, enchant, bewitch, please, entice, seduce, tempt. ➋ AMUSE, absorb, engross, engage, divert, entertain, distract, occupy.

behalf n
■ **on behalf of** ➊ IN THE INTERESTS OF, for the sake of, in support of, for the good of, on account of. ➋ REPRESENTING, in the name of, in place of.

behave v ➊ ACT, conduct oneself, perform, operate, function, acquit oneself; *formal* comport oneself. ➋ BE GOOD, be polite, mind one's manners, be obedient; *informal* mind one's Ps and Qs.

behaviour n CONDUCT, actions, demeanour, manners, ways, activity, functioning, performance, operation; *N. Amer.* deportment; *formal* comportment.

being n ➊ CREATURE, living thing, entity, animal, person, individual, human, mortal. ➋ EXISTENCE, life, living, animation, actuality, reality.

belated adj LATE, overdue, delayed, unpunctual, tardy, behind time, behindhand.
– OPPOSITES early.

belief n ➊ OPINION, judgement, view, thought, feeling, conviction, way of thinking, theory, notion, impression. ➋ TRUST, faith, credence, reliance, assurance, certainty, confidence, security, sureness. ➌ FAITH, creed, credo, doctrine, dogma,

persuasion, conviction, tenet, teaching, ideology.
– OPPOSITES doubt.

believe v ❶ ACCEPT, be convinced by, trust, subscribe to, rely on, swear to; *informal* swallow, buy, fall for, take as gospel. ❷ THINK, hold, suppose, reckon, be of the opinion, assume, presume, imagine, consider, conjecture, guess, hypothesize, theorize, maintain, understand, surmise, postulate.
– OPPOSITES disbelieve.

believer n ADHERENT, devotee, follower, supporter, disciple.
– OPPOSITES sceptic.

belittle n DISPARAGE, decry, slight, depreciate, deprecate, make light of, underestimate, underrate, undervalue, detract from, denigrate, downgrade, minimize, criticize, scoff at, sneer at.
– OPPOSITES praise.

belligerent adj ❶ AGGRESSIVE, argumentative, pugnacious, combative, antagonistic, confrontational, disputatious, bellicose, provocative, militant, quarrelsome, hot-tempered, quick-tempered, irascible, captious. ❷ WARRING, at war, hostile, battling, combatant, contending, militant, warmongering, warlike, martial.
– OPPOSITES peaceable.

belong v ❶ BE OWNED BY, be the property of, be held by. ❷ BE A MEMBER OF, be part of, be one of, be connected with, be associated with, be affiliated to, be allied to, be included in, be an adherent of. ❸ HAVE A PLACE, be supposed to be. ❹ BE AT HOME, be suited, be welcome, fit in, be accepted.

belongings pl n PROPERTY, possessions, things, effects, goods, chattels, paraphernalia, appurtenances, accoutrements, impedimenta; *informal* stuff, gear, junk.

beloved adj LOVED, adored, dear, dearest, cherished, worshipped, treasured, prized, precious, sweet, idolized, darling.
– OPPOSITES hated.
▶ n SWEETHEART, lover, love, girlfriend, boyfriend, inamorata, inamorato; *archaic* paramour.

belt n ❶ GIRDLE, sash, waistband, band, cummerbund, girth; *poetic/literary* cincture. ❷ STRIP, stretch, band, stripe, streak, bar, region, zone, area, district, tract, extent.
▶ v HIT, strike, beat, thump, cuff; *informal* whack, wallop. See also HIT (1).

bemused adj BEWILDERED, dazed, confused, stunned, muddled, puzzled, perplexed, baffled, befuddled, stupefied, amazed, astounded, astonished, overwhelmed, disconcerted.

bend v ❶ CURVE, crook, make crooked, arch, bow, twist, flex, warp, fold, contort, mould, shape. ❷ TURN, curve, twist, curl, veer, swerve, loop, diverge, deviate, wind, coil, spiral, incurvate. ❸ STOOP, lean, crouch, bow, hunch, duck.
– OPPOSITES straighten.

▶ n CURVE, corner, turn, twist, arc, angle, loop, coil, spiral, crook, swerve, deflection, deviation, zigzag, dog-leg.
– OPPOSITES straight.

beneath prep ❶ BELOW, under, underneath, lower than. ❷ INFERIOR TO, lower than, subservient to, subordinate to, secondary to. ❸ UNWORTHY OF, not proper for, degrading to, undignified for, unsuitable for, inappropriate for, unbecoming for.
– OPPOSITES above.

benefactor n HELPER, supporter, sponsor, patron, backer, donor, promoter, subsidizer, subscriber, well-wisher, sympathizer, philanthropist, fairy godmother; *informal* angel.

beneficial adj ADVANTAGEOUS, profitable, helpful, useful, worthwhile, valuable, gainful, healthy, rewarding, fruitful, productive, salutary, salubrious, wholesome, improving, serviceable, propitious, promising, favourable, obliging, accommodating, nutritious, nourishing, nurturing.
– OPPOSITES disadvantageous.

beneficiary n HEIR, heiress, inheritor, recipient, legatee, payee, assignee, receiver, successor.

benefit n ❶ ADVANTAGE, asset, blessing, boon, plus, plus point; *informal* perk; *formal* perquisite. ❷ GOOD, well-being, advantage, interest, profit, gain, welfare,

convenience, prosperity, good fortune, aid, assistance, help, service, privilege, betterment. ❸ AID, allowance, subsidy, grant, payment, assistance; *Brit. informal* dole.
– OPPOSITES disadvantage, detriment.

▶ v ❶ HELP, profit, be advantageous to, be good for, serve, aid, assist, advance, further, promote, advantage, forward, boost, avail, enhance, improve, better. ❷ GAIN, profit, do well, reap benefits/reward, prosper, put to good use, do well out of; *informal* cash in.
– OPPOSITES damage, suffer.

benevolent adj KIND, kind-hearted, kindly, generous, warm-hearted, caring, benign, amiable, friendly, beneficent, liberal, magnanimous, bountiful, humane, humanitarian, altruistic, philanthropic, compassionate, sympathetic, considerate, thoughtful, obliging, well meaning, helpful.
– OPPOSITES malicious, unkind.

benign adj ❶ KINDLY, benevolent, kind-hearted, kind, generous, cordial, genial, amiable, warm, gentle, tolerant, gracious, friendly, accommodating. ❷ FAVOURABLE, auspicious, propitious, opportune, lucky, advantageous, helpful, providential, suitable, appropriate, healthy, wholesome, health-giving, salubrious, pleasant, refreshing, agreeable, mild, temperate, balmy. ❸ NON-MALIGNANT,

curable, treatable, remediable, innocent, harmless.
– OPPOSITES unfriendly, unfavourable, malignant.

bent adj **1** CURVED, crooked, twisted, angled, bowed, arched, warped, distorted, contorted, folded, coiled, buckled, hunched. **2** CORRUPT, dishonest, fraudulent, criminal, untrustworthy, unprincipled, immoral; *informal* crooked.
– OPPOSITES straight, honest.
▶ n TENDENCY, inclination, predisposition, leaning, talent, gift, flair, ability, aptitude, penchant, predilection, propensity, proclivity.

bequeath v LEAVE (IN ONE'S WILL), will, make over, pass on, hand on/down, transfer, donate, give, bestow on, confer on, endow with.

bequest n LEGACY, inheritance, endowment, settlement, estate, heritage.

bereavement n DEATH IN THE FAMILY, loss, passing (away), demise; *formal* decease.

berserk adj MAD, crazy, insane, out of one's mind, hysterical, frenzied, crazed, demented, maniacal, manic, frantic, raving, wild, amok, on the rampage; *informal* off the deep end, ape, bananas, bonkers; *Brit. informal* spare.

berth n **1** BUNK, bed, cot, hammock. **2** MOORING, dock, quay, pier.
▶ v DOCK, moor, land, tie up, make fast.

beseech v IMPLORE, beg, entreat, plead with, appeal to, call on, supplicate, importune, pray to, ask, petition.

besiege v **1** LAY SIEGE TO, beleaguer, blockade. **2** SURROUND, mob, crowd round, swarm round, ring, encircle.

best adj FINEST, greatest, top, foremost, leading, pre-eminent, premier, prime, first, supreme, of the highest quality, superlative, par excellence, unrivalled, second to none, without equal, nonpareil, unsurpassed, peerless, matchless, unparalleled, unbeatable, optimum, optimal, ultimate, ideal, perfect; *informal* star, number-one.
– OPPOSITES worst.
▶ n FINEST, top, cream, choice, prime, elite, crème de la crème, flower, jewel in the crown; *informal* pick of the bunch.

bestial adj SAVAGE, animal, brutish, brutal, barbaric, cruel, vicious, violent, inhuman, depraved, degenerate.
– OPPOSITES civilized, humane.

bestow v CONFER, grant, accord, afford, endow with, vest in, present, award.

bet v WAGER, gamble, stake, risk, venture, hazard, chance, put/lay money, speculate; *Brit. informal* have a flutter, have a punt.
▶ n WAGER, gamble, stake, ante; *Brit. informal* flutter, punt.

betray v **1** BREAK ONE'S PROMISE TO, be disloyal to, be unfaithful to, break faith with, play someone false, inform on/against, give away, denounce, sell out, stab in the back; *informal* split on, rat on, peach on, stitch up, do the dirty on, sell down the river, squeal on; *Brit. informal* grass on, shop, sneak on; *N. Amer. informal* finger. ❷ REVEAL, disclose, divulge, tell, give away, leak, let slip, let out, blurt out; *informal* blab, spill.

better adj ❶ SUPERIOR, finer, of higher quality; *informal* a cut above, streets ahead, head and shoulders above. ❷ WELL, healthy, cured, healed, recovered, recovering, on the road to recovery; *informal* on the mend.
– OPPOSITES worse, inferior.
▶ v *see* IMPROVE (1).

beware v BE ON YOUR GUARD, watch out, look out, mind out, be alert, be on the lookout, keep your eyes open/peeled, keep an eye out, take care, be careful, be cautious, have a care, watch your step.

bewilder v BAFFLE, mystify, bemuse, perplex, puzzle, confuse, nonplus; *informal* flummox, stump, beat, fox, discombobulate.

bewitch v CAPTIVATE, enchant, entrance, cast/put a spell on, enrapture, charm, beguile, fascinate, enthral.

bias n PREJUDICE, partiality, partisanship, favouritism, unfairness, one-sidedness, tendency, inclination, predilection, bigotry, intolerance, discrimination.
– OPPOSITES impartiality.

▶ v PREJUDICE, influence, colour, sway, predispose, distort, skew.

biased adj PREJUDICED, partial, partisan, one-sided, blinkered, jaundiced, distorted, warped, twisted, skewed, bigoted, intolerant, discriminatory.
– OPPOSITES impartial.

bid v OFFER, put up, tender, proffer, propose.
▶ n ❶ OFFER, tender, proposal. ❷ ATTEMPT, effort, endeavour, try; *informal* crack, go, shot, stab.
■ bid for TRY TO GET, go for, make a pitch for, make a bid for.

big adj LARGE, great, of considerable size, sizeable, substantial, goodly, tall, high, huge, immense, enormous, colossal, massive, mammoth, broad, vast, prodigious, gigantic, giant, monumental, stupendous, gargantuan, man-size, king-size, outsize, considerable; *informal* whopping, mega, astronomical, humongous; *Brit. informal* ginormous.
– OPPOSITES small.

bigot n DOGMATIST, partisan, sectarian, racist, sexist, chauvinist.

bigoted adj PREJUDICED, biased, one-sided, sectarian, discriminatory, opinionated, dogmatic, intolerant, narrow-minded, blinkered, racist, sexist, chauvinistic, jingoistic.
– OPPOSITES open-minded.

bill n ❶ INVOICE, account, statement; *N. Amer.* check; *informal* tab. ❷ DRAFT LAW, proposed legislation, measure.

▶ v INVOICE, charge, debit, send a statement to.

billow v ❶ PUFF UP / OUT, balloon (out), swell, fill (out), belly out. ❷ SWIRL, spiral, roll, undulate, eddy, pour, flow.

bind v ❶ TIE (UP), fasten (together), hold together, secure, make fast, attach, rope, strap, lash, truss, tether. ❷ BANDAGE, dress, cover, wrap, strap up, tape up. ❸ UNITE, join, bond, knit.
– OPPOSITES untie, separate.

binding adj IRREVOCABLE, unalterable, inescapable, unbreakable, contractual, compulsory, obligatory, mandatory.

birth n ❶ CHILDBIRTH, delivery, nativity, birthing; dated confinement. ❷ BEGINNING(S), emergence, genesis, dawn, rise, start. ❸ ANCESTRY, lineage, blood, descent, parentage, family, extraction, origin, genealogy, stock.
– OPPOSITES death, demise, end.

■ **give birth to** HAVE, bear, produce, be delivered of, bring into the world; N. Amer. birth; informal drop.

bisect v CUT IN HALF, halve, divide/cut/split in two, cross, intersect.

bit n ❶ PIECE, portion, segment, section, part, fragment, scrap, shred, crumb, grain, speck, snippet, snatch, spot, drop, pinch, dash, soupçon, morsel, iota, jot, whit, atom, particle, trace, touch, suggestion, hint;

informal smidgen, tad. ❷ MOMENT, minute, second, (little) while; informal sec, jiffy; Brit. informal mo, tick.
– OPPOSITES lot.

■ **bit by bit** GRADUALLY, little by little, in stages, step by step, piecemeal, slowly.

bite v ❶ SINK ONE'S TEETH INTO, chew, munch, nibble at, gnaw, crunch, champ, tear at. ❷ GRIP, hold, get a purchase. ❸ TAKE EFFECT, be effective, work, act, have results.
▶ n ❶ CHEW, munch, nibble, gnaw, nip. ❷ SNACK, mouthful, refreshments; informal a little something. ❸ PIQUANCY, pungency, spiciness, tang, zest, sharpness, tartness; informal kick, punch.

biting adj see COLD (1), SCATHING.

bitter adj ❶ ACRID, tart, sour, sharp, acid, unsweetened, harsh, biting, acerbic, astringent, pungent, vinegary, acetous, unpleasant. ❷ RESENTFUL, angry, sullen, embittered, sour, sore, rancorous, acerbic, acrimonious, peevish, petulant, spiteful, malicious, vicious, sharp, waspish, piqued, jaundiced, jealous, envious, indignant, morose, begrudging, crabbed.
– OPPOSITES sweet, happy.

bizarre adj EXTRAORDINARY, outlandish, eccentric, fantastic, surreal, freakish, grotesque, peculiar, odd, strange, curious, abnormal, weird, unusual, uncommon, outré, unconventional, queer, aberrant,

deviant, ludicrous, droll; *informal* offbeat, oddball, way-out, wacky; *Brit. informal, dated* rum.
– OPPOSITES ordinary.

black adj JET, ebony, sable, inky, sooty, pitch-black, pitch-dark, dark, dusky, coal-black, funereal, raven; *poetic/literary* Stygian.

blacken v DARKEN, make dark, dirty, smudge, stain, soil, begrime, befoul.

blame v ❶ ACCUSE, hold responsible, condemn, find guilty, find fault with, criticize, censure, reprimand, reproach, admonish, reprove, reprehend, scold, upbraid, chide, berate, take to task. ❷ ATTRIBUTE, ascribe, impute, pin on.
▶ n ❶ RESPONSIBILITY, accountability, guilt, fault, culpability, liability, onus. ❷ CRITICISM, condemnation, censure, accusation, incrimination, stricture, reproach, reproof, recrimination, reprimand, indictment, complaint, berating; *informal* stick, rap; *formal* castigation.

blameless adj INNOCENT, faultless, guiltless, in the clear, irreproachable, unimpeachable, above reproach, upright, moral, virtuous, unoffending, impeccable, stainless, unblemished.
– OPPOSITES guilty.

bland adj ❶ TASTELESS, insipid, flavourless, mild. ❷ DULL, boring, uninspired, uninspiring, unoriginal, unexciting, tedious, nondescript, trite, vapid, mediocre, humdrum, weak.
– OPPOSITES tangy, interesting.

blank adj ❶ BARE, plain, clean, unmarked, empty, vacant, clear, void, unfilled, spotless. ❷ EXPRESSIONLESS, inscrutable, impassive, unresponsive, deadpan, poker-faced, indifferent, vacant, empty, uncomprehending, vacuous, glazed, emotionless, uninterested. ❸ EMPTY, vacant, at a loss, nonplussed, confused, baffled, bewildered, lost, dumbfounded, uncomprehending, puzzled, perplexed.
– OPPOSITES full, expressive.
▶ n GAP, void, space, vacancy, emptiness, vacuum, nothingness, vacuity.

blasphemous adj PROFANE, sacrilegious, irreligious, impious, irreverent, ungodly, godless, sinful, disrespectful, unholy.
– OPPOSITES reverent.

blasphemy n ❶ SACRILEGE, profanity, impiety, impiousness, irreverence, irreligiousness, profaneness, ungodliness, desecration, unholiness, execration. ❷ OATH, curse, swear word, profanity.

blast n ❶ GUST, draught, rush, gale, storm, squall, blow. ❷ EXPLOSION, detonation, blowing up, discharge, burst, bang, eruption.
▶ v ❶ BLOW UP, blow to pieces, explode, shatter, demolish, burst, ruin. ❷ BOOM, roar, blare, screech, trumpet.

blatant adj FLAGRANT, glaring, obvious, unconcealed, undisguised, overt, manifest, brazen, shameless, unembarrassed, barefaced, naked, sheer, conspicuous, prominent, obtrusive, apparent, stark, unmistakable, unmitigated, outright, out-and-out.
– OPPOSITES discreet, inconspicuous.

blaze n ❶ FIRE, conflagration, burning, flame, inferno. ❷ BEAM, gleam, glitter, shine, radiance, dazzle, brightness, brilliance, flash, flare.
▶ v ❶ BURN, be on fire, be ablaze, flame, catch fire, flare up, burst into flame. ❷ SHINE, gleam, glimmer, dazzle, beam, flare, flash, glitter.

bleach v FADE, blanch, discolour, turn white/pale, etiolate, decolorize, lighten, whiten, peroxide.

bleak adj ❶ DESOLATE, bare, barren, forbidding, exposed, cold, unwelcoming, unsheltered, waste, desert, windswept, windy, arid, uncultivated, wild, dreary, lonely, grim. ❷ DISMAL, dreary, gloomy, depressing, melancholy, wretched, hopeless, sombre, discouraging, disheartening, unpromising, comfortless, miserable, cheerless, joyless.
– OPPOSITES lush, promising.

bleary adj BLURRED, blurry, dim, unclear, indistinct, fuzzy, cloudy, clouded, foggy, misty, hazy, filmy, smeary, obscured,

fogged, murky, watery, rheumy.
– OPPOSITES clear.

blemish n DEFECT, stain, flaw, fault, disfigurement, imperfection, deformity, ugliness, blot, mark, smear, blotch, crack, chip, taint.
▶ v SPOIL, mar, damage, injure, flaw, mark, stain, taint, impair, disfigure, discolour, tarnish, blot, deface, sully, besmirch.

blend v ❶ MIX, combine, intermix, mingle, amalgamate, unite, commix, commingle, merge, compound, fuse, coalesce, integrate, homogenize, synthesize, meld, alloy; technical admix. ❷ HARMONIZE, complement, fit, suit, go with.
▶ n MIXTURE, mix, combination, amalgam, compound, fusion, union, amalgamation, synthesis, composite, alloy, melange, concoction.

bless v ❶ SANCTIFY, consecrate, hallow, dedicate, anoint, make sacred. ❷ GLORIFY, extol, praise, exalt, adore; formal laud.
– OPPOSITES curse.

blessed adj ❶ SACRED, holy, divine, venerated, consecrated, hallowed, sanctified, beatified, revered. ❷ HAPPY, fortunate, blissful, lucky, favoured, joyful, joyous, glad, cheerful, contented; poetic/literary blithe. ❸ WONDERFUL, marvellous, welcome, longed for.
– OPPOSITES cursed, wretched.

blessing n ❶ BENEDICTION, consecration, dedication, prayer, grace, thanksgiving,

commendation, invocation.
2 APPROVAL, permission, consent, sanction, backing, endorsement, assent, support, concurrence, agreement, encouragement, approbation; *informal* go-ahead, the green light. **3** GODSEND, boon, gift, favour, benefit, advantage, asset, comfort, convenience, help, bit of luck.
– OPPOSITES veto.

blight n **1** DISEASE, plague, pestilence, fungus, infestation, canker, mildew. **2** AFFLICTION, misfortune, plague, disaster, calamity, trouble, ruin, catastrophe, curse, bane, scourge, tribulation, woe.
▶ v RUIN, destroy, spoil, shrivel, wither, crush, blast, mar.

blind adj **1** SIGHTLESS, unseeing, visually impaired, visionless, partially sighted, purblind. **2** OBTUSE, blinkered, imperceptive, unaware, insensible, insensitive, unseeing, heedless, careless, unobservant, oblivious, indifferent, neglectful, slow, slow-witted, dense, stupid. **3** UNCRITICAL, unthinking, unreasoning, undiscerning, unreasoned, irrational, indiscriminate, injudicious, partial, prejudiced, biased.
▶ v MAKE BLIND, deprive of sight, blinker, blindfold.
2 DAZZLE, deceive, delude, beguile, infatuate, confuse, bewilder, hoodwink; *informal* pull the wool over someone's eyes.
▶ n SHUTTER, shade, curtain, screen.

bliss n JOY, ecstasy, delight, rapture, euphoria, elation, happiness, pleasure, gladness, blessedness, beatitude, heaven, paradise, seventh heaven.
– OPPOSITES misery.

bloated adj SWOLLEN, distended, puffy, puffed up, inflated, enlarged, expanded, dilated.

blob n DROP, droplet, globule, dollop, gobbet, bubble, ball, bead, daub, blotch, dab, spot, splash, blot, smudge, smear; *informal* glob.

block v **1** CLOG, choke, jam, close, obstruct, constrict, stop up, plug, dam, bung up, barricade, bar. **2** HINDER, prevent, obstruct, hamper, impede, bar, frustrate, thwart, check, resist, deter, oppose, arrest, stop, halt, scotch, stonewall.
▶ n **1** BLOCKADE, barrier, barricade, obstacle, bar, hindrance, impediment, obstruction, deterrent, check, stumbling block, difficulty, drawback, hitch. **2** BAR, piece, chunk, hunk, cake, lump, mass, slab, ingot, brick. **3** GROUP, set, batch, section, quantity.

blockage n OBSTRUCTION, congestion, constriction, stoppage, occlusion, block, impediment, jam, bottleneck.

blood n **1** GORE, vital fluid; *poetic/literary* lifeblood, ichor. **2** ANCESTRY, lineage, family, descent, birth, extraction, pedigree, origin, genealogy, inheritance, stock, race, kinship.

blood-curdling adj TERRIFY-

ING, horrifying, spine-chilling, chilling, frightening, fearful, dreadful, terrible, horrendous, horrific, appalling, frightful.

bloodshed n KILLING, carnage, slaughter, murder, massacre, butchery, bloodletting, bloodbath; *poetic/literary* slaying.

bloodthirsty adj SAVAGE, cruel, murderous, ferocious, homicidal, vicious, brutal, ruthless, barbaric, barbarous, inhuman, sadistic, bloody, slaughterous, violent, warlike, bellicose; *archaic* sanguinary.

bloody adj ❶ BLEEDING, bloodstained, blood-soaked, blood-spattered, unstaunched, raw. ❷ SAVAGE, fierce, gory, cruel, slaughterous; *archaic* sanguinary.

bloom n ❶ BLOSSOM, flower, floret. ❷ FRESHNESS, radiance, lustre, glow, sheen, flush, perfection, blush, beauty. ❸ PERFECTION, prime, heyday, vigour, strength, flourishing.
▶ v ❶ FLOWER, blossom, burgeon, bud. ❷ FLOURISH, prosper, thrive, be healthy, be happy, do well.

blot n ❶ SPOT, smudge, speck, blotch, stain, mark, dot, patch, blob, smear; *Brit. informal* splodge. ❷ BLEMISH, imperfection, eyesore, defect, stain, fault, flaw, taint, ugliness.
▶ v MARK, stain, dot, speckle, smudge, spoil, blotch, spot, spatter, bespatter, disfigure; *poetic/literary* besmirch.

■ **blot out** OBLITERATE, erase, efface, wipe out, delete,

expunge, destroy, obscure, conceal, darken, dim, shadow.

blotchy adj SPOTTED, speckled, blotted, discoloured, patchy, smudged, uneven, streaked, stained, blotched, spattered.

blow[1] n WIND, gale, breeze, blast, gust, storm, tempest.
▶ v ❶ PUFF, blast, gust, flurry, bluster. ❷ WAFT, flutter, buffet, whirl, whisk, sweep, drive, carry, transport, convey. ❸ BREATHE, breathe out, exhale, puff, pant, gasp, whistle. ❹ SOUND, play, blare, toot, blast.
■ **blow over** SUBSIDE, die down, pass, cease, settle, end, vanish.
blow up ❶ EXPLODE, shatter, burst, detonate, go off, blast, erupt. ❷ INFLATE, pump up, expand, swell, distend, puff up. ❸ ENLARGE, magnify, heighten, exaggerate, overstate, embroider, colour, improve on. ❹ LOSE ONE'S TEMPER, rage, fume, erupt, go wild; *informal* blow one's top, hit the roof, fly off the handle.

blow[2] n ❶ HIT, bang, knock, stroke, slap, smack, punch, buffet, rap, impact, jolt; *informal* whack, wallop, clout, bash, belt, biff, thwack. ❷ AFFLICTION, misfortune, shock, upset, disaster, calamity, catastrophe, grief, disappointment, setback, reversal, bombshell.

blueprint n DESIGN, plan, draft, prototype, model, pattern, scheme, sketch, diagram, outline, layout, representation.

bluff[1] v TRICK, deceive, mislead, hoodwink, hoax, take in, dupe,

delude, fool, sham, feign, fake, lie; *poetic/literary* cozen.
▶ n BLUSTER, deceit, deception, trickery, fraud, fake, front, facade, pretence, sham, subterfuge, humbug.

bluff² adj BLUNT, straightforward, frank, candid, outspoken, direct, hearty, rough.

blunder v ❶ MAKE A MISTAKE, slip, err, be in error, miscalculate, misjudge, mismanage, bungle; *informal* slip up, screw up, botch, blow it, put one's foot in it. ❷ STUMBLE, stagger, lurch, flounder, be clumsy.
▶ n ERROR, fault, mistake, slip, miscalculation, misjudgement, false/wrong move, faux pas, oversight, inaccuracy, gaffe; *informal* slip-up, boo-boo, howler, clanger; *Brit. informal* boob, cockup.

blunt adj ❶ DULL, edgeless, unsharpened, unpointed, rounded. ❷ DIRECT, frank, forthright, bluff, outspoken, plainspoken, unceremonious, undiplomatic, tactless, rude, brusque, curt, abrupt, insensitive; *informal* upfront.
– OPPOSITES sharp.
▶ v DULL, take the edge off, deaden, weaken, dampen, allay, abate, lessen, appease, impair.

blur v SMEAR, besmear, smudge, mist, cloud, fog, befog, bedim, blear, becloud, obscure, mask.

blurred adj INDISTINCT, blurry, hazy, misty, cloudy, foggy, fuzzy, vague, unfocused, unclear, obscure, ill-defined,

nebulous, dim, faint, smeary, smudged.
– OPPOSITES clear.

blurt
■ **blurt out** SAY, utter, let slip, blab, disclose, reveal, let out, divulge, tell, babble, exclaim; *informal* spill the beans, let the cat out of the bag, give the game away.

blush v REDDEN, go red/pink, flush, colour, crimson, glow, be ashamed, be embarrassed.

bluster v ❶ BLOW, storm, rage, blast, gust, roar. ❷ BOAST, bluff, brag, swagger, show off, vaunt, lord it, hector, bully, domineer, threaten, rant, harangue, be overbearing; *informal* throw one's weight about.
▶ n BOASTING, bravado, bluff, bombast, bragging, braggadocio, hectoring, domineering, swagger.

blustery adj STORMY, windy, gusty, squally, wild, tempestuous, violent.
– OPPOSITES calm.

board n ❶ PLANK, beam, panel, slat, timber, sheet, block. ❷ FOOD, meals, sustenance, provisions, keep. ❸ PANEL, committee, council, directorate.
▶ v ❶ GET ON, get aboard/on board, enter, embark, mount. ❷ LODGE, stay, live, room, billet.

boast v ❶ BRAG, swank, crow, swagger, vaunt, show off, exaggerate, bluster, blow one's own trumpet, pat oneself on the back; *informal* talk big. ❷ POSSESS, have, own, pride oneself on, take pride in, enjoy, benefit from, exhibit, display.

▶ n ❶ BRAG, self-praise, vaunt, overstatement; *informal* swank.
❷ PRIDE, treasure, joy, gem; *informal* pride and joy, apple of someone's eye.

boastful adj CONCEITED, bragging, vain, arrogant, cocky, egotistical, proud, swaggering, swollen-headed, blustering, vaunting, braggart, overbearing; *informal* swanky, big-headed; *poetic/literary* vainglorious.
– OPPOSITES modest.

bob v BOUNCE, dip, jump, nod, leap, hop, jerk, jolt, quiver, wobble, toss, shake, oscillate.

bodily adj CORPOREAL, physical, carnal, corporal, fleshly, material, substantial, tangible, incarnate.

body n ❶ FIGURE, frame, form, physique, shape, build, anatomy, skeleton, trunk, torso.
❷ CORPSE, carcass, remains, relics, mummy; *Medicine* cadaver; *informal* stiff. ❸ SET, group, band, party, company, crowd, number, assembly, association.
❹ ACCUMULATION, collection, quantity, mass, corpus.

bog n MARSH, swamp, marshland, fen, quagmire, morass, mire, slough, mud.

■ **bog down** MIRE, slow, hamper, hinder, obstruct, impede, delay, stall, detain, entangle, ensnare, embroil, swamp, overwhelm.

bogus adj COUNTERFEIT, fake, sham, false, spurious, forged, fraudulent, artificial, pre-

tended, pretend, pseudo, imitation, mock, inauthentic, suppositious, soi-disant; *informal* phoney.
– OPPOSITES genuine.

boil v ❶ BUBBLE, seethe, simmer, stew, heat, cook, effervesce, foam, fizz, steam.
❷ RAGE, fume, seethe, storm, rant, rave, fulminate, flare up.

boisterous adj ❶ LIVELY, bouncy, playful, exuberant, frisky, romping, unruly, disorderly, rough, wild, irrepressible, undisciplined, spirited, animated, obstreperous, riotous, rollicking, uproarious, rowdy, noisy; *Brit. informal* rumbustious. ❷ ROUGH, choppy, stormy, wild, squally, breezy, turbulent, tempestuous, raging, gusty, blustery.
– OPPOSITES restrained, calm.

bold adj ❶ DARING, brave, adventurous, dauntless, unafraid, courageous, plucky, intrepid, audacious, fearless, valiant, gallant, hardy, heroic, valorous, undaunted, confident, venturesome, enterprising, daredevil, reckless, resolute.
❷ FORWARD, audacious, presumptuous, impudent, pert, impertinent, brazen, shameless, immodest, insolent, brash, cheeky, rude, barefaced, blatant, unashamed; *informal* saucy.
❸ STRIKING, eye-catching, prominent, pronounced, conspicuous, noticeable, emphatic, obvious, vivid, bright, showy, flashy, strong, distinct, marked.
– OPPOSITES timid, modest, faint, subdued.

bolster n CUSHION, pillow, support, prop, stay, rest.
▶ v SUPPORT, prop up, shore up, hold up, reinforce, buttress, strengthen, boost, maintain, build up, aid, assist, augment.

bolt n ❶ BAR, latch, lock, catch, fastening, pin, peg, rivet, rod. ❷ FLASH, streak, flare, shaft, burst. ❸ ARROW, dart, missile, projectile, shaft. ❹ RUN, dash, sprint, dart, rush, bound, escape.
▶ v ❶ BAR, lock, fasten, secure, rivet, pin, nail, clamp. ❷ RUN, dash, sprint, dart, rush, hurtle, hurry, fly, flee, run for it, escape, abscond; Brit. informal scarper, do a bunk. ❸ GOBBLE, guzzle, wolf, stuff, gulp, cram, devour.

bombard v ❶ SHELL, bomb, blitz, strafe, blast, pound, fire at, attack, assault, assail, batter. ❷ BADGER, pester, harass, bother, hound, plague, besiege, beset, assail, importune, belabour.

bombardment n ASSAULT, attack, bombing, shelling, strafing, blitz, air raid, cannonade, fusillade, barrage, broadside.

bombastic adj POMPOUS, pretentious, grandiose, grandiloquent, turgid, verbose, ranting, extravagant, magniloquent, blustering, ostentatious, affected, inflated, periphrastic.

bonanza n WINDFALL, godsend, bonus, boom, plenty, cornucopia, surplus, amplitude, sufficiency.

bond n ❶ CHAIN, fetter, rope, cord, shackle, manacle, tie, restraint, restriction, limitation, harness, straitjacket. ❷ LINK, connection, tie, attachment, affinity, union, relation, relationship, closeness, intimacy, nexus, ligature.
▶ v UNITE, join, bind, connect, link, attach, fasten, secure, stick, glue, fuse, weld, blend, merge.

bondage n SLAVERY, servitude, enslavement, subjection, captivity, oppression; historical serfdom, vassalage, thraldom.
– OPPOSITES freedom.

bonus n ❶ GAIN, advantage, extra, plus, benefit, boon. ❷ GIFT, gratuity, tip, present, bounty, reward, commission, honorarium; informal perk.

bony adj THIN, skinny, scrawny, angular, lean, skeletal, emaciated, cadaverous, gaunt, rawboned.
– OPPOSITES plump.

book n VOLUME, tome, work, title, publication, paperback, hardback, folio, edition, copy.
▶ v RESERVE, engage, charter, secure, bag, order, sign up, arrange, organize, schedule, programme.

bookish adj STUDIOUS, scholarly, scholastic, learned, erudite, highbrow, bluestocking, intellectual, academic, literary, pedantic, impractical; informal brainy, egghead.

booklet n LEAFLET, pamphlet, brochure, notebook.

boom n ❶ CRASH, bang, report,

explosion, blast, rumble, roar, thunder, reverberation. ❷ BOOST, surge, increase, upturn, improvement, growth, expansion, spurt, upsurge, success, bonanza, prosperity, advance, popularity, development.
– OPPOSITES decline.
▶ v RESOUND, reverberate, rumble, roar, thunder, bang, blast.

boorish adj RUDE, crude, loutish, churlish, unrefined, coarse, ill-mannered, impolite, uncouth, gross, oafish, uncultured, philistine, unsophisticated, vulgar, ignorant, indelicate, insensitive; Brit. informal yobbish.
– OPPOSITES refined.

boost v ❶ LIFT, raise, push, thrust, elevate, support, hoist, heave, shove. ❷ ENCOURAGE, support, uplift, increase, raise, heighten, promote, further, advance, improve, foster, assist, expand, enlarge, develop, facilitate, sustain; informal hike up, jack up.
▶ n ❶ PUSH, shove, lift, thrust, helping hand. ❷ IMPETUS, impulse, encouragement, support, increase, expansion, rise, improvement, advance, stimulus; informal shot in the arm.

boot v KICK, knock, punt.

booth n ❶ STALL, stand, kiosk, counter. ❷ CUBICLE, compartment, enclosure, hut, carrel.

booty n LOOT, plunder, haul, spoils, gains, prizes, profits,

takings, pickings, winnings; informal swag, boodle, the goods.

border n ❶ EDGE, perimeter, verge, boundary, limit, margin, periphery, brink, fringe, hem, brim, rim, skirt, surround. ❷ FRONTIER, boundary, borderline, limit.
▶ v ❶ BE NEXT / ADJACENT TO, be close to, neighbour, adjoin, abut, touch, join, connect, edge, skirt, bound. ❷ EDGE, fringe, hem, trim, bind, decorate, rim.
■ **border on** VERGE ON, approach, come close to, approximate, be near/similar to, resemble.

bore¹ v PIERCE, penetrate, drill, puncture, perforate, burrow, tap, tunnel, mine, dig out, sink.

bore² v BE TEDIOUS TO, weary, tire, fatigue, exhaust, depress, jade, pall on, send to sleep, leave cold, bore to tears, bore to death; informal turn off.
– OPPOSITES interest, amuse.

boring adj TEDIOUS, dull, uninteresting, uninspiring, unexciting, unstimulating, monotonous, unvaried, repetitive, dreary, humdrum, commonplace, flat, lacklustre, dry, dry as dust, stale, soporific, dead, soul-destroying, tiring, tiresome, wearisome; informal deadly.
– OPPOSITES interesting, amusing.

borrow v ❶ ASK FOR THE LOAN OF, beg, be lent, take as a loan, have temporarily, lease, hire; informal cadge, scrounge, bum;

N. Amer. informal mooch. ❷ COPY, plagiarize, take, imitate, adopt, appropriate, commandeer, steal, pirate, purloin, help oneself to; informal filch, grab; Brit. informal nick, pinch.
– OPPOSITES lend.

boss n HEAD, chief, leader, supervisor, manager, director, employer, superintendent, foreman, overseer, controller, master; informal numero uno; Brit. informal gaffer, governor; N. Amer. informal head honcho.
▶ V ORDER ABOUT / AROUND, give orders/commands to, control, bully, push around, domineer, dominate; informal throw one's weight about.

bossy adj DOMINEERING, overbearing, dictatorial, high-handed, authoritarian, autocratic, tyrannical, despotic, assertive, pushy, imperious, oppressive, bullying, lordly, officious, hectoring.
– OPPOSITES submissive.

botch v BUNGLE, make a mess of, do badly, spoil, muff, mismanage, fumble; informal mess/screw up, make a hash of; Brit. informal cock up.

bother v ❶ DISTURB, trouble, worry, pester, harass, annoy, upset, irritate, vex, inconvenience, plague, torment, nag, molest; informal hassle, get in someone's hair. ❷ DISTRESS, worry, concern, trouble, perturb, disconcert.
▶ n ❶ NUISANCE, annoyance, irritation, pest, trouble, worry, vexation. ❷ TROUBLE, disturb-

ance, commotion, disorder, uproar, fighting, violence, furore, brouhaha.

bottle n FLASK, container, carafe, pitcher, decanter, flagon, phial, magnum, jeroboam, carboy, demijohn.
■ **bottle up** see SUPPRESS (2).

bottleneck n NARROWING, constriction, obstruction, congestion, blockage, jam, hold-up.

bottom n ❶ BASE, foundation, basis, support, substructure, pedestal, substratum, underpinning. ❷ LOWEST POINT, foot, base, nadir. ❸ UNDERNEATH, underside, lower side, belly. ❹ BUTTOCKS, rear end, rear, seat, rump; informal backside, behind; Brit. informal bum, arse, jacksie; N. Amer. informal butt, fanny; humorous posterior.
– OPPOSITES top, surface.
▶ adj LOWEST, deepest, least, last, minimum.

bottomless adj ❶ DEEP, immeasurable, fathomless, unfathomable, unplumbable. ❷ UNLIMITED, inexhaustible, infinite, boundless.

bounce v JUMP, leap, spring, bob, rebound, skip, recoil, ricochet, jounce.
▶ n SPRINGINESS, spring, elasticity, give, resilience.

bound¹ adj ❶ CERTAIN, sure, definite, very likely, fated, predestined. ❷ OBLIGATED, obliged, required, forced, compelled, constrained, duty-bound. ❸ TIED, tied up, roped, tethered, fettered, secured.

■ **bound for** GOING / TRAVELLING TOWARDS, going to, heading for, making for, off to.

bound² v LEAP, jump, spring, skip, hop, vault, bounce, hurdle, bob, gambol, romp, prance, caper.

boundary n FRONTIER, border, limit, edge, dividing line, perimeter, verge, margin, threshold, bounds, periphery, fringe, borderline, brink, extremity.

boundless adj LIMITLESS, unlimited, infinite, endless, unbounded, unending, neverending, without end, unrestricted, inexhaustible, immeasurable, incalculable, vast, great, immense.
– OPPOSITES limited, restricted.

bountiful adj ABUNDANT, plentiful, ample, superabundant, copious, lavish, profuse, princely; *poetic/literary* plenteous, bounteous.
– OPPOSITES mean, meagre.

bounty n ❶ REWARD, recompense, remuneration, gratuity, tip, premium, bonus. ❷ GENEROSITY, munificence, altruism, largesse, benevolence, kindness, philanthropy.

bouquet n ❶ BUNCH OF FLOWERS, spray, posy, wreath, garland, nosegay, corsage, buttonhole. ❷ SMELL, aroma, odour, fragrance, scent, perfume; *poetic/literary* redolence.

bout n ❶ MATCH, contest, fight, engagement, round, competition, encounter, struggle; *informal* set-to. ❷ ATTACK, spell, fit, period, paroxysm.

bow v INCLINE THE HEAD / BODY, curtsy, bob, stoop, make obeisance, genuflect, bend the knee, prostrate oneself, kowtow, salaam.

bowl¹
■ **bowl over** ❶ KNOCK DOWN, bring, down, floor, fell. ❷ ASTOUND, amaze, astonish, stagger, dumbfound, stun, surprise; *informal* flabbergast.

bowl² n BASIN, dish, pan, container, vessel.

box¹ n CONTAINER, receptacle, crate, case, carton, pack, package, chest, trunk, bin, coffer, casket.

box² v FIGHT, spar, punch, thump, cuff, batter, pummel; *informal* belt, sock, clout, whack, slug, slam.

boxer n FIGHTER, pugilist, sparring partner, prizefighter.

boy n YOUTH, lad, youngster, stripling, schoolboy; *informal* kid, whippersnapper.

boycott v ❶ SHUN, ostracize, stay away from, avoid, spurn, reject, eschew, send to Coventry, blackball, blacklist. ❷ BAN, bar, prohibit, embargo, proscribe, blacklist, debar.

brace v ❶ STRENGTHEN, support, reinforce, shore up, prop up, buttress. ❷ STEADY, secure, stabilize, make fast. ❸ PREPARE, ready, fortify, tense.

brag v BOAST, show off, blow one's own trumpet, crow, sing one's own praises.

brain n ❶ CEREBRUM, cerebral matter, encephalon; *informal* grey matter. ❷ INTELLIGENCE, intellect, mind, sense, cleverness, wit, understanding, acumen; *informal* nous, savvy.

brainy adj CLEVER, intelligent, bright, brilliant, gifted; *informal* smart.
– OPPOSITES stupid.

branch n ❶ BOUGH, limb, stem, twig, shoot, sprig, arm. ❷ DEPARTMENT, division, subdivision, section, subsection, part, wing, office.
▶ v FORK, divide, diverge, separate, bifurcate, split, subdivide.
■ **branch out** EXTEND, spread out, diversify, expand, proliferate, multiply.

brand n ❶ MAKE, variety, line, trade name, trademark. ❷ KIND, type, sort, variety, style, stamp, cast.
▶ v ❶ STAMP, mark, burn, scorch, sear, tag, identify. ❷ STIGMATIZE, characterize, mark, taint, vilify, disgrace, discredit, denounce.

brandish v FLOURISH, wave, wield, raise, swing, display, shake, wag, flaunt, show off.

brash adj BOLD, self-confident, cocky, audacious, assertive, brazen, aggressive, forward, insolent, impudent, bumptious.
– OPPOSITES meek.

bravado n BLUSTER, swaggering, arrogance, boldness, audacity, bombast, braggadocio.

brave adj COURAGEOUS, valiant, fearless, intrepid, plucky, unafraid, heroic, bold, daring, resolute, indomitable, audacious, unshrinking, determined, undaunted, lionhearted, spirited, dauntless, gallant, valorous, stalwart, doughty, stout-hearted, venturesome, game; *informal* gutsy, spunky.
– OPPOSITES cowardly, fearful.

bravery n COURAGE, courageousness, fearlessness, pluck, pluckiness, intrepidity, boldness, heroism, audacity, daring, nerve, fortitude, resolution, grit, spirit, dauntlessness, mettle, valour, tenacity, doughtiness, hardihood; *informal* guts, spunk; *Brit. informal* bottle.
– OPPOSITES cowardice.

brawl n FIGHT, scuffle, fracas, rumpus, altercation, clash, free-for-all, tussle, brouhaha, quarrel, wrangle, commotion, uproar, ruckus; *informal* punch-up, scrap; *dated* affray.
▶ v SEE FIGHT v (1).

brawny adj MUSCULAR, powerful, burly, strong, powerfully built, robust, sturdy, strapping, sinewy.
– OPPOSITES scrawny, puny.

brazen adj BOLD, shameless, unashamed, unabashed, audacious, defiant, brash, forward, pushy, presumptuous, brassy, impudent, insolent, cheeky, immodest, pert; *informal* saucy.
– OPPOSITES reserved, modest.

breach n ❶ BREAK, rupture, split, opening, crack, gap, hole, fissure, rent, fracture, rift, cleft, aperture, gulf, chasm. ❷ BREAKING, violation, infringement,

contravention, transgression, infraction. ❸ BREAKING OFF, severance, estrangement, parting, parting of the ways, rift, split, falling-out, schism, alienation, disaffection, quarrel, discord.
▸ v ❶ BREAK THROUGH, split, rupture, open up, burst through, make a gap in. ❷ BREAK, contravene, violate, infringe, transgress against, defy, disobey, flout.

break v ❶ SMASH, crack, shatter, split, burst, fracture, fragment, split, burst, fracture, fragment, splinter, crash, snap, rend, tear, divide, sever, separate, part, demolish, disintegrate. ❷ VIOLATE, contravene, infringe, breach, disobey, defy, flout, transgress against. ❸ STOP, take a break, pause, rest, discontinue, give up; informal knock off, take five. ❹ BEAT, surpass, outdo, better, exceed, outstrip, top, cap.
– OPPOSITES repair, mend, obey.
▸ n ❶ CRACK, hole, gap, opening, chink, split, fissure, tear, rent, gash, rupture, rift, chasm, cleft. ❷ INTERVAL, pause, stop, halt, intermission, rest, respite, breathing space, interlude; informal breather, let-up, time out. ❸ BREACH, split, rupture, rift, discontinuation, schism, disaffection, alienation.

■ **break away** LEAVE, break with, separate from, part company with, detach oneself from, secede from. **break down** ❶ STOP WORKING, give out, go wrong, malfunction, conk out; Brit. informal pack up ❷ See ANALYSE. ❸ See COLLAPSE v (3). **break in** see INTERRUPT (1). **break off** END, bring to an end, finish, cease, discontinue, call a halt to, suspend. **break out** see ESCAPE v (1). **break up** ❶ See DISPERSE. ❷ See SEPARATE v (4).

breakdown n ❶ STOPPAGE, failure, malfunctioning, seizing up; informal conking out. ❷ COLLAPSE, failure, disintegration, foundering, falling through. ❸ ANALYSIS, classification, itemization, categorization, explanation, examination, dissection.

breakthrough n ADVANCE, step/leap forward, leap, quantum leap, discovery, find, invention, innovation, development, improvement, revolution.

breast n BUST, bosom, chest, front, thorax; informal boob, knocker.

breath n ❶ INHALATION, pant, gasp, gulp of air, inspiration, exhalation, expiration. ❷ PUFF, waft, gust, breeze.

breathe v ❶ INHALE, EXHALE, respire, puff, pant, gasp, wheeze, gulp. ❷ WHISPER, murmur, purr, sigh, say.

breathless adj OUT OF BREATH, panting, wheezing, wheezy, puffing, gasping, winded, choking.

breathtaking adj SPECTACULAR, magnificent, impressive, awesome, awe-inspiring, astounding, exciting, astonishing, amazing, thrilling, stunning; *informal* out of this world.

breed v ❶ REPRODUCE, procreate, multiply, give birth, bring forth young, propagate; *poetic/literary* beget. ❷ PRODUCE, bring about, give rise to, create, generate, stir up, engender, make for, foster, arouse, induce, originate, occasion.
▶ n ❶ FAMILY, variety, type, kind, class, strain, stock, line. ❷ STOCK, species, race, lineage, extraction, pedigree.

breeze n BREATH OF WIND, gentle wind, draught, puff of air, gust, flurry, current of air; *poetic/literary* zephyr.

breezy adj WINDY, blowy, blustery, gusty, squally, fresh.

brevity n SHORTNESS, briefness, conciseness, concision, terseness, compactness, pithiness, succinctness, economy, curtness, condensation, pointedness.

brew v ❶ MAKE, prepare, infuse, ferment, mash. ❷ BE IMMINENT, loom, gather, form, be threatening, be impending, impend.
▶ n DRINK, beverage, liquor, ale, beer, tea, infusion, mixture, potion.

bribe v CORRUPT, entice, suborn, get at, buy off, pay off; *informal* grease someone's palm, sweeten, fix, square.
▶ n INDUCEMENT, enticement, incentive; *informal* backhander, sweetener, graft, kickback.

bridge n ❶ ARCH, span, overpass, flyover, viaduct. ❷ BOND,

link, tie, connection, cord, binding.
▶ v SPAN, cross, go over, pass over, traverse, extend across, reach across, arch over.

brief adj ❶ CONCISE, short, succinct, to the point, terse, economic, abbreviated, pithy, pointed, curt, crisp, condensed, compressed, sparing, thumbnail, epigrammatic. ❷ SHORT-LIVED, short, fleeting, momentary, temporary, impermanent, passing, fading, transitory, ephemeral, transient.
– OPPOSITES long.
▶ v INSTRUCT, inform, direct, guide, advise, enlighten, prepare, prime; *informal* fill in, put in the picture, give someone the low-down.
▶ n ❶ INFORMATION, advice, instructions, directions, guidance, briefing, preparation, priming, intelligence; *informal* low-down, rundown. ❷ ARGUMENT, case, proof, defence, evidence, contention, demonstration.

briefly adv ❶ CONCISELY, succinctly, to the point, tersely, sparingly, economically. ❷ FLEETINGLY, temporarily, momentarily, ephemerally. ❸ IN SHORT, in brief, to cut a long story short, in a word, in a nutshell, in essence.

briefs pl n UNDERPANTS, pants, Y-fronts, knickers; *Brit.* cami-knickers; *N. Amer.* shorts; *informal* panties.

bright adj ❶ SHINING, brilliant, vivid, intense, blazing,

dazzling, beaming, sparkling, glittering, gleaming, radiant, glowing, glistening, shimmering, luminous, lustrous, incandescent. ❷ VIVID, intense, rich, brilliant, bold, glowing. ❸ CLEAR, cloudless, unclouded, sunny, pleasant, clement. ❹ INTELLIGENT, clever, sharp, quick-witted, astute, acute, ingenious, resourceful, accomplished; *informal* brainy, smart. ❺ PROMISING, optimistic, favourable, hopeful, auspicious, propitious, encouraging, lucky, golden.
– OPPOSITES dark, dull, stupid.

brighten v ❶ MAKE BRIGHT / BRIGHTER, light up, lighten, illuminate, irradiate; *poetic/literary* illumine. ❷ CHEER UP, gladden, liven up, enliven, perk up, animate; *informal* buck up, pep up.

brilliant adj ❶ BRIGHT, shining, intense, radiant, beaming, gleaming, sparkling, dazzling, lustrous. ❷ CLEVER, intelligent, astute, masterly, inventive, resourceful, discerning; *informal* smart. ❸ EXCELLENT, superb, very good, outstanding, exceptional; *Brit. informal* brill, smashing.
– OPPOSITES dull, bad.

brim n RIM, lip, edge, brink, margin, circumference, perimeter, verge.
▶ V BE FULL, be filled up, be full to capacity, overflow, run over, well over.

bring v ❶ FETCH, carry, bear, take, convey, transport, deliver, lead, guide, conduct, usher,

escort. ❷ CAUSE, create, produce, result in, engender, give rise to, precipitate, occasion, wreak, effect, contribute to.
■ **bring about** *see* sense (2) above. **bring in** *see* EARN (1). **bring off** *see* ACHIEVE. **bring up** ❶ *see* RAISE (3). ❷ *see* BROACH (2).

brink n ❶ EDGE, verge, margin, limit, rim, extremity, boundary, fringe. ❷ VERGE, edge, threshold, point.

brisk adj ❶ QUICK, rapid, fast, swift, speedy, energetic, lively, vigorous, sprightly, spirited. ❷ ABRUPT, brusque, nononsense, sharp, curt, crisp; *informal* snappy.
– OPPOSITES slow, leisurely.

bristle n HAIR, stubble, whisker, prickle, spine, quill, thorn, barb.
▶ V GROW ANGRY / INDIGNANT, be irritated, bridle, flare up, draw oneself up, rear up.

brittle adj ❶ BREAKABLE, hard, crisp, fragile, frail, delicate; *formal* frangible. ❷ EDGY, nervous, on edge, tense, stiff; *informal* uptight.
– OPPOSITES flexible, relaxed.

broach v ❶ PIERCE, puncture, tap, draw off. ❷ INTRODUCE, raise, bring up, mention, suggest, open, put forward, propound.

broad adj ❶ WIDE, large, extensive, vast, spacious, expansive, sweeping, boundless, ample, capacious, open. ❷ WIDERANGING, wide, general, comprehensive, inclusive, encyclopedic, all-embracing, universal, unlimited. ❸ GENERAL, non-

specific, unspecific, imprecise, vague, loose, sweeping.
– OPPOSITES narrow.

broadcast v ❶ TRANSMIT, relay, send out, put on the air, beam, televise, telecast. ❷ AN-NOUNCE, make public, report, publicize, publish, advertise, proclaim, air, spread, circulate, disseminate, promulgate.
▶ n PROGRAMME, show, transmission, telecast.

broaden v ❶ WIDEN, make broader, extend, spread, enlarge. ❷ EXPAND, widen, enlarge, extend, increase, augment, add to, develop, amplify, swell.

broad-minded adj OPEN-MINDED, liberal, tolerant, unprejudiced, flexible, unbiased, undogmatic, catholic, fair, progressive, freethinking, enlightened, permissive.
– OPPOSITES narrow-minded.

brochure n BOOKLET, catalogue, prospectus, leaflet, pamphlet, handbill, handout, advertisement.

broke adj PENNILESS, insolvent, bankrupt, poverty-stricken, impoverished, impecunious, destitute, indigent, ruined; informal flat broke, strapped for cash, cleaned out, on one's uppers; Brit. informal skint, stony broke.

broken-hearted adj GRIEF-STRICKEN, desolate, despairing, devastated, inconsolable, miserable, overwhelmed, wretched, forlorn, woeful, crestfallen.

brood n OFFSPRING, young,

family, clutch, nest, litter, children, youngsters.
▶ v ❶ WORRY, agonize, fret, dwell on, meditate, mull over. ❷ SIT ON, hatch, incubate.

brook¹ n STREAM, streamlet, channel, rivulet, runnel; N. English beck; Scottish & N. English burn; N. Amer. & Austral./NZ creek.

brook² v TOLERATE, stand, bear, allow.

browbeat v BULLY, force, coerce, intimidate, compel, badger, hector, harangue, terrorize, tyrannize.

brown adj ❶ HAZEL, chestnut, nut-brown, brunette, chocolate, coffee, walnut, ochre, sepia, mahogany, russet, umber, burnt sienna, dun, khaki, beige, tan. ❷ TANNED, sunburnt, browned, bronze, bronzed, swarthy.
▶ v GRILL, toast, sear, seal.

browse v ❶ LOOK THROUGH, skim, scan, glance at, thumb through, leaf through, peruse. ❷ GRAZE, feed, eat, crop, nibble.

bruise n CONTUSION, swelling, bump, mark, blemish, welt.
▶ v CONTUSE, injure, blacken, mark, discolour, make black and blue.

brunt n IMPACT, full force, burden, shock, thrust, violence, pressure, strain, stress, repercussions, consequences.

brush n ❶ BROOM, sweeper, besom, whisk. ❷ ENCOUNTER, clash, confrontation, conflict, skirmish, tussle, fight, engagement.
▶ v ❶ SWEEP, clean, groom,

buff. ❷ TOUCH, graze, kiss, glance, contact.

■ **brush aside** *see* DISMISS (1).
brush off *see* REBUFF V.

brusque adj ABRUPT, curt, blunt, short, terse, caustic, gruff, rude, discourteous, impolite.
– OPPOSITES polite.

brutal adj SAVAGE, cruel, vicious, sadistic, violent, bloodthirsty, ruthless, callous, murderous, heartless, merciless, pitiless, remorseless, inhuman, barbarous, barbaric, ferocious, wild, brutish, bestial.
– OPPOSITES gentle.

brute n ❶ ANIMAL, beast, creature. ❷ SAVAGE, monster, animal, sadist, barbarian, fiend, devil, lout, oaf, boor; *informal* swine.
▶ adj CRUDE, rough, mindless, physical, unfeeling.

bubble n GLOBULE, bead, drop, air pocket.
▶ v FIZZ, foam, froth, gurgle, effervesce, sparkle, boil, simmer, seethe, percolate.

bubbly adj ❶ FIZZY, foamy, frothy, effervescent, sparkling, sudsy. ❷ VIVACIOUS, lively, animated, sparkling, excited, effervescent, bouncy, ebullient, elated.

bucket n PAIL, pitcher, can, scuttle.

buckle n ❶ CLASP, fastener, clip, catch, fastening, hasp. ❷ KINK, warp, distortion, wrinkle, bulge.
▶ v ❶ FASTEN, hook, secure, do

up, strap, tie, clasp, clip. ❷ BEND, twist, contort, warp, crumple, distort.

bud n SHOOT, sprout.
▶ v SPROUT, germinate, shoot, burgeon.

budge v ❶ MOVE, shift, stir, yield, go, proceed. ❷ PERSUADE, convince, influence, sway, bend.

budget n FINANCIAL PLAN, estimate, statement, account, allowance, means, resources.
▶ v ❶ PLAN, allow, set aside, allocate, save. ❷ PLAN, schedule, allocate, ration, apportion, allot.

buff[1] n POLISH, shine, rub, smooth, burnish.

buff[2] n FAN, enthusiast, aficionado, devotee, admirer, expert; *informal* freak, nut.

buffer n BULWARK, fender, bumper, cushion, guard, safeguard, shield, screen, intermediary.

buffet[1] n CAFE, cafeteria, snack bar, refreshment counter/stall.

buffet[2] v BATTER, strike, knock against, hit, bang, beat against.

buffoon n FOOL, idiot, dot, nincompoop; *informal* dope, chump, numbskull, halfwit; *Brit. informal* nitwit.

bug n ❶ INSECT, flea, mite; *informal* creepy-crawly; *Brit. informal* minibeast. ❷ GERM, virus, bacterium, microbe, microorganism. ❸ ILLNESS, sickness, disease, infection, disorder, upset, complaint; *Brit. informal* lurgy. ❹ FAULT, flaw, defect, error, imperfection, failing, obstruction; *informal* gremlin.

▶v **1** TAP, wiretap, listen in on, intercept, spy on. **2** *see* ANNOY.

build v CONSTRUCT, make, erect, put up/together, assemble, set up, manufacture, fabricate, raise, form.
▶n PHYSIQUE, body, frame, shape.
■ **build up** *see* INTENSIFY.

building n STRUCTURE, construction, edifice, pile, erection.

build-up n GROWTH, increase, expansion, enlargement, accumulation, escalation, development.

bulbous adj DISTENDED, bulging, swollen, rotund, convex, bloated, spherical, rounded.

bulge v SWELL, swell out, project, protrude, stick out, balloon, jut out, enlarge, billow, distend, bloat.
▶n SWELLING, bump, protuberance, protrusion, lump, knob, projection, prominence, distension.

bulk n **1** SIZE, volume, quantity, weight, extent, mass, substance, magnitude, dimensions, amplitude. **2** MAJORITY, preponderance, greater part, mass, body, generality.

bulky adj UNWIELDY, awkward, large, big, substantial, massive, immense, voluminous, weighty, ponderous; *informal* hulking.

bulldoze v **1** DEMOLISH, flatten, level, raze. **2** FORCE, push, shove, drive, propel.

bulletin n REPORT, announcement, statement, newsflash, account, message, communi-

qué, communication, dispatch, notification.

bullish adj OPTIMISTIC, hopeful, confident, positive, assured, cheerful, sanguine.

bully n INTIMIDATOR, persecutor, oppressor, browbeater, tyrant, tormentor, bully boy, thug; *informal* tough.
▶v INTIMIDATE, coerce, browbeat, oppress, domineer, persecute, torment, pressurize, pressure, terrorize, tyrannize, cow; *informal* push around.

bulwark n **1** RAMPART, embankment, fortification, bastion, redoubt, outwork, breastwork. **2** SUPPORT, defence, guard, protection, safeguard.

bumbling adj CLUMSY, awkward, blundering, incompetent, bungling, inept, inefficient, stumbling, lumbering, foolish.

bump v **1** HIT, bang, strike, knock, jar, crash into, collide with, smash into. *See also* HIT (1). **2** BOUNCE, jolt, shake, jerk, rattle, jounce.
▶n **1** BANG, crash, thud, thump, knock, smash, collision. **2** LUMP, swelling, contusion, injury, protrusion, bulge, projection, protuberance, hump, knob, distension.
■ **bump into** *see* MEET (1).

bumpkin n YOKEL, clodhopper, peasant, rustic, country cousin; *N. Amer. informal* hillbilly, hick, hayseed, rube.

bumptious adj SELF-IMPORTANT, conceited, arrogant,

cocky, full of oneself, overconfident, brash, overbearing, puffed up, self-opinionated, egotistical, immodest, boastful, presumptuous, pompous, officious, swaggering, forward, pushy; *informal* big-headed.
– OPPOSITES modest.

bumpy adj ❶ ROUGH, uneven, rutted, potholed, pitted, lumpy, knobby. ❷ JOLTING, jarring, bouncy, jerky, rough.
– OPPOSITES smooth.

bunch n ❶ COLLECTION, cluster, batch, set, quantity, bundle, heap, sheaf, clump. ❷ BOUQUET, spray, posy, sheaf, corsage, nosegay. ❸ GROUP, crowd, party, band, gathering, swarm, gang, flock, mob, knot, cluster, multitude.
▶ v GATHER, cluster, huddle, group, flock, mass, cram, pack, herd, bundle.
– OPPOSITES disperse.

bundle n BATCH, pile, collection, heap, stack, bunch, parcel, bale, sheaf, mass, quantity, accumulation.
▶ v ❶ TIE, tie up, wrap, bind, fasten together, pack, parcel, roll, truss. ❷ PUSH, shove, hurry, hustle, rush, thrust, throw.

bungle v MAKE A MESS OF, mismanage, spoil, ruin, blunder, muff, mar; *informal* screw up, foul up, mess up, louse up, botch, make a hash of, muck up; *Brit. informal* cock up.

bungling adj CLUMSY, incompetent, inept, unskilful, blundering, maladroit; *informal* ham-fisted, cack-handed.

buoy n FLOAT, marker, beacon.

buoyant adj ❶ FLOATING, afloat, floatable, light. ❷ *See* CHEERFUL (1).

burden n ❶ LOAD, weight, cargo, freight. ❷ RESPONSIBILITY, duty, obligation, onus, charge, care, worry, anxiety, problem, trouble, difficulty, strain, stress, affliction, weight, trial, tribulation, encumbrance, millstone, cross, albatross.
▶ v ❶ LOAD, overload, weigh down, encumber, hamper. ❷ TROUBLE, worry, oppress, bother, distress, afflict, torment, strain, tax, overwhelm, saddle, encumber; *informal* land.

bureau n ❶ AGENCY, office, department, service. ❷ DESK, writing desk, writing table.

bureaucracy n OFFICIALDOM, officials, administration, civil servants, civil service, government, directorate, regulations, paperwork, red tape.

burglar n HOUSEBREAKER, thief, robber, raider, looter, cat burglar, intruder; *N. Amer. informal* second-story man.

burglary n HOUSEBREAKING, breaking and entering, breaking in, break-in, forced/forcible entry, theft, robbery.

burial n INTERMENT, burying, entombment, funeral, obsequies; *formal* exequies.
– OPPOSITES exhumation.

burly adj WELL BUILT, muscular, brawny, stout, thickset, stocky, sturdy, big, powerful, strong, strapping, hefty, athletic.

tough, husky; *informal* beefy, hulking.
– OPPOSITES puny.

burn v ❶ BE ON FIRE, be alight, be ablaze, go up, blaze, be aflame, smoulder, flare, flash, glow, smoke, flicker. ❷ SET ON FIRE, set fire to, set alight, ignite, light, kindle, put a match to, incinerate, reduce to ashes, cremate, consume, sear, char, scorch.

burning adj ❶ ON FIRE, blazing, ablaze, aflame, alight, flaring, glowing, smouldering, ignited, flickering, scorching, incandescent; *poetic/literary* afire. ❷ STINGING, smarting, biting, prickling, irritating, searing, caustic, corrosive, painful. ❸ INTENSE, eager, passionate, fervent, ardent, fervid. ❹ IMPORTANT, crucial, significant, urgent, pressing, critical, compelling, vital, essential, acute, pivotal.

burnish v POLISH, shine, brighten, rub, buff, buff up, smooth.

burrow n TUNNEL, hole, hollow, excavation, lair, den, earth, warren, set.
▶ v DIG, tunnel, excavate, mine, hollow out, gouge out, scoop out.

burst v ❶ SPLIT, break open, rupture, crack, shatter, explode, give way, fracture, disintegrate, fragment, fly open. ❷ RUSH, thrust, shove, push, dash, run, erupt, surge.

bury v ❶ INTER, lay to rest, entomb, consign to the grave; *informal* plant. ❷ CONCEAL, hide,

cover with, submerge, tuck, sink, cup.
– OPPOSITES exhume.

bush n ❶ SHRUB, thicket, undergrowth, shrubbery. ❷ SCRUB, brush, wilds, backwoods; *Austral/NZ* outback.

bushy adj THICK, shaggy, dense, tangled, hairy, bristly, fuzzy, luxuriant, unruly, untidy, spreading.

business n ❶ OCCUPATION, profession, line, career, job, trade, vocation, work, employment, pursuit, métier. ❷ TRADE, commerce, industry, buying and selling, trading, merchandising, trafficking, bargaining, dealing, transactions. ❸ COMPANY, firm, enterprise, corporation, concern, organization, venture, shop, establishment, partnership. ❹ CONCERN, affair, responsibility, duty, function, task, assignment, obligation, problem. ❺ AFFAIR, matter, thing, case, set of circumstances, issue.

businesslike adj ❶ PROFESSIONAL, efficient, organized, methodical, systematic, well ordered, practical, thorough, painstaking, meticulous, correct. ❷ ROUTINE, conventional, unimaginative, prosaic, down-to-earth, workaday.
– OPPOSITES unprofessional, disorganized.

bust[1] n BREASTS, bosom, chest, torso; *informal* boobs, knockers.

bust[2] v ❶ BREAK, destroy, wreck, rupture, fracture, crack. ❷ ARREST, capture, catch, seize;

informal pinch, nab, collar; *Brit. informal* nick.

bustle n ACTIVITY, flurry, stir, restlessness, movement, hustle, hurly-burly, busyness, commotion, tumult, excitement, agitation, fuss; *informal* to-do.
▶ v HURRY, rush, dash, scurry, dart, hasten, scramble, fuss, scamper, flutter; *informal* tear.

busy adj ❶ ACTIVE, industrious, tireless, energetic, hectic, strenuous, full, bustling, exacting; *informal* on the go. ❷ OCCUPIED, working, engaged, at work, on duty, otherwise engaged; *informal* tied up. ❸ ORNATE, over-elaborate, over-decorated, fussy, cluttered.
– OPPOSITES idle, simple.

busybody n MEDDLER, interferer, troublemaker, mischiefmaker, gossip, scandalmonger, muckraker; *informal* snooper, nosy parker.

butt[1] v KNOCK, strike, shove, ram, bump, push, thrust, prod, poke, jab, thump, buffet.
■ **butt in** INTERRUPT, intrude, interfere in; *informal* stick one's nose/oar in.

butt[2] n TARGET, victim, object, subject, scapegoat, dupe.

butt[3] n ❶ HANDLE, shaft, hilt, haft. ❷ STUB, end, remnant, tail end; *Brit. informal* fag end.

buttocks n CHEEKS, rump, behind, hindquarters, seat; *Brit.* bottom; *informal* BTM, backside, derrière; *Brit. informal* bum, arse; *N. Amer. informal* butt, fanny; *humorous* posterior, fundament.

buttonhole v ACCOST, waylay, importune, detain, grab, catch, take aside.

buttress n SUPPORT, prop, reinforcement, strut, stanchion, pier.
▶ v STRENGTHEN, support, reinforce, prop up, shore up, brace, underpin, uphold, defend, back up.

buxom adj BIG-BREASTED, bigbosomed, full-figured, voluptuous, well rounded, Rubenesque, plump, robust, shapely, ample; *informal* busty, well endowed.

buy v PURCHASE, pay for, get, acquire, obtain, come by, procure, invest in.
– OPPOSITES sell.
▶ n PURCHASE, acquisition, bargain, deal.
– OPPOSITES sale.

buzz v HUM, murmur, drone, whirr, whisper; *poetic/literary* susurrate.

bygone adj PAST, departed, dead, gone, former, previous, one-time, forgotten, lost, old, antiquated, ancient, obsolete, outmoded.

bypass v ❶ GO ROUND, make a detour round, pass round. ❷ CIRCUMVENT, avoid, evade, get round, pass over, ignore, skirt, sidestep, miss out, go over the head of, short-circuit.

bystander n ONLOOKER, spectator, eyewitness, witness, watcher, viewer, passer-by.

Cc

cabin n **①** HUT, shack, shed, chalet, lodge, shelter, bothy. **②** BERTH, compartment, stateroom, sleeping quarters, saloon, deckhouse.

cable n ROPE, cord, wire, line, lead, hawser, mooring line, chain, guy.

cache n HOARD, store, supply, collection, fund; *informal* stash.

cacophonous adj DISCORDANT, atonal, dissonant, noisy, raucous, harsh, unmusical. – OPPOSITES harmonious.

cacophony n DISCORDANCE, dissonance, atonality, noise, racket, din, row, caterwauling, jangle, tumult, stridency, raucousness.

cadaverous adj CORPSE-LIKE, death-like, gaunt, haggard, drawn, emaciated, skeletal, hollow-eyed, ashen, pale, wan, ghostly.

cadence n RHYTHM, beat, pulse, tempo, measure, metre, swing, lilt, intonation, inflection, accent, modulation.

cafe n CAFETERIA, snack bar, buffet, coffee bar/shop/house, tea room/shop, diner, bistro, restaurant, brasserie.

cage n PEN, enclosure, pound, coop, lock-up, hutch, aviary. ▶ v *see* CONFINE (1).

cagey adj GUARDED, secretive, cautious, non-committal, wary, careful, chary, wily.

cajole v COAX, wheedle, beguile, seduce, persuade, flatter, humour, lure, entice, tempt, inveigle; *informal* sweet-talk, soft-soap, butter up.

cake n **①** BUN, gateau, pastry. **②** BLOCK, bar, slab, piece, lump, cube, mass, loaf, chunk. ▶ v **①** HARDEN, solidify, thicken, dry, bake, congeal, coagulate, consolidate. **②** COVER, coat, plaster, encrust, clog.

calamitous adj DISASTROUS, catastrophic, devastating, cataclysmic, ruinous, dire, dreadful, terrible, tragic, fatal, wretched, woeful, ghastly, unfortunate.

calamity n DISASTER, catastrophe, tragedy, misfortune, cataclysm, accident, devastation, misadventure, mischance, mishap, ruin, tribulation, woe.

calculate v **①** WORK OUT, estimate, determine, compute, count up, figure out, reckon up, evaluate, total. **②** ESTIMATE, gauge, judge, measure, weigh up, reckon, rate. **③** DESIGN, plan, aim, intend.

calculated adj *see* DELIBERATE adj (1).

calculating adj *see* CRAFTY.

calibre n **①** QUALITY, worth, stature, distinction, ability, merit, talent, capability, excellence, competence, capacity, endowments, gifts, strengths, scope. ❷ BORE, gauge, diameter, size.

call v ❶ CRY, cry out, shout, bellow, exclaim, yell, scream, roar, shriek. ❷ TELEPHONE, phone, call up; *Brit.* ring; *informal* buzz, give someone a buzz/tinkle; *Brit. informal* give someone a ring. ❸ VISIT, pay a visit/call, call on, stop by; *informal* drop in/by, pop in. ❹ CONVENE, summon, assemble, announce, order; *formal* convoke. ❺ NAME, christen, baptize, entitle, dub, designate, describe as, label, term. ❻ SEND FOR, summon, ask for, contact, order, fetch, bid. ❼ AWAKEN, wake, arouse, rouse.
▶ n ❶ CRY, shout, exclamation, yell, scream, shriek, roar, bellow. ❷ PLEA, request, appeal, order, command, summons. ❸ NEED, occasion, reason, cause, justification, grounds, excuse. ❹ DEMAND, requirement, request, need, want, requisition. ■ **call for** NEED, require, be grounds for, justify, necessitate, demand, entail. **call off** *see* CANCEL.

calling n VOCATION, occupation, job, line, line of work, career, profession, métier, business, work, employment, trade, craft, pursuit, province, field.

callous adj INSENSITIVE, unfeeling, hard, hardened, heartless, hard-hearted, hard-bitten, tough, cold, cool, stony-hearted, cruel, uncaring,

unsympathetic, indifferent, unresponsive, dispassionate, unconcerned, unsusceptible, merciless, pitiless, soulless; *informal* hard-nosed, hard-boiled.
– OPPOSITES compassionate.

callow adj IMMATURE, inexperienced, naive, unsophisticated, innocent, uninitiated, raw, green, young, adolescent; *informal* wet behind the ears.
– OPPOSITES mature, experienced.

calm adj ❶ COMPOSED, relaxed, collected, cool, controlled, restrained, self-controlled, self-possessed, quiet, tranquil, unruffled, serene, unexcited, unflappable, undisturbed, imperturbable, unemotional, unmoved, impassive, undemonstrative, poised, level-headed, patient, equable, stoical, pacific; *informal* laid-back, together. ❷ STILL, windless, mild, tranquil, balmy, quiet, peaceful, restful, undisturbed, halcyon.
– OPPOSITES excitable, stormy.
▶ v ❶ SOOTHE, quieten, pacify, hush, tranquillize, mollify, appease, allay, alleviate, assuage. ❷ QUIETEN, settle, settle down, die down, still.
– OPPOSITES agitate.
▶ n ❶ COMPOSURE, coolness, self-control, tranquillity, serenity, quietness, peace, peacefulness, harmony, restfulness, repose. ❷ STILLNESS, tranquillity, serenity, quietness, quietude.

calumny n SLANDER, libel, defamation, misrepresentation, false accusation, insult, abuse, denigration, vilification, vituperation, aspersions, backbiting, detraction, disparagement, deprecation, revilement, obloquy, smear campaign; *informal* mud-slinging.

camouflage n DISGUISE, mask, screen, cover, protective colouring, cloak, cover-up, front, false front, guise, facade, blind, concealment, masquerade, subterfuge.
▶ v DISGUISE, hide, conceal, mask, screen, cloak, veil, cover, cover up, obscure.

camp¹ n ENCAMPMENT, settlement, campsite, camping ground, tents, bivouac, cantonment.

camp² adj EFFEMINATE, effete, mincing, affected, artificial, mannered, posturing, studied.
– OPPOSITES macho.

campaign n ❶ BATTLE, war, offensive, expedition, attack, crusade. ❷ DRIVE, push, operation, plan, promotion, strategy, movement, manoeuvre.
▶ v FIGHT, battle, work, crusade, push, strive, struggle.

cancel v ❶ CALL OFF, scrap, drop, axe, abandon, stop, discontinue. ❷ ANNUL, declare void, invalidate, quash, nullify, set aside, retract, negate, countermand, rescind, revoke, repudiate, abrogate, abolish.
– OPPOSITES confirm.
■ **cancel out** COUNTERBALANCE, offset, counteract, neutralize, redeem.

cancer n MALIGNANT GROWTH,

cancerous growth, tumour, malignancy; *technical* carcinoma, sarcoma.

candid adj FRANK, open, honest, truthful, direct, plainspoken, blunt, straightforward, straight from the shoulder, outspoken, sincere, forthright, no-nonsense, unequivocal, undisguised, bluff, brusque.
– OPPOSITES guarded.

candidate n APPLICANT, contender, nominee, contestant, competitor, runner, entrant, aspirant, possibility.

candour n FRANKNESS, honesty, truthfulness, openness, directness, bluntness, outspokenness, sincerity, forthrightness.

canny adj SHREWD, sharp, astute, discerning, penetrating, clever, perspicacious, judicious, wise, sagacious, circumspect.
– OPPOSITES foolish.

canopy n AWNING, shade, sunshade, cover, tarpaulin.

canvass v ❶ SEEK VOTES, solicit votes, campaign, electioneer, drum up support, persuade, convince. ❷ INVESTIGATE, survey, find out, enquire into, look into, examine, scrutinize, explore, study, analyse, evaluate.
▶ v SURVEY, poll, opinion poll, census, investigation, market research.

canyon n RAVINE, valley, gorge, gully, defile, chasm, gulf, abyss.

capability n ABILITY, capacity, potential, aptitude, faculty, facility, power, skill, skilfulness, competence, efficiency, effectiveness, proficiency, adeptness.

capable adj ABLE, competent, effective, efficient, proficient, accomplished, talented, gifted, adept, skilful, experienced, practised, expert, masterly, qualified, adequate, clever, intelligent; *informal* smart.
– OPPOSITES incapable, incompetent.

■ **capable of** UP TO, equal to, inclined to, disposed to, liable to, prone to, likely to.

capacity n ❶ SPACE, room, size, scope, extent, volume, largeness, dimensions, proportions, magnitude, ampleness, amplitude. ❷ ABILITY, capability, aptitude, facility, competence, competency, potential, proficiency, skill, talent, accomplishment, cleverness, intelligence. ❸ POSITION, role, job, post, office, function, responsibility, appointment, province.

cape[1] n CLOAK, shawl, wrap, coat, robe, cope.

cape[2] n HEADLAND, point, promontory, peninsula, neck, tongue.

caper v FROLIC, romp, skip, gambol, cavort, prance, dance, jig, leap, hop, jump, bound, spring, bounce.

capital n ❶ FIRST CITY, seat of government, metropolis. ❷ MONEY, funds, finance, cash, wealth, principal, savings, resources, means, assets, reserves, property, wherewithal.
▶ adj UPPER-CASE, block.

capitulate v SURRENDER, yield, give in/up, back down, submit, concede, throw in the towel/sponge, succumb, cave in, relent, accede, acquiesce.
– OPPOSITES resist.

caprice n WHIM, impulse, fancy, vagary, notion, fad, quirk.

capricious adj FICKLE, unpredictable, impulsive, changeable, inconstant, mercurial, whimsical, volatile, erratic, variable, wayward, fitful, quirky, fanciful, uncertain, irregular, unreliable.
– OPPOSITES stable, consistent.

capsize v OVERTURN, turn over, upset, upend, tip over, knock over, keel over, turn turtle, invert.

capsule n PILL, tablet, caplet, lozenge; *informal* tab.

captain n ❶ COMMANDER, master, officer in charge; *informal* skipper. ❷ CHIEF, head, leader, principal; *informal* boss.

caption n HEADING, title, wording, head, legend, inscription, description.

captious adj CRITICAL, criticizing, carping, fault-finding, quibbling, cavilling; *informal* nit-picking.
– OPPOSITES forgiving.

captivate v CHARM, delight, enchant, bewitch, fascinate, dazzle, beguile, entrance,

enrapture, attract, hypnotize, mesmerize, enthral, allure, win, infatuate, seduce, ravish, ensnare, steal someone's heart.
– OPPOSITES repel, bore.

captive adj IMPRISONED, locked up, caged, incarcerated, jailed, confined, detained, taken prisoner, interned, penned up, captured, ensnared, restrained, in captivity, in bondage; *informal* under lock and key.
– OPPOSITES free.
▶ n PRISONER, detainee, prisoner-of-war, convict, internee, slave; *informal* jailbird, con.

captivity n IMPRISONMENT, custody, detention, confinement, internment, incarceration, restraint, constraint, committal, bondage, slavery, servitude, enslavement, subjugation, subjection; *historical* thraldom.
– OPPOSITES freedom.

capture v CATCH, arrest, apprehend, take prisoner, take into custody, seize, trap, take, lay hold of, take captive; *informal* nab, pinch, collar, lift, bag; *Brit. informal* nick.
– OPPOSITES free, liberate.
▶ n ARREST, apprehension, detention, imprisonment, seizure, trapping.

car n MOTOR CAR, motor, automobile; *informal* wheels; *N. Amer. informal* auto.

carcass n ❶ BODY, corpse, remains; *Medicine* cadaver; *informal* stiff. ❷ FRAME, framework, skeleton, remains, structure, shell, hulk.

cardinal adj FUNDAMENTAL, basic, main, chief, primary, prime, principal, paramount, key, essential.
– OPPOSITES unimportant.

care n ❶ WORRY, anxiety, sadness, trouble, stress, unease, distress, disquiet, sorrow, anguish, grief, woe, hardship, tribulation, affliction, responsibility, pressure, strain, burden. ❷ CAREFULNESS, attention, thought, regard, thoroughness, conscientiousness, pains, vigilance, accuracy, precision, meticulousness, fastidiousness, punctiliousness, mindfulness, solicitude, forethought, heed. ❸ CHARGE, supervision, custody, protection, safe keeping, guardianship, control, management, ministration, wardship.
– OPPOSITES happiness, inattention, carelessness.
▶ v MIND, be concerned, be interested, worry oneself, bother, trouble, have regard.
■ **care for** see LOVE v (1), LOOK AFTER.

career n PROFESSION, occupation, job, vocation, calling, livelihood, employment, work, métier.

carefree adj CHEERFUL, lighthearted, happy, nonchalant, unworried, untroubled, cheery, happy-go-lucky, jolly, merry, buoyant, easy-going, relaxed, unconcerned, breezy, jaunty, insouciant, blithe; *informal* upbeat, laid-back.
– OPPOSITES worried, miserable.

careful adj ❶ CAUTIOUS, alert, attentive, watchful, aware, vigilant, wary, on one's guard, prudent, heedful, circumspect, mindful, observant, chary. ❷ CONSCIENTIOUS, painstaking, meticulous, diligent, attentive, accurate, precise, scrupulous, fastidious, punctilious, methodical, organized, systematic, thorough, well organized.
– OPPOSITES careless.

careless adj ❶ INATTENTIVE, thoughtless, negligent, unthinking, irresponsible, lax, slipshod, sloppy, forgetful, absent-minded, remiss. ❷ CURSORY, perfunctory, hasty, inaccurate, disorganized, slapdash, slipshod, sloppy, messy. ❸ THOUGHTLESS, unthinking, insensitive, indiscreet, unguarded, ill-considered, reckless, rash, imprudent.
– OPPOSITES careful.

caress v FONDLE, stroke, smooth, touch, pet, cuddle, pat, nuzzle, kiss, embrace, hug.

caretaker n JANITOR, superintendent, porter, warden, watchman, keeper, steward, curator, concierge.

careworn adj see WEARY adj (1).

cargo n FREIGHT, payload, load, consignment, contents, goods, merchandise, baggage, shipment, boatload, lorryload, truckload, lading.

caricature n PARODY, mimicry, lampoon, distortion, burlesque, travesty, cartoon, satire, farce; informal take-off, send-up.

▶ v PARODY, mimic, lampoon, mock, ridicule, distort, satirize, burlesque; informal take off, send up.

carnage n SLAUGHTER, massacre, mass murder, butchery, bloodbath, bloodshed, holocaust, pogrom.

carnal adj SEXUAL, sensual, erotic, fleshly, lustful, lewd, lecherous, lascivious, libidinous, coarse, gross, prurient, salacious, lubricious.

carnival n FESTIVAL, celebration, fair, fiesta, fête, gala, jamboree, festivity, revelry.

carouse v MAKE MERRY, party, go on a spree, binge, roister, overindulge; informal live it up, paint the town red, go on a bender.

carp v COMPLAIN, find fault, criticize, quibble, grumble, object, reproach, censure, cavil, nag; informal nit-pick, gripe, go on.

carpenter n WOODWORKER, cabinetmaker, joiner; Brit. informal chippy.

carriage n ❶ COACH, vehicle. ❷ BEARING, posture, stance, gait, manner, presence, air, demeanour, mien, behaviour, conduct; Brit. deportment; formal comportment. ❸ TRANSPORT, transportation, freight, conveyance, delivery, carrying.

carry v ❶ CONVEY, transport, move, transfer, take, bring, fetch, bear, haul, shift, transmit, relay, manhandle; informal lug, cart. ❷ SUPPORT, bear,

sustain, maintain, hold up, shoulder. ❸ AFFECT, influence, have an effect on, stimulate, motivate, spur on, drive, impel, urge. ❹ INVOLVE, lead to, result in, require, entail, demand.
■ **carry on** see CONTINUE. **carry out** see DO (1).

cart n BARROW, wheelbarrow, handcart, pushcart.
▶ v see CARRY (1).

carton n BOX, container, package, case, packet, pack.

cartoon n ❶ CARICATURE, parody, lampoon, burlesque, satire; informal send-up, take-off. ❷ ANIMATED FILM, animation, comic strip, photostory.

cartridge n ❶ CASE, container, cylinder, capsule, cassette, magazine. ❷ ROUND, shell.

carve v ❶ SCULPT, sculpture, chisel, cut, hew, whittle, form, shape, fashion, mould. ❷ ENGRAVE, etch, incise, notch, cut in. ❸ SLICE, cut up.
■ **carve up** see DIVIDE (3).

cascade n WATERFALL, falls, shower, fountain, torrent, flood, deluge, outpouring, avalanche, cataract.
▶ v GUSH, pour, surge, spill, overflow, tumble, descend.

case[1] n ❶ SITUATION, occasion, context, circumstances, instance, position, conditions, event, occurrence, predicament, contingency, plight. ❷ INSTANCE, example, occurrence, occasion, illustration, specimen. ❸ TRIAL, proceedings, lawsuit, action, suit. ❹ PATIENT, victim, sufferer, invalid.

case[2] n CONTAINER, box, receptacle, canister, crate, carton, pack, suitcase, trunk, luggage, baggage.

cash n MONEY, funds, finance, capital, resources, currency, change, notes, coins, legal tender; informal dough, bread, moolah; Brit. informal readies, the ready.
▶ v EXCHANGE, change, turn into money/cash, realize; Brit. encash.

cashier n TELLER, clerk, banker, treasurer, purser, bursar, controller.

cask n BARREL, keg, vat, butt, tub, vessel, tun, hogshead, firkin, pipe.

cast v ❶ THROW, toss, fling, pitch, hurl, sling, lob, launch, let fly; informal chuck, heave. ❷ EMIT, give off, send out, shed, radiate, diffuse, spread. ❸ MOULD, form, fashion, sculpt, model.
▶ n ❶ FIGURE, shape, mould, form, sculpture. ❷ SORT, kind, type, style, stamp.

caste n CLASS, order, rank, level, grade, position, station, place, status, standing, grading.

castle n FORTRESS, fort, citadel, stronghold, fortification, keep, palace, chateau, tower.

casual adj ❶ INDIFFERENT, careless, lax, unconcerned, uninterested, unenthusiastic, easy-going, nonchalant, offhand, throwaway, relaxed, apathetic, lackadaisical, blasé, insouciant, unprofessional; informal laid-back. ❷ SLIGHT,

superficial, shallow.
❸ TEMPORARY, part-time, free-lance, irregular. ❹ ACCIDENTAL, chance, unintentional, un-planned, unexpected, unfore-seen, unanticipated, fortuitous, serendipitous, incidental.
❺ INFORMAL, relaxed, leisure, unceremonious; *informal* sporty.
– OPPOSITES diligent, perman-ent, deliberate, formal.

casualty n FATALITY, victim, sufferer, dead/wounded/in-jured person.

cat n FELINE, tomcat, tom, kitten; *informal* pussy, pussy cat, puss, kitty; *Brit. informal* moggie, mog.

catalogue n LIST, record, register, inventory, index, dir-ectory, roll, table, guide, classi-fication, calendar, schedule.
▶ v LIST, file, classify, categorize, register, record, make an inventory of, alphabetize.

catapult v LAUNCH, hurl, propel, shoot, fling, fire. *See also* THROW (1).

cataract n WATERFALL, falls, cascade, rapids, torrent, down-pour.

catastrophe n DISASTER, calamity, cataclysm, tragedy, misfortune, blow, mishap, mis-adventure, reverse, debacle, fiasco, trouble, trial, adversity, affliction.

catch v ❶ GRASP, seize, grab, clutch, grip, hold, pluck, clench, intercept, snare, trap, receive, acquire. ❷ CAPTURE, apprehend, arrest, seize, take prisoner, lay hold of, trap,

snare; *informal* collar, nab, pinch; *Brit. informal* nick. ❸ HEAR, under-stand, follow, grasp, compre-hend, make out, take in, discern, perceive, fathom.
❹ CONTRACT, get, develop, become infected by, suffer from, succumb to; *Brit.* go down with.
▶ n ❶ BOLT, lock, fastening, fastener, clasp, hasp, hook, clip, latch, snib. ❷ SNAG, dis-advantage, drawback, diffi-culty, hitch, fly in the ointment, stumbling block, trick, snare. ❸ YIELD, take, haul, bag, net, prize.
■ catch on ❶ BECOME POPULAR, come into fashion, succeed, become all the rage; *informal* become trendy. ❷ *See* UNDER-STAND (1).

catching adj CONTAGIOUS, infectious, communicable, transmissible, transmittable.

catchy adj MEMORABLE, popu-lar, haunting, appealing, cap-tivating, melodious, singable.

categorical adj UNQUALIFIED, unconditional, unequivocal, unambiguous, unreserved, definite, absolute, explicit, emphatic, positive, express, firm, direct, conclusive, decided, forceful, downright, utter, out-and-out.
– OPPOSITES equivocal, tentative.

category n CLASS, group, classification, grouping, type, sort, kind, variety, grade, order, rank, division, heading, section, department.

cater

■ **cater for ❶** FEED, provide food for, provision, serve, cook for; *dated* victual. **❷** TAKE INTO ACCOUNT / CONSIDERATION, allow for, bear in mind, make provision for, have regard for.

catholic adj WIDE, broad,
wide-ranging, all-embracing, general, comprehensive, varied, all-inclusive, eclectic, universal.
– OPPOSITES narrow.

cattle n COWS, bovines, livestock, stock, bulls, heifers, calves, bullocks, steers.

cause n ❶ ORIGIN, source, root,
beginning, genesis, occasion, mainspring, author, originator, creator, produce, agent, prime mover, maker. **❷** REASON, basis, grounds, justification, call, motive, motivation.
❸ PRINCIPLE, ideal, belief, conviction, object, end, aim, objective, purpose, charity.
▶ v ❶ BRING ABOUT, produce, create, make happen, give rise to, lead to, result in, provoke, originate, generate, engender, arouse, effect, occasion, precipitate, induce. **❷** FORCE, make, compel, induce.

caustic adj ❶ CORROSIVE, acid,
corroding, burning, destructive, mordant, acrid. **❷** CUTTING, biting, sarcastic, stinging, scathing, virulent, waspish, trenchant, pungent, astringent, acidulous, acrimonious, mordant.
– OPPOSITES gentle, mild.

caution n ❶ CARE, carefulness,
attention, alertness, wariness, prudence, watchfulness, vigilance, heed, heedfulness, guardedness, circumspection, discretion, forethought, mindfulness. **❷** WARNING, reprimand, admonition, injunction; *informal* dressing-down; *Brit. informal* ticking-off.
▶ v ❶ WARN, advise, urge, counsel, inform, alert, forewarn, admonish. **❷** REPRIMAND, admonish, warn, give a warning to, censure; *informal* tell off; *Brit. informal* tick off.

cautious adj CAREFUL, wary,
prudent, guarded, alert, circumspect, watchful, vigilant, mindful, shrewd, chary, tactful, non-committal, tentative; *informal* cagey.
– OPPOSITES incautious, reckless.

cavalier adj OFFHAND,
arrogant, haughty, disdainful, supercilious, insolent, condescending, lofty, patronizing.

cave n CAVERN, hollow, grotto,
pothole, cavity, dugout, underground chamber.
■ **cave in** *see* COLLAPSE.

cavity n HOLE, hollow, crater,
pit, orifice, gap, dent, aperture.

cease v STOP, finish, end,
bring to a halt, halt, break off, discontinue, conclude, suspend, terminate, desist, leave off, refrain from; *informal* quit, knock off, lay off.
– OPPOSITES start, begin.

ceaseless adj UNENDING,
endless, constant, continual, continuous, non-stop,

perpetual, never-ending, incessant, persistent, relentless, unremitting, interminable, everlasting, untiring, chronic.
– OPPOSITES intermittent.

celebrate v ❶ ENJOY ONESELF, rejoice, make merry, revel, party; *informal* go out on the town, paint the town red, whoop it up. ❷ COMMEMORATE, remember, honour, observe, make, keep, toast, drink to. ❸ PERFORM, officiate at, observe.

celebrated adj *see* FAMOUS.

celebration n ❶ PARTY, festival, carnival, gala, fête, festivity, revelry, merrymaking, jollification, spree; *informal* bash, shindig; *Brit. informal* beanfeast, rave-up. ❷ COMMEMORATION, remembrance, observance, honouring, keeping.

celebrity n ❶ *See* FAME. ❷ FAMOUS PERSON, star, dignitary, luminary, notable, personage; *informal* bigwig, big shot, big noise.

celestial adj ❶ ASTRONOMICAL, cosmic, heavenly, stellar, interstellar, extraterrestrial. ❷ DIVINE, heavenly, supernatural, transcendental, godlike, ethereal, sublime, spiritual, immortal, angelic, seraphic, cherubic.

celibacy n CHASTITY, purity, abstinence, self-denial, asceticism, virginity, bachelorhood, spinsterhood, monasticism,

monkhood, nunhood, continence, abnegation.

celibate adj CHASTE, pure, abstinent, virgin, immaculate, continent.

cell n ❶ ENCLOSURE, dungeon, lock-up, cubicle, room, apartment, chamber, stall. ❷ CAVITY, compartment, hole, unit.

cement n ADHESIVE, glue, paste, bonding, binder.

cemetery n GRAVEYARD, burial ground, churchyard, necropolis.

censor v EXPURGATE, bowdlerize, cut, delete, edit, remove, make cuts/changes to, amend, prohibit, forbid, ban.

censorious adj CRITICAL, hypercritical, disapproving, condemnatory, judgemental, moralistic, fault-finding, captious, carping, cavilling.

censure v CRITICIZE, blame, disapprove of, denounce, reprove, rebuke, reproach, reprimand, upbraid, berate, scold, chide, reprehend; *informal* tell off; *Brit. informal* tick off, carpet; *formal* castigate.
▶ n CRITICISM, blame, condemnation, denunciation, disapproval, reproval, reproof, reproach, rebuke, reprimand, scolding, berating, upbraiding, obloquy, reprehension, vituperation; *informal* talking-to, dressing-down; *formal* castigation.

central adj ❶ MIDDLE, mid, median, mean, mesial. ❷ MAIN, chief, principal, foremost, basic, fundamental, key,

essential, primary, pivotal, core, focal, cardinal.
– OPPOSITES side, outer, subordinate.

centralize v CONCENTRATE, centre, consolidate, condense, amalgamate, unify, incorporate, streamline, focus, rationalize.

centre n MIDDLE, middle point, heart, core, nucleus, midpoint, hub, kernel, focus, focal point, pivot, inside, interior.
– OPPOSITES periphery.
▶ v CONCENTRATE, focus, converge, close in, pivot.

ceremonial adj FORMAL, official, ritual, ritualistic, celebratory, liturgical, stately, dignified, solemn.

ceremonious adj DIGNIFIED, majestic, imposing, impressive, solemn, stately, formal, courtly, scrupulous, precise, punctilious, deferential, stiff, rigid.
– OPPOSITES casual.

ceremony n ❶ RITE, service, ritual, sacrament, formality, observance, celebration, commemoration, function, event, parade. ❷ FORMALITY, pomp, decorum, formalities, niceties, etiquette, propriety, ritual, attention to detail, protocol, punctiliousness, pageantry, grandeur, ceremonial.

certain adj ❶ SURE, confident, convinced, satisfied, persuaded, assured, unwavering, secure, unshaken. ❷ ASSURED, inevitable, definite, destined, inescapable, bound to happen,

inexorable, unarguable, ineluctable. ❸ DEFINITE, sure, sound, reliable, dependable, trustworthy, unquestionable, beyond question, evident, plain, clear, indubitable, undeniable, obvious, undisputed, incontrovertible, incontestable, conclusive, infallible, foolproof; informal sure-fire. ❹ PARTICULAR, specific, precise, special, individual.
– OPPOSITES doubtful, possible, unlikely.

certainly adv DEFINITELY, surely, assuredly, undoubtedly, undeniably, obviously, plainly, clearly.

certainty n ❶ SURENESS, authority, positiveness, confidence, assurance, assuredness, conviction, reliability, conclusiveness, authoritativeness, validity. ❷ FACT, inevitability, foregone conclusion, indubitability; informal sure thing; Brit. informal dead cert.
– OPPOSITES uncertainty.

certificate n CERTIFICATION, authorization, document, licence, warrant, credentials, pass, permit, guarantee, voucher, diploma, qualification, testimonial.

certify v ❶ AUTHENTICATE, document, verify, validate, confirm, bear witness to, attest to, testify to, substantiate, corroborate, endorse, vouch for, ratify, warrant. ❷ ACCREDIT, license, recognize, authorize, qualify, give a certificate/diploma to.

cessation n END, finish, termination, conclusion, halt, pause, break, respite, let-up.

chain n ❶ SHACKLE, fetter, manacle, bonds, coupling, link. ❷ SERIES, succession, progression, sequence, string, set, cycle, line, row, concatenation.
▶ v FASTEN, secure, tie, bind, tether, shackle, fetter, manacle, handcuff, hitch.

chair v PRESIDE OVER, lead, direct, manage, control, oversee, supervise.

chalky adj WHITE, pale, wan, pallid, ashen, pasty, waxen, blanched, bleached, colourless.

challenge v ❶ DARE, summon, invite, throw down the gauntlet to, defy. ❷ QUESTION, dispute, call into question, protest against, object to, take exception to, disagree with, argue against, contest, oppose, query, demur against, impugn. ❸ STIMULATE, test, tax, inspire, excite, arouse, spur on.

challenging adj STIMULATING, exciting, inspiring, testing, thought-provoking.
– OPPOSITES easy.

chamber n ❶ ROOM, cubicle, bedroom, bedchamber, boudoir. ❷ CAVITY, compartment, hollow, cell.

champion n ❶ WINNER, prizewinner, medallist, recordbreaker, victor, title-holder, conqueror, hero. ❷ SUPPORTER, defender, upholder, advocate, backer, patron, protector, vindicator. ❸ KNIGHT, hero, warrior, contender, fighter, man-at-arms, paladin.
▶ adj WINNING, victorious, unrivalled, leading, great, supreme, record-breaking.
▶ v DEFEND, support, uphold, stand up for, back, advocate, promote, espouse.

chance n ❶ ACCIDENT, coincidence, luck, fate, destiny, fluke, providence, fortune, serendipity, fortuity. ❷ POSSIBILITY, likelihood, prospect, probability, likeliness, odds, conceivability. ❸ OPPORTUNITY, time, occasion, turn, opening; informal shot.
▶ adj ACCIDENTAL, unforeseen, unexpected, coincidental, lucky, unplanned, unintended, unintentional, unpremeditated, casual, inadvertent, unanticipated, unforeseeable, random, haphazard, unlooked for, fortuitous, serendipitous, adventitious, fluky.
– OPPOSITES intentional, deliberate.
▶ v ❶ See HAPPEN. ❷ See RISK v (2, 3).
■ **chance on/upon** MEET, encounter, come across, stumble on; informal bump into, run into.

chancy adj RISKY, dangerous, hazardous, unsafe, uncertain, precarious, perilous, insecure, speculative, unpredictable; informal dicey; Brit. informal dodgy.
– OPPOSITES safe.

change v ❶ ALTER, adjust, transform, modify, convert, vary, amend, rearrange, reorganize, remodel, reform, reconstruct, restyle, recast, tailor, transmute, accustom, metamorphose, transmogrify, permutate, permute. ❷ BE CHANGED, alter, be transformed, evolve, develop, move on, mutate, shift, do an about-face, do a U-turn; Brit. informal chop and change. ❸ EXCHANGE, swap, switch, substitute, replace, trade, interchange, barter, transpose. ▶ n ❶ ALTERATION, modification, adaptation, difference, transformation, conversion, variation, development, remodelling, reorganization, rearrangement, reconstruction, shift, transition, metamorphosis, mutation, transmutation, transmogrification, innovation, vicissitude, permutation. ❷ EXCHANGE, switch, swap, trade, substitution, interchange, bartering. ❸ COINS, silver, small change, cash, petty cash.

changeable adj VARIABLE, changing, varying, shifting, vacillating, fluctuating, volatile, capricious, wavering, unstable, unsteady, irregular, erratic, unreliable, inconsistent, unpredictable, fickle, inconstant, mercurial, fluid, fitful, kaleidoscopic, protean, mutable, chequered, vicissitudinous.
– OPPOSITES constant.

channel n ❶ PASSAGE, sea passage, strait, narrow, neck, waterway, watercourse, fiord. ❷ GUTTER, furrow, groove, conduit, duct, culvert, ditch, gully. ❸ PATH, route, direction, way, approach, course. ❹ MEDIUM, means, agency, vehicle, route.

▶ v CONVEY, conduct, transmit, transport, guide, direct.

chant n SONG, hymn, chorus, carol, psalm.
▶ v INTONE, recite, sing, cantillate.

chaos n DISORDER, anarchy, mayhem, bedlam, pandemonium, turmoil, tumult, uproar, disruption, upheaval, confusion, disarray, lawlessness, riot, disorganization.
– OPPOSITES order.

chaotic adj ANARCHIC, in chaos, disordered, disorganized, confused, disorderly, unruly, uncontrolled, tumultuous, jumbled, upset, askew, disrupted, in disarray, awry, lawless, riotous, ungovernable, rebellious, orderless; informal topsy-turvy, haywire, higgledy-piggledy; Brit. informal shambolic.
– OPPOSITES disorderly.

character n ❶ PERSONALITY, nature, disposition, temperament, temper, make-up, constitution, cast, attributes, bent, complexion. ❷ STRENGTH, honour, integrity, moral fibre, uprightness, rectitude, fortitude, backbone. ❸ ECCENTRIC, original, individual, oddity; informal oddball, odd fellow, queer fish; informal, dated card. ❹ PERSON, individual, human being; informal fellow, guy, type, sort, customer; Brit. informal bloke, chap. ❺ REPUTATION, name, standing, position, status. ❻ TYPE, sign, symbol, mark, figure, hieroglyph, cipher, ideogram.

characteristic n QUALITY, attribute, feature, trait, property, peculiarity, quirk, mannerism, idiosyncrasy, hallmark, trademark.
▶ adj TYPICAL, distinctive, distinguishing, particular, special, individual, peculiar, specific, representative, symbolic, idiosyncratic, symptomatic.

characterize v PORTRAY, depict, describe, present, identify, draw, brand, typify, delineate, denote, indicate, specify, designate.

charade n PRETENCE, travesty, mockery, fake, sham, deception, pose, farce, absurdity, parody, pantomime, play-acting, masquerade.

charge v ❶ ASK IN PAYMENT, ask, ask for, expect, make someone pay, impose, levy, require. ❷ ACCUSE OF, arraign, indict, prosecute, impute, blame, incriminate. ❸ ATTACK, storm, assault, rush, open fire on, assail, fall on; *informal* lay into, wade into. ❹ ENTRUST, burden, impose on, give, load, encumber, saddle. ❺ FILL, load, imbue, instil, suffuse, permeate, pervade.
– OPPOSITES absolve.
▶ n ❶ COST, rate, price, amount, fee, payment, expense, outlay, expenditure, levy, toll, terms, dues. ❷ ACCUSATION, allegation, indictment, arraignment, impeachment, citation, imputation, blame, incrimination.

❸ ATTACK, assault, offensive, storming, raid, strike, onrush, onslaught, sally, incursion, sortie. ❹ CARE, custody, responsibility, protection, supervision, safe keeping, keeping, trust, guardianship, surveillance.

charitable adj ❶ GENEROUS, kind, giving, philanthropic, magnanimous, liberal, munificent, bountiful, open-handed, benevolent. ❷ LIBERAL, generous, tolerant, understanding, broad-minded, sympathetic.
– OPPOSITES uncharitable.

charity n ❶ DONATIONS, contributions, handouts, financial assistance, funding, endowments, almsgiving, philanthropy, benefaction. ❷ COMPASSION, humanity, goodwill, kindliness, sympathy, love, tolerance, thoughtfulness, generosity, altruism, humanitarianism, benevolence.

charm n ❶ ATTRACTIVENESS, attraction, appeal, allure, fascination, desirability, charisma, lure, delightfulness, captivation, allurement. ❷ SPELL, magic words, incantation, sorcery, witchcraft, wizardry. ❸ AMULET, trinket, talisman, mascot.
▶ v DELIGHT, please, attract, captivate, fascinate, win over, bewitch, beguile, enchant, seduce, hypnotize, mesmerize, enthral, intrigue, disarm, enamour, allure, draw.
– OPPOSITES repel.

chart n GRAPH, table, diagram, map, plan, blueprint, guide, scheme, tabulation.
▸ v MAP, map out, plot, graph, delineate, sketch, draft.

chase v PURSUE, run/go after, follow, hunt, hound, track, trail, tail.

chasm n ABYSS, ravine, pit, canyon, opening, void, crater, crevasse, gap, fissure, rift.

chaste adj ❶ CELIBATE, virginal, abstinent, pure, innocent, virtuous, undefiled, moral, immaculate, unmarried. ❷ VIRTUOUS, good, pure, innocent, decent, moral, modest, wholesome, upright, righteous, becoming, restrained, unsullied.
– OPPOSITES promiscuous.

chastity n CHASTENESS, celibacy, abstinence, virginity, self-restraint, self-denial, virtue, purity, innocence, continence, sinlessness.

chat v TALK, gossip, chatter, have a conversation with, converse, prattle, jabber.
▸ n TALK, gossip, conversation, heart-to-heart; informal confab, chinwag; Brit. informal natter.

chatty adj TALKATIVE, garrulous, loquacious, voluble, effusive, gushing, gossipy.
– OPPOSITES taciturn.

chauvinism n JINGOISM, prejudice, bigotry, bias, machismo.

cheap adj ❶ INEXPENSIVE, low-cost, low-priced, economical, reasonable, bargain, economy, reduced, marked down, discounted, sale; informal bargain-basement, knock-down. ❷ POOR-QUALITY, inferior, shoddy, common, tawdry, tatty, paltry, worthless, second-rate, gimcrack; informal tacky, trashy. ❸ DESPICABLE, contemptible, tasteless, unpleasant, unworthy, mean, low, base, sordid, vulgar.
– OPPOSITES expensive.

cheapen v DEGRADE, debase, belittle, demean, devalue, denigrate, discredit, prostitute, lower the tone of.

cheat v ❶ DECEIVE, trick, swindle, take in, defraud, dupe, hoodwink, double-cross, take advantage of, exploit, gull; informal rip off, take for a ride, con, diddle, bamboozle, finagle, bilk, fleece. ❷ AVOID, elude, evade, dodge, escape, shun, eschew.
▸ n ❶ CHEATER, swindler, fraud, confidence trickster, deceiver, trickster, double-crosser, impostor, crook, hoaxer, rogue, charlatan, mountebank, shark; informal con man, phoney; Brit. informal twister. ❷ SWINDLE, fraud, deception, deceit, trick, trickery, ruse, misrepresentation, chicanery, imposture, artifice; informal con, rip-off, fiddle, racket; Brit. informal swizz.

check v ❶ EXAMINE, inspect, look over/at, scrutinize, test, monitor, investigate, probe, enquire into, study; informal give the once-over to. ❷ STOP, halt, arrest, bring to a standstill, slow down, brake, obstruct,

inhibit, bar, impede, block, retard, curb, delay, thwart.
► n ❶ EXAMINATION, inspection, scrutiny, test, monitoring, investigation, enquiry, probe, study; *informal* once-over, going-over. ❷ STOP, stoppage, halt, obstruction, break, slowing down, slowdown, delay, interruption, suspension, hiatus, retardation.

cheek n IMPUDENCE, impertinence, insolence, effrontery, boldness, audacity, temerity, brazenness; *informal* brass, neck, gall, lip; *Brit. informal* sauce.

cheeky adj IMPUDENT, impertinent, insolent, disrespectful, insulting, impolite, presumptuous, mocking, irreverent, forward, pert; *informal* saucy; *N. Amer. informal* sassy.
– OPPOSITES respectful.

cheep v CHIRP, chirrup, tweet, twitter, warble, trill.

cheer v ❶ ACCLAIM, applaud, hail, hurrah, encourage, clap, shout/yell at. ❷ MAKE CHEERFUL, please, hearten, gladden, brighten, buoy up, comfort, console, buoy up, solace, uplift; *informal* buck up.
► n ❶ ACCLAIM, acclamation, applause, hurray, hurrah, ovation, plaudit, shout, shouting, hailing, clapping, encouragement, approval. ❷ CHEERFULNESS, happiness, gladness, merriment, glee, mirth, gaiety, joy, pleasure, jubilation, rejoicing, festivity, revelry.
■ **cheer up** BRIGHTEN, liven up, perk up, rally, take heart.

cheerful adj ❶ HAPPY, bright, glad, merry, sunny, joyful, delighted, good-humoured, jolly, animated, buoyant, light-hearted, carefree, gleeful, breezy, cheery, jaunty, perky, smiling, laughing, optimistic, hopeful, positive, in good spirits, sparkling, happy-go-lucky, sprightly, rapturous; *informal* chirpy; *poetic/literary* blithe. ❷ BRIGHT, sunny, cheering, pleasant, agreeable, friendly, happy.
– OPPOSITES sad, cheerless, dull.

cheerless adj GLOOMY, miserable, dreary, dull, dismal, depressing, bleak, drab, grim, austere, dark, dingy, desolate, sombre, uninviting, forbidding, melancholy, comfortless, forlorn, joyless, disconsolate, funereal, woeful.
– OPPOSITES cheerful, bright.

cheery adj CHEERFUL, happy, bright, merry, glad, in good spirits. *See also* CHEERFUL (1).
– OPPOSITES sad.

chemist n PHARMACIST, pharmacy; *N. Amer.* drugstore; *archaic* apothecary.

chequered adj MIXED, varied, diverse, diversified, eventful.

cherish v ❶ TREASURE, prize, hold dear, love, adore, dote on, idolize, cosset, nurture, look after, protect, value. ❷ HAVE, entertain, harbour, cling to, nurture, foster.
– OPPOSITES neglect.

chest n ❶ BREAST, thorax, sternum, ribcage. ❷ BOX, crate, case, trunk, container, coffer, casket.

chew v BITE, crunch, gnaw, masticate, champ, grind.

chic adj STYLISH, fashionable, smart, elegant, modish, voguish.

chief n ❶ CHIEFTAIN, head, headman, ruler, leader, overlord, suzerain. ❷ HEAD, ruler, principal, leader, director, manager, supervisor, superintendent, senior, director, manager, chairman, chairperson, chief executive, proprietor, master, mistress, overseer, foreman, controller, captain, commander; *informal* boss, kingpin, top dog, big cheese, bigwig, number one, supremo; *Brit. informal* gaffer, governor.
▸ adj ❶ SUPREME, foremost, principal, highest, leading, pre-eminent, senior, superior, premier, head, directing, grand, top. ❷ MAIN, principal, most important, cardinal, key, primary, prime, central, fundamental, predominant, foremost, vital, paramount, uppermost.
– OPPOSITES minor, subordinate.

chiefly adv MAINLY, principally, primarily, in the main, predominantly, especially, particularly, mostly, essentially, on the whole, for the most part, above all.

child n ❶ BOY, GIRL, youngster, young person, infant, baby, toddler, tot, tiny tot, youth, adolescent, juvenile, minor; *Scottish* bairn; *informal* kid,

nipper, shaver, brat, guttersnipe; *Brit. informal* sprog. ❷ SON, DAUGHTER, offspring, progeny, descendant, scion; *Law* issue.

childbirth n LABOUR, delivery, confinement, parturition, accouchement.

childhood n YOUTH, infancy, babyhood, boyhood, girlhood, adolescence, minority; *informal* teens, pre-teens.

childish adj IMMATURE, infantile, juvenile, puerile, irresponsible, foolish, jejune. See also SILLY (1).
– OPPOSITES mature.

childlike adj INNOCENT, simple, unsophisticated, trusting, gullible, naive, ingenuous, guileless, artless, unaffected, credulous.

chill v COOL, freeze, refrigerate, make cold/cool.
– OPPOSITES heat.
▸ n ❶ COOLNESS, chilliness, coldness, iciness, rawness, frigidity, nip, bite. ❷ COLDNESS, coolness, aloofness, unfriendliness, hostility, distance, unresponsiveness.
– OPPOSITES warmth.

chilly adj ❶ COLD, cool, icy, freezing, chill, fresh, sharp, biting, raw, brisk, penetrating, wintry, frigid. ❷ UNFRIENDLY, cool, cold, aloof, distant, unresponsive, reserved, unsympathetic, unwelcoming, hostile, remote, frigid.
– OPPOSITES warm, friendly.

chime v RING, peal, toll, strike, sound, clang, tinkle, resound.
▸ n PEAL, striking, tolling.

china n ❶ DISHES, tableware, dinner/tea service. ❷ PORCELAIN.

chink n ❶ CRACK, gap, cleft, rift, slit, fissure, crevice, split, opening, aperture, cranny, cavity.

chip n ❶ SHARD, flake, fragment, splinter, paring, sliver, bit, fleck, shred, scrap, snippet. ❷ NICK, crack, notch, snick, scratch, splinter, gash, fault, flaw, dent.
▶ v ❶ NICK, crack, notch, scratch, splinter, gash, damage, snick. ❷ CHISEL, whittle, hew.

chivalrous adj ❶ COURTEOUS, polite, gallant, gentlemanly, gracious, well mannered, thoughtful, protective. ❷ COURTLY, knightly, courageous, brave, valiant, heroic, daring, intrepid, honourable, just, fair, constant, true, magnanimous.
– OPPOSITES rude, boorish.

choice n ❶ SELECTION, option, choosing, preference, picking, election, adoption. ❷ ALTERNATIVE, option, possibility, solution, answer, way out. ❸ VARIETY, range, selection, assortment, mixture, store, supply, display, array, miscellany.
▶ adj BEST, excellent, superior, first-rate, first-class, prize, prime, select, special, exclusive, rare, hand-picked.
– OPPOSITES inferior.

choke v ❶ STRANGLE, asphyxiate, throttle, suffocate, smother, stifle. ❷ GAG, gasp, retch, struggle for air, asphyxi-

ate, suffocate. ❸ CLOG, congest, jam, block, obstruct, fill up, constrict, plug, stop up.
■ **choke back** see SUPPRESS (2).

choose v ❶ SELECT, pick, pick on/out, decide on, opt for, settle on, agree on, fix on, plump for, prefer, designate, elect, single out, adopt, espouse, hand-pick, name, nominate, vote for, show a preference for.

choosy adj FUSSY, particular, discriminating, exacting, finicky, pernickety, fastidious, hard to please, selective, discerning; informal picky.

chop v ❶ CUT DOWN, fell, hack down, hew, bring down, saw down, lop, split. ❷ CUT UP, dice, cube, fragment, crumble. ❸ See CUT (2).

choppy adj ROUGH, turbulent, stormy, squally, blustery, tempestuous.
– OPPOSITES calm.

chorus n ❶ CHOIR, ensemble, choral group, choristers, singers, vocalists. ❷ REFRAIN, response.

christen v BAPTIZE, anoint, name, dub, call, designate, style, term.

chronic adj ❶ PERSISTENT, long-lasting, long-standing, lingering, continual, constant, incessant, deep-rooted, deepseated, ingrained. ❷ HABITUAL, inveterate, confirmed, hardened. ❸ BAD, dreadful, appalling, awful, atrocious.
– OPPOSITES acute.

chronicle n RECORD, account,

history, story, description, calendar, annals, narrative, journal, archive, log.
▶ v RECORD, report, document, set down, relate, tell about, register.

chronological adj CONSECUTIVE, in sequence, sequential, ordered, historical, serial, progressive.

chubby adj PLUMP, tubby, flabby, dumpy, paunchy, fleshy, stout, portly, rotund. *See also* FAT (1).
– OPPOSITES skinny.

chunk n LUMP, piece, block, hunk, slab, square, portion, mass, wedge; *informal* dollop.

church n PLACE OF WORSHIP, house of God, cathedral, chapel, abbey, minster, temple, tabernacle, mosque, synagogue.

churlish adj RUDE, impolite, boorish, oafish, ill-mannered, discourteous, surly, curt, sullen, brusque.
– OPPOSITES polite.

churn v ❶ BEAT, whip up, agitate, stir up, shape up, disturb. ❷ SEETHE, foam, boil, froth, swirl, toss, convulse.

cinema n FILMS, movies, pictures, motion pictures; *informal* silver screen, big screen.

circle n ❶ RING, disc, round, loop, circumference, ball, globe, sphere, orb. ❷ GROUP, circle of friends, set, company, crowd, ring, coterie, clique, assembly, fellowship, class.
▶ v ❶ MOVE ROUND, revolve, rotate, orbit, circumnavigate,

wheel, gyrate, whirl, pivot, swivel. ❷ SURROUND, ring, encircle, enclose, envelop, hedge in, hem in, gird, belt, circumscribe.

circuit n LAP, round, cycle, loop, circumference, turn, ambit.

circuitous adj WINDING, indirect, meandering, roundabout, twisting, tortuous, rambling, zigzag, labyrinthine, maze-like, serpentine.
– OPPOSITES direct.

circular adj ROUND, spherical, spheroid, ring-shaped, globular, annular.
▶ n PAMPHLET, leaflet, notice, advertisement.

circulate v ❶ SPREAD, spread round, make known, broadcast, publish, distribute, give out, disseminate, propagate, issue, pronounce, advertise; *informal* put about. ❷ MOVE / GO ROUND, flow, revolve, rotate, whirl, gyrate.

circumference n PERIMETER, border, boundary, periphery, bounds, limits, confines, edge, rim, verge, margin, fringe, outline, skirt, circuit, compass, extremity.

circumspect adj CAUTIOUS, wary, careful, guarded, vigilant, watchful, prudent, suspicious, apprehensive, observant, leery, chary, judicious, politic.
– OPPOSITES unguarded.

circumstances pl n ❶ SITUATION, set of affairs, conditions, facts, position, context, occurrence, event, background,

particulars, surroundings.
❷ STATE, situation, conditions, financial position, plight, predicament, means, resources, station.

circumstantial adj INDIRECT, incidental, presumed, conjectural, inferential.

citadel n FORTRESS, fort, fortification, stronghold, bastion, castle, tower, keep, fastness.

citation n QUOTATION, quote, reference, extract, excerpt, allusion, passage, source.

cite v QUOTE, mention, refer to, allude to, name, adduce, specify, excerpt, extract.

citizen n SUBJECT, national, native, passport-holder, resident, inhabitant, denizen, dweller, householder, taxpayer, voter, freeman, freewoman, burgher, burgess.

city n TOWN, conurbation, metropolis, urban area, municipality; informal concrete jungle, urban sprawl.

civil adj ❶ POLITE, courteous, well mannered, well bred, gentlemanly, ladylike, refined, urbane, polished, cultured, cultivated, cordial, civilized, genial, pleasant. ❷ CIVIC, public, municipal, community, local.
– OPPOSITES rude.

civility n COURTESY, politeness, courteousness, good manners, graciousness, cordiality, pleasantness, geniality, affability, amiability, urbanity, gallantry.
– OPPOSITES rudeness.

civilization n ❶ DEVELOP-

MENT, advancement, progress, enlightenment, culture, cultivation, refinement, sophistication. ❷ SOCIETY, culture, community, nation, country, people, way of life.

civilize v ENLIGHTEN, educate, cultivate, instruct, improve, refine, polish, domesticate, socialize, humanize, edify.

civilized adj ENLIGHTENED, advanced, developed, cultured, cultivated, educated, sophisticated, refined, sociable, urbane, well behaved.
– OPPOSITES uncivilized, barbarous.

claim v ❶ DEMAND, request, ask for, lay claim to, require, insist on, command, exact, requisition. ❷ PROFESS, maintain, state, declare, assert, allege, protest, insist, contend, hold, avow, affirm, postulate; formal aver.

clairvoyant noun PSYCHIC, fortune teller, crystal-gazer; medium, spiritualist; telepath.

clamber v SCRAMBLE, climb, scrabble, scale, ascend, mount, shin, shinny, claw one's way.

clammy adj MOIST, damp, humid, sweaty, sticky, close, muggy, dank.

clamour n NOISE, uproar, outcry, racket, row, din, shouts, shouting, yelling, babel, commotion, hubbub, hullabaloo, brouhaha, vociferation.
▶ v SHOUT, yell, call/cry out, exclaim.

clamp n VICE, press, brace, clasp, fastener, hasp.

▶ v GRIP, hold, press, squeeze, clench, fix, secure, make fast.

clandestine adj SECRET, undercover, surreptitious, furtive, concealed, hidden, underhand, cloak-and-dagger.

clarify v ❶ MAKE CLEAR, explain, clear up, make plain, illuminate, resolve, throw light on, make simple, simplify. ❷ PURIFY, refine.
– OPPOSITES confuse.

clash v ❶ BANG, strike, crash, clang, clatter, rattle, jangle. ❷ FIGHT, contend, quarrel, wrangle, do battle, feud, grapple, cross swords. ❸ See COINCIDE (1).

clasp n ❶ CATCH, fastener, fastening, clip, hook, buckle, pin, hasp. ❷ EMBRACE, hug, cuddle, hold, grip, grasp.
▶ v EMBRACE, hug, squeeze, clutch, grip, grasp, hold.

class n ❶ CATEGORY, group, sort, type, kind, set, division, order, rank, classification, grade, section, denomination, species, genus, genre, domain. ❷ SOCIAL ORDER / DIVISION, rank, stratum, level, status, standing, station, group, grouping, caste, lineage, pedigree, descent. ❸ QUALITY, excellence, distinction, ability, stylishness, elegance, chic.
▶ v see CLASSIFY.

classic adj ❶ EXCELLENT, memorable, notable, lasting, brilliant, finest, first-rate, first-class, outstanding, exemplary, consummate, masterly, legendary, immortal. ❷ TYPICAL,

archetypal, definitive, standard, model, stock, prototypical, paradigmatic, copybook. ❸ TRADITIONAL, simple, timeless, ageless, enduring, abiding, long-lasting, time-honoured, long-established.
▶ n MASTERPIECE, master work, great work, standard work.

classical adj ❶ ANCIENT, Greek, Grecian, Hellenic, Attic, Roman, Latin. ❷ SERIOUS, symphonic, traditional, highbrow. ❸ ELEGANT, balanced, well proportioned, symmetrical, austere, pure, simple, plain, harmonious, restrained.

classification n CATEGORIZATION, ordering, organization, grouping, arrangement, grading, systemization, codification, tabulation, taxonomy.

classify v CATEGORIZE, class, arrange, order, sort, organize, group, catalogue, systematize, type, rank, index, file, bracket.

clause n SECTION, subsection, paragraph, article, item, point, passage, part, heading, provision, proviso, stipulation, note.

claw n NAIL, talon, pincer, nipper, chela.
▶ v SCRATCH, tear, scrape, lacerate, rip, maul.

clean adj ❶ UNSTAINED, spotless, unsoiled, unblemished, unsullied, immaculate, speckless, hygienic, sanitary, disinfected, sterile, sterilized, washed, cleansed, laundered, scrubbed. ❷ PURE, clear, unpolluted, natural, unadulterated, uncontaminated, untainted.

❸ GOOD, upright, virtuous, pure, decent, respectable, moral, upstanding, exemplary, chaste, undefiled. ❹ UNUSED, unmarked, blank, untouched, new, vacant, void. ❺ FAIR, honest, sporting, sportsmanlike, honourable.
– OPPOSITES dirty.

▶ v WASH, cleanse, wipe, sponge, scour, swab, dry-clean, launder, tidy, vacuum, hoover, dust, mop, sweep.
– OPPOSITES dirty, soil.

cleanse v WASH, clean, bathe, rinse, disinfect.

clear adj ❶ BRIGHT, cloudless, fine, fair, light, sunny, sunshiny. ❷ TRANSPARENT, translucent, limpid, pellucid, crystalline, diaphanous. ❸ OBVIOUS, plain, evident, apparent, sure, definite, unmistakable, beyond question, indisputable, patent, manifest, incontrovertible, irrefutable, palpable. ❹ COMPREHENSIBLE, plain, intelligible, understandable, lucid, coherent, distinct. ❺ OPEN, empty, unobstructed, unimpeded, free, unhindered, unlimited. ❻ UNTROUBLED, undisturbed, innocent, guiltfree, guiltless, clean, peaceful, tranquil, serene, sinless, stainless.
– OPPOSITES cloudy, opaque, vague, incoherent.

▶ adv ❶ AWAY FROM, at a distance from, apart from, out of contact with. ❷ COMPLETELY, entirely, fully, wholly, thoroughly.

▶ v ❶ UNBLOCK, unclog, unstop, clean out, free. ❷ EMPTY, vacate, evacuate. ❸ ACQUIT, absolve, discharge, let go, exonerate, vindicate, excuse, pardon. ❹ JUMP, vault, leap, hop, pass over. ❺ AUTHORIZE, sanction, give consent to, approve, permit, allow, pass; informal give the go-ahead to.

■ **clear up** see EXPLAIN (1).

clearance n ❶ CLEARING, removal, emptying, evacuation, eviction, depopulation, withdrawal. ❷ GAP, space, headroom, allowance, margin, leeway, room to spare. ❸ AUTHORIZATION, permission, consent, sanction, leave, endorsement; informal go-ahead, green light.

clear-cut adj DEFINITE, specific, precise, explicit, unequivocal.

clearly adv OBVIOUSLY, plainly, undoubtedly, undeniably, surely, certainly, incontestably, patently, incontrovertibly.

cleave v SPLIT, crack, lay open, divide, hew, hack, chop/slice up, sever, sunder, rend.

cleft n SPLIT, crack, fissure, gap, crevice, rift, break, fracture.

clemency n MERCY, leniency, compassion, kindness, humanity, pity, sympathy, fairness, magnanimity, moderation, indulgence.
– OPPOSITES ruthlessness.

clench v GRIP, grasp, clutch, hold, seize, clamp, squeeze.

clergyman n MINISTER, priest, pastor, preacher, vicar, rabbi, imam, cleric, churchman, churchwoman, man of the cloth, bishop, archbishop, cardinal, prelate, ecclesiastic, divine.

clerical adj ❶ OFFICE, secretarial. ❷ ECCLESIASTICAL, spiritual, priestly, episcopal, churchly, pastoral, canonical, rabbinical, sacerdotal, apostolic, prelatic.

clever adj ❶ INTELLIGENT, bright, sharp, quick-witted, quick, gifted, talented, brilliant, able, capable, knowledgeable, educated, sagacious; *informal* brainy, smart. ❷ SHREWD, cunning, ingenious, astute, skilful, skilled, resourceful, wily, inventive, subtle, canny, artful, adroit, guileful; *informal* foxy; *N. Amer. informal* cute. ❸ DEXTEROUS, skilful, deft, nimble, handy.
– OPPOSITES stupid, awkward.

cliché n HACKNEYED / WELL-WORN PHRASE, platitude, commonplace, banality, truism, saw, maxim; *informal* old chestnut.

click v ❶ CLINK, clack, snap, tick. ❷ BECOME CLEAR, make sense, fall into place, come home to one. ❸ TAKE TO EACH OTHER, get on, feel a rapport, be compatible, be on the same wavelength; *informal* hit it off. ❹ BE SUCCESSFUL, prove popular, succeed, be a success, go down well.

client n CUSTOMER, patron, regular, buyer, purchaser, shopper, consumer, user, patient.

cliff n PRECIPICE, rock face, crag, bluff, escarpment, scar, scarp, promontory, tor.

climate n ATMOSPHERE, mood, environment, temper, spirit, feeling, ambience, aura, ethos.

climax n CULMINATION, high point, crowning point, height, peak, pinnacle, summit, top, highlight, acme, zenith, apex, apogee, ne plus ultra.
– OPPOSITES anticlimax, nadir.

climb v ❶ GO UP, ascend, mount, scale, clamber up, shin up. ❷ RISE, increase, shoot up, soar. ❸ SLOPE UPWARD, incline, bank.
– OPPOSITES descend, fall.
■ **climb down** ❶ DESCEND, go down, shin down. ❷ BACK DOWN, retreat, retract, eat one's words, eat humble pie.

clinch v COMPLETE, settle, secure, seal, set the seal on, confirm, conclude, assure, cap, close, wind up.

cling v STICK, adhere, hold, grip, clasp, clutch.
■ **cling to** EMBRACE, clutch, hold on to, grasp, grip, cleave to.

clinic n MEDICAL CENTRE, health centre, infirmary, surgery, sickbay.

clip¹ v PIN, staple, fasten, fix, attach, hold.
▸ n FASTENER, clasp, pin.

clip² v CUT, crop, trim, snip, shear, prune.
▸ n EXCERPT, cutting, snippet, fragment, portion, bit, passage, section, trailer.

clique n COTERIE, in-crowd, set,

group, gang, faction, band, ring, fraternity.

cloak n ❶ CAPE, robe, wrap, poncho, mantle. ❷ COVER, screen, mask, veil, shroud, cloud, shield, camouflage, disguise.
▶ v HIDE, conceal, cover, screen, mask, veil, shroud, shield, camouflage, obscure, disguise.

clog v OBSTRUCT, block, jam, congest, stop up, plug, dam, bung up, impede, hinder, hamper.

close¹ adj ❶ NEAR, adjacent, neighbouring, in close proximity, adjoining, abutting, hard by. ❷ SIMILAR, like, alike, near, comparable, corresponding, akin, parallel. ❸ ACCURATE, precise, near, true, faithful, literal, conscientious. ❹ INTIMATE, devoted, loving, inseparable, bosom, close-knit, confidential. ❺ DENSE, condensed, crowded, compact, packed, solid, tight, cramped, congested, squeezed. ❻ HARD-FOUGHT, well matched, evenly matched, sharply contested; informal neck-and-neck, nose-to-nose, fifty-fifty. ❼ CAREFUL, keen, rigorous, thorough, vigilant, alert, concentrated, minute, detailed, intent, assiduous, painstaking, searching. ❽ HUMID, muggy, airless, stuffy, suffocating, oppressive, stifling, musty, unventilated; Brit. informal fuggy. ❾ MEAN, miserly, parsimonious, niggardly, penny-pinching, near; informal tight-fisted, tight, stingy.
– OPPOSITES distant, remote.

close² v ❶ SHUT, slam, fasten, secure, lock, bolt, bar, latch. ❷ SEAL OFF, stop up, obstruct, block, clog, choke. ❸ END, bring to an end, conclude, finish, terminate, wind up, adjourn, discontinue. ❹ NARROW, lessen, grow smaller, dwindle, reduce.
– OPPOSITES open.

closet n CUPBOARD, wardrobe, cabinet, locker, storage room.
▶ v SEQUESTER, cloister, seclude, confine, isolate.
▶ adj SECRET, undisclosed, hidden, concealed, furtive.

clot n LUMP, clump, mass, obstruction, thrombus; informal glob.
▶ v COAGULATE, set, congeal, solidify, thicken, jell, cake, curdle.

cloth n FABRIC, material, textile, stuff.

clothe v DRESS, attire, garb, robe, outfit, fit out, turn out, deck out, rig out, drape, accoutre; informal doll up, kit out; archaic apparel.
– OPPOSITES undress.

clothes pl n GARMENTS, clothing, dress, attire, costume, garb, wardrobe, outfit, finery, ensemble, vestments; informal get-up, gear, togs, weeds; Brit. informal clobber; formal apparel; dated raiment.

cloud n ❶ HAZE, pall, shroud, cloak, screen, cover. ❷ SHADOW, threat, gloom, darkness.

cloudy adj ❶ OVERCAST, dark, grey, hazy, sombre, leaden, heavy, gloomy, dim, sunless, starless. ❷ OPAQUE, murky,

muddy, milky, turbid.
❸ BLURRED, vague, indistinct, hazy, obscure, confused, muddled, nebulous.
– OPPOSITES cloudless, clear.

clown n ❶ JESTER, fool, buffoon, harlequin, pierrot.
❷ JOKER, comedian, comic, humorist, funny man, wag, wit, prankster.

club¹ n SOCIETY, group, association, organization, circle, set, league, union, federation, fellowship, fraternity, brotherhood, sisterhood, sorority.
■ **club together** COMBINE, join forces, pool resources, divide costs; informal have a whip-round.

club² n CUDGEL, baton, truncheon, bludgeon, staff; Brit. informal cosh.
▶ v see HIT (1).

clue n SIGN, lead, hint, indication, indicator, suggestion, pointer, evidence, information, guide, tip, tip-off, suspicion, trace, inkling.

clump n CLUSTER, bunch, bundle, collection, mass, assembly, assemblage. See also GROUP n (2).

clumsy adj ❶ AWKWARD, uncoordinated, ungainly, blundering, inept, bungling, bumbling, maladroit, fumbling, lumbering, heavy-handed, unhandy, unskilful, inexpert, graceless, ungraceful; informal cackhanded, ham-fisted, butterfingered, like a bull in a china shop. ❷ UNWIELDY, awkward, cumbersome, bulky, heavy,

solid, inconvenient, inelegant, ponderous; informal hulking.
❸ CRUDE, boorish, crass, inappropriate, ill-judged, tactless, graceless, insensitive, uncouth, inept, gauche, unpolished.
– OPPOSITES graceful, adroit.

cluster n BUNCH, clump, group, collection, gathering, crowd, assembly, assemblage, knot.
▶ v GATHER, collect, assemble, congregate, group, come together, flock together.

clutch v GRIP, grasp, clasp, cling to, hang on to, clench.
■ **clutch at** GRAB, seize, catch at, snatch at, claw at, reach for.

clutches pl n HANDS, power, control, hold, grip, grasp, claws, possession, keeping, custody.

clutter n MESS, jumble, litter, disorder, junk, untidiness, chaos, confusion, heap, odds and ends, hotchpotch, tangle.
▶ v LITTER, make untidy, make a mess of, be strewn about, be scattered about; informal mess up.

coach¹ n BUS, carriage; dated omnibus; historical charabanc.

coach² n INSTRUCTOR, trainer, teacher, tutor, mentor.
▶ v INSTRUCT, train, teach, tutor, guide, prepare, direct, drill, cram, prime, put someone through their paces.

coagulate v CONGEAL, clot, thicken, set, gel, solidify, stiffen, curdle.

coalesce v COMBINE, unite, join together, blend, fuse,

amalgamate, integrate, affiliate, commingle.

coalition n UNION, alliance, league, affiliation, association, federation, bloc, confederacy, amalgamation, merger, conjunction, fusion.

coarse adj ❶ ROUGH, uneven, harsh, lumpy, bristly, prickly, gritty, hairy, shaggy, scratchy. ❷ RUDE, ill-mannered, uncivil, boorish, loutish, uncouth, crass, churlish. ❸ VULGAR, indecent, obscene, crude, smutty, offensive, indelicate, bawdy, immodest, unrefined, earthy, ribald, lewd, improper, foul, prurient, pornographic; *informal* blue, raunchy.
– OPPOSITES fine, refined.

coast n SHORE, seashore, coastline, shoreline, beach, foreshore, seaboard, water's edge; *poetic/literary* strand.
▶ v GLIDE, cruise, freewheel, drift, taxi, sail, skim, slide.

coat n ❶ JACKET, overcoat. ❷ FUR, hair, wool, fleece, hide, pelt. ❸ LAYER, covering, coating, overlay, film, patina, veneer, wash, glaze, finish, membrane.
▶ v *see* COVER v (1).

coax v CAJOLE, persuade, wheedle, beguile, inveigle, talk into, induce, entice, win over, prevail upon; *informal* sweet-talk, soft-soap.

cocky adj ARROGANT, conceited, egotistical, vain, swollen-headed, cocksure, swaggering, brash.
– OPPOSITES modest.

code n ❶ CIPHER, secret writing, cryptograph. ❷ SYSTEM, laws, rules, regulations, rule book.

coerce v FORCE, compel, pressure, pressurize, drive, bully, intimidate, frighten, terrorize, browbeat, impel, constrain, oblige; *informal* lean on, twist someone's arm, strong-arm, put the screws on.

coffer n BOX, chest, case, casket, strongbox, safe, trunk, cabinet.

cogent adj CONVINCING, persuasive, compelling, forceful, effective, conclusive, indisputable, sound, unanswerable, powerful, strong, weighty, potent, influential, telling, authoritative, well argued.
– OPPOSITES unconvincing.

coherent adj LOGICAL, rational, reasoned, consistent, lucid, articulate, systematic, orderly, structured, well structured, well ordered, cohesive, organized, comprehensible, intelligible, unified, integrated.
– OPPOSITES incoherent, muddled.

cohort n TROOP, brigade, squad, squadron, group, company, body, band, legion, column.

coil v LOOP, wind, spiral, curl, twist, snake, turn, wreathe, entwine, twine, convolute.

coin n ❶ PIECE, bit. ❷ CHANGE, small/loose change, silver, copper, coppers, coinage, specie.
▶ v ❶ MINT, stamp, mould, die, forge. ❷ INVENT, create, make up, devise, conceive, originate,

introduce, think/dream up, formulate, concoct, produce, fabricate.

coincide v ❶ OCCUR SIMULTANEOUSLY, fall together, be concurrent, concur, coexist, synchronize, happen together, clash. ❷ AGREE, accord, match, correspond, concur, square, tally, harmonize.

coincidence n CHANCE, accident, luck, fluke, fortuity, serendipity.

coincidental adj ACCIDENTAL, chance, unintentional, unplanned, lucky, casual, fortuitous, serendipitous.

cold adj ❶ CHILLY, cool, freezing, bitter, icy, chill, wintry, frosty, raw, perishing, biting, glacial, numbing, piercing, frigid, inclement, windy, Siberian, crisp, sunless, polar; *informal* nippy; *Brit. informal* parky. ❷ SHIVERY, shivering, cool, chilly, chilled, freezing, frozen, frozen stiff, frostbitten. ❸ DISTANT, reserved, aloof, remote, unfriendly, unresponsive, unfeeling, unemotional, indifferent, dispassionate, stand-offish, frigid, glacial, passionless, unmoved, unexcitable, phlegmatic, lukewarm, apathetic, spiritless, unsympathetic, uncaring, heartless, callous, cold-hearted, stony-hearted, inhospitable.
– OPPOSITES hot, warm.

cold-blooded adj RUTHLESS, callous, savage, inhuman, barbaric, heartless, pitiless, merciless, hard-hearted.
– OPPOSITES kind, humane.

collaborate v ❶ COOPERATE, work together, join forces, join, unite, combine; *informal* team up, pull together. ❷ COLLUDE, connive, turn traitor, conspire, fraternize; *informal* rat.

collaborator n ❶ COWORKER, colleague, associate, fellow worker, partner, helper, confederate, accomplice, team mate, co-author; *humorous* partner in crime. ❷ TRAITOR, turncoat, quisling, colluder, fraternizer, conspirator; *informal* Judas, blackleg.

collapse v ❶ FALL IN / DOWN, cave in, give way, crumple, disintegrate, subside, buckle, tumble down, fall to pieces, come apart, break up, fold up, sink, give in. ❷ FAINT, pass out, black out, fall down, lose consciousness, fall unconscious, swoon; *informal* keel over. ❸ BREAK DOWN, fail, fold, fall through, founder, come to nothing, disintegrate, fall flat, miscarry, crash; *informal* flop.
▶ n ❶ CAVE-IN, fall-in, subsidence, disintegration, break-up. ❷ FAINTING, loss of consciousness, swoon. ❸ BREAKDOWN, failure, disintegration, foundering.

collate v ARRANGE, put in order, order, sort, categorize.

colleague n CO-WORKER, fellow worker, associate, workmate, partner, collaborator, confederate.

collect v ❶ PUT TOGETHER, gather, accumulate, pile up, assemble, stockpile, amass, store,

hoard, put by, save, reserve, heap up, aggregate. ❷ COME TOGETHER, gather, assemble, congregate, converge, mass, flock together, convene, rally. ❸ RAISE, gather, solicit, obtain, acquire, secure. ❹ FETCH, call for, go and get, pick up, bring.
– OPPOSITES disperse.

collected adj COMPOSED, COOL, poised, unperturbed, serene, unruffled, unshaken. *See also* CALM adj (1).

collection n ❶ ACCUMULATION, pile, stockpile, store, stock, supply, heap, hoard, mass, conglomeration, array, aggregation. ❷ DONATIONS, contributions, gifts, offerings, alms.

collective adj JOINT, united, combined, shared, common, cooperative, concerted, collaborative, corporate, aggregate.
– OPPOSITES individual.

college n UNIVERSITY, polytechnic, institute, college of further education, school, conservatory.

collide v CRASH, come into collision, bang into, smash into, knock into, run into, slam into, cannon into.

collision n CRASH, impact, accident, smash, pile-up, bump, scrape, knock, clash, wreck.

colloquial adj CONVERSATIONAL, informal, casual, familiar, chatty, everyday, idiomatic, demotic, vernacular.
– OPPOSITES formal.

collusion n COMPLICITY, connivance, collaboration, secret

understanding, plotting, intrigue; *informal* cahoots.

colonize v OCCUPY, settle, populate, people, subjugate, pioneer, open up, found.

colony n ❶ DEPENDENCY, possession, settlement, territory, province, dominion, protectorate, satellite state. ❷ COMMUNITY, group, ghetto, quarter.

colossal adj ENORMOUS, huge, immense, gigantic, vast, massive, mammoth, gargantuan, monumental, prodigious, monstrous, titanic, mountainous, towering, elephantine, Brobdingnagian.
– OPPOSITES small.

colour n ❶ HUE, tint, shade, tone, tinge, coloration, colouring, pigmentation, pigment. ❷ PINKNESS, rosiness, redness, ruddiness, blush, flush, glow, bloom.
▶ v ❶ TINT, dye, paint, colourwash, tinge, stain, shade, pigment. ❷ INFLUENCE, affect, prejudice, distort, bias, slant, taint, sway, pervert, warp.

colourful adj ❶ BRIGHT, vivid, intense, brilliant, vibrant, multi-coloured, deep-coloured, iridescent, psychedelic, gaudy, variegated. ❷ VIVID, graphic, lively, interesting, animated, rich, striking, picturesque, stimulating, telling. ❸ INTERESTING, eccentric, unusual, flamboyant, dynamic, flashy.
– OPPOSITES colourless, dull.

colourless adj ❶ UNCOLOURED, achromatic, white, bleached, faded. ❷ DULL,

boring, uninteresting, tame, lifeless, dreary, insipid, lacklustre, characterless, vapid, vacuous.
– OPPOSITES colourful.

column n ❶ PILLAR, post, support, upright, shaft, pilaster, obelisk, caryatid. ❷ LINE, row, file, queue, procession, train, rank, string, progression, cavalcade. ❸ ARTICLE, piece, item, feature, editorial, leader, leading article.

comb v ❶ GROOM, arrange, tidy, smarten up, spruce up, untangle, curry, dress. ❷ SEARCH, hunt through, scour, ransack, rummage, rake, sift, go over with a fine-tooth comb.

combat n BATTLE, fighting, conflict, hostilities, fight, clash, skirmish, duel, contest, engagement, encounter.
▶ v FIGHT, battle against, oppose, resist, contest, make a stand against, stand up to, grapple with, struggle against, tackle, withstand, defy, strive against.
See also FIGHT v.

combative adj AGGRESSIVE, belligerent, pugnacious, bellicose, quarrelsome, argumentative, antagonistic, contentious, truculent.
– OPPOSITES conciliatory.

combination n ❶ BLEND, mixture, compound, amalgamation, amalgam, mix, alloy, composite, aggregate, fusion, marriage, synthesis, concoction. ❷ UNION, association, alliance, federation, merger, grouping, confederation,

confederacy, cooperation, coalition, partnership, league, consortium, syndication.

combine v ❶ JOIN, join forces, unite, form an alliance, get together, cooperate, ally, pool resources, associate, unify, integrate; informal team up, gang together, club together. ❷ MIX, blend, add together, fuse, compound, mingle, merge, amalgamate, bind, alloy, bond, incorporate, synthesize, interweave.
– OPPOSITES separate, part.

combustible adj FLAMMABLE, inflammable, incendiary, explosive.
– OPPOSITES incombustible.

come v ❶ MOVE TOWARDS, approach, advance, draw near, near, reach, bear down on, close in on. ❷ ARRIVE, appear, turn up, put in an appearance, materialize; informal show up, fetch up, blow in. ❸ BE AVAILABLE, be made, be produced, be on offer.
– OPPOSITES go, leave.
■ **come about** see HAPPEN. **come across** see MEET (1), FIND (1). **come clean** see CONFESS. **come off** see SUCCEED (2). **come out with** see SAY (2).

comedian n ❶ COMIC, stand-up comedian, humorist. ❷ WIT, wag, joker, clown, jester; informal laugh; informal, dated card.

comedy n HUMOUR, joking, funniness, wit, wittiness, fun, farce, hilarity, levity, slapstick, clowning, buffoonery, facetiousness, drollery.

comfort n ❶ EASE, well-being, affluence, contentment, tranquillity, luxury, opulence, serenity, repose, cosiness, plenty, sufficiency. ❷ SOLACE, help, support, sympathy, consolation, succour, cheer, condolence, relief, easement, alleviation, gladdening.
– OPPOSITES discomfort, grief, pain.

▶ v HELP, support, bring comfort to, console, sympathize with, solace, reassure, succour, cheer, soothe, hearten, gladden, assuage.
– OPPOSITES distress.

comfortable adj ❶ WELL FITTING, snug, loose-fitting, roomy. ❷ cosy, homely, snug, relaxing, tranquil. ❸ PLEASANT, well off, affluent, prosperous, well-to-do, luxurious, opulent, free from hardship, untroubled, happy, contented.
– OPPOSITES uncomfortable.

comic adj FUNNY, humorous, amusing, entertaining, comical, witty, hilarious, farcical, jocular, hysterical, diverting, joking, droll, zany, side-splitting, ridiculous, facetious, whimsical, uproarious, waggish; informal rich, priceless.
– OPPOSITES serious.

▶ n see COMEDIAN.

command v ❶ ORDER, give orders to, direct, instruct, charge, require, prescribe, ordain, demand, compel, bid, summon, enjoin; formal adjure.

❷ BE IN CHARGE OF, have charge of, control, have control of, lead, head, rule, direct, supervise, manage, govern, preside over, superintend.

▶ n ❶ ORDER, instruction, decree, directive, edict, direction, dictate, injunction, requirement, prescription, bidding, mandate, fiat, commandment, precept. ❷ CHARGE, control, authority, power, direction, mastery, government, management, supervision, administration, dominion, sway, domination, ascendancy. ❸ KNOWLEDGE, grasp, mastery.

commander n LEADER, head, chief, director, officer-in-charge; informal boss, top dog, kingpin, big cheese. See also CHIEF.

commemorate v CELEBRATE, remember, honour, salute, mark, memorialize, pay tribute to, pay homage to, immortalize, solemnize.

commence v BEGIN, start, initiate, originate, embark on, go ahead, inaugurate, launch; informal set the ball rolling, get the show on the road.
– OPPOSITES finish, end, conclude.

commend v PRAISE, applaud, speak highly of, acclaim, extol, compliment, approve of, eulogize; formal laud.
– OPPOSITES criticize.

commendable adj ADMIRABLE, praiseworthy, laudable, creditable, worthy, estimable,

meritorious, reputable, deserving.
– OPPOSITES reprehensible.

comment v ❶ SAY, observe, state, remark, speak, express an opinion on, interpose, interject, opine. ❷ EXPLAIN, annotate, write notes, interpret, elucidate, clarify, shed light on.
▶ n ❶ REMARK, opinion, observation, view, statement, reaction, criticism, animadversion. ❷ NOTE, annotation, explanation, interpretation, footnote, gloss, exposition, interpolation, marginalia.

commentary n ❶ NARRATION, description, account, review, analysis. ❷ ANNOTATION, notes, interpretation, analysis, critique, elucidation, exegesis.

commerce n BUSINESS, trade, trading, dealing, dealings, financial transactions, buying and selling, merchandising, trafficking.

commercial adj ❶ BUSINESS, trade, profit-making, marketing, mercantile, merchandising, sales. ❷ PROFIT-ORIENTATED, materialistic, mercenary, mercantile.
▶ n ADVERTISEMENT, advertising break; informal ad, plug; Brit. informal advert.

commission n ❶ TASK, employment, piece of work, work, duty, charge, mission, responsibility. ❷ PERCENTAGE, brokerage, share, fee, compensation; informal cut, rake-off. ❸ PERFORMANCE, perpetration, execution, committal.

▶ v ❶ ENGAGE, employ, appoint, contract, book, authorize. ❷ ORDER, place an order for, contract for, pay for, authorize.

commit v ❶ PERFORM, carry out, perpetrate, enact, effect, do. ❷ ENTRUST, trust, deliver, hand over, give, consign, assign, transfer.
■ **commit oneself** PROMISE, pledge, engage, bind oneself, obligate oneself, covenant.

commitment n ❶ DEDICATION, involvement in, devotion, zeal, loyalty, allegiance, adherence. ❷ PROMISE, pledge, undertaking, vow, assurance, guarantee, covenant. ❸ OBLIGATION, duty, responsibility, undertaking, appointment, arrangement, liability, task, engagement, tie.

committed adj DEDICATED, enthusiastic, devoted, keen, passionate, resolute, earnest, single-minded, whole-hearted, unwavering, ardent, zealous; informal card-carrying.
– OPPOSITES apathetic.

common adj ❶ ORDINARY, average, normal, conventional, typical, unexceptional, plain, commonplace, run-of-the-mill, simple, habitual, undistinguished, unsurprising, pedestrian, humdrum, everyday, workaday, customary, stock; Brit. informal common or garden. ❷ WIDESPREAD, general, universal, popular, accepted, prevalent, prevailing, shared, public, communal, collective. ❸ VULGAR, coarse, rude,

uncouth, unrefined, boorish, churlish, inferior, disreputable, lower-class, plebeian, lowly, proletarian; *Brit. informal* yobbish.
– OPPOSITES exceptional, rare, refined.
▶ n PARK, heath, parkland.

commonplace adj ORDINARY, unexceptional, undistinguished, routine, pedestrian, mediocre, dull, uninteresting, humdrum, trite, hackneyed.
– OPPOSITES remarkable.

commotion n DISTURBANCE, racket, uproar, disorder, chaos, tumult, clamour, pandemonium, rumpus, hubbub, riot, fracas, hullabaloo, row, furore, brouhaha, confusion, upheaval, disruption, bother, turmoil, agitation, contretemps, excitement, fuss, disquiet, ferment, bustle, hustle and bustle; *informal* to-do, bedlam, stir, palaver.

communal adj COMMON, collective, shared, joint, general, public, community, cooperative.
– OPPOSITES individual, private.

communicable adj INFECTIOUS, contagious, catching, transmittable, transmissible, transferable.

communicate v ❶ MAKE KNOWN, pass on, convey, spread, impart, get across, publish, transmit, broadcast, announce, report, relay, disseminate, proclaim, promulgate, divulge, disclose, express, mention, reveal, intimate, transfer.
❷ GET ONE'S IDEAS / MESSAGE ACROSS, talk, get in touch, converse, confer, correspond, commune, have dealings, interface. ❸ TRANSMIT, pass on, spread, give, infect with, transfer. ❹ CONNECT, be connected to, lead to, adjoin, abut on.

communication n ❶ CONTACT, interaction, getting in touch, link, dissemination, communion. ❷ MESSAGE, dispatch, letter, report, statement, news, information, data, intelligence, word.

communicative adj TALKATIVE, chatty, open, frank, candid, expansive, forthcoming, voluble, loquacious, informative, conversational.
– OPPOSITES uncommunicative, reserved.

communion n EMPATHY, rapport, sympathy, affinity, closeness, togetherness, unity, accord, fellowship, harmony, fusion; *formal* concord.

commute v ❶ TRAVEL TO AND FROM, travel back and forth, shuttle. ❷ LESSEN, reduce, shorten, curtail, mitigate, modify.

compact¹ adj ❶ DENSE, compressed, condensed, packed close, tight-packed, solid, firm, close, consolidated. ❷ CONCISE, succinct, terse, brief, condensed, pithy, to the point, epigrammatic, abridged, abbreviated, compendious. ❸ SMALL, neat, portable, handy.
– OPPOSITES loose, rambling, large.

compact² n AGREEMENT, contract, pact, covenant, treaty, alliance, bargain, deal, settlement, entente.

companion n ❶ ESCORT, friend, partner, consort, chaperone, confederate, colleague, associate, ally, crony, comrade. ❷ COUNTERPART, fellow, match, twin, complement, mate.

companionship n FRIENDSHIP, company, fellowship, togetherness, society, camaraderie, intimacy, rapport, comradeship.

company n ❶ BUSINESS, firm, organization, corporation, conglomerate, consortium, concern, enterprise, house, establishment, partnership, syndicate. ❷ See COMPANIONSHIP. ❸ VISITORS, callers, guests. ❹ GROUP, band, party, body, association, society, troupe, fellowship, circle, collection, league, crew, guild. ❺ ASSEMBLY, gathering, audience, crowd, group, throng.

comparable adj SIMILAR, like, parallel, analogous, related, equivalent, matching, compatible, commensurate, corresponding, proportionate, proportional, cognate.
– OPPOSITES dissimilar.

compare v ❶ CONTRAST, make a comparison between, measure against, juxtapose, differentiate, collate. ❷ BEAR COMPARISON, be comparable, be the equal, be on a par, be in the same class, compete, approach, match, come up to; informal hold a candle to.

comparison n ❶ CONTRAST, juxtaposition, correlation, distinction, collation, differentiation. ❷ RESEMBLANCE, likeness, similarity, correlation, analogy, comparability.

compassionate adj TENDER, gentle, kindly, softhearted, understanding, sympathetic, humane, pitying, lenient, charitable, benevolent.

compatible adj ❶ WELL SUITED, suited, like-minded, in agreement, in tune, of the same mind, in harmony. ❷ CONSISTENT, in keeping, reconcilable, consonant, congruent, congruous.
– OPPOSITES incompatible.

compel v FORCE, make, coerce, drive, pressure, pressurize, order, constrain, impel, oblige, press, necessitate, urge; informal put the screws on, strong-arm, railroad, bulldoze.

compelling adj ❶ FASCINATING, gripping, enthralling, hypnotic, mesmerizing. ❷ CONVINCING, telling, forceful, powerful, weighty, conclusive, irrefutable, cogent.
– OPPOSITES boring, weak.

compensate v ❶ RECOMPENSE, repay, reimburse, make amends, make up for, atone, redress, make restitution, make reparation, make good, expiate, requite. ❷ OFFSET, counterbalance, counteract, balance, cancel out, neutralize, counterpoise, nullify.

compensation n ❶ RECOMPENSE, damages, repayment, reimbursement, indemnification, requital. ❷ AMENDS, restitution, redress, atonement, expiation.

compete v ❶ TAKE PART, be a contestant, participate, enter, go in for; *informal* throw one's hat in the ring. ❷ CONTEND, struggle, fight, oppose, rival, be in competition, vie, strive.
– OPPOSITES cooperate.

competent adj CAPABLE, able, proficient, skilful, skilled, adept, accomplished, qualified, expert, efficient, effective, trained, workmanlike.
– OPPOSITES incompetent, inept.

competition n ❶ CONTEST, match, game, heat, tournament, championship, event, meet, quiz, race, rally, trial, challenge. ❷ CONTENTION, opposition, rivalry, contest, struggle, vying, strife.

competitive adj ❶ AMBITIOUS, aggressive, combative, antagonistic, hard-fought, keen, cut-throat, lively, contentious. ❷ REASONABLE, moderate, fair, comparable, similar, average.
– OPPOSITES uncompetitive.

competitor n ❶ CONTESTANT, contender, challenger, participant, candidate. ❷ RIVAL, opponent, adversary, antagonist, opposition.

compile v COLLECT, gather, accumulate, amass, assemble, put together, marshal, organize, arrange, collate, anthologize.

complain v ❶ CRITICIZE, make/lodge a complaint, find fault, carp, make a fuss; *informal* kick up a fuss. ❷ GRUMBLE, whine, lament, bewail; *informal* moan, gripe, grouch, grouse, bellyache, bitch.

complaint n ❶ GRIEVANCE, criticism, protest, accusation, charge, remonstrance, objection, grumble; *informal* gripe, grouse, moan, beef, whine, whinge. ❷ ILLNESS, disease, sickness, ailment, disorder, affliction, malady, infection, malaise. *See also* ILLNESS.

complement n ❶ COMPANION, addition, supplement, accessory, finishing/final touch. ❷ AMOUNT, total, allowance, aggregate, load, capacity, quota.
▶ v COMPLETE, round/set off, go well with, add the finishing/final touch to, supplement.

complementary adj MATCHING, finishing, perfecting, interdependent, reciprocal.

complete adj ❶ ENTIRE, whole, full, total, intact, comprehensive, undivided, uncut, unshortened, unabridged, unexpurgated. ❷ FINISHED, completed, accomplished, achieved, done, concluded, ended, finalized. ❸ ABSOLUTE, utter, total, out-and-out, downright, thorough, thoroughgoing, unmitigated, unqualified, sheer, rank, dyed-in-the-wool.
– OPPOSITES incomplete, partial, unfinished.

▶ v **①** FINISH, conclude, end,
accomplish, achieve, do,
perform, execute, fulfil, effect,
discharge, realize, settle,
clinch; *informal* wrap up, polish
off. **②** ROUND OFF, finish off,
make perfect, crown, cap, add
the final/finishing touch.

completely adv TOTALLY,
utterly, absolutely, thoroughly,
quite, wholly, altogether.

complex adj **①** COMPLICATED,
difficult, intricate, convoluted,
involved, knotty, puzzling,
perplexing, cryptic, problematic, enigmatic, tortuous,
labyrinthine; *informal* tricky.
② COMPOSITE, compound,
elaborate, multiple, manifold,
heterogeneous, multiplex.
– OPPOSITES simple, elementary.

complicate v MAKE DIFFICULT,
confuse, make involved/intri-
cate, muddle, jumble, entangle,
compound; *informal* snarl up,
screw up.
– OPPOSITES simplify.

complicated adj *see* COMPLEX
(1).

complication n **①** PROBLEM,
difficulty, obstacle, snag, drawback, setback. **②** CONFUSION, difficulty, complexity, muddle,
intricacy.

compliment n PRAISE, tribute, admiration, flattery, commendation, congratulations,
accolade, honour, plaudits,
bouquet, testimonial, eulogy,
panegyric; *formal* encomium.
▶ v CONGRATULATE, praise, speak
highly of, commend, flatter,

acclaim, honour, pay tribute to,
salute, admire, sing someone's
praises, extol, felicitate, eulogize; *formal* laud.
– OPPOSITES insult, criticize.

complimentary adj CON-
GRATULATORY, admiring, approving, appreciative, flattering,
commendatory, eulogistic,
panegyrical; *formal* encomiastic,
laudatory.
– OPPOSITES insulting,
abusive.

comply v OBEY, conform to,
observe, abide by, keep to,
adhere to, assent to, consent to,
agree with, accord with, acquiesce in, follow, respect, yield,
submit, defer to.
– OPPOSITES disobey, ignore.

component n PART, piece,
element, bit, section, constituent, ingredient, unit, item,
module.

compose v **①** WRITE, make
up, create, think up, produce,
devise, invent, concoct,
compile, fashion, formulate.
② COMPRISE, form, make up,
constitute. **③** CALM, quiet,
collect, control, soothe, pacify,
assuage, still.

composed adj *see* CALM adj (1).

composition n **①** STRUC-
TURE, make-up, organization,
layout, configuration, constitution, character, formulation.
② STORY, article, essay, poem,
novel, work of art, piece, work,
opus. **③** ARRANGEMENT, proportions, balance, harmony,
symmetry.

compound n BLEND, mixture,

amalgam, combination, fusion, alloy, conglomerate, synthesis, medley, hybrid; *technical* admixture.

▶ adj COMPOSITE, blended, complex, fused, conglomerate.

▶ v **1** *See* COMBINE. **2** WORSEN, make worse, add to, exacerbate, aggravate, magnify, intensify, heighten.

comprehend v UNDERSTAND, grasp, take in, follow, appreciate, see, realize, assimilate, fathom, perceive, discern, apprehend; *Brit. informal* twig.

comprehensible adj UNDERSTANDABLE, clear, straightforward, intelligible, self-explanatory, lucid, explicit, discernible, graspable, fathomable.

– OPPOSITES incomprehensible.

comprehensive adj COMPLETE, all-inclusive, full, all-embracing, total, encyclopedic, wholesale, universal, exhaustive, detailed, thorough, extensive, widespread, broad, wide-ranging, far-reaching, blanket, umbrella, catholic.

– OPPOSITES selective.

compress v **1** COMPACT, squeeze, press down/together, crush, squash, flatten, cram, condense, constrict, tamp; *informal* jam together. **2** SHORTEN, abbreviate, abridge, reduce, contract, summarize, truncate.

– OPPOSITES expand.

comprise v **1** CONSIST OF, include, contain, be composed of, take in, embrace, encompass.

2 MAKE UP, form, constitute, compose.

compromise v **1** COME TO AN UNDERSTANDING, make concessions, strike a balance, meet halfway, come to terms, make a deal, give and take, find the middle ground, find a happy medium, reach a formula, negotiate a settlement. **2** DAMAGE, injure, undermine, discredit, dishonour, bring into disrepute, shame, embarrass, endanger, jeopardize, imperil, weaken.

▶ n UNDERSTANDING, deal, balance, concession, happy medium, trade-off, middle course, give and take, adjustment.

compulsion n **1** OBLIGATION, force, constraint, duress, coercion, pressure, oppression. **2** URGE, need, desire, drive, necessity, addiction, preoccupation, obsession.

compulsive adj **1** UNCONTROLLABLE, obsessive, irresistible, compelling, overwhelming, driving, urgent, besetting. **2** OBSESSIONAL, obsessive, addicted, habitual, incorrigible, incurable, dependent, out of control; *informal* hooked.

compulsory adj OBLIGATORY, mandatory, required, binding, forced, necessary, essential, unavoidable, inescapable, requisite, prescribed, set, statutory, de rigueur, stipulated.

– OPPOSITES optional.

compunction n REMORSE, regret, guilt, scruples, qualms,

contrition, pangs of
conscience, penitence, repentance, contriteness.

compute v CALCULATE, count,
add up, work out, reckon, determine, total, figure out, estimate, tally, measure, evaluate,
rate, enumerate, sum.

comrade n FRIEND, companion, colleague, partner, associate, confederate, co-worker,
fellow worker, teammate, ally;
informal pal; *Brit. informal* mate.

con v DECEIVE, swindle, trick,
cheat, mislead, hoodwink,
delude; *informal* bamboozle.

conceal v ❶ HIDE, cover, keep
hidden, keep out of sight, obscure, screen, mask, disguise,
camouflage, shelter, bury, tuck
away. ❷ KEEP SECRET, hide, keep
dark, cover up, hush up, dissemble; *informal* keep the lid on.
– OPPOSITES reveal, expose.

concealed adj *see* HIDDEN.

concede v ❶ ADMIT, acknowledge, accept, allow, grant,
accede, confess, recognize,
own. ❷ GIVE UP, yield, surrender, hand over, relinquish, cede.
– OPPOSITES deny, retain.

conceit n PRIDE, arrogance,
vanity, egotism, self-importance, self-satisfaction, self-
admiration, boasting, swagger,
narcissism; *poetic/literary* vain-
glory.
– OPPOSITES humility.

conceited adj PROUD, arrogant, vain, self-important,
swollen-headed, haughty, immodest, egotistical, egocentric,
self-satisfied, smug, cocky,

boastful, swaggering, narcissistic, supercilious, overweening,
complacent, bumptious; *informal*
big-headed, stuck up, toffee-
nosed, snooty; *poetic/literary*
vainglorious.
– OPPOSITES modest, humble.

conceivable adj CREDIBLE,
believable, thinkable, imaginable, possible, understandable,
comprehensible.
– OPPOSITES inconceivable.

conceive v ❶ BECOME PREG-
NANT, be impregnated. ❷ THINK
UP, formulate, create, work out,
form, devise, originate, produce, frame, draw up, develop,
imagine, dream up, contrive,
envisage; *informal* cook up.

concentrate v ❶ GIVE ONE'S
ATTENTION TO, be absorbed in,
focus on, be engrossed in, put
one's mind to, consider closely.
❷ COLLECT, gather, crowd, mass,
accumulate, congregate, amass,
cluster, converge, rally. ❸ CON-
DENSE, reduce, compress, boil
down, distil.
– OPPOSITES disperse, dilute.

concentrated adj INTENSIVE,
intense, rigorous, vigorous,
all-out.
– OPPOSITES half-hearted.

concern n ❶ WORRY, anxiety,
disquiet, distress, apprehension, disturbance, perturbation. ❷ INTEREST, importance,
relevance, bearing, applic-
ability. ❸ AFFAIR, matter of
interest, department, involvement, business, responsibility,
duty, job, task, occupation.
❹ BUSINESS, company, firm,

enterprise, organization, corporation, establishment.
– OPPOSITES indifference.
▶ v ❶ AFFECT, be the business of, be relevant to, involve, apply to, be of interest to, touch. ❷ WORRY, disturb, trouble, bother, make anxious, perturb, distress.

concerned adj ❶ INVOLVED, implicated, relevant, party to, connected, interested. ❷ WORRIED, disturbed, anxious, upset, bothered, apprehensive, uneasy, distressed, perturbed, exercised.

concerning prep ABOUT, relating to, regarding, as regards, involving, with reference to, with respect to, in the matter of, re, apropos.

concerted adj JOINT, combined, united, collective, coordinated, collaborative, cooperative, synchronized.

conciliate v PLACATE, calm down, appease, pacify, mollify, assuage, soothe.
– OPPOSITES provoke.

concise adj SUCCINCT, brief, short, compact, condensed, terse, compressed, to the point, pithy, laconic, epigrammatic, synoptic, compendious.
– OPPOSITES lengthy, wordy.

conclude v ❶ END, finish, come/bring to an end, halt, stop, cease, terminate, discontinue; informal wind up. ❷ COME TO A CONCLUSION, deduce, infer, gather, judge, assume, presume, suppose, conjecture, surmise.
– OPPOSITES start.

conclusion n ❶ END, finish, halt, stop, close, completion, termination, cessation, culmination, discontinuance. ❷ DEDUCTION, inference, decision, opinion, judgement, verdict, conviction, assumption, presumption, interpretation, resolution, solution.
– OPPOSITES beginning.

conclusive adj DECISIVE, definitive, certain, incontestable, unquestionable, unequivocal, final, clinching, ultimate, categorical, irrefutable, convincing, cogent.
– OPPOSITES inconclusive.

concoct v INVENT, devise, think up, dream up, put together, plan, fabricate, formulate, form, hatch, plot, forge, design, fashion, brew; informal cook up.

concrete adj ACTUAL, real, definite, genuine, factual, substantial, solid, physical, visible, material, tangible, palpable, specific, objective, firm, existing.
– OPPOSITES abstract, unreal.

concur v AGREE, assent, acquiesce, accord, be of the same mind.
– OPPOSITES disagree.

concurrent adj SIMULTANEOUS, parallel, coexisting, overlapping, coexistent, coincident, contemporaneous, synchronous, side by side.

condemn v ❶ DENOUNCE, criticize, censure, damn, deplore, berate, reprove, upbraid, reproach, blame, reprehend,

deprecate, disapprove of, disparage, revile, execrate, decry, reprobate; informal slam; Brit. informal slate; formal castigate. **❷** SENTENCE, pass sentence on, convict. **❸** DAMN, doom, compel, coerce, impel.
– OPPOSITES praise, acquit.

condense v **❶** SHORTEN, abridge, abbreviate, cut, reduce, compress, curtail, summarize, contract, compact, synopsize, encapsulate. **❷** THICKEN, concentrate, reduce, distil, solidify, coagulate.
– OPPOSITES lengthen.

condescend v DEIGN, lower oneself, stoop, descend, unbend, humble/demean oneself.

condescending adj PATRONIZING, supercilious, disdainful, superior, snobbish, lofty, lordly; informal snooty, snotty, toffee-nosed.

condition n **❶** STATE, state of affairs, situation, circumstance, position, predicament, plight, quandary. **❷** SHAPE, fitness, health, state of health, order, trim; informal nick, fettle, kilter. **❸** RESTRICTION, proviso, provision, stipulation, prerequisite, rule, limitation, terms, limit. **❹** DISEASE, illness, disorder, complaint, problem, ailment, malady.
▶ v TRAIN, accustom, habituate, adapt, influence, mould, determine, govern, educate, inure.

conditional adj PROVISIONAL, dependent, contingent, qualified, limited, restricted,

provisory; informal with strings attached.
– OPPOSITES unconditional.

condone v ALLOW, tolerate, excuse, pardon, make allowances for, forgive, overlook, disregard, turn a blind eye to, let pass; informal wink at.
– OPPOSITES condemn.

conducive adj CONTRIBUTORY, helpful, favourable, useful, instrumental, advantageous, supportive, beneficial.

conduct n **❶** BEHAVIOUR, actions, habits, practices, bearing, manners; N. Amer. deportment; formal comportment. **❷** RUNNING, handling, operation, direction, management, organization, administration, control, regulation, guidance, supervision, leadership.
▶ v **❶** BEHAVE, act, acquit, deport; formal comport. **❷** DIRECT, run, manage, administer, be in charge of, lead, organize, handle, control, supervise, regulate, preside over. **❸** SHOW, guide, lead, escort, accompany, take.

confer v **❶** BESTOW, present, award, grant, give, hand out, invest, accord. **❷** TALK, have discussions, exchange views, consult, debate, deliberate, compare notes, converse, seek advice; informal put their/your/our heads together.

conference n MEETING, seminar, discussion, deliberation, convention, council, congress, forum, symposium, colloquium, convocation.

confess v ADMIT, acknowledge, own up to, make known, disclose, reveal, divulge, accept responsibility, make a clean breast of, unburden oneself, come clean; *informal* spill the beans, get something off one's chest, blurt out, fess up.

confidant n FRIEND, crony, intimate, alter ego; *informal* pal, chum; *Brit. informal* mate.

confide v CONFESS, reveal, disclose, tell, divulge, admit, unburden oneself, unbosom oneself, open one's heart.

confidence n ❶ BELIEF, reliance, faith, certainty, trust, credence, dependence. ❷ SELF-ASSURANCE, self-confidence, self-reliance, self-possession, nerve, poise, courage, boldness, conviction, panache, composure, mettle, fortitude, verve.
– OPPOSITES distrust, uncertainty, doubt.

confident adj ❶ CERTAIN, sure, convinced, positive, sanguine. ❷ SELF-ASSURED, self-possessed, self-confident, unafraid, fearless, secure, bold, assertive, cocksure.
– OPPOSITES uncertain.

confidential adj ❶ SECRET, top secret, private, classified, restricted, off the record, suppressed, personal, intimate. ❷ CLOSE, trusted, intimate, faithful, reliable, trustworthy.

confine v ❶ ENCLOSE, cage, lock up, imprison, detain, jail, shut up, intern, hold captive, incarcerate, restrain, impound, keep, pen, coop up, box up, immure, wall up. ❷ RESTRICT, limit, keep within the limits of, circumscribe, curb.
– OPPOSITES free.

confirm v ❶ VERIFY, prove, bear out, corroborate, validate, endorse, authenticate, establish, substantiate, give credence to, evidence. ❷ RATIFY, endorse, approve, sanction, authorize, underwrite, warrant, accredit. ❸ GUARANTEE, assure, affirm, promise, pledge, assert, reassert.
– OPPOSITES contradict, deny.

confiscate v SEIZE, impound, take possession of, remove, take away, appropriate, commandeer, expropriate, sequester, sequestrate, arrogate.

conflict n ❶ DISPUTE, quarrel, squabble, wrangle, feud, hostility, disagreement, dissension, discord, friction, antagonism, strife, contention; *informal* row. ❷ WAR, battle, fight, warfare, clash, engagement, encounter, hostilities, combat, struggle. ❸ CLASH, incompatibility, incongruity, mismatch, variance, divergence, inconsistency.
– OPPOSITES agreement, peace, harmony.
▶ v CLASH, differ, disagree, be at odds, be in opposition, be at variance, be incompatible, contrast, oppose each other, collide.
– OPPOSITES agree.

conform v ❶ COMPLY, obey the rules, adapt, adjust, be conventional; *informal* run with

the pack, swim with the stream. ❷ FIT, match, agree with, correspond to, tally with, square with, accord with.
– OPPOSITES rebel, differ.

conformity n ❶ CONVENTIONALITY, traditionalism, orthodoxy. ❷ COMPLIANCE, obedience, observance, adaptation, adjustment, accommodation.

confront v FACE, face up to, tackle, stand up to, defy, challenge, take on, resist, attack, assault, accost, waylay, meet head on.
– OPPOSITES avoid.

confuse v ❶ BEWILDER, puzzle, perplex, bemuse, baffle, mystify, befuddle, disorientate, disorient, agitate, nonplus; *informal* rattle, throw, flummox. ❷ MUDDLE, mix up, jumble, tangle up, disorder; *informal* snarl up. ❸ MISTAKE, mix/muddle up.
– OPPOSITES enlighten, simplify.

confused adj ❶ UNCLEAR, hazy, indistinct, foggy, obscure, garbled, incoherent, woolly. ❷ MUDDLED, jumbled, untidy, disordered, disorderly, out of order, chaotic, disorganized, upset, disarranged; *informal* topsy-turvy, at sixes and sevens, higgledy-piggledy. ❸ BEWILDERED, disorientated, disoriented, flustered, befuddled, addled, unbalanced, unhinged, demented, at sea, nonplussed; *informal* in a tizzy, discombobulated.
– OPPOSITES clear, orderly.

confusion n ❶ BEWILDERMENT, perplexity, bafflement, puzzlement, mystification, bemusement, muddle, disorientation, befuddlement, distraction. ❷ MUDDLE, jumble, mess, untidiness, disorder, chaos, turmoil, shambles, disorderliness, disorganization, disturbance, fuss, upheaval, commotion, uproar, pandemonium.
– OPPOSITES clarity, order.

congeal v SOLIDIFY, coagulate, thicken, clot, set, harden, cake, jell, condense, coalesce, curdle.

congenial adj AGREEABLE, friendly, pleasant, amiable, amicable, nice, kindly, good-natured, companionable, sympathetic, like-minded, pleasing, understanding, well suited, kindred.
– OPPOSITES unfriendly, unpleasant.

congenital adj ❶ HEREDITARY, inherited, innate, constitutional, inborn, inbred. ❷ INVETERATE, utter, complete, thoroughgoing, dyed-in-the-wool.

congested adj ❶ BLOCKED, clogged, choked, plugged, stopped up. ❷ PACKED, jammed, overcrowded, crowded, blocked, obstructed, overflowing, teeming.
– OPPOSITES clear.

congratulate v COMPLIMENT, offer good wishes to, wish joy to, praise, felicitate.
– OPPOSITES criticize.

congregate v GATHER, assemble, come together, collect, mass, group, convene, flock together, converge, meet, crowd, cluster, throng, swarm, rendezvous, muster, rally, foregather.
– OPPOSITES disperse.

conjecture n GUESS, suspicion, theory, hypothesis, presumption, presupposition, notion, fancy, surmise, inference; informal guesstimate.

connect v ❶ ATTACH, link, fix, couple, affix, clamp, secure, tie, rivet, fuse, solder, weld. ❷ ASSOCIATE, link, relate to, equate, identify, bracket, draw a parallel with.
– OPPOSITES separate.

connection n ❶ ATTACHMENT, fastening, coupling, clamp, joint, clasp. ❷ LINK, relationship, association, relation, correspondence, parallel, analogy.

connive v CONSPIRE, collude, be in collusion with, collaborate, plot, scheme, abet, be a party to, intrigue.

connotation n NUANCE, undertone, intimation, hint, suggestion, implication, allusion, insinuation, reference.

conquer v ❶ DEFEAT, beat, vanquish, overpower, overthrow, subdue, rout, trounce, subjugate, triumph over, overwhelm, crush, overrun, prevail over, quell, worst; informal thrash, lick. ❷ SEIZE, occupy, invade, annex, overrun, win, appropriate. ❸ OVERCOME, master, get the better of, surmount, quell, vanquish.

conquest n ❶ VICTORY, beating, defeat, overthrow, overpowering, subjugation, trouncing, rout, triumph, mastery, crushing. ❷ OCCUPATION, seizure, possession, annexation, invasion, overrunning, appropriation. ❸ ADMIRER, worshipper, fan, adherent, follower, supporter.

conscience n MORAL SENSE, morals, principles, ethics, scruples, standards, qualms, reservations, misgivings.

conscientious adj DILIGENT, careful, meticulous, thorough, attentive, precise, accurate, exact, punctilious, dedicated, hard-working, painstaking, scrupulous, rigorous, detailed.
– OPPOSITES casual.

conscious adj ❶ AWAKE, aware, alert, sentient, responsive. ❷ DELIBERATE, premeditated, intentional, intended, on purpose, calculated, voluntary, studied, knowing, volitional.
– OPPOSITES unconscious.

consecrate v SANCTIFY, bless, make holy/sacred, devote, hallow.

consecutive adj SUCCESSIVE, succeeding, following, in sequence, sequential, serial, in turn, progressive, continuous, uninterrupted, unbroken, chronological.

consensus n AGREEMENT, common consent, consent, unanimity, harmony, unity, concurrence; formal concord.
– OPPOSITES disagreement.

consent n AGREEMENT, assent, acceptance, approval, permission, acquiescence, sanction, compliance, concurrence; *informal* go-ahead, green light.
▶ v AGREE TO, accept, approve, go along with, acquiesce in, accede to, concede to, yield to, give in to, submit to, comply with, abide by, concur with.
– OPPOSITES dissent, refuse.

consequence n ❶ RESULT, effect, outcome, aftermath, repercussion, upshot, reverberation, by-product, event, issue, end. ❷ IMPORTANCE, significance, note, value, concern, substance, weight, import, moment, portent.
– OPPOSITES cause.

consequent adj RESULTING, subsequent, following, ensuing, resultant, consequential, successive, sequential.

conservation n PRESERVATION, protection, safe keeping, safeguarding, saving, guarding, care, charge, custody, husbandry, upkeep, maintenance.
– OPPOSITES destruction.

conservative adj ❶ RIGHT-WING, reactionary, Tory; *N. Amer.* Republican. ❷ CONVENTIONAL, traditional, reactionary, orthodox, cautious, prudent, careful, moderate, middle-of-the-road, unadventurous, temperate, stable, unchanging, old-fashioned, hidebound, sober. ❸ MODERATE, reasonable, cautious.
– OPPOSITES radical.

conserve v PRESERVE, save, keep, protect, take care of, use sparingly, husband, hoard, store up, nurse.
– OPPOSITES squander, waste.

consider v ❶ THINK ABOUT, weigh up, give thought to, examine, study, ponder, contemplate, deliberate over, mull over, meditate on, ruminate over, chew over, turn over in one's mind. ❷ THINK, believe, regard as, deem, hold to be, judge, rate.

considerable adj ❶ SUBSTANTIAL, sizeable, appreciable, tolerable, goodly, fair, reasonable, ample, plentiful, abundant, marked, noticeable, comfortable, decent, great, lavish. ❷ DISTINGUISHED, noteworthy, noted, important, significant, influential, illustrious, renowned.
– OPPOSITES negligible.

considerate adj THOUGHTFUL, kind, helpful, concerned, attentive, solicitous, kindly, unselfish, compassionate, sympathetic, charitable, patient, generous, obliging, accommodating, neighbourly, altruistic.
– OPPOSITES thoughtless.

consign v HAND OVER, give over, deliver, send, pass on, transfer, assign, entrust, commend, remit, bequeath.

consignment n LOAD, batch, delivery, shipment, cargo, container load.

consist v BE COMPOSED OF, be made up of, comprise, contain, include, incorporate, add up to, involve, embody.

consistent adj ❶ CONSTANT, unchanging, unvarying, undeviating, steady, dependable, steadfast, stable, reliable, faithful, uniform, true to type. ❷ COMPATIBLE, conforming to, consonant, agreeing, congruous, accordant.
– OPPOSITES inconsistent.

consolation n COMFORT, sympathy, solace, compassion, pity, commiseration, relief, help, support, cheer, encouragement, soothing, assuagement, alleviation.

consolidate v MAKE STRONGER, strengthen, make secure, secure, make stable, stabilize, reinforce, fortify, cement.
– OPPOSITES weaken.

consort
■ **consort with** ASSOCIATE WITH, keep company with, mix with, spend time with, fraternize with, have dealings with; informal hang around with.

conspicuous adj CLEAR, visible, obvious, evident, apparent, prominent, notable, noticeable, marked, plain, unmistakable, observable, recognizable, discernible, perceptible, distinguishable, manifest, patent, vivid, striking, glaring, blatant, flagrant, obtrusive, showy, bold, ostentatious, eminent.
– OPPOSITES inconspicuous, unobtrusive.

conspiracy n PLOT, scheme, plan, stratagem, machinations, cabal, intrigue, collusion, connivance, machination, treason.

conspirator n PLOTTER, conspirer, schemer, intriguer, colluder, collaborator, confederate, traitor; informal wheeler-dealer.

conspire v PLOT, scheme, form conspiracy, hatch a plot, intrigue, collude, collaborate, connive, combine, be in league; informal be in cahoots.

constant adj ❶ EVEN, regular, uniform, stable, steady, unchanging, fixed, consistent, invariable, unvarying, sustained, immutable. ❷ CONTINUAL, unending, non-stop, sustained, incessant, endless, unceasing, perpetual, persistent, interminable, unflagging, unremitting, relentless, unrelenting. ❸ LOYAL, faithful, devoted, dependable, staunch, true, trustworthy, trusty, resolute, steadfast, unwavering, unswerving.
– OPPOSITES variable, fickle.

consternation n DISMAY, anxiety, bewilderment, distress, alarm, surprise, astonishment, amazement, confusion, mystification, panic, fear, fright, dread, horror, trepidation, shock, terror, awe.

construct v BUILD, make, assemble, erect, set up, manufacture, produce, put together, fabricate, fashion, forge, establish, raise, elevate, engineer, form.
– OPPOSITES demolish.

construction n ❶ BUILDING, assembly, erection, manufacture, fabrication, elevation. ❷ STRUCTURE, building, edifice, framework. ❸ INTERPRETATION, meaning, reading, explanation, inference.

constructive adj USEFUL, helpful, productive, practical, positive, valuable, worthwhile, beneficial, creative.
– OPPOSITES destructive, negative.

consult v ❶ CONFER, discuss, talk, talk over, speak to, exchange views, deliberate; *informal* put heads together, talk turkey. ❷ ASK, seek advice from, call in, turn to, take counsel from.

consume v ❶ EAT, drink, swallow, ingest, devour, guzzle; *informal* gobble, tuck into; *Brit. informal* scoff. ❷ USE, utilize, expend, deplete, absorb, exhaust, waste, squander, drain, dissipate.

contact v ❶ COMMUNICATE WITH, get/be in touch with, be in communication with, approach, write to, phone, call, ring up, speak to, reach, get hold of, notify, sound out.
▶ n TOUCH, proximity, exposure, joining, junction, contiguity, tangency.

contagious adj CATCHING, communicable, transmittable, transmissible, infectious, spreadable, pandemic.

contain v ❶ HOLD, carry, have capacity for, accommodate, seat. ❷ INCLUDE, comprise, take in, embrace, incorporate, involve. ❸ RESTRAIN, hold in/back, control, keep in check, keep under control, suppress, repress, curb, stifle.

container n RECEPTACLE, vessel, holder, repository.

contaminate v ADULTERATE, pollute, debase, defile, corrupt, taint, dirty, infect, foul, spoil, tarnish, sully, soil, stain, befoul.

contemplate v ❶ THINK ABOUT, meditate over/on, consider, ponder over/on, reflect over/on, muse on, dwell on, deliberate over, ruminate over, cogitate on. ❷ ENVISAGE, think about, consider, intend, plan, propose, foresee, expect to. ❸ LOOK AT, view, regard, examine, inspect, observe, scrutinize, survey, eye.

contemplative adj THOUGHTFUL, pensive, reflective, meditative, ruminative, musing, intent, rapt, lost in thought.

contemporary adj ❶ CURRENT, modern, present-day, up to date, latest, fashionable, recent, newest; *informal* trendy, with it. ❷ CONTEMPORANEOUS, concurrent, coexistent, coeval, synchronous.
– OPPOSITES old-fashioned.

contempt n SCORN, disdain, disgust, loathing, abhorrence, detestation, disrespect, derision, mockery, condescension. *See also* HATRED.
– OPPOSITES admiration.

contemptible adj DESPICABLE, detestable, beneath

contempt, disgraceful, loathsome, odious, ignominious, lamentable, pitiful, discreditable, low, mean, shameful, abject, unworthy, worthless, base, vile, shabby, cheap, sordid, wretched, degenerate.
– OPPOSITES admirable.

contemptuous adj SCORNFUL, disdainful, insulting, disrespectful, derisive, derisory, insolent, mocking, sneering, jeering, belittling, dismissive, condescending, patronizing, haughty, lofty, supercilious, arrogant, superior, snide, imperious; *informal* snooty, high and mighty, snotty; *formal* contumelious.
– OPPOSITES respectful, admiring.

contend v ❶ COMPETE, oppose, challenge, contest, vie, clash, strive, struggle, grapple, tussle, wrestle. ❷ COPE WITH, face, grapple with, take on. ❸ STATE, declare, assert, maintain, hold, claim, profess, allege, affirm; *formal* aver.

content¹ n see CONTENTMENT.
▶ adj see CONTENTED.
▶ v see SATISFY (2).

content² n CONSTITUENT, part, ingredient, element.

contented adj SATISFIED, content, pleased, happy, cheerful, glad, gratified, fulfilled, at ease, at peace, comfortable, relaxed, serene, tranquil, unworried, untroubled, uncomplaining, complacent.
– OPPOSITES discontented, dissatisfied.

contentment n SATISFACTION, content, contentedness, happiness, pleasure, cheerfulness, gladness, gratification, fulfilment, relaxation, ease, comfort, peace, serenity, equanimity, tranquillity, complacency.
– OPPOSITES dissatisfaction.

contest n ❶ See COMPETITION (1). ❷ STRUGGLE, conflict, clash, fight, combat, tussle, skirmish.
▶ v ❶ COMPETE FOR, contend for, fight for/over, vie for, battle for, struggle for, tussle over; *informal* make a bid for. ❷ CHALLENGE, question, call into question, oppose, doubt, dispute, object to, query, resist.

contestant n COMPETITOR, entrant, candidate, contender, participant, rival, opponent, adversary, player.

context n CIRCUMSTANCES, situation, conditions, state of affairs, background, environment, setting, frame of reference, framework, surroundings, milieu.

contingency n EVENT, eventuality, incident, happening, occurrence, juncture, accident, chance, possibility, emergency, uncertainty, fortuity.

continual adj ❶ CONSTANT, perpetual, endless, interminable. *See also* CONTINUOUS. ❷ FREQUENT, regular, constant, habitual, persistent, recurrent, repeated.
– OPPOSITES occasional, temporary.

continue v ❶ CARRY ON, go on,

keep on, persist, persevere, stay, endure, remain, survive, last, sustain, linger; *informal* stick at. ❷ PROLONG, extend, sustain, maintain, protract, perpetuate. ❸ RESUME, carry on with, recommence, restart, start again, return to, take up.
– OPPOSITES stop.

continuous adj CONSTANT, uninterrupted, non-stop, perpetual, sustained, ceaseless, incessant, relentless, unceasing, unremitting, endless, neverending, interminable, lasting, everlasting, unbroken.
– OPPOSITES sporadic, intermittent.

contour n OUTLINE, silhouette, profile, figure, shape, form, line, curve.

contract n AGREEMENT, pact, arrangement, settlement, covenant, compact, understanding, treaty, bargain, deal, convention, concordat, entente.
▶ v ❶ GET / BECOME / MAKE SMALLER, shrink, reduce, shrivel, narrow, tighten, draw in, constrict, tense, diminish, decrease, shorten, compress, curtail, concentrate, abbreviate, abridge. ❷ AGREE, arrange, come to terms, reach an agreement, negotiate, bargain, strike a bargain, engage, settle, covenant. ❸ CATCH, develop, get, become infected with; *Brit.* go down with.
– OPPOSITES expand.

contradict v SAY THE OPPOSITE OF, oppose, challenge, counter,

be at variance with, clash with, dissent from, rebut, refute, controvert, impugn, confute.
– OPPOSITES agree.

contradictory adj OPPOSING, opposite, opposed, conflicting, clashing, contrasting, incompatible, inconsistent, irreconcilable, dissenting, contrary, antithetical.

contraption n DEVICE, machine, mechanism, gadget, contrivance, apparatus, appliance; *informal* whatsit, thingamajig, thingamabob, thingummy, whatchamacallit, gizmo, doodah.

contrary adj ❶ OPPOSING, opposite, contradictory, conflicting, contrasting, clashing, incompatible, irreconcilable, inconsistent, incongruous, antithetical. ❷ AWKWARD, wilful, perverse, obstinate, stubborn, headstrong, wayward, intractable, unaccommodating, recalcitrant, intransigent, refractory, cantankerous; *informal* pigheaded, cussed; *Brit. informal* stroppy.
– OPPOSITES compatible, accommodating.

contrast n DIFFERENCE, dissimilarity, disparity, distinction, differentiation, divergence, opposition, dissimilitude.
▶ v ❶ COMPARE, set side by side, juxtapose, distinguish, differentiate, discriminate. ❷ FORM A CONTRAST, differ, contradict, clash, conflict, be at variance, be contrary, diverge.

contribute v **1** GIVE, donate, provide, subscribe, present, hand out, supply, grant, endow, bestow, confer, furnish; *informal* chip in. **2** LEAD TO, be conducive to, be instrumental in, help, add to, promote, advance; *informal* have a hand in.

contribution n **1** DONATION, gift, subscription, offering, present, grant, allowance, subsidy, endowment; *informal* handout. **2** PARTICIPATION, input; *informal* one's pennyworth.

contrite adj PENITENT, repentant, remorseful, regretful, sorry, conscience-stricken, guilt-stricken, chastened, in sackcloth and ashes.
– OPPOSITES unrepentant.

control n **1** AUTHORITY, power, charge, management, command, direction, rule, government, supervision, oversight, regulation, jurisdiction, dominance, mastery, leadership, reign, supremacy, sway, superintendence, guidance. **2** LIMITATION, restriction, regulation, check, restraint, curb, brake. **3** INSTRUMENT, switch, dial, knob, lever.
▶ v **1** BE IN CHARGE OF, be in control of, manage, head, direct, command, rule, govern, oversee, dominate, preside over, conduct, reign over; *informal* be the boss of, be in the driver's seat, be in the saddle. **2** REGULATE, restrain, keep in check, restrict, curb, hold back, contain, limit, subdue, bridle.

controversial adj DISPUTED, contentious, at issue, open to question/discussion, disputable, debatable, under discussion, problematical, doubtful, questionable, contended, incontrovertible.

controversy n DISPUTE, argument, debate, disagreement, dissension, contention, altercation, wrangle, wrangling, quarrelling, squabbling, bickering, war of words, polemic.

convalesce v GET BETTER, recover, recuperate, improve, return to health, be on the mend, regain strength.

convene v **1** CALL, call together, summon, round up, rally; *formal* convoke. **2** ASSEMBLE, gather, meet, collect, congregate, muster.

convenient adj **1** SUITABLE, suited, appropriate, fitting, fit, favourable, advantageous, opportune, timely, well timed, expedient, useful, serviceable. **2** ACCESSIBLE, nearby, close at hand, handy, at hand, within reach, just round the corner.
– OPPOSITES inconvenient.

convention n **1** *See* ASSEMBLY. **2** PROTOCOL, formality, code, custom, tradition, practice, usage, etiquette, propriety.

conventional adj **1** ACCEPTED, expected, customary, usual, normal, standard, regular, correct, proper, orthodox, traditional, prevailing, prevalent, conformist, decorous, conservative, formal,

ritual. ❷ COMMONPLACE, common, run-of-the-mill, everyday, prosaic, routine, stereotyped, pedestrian, hackneyed, unoriginal, clichéd, trite, platitudinous, bourgeois; Brit. informal common or garden.
– OPPOSITES unconventional.

converge v MEET, intersect, join, merge, unite, come together, become one, coincide, concur.
– OPPOSITES diverge, separate.

conversant adj ACQUAINTED WITH, familiar with, knowledgeable about, well versed in, informed about, apprised of, au fait with, experienced in, proficient in, practised in, skilled in; informal well up on.

conversation n TALK, discussion, chat, dialogue, communication, gossip, exchange of views, conference, tête-a-tête, discourse, colloquy, intercourse, heart to heart, palaver; informal powwow, confab, chinwag; Brit. informal natter.

convert v ❶ CHANGE, transform, alter, modify, reshape, refashion, remodel, remake, rebuild, reorganize, metamorphose, transfigure, transmogrify, transmute. ❷ CONVINCE, persuade, reform, re-educate, baptize, save, proselytize.

convey v ❶ TRANSPORT, carry, bring, fetch, take, move, deliver, bear, shift, transfer, ship, conduct, transmit; informal cart, lug. ❷ TRANSMIT,

communicate, pass on, send, make known, tell, announce, relate, impart, hand on, dispatch, reveal, disclose.

convict v PRISONER, criminal, offender, felon, law-breaker, malefactor; informal jailbird, con, old lag.
▶ v DECLARE / FIND GUILTY, sentence, condemn.
– OPPOSITES acquit.

conviction n ❶ CONFIDENCE, assurance, belief, certainty, persuasion, firmness, earnestness, certitude. ❷ BELIEF, view, principle, opinion, thought, idea, creed, tenet, persuasion.
– OPPOSITES uncertainty.

convince v PERSUADE, prove to, satisfy, assure, talk round, bring round, win over, sway.

convincing adj PERSUASIVE, powerful, plausible, credible, conclusive, cogent, incontrovertible.
– OPPOSITES unconvincing.

convivial adj FRIENDLY, genial, cordial, sociable, affable, amiable, congenial, agreeable, jolly, cheerful.

convoy n GROUP, company, line, fleet, cortège, caravan, assemblage.
▶ v ESCORT, accompany, attend, protect, guard, defend, guide, shepherd, flank.

cook v PREPARE, make, put together, concoct, improvise.

cool adj ❶ CHILLED, chilly, fresh, refreshing, unheated, breezy, draughty; informal nippy. See also COLD (1). ❷ CALM, relaxed, composed, collected, self-possessed,

level-headed, self-controlled, unexcited, unmoved, unperturbed, unruffled, unemotional, placid, serene. ❸ ALOOF, distant, reserved, stand-offish, unfriendly, offhand, indifferent, uninterested, undemonstrative, unwelcoming, uncommunicative, chilly, frigid, impassive, dispassionate. ❹ SOPHISTICATED, urbane, cosmopolitan, elegant.
– OPPOSITES warm.
▶ v ❶ CHILL, refrigerate, freeze. ❷ LESSEN, diminish, reduce, dampen, abate, moderate, temper, soothe, assuage, allay, mollify.
– OPPOSITES heat, inflame.

cooperate v WORK TOGETHER, join forces, unite, help each other, act jointly, combine, collaborate, pool resources, conspire, connive, coordinate; *informal* pull together, pitch in, play ball.

cooperative adj ❶ JOINT, united, shared, unified, combined, concerted, collective, collaborative, coordinated. ❷ HELPFUL, of assistance, obliging, accommodating, supportive, responsive, willing.
– OPPOSITES uncooperative.

coordinate v ARRANGE, organize, order, integrate, correlate, systematize, synchronize, harmonize.

cope v MANAGE, succeed, survive, carry on, get through, get on, get by, subsist, come through; *informal* make out.
■ **cope with** HANDLE, deal with, take care of, contend with, grapple with, struggle with.

copious adj ABUNDANT, plentiful, ample, profuse, full, extensive, generous, lavish, superabundant, rich, liberal, bountiful, exuberant, luxuriant, overflowing, abounding; *poetic/literary* plenteous, bounteous.
– OPPOSITES scarce.

copy n ❶ REPRODUCTION, imitation, replica, likeness, representation, twin, counterfeit, forgery, fake, sham. ❷ DUPLICATE, facsimile, carbon, carbon copy, photocopy, transcript; *trademark* Xerox, photostat.
▶ v ❶ IMITATE, mimic, emulate, mirror, echo, follow, simulate, ape, parrot. ❷ DUPLICATE, photocopy, xerox, photostat. ❸ REPRODUCE, replicate, forge, counterfeit.

cord n STRING, rope, twine, cable, line, ligature.

cordon n BARRIER, line, chain, ring, picket line.
■ **cordon off** CLOSE OFF, fence off, shut off, separate off, isolate, enclose, encircle, surround, picket.

core n CENTRE, heart, nucleus, nub, kernel, crux, essence, heart of the matter, substance, gist, pith; *informal* nitty-gritty.

corner n ❶ BEND, angle, curve, turn, crook. ❷ JUNCTION, turn, intersection, crossroads, fork, convergence. ❸ NOOK, cranny, recess, crevice, hideaway, niche, cavity, hole; *informal* hidey-hole.

▶ v TRAP, capture, run to earth, bring to bay.

corpse n BODY, remains, cadaver, carcass; *informal* stiff.

correct adj **❶** RIGHT, accurate, true, actual, exact, precise, unerring, faithful, strict, faultless, flawless, confirmed, verified; *informal* on the mark; *Brit. informal* spot on, bang on. **❷** PROPER, suitable, appropriate, accepted, fit, fitting, seemly, apt, approved, conventional, usual, customary.
– OPPOSITES wrong, incorrect, improper.
▶ v **❶** RECTIFY, amend, set right, remedy, repair, emend, redress, cure, improve, better. **❷** ADJUST, regulate, fix, set, standardize, normalize. **❸** See REPRIMAND V.

correspond v **❶** AGREE, be in agreement, accord, concur, coincide, conform, match, fit together, square, tally, dovetail, correlate. **❷** EXCHANGE LETTERS, write to, communicate, keep in touch/contact.

correspondence n LETTERS, mail, post, notes, messages.

corroborate v CONFIRM, verify, bear out, authenticate, validate, certify, endorse, ratify, substantiate, uphold, attest to; *informal* back up.

corrode v **❶** EAT AWAY, wear away, erode, abrade, destroy, consume, rust, oxidize. **❷** WEAR AWAY, rust, deteriorate, disintegrate, crumble, fragment.

corrugated adj FURROWED,

ridged, wrinkled, creased, grooved, crinkled, ribbed, channelled, puckered, fluted.

corrupt adj **❶** DISHONEST, fraudulent, unscrupulous, dishonourable, untrustworthy, venal; *informal* crooked, bent, shady. **❷** IMMORAL, depraved, wicked, evil, sinful, degenerate, perverted, dissolute, debauched, decadent, abandoned, lascivious, lecherous.
– OPPOSITES honest, pure.
▶ v **❶** BRIBE, buy, buy off, pay off, suborn, induce, lure, entice; *informal* grease someone's palm. **❷** DEPRAVE, pervert, warp, debauch, lead astray.

cosmic adj **❶** UNIVERSAL, worldwide. **❷** VAST, huge, enormous, immense, immeasurable, infinite, limitless.

cosmopolitan adj **❶** INTERNATIONAL, global, universal. **❷** SOPHISTICATED, liberal, urbane, worldly, wordly-wise, well travelled.
– OPPOSITES parochial.

cost n PRICE, charge, amount, rate, value, quotation, payment, expense, outlay; *informal* damage.
▶ v BE PRICED AT, be worth, come to, fetch, amount to, realize; *informal* set someone back.

costly adj **❶** EXPENSIVE, dear, exorbitant, extortionate, extravagant; *informal* steep. **❷** DISASTROUS, harmful, ruinous, catastrophic, pyrrhic.
– OPPOSITES cheap, inexpensive.

cosy adj COMFORTABLE, snug,

restful, warm, relaxed, homely, sheltered, secure, safe; *informal* comfy, snug as a bug.
– OPPOSITES uncomfortable.

counsel n ❶ *See* ADVICE. ❷ *See* LAWYER.
▶ v ADVISE, guide, direct, recommend, warn, admonish, caution.

count v ❶ ADD UP, keep a count of, calculate, work out, total, estimate, reckon up, enumerate, check, tally, compute, tell; *informal* tot up. ❷ REGARD, consider, think, look upon, hold, judge, deem. ❸ MATTER, be of account, signify, enter into consideration, mean anything, amount to anything, rate.
■ **count on** *see* RELY ON.

countenance n FACE, features, expression, look, mien, appearance, visage, air.
▶ v *see* PERMIT V, STAND V (4).

counter[1] n ❶ TOP, surface, worktop, table, checkout, stand. ❷ TOKEN, disc, piece, marker, wafer, man.

counter[2] v OPPOSE, resist, combat, dispute, argue against, rebut, contradict, retaliate, ward off, parry; *informal* hit back at, come back at.

counteract v OFFSET, balance, counterbalance, neutralize, act counter to, be an antidote to, oppose, work against, thwart, negate, annul, impede, hinder, invalidate, countervail.

counterbalance v BALANCE, compensate for, make up for,

offset, neutralize, equalize, set off, undo, counterpoise.

counterfeit adj FAKE, faked, forged, copied, imitation, pseudo, fraudulent, sham, bogus, spurious, feigned, ersatz; *informal* phoney.
– OPPOSITES genuine.
▶ n FAKE, copy, forgery, imitation, reproduction, fraud, sham.
▶ v FAKE, copy, imitate, reproduce, simulate, feign, falsify, pretend.

counterpart n EQUIVALENT, equal, opposite number, parallel, complement, match, twin, mate, fellow, analogue, correlative, copy, duplicate.

countless adj INNUMERABLE, incalculable, infinite, immeasurable, endless, limitless, without limit/end, untold, inexhaustible, boundless, myriad, legion, no end of.

country n ❶ STATE, nation, realm, kingdom, land, territory, power, commonwealth, domain, people, principality. ❷ LAND, terrain, landscape, territory, scenery, region, area, district, neighbourhood.

coupon n VOUCHER, token, ticket, slip, stub, certificate.

courage n BRAVERY, fearlessness, valour, heroism, intrepidity, pluck, nerve, grit, boldness, daring, audacity, mettle, spirit, fortitude, firmness, resolution, tenacity, determination, lion-heartedness, gallantry, stout-heartedness, dauntlessness, indomitability,

hardihood, fibre; *informal* guts, spunk; *Brit. informal* bottle.
– OPPOSITES cowardice, fear.

courageous adj BRAVE, fearless, heroic, bold, daring, plucky, audacious, unshrinking, dauntless, lionhearted, intrepid, valiant, valorous, gallant, tenacious, indomitable, resolute, determined, game, spirited, stouthearted, undaunted, stalwart.
– OPPOSITES cowardly.

course n ❶ ROUTE, way, track, direction, path, trail, line, road, passage, lane, tack, trajectory, circuit, ambit, orbit. ❷ WAY, method, line of action, procedure, process, system, policy, programme, regimen. ❸ DURATION, passing, passage, period, lapse, term, span. ❹ CLASSES, lectures, curriculum, schedule, syllabus, programme.

court n ❶ LAW COURT, court of law, tribunal, forum, bench, chancery, assizes. ❷ ATTENDANTS, household, retinue, entourage, train, suite. ❸ HOMAGE, suit, wooing, courtship, respects, blandishments.
▶ v ❶ WOO, pursue, run after, go out with; *informal* date, go steady (with). ❷ INVITE, risk, provoke, lead to, cause, bring on, elicit.

courteous adj POLITE, well mannered, civil, gentlemanly, gracious, mannerly, well bred, civilized, urbane.
– OPPOSITES discourteous, rude.

courtier n ATTENDANT, follower, steward, page, squire, cup-bearer, train-bearer, liegeman.

cove n BAY, inlet, sound, creek, bight, anchorage; *Scottish* firth.

cover v ❶ PLACE OVER, spread over, protect, shield, shelter, conceal, coat, extend over, cloak, overlay, blanket, carpet, drape, overlie, overspread, shroud, surface, veil, enclose, mask, screen, obscure, enshroud, house, secrete, bury, hide, submerge, layer, film, mantle, pave, clothe, wrap, swaddle, attire, garb, robe, encase, sheathe. ❷ DEAL WITH, involve, take in, contain, encompass, embrace, incorporate, treat, examine, survey. ❸ REPORT, write up, describe, tell of, give an account of, give details of, investigate.
▶ n ❶ COVERING, surface, top, lid, cap, screen, layer, coat, coating, carpet, canopy, crust, mantle, blanket, overlay, mask, cloak, veil, film, sheath, shield, veneer, wrapping, housing, cocoon, casing, cladding, skin, tarpaulin, encrustation, rind. ❷ DISGUISE, front, camouflage, pretence, facade, false front, smokescreen, windowdressing, pretext, cloak, veil, mask. ❸ INSURANCE, protection, compensation, indemnity, indemnification.

covert adj SECRET, concealed, hidden, surreptitious, furtive, stealthy, private, underground.
– OPPOSITES overt.

covet v DESIRE, want, wish for, long/yearn for, crave, hanker after, lust after, thirst for, hunger for, set one's heart on, aspire to, aim for, envy, begrudge.

cowardly adj FEARFUL, timid, timorous, faint-hearted, spineless, lily-livered, chicken-hearted, craven, base, shrinking, pusillanimous, afraid of one's shadow, submissive, unheroic, unchivalrous, ungallant; *informal* chicken, yellow, yellow-bellied, gutless, wimpish.
– OPPOSITES brave, courageous.

cower v CRINGE, shrink, flinch, draw back, recoil, crouch, wince, slink, blench, quail, quake, tremble, quiver, grovel, skulk.

coy adj COQUETTISH, arch, kittenish, evasive, shy, modest, unforthcoming, demure, bashful, reticent, diffident, retiring, self-effacing, hesitant, shrinking, withdrawn, timid, prudish, lacking confidence, unsure.
– OPPOSITES brazen.

crack n ❶ FRACTURE, break, chip, split, fissure, crevice, breach, rupture, rift, chink, gap, cavity, slit, cleft, cranny. ❷ ATTEMPT, try, shot, opportunity; *informal* go, stab. ❸ See JOKE n (1).
▶ v ❶ FRACTURE, break, fragment, chip, split, splinter, snap. ❷ BREAK DOWN, give way, collapse, yield, succumb; *informal* go

to pieces, come apart at the seams.

cradle n ❶ CRIB, cot, carrycot, bassinet. ❷ BIRTHPLACE, source, fount, wellspring, beginnings, nursery.
▶ v HOLD, rock, nestle, shelter, support.

craft n ❶ SKILL, skilfulness, expertise, ability, mastery, artistry, art, technique, aptitude, dexterity, talent, flair, knack, genius. ❷ TRADE, occupation, vocation, calling, pursuit, business, line, work, employment. ❸ VESSEL, ship, boat, aircraft, plane, spacecraft.

crafty adj CUNNING, artful, calculating, designing, scheming, wily, sly, devious, tricky, foxy, shrewd, astute, canny, sharp, Machiavellian, shifty, guileful, deceitful, duplicitous, insidious, treacherous, fraudulent, underhand; *informal* crooked.
– OPPOSITES honest.

crag n CLIFF, bluff, escarpment, scarp, ridge, peak, pinnacle, tor.

cram v ❶ STUFF, push into, force into, pack in, ram down, press into, squeeze into, compress, compact, condense. ❷ See STUDY (1).

cramped adj CONFINED, crowded, packed, narrow, small, restricted, limited, uncomfortable, closed in, hemmed in, tight, overfull, squeezed, jammed in, congested.
– OPPOSITES spacious.

crash v ❶ COLLIDE WITH, bump

into, smash into, plough into, pitch into, jolt, jar. ❷ FALL, topple, tumble, overbalance, pitch, plunge, hurtle, lurch.
▶ n ❶ COLLISION, accident, smash, pile-up, bump; *Brit. informal* prang. ❷ CLASH, clang, clank, bang, smash, clangour, racket, din, boom, explosion. ❸ COLLAPSE, failure, fall, plummet, ruin, downfall, depression, debacle.

crate n BOX, case, chest, carton, basket, hamper, receptacle.

crater n HOLE, hollow, pit, cavity, depression, dip, chasm, abyss.

crawl v ❶ CREEP, move on hands and knees, go on all fours, slither, squirm, wriggle, writhe, worm one's way, sneak. ❷ FAWN, flatter, grovel, cringe, toady; *informal* suck up.

craze n TREND, fashion, fad, vogue, enthusiasm, passion, obsession, mania, fixation, whim, fascination, preoccupation, rage, infatuation.

crazy adj ❶ MAD, insane, unbalanced, demented, lunatic, crazed, of unsound mind, deranged, unhinged, touched, berserk; *informal* batty, loony, nuts, cuckoo, bonkers, mental, round the bend/twist; *Brit. informal* potty. ❷ ABSURD, idiotic, stupid, ridiculous, silly, foolish, peculiar, odd, strange, queer, eccentric, bizarre, weird, fantastic, inane, fatuous, unwise, preposterous; *informal* half-baked; *Brit. informal* potty. ❸ ENTHUSIASTIC, mad, keen,

passionate, smitten, fanatical, devoted, fervent, excited.
– OPPOSITES sensible, uninterested.

cream n LOTION, paste, ointment, salve, unguent, liniment, emulsion.

crease n WRINKLE, furrow, line, fold, crinkle, ridge, corrugation, pucker, ruck, pleat, tuck.
▶ v CRUMPLE, wrinkle, rumple, crinkle, ruck up, pucker, ridge, furrow, corrugate, pleat, tuck.

create v ❶ PRODUCE, originate, generate, design, establish, set up, invent, make, build, construct, develop, initiate, engender, frame, fabricate, erect, found, institute, constitute, inaugurate, shape, form, mould, forge, concoct, hatch. ❷ BRING INTO BEING, give birth/life to, father, sire, spawn, procreate; *poetic/literary* beget. ❸ RESULT IN, make, produce, bring about, give rise to, lead to.
– OPPOSITES destroy.

creative adj INVENTIVE, imaginative, original, artistic, inspired, visionary, talented, gifted, resourceful, ingenious, clever, productive, fertile, fecund.

creator n ❶ INVENTOR, originator, author, maker, designer, initiator, deviser, producer, manufacturer, architect, builder, prime mover, parent, generator; *poetic/literary* begetter. ❷ GOD, the Almighty.

creature n ❶ ANIMAL, beast, being, living thing, organism;

N. Amer. informal critter. **②** PERSON, human being, individual, character, soul, mortal; *informal* fellow. **③** LACKEY, minion, puppet, toady, sycophant, hireling, retainer, dependant, hanger-on, vassal.

credentials pl n DOCUMENTS, references, documentation, qualifications, certificate, diploma, testimonial, warrant, licence, permit, card, voucher, passport, letter of introduction.

credible adj **❶** BELIEVABLE, plausible, convincing, likely, conceivable, imaginable, persuasive, tenable. **❷** ACCEPTABLE, reliable, trustworthy, dependable.
– OPPOSITES incredible, untrustworthy.

credit n **❶** PRAISE, acclaim, approval, commendation, acknowledgement, tribute, kudos, glory, recognition, esteem, regard, respect, merit, veneration; *formal* laudation. **②** FINANCIAL STANDING / STATUS, solvency.
▶ v **❶** BELIEVE, accept, trust, have faith in, rely on, depend on, put confidence in; *informal* fall for, swallow, buy. **②** ASCRIBE TO, attribute to, assign to, give credit to, accredit to, impute to, chalk up to, put down to.

creditable adj PRAISEWORTHY, admirable, commendable, laudable, meritorious, exemplary, worthy, respectable, reputable, estimable, honourable, deserving.
– OPPOSITES discreditable.

credulous adj GULLIBLE, easily taken in, over-trusting, naive, unsuspicious, uncritical; *informal* green, wet behind the ears.
– OPPOSITES suspicious.

creed n BELIEF, principle, teaching, doctrine, dogma, tenet, catechism, article of faith.

creek n INLET, bay, cove, estuary, bight; *Scottish* firth.

creep v CRAWL, move on hands and knees, go on all fours, slither, squirm, wriggle, writhe, move stealthily, sneak, tiptoe, slink, skulk, worm one's way.
▶ n SYCOPHANT, toady, fawner, sneak; *informal* bootlicker.

creepy adj HORRIFYING, horrific, horrible, frightening, scary, terrifying, hair-raising, awful, disturbing, eerie, sinister, weird, nightmarish, macabre, ominous, menacing, threatening, disgusting, repellent, repulsive, revolting.

crest n **❶** COMB, tuft, cockscomb, plume. **②** SUMMIT, top, peak, crown, brow, apex, ridge, heights. **③** BADGE, emblem, regalia, insignia, device, coat of arms, seal, shield, sign, symbol.

crestfallen adj DOWNCAST, dejected, depressed, glum, downhearted, disheartened, discouraged, dispirited, despondent, disconsolate; *informal* down in the dumps, in the doldrums.
– OPPOSITES cheerful.

crevice n FISSURE, cleft, crack, cranny, split, rift, slit, gash, rent, fracture, opening, gap, hole, interstice.

crick n PAIN, cramp, twinge, spasm, pang, stiffness.

crime n ❶ OFFENCE, violation, felony, misdemeanour, misdeed, wrong, transgression, fault, injury; archaic trespass.
❷ LAWBREAKING, illegality, misconduct, wrongdoing, delinquency, villainy, wickedness, evil; Law malfeasance.

criminal adj ❶ UNLAWFUL, illegal, illicit, lawless, felonious, delinquent, indictable, culpable, wrong, villainous, corrupt, evil, wicked, iniquitous, nefarious; informal crooked, bent. ❷ DEPLORABLE, scandalous, shameful, reprehensible, senseless, foolish, ridiculous, sinful, immoral.
– OPPOSITES lawful, commendable.
▶ n OFFENDER, lawbreaker, wrongdoer, malefactor, felon, delinquent, miscreant, culprit, villain, gangster, racketeer, hoodlum, bandit, transgressor, sinner; informal crook, con, baddy; archaic trespasser.

cringe v COWER, shrink, draw back, quail, flinch, recoil, start, shy, dodge, duck, crouch, wince, tremble, quiver, shake.

cripple v ❶ DISABLE, incapacitate, lame, debilitate, impair, damage, maim, weaken, enfeeble, paralyse. ❷ DAMAGE, injure, ruin, destroy, weaken, hamstring, enfeeble, paralyse, bring to a standstill.

crisis n EMERGENCY, disaster, catastrophe, calamity, predicament, plight, mess, trouble,

difficulty, extremity, dilemma, quandary, exigency; informal fix, pickle, scrape.

crisp adj ❶ BRITTLE, breakable, crunchy, crispy, friable.
❷ BRISK, decisive, vigorous, brusque, curt, abrupt.
– OPPOSITES limp, soft, rambling.

criterion n MEASURE, standard, benchmark, norm, yardstick, scale, touchstone, barometer, exemplar, canon.

critic n ❶ REVIEWER, commentator, pundit, arbiter, judge, evaluator. ❷ ATTACKER, faultfinder, detractor, reviler, vilifier, carper, backbiter; informal knocker, nit-picker.

critical adj ❶ CENSORIOUS, disapproving, disparaging, derogatory, fault-finding, carping, depreciatory, niggling, cavilling, judgemental, uncomplimentary, scathing, unfavourable, captious; informal nit-picking. ❷ EVALUATIVE, analytic, interpretative, expository, explanatory, explicative, elucidative, annotative. ❸ CRUCIAL, decisive, pivotal, key, important, vital, urgent, pressing. ❹ DANGEROUS, grave, serious, risky, perilous, hazardous, precarious.
– OPPOSITES complimentary, unimportant.

criticism n ❶ CONDEMNATION, censure, disapproval, disparagement, fault-finding, reproof, carping, cavilling, captiousness, animadversion; informal nit-picking, brickbats, flak,

knocking, slamming. **❷** EVALU-
ATION, comment, commentary,
assessment, appreciation, appraisal, analysis, interpretation, judgement, elucidation,
explication, annotation.

criticize v FIND FAULT WITH,
censure, denounce, condemn,
disapprove of, disparage, cast
aspersions on, snipe at,
impugn, scold, decry, carp at,
cavil at, excoriate, animadvert
on; *informal* nit-pick, pick holes
in, knock, slam, pan, lash, get
at, pitch into, rap, flay, hand
out brickbats; *Brit. informal* slate.
– OPPOSITES praise.

crockery n DISHES, tableware,
pottery, porcelain, china,
earthenware.

crook n **❶** *See* CRIMINAL. **❷** BEND,
curve, curvature, angle, bow,
hook.

crooked adj **❶** *See* CRIMINAL adj
(1). **❷** BENT, curved, twisted,
warped, contorted, angled,
bowed, irregular, hooked,
flexed, winding, twisting,
zigzag, misshapen, out of
shape, lopsided, off-centre,
meandering, sinuous, tortuous,
serpentine.
– OPPOSITES straight.

crop n HARVEST, growth, yield,
produce, vintage, fruits,
gathering, reaping.
▸ v CUT, trim, clip, shear, lop,
snip, prune, mow, graze,
nibble, browse.

cross n **❶** AFFLICTION, trouble,
worry, burden, trial, disaster,
tribulation, misfortune,
misery, adversity, woe, pain,

suffering, catastrophe, calamity. **❷** HYBRID, mixture, crossbreed, amalgam, blend, combination, mongrel.
▸ v **❶** GO ACROSS, span, stretch/
extend across, pass over,
bridge, ford, traverse. **❷** INTER-
SECT, meet, join, converge,
criss-cross, interweave, intertwine. **❸** OPPOSE, resist, thwart,
frustrate, obstruct, foil,
impede, hinder, hamper,
check, contradict.
▸ adj ANNOYED, irritated, vexed,
bad-tempered, short-tempered,
irascible, touchy, fractious,
peevish, crotchety, grouchy,
querulous, cantankerous, testy,
waspish; *informal* snappy.
– OPPOSITES pleased, good-
humoured.
■ **cross out** *see* DELETE.

crossing n **❶** JUNCTION, crossroads, intersection. **❷** PEDES-
TRIAN / PELICAN CROSSING, underpass, subway, level crossing,
bridge, ford, causeway, flyover.

crouch v SQUAT, bend, duck,
stoop, hunch over, hunker,
cower, cringe.

crowd n **❶** HORDE, throng,
mob, mass, multitude, host,
rabble, army, herd, flock, drove,
swarm, troupe, pack, press,
crush, flood, assembly, gathering, collection, congregation,
convention. **❷** AUDIENCE, house,
turnout, gate, attendance,
spectators, viewers, listeners.
▸ v **❶** GATHER, cluster, flock,
swarm, throng, huddle, concentrate, foregather. **❷** PRESS,
push, shove, thrust, jostle,

elbow, squeeze, pile, pack, cram, jam, bundle, stuff.

crowded adj FULL, busy, packed, congested, overflowing, teeming, swarming, crammed, thronged, populous; *informal* jam-packed, full to bursting.
– OPPOSITES empty.

crown n ❶ ROYALTY, monarchy, monarch, king, queen, emperor, empress. ❷ TOP, crest, summit, apex, tip, head, pinnacle.
▶ v ❶ INVEST, enthrone, inaugurate, install, induct, anoint. ❷ CAP, be the culmination/climax of, round off, complete, perfect, conclude, top off.

crucial adj IMPORTANT, vital, critical, decisive, pivotal, central, urgent, pressing, high-priority, essential.
– OPPOSITES unimportant.

crude adj ❶ RAW, unrefined, natural, coarse, unprocessed, unpolished. ❷ ROUGH, primitive, rudimentary, rough and ready, unpolished, makeshift, rough-hewn, unskilful, amateurish, clumsy, inartistic, awkward, inept. ❸ *see* VULGAR (1).
– OPPOSITES refined.

cruel adj BRUTAL, savage, barbaric, inhuman, barbarous, vicious, ferocious, fierce, evil, callous, pitiless, fiendish, sadistic, venomous, cold-blooded, ruthless, merciless, unrelenting, implacable, remorseless, unfeeling, heartless, malevolent, inhumane, severe, harsh, stern, stony-hearted, hard-hearted, flinty, bestial, tyrannical.
– OPPOSITES kind, merciful.

cruelty n BRUTALITY, savagery, savageness, inhumanity, barbarism, barbarousness, viciousness, ferocity, fierceness, callousness, heartlessness, evil, fiendishness, sadism, ruthlessness, pitilessness, relentlessness, severity, harshness, inclemency.
– OPPOSITES kindness, compassion.

cruise n TRIP, voyage, sail.
▶ v SAIL, voyage, journey, drift, coast.

crumb n BIT, fragment, morsel, particle, grain, speck, scrap, snippet, atom, sliver.

crumble v ❶ CRUSH, break up, pulverize, pound, grind, powder, fragment. ❷ DISINTE-GRATE, fall apart, break down/up, collapse, deteriorate, decompose, rot, rot away, perish.

crumple v CRUSH, crease, rumple, wrinkle, crinkle, fold, pucker, dent, mangle.

crunch v BITE, chew, gnaw, masticate, champ, chomp, munch, crush, grind, pulverize.

crusade n CAMPAIGN, drive, movement, push, struggle, cause, war.
▶ v FIGHT, campaign, work, take up arms, take up a cause.

crush v ❶ SQUASH, squeeze, press, mash, compress, mangle, pound, pulverize, smash, crunch, grind, pulp, shiver. ❷ PUT DOWN, defeat,

suppress, subdue, overpower, overwhelm, quash, stamp out, conquer, extinguish. **❸** HUMILIATE, mortify, shame, abash, chagrin.
▶ n CROWD, jam, congestion.

crust n CASING, outer layer, rind, shell, husk, covering, skin, encrustation, scab, concretion.

crusty adj CRISP, crispy, brittle, hard, well done, friable.

cry v **❶** WEEP, sob, wail, snivel, blubber, whimper, whine, bawl, howl. **❷** CALL OUT, yell, exclaim, screech, bellow, howl.
▶ n **❶** SOB, wail, blubbering, keening. **❷** CALL, exclamation, scream, screech, yell, shout, bellow, howl.

crypt n TOMB, vault, burial chamber, sepulchre, catacomb, undercroft.

cryptic adj MYSTERIOUS, obscure, enigmatic, arcane, esoteric, puzzling, perplexing, secret, concealed, coded, unintelligible, hidden, unclear, veiled.
– OPPOSITES clear.

cuddle v HUG, embrace, clasp, fondle, pet, snuggle, nestle, curl up, enfold, nurse, dandle; informal canoodle, neck, smooch.

cudgel n CLUB, bludgeon, stick, truncheon, blackjack, baton, bat, bastinado; Brit. informal cosh.
▶ v BLUDGEON, club, beat, strike, pound, pummel, thrash, thump; informal clobber, thwack; Brit. informal cosh.

cue n SIGNAL, sign, hint, indica-

tion, suggestion, reminder, intimation.

culminate v PEAK, come to/ reach a climax, come to an end, come to a head, end, finish, close, conclude, terminate; informal wind up.

culpable adj GUILTY, in the wrong, at fault, blameworthy, to blame, answerable, wrong, reprehensible, reproachable, sinful.
– OPPOSITES blameless, innocent.

culprit n GUILTY PARTY, person responsible, sinner, evil-doer, miscreant, lawbreaker, criminal, delinquent, reprobate, transgressor, malefactor.

cult n **❶** SECT, church, religion, body, denomination, faith, belief, persuasion. **❷** CRAZE, fashion, fad, vogue, trend, obsession.

cultivate v **❶** TILL, farm, work, plough, dig, prepare, fertilize. **❷** EDUCATE, improve, better, develop, train, civilize, enlighten, refine, elevate, enrich. **❸** WOO, court, pursue, ingratiate oneself with, curry favour with; informal butter up, suck up to. **❹** FOSTER, develop, pursue, devote oneself to, encourage, support, further, aid.

cultivated adj see CULTURED.

cultural adj ARTISTIC, aesthetic, educational, improving, educative, enlightening, intellectual, civilizing, elevating, broadening, developmental.

culture n **❶** CULTIVATION, enlightenment, education,

accomplishment, edification, erudition, refinement, polish, sophistication, urbanity, discernment, discrimination, good taste, breeding, politeness, savoir faire. ❷ CIVILIZATION, way of life, lifestyle, customs, habits, ways, mores.

cultured adj ARTISTIC, cultivated, educated, learned, enlightened, intellectual, knowledgeable, highbrow, scholarly, well informed, well read, erudite, accomplished, well versed, refined, genteel, polished, sophisticated, urbane.

cunning adj ❶ CRAFTY, devious, wily, sly, artful, shrewd, astute, knowing, sharp, Machiavellian, deceitful, shifty, guileful; *informal* tricky, foxy. ❷ CLEVER, ingenious, resourceful, inventive, imaginative, skilful, deft, subtle, adroit.
– OPPOSITES ingenuous.
▶ n ❶ CRAFTINESS, artfulness, wiliness, slyness, shrewdness, guile, astuteness, sharpness. ❷ CLEVERNESS, ingenuity, resourcefulness, inventiveness, skill, deftness, adroitness, finesse, capability.

cup n ❶ MUG, teacup, beaker, tumbler, tankard, wine glass, chalice, goblet. ❷ TROPHY, prize, award.

curator n KEEPER, caretaker, custodian, guardian, conservator, steward.

curb v RESTRAIN, check, keep in check, control, contain, hold back, repress, suppress, moderate, dampen, put a brake on, impede, retard, subdue, bridle, muzzle.
– OPPOSITES encourage.

curdle v CONGEAL, turn, coagulate, clot, solidify, thicken, condense.

cure n REMEDY, antidote, treatment, therapy, alleviation, medicine, restorative, panacea, corrective.
▶ v ❶ HEAL, make better, rehabilitate, remedy, put right, repair, fix, restore, palliate, rectify, relieve. ❷ PRESERVE, smoke, salt, dry, kipper, pickle.
– OPPOSITES aggravate.

curiosity n INQUISITIVENESS, interest, questioning, prying, meddling; *informal* snooping, nosiness.

curious adj ❶ INQUISITIVE, inquiring, interested, searching, querying, questioning, interrogative, puzzled, intrusive, prying, interfering; *informal* snooping. ❷ See STRANGE (1).
– OPPOSITES incurious.

curl v ❶ SPIRAL, coil, bend, twist, wind, loop, twirl, wreathe, meander, snake, corkscrew. ❷ CRIMP, perm, crinkle, frizz, wave.
▶ n ❶ SPIRAL, twist, coil, whorl, helix. ❷ RINGLET, coil, kink, wave, curlicue, corkscrew.

curly adj CURLED, crimped, kinked, crinkly, wavy, frizzy, permed, fuzzy.
– OPPOSITES straight.

current adj PRESENT, present-day, contemporary, up to date, up to the minute, existing, modern, fashionable, popular,

prevailing, prevalent, accepted, common, general, widespread, rife; *informal* trendy, now, in.
– OPPOSITES obsolete.
▶ n FLOW, stream, tide, river, channel, drift, jet, draught, undercurrent, undertow.

curse n ❶ DAMNATION, execration, imprecation, evil eye, malediction, anathema; *informal* jinx. ❷ SWEAR WORD, obscenity, oath, profanity, expletive, blasphemy, bad language.
▶ v ❶ PUT A CURSE ON, damn, execrate, put the evil eye on, anathematize. ❷ SWEAR, use bad/foul language, utter oaths, blaspheme, be foul-mouthed.

cursory adj HASTY, rapid, hurried, quick, perfunctory, slapdash, casual, superficial, desultory, fleeting, passing, ephemeral, transient.
– OPPOSITES thorough.

curt adj TERSE, abrupt, brusque, blunt, short, sharp, crisp, tart, gruff, uncommunicative, laconic, offhand, rude, summary, impolite, unceremonious, ungracious, uncivil, brief, concise, succinct, pithy, compact; *informal* snappy, snappish.
– OPPOSITES expansive.

curtail v REDUCE, shorten, cut, cut back/down, decrease, lessen, diminish, slim down, tighten up, pare down, trim, dock, lop, truncate, abridge, abbreviate, contract, compress, shrink.
– OPPOSITES lengthen, expand.

curtain n DRAPE, hanging, blind, screen.

curtsy v BOW, genuflect, bend the knee, bob, salaam.

curve n ❶ BEND, arch, arc, bow, turn, loop, hook, crescent, spiral, twist, swirl, whorl, corkscrew, curvature, undulation, camber, meander.
▶ v ❶ BEND, arc, arch, bow, turn, swerve, twist, wind, hook, loop, spiral, coil, meander, snake, swirl, bulge, camber, inflect, incurve.

curved adj BENT, arched, rounded, bowed, twisted, crooked, humped, concave, serpentine, whorled, undulating, tortuous, sinuous.
– OPPOSITES straight.

cushion n PILLOW, bolster, pad, headrest, hassock, mat, squab, pillion, scatter cushion, beanbag.
▶ v ❶ PILLOW, bolster, cradle, support, prop up. ❷ SOFTEN, lessen, diminish, mitigate, allay, deaden, muffle, stifle.

custody n ❶ CARE, charge, guardianship, keeping, safe keeping, protection, supervision, superintendence, control, tutelage. ❷ DETENTION, imprisonment, incarceration, confinement, restraint, constraint, duress.

custom n ❶ HABIT, practice, routine, way, policy, rule, convention, procedure, ritual, ceremony, form, usage, observance, fashion, mode, style. ❷ TRADE, business, patronage, support, customers, buyers.

customary adj USUAL, accustomed, regular, typical, common, habitual, traditional, routine, fixed, set, established, familiar, everyday, prevailing, confirmed, normal, ordinary, expected, favourite, popular, stock, well worn; *poetic/literary* wonted.
– OPPOSITES unusual, exceptional.

customer n BUYER, purchaser, shopper, consumer, patron, client.

cut v ❶ GASH, slash, lacerate, slit, nick, pierce, notch, penetrate, wound, lance, incise, score. ❷ CARVE, slice, chop, sever, divide, cleave. ❸ SHAPE, fashion, form, mould, chisel, carve, sculpt, chip away, whittle. ❹ TRIM, clip, crop, snip, shear, dock, shave, pare, mow. ❺ REDUCE, decrease, lessen, lower, diminish, contract, prune, curb, curtail, slash, rationalize, economize on. ❻ SHORTEN, abridge, condense, abbreviate, contract, compact, precis, summarize.
▶ n ❶ GASH, laceration, slash, incision, slit. ❷ CUTBACK, decrease, reduction, curtailment, contraction. ❸ SHARE, portion, proportion.

cutting adj WOUNDING, hurtful, caustic, acid, barbed, acrimonious, sarcastic, spiteful, sardonic, vicious, malicious, sharp, trenchant, mordant.

cycle n ❶ SERIES, sequence, succession, round, run, rotation. ❷ BICYCLE, bike, tandem, tricycle, monocycle.

cynical adj SCEPTICAL, pessimistic, doubting, unbelieving, disbelieving, distrustful, suspicious, misanthropic, critical, sardonic, scoffing.
– OPPOSITES optimistic.

Dd

dab v PAT, blot, press, touch, smudge, besmear, bedaub.
▶ n ❶ PAT, blot, press, touch, smudge. ❷ BIT, speck, touch, trace, dash, drop, tinge, suggestion, hint, modicum.

dabble v ❶ PADDLE, dip, splash, slosh. ❷ FLIRT WITH, toywith, dally with, dip into.

dabbler n DILETTANTE, amateur, trifler.

daily adj ❶ EVERYDAY, quotidian, diurnal. ❷ COMMON, regular, commonplace, usual, habitual, customary.
▶ adv EVERY DAY, once a day, day after day, day by day, per diem.

dainty adj ❶ PETITE, delicate, neat, exquisite, graceful, elegant, trim, pretty, fine, refined. ❷ PARTICULAR, discriminating, fastidious, fussy, choosy,

finicky, refined, scrupulous, meticulous, squeamish, nice. ❸ TASTY, delicious, appetizing, palatable, choice, savoury, flavoursome, luscious, juicy, succulent.
– OPPOSITES unwieldy, undiscriminating, unpalatable.
▶ n TITBIT, delicacy, confection, sweetmeat, bonne bouche.

dally v DAWDLE, loiter, delay, linger, take one's time, loaf, saunter, procrastinate, waste time; informal dilly-dally, hang about; archaic tarry.
– OPPOSITES hurry.

dam n BARRIER, wall, obstruction, barricade, embankment, barrage, bank, weir.
▶ v BLOCK, obstruct, hold back, check, stop, staunch, stem.

damage n ❶ HARM, injury, destruction, hurt, impairment, defacement, abuse, defilement, vandalism, ruin, devastation, havoc, detriment, mischief, outrage, accident, loss, suffering. ❷ COST, charge, expense, bill, total.
▶ v HARM, injure, do damage to, spoil, vandalize, destroy, wreck, ruin, mar, deface, devastate, defile, play havoc with, do mischief to, mutilate, impair, disable, sabotage, warp.

damaging adj SEE HARMFUL.

damn v ❶ CURSE, execrate, anathematize, imprecate. ❷ CRITICIZE, censure, condemn, attack, flay; informal pan, slam, knock, blast, take apart; Brit. informal slate.
– OPPOSITES bless, praise.

damning adj INCRIMINATING, condemnatory, condemning, implicating, accusatorial.

damp adj ❶ MOIST, soggy, wettish, dank. ❷ RAINY, wettish, drizzly, humid, clammy, muggy, misty, foggy, vaporous.
– OPPOSITES dry.
▶ v ❶ MOISTEN, dampen, sprinkle, humidify. ❷ DISCOURAGE, dampen, check, curb, restrain, stifle, inhibit; informal put a damper on, pour cold water on. ❸ REDUCE, lessen, diminish, decrease, moderate.

dance v CAPER, trip, jig, skip, prance, cavort, hop, frolic, gambol, jump, leap, romp, bounce, whirl, spin.

dandy n FOP, man about town, boulevardier; informal sharp dresser; dated beau, popinjay, blade; archaic coxcomb.

danger n ❶ RISK, peril, hazard, jeopardy, endangerment, precariousness, insecurity, instability. ❷ CHANCE, possibility, threat, risk.
– OPPOSITES safety.

dangerous adj ❶ RISKY, perilous, unsafe, hazardous, precarious, insecure, exposed, defenceless, uncertain, unsound, critical, alarming; informal hairy, chancy. ❷ MENACING, threatening, ruthless, nasty, violent, desperate, treacherous, unmanageable, wild, volatile.
– OPPOSITES safe, harmless.

dangle v ❶ HANG, swing, sway, trail, droop, flap, wave. ❷ TEMPT

WITH, entice with, lure with, hold out.

dank adj DAMP, wet, moist, humid, clammy, chilly.
– OPPOSITES dry.

dappled adj SPOTTED, marked, mottled, flecked, stippled, freckled, dotted, streaked, patchy, marbled, blotchy, blotched, piebald, motley, brindled, pinto, variegated, particoloured.

dare v ❶ RISK, hazard, venture, have the courage, take the risk, be brave enough, make bold. ❷ CHALLENGE, provoke, goad, taunt.

daring adj BOLD, adventurous, brave, courageous, audacious, intrepid, fearless, undaunted, unshrinking, rash, reckless, foolhardy.

dark adj ❶ BLACK, pitch-black, pitch-dark, jet-black, inky, unlit, shadowy, shady, murky, dim, indistinct, dingy, foggy, misty, cloudy, overcast, sunless, gloomy, funereal. ❷ DARK-SKINNED, sallow, swarthy, black, olive-skinned, ebony, tanned, bronzed. ❸ MOODY, brooding, angry, sullen, dour, glum, morose, sulky, frowning, glowering, forbidding, ominous. ❹ EVIL, wicked, villainous, sinful, iniquitous, vile, base, foul, horrible, atrocious, nefarious, fiendish, satanic, damnable. ❺ See MYSTERIOUS.
– OPPOSITES light, pale, cheerful.

darken v ❶ GROW DARK / DARKER, blacken, cloud over, dim, grow dim. ❷ MAKE DARK / DARKER, blacken, black, dim, shade, overshadow, eclipse.
– OPPOSITES lighten, brighten.

darling n ❶ DEAR, dearest, sweetheart, love, beloved, honey. ❷ CHARMER, pet, sweetheart; informal sweetie, poppet.

dart n ARROW, bolt, missile.
▶ v RUSH, dash, bolt, sprint, run, race, hurtle, fly, bound, flash, shoot, leap, spring, scuttle, flit; informal scoot, zip, whizz.

dash v ❶ RUSH, run, hurry, race, sprint, tear, speed, fly, dart, bolt, hasten. ❷ SHATTER, destroy, ruin, spoil, frustrate, thwart, blight, baulk, check.
▶ n ❶ RUSH, bolt, run, race, flight, dart, sprint, sortie, spurt. ❷ BIT, pinch, drop, sprinkling, touch, trace, tinge.

dashing adj DEBONAIR, stylish, lively, spirited, dynamic, energetic, animated, gallant, bold, daring, swashbuckling, dazzling.

data pl n INFORMATION, facts, figures, details, statistics, material, input.

date n ❶ DAY, point in time. ❷ MEETING, appointment, engagement, rendezvous, assignation; poetic/literary tryst. ❸ PARTNER, escort, girlfriend, boyfriend; dated beau.

dated adj OUT OF DATE, outdated, old-fashioned, outmoded, antiquated; informal old hat.
– OPPOSITES up to date, modern.

daunt v INTIMIDATE, frighten, overawe, scare, alarm, dismay, unnerve, abash, cow, dishearten, dispirit.

dawdle v LOITER, delay, move slowly, linger, take one's time, waste time, idle, dally, straggle, trail behind, potter about, move at a snail's pace.
– OPPOSITES hurry, hasten.

dawn n ❶ DAYBREAK, break of day, sunrise, first light, cockcrow. ❷ BEGINNING, start, birth, rise, commencement, onset, advent, arrival, appearance, emergence, origin, inception, genesis, unfolding, development.
– OPPOSITES dusk.

day n ❶ DAYTIME, daylight, daylight hours, broad daylight. ❷ PERIOD, time, epoch, age, era, generation.

daze v STUN, stupefy, confuse, bewilder, befuddle, addle, numb, benumb, paralyse.

dazzle v ❶ BLIND, bedazzle, daze. ❷ OVERPOWER, overwhelm, overawe, awe, stagger, fascinate, dumbfound, amaze, astonish.

dead adj ❶ DECEASED, lifeless, gone, passed on/away, departed, no more, late, inanimate, defunct; *informal* done for. ❷ OBSOLETE, extinct, outmoded, outdated, lapsed, inactive. ❸ DULL, boring, uninteresting, tedious, uneventful, flat, wearisome, humdrum, stale, moribund, vapid.
– OPPOSITES alive, lively.

▶ adv COMPLETELY, totally, absolutely, entirely, utterly, thoroughly, categorically.

deaden v ❶ DESENSITIZE, numb, anaesthetize, paralyse, dull. ❷ REDUCE, suppress, moderate, blunt, dull, muffle, diminish, mitigate, alleviate, smother, stifle.

deadlock n STALEMATE, impasse, stand-off, standstill, halt, stop.

deadly adj FATAL, lethal, dangerous, destructive, toxic, poisonous, venomous, virulent, noxious. *See also* HARMFUL (1).
– OPPOSITES harmless.

deafening adj LOUD, earsplitting, thunderous, resounding, ringing, reverberating.

deal n ❶ AGREEMENT, transaction, arrangement, contract, bargain, understanding, settlement, compact, pact. ❷ AMOUNT, quantity, volume.
▶ v ❶ TRADE, do business, buy and sell, traffic. ❷ DISTRIBUTE, share out, allocate, divide out, hand out, dole out, apportion, mete out. ❸ ADMINISTER, deliver, give, direct, aim.
■ **deal with** ATTEND TO, see to, take care of, cope with, handle, manage, tackle.

dealer n TRADER, broker, retailer, wholesaler, supplier, purveyor, distributor, vendor, tradesman, merchant, trafficker, pedlar.

dear adj ❶ BELOVED, loved, adored, cherished, intimate, close, esteemed, respected. ❷ EXPENSIVE, costly, overpriced,

exorbitant, high-priced; *informal* pricey, steep.
- OPPOSITES cheap.

dearth n LACK, scarcity, scareness, shortage, deficiency, insufficiency, paucity.
- OPPOSITES abundance.

death n ❶ DYING, demise, end, final exit, passing on/away. ❷ KILLING, murder, massacre, slaughter; *poetic/literary* slaying.
- OPPOSITES life.

debacle n FIASCO, disaster, catastrophe, failure, collapse, ruin, defeat, rout, havoc.

debase v DEGRADE, devalue, demean, disgrace, dishonour, shame, discredit, cheapen, humble, humiliate, diminish, ruin, soil, sully, vulgarize.
- OPPOSITES enhance.

debatable adj ARGUABLE, questionable, open to question, disputable, controversial, contentious, doubtful, open to doubt, dubious, uncertain, unsure, undecided, borderline, moot.
- OPPOSITES certain.

debate n ARGUMENT, dispute, discussion, difference of opinion, altercation, disputation, wrangle, controversy, war of words, polemic.
▶ v ARGUE, dispute, argue the pros and cons of, discuss, bandy words, wrangle, contend, moot; *informal* kick around.

debauched adj DEGENERATE, dissipated, dissolute, immoral, abandoned, promiscuous, wanton.
- OPPOSITES wholesome.

debris n RUBBLE, wreckage, detritus, rubbish, litter, waste, flotsam, remains, ruin, fragments.

debt n ❶ BILL, account, money owing, score, tally, dues, arrears. ❷ OBLIGATION, liability, indebtedness.

decamp v RUN OFF / AWAY, make off, flee, take off, abscond, escape; *informal* cut and run, skedaddle, vamoose, skip, hightail it; *Brit. informal* do a moonlight flit.

decay v ❶ ROT, decompose, go bad, putrefy, spoil, perish, corrode. ❷ DEGENERATE, decline, deteriorate, fail, wane, ebb, dwindle, crumble, disintegrate, wither, die, atrophy.

deceit n DECEPTION, cheating, dishonesty, duplicity, double-dealing, fraud, fraudulence, trickery, subterfuge, untruthfulness, duping, chicanery, underhandedness, cunning, wiliness, dissimulation, pretence, artifice, treachery.
- OPPOSITES honesty.

deceitful adj DECEPTIVE, misleading, fraudulent, double-dealing, sneaky, treacherous, untruthful, dishonest, underhand, false, untrustworthy, lying, unfaithful, two-faced, duplicitous, mendacious, insincere, disingenuous, sham, bogus, spurious, perfidious; *informal* crooked, tricky.
- OPPOSITES honest.

deceive v MISLEAD, take in, fool, delude, misguide, lead on, trick, hoodwink, dupe, hoax, swindle, outwit, ensnare, entrap, double-cross, gull; *informal* con, take for a ride, pull someone's leg, pull the wool over someone's eyes, pull a fast one on, bamboozle, diddle.

decelerate v SLOW DOWN, go slower, reduce speed, brake, put the brakes on, ease up.
– OPPOSITES accelerate.

decent adj ❶ PROPER, acceptable, respectable, correct, appropriate, seemly, fitting, fit, suitable, modest, becoming, tasteful, decorous, pure. ❷ HONEST, trustworthy, dependable, respectable, worthy, upright, kind, thoughtful, obliging, helpful, generous, courteous, civil. ❸ SUFFICIENT, acceptable, reasonable, adequate, ample.
– OPPOSITES indecent.

deception n ❶ TRICK, ruse, dodge, subterfuge, fraud, cheat, swindle, sham, pretence, bluff, stratagem, confidence trick, imposture; *informal* con. ❷ See DECEIT.

deceptive adj ❶ MISLEADING, false, illusory, ambiguous, unreliable, wrong, distorted, deceiving, delusive, spurious, treacherous. ❷ See DECEITFUL.
– OPPOSITES genuine.

decide v ❶ COME TO A DECISION, reach/make a decision, make up one's mind, resolve, choose, come to a conclusion, conclude, commit oneself, opt for, select. ❷ JUDGE, adjudicate, arbitrate, make a judgement on, make a ruling, give a verdict.

decided adj CLEAR, distinct, definite, obvious, certain, marked, pronounced, emphatic, categorical, unequivocal.

decision n CONCLUSION, resolution, judgement, verdict, pronouncement, determination, outcome, findings.

decisive adj ❶ DETERMINED, resolute, firm, sure, purposeful, unhesitating, unswerving, unwavering, unfaltering, incisive, emphatic. ❷ DECIDING, determining, conclusive, final, critical, crucial, significant, influential.
– OPPOSITES irresolute, inconclusive.

declaration n ❶ STATEMENT, announcement, proclamation, pronouncement, broadcast, promulgation, edict, notification, manifesto. ❷ ASSERTION, protestation, insistence, profession, claim, allegation, avowal, contention, affirmation, swearing; *formal* averment.

declare v STATE, announce, proclaim, make known, assert, pronounce, broadcast, report, trumpet, profess, claim, allege, affirm, maintain, swear, emphasize, insist, avow, attest.

decline v ❶ REFUSE, turn down, reject, say no, rebuff, forgo, send one's regrets; *informal* give the thumbs down to. ❷ LESSEN, decrease, dwindle, wane, fade, ebb, fall/taper off, tail off, flag, abate. ❸ DETERIORATE, diminish, weaken, fail,

degenerate, wither, fade away, sink.
– OPPOSITES accept, flourish, increase.
▶ n DECREASE, reduction, lessening, downturn, downswing, slump, plunge, diminution, ebb, waning, falling-off, deterioration, degeneration; *informal* nosedive.

decode v DECIPHER, unravel, make out, unscramble, solve, explain, interpret, read; *informal* crack, figure out.
– OPPOSITES encode.

decompose v ROT, decay, putrefy, go bad, go off, break down, disintegrate, fester.

decor n DECORATION, furnishings, furbishing, colour scheme, ornamentation.

decorate v ❶ ADORN, ornament, festoon, beautify, prettify, embellish, garnish, trim, enhance, garland. ❷ PAINT, wallpaper, paper, renovate, refurbish, furbish; *informal* do up. ❸ HONOUR, give a medal to, pin a medal on, confer an award on.

decoration n ❶ ADORNMENT, ornamentation, embellishment, beautification, prettification, enhancement. ❷ ORNAMENT, trinket, bauble, frill, flourish, frippery, knick-knack, tinsel, trimming. ❸ MEDAL, award, order, badge, star, ribbon, laurel, colours, insignia.

decorative adj ORNAMENTAL, ornate, fancy, elaborate.

decorous adj PROPER,

seemly, decent, becoming, fitting, tasteful, in good taste, correct, appropriate, suitable, presentable, apt, apposite, polite, well mannered, well behaved, refined, genteel, well bred, respectable, dignified.
– OPPOSITES indecorous, unseemly.

decorum n PROPRIETY, decency, correctness, appropriateness, seemliness, respectability, good taste, politeness, courtesy, refinement, breeding, etiquette, protocol, conformity, good form; *informal* the thing to do.

decoy n LURE, bait, temptation, diversion, distraction, snare, trap, inducement, attraction, enticement.
▶ v LURE, attract, tempt, seduce, inveigle, draw, lead, ensnare, entrap, snare, trap, trick.

decrease v ❶ LESSEN, reduce, grow less, diminish, drop, fall off, decline, contract, dwindle, shrink, lower, cut down/back, curtail. ❷ DIE DOWN, abate, subside, let up, slacken, ebb, wane, taper off, peter out, tail off.
– OPPOSITES increase.
▶ n REDUCTION, drop, lessening, decline, falling-off, downturn, cutback, diminution, curtailment, contraction, shrinkage.
– OPPOSITES increase.

decree n ❶ EDICT, order, law, statute, act, ordinance, regulation, injunction, rule, enactment, command,

mandate, proclamation, precept, dictum. ❷ RULING, verdict, judgement, decision, finding.
▶ v ORDAIN, rule, order, command, dictate, lay down, prescribe, pronounce, declare, proclaim, direct, determine, decide, promulgate, enact, adjudge, enjoin.

decrepit adj DILAPIDATED, battered, ramshackle, derelict, broken-down, run down, worn out, rickety, antiquated; *informal* the worse for wear, on its last legs.
– OPPOSITES sound.

dedicate v ❶ DEVOTE, commit, give, give over, pledge, surrender. ❷ INSCRIBE, address, assign, name.

dedicated adj COMMITTED, devoted, wholehearted, enthusiastic, keen, zealous, single-minded, sworn.

deduce v CONCLUDE, come to the conclusion that, infer, gather, work out, reason, understand, come to understand, surmise, divine, assume, presume, glean; *informal* put two and two together; *Brit. informal* suss out.

deduct v SUBTRACT, take away, take off, withdraw, remove, discount, abstract.
– OPPOSITES add.

deduction n ❶ CONCLUSION, inference, reasoning, assumption, presumption, findings, result. ❷ SUBTRACTION, reduction, decrease, taking off, removal, withdrawal, discount.

deed n ❶ ACT, action, feat,

exploit, performance, undertaking, effort, accomplishment, enterprise, achievement, endeavour, stunt. ❷ DOCUMENT, title, contract, instrument, indenture.

deep adj ❶ FATHOMLESS, bottomless, yawning, cavernous, profound, unplumbed, abyssal. ❷ PROFOUND, extreme, intense, great, deep-seated, deep-rooted, grave. ❸ INTENSE, heartfelt, fervent, ardent, impassioned. ❹ LOW, low-pitched, bass, rich, powerful, resonant, sonorous, rumbling, booming, resounding.
– OPPOSITES shallow, light, high.

deface v SPOIL, disfigure, blemish, mar, deform, ruin, sully, tarnish, damage, mutilate, vandalize, injure, uglify.

defame v SLANDER, libel, blacken someone's name, cast aspersions on, smear, malign, insult, speak evil of, vilify, traduce, besmirch, drag through the mud, defile, stigmatize, disparage, denigrate.

defeat v ❶ BEAT, conquer, get the better of, win a victory over, vanquish, rout, trounce, overcome, overpower, overwhelm, crush, quash, subjugate, subdue, quell; *informal* thrash, wipe the floor with, lick, smash, clobber, zap. ❷ BAFFLE, puzzle, perplex, confound, frustrate. ❸ REJECT, throw out, outvote.
– OPPOSITES lose.
▶ n CONQUEST, beating, van-

quishing, thrashing, rout, overpowering, overthrow, reverse, setback, subjugation, humiliation, failure, repulse; *informal* drubbing, licking.

defect[1] n FAULT, flaw, imperfection, deficiency, shortcoming, weak spot/point, weakness, mistake, error, failing, inadequacy, omission, absence, snag, kink, deformity, blemish, crack, break, tear, scratch; *informal* bug.

defect[2] v DESERT, change sides, go over, apostatize.

defective adj FAULTY, flawed, imperfect, malfunctioning, broken, in disrepair, inadequate, deficient, incomplete, weak, unsatisfactory, cracked, torn, scratched, insufficient, wanting.
– OPPOSITES intact.

defence n ❶ PROTECTION, guard, shield, security, safeguard, cover, shelter, fortification, screen, resistance, deterrent. ❷ JUSTIFICATION, argument, apology, apologia, vindication, plea, explanation, excuse, extenuation, exoneration.

defenceless adj VULNERABLE, helpless, exposed, weak, powerless, unguarded, unprotected, unarmed, open to attack, wide open.

defend v ❶ PROTECT, guard, watch over, safeguard, keep from harm, preserve, secure, shelter, screen, shield, cover, fight for. ❷ JUSTIFY, argue for, speak on behalf of, make a case

for, give reasons for, plead for, champion, stand up for, explain, exonerate.
– OPPOSITES attack.

defendant n ACCUSED, prisoner at the bar, respondent, appellant, litigant.

defensive adj ❶ PROTECTIVE, watchful, shielding, opposing. ❷ OVERSENSITIVE, prickly, apologetic, thin-skinned.
– OPPOSITES offensive.

defer v POSTPONE, put off, delay, adjourn, hold over, suspend, stay, hold in abeyance, prorogue; *informal* put on ice, shelve.

deference n RESPECT, reverence, homage, veneration, dutifulness, consideration, regard, attentiveness, attention, thoughtfulness.

defiant adj CHALLENGING, aggressive, provocative, rebellious, disobedient, uncooperative, insolent, resistant, insubordinate, mutinous, obstinate, headstrong, antagonistic, refractory, contemptuous, scornful, bold, brazen, daring, audacious, truculent, unruly, self-willed.

deficiency n ❶ LACK, shortage, scarcity, scantiness, want, dearth, insufficiency, inadequacy, deficit, absence, paucity. ❷ See DEFECT[1].

defile v CORRUPT, contaminate, taint, tarnish, pollute, foul, dirty, soil, sully, pervert, infect, besmirch, desecrate, dishonour.

define v ❶ EXPLAIN, give the meaning of, spell out,

elucidate, describe, interpret, expound, clarify. ❷ MARK OUT / OFF, fix, establish, determine, settle, bound, demarcate, delineate, delimit, circumscribe, describe.

definite adj ❶ SPECIFIC, precise, particular, exact, well defined, clear, clear-cut, explicit, fixed, established, confirmed, determined, express. ❷ CERTAIN, sure, decided, positive, settled, guaranteed, assured, conclusive, final. ❸ FIXED, marked, delimited, demarcated, circumscribed.
− OPPOSITES indefinite, uncertain, indeterminate.

definitely adv CERTAINLY, surely, for sure, without doubt/ question, beyond any doubt, undoubtedly, indubitably, positively, absolutely, undeniably, unmistakably, plainly, clearly, obviously, decidedly.

definition n ❶ MEANING, description, elucidation, exposition, interpretation, clarification. ❷ SHARPNESS, clearness, clarity, distinctness, focus, precision.

definitive adj CONCLUSIVE, authoritative, final, decisive, unconditional, unqualified, absolute, categorical, settled, official, ultimate, decided, agreed, standard, complete, correct.

deflect v TURN ASIDE, turn, divert, parry, fend off, ward off, intercept, glance off, veer, swerve, deviate, switch, avert, sidetrack.

deformed adj MISSHAPEN, malformed, distorted, contorted, twisted, crooked, crippled, maimed, disfigured, damaged, mutilated, marred, warped, gnarled, mangled, perverted, corrupted, depraved.

defraud v CHEAT, swindle, rob, trick, fool; informal rip off, fleece, con, gyp.

deft adj DEXTEROUS, nimble, adroit, agile, skilful, skilled, adept, proficient, able, clever, expert, quick.
− OPPOSITES clumsy, maladroit.

defy v ❶ DISOBEY, disregard, rebel, ignore, flout, deride, slight, scorn; informal thumb one's nose at, scoff at, snap one's fingers at. ❷ RESIST, stand up to, confront, face, repel, repulse, thwart, frustrate, foil, withstand, brave; informal meet head-on.
− OPPOSITES obey.

degenerate adj see DE-BAUCHED.
▶ v DETERIORATE, decline, worsen, decay, rot, regress, fail, fall off, sink, slide, slip; informal go to the dogs, go to pot, hit the skids.
− OPPOSITES improve.

degrade v ❶ DEBASE, discredit, cheapen, belittle, demean, lower, devalue, reduce, shame, disgrace, dishonour, humble, humiliate, abase, mortify; formal vitiate. ❷ DEMOTE, downgrade, strip of rank, cashier, unseat, dethrone.
− OPPOSITES dignify.

degree n ❶ LEVEL, stage, grade, step, rung, point, mark, measure, gradation, limit. ❷ EXTENT, measure, magnitude, level, amount, intensity, quality, proportion, ratio.

deign v CONDESCEND, lower oneself, stoop, think/see fit, deem worthy, consent.

deity n GOD, goddess, supreme being, divinity, godhead, divine being, demiurge.

dejected adj DEPRESSED, dispirited, discouraged, disheartened, downhearted, crestfallen, downcast, disappointed, unhappy, sad, miserable, despondent, forlorn, woebegone, disconsolate, morose; *informal* down in the dumps, blue, long-faced.
– OPPOSITES cheerful.

delay v ❶ POSTPONE, put off, hold over, adjourn, defer, stay, hold in abeyance; *informal* shelve, put on ice, put on the back burner. ❷ HOLD UP / BACK, detain, hinder, obstruct, hamper, impede, check, restrain, arrest; *informal* bog down. ❸ LINGER, loiter, dawdle, dally, lag/fall behind, procrastinate; *informal* dilly-dally; *archaic* tarry.
– OPPOSITES advance, hurry.
▶ n ❶ POSTPONEMENT, adjournment, deferment, suspension, stay. ❷ HOLD-UP, wait, setback, check, stoppage, halt, interruption, detention, hindrance, obstruction, impediment.

delegate v ❶ APPOINT, designate, nominate, name, depute, commission, mandate, choose, select, elect, ordain. ❷ PASS ON, hand over, transfer, give, entrust, assign, commit.
▶ n REPRESENTATIVE, agent, envoy, legate, emissary.

delegation n DEPUTATION, legation, mission, commission, embassy.

delete v ERASE, cross out, rub out, cut out, cancel, edit out, remove, take out, expunge, obliterate, blue-pencil, efface.

deliberate adj ❶ INTENTIONAL, planned, intended, calculated, considered, designed, studied, conscious, purposeful, wilful, premeditated, pre-arranged, preconceived, aforethought. ❷ CAREFUL, unhurried, cautious, thoughtful, steady, regular, measured, unwavering, unhesitating, unfaltering, determined, resolute, ponderous, laborious.
– OPPOSITES unintentional, hasty.
▶ v see THINK (3).

deliberately adv INTENTIONALLY, on purpose, purposefully, by design, knowingly, wittingly, consciously, premeditatedly, calculatingly; *informal* in cold blood.

delicate adj ❶ FINE, fragile, dainty, exquisite, slender, slight, elegant, graceful, flimsy, wispy, gossamer. ❷ FRAIL, sickly, weak, unwell, in poor health, infirm, ailing, debilitated. ❸ CAREFUL, sensitive, tactful, discreet, considerate, diplomatic, politic. ❹ SUBTLE, subdued, muted, pastel, pale,

understated. ❺ DIFFICULT, awkward, tricky, sensitive, critical, precarious; *informal* ticklish, touchy. ❻ DEFT, skilled, skilful, expert.
– OPPOSITES coarse, robust.

delicious adj ❶ APPETIZING, tasty, delectable, mouth-watering, savoury, palatable, luscious, flavoursome, tooth-some, ambrosial; *informal* yummy, scrumptious.
❷ DELIGHTFUL, enchanting, enjoyable, pleasant, agreeable, charming, pleasurable, enter-taining, amusing, diverting.
– OPPOSITES revolting, disgusting.

delight n JOY, pleasure, happiness, gladness, bliss, ecstasy, rapture, elation, jubilation, satisfaction, excitement, enter-tainment, amusement, trans-ports.
– OPPOSITES dismay.
▶ v PLEASE, gladden, thrill, cheer, gratify, enchant, excite, transport, captivate, charm, entertain, amuse, divert.
– OPPOSITES dismay, displease.

delighted adj *see* HAPPY (1, 2).

delightful adj PLEASING, agree-able, enjoyable, pleasant, pleasurable, amusing, enter-taining, diverting, gratifying, delectable, enchanting, captiv-ating, entrancing, ravishing, attractive, beautiful, engaging, winning, joyful, exciting, thrilling.

delinquent n OFFENDER, wrongdoer, lawbreaker, crim-inal, hooligan, culprit, ruffian, hoodlum, miscreant, transgres-sor, malefactor; *Brit.* tearaway.

delirious adj ❶ RAVING, inco-herent, babbling, light-headed, irrational, deranged, demen-ted, unhinged, insane; *informal* off one's head. ❷ ECSTATIC, eu-phoric, carried away, wild with excitement, frantic, trans-ported.

deliver v ❶ DISTRIBUTE, carry, bring, take, transport, convey, send, dispatch, remit. ❷ GIVE, give voice to, pronounce, enun-ciate, announce, proclaim, de-clare, read, recite, broadcast, promulgate. ❸ SET FREE, save, liberate, free, release, rescue, set loose, emancipate, redeem. ❹ DIRECT, aim, give, deal, ad-minister, inflict, throw, pitch.

delivery n ❶ DISTRIBUTION, transport, carriage, convey-ance, dispatch. ❷ CONSIGNMENT, batch, load. ❸ ENUNCIATION, articulation, intonation, elocu-tion, utterance, presentation. ❹ CHILDBIRTH, labour, confine-ment, parturition.

deluge n FLOOD, downpour, inundation, spate, rush.
▶ v FLOOD, inundate, swamp, engulf, drown, submerge, soak, drench, douse, overwhelm.

delusion n MISCONCEPTION, illusion, fallacy, misapprehen-sion, mistake, misunder-standing, hallucination, fantasy, fancy.

delve v SEARCH, rummage, dig into, hunt through, investigate, probe, examine.

demand v ❶ ASK FOR, request, insist on, press for, urge, clamour for, claim, lay claim to. ❷ EXPECT, impose, insist on, order, requisition. ❸ REQUIRE, need, necessitate, involve, want, call for, cry out for. ❹ ASK, inquire, question, interrogate.
▶ n ❶ REQUEST, entreaty, claim, requisition. ❷ REQUIREMENT, need, necessity, claim, imposition, exigency. ❸ INQUIRY, question, interrogation, challenge.

demanding adj *see* DIFFICULT (1).

demean v DEGRADE, lower, debase, devalue, humble, abase, humiliate, disgrace, shame, belittle.

demeanour n AIR, appearance, bearing, conduct, behaviour, mien, deportment, carriage; *formal* comportment.

demolish v KNOCK DOWN, pull/tear down, flatten, bring down, raze, level, bulldoze, wreck, topple, dismantle, break up, pulverize.
– OPPOSITES build.

demonic adj HELLISH, diabolical, satanic, infernal, evil, wicked, fiendish.
– OPPOSITES angelic.

demonstrable adj PROVABLE, verifiable, indisputable, incontrovertible, irrefutable, conclusive, undeniable, unquestionable, confirmable, attestable, evincible.

demonstrate v ❶ SHOW, indicate, display, exhibit, manifest, evince, evidence.
❷ PROVE, indicate, show, determine, confirm, validate, verify, establish. ❸ PROTEST, march, parade, rally, picket.

demonstration n ❶ EXPLANATION, exposition, illustration, description. ❷ INDICATION, confirmation, substantiation, verification, validation, affirmation. ❸ PROTEST, march, parade, rally, vigil, lobby, picket; *informal* demo, sit-in.

demonstrative adj EMOTIONAL, unrestrained, expressive, open, effusive, expansive, gushing, affectionate, loving, warm.
– OPPOSITES undemonstrative, reserved.

demoralize v DISCOURAGE, dishearten, dispirit, depress, crush, shake, undermine.
– OPPOSITES hearten.

demure adj MODEST, unassuming, bashful, retiring, shy, meek, diffident, reticent, timid, shrinking, timorous, sober.
– OPPOSITES brazen.

denial n ❶ CONTRADICTION, repudiation, disaffirmation, negation, dissent, abjuration. ❷ REFUSAL, rejection, dismissal, veto, repulse; *informal* thumbs down.
– OPPOSITES confession.

denigrate v DISPARAGE, belittle, diminish, deprecate, detract from, decry, defame, slander, libel, cast aspersions on, malign, vilify, besmirch, abuse, revile; *informal* bad-mouth, put down.
– OPPOSITES praise.

denomination n ❶ CREED,
faith, church, sect, persuasion,
communion, order, school.
❷ CATEGORY, type, classification,
group, grouping.

denote v BE A SIGN OF, indicate,
mean, stand for, signify,
represent, symbolize, express,
betoken.

denounce v ❶ CONDEMN,
attack, criticize, censure, decry,
fulminate against, inveigh
against, revile; formal castigate.
❷ ACCUSE, inform against,
incriminate, implicate, charge,
inculpate, indict, impeach.

dense adj ❶ TIGHTLY PACKED,
close-packed, crowded,
jammed together, crammed,
compressed, compacted,
closely set. ❷ CONCENTRATED,
heavy, condensed, thick,
viscous, impenetrable, opaque.
❸ STUPID, slow-witted, slow,
dull-witted, obtuse, block-
headed; informal thick, dim.
– OPPOSITES sparse, light,
clever.

deny v ❶ REPUDIATE, dispute,
reject, contradict, disagree
with, disclaim, dissent from,
negate, disaffirm, abjure, controvert. ❷ REFUSE, reject, turn
down, decline, dismiss,
repulse, veto; informal give the
thumbs down to, give the red
light to.
– OPPOSITES admit, allow,
grant.

depart v ❶ LEAVE, go, take
one's leave/departure, withdraw, absent oneself, set off,
start out, get under way, quit,
make an exit, decamp, retire,
retreat; informal make tracks,
shove off, split, vamoose, hightail it. ❷ See DEVIATE.

departed adj DEAD, deceased,
late, gone, passed away/on.

department n ❶ SECTION,
division, unit, branch, office,
bureau, agency, compartment.
❷ AREA OF RESPONSIBILITY, area,
concern, sphere, line, province,
domain, field, realm, jurisdiction.

departure n LEAVING, going,
starting out, embarkation,
escape, exit, withdrawal,
retreat, retirement.
– OPPOSITES arrival.

depend v ❶ BE DEPENDENT ON,
turn/hinge on, be subject to,
rest on, be contingent on, revolve around, be influenced by.
❷ RELY ON, count/bank on, trust
in, put one's faith in, swear by,
be sure of, be supported by.

dependable adj RELIABLE,
trustworthy, trusty, faithful,
steady, responsible, sure,
stable, unfailing, sound.
– OPPOSITES unreliable.

dependent adj ❶ DEPENDING
ON, conditional on, contingent
on, subject to, determined by,
connected with, relative to.
❷ RELYING ON, reliant on, supported by, sustained by. ❸ RELI-
ANT, helpless, weak,
defenceless, vulnerable.
– OPPOSITES independent.

depict v PORTRAY, represent,
draw, paint, sketch, illustrate,
delineate, outline, reproduce,
render, describe, set out,

relate, detail, narrate, recount, chronicle.

deplete v EXHAUST, use up, consume, expend, spend, drain, empty, milk.
– OPPOSITES augment, increase.

deplorable adj DISGRACEFUL, shameful, reprehensible, scandalous, shocking, dishonourable, discreditable, despicable, contemptible, blameworthy, abominable, lamentable, dire, pitiable, calamitous, base, sordid, vile, execrable, opprobrious.
– OPPOSITES admirable.

deplore v ❶ See CONDEMN (1). ❷ BE SCANDALIZED BY, be shocked by, be offended by, disapprove of, abhor.
– OPPOSITES applaud.

deploy v ❶ ARRANGE, position, dispose, distribute, station. ❷ USE, utilize, set out/up, bring into play, have recourse to.

deport v EXPEL, banish, evict, transport, oust, expatriate, extradite.

depose v UNSEAT, oust, remove, dismiss, dethrone, discharge, cashier; informal sack, fire, give someone the boot; Brit. informal give someone the push.

deposit n ❶ DOWN PAYMENT, instalment, retainer, security, pledge, stake. ❷ SEDIMENT, accumulation, layer, precipitation, deposition, sublimate, dregs, silt, alluvium.
▶ v ❶ BANK, lodge, consign, entrust, store, hoard, stow, put away, lay in; informal squirrel away. ❷ PUT, place, lay, drop, let fall; informal dump, park.

depot n ❶ STATION, garage, terminus, terminal. ❷ STORE, storehouse, warehouse, repository, depository, magazine, arsenal, cache.

deprave v CORRUPT, debauch, lead astray, pervert, debase, degrade, defile, pollute, contaminate.

depraved adj see CORRUPT adj (2).

depreciate v ❶ DECREASE IN VALUE, lose value, decline in price. ❷ See DISPARAGE.

depress v ❶ SADDEN, make gloomy/despondent, dispirit, dishearten, discourage, weigh down, grieve, oppress, dampen someone's spirits, burden. ❷ SLOW DOWN/UP, weaken, lower, reduce, impair, enfeeble, drain, sap, debilitate, devitalize.
– OPPOSITES cheer.

depressed adj see SAD (1).

depression n ❶ SADNESS, unhappiness, despair, gloom, dejection, downheartedness, despondency, melancholy, desolation, moodiness, moroseness, pessimism; informal the dumps, the blues. ❷ HOLLOW, indentation, cavity, dip, valley, pit, hole, bowl, excavation, concavity. ❸ RECESSION, slump, slowdown, stagnation, decline.
– OPPOSITES happiness, boom.

deprive v DISPOSSESS, take away from, strip, deny, expropriate, divest, wrest, rob.

deprived adj see POOR (1).

deputize v TAKE THE PLACE OF, stand in for, act for, do someone's job, substitute for, take over from, replace, cover for, understudy.

deputy n SUBSTITUTE, representative, stand-in, delegate, envoy, proxy, agent, ambassador, commissioner, legate.

derelict adj ❶ ABANDONED, deserted, neglected, rejected, discarded, forsaken, relinquished, cast off. ❷ DILAPIDATED, ramshackle, tumbledown, run down, broken-down, in disrepair, crumbling, rickety.
▶ n VAGRANT, beggar, down and out, tramp, outcast; N. Amer. hobo; Brit. informal dosser.

deride v MOCK, ridicule, jeer at, scoff at, sneer at, make fun of, poke fun at, laugh at, scorn, lampoon, satirize, taunt, insult, rag, tease, chaff, disparage, slight, vilify; informal pooh-pooh.

derogatory adj DISPARAGING, deprecatory, depreciatory, detracting, disapproving, unflattering, insulting, defamatory.
– OPPOSITES complimentary.

descend v ❶ GO / COME DOWN, climb down, fall, drop, sink, subside, plunge, plummet, tumble, slump. ❷ GET DOWN, get off, alight, disembark, dismount, detrain, deplane.
– OPPOSITES ascend.

descent n ❶ SLOPE, incline, dip, drop, gradient, declivity, slant. ❷ ANCESTRY, parentage, origins, lineage, extraction, heredity, genealogy, succession, stock, line, pedigree, blood, strain.
– OPPOSITES ascent.

describe v ❶ GIVE DETAILS OF, detail, tell, narrate, put into words, express, recount, relate, report, set out, chronicle, illustrate, characterize, portray, depict. ❷ DRAW, mark out, delineate, outline, trace, sketch.

description n ACCOUNT, statement, report, chronicle, narration, recounting, commentary, explanation, illustration, designation, characterization, portrayal, depiction, elucidation, relation.

descriptive adj DETAILED, graphic, vivid, striking, expressive, illustrative, depictive, pictorial.

desecrate v DEFILE, profane, blaspheme, pollute, treat sacrilegiously, contaminate, befoul, infect, debase, degrade, dishonour.
– OPPOSITES honour.

desert[1] v ❶ ABANDON, forsake, give up, leave, turn one's back on, betray, jilt, strand, leave stranded, maroon, neglect, shun, relinquish; informal walk out on, leave in the lurch, leave high and dry. ❷ ABSCOND, defect, run away, flee, decamp, bolt, depart, quit; informal go AWOL, turn tail, take French leave.

desert[2] adj ARID, dry, parched, scorched, torrid.
▶ n WASTELAND, wilderness, barrenness, wilds.

deserted adj ABANDONED, empty, neglected, vacant, uninhabited, unoccupied, untenanted, desolate, lonely, solitary, godforsaken.
– OPPOSITES crowded.

deserter n ❶ ABSCONDER, runaway, defector, fugitive, truant, escapee. ❷ RENEGADE, turncoat, traitor, betrayer, apostate; *informal* rat.

deserve v MERIT, warrant, be worthy of, rate, justify, earn, be entitled to, have a right to, have a claim on.

deserving adj *see* WORTHY.

design n ❶ PLAN, blueprint, drawing, sketch, outline, map, plot, diagram, draft, scheme, model. ❷ PATTERN, style, arrangement, composition, configuration, shape. ❸ INTENTION, aim, purpose, plan, objective, goal, end, target, point, hope, desire, wish, aspiration.
▶ v ❶ PLAN, draw, sketch, outline, map out, block out, delineate, draft, depict. ❷ CREATE, invent, think up, originate, conceive, fashion. ❸ INTEND, aim, contrive, plan, tailor, mean, destine.

designer n CREATOR, inventor, deviser, originator, architect, author.

desire v WISH FOR, want, long for, yearn for, thirst for, hunger after, crave, ache for, set one's heart on, hanker after, fancy, have a fancy for, covet, aspire to; *informal* have a yen for. ❷ LUST AFTER, burn for; *informal* have the hots for.
▶ n ❶ WISH, want, fancy, inclination, preference, longing, yearning, craving, eagerness, enthusiasm, hankering, predilection, aspiration. ❷ LUST, lustfulness, passion, lechery, sexual appetite, libido, sensuality, sexuality, lasciviousness, salaciousness, libidinousness; *informal* the hots.

desolate adj ❶ ABANDONED, deserted, barren, uninhabited, unoccupied, lonely, isolated, bare, desert, bleak, depopulated, forsaken, unfrequented, remote, cheerless, dismal, godforsaken. ❷ SAD, unhappy, miserable, broken-hearted, wretched, downcast, dejected, downhearted, melancholy, gloomy, depressed, forlorn, disconsolate, despondent, distressed, grieving, bereft.
– OPPOSITES populous, joyful.

despair n HOPELESSNESS, depression, dejection, despondency, pessimism, melancholy, gloom, misery, wretchedness, distress, anguish.
▶ v LOSE HOPE, give up hope, give up, lose heart, be discouraged, resign oneself.

desperate adj ❶ RECKLESS, rash, foolhardy, risky, hazardous, daring, wild, imprudent, incautious, injudicious, ill-conceived, precipitate. ❷ URGENT, pressing, acute, critical, crucial, drastic, serious, grave, dire, extreme, great. ❸ BAD, appalling, grave, intolerable, deplorable, lamentable.

despise v DISDAIN, scorn, hate, detest, loathe, be contemptuous of, abhor, abominate, look down on, deride, spurn, shun, scoff at, jeer at, mock, revile, execrate, undervalue.
– OPPOSITES admire.

despondent adj DOWNCAST, miserable, sad, sorrowful, disheartened, discouraged, disconsolate, low-spirited, dispirited, downhearted, in despair, despairing, melancholy, gloomy, glum, morose, woebegone.
– OPPOSITES cheerful, happy.

despotic adj AUTOCRATIC, dictatorial, tyrannical, authoritarian, absolute, oppressive, totalitarian, domineering, imperious, arrogant, high-handed, arbitrary.

destination n JOURNEY'S END, stop, terminus, port of call, goal.

destined adj ❶ BOUND FOR, en route for, heading for/towards, directed towards, scheduled for. ❷ FATED, ordained, preordained, predestined, predetermined, doomed, certain, sure, bound.

destiny n ❶ FATE, lot, portion, due, future, doom. ❷ CHANCE, fortune, predestination, luck, fate, karma, kismet.

destitute adj PENNILESS, impoverished, poverty-stricken, poor, impecunious, penurious, indigent, insolvent, deprived, down-and-out, beggarly; *informal*

on one's uppers; *Brit. informal* skint.
– OPPOSITES rich, wealthy.

destroy v ❶ DEMOLISH, wreck, smash, annihilate, knock down, pull down, tear down, level, raze, shatter, dismantle, blow up, wipe out, bomb, torpedo, ruin, spoil, devastate, lay waste to, ravage, wreak havoc on, extinguish, vaporize, extirpate. ❷ KILL, slaughter, put to sleep, exterminate, wipe out, massacre, liquidate, decimate.
– OPPOSITES build, construct.

destruction n ❶ DEMOLITION, annihilation, devastation, levelling, razing, blowing up, wiping out, tearing down, ruination, desolation, ruin, havoc, termination, extinction. ❷ KILLING, slaughter, massacre; *poetic/literary* slaying.

destructive adj ❶ RUINOUS, devastating, disastrous, catastrophic, calamitous, cataclysmic, fatal, deadly, dangerous, lethal, damaging, noxious, pernicious, injurious, harmful, detrimental, deleterious. ❷ NEGATIVE, adverse, unfavourable, contrary, antagonistic, hostile, unfriendly, derogatory, disparaging, disapproving, undermining.
– OPPOSITES constructive.

desultory adj HALF-HEARTED, rambling, aimless, irregular, fitful, haphazard, erratic, inconsistent.
– OPPOSITES keen.

detach v DISCONNECT, unfasten, remove, undo, take off, release,

unhitch, separate, uncouple, loosen, free, sever, tear off, disengage, part.
– OPPOSITES attach.

detached adj DISPASSIONATE, impersonal, indifferent, aloof, unconcerned, reserved, remote, cool.
– OPPOSITES passionate, involved.

detail n ❶ ITEM, point, particular, factor, nicety, fact, element, aspect, circumstance, intricacy, feature, respect, attribute, component, part, unit. ❷ UNIT, detachment, task force, patrol.

detailed adj FULL, comprehensive, exhaustive, thorough, all-inclusive, itemized, precise, exact, specific, meticulous, particularized.
– OPPOSITES general.

detain v ❶ DELAY, hold up/back, keep, slow down/up, hinder, impede, check, retard, inhibit, stay. ❷ PUT / KEEP IN CUSTODY, imprison, confine, lock up, jail, incarcerate, intern, restrain, hold, arrest, impound; *informal* collar; *Brit. informal* nick.

detect v ❶ FIND OUT, discover, turn up, uncover, bring to light, expose, unearth, reveal, unmask, unveil; *informal* track down, ferret out. ❷ NOTICE, note, perceive, discern, make out, observe, spot, become aware of, recognize, distinguish, identify, catch, sense, see, smell.

detective n INVESTIGATOR, police officer; *informal* private

eye, sleuth, tec, dick; *N. Amer. informal* gumshoe.

detention n CUSTODY, confinement, imprisonment, incarceration, internment, detainment, arrest, quarantine.

deter v PREVENT, put off, stop, discourage, talk out of, dissuade, check, restrain, caution, frighten, intimidate, daunt, scare off, warn against, prohibit, hinder, impede, obstruct.
– OPPOSITES encourage.

deteriorate v ❶ GET WORSE, worsen, decline, degenerate, go downhill, sink, slip, lapse, fall, drop; *informal* go to the dogs, go to pot. ❷ DISINTEGRATE, crumble, fall apart, fall to pieces, break up, decay, decompose.
– OPPOSITES improve.

determination n FIRMNESS, persistence, resoluteness, tenacity, perseverance, steadfastness, single-mindedness, resolve, drive, fortitude, dedication, backbone, stamina, mettle, conviction, doggedness, stubbornness, intransigence, obduracy, push, thrust, pertinacity; *informal* grit, guts.

determine v ❶ DECIDE, agree on, fix, settle, establish, judge, arbitrate, decree, ordain. ❷ FIND OUT, discover, learn, establish, calculate, work out, check, ascertain, verify. ❸ AFFECT, influence, act/work on, regulate, decide, condition, direct, control, rule, dictate, govern, form, shape.

determined adj FIRM, resolute, purposeful,

single-minded, steadfast, tenacious, strong-willed, dedicated, persistent, persevering, dogged, unflinching, tough, assertive, mettlesome, plucky, unwavering, stubborn, obdurate, intransigent, indomitable, inflexible.
– OPPOSITES irresolute, hesitant.

deterrent n DISINCENTIVE, inhibition, restraint, discouragement, curb, check, impediment, hindrance, obstacle, block, obstruction, barrier, warning, threat.
– OPPOSITES incentive.

detest v LOATHE, hate, abhor, despise, abominate, execrate.
See also HATE v (1).
– OPPOSITES love.

detestable adj LOATHSOME, abhorrent, hateful, odious, despicable, contemptible, disgusting, repugnant, distasteful, abominable.

detract v TAKE AWAY FROM, diminish, reduce, lessen, lower, devalue.

detrimental adj HARMFUL, damaging, injurious, hurtful, destructive, pernicious, deleterious, inimical, prejudicial, unfavourable.
– OPPOSITES benign.

devastate v ① DESTROY, ruin, lay waste to, demolish, wreck, flatten, obliterate, level, raze, annihilate, ravage, despoil, sack. ② See DISMAY v (1).

develop v ① GROW, evolve, mature, improve, expand, spread, enlarge, advance, progress, flourish, prosper, make headway. ② ELABORATE, unfold, work out, enlarge on, expand, broaden, add to, augment, amplify, dilate on, magnify, supplement, reinforce. ③ ACQUIRE, begin to have, contract, pick up, get. ④ BEGIN, start, come about, follow, happen, result, ensue, break out.

development n ① GROWTH, evolution, advance, improvement, expansion, spread, progress, maturing, furtherance, extension, headway. ② EVENT, turn of events, occurrence, happening, incident, circumstance, situation, issue, outcome, upshot. ③ ESTATE, complex, building, structure, conglomeration.

deviate v DIVERGE, branch off, turn aside, depart from, make a detour, digress, deflect, differ, vary, change, veer, swerve, wander, bend, drift, stray, tack, slew.

device n ① APPLIANCE, gadget, implement, tool, utensil, piece of equipment, apparatus, instrument, machine, contraption, contrivance, invention; informal gizmo. ② SCHEME, ploy, plan, plot, stratagem, trick, deception, artifice, ruse, dodge, stunt, gambit, subterfuge, manoeuvre, expedient, fraud, imposture. ③ EMBLEM, symbol, insignia, crest, coat of arms, seal, badge, token, motif, design, figure, motto, slogan, legend.

devilish adj DEMONIC, diabolical, fiendish, satanic, infernal, hellish, demoniacal.

devious adj ❶ CUNNING, underhand, sly, crafty, wily, artful, scheming, designing, calculating, deceitful, dishonest, double-dealing, guileful, treacherous, furtive, secretive; *informal* slippery, crooked.
❷ INDIRECT, roundabout, circuitous, rambling, winding, tortuous, wandering, erratic, digressive.
– OPPOSITES honest, direct.

devise v CREATE, invent, originate, concoct, contrive, plan, form, formulate, plot, scheme, compose, frame, construct, think up, imagine, fabricate, hatch, put together, prepare.

devoted adj COMMITTED, faithful, loyal, true, dedicated, staunch, devout, steadfast, constant, unswerving, zealous.

devotee n FAN, enthusiast, admirer, follower, adherent, disciple, supporter, champion, advocate, fanatic, zealot; *informal* buff, freak.

devotion n FAITHFULNESS, loyalty, steadfastness, commitment, staunchness, allegiance, dedication, devoutness, fervour, zeal.
– OPPOSITES disloyalty, indifference.

devour v EAT GREEDILY, consume, swallow, gorge oneself on, guzzle down, feast on; *informal* tuck into, pig out on.

devout adj PIOUS, religious, godly, churchgoing, reverent, holy, righteous, orthodox, saintly.
– OPPOSITES impious.

dexterity n DEFTNESS, adroitness, nimbleness, agility, skilfulness, adeptness, expertise, talent, craft, mastery, finesse.

diabolical adj ❶ DEVILISH, demonic, fiendish, satanic, infernal, hellish, demoniacal.
❷ VERY BAD, horrible, dreadful, appalling, shocking, outrageous, atrocious.

diagnose v IDENTIFY, detect, find, determine, recognize, distinguish, isolate, pinpoint.

diagonal adj CROSSWAYS, crosswise, slanting, slanted, sloping, oblique, angled, cornerways, cornerwise.

diagram n PLAN, picture, representation, blueprint, sketch, illustration, outline, draft, table, chart, figure.

dialect n REGIONAL LANGUAGE, vernacular, patois, regionalism, localism, provincialism; *informal* lingo.

dialogue n CONVERSATION, talk, chat, communication, debate, argument, exchange of views, discussion, conference, discourse, parley, colloquy, interlocution, palaver; *informal* powwow, chinwag, rap session.

diary n JOURNAL, chronicle, account, record, log, history, annals, calendar.

dictate v ❶ READ ALOUD, read out, speak, say, utter, recite.
❷ ORDER, command, decree,

ordain, direct, enjoin, give orders, order about, impose one's will, domineer, lay down the law; *informal* boss about, throw one's weight about.

dictator n ABSOLUTE RULER, despot, autocrat, tyrant, oppressor.

dictatorial adj TYRANNICAL, oppressive, despotic, overbearing, domineering, repressive, imperious, high-handed, authoritarian, totalitarian, peremptory, dogmatic, arbitrary, fascistic; *informal* bossy.

diction n ENUNCIATION, articulation, elocution, pronunciation, intonation, inflection, delivery.

dictum n UTTERANCE, pronouncement, direction, injunction, statement, dictate, command, order, decree, edict.

die v ❶ EXPIRE, perish, pass on/away, lose one's life, meet one's end, lay down one's life, breathe one's last, be no more, go to one's last resting place; *informal* give up the ghost, kick the bucket, bite the dust, be pushing up daisies, croak, turn up one's toes, cash in one's chips, pop off; *Brit. informal* snuff it, pop one's clogs. ❷ COME TO AN END, end, pass, disappear, vanish, fade, decline, ebb, dwindle, melt away, wane, wither, subside. ❸ FAIL, break down, halt, stop, lose power.
– OPPOSITES live.

diehard adj INTRANSIGENT, inflexible, uncompromising, indomitable, unyielding, rigid, immovable, adamant,

dyed-in-the-wool, conservative, reactionary.

differ v ❶ BE DIFFERENT, vary, contrast, diverge, be dissimilar, be distinguishable. ❷ DISAGREE, be in dispute, dissent, be at variance, oppose, take issue, contradict, dispute, conflict, clash, quarrel, argue, wrangle, squabble, quibble, altercate.
– OPPOSITES agree.

difference n ❶ DISSIMILARITY, contrast, distinction, variance, variation, divergence, deviation, contradiction, disparity, imbalance, incongruity, dissimilitude, differentiation, antithesis, nonconformity, contrariety. ❷ DIFFERENCE OF OPINION, dispute, disagreement, argument, debate, misunderstanding, quarrel, altercation, wrangle, clash, contretemps, feud, vendetta; *informal* row, tiff, set-to. ❸ BALANCE, remainder, rest, residue, excess.
– OPPOSITES similarity.

different adj ❶ DISSIMILAR, contrasting, diverse, disparate, divergent, incompatible, opposed, inconsistent, at variance, at odds, clashing, conflicting, discrepant, unlike. ❷ CHANGED, altered, modified, transformed, metamorphosed. ❸ VARIOUS, several, many, numerous, sundry, assorted, diverse. ❹ UNUSUAL, uncommon, out of the ordinary, distinctive, rare, unique, novel, special, remarkable, singular, noteworthy, unconventional, atypical, strange, odd, bizarre.
– OPPOSITES similar, ordinary.

difficult adj ❶ HARD, demanding, laborious, onerous, burdensome, tough, strenuous, arduous, exhausting, exacting, tiring, wearisome, back-breaking, painful, oppressive; *informal* no picnic. ❷ COMPLEX, complicated, hard, problematic, intricate, involved, puzzling, baffling, perplexing, knotty, thorny, delicate, obscure, abstruse, enigmatic, abstract, recondite, profound, deep. ❸ TROUBLESOME, demanding, tiresome, unmanageable, intractable, perverse, recalcitrant, obstreperous, refractory, fractious, uncooperative, unamenable. ❹ INCONVENIENT, ill-timed, unfavourable.
– OPPOSITES easy, simple.

difficulty n ❶ PROBLEM, complication, snag, hitch, obstacle, hindrance, hurdle, pitfall, impediment, obstruction, barrier. ❷ PROTEST, objection, complaint, gripe, demur, cavil. ❸ PREDICAMENT, quandary, dilemma, plight, distress, embarrassment, trouble, straits; *informal* fix, jam, spot, scrape. ❹ HARDSHIP, trial, tribulation, ordeal, exigency.

diffident adj SHY, modest, bashful, sheepish, unconfident, timid, unassertive, fearful, timorous, shrinking, apprehensive, reserved, withdrawn, hesitant, tentative, reluctant, doubtful, unsure, insecure, unobtrusive, self-effacing, unassuming, humble, meek, distrustful, suspicious.
– OPPOSITES bold, assertive.

diffuse adj ❶ SPREAD OUT, scattered, dispersed, diffused. ❷ WORDY, verbose, long-winded, prolix, discursive, rambling, wandering, meandering, digressive, circumlocutory; *informal* waffly.
– OPPOSITES concentrated, concise.

dig v ❶ CULTIVATE, turn over, work, spade, till, harrow, fork over. ❷ EXCAVATE, dig out, burrow, mine, quarry, hollow out, scoop out, tunnel, gouge. ❸ POKE, nudge, prod, jab, thrust, punch.
■ **dig up** EXHUME, unearth, disinter.

digest v ❶ ABSORB, assimilate, break down, dissolve, process, macerate. ❷ UNDERSTAND, take in, absorb, comprehend, grasp, master, consider, think about, mull over, weigh up.
▶ n SUMMARY, abstract, precis, outline, review, compendium, abridgement, epitome.

dignified adj FORMAL, grave, solemn, stately, noble, decorous, reserved, ceremonious, courtly, majestic, august, lofty, exalted, regal, lordly, imposing, grand, impressive.
– OPPOSITES undignified.

dignitary n LUMINARY, worthy, notable, VIP, big name, leading light, celebrity, star, lion, pillar of society; *informal* somebody, bigwig, big shot, big noise, celeb, top brass, lord/lady muck; *N. Amer. informal* big wheel.

dignity n STATELINESS, nobleness, nobility, formality,

solemnity, gravity, gravitas, decorum, propriety, respectability, reserve, courtliness, ceremoniousness, majesty, augustness, loftiness, exaltedness, regality, grandeur, lordliness, impressiveness.

digress v STRAY FROM THE POINT, get off the subject, go off at a tangent, ramble, wander, deviate, turn aside, depart, drift, meander, maunder; *informal* lose the thread.

dilapidated adj RUN-DOWN, ramshackle, broken-down, in ruins, ruined, tumbledown, falling to pieces, falling apart, in disrepair, shabby, battered, rickety, shaky, crumbling, decayed, decrepit, worn out, neglected, uncared for.

dilate v ENLARGE, widen, expand.
– OPPOSITES contract.

dilemma n DIFFICULTY, problem, quandary, predicament, puzzle, plight, trouble, perplexity, confusion, embarrassment; *informal* catch-22, tight spot.
■ **in a dilemma** on the horns of a dilemma, between the devil and the deep blue sea, between a rock and a hard place, in a cleft stick.

diligent adj ASSIDUOUS, industrious, conscientious, hardworking, painstaking, meticulous, thorough, careful, attentive, heedful, earnest, studious, persevering, persistent, tenacious, zealous, active, busy, untiring, tireless, indefat-

igable, dogged, plodding, laborious.
– OPPOSITES lazy.

dilute v WATER DOWN, weaken, thin out, cut, adulterate, mix.
– OPPOSITES concentrate.

dim adj ❶ DULL, muted, faint, weak, feeble, pale, dingy, lustreless. ❷ DARK, gloomy, badly lit, poorly lit, dingy, dismal. ❸ VAGUE, ill-defined, indistinct, unclear, shadowy, blurred, blurry, fuzzy, imperceptible, obscured, nebulous, bleary, obfuscated. ❹ See STUPID (1).
– OPPOSITES bright, clear.
▶ v ❶ DIP, turn down, lower. ❷ GROW DARKER, darken, cloud over.
– OPPOSITES brighten.

dimension n ❶ SIZE, extent, length, width, area, volume, capacity, proportions. ❷ ASPECT, facet, side, feature, element.

diminish v ❶ LESSEN, grow less, decrease, reduce, shrink, contract, abate, grow weaker, lower, curtail, cut, narrow, constrict, truncate. ❷ SUBSIDE, wane, recede, dwindle, slacken, fade, decline, peter out. ❸ DISPARAGE, denigrate, belittle, deprecate, devalue, detract from, cheapen, defame, vilify.
– OPPOSITES increase, boost.

diminutive adj SMALL, tiny, little, petite, minute, miniature, microscopic, undersized, dwarfish.
– OPPOSITES enormous.

din n NOISE, uproar, row, racket, commotion, hullabaloo, tumult, hubbub, clamour, outcry, shouting, yelling, pandemonium, bedlam, rumpus, brouhaha, babel.

dingy adj DARK, dull, dim, gloomy, drab, dismal, dreary, cheerless, dusky, sombre, murky, smoggy, dirty, sooty, grimy, discoloured, faded, shabby, worn, seedy, rundown, tacky.
– OPPOSITES bright.

dip v ❶ GO DOWN, descend, sink, subside, fall, drop, decline, sag, droop. ❷ IMMERSE, plunge, submerge, duck, dunk, lower, sink, soak, drench, steep, bathe.
– OPPOSITES rise.
▶ n ❶ SWIM, bathe, plunge, dive, paddle. ❷ HOLLOW, hole, basin, concavity, depression, declivity, slope, incline, slant.

diplomacy n TACTFULNESS, tact, discretion, subtlety, sensitivity, delicacy, politeness, finesse, prudence, judiciousness, cleverness, artfulness, cunning, care, skill.

diplomatic adj TACTFUL, subtle, discreet, careful, delicate, sensitive, thoughtful, considerate, prudent, judicious, polite, politic, clever, skilful, artful.
– OPPOSITES tactless.

dire adj TERRIBLE, dreadful, awful, appalling, frightful, horrible, atrocious, grim, cruel, disastrous, ruinous, wretched, miserable, woeful, calamitous, catastrophic.

direct adj ❶ STRAIGHT,

uncircuitous, unswerving, undeviating. ❷ NON-STOP, straight through, through, uninterrupted, unbroken. ❸ FRANK, blunt, straightforward, straight to the point, straight, clear, plain, explicit, candid, open, honest, sincere, unambiguous, unequivocal, outspoken, plain-spoken, forthright, matter-of-fact.
– OPPOSITES indirect.
▶ v ❶ SHOW THE WAY, give directions, guide, steer, lead, conduct, usher, navigate, pilot. ❷ BE IN CHARGE OF, lead, run, command, control, supervise, oversee, superintend, regulate, govern, conduct, handle, preside over, mastermind, orchestrate; informal call the shots. ❸ AIM AT, address to, intend/ mean for, destine for, point at, train on, fix on. ❹ COMMAND, order, instruct, charge, bid, enjoin; formal adjure.

directive n COMMAND, direction, order, instruction, charge, bidding, injunction, ruling, regulation, dictate, decree, edict, notice, ordinance, prescription, mandate, fiat.

director n MANAGER, administrator, executive, head, chief, chairperson, leader, governor, president, superintendent, supervisor, overseer; informal boss; Brit. informal gaffer.

dirge n LAMENT, elegy, requiem, keen, funeral song, threnody.

dirt n ❶ GRIME, dust, soot, muck, mud, filth, sludge, slime, ooze, waste, dross, pollution,

smudge, stain, tarnish; *informal* crud; *Brit. informal* gunge.
❷ EARTH, soil, clay, silt, loam.
❸ *See* OBSCENITY (1).

dirty adj ❶ UNCLEAN, filthy, stained, grimy, soiled, grubby, messy, dusty, mucky, sooty, muddy, bedraggled, slimy, polluted, sullied, foul, smudged, tarnished, defiled, spotted; *informal* cruddy, yucky; *Brit. informal* grotty, gungy. ❷ OBSCENE, indecent, vulgar, ribald, salacious, smutty, coarse, bawdy, suggestive, prurient, lewd, lascivious, licentious. ❸ UNFAIR, unsporting, dishonourable, dishonest, unscrupulous, illegal, deceitful, double-dealing, treacherous; *informal* crooked. ❹ MALEVOLENT, bitter, angry, annoyed, resentful, indignant, offended, smouldering.
– OPPOSITES clean.
▶ v SOIL, stain, muddy, begrime, blacken, mess up, spatter, smudge, smear, spot, splash, sully, pollute, foul, defile; *poetic/literary* besmirch.
– OPPOSITES clean.

disability n HANDICAP, infirmity, impairment, affliction, disorder, complaint, ailment, illness, malady, disablement.

disable v INCAPACITATE, impair, damage, injure, cripple, lame, handicap, debilitate, indispose, weaken, enfeeble, render infirm, immobilize, paralyse, hamstring, maim, prostrate, mutilate.

disadvantage n ❶ DRAW-BACK, snag, weak point, down-side, fly in the ointment, weakness, flaw, defect, fault, handicap, liability, trouble, hindrance, obstacle; *informal* minus. ❷ DETRIMENT, prejudice, harm, damage, loss, injury, hurt.
– OPPOSITES advantage.

disaffected adj ALIENATED, estranged, unfriendly, disunited, dissatisfied, disgruntled, discontented, disloyal, rebellious, mutinous, seditious, hostile, antagonistic; *informal* up in arms.
– OPPOSITES contented.

disagree v ❶ DIFFER, fail to agree, be in dispute, dissent, be at variance/odds, quarrel, argue, bicker, wrangle, squabble, dispute, debate, take issue; *informal* have words, fall out. ❷ BE DIFFERENT, be dissimilar, vary, conflict, clash, contrast, diverge.
– OPPOSITES agree.

disagreeable adj UNPLEASANT, objectionable, disgusting, horrible, nasty, dreadful, hateful, detestable, offensive, repulsive, obnoxious, odious, repellent, revolting, sickening.
– OPPOSITES pleasant.

disallow v REJECT, say no to, refuse, dismiss, forbid, prohibit, veto, embargo, proscribe, rebuff, repel, repudiate, repulse, ban, bar, cancel, disclaim, disown, abjure, disavow.

disappear v ❶ VANISH, pass from sight, be lost to view, fade, recede, dematerialize, evaporate. ❷ *See* LEAVE¹ v (1). ❸ DIE OUT, come to an end, end, pass away,

vanish, expire, perish, fade away, leave no trace, pass into oblivion.
– OPPOSITES appear.

disappoint V LET DOWN, fail, dishearten, depress, dispirit, upset, sadden, chagrin, dash someone's hopes, dismay, chagrin, disgruntle, disenchant, disillusion, dissatisfy, vex.
– OPPOSITES delight.

disappointed adj SADDENED, let down, disheartened, downhearted, downcast, depressed, despondent, dispirited, disenchanted, disillusioned.
– OPPOSITES pleased.

disapproval n DISAPPROBATION, displeasure, criticism, blame, censure, condemnation, dislike, disfavour, discontent, dissatisfaction, reproach, reproof, remonstration, deprecation, animadversion.
– OPPOSITES approval.

disapprove V FIND UNACCEPTABLE, dislike, deplore, have a poor opinion of, be displeased with, frown on, criticize, look askance at, censure, condemn, denounce, object to, take exception to, reprove, remonstrate, disparage, deprecate; *informal* take a dim view of, look down one's nose at.
– OPPOSITES approve.

disarray n DISORDER, confusion, untidiness, chaos, mess, muddle, clutter, jumble, mixup, tangle, shambles, dishevelment; *Scottish* guddle.
– OPPOSITES tidiness.

disaster n CATASTROPHE,

calamity, cataclysm, tragedy, act of God, accident, mishap, misadventure, mischance, stroke of bad luck, heavy blow, shock, adversity, trouble, misfortune, ruin, ruination.
– OPPOSITES success.

disastrous adj CATASTROPHIC, cataclysmic, calamitous, devastating, tragic, dire, terrible, shocking, appalling, dreadful, harmful, black, ruinous, unfortunate, unlucky, ill-fated, illstarred, injurious, detrimental, hapless.
– OPPOSITES successful.

disbelieve V REJECT, discount, give no credence to, be incredulous, question, suspect, challenge, scoff at, mistrust, distrust.
– OPPOSITES believe.

discard V THROW OUT / AWAY, dispose of, get rid of, jettison, toss out, dispense with, scrap, cast aside, reject, repudiate, abandon, relinquish, forsake, shed; *informal* have done with, dump, ditch.
– OPPOSITES keep.

discern V SEE, notice, observe, perceive, make out, distinguish, detect, recognize, determine.

discernible adj VISIBLE, noticeable, observable, perceptible, perceivable, detectable, recognizable, apparent, obvious, clear, manifest, conspicuous, patent.

discerning adj DISCRIMINATING, astute, shrewd, ingenious, clever, perceptive, penetrating, perspicacious, percipient, judicious, sensitive, knowing.

discharge v ❶ EMIT, exude, release, give off, eject, send out, leak, dispense, void, gush, excrete, ooze, belch, secrete, spew, spit out. ❷ DISMISS, expel, get rid of, oust, cashier; *informal* fire, sack, axe, send packing, give someone the boot, boot out. ❸ FIRE, shoot, let off, set off, detonate. ❹ SET FREE, free, release, liberate, acquit, clear, absolve, exonerate, pardon, emancipate, exculpate. ❺ CARRY OUT, perform, do, accomplish, achieve, fulfil, execute.

disciple n APOSTLE, follower, supporter, adherent, devotee, advocate, student, pupil, believer, proponent, partisan, votary.

disciplinarian n MARTINET, authoritarian, hard taskmaster, tyrant, despot, stickler for order, autocrat, dictator, hard-liner; *informal* slave-driver.

discipline n ❶ CONTROL, self-control, self-restraint, strictness, restraint, orderliness, regulation, direction, restriction, limitation, check, curb. ❷ PUNISHMENT, correction, chastisement, penalty, reprimand, rebuke, reproof. ❸ FIELD OF STUDY, subject, area, course, speciality, specialty.
▶ v ❶ CONTROL, restrain, regulate, restrict, govern, limit, check, curb. ❷ PUNISH, chastise, correct, penalize, reprimand, rebuke, reprove; *formal* castigate.

disclaim v DENY, renounce, repudiate, reject, refuse, decline, disown, abandon, abjure; *informal* wash one's hands of.

disclose v REVEAL, divulge, tell, impart, communicate, broadcast, unveil, leak, let slip, blurt out.

discolour v STAIN, soil, mark, streak, spot, tarnish, tinge, fade, bleach.

discomfort n ❶ PAIN, ache, soreness, irritation, pang, throb, smart. ❷ HARDSHIP, unpleasantness, trouble, distress.

disconcert v UNSETTLE, shake, disturb, take aback, perturb, ruffle, upset, agitate, worry, discomfit, discompose, confound, throw off balance, distract, confuse, nonplus; *informal* throw, put someone off their stroke, faze, rattle.

disconnect v UNDO, detach, disengage, uncouple, unfasten, unhook, unhitch, unplug, cut off, break off, sever, part, turn off, switch off.
– OPPOSITES connect.

disconnected adj DISJOINTED, confused, garbled, jumbled, mixed up, incoherent, unintelligible, rambling, disordered, wandering.

discontented adj DISSATISFIED, displeased, disgruntled, unhappy, miserable, disaffected; *informal* fed up, browned off, hacked off; *Brit. informal* cheesed off.

discord n ❶ DISAGREEMENT, dispute, argument, conflict, friction, strife, opposition,

hostility, disharmony, incompatibility, disunity. *See also* QUARREL n. ❷ DISHARMONY, dissonance, cacophony.
– OPPOSITES harmony.

discordant adj ❶ CONFLICTING, differing, contrary, opposed, opposing, opposite, contradictory, contentious, hostile, divergent, incompatible, incongruous. ❷ DISSONANT, atonal, tuneless, cacophonous, inharmonious, jangling, grating, jarring, harsh, strident, shrill.
– OPPOSITES harmonious.

discount n REDUCTION, price cut, rebate, concession; *informal* mark-down.
▶ v DISREGARD, ignore, dismiss, overlook, pass over, pay no attention to, take no notice of, gloss over, brush off.

discourage v ❶ DISHEARTEN, dispirit, depress, demoralize, deject, disappoint, disenchant, dismay, cast down, frighten, put off, scare, daunt, intimidate, cow, unnerve, unman; *informal* pour cold water on. ❷ DISSUADE, put off, deter, talk out of, advise against, urge against, caution against, restrain, inhibit, divert from. ❸ OPPOSE, disapprove of, repress, deprecate; *informal* put a damper on.
– OPPOSITES encourage.

discouragement n ❶ OPPOSITION, disapproval, repression, deprecation. ❷ DETERRENT, disincentive, impediment, hindrance,

obstacle, barrier, curb, damper, check, restraint, constraint.
– OPPOSITES encouragement.

discourse n ❶ ADDRESS, speech, lecture, oration, sermon, homily, paper, essay, treatise, dissertation, paper, study, disquisition. ❷ *See* CONVERSATION.
▶ v *see* SPEAK (1), TALK v (1).

discover v ❶ FIND, come across/upon, locate, stumble upon, chance upon, light upon, bring to light, unearth, uncover, turn up; *informal* dig up. ❷ FIND OUT, come to know, learn, realize, detect, ascertain, determine, recognize, see, spot, notice, perceive; *informal* get wise to; *Brit. informal* twig. ❸ INVENT, devise, originate, pioneer, conceive of, contrive.

discoverer n ❶ INVENTOR, originator, pioneer, deviser, designer, initiator. ❷ FOUNDER, explorer, pioneer.

discovery n ❶ DETECTION, recognition, disclosure, finding, determination, revelation. ❷ INNOVATION, invention, breakthrough, finding, find.

discredit v ❶ ATTACK, denigrate, disparage, defame, slur, slander, libel, detract from, cast aspersions on, vilify, bring into disrepute, deprecate, decry, dishonour, devalue, degrade, belittle, disgrace, censure. ❷ DISPROVE, invalidate, refute, dispute, challenge, reject, deny.

discreet adj CAREFUL, circumspect, cautious, wary, guarded, sensitive, prudent, judicious, chary, tactful, reserved,

diplomatic, muted, understated, delicate, considerate, politic, wise, sensible, sagacious.
– OPPOSITES indiscreet, tactless.

discrepancy n INCONSISTENCY, disparity, deviation, variance, variation, divergence, incongruity, difference, disagreement, dissimilarity, conflict, discordance, gap, lacuna.
– OPPOSITES similarity.

discretionary adj OPTIONAL, voluntary, open, open to choice, elective, non-mandatory, unrestricted, volitional.
– OPPOSITES compulsory.

discriminate v ❶ DISTINGUISH, differentiate, tell the difference, tell apart, separate, discern. ❷ BE BIASED AGAINST, show prejudice against/towards, treat differently, favour.

discriminating adj see PERCEPTIVE.

discrimination n
❶ DISCERNMENT, good taste, taste, perception, penetration, perspicacity, shrewdness, astuteness, acumen, judgement, refinement, sensitivity, insight, subtlety, cultivation, artistry. ❷ PREJUDICE, bias, intolerance, bigotry, narrowmindedness, favouritism, chauvinism, racism, sexism, unfairness.

discuss v TALK OVER, talk/chat about, debate, argue about/over, exchange views about, converse about, deliberate, consider, go into, examine,

review, analyse, weigh up, consult about, ventilate; *informal* kick about, thrash out.

discussion n CONVERSATION, talk, dialogue, chat, argument, dispute, conference, debate, discourse, exchange of views, seminar, consultation, symposium, deliberation, review, analysis; *informal* confab. *See also* TALK n (1).

disdainful adj SCORNFUL, contemptuous, derisive, sneering, disparaging, arrogant, proud, supercilious, haughty, superior, lordly, pompous, snobbish, aloof, indifferent.
– OPPOSITES respectful.

disease n see ILLNESS.

diseased adj UNHEALTHY, unwell, sick, sickly, infected, abnormal, blighted, unsound, cankerous. *See also* ILL adj (1).

disembark v LAND, arrive, get off, step off, alight, go ashore, deplane, detrain.
– OPPOSITES embark.

disfigure v MUTILATE, deface, deform, blemish, scar, spoil, mar, damage, injure, maim, vandalize, ruin, make ugly, uglify.

disgrace n ❶ SHAME, humiliation, dishonour, scandal, ignominy, degradation, discredit, infamy, debasement. ❷ SCANDAL, black mark, stain, blemish, stigma, blot, smear.
– OPPOSITES honour.

disgraceful adj SCANDALOUS, outrageous, shocking, shameful, dishonourable, disreputable, contemptible, despicable,

ignominious, reprehensible, improper, unseemly.
– OPPOSITES admirable.

disgruntled adj DISSATISFIED, displeased, unhappy, discontented, annoyed, exasperated, irritated, vexed, grumpy, testy, petulant; informal fed up; Brit. informal cheesed off.

disguise n CAMOUFLAGE, costume, pretence, mask, cover, cloak; informal get-up, smokescreen.
▶ v ➊ DRESS UP, camouflage, cover up, conceal, hide, mask, veil, cloak, shroud. ➋ COVER UP, falsify, misrepresent, fake, feign, dissemble, dissimulate, varnish.

disgust n REVULSION, repugnance, repulsion, aversion, abhorrence, loathing, detestation, distaste, nausea.
▶ v SICKEN, nauseate, revolt, repel, put off, offend, outrage, shock, appal, scandalize, displease, dissatisfy, annoy, anger; informal turn someone's stomach.

dish n ➊ PLATE, platter, bowl, basin, container, receptacle, salver. ➋ FOOD, recipe, fare, concoction, item on the menu.
■ **dish up** SERVE, serve up, spoon, ladle, scoop.

dishearten v DISCOURAGE, dispirit, depress, crush, sadden, disappoint, deter, weigh down; informal put a damper on.
– OPPOSITES encourage.

dishevelled adj UNTIDY, rumpled, messy, scruffy, bedraggled, disordered, disarranged, tousled, unkempt, slovenly, uncombed, slatternly, blowsy, frowzy.
– OPPOSITES tidy, neat.

dishonest adj UNTRUTHFUL, deceitful, lying, underhand, cheating, fraudulent, false, misleading, dishonourable, unscrupulous, unprincipled, corrupt, deceptive, crafty, cunning, designing, mendacious, double-dealing, two-faced, treacherous, perfidious, unfair, unjust, unethical, disreputable, rascally, knavish, roguish; informal crooked, shady, bent, slippery.
– OPPOSITES honest.

dishonour n DISGRACE, shame, humiliation, discredit, blot, blemish, stigma, scandal, infamy, ignominy, disrepute, disfavour, abasement, odium, opprobrium, obloquy.
▶ v DISGRACE, bring shame to, shame, discredit, degrade, humiliate, sully, stain, stigmatize, insult, abuse, affront, slight, offend.

dishonourable adj ➊ UNPRINCIPLED, unscrupulous, untrustworthy, corrupt, treacherous, perfidious, traitorous, disreputable, discreditable; informal shady; archaic blackguardly. ➋ DISGRACEFUL, shameful, ignoble, shameless, ignominious, contemptible, blameworthy, despicable, reprehensible, base.
– OPPOSITES honourable.

disillusion v DISABUSE, disenchant, shatter someone's

illusions, open someone's eyes, set straight, enlighten, disappoint; *informal* make sadder and wiser.

disinclined adj RELUCTANT, unenthusiastic, unwilling, hesitant, loath, averse, resistant, antipathetic, opposed, recalcitrant, not in the mood.

disinfect v STERILIZE, sanitize, clean, cleanse, purify, fumigate, decontaminate.

disingenuous adj INSINCERE, deceitful, feigned, underhand, duplicitous, two-faced, false, untruthful, artful, cunning, wily, scheming, calculating.

disintegrate v FALL APART, fall to pieces, break up, break apart, shatter, crumble, come apart, crack up, smash, splinter, decompose, decay, rot, dissolve, degenerate, erode, moulder.

disinterested adj UNBIASED, unprejudiced, impartial, detached, objective, dispassionate, impersonal, open-minded, neutral, fair, just, even-handed.
– OPPOSITES biased, partial.

disjointed adj INCOHERENT, rambling, unconnected, disconnected, wandering, disorganized, confused, muddled, jumbled, disordered, aimless, directionless, uncoordinated, fitful, spasmodic, dislocated, discontinuous.
– OPPOSITES coherent.

dislike v HAVE NO LIKING FOR, have an aversion to, regard with distaste, feel hostility towards, be unable to stomach, have no taste for, object to, hate, detest, loathe, abominate, abhor, despise, scorn, execrate, shun, have a grudge against.
– OPPOSITES like.
▶ n AVERSION, distaste, disapproval, animosity, hostility, antipathy, hate, antagonism, detestation, loathing, disgust, repugnance, enmity, abhorrence, animus.

dislocate v DISPLACE, put out, disjoint, disengage, disconnect, put out of joint; *Medicine* luxate.

disloyal adj UNFAITHFUL, faithless, false, untrue, inconstant, untrustworthy, treacherous, traitorous, perfidious, disaffected, seditious, subversive, unpatriotic, renegade, apostate, dissident, double-dealing, two-faced, deceitful.
– OPPOSITES loyal.

disloyalty n UNFAITHFULNESS, faithlessness, infidelity, breaking of faith, breach of trust, falseness, falsity, inconstancy, untrustworthiness, treachery, treason, perfidiousness, disaffection, sedition, subversion, apostasy, dissidence, double-dealing.
– OPPOSITES loyalty.

dismal adj GLOOMY, sad, bleak, miserable, wretched, drab, dreary, dingy, cheerless, desolate, depressing, grim, funereal, uninviting.
– OPPOSITES cheerful, bright.

dismantle v TAKE APART, take to pieces, disassemble, pull

apart, strip down, tear down, demolish.
– OPPOSITES assemble.

dismay n DISAPPOINTMENT, distress, consternation, discouragement, anxiety, apprehension, gloom, horror, agitation.
– OPPOSITES pleasure, relief.
▶ v ❶ DISCOURAGE, dishearten, dispirit, put off, depress, disappoint, daunt, abash, cast down, devastate. ❷ SHOCK, horrify, take aback, startle, alarm, frighten, scare, surprise, disturb, perturb, upset, unsettle, unnerve.
– OPPOSITES encourage.

dismiss v ❶ BANISH, put away, lay/set aside, reject, drop, put out of one's mind, brush aside, think no more of, spurn, repudiate; informal pooh-pooh. ❷ EXPEL, discharge, give notice to, lay off, make redundant, remove, oust, cashier; informal sack, fire, boot out, give the boot/push to, give someone their marching orders, send packing. ❸ DISPERSE, send away, disband, let go, release, free, discharge.

disobedient adj INSUBORDINATE, rebellious, defiant, unruly, wayward, undisciplined, mutinous, recalcitrant, intractable, wilful, refractory, fractious, obdurate, stubborn, obstreperous, disorderly, delinquent, uncontrollable, disruptive, wild, noncompliant, perverse, naughty, mischievous, contrary; formal contumacious.
– OPPOSITES obedient.

disobey v DEFY, not comply with, disregard, ignore, oppose, contravene, flout, infringe, resist, overstep, rebel against, transgress, violate; informal fly in the face of.

disobliging adj UNHELPFUL, uncooperative, unaccommodating, unfriendly, unsympathetic, discourteous, uncivil.
– OPPOSITES helpful.

disorder n ❶ MESS, untidiness, chaos, muddle, clutter, jumble, confusion, disorderliness, disarray, disorganization, shambles. ❷ DISTURBANCE, disruption, riot, tumult, fracas, rumpus, unrest. ❸ DISEASE, complaint, affliction, illness, sickness, malady.
– OPPOSITES tidiness, peace.

disorderly adj ❶ See UNTIDY. ❷ See UNDISCIPLINED (1).

disorganized adj CONFUSED, disorderly, untidy, chaotic, jumbled, muddled, in disarray, unsystematic, haphazard, random, unorganized, scatterbrained, unmethodical, careless, sloppy, slipshod, slapdash, messy, hit-or-miss, aimless, unplanned, unstructured; Brit. informal shambolic.
– OPPOSITES organized, systematic.

disown v RENOUNCE, repudiate, reject, abandon, forsake, disclaim, disavow, deny, disallow, abnegate, disinherit; informal turn one's back on.

disparage v BELITTLE, slight, deprecate, denigrate, depreciate, dismiss, ridicule,

malign, scorn, insult, impugn, vilify, traduce; *informal* put down, bad-mouth; *Brit. informal* rubbish.
– OPPOSITES praise.

disparity n DISCREPANCY, difference, dissimilarity, contrast, gap, inequality, unevenness, inconsistency, imbalance, incongruity.

dispassionate adj CALM, level-headed, cool, unflappable, unruffled, collected, nonchalant, sober, equable, serene, unperturbed, detached, objective, disinterested, indifferent.
– OPPOSITES emotional.

dispatch v ❶ SEND, post, mail, forward, transmit, consign, remit, convey. ❷ *See* KILL (1).
▶ n LETTER, message, bulletin, communication, report, account, missive, document.

dispense v ❶ DISTRIBUTE, hand out, share out, measure out, divide out, dole out, allocate, assign, apportion, allot, supply, disburse, bestow, mete out, confer. ❷ MAKE UP, prepare, mix, supply.
■ **dispense with** OMIT, do without, waive, forgo, give up, relinquish, renounce.

disperse v ❶ GO SEPARATE WAYS, break up, disband, separate, scatter, dissolve, leave, vanish, melt away. ❷ DRIVE AWAY, break up, scatter, dissipate, dispel, banish.
– OPPOSITES gather.

displace v ❶ REMOVE, dismiss, discharge, depose,

dislodge, eject, expel, force out; *informal* sack, fire. ❷ REPLACE, take the place of, take over from, succeed, oust, supersede, supplant.

display v ❶ PUT ON SHOW / VIEW, show, exhibit, present, unveil, set forth, demonstrate, advertise, publicize. ❷ MANIFEST, show, evince, betray, show evidence of, reveal, disclose.
– OPPOSITES conceal, hide.
▶ n ❶ EXHIBITION, show, exhibit, presentation, demonstration, array. ❷ SPECTACLE, show, parade, pageant.

displease v ANNOY, irritate, anger, put out, dissatisfy, irk, vex, offend, pique, gall, nettle, incense, exasperate, disgust, perturb; *informal* aggravate.

dispose v ❶ ARRANGE, order, position, place, range, line up, array, marshal, organize, group, rank, regulate. ❷ INCLINE, make willing, predispose, make, prompt, lead, induce, motivate.
■ **dispose of** *see* DISCARD.

disposed adj INCLINED, willing, predisposed, minded, of a mind to, in the mood to, prepared, ready, prone, liable, given, apt.

disprove v PROVE FALSE, invalidate, refute, negate, confute, rebut, give the lie to, deny, contradict, discredit, controvert, expose, demolish.
– OPPOSITES prove.

dispute n ARGUMENT, quarrel, altercation, clash, wrangle, squabble, feud, disturbance, fracas, brawl; *informal* row.

▶ v ❶ DEBATE, discuss, argue, disagree, clash, quarrel, bicker, wrangle, squabble. ❷ QUESTION, call into question, challenge, contest, doubt, deny, object to, oppose, controvert, impugn, gainsay.
– OPPOSITES agree.

disqualify v RULE OUT, bar, exclude, reject, turn down, prohibit, debar, preclude.

disquiet n UNEASINESS, anxiety, nervousness, agitation, upset, worry, concern, distress, alarm, fear, fretfulness, dread, foreboding.
– OPPOSITES calm.

disregard v IGNORE, pay no attention to, take no notice of, neglect, discount, set aside, brush aside, overlook, turn a blind eye to, pass over, forget, gloss over, make light of, play down, laugh off, skip, snub, cold-shoulder; informal pooh-pooh.
– OPPOSITES attention.

disrepair n DILAPIDATION, decay, collapse, shabbiness, ruin, deterioration, decrepitude.

disreputable adj INFAMOUS, notorious, dishonourable, dishonest, unprincipled, villainous, corrupt, unworthy, questionable, unsavoury, contemptible, unscrupulous, despicable, disgraceful, reprehensible, discreditable, shocking, outrageous, scandalous.
– OPPOSITES reputable.

disrespectful adj IMPOLITE, discourteous, ill-mannered, rude, uncivil, irreverent, insolent, inconsiderate, impertinent, impudent, cheeky, scornful, contemptuous, insulting, churlish, derisive, uncomplimentary.
– OPPOSITES respectful.

disrupt v UPSET, interrupt, break up, throw into disorder, cause turmoil in, disturb, interfere with, obstruct, impede, hamper, unsettle; Brit. throw a spanner in the works.

dissatisfaction n DISCONTENT, displeasure, disappointment, disapproval, frustration, unhappiness, dismay, disquiet, annoyance, irritation, anger, exasperation, resentment, malaise, restlessness, disapprobation.
– OPPOSITES satisfaction.

dissatisfied adj DISCONTENTED, displeased, disgruntled, unsatisfied, disapproving, disappointed, frustrated, unhappy, angry, vexed, irritated, annoyed, resentful, restless, unfulfilled.
– OPPOSITES satisfied.

disseminate v SPREAD, circulate, broadcast, publish, publicize, proclaim, promulgate, propagate, dissipate, scatter, distribute, disperse, diffuse, bruit abroad.

dissident n DISSENTER, rebel, objector, protestor, nonconformist, recusant, apostate.
– OPPOSITES conformist.

dissimilar adj DIFFERENT, distinct, unlike, varying,

dissipate v ❶ DISPERSE, scatter, drive away, dispel, dissolve. ❷ SQUANDER, waste, fritter away, misspend, deplete, use up, consume, run through.

dissipated adj see DEBAUCHED.

dissociate v SEPARATE, set apart, segregate, isolate, detach, disconnect, sever, divorce.
– OPPOSITES associate.

dissolve v ❶ LIQUEFY, become liquid, melt, deliquesce. ❷ END, bring to an end, break up, terminate, discontinue, wind up, disband, suspend. ❸ BE OVERCOME WITH, break into, collapse into.

dissuade v PERSUADE AGAINST, advise against, warn against, put off, stop, talk out of, argue out of, discourage from, deter from, divert, turn aside from.
– OPPOSITES persuade.

distance n ❶ SPACE, extent, interval, gap, separation, span, stretch, measurement, length, width, breadth, depth, range, mileage. ❷ ALOOFNESS, reserve, coolness, remoteness, reticence, coldness, stiffness, frigidity, restraint, formality, unresponsiveness, unfriendliness; *informal* stand-offishness.
■ **distance oneself** SEPARATE ONESELF, dissociate oneself, keep one's distance, set oneself apart, remove oneself, stay away, keep away, detach oneself, be unfriendly.

disparate, unrelated, divergent, deviating, diverse, various, contrasting, mismatched.
– OPPOSITES similar.

distant adj ❶ FAR, faraway, far-off, remote, out of the way, outlying, far-flung, inaccessible. ❷ AWAY, off, apart, separated, dispersed, scattered. ❸ RESERVED, aloof, uncommunicative, remote, withdrawn, unapproachable, restrained, reticent, cool, cold, stiff, formal, unfriendly, unresponsive, haughty, condescending.
– OPPOSITES close, friendly.

distasteful adj DISAGREEABLE, unpleasant, displeasing, undesirable, off-putting, objectionable, offensive, obnoxious, repugnant, disgusting, unsavoury, revolting, nauseating, sickening, loathsome, abhorrent, detestable.
– OPPOSITES pleasant.

distinct adj ❶ CLEAR, clear-cut, well defined, marked, sharp, decided, visible, perceptible, definite, unmistakable, obvious, recognizable, plain, plain as day, evident, apparent, manifest, patent, unambiguous, palpable, unequivocal. ❷ SEPARATE, individual, different, unconnected, contrasting, discrete, disparate, dissimilar, detached, unassociated.
– OPPOSITES indistinct, vague.

distinction n ❶ CONTRAST, difference, dissimilarity, division, dividing line, separation, differentiation, contradistinction, peculiarity. ❷ NOTE, consequence, importance, account, significance, greatness, prestige, eminence, prominence, renown, fame, celebrity, mark, honour, merit,

worth, excellence, name, rank, quality, superiority.
–OPPOSITES similarity, mediocrity.

distinctive adj DISTINGUISHING, characteristic, typical, individual, particular, special, peculiar, different, uncommon, unusual, remarkable, singular, extraordinary, noteworthy, original, idiosyncratic.
–OPPOSITES ordinary.

distinguish v ❶ TELL APART, differentiate, discriminate, tell the difference between, decide between, determine. ❷ SET APART, single out, separate, characterize, individualize. ❸ MAKE OUT, see, perceive, discern, observe, notice, recognize, pick out, espy.

distinguished adj FAMOUS, renowned, well known, prominent, famed, noted, notable, illustrious, celebrated, respected, acclaimed, esteemed, legendary.
–OPPOSITES obscure.

distort v ❶ TWIST, bend, warp, contort, buckle, deform, misshape, mangle, wrench. ❷ MISREPRESENT, pervert, twist, falsify, slant, bias, colour, tamper with, alter, change, garble.

distract v ❶ DIVERT, deflect, sidetrack, interrupt, interfere, draw away, turn aside. ❷ AMUSE, entertain, divert, beguile, engage, occupy. ❸ CONFUSE, bewilder, disturb, fluster, agitate, disconcert, discompose, harass, annoy, trouble; informal hassle.

distracted adj see DISTRAUGHT.

distraction n ❶ DIVERSION, interruption, disturbance, interference, obstruction. ❷ CONFUSION, bewilderment, agitation, befuddlement, harassment. ❸ AMUSEMENT, diversion, entertainment, recreation, pastime, divertissement.

distraught adj DISTRESSED, disturbed, excited, overcome, overwrought, frantic, distracted, beside oneself, wild, hysterical, grief-stricken, mad, maddened, insane, crazed, deranged; informal out of one's mind, worked up.
–OPPOSITES calm.

distress n ❶ ANGUISH, suffering, pain, agony, affliction, torment, misery, wretchedness, torture, sorrow, grief, sadness, discomfort, heartache, desolation, trouble, worry, anxiety, uneasiness, perturbation, angst. ❷ HARDSHIP, adversity, trouble, misfortune, poverty, need, destitution, privation, impoverishment, indigence, penury, beggary, dire straits.
–OPPOSITES happiness, prosperity.
▶ v UPSET, pain, trouble, worry, bother, disturb, perturb, torment, grieve, sadden, make miserable, vex, shock, scare, alarm.
–OPPOSITES calm.

distribute v ❶ GIVE OUT, hand out, share out, divide out, dole out, measure out, parcel out, mete out, allocate, allot, issue, dispense, apportion, administer, deal out, dish out, assign, dispose. ❷ CIRCULATE, pass around, hand out, deliver, convey, transmit. ❸ DISSEMINATE, disperse, scatter, strew, spread, sow, diffuse.

district n AREA, region, place, locality, neighbourhood, sector, vicinity, quarter, territory, domain, precinct, province, zone, ward, department, parish, community.

distrust v MISTRUST, be suspicious of, have doubts about, doubt, be wary/chary of, have misgivings about, question, wonder about, suspect, disbelieve; informal be leery of.
– OPPOSITES trust.

disturb v ❶ INTERRUPT, distract, bother, trouble, intrude on, butt in on, interfere with, harass, plague, pester, hinder; informal hassle. ❷ MUDDLE, disorder, disarrange, confuse, throw into confusion; informal jumble up, mess about with. ❸ CONCERN, trouble, worry, perturb, upset, fluster, agitate, discomfit, alarm, frighten, dismay, distress, unsettle, ruffle.

disturbed adj ❶ UPSET, troubled, worried, concerned, agitated, alarmed, dismayed, unsettled, ruffled. ❷ UNBALANCED, disordered, maladjusted, neurotic, psychotic; informal screwed up.

disused adj UNUSED, neglected, abandoned, discontinued, obsolete, superannuated, withdrawn, discarded, idle, closed.

ditch n TRENCH, channel, dyke, canal, drain, gutter, gully, moat, furrow, rut.
▶ v THROW OUT, abandon, discard, drop, jettison, scrap, get rid of, dispose of; informal dump.

dive v PLUNGE, plummet, jump, leap, bound, spring, nosedive, fall, descend, submerge, drop, swoop, dip, pitch, bellyflop.

diverge v SEPARATE, fork, branch off, radiate, spread out, bifurcate, divide, split, part, go off at a tangent, divaricate, ramify.
– OPPOSITES converge.

diverse adj ASSORTED, various, miscellaneous, mixed, varied, diversified, variegated, heterogeneous, different, differing, distinct, unlike, dissimilar, distinctive, contrasting, conflicting.

diversify v BRANCH OUT, expand, bring variety to, develop, extend, enlarge, spread out, vary, mix, change, transform.

diversion n ❶ DETOUR, deviation, alternative route. ❷ AMUSEMENT, entertainment, distraction, fun, relaxation, recreation, pleasure, enjoyment, delight, divertissement.

divert v ❶ DEFLECT, turn aside, change the course of, redirect, draw away, switch, sidetrack. ❷ AMUSE, entertain, distract, delight, beguile, give pleasure to, enchant, interest, occupy, absorb, engross.

diverting adj AMUSING, entertaining, distracting, fun, enjoyable, pleasurable, interesting, absorbing, engrossing.
– OPPOSITES boring.

divide v ❶ SPLIT, cut up, separate, sever, halve, bisect, sunder, rend, part, segregate, partition, detach, disconnect, disjoin. ❷ BRANCH, fork, diverge, split in two. ❸ SHARE OUT, allocate, allot, apportion, distribute, dispense, hand out, dole out, measure out, parcel out, carve up. ❹ BREAK UP, separate, alienate, split up, disunite, set/pit against one another, set at odds, come between, sow dissension.
– OPPOSITES unite.

divine[1] adj ❶ HEAVENLY, celestial, holy, angelic, spiritual, saintly, seraphic, sacred, consecrated, godlike, godly, supernatural. ❷ LOVELY, beautiful, wonderful, glorious, marvellous, admirable; *informal* super, stunning.
– OPPOSITES mortal.

divine[2] v FORETELL, predict, foresee, forecast, presage, augur, portend, prognosticate.

divinity n ❶ DIVINE NATURE, divineness, deity, godliness, holiness, sanctity. ❷ THEOLOGY, religious studies, religion, scripture.

division n ❶ DIVIDING LINE, boundary, limit, border, partition, demarcation, frontier, margin. ❷ SECTION, part,

portion, slice, fragment, chunk, component, share, compartment, category, class, group, family, grade. ❸ BRANCH, department, section, arm, sector, unit. ❹ DISAGREEMENT, conflict, dissension, discord, difference of opinion, feud, breach, rupture, split, variance, disunion, estrangement, alienation, schism.

divorce n BREAK-UP, split, dissolution, annulment, separation, breach, rupture.
▶ v BREAK UP, split up, separate, part, annul/end the marriage.

dizzy adj LIGHT-HEADED, giddy, faint, shaky, off balance, reeling, staggering; *informal* weak at the knees, wobbly, woozy.

do v ❶ PERFORM, carry out, undertake, execute, accomplish, discharge, achieve, implement, complete, finish, bring about, effect, produce, engineer. ❷ ACT, behave, conduct oneself; *formal* comport oneself. ❸ BE ENOUGH, be adequate, suffice, be sufficient, be satisfactory, serve the purpose, fit the bill, pass muster, measure up. ❹ GRANT, bestow, render, pay, give, afford. ❺ GET ON / ALONG, progress, fare, make out, manage, continue.

docile adj AMENABLE, compliant, tractable, manageable, accommodating, obedient, pliant, biddable, submissive, dutiful, malleable.
– OPPOSITES disobedient.

dock[1] n PIER, quay, wharf,

jetty, berth, harbour, port, slipway, marina, waterfront.

dock² v ❶ CUT, shorten, crop, lop, truncate. ❷ DEDUCT, subtract, remove, take off.

doctor n PHYSICIAN, medical practitioner, GP, general practitioner, consultant, registrar; *informal* medic, doc; *Brit. informal* quack.

doctrine n CREED, belief, teaching, credo, dogma, conviction, tenet, principle, maxim, axiom, precept, article of faith, canon, theory, thesis, orthodoxy, postulate.

document n PAPER, form, certificate, record, report, deed, voucher, charter, instrument, licence, parchment, visa, warrant.
▶ v RECORD, detail, report, register, chart, cite, instance.

documentary adj ❶ DOCU-MENTED, recorded, written, registered. ❷ FACTUAL, non-fiction, true-to-life, real-life, realistic.

dodge v ❶ DART, duck, dive, swerve, veer, jump, move aside. ❷ EVADE, avoid, elude, fend off, parry, fudge, escape, steer clear of, shun, shirk, deceive, trick.
▶ n RUSE, ploy, stratagem, trick, subterfuge, wile, deception, manoeuvre, contrivance, expedient; *Brit. informal* wheeze.

dog n HOUND, bitch, cur, mongrel, tyke, pup, puppy, whelp; *informal* doggy, pooch, mutt, bow-wow.
▶ v FOLLOW, pursue, track,

shadow, trail, hound, plague, trouble, haunt.

dogged adj DETERMINED, obstinate, stubborn, tenacious, relentless, single-minded, unflagging, unwavering, persistent, obdurate, firm, steadfast, staunch.

dogmatic adj OPINIONATED, peremptory, assertive, insistent, pushy, emphatic, categorical, authoritarian, domineering, imperious, arrogant, overbearing, dictatorial, intolerant, biased, prejudiced.

dole n BENEFIT, welfare, social security, income support.
■ **dole out** *see* DISTRIBUTE (1).

doleful adj MOURNFUL, sad, sorrowful, dejected, depressed, miserable, disconsolate, wretched; *informal* blue, down in the dumps.

domestic adj ❶ HOME, family, household, private. ❷ DOMESTI-CATED, tame, pet, trained; *Brit.* house-trained; *N. Amer.* housebroken.

domesticate v ❶ TAME, train, break in; *Brit.* house-train; *N. Amer.* housebreak. ❷ NATURAL-IZE, acclimatize, habituate, accustom, familiarize, assimilate.

dominant adj ❶ COMMANDING, ruling, controlling, presiding, governing, supreme, ascendant, domineering, most influential, most assertive, authoritative. ❷ CHIEF, most important, predominant, main, leading, principal, paramount,

pre-eminent, primary, outstanding, prevailing.
– OPPOSITES submissive.

dominate v ❶ RULE, govern, control, exercise control over, have the whip hand, command, direct, preside over, have mastery over, domineer, tyrannize, intimidate; *informal* call the shots, have under one's thumb, be in the driver's seat, wear the trousers. ❷ OVERLOOK, tower above, stand over, project over, hang over, loom over, bestride.

domineering adj OVERBEARING, authoritarian, autocratic, imperious, high-handed, peremptory, arrogant, dictatorial, haughty, masterful, forceful, pushy, tyrannical, despotic, oppressive, iron-fisted; *informal* bossy.
– OPPOSITES meek, servile.

donate v GIVE, contribute, present, make a gift of, hand over, grant, subscribe; *informal* chip in, kick in.

donation n CONTRIBUTION, gift, subscription, present, grant, offering, gratuity, charity, benefaction, largesse.

donor n CONTRIBUTOR, giver, benefactor, benefactress, supporter, backer, philanthropist; *informal* angel.

doom n ❶ RUIN, ruination, downfall, destruction, disaster, catastrophe, annihilation, extinction, death, termination, quietus. ❷ FATE, destiny, fortune, lot, portion.
▶ v DESTINE, condemn, ordain, preordain, consign, predestine.

doomed adj DAMNED, cursed, hopeless, accursed, ill-fated, ill-starred, ruined, bedevilled.

door n ❶ DOORWAY, portal, entrance, exit, way out, barrier. ❷ ENTRY, entrance, opening, access, gateway, way, path, road, ingress.

dormant adj ❶ SLEEPING, asleep, hibernating, resting, slumbering, inactive, inert, comatose, quiescent. ❷ HIDDEN, latent, potential, untapped, unused.
– OPPOSITES awake, active.

dose n ❶ AMOUNT, quantity, measure, portion, draught. ❷ BOUT, attack, spell.

dot n SPOT, speck, fleck, point, mark, dab, particle, atom, iota, jot, mote, mite.

dote
■ **dote on** ADORE, idolize, love, treasure, prize, make much of, lavish affection on, indulge, spoil, pamper.

double adj ❶ DUPLICATE, twinned, twin, paired, in pairs, dual, coupled, twofold. ❷ AMBIGUOUS, dual, ambivalent, equivocal, double-edged.
▶ n TWIN, clone, lookalike, doppelgänger, duplicate, replica, copy, facsimile, counterpart, match, mate, fellow; *informal* spitting image, dead ringer.

double-cross v BETRAY, cheat, defraud, trick, mislead, deceive, swindle, hoodwink; *informal* two-time, take for a ride.

doubt v ❶ BE SUSPICIOUS OF,

suspect, distrust, mistrust, have misgivings about, feel uneasy about, call into question, question, query. ❷ HAVE DOUBTS, be dubious, be undecided, lack conviction, have scruples.
– OPPOSITES trust.

▶ n ❶ DISTRUST, mistrust, suspicion, scepticism, lack of confidence, uneasiness, reservations, misgivings, qualms. ❷ UNCERTAINTY, indecision, hesitancy, hesitation, vacillation, wavering, irresolution, lack of conviction.

doubtful adj ❶ IN DOUBT, uncertain, unsure, improbable, unlikely. ❷ DISTRUSTFUL, mistrustful, doubting, suspicious, sceptical, having reservations, apprehensive, uneasy, questioning, unsure, incredulous. ❸ UNCERTAIN, dubious, open to question, questionable, debatable, inconclusive, unresolved, unconfirmed. ❹ UNCLEAR, dubious, ambiguous, equivocal, obscure, vague, nebulous. ❺ SUSPECT, dubious, suspicious, questionable, under suspicion, unreliable, disreputable.
– OPPOSITES certain.

dour adj MOROSE, unsmiling, gloomy, sullen, sour, gruff, churlish, uncommunicative, unfriendly, forbidding, grim, stern, austere, severe, harsh, dismal, dreary.
– OPPOSITES cheerful.

dowdy adj FRUMPISH, drab, dull, unfashionable, inelegant, unstylish, slovenly, shabby, dingy, untidy, frowzy.
– OPPOSITES smart.

downcast adj see DEJECTED.

downright adv COMPLETELY, totally, absolutely, utterly, thoroughly, profoundly, categorically, positively.

downward adj DECLINING, descending, falling, downhill, going down, earthbound.
– OPPOSITES upward.

drab adj ❶ DULL, colourless, grey, mousy, dingy, dreary, cheerless, gloomy, sombre, depressing. ❷ UNINTERESTING, boring, tedious, dry, dreary, lifeless, lacklustre, uninspired.
– OPPOSITES bright, interesting.

draft n ❶ OUTLINE, plan, rough version, skeleton, abstract, notes. ❷ MONEY ORDER, cheque, bill of exchange, postal order.

drag v ❶ PULL, haul, draw, tug, yank, trail, tow, lug. ❷ GO ON TOO LONG, go on and on, become tedious, pass slowly, be boring, crawl, creep.

■ **drag out** PROTRACT, prolong, draw out, spin out, stretch out, lengthen, extend.

drain v ❶ DRAW OFF, extract, remove, pump out, bleed, milk, tap, filter. ❷ FLOW OUT, seep out, leak, trickle, ooze, well out, discharge, exude, effuse. ❸ USE UP, exhaust, deplete, consume, sap, bleed, tax, strain.

▶ n TRENCH, channel, duct, sewer, gutter, ditch, culvert, pipe, outlet, conduit.

dramatic adj ❶ THEATRICAL, stage, thespian, dramaturgical. ❷ EXCITING, sensational, startling, spectacular, thrilling, tense, suspenseful, electrifying, stirring, affecting. ❸ STRIKING, impressive, vivid, breathtaking, moving, affecting, graphic.

dramatist n PLAYWRIGHT, scriptwriter, screenwriter, dramaturge.

dramatize v ❶ ADAPT, put into dramatic form. ❷ EXAGGERATE, make a drama of, overstate, overdo; *informal* ham it up, lay it on thick.

drape v COVER, envelope, swathe, blanket, cloak, veil, shroud, decorate, adorn, deck, festoon, array, overlay.
▶ n CURTAIN, drapery, screen, hanging, tapestry, valance.

drastic adj SEVERE, extreme, strong, vigorous, draconian, desperate, radical, dire, harsh, forceful, rigorous, sharp.

draw v ❶ PULL, haul, drag, tug, yank, tow, trail, lug. ❷ ATTRACT, lure, entice, invite, engage, interest, win, capture, captivate, tempt, seduce, fascinate, allure. ❸ SKETCH, portray, depict, delineate, make a drawing of, represent, paint, design, trace, map out, chart, mark out. ❹ PULL OUT, take out, bring out, extract, withdraw, unsheathe.
▶ n ❶ LURE, attraction, pull, enticement, allure, magnetism. ❷ LOTTERY, raffle, sweepstake. ❸ TIE, dead heat, stalemate.
■ **draw on** MAKE USE OF, have

recourse to, exploit, employ, rely on. **draw out** EXTEND, protract, prolong, lengthen, drag out, spin out.

drawback n DISADVANTAGE, catch, problem, snag, difficulty, trouble, flaw, hitch, fly in the ointment, stumbling block, handicap, obstacle, impediment, hindrance, barrier, hurdle, deterrent, nuisance, defect.
– OPPOSITES benefit.

drawing n PICTURE, sketch, illustration, portrayal, representation, depiction, composition, study, outline, diagram.

dread n FEAR, fearfulness, terror, alarm, nervousness, uneasiness, anxiety, apprehension, trepidation, horror, concern, foreboding, dismay, perturbation; *informal* blue funk, the heebie-jeebies.
▶ v FEAR, be afraid of, be terrified by, worry about, have forebodings about, shrink from, flinch from; *informal* have cold feet about.

dreadful adj ❶ TERRIBLE, horrible, frightful, awful, dire, frightening, terrifying, distressing, alarming, shocking, appalling, harrowing, ghastly, fearful, hideous, gruesome, horrendous, calamitous, grievous. ❷ NASTY, unpleasant, disagreeable, repugnant, distasteful, odious.
– OPPOSITES pleasant, agreeable.

dream n ❶ VISION, nightmare, hallucination, fantasy, day-

dream, reverie, illusion, delusion. ❷ AMBITION, aspiration, goal, design, plan, aim, hope, desire, wish, daydream, fantasy.
▶ v ❶ DAYDREAM, be in a reverie, be in a trance, be lost in thought, muse, be preoccupied. ❷ THINK, consider, conceive, suppose, visualize.
■ **dream up** THINK UP, invent, concoct, devise, create, hatch; *informal* cook up.

dreamy adj ❶ DREAMLIKE, vague, dim, hazy, shadowy, misty, faint, indistinct, unclear.

dreary adj ❶ DULL, drab, uninteresting, colourless, lifeless, dry, flat, tedious, boring, humdrum, monotonous, wearisome, routine, unvaried.
– OPPOSITES interesting.

drench v SOAK, drown, saturate, flood, inundate, steep, permeate, douse, souse, wet, slosh.

dress n ❶ FROCK, gown, garment, robe. ❷ CLOTHES, garments, attire, costume, outfit, ensemble, garb; *informal* get-up, togs, duds.
▶ v ❶ CLOTHE, attire, garb, fit out, turn out, robe, accoutre; *archaic* apparel. ❷ BANDAGE, bind up, cover.
– OPPOSITES undress.

dribble v ❶ DROOL, slaver, slobber; *Scottish* slabber. ❷ DRIP, trickle, leak, run, ooze, seep, exude.

drift v ❶ BE CARRIED ALONG, float, coast, be borne, be wafted. ❷ WANDER, roam, rove, meander, stray. ❸ PILE UP, accumulate, gather, form heaps, bank up, amass.
▶ n ❶ GIST, essence, substance, meaning, significance, import, purport, tenor. ❷ PILE, heap, bank, mound, mass, accumulation.

drill v ❶ TRAIN, instruct, coach, teach, exercise, rehearse, ground, inculcate, discipline; *informal* put someone through their paces. ❷ BORE A HOLE IN, pierce, penetrate, puncture, perforate.
▶ n ❶ TRAINING, instruction, coaching, teaching, indoctrination. ❷ PROCEDURE, routine, practice.

drink v ❶ SWALLOW, sip, gulp down, drain, guzzle, imbibe, quaff, partake of; *informal* swig, swill, toss off. ❷ TAKE ALCOHOL, indulge, imbibe, tipple; *informal* booze, take a drop, hit the bottle, knock back a few.
▶ n ❶ SWALLOW, gulp, sip, draught; *informal* swill, swig. ❷ ALCOHOL, liquor, spirits; *informal* booze, the hard stuff, hooch.

drip v DRIBBLE, trickle, drizzle, leak, ooze, splash, sprinkle; *informal* plop.
▶ n DROP, dribble, splash, trickle, leak, bead.

drive v ❶ OPERATE, steer, handle, guide, direct, manage. ❷ MOVE, herd, get going, urge, press, impel, push, round up. ❸ FORCE, make, compel, coerce, oblige, impel, pressure, goad, spur, prod. ❹ HAMMER, thrust,

ram, strike, bang, sink, plunge.
▶n ❶ TRIP, run, outing, journey, jaunt, tour, excursion; *informal* spin, joyride. ❷ ENERGY, determination, enthusiasm, industry, vigour, push, motivation, persistence, keenness, enterprise, initiative, aggressiveness, zeal, verve; *informal* get-up-and-go, pizzazz, zip. ❸ CAMPAIGN, effort, push, crusade.

drop v ❶ FALL, descend, plunge, dive, plummet, tumble, dip, sink, subside, swoop. ❷ DECREASE, fall, lessen, diminish, dwindle, sink, plunge, plummet. ❸ LEAVE, finish with, desert, abandon, jilt, reject, discard, renounce, disown; *informal* ditch, chuck, run out on. ❹ FALL DOWN, collapse, faint, swoon, drop/fall dead.
– OPPOSITES rise, increase.
▶n ❶ DROPLET, globule, bead, bubble, blob, spheroid, oval. ❷ BIT, dash, trace, pinch, dap, speck, modicum, dribble, splash, trickle, sprinkle. ❸ DECREASE, fall, decline, reduction, cut, lowering, depreciation, slump. ❹ INCLINE, slope, descent, declivity, plunge, abyss, chasm, precipice, cliff.

drown v ❶ FLOOD, submerge, inundate, deluge, swamp, engulf, drench. ❷ BE LOUDER THAN, muffle, overpower, overwhelm, stifle.

drowsy adj SLEEPY, tired, lethargic, weary, dozy, dozing,

sluggish, somnolent, heavy-eyed; *informal* dopey.
– OPPOSITES alert.

drug n ❶ MEDICINE, medication, medicament, remedy, cure, panacea; *informal* magic bullet; *dated* physic. ❷ NARCOTIC, opiate; *informal* dope, junk.
▶v ANAESTHETIZE, tranquillize, sedate, knock out, render unconscious, stupefy, poison, narcotize, befuddle; *informal* dope.

drum v TAP, beat, rap, knock, tattoo, strike, thrum.

drunk adj INTOXICATED, inebriated, blind drunk, the worse for drink, under the influence, befuddled, merry, tipsy, incapable, tight; *informal* tiddly, squiffy, plastered, smashed, paralytic, sloshed, blotto, sozzled, drunk as a lord, pie-eyed, three sheets to the wind, well oiled, stewed, pickled, tanked up, steaming, out of it, one over the eight, canned, tired and emotional; *Brit. informal* legless, bevvied.
– OPPOSITES sober.
▶n DRUNKARD, heavy drinker, alcoholic, dipsomaniac, inebriate; *informal* soak, boozer, alky, lush, wino.

dry adj ❶ ARID, parched, dehydrated, scorched, waterless, moistureless, desiccated, withered, shrivelled, wizened, rainless, torrid, barren, unproductive, sterile. ❷ DULL, uninteresting, boring, tedious, dreary, monotonous, tiresome, wearisome, flat,

unimaginative, prosaic, humdrum. ❸ COOL, cold, indifferent, aloof, unemotional, remote, impersonal.
– OPPOSITES wet.
▶ v ❶ DRY UP, mop, blot, towel, drain. ❷ MAKE DRY, dry up, parch, scorch, dehydrate, sear, desiccate, wither, wilt, shrivel, mummify.

dub v CALL, name, christen, designate, term, entitle, style, label, tag, nickname, denominate, nominate.

dubious adj ❶ DOUBTFUL, uncertain, unsure, hesitant, undecided, wavering, vacillating, irresolute, suspicious, sceptical; *informal* iffy. ❷ SUSPICIOUS, questionable, suspect, untrustworthy, unreliable, undependable; *informal* shady, fishy, iffy.
– OPPOSITES certain, trustworthy.

duck v ❶ BEND, bob down, crouch, stoop, squat, hunch down, hunker down. ❷ IMMERSE, submerge, dip, plunge, douse, souse, dunk.

duct n PIPE, tube, conduit, channel, passage, canal, culvert.

due adj ❶ OWING, owed, payable, outstanding, receivable. ❷ DESERVED, merited, earned, justified, appropriate, fitting, suitable, right. ❸ PROPER, correct, rightful, fitting, appropriate, apt, adequate, ample, satisfactory, requisite, apposite.

dull adj ❶ DRAB, dreary, sombre,

dark, subdued, muted, toned down, lacklustre, lustreless, faded, washed out. ❷ OVERCAST, cloudy, gloomy, dismal, dreary, dark, leaden, murky, sunless, lowering. ❸ UNINTERESTING, boring, tedious, tiresome, wearisome, dry, monotonous, flat, bland, unimaginative, humdrum, prosaic, vapid. ❹ MUTED, muffled, indistinct, feeble, deadened.
– OPPOSITES bright, interesting.

dumbfound v ASTOUND, amaze, astonish, startle, surprise, stun, stagger, take aback, bewilder, overwhelm, confound, baffle, confuse, disconcert; *informal* throw, knock sideways; *Brit. informal* knock for six.

dummy n ❶ MODEL, mannequin, figure, doll. ❷ COPY, reproduction, imitation, representation, sample, substitute, counterfeit, sham. ❸ See IDIOT.

dump v ❶ DISPOSE OF, get rid of, discard, throw away/out, scrap, jettison. ❷ LEAVE, abandon, desert, walk out on, forsake; *informal* leave in the lurch.
▶ n ❶ TIP, rubbish dump, scrapyard, junkyard. ❷ PIGSTY, hovel, slum, shack; *informal* hole.

dunce n FOOL, dolt, idiot, ass, ignoramus, imbecile, simpleton; *informal* chump, booby, nincompoop, ninny, dunderhead, blockhead, fathead, halfwit, cretin, moron, dummy, numbskull, dimwit; *Brit. informal* twerp, clot, twit, nitwit.

duplicate n ❶ REPLICA, copy, reproduction, likeness, twin, double, clone, match; *informal* lookalike, spitting image, dead ringer. ❷ COPY, carbon copy, photocopy; *trademark* photostat, Xerox.
▶ adj MATCHING, twin, identical, corresponding, second, paired.
▶ v ❶ COPY, photocopy, reproduce, replicate, clone, photostat, xerox. ❷ REPEAT, do again, replicate, perform again.

duplicity n DECEITFULNESS, double-dealing, dishonesty, two-facedness, trickery, guile, chicanery, artifice.

durable adj ❶ LONG-LASTING, hard-wearing, strong, sturdy, tough, resistant, imperishable. ❷ LASTING, long-lasting, enduring, persistent, abiding, continuing, stable, constant, firm, permanent, unchanging, dependable, reliable.
– OPPOSITES flimsy, ephemeral.

dusk n TWILIGHT, sunset, sundown, nightfall, evening, dark.

dust n ❶ DIRT, grime, powder, soot. ❷ EARTH, soil, clay, ground, dirt.

dusty adj ❶ DUST-COVERED, dirty, grimy, grubby, unclean, sooty, undusted. ❷ POWDERY, chalky, crumbly, sandy, fine, friable.

dutiful adj CONSCIENTIOUS, obedient, submissive, compliant, deferential, respectful, filial, reverent, reverential, devoted, considerate, thoughtful, pliant, docile.
– OPPOSITES disrespectful, remiss.

duty n ❶ RESPONSIBILITY, obligation, service, loyalty, allegiance, obedience, faithfulness, respect, deference, fidelity, homage. ❷ TASK, job, assignment, requirement, responsibility, obligation, mission, commission, function, office, charge, role, burden, onus. ❸ TAX, levy, tariff, excise, toll, fee, impost.

dwarf v TOWER OVER, overshadow, dominate, stand head and shoulders above, diminish, minimize.

dwell v LIVE, reside, stay, lodge; *informal* hang out; *formal* abide.

dwindle v BECOME / GROW LESS, diminish, decrease, lessen, shrink, contract, fade, wane.
– OPPOSITES increase, grow.

dye n COLOUR, shade, tint, hue.
▶ v COLOUR, tint, stain, pigment, shade.

dynamic adj ENERGETIC, active, lively, spirited, aggressive, pushy, enthusiastic, driving, eager, motivated, zealous, alive, vigorous, strong, forceful, powerful, high-powered, potent, vital, effective; *informal* go-ahead, go-getting, zippy, peppy.

Ee

eager adj **❶** KEEN, enthusiastic, avid, fervent, impatient, zealous, passionate, wholehearted, earnest, diligent, ambitious, enterprising; *informal* bright-eyed and bushy-tailed, raring to go. **❷** LONGING, yearning, anxious, intent, agog, wishing, desirous, hopeful, thirsty, hungry, greedy; *informal* dying, itching, hot.
– OPPOSITES indifferent, apathetic.

early adv **❶** AHEAD OF TIME, too soon, beforehand, before the appointed time, prematurely. **❷** IN GOOD TIME, ahead of schedule, before the appointed time.
– OPPOSITES late.
▶ adj **❶** ADVANCED, forward, premature, untimely, precocious. **❷** PRIMITIVE, primeval, prehistoric, primordial.
– OPPOSITES overdue.

earn v **❶** GET, make, receive, obtain, draw, clear, collect, bring in, take home, gross, net; *informal* pull in, pocket. **❷** GAIN, win, attain, merit, achieve, rate, secure, obtain, deserve, be entitled to, be worthy of, warrant.

earnest adj **❶** SERIOUS, solemn, grave, intense, thoughtful, studious, staid, diligent, steady, hard-working, committed, dedicated, assiduous, keen, zealous. **❷** SINCERE, fervent, intense, ardent, passionate, heartfelt, wholehearted, enthusiastic, urgent, zealous, fervid, warm.
– OPPOSITES flippant.

earnings pl n INCOME, salary, wage, pay, remuneration, fee, stipend, emolument, honorarium.

earth n SOIL, clay, loam, turf, clod, dirt, sod, ground.

earthly adj **❶** WORLDLY, temporal, secular, mortal, human, material, materialistic, nonspiritual, mundane, carnal, fleshly, physical, corporeal, gross, sensual, base, sordid, vile, profane. **❷** POSSIBLE, feasible, conceivable, imaginable, likely.
– OPPOSITES spiritual.

earthy adj **❶** UNSOPHISTICATED, down-to-earth, unrefined, homely, simple, plain, unpretentious, natural, uninhibited, rough, robust. **❷** CRUDE, bawdy, coarse, ribald, indecent, obscene, indecorous; *informal* blue.

ease n **❶** EFFORTLESSNESS, no difficulty, simplicity, deftness, proficiency, facility, adroitness, dexterity, mastery. **❷** COMFORT, contentment, enjoyment, content, affluence, wealth, prosperity, luxury, opulence. **❸** PEACE, peacefulness, calmness, tranquillity, compos-

ure, serenity, restfulness, quiet, security.
– OPPOSITES difficulty.
▶ v ❶ LESSEN, mitigate, reduce, lighten, diminish, moderate, ameliorate, relieve, assuage, allay, soothe, palliate, appease. ❷ GUIDE, manoeuvre, edge, inch, steer, glide, slip. ❸ COMFORT, console, soothe, solace, calm, quieten, pacify.
– OPPOSITES aggravate.

easy adj ❶ SIMPLE, uncomplicated, straightforward, undemanding, effortless, painless, trouble-free, facile; *informal* idiot-proof. ❷ NATURAL, casual, informal, unceremonious, easy-going, amiable, unconcerned, affable, carefree, nonchalant, composed, urbane, insouciant, suave; *informal* laid-back. ❸ UNTROUBLED, unworried, relaxed, at ease, calm, tranquil, composed, serene, comfortable, contented, secure. ❹ MODERATE, steady, regular, undemanding, leisurely, unhurried.
– OPPOSITES difficult, formal, uneasy.

easy-going adj EVEN-TEMPERED, relaxed, carefree, happy-go-lucky, placid, serene, nonchalant, insouciant, tolerant, undemanding, amiable, patient, understanding, imperturbable; *informal* laid-back, together.
– OPPOSITES intolerant.

eat v CONSUME, devour, swallow, chew, munch, gulp down, bolt, wolf, ingest; *informal* tuck into, put away; *Brit. informal* scoff.

■ **eat away** ERODE, wear away, corrode, gnaw away, dissolve, waste away, rot, decay, destroy.

eavesdrop v LISTEN IN, spy, monitor, tap, wire-tap, overhear; *informal* bug, snoop.

ebb v ❶ GO OUT, flow back, retreat, fall back, draw back, recede, abate, subside. ❷ *See* DECLINE v (2, 3).

ebullience n EXUBERANCE, buoyancy, high spirits, exhilaration, elation, euphoria, high-spiritedness, jubilation, animation, sparkle, vivacity, zest, irrepressibility.

eccentric adj ODD, strange, queer, peculiar, unconventional, idiosyncratic, quirky, bizarre, weird, outlandish, irregular, uncommon, abnormal, freakish, aberrant, anomalous, capricious, whimsical; *informal* offbeat, way-out, dotty, nutty, screwy.
– OPPOSITES ordinary, conventional.
▶ n CHARACTER, oddity, crank; *informal* queer fish, weirdo, oddball, nut; *Brit. informal* nutter; *N. Amer. informal* screwball.

echo v ❶ REVERBERATE, resound, ring, repeat, reflect. ❷ COPY, imitate, repeat, reproduce, reiterate, mirror, parrot, reflect, parallel, parody, ape.

eclipse v ❶ BLOCK, cover, blot out, obscure, conceal, cast a shadow over, darken, shade, veil, shroud. ❷ OUTSHINE, overshadow, dwarf, put in the shade, surpass, exceed, outstrip, transcend.

economical adj ❶ THRIFTY, sparing, careful, prudent, frugal, scrimping, mean, niggardly, penny-pinching, parsimonious; *informal* stingy; *Brit. informal* tight. ❷ CHEAP, inexpensive, reasonable, low-price, low-cost, budget.
– OPPOSITES extravagant.

economize v BUDGET, cut back, scrimp, save, be economical, be sparing, retrench; *informal* cut corners, tighten one's belt, draw in one's horns.

economy n ❶ WEALTH, resources, financial state. ❷ THRIFTINESS, carefulness, prudence, frugality, thrift, care, restraint, meanness, stinginess, miserliness, niggardliness, parsimony, penny-pinching, husbandry, conservation.

ecstasy n BLISS, delight, rapture, joy, joyousness, happiness, elation, euphoria, jubilation, exultation, transports of delight, rhapsodies; *informal* seventh heaven, cloud nine.
– OPPOSITES misery.

ecstatic adj BLISSFUL, enraptured, rapturous, joyful, joyous, overjoyed, jubilant, gleeful, exultant, elated, in transports of delight, delirious in a frenzy of delight, rhapsodic, orgasmic, transported; *informal* on cloud nine, in seventh heaven, over the moon.
– OPPOSITES miserable.

eddy n WHIRL, whirlpool, vortex, maelstrom, swirl, countercurrent, counterflow.
▶ v SWIRL, whirl, spin, turn.

edge n ❶ BORDER, boundary, side, rim, margin, fringe, outer limit, extremity, verge, brink, lip, contour, perimeter, periphery, parameter, ambit. ❷ STING, bite, sharpness, severity, pointedness, acerbity, acidity, acrimony, virulence, trenchancy, pungency. ❸ ADVANTAGE, lead, superiority, upper hand, whip hand, dominance, ascendancy; *informal* head start.
▶ v ❶ TRIM, hem, border, fringe, rim, bind, verge. ❷ INCH, creep, sidle, steal, ease, elbow, worm, work, sidestep.

edgy adj NERVOUS, nervy, tense, anxious, apprehensive, on tenterhooks, uneasy, irritable, touchy, irascible, tetchy; *informal* twitchy, uptight.
– OPPOSITES calm.

edit v REVISE, correct, emend, polish, check, modify, rewrite, rephrase, prepare, adapt, amend, alter.

edition n ❶ ISSUE, number, version, printing. ❷ PRINTING, impression, publication, issue.

educate v TEACH, instruct, tutor, coach, school, train, drill, inform, enlighten, inculcate, prime, indoctrinate, edify, cultivate, develop, improve, prepare, rear, nurture, foster.

educated adj LITERATE, well read, informed, knowledgeable, learned, enlightened,

erudite, cultivated, refined, cultured, schooled.
– OPPOSITES illiterate, ignorant.

education n ❶ TEACHING, schooling, instruction, tuition, training, tutelage, enlightenment, edification, cultivation, development, improvement, preparation, indoctrination, drilling. ❷ LITERACY, knowledge, scholarship, letters, cultivation, refinement, culture.

eerie adj UNCANNY, unearthly, ghostly, mysterious, strange, weird, unnatural, frightening, chilling, fearful, spine-chilling, blood-curdling, spectral; informal spooky, scary, creepy.

effect n ❶ RESULT, outcome, consequence, upshot, repercussion, impact, aftermath, conclusion, issue, fruit. ❷ EFFECTIVENESS, success, influence, efficacy, weight, power. ❸ SENSE, meaning, drift, essence, tenor, significance, import, purport.
▸ v BRING ABOUT, carry out, execute, initiate, cause, make, create, produce, perform, achieve, accomplish, complete, fulfil, implement, actuate.

effective adj ❶ SUCCESSFUL, competent, productive, capable, able, efficient, useful, efficacious, adequate, active. ❷ VALID, in force, in operation, operative, active, effectual. ❸ FORCEFUL, powerful, telling, cogent, compelling, persuasive, convincing, moving.
– OPPOSITES ineffective.

effeminate adj WOMANISH, unmanly, girlish, effete, weak, camp; informal wimpish, sissy, pansy-like.
– OPPOSITES manly, virile.

efficient adj WELL ORGANIZED, organized, capable, competent, effective, productive, proficient, adept, skilful, businesslike, workmanlike.
– OPPOSITES inefficient.

effigy n IMAGE, likeness, statue, bust, model, dummy, representation, carving.

effort n ❶ EXERTION, force, power, energy, work, application, muscle, labour, striving, endeavour, toil, struggle, strain, stress; informal elbow grease. ❷ ATTEMPT, try, endeavour; informal go, shot, crack, stab. ❸ ACHIEVEMENT, accomplishment, attainment, creation, result, production, feat, deed, opus.

effrontery n IMPERTINENCE, insolence, impudence, cheek, audacity, temerity, presumption, gall, rashness, bumptiousness; informal nerve, neck, brass neck.

effusive adj GUSHING, unrestrained, extravagant, fulsome, lavish, enthusiastic, expansive, profuse, demonstrative, exuberant; verbose, wordy, long-winded; informal over the top, OTT.

egotistic, egotistical adj EGOCENTRIC, self-absorbed, egoistic, narcissistic, conceited, vain, proud, arrogant, self-important, boastful, superior, bragging, self-admiring.

eject v ❶ EMIT, discharge, expel, cast out, exude, excrete, spew out, disgorge, spout, vomit, ejaculate. ❷ EVICT, expel, turn out, put out, remove, oust, banish, deport, exile; *informal* kick out, chuck out, turf out, boot out.

elaborate adj ❶ COMPLICATED, detailed, complex, involved, intricate, studied, painstaking, careful. ❷ COMPLEX, detailed, ornate, fancy, showy, fussy, ostentatious, extravagant, baroque, rococo.
– OPPOSITES simple.
■ **elaborate on** EXPAND ON, enlarge on, flesh out, amplify, add detail to, expatiate on.

elastic adj STRETCHY, stretchable, flexible, springy, pliant, pliable, supple, yielding, rubbery, plastic, resilient.
– OPPOSITES rigid.

elderly adj OLD, aging, aged, ancient, superannuated, long in the tooth, past one's prime; *Biology* senescent; *informal* getting on, over the hill.
– OPPOSITES young, youthful.

elect v VOTE FOR, cast one's vote for, choose by ballot, choose, pick, select, appoint, opt for, plump for, decide on, designate.

election n BALLOT, poll, vote, referendum, plebiscite, general election.

electric adj ❶ ELECTRICALLY OPERATED, battery-operated; *Brit.* mains-powered. ❷ EXCITING, charged, tense, thrilling, stirring, galvanizing, stimulating, jolting.

electrify v THRILL, excite, startle, arouse, rouse, stimulate, move, stir, animate, fire, charge, invigorate, galvanize.

elegant adj STYLISH, graceful, tasteful, artistic, fashionable, cultured, beautiful, lovely, charming, exquisite, polished, cultivated, refined, suave, debonair, modish, dignified, luxurious, sumptuous, opulent.
– OPPOSITES inelegant.

element n ❶ PART, piece, ingredient, factor, feature, component, constituent, segment, unit, member, subdivision, trace, detail, module. ❷ ENVIRONMENT, habitat, medium, milieu, sphere, field, domain, realm, circle, resort, haunt.

elementary adj ❶ BASIC, introductory, preparatory, fundamental, rudimentary, primary. ❷ EASY, simple, straightforward, uncomplicated, facile, simplistic.
– OPPOSITES advanced, difficult.

elevate v ❶ RAISE, lift, hoist, hike. ❷ PROMOTE, upgrade, advance, prefer, exalt, aggrandize.
– OPPOSITES lower, demote.

elevated adj ❶ RAISED, upraised, lifted up, aloft, high up. ❷ HIGH, great, grand, lofty, dignified, noble, exalted, magnificent, inflated. ❸ LOFTY, exalted, inflated, pompous, bombastic, orotund, fustian.

elf n FAIRY, pixie, sprite, goblin, hobgoblin, imp, puck, troll.

elicit v BRING OUT, draw out, obtain, extract, extort, exact, wrest, evoke, derive, educe, call forth.

eligible adj SUITABLE, fitting, fit, appropriate, proper, acceptable, qualified, worthy, authorized, competent, allowed.
– OPPOSITES ineligible.

elite n ❶ THE BEST, the pick, the cream, the elect. ❷ ARISTOCRACY, nobility, gentry, high society, beau monde; informal beautiful people, jet set.

eloquent adj ARTICULATE, expressive, well spoken, fluent, silver-tongued, smooth-tongued, well expressed, vivid, graphic, pithy, persuasive, glib, forceful, effective, plausible.
– OPPOSITES inarticulate, tongue-tied.

elude v AVOID, dodge, evade, lose, escape, duck, flee, circumvent; informal shake off, give the slip to, throw off the scent, slip away from.

elusive adj ❶ DIFFICULT TO FIND / CATCH, slippery, evasive; informal shifty, cagey. ❷ EVASIVE, ambiguous, misleading, equivocal, deceptive, baffling, puzzling, fraudulent.

emaciated adj THIN, skinny, wasted, skeletal, gaunt, anorexic, starved, scrawny, cadaverous, shrunken, haggard, withered, shrivelled, drawn, pinched, wizened, attenuated, atrophied.
– OPPOSITES fat.

emancipate v FREE, set free, liberate, release, let loose, deliver, unchain, discharge, unfetter, unshackle, unyoke; historical manumit.

emasculate v WEAKEN, enfeeble, debilitate, erode, undermine, cripple, pull the teeth of; informal water down.

embargo n BAN, bar, prohibition, stoppage, proscription, restriction, restraint, blockage, check, barrier, obstruction, impediment, hindrance.

embarrass v MAKE UNCOMFORTABLE / AWKWARD, make self-conscious, upset, disconcert, discomfit, discompose, confuse, fluster, agitate, distress, chagrin, shame, humiliate, abash, mortify, discountenance, nonplus; informal show up, put one on the spot.

embed v INSERT, drive in, hammer in, ram in, sink, implant, plant, set/fix in, root.

embellish v DECORATE, adorn, ornament, dress up, beautify, festoon, enhance, garnish, trim, gild, varnish, embroider, deck, bedeck, emblazon, bespangle; informal tart up.

embezzle v STEAL, rob, thieve, pilfer, misappropriate, pocket, appropriate, purloin, abstract; informal filch, put one's hand in the till, rip off; formal peculate.

emblazon v DECORATE, adorn, ornament, embellish, illuminate, colour, paint.

emblem n CREST, insignia, badge, symbol, sign, device, representation, token, image, figure, mark.

embody v ❶ PERSONIFY, represent, symbolize, stand for, typify, exemplify, incarnate, manifest, incorporate, realize, reify. ❷ INCORPORATE, combine, bring together, comprise, include, collect, contain, integrate, constitute, consolidate, encompass, assimilate, systematize.

embrace v ❶ TAKE/HOLD IN ONE'S ARMS, hold, hug, cuddle, clasp, squeeze, clutch, seize, grab, enfold, enclasp, encircle; informal canoodle with, neck with. ❷ WELCOME, accept, take up, adopt, espouse.

emerge v ❶ COME OUT, come into view, appear, become visible, surface, crop up, spring up, materialize, arise, proceed, issue, come forth, emanate. ❷ BECOME KNOWN, come out, come to light, become apparent, transpire, come to the fore.

emergency n CRISIS, difficulty, predicament, danger, accident, quandary, plight, dilemma, crunch, extremity, exigency; informal pickle.

eminence n IMPORTANCE, greatness, prestige, reputation, fame, distinction, renown, pre-eminence, prominence, illustriousness, rank, standing, note, station, celebrity.

eminent adj IMPORTANT, great, distinguished, well known, celebrated, famous, renowned, noted, prominent, esteemed, noteworthy, pre-eminent, outstanding, superior, high-ranking, exalted, revered, elevated, august, paramount.
– OPPOSITES unimportant.

emit v DISCHARGE, give out/off, throw out, issue, disgorge, vent, vomit, send forth, eject, spew out, emanate, radiate, ejaculate, exude, ooze, leak, excrete.

emotional adj ❶ PASSIONATE, demonstrative, feeling, hot-blooded, warm, responsive, tender, loving, sentimental, ardent, fervent, sensitive, excitable, temperamental, melodramatic. ❷ MOVING, touching, affecting, poignant, emotive, tear-jerking, pathetic, heart-rending, soul-stirring, impassioned.
– OPPOSITES unfeeling.

emotive adj SENSITIVE, delicate, controversial, touchy, awkward.

emphasis n ❶ STRESS, attention, importance, priority, weight, significance, prominence, urgency, force, insistence, accentuation, pre-eminence, import, mark. ❷ ACCENT, stress, accentuation, weight.

emphasize v LAY / PUT STRESS ON, stress, accent, dwell on, focus on, underline, accentuate, call attention to, highlight, give prominence to, point up, spotlight, insist on, play up, feature, intensify, strengthen, heighten, deepen, underscore.
– OPPOSITES understate, minimize.

emphatic adj ❶ FORCEFUL,

forcible, categorical, unequivocal, definite, decided, certain, determined, absolute, direct, earnest, energetic, vigorous. **❷** MARKED, pronounced, decided, positive, distinct, distinctive, unmistakable, important, significant, striking, strong, powerful, resounding, telling, momentous.
– OPPOSITES hesitant.

employ v **❶** HIRE, engage, take on, sign up, put on the payroll, enrol, apprentice, commission, enlist, retain, indenture. **❷** USE, make use of, utilize, apply, exercise, bring to bear.

employed adj **❶** WORKING, in work, in employment, in a job. **❷** OCCUPIED, busy, engaged, preoccupied.
– OPPOSITES unemployed, unoccupied.

employee n WORKER, member of staff, hand, hired hand, hireling, labourer, assistant.

employer n MANAGER, owner, proprietor, patron, contractor, director; Brit. informal gaffer, governor.

empower v **❶** AUTHORIZE, license, certify, accredit, qualify, sanction, warrant, commission, delegate. **❷** ALLOW, enable, give strength to, equip.

empty adj **❶** UNFILLED, vacant, unoccupied, hollow, void, uninhabited, bare, desolate, unadorned, barren, blank, clear. **❷** MEANINGLESS, futile, ineffective, ineffectual, useless, worthless, insubstantial, fruitless,

idle. **❸** PURPOSELESS, aimless, hollow, barren, senseless, unsatisfactory, banal, inane, frivolous, trivial, worthless, valueless, profitless. **❸** BLANK, expressionless, vacant, deadpan, vacuous, absent.
– OPPOSITES full.
▶ v VACATE, clear, evacuate, unload, unburden, void, deplete, sap.

enable v ALLOW, permit, make possible, give the means to, equip, empower, facilitate, prepare, entitle, authorize, sanction, fit, license, warrant, validate, accredit, delegate, legalize.
– OPPOSITES prevent.

enchant v BEWITCH, hold spellbound, fascinate, charm, captivate, entrance, beguile, enthral, hypnotize, mesmerize, enrapture, delight, enamour.

enchanting adj BEWITCHING, charming, delightful, attractive, appealing, captivating, irresistible, fascinating, engaging, endearing, entrancing, alluring, winsome, ravishing.

enclose v **❶** SURROUND, circle, hem in, ring, shut in, hedge in, wall in, confine, encompass, encircle, circumscribe, encase, gird. **❷** INCLUDE, send with, put in, insert, enfold.

enclosure n COMPOUND, yard, pen, pound, ring, fold, paddock, stockade, corral, run, sty, cloister, close, kraal.

encompass v INCLUDE, cover, embrace, contain, comprise,

take in, incorporate, envelop, embody.

encounter v ❶ MEET, run into/across, come upon, stumble across, chance upon, happen upon; *informal* bump into. ❷ BE FACED WITH, contend with, confront, tussle with.
▶ n FIGHT, battle, clash, conflict, confrontation, engagement, skirmish, scuffle, tussle, brawl; *informal* run-in, set-to, brush.

encourage v ❶ CHEER, rally, stimulate, motivate, inspire, stir, incite, hearten, animate, invigorate, embolden; *informal* buck up. ❷ URGE, persuade, prompt, influence, exhort, spur, goad, egg on. ❸ PROMOTE, advance, foster, help, assist, support, aid, advocate, back, boost, abet, forward, strengthen.
– OPPOSITES discourage.

encroach v TRESPASS, intrude, invade, infringe, infiltrate, overrun, impinge, usurp, appropriate; *informal* tread on someone's toes, muscle in on, invade someone's space.

encumber v INCONVENIENCE, constrain, handicap, hinder, impede, obstruct, retard, check, restrain.

encyclopedic adj COMPREHENSIVE, complete, wide-ranging, all-inclusive, exhaustive, all-embracing, thorough, universal, all-encompassing, compendious, vast.

end n ❶ ENDING, finish, close, conclusion, cessation, termination, completion, resolution,

climax, finale, culmination, denouement, epilogue, expiry; *informal* wind-up, pay-off. ❷ EDGE, border, boundary, limit, extremity, margin, point, tip, extent. ❸ REMAINDER, remnant, fragment, vestige, left-over. ❹ AIM, goal, purpose, intention, objective, design, motive, aspiration, intent, object.
– OPPOSITES beginning, start.
▶ v ❶ COME TO AN END, finish, stop, close, cease, conclude, terminate, discontinue, break off, fade away, peter out; *informal* wind up. ❷ BRING TO AN END, finish, stop, cease, conclude, close, terminate, break off, complete, dissolve, resolve.
– OPPOSITES begin, start.

endanger v THREATEN, put at risk, put in danger, jeopardize, imperil, risk, expose, hazard, compromise.
– OPPOSITES protect.

endearing adj CHARMING, adorable, lovable, attractive, engaging, disarming, appealing, winning, sweet, captivating, enchanting, winsome.

endearment n ❶ SWEET TALK, sweet nothings, soft words, blandishments. ❷ AFFECTION, love, fondness, liking, attachment.

endeavour v TRY, attempt, strive, venture, aspire, undertake, struggle, labour, essay; *informal* work at, have a go/stab at.

endless adj ❶ UNENDING, unlimited, infinite, limitless, boundless, continual, perpet-

ual, constant, everlasting, unceasing, unfading, interminable, incessant, measureless, untold, incalculable. ❷ CONTINUOUS, unbroken, uninterrupted, never-ending, whole, entire. ❸ NON-STOP, interminable, overlong, unremitting, monotonous, boring.
– OPPOSITES finite, limited.

endorse v ❶ SIGN, countersign, validate, autograph, superscribe, underwrite. ❷ APPROVE, support, back, favour, recommend, advocate, champion, subscribe to, uphold, authorize, sanction, ratify, affirm, warrant, confirm, vouch for, corroborate.

endow v PROVIDE, give, present, confer, bestow, gift, enrich, supply, furnish, award, invest; *poetic/literary* endue.

endurance n ❶ STAMINA, staying power, perseverance, tenacity, fortitude, durability, continuance, longevity. ❷ TOLERATION, sufferance, forbearance, acceptance, patience, resignation.

endure v ❶ LAST, continue, persist, remain, live on, hold on, survive, abide; *archaic* bide, tarry. ❷ STAND, bear, put up with, tolerate, suffer, abide, submit to, countenance, stomach, swallow; *Brit. informal* stick; *formal* brook.
– OPPOSITES fade.

enemy n ADVERSARY, opponent, foe, rival, antagonist, competitor.
– OPPOSITES friend.

energetic adj ❶ ACTIVE, lively, vigorous, strenuous, dynamic, brisk, spirited, animated, vibrant, sprightly, vital, tireless, indefatigable; *informal* zippy, peppy, bright-eyed and bushy-tailed. ❷ FORCIBLE, forceful, determined, aggressive, emphatic, driving, powerful, effective, potent.
– OPPOSITES lethargic.

energy n VIGOUR, strength, stamina, power, forcefulness, drive, push, exertion, enthusiasm, life, animation, liveliness, vivacity, vitality, spirit, spiritedness, fire, zest, exuberance, buoyancy, verve, dash, sparkle, effervescence, brio, ardour, zeal, passion, might, potency, effectiveness, efficiency, efficacy, cogency; *informal* vim, zip, zing.

enfold v ENCLOSE, fold, envelop, encircle, swathe, shroud, swaddle.

enforce v ❶ APPLY, carry out, administer, implement, bring to bear, impose, prosecute, execute, discharge, fulfil. ❷ FORCE, compel, insist on, require, coerce, necessitate, urge, exact.

engage v ❶ EMPLOY, hire, take on, appoint, enlist, enrol, commission. ❷ OCCUPY, absorb, hold, engross, grip, secure, preoccupy, fill. ❸ TAKE PART, enter into, become involved in, undertake, embark on, set about, join in, participate in, tackle, launch into. ❹ FIT TOGETHER, join

together, mesh, intermesh, interconnect.
– OPPOSITES dismiss.

engender v CAUSE, produce, create, bring about, give rise to, lead to, arouse, rouse, provoke, excite, incite, induce, generate, instigate, effect, hatch, occasion, foment; *formal* effectuate.

engine n MOTOR, mechanism, machine, power source, generator.

engineer v BRING ABOUT, cause, plan, plot, contrive, devise, orchestrate, mastermind, originate, manage, control, superintend, direct, conduct, handle, concoct.

engrave v INSCRIBE, etch, carve, cut, chisel, imprint, impress, mark.

enhance v ADD TO, increase, heighten, stress, emphasize, strengthen, improve, augment, boost, intensify, reinforce, magnify, amplify, enrich, complement.

enjoy v ❶ TAKE PLEASURE IN, delight in, appreciate, like, love, rejoice in, relish, revel in, savour, lap up, luxuriate in; *informal* fancy. ❷ HAVE, possess, benefit from, own, have the advantage of, be blessed with.
– OPPOSITES dislike.

■ **enjoy oneself** HAVE FUN, have a good time, make merry, celebrate, party, have the time of one's life; *informal* have a ball, let one's hair down.

enjoyable adj ENTERTAINING, amusing, delightful, diverting, satisfying, gratifying, pleasant,
lovely, agreeable, pleasurable, fine, good, great, nice.
– OPPOSITES boring, disagreeable.

enlarge v MAKE BIGGER / LARGER, expand, extend, add to, augment, amplify, supplement, magnify, multiply, widen, broaden, lengthen, elongate, deepen, thicken, distend, dilate, swell, inflate.

enlighten v INFORM, make aware, advise, instruct, teach, educate, tutor, illuminate, apprise, counsel, edify, civilize, cultivate.

enlist v ❶ ENROL, sign up, conscript, recruit, hire, employ, take on, engage, muster, obtain, secure. ❷ JOIN, join up, enrol in, sign up for, enter into, volunteer for.

enliven v BRIGHTEN UP, cheer up, perk up, hearten, gladden, excite, stimulate, exhilarate, invigorate, revitalize, buoy up, give a boost to, wake up, rouse, refresh; *informal* jazz up, ginger up, light a fire under.

enormous adj HUGE, immense, massive, vast, gigantic, colossal, mammoth, astronomic, gargantuan, mountainous, prodigious, tremendous, stupendous, titanic, excessive, Herculean, Brobdingnagian; *informal* jumbo.
– OPPOSITES tiny.

enough adj SUFFICIENT, adequate, ample, abundant.
– OPPOSITES insufficient, inadequate.

enquire v see INQUIRE.

enrage v MADDEN, infuriate, incense, exasperate, provoke, annoy, irritate, inflame, incite, irk, agitate; *informal* make someone's hackles rise, make someone's blood boil, get someone's back up; *Brit. informal* wind up.
– OPPOSITES placate.

enrapture v DELIGHT, thrill, captivate, charm, fascinate, enchant, beguile, bewitch, entrance, enthral, transport, ravish; *informal* blow someone's mind, turn on.

ensue v FOLLOW, come next/after, result, occur, happen, turn up, arise, transpire, proceed, succeed, issue, derive, stem, supervene; *poetic/literary* come to pass, befall.

ensure v MAKE CERTAIN, make sure, guarantee, confirm, certify, secure, effect, warrant.

entail v INVOLVE, require, call for, necessitate, demand, impose, cause, bring about, produce, result in, lead to, give rise to, occasion.

enter v ❶ COME / GO INTO, pass/move into, invade, infiltrate, penetrate, pierce, puncture. ❷ BEGIN, start, commence, embark on, engage in, undertake, venture on. ❸ TAKE PART IN, participate in, go in for, gain entrance/admittance to. ❹ SUBMIT, put forward, present, proffer, register, tender. ❺ RECORD, register, put down, note, mark down, document, list, file, log.

enterprise n ❶ VENTURE, undertaking, project, operation, endeavour, task, effort, plan, scheme, campaign. ❷ RESOURCEFULNESS, initiative, drive, push, enthusiasm, zest, energy, vitality, boldness, audacity, courage, imagination, spirit, spiritedness, vigour; *informal* get-up-and-go, vim, oomph. ❸ BUSINESS, firm, industry, concern, operation, corporation, establishment, house.

enterprising adj RESOURCEFUL, entrepreneurial, energetic, determined, ambitious, purposeful, pushy, adventurous, audacious, bold, daring, active, vigorous, imaginative, spirited, enthusiastic, eager, keen, zealous, vital, courageous, intrepid; *informal* go-ahead, up-and-coming, peppy.

entertain v ❶ AMUSE, divert, delight, please, charm, cheer, interest, beguile, engage, occupy. ❷ PLAY HOST / HOSTESS, receive guests, provide hospitality, have people round, have company, keep open house, hold/throw a party. ❸ CONSIDER, give consideration to, take into consideration, give some thought to, think about/over, contemplate, weigh up, ponder, muse over, bear in mind.

entertainment n ❶ AMUSEMENT, fun, enjoyment, recreation, diversion, distraction, pastime, hobby, sport. ❷ SHOW, performance, concert, play, presentation, spectacle, pageant.

enthralling adj CAPTIVATING, enchanting, spellbinding,

fascinating, bewitching, gripping, riveting, charming, delightful, intriguing, mesmerizing, hypnotic.

enthusiasm n EAGERNESS, keenness, fervour, ardour, passion, zeal, warmth, vehemence, zest, fire, excitement, exuberance, ebullience, avidity, wholeheartedness, commitment, devotion, fanaticism, earnestness.
– OPPOSITES apathy.

enthusiast n SUPPORTER, follower, fan, devotee, lover, admirer, fanatic, zealot, aficionado; *informal* buff, freak.

enthusiastic adj EAGER, keen, fervent, ardent, passionate, warm, zealous, vehement, excited, spirited, exuberant, ebullient, avid, wholehearted, hearty, committed, devoted, fanatical, earnest; *informal* mad about.
– OPPOSITES apathetic, indifferent.

entice v TEMPT, lure, seduce, inveigle, lead on/astray, beguile, coax, wheedle, cajole, decoy, bait.

entire adj ❶ WHOLE, complete, total, full, continuous, unbroken. ❷ INTACT, undamaged, unbroken, sound, unmarked, perfect, unimpaired, unblemished, unspoiled.
– OPPOSITES partial.

entirely adv COMPLETELY, absolutely, totally, fully, wholly, altogether, utterly, in every respect, without exception, thoroughly, perfectly.

entitle v ❶ GIVE THE RIGHT TO, make eligible, qualify, authorize, allow, sanction, permit, enable, empower, warrant, enfranchise, accredit. ❷ CALL, name, term, style, dub, designate.

entity n BEING, body, person, creature, individual, organism, object, thing, article, substance, quantity, existence.

entourage n RETINUE, escort, cortège, train, suite, bodyguard, attendants, companions, followers, associates; *informal* groupies.

entrails pl n INTESTINES, internal organs, bowels, vital organs, viscera; *informal* guts, insides, innards.

entrance n ❶ WAY IN, entry, means of entry/access, access, door, doorway, gate, gateway, drive, driveway, foyer, lobby, porch, threshold, portal. ❷ COMING IN, entry, appearance, arrival, introduction, ingress. ❸ ADMISSION, entry, permission to enter, right of entry, access, ingress.
– OPPOSITES exit, departure.

entrant n ❶ NEWCOMER, beginner, new arrival, probationer, trainee, novice, tyro, initiate, neophyte; *informal* cub, rookie; *N. Amer. informal* greenhorn. ❷ CONTESTANT, competitor, participant, player, candidate, applicant, rival, opponent.

entreat v BEG, implore, plead with, appeal to, petition, solicit, pray, crave, exhort, enjoin, importune, supplicate; *poetic/literary* beseech.

entrenched adj DEEP-SEATED, deep-rooted, rooted, well established, fixed, set, firm, ingrained, unshakeable, immovable, indelible, dyed in the wool.

envelop v ENFOLD, cover, wrap, swathe, swaddle, cloak, blanket, surround, engulf, encircle, encompass, conceal, hide, obscure.

envelope n WRAPPER, wrapping, cover, covering, case, casing, jacket, shell, sheath, skin, capsule, holder, container.

enviable adj EXCITING ENVY, desirable, covetable, worth having, tempting, excellent, fortunate, lucky, favourable.

envious adj JEALOUS, covetous, desirous, green-eyed, green, grudging, begrudging, resentful, bitter, jaundiced; *informal* green with envy.

environment n SURROUNDINGS, habitat, territory, domain, medium, element, milieu, situation, location, scene, locale, background, conditions, circumstances, setting, context, atmosphere, ambience, mood.

envisage v PREDICT, foresee, imagine, visualize, picture, anticipate, envision, contemplate, conceive of, think of, dream of.

envy n ENVIOUSNESS, jealousy, covetousness, desire, cupidity, longing, resentment, bitterness, resentfulness, discontent, spite, dissatisfaction.
▶ v BE ENVIOUS OF, be jealous of, covet, be covetous of, begrudge, grudge, resent.

ephemeral adj FLEETING, short-lived, transitory, transient, momentary, brief, short, temporary, passing, impermanent, evanescent, fugitive.
– OPPOSITES permanent.

epidemic n OUTBREAK, pandemic, plague, scourge, upsurge, wave, upswing, upturn, increase, growth, rise, mushrooming.
▶ adj RIFE, rampant, widespread, extensive, wide-ranging, prevalent, sweeping, predominant.

episode n ❶ PART, instalment, chapter, section, passage, scene. ❷ INCIDENT, occurrence, event, happening, experience, adventure, matter, occasion, affair, business, circumstance, interlude.

epitome n PERSONIFICATION, embodiment, essence, quintessence, archetype, representation, model, typification, example, exemplar, prototype.

epoch n ERA, age, period, time, date.

equal adj ❶ IDENTICAL, alike, like, comparable, commensurate, equivalent, the same as, on a par with. ❷ EVEN, evenly matched, balanced, level, evenly proportioned; *Brit.* level pegging; *informal* fifty-fifty, neck and neck. ❸ CAPABLE OF, up to, fit for, good enough for, adequate for, sufficient for, suited, ready for.

▶ n EQUIVALENT, match, parallel, peer, twin, alter ego, counterpart.

▶ v ❶ BE EQUAL / LEVEL WITH, be equivalent to, match, measure up to, equate with, vie with, rival, emulate. ❷ MATCH, reach, achieve, parallel, come up to, measure up to.

equality n ❶ SAMENESS, identity, parity, likeness, similarity, uniformity, evenness, levelness, balance, correspondence, comparability. ❷ FAIRNESS, justice, justness, impartiality, egalitarianism, even-handedness.

– OPPOSITES inequality.

equanimity n COMPOSURE, presence of mind, self-control, self-possession, level-headedness, equilibrium, poise, aplomb, sangfroid, calmness, calm, coolness, serenity, placidity, tranquillity, phlegm, imperturbability, unflappability.

– OPPOSITES anxiety.

equilibrium n ❶ BALANCE, stability, steadiness, evenness, symmetry, equipoise, counterpoise. ❷ See EQUANIMITY.

equip v FIT OUT, rig out, provide, supply, furnish, prepare, stock, arm, attire, array, dress, outfit, accoutre, endow; informal kit out.

equitable adj FAIR, fairminded, just, even-handed, right, rightful, proper, reasonable, honest, impartial, unbiased, unprejudiced, openminded, non-discriminatory, disinterested, dispassionate.

– OPPOSITES inequitable, unfair.

equivalent adj EQUAL, identical, similar, the same, alike, like, comparable, corresponding, commensurate, matching, interchangeable, on a par, tantamount, synonymous, homologous.

– OPPOSITES different, dissimilar.

equivocal adj AMBIGUOUS, ambivalent, vague, unclear, obscure, roundabout, noncommittal, hazy, oblique, evasive, misleading, duplicitous, indeterminate, uncertain.

– OPPOSITES unequivocal.

era n AGE, epoch, period, time, eon, generation, stage, cycle, season.

eradicate v REMOVE, get rid of, wipe out, eliminate, do away with, extirpate, abolish, annihilate, stamp out, obliterate, extinguish, excise, expunge, destroy, kill.

erase v DELETE, rub out, wipe out, remove, cross out, strike out, blot out, efface, expunge, obliterate, cancel.

erect adj ❶ UPRIGHT, straight, vertical. ❷ RIGID, stiff, hard, firm.

▶ v BUILD, construct, put up, assemble, put together, raise, elevate, mount.

erode v WEAR AWAY, wear, eat away at, corrode, abrade, gnaw away at, grind down, consume, devour, spoil, disintegrate, destroy, excoriate.

erotic adj AROUSING, stimulating, aphrodisiac, exciting, titillating, seductive, sensual, sexy, carnal, salacious, suggestive, pornographic; *informal* steamy.

err v BE WRONG, be incorrect, make a mistake, be mistaken, blunder, misjudge, miscalculate, misunderstand, misconstrue, get it wrong, be wide of the mark; *informal* be barking up the wrong tree, slip up; *Brit. informal* boob.

errand n TASK, job, commission, chore, assignment, undertaking, message, charge, mission.

erratic adj ❶ INCONSISTENT, variable, irregular, unstable, unpredictable, unreliable, capricious, whimsical, fitful, wayward, abnormal, eccentric, aberrant, deviant. ❷ WANDERING, meandering, wavering, directionless, haphazard.
– OPPOSITES consistent.

error n ❶ MISTAKE, inaccuracy, miscalculation, blunder, fault, flaw, oversight, misprint, erratum, misinterpretation, misreading, fallacy, misconception, delusion; *Brit. literal; informal* slip-up, boo-boo, howler, typo; *Brit. informal* boob; *Brit. informal, dated* bloomer. ❷ WRONGNESS, misconduct, misbehaviour, lawlessness, criminality, delinquency, sinfulness, evil.

erupt v ❶ EJECT, gush, pour forth, spew, vent, boil over,

vomit. ❷ BREAK OUT, flare up, blow up, explode.

escalate v GROW, increase, be stepped up, mushroom, intensify, heighten, accelerate, be extended, be magnified, be amplified.

escapade n STUNT, prank, adventure, caper, romp, frolic, fling, spree, antics; *informal* lark, scrape, shenanigans.

escape v ❶ GET AWAY, break out, run away, break free, flee, bolt, abscond, decamp, fly, steal away, slip away; *informal* skedaddle, vamoose, fly the coop; *Brit. informal* do a bunk, do a runner. ❷ AVOID, evade, dodge, elude, circumvent, sidestep, steer clear of, shirk; *informal* duck, bilk; *Brit. informal* skive (off). ❸ LEAK, seep, pour out, gush, spurt, issue, flow, discharge, emanate, drain.
▶ n ❶ BREAKOUT, getaway, flight. ❷ AVOIDANCE, evasion, dodging, eluding, elusion, circumvention. ❸ LEAK, leakage, seepage, gush, spurt, issue, flow, discharge, outflow, emanation, efflux.

escort n ❶ ENTOURAGE, retinue, attendants, train, cortège, bodyguard, protector, convoy, defender, contingent. ❷ PARTNER, companion, gigolo, hostess, geisha; *informal* date; *dated* beau.
▶ v ❶ ACCOMPANY, guide, conduct, lead, usher, shepherd, guard, protect, safeguard, defend. ❷ PARTNER, accompany, take out, go out with, attend on.

esoteric adj ABSTRUSE, obscure, cryptic, arcane, recondite, abstract, mysterious, hidden, secret, mystic, magical, occult, cabbalistic.

essence n ❶ FUNDAMENTAL NATURE, substance, crux, quintessence, heart, lifeblood, kernel, marrow, pith, reality, actuality; *Philosophy* quiddity. ❷ EXTRACT, concentrate, distillate, tincture, elixir, abstraction.

essential adj ❶ NECESSARY, important, indispensable, vital, crucial, needed, requisite. ❷ BASIC, fundamental, chief, intrinsic, inherent, innate, elemental, characteristic, principal, cardinal.
– OPPOSITES unimportant.

establish v ❶ SET UP, found, institute, form, start, begin, bring about, create, inaugurate, organize, build, construct, install, plant. ❷ PROVE, show to be true, show, demonstrate, confirm, attest to, certify, verify, evidence, substantiate, corroborate, validate, authenticate, ratify.
– OPPOSITES disprove.

established adj ACCEPTED, official, proven, settled, conventional, traditional, fixed, entrenched, inveterate, dyed in the wool.

establishment n ❶ FORMATION, foundation, founding, setting up, creation, inception, inauguration, building, construction, organization, installation. ❷ RESIDENCE, house,

household, home, estate; *formal* dwelling, abode, domicile. ❸ FIRM, business, company, shop, store, concern, office, factory, organization, enterprise, corporation, conglomerate.

estate n ❶ PROPERTY, landholding, lands, manor, domain. ❷ AREA, piece of land, region, tract, development. ❸ ASSETS, resources, effects, possessions, belongings, wealth, fortune, property.

esteem v RESPECT, admire, value, honour, look up to, think highly of, revere, venerate, appreciate, favour, approve of, like, love, cherish, prize, treasure.

estimate v WORK OUT, calculate, assess, gauge, reckon, weigh up, evaluate, judge, appraise, guess, compute.
▶ n ❶ ESTIMATION, valuation, costing, assessment, appraisal, evaluation. ❷ OPINION, estimation, judgement, consideration, thinking, mind, point of view, viewpoint, feeling, conviction, deduction, conclusion, guess, conjecture, surmise.

estimation n see ESTIMATE n (2).

estrangement n ALIENATION, parting, separation, divorce, break-up, split, breach, severance, division, hostility, antagonism, antipathy, disaffection.

estuary n RIVER MOUTH; *Scottish* firth.

eternal adj ENDLESS, everlasting, never-ending, without end, immortal, infinite, enduring, deathless, undying, permanent, indestructible, imperishable, immutable, ceaseless, incessant, constant, continuous, unchanging, unremitting, interminable, relentless, perpetual.

eternity n IMMORTALITY, afterlife, everlasting life, the hereafter, the next world, heaven, paradise, nirvana.

ethical adj MORAL, honourable, upright, righteous, good, virtuous, decent, principled, honest, just, fair, right, correct, proper, fitting, seemly, high-minded, decorous.
– OPPOSITES unethical, immoral.

euphoric adj ELATED, joyful, ecstatic, jubilant, enraptured, rapturous, blissful, exhilarated, gleeful, excited, high-spirited, exalted, buoyant, intoxicated, merry; *informal* on cloud nine, in seventh heaven, over the moon, on a high.

evacuate v ❶ LEAVE, abandon, vacate, move out of, pull out of, quit, withdraw from, retreat from, flee, depart from, go away from, retire from, decamp from, desert, forsake. ❷ EXPEL, excrete, eject, discharge, eliminate, void, purge, drain.

evade v ❶ AVOID, dodge, escape from, elude, circumvent, sidestep, shake off, keep out of the way of, keep one's distance from, steer clear of,

shun, shirk; *informal* duck, give the slip to, chicken out of. ❷ DODGE, avoid, parry, fend off, quibble about, fudge, not give a straight answer to; *informal* duck, cop out of.

evaluate v ASSESS, put a price on, appraise, weigh up, size up, gauge, judge, rate, estimate, rank, calculate, reckon, measure, determine.

evaporate v ❶ BECOME VAPOUR, vaporize, volatilize. ❷ DRY, dry up/out, dehydrate, desiccate, sear, parch. ❸ VANISH, fade, disappear, melt away, dissolve, dissipate.

evasive adj EQUIVOCAL, equivocating, prevaricating, quibbling, indirect, roundabout, circuitous, oblique, cunning, artful, casuistic; *informal* cagey, waffling.

even adj ❶ FLAT, level, smooth, plane, uniform, flush, true. ❷ CONSTANT, steady, uniform, consistent, stable, unvarying, unchanging, unwavering, regular, unfluctuating. ❸ EQUAL, identical, the same, alike, like, similar, comparable, commensurate, parallel, on a par.
– OPPOSITES bumpy, uneven.
▶ adv ❶ YET, still, more so, all the more, all the greater. ❷ AT ALL, so much as, hardly, barely, scarcely.
▶ v ❶ SMOOTH, level, flatten, make flush. ❷ EQUALIZE, make equal, make the same, balance up, standardize, regularize.

evening n NIGHT, close of day,

twilight, dusk, nightfall, sunset, sundown.

event n ❶ OCCASION, affair, business, matter, occurrence, happening, episode, circumstance, fact, eventuality, experience, phenomenon. ❷ COMPETITION, contest, fixture, engagement, game, tournament, round, bout, race. ❸ END, conclusion, outcome, result, upshot, consequence, effect, aftermath.

eventful adj BUSY, action-packed, lively, full, active, important, noteworthy, memorable, notable, remarkable, outstanding, fateful, momentous, significant, crucial, historic, critical, decisive, consequential.
– OPPOSITES uneventful, dull, insignificant.

eventual adj FINAL, closing, concluding, end, last, ultimate, resulting, resultant, later, ensuing, consequent, subsequent.

eventually adv IN THE END, ultimately, finally, at the end of the day, in the long run, when all is said and done, one day, some day, sooner or later, sometime.

everlasting adj NEVER-ENDING, endless, without end, eternal, perpetual, undying, immortal, deathless, indestructible, abiding, enduring, infinite, boundless, timeless.

evermore adv FOREVER, always, for all time, endlessly, without end, ceaselessly, unceasingly, constantly.

evict v TURN OUT, throw out, eject, expel, remove, oust, dispossess, dislodge; *informal* throw out on the streets, throw someone out on their ear, chuck out, kick/turf out, give the heave-ho to, give the bum's rush to.

evidence n ❶ PROOF, verification, confirmation, substantiation, corroboration, authentication, support, grounds. ❷ TESTIMONY, sworn statement, deposition, declaration, allegation, affidavit, attestation.

evident adj OBVIOUS, clear, apparent, plain, unmistakable, noticeable, conspicuous, perceptible, visible, discernible, transparent, manifest, patent, tangible, palpable, indisputable, undoubted, incontrovertible, incontestable.

evil adj ❶ WICKED, wrong, bad, immoral, sinful, corrupt, vile, base, depraved, iniquitous, heinous, villainous, nefarious, sinister, reprobate, vicious, atrocious, malevolent, demonic, malicious, devilish, diabolic. ❷ BAD, harmful, injurious, destructive, deleterious, pernicious, mischievous, malignant, venomous, noxious. ❸ UNFAVOURABLE, adverse, unfortunate, unhappy, disastrous, catastrophic, ruinous, calamitous, unpropitious, inauspicious, dire, woeful.
– OPPOSITES good.
▶ n ❶ WICKEDNESS, wrong, bad, wrongdoing, sin, sinfulness, immorality, vice, iniquity,

vileness, baseness, corruption, depravity, villainy, malevolence, devilishness. ❷ HARM, hurt, pain, misery, sorrow, suffering, disaster, misfortune, catastrophe, ruin, calamity, affliction, woe.
– OPPOSITES goodness.

evoke v BRING ABOUT, cause, produce, bring forth, induce, arouse, excite, awaken, give rise to, stir up, stimulate, kindle, elicit, educe, summon up, call forth, conjure up, invoke, raise.

evolution n DEVELOPMENT, progress, growth, progression, unrolling, expansion, natural selection, Darwinism.

evolve v DEVELOP, grow, progress, emerge, mature, expand, unfold, unroll, open out, work out.

exacerbate v AGGRAVATE, make worse, worsen, intensify; informal add fuel to the fire, put salt on the wound.

exact adj ❶ ACCURATE, precise, correct, faithful, close, true, unerring, literal, strict; informal on the nail; Brit. informal spot on, bang on; formal veracious. ❷ CAREFUL, precise, meticulous, painstaking, methodical, conscientious, punctilious, rigorous, scrupulous, exacting.
– OPPOSITES inaccurate, careless.
▸ v REQUIRE, demand, extract, extort, insist on, request, compel, call for, command, impose, wring, wrest, squeeze.

exacting adj see DIFFICULT (1).

exaggerate v OVERSTATE, overemphasize, overstress, overestimate, overvalue, magnify, embellish, amplify, embroider, colour, add colour, over-elaborate, aggrandize, overdraw, hyperbolize; informal make a mountain out of a molehill, lay it on thick, lay it on with a trowel.
– OPPOSITES understate, minimize.

exalted adj ❶ HIGH, high-ranking, lofty, grand, eminent, elevated, prestigious, august. ❷ ELATED, exultant, jubilant, triumphant, joyful, rapturous, ecstatic, blissful, rhapsodic, transported.

examination n ❶ STUDY, inspection, scrutiny, investigation, review, analysis, research, observation, exploration, consideration, appraisal. ❷ CHECK-UP, inspection, observation, assessment. ❸ QUESTIONING, cross-examination, cross-questioning.

examine v ❶ LOOK AT / INTO, study, investigate, inquire into, survey, analyse, review, research, explore, sift, probe, check out, consider, appraise, weigh, weigh up, scan, inspect, vet. ❷ INSPECT, look at, check over, assess, observe, give a check-up to, scrutinize. ❸ PUT QUESTIONS TO, question, interrogate, quiz, test, cross-examine, cross-question; informal give the third-degree to, grill, pump.

example n ❶ SAMPLE, specimen, instance, representative, case, case in point, illustration. ❷ MODEL, pattern, ideal, standard, paradigm, criterion.

exasperate v ANGER, infuriate, annoy, irritate, madden, incense, enrage, provoke, irk, vex, gall, pique, try someone's patience; *informal* get on someone's nerves, make someone's blood boil, bug, needle, get to, rile.

excavate v DIG, dig out, quarry, mine, burrow, hollow out, scoop out, gouge, cut out, unearth.

exceed v BE GREATER THAN, surpass, beat, outdo, outstrip, outshine, transcend, go beyond, better, pass, top, cap, overshadow, eclipse.

exceedingly adv EXTREMELY, very, extraordinarily, unusually, tremendously, enormously, vastly, greatly, highly, supremely, hugely, inordinately, superlatively.

excellence n EMINENCE, merit, pre-eminence, distinction, greatness, fineness, quality, superiority, transcendence, supremacy, value, worth, skill.

excellent adj VERY GOOD, firstrate, first-class, of a high standard, of high quality, great, fine, distinguished, superior, superb, outstanding, marvellous, eminent, pre-eminent, noted, notable, supreme, admirable, superlative, sterling, worthy, prime, select, model,

exemplary, consummate, remarkable; *informal* A1, top-notch, ace, tip-top, super; *Brit. informal* smashing, brilliant, brill.
– OPPOSITES poor, inferior.

except prep WITH THE EXCEPTION OF, excepting, excluding, besides, leaving out, barring, bar, other than, omitting, saving, save.

exception n ❶ EXCLUSION, omission. ❷ SPECIAL CASE, anomaly, irregularity, peculiarity, oddity, deviation, departure, quirk, freak.
■ take exception OBJECT, be offended, take offence, resent, take umbrage, demur, disagree, cavil.

exceptional adj ❶ UNUSUAL, uncommon, abnormal, out of the ordinary, atypical, rare, odd, anomalous, singular, peculiar, inconsistent, aberrant, deviant, divergent. ❷ UNUSUALLY GOOD, excellent, extraordinary, remarkable, outstanding, special, phenomenal, prodigious.
– OPPOSITES normal, usual, average.

excerpt n EXTRACT, quote, citation, quotation, passage, selection, highlight, part, section, fragment, piece, portion.

excess n ❶ SURPLUS, overabundance, glut, surfeit, superfluity, plethora, superabundance, overkill. ❷ REMAINDER, residue, leftovers, overflow, overload. ❸ IMMODERATION, lack of restraint, overindulgence,

intemperance, debauchery, dissipation, dissolution.
– OPPOSITES shortage, moderation.
▶ adj EXTRA, additional, too much, surplus, spare, superfluous, redundant.

excessive adj TOO MUCH, immoderate, extravagant, lavish, superabundant, unreasonable, undue, uncalled for, extreme, inordinate, unjustifiable, unwarranted, unnecessary, needless, disproportionate, exorbitant, outrageous, intemperate, unconscionable.

exchange v TRADE, swap, barter, interchange, reciprocate, bandy.
▶ n TRADE, trade-off, barter, swapping, traffic, dealings, interchange, giving and taking, reciprocity.

excise v ❶ CUT OUT / OFF, remove, eradicate, extirpate; *technical* resect. ❷ DELETE, remove, cut out, cross/strike out, erase, expunge, eliminate, blue-pencil, expurgate, bowdlerize.

excitable adj TEMPERAMENTAL, emotional, highly strung, nervous, edgy, mercurial, volatile, tempestuous, hot-tempered, quick-tempered, hot-headed, passionate, fiery, irascible, testy, moody, choleric.
– OPPOSITES calm.

excite v ❶ STIMULATE, animate, rouse, arouse, move, thrill, inflame, provoke, stir up, electrify, intoxicate, titillate, discompose; *informal* turn on, get

going, work up; *Brit. informal* wind up. ❷ BRING ABOUT, cause, rouse, arouse, awaken, incite, provoke, stimulate, kindle, evoke, stir up, elicit, engender, foment, instigate.

excited adj AROUSED, animated, stimulated, thrilled, agitated, impassioned, hysterical, frenzied, delirious, enthusiastic, lively, exuberant, exhilarated, overwrought, feverish, wild; *informal* wound up, high, turned on.
– OPPOSITES calm, indifferent.

excitement n ❶ ANIMATION, enthusiasm, passion, agitation, emotion, exhilaration, anticipation, elation, feverishness, ferment, tumult, discomposure, perturbation. ❷ THRILL, adventure, stimulation, pleasure; *informal* kick. ❸ AROUSAL, stimulation, awakening, evocation, kindling.

exciting adj THRILLING, exhilarating, stimulating, gripping, dramatic, stirring, intoxicating, rousing, electrifying, invigorating, spine-tingling, riveting, moving, inspiring, provocative, titillating, sensational.
– OPPOSITES boring, uninteresting.

exclaim v CALL, cry, call/cry out, shout, yell, roar, bellow, shriek, proclaim, utter, vociferate; *dated* ejaculate.

exclamation n CALL, cry, shout, yell, roar, bellow, shriek, utterance, interjection, expletive; *dated* ejaculation.

exclude v ❶ BAR, debar, keep

out, shut out, prohibit, forbid, prevent, disallow, refuse, ban, veto, blackball, proscribe, interdict, stand in the way of. ❷ ELIMINATE, rule out, preclude, reject, set aside, omit, pass over, leave out, ignore, repudiate, except. ❸ BE EXCLUSIVE OF, not include, not be inclusive of, omit, leave out.
– OPPOSITES include.

exclusive adj ❶ SELECT, selective, restrictive, restricted, private, closed, limited, discriminating, cliquish, snobbish, fashionable, chic, elegant, upmarket; *informal* ritzy; *Brit. informal* posh, swish. ❷ NOT INCLUDING, excluding, with the exception of, except for, not counting, leaving out, omitting.
– OPPOSITES inclusive.

excommunicate v EXCLUDE, expel, cast out, banish, eject, remove, bar, debar, proscribe, anathematize, interdict, repudiate.

excrement n WASTE MATTER, excreta, faeces, stools, droppings, ordure, dung, manure.

excrete v DEFECATE, urinate, pass, void, discharge, eject, evacuate, expel, eliminate, emit.

excruciating adj AGONIZING, unbearable, insufferable, harrowing, searing, acute, piercing, racking, torturous, severe, intense.

excusable adj FORGIVABLE, pardonable, defensible, justifiable, understandable, condonable, venial.

excuse n ❶ EXPLANATION, reason, grounds, justification, defence, apology, vindication, mitigation, mitigating circumstances. ❷ PRETEXT, pretence, cover-up, front, subterfuge, fabrication, evasion. ❸ APOLOGY, travesty, mockery, pitiful example.
▶ v ❶ FORGIVE, pardon, absolve, acquit, exonerate, make allowances for, bear with, tolerate, indulge, exculpate. ❷ LET OFF, exempt, spare, release, absolve, relieve, free, liberate.
– OPPOSITES condemn.

execute v ❶ PUT TO DEATH, kill, carry out a sentence of death. ❷ CARRY OUT, accomplish, perform, implement, effect, bring off, achieve, complete, fulfil, enact, enforce, put into effect, do, engineer, prosecute, discharge, realize, attain, render.

exemplary adj MODEL, ideal, perfect, excellent, admirable, commendable, faultless, praiseworthy, laudable, honourable, meritorious.

exemplify v TYPIFY, personify, epitomize, represent, embody, illustrate, show, demonstrate, symbolize.

exempt v FREE FROM, release from, make an exception for, exclude from, excuse from, absolve from, spare, liberate from, relieve of, discharge from, dismiss from; *informal* let off.

exercise n ❶ ACTIVITY, exer-

tion, effort, action, work, movement, training, gymnastics, sports, aerobics, callisthenics, keep-fit, workout, warm-up, limbering up, drill. ❷ EMPLOYMENT, use, application, utilization, implementation, practice, operation, exertion, discharge.
▶ v ❶ WORK OUT, train, do exercises, exert oneself, drill. ❷ EMPLOY, use, make use of, utilize, apply, implement, exert. ❸ WORRY, disturb, trouble, perplex, distress, preoccupy, annoy, make uneasy, perturb, vex.

exert v ❶ EMPLOY, exercise, use, make use of, utilize, apply, wield, bring to bear, set in motion, expend, spend. ❷ APPLY ONESELF, make an effort, spare no effort, try hard, do one's best, give one's all, strive, endeavour, struggle, labour, toil, strain, work, push, drive; informal put one's back into it.

exhaust v ❶ TIRE, wear out, fatigue, drain, weary, sap, debilitate, prostrate, enfeeble, disable; informal knock out; Brit. informal knacker, fag out; N. Amer. informal poop. ❷ USE UP, deplete, consume, finish, expend, run through, waste, squander, dissipate, fritter away; informal blow.
– OPPOSITES invigorate, replenish.

exhausting adj TIRING, fatiguing, wearing, gruelling, punishing, strenuous, arduous, back-breaking, taxing, laborious, enervating, sapping, debilitating.

exhaustion n TIREDNESS, fatigue, weariness, weakness, collapse, debility, prostration, faintness, lassitude, enervation.

exhaustive adj ALL-INCLUSIVE, comprehensive, intensive, all-out, in-depth, total, all-embracing, thorough, encyclopedic, complete, full, thoroughgoing, extensive, profound, far-reaching, sweeping.
– OPPOSITES perfunctory.

exhibit v ❶ PUT ON DISPLAY, show, display, demonstrate, set out/forth, present, model, expose, air, unveil, flaunt, parade. ❷ SHOW, express, indicate, reveal, display, demonstrate, betray, give away, disclose, manifest, evince, evidence.

exhibition n DISPLAY, show, fair, demonstration, presentation, exposition, spectacle.

exhilarate v MAKE HAPPY, elate, delight, gladden, brighten, enliven, excite, thrill, animate, invigorate, lift, perk up, stimulate, raise someone's spirits, revitalize, exalt, inspirit; informal pep up.

exhilaration n ELATION, joy, happiness, delight, gladness, high spirits, excitement, gaiety, glee, animation, vivacity, exaltation, mirth, hilarity.

exhort v URGE, persuade, press, encourage, prompt, sway, advise, counsel, incite, goad, stimulate, push, entreat, bid, enjoin, admonish, warn.

exile v BANISH, deport, expatriate, expel, drive out, eject, oust, uproot.
▶ n ❶ BANISHMENT, deportation, expatriation, uprooting, separation. ❷ EXPATRIATE, deportee, refugee, displaced person, outcast, pariah.

exist v ❶ LIVE, be, have existence, have being, have life, breathe, draw breath, subsist, be extant, be viable. ❷ SURVIVE, live, stay alive, subsist, eke out a living.
– OPPOSITES die.

existing adj IN EXISTENCE, existent, extant, living, surviving, remaining, enduring, prevailing, abiding, present, current.

exit n ❶ WAY OUT, door, doorway, gate, gateway, opening, egress, portal. ❷ DEPARTURE, withdrawal, leaving, going, retirement, leave-taking, retreat, flight, exodus, farewell, adieu.
– OPPOSITES entrance, arrival.

exonerate v ABSOLVE, clear, acquit, discharge, vindicate, exculpate, dismiss, let off, excuse, pardon, justify.
– OPPOSITES incriminate.

exorbitant adj EXCESSIVE, unreasonable, extortionate, extreme, immoderate, outrageous, inordinate, preposterous, monstrous, unwarranted, undue, unconscionable.
– OPPOSITES moderate.

exotic adj ❶ FOREIGN, tropical, imported, alien, novel, introduced, external, extraneous.

❷ STRIKING, outrageous, colourful, extraordinary, sensational, extravagant, unusual, remarkable, astonishing, strange, outlandish, bizarre, peculiar, impressive, glamorous, fascinating, mysterious, curious, different, unfamiliar.

expand v ❶ GROW/BECOME / MAKE LARGER, enlarge, increase in size, swell, inflate, magnify, amplify, add to, distend, lengthen, heighten, broaden, thicken, prolong, stretch, extend, multiply, dilate. ❷ OPEN OUT, spread out, unfold, unfurl, unravel, unroll.
– OPPOSITES contract.

expanse n AREA, stretch, region, tract, extent, breadth, space, sweep, field, plain, surface, extension.

expansive adj SOCIABLE, outgoing, friendly, affable, talkative, communicative, uninhibited, open, frank, genial, extrovert, garrulous, loquacious.

expect v ❶ SUPPOSE, assume, believe, imagine, think, presume, surmise, calculate, conjecture; informal reckon. ❷ ANTICIPATE, envisage, predict, forecast, await, look for, look forward to, watch for, hope for, contemplate, bargain for, have in prospect. ❸ DEMAND, insist on, require, count on, rely on, call for, look for, wish, want, hope for.

expectant adj ❶ HOPEFUL, eager, anticipating, anticipatory, ready, watchful, in suspense, anxious, on tenter-hooks; *informal* keyed up. **❷** PREGNANT, expecting, in the family way; *technical* gravid.

expectation n **❶** ASSUMPTION, belief, supposition, presumption, assurance, conjecture, surmise, reckoning, calculation, confidence. **❷** PROSPECTS, hopes, outlook, good fortune.

expedient adj CONVENIENT, useful, pragmatic, advantageous, beneficial, profitable, gainful, practical, desirable, appropriate, suitable, advisable, apt, fit, effective, helpful, politic, judicious, timely, opportune, propitious.
▶ n MEANS, measure, stratagem, plan, scheme, plot, manoeuvre, trick, ploy, ruse, device, artifice, contrivance, invention.

expel v **❶** EVICT, banish, oust, drive out, exile, throw out, cast out, expatriate, deport, proscribe, outlaw; *informal* chuck out, kick out, boot out, turf out, heave out, send packing, give the bum's rush to. **❷** DISCHARGE, eject, eliminate, excrete, evacuate, void, belch, spew out.

expend v SPEND, pay out, lay out, disburse, lavish, squander, waste, fritter away, use up, consume, exhaust, deplete, sap, empty, finish off.

expendable adj DISPOSABLE, dispensable, replaceable, non-essential, inessential, unimportant.
– OPPOSITES indispensable.

expense n COST, price, outlay, payment, expenditure, outgoings, charge, amount, fee, rate, figure, disbursement.

expensive adj OVERPRICED, exorbitant, steep, costly, dear, high-priced, extortionate, extravagant, lavish. See also EXORBITANT.
– OPPOSITES cheap.

experience n **❶** FAMILIARITY, knowledge, involvement, practice, practical knowledge, participation, contact, acquaintance, exposure, observation, understanding. **❷** EVENT, incident, occurrence, happening, affair, episode, adventure, encounter, circumstance, test, trial, case, ordeal.
▶ v HAVE EXPERIENCE OF, undergo, encounter, meet, feel, become familiar with, come into contact with, go through, live through, suffer, sustain.

experienced adj PRACTISED, proficient, accomplished, skilful, seasoned, trained, expert, competent, adept, capable, knowledgeable, qualified, well versed, professional, mature, veteran, master.
– OPPOSITES novice.

experiment n TEST, investigation, trial, trial run, try-out, examination, observation, enquiry, demonstration, venture.
▶ v CONDUCT EXPERIMENTS, carry out tests/trials, conduct research, test, examine, investigate, explore, observe.

experimental adj TRIAL, exploratory, pilot, tentative,

speculative, preliminary, under review.

expert n AUTHORITY, specialist, professional, master, adept, pundit, maestro, virtuoso, connoisseur; *informal* old hand, ace, wizard, buff, pro; *Brit. informal* dab hand.

▸ adj ACCOMPLISHED, brilliant, competent, adept, master, able, proficient, skilful, experienced, practised, qualified, knowledgeable, capable, specialist, adroit, deft, dexterous, clever; *informal* crack, top-notch, wizard.
– OPPOSITES incompetent.

expire v ❶ RUN OUT, lapse, finish, end, come to an end, terminate, conclude, discontinue, stop, cease. ❷ *See* DIE (1).

explain v ❶ DESCRIBE, give an explanation of, make clear/plain, teach, illustrate, demonstrate, define, spell out, interpret, clear up, throw light on, clarify, elucidate, explicate, decipher, expound, decode, delineate, expose, resolve, solve, gloss, unravel, unfold; *informal* get across. ❷ ACCOUNT FOR, justify, give a reason for, give a justification for, excuse, defend, vindicate, legitimize, rationalize, mitigate.

explanation n ❶ DESCRIPTION, interpretation, elucidation, explication, demonstration, definition, clarification, decoding, expounding, illustration, exposure, resolution, solution. ❷ ACCOUNT, justification, reason, excuse, defence,

apology, vindication, mitigation, apologia.

explanatory adj EXPOSITORY, descriptive, interpretative, illustrative, demonstrative, elucidative, elucidatory, explicative, justificatory, exegetic.

expletive n SWEAR WORD, oath, curse, obscenity, epithet, exclamation, four-letter word, dirty word.

explicit adj ❶ CLEAR, understandable, detailed, crystal-clear, direct, plain, obvious, precise, exact, straightforward, definite, categorical, specific, unequivocal, unambiguous. ❷ UNRESTRAINED, unreserved, uninhibited, open, candid, frank, direct, full-frontal, no holds barred.
– OPPOSITES vague, implicit.

explode v ❶ BLOW UP, detonate, go off, erupt, burst, fly apart, fly into pieces; *informal* go bang. ❷ DISPROVE, invalidate, refute, discredit, debunk, repudiate, belie, give the lie to, ridicule; *informal* blow up, blow sky-high, knock the bottom from.

exploit v ❶ MAKE USE OF, use, put to use, utilize, turn/put to good use, profit from/by, turn to account, capitalize on, make capital out of; *informal* milk, cash in on. ❷ TAKE ADVANTAGE OF, abuse, impose on, misuse; *informal* take for a ride, walk all over, put one over on.
▸ n FEAT, deed, adventure, stunt, achievement, accomplishment, attainment.

explore v ❶ TRAVEL, tour, range over, traverse, survey, inspect, scout, reconnoitre, prospect. ❷ INVESTIGATE, look into, enquire into, consider, examine, scrutinize, research, study, review, take stock of.

explosion n ❶ BLAST, bang, detonation, eruption, discharge, boom, rumble, report, thunder, crash, clap, crack. ❷ OUTBURST, flare-up, fit, outbreak, eruption, paroxysm.

explosive adj ❶ VOLATILE, unstable, inflammable, eruptive. ❷ TENSE, charged, serious, critical, dangerous, hazardous, overwrought, ugly, volcanic.

exponent n ❶ ADVOCATE, supporter, upholder, backer, defender, champion, spokesperson, promoter, proponent, propagandist. ❷ PRACTITIONER, performer, interpreter, player, presenter, executant.

expose v ❶ UNCOVER, bare, lay bare, strip, reveal, denude. ❷ REVEAL, show, display, exhibit, make obvious, disclose, manifest, unveil. ❸ DISCLOSE, bring to light, reveal, uncover, divulge, let out, denounce, unearth, unmask, detect, betray; *informal* spill the beans on, blow the whistle on.
– OPPOSITES cover, conceal.

express v COMMUNICATE, convey, put across/over, utter, voice, air, articulate, state, give vent to, phrase, word, put into words, indicate, show, demonstrate, reveal.

expression n ❶ STATEMENT, utterance, pronouncement, assertion, proclamation, articulation, voicing. ❷ WORD, phrase, term, choice of words, turn of phrase, wording, language, phrasing, speech, diction, idiom, style, delivery, intonation; *formal* locution. ❸ LOOK, countenance, appearance, air, mien, aspect. ❹ FEELING, emotion, passion, intensity, power, force, imagination, artistry, poignancy, depth, spirit, vividness, ardour.

expressionless adj
❶ BLANK, deadpan, inscrutable, emotionless, impassive, poker-faced, straight-faced, vacuous. ❷ DULL, dry, boring, wooden, undemonstrative, apathetic, devoid of feeling.
– OPPOSITES expressive.

expressive adj ❶ ELOQUENT, demonstrative, emotional, suggestive, telling, vivid. ❷ PASSIONATE, intense, emotional, moving, poignant, striking, eloquent, vivid, evocative, artistic, sympathetic.
– OPPOSITES expressionless, unemotional.

expressly adv ❶ ABSOLUTELY, explicitly, clearly, plainly, distinctly, specifically, unequivocally, precisely. ❷ SPECIALLY, especially, particularly, solely, specifically, singularly.

extend v ❶ EXPAND, increase, enlarge, lengthen, widen, broaden, stretch, draw out, elongate. ❷ INCREASE, widen, add to, expand, augment, enhance, develop, supplement,

amplify. ❸ PROLONG, increase, lengthen, protract, drag out, stretch out, spin out. ❹ OFFER, give, proffer, present, hold out, advance, impart. ❺ CONTINUE, stretch, carry on, run on, last, unroll, range.
– OPPOSITES contract, curtail.

extensive adj ❶ LARGE, sizeable, substantial, spacious, considerable, vast, immense. ❷ BROAD, wide, wide-ranging, comprehensive, thorough, complete, all-embracing, inclusive.
– OPPOSITES small, limited.

extent n ❶ LENGTH, area, expanse, stretch, range, scope. ❷ BREADTH, range, scope, degree, comprehensiveness, completeness, thoroughness.

exterior n OUTSIDE, surface, front, covering, facade, shell, skin.
▶ adj OUTER, outside, outermost, outward, external, surface, superficial.
– OPPOSITES interior.

exterminate v KILL, destroy, annihilate, eradicate, extirpate, abolish, eliminate; informal wipe out, bump off.

extinguish v ❶ PUT OUT, blow out, quench, smother, douse, snuff out, dampen down, stifle, choke off. ❷ DESTROY, kill, end, remove, annihilate, wipe out, eliminate, abolish, eradicate, erase, expunge, suppress, extirpate.
– OPPOSITES light, kindle.

extol v PRAISE, sing someone's praises, applaud, acclaim, pay tribute to, commend, exalt, congratulate, compliment, celebrate, glorify, eulogize; formal laud.
– OPPOSITES condemn.

extra adj ❶ ADDITIONAL, further, supplementary, supplemental, added, subsidiary, auxiliary, ancillary, other, accessory. ❷ SPARE, surplus, left over, excess, redundant, superfluous, reserve, unused.

extract v ❶ PULL OUT, draw out, take out, pluck out, wrench out, prise out, tear out, uproot, withdraw. ❷ EXTORT, exact, force, coerce, elicit, wring, wrest, squeeze.
▶ n ❶ CONCENTRATE, essence, distillate, juice, solution, decoction. ❷ EXCERPT, passage, cutting, clipping, abstract, citation, selection, quotation, fragment.

extraordinary adj ❶ EXCEPTIONAL, unusual, rare, uncommon, unique, singular, outstanding, striking, remarkable, phenomenal, marvellous, wonderful, signal, peculiar, unprecedented. ❷ AMAZING, surprising, unusual, remarkable, strange, astounding, odd. ❸ ODD, strange, curious, bizarre, unconventional, weird.
– OPPOSITES ordinary, commonplace.

extravagant adj ❶ SPENDTHRIFT, profligate, wasteful, lavish, reckless, imprudent, excessive, improvident, prodigal, thriftless. ❷ EXAGGERATED, excessive, unrestrained, outrageous, immoderate, preposterous, absurd, irrational, reckless, wild; *informal* over-the-top, OTT.

❸ EXORBITANT, excessive, unreasonable, extortionate, inordinate, immoderate, expensive, steep, dear, costly, overpriced.
– OPPOSITES thrifty, restrained.

extreme adj ❶ GREAT, greatest, acute, intense, severe, highest, utmost, maximum, supreme, high, ultimate, exceptional, extraordinary. ❷ SEVERE, harsh, Draconian, stringent, drastic, strict, stern, unrelenting, relentless, unbending, uncompromising, unyielding, radical, overzealous. ❸ FANATICAL, immoderate, intemperate, militant, radical, intransigent, extremist, exaggerated, excessive, unreasonable, overzealous, outrageous.
– OPPOSITES moderate.
▶ n MAXIMUM, highest point, pinnacle, climax, acme, zenith, apex, ne plus ultra.

extremely adv VERY, exceedingly, exceptionally, intensely, greatly, acutely, utterly, excessively, inordinately, markedly, extraordinarily, uncommonly, severely, terribly; *informal* awfully.

extrovert adj OUTGOING, extroverted, sociable, friendly, social, lively, cheerful, effervescent, exuberant.
– OPPOSITES introverted.

exuberant adj ❶ ELATED, exhilarated, cheerful, sparkling, full of life, animated, lively, high-spirited, spirited, buoyant, effervescent, vivacious, excited, ebullient, exultant, enthusiastic, irrepressible, energetic, vigorous, zestful; *informal* upbeat, bouncy. ❷ PROFUSE, luxuriant, lush, thriving, abundant, superabundant, prolific, teeming, lavish, copious, rich, plentiful, abounding, overflowing, rank.
– OPPOSITES depressed, meagre.

exultant adj JOYFUL, overjoyed, jubilant, triumphant, delighted, ecstatic, cock-a-hoop, gleeful, enraptured, transported.

eyeful n ❶ LOOK, good look, view, stare, gaze; *informal* load, gander; *Brit. informal* butcher's, shufti. ❷ VISION, dream, beauty, dazzler; *informal* stunner, knockout, sight for sore eyes, bobby-dazzler.

eyesore n BLEMISH, blot, scar, blight, disfigurement, defacement, defect, monstrosity, carbuncle, atrocity, disgrace, ugliness.

eyewitness n WITNESS, observer, onlooker, bystander, passer-by, spectator, watcher, viewer, beholder.

Ff

fabric n **❶** CLOTH, material, textile, stuff. **❷** STRUCTURE, make-up, framework, frame, constitution, essence.

fabricate v **❶** ASSEMBLE, construct, build, make, manufacture, erect, put together, form, produce, fashion, frame, shape. **❷** MAKE UP, invent, concoct, think up, hatch, devise, trump up, coin.

fabulous adj **❶** See MARVELLOUS. **❷** MYTHICAL, legendary, fantastical, imaginary, fictional, fictitious, unreal, made up, fanciful, apocryphal.

face n **❶** COUNTENANCE, visage, physiognomy, features, lineaments; _informal_ mug, clock, dial; _Brit. informal_ phizog, phiz. **❷** EXPRESSION, look, demeanour, air, aspect.
▶ v **❶** LOOK ON TO, overlook, look towards, give on to, be opposite to. **❷** ENCOUNTER, meet, confront, withstand, cope with, deal with, brazen out, defy, brave, oppose; _informal_ get to grips with, meet head-on. **❸** DRESS, finish, polish, smooth, level, coat, surface, clad, veneer.
– OPPOSITES evade.

facet n ASPECT, feature, characteristic, factor, element, angle, side, point, part.

facetious adj FLIPPANT, jocular, frivolous, light-hearted, tongue-in-cheek, waggish, jocose.
– OPPOSITES serious.

facile adj **❶** INSINCERE, superficial, glib, shallow, slick, urbane, suave, bland. **❷** EASY, simple, uncomplicated, unchallenging.

facility n **❶** EASE, effortlessness, skill, adroitness, smoothness, fluency, slickness. **❷** AMENITY, resource, service, benefit, convenience, equipment, aid, opportunity.

fact n **❶** TRUTH, actuality, reality, certainty, certitude. **❷** DETAIL, particular, information, point, item, factor, element, feature, circumstance, specific.
– OPPOSITES falsehood.

faction n GROUP, section, side, party, band, set, ring, division, contingent, lobby, camp, bloc, clique, coalition, confederacy, coterie, caucus, cabal, junta, ginger group, splinter group, pressure group; _informal_ gang, crew.

factor n ELEMENT, part, component, ingredient, constituent, point, detail, item, facet, aspect, feature, characteristic, consideration, influence, circumstance, thing, determinant.

factual adj REAL, realistic, true, fact-based, true-to-life, truthful, authentic, genuine, accurate, sure, exact, precise, honest, faithful, literal, matter-of-fact, verbatim, word-for-word, objective, unbiased, unprejudiced, unvarnished, unadorned, unadulterated, unexaggerated.
– OPPOSITES untrue, fictitious.

fad n CRAZE, mania, enthusiasm, vogue, fashion, trend, mode, fancy, whim.

fade v ❶ GROW PALE, lose colour, become paler, become bleached, become washed out, dull, dim, lose lustre. ❷ GROW LESS, dwindle, diminish, decline, die away, disappear, vanish, die, peter out, dissolve, melt away, grow faint, wane, fail, evanesce.
– OPPOSITES increase.

fail v ❶ NOT SUCCEED, be unsuccessful, fall through, be frustrated, break down, be defeated, be in vain, collapse, founder, misfire, meet with disaster, come to grief, come to nothing, run aground, go astray; informal come a cropper, bite the dust, fizzle out, miss the mark, not come up to scratch. ❷ GO BANKRUPT, collapse, crash, go under, become insolvent, go into receivership, cease trading, be closed, close down; informal fold, flop, go bust, go broke. ❸ LET DOWN, desert, neglect, abandon, forsake, disappoint. ❹ OMIT, neglect, forget, be unable.
– OPPOSITES succeed.

failing n FAULT, shortcoming, weakness, imperfection, defect, flaw, blemish, frailty, foible, drawback.
– OPPOSITES strength.

failure n ❶ FIASCO, vain attempt, defeat, debacle, blunder; informal botch, flop, washout. ❷ LOSER, incompetent, non-achiever, disappointment, ne'er-do-well; informal no-hoper, dud, flop, washout. ❸ OMISSION, neglect, negligence, dereliction, remissness, delinquency.
– OPPOSITES success.

faint adj ❶ INDISTINCT, unclear, obscure, dim, pale, faded, bleached. ❷ SOFT, muted, indistinct, low, weak, feeble, subdued, stifled, whispered. ❸ SLIGHT, small, remote, vague, minimal. ❹ DIZZY, giddy, lightheaded, muzzy, weak, weak-headed, vertiginous; informal woozy.
– OPPOSITES clear, loud.
▸ v LOSE CONSCIOUSNESS, black out, pass out, collapse, swoon; informal keel over, conk out, flake out.

fair[1] adj ❶ JUST, impartial, unbiased, unprejudiced, objective, even-handed, disinterested, dispassionate, equitable, detached, above board, lawful, legal, legitimate, proper, square; informal on the level. ❷ REASONABLE, tolerable, passable, satisfactory, respectable, decent, goodish, moderate, average, middling, adequate, sufficient, ample, so-so. ❸ BLOND / BLONDE, light, yellow,

golden, flaxen, light brown, strawberry blonde. ❹ BEAUTIFUL, pretty, lovely, attractive, good-looking; *Scottish & N. English* bonny; *poetic/literary* beauteous; *archaic* comely. ❺ FINE, dry, bright, clear, sunny, cloudless, unclouded.
– OPPOSITES unfair, ugly.

fair² n ❶ EXHIBITION, display, show, exhibit, exposition, expo. ❷ FESTIVAL, carnival, fête, gala.

fairly adv ❶ JUSTLY, equitably, impartially, even-handedly, without prejudice, objectively. ❷ REASONABLY, quite, pretty, passably, tolerably, moderately, satisfactorily, rather, somewhat, adequately.

faith n ❶ TRUST, belief, confidence, conviction, credence, reliance, credit, optimism, hopefulness. ❷ RELIGION, church, denomination, belief, creed, persuasion, teaching, doctrine, sect.
– OPPOSITES mistrust.

faithful adj ❶ LOYAL, devoted, constant, dependable, true, reliable, trustworthy, staunch, unwavering, unwavering, steadfast, dutiful, dedicated, committed. ❷ ACCURATE, true, exact, precise, close, strict, unerring; *Brit. informal* spot on, bang on.
– OPPOSITES unfaithful, inaccurate.

fake adj ❶ SHAM, imitation, false, counterfeit, forged, fraudulent, bogus, spurious, pseudo, mock, simulated, artificial, synthetic, reproduction,

ersatz; *informal* phoney. ❷ ASSUMED, affected, feigned, put on, pseudo, insincere; *informal* phoney.
– OPPOSITES genuine, authentic.
▶ n ❶ SHAM, imitation, forgery, counterfeit, copy, reproduction, hoax. ❷ FRAUD, charlatan, impostor, hoaxer, cheat, humbug, mountebank, quack; *informal* phoney.

fall v ❶ DROP, descend, come/go down, sink, plummet, cascade, gravitate. ❷ FALL DOWN / OVER, collapse, fall in a heap, trip, trip over, stumble, slip, tumble, slide, topple over, keel over, go head over heels, take a spill. ❸ DECREASE, dwindle, go down, grow less, diminish, plummet, depreciate, slump, deteriorate.
▶ n ❶ TUMBLE, trip, spill, stumble, slide, collapse. ❷ DOWNFALL, demise, collapse, ruin, failure, decline, deterioration, destruction, overthrow. ❸ DECREASE, lessening, cut, dip, reduction, depreciation, slump. ■ **fall apart** see DISINTEGRATE. **fall back** see RETREAT v (1). **fall back on** see RESORT TO, have recourse to, call into play, call upon, make use of, use, employ, rely on.

fallacy n MISCONCEPTION, false notion, error, mistake, misapprehension, miscalculation, delusion, misjudgement.

false adj ❶ UNTRUE, untruthful, fictitious, inaccurate, misleading, invented, concocted, fabricated, incorrect, wrong, faulty, erroneous, unfounded, invalid, forged, fraudulent, spurious.

❷ TREACHEROUS, disloyal, unfaithful, faithless, traitorous, two-faced, double-dealing, untrustworthy, deceitful, untrue, deceiving, deceptive, duplicitous, dishonourable, perfidious, dishonest, hypocritical, unreliable, unsound, lying, mendacious.
– OPPOSITES true, loyal, faithful.

falsehood n LIE, untruth, false statement, fib, falsification, fabrication, invention, piece of fiction, fairy story, exaggeration; informal whopper.
– OPPOSITES truth.

falsify v ALTER, doctor, tamper with, forge, counterfeit, distort, pervert, adulterate.

falter v ❶ HESITATE, waver, delay, drag one's feet, vacillate, shilly-shally, blow hot and cold, be undecided, sit on the fence, oscillate, fluctuate; Brit. hum and haw. ❷ STAMMER, stutter, speak haltingly.

fame n RENOWN, celebrity, eminence, notability, note, distinction, prominence, mark, esteem, importance, greatness, account, pre-eminence, glory, honour, illustriousness, stardom, reputation, repute, notoriety, infamy.
– OPPOSITES obscurity.

familiar adj ❶ WELL KNOWN, known, recognized, accustomed, common, customary, everyday, ordinary, commonplace, frequent, habitual, usual, repeated, stock, routine, mundane, run-of-the-mill, conventional, household; Brit. informal common or garden. ❷ OVERFAMILIAR, presumptuous, disrespectful, forward, bold, impudent, impertinent, intrusive, pushy.
– OPPOSITES unfamiliar.
■ **familiar with** ACQUAINTED WITH, knowledgeable about, informed about, expert in, conversant with, well up on, au fait with, at home with, no stranger to, au courant with.

family n ❶ HOUSEHOLD, ménage, clan, tribe. ❷ CHILDREN, offspring, progeny, brood, descendants; informal kids; Law issue, scions. ❸ ANCESTRY, extraction, parentage, pedigree, birth, background, descent, lineage, genealogy, line, bloodline, stock, dynasty, house, forebears, forefathers.

famine n ❶ STARVATION, hunger, lack of food. ❷ SCARCITY, shortage, insufficiency, lack, want, dearth, paucity, deficiency.

famished adj STARVING, starved, ravenous, hungry, undernourished.

famous adj WELL KNOWN, renowned, celebrated, famed, noted, prominent, notable, eminent, great, pre-eminent, distinguished, esteemed, respected, venerable, illustrious, acclaimed, honourable, exalted, glorious, remarkable, signal, popular, legendary, much publicized.
– OPPOSITES unknown, obscure.

fan n ADMIRER, follower, devotee, enthusiast, aficionado, disciple, adherent, supporter, backer, champion; informal buff, freak, nut, groupie.

fanatic n ❶ EXTREMIST, zealot, militant, activist, partisan, bigot, sectarian. ❷ DEVOTEE, addict, enthusiast, fan, lover.

fanatical adj ❶ EXTREMIST, extreme, zealous, radical, militant, sectarian, bigoted, dogmatic, prejudiced, intolerant, narrow-minded, partisan, rabid. ❷ ENTHUSIASTIC, eager, keen, fervent, passionate, obsessive, immoderate, frenzied, frenetic; informal wild, gung-ho.

fanciful adj ❶ UNREAL, imaginary, illusory, made up, fantastic, romantic, mythical, legendary, fairy-tale. ❷ IMAGINATIVE, inventive, whimsical, capricious, visionary, impractical.

fancy n ❶ DESIRE, urge, wish, want, yearning, longing, inclination, bent, hankering, impulse, fondness, liking, love, partiality, preference, taste, predilection, relish, penchant; informal yen, itch. ❷ IMAGINATION, creativity, conception, images, visualizations.
▶ v ❶ HAVE AN IDEA, think, guess, believe, suppose, reckon, suspect, conjecture, surmise. ❷ FIND ATTRACTIVE, be attracted to, be infatuated by, take to, desire, lust after; informal go for, be wild/mad about, have taken a shine to.
▶ adj ORNATE, elaborate, ornamented, decorative, embel-

lished, intricate, lavish, ostentatious, showy, luxurious, sumptuous; informal jazzy, snazzy, ritzy.

fantastic adj ❶ FANCIFUL, imaginary, unreal, illusory, romantic, make-believe, extravagant, irrational, wild, mad, absurd, incredible, strange, eccentric, whimsical. ❷ STRANGE, weird, queer, peculiar, outlandish, eccentric, bizarre, grotesque, freakish, fanciful, quaint, exotic, elaborate, ornate, intricate, rococo, baroque. ❸ See MARVELLOUS.
– OPPOSITES ordinary.

fantasy n ❶ IMAGINATION, fancy, creativity, invention, originality, vision, myth, romance. ❷ SPECULATION, fancy, daydreaming, reverie, flight of fancy, fanciful notion, dream, daydream, pipe dream.

far adv A LONG WAY, a great distance, a good way, afar.
▶ adj FARAWAY, far-flung, distant, remote, out of the way, far removed, outlying, inaccessible.
– OPPOSITES near.

farcical adj RIDICULOUS, ludicrous, absurd, laughable, preposterous, nonsensical, silly, foolish, asinine.

farewell n GOODBYE, adieu, leave-taking, parting, send-off, departure, departing.
▶ exclamation GOODBYE, so long, adieu, au revoir, see you, see you later; Brit. informal cheerio, cheers.

far-fetched adj IMPROBABLE, unlikely, implausible, remote,

incredible, unbelievable, doubtful, dubious, unconvincing, strained, laboured, fanciful, unrealistic; *informal* hard to take/swallow.
– OPPOSITES likely.

fascinate v CAPTIVATE, enchant, beguile, bewitch, infatuate, enthral, enrapture, entrance, hold spellbound, rivet, transfix, mesmerize, hypnotize, lure, allure, tempt, entice, draw, tantalize, charm, attract, intrigue, delight, absorb, engross.
– OPPOSITES bore, repel.

fashion n ❶ STYLE, vogue, trend, latest thing, taste, mode, craze, rage, fad, convention, custom, practice. ❷ CLOTHES, design, couture; *informal* rag trade. ❸ WAY, manner, style, method, system, mode, approach.
▶ v MAKE, build, construct, manufacture, create, devise, shape, form, mould, forge, hew, carve.

fashionable adj STYLISH, in fashion, up to date, up to the minute, contemporary, modern, voguish, in vogue, modish, popular, all the rage, trendsetting, latest, smart, chic, elegant; *informal* trendy, natty, with it, ritzy.
– OPPOSITES unfashionable.

fast adj ❶ QUICK, rapid, swift, speedy, brisk, hurried, breakneck, hasty, accelerated, flying, express, fleet; *informal* nippy. ❷ LOYAL, devoted, faithful, steadfast, firm, staunch, constant, lasting, unchanging, unwavering, enduring. ❸ LICENTIOUS, promiscuous, dissolute, loose, wanton. ❹ WILD, dissipated, debauched, dissolute, promiscuous, intemperate, immoderate, unrestrained, reckless, profligate, extravagant.
– OPPOSITES slow.
▶ adv ❶ QUICKLY, rapidly, swiftly, speedily, briskly, hastily, hurriedly, in a hurry, post-haste, expeditiously; *informal* hell for leather, like a shot, like a bat out of hell, lickety-split. ❷ FIRMLY, tightly, securely, immovably, fixedly.

fasten v ❶ BOLT, lock, secure, chain, seal. ❷ ATTACH, fix, affix, clip, pin, tack, stick. ❸ TIE, bind, tether, hitch, anchor, lash. ❹ DIRECT, aim, point, focus, fix, concentrate, rivet, zero in.

fastidious adj FUSSY, finicky, over-particular, critical, hard to please, overcritical, hypercritical; *informal* choosy, picky, pernickety.
– OPPOSITES easy-going.

fat adj ❶ PLUMP, stout, overweight, obese, heavy, large, solid, corpulent, tubby, chubby, portly, rotund, pudgy, flabby, pot-bellied, gross, paunchy, bloated, dumpy, bulky, fleshy, stocky, well fed, massive, elephantine; *informal* beefy, roly-poly. ❷ SUBSTANTIAL, large, major, sizeable, significant, considerable.
– OPPOSITES thin, lean.

fatal adj ❶ MORTAL, deadly, lethal, terminal, final, incurable. ❷ RUINOUS, disastrous, destructive, catastrophic, calamitous, cataclysmic. ❸ CRITICAL, fateful, decisive, crucial, pivotal, determining, momentous, important.

fatalism n STOICISM, resignation, acceptance.

fatality n DEATH, casualty, mortality, loss.

fate n ❶ DESTINY, providence, predestination, predetermination, kismet, chance, one's lot in life, the stars. ❷ FUTURE, outcome, issue, upshot, end.

father n MALE PARENT, paterfamilias, patriarch; *informal* dad, daddy, pop, poppa, pa, old boy, old man; *Brit. informal, dated* pater.

fathom v UNDERSTAND, comprehend, grasp, perceive, divine, penetrate, search out, get to the bottom of, ferret out.

fatigue n TIREDNESS, weariness, exhaustion, lethargy, prostration, lassitude, debility, listlessness, enervation.
– OPPOSITES vigour.
▶ v TIRE, tire out, weary, exhaust, wear out, drain, prostrate, enervate; *informal* take it out of, do in, whack; *Brit. informal* fag out; *N. Amer. informal* poop.

fatuous adj SILLY, foolish, stupid, senseless, nonsensical, idiotic, puerile, brainless, mindless, asinine, vacuous, moronic, witless.
– OPPOSITES sensible.

fault n ❶ DEFECT, flaw, imperfection, blemish, failing, weakness, weak point, deficiency, snag, error, mistake, inaccuracy, blunder, oversight. ❷ MISDEED, wrongdoing, offence, misdemeanour, sin, vice, misconduct, lapse, indiscretion, transgression, peccadillo; *archaic* trespass.
▶ v FIND FAULT WITH, criticize, complain about, censure, quibble about, find lacking, impugn; *informal* pick holes in.
■ **at fault** TO BLAME, in the wrong, culpable, responsible, accountable, answerable, blameworthy.

faultless adj ❶ PERFECT, flawless, without fault, unblemished, impeccable, accurate, correct, exemplary, model. ❷ INNOCENT, blameless, guiltless, above reproach, irreproachable, pure, sinless, unsullied.
– OPPOSITES imperfect.

faulty adj ❶ MALFUNCTIONING, defective, broken, out of order, damaged, unsound; *informal* on the blink, kaput. ❷ DEFECTIVE, flawed, unsound, wrong, inaccurate, incorrect, erroneous, fallacious, impaired, weak, invalid.
– OPPOSITES working, correct.

favour n ❶ SERVICE, good turn, kindness, courtesy, good deed. ❷ APPROVAL, approbation, good will, esteem, kindness, benevolence, friendliness. ❸ BACKING, support, patronage, aid, assistance, championship.
– OPPOSITES disservice, disfavour.
▶ v ❶ APPROVE OF, advocate,

recommend, support, back, endorse, sanction. **②** BE TO THE ADVANTAGE OF, be advantageous to, benefit, help, assist, aid, advance, abet, succour.
– OPPOSITES oppose.

favourable adj **①** APPROVING, good, enthusiastic, well disposed, commendatory. **②** ADVANTAGEOUS, in one's favour, beneficial, on one's side, helpful, good, hopeful, promising, fair, auspicious, propitious, opportune, timely, encouraging, conducive, convenient, suitable, fitting, appropriate. **③** GOOD, pleasing, agreeable, successful, positive.
– OPPOSITES unfavourable.

favourite adj BEST-LOVED, most-liked, favoured, preferred, chosen, ideal, treasured, pet, well liked.
▶ n FIRST CHOICE, pick, beloved, darling, idol, god, goddess, jewel; informal teacher's pet; Brit. informal blue-eyed boy.

fear n **①** FEARFULNESS, fright, terror, alarm, panic, trepidation, apprehensiveness, dread, nervousness, timidity, disquiet, trembling, anxiety, worry, unease, agitation, concern, foreboding, misgiving, doubt, angst, quaking, quivering, consternation, dismay, shivers, tremors; informal funk, blue funk, butterflies. **②** LIKELIHOOD, probability, chance, prospect, possibility.
▶ v BE AFRAID OF, be scared of, dread, live in fear of, go in terror of, take fright at, shudder at, shrink from, quail at, tremble at, have cold feet.

fearful adj **①** AFRAID, frightened, scared, terrified, apprehensive, alarmed, uneasy, nervous, tense, panicky, timid, faint-hearted, timorous, diffident, intimidated, hesitant, trembling, quaking, quivering, cowering, cowardly, pusillanimous; informal jumpy, jittery. **②** TERRIBLE, dreadful, appalling, frightful, ghastly, horrific, horrible, horrendous, shocking, awful, hideous, atrocious, monstrous, dire, grim, unspeakable, gruesome, distressing, harrowing, fearsome, alarming.
– OPPOSITES fearless.

fearless adj UNAFRAID, brave, courageous, intrepid, valiant, gallant, plucky, lion-hearted, stout-hearted, heroic, bold, daring, confident, game, audacious, indomitable, doughty, undaunted, unflinching, unshrinking, unabashed; informal gutsy, spunky.
– OPPOSITES fearful, cowardly.

fearsome adj see FEARFUL (2).

feasible adj PRACTICABLE, possible, achievable, doable, likely, attainable, workable, accomplishable, realizable, viable, reasonable, realistic, within reason.
– OPPOSITES impractical, impossible.

feast n **①** BANQUET, dinner, repast, junket, revels; informal blowout, spread, bash, thrash; Brit. informal beanfeast, beano.

❷ FEAST DAY, festival, saint's day, holy day, holiday, fête, gala, festivity.
▶ v **EAT ONE'S FILL OF**, gorge on, indulge in; *informal* stuff one's face with, stuff oneself with.

feat n DEED, act, action, exploit, achievement, accomplishment, performance, attainment, manoeuvre, move, stunt.

feather n PLUME, quill, pinion, plumule, pinna, plumage, down, hackles.

feature n ❶ ASPECT, characteristic, facet, side, point, attribute, quality, property, trait, mark, hallmark, trademark, peculiarity, idiosyncrasy. ❷ ARTICLE, piece, item, report, story, column.
▶ v ❶ PRESENT, give prominence to, promote, star, spotlight, highlight, emphasize, accentuate, play up. ❷ PLAY A PART, have a place, have prominence.

federation n CONFEDERATION, confederacy, league, alliance, coalition, union, syndicate, association, amalgamation, combination, entente, fraternity.

feeble adj ❶ WEAK, weakly, weakened, frail, infirm, sickly, puny, delicate, slight, failing, ailing, helpless, powerless, debilitated, decrepit, doddering, tottering, enfeebled, enervated, effete, etiolated. ❷ INADEQUATE, ineffectual, ineffective, weak, indecisive, wishy-washy. ❸ UNCONVINCING, unsuccessful, ineffective, inef-

fectual, poor, weak, futile, tame, paltry, slight.
– OPPOSITES strong.

feed v ❶ NOURISH, sustain, cater for, provide for, wine and dine. ❷ EAT, take nourishment, graze, browse. ❸ GIVE, supply, provide, furnish.

feel v ❶ TOUCH, stroke, caress, fondle, handle, finger, manipulate, paw, maul. ❷ BE AWARE OF, notice, be conscious of, perceive, observe, be sensible of. ❸ EXPERIENCE, undergo, have, know, go through, bear, endure, suffer. ❹ THINK, believe, consider, be of the opinion, hold, judge, deem.
■ **feel for** SYMPATHIZE WITH, be sorry for, pity, empathize with, feel compassion for, be moved by, weep for, grieve for, commiserate with.

feeling n ❶ SENSATION, sense, perception, awareness, consciousness. ❷ IDEA, suspicion, funny feeling, impression, notion, inkling, hunch, apprehension, presentiment, premonition, foreboding. ❸ SYMPATHY, pity, compassion, understanding, concern, sensitivity, tenderness, commiseration, empathy, fellow-feeling.

felicitous adj ❶ APT, well chosen, well expressed, well put, fitting, suitable, appropriate, pertinent, apposite, germane. ❷ HAPPY, joyful, fortunate, lucky, successful, prosperous.
– OPPOSITES inappropriate, unfortunate.

fell v ❶ CUT DOWN, chop down, saw down. ❷ KNOCK DOWN, bring down, knock out; *informal* deck, floor, lay out.

fellow n MAN, male, boy, person, individual; *informal* guy, character, customer, codger; *Brit. informal* bloke, chap.

feminine adj WOMANLY, girlish, ladylike, soft, delicate, gentle, tender, graceful, refined, modest.
– OPPOSITES masculine.

fence n BARRIER, railing, rail, paling, wall, hedge, barricade, rampart, stockade, palisade.
▶ v ❶ ENCLOSE, surround, encircle, circumscribe, encompass. ❷ SHUT IN, confine, pen, separate off, secure, imprison.

fend
■ **fend for oneself** PROVIDE FOR ONESELF, take care of oneself, get by, look after oneself, support, oneself, survive. **fend off** WARD OFF, stave off, parry, turn aside, keep off, divert, deflect, avert, defend oneself against, guard against, forestall.

ferment n ❶ FERMENTATION AGENT, yeast, mould, bacteria, leaven, leavening. ❷ FRENZY, furore, fever, tumult, commotion, uproar, agitation, turbulence, stir, confusion, fuss, brouhaha, hubbub, stew, hurly-burly, racket, imbroglio.
▶ v ❶ UNDERGO FERMENTATION, foam, froth, bubble, effervesce, seethe, boil, rise, work. ❷ EXCITE, inflame, agitate, incite.

ferocious adj ❶ FIERCE, savage, brutal, brutish, ruthless, cruel, pitiless, merciless, vicious, barbarous, violent, barbaric, inhuman, inexorable, bloodthirsty, murderous, wild, untamed, predatory, rapacious. ❷ INTENSE, very great, fierce, extreme, acute.
– OPPOSITES gentle.

ferry v CARRY, transport, convey, run, ship, shuttle, chauffeur.

fertile adj ❶ FRUITFUL, productive, rich, fecund. ❷ INVENTIVE, creative, original, ingenious, resourceful, productive, visionary, constructive.
– OPPOSITES sterile.

fertilize v ❶ ADD FERTILIZER TO, feed, enrich, mulch, dress, compost, top-dress. ❷ IMPREGNATE, inseminate, make pregnant, fecundate.

fertilizer n PLANT FOOD, manure, dung, compost, dressing, top-dressing, bonemeal, guano, marl.

fervent adj PASSIONATE, ardent, impassioned, intense, vehement, heartfelt, emotional, fervid, emotive, warm, devout, sincere, eager, zealous, earnest, enthusiastic, excited, animated, spirited; *poetic/literary* perfervid.
– OPPOSITES apathetic, unemotional.

fervour n PASSION, ardour, intensity, vehemence, emotion, warmth, devoutness, sincerity, eagerness, zeal, enthusiasm,

earnestness, excitement, animation, spirit, vigour.
– OPPOSITES apathy, indifference.

fester v ❶ SUPPURATE, run, discharge, ulcerate, rot, decay, go bad, go off, decompose, disintegrate, gather, come to a head. ❷ RANKLE, chafe, cause bitterness/resentment, gnaw.

festival n ❶ SAINT'S DAY, holy day, feast day, holiday, anniversary, day of observance. ❷ CARNIVAL, gala day, fête, celebrations, festivities.

festive adj JOYFUL, joyous, happy, jolly, merry, jovial, light-hearted, cheerful, cheery, jubilant, convivial, gleeful, mirthful, uproarious, rollicking, backslapping, celebratory, carnival, sportive, festal.

festoon v GARLAND, wreathe, hang, drape, decorate, adorn, ornament, array, deck, bedeck, swathe, beribbon.
▶ n GARLAND, wreath, chaplet, lei, swathe, swag.

fetch v ❶ GET, go and get, bring, carry, deliver, convey, transport, escort, conduct, lead, usher in. ❷ SELL FOR, realize, go for, bring in, yield, earn, cost, afford.

fetching adj ATTRACTIVE, charming, enchanting, sweet, winsome, captivating, fascinating, alluring.

feud n VENDETTA, conflict, quarrel, argument, hostility, enmity, strife, discord, bad blood, animosity, grudge, an-

tagonism, estrangement, schism, unfriendliness.

fever n FEVERISHNESS, high temperature, delirium; formal pyrexia.

feverish adj ❶ FEVERED, febrile, hot, burning. ❷ FRENZIED, excited, frenetic, agitated, nervous, overwrought, frantic, distracted, worked up, flustered, impatient, passionate.

few adj ❶ NOT MANY, hardly any, scarcely any, one or two, a handful of, a sprinkling of, a couple of, few and far between, infrequent, sporadic, irregular. ❷ SCARCE, rare, negligible, scant, thin on the ground.
– OPPOSITES many.

fiasco n FAILURE, disaster, debacle, catastrophe, mess, ruination, abortion; informal flop, washout.

fibre n THREAD, strand, tendril, filament, fibril.

fickle adj CAPRICIOUS, unpredictable, mercurial, changeable, variable, volatile, inconstant, unstable, vacillating, unsteady, unfaithful, faithless, undependable, inconsistent, irresolute, flighty, giddy, erratic, fitful, irregular, mutable.
– OPPOSITES constant, stable.

fiction n ❶ STORY TELLING, narration, romance, fable, fantasy, legend. ❷ FABRICATION, lie, piece of fiction, untruth, falsehood, invention, concoction, fib, improvisation, prevarication; informal cock and bull story, whopper.
– OPPOSITES fact.

fictional adj FICTITIOUS, invented, made up, imaginary, unreal, non-existent, make-believe, fabricated, mythical, fanciful.
– OPPOSITES real, actual.

fictitious adj ❶ INVENTED, made up, imaginary, imagined, untrue, false, apocryphal. ❷ FALSE, bogus, sham, counterfeit, fake, fabricated, spurious, concocted.
– OPPOSITES true, genuine.

fidelity n FAITHFULNESS, loyalty, devotedness, devotion, allegiance, commitment, constancy, trustworthiness, dependability, reliability, staunchness, obedience.
– OPPOSITES disloyalty.

fidget v ❶ MOVE RESTLESSLY, wriggle, squirm, twitch, jiggle; informal have ants in one's pants. ❷ FIDDLE WITH, play with, fuss with.

fidgety adj RESTLESS, restive, on edge, uneasy, nervous, nervy, twitchy; informal jittery, jumpy, like a cat on hot bricks.

field n ❶ PASTURE, meadow, grassland, paddock, sward; literary lea, mead, greensward; archaic glebe. ❷ AREA, area of activity, sphere, province, department, subject, discipline, line, speciality, domain, territory, regime. ❸ RANGE, scope, limits, confines, purview.

fiend n ❶ DEVIL, demon, evil spirit. ❷ BRUTE, monster, savage, beast, barbarian, sadist, ogre; archaic blackguard.

fiendish adj WICKED, cruel, savage, brutal, brutish, barbaric, barbarous, inhuman, vicious, bloodthirsty, ferocious, ruthless, heartless, pitiless, merciless, black-hearted, unfeeling, malevolent, villainous, odious, malignant, devilish, diabolical, demonic, satanic.

fierce adj ❶ FEROCIOUS, savage, wild, vicious, bloodthirsty, dangerous, brutal, cruel, murderous, menacing, threatening, slaughterous, terrible, grim, tigerish, wolfish, feral. ❷ PASSIONATE, intense, ardent, impassioned, fervent, fiery, uncontrolled, fervid. ❸ KEEN, strong, intense, relentless, cut-throat.
– OPPOSITES gentle, mild.

fight v ❶ ATTACK / ASSAULT EACH OTHER, hit each other, come to blows, exchange blows, grapple, scuffle, brawl, box, skirmish, tussle, collide, spar, joust, clash, wrestle, battle, do battle, give battle, war, wage war, go to war, make war, take up arms, combat, engage, meet; informal scrap. ❷ QUARREL, argue, feud, bicker, squabble, fall out, wrangle, dispute, be at odds, disagree, battle, altercate. ❸ OPPOSE, contest, take a stand against, object to, resist, defy, withstand, struggle against, take issue with.
▶ n ❶ BRAWL, scuffle, tussle, skirmish, struggle, fracas, battle, engagement, clash, conflict, combat, contest, encounter, exchange, brush; informal

set-to, scrap, punch-up, dust-up; *Law, dated* affray. **2** QUARREL, disagreement, difference of opinion, dispute, argument, altercation, feud.

■ **fight back ❶** DEFEND ONESELF, put up a fight, retaliate, counter-attack. **❷** SUPPRESS, repress, check, curb, restrain, contain, bottle up. **fight off** WARD OFF, beat off, stave off, repel, repulse, hold at bay, resist.

figurative adj METAPHORICAL, symbolic, allegorical, non-literal, representative, emblematic, imagistic.
– OPPOSITES literal.

figure n **❶** NUMBER, numeral, digit, integer, sum, value, symbol, cipher. **❷** COST, price, amount, value, total, sum, aggregate. **❸** SHAPE, form, outline, silhouette. **❹** BODY, physique, build, frame, torso, proportions. **❺** DIAGRAM, illustration, picture, drawing, sketch, chart, plan, map.
▶ v **❶** APPEAR, feature, play a part, be featured, be conspicuous. **❷** BE LIKELY, be probable, be understandable, make sense.

■ **figure out ❶** *See* CALCULATE. **❷** *See* UNDERSTAND (1).

file¹ n **❶** FOLDER, portfolio, box, document case, filing cabinet. **❷** DOSSIER, information, documents, records, data, particulars, case notes.
▶ v RECORD, enter, store, categorize, classify, put in place, put in order, put on record, pigeonhole.

file² n LINE, column, row, string, chain, queue.
▶ v WALK / MARCH IN A LINE, march, parade, troop, stream.

fill v **❶** OCCUPY ALL OF, crowd, overcrowd, congest, cram, pervade. **❷** PACK, load, stack, supply, furnish, provide, replenish, restock, refill. **❸** STOP UP, block up, plug, seal, bung up, close, clog. **❹** CARRY OUT, execute, perform, complete, fulfil.

film n **❶** MOVIE, picture, motion picture, video; *informal* flick. **❷** LAYER, coat, coating, covering, cover, dusting, sheet, blanket, skin, tissue, membrane, pellicle. **❸** HAZE, mist, cloud, blur, veil, murkiness.

filter n STRAINER, sieve, riddle, sifter, colander, gauze, netting.
▶ v STRAIN, sieve, sift, riddle, filtrate, clarify, purify, clear, refine.

filth n DIRT, muck, grime, mud, sludge, mire, slime, excrement, dung, manure, ordure, sewage, rubbish, refuse, garbage, trash, contamination, pollution; *informal* crud; *Brit. informal* gunge.

filthy adj DIRTY, unclean, mucky, muddy, slimy, murky, squalid, foul, nasty, polluted, contaminated, unwashed, grubby, dirt-encrusted, black, blackened, begrimed, rotten, decaying, smelly, fetid, putrid, faecal.
– OPPOSITES clean, spotless.

final adj **❶** LAST, closing, concluding, finishing, terminal, end, ultimate, eventual, end-

most. ❷ ABSOLUTE, conclusive, irrevocable, unalterable, incontrovertible, indisputable, decisive, definite, definitive, settled.
– OPPOSITES first.

finale n END, finish, close, conclusion, climax, culmination, denouement, last act, final scene, final curtain, epilogue; *informal* wind-up.

finalize v COMPLETE, conclude, settle, decide, agree on, work out, tie up, wrap up, put the finishing touches to, clinch, sew up.

finance n ❶ MONEY MATTERS, financial affairs, economics, commerce, business, investment, banking, accounting. ❷ MONEY, funds, cash, resources, assets, capital, wealth, wherewithal, revenue, stock. ▶ v PAY FOR, fund, back, support, subsidize, underwrite, capitalize, guarantee, provide capital for.

financial adj MONETARY, fiscal, pecuniary, economic, budgetary.

find v ❶ DISCOVER, come across, chance upon, stumble on, light on, bring to light, turn up, happen upon, come up with, hit upon, uncover, unearth, locate, lay one's hands on, encounter. ❷ OBTAIN, get, achieve, attain, acquire, gain, earn, procure. ❸ REALIZE, discover, learn, conclude, detect, observe, notice, note, perceive.

finding n DECISION, conclusion, verdict, judgement, pro-

nouncement, decree, order, recommendation.

fine adj ❶ EXCELLENT, first-class, first-rate, great, exceptional, outstanding, admirable, superior, magnificent, splendid, quality, beautiful, exquisite, choice, select, prime, supreme, rare; *informal* A1, top-notch; *Brit. informal, dated* top-hole. ❷ FAIR, dry, bright, clear, cloudless, sunny, balmy, clement. ❸ SHEER, light, lightweight, thin, flimsy, diaphanous, filmy, chiffony, gossamer, gauze-like, gauzy, transparent, translucent, airy, ethereal. ❹ ELEGANT, stylish, expensive, smart, chic, fashionable, modish, high-fashion, lavish. ❺ ALL RIGHT, satisfactory, acceptable, agreeable, convenient, suitable; *informal* OK.

finish v ❶ COMPLETE, conclude, accomplish, carry out, execute, discharge, deal with, do, get done, fulfil, achieve, attain, end, close, bring to a conclusion, finalize, terminate, round off, put the finishing touches to; *informal* wind up, wrap up, sew up, polish off, knock off. ❷ STOP, cease, give up, suspend, have done with, discontinue. ❸ USE, use up, consume, exhaust, empty, deplete, drain, expend, dispatch, dispose of.
– OPPOSITES start, begin.
▶ n ❶ END, completion, conclusion, close, closing, cessation, final act, finale, accomplishment, fulfilment, achievement, consummation, execution. ❷ SURFACE, veneer, coating,

texture, glaze, lustre, gloss,
polish, shine, patina.

finite adj LIMITED, restricted,
bounded, delimited, demarcated, subject to limitations,
determinate, measurable,
countable.
– OPPOSITES infinite.

fire n ❶ BLAZE, conflagration,
inferno, flames, combustion.
❷ GUNFIRE, sniping, bombardment, flak, shelling, barrage,
fusillade, salvo. ❸ PASSION, intensity, ardour, zeal, energy,
spirit, vivacity, sparkle, vigour,
fervour, enthusiasm.
▶ v ❶ SET FIRE TO, set on fire, set
alight, set ablaze, light, ignite,
kindle, put a match to.
❷ SHOOT, let off, discharge,
trigger. ❸ STIMULATE, animate,
arouse, rouse, stir up, excite,
enliven, inflame, inspire,
motivate, incite, galvanize,
electrify, impassion. ❹ DISMISS,
discharge, get rid of, oust,
depose, cashier; informal give
someone their marching
orders, show someone the door,
sack, give someone the sack,
axe, give someone the
bullet.

firebrand n TROUBLEMAKER,
agitator, rabble-rouser, demagogue, tub-thumper.

fireproof adj NON-FLAMMABLE,
non-inflammable, fireresistant, flame-resistant,
flame-retardant, incombustible, unburnable.
– OPPOSITES inflammable.

firm¹ adj ❶ HARD, hardened,
stiff, rigid, inflexible, unyielding, inelastic, resistant, solid,
solidified, compacted, compressed, condensed, dense,
close-grained, congealed,
frozen, set, jelled, stony.
❷ SETTLED, fixed, decided, definite, established, unalterable,
unchangeable. ❸ STRONG, vigorous, sturdy, powerful.
❹ CONSTANT, unchanging, enduring, abiding, durable, deeprooted, long-standing, longlasting, steady, stable, staunch.
❺ DETERMINED, resolute, decided,
resolved, unfaltering, unwavering, unflinching, unswerving,
unyielding, unbending, inflexible, obstinate, stubborn, obdurate, strict, intransigent,
unmalleable.
– OPPOSITES soft.

firm² n BUSINESS, company,
concern, establishment, organization, corporation, conglomerate, partnership; informal
outfit.

first adj ❶ INITIAL, earliest, original, introductory, opening,
primitive, premier, primordial,
primeval. ❷ BASIC, fundamental, rudimentary, key, cardinal,
primary, beginning.
– OPPOSITES last.
▶ adv ❶ AT FIRST, to begin with,
at the beginning, at the outset,
initially. ❷ FIRSTLY, before anything else, first and foremost,
in the first place.

fish v GO FISHING, angle, cast,
trawl.

fishy adj SUSPICIOUS, dubious,
questionable, doubtful, suspect, odd, queer, peculiar,

strange, not quite right; *informal* funny, shady, not kosher.

fit¹ adj **❶** WELL, healthy, in good health, in shape, in good shape, in good trim, in good condition, strong, robust, hale and hearty, sturdy, hardy, vigorous. **❷** CAPABLE, able, competent, good enough, adequate, ready, prepared, satisfactory, qualified, trained, equipped, worthy, eligible; *informal* up to scratch. **❸** FITTING, proper, seemly, decent, right, decorous, correct, apt, appropriate, suitable, apposite, relevant, pertinent.
– OPPOSITES unfit, inappropriate.
▶ v **❶** AGREE WITH, be in agreement with, accord with, concur with, correspond with, match, tally with, suit, go with, conform to, dovetail with, be consonant with, be congruent with. **❷** JOIN, connect, put together, put in place, fix, arrange, insert, adjust, shape.

fit² n **❶** CONVULSION, spasm, paroxysm, seizure, attack. **❷** BOUT, burst, outburst, outbreak.

fix v **❶** FASTEN, secure, attach, connect, join, couple, stick, glue, cement, pin, nail, screw, bolt, clamp, bind, tie, pinion, anchor, plant, embed, establish, position, station. **❷** DECIDE ON, settle, set, agree on, arrange, arrive at, determine, establish, name, specify. **❸** REPAIR, mend, put right, patch up, put to rights, restore, adjust, rectify, sort out, see to.
▶ n PREDICAMENT, difficulty,

quandary, plight, dilemma, trouble, muddle, mess, corner, tricky situation, tight spot; *informal* pickle, jam, hole, scrape; *Brit. informal* spot of bother.

fixation n OBSESSION, preoccupation, compulsion, complex, mania, monomania; *informal* hang-up, thing.

fizz v BUBBLE, effervesce, froth, sparkle, foam, fizzle, sputter.

fizzy adj BUBBLY, bubbling, sparkling, effervescent, gassy, carbonated.

flag¹ n STANDARD, ensign, banner, pennant, streamer, bunting, colours, pennon, gonfalon.

flag² v **❶** TIRE, become tired/weary, weaken, grow weak, lose one's strength. **❷** FADE, decline, fail, wane, diminish, ebb, decrease, taper off.

flagrant adj OBVIOUS, glaring, blatant, outrageous, shameless, disgraceful, shocking, scandalous, terrible, dreadful.

flair n **❶** ABILITY, capability, aptitude, facility, skill, talent, gift, knack, bent, genius. **❷** STYLE, panache, dash, elan, good taste, discrimination, discernment.

flap v FLUTTER, beat, thresh, thrash, wave, wag, agitate, waggle, swing, shake, oscillate.

flash v **❶** GLARE, beam, gleam, shine out, glint, sparkle, flicker, shimmer, twinkle, glimmer, glisten, scintillate, coruscate. **❷** SHOW OFF, flaunt, flourish, display, exhibit.

flat adj **❶** LEVEL, horizontal,

levelled, even, smooth, unbroken, plane. ❷ STRETCHED OUT, prone, spreadeagled, prostrate, supine, recumbent. ❸ DEFLATED, punctured, burst, collapsed, ruptured. ❹ MONOTONOUS, boring, dull, tedious, uninteresting, lifeless, dead, lacklustre, bland, insipid, vapid, prosaic. ❺ OUTRIGHT, direct, out-and-out, definite, positive, downright, firm, conclusive, utter, complete, categorical, unconditional.

flatten v ❶ LEVEL, level out/off, even out, smooth, compress, trample, press down, crush, squash, compact. ❷ DEMOLISH, tear down, knock down, raze, raze to the ground. ❸ KNOCK SOMEONE OFF THEIR FEET, knock to the ground, floor, prostrate, fell.

flatter v ❶ COMPLIMENT, praise, sing someone's praises, praise to excess, praise to the skies, pay court to, pay blandishments to, fawn upon, cajole, humour, flannel, wheedle; *informal* sweet-talk, soft-soap, butter up, lay it on thick, play up to.
– OPPOSITES insult.

flattering adj ❶ COMPLIMENTARY, adulatory, fulsome, laudatory, honeyed, sugary, ingratiating, cajoling. ❷ ENHANCING, becoming.
– OPPOSITES unflattering.

flattery n PRAISE, adulation, fulsomeness, unctuousness, fawning, puffery, cajolery, wheedling, compliments,

blandishments, honeyed words; *informal* sweet talk, soft soap, flannel.

flaunt v SHOW OFF, parade, display, exhibit, draw attention to, make a show of, wave, dangle, brandish.

flavour n ❶ TASTE, savour, tang, relish. ❷ FLAVOURING, seasoning, tastiness, tang, relish, piquancy, spiciness, zest. ❸ ATMOSPHERE, spirit, essence, nature, character, soul, quality, feel, feeling, ambience, tone, style.

flaw n ❶ SHORTCOMING, defect, imperfection, fault, failing, blemish, weakness, weak spot, foible. ❷ DEFECT, fault, crack, chip, fracture, break, crevice, fissure, rent, split, tear.
– OPPOSITES strength.

flawless adj ❶ PERFECT, impeccable, faultless. ❷ UNBLEMISHED, perfect, blemish-free, unmarred, unimpaired. ❸ PERFECT, whole, intact, sound, undamaged, unbroken.
– OPPOSITES imperfect, flawed.

flee v RUN AWAY, run off, make off, fly, take flight, beat a hasty retreat, bolt, abscond, retreat, depart hastily, make a quick exit, run for it, make a run for it, take off, take to one's heels, decamp, escape, make one's getaway, vanish; *informal* do a disappearing act, cut and run, beat it, skedaddle, split, scram, light out; *Brit. informal* scarper, do a bunk, do a runner.

fleeting adj BRIEF, short-lived, transient, momentary, rapid, swift, transitory, ephemeral, temporary, impermanent, here today and gone tomorrow, evanescent, fugitive, vanishing, flying, passing, flitting.
– OPPOSITES lasting.

flesh n MUSCLE, tissue, meat, brawn, body.

flexible adj ❶ BENDABLE, pliable, pliant, elastic, plastic, springy, mouldable, rubbery. ❷ SUPPLE, agile, limber, lithe, lissom, double-jointed. ❸ ADAPTABLE, adjustable, changeable, open to change, variable, open, open-ended, provisional, mutable. ❹ COOPERATIVE, accommodating, tractable, compliant, manageable, amenable, malleable, biddable, docile, submissive, yielding.
– OPPOSITES inflexible, rigid.

flick v ❶ STRIKE, hit, whip, rap, tap, touch. ❷ CLICK, switch, snap, flip.
■ **flick through** SKIM, glance over/through, browse through, thumb through.

flight n ❶ AVIATION, flying, air transport, aeronautics. ❷ FLOCK, group, skein, bevy, covey, migration.

flimsy adj ❶ INSUBSTANTIAL, fragile, frail, slight, makeshift, rickety, shaky, jerry-built, ramshackle, gimcrack. ❷ THIN, light, fine, delicate, lightweight, sheer, filmy, diaphanous, transparent, gossamer, gauzy. ❸ FEEBLE, weak, poor, inadequate, thin, unconvincing, transparent, implausible, unsatisfactory, trivial, shallow, paltry.
– OPPOSITES strong.

flinch v DRAW BACK, shrink back, pull back, start back, recoil, withdraw, shy away, cringe, cower, quail, crouch, wince, blench.
■ **flinch from** SHIRK, evade, avoid, shy away from, dodge, duck, baulk at.

fling v THROW, hurl, toss, pitch, cast, launch, catapult, propel, send flying, let fly, shy, lob; *informal* chuck, heave.

flippant adj FRIVOLOUS, glib, offhand, impertinent, insouciant, impudent, irreverent, superficial, carefree, thoughtless, shallow, cheeky, pert; *informal* flip.
– OPPOSITES serious.

flirt v CHAT UP, make eyes at, toy with, lead on, trifle with, dally with, tease.
▶ n COQUETTE, tease, vamp, heartbreaker, trifler, philanderer.

flirtatious adj PROVOCATIVE, teasing, coquettish, playful, amorous, philandering, come-hither.

float v ❶ STAY AFLOAT, be buoyant, sail, bob, glide, drift, slip. ❷ MOVE AIMLESSLY, drift, wander, meander; *N. Amer. informal* bum around.
– OPPOSITES sink.

flock n ❶ HERD, drove. ❷ FLIGHT, bevy, gaggle, skein. ❸ CROWD, gathering, assembly, group, company, collection, congregation, throng, mass, host, multitude, troop, convoy.

flog v WHIP, lash, horsewhip, flay, flagellate, birch, scourge, belt, cane, strap, thrash, beat, whack, wallop, chastise, trounce; *informal* tan someone's hide.

flood n ❶ DELUGE, torrent, inundation, spate, overflow, flash flood. ❷ ABUNDANCE, superabundance, profusion, glut, surfeit, plethora, superfluity; *informal* tons, heaps, loads.
– OPPOSITES trickle.
▶ v ❶ INUNDATE, deluge, pour over, immerse, submerge, swamp, drown, engulf, saturate. ❷ OVERSUPPLY, saturate, overfill, glut, overwhelm.
– OPPOSITES trickle.

floor n STOREY, level, tier, deck.

flop v ❶ COLLAPSE, slump, drop, fall, tumble, droop, sag, dangle. ❷ FAIL, be unsuccessful, be a disaster, miss the mark, founder, fall flat; *informal* bomb, go down like a lead balloon.
– OPPOSITES succeed.

florid adj ❶ RED, ruddy, flushed, high-coloured, rubicund, rubescent, erubescent. ❷ FLOWERY, over-elaborate, verbose, purple, grandiloquent.
– OPPOSITES pale, plain.

flounder v ❶ THRASH, struggle, blunder, stumble, fumble, grope. ❷ STRUGGLE, falter, be in difficulties, be confused, be in the dark, be out of one's depth.

flourish v ❶ BRANDISH, wave,

wield, swing, hold aloft, display, exhibit, flaunt, show off, parade, vaunt. ❷ THRIVE, grow, do well, develop, burgeon, bloom, blossom, bear fruit, flower, succeed, prosper.

flout v DEFY, disdain, scorn, show contempt for, scoff at, mock, laugh at, deride, ridicule, sneer at.
– OPPOSITES obey, observe.

flow v ❶ MOVE, course, run, go along, proceed, glide, stream, ripple, swirl, surge, sweep, roll, whirl, rush, drift, slide, trickle, gurgle. ❷ GUSH, stream, well, spurt, spout, squirt, spew, jet, spill, leak, seep, ooze, drip.
▶ n ❶ CURRENT, course, drift, stream, tide, spate. ❷ GUSH, stream, outflow, outpouring, welling.

flower n ❶ BLOOM, blossom, floweret, floret, annual, perennial. ❷ BEST, finest, pick, cream, elite.

fluctuate v ❶ RISE AND FALL, go up and down, see-saw, yo-yo, be unstable, vary, change, alter, swing, oscillate, ebb and flow, undulate. ❷ WAVER, vacillate, hesitate, change one's mind, blow hot and cold, shilly-shally, alternate, veer, teeter, totter; *Brit.* hum and haw.

fluent adj ❶ ARTICULATE, eloquent, silver-tongued, smooth-spoken, voluble. ❷ SMOOTH, flowing, fluid, natural, effortless, graceful, elegant, mellifluous, euphonious.
– OPPOSITES inarticulate.

fluff n DOWN, fuzz, lint, nap, pile, dust.

fluid adj ❶ LIQUID, liquefied, gaseous, gassy, melted, molten, running, flowing, uncongealed. ❷ SMOOTH, fluent, flowing, graceful, elegant, effortless, easy, natural. ❸ FLEXIBLE, open to change, adaptable, not fixed, adjustable, variable, mutable. ❹ UNSTABLE, likely to change, unsteady, fluctuating, shifting.
– OPPOSITES solid.
▶ n LIQUID, gas, solution.

flush v ❶ BLUSH, turn red, redden, colour, colour up, crimson, burn up, flame up, glow, suffuse with colour. ❷ WASH OUT, rinse out, cleanse, hose down, swab. ❸ EXPEL, eject.

fluster v AGITATE, ruffle, unsettle, upset, bother, put on edge, panic, disconcert, discompose, confuse, throw off balance, confound, nonplus; informal hassle, rattle, faze, throw into a tizz.

flutter v ❶ BEAT, flap, quiver, agitate, vibrate, ruffle. ❷ BAT, flicker, flit. ❸ FLAP, wave, flop, ripple, quiver, shiver, tremble.

fly v ❶ SOAR, take wing, take to the air, wing, wing its way, hover, swoop. ❷ DISPLAY, show, exhibit, wave, hoist, raise, hang out. ❸ DASH, race, rush, tear, bolt, zoom, dart, speed, hurry, career, hasten; informal hare off, be off like a shot. ❹ FLEE, run away, bolt, take flight, make off, abscond, beat a retreat, run for it, decamp, make one's escape; informal cut and run, skedaddle; Brit. informal scarper, do a bunk.

foam v FROTH, froth up, bubble, fizz, cream, lather, spume, effervesce.
▶ n FROTH, bubbles, fizz, head, spume, lather, effervescence, suds.

focus n ❶ CENTRE, central point, focal point, centre of attention, core, hub, pivot, magnet, cynosure. ❷ FOCAL POINT, point of conversion.
▶ v AIM, fix, concentrate, bring to bear, zero in on, zoom in on, centre, pinpoint, rivet.

foe n ENEMY, opponent, adversary, rival, antagonist, combatant, contestant.
– OPPOSITES friend.

fog n MIST, smog, haze, murk, murkiness, gloom; informal peasouper.

foggy adj ❶ MISTY, smoggy, dark, grey, dim, overcast, murky, hazy, gloomy. ❷ VAGUE, indistinct, cloudy, hazy, unclear, obscure, befuddled, confused, muddled, dazed.
– OPPOSITES clear.

foible n WEAKNESS, weak point, failing, shortcoming, flaw, blemish, defect, frailty, quirk, idiosyncrasy; informal hang-up.

foil v THWART, frustrate, stop, baffle, defeat, check, checkmate, circumvent, counter, baulk, disappoint, impede, obstruct, hamper, hinder.

fold n ❶ LAYER, pleat, overlap, turn, gather, crease, knife-edge.

2 WRINKLE, pucker, furrow, crinkle, crows feet.
▶ v **1** DOUBLE UP, turn under, turn up, bend, tuck, crease, gather, pleat, crimp, crumple. **2** WRAP, enfold, clasp, embrace, envelop, hug, squeeze. **3** FAIL, collapse, go out of business, go bankrupt, crash, go to the wall; *informal* go bust, go under, flop.

folk n PEOPLE, populace, population, citizenry, general public, public, clan, tribe.

follow v **1** GO / COME BEHIND, walk behind, go with, escort, accompany, keep pace with, attend, chase, pursue, run after, trail, shadow, hunt, stalk, track, dog, hound; *informal* tread on someone's heels, tail, tag after. **2** OBEY, observe, comply with, heed, conform to, pay attention to, stick to, adhere to, note, have regard to, mind, be guided by, accept, yield to. **3** RESULT FROM, arise from, be consequent on, develop from, ensue from, emanate from, issue from, proceed from, spring from, flow from. **4** UNDERSTAND, comprehend, take in, see, grasp, fathom, get, catch on to, appreciate. **5** BE A FOLLOWER OF, be a supporter of, be interested in, be devoted to, support, keep abreast of, keep up to date with.
■ **follow through** CONTINUE, complete, bring to completion, see something through. **follow up** INVESTIGATE, research, find out about, look into, check out, pursue.

following adj NEXT, ensuing,

succeeding, subsequent, successive.
▶ n SUPPORTERS, backers, fans, admirers, devotees, public, audience, adherents, patrons.

foment v INCITE, instigate, stir up, provoke, excite, arouse, encourage, initiate, agitate. *See also* STIMULATE.

fond adj **1** ADORING, devoted, loving, affectionate, caring, warm, tender, amorous, doting, indulgent. **2** FOOLISH, naive, deluded, delusory, absurd, vain, empty.
– OPPOSITES hostile.

fondle v CARESS, stroke, pat, pet, cuddle, hug, nuzzle.

food n NOURISHMENT, sustenance, nutriment, subsistence, diet, fare, menu, bread, board, provender, cooking, cuisine, foodstuffs, refreshments, edibles, meals, provisions, rations, stores, commons, comestibles, solids; *informal* nosh, grub, eats, chow; *Brit. informal* scoff; *dated* victuals.

fool n **1** IDIOT, dolt, dunce, ass, ignoramus, imbecile, simpleton; *informal* chump, booby, nincompoop, ninny, dunderhead, blockhead, fathead, halfwit, cretin, moron, dummy, numbskull, dimwit; *Brit. informal* twerp, clot, twit, nitwit. **2** DUPE, butt, laughing stock, gull, easy mark, cat's paw; *informal* stooge, sucker, pushover, sap, fall guy; *Brit. informal* mug.
▶ v **1** TRICK, deceive, hoax, make a fool of, dupe, take in, mislead, hoodwink, bluff,

delude, beguile, gull; *informal* con, bamboozle, kid, have on. ❷ PRETEND, make believe, feign, put on an act, sham, fake.

foolish adj SILLY, stupid, idiotic, senseless, brainless, dense, moronic, half-witted, doltish, imprudent, incautious, injudicious, irresponsible, mad, crazy, unwise, ill-advised, ill-considered; *informal* dotty, batty, nutty, dippy, screwy; *Brit. informal* daft, potty, barmy.
– OPPOSITES sensible.

foolproof adj INFALLIBLE, certain, sure, guaranteed, safe, dependable, trustworthy, neverfailing.

forbid v PROHIBIT, ban, bar, debar, outlaw, veto, proscribe, disallow, preclude, interdict, exclude, rule out, stop.
– OPPOSITES allow.

forbidden adj PROHIBITED, out of bounds, banned, outlawed, vetoed, proscribed, taboo, debarred, interdicted.

forbidding adj ❶ STERN, harsh, grim, hard, tough, hostile, unfriendly, disagreeable, nasty, mean, repellent, offputting. ❷ FRIGHTENING, ominous, threatening, menacing, sinister, daunting, foreboding.
– OPPOSITES friendly.

force n ❶ POWER, strength, vigour, energy, potency, muscle, might, effort, impact, exertion, pressure, stamina, vitality, stimulus, dynamism. ❷ COERCION, duress, compulsion, pressure, constraint, enforcement, violence; *informal*

arm-twisting. ❸ PERSUASIVENESS, validity, weight, effectiveness, influence, power, strength, vehemence, efficacy; *informal* punch, bite. ❹ DETACHMENT, unit, squad, squadron, battalion, division, regiment, army, patrol.
▶ v ❶ COMPEL, coerce, make, bring pressure on, use force on, pressure, pressurize, impel, drive, oblige, necessitate, constrain, urge, press-gang; *informal* use strong-arm tactics on, put the squeeze on. ❷ DRIVE, push, propel, thrust, shove, press. ❸ WREST, extract, extort, wring, drag.

forceful adj ❶ POWERFUL, vigorous, strong, potent, dynamic, energetic, assertive. ❷ PERSUASIVE, telling, convincing, compelling, effective, cogent, impressive, valid.
– OPPOSITES weak, unconvincing.

forecast v PREDICT, foretell, foresee, prophesy, forewarn, prognosticate, augur, divine, guess, conjecture, speculate, calculate.
▶ n PREDICTION, prophecy, prognostication, augury, prognosis, guess, conjecture, projection.

foregoing adj PRECEDING, prior, previous, former, above, aforesaid, antecedent, anterior.

foreign adj ❶ OVERSEAS, distant, remote, alien, exotic. ❷ STRANGE, unfamiliar, unknown, exotic, outlandish, odd, peculiar, curious. ❸ IRRELEVANT, unrelated, not pertinent,

unconnected, inappropriate, extraneous, outside, extrinsic, inappropriate.
– OPPOSITES domestic, native, familiar.

foreigner n ALIEN, non-native, immigrant, incomer, new-comer, stranger, outsider.
– OPPOSITES native.

foremost adj LEADING, principal, premier, top, first, primary, front, paramount, chief, main, most important, supreme, highest.

forerunner n PREDECESSOR, precursor, antecedent, ancestor, forefather, harbinger, herald, usher, advance guard.

foreshadow v FOREBODE, bode, presage, augur, portend, indicate, show, signify, point to, prefigure, promise.

foresight n FAR-SIGHTEDNESS, perspicacity, anticipation, forethought, presence of mind, preparedness, readiness, prescience, provision, discernment, care, caution.

forest n WOODLAND, wood, woods, trees, plantation.

forestall v PRE-EMPT, anticipate, intercept, thwart, frustrate, stave off, ward off, fend off, prevent, avert, hinder, impede, obstruct; informal steal a march on, get ahead of.

foretell v PREDICT, forecast, prophesy, foresee, forewarn, prognosticate, augur, divine. ❷ PRESAGE, augur, forebode, portend, foreshadow, prefigure, point to, indicate, betoken.

forethought n FORESIGHT, far-sightedness, anticipation, provision, circumspection, prudence, judiciousness, care, precaution.

forever adv ALWAYS, evermore, ever, for all time, until the end of time, eternally, perpetually; informal till the cows come home, till hell freezes over, for keeps, for good and all.

forfeit n FINE, penalty, confiscation, damages, loss, relinquishment.
▶ v GIVE UP, hand over, relinquish, be stripped of.

forge v ❶ BEAT INTO SHAPE, hammer out, shape, form, fashion, mould, cast, found, make, manufacture, frame, construct, create. ❷ FAKE, fabricate, falsify, counterfeit, copy, imitate.

forgery n FAKE, counterfeit, sham, fraud, imitation, reproduction; informal phoney.

forget v ❶ FAIL TO REMEMBER, lose track of, overlook, let slip. ❷ DISREGARD, put out of one's mind, ignore, let bygones be bygones. ❸ LEAVE BEHIND, omit to take, overlook.
– OPPOSITES remember.

forgetful adj ❶ ABSENT-MINDED, vague, apt to forget, abstracted, amnesiac. ❷ NEGLECTFUL, negligent, careless, heedless, unmindful, inattentive, lax, remiss, oblivious.

forgive v PARDON, excuse, absolve, exonerate, acquit, let off, let bygones be bygones, bury the hatchet, bear no malice, harbour no grudge; *informal* let someone off the hook.

forgiveness n PARDON, amnesty, reprieve, absolution, exoneration, acquittal, remission, clemency, tolerance, compassion, exculpation, indulgence, leniency.

forgiving adj MERCIFUL, lenient, magnanimous, understanding, compassionate, humane, clement, soft-hearted, forbearing, tolerant, mild.
– OPPOSITES unforgiving.

forgo v DO / DO WITHOUT, waive, renounce, sacrifice, relinquish, abjure, surrender, cede, abandon, yield, abstain from, refrain from, eschew; *formal* forswear.

fork v BRANCH, branch off, diverge, bifurcate, divide, split, separate, go separate ways, divaricate.

forlorn adj UNHAPPY, sad, miserable, wretched, pathetic, woebegone, disconsolate, lonely, cheerless, desolate, pitiable, pitiful, uncared for.

form n ❶ SHAPE, formation, configuration, structure, construction, conformation, arrangement, appearance, exterior. ❷ APPEARANCE, shape, character, guise, description, manifestation, semblance. ❸ TYPE, kind, sort, variety, species, genre, stamp, kidney, genus. ❹ STRUCTURE, organization, order, planning, symmetry, proportion, orderliness, framework, format. ❺ CONDITION, fitness, health, shape,

trim, fettle. ❻ APPLICATION, document, paper, sheet of paper.
▶ v ❶ MAKE, fashion, shape, model, mould, forge, construct, build, assemble, put together, set up, erect, produce, concoct. ❷ DEVISE, formulate, think up, plan, draw up, frame, hatch, forge, develop, organize, dream up. ❸ BRING ABOUT, set up, establish, found, organize, institute, inaugurate. ❹ TAKE SHAPE, appear, materialize, show, become visible, come into being. ❺ ACQUIRE, get into, contract, develop, get, pick up, grow into.

formal adj ❶ CORRECT, proper, conventional, reserved, aloof, remote, precise, exact, punctilious, stiff, unbending, inflexible, stand-offish, prim, stuffy, strait-laced. ❷ OFFICIAL, set, fixed, conventional, standard, regular, customary, approved, prescribed, pro forma, legal, lawful, ceremonial, ritual. ❸ ORDERLY, arranged, symmetrical, regular, methodical.
– OPPOSITES informal.

formation n ❶ ARRANGEMENT, pattern, order, grouping, configuration, structure, format, layout, disposition, design. ❷ ESTABLISHMENT, setting up, institution, founding, creation, inauguration. ❸ COMPOSITION, make-up, constitution, organization.

former adj ❶ PREVIOUS, prior, preceding, earlier, late, sometime, erstwhile, one-time, foregoing, antecedent, anterior, ci-devant; *formal* quondam.

❷ EARLIER, past, long past, bygone, long departed, long gone, old, ancient, of yore.

formidable adj ❶ INTIMIDATING, daunting, alarming, frightening, terrifying, horrifying, dreadful, awesome, fearsome, menacing, threatening, dangerous; *informal* scary. ❷ STRONG, powerful, impressive, mighty, great, redoubtable, terrific, indomitable, invincible. ❸ DIFFICULT, arduous, onerous, tough, mammoth, colossal, challenging, overwhelming, staggering.
– OPPOSITES weak, easy.

formula n ❶ FORM OF WORDS, set expression, wording, rubric, formulary. ❷ RECIPE, prescription, method, blueprint, procedure, convention, modus operandi, ritual, principles, rules, precepts, rubric.

formulate v ❶ DRAW UP, work out, plan, map out, prepare, compose, devise, think up, conceive, create, invent, coin, design. ❷ DEFINE, state clearly, set down, frame, give form to, specify, itemize, detail, indicate, systematize.

forsake v ❶ DESERT, abandon, leave, quit, jilt, throw over, cast off, discard, repudiate, reject, disown; *informal* leave in the lurch, leave flat. ❷ GIVE UP, renounce, relinquish, forgo, turn one's back on, repudiate, have done with, discard, set aside.

forthcoming adj ❶ FUTURE, coming, expected, prospective, imminent, impending.

❷ COMMUNICATIVE, informative, talkative, expansive, voluble, chatty, loquacious, open.

forthright adj DIRECT, frank, open, candid, blunt, outspoken, plain-speaking, plain-spoken, straightforward, honest.
– OPPOSITES evasive.

fortify v ❶ BUILD DEFENCES ROUND, protect, secure, garrison, cover, guard, buttress, shore up. ❷ STRENGTHEN, invigorate, energize, revive, embolden, give courage to, encourage, cheer, hearten, buoy up, reassure, make confident, brace, sustain.

fortitude n STRENGTH, firmness, courage, nerve, grit, backbone, bravery, pluck, mettle, fearlessness, valour, intrepidity, stout-heartedness, forbearance, tenacity, perseverance, resolution, resoluteness, determination.
– OPPOSITES cowardice.

fortunate adj LUCKY, blessed, favoured, in luck, having a charmed life, happy, felicitous, prosperous, well off, successful, flourishing; *informal* sitting pretty, born with a silver spoon in one's mouth; *Brit. informal* jammy.

fortune n ❶ WEALTH, affluence, treasure, opulence, prosperity, riches, property, assets, means, possessions. ❷ HUGE AMOUNT, mint, king's ransom; *informal* packet, bundle, bomb, pile. ❸ CHANCE, accident, luck, coincidence, happy chance,

fortuity, serendipity, contingency, providence.
– OPPOSITES pittance.

fortune-teller n SEER, soothsayer, prophet, prophetess, augur, diviner, sibyl, oracle, clairvoyant, astrologer.

forward adj ❶ ONWARD, advancing, progressing, progressive, frontal. ❷ ADVANCED, well advanced, early, premature, precocious. ❸ FRONT, at the front/fore, fore, frontal, foremost, head, leading, advance. ❹ BOLD, brash, brazen, audacious, presumptuous, cocky, familiar, assertive, confident, overweening, aggressive, pushy, thrusting, pert, impudent, impertinent, cheeky, insolent; informal brass-necked, fresh.
– OPPOSITES backward, shy.
▶ adv ❶ TOWARDS THE FRONT, onward, onwards, on, ahead, forth. ❷ OUT, into view, into the open, into public view.
▶ v ❶ SEND ON, pass on, dispatch, transmit, post, mail, ship, freight, deliver. ❷ ADVANCE, further, hasten, speed up, hurry along, accelerate, expedite, step up, aid, assist, help, encourage, foster, promote, favour, support, back, give backing to.

foster v ❶ ENCOURAGE, promote, further, stimulate, boost, advance, forward, cultivate, foment, help, aid, assist, support, uphold, back, give backing to, facilitate. ❷ BRING UP, rear, raise, care for, look after, take care of, mother,

parent. ❸ CHERISH, harbour, hold, entertain, nurse, nourish, nurture, sustain.

foul adj ❶ DISGUSTING, revolting, repulsive, nauseating, sickening, loathsome, odious, abominable, offensive, nasty. ❷ EVIL-SMELLING, stinking, high, rank, fetid; poetic/literary mephitic, noisome. ❸ IMPURE, contaminated, polluted, adulterated, infected, tainted, defiled, filthy, dirty, unclean. ❹ BLASPHEMOUS, profane, obscene, vulgar, offensive, coarse, filthy, indecent, indelicate, smutty, salacious, suggestive, off colour, low, ribald, lewd, scatological; informal blue. ❺ ABHORRENT, detestable, hateful, loathsome, despicable, contemptible, offensive, odious, disgusting, revolting, dishonourable, disgraceful, base, low, mean, sordid, vile, wicked, heinous, execrable, iniquitous, nefarious, infamous. ❻ UNFAIR, dishonourable, dishonest, underhand, unsportsmanlike, unsporting, dirty, unprincipled, unscrupulous, immoral, fraudulent; informal crooked.
▶ v DIRTY, soil, stain, blacken, muddy, begrime, smear, spatter, besmear, defile, pollute, contaminate, taint, sully; poetic/literary besmirch.

found v ESTABLISH, set up, institute, originate, initiate, bring into being, create, start, inaugurate, constitute, endow, organize, develop.

foundation n ❶ BASE,

bottom, substructure, bedrock, substratum, understructure, underpinning. ❷ BASIS, groundwork, principles, fundamentals, rudiments.
❸ ESTABLISHMENT, founding, institution, inauguration, initiation, constitution, endowment.

founder n ESTABLISHER, builder, constructor, maker, initiator, instigator, beginner, inventor, discoverer, framer, designer, architect, creator, author, originator, organizer, developer, generator, prime mover, father, patriarch.

fountain n ❶ SPRAY, jet, spout, well, fount, stream, fountainhead. ❷ SOURCE, fount, fountainhead, origin, wellspring, commencement, beginning, cause, birth, genesis, root, mainspring, derivation, inception, inspiration.

fractious adj BAD-TEMPERED, cross, irritable, ill-humoured, ill-natured, petulant, testy, querulous, touchy, irascible, sulky, sullen, morose; informal snappish.

fracture n BREAK, breakage, rupture, split, crack, fissure, cleft, rift, rent, chink, crevice, gap, opening, aperture.
▶ v BREAK, crack, split, rupture, splinter.

fragile adj ❶ FLIMSY, breakable, frail, delicate, insubstantial, brittle, dainty, fine. ❷ ILL, unwell, sickly, ailing, delicate, weak, infirm.
– OPPOSITES strong.

fragment n PIECE, part, particle, shred, chip, shard, sliver, splinter, scrap, bit, snip, snippet, wisp, tatter, remnant, remainder, fraction.
▶ v see BREAK v (1).

fragmentary adj INCOMPLETE, partial, piecemeal, disconnected, broken, disjointed, discontinuous, uneven, incoherent, scrappy, bitty, sketchy, unsystematic.
– OPPOSITES complete, whole.

fragrance n SCENT, smell, perfume, aroma, bouquet, balm, balminess; poetic/literary redolence.

fragrant adj SWEET-SMELLING, aromatic, scented, perfumed, balmy, odorous, odoriferous; poetic/literary redolent.
– OPPOSITES smelly.

frail adj ❶ FRAGILE, breakable, delicate, easily broken; formal frangible. ❷ WEAK, infirm, ill, unwell, sickly, ailing, delicate, slight, slender, puny, unsound.
– OPPOSITES strong, robust.

frame n ❶ STRUCTURE, framework, foundation, body, chassis, skeleton, scaffolding, shell, casing, support. ❷ BODY, physique, build, figure, shape, size, carcass. ❸ MOUNT, mounting, setting, border.
▶ v ❶ FORMULATE, put together, draw up, plan, think up, draft, map out, shape, compose, form, devise, create, establish, conceive. ❷ INCRIMINATE, fabricate charges/evidence against; Brit. informal fit up.

framework n ❶ See FRAME n

(1). ❷ ORDER, organization, frame, scheme, fabric.

frank adj ❶ CANDID, direct, straightforward, plain, plain-spoken, straight, outspoken, blunt, open, sincere, honest, truthful, artless, guileless, explicit, downright. ❷ OPEN, obvious, transparent, patent, undisguised, manifest, unmistakable, evident, noticeable, visible.
– OPPOSITES evasive.

frantic adj DISTRAUGHT, overwrought, panic-stricken, panicky, beside oneself, at one's wits' end, frenzied, wild, hysterical, frenetic, berserk, worked up, fraught, distracted, agitated, distressed, out of control, uncontrolled, unhinged, mad, crazed, out of one's mind, maniacal.
– OPPOSITES calm.

fraud n ❶ FRAUDULENCE, sharp practice, cheating, swindling, crookedness, embezzlement, trickery, deceit, double-dealing, duplicity, treachery, chicanery, imposture, skulduggery; informal monkey business. ❷ RUSE, trick, deception, swindle, hoax, subterfuge, wile, stratagem, artifice. ❸ IMPOSTOR, fake, sham, cheat, cheater, swindler, trickster, charlatan, quack, mountebank; informal phoney, con man.

fraudulent adj DISHONEST, cheating, swindling, criminal, deceitful, double-dealing, duplicitous, unscrupulous, dis-

honourable; informal crooked, shady, sharp.
– OPPOSITES honest.

fraught adj ❶ FILLED WITH, full of, attended by, teeming with, accompanied by. ❷ ANXIOUS, distraught, overwrought, agitated, worked up, distracted, distressed.

fray v ❶ UNRAVEL, wear, wear thin, wear out/away, become threadbare, become tattered/ragged. ❷ STRAIN, tax, overtax, irritate, put on edge, make edgy/tense.

freak n ❶ ABERRATION, abnormality, oddity, irregularity, monster, monstrosity, mutant, malformation. ❷ ODDITY, peculiar person; informal queer fish, odd bod, oddball, weirdo, nutcase, nut. ❸ FAN, enthusiast, fanatic, addict, aficionado, devotee; informal buff, fiend, nut.
▶ adj ABNORMAL, unusual, aberrant, atypical, exceptional, unaccountable, unpredictable, unforeseeable, bizarre, queer, odd, unparalleled, fluky.

free adj ❶ FREE OF CHARGE, complimentary, for nothing, without charge, gratis, at no cost, for free, on the house. ❷ AVAILABLE, unoccupied, at leisure, with time on one's hands, with time to spare. ❸ UNOCCUPIED, empty, vacant, available, spare, untaken, uninhabited. ❹ INDEPENDENT, self-governing, autonomous, sovereign, emancipated, democratic, enfranchised. ❺ AT LIBERTY, at large, loose, on the loose,

unconfined, unchained, unrestrained, unshackled, unfettered. ❻ UNOBSTRUCTED, unimpeded, clear, unblocked, unhampered. ❼ FAMILIAR, overfamiliar, bold, assertive, presumptuous, cocky, forward, cheeky, aggressive, impudent.
▶ v ❶ SET FREE, release, let go, set at liberty, liberate, turn loose, untie, unchain, unfetter, unshackle, uncage, unleash, deliver. ❷ RESCUE, release, extricate, get loose, disentangle, disengage, disencumber. ❸ EXEMPT, make exempt, excuse, except, relieve.
■ free off/from WITHOUT, devoid of, lacking in, exempt from, not liable to, safe from, immune to, unaffected by, clear of, unencumbered by, relieved of, released from, rid of.

freedom n ❶ LIBERTY, emancipation, release, deliverance, independence, autonomy, sovereignty, self-government, enfranchisement; *historical* manumission. ❷ SCOPE, latitude, flexibility, wide margin, elbow room, licence, facility, free rein. ❸ NATURALNESS, openness, lack of reserve, informality, lack of ceremony, spontaneity.
– OPPOSITES captivity.

freeze v ❶ ICE OVER / UP, glaciate, solidify, harden. ❷ CHILL, cool, make cold, deep-freeze. ❸ STAND STILL, stop dead, stop in one's tracks, go rigid, become motionless. ❹ FIX, hold, peg, suspend.

freezing adj BITTERLY COLD,

chilling, frosty, glacial, arctic, wintry, raw, biting, piercing, penetrating, cutting, numbing, Siberian.

freight n CARGO, load, consignment, lading, merchandise, goods.

frenzy n MADNESS, mania, insanity, wild excitement, wildness, hysteria, agitation, distraction, fit, seizure, paroxysm, outburst, spasm.

frequent adj ❶ MANY, numerous, several, repeated, recurrent, persistent, continuing, quite a lot/few. ❷ REGULAR, habitual, common, customary, usual, familiar, everyday, continual, constant, incessant.
– OPPOSITES infrequent.
▶ v VISIT, attend, haunt, patronize; *informal* hang out at.

fresh adj ❶ NATURAL, unprocessed, raw, newly harvested, crisp, unwilted, undried, uncured. ❷ NEW, brand new, recent, latest, up to date, modern, new-fangled, innovative, different, original, novel, unusual, unconventional, unorthodox. ❸ ENERGETIC, vigorous, invigorated, lively, vibrant, spry, sprightly, bright, alert, bouncing, refreshed, rested, restored, revived, fresh as a daisy; *informal* full of beans, bright-eyed and bushy-tailed. ❹ ADDITIONAL, more, further, extra, supplementary. ❺ HEALTHY, clear, bright, wholesome, blooming, glowing, fair, rosy, pink, ruddy. ❻ CLEAR, bright, cool, crisp, sparkling, pure, clean, refreshing.

❼ FAMILIAR, overfamiliar, forward, presumptuous, cocky, bold, audacious, brazen, cheeky, impudent, impertinent, insolent, disrespectful; *informal* brass-necked.

– OPPOSITES stale, old, tired.

fret v **❶** WORRY, be upset, be distressed, be anxious, agonize, pine, brood, mope, fuss, complain, grumble, whine. **❷** *See* ANNOY (2).

friction n **❶** ABRASION, attrition, rubbing, chafing, scraping, rasping. **❷** DISSENSION, dissent, disagreement, discord, strife, conflict, contention, dispute, argument, quarrelling, bickering, squabbling, hostility, rivalry, animosity, antagonism, resentment, bad feeling.

– OPPOSITES harmony.

friend n COMPANION, crony, bosom friend, comrade, playmate, soul mate, intimate, confidante, alter ego, ally, acquaintance, associate, familiar, shadow; *informal* pal, chum; *Brit. informal* mate; *N. Amer. informal* buddy.

– OPPOSITES enemy.

friendless adj ALONE, companionless, by oneself, lone, lonely, lonesome, with no one to turn to, solitary, with no ties, unattached, single, forlorn, unpopular, unloved, forsaken, deserted, ostracized, abandoned.

friendliness n AMIABILITY, affability, geniality, warmth, affection, companionability,

cordiality, conviviality, sociability, neighbourliness, approachability, communicativeness, good-naturedness, amenability, benevolence.

– OPPOSITES hostility.

friendly adj **❶** AMIABLE, affable, warm, genial, agreeable, companionable, cordial, convivial, sociable, hospitable, comradely, neighbourly, outgoing, approachable, accessible, communicative, open, unreserved, easy-going, good-natured, kindly, benign, amenable, well disposed, sympathetic, benevolent; *informal* chummy; *Brit. informal* matey. **❷** AMICABLE, close, cordial, congenial, intimate, familiar, peaceable, conciliatory.

– OPPOSITES unfriendly.

friendship n **❶** CLOSE RELATIONSHIP, companionship, intimacy, rapport, affinity, attachment, alliance, harmony, fellowship, mutual understanding, amity, comradeship. **❷** FRIENDLINESS, affability, amiability, warmth, geniality, cordiality, neighbourliness, good-naturedness, kindliness.

fright n **❶** FEAR, terror, alarm, horror, dread, fearfulness, apprehension, trepidation, consternation, dismay, disquiet, nervousness, panic; *informal* blue funk, jitters, heebie-jeebies, willies. **❷** SCARE, shock, shivers.

frighten v SCARE, terrify, startle, alarm, terrorize, give a shock to, shock, panic, appal, throw into a panic, unnerve, unman, intimidate, cow, daunt, dismay, make someone's blood run cold, freeze someone's blood; *informal* scare the living daylights out of, scare stiff, scare someone out of their wits, scare witless, make someone's hair stand on end, make someone's hair curl, throw into a blue funk, make someone jump out of their skin, spook; *Brit. informal* put the wind up.

frightful adj ❶ DREADFUL, terrible, horrible, horrid, hideous, ghastly, gruesome, grisly, macabre, grim, dire, abhorrent, revolting, repulsive, loathsome, odious, fearful, fearsome, terrifying, alarming, shocking, harrowing, appalling, daunting, unnerving. ❷ DISAGREEABLE, unpleasant, dreadful, horrible, terrible, awful, ghastly, insufferable, unbearable, annoying, irritating. ❸ VERY BAD, terrible, dreadful, awful, ghastly, nasty.

frigid adj ❶ COLD, icy, distant, austere, aloof, remote, unapproachable, forbidding, stiff, formal, unbending, cool, unfeeling, unemotional, unfriendly, hostile, unenthusiastic. ❷ PASSIONLESS, cold, unresponsive, passive. ❸ VERY COLD, bitterly cold, freezing, frozen, icy, frosty, chilly, wintry, arctic, glacial, Siberian, polar, gelid.

fringe n ❶ BORDER, frill, ruffle, gathering, trimming, tassels, edging. ❷ OUTER EDGE, edge, border, perimeter, periphery, margin, rim, limits, outskirts, verge.

frisky adj LIVELY, bouncy, active, playful, spirited, romping, rollicking, sportive, in high spirits, high-spirited, exuberant, joyful, sprightly, perky, jaunty; *informal* full of beans; *poetic/literary* frolicsome.

frivolity n ❶ LIGHT-HEARTEDNESS, gaiety, levity, fun, silliness, foolishness. ❷ EMPTY-HEADEDNESS, frivolousness, giddiness, flightiness, dizziness, flippancy, silliness, zaniness.

frivolous adj ❶ SILLY, flighty, foolish, dizzy, facetious, flippant, senseless, giddy, light-hearted, merry, superficial, shallow, empty-headed, feather-brained. ❷ FLIPPANT, ill-considered, inane, facetious, superficial, shallow; *informal* flip.
– OPPOSITES serious.

frolic v GAMBOL, cavort, skip, frisk, caper, cut capers, dance, leap, romp, trip, prance, hop, jump, bounce, rollick, sport, curvet.

▶ n ROMP, lark, antics, caper, escapade, prank, revels, spree, high jinks.

front n ❶ FACE, facade, frontage, fore, forepart, foremost part, forefront, foreground, anterior. ❷ HEAD, top, lead, beginning. ❸ FRONT LINE, vanguard, van, firing line. ❹ COVER, blind, facade, disguise, pretext, mask.
– OPPOSITES back.

▶ adj LEADING, lead, first, foremost.

■ **front on** FACE TOWARDS, look out on, overlook, lie opposite to.

frontier n BORDER, boundary, limit, edge, rim, bounds, confines, marches.

frosty adj ❶ FREEZING, frozen, cold, glacial, frigid, arctic, icy, wintry, bitter. ❷ UNFRIENDLY, cold, unwelcoming, unenthusiastic, icy, glacial.

froth n FOAM, fizz, lather, head, scum, effervescence, bubbles, suds, spume.

frown v ❶ SCOWL, glare, glower, knit one's brows, lower, lour; informal look daggers at, give a dirty look to. ❷ DISAPPROVE OF, view with dislike/disfavour, dislike, not take kindly to, not think much of, take a dim view of, look askance at.

frugal adj THRIFTY, economical, sparing, careful, prudent, abstemious, scrimping, niggardly, cheese-paring, penny-pinching, miserly, parsimonious; informal stingy.
– OPPOSITES extravagant, spendthrift.

fruitful adj ❶ FERTILE, fecund, potent, abundant, flourishing, lush, copious, bountiful; poetic/literary bounteous. ❷ USEFUL, worthwhile, productive, well spent, profitable, advantageous, beneficial, rewarding, gainful, successful, effective.
– OPPOSITES barren, futile, fruitless.

fruition n FULFILMENT, realization, materialization, achieve-

ment, attainment, success, completion, consummation, actualization, perfection, maturation, maturity, ripening.

fruitless adj FUTILE, useless, vain, in vain, to no avail, worthless, pointless, abortive, to no effect, idle, ineffectual, ineffective, inefficacious, unproductive, unrewarding, profitless, unsuccessful, unavailing.
– OPPOSITES fruitful, productive.

frustrate v ❶ DISCOURAGE, dishearten, dispirit, depress, dissatisfy, make, discontented, anger, annoy, vex, irritate, embitter, irk. ❷ DEFEAT, thwart, obstruct, impede, hamper, hinder, check, block, counter, foil, baulk, forestall, disappoint, baffle, stymie, stop, cripple, spoil, circumvent.

fudge v EVADE, dodge, avoid, shift ground about.

fuel v SUPPLY WITH FUEL, fire, stoke up, charge, power.

fugitive n ESCAPEE, runaway, deserter, refugee, renegade.
▶ adj TRANSIENT, transitory, fleeting, ephemeral, passing, impermanent, momentary, short-lived, short, brief, evanescent, fugacious.

fulfil v ❶ ACCOMPLISH, achieve, carry out, execute, perform, discharge, complete, implement, finish, conclude, effect; formal effectuate. ❷ SATISFY, realize, attain, consummate. ❸ CONFORM TO, satisfy, fill, answer, meet, comply with, obey.

full adj ❶ FILLED UP, filled, filled to the brim, brimming, overflowing, filled to capacity. ❷ CROWDED, packed, crammed, solid with people, chock-a-block, chock-full; *informal* jam-packed. ❸ SATISFIED, sated, gorged, replete, glutted, cloyed. ❹ COMPLETE, entire, whole, comprehensive, thorough, exhaustive, detailed, all-inclusive, all-encompassing, extensive, unabridged. ❺ BAGGY, voluminous, loose-fitting, capacious. ❻ RICH, deep, resonant, loud, strong; *informal* fruity.
– OPPOSITES empty, incomplete.

fully adv COMPLETELY, entirely, wholly, totally, thoroughly, in all respects, utterly, amply, satisfactorily.

fumble v ❶ FAIL TO CATCH, miss, drop, mishandle, misfield. ❷ GROPE, feel about, search blindly, scrabble about/around.

fume v BE ENRAGED, seethe, boil, be livid, rage, rant and rave, be furious, be incensed, flare up; *informal* be up in arms, get hot under the collar, fly off the handle, foam at the mouth, get all steamed up, flip one's lid, blow one's top.

fumes pl n VAPOUR, gas, exhaust, smoke, pollution, smog, fog.

fun n ❶ AMUSEMENT, entertainment, recreation, relaxation, enjoyment, pleasure, diversion, play, playfulness, tomfoolery, buffoonery, distraction, good time, jollification, merrymaking, junketing; *informal* living it up, skylarking. ❷ MERRIMENT, gaiety, mirth, laughter, hilarity, glee, cheerfulness, gladness, jollity, joy, high spirits, zest.
– OPPOSITES misery.
■ **make fun of** RIDICULE, deride, mock, scoff at, sneer at, taunt, jeer at, lampoon, parody; *informal* send up, rib, take off.

function n ❶ ROLE, capacity, responsibility, duty, task, job, post, situation, office, occupation, employment, business, charge, province, concern, activity, operation, mission. ❷ SOCIAL EVENT, gathering, affair, reception, party; *informal* do; *Brit. informal* beanfeast.
▶ v WORK, go, run, be in working order, operate.

functional adj ❶ PRACTICAL, useful, serviceable, utilitarian, working, workaday, hard-wearing. ❷ WORKING, in working order, going, running, operative, in commission.

fund n RESERVE, collection, pool, kitty, endowment, foundation, grant, investment, capital, savings.
▶ v FINANCE, pay for, back, subsidize, stake, endow, support.

fundamental adj BASIC, rudimentary, elemental, underlying, primary, cardinal, initial, original, prime, first, principal, chief, key, central, structural, organic, inherent, intrinsic,

vital, essential, important, indispensable, necessary.
– OPPOSITES unimportant.

fundamentally adv BASICALLY, at heart, at bottom, deep down, essentially, intrinsically.

funds pl n MONEY, ready money, cash, hard cash, capital, the wherewithal, means, assets, resources, savings; *informal* dough, bread; *Brit. informal* dosh.

funny adj ❶ AMUSING, comical, comic, humorous, hilarious, entertaining, diverting, laughable, hysterical, side-splitting, witty, jocular, riotous, droll, absurd, rich, facetious, ludicrous, ridiculous, farcical, risible, silly, slapstick, waggish. ❷ PECULIAR, odd, strange, curious, queer, bizarre, mysterious, suspicious, dubious; *informal* weird.
– OPPOSITES serious.

furious adj ❶ ENRAGED, very angry, raging, infuriated, livid, fuming, boiling, incensed, inflamed, frenzied, indignant, mad, maddened, wrathful, beside oneself, in high dudgeon; *informal* hot under the collar, up in arms, foaming at the mouth. ❷ VIOLENT, fierce, wild, intense, vehement, unrestrained, tumultuous, tempestuous, stormy, turbulent, boisterous.
– OPPOSITES calm.

furnish v ❶ PROVIDE WITH FURNITURE, fit out, outfit, appoint. ❷ SUPPLY, provide, give, present, offer, equip, grant, bestow, endow, provision.

furniture n FURNISHINGS, house fittings, effects, movables, appointments, chattels.

furore n COMMOTION, uproar, disturbance, hullabaloo, turmoil, tumult, brouhaha, tempest, stir, excitement, outburst, outcry; *informal* to-do.

furrow n ❶ GROOVE, trench, channel, rut, trough, ditch, seam, hollow. ❷ CREASE, line, wrinkle, crinkle, corrugation, crow's foot.

further adj ADDITIONAL, more, extra, supplementary, other, new, fresh.
▶ adv FURTHERMORE, moreover, what's more, also, besides, additionally, as well, to boot, on top of that, over and above that, by the same token.
▶ v ADVANCE, forward, facilitate, aid, assist, help, lend a hand to, promote, back, contribute to, encourage, foster, champion.

furthest adj FARTHEST, furthermost, most distant, most remote, outermost, outmost, extreme, uttermost, ultimate.

furtive adj SECRETIVE, secret, stealthy, surreptitious, clandestine, sneaky, sneaking, hidden, disguised, shifty, skulking, covert, cloaked, conspiratorial, sly, underhand, under the table, wily.
– OPPOSITES open, above board.

fury n ❶ ANGER, rage, wrath, madness, passion, frenzy; *poetic/literary* ire. ❷ FIERCENESS, violence, ferocity, intensity, force, power, severity, turbulence, tempestuousness.

fuse v COMBINE, amalgamate, join, put together, unite, blend, intermix, intermingle, merge, coalesce, integrate, meld, compound, agglutinate, weld, solder.

– OPPOSITES separate.

fuss n FLUSTER, agitation, excitement, bother, commotion, stir, confusion, uproar, tumult, upset, worry; *informal* palaver, storm in a teacup, flap, tizzy, stew.

▶ V BE WORRIED / AGITATED, worry, rush about, dash about; *informal* get worked up, be in a tizzy, flap, be in a stew, make a big thing out of it.

fussy adj ❶ PARTICULAR, over-particular, finicky, pernickety, fastidious, hard to please, difficult, exacting, demanding, selective, discriminating, faddish; *informal* choosy, picky, nit-picking; *Brit. informal* faddy.

❷ CLUTTERED, busy, over-decorated, ornate, overdone, over-elaborate, rococo, over-embellished.

futile adj USELESS, vain, in vain, to no avail, ineffectual, unsuccessful, unproductive, unprofitable, abortive, unavailing, inefficacious, barren, impotent, hollow.

– OPPOSITES fruitful.

future n ❶ TIME TO COME, time ahead, hereafter, coming times. ❷ PROSPECTS, expectations, anticipation, outlook, likely success/advancement.

▶ adj FORTHCOMING, coming, impending, approaching, prospective, expected, planned, destined, awaited.

fuzzy adj ❶ DOWNY, down-covered, frizzy, woolly, furry, fleecy, fluffy, linty, napped. ❷ OUT OF FOCUS, unfocused, blurred, blurry, indistinct, unclear, misty, distorted, ill-defined, bleary.

Gg

gadget n APPLIANCE, apparatus, device, contrivance, mechanism, instrument, tool, implement, invention, contraption; *informal* widget, gizmo.

gaffe n MISTAKE, blunder, slip, indiscretion, faux pas, solecism, gaucherie; *informal*

clanger, howler, boo-boo; *Brit. informal* boob; *Brit. informal, dated* bloomer.

gag n JOKE, witticism, jest, quip, funny remark, hoax, prank; *informal* crack, wisecrack.

gaiety n ❶ CHEERFULNESS, light-heartedness, merriment, glee, happiness, high spirits, glad-

ness, delight, joy, joyfulness, joyousness, pleasure, exuberance, elation, jollity, hilarity, mirth, joviality, liveliness, animation, vivacity, effervescence, buoyancy, sprightliness, exultation; *poetic/literary* blitheness. ❷ COLOURFULNESS, brightness, sparkle, brilliance, glitter, showiness, gaudiness, garishness.
– OPPOSITES gloom.

gain v ❶ OBTAIN, get, acquire, secure, procure, attain, build up, achieve, arrive at, come to have, win, capture, pick up, net, reap, gather. ❷ INCREASE IN, add on, get more of. ❸ CATCH UP WITH, get nearer to, close in on, narrow the gap between, overtake, come up to, approach. ❹ REACH, arrive at, get to, come to, attain.
– OPPOSITES lose.
▶ n ❶ INCREASE, addition, rise, augmentation, increment, accumulation, accretion. ❷ PROFIT, earnings, income, advantage, benefit, reward, yield, return, winnings, proceeds, dividend, interest, emolument; *informal* pickings.

gainful adj PROFITABLE, rewarding, remunerative, lucrative, productive, beneficial, fruitful, advantageous, worthwhile, useful.

gait n WALK, step, stride, pace, tread, manner of walking, bearing, carriage.

gale n STORM, tempest, hurricane, squall, tornado, cyclone, typhoon.

gallant adj ❶ CHIVALROUS, gentlemanly, courtly, courteous, polite, attentive, gracious, considerate, thoughtful, obliging, deferential. ❷ BRAVE, courageous, valiant, bold, daring, plucky, fearless, intrepid, dashing, heroic, lionhearted, mettlesome.
– OPPOSITES rude, cowardly.

galvanize v ELECTRIFY, shock, stir, startle, jolt, arouse, awaken, spur, prod, stimulate, invigorate, fire, animate, vitalize, energize, thrill, inspire.

gamble v ❶ BET, wager, lay a bet, place a wager, stake, game, try one's luck; *informal* punt; *Brit. informal* have a flutter. ❷ TAKE A CHANCE / RISK, speculate, venture; *informal* stick one's neck out, go out on a limb, take a flier.

game n ❶ PASTIME, diversion, recreation, entertainment, amusement, sport, play, distraction, frolic, romp, fun, merriment. ❷ MATCH, contest, tournament, meeting, event, round, bout. ❸ BUSINESS, line, trade, occupation, profession, industry, activity, calling. ❹ WILD ANIMALS, quarry, prey, big game.

gang n GROUP, band, company, crowd, gathering, pack, horde, mob, herd.

gangly adj LANKY, rangy, skinny, angular, spindly, awkward.

gangster n RACKETEER, crook, criminal, hoodlum, Mafioso, gang member, mobster, robber, brigand, bandit, desperado,

gap n ❶ OPENING, hole, aperture, cavity, space, breach, break, fracture, rift, fissure, rent, cleft, chink, crack, crevice, divide, cranny, orifice, interstice. ❷ PAUSE, break, intermission, interval, interlude, lull, respite, breathing space, rest, suspension, hiatus, recess. ❸ OMISSION, blank, lacuna, void, vacuity. ❹ DIFFERENCE, disparity, inconsistency, incompatibility, disagreement, divergence, breach, discrepancy, distance, division.

gape v ❶ STARE, gaze, goggle, ogle; *informal* gawk, rubberneck. ❷ OPEN WIDE, open up, yawn, part, split, crack.

garb n CLOTHES, garments, clothing, dress, attire, costume, outfit, wear, uniform, vestments, livery, trappings; *informal* gear, get-up, togs, rig-out, duds; *formal* apparel; *archaic* habit.
▶ v CLOTHE, dress, attire, array, robe, cover, outfit, fit; *informal* kit out, rig out; *archaic* apparel.

garbage n WASTE, rubbish, refuse, litter, debris, junk, filth, detritus, scraps, leftovers, remains, slops.

garble v DISTORT, twist, warp, slant, doctor, falsify, pervert, corrupt, misstate, misquote, misreport, misrepresent, misinterpret, misunderstand.

garish adj FLASHY, flash, showy, loud, gaudy, lurid, bold, glaring, brassy, tinselly, vivid, tawdry, tasteless, in poor taste, vulgar.
– OPPOSITES sober, tasteful.

garner v GATHER, collect, accumulate, heap, pile up, amass, stack up, assemble, hoard, stockpile, deposit, husband, reserve, save, preserve.

garrison n ❶ FORCE, detachment, unit, brigade, platoon, squadron. ❷ BARRACKS, base, fort, fortress, fortification, stronghold, camp, encampment, citadel.
▶ v STATION, post, assign, position, billet, send in.

garrulous adj TALKATIVE, chatty, verbose, loquacious, long-winded, effusive; *informal* mouthy, gabby.
– OPPOSITES taciturn.

gash v CUT, slash, tear, lacerate, wound, gouge, incise, slit, rend, split, rent, nick, cleave.

gasp v PANT, puff, puff and blow, blow, catch one's breath, gulp, choke, fight for breath, wheeze; *informal* huff and puff.

gate n BARRIER, door, gateway, doorway, access, entrance, exit, opening, turnstile, passage, egress, portal, wicket, postern.

gather v ❶ COME TOGETHER, collect, assemble, congregate, meet, group, cluster, mass, crowd, flock together, convene, foregather, muster, converge, accumulate. ❷ CALL TOGETHER, summon, assemble, collect, convene, round up, muster, marshal. ❸ COLLECT, accumulate, assemble, amass, store, garner, stockpile, heap up, pile

up, stack up, hoard; *informal* stash away. ❹ UNDERSTAND, be given to understand, believe, hear, learn, infer, deduce, conclude, come to the conclusion, surmise, assume. ❺ HARVEST, pick, collect, reap, glean, garner, cull, pluck. ❻ INCREASE, grow, rise, build, expand, enlarge, swell, extend, intensify, deepen, heighten, thicken.
– OPPOSITES disperse.

gathering n ASSEMBLY, congregation, company, collection, group, crowd, band, throng, mass, horde, meeting, convention, conclave, rally, congress, convocation.

gauche adj AWKWARD, clumsy, ungainly, bumbling, maladroit, lumbering, inept, inelegant, unpolished, graceless, unsophisticated, uncultured, uncultivated.
– OPPOSITES sophisticated, adroit.

gaudy adj see GARISH.

gauge n ❶ SIZE, measure, extent, degree, capacity, magnitude, height, width, thickness, span, bore. ❷ MEASURE, basis, standard, guide, guideline, touchstone, yardstick, benchmark, criterion, rule, norm, example, model, pattern, exemplar, sample, test, indicator.

gaunt adj ❶ HAGGARD, drawn, cadaverous, skeletal, emaciated, skinny, skin and bone, spare, bony, angular, lanky, lean, raw-boned, spindly, pinched, hollow-cheeked,

scrawny, scraggy, wasted, shrivelled, withered. ❷ BLEAK, barren, desolate, bare, dreary, dismal, forlorn, grim, stern, harsh, forbidding.
– OPPOSITES fat, lush.

gay adj HOMOSEXUAL, lesbian, homoerotic; *informal* queer; *Brit. informal* bent, poofy.
– OPPOSITES gloomy, heterosexual.

gaze v STARE, gape, take a good look, look fixedly, goggle, stand agog, watch in wonder, ogle, eye, contemplate; *informal* gawk, rubberneck, give the once-over.

gear n ❶ EQUIPMENT, tools, kit, apparatus, implements, tackle, appliances, utensils, supplies, accessories, paraphernalia, accoutrements, contrivances, trappings; *informal* stuff. ❷ BELONGINGS, possessions, things, luggage, baggage, kit, effects, goods, paraphernalia, impedimenta, chattels.

genealogy n FAMILY TREE, ancestry, pedigree, line, lineage, descent, parentage, birth, derivation, extraction, family, strain, stock, bloodline, heritage, roots.

general adj ❶ USUAL, customary, common, ordinary, normal, standard, regular, everyday, typical, conventional, habitual, run-of-the-mill. ❷ COMMON, accepted, widespread, shared, broad, wide, prevalent, prevailing, universal, popular, public, generic, extensive. ❸ UNIVERSAL, blanket, comprehensive,

all-inclusive, across-the-board, broad-ranging, broad, sweeping, indiscriminate, catholic, encyclopedic. ❹ MIXED, assorted, miscellaneous, diversified, variegated, composite, heterogeneous. ❺ BROAD, loose, rough, approximate, non-specific, vague, ill-defined, indefinite, inexact, imprecise.
– OPPOSITES unusual, specific, detailed.

generally adv ❶ USUALLY, in general, as a rule, normally, ordinarily, almost always, customarily, habitually, typically, regularly, for the most part, mainly, by and large, on average, on the whole, in most cases. ❷ COMMONLY, widely, extensively, universally, comprehensively.

generate v CAUSE, give rise to, produce, make, bring into being, create, engender, originate, initiate, occasion, arouse, whip up, propagate.

generosity n LIBERALITY, kindness, magnanimity, benevolence, munificence, open-handedness, bounty, hospitality, charitableness, lavishness.

generous adj ❶ LIBERAL, kind, magnanimous, benevolent, munificent, beneficent, bountiful, hospitable, open-handed, charitable, ungrudging, lavish, unstinting, free-handed, princely; *poetic/literary* bounteous. ❷ NOBLE, magnanimous, high-minded, honourable, good, unselfish, altruistic, unprejudiced, disinterested.

❸ ABUNDANT, liberal, plentiful, lavish, ample, rich, copious, superabundant, overflowing.
– OPPOSITES mean, selfish, meagre.

genial adj AMIABLE, affable, friendly, sociable, congenial, amicable, convivial, good-humoured, good-natured, agreeable, warm, pleasant, cordial, amenable, well disposed, cheerful, cheery, kind, kindly, benign, happy, sunny, jovial, easy-going, sympathetic.
– OPPOSITES unfriendly.

genius n ❶ BRILLIANT PERSON, mental giant, prodigy, virtuoso, master, mastermind, maestro, intellectual, intellect, expert, adept; *informal* brain, Einstein. ❷ BRILLIANCE, intelligence, cleverness, capability, flair, talent, aptitude, ability, capacity, endowment.

genteel adj ❶ RESPECTABLE, refined, patrician, ladylike, gentlemanly, well bred, aristocratic, noble, blue-blooded, well born. ❷ POLITE, well mannered, courteous, mannerly, civil, gracious, decorous, courtly, polished, cultivated, stylish, elegant.
– OPPOSITES uncouth.

gentle adj ❶ TENDER, kind, kindly, humane, benign, merciful, lenient, compassionate, tender-hearted, placid, sweet-tempered, mild, serene, soft, quiet, tranquil, still, peaceful, pacific, meek, dove-like. ❷ MILD, moderate, light, temperate, soft, balmy. ❸ SOFT,

tender, light, smooth, soothing. ❹ PLACID, docile, tame, biddable, tractable, manageable, meek, easily handled, broken, trained, schooled. ❺ GRADUAL, slight, easy, imperceptible.
– OPPOSITES cruel, fierce, rough.

genuine adj ❶ REAL, authentic, true, pure, actual, bona fide, veritable, sound, pukka, sterling, legitimate, lawful, legal, valid, original, unadulterated, unalloyed; *informal* kosher, honest-to-goodness. ❷ SINCERE, truthful, honest, frank, candid, open, natural, unaffected, artless, ingenuous; *informal* upfront.
– OPPOSITES fake, insincere.

germ n ❶ MICROBE, micro-organism, bacillus, bacterium, virus; *informal* bug. ❷ BEGINNING, start, genesis, seed, embryo, root, bud, origin, source, fount, fountain, rudiment.

gesture n SIGNAL, motion, sign, wave, indication, gesticulation.
▶ v GESTICULATE, signal, make a sign, motion, wave, indicate.

get v ❶ ACQUIRE, obtain, come by, come into possession of, secure, procure, buy, purchase. ❷ RECEIVE, be sent, be given. ❸ GO FOR, fetch, bring, collect, carry, transport, convey. ❹ EARN, be paid, make, bring in, clear, gross, net, take home, pocket; *informal* pull in. ❺ CAPTURE, seize, arrest, apprehend, take, trap, lay hold of, grab, bag, take captive, grasp;

informal collar, nab; *Brit. informal* nick. ❻ COMPREHEND, grasp, see, fathom, work out, follow; *informal* make head or tail of, catch on, get the hang of. ❼ PERSUADE, induce, coax, talk into, wheedle into, prevail upon, influence, sway, convince, win over. ❽ BECOME, grow, come to be, turn.
– OPPOSITES lose.

■ **get ahead** SUCCEED, do well, make good, be successful, prosper, flourish, rise in the world. **get at** ❶ FIND FAULT WITH, pick on, criticize, carp, nag, taunt. ❷ SUGGEST, mean, imply, hint, intend, lead up to. **get by** SURVIVE, cope, manage, subsist, exist, get along, fare, make both ends meet; *informal* keep one's head above water, make out. **get out of** AVOID, dodge, evade, shirk, escape.

getaway n ESCAPE, flight, breakout, break, absconding.

ghastly adj ❶ TERRIBLE, horrible, frightful, dreadful, awful, horrid, horrendous, hideous, shocking, grim, gruesome, terrifying, frightening. ❷ LOATHSOME, odious, nasty, contemptible, dreadful, appalling, foul. ❸ VERY BAD, serious, grave, critical, unforgivable, awful, terrible.

ghost n ❶ APPARITION, spectre, spirit, phantom, wraith, shade; *informal* spook; *poetic/literary* phantasm. ❷ SUGGESTION, hint, trace, glimmer, shadow, impression, semblance.

ghostly adj SPECTRAL,

phantom, ghost-like, wraithlike, unearthly, supernatural, other-wordly, illusory, insubstantial, shadowy, eerie, creepy, scary, weird, uncanny; *informal* spooky; *poetic/literary* phantasmal.

giant n COLOSSUS, behemoth, man mountain, titan, Goliath. ▶ adj GIGANTIC, enormous, huge, colossal, immense, vast, mammoth, gargantuan, titanic, elephantine, prodigious, stupendous, Brobdingnagian; *informal* jumbo.

gibe n *see* JIBE.

giddy adj DIZZY, faint, light-headed, unsteady, reeling, vertiginous; *informal* woozy.

gift n ❶ PRESENT, offering, donation, contribution, grant, bonus, bounty, largesse, boon, gratuity, benefaction, bequest, legacy, inheritance, endowment. ❷ TALENT, aptitude, flair, facility, knack, bent, ability, faculty, capacity, capability, skill, attribute, expertise, genius, mind for.

gifted adj TALENTED, brilliant, clever, bright, intelligent, ingenious, sharp, able, accomplished, capable, masterly, skilled, adroit, proficient, expert; *informal* smart. – OPPOSITES inept.

gigantic adj *see* GIANT adj.

giggle v TITTER, snigger, snicker, chuckle, chortle, laugh, cackle; *informal* tee-hee.

gingerly adv CAUTIOUSLY, warily, carefully, attentively, heedfully, vigilantly, watch-fully, guardedly, prudently, circumspectly, judiciously, suspiciously, hesitantly, reluctantly, timidly, timorously. – OPPOSITES recklessly.

girl n ❶ YOUNG WOMAN, female, young lady, miss; *Scottish & N. English* lass, lassie; *informal* chick, filly; *Brit. informal* bird; *N. Amer. informal* babe, broad; *Austral./NZ informal* sheila. ❷ GIRLFRIEND, lover, sweetheart, mistress, inamorata.

girth n CIRCUMFERENCE, perimeter, size, bulk, measure.

gist n ESSENCE, substance, drift, sense, crux, significance, idea, import, core, quintessence, nucleus, kernel, nub, pith, marrow, burden.

give v ❶ PRESENT, hand, hand over, bestow, donate, contribute, confer, turn over, award, grant, accord, leave, will, bequeath, make over, entrust, consign, vouchsafe. ❷ PROVIDE, supply, furnish, proffer, offer. ❸ PRODUCE, yield, afford, result in. ❹ CAUSE, be a source of, make, create. ❺ LET OUT, utter, emit, issue, voice.

■ **give away** REVEAL, disclose, divulge, let slip, leak, let out, expose, uncover. **give in** GIVE UP, surrender, admit defeat, concede, yield, capitulate, submit, comply, succumb, retreat; *informal* quit. **give off** EMIT, send out, throw out, discharge, exude, release, vent, produce. **give up** STOP, cease, leave off, desist from, swear off, renounce, abandon, discontinue, *informal* quit, cut out, chuck; *formal* forswear.

glad adj ❶ HAPPY, pleased, delighted, thrilled, gratified, overjoyed, elated, satisfied, contented; *informal* over the moon, tickled pink; *Brit. informal* chuffed. ❷ WILLING, eager, ready, prepared, happy, pleased. ❸ WELCOME, joyful, cheering, happy, cheerful, pleasing, gratifying.
– OPPOSITES unhappy, reluctant.

gladden v MAKE HAPPY, delight, cheer, cheer up, hearten, brighten up, raise someone's spirits, please, elate, buoy up, give a lift to; *informal* buck up.
– OPPOSITES sadden.

glamorous adj ❶ ALLURING, dazzling, smart, elegant, beautiful, lovely, attractive, charming, fascinating, exciting, beguiling, bewitching, enchanting, entrancing, irresistible, tantalizing. ❷ EXCITING, fascinating, stimulating, thrilling, glossy, glittering; *informal* ritzy, glitzy.
– OPPOSITES dowdy, boring.

glamour n ❶ BEAUTY, loveliness, attractiveness, allure, attraction, elegance, charm, fascination. ❷ EXCITEMENT, allure, charm, fascination, enchantment, captivation, magic, spell.

glance v LOOK QUICKLY / HURRIEDLY, take a quick look, glimpse, catch a glimpse, peek, peep, sneak a look.

glare v ❶ SCOWL, glower, frown, look threateningly, look daggers, give someone dirty looks, lour. ❷ DAZZLE, beam, flare, blaze, flame.

glaring adj ❶ DAZZLING, blazing, flaring. ❷ OBVIOUS, conspicuous, manifest, overt, patent, visible, flagrant, blatant, outrageous, egregious, gross.

glass n TUMBLER, flute, schooner, balloon, goblet, beaker.

glasses pl n SPECTACLES, eye-glasses, bifocals, sunglasses, monocle, lorgnette, pince-nez, field glasses, binoculars, opera glasses.

glassy adj ❶ SHINY, glossy, smooth, mirror-like, clear, transparent, translucent, limpid, pellucid. ❷ GLAZED, blank, expressionless, empty, vacant, deadpan, vacuous, fixed, unmoving, lifeless, motionless.

glaze v VARNISH, coat, polish, enamel, lacquer, gloss, burnish. ▶ n GLOSS, lustre, finish, lacquer, enamel.

gleam v SHINE, radiate, flash, glow, glint, flare, glisten, glitter, beam, shimmer, glimmer, sparkle, twinkle, scintillate. ▶ n ❶ BEAM, flash, glow, shaft, ray, flare, glint. ❷ LUSTRE, glow, shine, gloss, sheen, brightness, flash, brilliance, coruscation.

glee n MIRTH, merriment, gaiety, delight, joy, joyfulness, joyousness, gladness, happiness, pleasure, jollity, hilarity, jocularity, joviality, exhilaration, high spirits, cheerfulness, exaltation, elation, exuberance, liveliness, verve, triumph; *poetic/literary* blitheness.

glib adj SMOOTH-TALKING, fast-talking, slick, smooth, fluent, smooth-tongued, silver-tongued, plausible, talkative, voluble, loquacious, unctuous, having the gift of the gab; *informal* sweet-talking.
– OPPOSITES tongue-tied, inarticulate.

glimpse v CATCH SIGHT OF, catch a glimpse of, spot, spy, discern, make out, distinguish, notice, observe, sight, espy, descry.
▶ n GLANCE, brief look, peek, peep, look, sight, view.

glint v SHINE, sparkle, flash, twinkle, glitter, glimmer, blink, gleam, wink, shimmer, glisten, dazzle, scintillate.

glisten v SHINE, shimmer, sparkle, twinkle, flicker, glint, blink, wink, gleam, flash, scintillate, coruscate.

glitter v SPARKLE, twinkle, flicker, blink, wink, shimmer, glimmer, glint, flash, gleam.
▶ n ❶ SPARKLE, twinkle, flicker, blink, winking. ❷ SHOWINESS, flashiness, glamour, ostentation, pageantry, splendour, fanfare; *informal* razzle-dazzle, glitz, pizzazz.

gloat v RELISH, revel in, glory in, rejoice in, exult in, triumph over, crow about; *informal* rub it in.

global adj ❶ WORLDWIDE, universal, international, planetary. ❷ GENERAL, comprehensive, all-encompassing, exhaustive, encyclopedic, thorough, total, with no exceptions, across-the-board.

globule n BEAD, drop, ball, droplet, pearl, particle.

gloom n ❶ DIMNESS, darkness, dark, blackness, murkiness, shadowiness, shadiness, dullness, obscurity, dusk, twilight. ❷ SADNESS, melancholy, unhappiness, sorrow, woe, grief, despondency, misery, dejection, glumness, desolation, depression, despair, pessimism, hopelessness.
– OPPOSITES light, cheer.

gloomy adj ❶ DARK, overcast, cloudy, dull, sunless, dim, shadowy, black, unlit, murky, sombre, dismal, dreary, shady, dingy. ❷ SAD, melancholy, unhappy, miserable, sorrowful, despondent, woebegone, disconsolate, dejected, downcast, downhearted, glum, dispirited, desolate, depressed, blue, pessimistic, morose; *informal* down in the mouth.
– OPPOSITES bright, cheerful.

glorious adj ❶ ILLUSTRIOUS, celebrated, noble, famous, famed, renowned, distinguished, honoured, eminent, magnificent, excellent, majestic, splendid, resplendent, supreme, triumphant, sublime, victorious. ❷ BEAUTIFUL, bright, sunny, brilliant, perfect. ❸ MARVELLOUS, splendid, wonderful, delightful, enjoyable, pleasurable, fine, excellent, great; informal fab, terrific.

glory n ❶ EXALTATION, worship, adoration, honour, reverence, extolment, veneration, thanksgiving. ❷ DISTINCTION, fame, kudos, renown, honour, prestige, acclaim, illustriousness, credit, accolade, recognition; formal laudation. ❸ SPLENDOUR, resplendence, magnificence, grandeur, majesty, pomp, pageantry, beauty.
– OPPOSITES disgrace.
■ **glory in** EXULT IN, rejoice in, take pleasure in, be proud of, delight in, revel in, boast about, crow about, gloat about.

gloss n ❶ SHINE, sheen, lustre, gleam, brightness, brilliance, sparkle, polish, shimmer, burnish. ❷ FRONT, facade, disguise, mask, semblance, camouflage, show, veneer, surface.
■ **gloss over** EVADE, avoid, smooth over, conceal, hide, cover up, disguise, mask, veil, whitewash.

glossy adj SHINING, shiny, gleaming, bright, smooth, lustrous, glistening, brilliant, polished, burnished, glazed, silky, silken, sleek, waxed.
– OPPOSITES dull, lustreless.

glow v ❶ GLEAM, shine, glimmer, smoulder, shed a glow, light up. ❷ BLUSH, flush, redden, grow pink, go scarlet, colour, crimson, radiate, thrill, tingle.
▶ n ❶ GLEAM, glimmer, luminosity, incandescence, phosphorescence, lambency.

❷ BRIGHTNESS, vividness, colourful ness, brilliance, radiance, splendour, richness. ❸ BLUSH, rosiness, flush, pinkness, redness, crimson, reddening, scarlet, bloom.

glower v SCOWL, stare angrily, glare, frown, give someone black/dirty looks, look daggers, lour.
– OPPOSITES smile.

glowing adj ❶ LUMINOUS, bright, vivid, brilliant, radiant, rich, smouldering, incandescent, phosphorescent, aglow, lambent. ❷ FAVOURABLE, enthusiastic, complimentary, laudatory, adulatory, ecstatic, rhapsodic, eulogistic, panegyrical; informal rave.

glue n ADHESIVE, gum, fixative, paste, cement, epoxy resin, mucilage.
▶ v STICK, paste, gum, fix, affix, cement, bond, seal.

glum adj GLOOMY, melancholy, sad, despondent, miserable, dejected, downcast, downhearted, dispirited, depressed, in low spirits; informal down in the mouth.
– OPPOSITES cheerful.

glut n SURPLUS, excess, surfeit, over-abundance, superabundance, oversupply, overprovision, saturation, superfluity.
– OPPOSITES dearth.

glutinous adj STICKY, viscous, tacky, mucous, gummy, adhesive, viscid, glue-like, mucilaginous.

gluttonous adj GREEDY, voracious, insatiable, ravenous,

gormandizing; *informal* piggish, hoggish.

gnaw v CHEW, munch, bite, nibble, masticate, worry.

go v ❶ MOVE, proceed, progress, walk, pass, travel, journey, repair. ❷ LEAVE, go away, depart, withdraw, retire, set off, set out, decamp; *informal* beat it, scram. ❸ WORK, be in working order, function, operate, be operative, run, perform. ❹ BECOME, grow, get, come to be, turn. ❺ BELONG, have a place, fit in, be located, be situated, be found, lie, stand. ❻ STOP, cease, disappear, vanish, be no more, fade away, melt away. ❼ TURN OUT, work out, fare, progress, develop, result, end, end up, eventuate. ❽ MATCH, go together, be compatible, blend, suit each other, complement each other, harmonize, accord, be in accord.
▶ n TRY, attempt, turn, opportunity, effort, bid, endeavour, essay; *informal* shot, stab, crack, whirl, whack.
■ **go down** ❶ SINK, submerge, founder, go under. ❷ DECREASE, fall, drop, be reduced, decline, plummet. **go far** DO WELL, be successful, succeed, make progress, get on, get ahead, make a name for oneself, advance; *informal* set the world on fire. **go in for** ENGAGE IN, take part in, participate in, practise, pursue, take up, adopt, espouse, embrace. **go off** ❶ EXPLODE, detonate, blow up, erupt, burst; *informal* go bang. ❷ GO BAD, go stale, go sour, be rotten.

goad n STIMULUS, incentive, incitement, inducement, stimulation, impetus, motivation, pressure, spur, jolt, prod, poke.
▶ v PROMPT, stimulate, induce, motivate, spur, urge, chivvy.

go-ahead n PERMISSION, authorization, assent, consent, sanction, leave, confirmation, imprimatur; *informal* green light, OK, okay, thumbs up.
▶ adj ENTERPRISING, ambitious, pioneering, progressive; *informal* up-and-coming, go-getting.

goal n AIM, objective, end, purpose, ambition, target, design, intention, intent, aspiration, ideal.

go-between n INTERMEDIARY, mediator, middleman, liaison, contact, messenger, agent, broker, medium, dealer, factor, pander.

godforsaken adj DESOLATE, dismal, dreary, bleak, wretched, miserable, gloomy, deserted, abandoned, forlorn, neglected, remote, backward, in the back of beyond.

godless adj ATHEISTIC, agnostic, sceptical, faithless, pagan, heathen, ungodly, impious, irreligious, unrighteous, sinful, wicked, evil, depraved.

godsend n PIECE OF GOOD FORTUNE, stroke of luck, blessing, boon, windfall, bonanza, gift, benediction.
– OPPOSITES curse.

goggle v STARE, gape, gaze, ogle; *informal* gawk, rubberneck.

good adj ❶ VIRTUOUS, moral, ethical, righteous, right-

minded, right-thinking, honourable, upright, honest, high-minded, noble, worthy, admirable, estimable, exemplary.
2 SATISFACTORY, acceptable, good enough, passable, tolerable, adequate, fine, excellent; *informal* great, hunky-dory, OK.
3 WELL BEHAVED, well mannered, obedient, manageable, tractable, malleable. **4** CORRECT, right, proper, fitting, suitable, appropriate, decorous, seemly.
5 COMPETENT, capable, able, accomplished, skilful, efficient, adept, proficient, expert, excellent, first-rate, first-class; *informal* top-notch, tip-top, A1. **6** FINE, healthy, sound, robust, strong, vigorous. **7** KIND, kindly, kind-hearted, good-hearted, friendly, obliging, well disposed, charitable, gracious, sympathetic, benevolent, altruistic, benign.
8 WHOLESOME, healthy, nutritious, nutritional, beneficial.
9 DELICIOUS, tasty, appetizing; *informal* scrumptious, yummy.
10 VALID, legitimate, genuine, authentic, sound, bona fide.
11 CONSIDERABLE, substantial, goodly, sizeable, large, sufficient, ample; *informal* tidy.
12 FINE, fair, mild, clear, bright, cloudless, sunny, calm, balmy, tranquil, clement, halcyon.
– OPPOSITES bad.
▶ n **1** BENEFIT, advantage, gain, profit, interest, well-being, welfare. **2** VIRTUE, goodness, righteousness, morality, ethics, rectitude, honour, uprightness, honesty, integrity, probity, worth, merit.

goodbye exclamation FAREWELL, adieu, au revoir; *informal* bye, bye-bye, see you later, see you, so long, ciao; *Brit. informal* cheerio, cheers, ta-ta.

good-humoured adj AMIABLE, affable, easy-going, genial, cheerful, cheery, happy, pleasant, good-tempered.
– OPPOSITES grumpy.

good-looking adj ATTRACTIVE, handsome, pretty, lovely, beautiful, personable, well favoured; *archaic* comely, fair.

goodly adj CONSIDERABLE, substantial, sizeable, significant, large, great, ample, sufficient; *informal* tidy.
– OPPOSITES paltry.

good-natured adj KIND, kindly, kind-hearted, warm-hearted, generous, benevolent, charitable, friendly, helpful, accommodating, amiable, tolerant.

goods pl n PROPERTY, belongings, possessions, effects, things, paraphernalia, chattels, movables, appurtenances, trappings, accoutrements; *informal* stuff, gear.

gorge n CHASM, canyon, ravine, abyss, defile, pass, cleft, crevice, rift, fissure.

gorgeous adj **1** BEAUTIFUL, attractive, lovely, good-looking, sexy; *informal* stunning. **2** SPLENDID, magnificent, superb, grand, impressive, sumptuous, imposing, dazzling, brilliant, glittering, breathtaking.

gory adj BLOODY, bloodstained,

horrific, violent, bloodthirsty, brutal, murderous, savage.

gossip n ❶ RUMOURS, scandal, tittle-tattle, tattle, hearsay, whispering campaign; *informal* mud-slinging, dirt. ❷ GOSSIP-MONGER, rumour-monger, scandalmonger, busybody, babbler, chatterer, prattler.
▶ v SPREAD RUMOURS, chat, chit-chat, blather, blether, talk, tattle, babble, gabble, prattle, prate; *informal* chinwag, jaw, yack.

gouge v DIG, incise, chisel, gash, scoop, hollow.

govern v ❶ RULE, reign over, be in power over, exercise control over, hold sway over, preside over, administer, lead, be in charge of, control, command, direct, order, guide, manage, conduct, oversee, supervise, superintend, pilot, steer. ❷ CONTROL, restrain, keep in check, check, curb, hold back, keep back, rein in, bridle, subdue, constrain, arrest, contain. ❸ DETERMINE, decide, sway, rule, influence, have an influence on, be a factor in.

government n ADMINISTRATION, regime, parliament, ministry, executive, rule, leadership, command, direction, control, guidance, management, conduct, supervision, superintendence.

gown n DRESS, frock, garment, costume, garb, habit.

grab v ❶ GRASP, clutch, grip, clasp, lay hold of, catch hold of, take hold of, fasten upon;

informal collar. ❷ SEIZE, snatch, pluck, snap up, appropriate, capture; *informal* bag, nab.

grace n ❶ ELEGANCE, refinement, charm, attractiveness, beauty, loveliness, polish, suaveness, culture, cultivation, good taste, taste, tastefulness, smoothness, suppleness, fluidity. ❷ MANNERS, courtesy, decency, consideration, tact, breeding, decorum, propriety. ❸ FAVOUR, good will, generosity, kindness, kindliness, indulgence, benefaction, mercy, mercifulness, compassion, clemency. ❹ BLESSING, prayer, thanksgiving, thanks, benediction.
▶ v ADORN, decorate, ornament, embellish, enhance, beautify, prettify, set off, deck.

graceful adj ELEGANT, refined, smooth, agile, flowing, nimble, cultured, cultivated, polished, suave, charming, appealing, attractive, beautiful, lovely; *archaic* comely.
– OPPOSITES inelegant.

gracious adj ❶ COURTEOUS, cordial, kindly, kind-hearted, warm-hearted, benevolent, friendly, amiable, considerate, affable, pleasant, polite, civil, well mannered, chivalrous, charitable, indulgent, obliging, accommodating, beneficent, benign. ❷ ELEGANT, tasteful, comfortable, luxurious. ❸ MERCIFUL, compassionate, gentle, mild, humane, clement.

grade n ❶ LEVEL, degree, stage, echelon, rank, standing, station, position, order, class. ❷ CATEGORY, class, classification, type, brand. ❸ GRADIENT, slope, incline, hill, rise, bank, declivity.

▶ v CLASSIFY, class, categorize, sort, group, order, brand, size, rank, evaluate, rate, value, range, graduate.

gradient n SLOPE, incline, hill, rise, bank, acclivity, declivity, grade.

gradual adj PROGRESSIVE, regular, steady, even, moderate, slow, measured, unhurried, step-by-step, successive, continuous, systematic.
– OPPOSITES sudden, abrupt.

gradually adv SLOWLY, steadily, moderately, evenly, bit by bit, little by little, by degrees, step by step, inch by inch, piece by piece, drop by drop.

graduate v ❶ TAKE A DEGREE, receive one's degree, become a graduate. ❷ MARK OFF, measure off, divide into degrees, grade, calibrate. ❸ MOVE UP, progress, advance, gain promotion, be promoted.

graft n ❶ SHOOT, bud, scion, new growth, slip, sprout, splice. ❷ TRANSPLANT, implant, implantation.

grain n ❶ PARTICLE, granule, bit, piece, scrap, crumb, fragment, morsel, speck, trace, scintilla, mite, iota. ❷ TEXTURE, weave, fibre, pattern, nap.

grand adj ❶ IMPRESSIVE, imposing, magnificent, splendid, superb, striking, palatial, stately, large, monumental,

majestic. ❷ SPLENDID, sumptuous, luxurious, lavish, magnificent, opulent, princely. ❸ GREAT, noble, aristocratic, distinguished, august, illustrious, eminent, elevated, esteemed, celebrated, preeminent, leading, prominent, notable, renowned, famous.
– OPPOSITES unimpressive, lowly.

grandiose adj ❶ OVERAMBITIOUS, ambitious, extravagant, high-flown, high-sounding, pompous, flamboyant, pretentious; informal OTT. ❷ GRAND, impressive, magnificent, imposing, striking, splendid, superb, stately, majestic.
– OPPOSITES modest.

grant v ❶ AGREE TO, consent to, assent to, accede to, permit, give one's permission for, allow, concede, accord, vouchsafe. ❷ ACKNOWLEDGE, concede, accept, cede, yield, go along with.
▶ n AWARD, endowment, contribution, donation, allowance, subsidy, allocation, allotment, gift, present, subvention, sponsorship, honorarium; Brit. bursary.

granule n GRAIN, particle, fragment, crumb, bit, scrap, molecule, atom, mite, iota, jot.

graphic adj ❶ VIVID, striking, expressive, descriptive, illustrative, lively, forcible, detailed, well defined, well drawn, telling, effective, cogent, clear, lucid, explicit.
– OPPOSITES dull.

grapple v ❶ FIGHT WITH, wrestle with, struggle with, tussle with, clash with, engage with, close with, battle with, combat with, brawl with. ❷ TACKLE, face, cope with, deal with, handle, manage, confront, address oneself to, attack, get down to, come to grips with.

grasp v ❶ GRIP, clutch, hold, clasp, clench, grab, snatch, get/take hold of, seize. ❷ UNDERSTAND, comprehend, follow, see, take in, realize, apprehend, perceive; *informal* get, get the picture, get the drift, catch on.

grasping adj GREEDY, acquisitive, avaricious, rapacious, covetous, mean, parsimonious, niggardly, penny-pinching, selfish, possessive; *informal* grabby, tight-fisted, stingy.
– OPPOSITES generous.

grate v ❶ SHRED, pulverize, mince, grind, granulate, triturate. ❷ RASP, scrape, jar, scratch, grind, creak, rub, grit. ❸ IRRITATE, annoy, jar on, irk, vex, gall, rankle with, anger, rile, exasperate, chafe; *Brit.* rub up the wrong way; *informal* set someone's teeth on edge, get on someone's nerves, aggravate.

grateful adj THANKFUL, appreciative, obliged, indebted, obligated, beholden, filled with gratitude.
– OPPOSITES ungrateful.

gratify v PLEASE, make happy, delight, give pleasure to, gladden, satisfy, thrill; *informal* warm the cockles of the heart.

gratitude n GRATEFULNESS, thankfulness, thanks, appreciation, thanksgiving, indebtedness, acknowledgement, recognition, sense of obligation.
– OPPOSITES ingratitude.

gratuitous adj ❶ UNPROVOKED, unjustified, groundless, without cause, without reason, unfounded, baseless, uncalled for, unwarranted, unmerited, needless, unnecessary, superfluous. ❷ FREE, complimentary, voluntary, unpaid, unrewarded, unasked for, without charge, at no cost.

gratuity n TIP, bonus, gift, present, donation, reward, recompense, largesse.

grave adj ❶ SOLEMN, serious, earnest, sober, sombre, severe, unsmiling, long-faced, stonyfaced, grim-faced, grim, gloomy, preoccupied, thoughtful, pensive, subdued, muted, quiet, dignified, sedate, dour, staid. ❷ SERIOUS, important, significant, weighty, momentous, urgent, pressing, vital, crucial, life-and-death, acute, pivotal, perilous, hazardous, dangerous, threatening, menacing.
– OPPOSITES carefree, trivial.

graveyard n CEMETERY, burial ground, churchyard, memorial park, necropolis, charnel house; *informal* boneyard; *N. Amer.* potter's field.

gravitate v ❶ MOVE TOWARDS, head towards, be drawn to, be pulled towards, be attracted to, drift towards, lean towards, incline towards. **2** SINK, fall, drop, descend, precipitate, be precipitated, settle.

gravity n **1** SOLEMNITY, seriousness, earnestness, sobriety, sombreness, severity, grimness, thoughtfulness, pensiveness, sedateness, dignity, dourness, staidness. **2** SERIOUSNESS, importance, significance, momentousness, weightiness, acuteness, criticalness, consequence, perilousness, peril, hazard, danger.

graze v **1** BRUSH, touch, rub, glance off, shave, skim, kiss. **2** SCRAPE, abrade, skin, scratch, chafe, bark, bruise, contuse.

greasy adj **1** FATTY, fat, oily, buttery, oleaginous, sebaceous, adipose. **2** SLIPPERY, slippy, slimy. **3** SLIMY, oily, unctuous, smooth, smooth-tongued, glib, suave, slick, fawning, ingratiating, grovelling, sycophantic, toadying, flattering, gushing; informal smarmy.

great adj **1** LARGE, big, extensive, vast, immense, boundless, unlimited, huge, spacious, enormous, gigantic, colossal, mammoth, monstrous, prodigious, tremendous, stupendous. **2** MAJOR, main, most important, leading, chief, principal, capital, paramount, primary. **3** IMPRESSIVE, grand, magnificent, imposing, splendid, majestic, glorious, sumptuous. **4** PROMINENT, eminent, pre-eminent, distinguished, illustrious, august, celebrated, renowned, noted, notable, noteworthy, famous, famed, leading, top, high, high-ranking, noble. **5** GIFTED, talented, outstanding, remarkable, exceptional, first-rate, incomparable, expert, skilful, skilled, able, masterly, adept, proficient, adroit; informal crack, ace. **6** EXCELLENT, enjoyable, marvellous, wonderful, first-class, first-rate, fine, very good, admirable; informal fab, super.

greatly adv VERY MUCH, considerably, to a great extent, extremely, exceedingly, vastly, enormously, immensely, tremendously, hugely, markedly, mightily, remarkably, abundantly.

greed n **1** GLUTTONY, voraciousness, voracity, ravenousness, insatiability; informal hoggishness, piggishness, swinishness. **2** AVARICE, acquisitiveness, rapacity, covetousness, cupidity, miserliness, parsimony; informal tight-fistedness. **3** DESIRE, eagerness, avidity, hunger, craving, longing, enthusiasm, impatience.

greedy adj **1** GLUTTONOUS, voracious, ravenous, ravening, famished, gourmandizing, insatiable, omnivorous; informal piggish, hoggish, gutsy; archaic esurient. **2** AVARICIOUS, acquisitive, grasping, rapacious, grabbing, covetous, miserly, hoarding, niggardly, close-fisted, parsimonious; informal grabby, money-grubbing, tight-fisted. **3** EAGER, hungry, avid,

desirous, anxious, impatient, enthusiastic, longing, craving.
– OPPOSITES generous.

greenhouse n HOTHOUSE, glasshouse, conservatory.

greet v SAY HELLO TO, address, salute, hail, nod to, wave to, raise one's hat to, acknowledge, accost, receive, meet, welcome.

greeting n HELLO, salute, salutation, address, nod, wave, acknowledgement, welcome.

greetings pl n GOOD WISHES, best wishes, regards, kind regards, congratulations, compliments, respects.

grey adj ❶ CLOUDY, overcast, dull, dark, sunless, gloomy, dim, dreary, dismal, cheerless, depressing, misty, foggy, murky. ❷ DULL, uninteresting, boring, characterless, anonymous, colourless. ❸ UNCLEAR, doubtful, uncertain, indistinct, mixed.

grief n SORROW, mourning, mournfulness, bereavement, lamentation, misery, sadness, anguish, pain, distress, agony, suffering, affliction, heartache, heartbreak, brokenheartedness, heaviness of heart, trouble, woe, tribulation, desolation, trial, despondency, dejection, despair, remorse, regret.
– OPPOSITES joy, delight.

grievance n ❶ COMPLAINT, protest, charge, moan, axe to grind, bone to pick; informal grouse, gripe, beef. ❷ INJUSTICE, unfairness, injury, damage,

hardship, offence, affront, insult.

grieve v ❶ MOURN, lament, be sorrowful, sorrow, be sad, weep and wail, cry, sob, suffer, ache, be in anguish, be distressed, bemoan, bewail; informal eat one's heart out. ❷ HURT, wound, pain, sadden, break someone's heart, upset, distress, cause suffering to, crush.
– OPPOSITES rejoice.

grim adj ❶ STERN, forbidding, fierce, formidable, threatening, ferocious, menacing, harsh, sombre, cross, crabbed, churlish, morose, surly, ill-tempered, sour, implacable, cruel, ruthless, merciless. ❷ RESOLUTE, determined, firm, decided, obstinate, adamant, unyielding, unwavering, unfaltering, unshakeable, obdurate, inflexible, unrelenting, relentless, inexorable, dead set. ❸ DREADFUL, horrible, horrendous, terrible, horrid, dire, ghastly, awful, appalling, frightful, shocking, unspeakable, harrowing, grisly, hideous, gruesome, macabre.
– OPPOSITES amiable.

grimy adj DIRTY, grubby, stained, soiled, dusty, sooty, muddy, filthy, besmeared; poetic/literary besmirched.
– OPPOSITES clean.

grind v ❶ CRUSH, pound, pulverize, mill, powder, granulate, crumble, mash, smash, triturate, kibble, levigate. ❷ SHARPEN, file, whet, smooth, polish, sand. ❸ GNASH, grit, grate, scrape, rasp.

■ **grind down** OPPRESS, persecute, ill-treat, torture, torment, harass, harry.

grip v ❶ GRASP, clutch, hold, clasp, clench, take/lay hold of, grab, seize, catch, latch on to. ❷ ABSORB, engross, rivet, spellbind, hold spellbound, entrance, fascinate, enthral, hold, catch, mesmerize, hypnotize, compel.
▶ n ❶ GRASP, clutch, clasp, clench, handshake, clinch. ❷ UNDERSTANDING, comprehension, awareness, perception.

grisly adj GRUESOME, frightful, horrifying, horrid, grim, horrendous, awful, dreadful, terrible, fearful, disgusting, hideous, repulsive, revolting, repugnant, repellent, macabre, spine-chilling, sickening, appalling, loathsome, abhorrent, odious, abominable.
– OPPOSITES pleasant.

grit n ❶ GRAVEL, sand, dust, dirt. ❷ PLUCK, courage, bravery, mettle, backbone, spirit, gameness, fortitude, toughness, determination, resolution, tenacity; informal guts, spunk; Brit. informal bottle.

groan v ❶ MOAN, cry, call out, sigh, murmur, whine, whimper. ❷ COMPLAIN, grumble, object, lament; informal moan, grouse, gripe, beef, bellyache, bitch. ❸ CREAK, grate, squeak, screech.

groove n ❶ CHANNEL, furrow, trench, trough, canal, gouge,

rut, gutter, cutting, cut, score, rabbet, rebate. ❷ RUT, routine, habit, treadmill, daily grind.

grope v ❶ FEEL, fumble, move blindly, pick. ❷ FUMBLE FOR, fish for, scrabble for, cast about for, search for, hunt for, look for.

gross adj ❶ OBESE, massive, huge, immense, colossal, big, large, overweight, fat, corpulent, bloated, bulky, lumpish, cumbersome, unwieldy; informal hulking. ❷ COARSE, crude, vulgar, obscene, rude, lewd, ribald, bawdy, dirty, filthy, smutty, earthy, risqué, indecent, indelicate, improper, unseemly, impure, offensive, sexual, sensual, pornographic; informal blue. ❸ BOORISH, loutish, oafish, coarse, vulgar, crass, ignorant, unrefined, unsophisticated, uncultured, uncultivated, undiscriminating, tasteless, insensitive, unfeeling, imperceptive, callous; Brit. informal yobbish. ❹ FLAGRANT, blatant, glaring, outrageous, shocking, serious, egregious, manifest, obvious, plain, apparent. ❺ TOTAL, whole, entire, aggregate, before deductions, before tax.
– OPPOSITES slender, refined, net.
▶ v EARN, make, bring in, take home, rake in.

grotesque adj ❶ BIZARRE, weird, outlandish, freakish, strange, odd, peculiar, unnatural, surreal, macabre, queer, fantastic, whimsical, fanciful, ridiculous, ludicrous, absurd, incongruous, preposterous,

extravagant. ❷ DISTORTED, misshapen, twisted, deformed, malformed, misproportioned.
– OPPOSITES normal.

ground n ❶ EARTH, floor, terra firma; *informal* deck. ❷ SOIL, earth, dirt, land, terrain, clay, turf, loam, clod, sod, dust. ❸ PITCH, stadium, field, arena, park. *See also* GROUNDS.
▶ v ❶ BASE, establish, settle, set, found. ❷ TEACH, instruct, train, tutor, coach, educate, drill, school, prepare, familiarize with, acquaint with, inform.

groundless adj WITHOUT BASIS, baseless, without foundation, unfounded, unsupported, imaginary, illusory, false, unsubstantiated, unwarranted, unjustified, unjustifiable, uncalled for, unprovoked, without cause/reason, unreasonable, irrational, illogical, empty, idle, chimerical.

grounds pl n ❶ SURROUNDINGS, land, property, estate, acres, lawns, gardens, park, parkland, area, domain, holding, territory. ❷ REASON, cause, basis, base, foundation, justification, call, rationale, argument, premise, occasion, factor, excuse, pretext, motive, inducement. ❸ DREGS, deposit, lees, sediment, precipitate, settlings, grouts.

group n ❶ SET, lot, category, classification, class, bracket, family, species, genus, branch. ❷ COMPANY, band, party, body, gathering, congregation, assembly, collection, bunch, cluster, crowd, flock, pack, troop, gang, batch. ❸ FACTION, set, coterie, clique, circle. ❹ SOCIETY, association, league, guild, circle, club, work party.
▶ v ❶ CLASSIFY, class, categorize, sort, grade, rank, bracket. ❷ ASSEMBLE, collect, gather together, arrange, organize, marshal, range, line up, dispose. ❸ COLLECT, gather, assemble, cluster. ❹ GET TOGETHER, band together, associate, consort.

grouse v COMPLAIN, grumble, groan, protest; *informal* moan, gripe, bellyache, beef, bitch, grouch, whinge.

grovel v ❶ ABASE ONESELF, toady, fawn, flatter, curry favour, humble oneself, kowtow, bow and scrape, lick someone's boots; *informal* crawl, butter someone up. ❷ PROSTRATE ONESELF, fall on one's knees, crawl, creep, kneel, slither.

grow v ❶ GET BIGGER, get larger, get taller, stretch, lengthen, heighten, enlarge, extend, expand, spread, thicken, widen, fill out, swell, increase, multiply. ❷ DEVELOP, sprout, shoot up, spring up, germinate, bud, burgeon, flourish, thrive, pullulate. ❸ FLOURISH, thrive, prosper, succeed, progress, make progress, make headway, advance, improve, expand. ❹ ARISE, originate, stem, issue, spring. ❺ BECOME, come to be, get to be, get, turn, wax. ❻ PRODUCE, cultivate, farm, propagate, raise.
– OPPOSITES shrink.

grown-up n ADULT, grown man, grown woman, woman, mature man/woman.

growth n ❶ INCREASE, expansion, enlargement, development, augmentation, proliferation, multiplication, extension, evolution, magnification, amplification, growing, deepening, heightening, widening, thickening, broadening, swelling, aggrandizement. ❷ DEVELOPMENT, maturation, germination, burgeoning, sprouting, shooting up, blooming, vegetation, pullulation. ❸ EXPANSION, rise, progress, success, advance, advancement, improvement, headway. ❹ TUMOUR, lump, cancer, swelling, excrescence, intumescence, tumefaction.

grubby adj DIRTY, filthy, unwashed, grimy, messy, soiled, scruffy, shabby, untidy, unkempt, slovenly, sordid, squalid; informal mucky, cruddy; Brit. informal gungy.
– OPPOSITES clean.

grudge n RESENTMENT, spite, malice, bitterness, ill will, pique, umbrage, grievance, hard feelings, rancour, malevolence, venom, hatred, dislike, aversion, animosity, animus.
▶ v ❶ BEGRUDGE, give unwillingly, give reluctantly.
❷ RESENT, mind, take ill, begrudge, envy, be jealous of.

gruelling adj EXHAUSTING, tiring, fatiguing, wearying, taxing, demanding, trying, arduous, laborious, backbreaking, strenuous, punishing, crushing, draining, hard, difficult, harsh, severe, grinding, stiff, brutal, relentless, unsparing, inexorable.

gruesome adj GRISLY, ghastly, frightful, horrible, horrifying, horrid, horrendous, awful, dreadful, grim, terrible, fearful, hideous, disgusting, repulsive, revolting, repugnant, repellent, macabre, spine-chilling, sickening, appalling, shocking, abominable, loathsome, abhorrent, odious.

grumble v COMPLAIN, groan, protest, object, find fault, carp, whine; informal moan, grouse, gripe, bellyache, beef, bitch, grouch, whinge.

grumpy adj BAD-TEMPERED, surly, churlish, crotchety, tetchy, crabby, crusty, ill-natured, bearish; informal grouchy.
– OPPOSITES good-humoured.

guarantee n ❶ WARRANTY, warrant, covenant, bond, contract, guaranty. ❷ PLEDGE, promise, assurance, word, word of honour, oath, bond.
▶ v ❶ UNDERWRITE, sponsor, back, support, provide collateral for, vouch for, provide surety for. ❷ PROMISE, pledge, give a pledge, give an assurance, give one's word, swear.

guard v ❶ DEFEND, shield, safeguard, stand guard over, protect, watch over, cover, patrol, police, preserve, save, conserve, secure, screen, shelter. ❷ BEWARE, keep watch, be alert,

take care, be on the lookout; *informal* keep an eye out, keep one's eyes peeled/skinned.
▶ n ❶ DEFENDER, guardian, bodyguard, custodian, sentry, sentinel, watchman, night-watchman, lookout, scout, watch, picket, garrison, escort, convoy, patrol; *informal* minder. ❷ WARDER, jailer, keeper; *informal* screw.

guarded adj CAREFUL, cautious, circumspect, wary, chary, reluctant, non-committal, reticent, restrained, reserved, discreet, prudent; *informal* cagey.

guess n CONJECTURE, surmise, estimate, hypothesis, guesswork, theory, reckoning, judgement, supposition, feeling, assumption, inference, prediction, speculation, notion; *informal* guesstimate.
▶ v ❶ CONJECTURE, surmise, estimate, reckon, hypothesize, postulate, predict, speculate. ❷ SUPPOSE, believe, think, imagine, judge, consider, feel, suspect, dare say, fancy, divine, deem, surmise, reckon.

guest n ❶ VISITOR, caller, company. ❷ RESIDENT, boarder, lodger, patron, tenant.

guidance n ❶ DIRECTION, leadership, management, auspices, control, handling, conduct, government, charge, rule, teaching, instruction. ❷ ADVICE, counselling, counsel, direction, recommendation, suggestion, tip, hint, pointer, intelligence, information, instruction.

guide v ❶ LEAD, lead the way, conduct, show, usher, shepherd, direct, show the way, pilot, steer, escort, accompany, convoy, attend. ❷ CONTROL, direct, manage, steer, command, be in charge of, govern, rule, preside over, superintend, supervise, handle, regulate, manipulate, manoeuvre. ❸ ADVISE, give advice to, counsel, give counselling to, make suggestions/recommendations to, give someone pointers/tips, inform, instruct.
▶ n ❶ ESCORT, chaperone, leader, courier, pilot, usher, attendant, director. ❷ ADVISER, counsellor, mentor, tutor, teacher, guru, confidant. ❸ GUIDEBOOK, handbook, manual, ABC, instructions, key, catalogue.

guile n CUNNING, duplicity, craftiness, artfulness, craft, wiliness, artifice, foxiness, slyness, deception, deceit, underhandedness, double-dealing, trickery, trickiness, sharp practice, treachery, chicanery, skulduggery, fraud, gamesmanship, knavery.
– OPPOSITES candour.

guilty adj ❶ TO BLAME, blameworthy, culpable, blameable, at fault, responsible, censurable, convicted, criminal, reproachable, condemnable, erring, errant, wrong, delinquent, offending, sinful, wicked, evil, unlawful, illegal, illicit, reprehensible, felonious, iniquitous. ❷ REMORSEFUL, ashamed, con-

science-stricken, shamefaced, regretful, contrite, repentant, penitent, rueful, sheepish, hangdog, compunctious.
– OPPOSITES innocent, unrepentant.

guise n ❶ COSTUME, clothes, likeness, outfit, dress, appearance, style. ❷ PRETENCE, disguise, screen, cover, blind, appearance, form.

gulf n ❶ BAY, cove, inlet, bight. ❷ CHASM, abyss, hollow, pit, hole, opening, rift, cleft, fissure, split, crevice, gully, canyon, gorge, ravine.

gullible adj CREDULOUS, trustful, over-trustful, easily deceived, easily taken in, unsuspecting, unsuspicious, ingenuous, naive, innocent, simple, inexperienced, green, foolish, silly; *informal* wet behind the ears.
– OPPOSITES cynical, suspicious.

gulp v ❶ SWALLOW, quaff, toss off, drain one's glass; *informal* swig, swill. ❷ BOLT, wolf, gobble, guzzle, devour; *informal* tuck into. ❸ FIGHT BACK, suppress, stifle, smother, choke back, strangle.
▶ n SWALLOW, mouthful, draught; *informal* swig.

gunman n ARMED ROBBER, sniper, gangster, terrorist, assassin, murderer, killer, bandit; *informal* gunslinger, hit man, hired gun, trigger man, gunfighter; *N. Amer. informal* hood.

gurgle v BUBBLE, murmur, babble, burble, lap, splash, tinkle, plash, purl.

gush v ❶ STREAM, rush, spout, spurt, surge, jet, well, pour, burst, cascade, flood, flow, run, issue, emanate. ❷ BE EFFUSIVE, enthuse, wax lyrical, bubble over, get carried away, fuss, babble, prattle, jabber, gabble, blather, chatter, make too much, overstate the case.
▶ n STREAM, outpouring, spurt, jet, spout, rush, burst, surge, cascade, flood, torrent, spate, freshet.

gusto n ZEST, enthusiasm, relish, zeal, fervour, verve, enjoyment, delight, exhilaration, pleasure, appreciation, liking, fondness, appetite, savour, taste.
– OPPOSITES apathy, indifference.

gut n STOMACH, belly, abdomen, bowels, colon, intestines, entrails, vital organs, viscera; *informal* insides, innards.
▶ v ❶ EVISCERATE, disembowel, dress, clean, draw. ❷ STRIP, ransack, empty, plunder, loot, rob, rifle, ravage, sack, clear out, destroy, devastate, lay waste.

guts pl n COURAGE, bravery, valour, nerve, fortitude, pluck, mettle, spirit, boldness, audacity, daring, hardiness, toughness, forcefulness, will power, tenacity; *informal* grit, gumption, spunk; *Brit. informal* bottle.

gutter n DRAIN, sewer, sluice, culvert, conduit, pipe, duct, channel, trench, trough, ditch, furrow.

guttural adj HUSKY, throaty, gruff, gravelly, harsh, croaking, rasping, deep, low, rough, thick.

gyrate v ROTATE, revolve, wheel round, turn round, circle, whirl, pirouette, twirl, swirl, spin, swivel.

Hh

habit n ❶ CUSTOM, practice, wont, procedure, way, routine, matter of course, style, pattern, convention, policy, mode, rule. ❷ TENDENCY, propensity, predisposition, proclivity, penchant, leaning, bent, inclination, custom, practice, quirk. ❸ ADDICTION, dependence, weakness, obsession, fixation. ❹ COSTUME, dress, garb, attire, clothes, clothing, garments, livery, uniform; formal apparel.

habitable adj INHABITABLE, liveable in, usable, fit to live in, fit to occupy, tenantable.
– OPPOSITES uninhabitable.

habitual adj ❶ USUAL, customary, accustomed, regular, normal, set, fixed, established, routine, common, ordinary, familiar, traditional; poetic/literary wonted. ❷ PERSISTENT, constant, continual, repeated, recurrent, perpetual, non-stop, continuous, frequent. ❸ CONFIRMED, addicted, chronic, inveterate, hardened, ingrained.
– OPPOSITES unaccustomed, infrequent, occasional.

hackneyed adj BANAL, trite, overused, overworked, tired, worn out, time-worn, stale, clichéd, platitudinous, unoriginal, commonplace, common, unimaginative, pedestrian, prosaic, run-of-the-mill, stock, conventional; informal corny, old hat, played out.
– OPPOSITES fresh, original.

haggard adj GAUNT, drawn, pinched, hollow-cheeked, scraggy, scrawny, withered, exhausted, ghost-like, death-like, wan, pallid, ghastly, cadaverous, peaked, drained, careworn, emaciated, wasted, thin.
– OPPOSITES plump.

hail v ❶ GREET, salute, acknowledge, lift one's hat to. ❷ SIGNAL, make a sign, flag, flag down, wave down, call, shout to. ❸ See ACCLAIM.

hair n ❶ LOCKS, tresses, shock of hair, mop of hair, head of hair. ❷ COAT, fur, pelt, hide, wool, fleece, mane.

hair-raising adj SPINE-CHILLING, blood-curdling, terrifying, horrifying, petrifying, frightening, alarming, shocking, exciting, thrilling; *informal* scary, creepy.

hairy adj HIRSUTE, woolly, shaggy, bushy, fuzzy, bristly, fleecy, downy, bearded, unshaven, bewhiskered, stubbly.

half-hearted adj LUKEWARM, unenthusiastic, apathetic, indifferent, uninterested, unconcerned, cool, listless, unemotional, lacklustre, dispassionate, cursory, perfunctory, superficial, passive, neutral.
– OPPOSITES enthusiastic.

hallmark n MARK, trademark, stamp, sign, badge, device, symbol, indicator, indication.

hallucinate v IMAGINE THINGS, see things, have hallucinations, dream, fantasize, be delirious; *informal* be on a trip.

hallucination n ILLUSION, delusion, figment of the imagination, vision, fantasy, apparition, dream, mirage, chimera, delirium, phantasmagoria.

halt v ❶ COME TO A HALT, stop, come to a stop/standstill, pull up, draw up, wait. ❷ FINISH, stop, cease, break off, call it a day, desist, discontinue; *informal* knock off; *Brit.* informal down tools. ❸ BLOCK, arrest, terminate, stop, curb, put an end/stop to, bring to an end, crush, frustrate, obstruct, baulk, impede, hold back.
– OPPOSITES begin.
▶ n STOP, stoppage, cessation, close, end, standstill, pause,

interval, interlude, intermission, break, hiatus, rest, respite.

hammer v BEAT, batter, pound, pummel, hit, strike, cudgel, slap, bludgeon, club; *informal* wallop, clobber.

hamper v HINDER, obstruct, impede, hold back, inhibit, retard, slow down, hold up, restrain, block, check, frustrate, thwart, foil, curb, interfere with, cramp, restrict, bridle, handicap, stymie, hamstring, shackle, fetter, encumber, trammel, cumber; *Brit.* throw a spanner in the works.
– OPPOSITES expedite.

hand n ❶ FIST, palm; *informal* mitt, paw, duke. ❷ POINTER, indicator, needle. ❸ WORKER, workman, employee, operative, hired hand, labourer, artisan.
▶ v GIVE, pass, pass over, hand over, deliver, present.
■ **hand on/down** PASS ON / DOWN, bequeath, will, give, transfer. **hand out** DISTRIBUTE, give out, pass out, deal out, dole out, mete out, dispense, apportion, disseminate, disburse, dish out.

handicap n ❶ DISABILITY, impairment, abnormality, disadvantage, defect. ❷ IMPEDIMENT, disadvantage, hindrance, obstruction, obstacle, encumbrance, check, block, curb, barrier, stumbling block, constraint, restriction, limitation, drawback, shortcoming.
– OPPOSITES advantage.

▶ v DISADVANTAGE, put at a disadvantage, impede, hinder, impair, hamper, obstruct, check, block, encumber, curb, trammel, bridle, hold back, constrain, restrict, limit.

handiwork n ❶ HANDICRAFT, craft, craftsmanship. ❷ ACTION, achievement, work, doing, creation, design, product, production, result.

handle v ❶ TOUCH, feel, hold, finger, grasp, grip, pick up, lift, pat, caress, stroke, fondle, poke, maul; *informal* paw. ❷ COPE WITH, deal with, treat, manage, control. ❸ BE IN CHARGE OF, control, manage, administer, direct, guide, conduct, supervise, take care of. ❹ DRIVE, steer, operate, manoeuvre. ❺ DEAL IN, trade in, traffic in, market, sell, stock, carry.
▶ n SHAFT, grip, handgrip, hilt, haft, knob, stock, helve.

handsome adj ❶ GOOD-LOOKING, attractive, personable; *informal* dishy. ❷ ATTRACTIVE, good-looking, lovely, elegant, fine, personable, well formed, well proportioned, stately, dignified. ❸ GENEROUS, magnanimous, liberal, lavish, considerable, sizeable, large, ample, abundant, plentiful; *poetic/literary* bounteous.
– OPPOSITES ugly.

handy adj ❶ TO HAND, at hand, within reach, available, accessible, near, nearby, close, at one's fingertips, convenient; *informal* on tap. ❷ USEFUL, helpful, practicable, practical, ser-

viceable, functional, expedient, easy-to-use, neat, convenient. ❸ DEFT, dexterous, nimble-fingered, adroit, proficient, adept, skilful, skilled, expert, clever/good with one's hands.
– OPPOSITES inaccessible, useless, inept.

hang v ❶ BE SUSPENDED, dangle, swing, sway, be pendent. ❷ SEND TO THE GALLOWS, send to the gibbet, execute; *informal* string up. ❸ STICK UP, attach, fix, fasten on, paste, glue, cement. ❹ ADORN, decorate, deck, ornament, drape, cover, furnish.
■ **hang about/around** WAIT, linger, loiter, dally, waste time; *archaic* tarry. **hang back** HOLD BACK, stay back, stay in the background, be reluctant, hesitate, recoil, demur, shrink back. **hang on** WAIT, hold on, stop, stay, remain, persevere.

hang-up n FIXATION, preoccupation, obsession, phobia, problem; *informal* thing, bee in one's bonnet.

hanker
■ **hanker after/for** LONG FOR, have a longing for, yearn for, crave, desire, hunger for, thirst for, be bent on, covet, want, wish for, set one's heart on, pine for, lust after; *informal* be itching for, be dying for, have a yen for.

haphazard adj UNPLANNED, random, indiscriminate, undirected, unforeseen, chaotic, chance, unsystematic, unorganized, unmethodical, orderless, aimless, irregular,

slapdash, thrown together, careless, casual, hit-or-miss.
– OPPOSITES methodical, systematic.

hapless adj UNLUCKY, unfortunate, out of luck, ill-starred, forlorn, wretched, unhappy, woebegone; *informal* down on one's luck.
– OPPOSITES lucky.

happen v TAKE PLACE, occur, come about, present itself, arise, materialize, appear, come into being, chance, arrive, transpire, crop up, develop, eventuate, supervene; *poetic/literary* come to pass.

happening n OCCURRENCE, event, incident, occasion, affair, circumstance, action, case, phenomenon, eventuality, episode, experience, adventure, scene, proceedings, chance.

happiness n CHEERFULNESS, cheeriness, merriness, gaiety, good spirits, high spirits, light-heartedness, joy, joyfulness, glee, joviality, carefreeness, enjoyment, gladness, delight, exuberance, elation, ecstasy, bliss, blissfulness, euphoria, transports; *poetic/literary* blitheness.
– OPPOSITES unhappiness, sadness.

happy adj ❶ CHEERFUL, cheery, merry, in good/high spirits, joyful, joyous, light-hearted, jovial, gleeful, buoyant, carefree, untroubled, smiling, glad, delighted, elated, ecstatic, blissful, euphoric, overjoyed,

exuberant, in seventh heaven, floating/walking on air; *informal* over the moon, on cloud nine, on top of the world; *dated* gay; *poetic/literary* blithe. ❷ GLAD, pleased, delighted, contented, satisfied, gratified, thrilled. ❸ LUCKY, fortunate, advantageous, favourable, beneficial, opportune, helpful, timely, convenient, welcome, propitious, auspicious, felicitous, fortuitous. ❹ APPROPRIATE, fitting, apt, fit, good, right, proper, seemly.
– OPPOSITES unhappy, sad, displeased, unfortunate.

harangue v LECTURE, tirade, diatribe, speech, talk, sermon, exhortation, declamation, oration, address, homily, peroration; *informal* spiel.

harass v ❶ BOTHER, pester, annoy, exasperate, worry, fret, disturb, agitate, provoke, badger, hound, torment, plague, persecute, harry, tease, bait, nag, molest, bedevil; *informal* hassle, give someone a hard time, drive someone up the wall. ❷ HARRY, attack repeatedly, raid, beleaguer, press hard, oppress.

harassed adj STRESSED, under pressure, distraught, under stress, strained, worried, careworn, troubled, vexed, agitated, fretting; *informal* hassled.
– OPPOSITES carefree.

harbour n ❶ PORT, anchorage, dock, haven, marina. ❷ REFUGE, shelter, haven, sanctuary, retreat, asylum, sanctum, covert.

▶ v ❶ SHELTER, give shelter to, house, lodge, put up, take in, billet, provide refuge for, shield, protect, conceal, hide, secrete. ❷ NURSE, maintain, nurture, hold on to, cherish, cling to, retain, entertain.

hard adj ❶ FIRM, solid, compact, compacted, compressed, condensed, dense, rigid, stiff, unyielding, resistant, inflexible, unpliable, tough, strong, stony, unmalleable, closepacked, rock-like. ❷ STRENUOUS, arduous, heavy, tiring, fatiguing, exhausting, backbreaking, laborious, rigorous, exacting, formidable, tough, difficult, uphill, toilsome, Herculean. ❸ DIFFICULT, complicated, complex, involved, intricate, puzzling, perplexing, baffling, knotty, thorny, bewildering, insoluble, enigmatic, unfathomable, incomprehensible. ❹ HARSH, severe, stern, hard-hearted, cold, unfeeling, unsympathetic, grim, ruthless, oppressive, tyrannical, pitiless, merciless, unrelenting, unsparing, callous, cruel, vicious, implacable, obdurate, unyielding, unjust, unfair. ❺ UNPLEASANT, grim, harsh, difficult, disagreeable, uncomfortable, intolerable, unendurable, unbearable, insupportable, distressing, painful, disastrous, calamitous. ❻ FORCEFUL, violent, heavy, strong, powerful, fierce, harsh, sharp.
– OPPOSITES soft, easy.

harden v ❶ SOLIDIFY, become hard, set, stiffen, cake, congeal, clot, coagulate, bake, anneal. ❷ TOUGHEN, make insensitive/unfeeling, deaden, numb, benumb.

hard-hitting adj TOUGH, uncompromising, unsparing, strongly-worded, vigorous, straight-talking, blunt, frank, critical; informal pulling no punches.

hardly adv SCARCELY, barely, only just, just, almost not, with difficulty, with effort.
– OPPOSITES fully.

hardship n ADVERSITY, deprivation, privation, want, need, destitution, poverty, austerity, desolation, misfortune, distress, suffering, affliction, pain, misery, wretchedness, tribulation, trials, burdens, calamity, catastrophe, disaster, ruin, ruination, torment, torture; poetic/literary travail.
– OPPOSITES ease, comfort.

hardy adj HEALTHY, fit, strong, robust, sturdy, tough, rugged, vigorous, in good condition, resilient, lusty, stalwart, hale and hearty, fit as a fiddle, sound in body and limb, in fine fettle, in good kilter.
– OPPOSITES delicate.

harm n ❶ HURT, injury, pain, suffering, trauma, destruction, loss, ruin, havoc, adversity, disservice, abuse, damage, mischief, detriment, defacement, defilement, impairment. ❷ EVIL, badness, wrongdoing, wrong, wickedness, vice, iniquity, sin, sinfulness, immorality, nefariousness.

▶ v HURT, injure, wound, inflict pain/suffering on, abuse, maltreat, ill-treat, ill-use, molest, do violence to, destroy, damage, do mischief to, deface, defile, impair, spoil, mar, blemish.

harmful adj ❶ HURTFUL, injurious, wounding, abusive, detrimental, damaging, deleterious, disadvantageous, destructive, dangerous, pernicious, noxious, baneful, toxic. ❷ BAD, evil, wicked, malign, corrupting, subversive.

– OPPOSITES harmless.

harmless adj ❶ SAFE, innocuous, non-toxic, mild, nonirritant. ❷ INOFFENSIVE, innocuous, unoffending, innocent, blameless, gentle.

– OPPOSITES harmful.

harmonious adj ❶ MELODIOUS, tuneful, musical, harmonizing, sweet-sounding, mellifluous, dulcet, euphonious, symphonious, consonant. ❷ PEACEFUL, peaceable, friendly, amicable, cordial, amiable, agreeable, congenial, united, cooperative, in harmony, in tune, attuned, in accord, compatible, sympathetic.

– OPPOSITES discordant, hostile.

harmonize v ❶ BE IN ACCORD, coincide, agree, correspond, tally, be in unison, be congruent, be of one mind. ❷ RECONCILE, settle differences, restore harmony to, make peaceful,

patch up, negotiate peace between, heal the breach, pour oil on troubled waters.

harmony n ❶ AGREEMENT, accord, accordance, concordance, concurrence, unanimity, cooperation, unity, unison, oneness, amicability, good will, amity, affinity, rapport, sympathy, like-mindedness, friendship, fellowship, comradeship, peace, peacefulness. ❷ COMPATIBILITY, congruity, consonance, coordination, blending, balance, symmetry, suitability; *formal* concord. ❸ TUNE, melody, tunefulness, melodiousness, mellifluousness, euphony.

– OPPOSITES disagreement, incongruity, dissonance.

harrowing adj DISTRESSING, agonizing, excruciating, traumatic, heart-rending, heartbreaking, painful, racking, afflicting, chilling, disturbing, vexing, alarming, perturbing, unnerving, horrifying, terrifying.

harsh adj ❶ ABRUPT, brusque, blunt, curt, gruff, short, surly, concise, clipped, impolite, discourteous, uncivil, ungracious. ❷ CRUEL, brutal, savage, barbarous, hard-hearted, despotic, tyrannical, ruthless, unfeeling, merciless, pitiless, relentless, unrelenting, inhuman. ❸ SEVERE, stringent, stern, grim, austere, uncompromising, inflexible, punitive, draconian. ❹ GRATING, jarring, grinding, rasping, strident, jangling, raucous, ear-piercing, discordant, dissonant,

unharmonious. **⑤** ROUGH, coarse, guttural, hoarse, croaking, raucous, strident, gravelly. **⑥** BLEAK, grim, desolate, stark, severe, austere, barren, rough, wild, bitter, inhospitable, comfortless, spartan. **⑦** GARISH, gaudy, glaring, bold, loud, flashy, showy, crass, crude, vulgar.
– OPPOSITES lenient, gentle.

harvest n REAPING, crop, yield, produce, vintage, ingathering.
▶ v GATHER, gather in, reap, glean, pick, pluck, collect, amass, accumulate, garner.

hassle v ANNOY, badger, harass, hound, pester, bother, trouble, worry, torment, plague; informal give someone a hard time.
▶ n TROUBLE, bother, inconvenience, annoyance, nuisance, harassment, difficulty, problem, struggle, fight, quarrel, altercation, disagreement, dispute, wrangle, tussle.

haste n SPEED, swiftness, rapidity, rapidness, quickness, fastness, briskness, urgency, alacrity, promptness, dispatch, expeditiousness, promptitude, expedition, celerity, fleetness.

hasty adj **❶** SWIFT, rapid, quick, fast, speedy, hurried, hurrying, running, prompt, expeditious, brisk, urgent, fleet. **❷** QUICK, short, brief, rushed, short-lived, fleeting, transitory, cursory, perfunctory, superficial, slight. **❸** HURRIED, rushed, impetuous, reckless, rash, foolhardy, precipitate, impulsive,

headlong, thoughtless, heedless, careless, ill-conceived.
– OPPOSITES slow, cautious.

hatch v **❶** INCUBATE, brood, sit on, cover. **❷** DEVISE, concoct, contrive, plan, scheme, design, invent, formulate, originate, conceive, dream up, think up; informal cook up.

hate v **❶** LOATHE, detest, abhor, dislike, despise, abominate, execrate, have an aversion to, feel hostile towards, be unable to stand/bear, view with dislike, be sick of, be tired of, shudder at, be repelled by, recoil from. **❷** BE RELUCTANT, be unwilling, feel disinclined, be sorry, dislike, not have the heart, shy away from, flinch from.
– OPPOSITES love, relish.
▶ n see HATRED.

hateful adj DETESTABLE, loathsome, abhorrent, abominable, despicable, execrable, odious, revolting, repugnant, repellent, disgusting, obnoxious, offensive, insufferable, horrible, unpleasant, nasty, disagreeable, foul, vile, heinous.
– OPPOSITES admirable.

hatred n HATE, loathing, detestation, abhorrence, dislike, aversion, hostility, ill will, enmity, animosity, antagonism, antipathy, animus, revulsion, repugnance, odium, rancour, grudge, execration, abomination.
– OPPOSITES love.

haughty adj ARROGANT, proud, conceited, self-important, egot-

istical, vain, swollen-headed, overweening, overbearing, pompous, smug, presumptuous, condescending, supercilious, lofty, patronizing, snobbish, imperious, boastful, scornful, lordly, high-handed; *informal* snooty, on one's high horse, high and mighty, stuck up, hoity-toity, uppity, uppish.
– OPPOSITES modest, humble.

haul v DRAG, pull, tug, draw, heave, trail, lug, tow, take in tow, cart, carry, convoy, ship.

haunt v ❶ FREQUENT, visit regularly, patronize; *informal* hang out in. ❷ OBSESS, prey on someone's mind, prey on, torment, plague, disturb, trouble, worry, oppress, burden, beset, harry, weigh on, come back to, stay with.

have v ❶ OWN, possess, keep, keep for one's use, use, hold, retain. ❷ GET, be given, receive, accept, obtain, acquire, procure, secure, gain. ❸ CONTAIN, include, comprise, embrace, take in, incorporate, embody, comprehend. ❹ EXPERIENCE, undergo, go through, encounter, meet, find, be subjected to, submit to, suffer from, endure, tolerate, put up with. ❺ FEEL, entertain, have/keep/bear in mind, harbour, foster, nurse, cherish. ❻ GIVE BIRTH TO, bear, deliver, be delivered of, bring into the world, bring forth.
■ **have had it** BE FINISHED, be out, be defeated, have lost, have no chance, have no hope.
have to MUST, have got to, be

bound to, be obliged to, be forced to, be compelled to.

haven n REFUGE, shelter, sanctuary, asylum, retreat, sanctum, sanctum sanctorum, covert.

havoc n ❶ DEVASTATION, destruction, damage, ruination, ruin, rack and ruin, despoliation, waste, gutting, wreckage, desolation, disaster, catastrophe, cataclysm. ❷ CHAOS, disorder, confusion, disruption, disorganization, mayhem; *informal* shambles.

hazard n ❶ DANGER, peril, risk, jeopardy, threat, menace. ❷ CHANCE, accident, luck, contingency, fortuity, fortuitousness.
▶ v ❶ RISK, put at risk, endanger, expose to danger, imperil, put in jeopardy, jeopardize. ❷ VENTURE, put forward, proffer, offer, submit, advance, volunteer.

hazardous adj DANGEROUS, risky, perilous, fraught with danger/risk, chancy, uncertain, unpredictable, precarious, parlous, unsafe, insecure; *informal* dicey, hairy, tricky.
– OPPOSITES safe.

haze n MIST, mistiness, fog, cloud, cloudiness, smog, vapour.

hazy adj ❶ MISTY, foggy, cloudy, smoggy, overcast. ❷ VAGUE, indefinite, blurred, fuzzy, faint, confused, muddled, unclear, obscure, dim, indistinct, ill-defined.
– OPPOSITES clear.

head n ❶ SKULL, cranium; *informal* nut; *Brit. informal* bonce; *informal, dated* conk, noodle, noddle. ❷ MIND, intelligence, intellect, brain, brains, mentality, wit, sense, wisdom, reasoning, rationality, understanding. ❸ LEADER, chief, commander, director, manager, superintendent, controller, administrator, supervisor, principal, captain. ❹ FRONT, fore, forefront, van, vanguard.

▶ v ❶ LEAD, be at the head of, be in charge of, be in command/control of, command, control, run, supervise, rule, govern, guide. ❷ MAKE FOR, go to, go in the direction of, aim for, set out for, start out for, go towards, steer towards, make a beeline for.

■ **head off** DIVERT, intercept, deflect, turn aside, block off, cut off, forestall.

headlong adv ❶ HEAD FIRST, head on, on one's head. ❷ HASTILY, hurriedly, impatiently, without thinking, rashly, recklessly, wildly, prematurely, carelessly, precipitately, heedlessly.
– OPPOSITES cautiously.

headquarters n CENTRE OF OPERATIONS, base, command post, main office/branch, head office.

heal v ❶ CURE, make well, make better, remedy, treat, mend, restore, regenerate. ❷ RECUPERATE, get better/well, mend, be cured, be on the mend, improve, be restored. ❸ RECONCILE, patch up, settle, set right, put right, harmonize, conciliate.

health n ❶ HEALTHINESS, fitness, well-being, good condition, good shape, soundness, robustness, strength, vigour, fine fettle, salubrity. ❷ STATE OF HEALTH, constitution, physical state, shape, condition, form, tone.

healthy adj ❶ IN GOOD HEALTH, fit, in good condition, robust, strong, vigorous, hardy, flourishing, blooming, hale and hearty, hale; *informal* in the pink. ❷ HEALTH-GIVING, beneficial, invigorating, bracing, stimulating, refreshing, nutritious, nourishing, wholesome, good for one.
– OPPOSITES unhealthy.

heap n ❶ PILE, stack, mound, mass, stockpile, accumulation, collection, agglomeration, conglomeration, hoard, store, stock, supply. ❷ A LOT, lots, a great deal, abundance, plenty, a mint; *informal* oodles, loads, tons, pots, stacks; *Brit. informal* lashings.

▶ v PILE UP, stack, amass, stockpile, mound, accumulate, collect, assemble, hoard, store, stock up, set aside, lay by.

hear v ❶ TAKE IN, catch, perceive, overhear; *informal* get, latch on to. ❷ BE INFORMED, be told of, be made aware, receive information, find out, discover, learn, gather, pick up, hear tell, get wind of. ❸ TRY, judge, pass judgement on, adjudicate, examine, investigate, inquire into, consider.

hearing n INQUIRY, trial, inquest, investigation, review.

heart n ❶ PASSION, love, affection, emotions, feelings. ❷ TENDERNESS, compassion, sympathy, empathy, humanity, responsiveness, fellow feeling, goodwill, kindness, kindliness. ❸ SPIRIT, enthusiasm, keenness, eagerness, liveliness. ❹ ESSENCE, crux, substance, core, quintessence.

heartache n SORROW, grief, sadness, anguish, pain, hurt, agony, suffering, misery, wretchedness, despair, desolation, woe, despondency; *poetic/literary* dolour.
– OPPOSITES happiness.

heartbreaking adj SAD, pitiful, tragic, poignant, painful, agonizing, distressing, affecting, grievous, bitter, cruel, harsh, tear-jerking, harrowing, excruciating.

hearten v CHEER, raise someone's spirits, revitalize, energize, invigorate, animate, exhilarate, uplift, elate, comfort, encourage, buoy up; *informal* buck up, give someone a shot in the arm.

heartfelt adj DEEPLY FELT, deep, profound, wholehearted, sincere, earnest, honest, devout, genuine, unfeigned, ardent, fervent, passionate, warm, enthusiastic, eager.

heartless adj UNFEELING, unsympathetic, unkind, uncaring, unmoved, untouched, cold, cold-hearted, cold-blooded, hard-hearted, cruel, harsh, stern, hard, brutal, merciless, pitiless, ruthless.
– OPPOSITES compassionate.

heat n ❶ HOTNESS, warmth, warmness, torridness, torridity, sultriness, calefaction. ❷ PASSION, warmth, intensity, vehemence, ardour, fervour, fervency, zeal, eagerness, enthusiasm, animation, earnestness, excitement, agitation.
– OPPOSITES cold, apathy.
▶ v ❶ WARM, warm up, make hot/warm, reheat, cook. ❷ GROW HOT / WARM, become hotter/warmer.

heated adj VEHEMENT, passionate, fierce, angry, furious, stormy, tempestuous, frenzied, raging, intense, impassioned, violent, animated, inflamed, enraged.

heathen n UNBELIEVER, infidel, pagan, disbeliever, atheist, heretic, idolater/idolatress.
▶ adj PAGAN, godless, infidel, heathenish, irreligious, idolatrous, atheistic, heretical.

heave v ❶ LIFT, haul, tug, raise, hoist. ❷ THROW, cast, toss, fling, hurl, let fly, pitch; *informal* sling, chuck. ❸ VOMIT, gag, retch, *Brit.* be sick; *N. Amer.* get sick; *informal* throw up, puke.

heaven n ❶ PARADISE, the next life, the hereafter, the life to come, the next world, the afterlife, nirvana. ❷ ECSTASY, bliss, rapture, joy, happiness, contentment, seventh heaven.

❸ SKY, skies; *poetic/literary* firmament, empyrean, ether.
– OPPOSITES hell.

heavenly adj ❶ CELESTIAL, divine, angelic, seraphic, cherubic, beatific, blessed, holy, god-like, immortal, paradisiacal. ❷ DELIGHTFUL, pleasurable, enjoyable, marvellous, wonderful, gratifying, blissful, rapturous, sublime, glorious, divine. ❸ BEAUTIFUL, exquisite, perfect, superb, ravishing, enchanting, alluring.
– OPPOSITES hellish.

heavy adj ❶ WEIGHTY, bulky, hefty, big, large, substantial, massive, enormous, unwieldy, cumbersome, burdensome. ❷ ONEROUS, burdensome, oppressive, difficult, unbearable, intolerable. ❸ HARD, forceful, strong, severe, harsh, intense, sharp. ❹ OVERWEIGHT, fat, stout, obese, tubby, corpulent, paunchy, lumbering, bulky; *informal* hulking. ❺ SEVERE, intense, serious, grave.
– OPPOSITES light.

heavy-handed adj *see* CLUMSY (1, 3).

hectic adj BUSY, active, frantic, frenetic, frenzied, bustling, flurried, fast and furious, turbulent, tumultuous, confused, exciting, excited, wild.
– OPPOSITES leisurely.

hedge n ❶ HEDGEROW, row of bushes, quickset, barrier, screen, protection, windbreak. ❷ SAFEGUARD, guard, protection, shield, cover, insurance.
▶ v ❶ SURROUND, enclose, encir-
cle, circle, border, edge, skirt. ❷ EQUIVOCATE, prevaricate, be vague/ambivalent, be non-committal, dodge the question/issue, beat about the bush, sidestep the question/issue, temporize, quibble; *Brit.* hum and haw; *N. Amer. informal* waffle.

heed n ATTENTION, attentiveness, notice, note, regard, mindfulness, mind, respect, consideration, thought, care, caution, watchfulness, wariness, chariness.
▶ V PAY HEED / ATTENTION TO, attend to, take notice/note of, notice, note, bear in mind, be mindful of, mind, mark, take into account, follow, obey, adhere to, observe, take to heart, be alert to, be cautious of, watch out for.

heedful adj ATTENTIVE, careful, mindful, cautious, prudent, circumspect, wary, observant, watchful, vigilant, alert, on guard.
– OPPOSITES heedless.

heedless adj INATTENTIVE, unheeding, careless, incautious, unmindful, regardless, unthinking, thoughtless, unwary, oblivious, unobservant, negligent, neglectful, rash, reckless, foolhardy, precipitate.
– OPPOSITES heedful.

heft v LIFT, lift up, raise, hoist, hike up, heave, boost.

hefty adj ❶ HEAVY, bulky, big, large, stout, massive, huge, muscular, brawny, strapping, sturdy, solidly built, strong; *informal* beefy, hulking.

❷ SUBSTANTIAL, sizeable, huge, colossal, expensive.
– OPPOSITES light.

height n ❶ HIGHNESS, altitude, loftiness, elevation, tallness, stature. ❷ TOP, mountain top, hilltop, summit, peak, crest, crown, pinnacle, apex, vertex, apogee. ❸ PEAK, zenith, apex, culmination, crowning point, climax, consummation, perfection.

heighten v ❶ RAISE, make higher, lift, elevate. ❷ MAKE GREATER, intensify, raise, increase, add to, build up, augment, boost, strengthen, amplify, magnify, aggravate, enhance.
– OPPOSITES lower.

heinous adj ABOMINABLE, atrocious, abhorrent, odious, detestable, loathsome, hateful, wicked, monstrous, horrible, ghastly, shocking, flagrant, contemptible, reprehensible, despicable.

hellish adj ❶ DEMONIC, diabolical, devilish, fiendish, satanic, infernal. ❷ UNPLEASANT, nasty, disagreeable, horrible, horrid, awful.

help v ❶ ASSIST, aid, give someone a (helping) hand, lend a hand, guide, be of service to, be useful to, succour, befriend. ❷ SUPPORT, back, contribute to, promote, boost. ❸ SOOTHE, relieve, ameliorate, alleviate, mitigate, assuage, cure, heal, improve, ease.
▶ n ❶ ASSISTANCE, aid, service, helping hand, guidance, bene-

fit, advantage, support, backing, succour. ❷ RELIEF, alleviation, amelioration, mitigation, remedy, cure, improvement, ease, corrective, balm. ❸ SERVANT, maid, worker, hired help; Brit. informal daily.
■ **help oneself to** TAKE, appropriate, commandeer, steal, make free with; informal walk off with; Brit. informal pinch, nick.

helper n ASSISTANT, aide, deputy, adjutant, second-in-command, auxiliary, right-hand man/woman, henchman, colleague, associate, co-worker, partner, ally, collaborator.

helpful adj ❶ USEFUL, of use, of service, beneficial, valuable, advantageous, constructive, practical, productive, instrumental. ❷ SUPPORTIVE, kind, friendly, obliging, accommodating, cooperative, sympathetic, considerate, caring, neighbourly, charitable, benevolent.
– OPPOSITES useless, unhelpful.

helping n PORTION, serving, ration, piece, plateful, amount, share.

helpless adj ❶ WEAK, feeble, disabled, incapable, infirm, debilitated, powerless, dependent, unfit, invalid, bedridden, paralysed; informal laid up. ❷ DEFENCELESS, unprotected, vulnerable, exposed, abandoned, destitute, forlorn, desolate.
– OPPOSITES independent.

hem n BORDER, edge, edging,

trim, trimming, fringe, frill, flounce, valance.
▶ v ❶ BIND, edge, trim, fringe. ❷ BORDER, edge, skirt, surround, encircle, circle, enclose, encompass. ❸ SHUT IN, hedge in, close in, pen in, confine, constrain, restrict, limit, trap, keep within bounds.

herd n FLOCK, pack, mob, crowd, throng, swarm, press, multitude.
▶ v DRIVE, round up, assemble, collect, muster, shepherd, guide, lead, force, urge, goad.

hereditary adj ❶ GENETIC, congenital, innate, inborn, inherent, family, inbred, transmissible, transferable. ❷ INHERITED, handed down, bequeathed, willed, transferred, transmitted, family, ancestral.

heresy n APOSTASY, dissent, nonconformity, unorthodoxy, free thinking, dissidence, scepticism, agnosticism, atheism, heterodoxy, revisionism, idolatry, paganism.

heretic n DISSENTER, apostate, unbeliever, sceptic, agnostic, atheist, nonconformist, free thinker, renegade, revisionist, schismatic, pagan, idolater, recusant.

heretical adj DISSIDENT, sceptical, nonconformist, atheistical, agnostic, freethinking, unorthodox, heterodox, renegade, revisionist, schismatic, idolatrous, pagan, recusant.
– OPPOSITES orthodox.

heritage n HISTORY, tradition, background, ancestry, lineage,

descent, family, extraction, heredity, birth.

hermit n RECLUSE, solitary, anchorite, anchoress, eremite, stylite.

heroic adj ❶ BRAVE, courageous, valiant, intrepid, fearless, gallant, valorous, stouthearted, lion-hearted, bold, daring, undaunted, dauntless, manly, virile, doughty, chivalrous. ❷ LEGENDARY, mythological, classic, classical, fabulous. ❸ EPIC, epical, Homeric, grandiloquent, highflown, high-sounding, extravagant, grandiose, bombastic, rhetorical, pretentious, turgid, magniloquent, orotund, elevated.
– OPPOSITES cowardly.

heroism n BRAVERY, courage, courageousness, valour, intrepidity, fearlessness, gallantry, stout-heartedness, lion-heartedness, boldness, daring, dauntlessness, doughtiness, manliness, virility, mettle, spirit, fortitude, chivalry.

hesitant adj ❶ UNCERTAIN, unsure, doubtful, dubious, sceptical, irresolute, indecisive, vacillating, wavering, oscillating, shilly-shallying, stalling, delaying, disinclined, unwilling, half-hearted, lacking confidence, diffident, timid, shy. ❷ RELUCTANT, unwilling, disinclined, diffident, having qualms about.
– OPPOSITES determined, decisive.

hesitate v ❶ DELAY, pause,

hang back, wait, be uncertain, be unsure, be doubtful, be indecisive, vacillate, waver, dither, shilly-shally, dally, stall, temporize, dilly-dally. ❷ BE RELUCTANT, be unwilling, be disinclined, shrink from, hang back from, think twice about, baulk at, demur from, scruple to, have misgivings about, be diffident about. ❸ STAMMER, stumble, falter, fumble for words; *Brit.* hum and haw.

hew v ❶ CHOP, hack, axe, cut, saw, fell, lop, sever, trim, prune. ❷ CARVE, sculpt, sculpture, shape, fashion, form, model, whittle, chip, hammer, chisel, rough-hew.

hidden adj ❶ OUT OF SIGHT, secret, unseen, not visible, not on view, covered, concealed, masked, shrouded, unrevealed. ❷ SECRET, obscure, indistinct, indefinite, unclear, vague, cryptic, mysterious, covert, concealed, under wraps, abstruse, arcane, recondite, clandestine, ulterior, unfathomable, inexplicable, occult, mystical.
– OPPOSITES obvious.

hide v ❶ CONCEAL ONESELF, go into hiding, take cover, find a hiding place, lie low, keep out of sight, secrete oneself, go to ground, go underground, cover one's tracks; *informal* hole up. ❷ STOW AWAY, secrete, store away, lock up; *informal* stash. ❸ OBSCURE, block, obstruct, darken, eclipse, cloud. ❹ KEEP SECRET, keep dark, withhold, conceal, suppress, mask, veil, shroud, camouflage, disguise, hush up; *informal* keep mum about, keep under one's hat.
– OPPOSITES reveal.

hideous adj ❶ UGLY, unsightly, grotesque, monstrous, repulsive, repellent, revolting, gruesome, disgusting, grim, ghastly, macabre. ❷ AWFUL, horrible, horrific, horrendous, horrifying, frightful, shocking, dreadful, outrageous, monstrous, appalling, terrible, terrifying, heinous, abominable, foul, vile, odious, loathsome, contemptible, execrable.
– OPPOSITES beautiful.

hiding n BEATING, thrashing, whipping, caning, spanking, flogging, drubbing, battering; *informal* licking, walloping, tanning, whaling, lathering.

hierarchy n SOCIAL ORDER, ranking, grading, class system, pecking order.

high adj ❶ TALL, lofty, elevated, soaring, towering, steep. ❷ HIGH-RANKING, leading, top, powerful, important, prominent, eminent, principal, chief, influential, distinguished, notable, illustrious, exalted. ❸ INTENSE, strong, powerful, extreme, forceful, vigorous, potent, violent. ❹ DRUGGED, intoxicated, inebriated, delirious, hallucinating; *informal* stoned, on a trip, turned on.
– OPPOSITES low.

highbrow n INTELLECTUAL, scholar, genius, mastermind; *informal* egghead, brain; *Brit. informal* brainbox.

▶ adj INTELLECTUAL, scholarly, bookish, cultured, cultivated, educated, sophisticated; *informal* brainy.
– OPPOSITES lowbrow.

high-handed adj AUTOCRATIC, tyrannical, despotic, domineering, oppressive, overbearing, imperious, haughty, lordly; *informal* bossy.

hike v ❶ WALK, march, tramp, trek, trudge, plod, ramble, wander, backpack. ❷ HITCH UP, pull up, jack up, lift up. ❸ RAISE, increase, add to, put up, jack up.
▶ n WALK, march, tramp, trek, ramble, trudge, wander.

hilarious adj VERY FUNNY, extremely amusing, comical, uproarious, humorous, entertaining, side-splitting; *informal* priceless.

hill n ❶ ELEVATION, heights, hillock, hilltop, knoll, hummock, mound, mount, fell, ridge. ❷ SLOPE, incline, rise, gradient, ramp, acclivity, declivity.

hinder v IMPEDE, hamper, hold back, interfere with, delay, hold up, slow down, retard, obstruct, inhibit, handicap, hamstring, block, interrupt, check, trammel, forestall, curb, baulk, thwart, frustrate, baffle, foil, stymie, stop, bring to a halt, arrest, defer, abort, prevent, debar.
– OPPOSITES facilitate.

hindrance n IMPEDIMENT, obstacle, obstruction, interference, handicap, block, restraint, interruption, check,

bar, barrier, drawback, snag, difficulty, stumbling block, encumbrance, curb, stoppage, trammel, deterrent, prevention, debarment.
– OPPOSITES aid, help.

hinge
■ **hinge on** DEPEND ON, turn on, hang on, be contingent on, pivot on, revolve around, rest on, centre on.

hint n ❶ CLUE, inkling, suggestion, innuendo, tip-off, insinuation, implication, indication, mention, allusion, intimation, whisper, a word to the wise. ❷ TIP, pointer, advice, help, suggestion. ❸ TOUCH, trace, suggestion, dash, soupçon, sprinkling, tinge, whiff, breath, taste, scent.
▶ v SUGGEST, insinuate, imply, indicate, mention, allude to, intimate, let it be known, signal, refer to, make a reference to.

hire v ❶ RENT, lease, charter, engage. ❷ APPOINT, sign on, take on, engage, employ, secure someone's services, enlist, contract with.

historic adj FAMED, notable, famous, celebrated, renowned, momentous, significant, important, consequential, memorable, remarkable, outstanding, extraordinary, epoch-making, red-letter.

historical adj DOCUMENTED, recorded, factual, chronicled, archival, authentic, actual, attested, verified, confirmed.

history n ❶ ANNAL, records,

chronicles, account, study, tale, saga, narrative, recital, reports, memoirs, biography. ❷ LIFE STORY, background, antecedents, experiences, adventures, fortunes. ❸ THE PAST, former times, bygone days, yesterday, the old days, the good old days, time gone by, antiquity.

hit v ❶ STRIKE, smack, slap, punch, box, cuff, buffet, thump, batter, pound, pummel, thrash, hammer, bang, knock, club, swat; *informal* whack, wallop, bash, belt, clout, clip, clobber, sock, biff, swipe. ❷ RUN INTO, collide with, bang into, smash into, crash into, knock into, bump, meet head-on.

hoard v STORE, store up, stock up, stockpile, put by, put away, lay by, lay in, set aside, pile up, stack up, stow away, husband, save, buy up, accumulate, amass, heap up, collect, gather, squirrel away, garner.
▶ n STORE, stockpile, supply, reserve, fund, cache, reservoir, accumulation, heap, pile, mass, aggregation, conglomeration; *informal* stash.

hoarse adj CROAKY, croaking, gruff, rough, throaty, harsh, husky, gravelly, rasping, guttural, raucous, cracked.
– OPPOSITES smooth.

hoax n PRACTICAL JOKE, joke, prank, jest, trick, ruse, deception, fraud, imposture, cheat, swindle; *informal* con, fast one, spoof, scam.
▶ v TRICK, fool, deceive, hood-wink, delude, bluff, dupe, take in, cheat, swindle, defraud, gull; *informal* con, pull a fast one on, pull the wool over someone's eyes, take for a ride, spoof.

hobble v WALK WITH DIFFICULTY, limp, falter, shuffle, totter, stagger, reel; *Scottish* hirple.

hobby n INTEREST, pursuit, pastime, diversion, recreation, relaxation, sideline, divertissement, entertainment, amusement.

hold v ❶ CLASP, clutch, grasp, grip, clench, seize, cling to. ❷ BEAR, carry, take, support, hold up, buttress, keep up, sustain, prop up, brace, suspend. ❸ DETAIN, hold in custody, confine, impound, constrain, lock up, imprison, put behind bars, incarcerate. ❹ KEEP, maintain, occupy, engage, involve, absorb, engross, monopolize, catch, arrest, fascinate, rivet. ❺ CONTAIN, take, accommodate, have a capacity for. ❻ CALL, convene, assemble, conduct, run, preside over, officiate at.
▶ n ❶ GRIP, grasp, clutch, clasp. ❷ CONTROL, grip, power, dominance, influence, mastery, dominion, authority, ascendancy.
■ hold out STAND FAST, stand firm, resist, withstand, maintain one's position, stay put.
hold up DELAY, hinder, impede, obstruct, retard, slow down, set back, stop, bring to a halt, prevent.

holder n ❶ OWNER, possessor, bearer, proprietor, keeper, custodian, purchaser, incumbent; *Brit.* occupier. ❷ CONTAINER, case, casing, receptacle, stand, cover, covering, housing, sheath.

hole n ❶ OPENING, aperture, gap, orifice, space, breach, break, fissure, crack, rift, puncture, perforation, cut, incision, split, gash, rent, slit, vent, notch. ❷ PIT, crater, excavation, mine, shaft, dugout, cave, cavern, pothole, depression, hollow, chamber, pocket, cavity, dip.

holiness n SANCTITY, sanctitude, saintliness, sacredness, divineness, divinity, godliness, blessedness, spirituality, religiousness, piety, righteousness, goodness, virtue, purity, sanctimoniousness.

hollow adj ❶ EMPTY, vacant, not filled, not solid, hollowed out. ❷ SUNKEN, deep-set, indented, depressed, concave, caved in, cavernous, incurvate. ❸ MUFFLED, muted, low, dull, deep, rumbling, flat, dead, sepulchral. ❹ WORTHLESS, valueless, empty, profitless, fruitless, unprofitable, pointless, meaningless, insignificant, specious, pyrrhic. ❺ INSINCERE, false, dissembling, deceitful, sham, untrue, spurious.
– OPPOSITES solid.
▶ n INDENTATION, depression, concavity, dent, dip, dint, dimple, hole, crater, cavern, pit, cavity, well, trough.

holocaust n ❶ DEVASTATION, destruction, inferno, conflagra-

tion, demolition. ❷ GENOCIDE, mass murder, annihilation, massacre, carnage, slaughter, extermination, butchery, ethnic cleansing.

holy adj ❶ DEVOUT, God-fearing, pious, spiritual, religious, righteous, good, virtuous, moral, saintly, saintlike, sinless, pietistic. ❷ SACRED, blessed, blest, sanctified, consecrated, hallowed, sacrosanct, dedicated, venerated, divine, religious.
– OPPOSITES impious.

home n ❶ HOUSE, residence, habitation; *formal* dwelling, abode, domicile. ❷ HOMELAND, birth place, native land, fatherland, motherland, country of origin. ❸ HABITAT, environment, natural element, territory, ground, haunts, domain; *formal* abode.
■ **home in on** AIM AT, focus on, focus attention on, concentrate on, pinpoint, zero in on, zoom in on.

homeless adj OF NO FIXED ABODE, destitute, derelict, without a roof over one's head, down-and-out, vagrant, itinerant, nomadic, dispossessed, rootless.

homely adj ❶ COMFORTABLE, cosy, snug, welcoming, informal, relaxed, modest, unassuming, unpretentious, simple, natural, plain. ❷ PLAIN, unattractive, ugly, plain-featured, ill-favoured; *informal* not much to look at, short on looks.
– OPPOSITES grand, beautiful.

homicide n MURDER, manslaughter, killing, slaughter, assassination, patricide, matricide, infanticide; *poetic/literary* slaying.

homily n SERMON, lecture, speech, address, discourse, lesson, talk, oration.

homosexual adj GAY, lesbian, homoerotic; *informal* queer; *Brit. informal* bent, poofy.
– OPPOSITES heterosexual.

honest adj ❶ PRINCIPLED, upright, honourable, ethical, moral, righteous, right-minded, virtuous, good, worthy, decent, law-abiding, high-minded, upstanding, just, fair, truthful, incorruptible, true, trustworthy, trusty, reliable, conscientious, scrupulous, reputable, dependable, loyal, faithful; *formal* veracious. ❷ TRUTHFUL, frank, candid, direct, forthright, straightforward, open, genuine, plain-speaking, matter-of-fact, outspoken, blunt, undisguised, unfeigned, unequivocal.
– OPPOSITES dishonest.

honestly adv ❶ LAWFULLY, legally, legitimately, fairly, by fair means, honourably, decently, ethically, morally, without corruption; *informal* on the level, on the straight and narrow. ❷ SPEAKING TRUTHFULLY, truthfully, to be honest, speaking frankly, in all sincerity, candidly, frankly, openly, plainly, in plain language, to someone's face, without dissembling; *informal* straight out, straight up, Scout's honour.

honorary adj NOMINAL, titular, in name only, unofficial, ex officio, complimentary, unpaid.

honour n ❶ HONESTY, uprightness, integrity, ethics, morals, high principles, righteousness, virtue, rectitude, goodness, decency, probity, worthiness, worth, fairness, justness, justice, truthfulness, trustworthiness, reliability, dependability, faithfulness, fidelity. ❷ GLORY, prestige, renown, fame, illustriousness, notability, esteem, distinction, credit, kudos. ❸ ACCLAIM, acclamation, applause, accolades, tributes, homage, praise, compliments, eulogy, paeans, adoration, reverence, adulation.
– OPPOSITES dishonour.
▶ v ❶ ESTEEM, respect, hold in esteem, have a high regard for, admire, defer to, revere, venerate, worship, adore, idolize. ❷ ACCLAIM, applaud, pay homage to, pay tribute to, lionize, cheer, praise, eulogize. ❸ FULFIL, discharge, carry out, observe, keep, be true to, live up to.

honourable adj HONEST, upright, ethical, moral, principled, upstanding, righteous, right-minded, virtuous, good, decent, worthy, fair, just, true, truthful, trustworthy, trusty, reliable, dependable, faithful.

hook v ❶ FASTEN, secure, fix, close the clasp. ❷ SNARE, trap, ensnare, entrap, enmesh.

hooligan n THUG, vandal, lout, rowdy, delinquent, ruffian, mugger, hoodlum; *Brit.* tearaway; *informal* tough, yahoo; *Brit. informal* yob, yobbo.

hoop n RING, band, circle, loop, wheel, girdle.

hop v JUMP, leap, bound, spring, vault, bounce, skip, caper, dance, frisk.

hope n EXPECTATION, hopefulness, expectancy, anticipation, desire, longing, wish, wishing, craving, yearning, aspiration, ambition, dream, belief, assurance, confidence, assumption, conviction, faith, trust, optimism.
– OPPOSITES despair, pessimism.
▶ v BE HOPEFUL OF, expect, anticipate, look forward to, await, contemplate, desire, long, wish, crave, yearn, aspire, be ambitious, dream, believe, assume, have confidence, be convinced, rely on, count on, trust in.

hopeful adj ❶ FULL OF HOPE, expectant, optimistic, confident, positive, assured, buoyant, sanguine. ❷ ENCOURAGING, promising, heartening, reassuring, gladdening, optimistic, favourable, auspicious, propitious, cheerful, bright, pleasant, rosy.
– OPPOSITES hopeless.

hopefully adv ❶ WITH HOPE, full of hope, expectantly, optimistically, confidently, with assurance, buoyantly, sanguinely. ❷ IT IS TO BE HOPED THAT, with luck, all being well, if all goes well, probably, conceivably, feasibly.

hopeless adj ❶ WITHOUT HOPE, despairing, in despair, desperate, pessimistic, dejected, downhearted, despondent, demoralized, disconsolate, downcast, wretched, forlorn, suicidal, woebegone. ❷ IMPOSSIBLE, impracticable, futile, useless, vain, pointless, worthless, unattainable, unachievable, no-win. ❸ POOR, incompetent, inadequate, inferior, ineffective, ineffectual; *informal* no good, useless.
– OPPOSITES hopeful, accomplished.

horde n CROWD, throng, mob, mass, group, multitude, host, army, pack, gang, troop, drove, crew, band, flock, swarm, gathering, assembly.

horrible adj ❶ AWFUL, dreadful, terrible, horrid, horrifying, terrifying, frightful, fearful, horrendous, shocking, gruesome, hideous, grim, ghastly, harrowing, disgusting, revolting, repulsive, loathsome, abhorrent, detestable, hateful, abominable. ❷ DISAGREEABLE, nasty, unpleasant, obnoxious, odious, awful, dreadful, ghastly, frightful, hideous, revolting, appalling.
– OPPOSITES v pleasant.

horrify v SHOCK, appal, outrage, scandalize, disgust, revolt, repel, nauseate, sicken, offend, dismay; *informal* turn off.

horror n ❶ TERROR, fear, fearfulness, alarm, fright, dread, awe, panic, trepidation, apprehensiveness, uneasiness, nervousness, dismay, consternation. ❷ ABHORRENCE, abomination, loathing, hate, detestation, repulsion, revulsion, disgust, distaste, aversion, hostility, antipathy, animosity.

horse n STEED, mount, hack, cob, nag; Brit. informal gee-gee.

horseman, horsewoman n RIDER, equestrian, jockey, horse soldier, cavalryman, dragoon, cavalier, cowboy, cowgirl.

horseplay n CLOWNING, fooling, tomfoolery, buffoonery, pranks, antics, capers, high jinks, rough and tumble, skylarking; informal shenanigans, monkey business.

hospitable adj WELCOMING, generous, open-handed, sociable, friendly, bountiful, neighbourly, kind, warm, helpful.
– OPPOSITES inhospitable.

hospital n CLINIC, infirmary, health centre, medical centre, sanatorium, nursing home, hospice, sick bay.

host n ❶ PROPRIETOR, proprietress, landlord, landlady, innkeeper, hotel-keeper, hotelier. ❷ PRESENTER, compère, master of ceremonies, MC, anchorman, anchorwoman.

hostage n CAPTIVE, prisoner, pawn, pledge, security.

hostile adj ❶ OPPOSED, antagonistic, averse, ill-disposed, against, inimical; informal anti. ❷ AGGRESSIVE, angry, belligerent, bellicose, warlike, warring, militant, antagonistic, unfriendly, unkind, unsympathetic, malevolent, malicious, spiteful, wrathful. ❸ ADVERSE, unfavourable, inauspicious, unpropitious, disadvantageous.
– OPPOSITES favourable, friendly.

hostility n ❶ ANTAGONISM, opposition, ill will, aversion, animosity, enmity. ❷ AGGRESSION, belligerence, anger, bellicosity, militancy, antagonism, unfriendliness, unkindness, malevolence, spite, malice, wrath.
– OPPOSITES friendship.

hot adj ❶ HEATED, very warm, boiling, boiling hot, piping hot, scalding, red-hot, sizzling, steaming, scorching, roasting, searing, blazing hot, sweltering, blistering, baking, oven-like, torrid, sultry. ❷ SPICY, peppery, piquant, fiery, pungent, sharp, biting, acrid. ❸ VIOLENT, furious, heated, fierce, ferocious, stormy, tempestuous, savage.
– OPPOSITES cold, mild.

hot-headed adj HOT-TEMPERED, quick-tempered, short-tempered, fiery, excitable, volatile, hasty, rash, impetuous, impulsive, reckless, foolhardy, wild, unruly.

house n ❶ RESIDENCE, home, habitation; informal pad; Brit. informal gaff; formal dwelling, abode, domicile. ❷ FAMILY, clan, line, dynasty, lineage, ancestry.
▸ v ❶ ACCOMMODATE, lodge, put

up, take in, have room for, sleep, shelter, harbour. ❷ COVER, sheathe, protect, shelter, guard, contain, keep.

household n ❶ FAMILY, home, house, ménage, establishment. ▶ adj DOMESTIC, family, ordinary, everyday, common, usual, run-of-the-mill.

hover v ❶ FLOAT, fly, be suspended, hang, drift, be wafted, flutter. ❷ LINGER, loiter, hang about, wait, stay. ❸ VACILLATE, fluctuate, oscillate, alternate, see-saw; *Scottish* swither.

however adv NEVERTHELESS, be that as it may, nonetheless, notwithstanding, anyway, anyhow, regardless, despite that, still, yet, just the same, though.

howl v BAY, yowl, ululate, yelp, wail, bawl, scream, bellow, caterwaul, cry.

hub n ❶ PIVOT, axis, nave. ❷ CENTRE, middle, core, heart, focus, focal point.

huddle v ❶ CROWD, throng, press, pack, cluster, cram, herd, squeeze, gather, congregate. ❷ CURL UP, snuggle, cuddle, nestle, hunch up. ▶ n GATHERING, crowd, cluster, pack, press.

hue n ❶ COLOUR, tone, shade, tint, tinge, dye. ❷ COMPLEXION, cast, aspect, light.

hug v ❶ EMBRACE, cuddle, take in one's arms, hold close, enfold in one's arms, clasp/press to one's bosom, squeeze, snuggle against. ❷ KEEP

CLOSE TO, stay near, follow closely.

huge adj ENORMOUS, immense, great, massive, colossal, vast, prodigious, gigantic, giant, gargantuan, mammoth, monumental, monstrous, elephantine, bulky, extensive, mountainous, titanic, Brobdingnagian, Herculean; *informal* jumbo.
– OPPOSITES tiny.

hulk n ❶ WRECK, shipwreck, derelict, ruin, shell, skeleton, hull, frame. ❷ OAF, lout, lump, lubber.

hull n FRAMEWORK, body, frame, skeleton, structure, casing, covering.

hum v ❶ MURMUR, drone, vibrate, thrum, buzz, whirr, purr. ❷ SING, croon, whisper, mumble.

human adj ❶ MORTAL, physical, bodily, fleshly, carnal, corporal. ❷ KIND, kindly, considerate, understanding, sympathetic, compassionate, approachable, humane, accessible. ❸ FLESH AND BLOOD, fallible, weak, frail, vulnerable, erring.

humane adj KIND, kindly, kind-hearted, good, good-natured, compassionate, understanding, considerate, sympathetic, forgiving, merciful, lenient, forbearing, gentle, tender, mild, benign, clement, benevolent, charitable, generous, magnanimous, approachable, accessible.
– OPPOSITES cruel, inhumane.

humble adj ❶ MODEST,

unassuming, self-effacing, meek, unassertive, unpretentious, unostentatious, servile, docile, submissive, obsequious, subservient, deferential, over-respectful, slavish, sycophantic. **2** COMMON, ordinary, simple, poor, low-born, of low birth, low-ranking, low, lowly, inferior, plebeian, proletarian, base, mean, unrefined, vulgar, unimportant, insignificant, inconsequential, undistinguished, ignoble.
– OPPOSITES arrogant, important.

▶ v **1** HUMILIATE, mortify, subdue, chasten, shame, put to shame, abash, degrade. **2** DEFEAT, crush, trounce, rout, break, conquer, vanquish, overwhelm, bring someone to their knees.

humdrum adj COMMONPLACE, routine, run-of-the-mill, unvaried, unvarying, ordinary, everyday, mundane, monotonous, repetitious, dull, uninteresting, boring, tedious, banal, tiresome, wearisome.
– OPPOSITES remarkable.

humiliate v MORTIFY, shame, humble, put to shame, make ashamed, disgrace, embarrass, discomfit, chasten, subdue, deflate, abash, debase, abase, degrade, crush, demean; *informal* take someone down a peg or two, make someone eat humble pie, put down, show up; *N. Amer.* make someone eat crow.

humiliation n MORTIFICATION, loss of pride, humbling, disgrace, loss of face, dishonour,

indignity, discredit, embarrassment, discomfiture, affront, abasement, debasement, degradation, submission; *informal* put-down.

humility n HUMBLENESS, lack of pride, modesty, meekness, self-effacement, unpretentiousness, unobtrusiveness, diffidence, servility, submissiveness, obsequiousness, subservience, deference, sycophancy.
– OPPOSITES arrogance, pride.

humorous adj FUNNY, comic, comical, entertaining, witty, jocular, amusing, hilarious, side-splitting, rib-tickling, farcical, facetious, ridiculous, ludicrous, absurd, droll.
– OPPOSITES serious.

humour n **1** FUNNINESS, comic side, funny side, comical aspect, comedy, farce, jocularity, hilarity, ludicrousness, absurdness, absurdity, drollness. **2** COMEDY, jokes, joking, jests, jesting, wit, wittiness, witticisms, waggishness, pleasantries, buffoonery; *informal* gags, wisecracks. **3** MOOD, temper, temperament, frame of mind, state of mind, disposition, spirits.

hump n PROTRUSION, protuberance, projection, bulge, swelling, lump, bump, knob, hunch, mass, nodule, node, intumescence, tumefaction.
▶ v **1** HUNCH, arch, curve, curl up, crook. **2** CARRY, lift, lug, heave, shoulder, hoist.

hunch n **1** FEELING, presentiment, premonition, intuition, sixth sense, suspicion, inkling, impression, idea. ❷ *See* HUMP *n.*

hunger n ❶ HUNGRINESS, lack of food, starvation, ravenousness, emptiness, famine, voracity, greediness. ❷ LONGING, craving, yearning, desire, want, need, thirst, appetite, hankering, lust; *informal* itch.

hungry adj ❶ FAMISHED, famishing, ravenous, starving, starved, half-starved, empty, greedy, voracious; *dated* sharpset. ❷ LONGING, yearning, craving, in need/want of, eager, keen, desirous of, covetous of.
– OPPOSITES full.

hunt v ❶ CHASE, give chase, pursue, stalk, track, trail, follow, shadow, hound, tail. ❷ SEARCH FOR, look for, seek, try to find, scour for, forage for, fish for, rummage for, scrabble for.

hurdle n ❶ FENCE, barrier, railing, rail, wall, hedge, hedgerow, bar, barricade. ❷ OBSTACLE, barrier, hindrance, impediment, obstruction, stumbling block, snag, complication, difficulty, handicap.

hurl v THROW, fling, pitch, cast, toss, heave, fire, launch, let fly, shy, propel, project, dart, catapult; *informal* sling, chuck.

hurried adj ❶ QUICK, rapid, fast, swift, speedy, hasty, breakneck. ❷ HASTY, quick, swift, rushed, cursory, superficial, perfunctory, offhand, passing, fleeting, transitory.
– OPPOSITES slow.

hurry v ❶ MOVE QUICKLY, hurry up, be quick, make haste, hasten, speed, lose no time, press on, push on, run, dash, rush; *informal* go hell for leather, get a move on, put one's foot down, step on it, get cracking, shake a leg, go like a bat out of hell, hightail it, hotfoot it. ❷ SPEED UP, quicken, hasten, accelerate, expedite, urge on, drive on, push on, goad, prod, hustle.
– OPPOSITES dawdle.

hurt v ❶ BE SORE, be painful, cause pain, ache, smart, sting, nip, throb, tingle, burn. ❷ INJURE, wound, bruise, cut, scratch, lacerate, maim, damage, mutilate, disable, incapacitate, impair, debilitate. ❸ UPSET, sadden, grieve, wound, distress, pain, cut to the quick, sting, offend, give offence to, discompose. ❹ HARM, damage, spoil, blight, mar, blemish, impair.

hurtful adj ❶ UPSETTING, wounding, injurious, distressing, unkind, nasty, mean, spiteful, malicious, cutting, cruel, mischievous, offensive. ❷ HARMFUL, damaging, injurious, detrimental, deleterious, destructive, prejudicial, ruinous, inimical.

husband n SPOUSE, partner, consort, groom, bridegroom; *informal* hubby, old man; *Brit. informal* other half.

hush v SILENCE, quieten, quieten down, shush, shut up.
▶ n QUIET, quietness, silence,

stillness, still, peace, calm, tranquillity.

hustle v ❶ PUSH, shove, thrust, crowd, jostle, elbow, nudge, shoulder. ❷ *See* HURRY. ❸ COERCE, force, impel, pressure, badger, urge, goad, prod, spur, propel.

hut n SHED, lean-to, shack, cabin, shanty, hovel; *Scottish* bothy.

hygiene n CLEANLINESS, sanitation, public health, sanitary measures.

hygienic adj SANITARY, clean, germ-free, disinfected, sterilized, sterile, aseptic, unpolluted, uncontaminated, healthy, pure.
– OPPOSITES dirty, unsanitary.

hypnotic adj MESMERIC, mesmerizing, sleep-inducing, soporific, somniferous, numbing, sedative, stupefacient.

hypnotize v ❶ PUT UNDER, put out, send into a trance, mesmerize, put to sleep. ❷ FASCINATE, bewitch, entrance, beguile, spellbind, magnetize.

hypocrisy n INSINCERITY, falseness, sanctimoniousness, falsity, deceptiveness, deceit, deceitfulness, deception, dishonesty, duplicity, imposture, cant, two-facedness,

double-dealing, pretence, Pharisaism, pietism.
– OPPOSITES sincerity.

hypocritical adj FALSE, insincere, sanctimonious, fraudulent, deceitful, deceptive, dishonest, untruthful, lying, dissembling, duplicitous, two-faced, double-dealing, untrustworthy, perfidious, specious, spurious; *informal* phoney.

hypothesis n THEORY, thesis, theorem, proposition, axiom, premise, postulate, supposition, assumption, presumption, conjecture, speculation.

hypothetical adj ASSUMED, presumed, theoretical, putative, speculative, conjectured, imagined, notional, academic.

hysteria n HYSTERICS, frenzy, loss of control, agitation, madness, delirium; *informal* the screaming habdabs.

hysterical adj ❶ FRENZIED, in a frenzy, frantic, out of control, berserk, beside oneself, distracted, distraught, overwrought, agitated, in a panic, mad, crazed, delirious, raving. ❷ VERY FUNNY / AMUSING, hilarious, uproarious, side-splitting, comical, farcical, screamingly funny.
– OPPOSITES calm.

Ii

ice n FROZEN WATER, frost, icicle, iceberg, glacier, rime.

icy adj ❶ FREEZING, chill, chilly, frigid, frosty, biting, raw, bitter, arctic, glacial, Siberian, polar, gelid. ❷ FROZEN, ice-bound, frosty, rimy, glassy, slippery, slippy. ❸ COLD, cool, frigid, frosty, stiff, aloof, distant, unfriendly, unresponsive, uncommunicative, reserved, reticent, restrained.

idea n ❶ CONCEPT, thought, conception, conceptualization, image, abstraction, perception, notion. ❷ THOUGHT, theory, view, viewpoint, opinion, feeling, outlook, belief, judgement, conclusion. ❸ IMPRESSION, feeling, notion, suspicion, inkling. ❹ ESTIMATION, approximation, guess, surmise; *informal* guesstimate. ❺ PLAN, design, aim, scheme, intention, objective, object, purpose, end, goal, target.

ideal adj ❶ PERFECT, consummate, supreme, absolute, complete, flawless, exemplary, classic, archetypal, model, quintessential. ❷ UNATTAINABLE, utopian, unreal, impracticable, imaginary, ivory-towered, romantic, visionary, fanciful.
▶ n ❶ ARCHETYPE, prototype, model, pattern, exemplar, paradigm, example, criterion,
yardstick. ❷ PRINCIPLE, standard, moral value, morals, ethics.

idealistic adj IMPRACTICAL, utopian, perfectionist, visionary, romantic, quixotic, unrealistic; *informal* starry-eyed.
– OPPOSITES practical, realistic.

ideally adv IN A PERFECT WORLD, all things being equal, theoretically, hypothetically, in theory.

identical adj ❶ THE SAME, the very same, one and the same, selfsame. ❷ ALIKE, like, similar, much the same, indistinguishable, corresponding, matching, twin.
– OPPOSITES different.

identify v ❶ RECOGNIZE, single out, pick out, spot, point out, pinpoint, discern, distinguish, name; *informal* put the finger on. ❷ ESTABLISH, find out, ascertain, diagnose, select, choose. ❸ ASSOCIATE, connect, think of in connection with. ❹ RELATE TO, empathize with, sympathize with, have a rapport with, respond to, feel for.

identity n ❶ NAME, specification. ❷ PERSONALITY, self, selfhood, ego, individuality, distinctiveness, singularity, uniqueness. ❸ IDENTIFICATION, recognition, naming.

❹ SAMENESS, interchangeability, likeness, similarity, closeness, accordance.

ideology n DOCTRINE, creed, credo, teaching, dogma, theory, thesis, tenets, beliefs, opinions, principles, convictions, attitudes.

idiocy n STUPIDITY, foolishness, absurdity, inanity, fatuity, fatuousness, asininity, lunacy, craziness, insanity, dumbness; Brit. informal daftness.
– OPPOSITES sense.

idiom n ❶ PHRASE, expression, locution, turn of phrase, set phrase, fixed expression.
❷ LANGUAGE, style of speech, speech, talk, usage, parlance, vernacular, jargon, patois; informal lingo.

idiomatic adj COLLOQUIAL, informal, vernacular, natural.

idiosyncrasy n PECULIARITY, oddity, eccentricity, trait, singularity, mannerism, quirk, habit, characteristic, speciality, quality, feature.

idiot n FOOL, dolt, dunce, ass, ignoramus, imbecile, simpleton; informal chump, booby, nincompoop, ninny, dunderhead, blockhead, fathead, halfwit, cretin, moron, dummy, numbskull, dimwit; Brit. informal twerp, clot, twit, nitwit.

idiotic adj STUPID, foolish, senseless, absurd, fatuous, inane, asinine, unintelligent, half-witted, hare-brained, lunatic, crazy, insane, mad, moronic, dumb, irrational,
nonsensical, ridiculous; Brit. informal daft.
– OPPOSITES sensible.

idle adj ❶ LAZY, indolent, slothful, sluggish, apathetic, torpid, slow, shiftless, loafing, dronish. ❷ INOPERATIVE, not in operation, inactive, out of action, unused, mothballed. ❸ EMPTY, unfilled, unoccupied, vacant. ❹ GROUNDLESS, baseless, worthless, futile, casual. ❺ TRIVIAL, unimportant, insignificant, trifling, superficial, shallow, foolish, inane, fatuous.
– OPPOSITES industrious, busy.
▶ v ❶ WHILE, loaf, lounge, loiter, dawdle, fritter, dally, potter. ❷ DO NOTHING, laze, loaf, be inactive, mark time, shirk, slack, vegetate, take it easy, rest on one's oars.

idol n ❶ GOD, icon, effigy, image, graven image, fetish, likeness. ❷ HERO, heroine, favourite, darling, pet, beloved, star, superstar, apple of one's eye; Brit. informal blue-eyed boy/girl.

idolize v ❶ WORSHIP, bow down before, glorify, exalt, revere, deify. ❷ HERO-WORSHIP, worship, adulate, adore, love, look up to, admire, dote on, lionize, revere, venerate.

ignite v ❶ SET FIRE TO, light, set on fire, set alight, fire, kindle, inflame, touch off, put a match to. ❷ CATCH FIRE, catch, burst into flames, burn up, burn, flame up, kindle.
– OPPOSITES extinguish.

ignominious adj ❶ SHAME-FUL, dishonourable, disgraceful, humiliating, mortifying, discreditable, disreputable, undignified, infamous, ignoble, inglorious, scandalous, abject, sorry, base. ❷ CONTEMPTIBLE, despicable, offensive, revolting, wicked, vile, base, low.
– OPPOSITES glorious.

ignorance n UNFAMILIARITY, unconsciousness, lack of knowledge, inexperience, greenness, innocence; *poetic/literary* nescience.
– OPPOSITES knowledge.

ignorant adj ❶ UNAWARE OF, unfamiliar with, unconscious of, unacquainted with, uninformed about, unconversant with, unenlightened about, inexperienced in, blind to, unschooled in, naive about, innocent about; *informal* in the dark about. ❷ UNEDUCATED, unschooled, illiterate, unlettered, uninformed, unknowledgeable, unintelligent, stupid, benighted.
– OPPOSITES knowledgeable.

ignore v ❶ DISREGARD, pay no attention to, take no notice of, brush aside, pass over, shrug off, shut one's eyes to, be oblivious to, turn a blind eye to, turn a deaf ear to. ❷ SLIGHT, spurn, cold-shoulder, look right through, look past, turn one's back on, send to Coventry, cut, cut dead.
– OPPOSITES acknowledge.

ill adj ❶ SICK, unwell, not well, poorly, ailing, sickly, infirm, feeling bad, afflicted, indisposed, out of sorts, diseased, bedridden, invalided, weak, feeble; *Brit.* off colour; *informal* under the weather, laid up, queasy, funny, seedy; *Brit. informal, dated* queer. ❷ HOSTILE, unfriendly, antagonistic, acrimonious, belligerent, bellicose, unkind, spiteful, rancorous, malicious, resentful, malevolent, bitter. ❸ BAD, infamous, notorious, wicked, nefarious, vile, evil, foul, sinful, corrupt, depraved, degenerate.
– OPPOSITES healthy.
▶ adv BADLY, unfavourably, with disfavour, with disapproval, with hostility, unkindly, maliciously, spitefully.

ill-advised adj UNWISE, ill-considered, imprudent, incautious, injudicious, ill-judged, impolitic, misguided, foolish, foolhardy, rash, hasty, over-hasty, short-sighted, thoughtless, careless, reckless.

illegal adj UNLAWFUL, illegitimate, illicit, lawless, criminal, felonious, actionable, unlicensed, unauthorized, unsanctioned, unwarranted, unofficial, outlawed, banned, forbidden, barred, prohibited, proscribed, contraband, black-market, under the counter, bootleg.
– OPPOSITES legal.

illegible adj INDECIPHERABLE, unreadable, unintelligible, scrawled, scribbled, unclear, obscure, squiggly.
– OPPOSITES legible.

illegitimate adj ❶ ILLEGAL, illicit, unlawful, lawless, criminal, unauthorized, unsanctioned, irregular, invalid. ❷ BORN OUT OF WEDLOCK; *dated* love, born on the wrong side of the blanket; *archaic* bastard, natural. ❸ UNSOUND, illogical, invalid, incorrect, spurious.
– OPPOSITES legitimate.

ill-fated adj UNLUCKY, luckless, unfortunate, hapless, unhappy, doomed, blighted, ill-starred, ill-omened.

ill-judged adj *see* ILL-ADVISED.

illness n SICKNESS, ailment, disease, complaint, malady, disorder, affliction, disability, attack, indisposition, infection, contagion, ill health, poor health.

illogical adj UNSOUND, fallacious, unproved, invalid, specious, unreasonable, unreasoned, fallible, untenable, unscientific, casuistic, sophistic, inconsistent, incorrect, wrong, absurd, preposterous, meaningless, senseless.
– OPPOSITES logical.

ill-treat v TREAT BADLY, abuse, harm, injure, damage, handle roughly, mishandle, ill-use, maltreat, misuse; *informal* knock about.

illuminating adj INSTRUCTIVE, informative, enlightening, explanatory, revealing, helpful.

illusion n ❶ DELUSION, misapprehension, misconception, deception, false/mistaken impression, fallacy, error, misjudgement, fancy.
❷ HALLUCINATION, figment of the imagination, spectre, phantom, mirage, fantasy, will-o'-the-wisp; *poetic/literary* phantasm.

illusory adj FALSE, mistaken, deceptive, delusory, delusional, delusive, fallacious, erroneous, misleading, untrue, specious, unreal, imagined, imaginary, fancied, non-existent, fanciful, notional, chimerical, dreamlike.
– OPPOSITES genuine.

illustrate v ❶ ADD PICTURES TO, adorn, decorate, ornament, embellish. ❷ DEMONSTRATE, exemplify, show, point up, instance, make plain/clear, clarify, bring home, emphasize, interpret.

illustration n ❶ PICTURE, drawing, sketch, figure, plate, artwork. ❷ EXAMPLE, demonstration, typical case, case in point, instance, specimen, sample, exemplar, analogy.

image n ❶ LIKENESS, representation, painting, picture, portrait, effigy, figure, statue, sculpture, bust. ❷ DOUBLE, twin, replica, clone, copy, reproduction, counterpart, doppelgänger; *informal* spit, spitting image, ringer, dead ringer. ❸ FIGURE OF SPEECH, conceit, trope, expression.

imaginary adj UNREAL, non-existent, illusory, fanciful, unsubstantial, chimerical, notional, assumed, supposed, suppositious, fictitious, fictional, mythical, mythological,

made up, invented, hallucinatory, ghostly, spectral, dreamlike, visionary, shadowy; *poetic/literary* phantasmic.
– OPPOSITES real, actual.

imagination n ❶ CREATIVITY, vision, inspiration, inventiveness, originality, innovation, ingenuity, insight, fancifulness. ❷ ILLUSION, figment of the imagination, fancy, vision, dream, unreality.

imaginative adj CREATIVE, inventive, original, innovative, visionary, inspired, fanciful, resourceful, ingenious, enterprising, clever, whimsical.
– OPPOSITES unimaginative.

imagine v ❶ PICTURE, visualize, see in the mind's eye, envision, envisage, conjure up, dream about, dream up, think up, conceive, fantasize about, conceptualize, plan, scheme, project. ❷ ASSUME, presume, expect, suppose, think, believe, be of the opinion that, take it, gather, fancy, judge, deem, infer, deduce, conjecture, surmise, guess, reckon, suspect, realize.

imbue v FILL, impregnate, inject, inculcate, instil, ingrain, inspire, permeate, charge.

imitate v ❶ COPY, emulate, simulate, mirror, follow someone's example, take after, follow, follow suit, take a page from someone's book, follow in someone's footsteps, echo. ❷ MIMIC, ape, impersonate, do an impression of, parody, mock, caricature, burlesque,

travesty; *informal* send up, take off, spoof, do.

imitation n ❶ COPY, reproduction, forgery, fake, counterfeit, resemblance, emulation, duplication, likeness, replica, simulation. ❷ MIMICKING, mimicry, aping, impersonation, impression, parody, mockery, caricature, burlesque, travesty; *informal* send-up, take-off, spoof.
▶ adj ARTIFICIAL, simulated, synthetic, man-made, mock, sham, fake, reproduction, pseudo, ersatz; *informal* phoney.

immature adj ❶ UNRIPE, undeveloped, unformed, imperfect, unfinished, incomplete, half-grown, crude, raw, green, unfledged, untimely. ❷ CHILDISH, juvenile, adolescent, infantile, babyish, puerile, callow, jejune, inexperienced, green; *informal* wet behind the ears.
– OPPOSITES mature.

immediate adj ❶ INSTANT, instantaneous, prompt, swift, speedy, sudden, abrupt. ❷ NEAR, nearest, next, nextdoor, close, closest, adjacent, adjoining, abutting, contiguous, proximate. ❸ CURRENT, present, existing, actual, existent, extant, urgent, pressing.
– OPPOSITES delayed, distant.

immediately adv RIGHT AWAY, right now, straight away, at once, instantly, now, this minute, directly, promptly, without delay; *informal* before you can say Jack Robinson, pronto.

immense adj HUGE, vast,

massive, enormous, gigantic, colossal, giant, great, extensive, infinite, immeasurable, illimitable, monumental, tremendous, prodigious, elephantine, monstrous, titanic, Brobdingnagian; *informal* mega; *Brit. informal* ginormous.
– OPPOSITES tiny, minute.

immerse v ❶ SUBMERGE, plunge, dip, dunk, duck, sink, souse, soak, drench, imbue, saturate. ❷ ABSORB, engross, occupy, engage, preoccupy, involve, engulf, lose oneself in.

immigrant n SETTLER, alien, incomer, non-native, new arrival, migrant, naturalized citizen, expatriate.

imminent adj IMPENDING, approaching, close, fast-approaching, at hand, near, coming, forthcoming, on the way, about to happen, upon us, in the offing, on the horizon, in the air, brewing, threatening, menacing, looming.
– OPPOSITES distant.

immobile adj UNMOVING, motionless, immovable, still, static, at rest, stationary, at a standstill, stock-still, dormant, rooted, fixed to the spot, rigid, frozen, stiff, riveted, like a statue; *technical* immotile, immotive.

immobilize v STOP, halt, bring to a standstill, paralyse, put out of action, inactivate, disable, cripple, freeze, transfix.

immodest adj BOLD, brazen, forward, impudent, unblushing, shameless, wanton, improper, indecent, cheeky.

immoral adj BAD, wicked, evil, unprincipled, dishonest, unethical, sinful, impure, corrupt, iniquitous, depraved, vile, base, degenerate, debauched, abandoned, dissolute, villainous, nefarious, reprobate, indecent, lewd, licentious, pornographic, unchaste, bawdy, of easy virtue.
– OPPOSITES ethical, chaste.

immortal adj ❶ UNDYING, eternal, deathless, everlasting, never-ending, endless, imperishable, timeless, indestructible, unfading, perennial, evergreen, perpetual, lasting, enduring, constant, abiding, immutable, indissoluble; *poetic/literary* sempiternal, perdurable. ❷ FAMOUS, celebrated, renowned.
– OPPOSITES mortal.

immortalize v COMMEMORATE, memorialize, eternalize, eternize, perpetuate, exalt, glorify; *formal* laud.

immovable adj ❶ FIXED, set fast/firm, fast, firm, secure, stable, rooted, riveted, moored, anchored, stuck, jammed, stiff, unbudgeable. ❷ MOTIONLESS, unmoving, stationary, still, stock-still, at a standstill, dead still, statue-like. ❸ FIRM, adamant, steadfast, unwavering, unswerving, resolute, determined, tenacious, stubborn, dogged, obdurate, inflexible, unyielding, unbending, uncompromising, unshakeable, inexorable.

immune adj NOT SUBJECT TO, not liable to, protected from, safe from, unsusceptible to, secure against, exempt from, clear of, free from, absolved from, released from, excused from, relieved of, spared from, exempted from, unaffected by, resistant to, proof against.
– OPPOSITES liable, susceptible.

immunize v INOCULATE, vaccinate, protect, shield, safeguard.

impact n ❶ COLLISION, crash, contact, smash, striking, clash, bump, knock, bang, jolt, thump, whack, thwack, slam, smack, slap. ❷ INFLUENCE, effect, impression, results, consequences, repercussions.

impair v WEAKEN, lessen, decrease, reduce, blunt, diminish, enfeeble, debilitate, enervate, damage, mar, spoil, injure, harm, hinder, disable, cripple, impede, undermine; formal vitiate.
– OPPOSITES improve, enhance.

impart v PASS ON, convey, communicate, transmit, relate, tell, make known, report, disclose, reveal, divulge, proclaim, broadcast.

impartial adj UNBIASED, unprejudiced, disinterested, objective, detached, neutral, equitable, even-handed, fair, fair-minded, open-minded, non-partisan, without fear or favour, with no axe to grind.
– OPPOSITES biased, partisan.

impartiality n DETACHMENT, disinterest, objectivity, neutrality, even-handedness, fairness, justness, open-mindedness.

impassable adj ❶ CLOSE, blocked, obstructed, unnavigable, untraversable, impenetrable. ❷ INSURMOUNTABLE, insuperable, unconquerable.

impatient adj ❶ EAGER, keen, anxious, avid, desirous, yearning, longing. ❷ RESTLESS, restive, excitable, agitated, nervous, edgy, impetuous. ❸ ABRUPT, brusque, terse, short, irritated, angry, testy, short-tempered, quick-tempered, curt, querulous, peevish, intolerant; informal snappy.
– OPPOSITES patient.

impede v HINDER, obstruct, hamper, handicap, block, check, curb, bar, hold back, hold up, delay, interfere with, disrupt, retard, slow, slow down, brake, restrain, thwart, frustrate, baulk, stop; Brit. throw a spanner in the works.
– OPPOSITES facilitate.

impediment n HINDRANCE, obstruction, obstacle, handicap, block, stumbling block, check, encumbrance, bar, barrier, curb, brake, restraint, drawback, difficulty, snag, setback.

impel v URGE, press, exhort, force, oblige, constrain, necessitate, require, demand, make, apply pressure, pressure, pressurize, spur, goad, incite, prompt, chivvy, persuade, inspire.

impending adj *see* IMMINENT.

impenetrable adj ❶ IMPERVIOUS, impermeable, solid, dense, thick, hard, closed, sealed, resistant, waterproof, tight, unpierceable. ❷ IMPASSABLE, inaccessible, thick, dense, overgrown. ❸ INCOMPREHENSIBLE, baffling, puzzling, abstruse, obscure, inexplicable, unfathomable, recondite, inscrutable, enigmatic.

imperceptible adj UNNOTICEABLE, unobtrusive, unapparent, slight, small, gradual, subtle, faint, fine, inconsequential, tiny, minute, minuscule, microscopic, infinitesimal, undetectable, indistinguishable, indiscernible, invisible, indistinct, unclear, obscure, vague, indefinite, shadowy, inaudible, muffled, impalpable.
– OPPOSITES obvious.

imperceptibly adv UNNOTICEABLY, unobtrusively, unseen, gradually, slowly, subtly, undetectable, little by little, bit by bit.

imperfect adj ❶ FAULTY, flawed, defective, blemished, damaged, broken, impaired. ❷ DEFICIENT, inadequate, insufficient, rudimentary, limited, patchy, sketchy.
– OPPOSITES flawless.

imperfection n ❶ FAULT, flaw, defect, blemish, deformity, crack, break, scratch, cut, tear, stain, spot. ❷ FAILING,

foible, deficiency, weakness, weak point, shortcoming, fallibility, frailty, infirmity, peccadillo.

imperious adj OVERBEARING, overweening, domineering, peremptory, high-handed, assertive, commanding, authoritative, lordly, masterful, dictatorial, tyrannical.
– OPPOSITES humble.

impersonal adj ❶ OBJECTIVE, detached, disinterested, dispassionate, neutral, unbiased, unprejudiced, fair, equitable, even-handed. ❷ COLD, cool, aloof, frigid, stiff, rigid, wooden, starchy, stilted, stuffy, businesslike, bureaucratic, matter-of-fact.
– OPPOSITES biased.

impersonate v IMITATE, mimic, personate, ape, mock, parody, caricature, masquerade as, burlesque, pose as, pass oneself off as; *informal* take off, do.

impertinent adj INSOLENT, impudent, cheeky, rude, impolite, unmannerly, ill-mannered, uncivil, coarse, uncouth, crude, discourteous, disrespectful, bold, brazen, audacious, presumptuous, forward, pert, brash, shameless; *informal* saucy, brass-necked, fresh, flip.
– OPPOSITES polite.

imperturbable adj SELF-POSSESSED, composed, collected, calm, cool, tranquil, serene, unexcitable, unflappable, even-tempered, easy-going, at ease,

unruffled, untroubled, undismayed, unmoved, nonchalant.
– OPPOSITES nervous, excitable.

impetuous adj ❶ IMPULSIVE, hasty, impatient, excitable, headstrong, rash, reckless, foolhardy, wild, uncontrolled, eager, enthusiastic, spontaneous, passionate, ardent, zealous. ❷ HASTY, precipitate, impulsive, spontaneous, impromptu, spur-of-the-moment, unthinking, unplanned, ill-conceived, ill-considered, unreasoned, heedless, reckless, rash.
– OPPOSITES cautious.

impetus n ❶ MOMENTUM, energy, force, power, propulsion, motion. ❷ STIMULUS, motivation, incentive, inducement, inspiration, encouragement, influence, push, urging, pressing, spur, goading, goad, instigation, actuation.

impinge
■ **impinge on** ❶ ENCROACH ON, infringe, intrude on, invade, trespass on, violate, usurp, make inroads on, obtrude on. ❷ AFFECT, have an effect on, have a bearing on, impress, touch, exert influence on, bear upon.

implausible adj UNLIKELY, improbable, hard to believe, incredible, unbelievable, unimaginable, inconceivable, debatable, questionable, doubtful.
– OPPOSITES plausible.

implement n TOOL, utensil, appliance, instrument, gadget, device, apparatus, contrivance; *informal* gizmo.
▶ v CARRY OUT, fulfil, execute, perform, discharge, accomplish, achieve, realize, put into effect, bring about, effect, enforce.

implicate v INCRIMINATE, involve, compromise, accuse, charge, blame, entangle, impeach, inculpate.
– OPPOSITES absolve.

implication n ❶ INCRIMINATION, involvement, connection, entanglement, embroilment, association. ❷ SUGGESTION, inference, insinuation, innuendo, hint, allusion, reference, assumption, presumption.

implicit adj ❶ IMPLIED, indirect, inferred, unspoken, undeclared, unexpressed, unstated, tacit, understood, suggested. ❷ ABSOLUTE, complete, total, wholehearted, utter, unqualified, unconditional, unreserved, unquestioning, firm, steadfast.
– OPPOSITES explicit.

implore v BEG, appeal to, entreat, plead with, ask, pray, request, solicit, supplicate, importune, press, crave, plead for, appeal for; *poetic/literary* beseech.

imply v INSINUATE, hint, suggest, intimate, give to understand, signal, indicate.

impolite adj see RUDE (1).

important adj ❶ SIGNIFICANT, crucial, of great consequence/ import, far-reaching, critical,

pivotal, momentous, substantial, weighty, valuable, serious, grave, urgent, of great moment, consequential, salient, chief, main, principal, major, of concern, of interest, relevant, of value, necessary, essential. ❷ EMINENT, prominent, pre-eminent, leading, foremost, outstanding, distinguished, esteemed, notable, noteworthy, of note, influential, of influence, powerful, high-ranking, high-level, top-level, prestigious.
– OPPOSITES unimportant.

importunate adj PERSISTENT, insistent, dogged, unremitting, relentless, pertinacious, pressing, urgent, demanding, exacting, clamorous, entreating, solicitous, imprecatory.

importune v BEG, implore, plead with, appeal to, call upon, supplicate, petition, press; *poetic/literary* beseech.

impose v ❶ ENFORCE, apply, exact, levy, charge, lay on, set, establish, fix, ordain, introduce, promulgate, decree. ❷ FORCE, inflict, foist, thrust, obtrude.

imposing adj IMPRESSIVE, striking, grand, splendid, majestic, august, lofty, stately.

impossible adj ❶ NOT POSSIBLE, out of the question, inconceivable, unthinkable, unimaginable, impracticable, unattainable, unachievable, unobtainable, beyond one, hopeless. ❷ UNBELIEVABLE, incredible, absurd, ludicrous,

ridiculous, preposterous, outlandish. ❸ UNMANAGEABLE, intractable, recalcitrant, wayward, intolerable, unbearable.
– OPPOSITES possible, plausible.

impostor n DECEIVER, pretender, fake, fraud, sham, charlatan, mountebank, hoodwinker, bluffer, trickster, cheat, cheater, swindler, confidence man/woman, rogue; *informal* con man/woman, con artist.

impracticable adj IMPOSSIBLE, out of the question, unfeasible, unworkable, unattainable, unrealizable, unsuitable.
– OPPOSITES feasible, possible.

impractical adj ❶ USELESS, ineffective, ineffectual, unrealistic, impossible, unviable. ❷ UNREALISTIC, idealistic, romantic, quixotic, starry-eyed.
– OPPOSITES practical.

imprecise adj INEXACT, approximate, estimated, rough, inaccurate, incorrect. ❷ VAGUE, loose, hazy, blurred, indefinite, woolly, confused, ambiguous, equivocal.
– OPPOSITES precise.

impregnate v SUFFUSE, permeate, imbue, penetrate, fill, infuse, pervade, soak, steep, saturate, drench, inundate.

impress v ❶ MAKE AN IMPRESSION / IMPACT ON, move, sway, influence, affect, stir, rouse, excite, inspire, galvanize. ❷ STAMP, imprint, print, mark, engrave, emboss.

impression n ❶ EFFECT, influence, impact, sway, hold, power, control. ❷ MARK, indentation, dent, hollow, outline, stamp, imprint. ❸ FEELING, sense, sensation, perception, notion, idea, thought, belief, opinion, conviction, suspicion, inkling, intuition, hunch, funny feeling. ❹ IMPERSONATION, imitation, mimicry, parody, caricature, take-off, send-up, burlesque, travesty.

impressionable adj SUGGESTIBLE, susceptible, persuadable, receptive, responsive, sensitive, open, gullible, ingenuous, pliable, malleable, mouldable.

impressive adj IMPOSING, striking, magnificent, splendid, moving, touching, affecting, stirring, rousing, exciting, powerful, inspiring.
– OPPOSITES ordinary, unexciting.

imprison v PUT IN PRISON, send to prison, jail, lock up, take into custody, put under lock and key, put away, incarcerate, confine, shut in/up, intern, detain, constrain, immure; *informal* send down.

imprisonment n CUSTODY, incarceration, internment, confinement, detention, restraint; *Brit. informal* porridge.

improbable adj UNLIKELY, doubtful, questionable, dubious, implausible, far-fetched, unconvincing, unbelievable, incredible, ridiculous, ludicrous, preposterous.
– OPPOSITES probable.

impromptu adj UNREHEARSED, ad lib, unprepared, extempore, extemporized, extemporaneous, spontaneous, improvised, unscripted, unpremeditated, unstudied; *informal* off-the-cuff, off the top of one's head, on the spur of the moment.
– OPPOSITES rehearsed.

improper adj ❶ UNSEEMLY, unbecoming, indecorous, unfitting, indiscreet, injudicious. ❷ INDECENT, off colour, indelicate, risqué, suggestive, smutty, obscene, lewd, pornographic; *informal* blue. ❸ INCORRECT, inaccurate, wrong, erroneous, false, fallacious.
– OPPOSITES proper.

improve v ❶ MAKE BETTER, better, ameliorate, mend, amend, reform, rehabilitate, set/put right, correct, rectify, help, advance, upgrade, revamp, modernize; *informal* give something a facelift. ❷ GET / GROW BETTER, advance, come along, make headway, develop, progress, make progress, pick up, perk up, take a turn for the better, take on a new lease of life, rally, look up. ❸ GET BETTER, recuperate, be on the mend, turn the corner, recover, gain strength, convalesce.
– OPPOSITES worsen.

improvident adj UNTHRIFTY, thriftless, spendthrift,

wasteful, prodigal, extravagant, uneconomical, shiftless.
– OPPOSITES thrifty.

improvise v ❶ EXTEMPORIZE, ad lib; *informal* speak off the cuff, play it by ear, make it up as you go along. ❷ THROW / PUT TOGETHER, contrive, devise, concoct, rig, jury-rig.

impudent adj IMPERTINENT, insolent, cheeky, bold, audacious, brazen, cocky, pert, presumptuous, forward, bumptious, impolite, rude, disrespectful, ill-mannered, unmannerly, ill-bred, shameless, immodest; *informal* saucy, brass-necked.

impulse n ❶ DRIVE, urge, instinct, appetite, proclivity. ❷ STIMULUS, inspiration, stimulation, incitement, incentive, inducement, motivation.

impulsive adj ❶ HASTY, sudden, quick, precipitate, impetuous, impromptu, spontaneous, snap, ill-considered, unplanned, unpremeditated, thoughtless, rash, reckless. ❷ IMPETUOUS, rash, reckless, spontaneous, instinctive, passionate, intuitive, emotional, foolhardy, madcap, devil-may-care.
– OPPOSITES deliberate, cautious.

impure adj ❶ ADULTERATED, debased, contaminated, polluted, tainted, infected, dirty, foul, unclean, filthy, sullied, defiled, unwholesome, poisoned, feculent. ❷ LEWD, lustful, obscene, indecent, lecherous, ribald,

smutty, pornographic, improper, crude, vulgar, coarse, gross.
– OPPOSITES pure.

inaccessible adj UNREACHABLE, out of reach, cut off, beyond reach, unapproachable, impenetrable, unattainable, out of the way, isolated, lonely, remote, godforsaken, off the beaten track.
– OPPOSITES accessible.

inaccurate adj ❶ INCORRECT, wrong, erroneous, faulty, inexact, imprecise, out. ❷ WRONG, false, not true, erroneous, fallacious, not right, imperfect, flawed, defective, unsound, unreliable, wide of the mark; *informal* full of holes.
– OPPOSITES accurate.

inactive adj ❶ IMMOBILE, motionless, inert, stationary, idle, sluggish, slow, indolent, lazy, lifeless, slothful, lethargic, stagnant, vegetating, dilatory, torpid. ❷ INOPERATIVE, idle, out of service, unused, out of use, unoccupied, mothballed, unemployed. ❸ DORMANT, quiescent, latent, passive.

inadequate adj ❶ INSUFFICIENT, not enough, too little, too few, lacking, found wanting, deficient, short, in short supply, meagre, scanty, scant, niggardly, scarce, sparse, skimpy, sketchy, incomplete. ❷ INCAPABLE, incompetent, unfit, ineffective, ineffectual, inefficient, unskilful, inexpert, inept; *informal* not up to scratch.
– OPPOSITES adequate.

inadvertent adj ACCIDENTAL, unintentional, chance, unpremeditated, unplanned, unconscious, uncalculated, unwitting, involuntary.
– OPPOSITES deliberate.

inadvisable adj UNWISE, ill-advised, ill-judged, misguided, injudicious, imprudent, foolish, impolitic, inexpedient.
– OPPOSITES shrewd.

inanimate adj ❶ LIFELESS, without life, dead, inert, insentient, insensate, extinct, defunct. ❷ APATHETIC, spiritless, lazy, inactive, listless, lethargic, sluggish, torpid.
– OPPOSITES living.

inappropriate adj UNSUITABLE, unfitting, out of place, unseemly, unbecoming, improper, indecorous, inapposite, incongruous, out of keeping, inexpedient, inadvisable, injudicious, infelicitous, untimely.
– OPPOSITES appropriate.

inarticulate adj ❶ UNINTELLIGIBLE, incomprehensible, incoherent, unclear, indistinct, blurred, muffled, mumbled, muttered. ❷ POORLY SPOKEN, faltering, hesitating, halting, stumbling, stuttering, stammering. ❸ UNSPOKEN, unuttered, unexpressed, unvoiced, wordless, silent, mute, dumb, speechless, voiceless, soundless, taciturn, tongue-tied.
– OPPOSITES articulate.

inattentive adj ❶ NEGLECTFUL, negligent, remiss, forgetful, careless, thoughtless, heedless, indifferent, unconcerned, inconsiderate. ❷ DISTRACTED, preoccupied, absent-minded, daydreaming, wool-gathering, lost in thought; informal in a world of one's own, miles away, with one's head in the clouds, in a brown study.
– OPPOSITES attentive.

inauspicious adj UNPROPITIOUS, unpromising, unlucky, unfortunate, unhappy, infelicitous, unfavourable, ill-omened, ominous, ill-fated, ill-starred, untoward, untimely.
– OPPOSITES auspicious.

incapable adj ❶ INCOMPETENT, ineffective, ineffectual, inadequate, inefficacious, unfit, unfitted, unqualified, inept, inapt, useless, feeble; informal not up to scratch. ❷ UNABLE TO, not capable of, lacking the ability to.
– OPPOSITES capable.

inception n BEGINNING, commencement, start, starting point, outset, opening, debut, inauguration, initiation, institution, birth, dawn, origin, rise; informal kick-off.
– OPPOSITES end.

incessant adj UNCEASING, ceaseless, non-stop, endless, unending, never-ending, everlasting, eternal, constant, continual, perpetual, continuous, uninterrupted, unbroken, ongoing, unremitting, persistent, recurrent.
– OPPOSITES intermittent.

incident n ❶ EVENT, happening, occurrence, episode, experience, proceeding, adventure, occasion, circumstance, fact, matter. **2** DISTURBANCE, commotion, scene, row, fracas, contretemps, skirmish, clash, conflict, confrontation, brush.

incidental adj **1** ACCIDENTAL, by chance, chance, random, fortuitous. **2** RELATED, connected, associated, accompanying, attendant, concomitant, contingent. **3** SECONDARY, subsidiary, subordinate.

incise v CUT, cut into, make an incision in, slit, slit open, gash, slash, notch, nick, furrow.

incite v **1** INSTIGATE, provoke, foment, whip up, stir up, prompt. **2** ENCOURAGE, urge, egg on, goad, spur on, prod, stimulate, drive on, excite, arouse, agitate, inflame, stir up, provoke.
–OPPOSITES discourage.

inclination n **1** TENDENCY, leaning, propensity, proclivity, predisposition, weakness, penchant, predilection, partiality, preference, affinity, attraction, fancy, liking, fondness, affection, love. **2** BEND, bow, nod, lowing, stooping.

incline v **1** TEND, lean, swing, veer, have a preference for, be attracted to, have an affinity for. **2** BEND, slope, slant, bank, cant, bevel, tilt, lean, tip, list, stoop. ▶ n SLOPE, gradient, hill, drop, declivity, descent, ascent, ramp, rise.

■ **be inclined to** HAVE A TENDENCY TO, be liable to, be likely to, be predisposed to.

include v **1** CONTAIN, hold, take in, admit, incorporate, embrace, encompass, comprise, embody, comprehend, subsume. **2** ADD, insert, allow for, put in, enter, introduce, count in, take account of, build in, number, incorporate.
–OPPOSITES exclude.

incoherent adj UNCONNECTED, disconnected, disjointed, disordered, confused, mixed up, muddled, jumbled, scrambled, rambling, wandering, discursive, illogical, unintelligible, inarticulate, mumbled, muttered, stuttered, stammered.
–OPPOSITES coherent.

income n SALARY, pay, earnings, wages, remuneration, takings, profits, revenue, gains, proceeds, means.

incomparable adj BEYOND COMPARE, inimitable, unequalled, matchless, nonpareil, unrivalled, peerless, unparalleled, unsurpassed, superlative, supreme, transcendent.

incompatible adj **1** UNSUITED, mismatched, ill-assorted, incongruous, antagonistic, conflicting, antipathetic, discordant; Brit. like chalk and cheese. **2** CLASHING, discordant, jarring, inharmonious. **3** CONTRARY TO, differing from, at odds with, inconsistent with, in opposition to, diametrically opposed to.
–OPPOSITES compatible.

incompetent adj **1** INCAPABLE, inept, inefficient,

ineffectual, unqualified, unable, unfitted, unsuitable, useless, inadequate, deficient. **❷** INEXPERT, unskilful, inept, bungling, awkward, maladroit, clumsy, floundering, gauche; *informal* botched.
– OPPOSITES competent.

incomplete adj **❶** UNFINISHED, partial, unaccomplished, undone, undeveloped, unexecuted, unperformed. **❷** IMPERFECT, broken, defective, lacking, wanting, deficient. **❸** SHORTENED, deficient, curtailed, abridged, expurgated, bowdlerized.
– OPPOSITES complete.

incomprehensible adj **❶** UNINTELLIGIBLE, too difficult/hard, complicated, complex, involved, intricate; *informal* over one's head. **❷** ILLEGIBLE, indecipherable, unintelligible, unreadable.
– OPPOSITES intelligible, clear.

inconceivable adj UNIMAGINABLE, unthinkable, incomprehensible, incredible, unbelievable, implausible, impossible, out of the question, preposterous, ridiculous, ludicrous.
– OPPOSITES plausible.

inconclusive adj INDEFINITE, indeterminate, indecisive, undetermined, open to question, open to doubt, vague, unsettled, unresolved, questionable, ambiguous, equivocal, unestablished; *informal* up in the air.
– OPPOSITES conclusive.

incongruous adj OUT OF PLACE, inappropriate, incompatible, discordant, jarring, out of keeping, inconsistent, contrary, unsuited, at odds, in opposition, opposed, conflicting, irreconcilable, strange, odd, absurd, unsuitable.
– OPPOSITES appropriate, suitable.

inconsequential adj INSIGNIFICANT, negligible, unimportant, trivial, trifling, petty; *informal* piddling.
– OPPOSITES important.

inconsiderate adj THOUGHTLESS, unthinking, uncaring, heedless, unmindful, regardless, undiscerning, insensitive, tactless, uncharitable, unkind, ungracious, selfish, self-centred, egotistical.
– OPPOSITES considerate.

inconsistent adj **❶** INCOMPATIBLE, out of keeping, out of place, contrary, at odds, at variance, in opposition, conflicting, in conflict, irreconcilable, discordant, discrepant. **❷** UNSTABLE, unsteady, changeable, erratic, irregular, unpredictable, capricious, fickle, whimsical, mercurial, volatile.
– OPPOSITES consistent.

inconspicuous adj UNOBTRUSIVE, unnoticeable, indistinct, ordinary, plain, run-of-the-mill, unremarkable, undistinguished, unostentatious, unimposing, hidden, insignificant, quiet, retiring, unassuming, in the background; *informal* low-key.
– OPPOSITES conspicuous.

inconvenience n
❶ TROUBLE, bother, disruption, disturbance, vexation, worry, annoyance, disadvantage, difficulty, embarrassment.
❷ AWKWARDNESS, unwieldiness, cumbersomeness, unhandiness.
▶ v DISTURB, bother, trouble, worry, disrupt, put out, impose upon, burden, distract, annoy, discommode.

inconvenient adj ❶ AWKWARD, unsuitable, inappropriate, inopportune, disadvantageous, inexpedient, disturbing, troublesome, bothersome, tiresome, vexatious, annoying, embarrassing, ill-timed, untimely, unseasonable.
❷ UNWIELDY, cumbersome, awkward, unmanageable, unhandy, difficult.
– OPPOSITES convenient.

incorporate v ❶ INCLUDE, embrace, absorb, embody, assimilate, subsume. ❷ MERGE, coalesce, fuse, blend, mix, amalgamate, combine, unite, integrate, unify, compact.
– OPPOSITES exclude.

incorrect adj ❶ WRONG, inaccurate, erroneous, wide of the mark. ❷ MISTAKEN, inaccurate, faulty, inexact, untrue, false, fallacious, non-factual, flawed; *informal* full of holes. ❸ IMPROPER, unsuitable, indecorous, inappropriate, lacking in propriety, unseemly, ungentlemanly, unladylike.
– OPPOSITES correct.

incorrigible adj INVETERATE,

irredeemable, hardened, dyed-in-the-wool, incurable, irreformable, hopeless, beyond hope, beyond redemption, impenitent, uncontrite, unrepentant, obdurate, habitual, shameless.

incorruptible adj ❶ VIRTUOUS, honest, upright, honourable, moral, ethical, trustworthy, straight, unbribable, high-principled. ❷ IMPERISHABLE, indestructible, indissoluble, everlasting, non-biodegradable.
– OPPOSITES corrupt.

increase v ❶ GROW, become greater/larger/bigger, expand, extend, multiply, intensify, heighten, mount, escalate, mushroom, snowball, swell, wax. ❷ ADD TO, enhance, build up, enlarge, augment, expand, extend, spread, heighten, raise, intensify, strengthen, magnify, proliferate, inflate, step up.
– OPPOSITES decrease.
▶ n GROWTH, rise, enlargement, expansion, extension, increment, addition, development, intensification, escalation, heightening, boost, augmentation, snowballing, mushrooming, strengthening, magnification, inflation.
– OPPOSITES decrease.

incredible adj ❶ UNBELIEVABLE, hard to believe, beyond belief, far-fetched, inconceivable, unimaginable, unthinkable, impossible, implausible, highly unlikely, improbable, absurd, preposterous, questionable, dubious, doubtful,

fictitious, mythical. ❷ EXTRAORDINARY, wonderful, great, supreme, tremendous, marvellous, amazing, astounding, prodigious, awe-inspiring, awesome, superhuman; *informal* fantastic, fab, magic.
– OPPOSITES credible.

incredulous adj DISBELIEVING, unbelieving, sceptical, cynical, distrusting, distrustful, mistrusting, mistrustful, doubtful, doubting, dubious, unconvinced, suspicious, uncertain.
– OPPOSITES credulous.

incriminate v IMPLICATE, involve, inculpate, inform against, charge, blame, pin the blame on, accuse, indict, impeach, arraign, stigmatize, blacken someone's name; *informal* point the finger at, finger, rat on; *Brit. informal* grass on.

incumbent adj ❶ BINDING, obligatory, mandatory, necessary, compulsory. ❷ CURRENT, existing, present, in office, in power.

incur v BRING UPON ONESELF, expose oneself to, lay oneself open to, provoke, be liable to, contract, meet with, experience.

incurable adj ❶ UNTREATABLE, inoperable, beyond cure, fatal, terminal, irremediable. ❷ See INCORRIGIBLE.

indecent adj ❶ IMPROPER, suggestive, indelicate, impure, risqué, off colour, ribald, bawdy, foul, vulgar, gross, crude, obscene, dirty, smutty, coarse, lewd, lascivious, salacious, licentious, pornographic, scatological; *informal* blue, raunchy. ❷ UNSEEMLY, improper, inappropriate, unsuitable, unfitting, unacceptable, offensive, outrageous.
– OPPOSITES proper, seemly.

indecisive adj IRRESOLUTE, hesitant, in two minds, wavering, vacillating, ambivalent, undecided, uncertain, unresolved, sitting on the fence, blowing hot and cold.

indefatigable adj TIRELESS, untiring, unflagging, persistent, tenacious, dogged, assiduous, industrious, indomitable, relentless, unremitting.

indefensible adj ❶ INEXCUSABLE, unjustifiable, unpardonable, unforgivable, inexpiable. ❷ UNTENABLE, insupportable, flawed, faulty, implausible, specious, unarguable.

indefinite adj ❶ VAGUE, unclear, imprecise, inexact, ambiguous, ambivalent, equivocal, confused, evasive. ❷ INDETERMINATE, unspecified. ❸ BLURRED, ill-defined, indistinct, fuzzy, hazy, dim, vague, obscure.
– OPPOSITES definite.

indemnify v INSURE, underwrite, guarantee, protect, secure, make secure, give security to, endorse.

independence n ❶ SELF-GOVERNMENT, autonomy, self-determination, sovereignty, freedom, home rule, autarchy. ❷ FREEDOM, liberty, self-sufficiency, self-reliance.

independent adj ❶ SELF-GOVERNING, autonomous, free, sovereign, self-determining, non-aligned, neutral, autarchic. ❷ FREETHINKING, bold, liberated, individualistic, unconventional, unrestrained, untrammelled, unfettered, unconstrained. ❸ SEPARATE, unconnected, unrelated, unattached, distinct, individual. – OPPOSITES subservient, biased, related.

indescribable adj INEXPRESSIBLE, undefinable, beyond words/description, incommunicable, ineffable, unutterable, incredible, extraordinary, remarkable, prodigious.

indestructible adj UNBREAKABLE, imperishable, durable, enduring, infrangible, inextinguishable, perennial, deathless, undying, immortal, endless, everlasting. – OPPOSITES fragile.

indeterminate adj UNFIXED, indefinite, undetermined, unspecified, unstipulated, unknown, uncertain, unpredictable, uncounted, uncalculated.

index n KEY, guide, directory, catalogue, table of contents.

indicate v ❶ SHOW, demonstrate, exhibit, display, manifest, evince, express, make known, tell, state, reveal, disclose, register, record, signal, denote, betoken, suggest, imply. ❷ POINT TO / AT, designate, specify.

indication n ❶ SIGN, symptom, mark, manifestation, signal, omen, augury, portent, warning, hint. ❷ SHOW, demonstration, exhibition, display, manifestation, revelation, disclosure.

indicator n ❶ POINTER, needle, marker, meter, display. ❷ INDEX, guide, mark, sign, signal, symbol, signpost.

indifferent adj ❶ UNCONCERNED, apathetic, heedless, uncaring, uninterested, unimpressed, aloof, detached, distant, cold, cool, impassive, dispassionate, unresponsive, unemotional, emotionless, unmoved, unexcited, unfeeling, unsympathetic, callous. ❷ MEDIOCRE, middling, moderate, fair, not bad, passable, adequate, barely adequate, average, ordinary, commonplace, undistinguished, uninspired; *informal* so-so, OK. – OPPOSITES enthusiastic.

indigenous adj NATIVE, original, aboriginal, autochthonous.

indignant adj ANGRY, angered, irate, furious, incensed, infuriated, annoyed, irritated, wrathful, enraged, exasperated, heated, riled, in a temper, in high dudgeon, provoked, piqued, disgruntled, fuming, livid, mad, seeing red; *informal* miffed, in a huff, up in arms, huffy; *Brit. informal* narked.

indirect adj ❶ CIRCUITOUS, roundabout, wandering, meandering, winding, curving, tortuous, zigzag, divergent,

deviant. ❷ DISCURSIVE, oblique,
digressive, long-drawn-out,
rambling, circumlocutory,
periphrastic, allusive. ❸ BACK-
HANDED, devious, insidious,
underhand, sneaky, surreptitious.
– OPPOSITES direct.

indiscreet adj IMPRUDENT,
unwise, incautious, injudicious, ill-advised, ill-judged, ill-
thought-out, ill-considered,
foolish, impolitic, careless,
unwary, hasty, rash, reckless,
impulsive, precipitate, foolhardy, tactless, insensitive, undiplomatic.

indiscriminate adj ❶ UN-
SELECTIVE, undiscriminating,
uncritical, careless, aimless,
hit-or-miss, haphazard,
random, unsystematic, un-
methodical, sweeping, general,
broad-based, wholesale.
❷ JUMBLED, mixed, haphazard,
motley, miscellaneous, diverse,
varied, confused, mongrel,
chaotic, thrown together;
informal higgledy-piggledy.
– OPPOSITES systematic.

indispensable adj ESSEN-
TIAL, vital, crucial, imperative,
key, necessary, requisite,
needed, important, urgent,
pressing, high-priority, fundamental.
– OPPOSITES superfluous.

indisputable adj INCONTEST-
ABLE, incontrovertible, undeniable, irrefutable, un-
questionable, indubitable,
beyond dispute/question,
beyond the shadow of a doubt,

unassailable, certain, sure,
positive, definite, absolute,
final, conclusive.
– OPPOSITES debatable.

indistinct adj ❶ BLURRED,
fuzzy, out of focus, bleary,
hazy, misty, shadowy, dim,
obscure, indefinite, indistinguishable, barely perceptible.
❷ MUFFLED, muted, low,
muttered, mumbled, slurred.
– OPPOSITES distinct.

indistinguishable adj
IDENTICAL, alike, very similar,
interchangeable, the same;
informal like two peas in a pod.
– OPPOSITES different.

individual adj ❶ SINGLE, separate, lone, sole, solitary, distinct, distinctive, particular,
specific, peculiar, isolated.
❷ CHARACTERISTIC, distinctive,
peculiar, personal, personalized, own, private, special, singular, original, unique,
idiosyncratic.

indolent adj LAZY, idle, slothful, lethargic, slow-moving,
slack, lackadaisical, apathetic,
listless, inert, torpid.
– OPPOSITES active.

induce v ❶ PERSUADE, talk
into, get, prevail upon, move,
prompt, inspire, instigate, influence, press, urge, incite, encourage, impel, motivate,
inveigle, coax, wheedle.
❷ BRING ABOUT, bring on, cause,
produce, effect, create, give rise
to, generate, originate, engender, occasion, set in motion,
develop, lead to.

inducement n INCENTIVE,

indulge | inequitable

encouragement, attraction, bait, carrot, lure, reward, incitement, stimulus, spur, goad, impetus, motive, provocation; *informal* come-on.

indulge v PAMPER, spoil, coddle, mollycoddle, cosset, pander to, humour, go along with, baby, pet.

indulgent adj PERMISSIVE, easygoing, compliant, fond, doting, forbearing, compassionate, humane, kind, understanding, sympathetic, liberal, forgiving, lenient, merciful, clement.
– OPPOSITES intolerant.

industrious adj HARD-WORKING, diligent, assiduous, conscientious, sedulous, laborious, steady, busy, active, bustling, energetic, on the go, vigorous, determined, dynamic, indefatigable, tireless, persistent, pertinacious, zealous, productive.
– OPPOSITES idle, lazy.

industry n ❶ MANUFACTURING, production, fabrication, construction, business, trade, field, line, craft. ❷ INDUSTRIOUSNESS, diligence, assiduity, application, activity, energy, vigour, effort, determination, dynamism, tirelessness, persistence, zeal, pertinacity, productiveness, sedulousness, sedulity, conscientiousness.

ineffective adj ❶ UNAVAILING, useless, to no avail, ineffectual, worthless, unsuccessful, futile, fruitless, unproductive, profitless, abortive, inadequate, inefficient, inefficacious, impotent,

idle, feeble, weak, incompetent, inept, lame, barren, sterile. ❷ INCOMPETENT, inept, unproductive, inadequate, ineffectual, feeble, weak, impotent.
– OPPOSITES effective.

inelegant adj ❶ AWKWARD, clumsy, ungainly, ungraceful, graceless. ❷ UNREFINED, uncultured, uncultivated, unpolished, unsophisticated, unfinished, gauche, crude, uncouth, ill-bred, coarse, vulgar.
– OPPOSITES graceful, refined.

ineligible adj UNSUITABLE, unqualified, unfit, unfitted, inappropriate, unequipped, unacceptable, undesirable, disqualified.
– OPPOSITES eligible.

inept adj ❶ INCOMPETENT, incapable, unskilled, inexpert, clumsy, awkward, maladroit, heavy-handed; *informal* cack-handed. ❷ INAPPROPRIATE, badly timed, inapt, unsuitable, infelicitous.
– OPPOSITES competent, appropriate.

inequality n DISPARITY, imbalance, lack of balance, disproportion, variation, variability, difference, discrepancy, contrast, dissimilarity, unevenness, incongruity.
– OPPOSITES equality.

inequitable adj UNFAIR, unjust, prejudiced, biased, discriminatory, partisan, partial, preferential, one-sided, intolerant, bigoted.
– OPPOSITES fair.

inert adj ❶ UNMOVING, inactive, motionless, immobile, still, stock-still, stationary, static, lifeless, inanimate, unconscious, passive, out cold, comatose, dormant, dead. ❷ IDLE, inactive, indolent, slack, lazy, slothful, dull, sluggish, lethargic, stagnant, languid, lackadaisical, listless, torpid.
– OPPOSITES active.

inertia n INERTNESS, inactivity, inaction, motionlessness, immobility, stagnation, passivity, stasis, idleness, indolence, laziness, sloth, slothfulness, dullness, sluggishness, lethargy, languor, listlessness, torpor.
– OPPOSITES activity.

inescapable adj UNAVOIDABLE, inevitable, unpreventable, inexorable, assured, certain, bound to happen, ineludible, ineluctable.
– OPPOSITES avoidable.

inestimable adj IMMEASURABLE, measureless, incalculable, priceless, precious, invaluable, unparalleled, supreme, superlative.

inevitable adj UNAVOIDABLE, unpreventable, inexorable, inescapable, fixed, settled, irrevocable, fated, destined, predestined, ordained, decreed, out of one's hands, assured, certain, bound/sure to happen, for sure, necessary, ineluctable.
– OPPOSITES avoidable.

inexhaustible adj UNLIMITED, limitless, illimitable, infinite, boundless, endless, never-ending, unrestricted, bottomless, measureless, copious, abundant.
– OPPOSITES limited.

inexpensive adj see CHEAP (1).

inexperienced adj UNTRAINED, untutored, unqualified, undrilled, unpractised, amateur, unskilled, uninitiated, uninformed, ignorant, unacquainted, unversed, naive, unsophisticated, unfledged, untried, unseasoned, new, callow, immature, fresh, green, raw; *informal* wet behind the ears.

inexplicable adj UNEXPLAINABLE, unaccountable, incomprehensible, beyond comprehension, unintelligible, unfathomable, baffling, puzzling, mysterious, strange, weird, abstruse, enigmatic, inscrutable.
– OPPOSITES understandable.

infallible adj ❶ UNFAILING, foolproof, dependable, trustworthy, reliable, sure, certain; *informal* sure-fire. ❷ UNERRING, unfailing, error-free, faultless, flawless, impeccable, unimpeachable, perfect.
– OPPOSITES fallible.

infamous adj NOTORIOUS, disreputable, ill-famed, of ill-repute, iniquitous, ignominious, dishonourable, discreditable, villainous, wicked, evil, vile, nefarious.

infant n BABY, little child, little one, tot, toddler; *Scottish* bairn.

infantile adj CHILDISH, babyish,

puerile, immature, juvenile, adolescent.
– OPPOSITES mature.

infatuated adj BESOTTED, enamoured, captivated, bewitched, beguiled, spellbound, fascinated, enraptured, carried away, obsessed, swept off one's feet, smitten.

infatuation n PASSING FANCY, crush, fancy, passion, obsession, fixation, craze, mania.

infect v ❶ CONTAMINATE, pollute, taint, blight, spoil, mar. ❷ INFLUENCE, affect, imbue, infuse, stimulate, inspire, corrupt, pervert.

infectious adj ❶ CONTAGIOUS, infective, communicable, transmittable, transmissible, catching, spreading. ❷ GERM-LADEN, pestilential, contaminating, toxic, noxious, virulent, poisonous. ❸ CATCHING, spreading, contagious, communicable, irresistible, compelling.

infer v DEDUCE, conclude, work out, derive, reason, gather, understand, presume, conjecture, surmise, theorize, hypothesize; *informal* figure; *Brit. informal* suss.

inferior adj ❶ LOWER, lesser, subordinate, junior, secondary, subsidiary, ancillary, minor, subservient, lowly, humble, servile, menial. ❷ FAULTY, imperfect, defective, substandard, low-quality, low-grade, shoddy, cheap, reject, gimcrack; *Brit. informal* grotty. ❸ SECOND-RATE,

indifferent, mediocre, incompetent, poor, bad, awful.
– OPPOSITES superior.

infernal adj HELLISH, diabolical, devilish, demonic, demoniac, fiendish, satanic.

infest v SPREAD THROUGH, overrun, take over, pervade, permeate, penetrate, infiltrate, invade, swarm over, beset, plague.

infidelity n UNFAITHFULNESS, adultery, cheating, cuckoldry, affair, liaison, intrigue, amour.

infinite adj ❶ BOUNDLESS, unbounded, unlimited, limitless, without end, extensive, vast. ❷ COUNTLESS, without number, numberless, innumerable, immeasurable, incalculable, untold, uncountable, inestimable, indeterminable, vast, enormous, stupendous, prodigious. ❸ UNLIMITED, boundless, endless, unending, neverending, inexhaustible, interminable, absolute, total.
– OPPOSITES limited.

infinity n LIMITLESSNESS, boundlessness, unlimitedness, endlessness, infinitude.

infirm adj FEEBLE, enfeebled, weak, frail, debilitated, decrepit, disabled, in poor health, failing, ailing, doddery, lame, crippled.
– OPPOSITES fit.

inflame v INCITE, excite, arouse, rouse, stir up, work up, whip up, agitate, fire, ignite, kindle, foment, impassion, provoke, stimulate, actuate.
– OPPOSITES cool.

inflammable adj FLAMMABLE, combustible, burnable, ignitable, incendiary.
– OPPOSITES incombustible.

inflate v ❶ BLOW UP, pump up, puff up/out, dilate, distend, swell, aerate. ❷ EXAGGERATE, increase, extend, amplify, augment, expand, intensify.
– OPPOSITES deflate.

inflexible adj ❶ RIGID, stiff, non-flexible, unbendable, unyielding, taut, hard, firm, inelastic, unmalleable.
❷ UNCHANGEABLE, unalterable, immutable, unvarying, firm, fixed, hard and fast, uncompromising, stringent, rigorous, inexorable. ❸ ADAMANT, firm, immovable, unaccommodating, dyed-in-the-wool, stubborn, obdurate, obstinate, intractable, unbending, intolerant, relentless, merciless, pitiless, uncompromising, inexorable, steely, iron-willed.
– OPPOSITES flexible.

inflict v ADMINISTER, deal out, mete out, serve out, deliver, apply, lay on, impose, levy, exact, wreak.

influence n EFFECT, impact, control, sway, ascendancy, power, mastery, agency, guidance, domination, rule, supremacy, leadership, direction, pressure.
▶ v ❶ AFFECT, have an effect on, impact on, sway, bias, incline, motivate, determine, guide, control, change, alter, transform. ❷ PERSUADE, induce,

impel, incite, manipulate, prompt.

influential adj ❶ POWERFUL, important, leading, authoritative, controlling, dominant, predominant, prestigious.
❷ INSTRUMENTAL, guiding, significant, important, persuasive, telling, meaningful.
– OPPOSITES unimportant.

influx n RUSH, inflow, inundation, flood, invasion, intrusion, incursion, ingress, convergence.

inform v ❶ TELL, let know, advise, apprise, notify, announce to, impart to, relate to, communicate to, acquaint, brief, instruct, enlighten, make conversant, send word to; *informal* put in the picture, fill in, clue in, put wise, spill the beans to, tip off, tip the wink to, give the inside story to. ❷ DENOUNCE, betray, incriminate, inculpate; *informal* blab on, rat on, squeal on, tell on, blow the whistle on, put the finger on, finger, sell down the river, snitch on, peach on; *Brit. informal* grass on.

informal adj ❶ CASUAL, non-formal, unceremonious, unofficial, simple, unpretentious, everyday, relaxed, easy. ❷ COLLOQUIAL, vernacular, non-literary, simple, natural, unofficial, unpretentious; *informal* slangy.
– OPPOSITES formal.

information n ❶ DATA, facts. ❷ KNOWLEDGE, intelligence, news, notice, word, advice, counsel, instruction, enlightenment, tidings, message, report, communiqué, communication; *informal* info, gen, low-down, dope, inside story, bumf, dirt.

informative adj INSTRUCTIVE, illuminating, enlightening, edifying, educational, revealing, telling, communicative, newsy, chatty, gossipy.
– OPPOSITES uninformative.

informed adj KNOWLEDGEABLE, well briefed, posted, abreast of the facts, well versed, primed, up to date, au fait, au courant.

informer n INFORMANT, betrayer, traitor, Judas, whistle-blower; *informal* rat, squealer, stool pigeon, canary, snitch, peacher; *Brit. informal* grass, nark, snout.

infrequent adj RARE, occasional, irregular, sporadic, uncommon, unusual, exceptional, few and far between, intermittent; *informal* once in a blue moon.
– OPPOSITES frequent.

infringe v BREAK, disobey, violate, contravene, transgress, breach, disregard, take no notice of, defy, flout.

ingenious adj CLEVER, intelligent, shrewd, astute, sharp, bright, talented, brilliant, masterly, resourceful, inventive, creative, original, subtle, crafty, wily, cunning, skilful, adroit, deft, capable; *informal* smart.
– OPPOSITES stupid, unimaginative.

ingenuous adj OPEN, sincere, honest, frank, candid, direct, forthcoming, artless, guileless, simple, naive, innocent, genuine, unaffected, trustful, trusting, truthful, unsuspicious.
– OPPOSITES insincere, artful.

ingratiating adj SYCOPHANTIC, toadying, fawning, unctuous, obsequious, servile, crawling, flattering, wheedling; *informal* bootlicking.

inhabit v LIVE IN, dwell in, reside in, occupy, lodge in, tenant, make one's home in, settle in, people, populate.

inhabitant n RESIDENT, dweller, occupant, habitant, settler, native, tenant; *Brit.* occupier.

inherent adj ❶ INTRINSIC, innate, built-in, inseparable, essential, basic, fundamental, ingrained. ❷ INBORN, inbred, innate, hereditary, inherited, in the family, congenital, familial.

inherit v BE LEFT, be willed, be bequeathed, come into, fall heir to, succeed to, accede to, assume, take over.

inheritance n LEGACY, bequest, endowment, birthright, heritage, patrimony.

inhibit v IMPEDE, hold back, prevent, stop, hamper, hinder, obstruct, interfere with, curb, check, restrict, restrain, constrain, bridle, rein in, baulk, frustrate, arrest.
– OPPOSITES assist, encourage.

inhibited adj SHY, reticent, self-conscious, reserved, constrained, repressed,

embarrassed, tongue-tied, subdued, withdrawn; *informal* uptight.
– OPPOSITES uninhibited.

inhibition n ❶ OBSTRUCTION, prevention, stopping, hindrance, hampering, impediment, curb, check, restriction, restraint, frustration, arrest. ❷ SHYNESS, reticence, reserve, self-consciousness, repression, constraint, embarrassment.

inhospitable adj ❶ UNWELCOMING, unfriendly, unsociable, unsocial, antisocial, uncivil, discourteous, ungracious, ungenerous, cool, cold, chilly, aloof, unkind, unsympathetic, ill-disposed, hostile, inimical, xenophobic. ❷ BLEAK, bare, uninviting, barren, desolate, lonely, empty, forbidding, hostile.
– OPPOSITES hospitable.

initial adj FIRST, beginning, starting, commencing, opening, early, prime, primary, elementary, introductory, inaugural, foundational, inceptive.
– OPPOSITES final.

initiate v ❶ BEGIN, start, commence, open, institute, inaugurate, get under way, set in motion, lay the foundations of, launch, actuate, instigate, trigger off, originate, pioneer, sow the seeds of; *informal* start the ball rolling. ❷ TEACH, instruct, coach, tutor, school, train, prime, familiarize, indoctrinate.
– OPPOSITES finish.

initiative n ENTERPRISE,

resourcefulness, inventiveness, resource, originality, creativity, drive, push, dynamism, ambition, ambitiousness, verve, dash, leadership; *informal* get-up-and-go, pep, zip.

injunction n COMMAND, instruction, order, ruling, direction, directive, dictate, dictum, mandate, enjoinment, admonition, precept, ultimatum.

injure v HURT, harm, damage, wound, maim, cripple, lame, disable, mutilate, deform, mangle, impair, weaken, enfeeble, blight, blemish.

injurious adj HARMFUL, hurtful, damaging, deleterious, detrimental, disadvantageous, unfavourable, destructive, pernicious, ruinous, disastrous, calamitous, malignant.
– OPPOSITES innocuous.

injury n ❶ HARM, hurt, wounding, damage, impairment, affliction. ❷ WOUND, sore, cut, bruise, gash, laceration, abrasion, lesion, contusion, trauma.

injustice n UNFAIRNESS, unjustness, inequity, bias, prejudice, favouritism, partiality, one-sidedness, discrimination, partisanship.
– OPPOSITES justice.

inkling n HINT, clue, intimation, suggestion, indication, whisper, suspicion, insinuation, notion, glimmering; *informal* the foggiest idea, the foggiest.

innate adj INBORN, inbred, congenital, hereditary, inherited, inherent, intrinsic, ingrained, natural, native, indigenous.

inner adj INTERIOR, inside, central, middle, further in.
– OPPOSITES outer.

innocence n ❶ GUILTLESSNESS, blamelessness, irreproachability, clean hands. ❷ SIMPLENESS, ingenuousness, naivety, guilelessness, openness, credulity, inexperience, gullibility.
– OPPOSITES guilt.

innocent adj ❶ NOT GUILTY, guiltless, blameless, clear, in the clear, above suspicion, above reproach, unimpeachable, irreproachable. ❷ HARMLESS, innocuous, safe, unobjectionable, inoffensive, playful. ❸ SIMPLE, naive, ingenuous, unsophisticated, artless, guileless, childlike, frank, open, trustful, trusting, credulous, inexperienced, unworldly, green, gullible; informal wet behind the ears.
– OPPOSITES guilty.

innocuous adj ❶ SAFE, harmless, non-poisonous. ❷ INOFFENSIVE, harmless, unobjectionable, unexceptionable, mild, peaceful, bland, commonplace, insipid.

innuendo n INSINUATION, implication, suggestion, hint, overtone, allusion, inkling, imputation, aspersion.

innumerable adj VERY MANY, numerous, countless, untold, incalculable, numberless, unnumbered, infinite, myriad;

informal umpteen, masses, oodles.
– OPPOSITES few.

inquire v ASK, make inquiries about, investigate, question, query, research, look into, examine, explore, probe, scan, scrutinize, study.

inquiry n ❶ INVESTIGATION, examination, exploration, probe, review, search, scrutiny, scrutinization, inspection, study, interrogation. ❷ QUESTION, query.

inquisitive adj INQUIRING, questioning, probing, scrutinizing, curious, burning with curiosity, interested, intrusive, meddlesome, prying; informal nosy, nosy-parker, snooping.
– OPPOSITES uninterested.

insane adj MAD, crazy, deranged, demented, unhinged, out of one's mind, non compos mentis; informal not all there, bonkers, cracked, batty, bats, cuckoo, loopy, loony, nuts, nutty, screw, bananas, off one's rocker, round the bend; Brit. informal barmy, crackers, off one's trolley.
– OPPOSITES sane.

inscrutable adj ENIGMATIC, impenetrable, unreadable, cryptic, deadpan, sphinx-like, poker-faced.
– OPPOSITES transparent.

insecure adj ❶ VULNERABLE, open to attack, defenceless, unprotected, unguarded, exposed, in danger, dangerous, perilous, hazardous. ❷ UNCONFIDENT, lacking confidence, timid,

diffident, uncertain, unsure, doubtful, hesitant, anxious, fearful, apprehensive, worried.
– OPPOSITES secure.

insensitive adj ❶ IMPERVIOUS TO, immune to, oblivious to, unmoved by, indifferent to, proof against, insusceptible to, unaffected by, unreactive to. ❷ HEARTLESS, uncaring, unfeeling, callous, tactless, thick-skinned, unconcerned, unsympathetic.
– OPPOSITES sensitive.

insert v DRIVE IN, push in, put in, press in, stick in, thrust in, work in, slide in, slip in, tuck in, pop in.
– OPPOSITES extract.
▶ n INSERTION, inset, supplement, circular, advertisement, ad.

inside n ❶ INTERIOR, inner part, contents. ❷ STOMACH, abdomen, gut, intestines, viscera, entrails, bowels, vital organs.
▶ adj INTERIOR, inner, internal, innermost, inward, on the inside, intramural.

insidious adj SURREPTITIOUS, sneaky, cunning, crafty, stealthy, subtle, artful, Machiavellian, sly, wily, slick, deceitful, deceptive, underhand, double-dealing, duplicitous, dishonest, insincere, treacherous, perfidious; informal tricky.
– OPPOSITES straightforward.

insignificant adj UNIMPORTANT, trivial, trifling, negligible, inconsequential, of no consequence, not worth mentioning, nugatory, meagre, paltry, scanty, petty, insubstantial, flimsy, irrelevant, immaterial.
– OPPOSITES significant, important.

insincere adj UNTRUTHFUL, dishonest, deceptive, not candid, not frank, disingenuous, dissembling, dissimulating, pretended, devious, hypocritical, deceitful, duplicitous, underhand, double-dealing, false, faithless, disloyal, treacherous, two-faced, lying, mendacious, evasive, shifty, slippery.
– OPPOSITES sincere.

insinuate v IMPLY, hint, whisper, suggest, indicate, give the impression, intimate, mention.

insist v ❶ BE FIRM, stand one's ground, stand firm, make a stand, be resolute, be determined, be emphatic, not take no for an answer; formal brook no refusal. ❷ MAINTAIN, assert, state, declare, contend, pronounce, proclaim, avow, vow, swear, stress, reiterate; formal aver.

insistent adj FIRM, emphatic, determined, resolute, tenacious, persistent, unyielding, obstinate, dogged, unrelenting, unremitting, relentless, inexorable, importunate.

insolence n IMPERTINENCE, impudence, cheek, cheekiness, rudeness, disrespect, incivility, insubordination, contempt, abuse, offensiveness, audacity, boldness, brazenness, brashness, pertness, forwardness, effrontery, insults; informal gall, chutzpah; *Brit. informal* sauce, backchat.

insolent adj IMPERTINENT, impudent, cheeky, rude, ill-mannered, disrespectful, insubordinate, contemptuous, insulting, abusive, offensive, audacious, bold, brash, brazen, pert, forward; *informal* saucy, fresh.
– OPPOSITES respectful.

insoluble adj **①** UNSOLVABLE, baffling, unfathomable, indecipherable, perplexing, complicated, intricate, involved, impenetrable, inscrutable, enigmatic, obscure, mystifying, inexplicable, incomprehensible, mysterious. **②** INDISSOLUBLE.

insolvent adj BANKRUPT, ruined, penniless, impoverished, penurious, impecunious; *informal* gone bust, in the red, broke, strapped for cash.

inspect v EXAMINE, check, go over, look over, survey, scrutinize, vet, audit, study, pore over, view, scan, observe, investigate, assess, appraise; *informal* give the once-over to.

inspection n EXAMINATION, check, check-up, survey, scrutiny, view, scan, observation, investigation, probe, assessment, appraisal; *informal* once-over, look-see.

inspector n EXAMINER, checker, scrutinizer, scrutineer, auditor, surveyor, observer, investigator, overseer, supervisor, assessor, appraiser, critic.

inspiration n **①** STIMULUS, stimulation, motivation, fillip, encouragement, influence, muse, goad, spur, incitement, arousal. **②** CREATIVITY, originality, inventiveness, genius, insight, vision, afflatus. **③** BRIGHT IDEA, revelation, illumination, enlightenment.

inspire v **①** STIMULATE, motivate, encourage, influence, rouse, stir, goad, energize, galvanize, animate. **②** AROUSE, excite, touch off, spark off, ignite, kindle, give rise to, produce, bring about, prompt, instigate.

instability n **①** UNSTEADINESS, unsoundness, shakiness, frailty, flimsiness, insubstantiality. **②** IMPERMANENCE, temporariness, transience, inconstancy. **③** CAPRICIOUSNESS, volatility, changeableness, flightiness, vacillation, wavering, fitfulness, oscillation.
– OPPOSITES stability.

install v **①** PUT IN, insert, put in place, position, place, fix, locate, situate, station, lodge. **②** INVEST, ordain, establish, initiate, ensconce, induct, institute.
– OPPOSITES remove.

instalment n PART, portion, section, segment, chapter, episode, division.

instance n CASE, case in point, example, illustration, occasion, occurrence.
▶ v CITE, mention, name, specify, quote, adduce.

instant adj ❶ INSTANTANEOUS, immediate, prompt, rapid, sudden, abrupt. ❷ PRE-PREPARED, ready-prepared, ready-mixed, pre-cooked.
▶ n MOMENT, minute, second, split second, trice, twinkling, twinkling of an eye, flash; *informal* jiffy, tick, shake.

instigate v ❶ BRING ABOUT, start, initiate, generate, actuate, incite, provoke, inspire, foment, kindle, stir up, whip up. ❷ INCITE, encourage, egg on, urge, prompt, goad, prod, induce, impel, constrain, press, persuade, prevail upon, sway, entice.
– OPPOSITES discourage.

instigator n INCITER, prime mover, motivator, agitator, fomenter, troublemaker, mischief-maker, ringleader, leader.

instil v IMBUE, infuse, inculcate, introduce, inject, implant, insinuate, ingrain, indoctrinate, teach, drill, arouse.

instinct n ❶ NATURAL FEELING, tendency, inclination, intuition, sixth sense, inner prompting. ❷ TALENT, gift, ability, capacity, faculty, aptitude, knack, bent, trait, characteristic.

instinctive adj ❶ AUTOMATIC, reflex, mechanical, spontaneous, involuntary, impulsive, intuitive, unthinking, unpremeditated. ❷ INBORN, inbred, innate, inherent, natural, intuitive, untaught, unlearned.
– OPPOSITES learned.

institute v ❶ BEGIN, start, commence, set in motion, put into operation, initiate. ❷ FOUND, establish, launch, bring into being, set up, constitute, organize, develop, create, originate, pioneer.
▶ n INSTITUTION, establishment, organization, foundation, society, association, league, guild, consortium.

institutional adj ❶ ORGANIZED, established, bureaucratic, accepted, orthodox, conventional, customary, formal, systematic, methodical, orderly. ❷ UNIFORM, same, unvarying, unvaried, unchanging, monotonous, bland, dull, insipid. ❸ COLD, cheerless, clinical, dreary, drab, unwelcoming, uninviting, impersonal, formal, forbidding.

instruct v ❶ TELL, order, direct, command, bid, charge, enjoin, demand, require. ❷ TEACH, educate, tutor, coach, train, school, drill, ground, prepare, prime, guide, inform, enlighten, discipline, edify.

instruction n ❶ TEACHING, education, tutoring, tutelage, coaching, training, schooling, drilling, grounding, preparation, priming, guidance, information, enlightenment, edification, lessons, classes, lectures. ❷ DIRECTIVE, direction, briefing, order, command, charge, injunction, requirement, ruling, mandate.

instructive adj INFORMATIVE, educational, educative, enlightening, illuminating, revealing, useful, helpful, edifying, uplifting, informational, cultural, academic, didactic, doctrinal.

instructor n TEACHER, schoolmaster, schoolmistress, educator, lecturer, professor, tutor, coach, trainer, adviser, counsellor, guide, mentor, demonstrator.

instrument n IMPLEMENT, tool, appliance, apparatus, mechanism, utensil, gadget, contrivance, device, aid.

instrumental adj HELPFUL, of use, of help, of assistance, useful, of service, contributory, active, involved, influential, significant, important, valuable, beneficial.

insubordinate adj DEFIANT, rebellious, mutinous, disobedient, refractory, recalcitrant, undisciplined, ungovernable, uncontrollable, unmanageable, unruly, disorderly, seditious, riotous, insurgent, contumacious.
– OPPOSITES obedient.

insufferable adj INTOLERABLE, unbearable, unendurable, insupportable, impossible, dreadful, excruciating, grim, outrageous.
– OPPOSITES bearable.

insufficient adj INADEQUATE, deficient, in short supply, scarce, meagre, scant, scanty, too small/few/little, not enough, lacking, wanting, at a premium.
– OPPOSITES sufficient.

insular adj ❶ ISOLATED, detached, separate, solitary, insulated, self-sufficient. ❷ NARROW, narrow-minded, illiberal, prejudiced, biased, bigoted, provincial, blinkered, parochial, limited, restricted.
– OPPOSITES broad-minded.

insulate v ❶ COVER, wrap, encase, enwrap, envelop, pad, cushion, seal, heatproof, soundproof. ❷ SEPARATE, segregate, isolate, detach, cut off, keep apart, exclude, sequester, protect, shield.

insult n SLIGHT, affront, gibe, snub, barb, slur, dig, abuse, disparagement, depreciation, impugnment, revilement, insolence, rudeness, aspersions.
▶ v OFFEND, affront, slight, hurt someone's feelings, hurt, abuse, injure, wound, mortify, humiliate, disparage, discredit, depreciate, impugn, slur, revile.
– OPPOSITES compliment.

insuperable adj INSURMOUNTABLE, impassable, overwhelming, invincible, unconquerable, unassailable.

insure v ASSURE, indemnify, cover, underwrite, guarantee, warrant.

intact adj WHOLE, complete, entire, perfect, in one piece, sound, unbroken, undamaged, unblemished, faultless, flawless.
– OPPOSITES damaged.

intangible adj ❶ IMPALPABLE, untouchable, incorporeal, phantom, spectral, ghostly. ❷ INDEFINABLE, indescribable,

vague, subtle, unclear, obscure, mysterious.
– OPPOSITES tangible.

integral adj ❶ ESSENTIAL, necessary, indispensable, requisite, basic, fundamental, inherent, intrinsic, innate. ❷ ENTIRE, complete, whole, total, full, intact, unified, integrated, undivided.
– OPPOSITES peripheral, fragmented.

integrate v JOIN, unite, combine, amalgamate, consolidate, blend, incorporate, coalesce, fuse, merge, intermix, mingle, commingle, assimilate, homogenize, mesh, harmonize, concatenate.
– OPPOSITES separate.

integrity n ❶ HONESTY, uprightness, rectitude, righteousness, virtue, probity, morality, honour, goodness, decency, truthfulness, fairness, sincerity, candour. ❷ UNITY, wholeness, entirety, completeness, totality, cohesion.
– OPPOSITES dishonesty.

intellect n INTELLIGENCE, understanding, reason, comprehension, mind, brain, thought, sense, judgement.

intellectual adj ❶ MENTAL, cerebral, academic, rational, logical. ❷ INTELLIGENT, academic, well educated, well read, erudite, learned, bookish, donnish, highbrow, scholarly, studious.
▶ n INTELLECT, genius, thinker, mastermind, academic, don, man/woman of letters,

bluestocking, highbrow, pedant; informal egghead, bookworm.

intelligence n ❶ INTELLECT, mind, brain, brainpower, mental capacity, aptitude, reason, understanding, comprehension, acumen, wit, cleverness, brightness, sharpness, brilliance, quickness of mind, discernment, alertness, perception, perspicacity, penetration, sense, brains, sagacity; informal grey matter, nous. ❷ INFORMATION, news, notice, notification, knowledge, account, advice, rumour, facts, data, reports, tidings; informal gen, low-down, dope. ❸ SPYING, observation, information collection, investigation, surveillance.

intelligent adj CLEVER, bright, sharp, brilliant, quick, quickwitted, perceptive, penetrating, discerning, sagacious, thinking, well informed, educated, knowledgeable, enlightened; informal brainy, smart.

intelligentsia pl n INTELLECTUALS, academics, literati, cognoscenti, illuminati, highbrows, pedants, the enlightened.

intelligible adj UNDERSTANDABLE, comprehensible, clear, lucid, plain, explicit, unambiguous, legible, decipherable, straightforward, meaningful.
– OPPOSITES unintelligible, incomprehensible.

intemperate adj IMMODERATE, self-indulgent, excessive, inor-

dinate, extreme, extravagant, unreasonable, outrageous.
– OPPOSITES moderate.

intend v MEAN, plan, have in mind/view, propose, aim, resolve, be resolved, be determined, expect, purpose, contemplate, think of.

intense adj ❶ ACUTE, fierce, severe, extreme, harsh, strong, powerful, potent, vigorous, great, profound, deep, concentrated, consuming. ❷ EARNEST, ardent, eager, keen, enthusiastic, zealous, excited, impassioned, passionate, fervent, burning, fervid, consuming, vehement, fanatical. ❸ NERVOUS, nervy, tense, overwrought, fraught, highly strung, emotional.
– OPPOSITES mild.

intensify v STRENGTHEN, increase, deepen, heighten, enhance, add to, fuel, build up, reinforce, magnify, fan, extend, boost, augment, escalate, step up, aggravate, exacerbate, worsen, inflame, raise.
– OPPOSITES reduce, decrease.

intensive adj CONCENTRATED, in-depth, thorough, exhaustive, all-out, thoroughgoing, total, all-absorbing, high-powered, unremitting, comprehensive.
– OPPOSITES cursory.

intent adj ❶ CONCENTRATED, concentrating, fixed, steady, steadfast, absorbed, attentive, engrossed, focused, occupied, preoccupied, rapt, enrapt, wrapped up, observant, watchful, alert, earnest, committed,

intense. ❷ SET ON, bent on, committed to, firm about, determined to, resolved to; informal hell-bent on.

intention n ❶ AIM, purpose, objective, goal, intent, end, end in view, target, aspiration, wish, ambition, plan, design, resolve, resolution, determination. ❷ PREMEDITATION, design, plan, calculation, preconception.

intentional adj INTENDED, deliberate, meant, done on purpose, wilful, purposeful, planned, calculated, designed, premeditated, preconceived, predetermined, pre-arranged, considered, weighed up, studied.
– OPPOSITES accidental, inadvertent.

inter v BURY, entomb, consign to the grave, lay to rest; informal put six feet under.

intercept v CUT OFF, stop, deflect, head off, catch, check, arrest, block, obstruct, impede, interrupt, thwart.

intercourse n ❶ DEALINGS, trade, traffic, commerce, association, communication, connection, contact, correspondence, congress, communion. ❷ SEX, sexual intercourse, sexual relations, copulation, coitus, coition, carnal knowledge, lovemaking, sexual congress, congress, intimacy.

interest n ❶ ATTENTIVENESS, attention, absorption, engrossment, heed, regard, notice,

scrutiny, curiosity, inquisitiveness. **2** CURIOSITY, attraction, appeal, fascination, charm, allure. **3** CONCERN, importance, consequence, import, moment, significance, note, relevance, seriousness, weight, gravity, priority, urgency. **4** PASTIME, hobby, activity, diversion, amusement, pursuit, relaxation; *informal* thing, scene. **5** SHARE, stake, portion, claim, investment, involvement, participation, stock, equity.
– OPPOSITES boredom.
▶ V ATTRACT, absorb, hold/ engage someone's interest, engross, fascinate, rivet, grip, captivate, amuse, intrigue, arouse curiosity in, concern.
– OPPOSITES bore.

interested adj **1** ATTENTIVE, intent, absorbed, engrossed, curious, fascinated, riveted, gripped, captivated, intrigued. **2** CONCERNED, involved, implicated. **3** PARTIAL, involved, partisan, biased, prejudiced.
– OPPOSITES uninterested, disinterested.

interesting adj ABSORBING, engrossing, fascinating, riveting, gripping, compelling, compulsive, spellbinding, captivating, appealing, engaging, amusing, entertaining, stimulating, thought-provoking, diverting, exciting, intriguing.
– OPPOSITES boring, uninteresting.

interfere v **1** HINDER, inhibit, impede, obstruct, get in the way of, check, block, hamper, handicap, cramp, frustrate,

trammel, thwart, baulk.
2 MEDDLE WITH, butt into, pry into, intrude into, intervene in, get involved in, tamper with, intercede in; *informal* poke one's nose into, horn in, stick one's oar in.

interim adj TEMPORARY, provisional, pro tem, stopgap, caretaker, acting, makeshift, improvised.

interior adj INNER, internal, inside, inward.
– OPPOSITES exterior, outer.
▶ n **1** INSIDE, inner part, centre, middle, nucleus, core, heart. **2** HINTERLAND, centre, heartland.
– OPPOSITES exterior.

interject v INTRODUCE, interpose, interpolate, add, insinuate, intersperse.

interlude n INTERVAL, intermission, break, pause, recess, rest, respite, halt, stop, stoppage, breathing space, delay, wait, hiatus.

intermediary n MEDIATOR, go-between, broker, agent, middleman, arbitrator, negotiator.

intermediate adj HALFWAY, in-between, middle, in the middle, mid, midway, intervening, interposed, transitional, medial, median, intermediary.

interminable adj ENDLESS, never-ending, everlasting, incessant, ceaseless, unlimited, infinite, boundless, countless, untold, innumerable, incalculable, immeasurable, indeterminable.

intermittent adj FITFUL, spasmodic, irregular, sporadic, occasional, periodic, cyclic, recurrent, recurring, broken, discontinuous, on and off, erratic.
– OPPOSITES continuous.

internal adj ❶ INNER, inside, inward, interior. ❷ DOMESTIC, home, civil, interior, in-house.
– OPPOSITES external, foreign.

international adj WORLD-WIDE, cosmopolitan, global, universal, intercontinental.

interpolate v INSERT, interject, interpose, introduce, add, inject, insinuate, put in, work in, intercalate.

interpret v ❶ TRANSLATE, transliterate, transcribe, paraphrase. ❷ EXPLAIN, elucidate, expound, explicate, clarify, make clear, illuminate, shed light on, gloss, simplify, spell out. ❸ DECODE, decipher, solve, crack, unravel, untangle. ❹ UNDERSTAND, take, take to mean, read.

interrogate v QUESTION, put/ pose questions to, examine, cross-examine, give the third degree to, inquire of, quiz, probe; *informal* put the screws on, pump, grill.

interrogation n QUESTIONING, cross-examination, inquisition, investigation, grilling, probing, inquiry; *informal* the third degree.

interrogative adj INQUISITIVE, questioning, quizzical, inquiring, curious, investigative, inquisitorial, probing.

interrupt v ❶ CUT IN ON, break in on, barge in on, intrude on, butt in on, disturb, heckle, interfere with; *informal* chime in on, horn in on, muscle in on; *Brit. informal* chip in on. ❷ SUSPEND, discontinue, break, break off, hold up, delay, lay aside, leave off, postpone, stop, put a stop to, halt, bring to a halt/ standstill, cease, end, cancel, sever.

interruption n ❶ INTERFERENCE, disturbance, intrusion, butting in, obtrusion; *informal* horning in. ❷ SUSPENSION, discontinuance, breaking off, delay, postponement, stopping, halt, cessation. ❸ INTERMISSION, interval, interlude, break, pause, recess, gap, hiatus.

intersect v ❶ CUT ACROSS / THROUGH, cut in two, divide, bisect. ❷ CROSS, criss-cross, meet, connect.

intersection n JUNCTION, interchange, crossroads, roundabout, spaghetti junction.

interval n ❶ INTERLUDE, interim, intervening time, time, period, meantime, meanwhile, wait, space. ❷ INTERMISSION, break, half-time, pause, lull, respite, breather, breathing space, gap, hiatus, delay.

intervene v ❶ COME / OCCUR BETWEEN, occur, happen, arise, take place, ensue, supervene, succeed; *poetic/literary* come to pass. ❷ INTERCEDE, mediate, arbitrate, negotiate, step in, involve oneself, come into, interpose, interfere, intrude.

interview n ❶ APPRAISAL,

evaluation, discussion, meeting, talk, dialogue. ❷ AUDIENCE, question and answer session, exchange, dialogue, colloquy, interlocution.
▶ v TALK TO, have a discussion/dialogue with, confer with, question, put questions to, sound out, examine, interrogate, cross-examine, evaluate.

interweave v ❶ WEAVE, intertwine, twine, twist, interlace, braid, plait. ❷ INTERMINGLE, mingle, interlink, intermix, mix, blend, interlock, knit, connect, associate.

intimate¹ adj ❶ CLOSE, near, dear, nearest and dearest, cherished, bosom, familiar, confidential, warm, friendly, comradely, amicable. ❷ INFORMAL, warm, cosy, friendly, comfortable, snug. ❸ PERSONAL, private, confidential, secret, privy.
– OPPOSITES distant.

intimate² v ❶ ANNOUNCE, make known, state, tell, inform, communicate, impart. ❷ IMPLY, suggest, let it be known, hint, insinuate, give an inkling that, indicate, signal; *informal* tip someone the wink.

intimidate v FRIGHTEN, terrify, scare, alarm, terrorize, overawe, awe, cow, subdue, daunt, domineer, browbeat, bully, tyrannize, coerce, compel, bulldoze, pressure, pressurize, threaten; *informal* push around, lean on, twist someone's arm.

intolerable adj UNBEARABLE, unendurable, beyond endurance, insufferable, insupportable, not to be borne, more than one can stand, impossible, painful, excruciating, agonizing.

intolerant adj BIGOTED, illiberal, narrow-minded, narrow, parochial, provincial, insular, small-minded, prejudiced, biased, partisan, one-sided, warped, twisted, fanatical, chauvinistic, jingoistic, racist, xenophobic, sexist, ageist, homophobic.
– OPPOSITES tolerant.

intonation n PITCH, tone, timbre, cadence, lilt, inflection, accentuation, emphasis, stress.

intoxicate v ❶ INEBRIATE, make drunk, befuddle, fuddle, stupefy. ❷ EXHILARATE, elate, thrill, invigorate, animate, enliven, excite, arouse, inflame, enrapture.

intoxicated adj *see* DRUNK.

intractable adj UNMANAGEABLE, ungovernable, uncontrollable, stubborn, obstinate, obdurate, perverse, disobedient, indomitable, refractory, recalcitrant, insubordinate, rebellious, wild, unruly, rowdy.
– OPPOSITES manageable.

intricate adj ❶ TANGLED, entangled, ravelled, twisted, knotty, convoluted, involute, maze-like, labyrinthine, winding, serpentine, circuitous, sinuous, fancy, elaborate, ornate, Byzantine, rococo. ❷ COMPLEX, complicated, diffi-

cult, involved, perplexing, puzzling, thorny, mystifying, enigmatic, obscure.
– OPPOSITES simple.

intrigue v ❶ INTEREST, absorb, arouse someone's curiosity, attract, draw, pull, rivet someone's attention, rivet, fascinate, charm, captivate, divert, pique, titillate. ❷ PLOT, conspire, scheme, connive, manoeuvre, machinate, devise.
– OPPOSITES bore.
▶ n PLOT, conspiracy, collusion, cabal, scheme, ruse, stratagem, wile, dodge, artifice, manoeuvre, machination, trickery, sharp practice, double-dealing.

intrinsic adj INHERENT, inborn, inbred, congenital, natural, native, indigenous, constitutional, built-in, ingrained, implanted, basic, fundamental, elemental, essential, true, genuine, real, authentic.

introduce v ❶ PRESENT, make known, acquaint, make acquainted, announce, give an introduction to. ❷ PREFACE, precede, lead into, commence, start off, begin. ❸ BRING IN, bring into being, originate, launch, inaugurate, institute, initiate, establish, found, set in motion, organize, develop, start, begin, commence, usher in, pioneer. ❹ INSERT, inject, interject, interpose, interpolate, intercalate, add, bring, infuse, instil.

introduction n FOREWORD, preface, front matter, preamble, prologue, prelude, exordium, lead-in; informal intro, prelims.
– OPPOSITES afterword.

introductory adj ❶ PREFATORY, preliminary, precursory, lead-in, initiatory, opening, initial, starting. ❷ PREPARATORY, elementary, basic, basal, rudimentary, fundamental, initiatory.
– OPPOSITES closing.

introspective adj INWARD-LOOKING, inner-directed, introverted, self-analysing, self-examining, subjective, contemplative, reflective, meditative, musing, pensive, brooding, preoccupied.

intrude v ❶ INTERRUPT, push/thrust oneself in, gatecrash, barge in, encroach, butt in, interfere, obtrude. ❷ ENCROACH ON, invade, impinge on, infringe on, trespass on, obtrude on, violate.

intruder n ❶ BURGLAR, housebreaker, thief, raider, invader, prowler, trespasser. ❷ UNWELCOME GUEST / VISITOR, gatecrasher, interloper, infiltrator.

intuition n ❶ INSTINCT, sixth sense, divination, presentiment, clairvoyance, second sight, extrasensory perception, ESP. ❷ FEELING, feeling in one's bones, hunch, inkling, presentiment, foreboding.

inundate v ❶ FLOOD, deluge, overrun, swamp, submerge, engulf, drown, cover, saturate, soak. ❷ OVERWHELM, overpower, overburden, swamp, bog down, glut.

inure v HARDEN, toughen, season, temper, habituate, familiarize, accustom, naturalize, acclimatize.

invade v ❶ ATTACK, assail, assault, overrun, occupy, storm, take over, descend upon, make inroads on, raid, plunder. ❷ INTRUDE ON, obtrude on, encroach on, infringe on, trespass on, burst in on, violate.
– OPPOSITES withdraw.

invalid adj ❶ INOPERATIVE, legally void, null, null and void, void, not binding, nullified, revoked, rescinded, abolished. ❷ UNJUSTIFIED, unsubstantiated, unwarranted, untenable, illogical, irrational, unscientific, false, faulty, fallacious, spurious, unacceptable, inadequate, unconvincing, ineffectual, unsound, weak, useless, worthless.

invaluable adj PRICELESS, beyond price, inestimable, precious, costly, worth its weight in gold, worth a king's ransom.
– OPPOSITES worthless.

invariable adj UNCHANGING, changeless, unchangeable, constant, unvarying, unvaried, invariant, unalterable, immutable, fixed, stable, set, steady, unwavering, static, uniform, regular, consistent.
– OPPOSITES varied.

invariably adv ALWAYS, every/each time, on every occasion, at all times, without fail/exception, regularly, consistently, repeatedly, habitually,

unfailingly, infallibly, inevitably.

invasion n ❶ OVERRUNNING, occupation, incursion, offensive, attack, assailing, assault, raid, foray, onslaught, plundering. ❷ INTRUSION, obtrusion, encroachment, infringement, breach, infraction, trespass, violation.

inveigle v PERSUADE, talk into, cajole, wheedle, coax, beguile, tempt, decoy, lure, entice, seduce, deceive; informal sweet-talk.

invent v ❶ ORIGINATE, create, innovate, discover, design, devise, contrive, formulate, think up, conceive, come up with, hit upon, compose, frame, coin. ❷ MAKE UP, fabricate, concoct, hatch, trump up, forge; informal cook up.

invention n ❶ ORIGINATION, creation, innovation, discovery, design, contrivance, construction, coinage; informal brainchild. ❷ INVENTIVENESS, originality, creativity, creativeness, imagination, artistry, inspiration, ingenuity, resourcefulness, genius.

inventive adj ORIGINAL, creative, innovational, imaginative, artistic, inspired, ingenious, resourceful, innovative, gifted, talented, skilful, clever.
– OPPOSITES unimaginative.

inventor n ORIGINATOR, creator, innovator, discoverer, author, architect, designer, deviser, developer, initiator, coiner, father, prime mover, maker, framer, producer.

inventory n LIST, listing, checklist, catalogue, record, register, tally, account, description, statement.

inverse adj OPPOSITE, converse, contrary, reverse, counter.

invert v TURN UPSIDE DOWN, upturn, overturn, upset, turn turtle, capsize.

invest v **1** PUT / SINK MONEY INTO, lay out money on, provide capital for, fund, subsidize. **2** SPEND, expend, lay out, put in, use up, devote, contribute, donate, give. **3** VEST, endow, confer, bestow, grant, entrust, give, place.

investigate v INQUIRE INTO, make inquiries about, go/look into, research, probe, explore, search, scrutinize, study, examine, inspect, consider, sift, analyse; informal check out; Brit. informal suss out.

investigation n INQUIRY, fact-finding, search, scrutinization, scrutiny, research, probe, exploration, study, survey, review, examination, inspection, consideration, sifting, analysis, inquest, hearing, questioning, inquisition.

inveterate adj CONFIRMED, habitual, inured, hardened, chronic, die-hard, deep-dyed, dyed-in-the-wool, long-standing, addicted, hard-core, incorrigible.

invidious adj **1** DISCRIMINATORY, unfair, prejudicial, slighting, offensive, objectionable, deleterious, detrimental. **2** UNPLEASANT, awkward, unpopular, repugnant, hateful.
– OPPOSITES fair, pleasant.

invigorate v REVITALIZE, energize, fortify, strengthen, put new strength/life/heart in, brace, refresh, rejuvenate, enliven, liven up, animate, exhilarate, perk up, stimulate, motivate, rouse, excite, wake up, galvanize, electrify; informal pep up.
– OPPOSITES tire.

invincible adj **1** UNCONQUERABLE, undefeatable, unbeatable, unassailable, invulnerable, indestructible, impregnable, indomitable, unyielding, unflinching, dauntless. **2** INSUPERABLE, unsurmountable, overwhelming, overpowering.
– OPPOSITES vulnerable.

inviolable adj INALIENABLE, untouchable, unalterable, sacrosanct, sacred, holy, hallowed.

invisible adj UNSEEABLE, out of sight, undetectable, imperceptible, indiscernible, indistinguishable, unseen, unnoticed, unobserved, hidden, concealed, inconspicuous, unnoticeable.

invite v **1** ASK, bid, summon, request someone's company/presence. **2** ASK FOR, request, call for, solicit, look for, seek, appeal for, petition, summon. **3** CAUSE, bring on, bring upon oneself, induce, provoke.

inviting adj ATTRACTIVE, appealing, pleasant, agreeable,

delightful, engaging, tempting, enticing, alluring, irresistible, ravishing, seductive.
– OPPOSITES repellent.

invocation n CALL, prayer, request, petition, appeal, supplication, entreaty, solicitation, imploring, importuning; *poetic/literary* beseeching.

invoke v CALL FOR, call up, pray for, request, supplicate, entreat, solicit, beg, implore, importune, call on, petition, appeal to; *poetic/literary* beseech.

involuntary adj ❶ REFLEXIVE, reflex, automatic, mechanical, unconditioned, spontaneous, instinctive, instinctual, unconscious, unthinking, unintentional, uncontrolled.
❷ UNWILLING, against one's will/wishes, reluctant, grudging, forced, coerced, coercive, compelled, compulsory, obligatory.
– OPPOSITES deliberate, voluntary.

involve v ❶ ENTAIL, imply, mean, denote, betoken, connote, require, necessitate, presuppose. ❷ INCLUDE, count in, cover, embrace, take in, number, incorporate, encompass, comprise, contain, comprehend. ❸ INTEREST, be of interest to, absorb, engage, engage/hold someone's attention, rivet, grip, occupy, preoccupy, engross.
– OPPOSITES preclude, exclude.

involved adj COMPLICATED, difficult, intricate, complex, elaborate, confused, confusing,

mixed up, jumbled, tangled, entangled, convoluted, knotty, tortuous, labyrinthine, Byzantine.

iota n BIT, mite, speck, atom, jot, whit, particle, fraction, morsel, grain; *informal* smidgen.

ironic adj ❶ SATIRICAL, mocking, derisive, scornful, sardonic, wry, double-edged, sarcastic. ❷ PARADOXICAL, incongruous.

irrational adj ILLOGICAL, unreasonable, groundless, unsound, implausible, absurd, ridiculous, silly, foolish, senseless, nonsensical, muddled, confused, ludicrous, preposterous, crazy, demented, insane.
– OPPOSITES rational.

irrefutable adj INCONTROVERTIBLE, incontestable, indisputable, undeniable, unquestionable, beyond question, indubitable, beyond doubt, conclusive, decisive, definite.

irregular adj ❶ ASYMMETRIC, unsymmetrical, uneven, broken, jagged, ragged, serrated, crooked, curving, craggy. ❷ UNEVEN, unsteady, shaky, fitful, variable, erratic, spasmodic, wavering, fluctuating, aperiodic. ❸ INCONSISTENT, erratic, sporadic, variable, inconstant, desultory, haphazard, intermittent, occasional. ❹ OUT OF ORDER, against the rules, unofficial, unorthodox, unconventional, abnormal.

irrelevant adj IMMATERIAL, unrelated, unconnected, inapposite, inapt, inapplicable, non-germane, inappropriate, extraneous, beside the point, not to the point, out of place; *informal* nothing to do with it, neither here nor there.

irreparable adj BEYOND REPAIR, past mending, irreversible, irrevocable, irretrievable, irrecoverable, irremediable, incurable, ruinous.

irreplaceable adj PRICELESS, invaluable, precious, unique, worth its weight in gold, rare.

irrepressible adj ❶ INEXTINGUISHABLE, unquenchable, uncontainable, uncontrollable, unstoppable, unrestrained, unchecked, unbridled. ❷ BUOYANT, effervescent, ebullient, vivacious, animated, spirited, lively.

irresistible adj ❶ OVERWHELMING, overpowering, compelling, irrepressible, forceful, potent, imperative, urgent. ❷ FASCINATING, alluring, enticing, seductive, captivating, enchanting, ravishing, tempting, tantalizing.

irresolute adj UNCERTAIN, unsure, doubtful, dubious, undecided, indecisive, unresolved, undetermined, unsettled, vacillating, wavering, hesitant, hesitating, tentative, in two minds, oscillating.
– OPPOSITES resolute.

irresponsible adj ❶ UNDEPENDABLE, unreliable, untrustworthy, careless, reckless, rash, flighty, giddy, scatterbrained, erratic, hare-brained, feather-brained, immature. ❷ THOUGHTLESS, ill-considered, unwise, injudicious, careless, reckless, immature.
– OPPOSITES sensible.

irreverent adj ❶ DISRESPECTFUL, impertinent, insolent, impudent, rude, cheeky, discourteous, impolite, uncivil. ❷ IMPIOUS, irreligious, heretical, sacrilegious, ungodly, blasphemous, profane.
– OPPOSITES respectful.

irrevocable adj UNALTERABLE, unchangeable, irreversible, fixed, settled, fated, immutable, predetermined, predestined.

irrigation n WATERING, wetting, spraying, sprinkling, moistening, soaking, flooding, inundating.

irritable adj BAD-TEMPERED, ill-tempered, ill-humoured, irascible, cross, edgy, testy, touchy, crabbed, peevish, petulant, cantankerous, grumpy, grouchy, crusty, dyspeptic, choleric, splenetic; *informal* snappish, snappy.
– OPPOSITES good-humoured, cheerful.

irritate v ❶ ANNOY, vex, provoke, irk, nettle, get on someone's nerves, exasperate, infuriate, anger, enrage, incense, make someone's hackles rise, ruffle, disturb, put out, bother, pester, try someone's patience; *Brit.* rub up the wrong way; *informal* aggravate, peeve, get someone's goat, get someone's back up, get up someone's nose, drive up the wall, drive bananas. **❷** CHAFE, fret, rub, pain, hurt, inflame, aggravate.

irritation n **❶** IRRITABILITY, annoyance, impatience, vexation, exasperation, indignation, crossness, ill temper, anger, fury, rage, wrath, displeasure; *informal* aggravation; *poetic/literary* ire. **❷** SOURCE OF ANNOYANCE, annoyance, irritant, pest, nuisance, thorn in the flesh; *informal* pain in the neck, pain.

isolate v SET APART, segregate, cut off, separate, detach, abstract, quarantine, keep in solitude, sequester, insulate.

isolated adj **❶** ALONE, solitary, lonely, separated, exiled, forsaken, forlorn. **❷** REMOTE, out of the way, off the beaten track, outlying, secluded, hidden, unfrequented, lonely, desolate, godforsaken. **❸** SINGLE, solitary, unique, random, unrelated, unusual, uncommon, exceptional, abnormal, atypical, untypical, anomalous, freak.

issue n **❶** MATTER, matter in question, point at issue, question, subject, topic, affair, problem, bone of contention, controversy, argument. **❷** RESULT, outcome, decision, upshot, end, conclusion, consequence, termination, effect, denouement. **❸** EDITION, number, printing, print run, impression, copy, instalment, version. **❹** ISSUING, issuance, publication, circulation, distribution, supplying, supply, dissemination, sending out, delivery.
▶ v **❶** PUT OUT, give out, deal out, send out, distribute, circulate, release, disseminate, announce, proclaim, broadcast. **❷** COME OUT / FORTH, emerge, emanate, appear, pour out/forth, exude, gush, seep, ooze.

itch v **❶** TINGLE, prickle, tickle, be irritated, be itchy. **❷** LONG, have a longing, yearn, hanker, pine, ache, burn, hunger, thirst, lust, desire greatly, crave.
▶ n **❶** TINGLING, irritation, itchiness, prickling, tickling; *Medicine* formication, paraesthesia. **❷** GREAT DESIRE, longing, yearning, craving, hankering, ache, burning, hunger, thirst, lust; *informal* yen.

item n **❶** ARTICLE, thing, piece of merchandise, goods. **❷** POINT, detail, matter, consideration, particular, feature, circumstance, aspect, element, ingredient.

jab n POKE, prod, dig, nudge, elbow, thrust, stab, bump, tap, punch; *informal* sock, biff.

jacket n CASING, case, encasement, sheath, sheathing, envelope, cover, covering, wrapping, wrapper, wrap.

jaded adj TIRED, weary, fatigued, worn out, exhausted, spent; *informal* played out, bushed, done, done in; *Brit. informal* fagged out; *N. Amer. informal* pooped.
– OPPOSITES fresh.

jagged adj SERRATED, toothed, notched, indented, nicked, pointed, snaggy, spiked, barbed, uneven, rough, ridged, ragged, craggy, broken, cleft.
– OPPOSITES smooth.

jam v ❶ WEDGE, sandwich, insert, force, ram, thrust, push, stick, press, cram, stuff. ❷ CRAM, pack, crowd, squeeze, crush. ❸ BECOME STUCK, stick, stall, halt, stop.
▶ n ❶ TRAFFIC JAM, hold-up, obstruction, congestion, bottleneck, stoppage, gridlock. ❷ PREDICAMENT, plight, straits, trouble, quandary; *informal* fix, pickle, hole, spot, tight spot, scrape; *Brit. informal* spot of bother.

jar v ❶ GRATE, rasp, scratch, squeak, screech. ❷ GRATE ON, irritate, disturb, upset, discompose, irk, annoy, nettle, vex. ❸ CLASH, conflict, be in opposition, be at variance, be at odds.

jargon n CANT, slang, argot, idiom, usage, vernacular, dialect, patois; *informal* lingo.

jaundiced adj CYNICAL, pessimistic, sceptical, distrustful, suspicious, misanthropic, bitter, resentful, jealous, envious.

jaunt n TRIP, outing, excursion, expedition, tour, holiday, break, airing, stroll, ramble.

jaunty adj SPRIGHTLY, bouncy, buoyant, lively, breezy, perky, frisky, merry, blithe, carefree, joyful. See also HAPPY (1).

jazzy adj FLASHY, fancy, stylish, smart, gaudy; *informal* flash, snazzy.

jealous adj ❶ ENVIOUS, begrudging, grudging, resentful, green with envy, green-eyed, covetous, desirous, emulous. ❷ SUSPICIOUS, possessive, distrustful, mistrustful, doubting, insecure. ❸ PROTECTIVE, vigilant, watchful, heedful, mindful, careful, solicitous, on guard, wary.
– OPPOSITES trusting.

jeer v MOCK, ridicule, deride, taunt, gibe, scorn, cry down, hector, barrack, boo, hiss,

tease, scoff at, laugh at, sneer
at; *informal* knock.
– OPPOSITES cheer.

jeopardy n RISK, danger,
endangerment, peril, hazard,
precariousness, insecurity,
vulnerability, threat, menace.
– OPPOSITES safety.

jerk v ❶ PULL, yank, tug,
wrench, tweak, pluck. ❷ JOLT,
lurch, bump, jump, bounce,
jounce.
▸ n ❶ PULL, yank, tug, wrench,
tweak. ❷ JOLT, lurch, bump,
start, jar. ❸ *See* IDIOT.

jerky adj ❶ SPASMODIC, fitful,
convulsive, twitchy, shaking,
shaky, tremulous, uncon-
trolled. ❷ JOLTING, lurching,
bumpy, bouncy, jouncing,
rough; *informal* jumpy.
– OPPOSITES smooth.

jester n ❶ COMIC, comedian,
humorist, wag, wit. ❷ FOOL,
clown, buffoon, merry andrew,
harlequin, pantaloon.

jet n ❶ STREAM, gush, spurt,
spout, spray, rush, fountain,
spring. ❷ NOZZLE, spout, nose,
sprinkler, sprinkler head,
spray, rose, atomizer.
▸ v SHOOT, gush, spurt, spout,
well, rush, spray, squirt, spew,
stream, surge, flow, issue.

jetty n PIER, wharf, quay, harbour, dock, breakwater, mole,
groyne.

jewel n GEM, gemstone, precious stone, stone, brilliant;
informal sparkler, rock.

jib v BALK AT, recoil from, shrink
from, stop short of, refuse.

jibe n TAUNT, sneer, jeer,
mocking, sneering, scoffing,
scorn, derision, ridicule,
teasing, sarcasm; *informal*
dig.

jilt v REJECT, cast aside, discard,
throw over, leave, forsake;
informal ditch, dump, give the
brush-off to, give the heave-ho,
give the elbow.

jingle v ❶ CLINK, chink, jangle,
rattle, clank. ❷ TINKLE, ding, go
ding-dong, go ting-a-ling, ring,
chime.
▸ n DITTY, chorus, refrain, short
song, limerick, piece of doggerel, carol, melody, tune,
catchy tune.

job n ❶ WORK, piece of work,
task, undertaking, chore, assignment, venture, enterprise,
activity, business, affair.
❷ OCCUPATION, profession, trade,
employment, vocation, calling,
career, field of work, means of
livelihood, métier, pursuit,
position, post, situation, appointment. ❸ DUTY, task,
chore, errand, responsibility,
concern, role, charge, office,
commission, capacity, contribution.

jobless adj UNEMPLOYED,
without employment, out of
work, without work, workless,
idle, inactive, unoccupied.
– OPPOSITES employed.

jocular adj HUMOROUS, funny,
witty, comic, comical, facetious, joking, jesting, playful,
roguish, waggish, whimsical,
droll, jocose, teasing, sportive,
amusing, entertaining,

diverting, hilarious, farcical, laughable.
– OPPOSITES serious.

jog v ❶ GO JOGGING, run slowly, dogtrot, trot, canter, lope. ❷ NUDGE, prod, poke, push, elbow, tap. ❸ STIMULATE, activate, stir, arouse, prompt.

join v ❶ FASTEN, attach, tie, bind, couple, connect, unite, link, splice, yoke, knit, glue, cement, fuse, weld, solder. ❷ JOIN FORCES WITH, team up with, band together with, cooperate with, collaborate with, affiliate with. ❸ ENLIST, sign up, enrol, become a member of, enlist in, sign up for, enrol in. ❹ ADJOIN, conjoin, abut on, border, border on, touch, meet, verge on, reach to, extend to.
– OPPOSITES detach, leave.

joint n JOIN, junction, juncture, intersection, nexus, knot, seam, coupling.
▶ adj COMMON, shared, joined, mutual, combined, collective, cooperative, allied, united, concerted, consolidated.
– OPPOSITES separate.

jointly adv TOGETHER, in combination, in conjunction, as one, mutually, in partnership, cooperatively, in cooperation, in league, in collusion; informal in cahoots.

joke n ❶ JEST, witticism, quip, yarn, pun, sally; informal wisecrack, crack, gag, funny. ❷ PRACTICAL JOKE, prank, trick, hoax, jape; informal leg-pull, lark. ❸ LAUGHING STOCK, butt, figure of fun, target, fair game, Aunt Sally.
▶ v ❶ TELL JOKES, crack jokes, jest, banter, quip, wisecrack. ❷ FOOL, fool around, tease, pull someone's leg; informal kid, have someone on.

jolly adj MERRY, joyful, joyous, jovial, happy, glad, mirthful, gleeful, cheerful, cheery, carefree, buoyant, lively, bright, light-hearted, jocund, sprightly, elated, exuberant, exhilarated, jubilant, high-spirited, sportive, playful; dated gay; poetic/literary blithe.
– OPPOSITES miserable.

jolt v ❶ BUMP AGAINST, knock against, bump into, bang into, collide with, jostle, push, shove, elbow, nudge, jar. ❷ BUMP, bounce, jounce, start, jerk, lurch, jar. ❸ UPSET, disturb, perturb, shake, shake up, shock, stun, disconcert, discompose, disquiet, startle, surprise, astonish, amaze, stagger.

jostle v ❶ BUMP AGAINST, knock against, bump into, bang into, collide with, jolt, push, shove, elbow. ❷ PUSH, thrust, shove, press, squeeze, elbow, force.

jot n IOTA, whit, bit, scrap, fraction, atom, grain, particle, morsel, mite, speck, trace, trifle, tinge; informal smidgen, tad.

journal n ❶ DIARY, daybook, notebook, commonplace book, log, logbook, chronicle, record, register. ❷ PERIODICAL, magazine, trade magazine, review, publication. ❸ NEWSPAPER,

paper, daily newspaper, daily, weekly newspaper, weekly, gazette.

journalist n REPORTER, newspaperman/woman, newsman/woman, news hound, pressman/woman, feature writer, columnist, correspondent, contributor, commentator, reviewer, editor or subeditor; *informal* stringer, sub.

journey n TRIP, expedition, excursion, travels, tour, trek, voyage, cruise, safari, peregrination, roaming, roving, globetrotting, odyssey, pilgrimage, outing, jaunt.

▶ ▼ *see* TRAVEL (1).

jovial adj JOLLY, jocular, jocose, jocund, happy, cheery, cheery, glad, in good spirits, merry, mirthful, buoyant, animated, convivial, sociable, cordial; *dated* gay; *poetic/literary* blithe.

– OPPOSITES miserable.

joy n ❶ DELIGHT, pleasure, gladness, enjoyment, gratification, happiness, rapture, glee, bliss, ecstasy, elation, rejoicing, exultation, jubilation, euphoria, ravishment, transport, felicity. ❷ SOURCE OF JOY, treasure, prize, gem, jewel, pride and joy, delight. ❸ SUCCESS, satisfaction, good fortune, luck, achievement.

– OPPOSITES misery.

joyful adj ❶ OVERJOYED, elated, beside oneself, thrilled, delighted, pleased, gratified, happy, glad, gleeful, jubilant, ecstatic, exultant, euphoric,

enraptured; *informal* over the moon, in seventh heaven, on cloud nine, tickled pink; *poetic/literary* blithe. ❷ GLAD, happy, good, pleasing, cheering, gratifying, heart-warming. ❸ JOYOUS, happy, cheerful, merry, festive, celebratory; *dated* gay.

– OPPOSITES unhappy.

judge v ❶ ADJUDICATE, adjudge, umpire, referee, arbitrate, mediate. ❷ ASSESS, appraise, evaluate, weigh up, size up, gauge, examine, review, criticize, diagnose. ❸ ESTIMATE, assess, reckon, guess, surmise; *informal* guesstimate. ❹ CONSIDER, believe, think, form the opinion, deduce, gather, conclude.

▶ n ❶ MAGISTRATE, sheriff, His/Her/Your Honour; *Brit.* m'lud; *Brit. informal* beak. ❷ APPRAISER, assessor, evaluator, critic, expert. ❸ ADJUDICATOR, umpire, referee, arbiter, arbitrator, mediator.

judgement n ❶ DISCERNMENT, acumen, shrewdness, common sense, good sense, sense, perception, perspicacity, percipience, penetration, discrimination, wisdom, judiciousness, prudence, sagacity, understanding, intelligence, powers of reasoning. ❷ VERDICT, decision, adjudication, ruling, finding, opinion, conclusion, decree, sentence. ❸ OPINION, view, belief, conviction, estimation, evaluation, assessment, appraisal.

judicial adj ❶ JUDICIARY, juridical, judicatory, legal.

❷ JUDGELIKE, impartial, unbiased, critical, analytical, discriminating, discerning, perceptive.

judicious adj WISE, prudent, politic, sagacious, shrewd, astute, sensible, commonsense, sound, well advised, well considered, well judged, considered, thoughtful, expedient, practical, discerning, discriminating, informed, intelligent, clever, enlightened, logical, rational, discreet, careful, cautious, circumspect, diplomatic; *informal* smart.
– OPPOSITES injudicious, foolish.

jug n PITCHER, carafe, decanter, jar, urn, crock, vessel, receptacle, container.

juggle v CHANGE AROUND, alter, tamper with, falsify, fake, manipulate, manoeuvre, rig, massage; *informal* fix, doctor, cook.

juice n EXTRACT, sap, secretion, liquid, liquor, fluid, serum.

juicy adj ❶ SUCCULENT, moist, lush, sappy, watery, wet, flowing. ❷ RACY, risqué, spicy, sensational, thrilling, fascinating, colourful, exciting, vivid.
– OPPOSITES dry, dull.

jumble v DISORGANIZE, muddle, confuse, disarrange, disorder, dishevel, tangle, shuffle, mix, mix up, mingle, put in disarray, make a shambles of, throw into chaos.
▶ n CLUTTER, muddle, confusion, litter, mess, hodgepodge, hotchpotch, mishmash,

confused heap, miscellany, motley collection, mixture, medley, gallimaufry, farrago.

jump v ❶ SPRING, leap, bound, hop, bounce, skip, caper, gambol, frolic, frisk, cavort. ❷ LEAP OVER, vault, pole-vault, hurdle, clear, go over, sail over. ❸ START, flinch, jerk, recoil, twitch, quiver, shake, wince; *informal* jump out of one's skin. ❹ SET UPON, mug, pounce on, fall on, swoop down on, attack, assault.
▶ n ❶ SPRING, leap, vault, bound, hop, bounce, skip. ❷ HURDLE, fence, rail, hedge, obstacle, barrier, gate. ❸ GAP, break, hiatus, interruption, space, lacuna, breach, interval. ❹ START, flinch, jerk, twitch, quiver, shake, wince.

jumpy adj NERVOUS, nervy, edgy, on edge, agitated, fidgety, anxious, uneasy, restive, tense, alarmed, apprehensive, panicky; *informal* jittery.
– OPPOSITES calm.

junction n ❶ JOIN, joint, juncture, link, bond, connection, seam, joining, coupling, linking, welding, union. ❷ CROSSROADS, crossing, intersection, interchange.

juncture n POINT, point in time, time, stage, period, critical point, crucial moment, moment of truth, turning point, crisis, crux, extremity.

junior adj YOUNGER, subordinate, lesser, lower, minor, secondary, inferior.
– OPPOSITES senior, older.

junk n RUBBISH, refuse, litter, scrap, waste, garbage, trash, debris, leavings, leftovers, remnants, cast-offs, rejects, odds and ends, bric-a-brac, oddments.

▶ v THROW OUT, throw away, discard, get rid of, dispose of, scrap; informal dump.

just adj ❶ FAIR, fair-minded, equitable, even-handed, impartial, unbiased, objective, neutral, disinterested, unprejudiced, open-minded. ❷ VALID, sound, well founded, well grounded, justified, justifiable, warranted, defensible, reasonable.

– OPPOSITES unjust, undeserved.

justice n ❶ JUSTNESS, fairness, fair play, fair-mindedness, equitableness, equity, even-handedness, impartiality, lack of bias, objectivity, neutrality, disinterestedness, lack of prejudice, open-mindedness. ❷ VALIDITY, justification, soundness, reasonableness. ❸ AMENDS, recompense, redress,

compensation, reparation, requital, retribution, penalty, punishment.

– OPPOSITES injustice.

justifiable adj VALID, sound, well founded, lawful, legitimate, legal, tenable, right, defensible, supportable, sustainable, warrantable, reasonable, within reason, sensible, acceptable, plausible, vindicable.

justify v ❶ GIVE GROUNDS FOR, give reasons for, show just cause for, explain, give an explanation for, rationalize, defend, stand up for, uphold. ❷ WARRANT, substantiate, bear out, show to be reasonable, prove to be right, confirm.

jut v STICK OUT, project, protrude, poke out, bulge out, overhang, beetle.

juvenile adj ❶ YOUNG, junior, minor. ❷ CHILDISH, puerile, infantile, immature, inexperienced, callow, green, unsophisticated, naive; informal wet behind the ears.

Kk

keen adj ❶ EAGER, enthusiastic, willing, avid, earnest, intent, diligent, assiduous, conscientious, zealous, fervent, fervid, impatient, yearning; informal raring to, itching to. ❷ FOND OF, devoted to, eager for, hungry

for, thirsty for. ❸ ACUTE, sharp, discerning, perceptive, sensitive, discriminating. ❹ ASTUTE, sharp, quick-witted, sharp-witted, shrewd, perceptive, penetrating, perspicacious, clever, bright, intelligent, bril-

liant, wise, canny, sagacious; *informal* brainy, smart; *formal* sapient.
– OPPOSITES apathetic, stupid.

keep v ❶ CARRY ON, continue, maintain, persist, persevere. ❷ HOLD ON TO, keep hold of, retain; *informal* hang on to. ❸ SAVE UP, accumulate, store, hoard, amass, pile up, collect, garner. ❹ LOOK AFTER, keep in good order, tend, mind, maintain, keep up, manage, superintend. ❺ PROVIDE FOR, support, maintain, sustain, subsidize, feed, nurture. ❻ KEEP TO, abide by, comply with, fulfil, carry out, keep faith with, stand by, honour, obey, observe; *formal* effectuate. ❼ OBSERVE, hold, celebrate, commemorate, respect, ritualize, solemnize, ceremonialize. ❽ KEEP BACK, hold back, hold up, delay, detain, retard, hinder, obstruct, impede, hamper, constrain, check, block.
■ **keep at** ❶ PERSIST, persevere, be persistent, be pertinacious, carry on, keep going, continue, work away, see it through; *informal* stick at it, stay the distance, hang on in there. ❷ KEEP ON AT, keep after, go on at, chivvy, badger, harp on at, nag, harass. **keep back** WITHHOLD, keep secret, keep hidden, hide, conceal, suppress.

keeper n ❶ JAILER, warder, warden, guard, custodian, sentry; *informal* screw. ❷ CURATOR, conservator, attendant, caretaker, steward, superintendent, overseer, administrator.

keepsake n MEMENTO, souvenir, remembrance, reminder, token of remembrance, relic, favour.

kernel n ❶ SEED, nut, grain, germ. ❷ NUB, nucleus, core, centre, heart, marrow, pith, substance, essence, essential part, gist, quintessence; *informal* nitty-gritty, nuts and bolts.

key n ❶ ANSWER, solution, explanation, guide, clue, cue, pointer, interpretation, explication, clarification, exposition. ❷ TONE, pitch, timbre, tonality.

kick v ❶ BOOT, punt. ❷ RECOIL, spring back. ❸ GIVE UP, stop, abandon, leave off, desist from; *informal* quit.

kill v ❶ TAKE SOMEONE'S LIFE, murder, do away with, do to death, slaughter, butcher, massacre, assassinate, liquidate, wipe out, destroy, erase, eradicate, exterminate, dispatch, put to death, execute; *informal* bump off, do in, knock off, top; *poetic/literary* slay. ❷ DESTROY, put an end to, ruin, extinguish, scotch, quell. ❸ EXHAUST, overtire, tire out, fatigue, wear out, debilitate, enervate, prostrate, tax, overtax, strain; *Brit. informal* fag out. ❹ HURT, cause pain, cause discomfort, be uncomfortable, be painful.

killer n ❶ MURDERER, slaughterer, butcher, assassin, liquidator, destroyer, exterminator, executioner, gunman; *informal* hit man; *poetic/literary* slayer.

killing n ❶ MURDER,

manslaughter, homicide, slaughter, butchery, massacre, bloodshed, carnage, liquidation, destruction, extermination, execution. ❷ FINANCIAL SUCCESS, bonanza, fortune, windfall, gain, profit, booty, coup; *informal* bomb, clean-up.

killjoy n SPOILSPORT, dampener, damper; *informal* wet blanket, party-pooper.

kin n RELATIVES, relations, family, connections, folks, people, kindred, kith and kin, kinsfolk, kinsmen, kinswomen.

kind[1] n ❶ SORT, type, variety, brand, class, category, genus, species. ❷ NATURE, character, manner, aspect, disposition, humour, style, stamp, mould.

kind[2] adj ❶ KIND-HEARTED, kindly, generous, charitable, giving, benevolent, magnanimous, big-hearted, warm-hearted, altruistic, philanthropic, humanitarian, humane, tender-hearted, soft-hearted, gentle, mild, lenient, merciful, clement, pitying, forbearing, patient, tolerant, sympathetic, compassionate, understanding, considerate, helpful, thoughtful, good, nice, pleasant, benign, friendly, genial, congenial, amiable, amicable, cordial, courteous, gracious, good-natured, warm, affectionate, loving, indulgent, obliging, accommodating, neighbourly; *Brit. informal* decent; *poetic/literary* bounteous.

– OPPOSITES unkind, nasty.

kindle v ❶ LIGHT, set alight, set on fire, set fire to, ignite, start, torch. ❷ STIMULATE, rouse, arouse, excite, stir, awaken, inspire, inflame, incite, induce, provoke, actuate, activate, touch off.

– OPPOSITES extinguish.

kindred adj ❶ RELATED, connected, of the same blood, of the same family, consanguineous, cognate. ❷ LIKE, similar, resembling, corresponding, matching, congenial, allied.

kink n ❶ TWIST, bend, coil, corkscrew, curl, twirl, knot, tangle, entanglement. ❷ FLAW, defect, imperfection, hitch, snag, difficulty, complication.

kinky adj ❶ QUIRKY, peculiar, odd, strange, queer, bizarre, eccentric, idiosyncratic, weird, outlandish, unconventional, unorthodox, whimsical, capricious, fanciful. ❷ PERVERTED, warped, deviant, unnatural, abnormal, depraved, degenerate, lascivious, licentious, lewd, sadistic, masochistic.

kit n ❶ EQUIPMENT, apparatus, set of tools, tools, implements, instruments, utensils, tackle, supplies, paraphernalia, accoutrements, effects, trappings, appurtenances; *informal* gear, stuff. ❷ OUTFIT, clothing, dress, uniform, colours; *informal* rig-out, gear, strip.

■ **kit out** EQUIP, supply, provide, fit out, fix up, furnish, outfit, deck out, rig out, arm, accoutre.

knack n TALENT, aptitude, gift, flair, bent, forte, ability, capability, capacity, expertise, expertness, skill, genius, facility, propensity, dexterity, ingenuity, proficiency, competence, handiness.

knead v WORK, manipulate, press, squeeze, massage, rub, form, shape.

kneel v GET DOWN ON ONE'S KNEES, fall to one's knees, genuflect, bow, bow down, stoop, make obeisance, kowtow.

knife n BLADE, cutting tool.
▶ v STAB, pierce, run through, impale, bayonet, transfix, cut, slash, lacerate, wound. *See also* WOUND v.

knit v ❶ LOOP, weave, interweave, crochet. ❷ LINK, bind, unite, draw together, ally.

knob n ❶ DOORKNOB, handle, door handle, switch, on/off switch. ❷ BUMP, bulge, swelling, lump, knot, node, nodule, pustule, growth, tumour, protuberance, tumescence.

knock v ❶ TAP, rap, bang, pound, hammer. ❷ STRIKE, hit, slap, smack, box, punch, cuff, buffet, thump, thwack, batter, pummel. ❸ KNOCK INTO, bang into, bump into, collide with, run into, crash into, crash against, smash into, dash against, jolt. ❹ CRITICIZE, find fault with, take apart, take to pieces, pick holes in, run down, carp at, cavil at, deprecate,

belittle, disparage, censure, condemn.

knot n LOOP, twist, bend, intertwinement, interlacement, ligature.
▶ v TIE, loop, bind, secure, tether, lash, leash.

know v ❶ BE AWARE OF, notice, perceive, realize, be conscious of, be cognizant of, sense, recognize; *informal* latch on to. ❷ HAVE KNOWLEDGE OF, understand, comprehend, apprehend, be conversant with, be familiar with, be acquainted with. ❸ BE FAMILIAR WITH, be acquainted with, experience, undergo, go through. ❹ HAVE MET, be acquainted with, have dealings with, associate with, be friends with, socialize with, fraternize with, be intimate with, be close to, be on good terms with.

knowing adj ❶ ASTUTE, shrewd, perceptive, meaningful, well informed, significant, eloquent, expressive. ❷ AWARE, astute, shrewd, perceptive, sophisticated, worldly, worldly-wise. ❸ CONSCIOUS, intentional, intended, deliberate, wilful, purposeful, calculated, on purpose, by design.

knowledge n ❶ LEARNING, erudition, scholarship, letters, education, enlightenment, wisdom. ❷ UNDERSTANDING, grasp, comprehension, apprehension, cognition, adeptness, skill, expertise, proficiency; *informal* know-how.

❸ ACQUAINTANCESHIP, familiarity, conversance.

knowledgeable adj ❶ WELL INFORMED, informed, educated, learned, erudite, scholarly, well read, cultured, cultivated, enlightened. ❷ HAVING A KNOWLEDGE OF, acquainted with, familiar with, experienced in, expert in, conversant with, having an understanding of.
– OPPOSITES ill-informed.

known adj RECOGNIZED, acknowledged, admitted, declared, proclaimed, avowed, confessed, published, revealed.

LI

label n ❶ IDENTIFICATION TAG, tag, ticket, tab, sticker, marker, docket. ❷ EPITHET, name, nickname, title, sobriquet, designation, description, characterization; *formal* denomination.
▶ v ❶ ATTACH LABELS TO, tag, tab, ticket, stamp, mark, put stickers on, docket. ❷ DESCRIBE, designate, identify, classify, class, categorize, brand, call, name, term, dub.

laborious adj ❶ HARD, heavy, difficult, arduous, strenuous, fatiguing, tiring, wearying, wearisome, tedious. ❷ PAINSTAKING, careful, meticulous, diligent, assiduous, industrious, hard-working, scrupulous, persevering, pertinacious, zealous. ❸ LABOURED, strained, forced.
– OPPOSITES easy, natural.

labour n ❶ WORK, employment, job, toil, exertion, effort, industry, industriousness, hard work, hard labour, drudgery, slog, donkey work, sweat of one's brow; *poetic/literary* travail. ❷ TASK, job, chore, undertaking, commission, assignment, charge, venture. ❸ EMPLOYEES, workers, workmen, workforce, working people, hands, labourers. ❹ CHILDBIRTH, birth, parturition, delivery, contractions, labour pains; *poetic/literary* travail; *dated* confinement.
▶ v WORK HARD, work away, toil, slave away, drudge, grub away, plod on/away, grind/sweat away, struggle, exert oneself, work like a slave, work one's fingers to the bone, work like a Trojan; *poetic/literary* travail.

laboured adj ❶ DIFFICULT, strained, forced, heavy, awkward. ❷ CONTRIVED, affected, studied, stiff, strained, stilted, forced, unnatural, artificial, overdone, overworked, heavy, ponderous, ornate, elaborate, over-elaborate, intricate, convoluted, complex, laborious.

labyrinth n MAZE, warren,

network, convolution, entanglement.

labyrinthine adj ❶ MAZE-LIKE, meandering, winding, wandering, twisting, circuitous, tangled. ❷ INTRICATE, complicated, complex, involved, tortuous, convoluted, tangled, entangled, confusing, puzzling, perplexing, mystifying, bewildering.

lacerate v CUT, tear, gash, slash, cut open, rip, rend, mangle, mutilate, hurt, wound, injure, maim.

lack n ABSENCE, want, need, deprivation, deficiency, privation, dearth, insufficiency, shortage, scarcity, scarceness, paucity.
 – OPPOSITES plenty.
▶ v BE LACKING, be without, have need of, need, stand in need of, require, want, be short of, be deficient in, miss.

laconic adj BRIEF, concise, terse, succinct, short, elliptical, crisp, pithy, to the point, incisive, abrupt, blunt, curt.
 – OPPOSITES verbose.

laden adj LOADED, burdened, heavily laden, weighed down, weighted, encumbered, hampered, oppressed, taxed.

lady n ❶ WOMAN, female. ❷ NOBLEWOMAN, gentlewoman, aristocrat.

ladylike adj GENTEEL, refined, well bred, cultivated, polished, decorous, proper, correct, respectable, well mannered, courteous, polite, civil, gracious.
 – OPPOSITES coarse.

lag v FALL BEHIND, fall back, trail, not keep pace, bring up the rear, loiter, linger, dally, straggle, dawdle, hang back, delay, move slowly, drag one's feet.

laid-back adj RELAXED, at ease, easy, leisurely, unhurried, casual, easy-going, free and easy, informal, nonchalant, unexcitable, imperturbable, unflappable.
 – OPPOSITES tense.

lair n ❶ TUNNEL, dugout, hollow, cave, haunt. ❷ RETREAT, hideaway, refuge, sanctuary, sanctum, sanctum sanctorum.

lake n POND, tarn, pool, reservoir, lagoon; Scottish loch; N. Amer. bayou.

lame adj ❶ LIMPING, hobbling, halting, crippled, game, disabled, incapacitated, defective; Brit. informal gammy. ❷ WEAK, feeble, thin, flimsy, unconvincing, unsatisfactory, inadequate, insufficient, deficient, defective, ineffectual.

lament v ❶ MOURN, grieve, sorrow, wail, moan, groan, weep, cry, sob, complain, keen, ululate, howl, beat one's breast. ❷ COMPLAIN ABOUT, bemoan, bewail, deplore.

lamentable adj ❶ DEPLORABLE, regrettable, tragic, terrible, wretched, woeful, sorrowful, distressing, grievous. ❷ MISERABLE, pitiful, poor, meagre, low, unsatisfactory, inadequate; informal measly.

lamp n LANTERN, table lamp, standard lamp, night light, light bulb, headlight, headlamp, sidelight, fog light, fog lamp.

land n ❶ DRY LAND, ground, solid ground, earth, terra firma. ❷ GROUND, fields, open space, expanse, stretch, tract. ❸ PROPERTY, ground, acres, estate, realty, real estate. ❹ COUNTRY, nation, fatherland, motherland, state, realm, province, territory, district, region, area, domain.
▸ v ❶ TOUCH DOWN, alight, make a landing, come in to land. ❷ MAKE A LANDING, bring down, put down, take down. ❸ BERTH, dock, reach the shore, come ashore, disembark, debark. ❹ DEAL, deliver, deposit, give, catch; *informal* fetch.

landlady, landlord n ❶ INNKEEPER, hotel keeper, hotelier, host, mine host; *Brit.* publican, pub-owner. ❷ OWNER, proprietor, lessor, householder, freeholder.

landscape n COUNTRYSIDE, scene, scenery, outlook, view, aspect, prospect, vista, panorama, perspective.

landslide n ❶ AVALANCHE, landslip, rockfall. ❷ DECISIVE VICTORY, runaway victory, overwhelming majority.

language n ❶ SPEECH, speaking, talking, words, vocabulary, utterances, verbal expression, verbalization, vocalization, communication, conversation, discourse, interchange. ❷ TONGUE, speech, parlance, mother tongue, native tongue; *informal* lingo.

languid adj LANGUISHING, listless, languorous, lackadaisical, spiritless, vigourless, lacking energy, lethargic, torpid, idle, inactive, inert, indolent, lazy, sluggish, slow-moving, unenthusiastic, apathetic, indifferent.
– OPPOSITES energetic, vigorous.

languish v ❶ DROOP, flag, wilt, wither, fade, fail, weaken, decline, go into a decline, go downhill, waste away. ❷ WASTE AWAY, rot, decay, wither away, be abandoned, be neglected, be forgotten, be disregarded.
– OPPOSITES thrive.

languor n LISTLESSNESS, lethargy, torpor, idleness, inactivity, inertia, indolence, laziness, sluggishness, sleepiness, drowsiness, somnolence, dreaminess, relaxation.
– OPPOSITES vigour.

lank adj LIFELESS, lustreless, limp, straggling, straight, long.

lanky adj TALL, spindly, gangling, gangly, lean, thin, angular, scraggy, bony, gaunt, rawboned, gawky, rangy; *informal* weedy.
– OPPOSITES sturdy.

lap n ❶ CIRCUIT, circle, loop, orbit, round, compass, ambit. ❷ ROUND, tour, section, stage.

lapse n ❶ SLIP, error, mistake, blunder, failing, fault, failure, omission, oversight, negligence, dereliction; *informal* slip-up. ❷ INTERVAL, gap, pause, intermission, interlude, lull, hiatus, break, passage.

❸ DECLINE, downturn, fall, falling, falling away, slipping, drop, deterioration, worsening, degeneration, backsliding.
▸ v ❶ DECLINE, fall, fall off, drop, go downhill, deteriorate, worsen, degenerate, go to pot. ❷ BECOME VOID, become invalid, expire, run out, terminate, become obsolete. ❸ SLIDE, slip, drift, sink, subside, submerge.

larder n PANTRY, storage room, storeroom, store, still room, cooler, scullery.

large adj ❶ BIG, great, of considerable size, sizeable, substantial, goodly, tall, high, huge, immense, enormous, colossal, massive, mammoth, vast, prodigious, gigantic, giant, monumental, stupendous, gargantuan, man-size, king-size, giant-size, outsize, considerable; informal jumbo, whopping. ❷ BURLY, big, heavy, bulky, thickset, powerfully built, heavy-set, chunky, strapping, hefty, ample, fat, obese, corpulent; informal hulking. ❸ ABUNDANT, copious, plentiful, ample, liberal, generous. ❹ WIDE, wide-ranging, large-scale, broad, extensive, far-reaching, sweeping, comprehensive, exhaustive.
– OPPOSITES small.
■ **at large** AT LIBERTY, free, unconfined, unrestrained, roaming, on the loose, on the run, fugitive.

largely adv TO A LARGE EXTENT, to a great degree, chiefly, for the most part, mostly, mainly, in the main, principally, in great measure.

lascivious adj LEWD, lecherous, lustful, licentious, promiscuous, libidinous, prurient, salacious, lubricious, concupiscent, debauched, depraved, degenerate, dissolute, dissipated.

lash v WHIP, horsewhip, scourge, birch, switch, flog, flail, flagellate, thrash, beat, strike, batter, hammer; informal wallop, whack.

last[1] adj ❶ FINAL, closing, concluding, ending, finishing, terminating, ultimate, terminal. ❷ HINDMOST, rearmost, at the end, at the back, final, aftermost. ❸ LEAST LIKELY, most unlikely, least suitable, least wanted, least favourite. ❹ LATEST, most recent.

last[2] v ❶ CONTINUE, go on, carry on, remain, persist, keep on. ❷ SURVIVE, exist, live, subsist, hold on, hold out. ❸ LAST LONG, wear well, stand up to wear, keep, endure.

late adj ❶ BEHIND SCHEDULE, behind, not on time, tardy, overdue, delayed, dilatory, slow. ❷ DECEASED, dead, departed, defunct, non-extant. ❸ FORMER, previous, preceding, past, prior.
– OPPOSITES punctual.

latent adj DORMANT, quiescent, inactive, passive, hidden, unrevealed, concealed, unapparent, indiscernible, imperceptible, invisible, covert, undeveloped, unrealized, potential, possible.
– OPPOSITES evident.

lateral adj SIDEWISE, sideways, sidelong, sideward, edgewise, edgeways, indirect, oblique, slanting.

latitude n ❶ PARALLEL.
❷ SCOPE, freedom of action, freedom, liberty, free play, carte blanche, leeway, elbow room, licence, indulgence.
– OPPOSITES longitude, restriction.

latter adj ❶ LAST-MENTIONED, second-mentioned, second of the two, second. ❷ LATER, hindmost, closing, end, concluding, final.
– OPPOSITES former.

laudable adj PRAISEWORTHY, commendable, admirable, worthy of admiration, meritorious, deserving, creditable, worthy, estimable, of note, noteworthy, exemplary, excellent.
– OPPOSITES shameful.

laugh v CHUCKLE, chortle, guffaw, giggle, titter, snigger, tee-hee, burst out laughing, roar/hoot with laughter, shake/be convulsed with laughter, split one's sides, be rolling in the aisles, be doubled up; *informal* be in stitches, die laughing, be creased up, fall about, crack up, break up.
■ **laugh at** MOCK, ridicule, deride, scoff at, jeer at, sneer at, make fun of, poke fun at, make a fool of, lampoon, satirize, taunt, tease; *informal* send up, take the mickey out of.

laughter n LAUGHING, chuckling, chortling, guffawing, giggling, tittering, sniggering, amusement, entertainment, humour, mirth, merriment, gaiety, hilarity, glee, light-heartedness; *poetic/literary* blitheness.

launch v ❶ FIRE, discharge, propel, project, send forth, throw, cast, hurl, let fly, blast off. ❷ SET IN MOTION, get going, begin, start, commence, embark upon, initiate, instigate, institute, inaugurate, establish, set up, organize, introduce, usher in.

lavatory n TOILET, public convenience, cloakroom, powder room, privy, urinal, latrine; *Brit.* WC, ladies, gents; *N. Amer.* bathroom, washroom, rest room; *Nautical* head; *informal* little girls' room, little boys' room; *Brit. informal* loo, bog, khazi, lav; *N. Amer. informal* can, john; *dated* water closet.

lavish adj ❶ COPIOUS, abundant, superabundant, plentiful, profuse, prolific, unlimited.
❷ EXTRAVAGANT, excessive, immoderate, wasteful, squandering, profligate, prodigal, thriftless, improvident, intemperate, unrestrained. ❸ GENEROUS, liberal, bountiful, open-handed, unstinting, free, munificent, extravagant. ❹ LUXURIANT, lush, gorgeous, sumptuous, costly, opulent, pretentious, showy.
– OPPOSITES meagre.
▶ v HEAP, shower, pour, deluge, give freely, give generously, bestow freely, waste, squander, dissipate.

law n ❶ STATUTE, regulation,

rule, enactment, act, decree, edict, command, order, ordinance, commandment, directive, pronouncement, covenant. ❷ PRINCIPLE, precept, standard, criterion, formula, tenet, doctrine, canon. ❸ GENERALIZATION, general truth, axiom, maxim, truism. ❹ LITIGATION, legal action, legal proceedings, lawsuit.

law-abiding adj LAWFUL, righteous, honest, honourable, upright, upstanding, good, virtuous, orderly, peaceable, peaceful, dutiful, duteous, obedient, compliant, complying.
– OPPOSITES lawless.

lawful adj ❶ LEGAL, legitimate, licit, just, valid, permissible, allowable, rightful, proper, constitutional, legalized, sanctioned, authorized, warranted, approved, recognized. ❷ see LAW-ABIDING.
– OPPOSITES illegal.

lawless adj ❶ WITHOUT LAW AND ORDER, anarchic, disorderly, ungoverned, unruly, insurrectionary, insurgent, revolutionary, rebellious, insubordinate, riotous, mutinous, seditious, terrorist. ❷ UNLAWFUL, illegal, lawbreaking, illicit, illegitimate, criminal, felonious, miscreant, transgressing, violating.
– OPPOSITES orderly, legal.

lawyer n SOLICITOR, legal practitioner, legal adviser, barrister, advocate, counsel, Queen's Counsel, QC; informal brief; N. Amer. attorney.

lax adj SLACK, slipshod, negligent, neglectful, remiss, careless, heedless, unmindful, inattentive, casual, easy-going, lenient, permissive, indulgent, overindulgent, complaisant, over-tolerant.

laxative n PURGATIVE, aperient, cathartic, senna, ipecacuanha, castor oil.

lay v ❶ SET, deposit, plant, settle, position. ❷ POSITION, set out, arrange, dispose. ❸ ATTRIBUTE, assign, ascribe, allocate, allot, impute. ❹ IMPOSE, inflict, encumber, saddle, tax, charge, burden, apply.
■ **lay aside** PUT ASIDE, put to one side, keep, save, store. **lay down** ❶ SURRENDER, relinquish, give up, yield, cede, turn over. ❷ SET DOWN, stipulate, prescribe, order, command, ordain, postulate, demand, proclaim, assert, maintain. **lay in** STOCK UP WITH / ON, stockpile, store, accumulate, amass, heap up, hoard, collect.

layabout n GOOD-FOR-NOTHING, ne'er-do-well, do-nothing, idler, loafer, lounger, shirker, wastrel, sluggard, laggard; informal waster; Brit. informal skiver.

layman n AMATEUR, non-professional, dilettante.

laze v IDLE, do nothing, loaf, lounge, lounge about, loll around, waste time, fritter away time.

laziness n IDLENESS, indolence, slothfulness, sloth,

inactivity, inertia, lethargy, languor, remissness, laxity.

lazy adj IDLE, indolent, slothful, work-shy, inactive, inert, sluggish, lethargic, languorous, listless, torpid, slow-moving, remiss, negligent, lax.
– OPPOSITES industrious.

lead v ❶ GUIDE, show someone the way, conduct, lead the way, usher, escort, steer, pilot. ❷ CAUSE, induce, prompt, move, incline, dispose, predispose, persuade, sway, influence, prevail upon, bring round. ❸ BE AT THE HEAD OF, be at the front of, head. ❹ COMMAND, direct, govern, rule, manage, be in charge of, regulate, preside over, head, supervise, superintend, oversee; informal head up. ❺ BE IN THE LEAD, be in front, be out in front, be ahead, be first, come first, precede. ❻ HAVE, live, pass, spend, experience, undergo.
▶ n ❶ LEADING POSITION / PLACE, first place, advance position, van, vanguard. ❷ MARGIN, gap, interval. ❸ EXAMPLE, model, pattern, standard of excellence. ❹ LEADING ROLE, star/starring role, star part, title role, principal part. ❺ LEASH, tether, rein, cord, rope, chain.
■ **lead off** BEGIN, start, start off, commence, open; informal kick off. **lead to** CAUSE, result in, bring on, call forth, provoke, contribute to. **lead up to** PREPARE THE WAY FOR, pave the way for, open the way for, do the groundwork for, work round/up to, make overtures about.

make advances about, hint at, approach the subject of, introduce the subject of.

leader n ❶ RULER, head, chief, commander, director, governor, principal, captain, manager, superintendent, supervisor, overseer, foreman, kingpin; informal boss, number one, skipper. ❷ PACESETTER, pacemaker, trendsetter, front runner, innovator, pioneer, trailblazer, pathfinder, groundbreaker, originator.
– OPPOSITES follower, supporter.

leading adj CHIEF, main, most important, principal, foremost, supreme, paramount, dominant, superior, first-rate, greatest, best, outstanding, preeminent; informal number-one.
– OPPOSITES subordinate, minor.

leaflet n PAMPHLET, booklet, brochure, handbill, flyer, bill, circular; Brit. informal advert.

league n ALLIANCE, confederation, confederacy, federation, union, association, coalition, combine, consortium, affiliation, guild, corporation, conglomerate, cooperative, partnership, fellowship, syndicate, band, group.

leak n ❶ DRIP, leaking, leakage, escape, seeping, seepage, oozing, percolation, discharge. ❷ OPENING, crack, crevice, chink, fissure, puncture, cut, gash, slit, rent, break, rift. ❸ DISCLOSURE, divulgence, revelation, uncovering.

▶ v ❶ ESCAPE, drip out, seep out/through, ooze out, exude, discharge, issue, gush out.
❷ DISCLOSE, divulge, reveal, make known, make public, impart, pass on, relate, give away, let slip; *informal* let the cat out of the bag, spill the beans about; take the lid off.

lean v ❶ BE SUPPORTED, be propped up, recline, repose.
❷ INCLINE, bend, slant, tilt, be at an angle, slope, bank, list, heel.
❸ INCLINE TOWARDS, tend towards, have a tendency towards, have a propensity for, have a proclivity for, have a preference for, be attracted to, have a liking for, gravitate towards, have an affinity with.
❹ DEPEND ON, be dependent on, rely on, count on, pin one's faith on, have faith in, trust, have every confidence in.

leaning n TENDENCY, inclination, bent, proclivity, propensity, penchant, predisposition, predilection, proneness, partiality, preference, bias, attraction, liking, fondness, taste.

leap v ❶ JUMP, bound, bounce, hop, skip, romp, caper, spring, frolic, frisk, cavort, gambol, dance. ❷ JUMP OVER, jump, vault over, vault, spring over, bound over, hurdle, clear, cross over, sail over. ❸ INCREASE RAPIDLY, soar, rocket, skyrocket, shoot up, escalate, mount.

learn v ❶ ACQUIRE A KNOWLEDGE OF, gain an understanding of, acquire skill in, become competent in, grasp, master, take in, absorb, assimilate, pick up.
❷ LEARN BY HEART, get by heart, memorize, commit to memory, become word-perfect in, get off pat. ❸ DISCOVER, find out, detect, become aware of, gather, hear, be informed, have it brought to one's attention, understand, ascertain, discern, perceive, get word of, get wind of.

learned adj ERUDITE, scholarly, well educated, knowledgeable, well read, widely read, well versed, well informed, lettered, cultured, intellectual, academic, literary, bookish.
– OPPOSITES ignorant.

learner n BEGINNER, trainee, apprentice, pupil, student, novice, tyro, neophyte, initiate; *informal* rookie; *N. Amer. informal* greenhorn.
– OPPOSITES veteran.

lease v ❶ RENT, hire, charter.
❷ LET, let out, rent, rent out, hire, hire out, sublet.

leash n ❶ LEAD, rein, tether, rope, cord, chain. ❷ REIN, curb, control, check, restraint, hold.

leathery adj ❶ WRINKLED, wizened, weather-beaten, rough, rugged, coriaceous. ❷ TOUGH, hard, hardened.

leave[1] v ❶ DEPART, go away, go, withdraw, retire, take oneself off, exit, take one's leave, make off, pull out, quit, be gone, decamp, disappear, say one's farewells/goodbyes; *informal* push off, shove off, cut, split, vamoose; *Brit. informal* do a bunk. ❷ SET OFF, set sail.
❸ ABANDON, desert, forsake, give

up, discard, turn one's back on, leave in the lurch; *informal* quit. ❹ LEAVE BEHIND, forget, mislay. ❺ ASSIGN, allot, consign, hand over, give over, refer, commit, entrust. ❻ BEQUEATH, will, endow, hand down, transfer, convey. ❼ CAUSE, leave behind, produce, generate, result in.

■ **leave out** MISS OUT, omit, fail to include, overlook.

leave² n ❶ PERMISSION, consent, authorization, sanction, warrant, dispensation, concession, indulgence. ❷ HOLIDAY, vacation, break, time off, furlough, sabbatical, leave of absence; *informal* hols, vac. ❸ LEAVING, leave-taking, departure, parting, withdrawal, exit, farewell, goodbye, adieu.

lecherous adj LUSTFUL, promiscuous, carnal, sensual, licentious, lascivious, lewd, salacious, libertine, libidinous, lubricious, concupiscent, debauched, dissolute, wanton, intemperate, dissipated, degenerate, depraved; *informal* horny, raunchy.
– OPPOSITES chaste.

lecture n ❶ TALK, speech, address, discourse, disquisition, lesson, sermon, homily. ❷ SCOLDING, reprimand, rebuke, reproof, reproach, remonstration, upbraiding, berating, tirade, diatribe; *informal* dressing-down, telling-off, talking-to.
▶ v ❶ TEACH, tutor in, instruct in, give instruction in, give lessons in. ❷ SCOLD, reprimand,

rebuke, reprove, reproach, remonstrate with, upbraid, berate; *formal* castigate.

lecturer n TEACHER, college teacher, tutor, reader, instructor, academic, academician.

ledge n SHELF, sill, mantel, mantelpiece, mantelshelf, projection, protrusion, overhang, ridge, step.

leer v OGLE, look lasciviously at, look suggestively at, eye, wink at, watch, stare, goggle, sneer, smirk grin; *informal* give someone the glad eye, give someone the once-over.

left adj ❶ LEFT-HAND, sinistral; *Nautical* port; *Heraldry* sinister. ❷ LEFT-WING, leftist, socialist, radical, progressive, liberal, communist, communistic.
– OPPOSITES right.

leg n ❶ LOWER LIMB, limb, member, shank; *informal* stump, peg, pin. ❷ SUPPORT, upright, prop, brace, underpinning. ❸ PART, portion, segment, section, bit, stretch, stage, lap.

legal adj ❶ LAWFUL, legitimate, licit, legalized, valid, right, proper, sound, permissible, permitted, allowable, allowed, above board, admissible, acceptable, authorized, sanctioned, warranted, licensed; *informal* legit. ❷ JUDICIAL, juridical, forensic.
– OPPOSITES illegal.

legalize v MAKE LEGAL, decriminalize, legitimize, legitimatize, legitimate, validate, ratify, permit, allow, admit, accept, authorize, sanction, warrant, license.

legend n MYTH, saga, epic, folk tale, folk story, traditional story, tale, story, narrative, fable, romance.

legendary adj ❶ MYTHICAL, heroic, traditional, fabled, fictitious, fictional, storybook, romantic, fanciful, fantastical, fabulous. ❷ CELEBRATED, acclaimed, illustrious, famous, famed, renowned, well known, popular, immortal.

legitimate adj ❶ LEGAL, lawful, licit, within the law, going by the rules; informal legit. ❷ LAWFUL, rightful, genuine, authentic, real, true, proper, correct, authorized, sanctioned, warranted, acknowledged, recognized, approved. ❸ VALID, sound, admissible, acceptable, well founded, justifiable, reasonable, plausible, credible, believable, reliable, logical, rational.
– OPPOSITES illegitimate.

legitimize v LEGALIZE, pronounce lawful, declare legal, legitimate, decriminalize, validate, permit, warrant, authorize, sanction, license, give the stamp of approval to.

leisure n FREE TIME, spare time, idle hours, inactivity, time off, relaxation, recreation, freedom, holiday, vacation, breathing space, respite; informal time to kill.

leisurely adj UNHURRIED, relaxed, easy, easy-going, gentle, comfortable, restful, slow, lazy, lingering; informal laid-back.
– OPPOSITES hurried.

lend v ❶ LOAN, give someone the loan of, let someone have the use of, advance. ❷ IMPART, add, give, bestow, confer, provide, supply, furnish.
– OPPOSITES borrow.

length n ❶ DISTANCE, extent, linear measure, span, reach. ❷ PERIOD, stretch, duration, term, span. ❸ PIECE, portion, section, measure, segment, swatch.

lengthen v ❶ MAKE LONGER, elongate, let down. ❷ GROW LONGER, get longer, draw out, stretch. ❸ PROLONG, make longer, increase, extend, expand, protract, stretch out, draw out.
– OPPOSITES shorten.

lengthy adj LONG, long-lasting, prolonged, extended, protracted, long-drawn-out.
– OPPOSITES short.

lenient adj MERCIFUL, clement, sparing, moderate, compassionate, humane, forbearing, tolerant, liberal, magnanimous, indulgent, kind, gentle, easy-going, mild.
– OPPOSITES severe.

less adj SMALLER, slighter, not so much, not so great.
▶ pron A SMALLER AMOUNT, not so much.
▶ adv TO A LESSER DEGREE, to a smaller extent, not so much.
▶ prep MINUS, subtracting, excepting, without.

lessen v ❶ GROW LESS, abate, decrease, diminish, subside, moderate, slacken, die down, let up, ease off, tail off, ebb, wane. ❷ RELIEVE, soothe, allay, assuage, alleviate, palliate, ease, dull, deaden, blunt, take the edge off.
– OPPOSITES increase.

lesson n ❶ CLASS, period of instruction, exercise, school-work, homework, assignment, task. ❷ EXAMPLE, warning, deterrent, message, moral, precept.

let v ❶ ALLOW, permit, give permission to, give leave to, authorize, sanction, grant, license, assent to, consent to, agree to; *informal* give the thumbs up to, give the go-ahead to, give the green light to. ❷ LET OUT, rent, rent out, lease, hire, sublet.
■ **let down** FAIL, disappoint, disillusion, forsake, abandon, desert, leave, betray, leave in the lurch. **let off** ❶ EXPLODE, detonate. ❷ ACQUIT, release, discharge, reprieve, absolve, exonerate, pardon, forgive, exempt, spare. **let up** LESSEN, abate, decrease, diminish, subside, moderate, slacken, die down, ease off, tail off, ebb, wane.

let-down n DISAPPOINTMENT, disillusionment, fiasco, anticlimax; *informal* washout.

lethal adj FATAL, deadly, mortal, death-dealing, murderous, poisonous, toxic, dangerous, virulent, noxious, destructive, disastrous, calamitous, ruinous.
– OPPOSITES harmless.

lethargic adj SLUGGISH, inactive, slow, slothful, torpid, listless, languid, apathetic, passive, weary, enervated, fatigued, sleepy, indolent, dull, comatose.
– OPPOSITES energetic.

lethargy n SLUGGISHNESS, inertia, inactivity, slowness, sloth, idleness, torpor, torpidity, lifelessness, dullness, listlessness, languor, languidness, apathy, passivity, weariness, lassitude, fatigue, sleepiness, drowsiness, somnolence, narcosis.
– OPPOSITES energy.

letter n ❶ CHARACTER, sign, symbol. ❷ MESSAGE, note, line, missive, epistle, dispatch.

level adj ❶ FLAT, smooth, even, uniform, plane, flush, horizontal. ❷ EVEN, uniform, regular, consistent, constant, stable, steady, unchanging, unvarying, unfluctuating. ❸ EQUAL, on a level, close together, neck and neck, level-pegging, side by side, on a par, with nothing to choose between them.
– OPPOSITES uneven, unsteady, unequal.
▶ n ❶ HEIGHT, highness, altitude, elevation. ❷ LEVEL OF ACHIEVEMENT, position, rank, standing, status, station, degree, grade, stage, standard. ❸ LAYER, stratum, bed.
▶ v ❶ LEVEL OUT, make level, even off, even out, make flat,

flatten, smooth, smooth out, plane. **②** RAZE, raze to the ground, pull down, knock down, tear down, demolish, flatten, bulldoze, lay waste, destroy.

liable adj **①** RESPONSIBLE, accountable, answerable, chargeable, blameworthy, at fault, censurable. **②** EXPOSED, open, subject, susceptible, vulnerable, in danger of, at risk of. **③** APT, likely, inclined, tending, disposed, predisposed, prone.

liar n FIBBER, perjurer, falsifier, false witness, fabricator, deceiver, spinner of yarns.

libel n DEFAMATION, denigration, vilification, disparagement, aspersions, calumny, slander, false report, traducement, obloquy, abuse, slur, smear; *formal* derogation, calumniation.
▶ v DEFAME, vilify, blacken someone's name, denigrate, disparage, cast aspersions on, slander, traduce, abuse, revile, malign, slur, smear, fling mud at; *formal* derogate, calumniate.

libellous adj DEFAMATORY, denigratory, vilifying, disparaging, derogatory, slanderous, false, misrepresentative, traducing, abusive, reviling, malicious, scurrilous, muckraking.

liberal adj **①** ABUNDANT, copious, ample, plentiful, lavish, profuse, munificent, bountiful, rich, handsome, generous. **②** GENEROUS, magnanimous,

open-handed, unsparing, unstinting, lavish, munificent, bountiful, big-hearted, kind, philanthropic, charitable, altruistic, unselfish; *poetic/literary* bounteous. **③** UNPREJUDICED, unbiased, unbigoted, impartial, disinterested, broad-minded, enlightened, catholic, indulgent, permissive. **④** LOOSE, flexible, free, general, inexact, imprecise. **⑤** ADVANCED, forward-looking, progressive, reformist, radical, latitudinarian.
– OPPOSITES conservative.

liberate v SET FREE, free, release, let out, let go, discharge, set loose, unshackle, unfetter, unchain, deliver, rescue, emancipate, unyoke; *historical* manumit.

liberty n **①** FREEDOM, independence, autonomy, sovereignty, self-government, self-rule. **②** LIBERATION, freeing, release, discharge, deliverance, emancipation; *historical* manumission.
■ **at liberty** FREE, loose, on the loose, at large, unconfined.

licence n **①** PERMIT, certificate, credentials, document, documentation, pass. **②** PERMISSION, leave, liberty, freedom, consent, authority, authorization, sanction, approval, warranty.

license v **①** GRANT A LICENCE TO, authorize, warrant, accredit, charter, franchise. **②** GIVE PERMISSION TO, permit, allow, grant leave to, entitle, give the

freedom to, sanction, give one's approval to, empower.
– OPPOSITES ban.

lid n COVER, top, cap, cork, stopper, plug.

lie¹ n UNTRUTH, falsehood, fib, white lie, fabrication, made-up story, trumped-up story, invention, piece of fiction, falsification, falsity, fairy story, cock and bull story, dissimulation, departure from the truth; *informal* terminological inexactitude, tall tale, whopper.
▶ v TELL A LIE, perjure oneself, fib, fabricate, invent/make up a story, falsify, dissemble, dissimulate, prevaricate, depart from the truth, be economical with the truth, bear false witness.

lie² v ❶ RECLINE, be recumbent, be prostrate, be supine, be prone, be stretched out, sprawl, rest, repose, relax, lounge, loll. ❷ BE, be situated, be located, be placed, be positioned, be found. ■ **lie in** CONSIST, be inherent, inhere, be present, exist, reside. **lie low** HIDE, go into hiding, hide out, conceal oneself, keep out of sight, keep a low profile, take cover, go to earth, go to ground, go underground; *informal* hole up.

life n ❶ EXISTENCE, being, animation, aliveness, viability. ❷ LIVING THINGS, living beings, living creatures, human/animal/plant life, fauna, flora. ❸ PERSON, human being, individual, mortal, soul. ❹ LIFETIME, days, duration of life, course of life, lifespan, time on earth, existence, career; *informal* one's born days.

lifeless adj ❶ DEAD, deceased, gone, cold, defunct. ❷ BARREN, sterile, bare, desolate, stark, arid, unproductive, uncultivated, empty, uninhabited, unoccupied. ❸ SPIRITLESS, lacking vitality, lacklustre, apathetic, uninspired, colourless, dull, flat, stiff, wooden, tedious, uninspiring.
– OPPOSITES alive, lively.

lifelike adj TRUE-TO-LIFE, realistic, photographic, faithful, authentic, exact, vivid, graphic, natural.
– OPPOSITES unrealistic.

lift v ❶ PICK UP, uplift, hoist, heave up, raise, raise up, heft. ❷ REMOVE, raise, withdraw, revoke, cancel, annul, void, countermand, relax, end, stop, terminate. ❸ STEAL, thieve, rob, pilfer, purloin, pocket, take, appropriate; *informal* filch, swipe; *Brit. informal* pinch, nick.

light¹ n ❶ ILLUMINATION, luminescence, luminosity, shining, gleaming, brightness, brilliance, blaze, glare, incandescence, effulgence, refulgence, lambency, radiance, lustre. ❷ DAYLIGHT, daylight hours, daytime, day, hours of sunlight. ❸ ASPECT, angle, slant, approach, viewpoint, point of view.
▶ v ❶ SET BURNING, set fire to, set a match to, ignite, kindle. ❷ ILLUMINATE, brighten, lighten, irradiate, flood with light,

floodlight; *poetic/literary* illumine.

▶ adj **1** FULL OF LIGHT, bright, well lit, well illuminated, sunny. **2** LIGHT-COLOURED, light-toned, pale, pastel, whitish, faded, bleached.

light² adj **1** LIGHTWEIGHT, underweight, portable. **2** thin, flimsy, insubstantial, delicate, floaty, gossamer. **3** GENTLE, slight, delicate, soft, weak, faint, indistinct. **4** MODERATE, easy, simple, undemanding, untaxing, effortless, facile; *informal* cushy. **5** LIGHT-HEARTED, entertaining, diverting, recreational, amusing, humorous, funny, frivolous, superficial, trivial, trifling.
– OPPOSITES heavy.

lighten¹ v MAKE LIGHTER, lessen, reduce, ease, alleviate, mitigate, allay, relieve, assuage, ameliorate.
– OPPOSITES increase.

lighten² v **1** BECOME LIGHTER, grow brighter, brighten. **2** MAKE LIGHTER, make brighter, brighten, light up, illuminate, shed light on, cast light on, irradiate.
– OPPOSITES darken.

lightly adv **1** SLIGHTLY, thinly, softly, gently. **2** SPARINGLY, sparsely, slightly. **3** AIRILY, carelessly, heedlessly, uncaringly, indifferently, thoughtlessly, flippantly, frivolously, slightingly.

like¹ v **1** BE FOND OF, have a liking for, be attracted to, be keen on, love, adore, have a soft spot for. **2** ENJOY, be keen on, find/take pleasure in, be partial to, love, adore, find agreeable, delight in, relish, revel in; *informal* get a kick from. **3** WISH, want, desire, prefer, had sooner, had rather.
– OPPOSITES dislike.

like² adj SIMILAR, comparable, corresponding, resembling, analogous, parallel, equivalent, of a kind, identical, matching, akin.
– OPPOSITES dissimilar.

▶ prep **1** IN THE SAME WAY AS, in the manner of, in a similar way to, after the fashion of, along the lines of. **2** TYPICAL OF, characteristic of, in character with.
▶ n EQUAL, match, counterpart, fellow, twin, mate, parallel, peer, compeer.

likeable adj PLEASANT, nice, friendly, agreeable, amiable, genial, charming, engaging, pleasing, appealing, winning, attractive, winsome, lovable, adorable.
– OPPOSITES unpleasant.

likelihood n LIKELINESS, probability, good chance, chance, prospect, good prospect, possibility.

likely adj **1** PROBABLE, possible, to be expected, on the cards, odds-on. **2** APT, inclined, tending, liable, prone. **3** SUITABLE, appropriate, fit, fitting, acceptable, proper, right, qualified, relevant, reasonable. **4** PROMISING, talented, gifted; *informal* up-and-coming.
– OPPOSITES unlikely.

liken v COMPARE, equate, analogize, draw an analogy between, draw a parallel between, parallel, correlate, link, associate.

likeness n ❶ RESEMBLANCE, similarity, sameness, similitude, correspondence, analogy. ❷ GUISE, semblance, appearance, outward form, form, shape, character. ❸ PICTURE, drawing, sketch, painting, portrait, photograph, study, representation, image, bust, statue, statuette, sculpture.

liking n FONDNESS, love, affection, desire, preference, partiality, penchant, bias, weakness, weak spot, soft spot, appreciation, taste, predilection, fancy, inclination, bent, leaning, affinity, proclivity, propensity, proneness, tendency.
– OPPOSITES dislike, aversion.

limb n ❶ ARM, leg, wing, member, extremity, appendage. ❷ BRANCH, bough.

limelight n FOCUS OF ATTENTION, public attention, public notice, public eye, public recognition, publicity, fame, renown, celebrity, stardom, notability, eminence, prominence, spotlight.

limit n ❶ BOUNDARY, border, bound, frontier, edge, perimeter, confines, periphery. ❷ MAXIMUM, ceiling, limitation, restriction, curb, check, restraint.
▶ v ❶ PLACE A LIMIT ON, restrict, curb, check, keep within bounds, hold in check, restrain, confine, control, ration,

reduce. ❷ RESTRICT, curb, restrain, constrain, hinder, impede, hamper, check, trammel.

limitation n ❶ RESTRICTION, curb, restraint, constraint, qualification, control, check, hindrance, impediment, obstacle, obstruction, bar, barrier, block, deterrent. ❷ INABILITY, incapability, incapacity, defect, frailty, weakness.

limited adj RESTRICTED, scanty, sparse, cramped, narrow, basic, minimal, little, inadequate, insufficient.
– OPPOSITES ample, boundless.

limitless adj ❶ INFINITE, endless, never-ending, interminable, immense, vast, extensive, measureless. ❷ UNLIMITED, boundless, unbounded, illimitable, infinite, endless, unceasing, interminable, inexhaustible, constant, perpetual.

limp adj ❶ FLOPPY, drooping, droopy, soft, flaccid, flabby, loose, slack. ❷ TIRED, fatigued, weary, exhausted, worn out, lethargic, enervated, feeble, frail, puny, debilitated. ❸ WEAK, characterless, ineffectual, insipid, wishy-washy, vapid; *informal* wet.
– OPPOSITES stiff.

line n ❶ RULE, bar, score, underline, underscore, stroke, slash. ❷ BAND, stripe, strip, belt, seam. ❸ FURROW, wrinkle, crease, crow's foot, groove, scar. ❹ OUTLINE, contour, con-

figuration, shape, figure, delineation, silhouette, profile. **❺** BOUNDARY, boundary line, limit, border, borderline, frontier, edge, margin, perimeter, periphery. **❻** ROW, queue, procession, column, file, string, chain, array; *Brit. informal* crocodile. **❼** LINEAGE, descent, ancestry, parentage, family, extraction, heritage, stock, strain, race, breed. **❽** ROPE, string, cord, cable, wire, thread, twine, strand, filament.
▶ BORDER, edge, fringe, bound, skirt, hem, rim, verge.
■ **line up** FORM A LINE, get into rows/columns, file, form a queue, queue up, group together, fall in.

linger v **❶** STAY, remain, wait around, hang around, delay, dawdle, loiter, dally, take one's time; *informal* dilly-dally; *archaic* tarry. **❷** PERSIST, continue, remain, stay, hang around, be protracted, endure.

link n **❶** CHAIN RING, loop, connection, connective, coupling, joint, knot. **❷** COMPONENT, constituent, element, part, piece, member, division. **❸** CONNECTION, relationship, relatedness, association, tie-up. **❹** BOND, tie, attachment, connection, relationship, association, affiliation, mutual interest.
▶ v **❶** CONNECT, fasten together, attach, bind, unite, couple, yoke. **❷** JOIN, connect, associate, relate, bracket.
− OPPOSITES detach, separate.

lip n EDGE, rim, brim, margin, border, verge, brink.

liquid n FLUID, liquor, solution, juice, sap.

liquidate v **❶** CONVERT TO CASH, cash, cash in, sell off, sell up, realize. **❷** KILL, murder, put to death, do away with, assassinate, put an end to, eliminate, dispatch, finish off, destroy, obliterate; *informal* do in, bump off, rub out, wipe out.

liquidize v BLEND, crush, purée, pulverize, process.

list[1] n CATALOGUE, inventory, record, register, roll, file, index, directory, listing, enumeration, table, tabulation, schedule, syllabus, calendar, programme, series.
▶ v NOTE DOWN, write down, record, register, set down, enter, itemize, enumerate, catalogue, file, tabulate, schedule, chronicle, classify, alphabetize.

list[2] v LEAN, lean over, tilt, tip, heel, heel over, careen, cant, incline, slant, slope.

listen v PAY ATTENTION TO, be attentive to, hear, attend, hark, give ear to, lend an ear to, hang on someone's words, keep one's ears open, prick up one's ears; *informal* be all ears, pin back one's ears.

listless adj LANGUID, lethargic, languishing, enervated, lackadaisical, spiritless, lifeless, inactive, inert, indolent, apathetic, passive, dull, heavy, sluggish, slothful, limp, languorous, torpid, supine, indifferent, uninterested, impassive.
− OPPOSITES energetic.

literal adj WORD-FOR-WORD, verbatim, line-for-line, exact, precise, faithful, close, strict, undeviating, true, accurate.

literary adj ❶ WELL READ, widely read, educated, well educated, scholarly, learned, intellectual, cultured, erudite, bookish, studious, lettered. ❷ FORMAL, poetic.

literate adj ❶ ABLE TO READ AND WRITE, educated, schooled. ❷ EDUCATED, well educated, well read, scholarly, learned, intellectual, erudite, cultured, cultivated, knowledgeable, well informed. ❸ WELL WRITTEN, stylish, polished, articulate, lucid, eloquent.

literature n ❶ WRITTEN WORKS, writings, printed works, published works, letters. ❷ PRINTED MATTER, brochure, leaflet, pamphlet, circular, information, data, facts; informal bumf.

lithe adj AGILE, flexible, supple, limber, loose-limbed, pliant, pliable, lissom.

litigation n LAWSUIT, legal case, case, legal dispute, legal contest, legal action, legal proceedings, suit, suit at law.

litter n ❶ RUBBISH, debris, refuse, junk, odds and ends, fragments, detritus, flotsam; N. Amer. trash, garbage. ❷ BROOD, young, offspring, progeny, family. ❸ STRETCHER, portable bed/couch, palanquin.
▶ v MAKE UNTIDY, mess up, make a mess of, clutter up, throw into disorder, disarrange; informal make a shambles of.

little adj ❶ SMALL, short, slight, petite, tiny, wee, miniature, mini, diminutive, minute, infinitesimal, microscopic, minuscule, young, dwarf, midget, pygmy, bantam; informal teeny, teeny-weeny, pint-sized. ❷ UNIMPORTANT, insignificant, minor, trivial, trifling, petty, paltry, inconsequential, negligible, nugatory. ❸ HARDLY ANY, small, scant, meagre, skimpy, sparse, insufficient, exiguous; informal piddling.
– OPPOSITES big, important.
▶ adv HARDLY, barely, scarcely, not much, only slightly, only just.

liturgy n RITUAL, worship, service, ceremony, rite, observance, celebration, office, sacrament.

live adj ❶ ALIVE, living, having life, breathing, animate, vital, existing, existent; informal in the land of the living. ❷ NOT PRERECORDED, unedited, with an audience. ❸ CHARGED, connected, active, switched on. ❹ CURRENT, topical, active, prevalent, important, lively, vital, pressing, burning, pertinent, controversial, debatable, unsettled.
– OPPOSITES dead.

livelihood n LIVING, subsistence, means of support, income, keep, maintenance, sustenance, upkeep, work, employment, occupation, trade, profession, career.

lively adj ❶ FULL OF LIFE, active, animated, energetic, alive,

vigorous, alert, spirited, high-spirited, vivacious, enthusiastic, keen, cheerful, buoyant, sparkling, bouncy, perky, sprightly, spry, frisky, agile, nimble; *informal* chirpy, chipper, peppy. ❷ BRISK, quick, rapid, swift, speedy, vigorous. ❸ ANIMATED, spirited, stimulating, heated, enthusiastic, forceful. ❹ BUSY, crowded, bustling, hectic, swarming, teeming, astir, buzzing, thronging.
– OPPOSITES apathetic.

liven

■ liven up ENLIVEN, put some life into, brighten up, cheer up, perk up, put some spark into, add some zest to, give a boost to, animate, vitalize, vivify; *informal* pep up; *Brit. informal* hot up.

living adj ALIVE, live, having life, breathing, animate, vital, existing, existent; *informal* in the land of the living.
▶ n LIVELIHOOD, subsistence, means of support, income, keep, maintenance, sustenance, upkeep, job, work, employment, occupation.

load n ❶ CARGO, freight, charge, burden, lading, contents, consignment, shipment, lorryload, shipload, containerload, busload. ❷ BURDEN, onus, weight, responsibility, duty, charge, obligation, tax, strain, trouble, worry, encumbrance, affliction, oppression, handicap, trial, tribulation, cross, millstone, albatross, incubus.
▶ v ❶ FILL, fill up, lade, freight, charge, pack, pile, heap, stack,

stuff, cram. ❷ BURDEN, weigh down, weight, saddle, charge, tax, strain, encumber, hamper, handicap, overburden, overwhelm, oppress, trouble, worry. ❸ PRIME, charge, fill. ❹ WEIGHT, add weight to, bias, rig.

loaf v LAZE, lounge, do nothing, idle, lie around, hang about, waste time, fritter away time, take things easy, twiddle one's thumbs, sit on one's hands.

loan n ADVANCE, credit, mortgage.
▶ v LEND, advance, give credit, give on loan, let out.

loath adj RELUCTANT, unwilling, disinclined, not in the mood, against, averse, opposed, resisting.
– OPPOSITES eager.

loathe v HATE, detest, abhor, despise, abominate, have an aversion to, not be able to bear, dislike, shrink from, recoil from, feel repugnance towards, be unable to stomach, execrate.
– OPPOSITES like, love.

loathing n HATRED, hate, detestation, abhorrence, aversion, abomination, repugnance, disgust, revulsion, odium, antipathy, dislike, ill will, enmity, execration.

loathsome adj HATEFUL, detestable, abhorrent, odious, repugnant, disgusting, repulsive, revolting, nauseating, abominable, vile, nasty, obnoxious, horrible, offensive, disagreeable, despicable, contemptible, reprehensible, execrable; *informal* yucky.

local n ❶ LOCAL PERSON, native, inhabitant, resident, parishioner. ❷ BAR, inn, tavern; *Brit.* PUB, public house; *informal* watering hole; *Brit. informal* boozer.

locale n PLACE, site, spot, position, location, venue, area, neighbourhood, locality, setting, scene.

locality n ❶ VICINITY, surrounding area, area, neighbourhood, district, region, environs, locale. ❷ LOCATION, position, place, whereabouts, bearings; *technical* locus.

localize v CONFINE, restrict, contain, limit, circumscribe, delimit.

locate v ❶ FIND, find out, discover, identify, pinpoint, detect, uncover, track down, run to earth, unearth, hit upon, come across, reveal, pin down. ❷ SITUATE, site, position, place, put, build, establish, station, set, fix, settle.

location n POSITION, place, situation, whereabouts, bearings, site, spot, point, scene, setting, venue, locale; *technical* locus.

lock v ❶ BOLT, fasten, bar, secure, make secure, padlock. ❷ JAM, become immovable, become rigid.
– OPPOSITES unlock.
▶ n BOLT, catch, fastener, clasp, bar, hasp.
■ **lock up** *see* IMPRISON.

locker n CUPBOARD, compart-

ment, cabinet, cubicle, storeroom, storage room.

lodge v ❶ BOARD, have lodgings, put up, reside, dwell, sojourn, stop; *informal* have digs. ❷ REGISTER, submit, put forward, place, file, lay, put on record, record. ❸ BECOME FIXED, become embedded, become implanted, stick, become caught, come to rest.

lofty adj ❶ TOWERING, soaring, tall, high, elevated, sky-high, sky-scraping. ❷ ARROGANT, haughty, proud, self-important, conceited, overweening, disdainful, supercilious, condescending, patronizing, lordly, snobbish, scornful, contemptuous, insulting, cavalier; *informal* high and mighty, stuck up, snooty, toffee-nosed, uppity. ❸ NOBLE, exalted, grand, sublime, imposing, esoteric.
– OPPOSITES low, modest, base.

log n ❶ BLOCK, piece, chunk, billet, stump, trunk, branch, bole. ❷ LOGBOOK, record, register, journal, diary, daybook, chart, account, tally.

logic n ❶ LINE OF REASONING, reasoning, argument, argumentation. ❷ REASON, sound judgement, judgement, wisdom, sense, good sense, common sense, rationale, relevance, coherence.

logical adj ❶ REASONED, well reasoned, rational, sound, cogent, coherent, clear, consistent, relevant. ❷ MOST LIKELY, likeliest, plausible, obvious.

❸ REASONING, thinking, straight-thinking, rational, consistent.
– OPPOSITES illogical.

loiter v HANG AROUND / ABOUT, linger, wait, skulk, loaf, lounge, idle, waste time, dawdle, take one's time, go at a snail's pace, dally, stroll, saunter, delay, loll.

lone adj SINGLE, solitary, sole, unaccompanied.

lonely adj ❶ FRIENDLESS, companionless, lonesome, forlorn, forsaken, abandoned, rejected, isolated, outcast, sad, unhappy, despondent. ❷ DESOLATE, barren, isolated, out of the way, remote, secluded, off the beaten track, deserted, uninhabited, unfrequented, unpopulated, godforsaken.
– OPPOSITES popular, crowded.

long[1] adj ❶ LENGTHY, extended, extensive, stretched out, spread out. ❷ PROLONGED, lengthy, protracted, extended, long-drawn-out, spun out, dragged out, interminable.
– OPPOSITES short.

long[2]
■ **long for** WISH FOR, desire, want, yearn for, crave, hunger for, thirst for, covet, lust after, hope for, dream of, pine for, eat one's heart out over, have a fancy for, hanker for/after; *informal* itch for, have a yen for.

longing n WISH, desire, wanting, yearning, craving, hunger, thirst, covetousness, lust, hope, dream, aspiration, pining, fancy, urge, hankering; *informal* itch, yen.

look v ❶ SEE, take a look, glance, fix one's gaze, focus, observe, view, regard, eye, take in, watch, examine, study, inspect, scan, scrutinize, survey, check, contemplate, consider, pay attention to, run the eyes over, peep, peek, glimpse, gaze, stare, gape, ogle; *informal* take a gander, have a squint, gawp, rubberneck; *Brit. informal* take a butcher's, take a dekko, take a shufti; *N. Amer. informal* eyeball. ❷ SEEM, seem to be, appear, appear to be, give every appearance/indication of being, look to be, strike someone as being. ❸ FACE, overlook, front, front on, give on to.
▶ n ❶ SIGHT, glance, observation, view, examination, study, inspection, scan, survey, peep, peek, glimpse, gaze, stare, gape, ogle; *informal* eyeful, gander, look-see, once-over, squint; *Brit. informal* butcher's, dekko, shufti. ❷ EXPRESSION, face, countenance, features, mien.
■ **look after** TAKE CARE OF, care for, attend to, tend, mind, keep an eye on, watch, sit with, nurse, take charge of, supervise, protect, guard. **look down on** REGARD WITH CONTEMPT, scorn, disdain, hold in disdain, sneer at, spurn, disparage, despise; *informal* look down one's nose at, turn up one's nose at. **look for** SEARCH FOR, hunt for, seek, look around for, cast about for, forage for.

loom v ❶ APPEAR, emerge, become visible, take shape,

materialize, reveal itself. ❷ BE IMMINENT, impend, be close, be ominously close, threaten, menace.

loop n COIL, hoop, noose, circle, ring, oval, spiral, curl, twirl, whorl, twist, convolution.
▶ v FORM A HOOP WITH, make a circle with, bend into spirals/whorls.

loophole n LET-OUT CLAUSE, means of avoidance, means of escape, escape clause, escape route, ambiguity, omission.

loose adj ❶ AT LARGE, at liberty, free, on the loose, unconfined, untied, unchained, untethered, unsecured, unshackled, unfastened, unrestricted, unbound, freed, let go, liberated, released, set loose. ❷ WOBBLY, not secure, insecure, rickety, unsteady, movable. ❸ UNTIED, unpinned, hanging free, flowing, floppy. ❹ LOOSE-FITTING, easy-fitting, generously cut, slack, baggy, saggy, sloppy. ❺ INEXACT, imprecise, vague, indefinite, ill-defined, broad, general, non-specific.
■ **let loose** SET FREE, unloose, turn loose, set loose, untie, unchain, untether, unfasten, detach, unleash, let go, release, free, liberate.

loosen v ❶ SLACKEN, slack, unstick, work loose, work free. ❷ LOOSE, relax, slacken, weaken, lessen, moderate.
– OPPOSITES tighten.
■ **loosen up** RELAX, ease up/off; informal let up, hang loose, lighten up.

loot n BOOTY, spoils, plunder, haul, stolen goods, pillage, prize; informal swag, the goods, hot goods, boodle.
▶ v PLUNDER, pillage, rob, burgle, steal from, ransack, sack, maraud, ravage, despoil.

lop v CUT OFF, chop, chop off, hack off, prune, sever, clip, dock, crop, remove, detach.

lose v ❶ MISLAY, misplace, fail to keep/retain, fail to keep sight of, drop, forget. ❷ BE DEPRIVED OF, suffer the loss of. ❸ ESCAPE FROM, evade, elude, dodge, give the slip to, shake off, throw off, throw off the scent, duck, get rid of. ❹ SUFFER DEFEAT, be defeated, be the loser, be worsted, get/have the worst of it, be beaten, be conquered, be vanquished, be trounced, come off second-best, fail, come to grief, meet one's Waterloo; informal come a cropper.

loser n RUNNER-UP, also-ran, the defeated, the vanquished, failure, born loser; informal flop, dud, non-starter, no-hoper, washout.
– OPPOSITES winner, success.

loss n ❶ MISLAYING, misplacement, dropping, forgetting. ❷ LOSING, deprivation, privation, forfeiture, bereavement, disappearance, waste, squandering, dissipation. ❸ CASUALTY, fatality, dead, death toll, number killed. ❹ DEFICIT, debit, debt, lack of profit, deficiency, losing, depletion.

lost adj ❶ MISSING, strayed, gone missing/astray, mislaid, misplaced, vanished, disappeared, forgotten. ❷ STRAY, astray, off course, off-track, disorientated, having lost one's bearings, adrift, going round in circles, at sea. ❸ MISSED, passed, forfeited, neglected, wasted, squandered, dissipated, gone by the board; *informal* down the drain.

lotion n CREAM, salve, ointment, moisturizer, balm, emollient, lubricant, unguent, liniment, embrocation, pomade, hand lotion, body lotion.

lottery n DRAW, raffle, sweepstake, game of chance, gamble, drawing of lots, bingo, tombola.

loud adj ❶ BLARING, booming, noisy, deafening, resounding, reverberant, sonorous, stentorian, roaring, thunderous, tumultuous, clamorous, headsplitting, ear-splitting, earpiercing, piercing, strident, harsh, raucous. ❷ BRASH, brazen, bold, loud-mouthed, vociferous, raucous, aggressive, pushy, coarse, crude, rough, crass, vulgar, brassy. ❸ GARISH, gaudy, flashy, bold, flamboyant, lurid, glaring, showy, obtrusive, vulgar, tawdry, tasteless, meretricious; *informal* flash, kitsch, camp, tacky; *Brit. informal* naff.
– OPPOSITES quiet.

lounge v LAZE, lie, lie around, recline, relax, take it easy, sprawl, slump, loll, repose, loaf, idle, loiter, hang about,
linger, skulk, waste time; *informal* hang out.
▶ n SITTING ROOM, drawing room, living room, parlour.

lousy adj ❶ VERY BAD, poor, incompetent, inadequate, unsatisfactory, inferior, careless, second-rate, terrible, miserable; *informal* rotten, no-good, poxy; *Brit. informal* duff. ❷ DIRTY, low, mean, base, despicable, contemptible, hateful, detestable, loathsome, vile, wicked, vicious.

lout n BOOR, oaf, dolt, churl, bumpkin, yahoo, barbarian; *informal* slob, clodhopper; *Brit. informal* yob, yobbo; *N. Amer. informal* lummox.

lovable adj ADORABLE, dear, sweet, cute, charming, lovely, likeable, attractive, delightful, captivating, enchanting, engaging, bewitching, pleasing, appealing, winsome, winning, endearing, warm-hearted, cuddly.
– OPPOSITES hateful, loathsome.

love n ❶ BE IN LOVE WITH, be fond of, feel affection for, be attracted to, be attached to, care fore, hold dear, adore, think the world of, dote on, worship, idolize, treasure, prize, cherish, be devoted to, desire, want, be infatuated with, lust after, long for, yearn for, adulate; *informal* have a crush on, lech after, have the hots for, be soft on; *Brit. informal* fancy. ❷ LIKE, have a liking for, have a weakness for, be partial to, have a soft spot

for, be addicted to, enjoy, find enjoyment in, relish, savour, appreciate, take pleasure in, delight in; *informal* get a kick out of, have a thing about.
– OPPOSITES hate.

▶ n ❶ AFFECTION, fondness, care, concern, attachment, regard, warmth, intimacy, devotion, adoration, passion, ardour, desire, lust, yearning, infatuation, adulation. ❷ LIKING FOR, weakness for, partiality for, enjoyment of, appreciation of, delight in, relish, passion for. ❸ BELOVED, loved one, true love, love of one's life, dear, dearest, dear one, darling, sweetheart, sweet, sweet one, angel, lover, inamorato/inamorata.

love affair n AFFAIR, romance, relationship, liaison, amour, intrigue, affair of the heart, affaire de cœur.

lovely adj ❶ BEAUTIFUL, pretty, attractive, good-looking, glamorous, handsome, sweet, fair, charming, adorable, enchanting, engaging, bewitching, winsome, seductive, ravishing; *archaic* comely. ❷ DELIGHTFUL, pleasant, nice, agreeable, pleasing, marvellous, wonderful; *informal* fabulous, terrific.
– OPPOSITES ugly, horrible.

lover n ❶ BOYFRIEND, girlfriend, mistress, lady-love, other man, other woman, beau, loved one, beloved, sweetheart, inamorato/inamorata; *informal* bit on the side, bit of fluff, toy boy,

fancy man, fancy woman; *archaic* paramour. ❷ ADMIRER, devotee, fan, enthusiast, aficionado; *informal* buff, freak.

loving adj AFFECTIONATE, fond, devoted, caring, adoring, doting, solicitous, demonstrative, tender, warm, warm-hearted, friendly, kind, sympathetic, charitable, cordial, amiable, amorous, ardent, passionate.

low adj ❶ SHORT, small, little, squat, stubby, stunted, truncated, dwarfish, knee-high. ❷ SPARSE, meagre, scarce, scanty, scant, few, little, deficient, inadequate, paltry, measly, trifling, reduced, depleted, diminished. ❸ DEPRESSED, dejected, despondent, disheartened, downhearted, downcast, gloomy, glum, unhappy, sad, miserable, blue, morose, moody, heavy-hearted, forlorn; *informal* fed up, down in the mouth, down in the dumps; *Brit. informal* brassed off, cheesed off. ❹ LOW-GRADE, inferior, substandard, below par, second-rate, deficient, defective, wanting, lacking, inadequate, mediocre, unacceptable, worthless. ❺ UNFAVOURABLE, poor, bad, adverse, hostile, negative.

lower[1] adj ❶ LESSER, lower-level, lower-grade, subordinate, junior, inferior, minor, secondary. ❷ CHEAPER, reduced, de-

creased, lessened, cut, slashed, curtailed, pruned.
– OPPOSITES higher.

lower² v ❶ LET DOWN, take down, haul down, drop, let fall, let sink. ❷ SOFTEN, quieten, hush, tone down, muffle, turn down, mute. ❸ DEGRADE, debase, demean, downgrade, discredit, devalue, dishonour, disgrace, belittle, humble, humiliate, disparage. ❹ REDUCE, bring down, decrease, lessen, cut, slash, curtail, prune. ❺ ABATE, die down, subside, let up, moderate, slacken, dwindle, lessen, ebb, fade away, wane, taper off, lull.
– OPPOSITES raise.

lowly adj ❶ HUMBLE, low-born, low-ranking, plebeian, peasant, poor, common, ordinary, inferior, subordinate. ❷ ORDINARY, simple, plain, commonplace, run-of-the-mill, modest, unambitious, unpretentious, unaspiring.
– OPPOSITES aristocratic, exalted.

loyal adj FAITHFUL, true, true-hearted, tried and true, trusted, trustworthy, trusty, true-blue, steadfast, staunch, dependable, reliable, devoted, dutiful, patriotic, constant, unchanging, unwavering, unswerving, firm, stable.
– OPPOSITES disloyal, treacherous.

loyalty n FAITHFULNESS, fidelity, allegiance, trueness, true-heartedness, trustiness, trustworthiness, steadfastness, staunchness, dependability, reliability, devotion, duty, patriotism, constancy, stability; historical fealty.
– OPPOSITES disloyalty, treachery.

lucid adj ❶ CLEAR, clear-cut, crystal-clear, comprehensible, intelligible, understandable, plain, simple, direct, straightforward, graphic, explicit. ❷ SANE, rational, in one's right mind, in possession of one's faculties, of sound mind, compos mentis, sensible, clear-headed.
– OPPOSITES confusing.

luck n ❶ FATE, fortune, destiny, chance, fortuity, accident, hazard, serendipity. ❷ GOOD LUCK, good fortune, success, prosperity, advantage, advantageousness, felicity; informal lucky break.

lucky adj ❶ FORTUNATE, blessed with good luck, favoured, born under a lucky star, charmed, successful, prosperous, happy, advantaged. ❷ FORTUITOUS, fortunate, providential, advantageous, timely, opportune, expedient, auspicious, propitious.
– OPPOSITES unlucky.

lucrative adj PROFITABLE, profit-making, moneymaking, paying, high-income, well paid, high-paying, gainful, remunerative, productive, fat, fruitful, rewarding, worthwhile.
– OPPOSITES unprofitable.

ludicrous adj ABSURD, ridiculous, laughable, risible,

derisible, comic, comical, farcical, silly, crazy, zany, nonsensical, odd, outlandish, eccentric, incongruous, preposterous.
– OPPOSITES sensible.

lull v SOOTHE, quiet, hush, silence, calm, still, quell, assuage, allay, ease, alleviate, pacify.
▶ n RESPITE, interval, break, hiatus, let-up, calm, calmness, stillness, quiet, quietness, tranquillity, silence, hush.

lumber v CLUMP, stump, plod, trudge, stamp, shuffle, shamble, stumble, waddle, lump along.

lumbering adj AWKWARD, clumsy, heavy-footed, blundering, bumbling, inept, maladroit, ungainly, like a bull in a china shop, ungraceful, lumpish, ponderous; informal clodhopping.
– OPPOSITES graceful, agile.

luminous adj ILLUMINATED, shining, bright, brilliant, radiant, dazzling, glowing, effulgent, luminescent, phosphorescent, vivid, resplendent.

lump n ❶ CHUNK, wedge, hunk, piece, mass, cake, nugget, ball, dab, pat, clod, gobbet, wad, clump, cluster, mound; Brit. informal gob. ❷ BUMP, swelling, bruise, bulge, protuberance, growth, carbuncle, tumour, tumescence, node.

lunacy n INSANITY, madness, mental illness/derangement, dementia, dementedness, loss of reason, unsoundness of mind, mania, frenzy, psychosis; informal craziness.
– OPPOSITES sanity.

lunatic n MANIAC, madman, madwoman, imbecile, idiot, psychopath; informal loony, nut, nutcase, head case, headbanger, psycho; Brit. informal nutter; N. Amer. informal screwball.

lunge v ❶ SPRING, jump, leap, bound, dash, charge, pounce, dive. ❷ STAB, jab, poke, thrust at, pitch into, lash out at, take a swing at, aim a blow at; informal take a swipe at.

lurch v STAGGER, sway, reel, weave, stumble, totter.

lure v ENTICE, cajole, attract, induce, inveigle, decoy, draw, lead, allure, tempt, seduce, beguile, ensnare.

lurid adj ❶ BRILLIANT, glaring, flaming, dazzling, glowing, intense, vivid, showy, gaudy. ❷ SENSATIONAL, melodramatic, exaggerated, extravagant, graphic, explicit, unrestrained, shocking, startling.
– OPPOSITES muted, restrained.

lurk v SKULK, lie in wait, lie low, hide, conceal oneself, take cover, crouch, sneak, slink, prowl, steal, tiptoe.

luscious adj JUICY, sweet, succulent, mouth-watering, tasty, appetizing, delectable, palatable, toothsome, nectar-like; informal scrumptious, yummy.

lush adj ❶ LUXURIANT, abundant, profuse, exuberant, dense, thick, riotous, overgrown, prolific, rank, flourishing, verdant, green. ❷ LUXURIOUS, sumptuous, grand, palatial, opulent, lavish, elaborate, extravagant; *informal* plush, ritzy.

lustful adj LECHEROUS, lascivious, lewd, libidinous, licentious, salacious, prurient, concupiscent, wanton, unchaste, hot-blooded, passionate, sensual, sexy; *informal* horny; *Brit. informal* randy.
– OPPOSITES chaste.

lusty adj ❶ HEALTHY, strong, vigorous, robust, hale and hearty, hearty, energetic, lively, blooming, rugged, sturdy, tough, stalwart, brawny, hefty, husky, burly, solidly built, powerful, virile, red-blooded. ❷ LOUD, vigorous, hearty, powerful, forceful.

luxuriant adj ❶ LUSH, abundant, profuse, exuberant, dense, thick, riotous, overgrown, prolific, teeming, verdant. ❷ ORNATE, elaborate, fancy, adorned, decorated, embellished, embroidered, extravagant, flamboyant, ostentatious, showy, baroque, rococo.

luxurious adj OPULENT, affluent, sumptuous, expensive, rich, costly, de luxe, lush, grand, splendid, magnificent, lavish, well appointed, comfortable, extravagant, ornate, fancy; *informal* plush, ritzy, swanky; *Brit. informal* posh.
– OPPOSITES spartan.

luxury n ❶ LUXURIOUSNESS, opulence, affluence, sumptuousness, grandeur, splendour, magnificence, lavishness, lap of luxury, bed of roses. ❷ EXTRA, non-essential, frill, extravagance, indulgence, treat, refinement.
– OPPOSITES simplicity, necessity.

lying n UNTRUTHFULNESS, fabrication, fibbing, perjury, falseness, falsity, dishonesty, mendacity, storytelling, dissimulation, dissembling, prevarication, deceit, guile; *informal* crookedness.
▶ adj UNTRUTHFUL, fabricating, false, dishonest, mendacious, dissimulating, dissembling, prevaricating, deceitful, guileful, double-dealing, two-faced; *informal* crooked.
– OPPOSITES truthful.

lyrical adj RHAPSODIC, effusive, rapturous, ecstatic, euphoric, carried away, emotional, impassioned.
– OPPOSITES unenthusiastic.

Mm

macabre adj GRUESOME, grisly, grim, gory, morbid, ghastly, hideous, horrific, horrible, horrifying, horrendous, frightening, frightful, fearsome, shocking, dreadful.

machine n APPLIANCE, apparatus, instrument, tool, device, contraption, gadget, mechanism, engine, motor, vehicle, car, bicycle, motor cycle, aeroplane.

machismo n MASCULINITY, manliness, virility, toughness, male chauvinism, sexism.

mad adj ❶ INSANE, deranged, crazy, demented, of unsound mind, crazed, lunatic, non compos mentis, unbalanced, unhinged, unstable, distracted, manic, frenzied, raving, distraught, frantic, hysterical, delirious, psychotic; *informal* not quite right, mad as a hatter, mad as a March hare, foaming at the mouth, off one's head, out of one's mind, off one's nut, nuts, nutty, off one's rocker, round the bend, raving mad, batty, bonkers, crackpot, cuckoo, loopy, loony, bananas, loco, dippy, screwy, with a screw loose, off the wall, not all there, not right upstairs; *Brit. informal* barmy, crackers, round the twist, not the full shilling, off one's trolley. ❷ *See* ANGRY. ❸ FOOLISH, insane, stupid,

lunatic, foolhardy, idiotic, crackbrained, irrational, unreasonable, illogical, senseless, nonsensical, absurd, impractical, silly, inane, asinine, ludicrous, wild, unwise, imprudent, preposterous. ❹ *see* ENTHUSIASTIC.
– OPPOSITES sane, sensible.

madden v ANGER, infuriate, enrage, incense, exasperate, irritate, inflame, annoy, provoke, upset, agitate, vex, irk, pique, gall, make someone's hackles rise, make someone's blood boil; *informal* make someone see red, get someone's back up.

madman n MANIAC, lunatic, psychopath; *informal* loony, nut, nutcase, head case, headbanger, psycho; *Brit. informal* nutter; *N. Amer. informal* screwball.

madness n INSANITY, craziness, dementia, mental illness, derangement, dementedness, instability of mind, unsoundness of mind, lunacy, distraction, mania, frenzy, psychosis.
– OPPOSITES sanity, calm.

magazine n PERIODICAL, journal, publication, supplement, colour supplement; *informal* glossy.

magic n ❶ SORCERY, witchcraft, wizardry, enchantment,

spell-working, necromancy, the supernatural, occultism, the occult, black magic, black art, voodoo, hoodoo, thaumaturgy. ❷ SLEIGHT OF HAND, legerdemain, conjuring, illusion, prestidigitation, deception, trickery, juggling.
▶ adj ❶ MAGICAL, enchanting, entrancing, spellbinding, fascinating, captivating, charming, glamorous, magnetic, irresistible, hypnotic. ❷ MARVELLOUS, wonderful, excellent; *informal* terrific, fab; *Brit. informal* brilliant, brill.

magician n SORCERER, sorceress, witch, wizard, warlock, enchanter, enchantress, spell-worker, spell-caster, necromancer, thaumaturge.

magnanimity n GENEROSITY, charitableness, charity, benevolence, beneficence, open-handedness, big-heartedness, kindness, munificence, bountifulness, largesse, altruism, philanthropy, unselfishness, selflessness, self-sacrifice, mercy, leniency.
– OPPOSITES meanness, selfishness.

magnanimous adj GENEROUS, charitable, benevolent, beneficent, open-handed, big-hearted, great-hearted, kind, kindly, munificent, bountiful, liberal, altruistic, philanthropic, noble, unselfish, selfless, self-sacrificing, ungrudging, unstinting, forgiving, merciful, lenient, indulgent.
– OPPOSITES mean.

magnificent adj ❶ SPLENDID, resplendent, grand, grandiose, impressive, imposing, striking, glorious, superb, majestic, august, noble, stately, exalted, awe-inspiring, royal, regal, kingly, princely, sumptuous, opulent, luxurious, lavish, rich, brilliant, radiant, elegant, gorgeous; *informal* ritzy; *Brit. informal* posh. ❷ EXCELLENT, masterly, skilful, virtuoso, splendid, impressive, fine, marvellous, wonderful.
– OPPOSITES ordinary, poor.

magnify v ❶ AUGMENT, enlarge, expand, amplify, intensify, heighten, deepen, broaden, widen, dilate, boost, enhance. ❷ EXAGGERATE, overstate, overdo, overemphasize, overplay, dramatize, colour, embroider, embellish, enhance, inflate, make a mountain out of a molehill.
– OPPOSITES minimize.

magnitude n SIZE, extent, measure, proportions, dimensions, volume, weight, quantity, mass, bulk, amplitude, capacity.

mail n POST, letters, packages, parcels, correspondence.

main adj HEAD, chief, principal, leading, foremost, most important, central, prime, premier, primary, supreme, predominant, pre-eminent, paramount, cardinal, crucial, vital, critical, pivotal, urgent.
– OPPOSITES minor.

mainly adv FOR THE MOST PART, mostly, in the main, on the whole, largely, by and large, to a large extent, to a great degree, predominantly, chiefly, principally, substantially, overall, in general, generally, usually, commonly, as a rule.

maintain v ❶ CONTINUE, keep going, keep up, keep alive, keep in existence, carry on, preserve, conserve, prolong, perpetuate, sustain. ❷ KEEP IN GOOD CONDITION, keep in repair, keep up, conserve, preserve, keep intact, care for, take good care of, look after. ❸ SUPPORT, provide for, keep, finance, feed, nurture, nourish, sustain. ❹ INSIST ON, hold to, declare, assert, state, announce, affirm, avow, profess, claim, allege, contend; *formal* aver.

maintenance n ❶ UPKEEP, repairs, preservation, conservation, care. ❷ ALIMONY, support, allowance, keep, upkeep, subsistence.

majestic adj REGAL, royal, kingly, queenly, princely, imperial, noble, lordly, august, exalted, awesome, elevated, lofty, stately, dignified, distinguished, magnificent, grand, splendid, resplendent, glorious, impressive, imposing, marvellous, superb, proud.

major adj ❶ GREATEST, best, most important, leading, foremost, chief, main, outstanding, first-rate, notable, eminent, pre-eminent, supreme. ❷ IMPORTANT, significant, crucial, vital, great, weighty, paramount, utmost,

prime. ❸ SERIOUS, radical, complicated.
– OPPOSITES minor.

majority n ❶ LARGER PART / NUMBER, greater part/number, most, more than half, bulk, mass, main body, preponderance, lion's share. ❷ LEGAL AGE, coming-of-age, seniority, adulthood, manhood, womanhood, maturity, age of consent.
– OPPOSITES minority.

make v ❶ BUILD, construct, assemble, put together, put up, erect, manufacture, produce, fabricate, create, form, fashion, model, mould, shape, forge. ❷ FORCE TO, compel to, coerce into, press into, drive into, pressure into, pressurize into, oblige to, require to, prevail upon to, dragoon into, impel to, constrain to, urge to; *informal* railroad into, put the heat on, put the screws on, use strong-arm tactics on. ❸ CAUSE, create, give rise to, produce, bring about, generate, engender, occasion, effect. ❹ CREATE, appoint, designate, name, nominate, select, elect, vote in, install, invest, ordain, assign. ❺ GAIN, acquire, obtain, get, realize, secure, win, earn, net, gross, clear, bring in, take home, pocket. ❻ PREPARE, get ready, put together, concoct, cook; *informal* whip up. ❼ COME TO, add up to, total, amount to. ❽ GIVE, deliver, utter, give voice to, enunciate, recite, pronounce. ❾ BE, act as, serve as, constitute, perform the function of, play the part of, represent, embody.

▶ n BRAND, label, sort, type, variety, style, mark, marque.

make-believe n PRETENCE, fantasy, daydreaming, dreaming, fabrication, play-acting, charade, masquerade.
▶ adj PRETENDED, feigned, made up, fantasy, dream, imagined, imaginary, unreal, fictitious, mock, sham, pretend.

maker n MANUFACTURER, builder, constructor, producer, creator, fabricator, author, architect, framer.

makeshift adj STOPGAP, make-do, provisional, temporary, rough and ready, substitute, improvised, standby, jerry-built, thrown together.

malice n MALEVOLENCE, maliciousness, malignity, malignancy, evil intentions, ill will, ill feeling, animosity, animus, hostility, enmity, bad blood, hatred, hate, spite, spitefulness, vindictiveness, rancour, bitterness, grudge, venom, spleen, defamation; informal bitchiness, cattiness.
– OPPOSITES benevolence.

malicious adj MALEVOLENT, malign, malignant, evil, evil-intentioned, ill-natured, hostile, spiteful, baleful, vindictive, rancorous, bitter, venomous, pernicious, hurtful, destructive, defamatory; informal bitchy, catty.
– OPPOSITES friendly.

malign v SLANDER, libel, defame, smear, blacken someone's name/character, vilify, speak ill of, spread lies about, cast aspersions on, misrepresent, traduce, denigrate; formal calumniate.
– OPPOSITES praise.

malnutrition n UNDERNOURISHMENT, lack of food, starvation, famine, anorexia.

maltreat v TREAT BADLY, ill-treat, ill-use, mistreat, misuse, abuse, handle/treat roughly, bully, injure, harm, hurt, molest.

maltreatment n ILL-TREATMENT, ill use, mistreatment, abuse, rough handling, mishandling, manhandling, bullying, injury, harm.

manage v ❶ BE IN CHARGE OF, run, be head of, head, direct, control, preside over, lead, govern, rule, command, superintend, supervise, oversee, administer, organize, conduct, handle, guide, be at the helm of; informal head up. ❷ SUCCEED IN, contrive, engineer, bring about/off, achieve, accomplish, effect. ❸ COPE, deal with the situation, get along/on, carry on, survive, make do.

manageable adj ❶ EASY, doable, practicable, possible, feasible, viable. ❷ CONTROLLABLE, governable, tractable, pliant, compliant, docile, accommodating, amenable, yielding, submissive.
– OPPOSITES unmanageable.

management n ❶ MANAGERS, employers, owners, proprietors, directors, board of directors, board, directorate, executives, administration;

informal bosses, top brass.
2 RUNNING, charge, care, direction, leadership, control, governing, ruling, command, superintendence, supervision, administration.

mandatory adj OBLIGATORY, compulsory, binding, required, requisite, essential, imperative, necessary.
– OPPOSITES voluntary.

mangle v MUTILATE, hack, cut about, lacerate, maul, tear at, rend, butcher, disfigure, deform.

mangy adj **1** SCABBY, scaly, diseased. **2** SHABBY, motheaten, worn, shoddy, dirty, mean, squalid, filthy, seedy; *Brit. informal* grotty.

manhandle v **1** HANDLE ROUGHLY, push, pull, shove, maul, mistreat, ill-treat, abuse, injure, damage, beat, batter; *informal* knock about, rough up. **2** HEAVE, haul, push, shove, pull, tug, manoeuvre; *informal* hump.

mania n **1** FRENZY, violence, wildness, hysteria, raving, derangement, dementia. **2** OBSESSION, compulsion, fixation, fetish, fascination, preoccupation, passion, enthusiasm, urge.

maniac n *see* MADMAN.

manifest adj OBVIOUS, clear, plain, apparent, patent, noticeable, perceptible, visible, transparent, conspicuous, unmistakable, distinct, blatant, glaring.
– OPPOSITES secret.
▶ v *see* SHOW v (1, 3).

manifestation n **1** DISPLAY, show, exhibition, demonstration, presentation, exposition, illustration, exemplification, indication, declaration, expression, profession. **2** EVIDENCE, proof, testimony, substantiation, sign, indication, mark, symbol, token, symptom.

manifold adj MULTIFARIOUS, multiple, numerous, many, several, multitudinous, various.

manipulate v **1** HANDLE, wield, ply, work. **2** INFLUENCE, control, use to one's advantage, exploit, manoeuvre, direct, guide, pull the strings. **3** JUGGLE, massage, falsify, doctor, tamper with, fiddle with, tinker with.

manipulator n HANDLER, wielder, operator.

mankind n MAN, homo sapiens, the human race, the human species, humankind, human beings, humans, people.

manly adj MASCULINE, all-male, macho, virile, strong, robust, vigorous, muscular, powerful, well built, strapping, sturdy, rugged, tough.
– OPPOSITES effeminate.

manner n **1** WAY, means, method, system, approach, technique, procedure, process, methodology, routine, practice, fashion, mode, style, habit, custom. **2** AIR, appearance, demeanour, aspect, mien, bearing, deportment, cast, behaviour, conduct. **3** KIND, sort, type, variety, form, nature, breed, brand, stamp, class, category.

mannerism n HABIT, characteristic, trait, idiosyncrasy, quirk, foible, peculiarity.

manoeuvre n ❶ MOVEMENT, move, measure. ❷ TRICK, stratagem, tactic, machination, manipulation, artifice, subterfuge, device, dodge, ploy, ruse, scheme, plan, plot, intrigue; *informal* wangle.
▶ v ❶ MOVE, work, negotiate, steer, guide, direct, manipulate. ❷ SCHEME, intrigue, plot, use trickery/artifice, machinate; *informal* pull strings.

manufacture v MAKE, produce, mass-produce, build, construct, assemble, put together, create, fabricate, turn out, process, form, fashion, model, mould, shape, forge.

manufacturer n MAKER, producer, builder, constructor, creator, fabricator, factory owner, industrialist, captain of industry.

many adj A LOT OF, lots of, numerous, innumerable, a large/great number of, countless, scores of, myriad, great quantities of, multitudinous, multiple, copious, abundant.
– OPPOSITES few.

mar v SPOIL, detract from, impair, damage, ruin, wreck, disfigure, blemish, scar, deface, harm, hurt, injure, deform, mutilate, maim, mangle.
– OPPOSITES enhance.

marauder n RAIDER, plunderer, pillager, looter, ravager, robber, pirate, freebooter.

march n WALK, step, pace, stride, tramp, hike, demonstration, parade, procession; *informal* demo.

margin n ❶ EDGE, side, verge, border, perimeter, boundary, limits, periphery, brim. ❷ LEEWAY, latitude, scope, room, room for manoeuvre, space, allowance, extra, surplus.

marginal adj SLIGHT, small, tiny, minute, low, minor, insignificant, minimal, negligible.

maritime adj NAVAL, marine, nautical, seafaring, seagoing.

mark n ❶ STAIN, blemish, blot, smear, trace, spot, speck, dot, blotch, smudge, bruise, scratch, scar, dent, pit, pock, chip, notch, nick, line, score, cut, incision, gash; *informal* splotch. ❷ MARKER, guide, pointer, landmark, direction post, signpost, milestone, waymark. ❸ SIGN, symbol, indication, symptom, feature, token, badge, emblem, evidence, proof, clue, hint.
▶ v ❶ STAIN, smear, smudge, scratch, scar, dent, chip, notch, score, cut, gash. ❷ PUT ONE'S NAME ON, initial, label, tag, stamp, brand, earmark. ❸ CORRECT, assess, evaluate, appraise, grade. ❹ CELEBRATE, commemorate, honour, observe, recognize, acknowledge, solemnize.

marked adj PRONOUNCED, decided, striking, clear, glaring, blatant, unmistakable, remarkable, prominent, signal, conspicuous, noticeable.
– OPPOSITES inconspicuous.

maroon v ABANDON, forsake, leave behind, desert, strand, leave stranded, leave isolated.

marriage n ❶ MARRIED STATE, matrimony, holy matrimony, wedlock, conjugal bond, union, match. ❷ MARRIAGE CEREMONY, wedding, wedding ceremony, nuptials. ❸ ALLIANCE, union, merger, unification, amalgamation, combination, affiliation, association, connection, coupling; informal hook-up.

marry v BE MARRIED, wed, be wed, become man and wife, become espoused; informal tie the knot, walk down the aisle, take the plunge, get spliced, get hitched, get yoked.

marsh n MARSHLAND, bog, peat bog, swamp, swampland, morass, mire, quagmire, quag, slough, fen, fenland; N. Amer. bayou.

marshal v GATHER TOGETHER, assemble, collect, muster, draw up, line up, align, set/put in order, arrange, deploy, dispose.

martial adj MILITANT, warlike, combative, belligerent, bellicose, aggressive, pugnacious.

marvel n WONDER, amazing thing, prodigy, sensation, spectacle, phenomenon, miracle.

■ **marvel at** BE AMAZED BY, be filled with amazement at, be awed by, be full of wonder at, wonder at.

marvellous adj ❶ AMAZING, astounding, astonishing, awesome, breathtaking, sensational, remarkable, spectacular, stupendous, phenomenal, prodigious, miraculous, extraordinary; poetic/literary wondrous. ❷ EXCELLENT, splendid, wonderful, magnificent, superb, glorious, great; informal super, fantastic, terrific, fabulous, awesome, ace, mean, bad, wicked; Brit. informal smashing.

masculine adj MALE, manly, manlike, virile, all-male, robust, vigorous, muscular, strapping, rugged, macho. – OPPOSITES feminine.

mash v CRUSH, pulp, purée, smash, squash, pound, beat. ▶ n PULP, mush, paste, purée, slush, pap.

mask n DISGUISE, guise, concealment, cover, cover-up, cloak, camouflage, veil, screen, front, false front, facade, blind, semblance, false colours, pretence. ▶ v DISGUISE, hide, conceal, cover up, obscure, cloak, camouflage, veil, screen.

mass n ❶ CONCENTRATION, conglomeration, aggregation, assemblage, collection. ❷ MAJORITY, greater part, major part, most, bulk, main body, preponderance. ▶ adj WHOLESALE, universal, widespread, general, large-scale, extensive, pandemic, popular. ▶ v AMASS, accumulate, assemble, gather, collect, draw together, join together.

massacre v see KILL (1).

massage v RUB, knead, pummel, manipulate.

master n LORD, overlord, ruler, overseer, superintendent, director, manager, controller, governor, commander, captain, chief, head, headman, principal, owner, employer; *informal* boss, top dog, big cheese.
▶ v ❶ CONQUER, vanquish, defeat, overcome, overpower, subdue, subjugate, govern, quell, quash, suppress, control, curb, check, bridle, tame. ❷ LEARN, become proficient in, grasp; *informal* get the hang of, get clued up about.

masterful adj AUTHORITATIVE, powerful, controlling, domineering, dictatorial, overbearing, overweening, imperious, peremptory, high-handed, arrogant, haughty.
– OPPOSITES weak.

masterly adj EXPERT, adept, clever, skilful, deft, adroit, skilled, dexterous, accomplished, polished; *informal* ace.
– OPPOSITES inept.

mastermind v DIRECT, manage, plan, organize, arrange, engineer, conceive, devise, forge, originate, initiate, think up, come up with; *informal* be the brains behind.

masterpiece n MAGNUM OPUS, masterwork, chef-d'œuvre, work of art, creation, pièce de resistance.

match v ❶ COMPLEMENT, blend with, harmonize with, go with, tone with, coordinate with, team with, tally with, correspond to, accord with. ❷ BE EQUAL TO, be a match for, measure up to, rival, vie with, compete with, compare with. ❸ PAIR UP, mate, couple, unite, join, combine, link, ally; *informal* hitch up, yoke.

matching adj CORRESPONDING, equivalent, parallel, analogous, complementary, the same, paired, twin, coupled, double, duplicate, identical, like.
– OPPOSITES different.

mate n ❶ FRIEND, companion, comrade, crony; *informal* pal, chum; *N. Amer. informal* buddy. ❷ ASSISTANT, helper, apprentice, subordinate.
▶ v BREED, copulate, couple.

material n ❶ MATTER, substance, stuff, medium, constituent elements. ❷ FABRIC, cloth, stuff, textile. ❸ DATA, information, facts, facts and figures, evidence, details.
▶ adj CORPOREAL, physical, bodily, fleshly, tangible, substantial, concrete.

materialize v ❶ COME INTO BEING, happen, occur, come about, take place; *poetic/literary* come to pass. ❷ APPEAR, turn up, become visible, come into view, come into sight, show oneself/itself, come to light, emerge.

matrimonial adj MARITAL, conjugal, connubial, nuptial, spousal.

matter n ❶ MATERIAL, substance, stuff. ❷ AFFAIR, business, proceeding, situation, circumstance, event, happening,

occurrence, incident, occasion, experience. ❸ SUBJECT, topic, issue, question, point, case.
▶ V BE OF IMPORTANCE, be of consequence, make a difference, signify, be relevant, carry weight, count.

mature adj ❶ ADULT, grown up, grown, fully grown, full-grown, of age. ❷ RIPE, ripened, mellow, ready, seasoned.
– OPPOSITES immature.
▶ V GROW UP, develop fully, become adult, reach adulthood, come of age.

maverick n NONCONFORMIST, rebel, dissenter, dissident, individualist, bohemian, eccentric.
– OPPOSITES conformist.

maxim n APHORISM, proverb, adage, saw, saying, axiom, precept, epigram, gnome.

maximum n MOST, utmost, uttermost, upper limit, ceiling, top, summit, peak, apogee, acme.
▶ adj HIGHEST, greatest, biggest, largest, topmost, most, utmost, supreme.
– OPPOSITES minimum.

mayhem n HAVOC, disorder, confusion, chaos, bedlam.

meadow n FIELD, grassland, pasture, paddock, lea.

meagre adj PALTRY, sparse, scant, scanty, spare, inadequate, insufficient, insubstantial, skimpy, miserly, niggardly, pathetic; informal stingy.
– OPPOSITES abundant.

mean[1] v ❶ INDICATE, signify, express, convey, denote, designate, stand for, represent, symbolize, portend, connote, imply, purport, suggest, allude to, intimate, hint at, insinuate, drive at. ❷ INTEND, have in mind, have in view, contemplate, set out, aim, aspire, desire, want, wish. ❸ INVOLVE, entail, lead to, result in, give rise to, bring about, cause.

mean[2] adj ❶ MISERLY, niggardly, parsimonious, close-fisted, penny-pinching, grasping, greedy, avaricious, ungenerous, illiberal, close, near; informal stingy, tight, tight-fisted, mingy. ❷ NASTY, disagreeable, unpleasant, unfriendly, offensive, obnoxious, cross, ill-natured, bad-tempered, irritable, churlish, surly, cantankerous, crotchety, crabbed. ❸ LOW, lowly, low-born, humble, modest, common, ordinary, base, proletarian, plebeian, obscure.
– OPPOSITES generous, kind, noble.

meander v WIND, zigzag, snake, curve, turn, bend.

meaning n ❶ DEFINITION, explanation, interpretation, elucidation, explication. ❷ SIGNIFICANCE, point, value, worth, consequence, account.

meaningful adj ❶ SIGNIFICANT, important, serious, sincere, in earnest. ❷ POINTED, significant, suggestive, eloquent, expressive, pregnant.
– OPPOSITES meaningless.

meaningless adj ❶ SENSELESS, unintelligible, incomprehensible, incoherent.

❷ POINTLESS, senseless, purposeless, motiveless, irrational. ❸ EMPTY, futile, pointless, aimless, valueless, worthless, trivial, insignificant. – OPPOSITES meaningful.

means pl n ❶ WAY, method, expedient, process, mode, manner, agency, instrument, instrument, channel, avenue, course.

meanwhile adv ❶ IN THE MEANTIME, for the time being, for now, for the moment, in the interim, in the interval. ❷ AT THE SAME TIME, simultaneously, concurrently, coincidentally.

measure n ❶ SIZE, dimension, proportions, magnitude, amplitude, mass, bulk, volume, capacity, quantity, weight. ❷ RULE, ruler, tape measure, gauge, meter, scale, level, yardstick. ❸ SHARE, portion, division, allotment, part, piece, quota, lot, ration, percentage; informal rake-off. ❹ ACTION, act, course, course of action, deed, proceeding, procedure, step, means, expedient. ▶ V CALCULATE, compute, estimate, quantify, weigh, size, evaluate, rate, assess, appraise, gauge, measure out, determine, judge, survey.

measured adj CAREFULLY CHOSEN, selected with care, well thought out, studied, calculated, planned, considered, deliberate, reasoned.

mechanical adj ❶ AUTOMATED, automatic, machine-driven, motor-driven, power-driven. ❷ AUTOMATIC, unthinking, unconscious, unfeeling, unemotional, cold, involuntary, instinctive, routine, habitual. – OPPOSITES manual.

mechanism n ❶ MACHINE, apparatus, appliance, tool, device, instrument, contraption, contrivance. ❷ PROCESS, procedure, system, operation, method, means, medium, agency, channel.

meddle V INTERFERE, butt in, intrude, intervene, interlope, pry, nose; informal stick one's nose in, horn in, snoop.

mediate V ARBITRATE, negotiate, conciliate, intervene, intercede, interpose, moderate, umpire, referee, act as peacemaker, reconcile, restore harmony, make peace, bring to terms, step in.

mediator n ARBITRATOR, arbiter, negotiator, go-between, middleman, intermediary, honest broker, peacemaker, intervenor, interceder, moderator, umpire, referee, judge, conciliator, reconciler.

medicinal adj MEDICAL, therapeutic, curative, healing, remedial, restorative, health-giving, analeptic.

medicine n ❶ MEDICATION, medicament, drug, remedy, cure; archaic physic. ❷ MEDICAL SCIENCE, practice of medicine, healing art.

mediocre adj ❶ INDIFFERENT, average, middle-of-the-road, middling, ordinary,

commonplace, pedestrian, run-of-the-mill, tolerable, passable, adequate, uninspired, undistinguished, unexceptional; *informal* so-so, fair-to-middling, nothing to write home about, no great shakes. **②** INFERIOR, second-rate, second-class, low-grade, poor, shabby, minor.
– OPPOSITES exceptional.

meditate v CONTEMPLATE, think about/over, muse on/about, ponder on/over, consider, concentrate on, reflect on, deliberate about/on, ruminate about/on/over, brood over, mull over, be in a brown study over.

meditation n CONTEMPLATION, thought, musing, pondering, consideration, reflection, deliberation, rumination.

medium n **①** MEDIAN, midpoint, middle, centre point, average, norm, standard, middle course, compromise, happy medium, golden mean. **②** MEANS, agency, channel, avenue, vehicle, organ, instrument.
▶ adj MIDDLE, mean, medial, median, midway, midpoint, intermediate.

meek adj DOCILE, modest, humble, unassuming, unpretentious, submissive, yielding, unresisting, patient, long-suffering, forbearing, resigned, gentle, peaceful, compliant, acquiescent, deferential, weak, timid, frightened, spineless, spiritless; *informal* weak-kneed.
– OPPOSITES assertive.

meet v **①** ENCOUNTER, come face to face with, make contact with, run into, run across, come across, come upon, chance upon, happen upon, light upon; *informal* bump into. **②** COME TOGETHER, abut, adjoin, join, link up, unite, connect, touch, converge, intersect. **③** GATHER, assemble, come together, foregather, congregate, convene, muster, rally; *formal* convoke.
– OPPOSITES avoid.

meeting n **①** ENCOUNTER, contact, assignation, rendezvous; *poetic/literary* tryst. **②** GATHERING, assembly, conference, congregation, convention, convocation, conclave; *informal* get-together. **③** ABUTMENT, junction, conjunction, union, convergence, confluence, concourse, intersection. **④** MEET, race meeting, athletics meeting, sports meeting.

melancholy adj DESPONDENT, dejected, depressed, down, downhearted, downcast, disconsolate, glum, gloomy, sunk in gloom, miserable, dismal, dispirited, low, in low spirits, in the doldrums, blue, mournful, lugubrious, woeful, woebegone, doleful, sorrowful, unhappy, heavy-hearted, low-spirited, sombre, pessimistic; *informal* down in the dumps, down in the mouth.
– OPPOSITES cheerful.

mellifluous adj SWEET, sweet-sounding/toned, dulcet, honey-eyed, mellow, soft, soothing, smooth, silvery, euphonious, musical.

mellow adj ❶ MATURE, well matured, soft, juicy, tender, luscious, sweet. ❷ GENTLE, easy-going, pleasant, kindly, kind-hearted, amicable, amiable, good-natured, affable, gracious. ❸ GENIAL, jovial, jolly, cheerful, happy, merry.

melodious adj MELODIC, musical, tuneful, harmonious, lyrical, dulcet, sweet, sweet-sounding, sweet-toned, silvery, silvery-toned, euphonious.
– OPPOSITES discordant.

melodramatic adj THEATRICAL, stagy, overdramatic, histrionic, over-sensational, extravagant, exaggerated, overdone, overemotional; informal actressy, camp, hammy.

melody n TUNE, air, strain, music, refrain, theme, song.

melt v DISSOLVE, deliquesce, thaw, unfreeze, defrost, soften, fuse.

member n ❶ ADHERENT, associate, fellow. ❷ ORGAN, limb, appendage, extremity.

memorable adj UNFORGETTABLE, not to be forgotten, momentous, significant, historic, notable, noteworthy, important, consequential, remarkable, outstanding, extraordinary, striking, impressive, distinctive, distinguished.
– OPPOSITES forgettable.

memorial n MONUMENT, statue, plaque, shrine, tombstone.

memorize v COMMIT TO

MEMORY, remember, learn by heart, get by heart, learn off, learn, learn by rote.

memory n ❶ RECOLLECTION, remembrance, powers of recall, recall, powers of retention, retention. ❷ COMMEMORATION, remembrance, honour, tribute.

menace n THREAT, danger, hazard, jeopardy.
▸ v THREATEN, intimidate, frighten, scare, alarm, terrify, bully, browbeat, cow, terrorize.

mend v ❶ REPAIR, fix, put back together, patch up, restore, rehabilitate, renew, renovate, make whole, make well, cure, heal. ❷ GET BETTER, recover, recuperate, improve, be well, be cured. ❸ PUT RIGHT, set straight, rectify, put in order, correct, amend, emend, improve.

menial adj LOWLY, humble, low-grade, low-status, unskilled, routine, humdrum, boring, dull.
– OPPOSITES elevated.
▸ n SERVANT, domestic, drudge, underling, lackey, flunkey; Brit. informal dogsbody, skivvy.

mentality n ❶ CAST OF MIND, frame of thinking, turn of mind, way of thinking, mind, psychology, mental attitude, outlook, character, disposition, make-up. ❷ INTELLECT, intellectual capabilities, intelligence, IQ, brainpower, brains, mind, comprehension, understanding; informal grey matter.

mention v REFER TO, allude to, touch on, speak briefly of,

hint at. ❷ SAY, state, name, cite, quote, call attention to, adduce. ❸ TELL, speak about/of, utter, communicate, let someone know, disclose, divulge, breathe a word of, reveal, intimate, whisper; *informal* let on about.
▶ n REFERENCE, allusion, observation, remark, statement, announcement, indication.

mentor n ADVISER, counsellor, guide, guru, spiritual leader, confidant, teacher, tutor, coach, instructor.

mercenary adj MONEY-ORIENTED, grasping, greedy, acquisitive, avaricious, covetous, bribable, venal; *informal* money-grubbing.

merchandise n GOODS, wares, stock, commodities, produce, vendibles.

merchant n TRADER, dealer, trafficker, wholesaler, broker, seller, salesman/woman/person, vendor, retailer, shopkeeper, distributor.

merciful adj LENIENT, clement, compassionate, pitying, forgiving, forbearing, sparing, humane, mild, soft-hearted, tender-hearted, kind, sympathetic, liberal, tolerant, generous, beneficent, benignant.
– OPPOSITES merciless, cruel.

merciless adj UNMERCIFUL, ruthless, relentless, inexorable, harsh, pitiless, unforgiving, unsparing, unpitying, implacable, barbarous, inhumane, inhuman, hard-hearted, heartless, callous, cruel, unsympathetic, unfeeling, illiberal, intolerant, rigid, severe, stern.
– OPPOSITES merciful, compassionate.

mercy n LENIENCY, clemency, compassion, pity, charity, forgiveness, forbearance, quarter, humanity, humaneness, mildness, soft-heartedness, tender-heartedness, kindness, sympathy, liberality, tolerance, generosity, beneficence, benignancy.
– OPPOSITES severity, cruelty.

mere adj NOTHING MORE THAN, no better than, no more important than, just a, only a, pure and simple.

merge v ❶ JOIN TOGETHER, join forces, amalgamate, unite, combine, incorporate, coalesce, team up. ❷ BLEND, fuse, mingle, mix, intermix, homogenize.
– OPPOSITES separate.

merit n ❶ EXCELLENCE, goodness, quality, worth, worthiness, value. ❷ GOOD POINT, strong point, advantage, asset, plus.
▶ v DESERVE, be deserving of, earn, be worthy of, be worth, be entitled to, have a right to, have a claim to, warrant, rate, incur.

merriment n CHEERFULNESS, gaiety, high-spiritedness, high spirits, buoyancy, carefreeness, levity, sportiveness, joy, joyfulness, joyousness, jolliness, jollity, rejoicing, conviviality, festivity, merrymaking, revelry, mirth, glee, gleefulness, laughter, hilarity, amusement, fun.
– OPPOSITES misery.

merry adj CHEERFUL, cheery, in good spirits, high-spirited, light-hearted, buoyant, carefree, sportive, joyful, joyous, rejoicing, jolly, jocund, convivial, festive, mirthful, gleeful, happy, glad, laughing; *dated* gay; *poetic/literary* frolicsome.
– OPPOSITES miserable.

mesh n ❶ NETTING, net, tracery, web, lattice, latticework, lacework, trellis, reticulation, plexus. ❷ TANGLE, entanglement, web, snare, trap.
▶ v ❶ BE ENGAGED, connect, interlock. ❷ HARMONIZE, fit together, go together, coordinate, match, be on the same wavelength, dovetail.

mesmerize v ❶ HYPNOTIZE, put into a trance, put under. ❷ HOLD SPELLBOUND, spellbind, entrance, enthral, bewitch, captivate, enchant, fascinate, grip, magnetize, hypnotize.

mess n ❶ DISORDER, untidiness, disarray, dirtiness, filthiness, clutter, shambles, litter, jumble, muddle, chaos, confusion, disorganization, turmoil. ❷ PLIGHT, predicament, tight spot, tight corner, difficulty, trouble, quandary, dilemma, muddle, mix-up, confusion, imbroglio; *informal* jam, fix, pickle, stew, hole. ❸ MUDDLE, bungle; *informal* botch, screw-up; *Brit. informal* cock-up.

■ **mess up** ❶ DIRTY, befoul, litter, pollute, clutter up, disarrange, throw into disorder, dishevel; *poetic/literary* besmirch. ❷ BUNGLE, muff, make a mess of, mar, spoil, ruin; *informal* botch,

make a hash of, muck up, foul up, screw up; *Brit. informal* cock up, make a muck of.

message n ❶ COMMUNICATION, piece of information, news, word, tidings, note, memorandum, letter, missive, bulletin, communiqué, dispatch, memo. ❷ MEANING, import, idea, point, purport, intimation, theme, moral.

messenger n MESSAGE-BEARER, courier, errand boy/girl, runner, envoy, emissary, agent, go-between, herald, harbinger.

messy adj UNTIDY, disordered, dirty, filthy, grubby, slovenly, cluttered, littered, muddled, in a muddle, chaotic, confused, disorganized, sloppy, in disarray, disarranged, dishevelled, unkempt; *Brit. informal* shambolic.
– OPPOSITES orderly.

metamorphosis n TRANS-FORMATION, transfiguration, change, alteration, conversion, changeover, mutation, transmutation, sea change; *informal* transmogrification.

method n ❶ PROCEDURE, technique, system, practice, modus operandi, process, approach, way, course of action, scheme, plan, rule, arrangement, form, style, manner, mode. ❷ ORDER, orderliness, sense of order, organization, arrangement, structure, form, planning, plan, design, purpose, pattern, regularity.

methodical adj ORDERLY, well ordered, organized, systematic, structured, logical,

well regulated, planned, efficient, businesslike.
– OPPOSITES disorganized.

meticulous adj CONSCIENTIOUS, careful, scrupulous, punctilious, painstaking, demanding, exacting, thorough, perfectionist, fastidious, particular.
– OPPOSITES careless, slapdash.

microscopic adj INFINITESIMAL, minuscule, tiny, minute.
– OPPOSITES massive.

middle adj MID, mean, medium, medial, median, midway, halfway, central, equidistant, intermediate, intermediary.
▶ n MEAN, median, mid-point, halfway point, centre, dead centre.

middling adj AVERAGE, medium, ordinary, fair, moderate, adequate, passable, tolerable, mediocre, indifferent, run-of-the-mill, unexceptional, unremarkable; *informal* fair-to-middling, so-so.

might n FORCE, power, strength, mightiness, powerfulness, forcefulness, potency, toughness, robustness, sturdiness, muscularity.

mighty adj ❶ FORCEFUL, powerful, strong, potent, tough, robust, sturdy, muscular, strapping, vigorous, energetic. ❷ HUGE, massive, vast, enormous, colossal, giant, gigantic, monumental, mountainous, towering.
– OPPOSITES puny, tiny.

migrant adj MIGRATORY, wandering, drifting, nomadic, itinerant, peripatetic, vagrant.

mild adj ❶ TENDER, gentle, soft, soft-hearted, tender-hearted, sensitive, sympathetic, warm, compassionate, humane, forgiving, conciliatory, forbearing, placid, meek, docile, calm, tranquil, serene, peaceful, peaceable, good-natured, amiable, affable, genial, easy, easy-going, mellow. ❷ GENTLE, soft, moderate, warm, balmy. ❸ BLAND, insipid, tasteless.
– OPPOSITES cruel, harsh, spicy.

milieu n ENVIRONMENT, surroundings, background, setting, scene, location, sphere, element.

militant adj AGGRESSIVE, combative, pugnacious, fighting, warring, combating, contending, embattled, in arms, belligerent, bellicose.
– OPPOSITES peaceful.
▶ n ACTIVIST, extremist, partisan.

military adj ARMY, service, soldierly, soldier-like, armed, martial.
▶ n ARMY, armed forces, services, militia, soldiery, navy, air force, marines.

militate
■ **militate against** OPERATE AGAINST, go against, count against, tell against, weigh against, be detrimental to, be disadvantageous to, be to the disfavour of, be counter to the interests of, conflict with the interests of.

milk v ❶ DRAW, draw off, express, siphon, tap, drain, extract. ❷ EXPLOIT, take advantage of, impose on, bleed, suck dry.

milky adj WHITE, milk-white, whitish, creamy, pearly, nacreous, ivory, alabaster, off-white, clouded, cloudy.

mill n FACTORY, plant, foundry, works, workshop, shop, industrial centre.
　▶ v GRIND, pulverize, pound, crush, powder, crunch, granulate; technical comminute, triturate.
　■ **mill about/around** MOVE AROUND, wander around, amble, meander, crowd, swarm, throng.

mimic v ❶ IMPERSONATE, give an impersonation of, imitate, copy, ape, caricature, parody; informal take off. ❷ RESEMBLE, look like, have/take on the appearance of, echo, mirror, simulate.
　▶ n MIMICKER, impersonator, impressionist, imitator, parodist, copyist, parrot, ape.

mince v CHOP/CUT INTO TINY PIECES, grind, crumble, hash.

mind n ❶ BRAIN, head, seat of intellect, psyche, ego, subconscious. ❷ BRAINPOWER, powers of thought, intellect, intellectual capabilities, mentality, intelligence, powers of reasoning, brain, brains, wits, understanding, comprehension, sense, ratiocination; informal grey matter. ❸ OPINION, way of thinking, thoughts, outlook, view, viewpoint, point of view, belief, judgement, attitude, feeling, sentiment. ❹ GENIUS, intellect, intellectual, thinker; informal brain, egghead.
　▶ v ❶ BE OFFENDED BY, take offence at, object to, care about, be bothered by, be upset by, be affronted by, resent, dislike, disapprove of, look askance at. ❷ TAKE HEED OF, heed, pay heed to, pay attention to, attend to, concentrate on, listen to, note, mark, observe, respect, obey, follow, comply with, adhere to. ❸ LOOK AFTER, take care of, attend to, tend, have charge of, keep an eye on, watch.
　■ **never mind** DO NOT BOTHER ABOUT, pay no attention to, do not worry about, disregard, forget, do not take into consideration, do not give a second thought to.

mindful adj PAYING ATTENTION TO, heedful of, watchful of, careful of, wary of, chary of, cognizant of, aware of, conscious of, alert to, alive to, sensible of.
　– OPPOSITES heedless.

mindless adj STUPID, foolish, senseless, witless, empty-headed, unintelligent, dull, slow-witted, obtuse; informal birdbrained, dumb, dopey, moronic.
　– OPPOSITES intelligent.

mine n ❶ COLLIERY, pit, quarry, lode, vein, deposit, coal mine. ❷ SOURCE, reservoir, repository, store, storehouse, wealth.
　▶ v EXCAVATE, quarry for, dig for, dig up, extract, unearth.

mingle v ❶ MIX, blend, combine, compound, homogenize, merge, unite, join, amalgamate, fuse. ❷ CIRCULATE, socialize, hobnob, fraternize, meet people.
– OPPOSITES separate.

miniature adj SMALL-SCALE, scaled down, mini, midget, baby, toy, pocket, dwarf; *informal* pint-sized.
– OPPOSITES giant.

minimal adj MINIMUM, least, smallest, slightest, nominal, token.
– OPPOSITES maximum.

minimize v ❶ KEEP AT / TO A MINIMUM, reduce, decrease, curtail, cut back on, prune, slash. ❷ BELITTLE, make light of, decry, discount, play down, deprecate, depreciate, underestimate, underrate.
– OPPOSITES maximize, exaggerate.

minimum n LOWEST LEVEL, bottom level, bottom, depth, nadir, least, lowest, slightest.
▶ adj MINIMAL, lowest, smallest, littlest, least, least possible, slightest.
– OPPOSITES maximum.

minion n LACKEY, flunkey, henchman, creature, toady, underling, hireling, servant, dependant, hanger-on, parasite.

minor adj LESSER, insignificant, unimportant, inconsequential, inferior, trivial, negligible, trifling, lightweight, subordinate.
– OPPOSITES major.

mint n FORTUNE, small fortune, vast sum, king's ransom; *informal* pile, stack, heap, packet, bundle.
▶ adj BRAND NEW, as new, unused, perfect, unblemished, undamaged, fresh.
▶ v STAMP, punch, die, cast, strike, coin, make, manufacture, produce.

minute adj TINY, minuscule, microscopic, miniature, diminutive, Lilliputian, little, small.
– OPPOSITES gigantic, huge.

minutely adv IN DETAIL, exhaustively, meticulously, punctiliously, painstakingly, closely.

miracle n WONDER, marvel, prodigy, phenomenon.

miraculous adj SUPERNATURAL, fantastic, magical, inexplicable, unaccountable, preternatural, superhuman, thaumaturgic, phenomenal, prodigious, wonderful, remarkable; *poetic/literary* wondrous.

mire n MARSH, bog, swamp, morass, quagmire, quag, slough, fen, fenland; *N. Amer.* bayou.
▶ v SINK, sink down, bog down, stick in the mud.

mirror v REFLECT, imitate, emulate, simulate, copy, follow, mimic, echo, ape, parrot, impersonate.

mirth n GAIETY, merriment, high spirits, cheerfulness, cheeriness, hilarity, glee, laughter, jocularity.

misapprehension n
MISUNDERSTANDING, misinterpretation, misconstruction, misreading, misjudgement, misconception, the wrong idea, a false impression, delusion.

misappropriate v EMBEZZLE, steal, thieve, swindle, pocket, help oneself to; Brit. informal nick, pinch; formal peculate.

misbehave v BEHAVE BADLY, be bad, be naughty, be disobedient, get up to mischief, misconduct oneself, be guilty of misconduct, be badmannered, show bad/poor manners, be rude, fool around; informal carry on, act up.

misbehaviour n MISCONDUCT, bad behaviour, disorderly conduct, badness, naughtiness, mischief, mischievousness, delinquency, misdeed, misdemeanour, bad/poor manners, rudeness; informal carrying on, acting up, shenanigans.

miscalculate v CALCULATE WRONGLY, make a mistake, go wrong, err, blunder, be wide of the mark; informal slip up, make a boo-boo; Brit. informal boob.

miscarriage n ❶ FAILURE, foundering, ruination, nonfulfilment, misfiring, breakdown, mismanagement, perversion, thwarting, frustration. ❷ SPONTANEOUS ABORTION, termination.

miscarry v ❶ HAVE A MISCARRIAGE, abort, lose the baby. ❷ GO WRONG, go awry, go amiss, be unsuccessful, fail, misfire, founder, come to nothing, come

to grief, meet with disaster, fall through, be ruined, fall flat.
– OPPOSITES succeed.

miscellaneous adj VARIED, assorted, mixed, diverse, sundry, variegated, diversified, motley, multifarious, jumbled, confused, indiscriminate, heterogeneous.

miscellany n ASSORTMENT, mixture, mixed bag, variety, collection, medley, pot-pourri, conglomeration, jumble, confusion, mix, mishmash, hotchpotch, hodgepodge, pastiche, patchwork, farrago, gallimaufry.

mischief n ❶ MISCHIEVOUSNESS, naughtiness, badness, bad behaviour, misbehaviour, misconduct, pranks, wrongdoing, delinquency; informal monkey business, shenanigans. ❷ HARM, hurt, injury, damage, disruption, trouble.

mischievous adj
❶ NAUGHTY, bad, badly behaved, misbehaving, disobedient, troublesome, vexatious, playful, rascally, roguish, delinquent; poetic/literary frolicsome. ❷ PLAYFUL, teasing, impish, roguish, waggish, arch.
– OPPOSITES well behaved.

misconception n see MISAPPREHENSION.

miserable adj ❶ UNHAPPY, sorrowful, dejected, depressed, downcast, downhearted, down, despondent, disconsolate, desolate, wretched, glum, gloomy, dismal, blue, melancholy, low-spirited, mournful,

woeful, woebegone, sad, doleful, forlorn, crestfallen; *informal* down in the mouth, down in the dumps. ❷ WRETCHED, mean, poor, shabby, squalid, filthy, foul, sordid, seedy, dilapidated. ❸ MEAGRE, paltry, scanty, low, poor, niggardly, pathetic. ❹ UNPLEASANT, disagreeable, displeasing, uncomfortable, wet, rainy, stormy.
– OPPOSITES happy.

miserly adj MEAN, niggardly, parsimonious, close-fisted, penny-pinching, cheese-paring, penurious, grasping, greedy, avaricious, ungenerous, illiberal, close, near; *informal* stingy, mingy, tight, tight-fisted, money-grabbing; *N. Amer. informal* cheap.
– OPPOSITES generous.

misery n ❶ DISTRESS, wretchedness, hardship, suffering, affliction, anguish, torment, torture, agony, pain, discomfort, deprivation, poverty, grief, sorrow, heartbreak, despair, depression, dejection, desolation, gloom, melancholy, woe, sadness, unhappiness. ❷ MISFORTUNE, trouble, adversity, affliction, ordeal, pain, sorrow, burden, load, blow, trial, tribulation, woe, torment, catastrophe, calamity, disaster.
– OPPOSITES happiness.

misfortune n ❶ BAD LUCK, ill luck, ill fortune, poor/hard luck, accident, misadventure, mischance. ❷ MISHAP, trouble, setback, reverse, adversity, misadventure, blow, failure, accident, disaster, tragedy,

affliction, sorrow, misery, woe, trial, tribulation, catastrophe, calamity.

misgiving n QUALM, doubt, reservation, suspicion, apprehension, unease, uncertainty.

misguided adj MISTAKEN, deluded, erroneous, fallacious, wrong, unwarranted, uncalled for, misplaced, ill-advised, unwise, injudicious, imprudent, foolish.

mishap n ACCIDENT, trouble, setback, reverse, adversity, misadventure, misfortune, stroke of bad luck, blow, disaster, trial, tribulation, catastrophe, calamity.

mislay v LOSE, misplace, lose track of, miss, be unable to find.
– OPPOSITES find.

mislead v MISINFORM, misdirect, delude, take in, deceive, fool, hoodwink, lead astray, throw off the scent, send on a wild-goose chase; *informal* lead up the garden path, take for a ride, pull the wool over someone's eyes.

misleading adj *see* DECEPTIVE.

miss v ❶ FAIL TO ATTEND, be too late for, absent oneself from, skip, be absent from, play truant from, take French leave from. ❷ FAIL TO SEIZE / GRASP, let slip, let go, pass up, overlook, disregard. ❸ REGRET THE ABSENCE / LOSS OF, feel the loss of, feel nostalgic for, long to see, long for, pine for, yearn for, ache for.

misshapen adj DEFORMED, malformed, ill-proportioned,

misproportioned, twisted, distorted, contorted, warped, curved, crooked, wry, bent, hunchbacked.

missing adj LOST, mislaid, misplaced, nowhere to be found, absent, not present, gone, gone astray, unaccounted for.
– OPPOSITES present.

mission n ❶ ASSIGNMENT, commission, task, job, errand, sortie, operation, work, chore, undertaking, duty, charge, trust. ❷ VOCATION, calling, pursuit, goal, aim, quest. ❸ DELEGATION, deputation, commission, legation.

mistake n ERROR, fault, inaccuracy, slip, blunder, miscalculation, misunderstanding, oversight, gaffe, faux pas, solecism, misapprehension, misreading; informal slip-up, booboo, howler; Brit. informal boob; Brit. informal, dated bloomer.
▶ v GET WRONG, misunderstand, misapprehend, misinterpret, misconstrue, misread.
■ **be mistaken** BE WRONG, be in error, be at fault, be under a misapprehension, be misinformed, be misguided, be wide of the mark, be barking up the wrong tree, get the wrong end of the stick. **mistake for** TAKE FOR, mix up with, confuse with, misinterpret as.

mistakenly adv BY MISTAKE, wrongly, in error, erroneously, incorrectly, falsely, fallaciously, misguidedly.
– OPPOSITES correctly.

mistreat v MALTREAT, treat badly, ill-treat, ill-use, misuse, abuse, mishandle, harm, hurt, molest; informal beat up, rough up.

mistress n LOVER, girlfriend, partner, lady-love, kept woman, inamorata; archaic paramour, concubine.

mistrust v FEEL MISTRUSTFUL OF, distrust, feel distrustful of, have doubts about, be suspicious of, suspect, have reservations about, have misgivings about, be wary of, have no confidence in, question, doubt, lack faith in.
– OPPOSITES trust.

misty adj HAZY, foggy, cloudy, blurred, fuzzy, dim, indistinct, vague, obscure, nebulous.
– OPPOSITES clear.

misunderstand v MISAPPREHEND, misinterpret, misconstrue, misread, get the wrong idea, receive a false impression; informal get the wrong end of the stick, be barking up the wrong tree.

misunderstanding n
❶ MISAPPREHENSION, mistake, error, mix-up, misinterpretation, misconstruction, misreading, misconception, misbelief, the wrong idea, a false impression; informal the wrong end of the stick.
❷ DISAGREEMENT, difference of opinion, falling-out, clash of views, dispute, quarrel, argument, squabble, conflict; informal spat, scrap, tiff.

misuse v ❶ PUT TO WRONG USE, misapply, misemploy, abuse,

squander, waste, dissipate.
2 MALTREAT, mistreat, treat badly, ill-treat, ill-use, abuse, mishandle, manhandle, harm, hurt, bully, molest, beat up, rough up.
▶ n **1** WRONG USE, misapplication, misemployment, abuse, squandering, waste, dissipation. **2** MISUSAGE, malapropism, barbarism, catachresis. **3** MALTREATMENT, mistreatment, ill-treatment, ill use, abuse, rough handling, mishandling, manhandling, bullying, injury, harm, molesting.

mitigate v ALLEVIATE, reduce, diminish, lessen, weaken, attenuate, allay, assuage, palliate, appease, soothe, relieve, ease, soften, temper, mollify, lighten, still, quieten, quiet, tone down, moderate, modify, extenuate, calm, lull, pacify, placate, tranquillize.
– OPPOSITES aggravate.

mix v **1** BLEND, combine, mingle, compound, homogenize, alloy, merge, unite, join, amalgamate, fuse, coalesce, interweave. **2** SOCIALIZE, mingle, associate with others, meet people.
– OPPOSITES separate.
▶ n MIXTURE, blend, combination, compound, alloy, merger, union, amalgamation, fusion.
■ **mix up 1** CONFUSE, muddle up, mistake, scramble. **2** INVOLVE, implicate, entangle, embroil, draw into, incriminate.

mixed adj **1** ASSORTED, varied,

miscellaneous, diverse, diversified, motley, heterogeneous.
2 HYBRID, cross-bred, interbred, mongrel. **3** AMBIVALENT, equivocal, unsure, uncertain.
– OPPOSITES homogeneous.

mixture n **1** COMPOUND, blend, mix, brew, combination, concoction, alloy. **2** ASSORTMENT, variety, melange, collection, medley, pot-pourri, conglomeration, jumble, mix, mishmash, hotchpotch, pastiche, farrago, mixed bag. **3** CROSS, crossbreed, mongrel, hybrid.

moan n GROAN, lament, lamentation, wail, whimper, whine.
▶ v **1** GROAN, wail, whimper, whine. **2** COMPLAIN, whine, carp; informal grouse, gripe, grouch, whinge, beef.

mob n CROWD, horde, multitude, rabble, mass, body, throng, host, gang, gathering, assemblage.
▶ v CROWD AROUND, swarm around, surround, besiege, jostle.

mobile adj **1** ABLE TO MOVE, moving, walking, motile, ambulatory. **2** TRANSPORTABLE, portable, travelling, peripatetic, locomotive. **3** EXPRESSIVE, animated, ever-changing, changeable.
– OPPOSITES immobile.

mobilize v **1** MUSTER, rally, marshal, assemble, call to arms, organize, make ready, prepare, ready. **2** GET READY, prepare, ready oneself.

mock v RIDICULE, jeer at, sneer at, deride, scorn, make fun of, poke fun at, laugh at, tease, taunt, twit, chaff, gibe at, insult; *informal* rag, kid, rib, take the mickey out of.

▶ adj IMITATION, artificial, simulated, synthetic, ersatz, so-called, fake, sham, false, spurious, bogus, counterfeit, forged, pseudo, pretended.

mockery n ❶ RIDICULE, jeering, derision, contempt, scorn, disdain, gibe, insult; *informal* ribbing. ❷ PARODY, travesty, caricature, lampoon, burlesque.

mocking adj SNEERING, derisive, derisory, contemptuous, scornful, disdainful, sardonic, insulting, satirical.

model n ❶ REPLICA, representation, mock-up, copy, dummy, imitation, facsimile, image. ❷ PROTOTYPE, archetype, type, mould, original, pattern, design, paradigm, sample, example, exemplar. ❸ STYLE, design, mode, form, mark, version, type, variety, kind, sort. ❹ IDEAL, paragon, perfect example, perfect specimen, exemplar, epitome, nonpareil, acme.

moderate adj ❶ MIDDLE-OF-THE-ROAD, non-radical. ❷ REASONABLE, within reason, within due limits, fair, just. ❸ NOT GIVEN TO EXCESSES, restrained, controlled, temperate, sober, steady. ❹ AVERAGE, middling, ordinary, fair, fairish, modest, tolerable, passable, adequate.
– OPPOSITES immoderate.

▶ v ❶ ABATE, let up, die down, calm down, lessen, decrease, diminish, slacken. ❷ LESSEN, decrease, diminish, mitigate, alleviate, allay, assuage, ease, palliate.

moderately adv QUITE, rather, somewhat, fairly, reasonably, to a certain degree, to some extent, within reason, within limits.

modern adj ❶ CONTEMPORARY, present-day, present, current, twentieth-century, existing, existent. ❷ UP TO DATE, up to the minute, fashionable, in fashion, in style, in vogue, voguish, modish, the latest, new, newfangled, fresh, advanced, progressive; *informal* trendy, with it.
– OPPOSITES old-fashioned.

modernize v MAKE MODERN, update, bring up to date, renovate, remodel, remake, redo, refresh, revamp, rejuvenate; *informal* do over.

modest adj ❶ SELF-EFFACING, humble, unpretentious, unassuming, free from vanity. ❷ SHY, bashful, self-conscious, diffident, reserved, retiring, reticent, quiet, coy, embarrassed, blushing, timid, fearful, meek. ❸ MODERATE, fair, tolerable, passable, adequate, satisfactory, acceptable, unexceptional, small, limited.
– OPPOSITES conceited, grand.

modesty n ❶ LACK OF VANITY, humility, self-effacement, lack of pretension, unpretentiousness. ❷ SHYNESS, bashfulness, self-consciousness, reserve, reticence, timidity, meekness.

modify v ALTER, change, adjust, adapt, revise, recast, reform, reshape, refashion, rework, remould, redo, revamp, reorganize, refine, transform.

moist adj WET, damp, clammy, humid, dank, rainy, drizzly, dewy, soggy, succulent, juicy, soft, spongy.

moisture n WATER, liquid, wetness, wet, dampness, damp, humidity, dankness, rain, dew, drizzle, perspiration, sweat.

molest v PESTER, annoy, plague, torment, harass, badger, harry, persecute, bother, worry, trouble, provoke; *informal* bug, needle, hassle.

mollify v CALM DOWN, pacify, placate, appease, soothe, quiet.
– OPPOSITES enrage.

moment n ❶ SHORT TIME, minute, second, instant; *informal* tick, jiffy. ❷ POINT IN TIME, time, instant, minute, juncture, stage.

momentary adj BRIEF, short, short-lived, fleeting, passing, transient, transitory, ephemeral, evanescent, temporary, impermanent.
– OPPOSITES lengthy.

momentous adj CRUCIAL, critical, vital, decisive, pivotal, serious, grave, important, significant, consequential, fateful, historic; *informal* earth-shattering.
– OPPOSITES insignificant.

momentum n IMPETUS, impulse, propulsion, thrust, push, driving power, drive, power, energy, force.

money n CASH, hard cash, ready money, finance, capital, funds, banknotes, currency, coin, coinage, silver, copper, legal tender, specie; *informal* wherewithal, dough, bread, loot, the necessary, the needful, shekels, tin, gelt, moolah, filthy lucre; *Brit. informal* dosh, brass, lolly, spondulicks, the ready, readies; *N. Amer. informal* mazuma.

monitor n DETECTOR, scanner, recorder, security camera, observer, watchdog, overseer, supervisor, invigilator.
▶ v OBSERVE, scan, record, survey, follow, keep an eye on, keep track of, check, oversee, supervise, invigilate.

monopolize v ❶ CORNER, control, take over, have sole rights in. ❷ DOMINATE, take over, not let anyone else take part in.
– OPPOSITES share.

monotonous adj UNVARYING, lacking/without variety, unchanging, repetitious, all the same, uniform, routine, humdrum, run-of-the-mill, commonplace, mechanical, uninteresting, unexciting, prosaic, wearisome, dull, boring, tedious, tiresome.
– OPPOSITES varied, interesting.

monster n ❶ FIEND, beast, brute, barbarian, savage, villain, ogre, devil, demon.

❷ MONSTROSITY, malformation, abortion, freak, freak of nature, mutant.

monstrous adj ❶ MALFORMED, unnatural, abnormal, grotesque, gruesome, repellent, freakish, mutant. ❷ OUTRAGEOUS, shocking, disgraceful, scandalous, atrocious, heinous, evil, abominable, terrible, horrible, dreadful, hideous, foul, vile, nasty, ghastly, odious, loathsome, intolerable, contemptible, despicable, vicious, cruel, savage.
– OPPOSITES lovely.

monument n ❶ MEMORIAL, statue, shrine, reliquary, sepulchre, mausoleum, cairn, obelisk, dolmen, cromlech, megalith. ❷ COMMEMORATION, memorial, remembrance, reminder, testament, witness, token.

monumental adj ❶ GREAT, huge, enormous, immense, vast, exceptional, extraordinary, tremendous, stupendous, prodigious, staggering. ❷ MASSIVE, impressive, striking, remarkable, magnificent, awe-inspiring, marvellous, majestic, stupendous, prodigious.

mood n HUMOUR, temper, disposition, frame of mind, state of mind, spirit, tenor, vein.

moody adj TEMPERAMENTAL, changeable, unpredictable, volatile, mercurial, unstable, unsteady, erratic, fitful, impulsive, capricious.

moon v LANGUISH, idle, mope,

daydream, be in a reverie, be in a brown study.

moot adj DEBATABLE, open to question, open, doubtful, disputable, arguable, contestable, controversial, unresolved, undecided.

moral n LESSON, teaching, message, meaning, significance, point.

morale n CONFIDENCE, heart, spirit, hope, hopefulness, optimism, determination, zeal.

morality n MORALS, moral code, moral standards, ethics, principles of right and wrong, standards/principles of behaviour.

morbid adj GRUESOME, grisly, macabre, hideous, dreadful, horrible, unwholesome.
– OPPOSITES wholesome.

more adv TO A GREATER EXTENT, further, longer, some more.
▶ pron ADDITIONAL AMOUNT / NUMBER, greater quantity/part, addition, supplement, extra, increase, increment.
– OPPOSITES less.

moreover adv BESIDES, furthermore, further, what is more, in addition, also, as well, into the bargain, to boot.

moron n FOOL, idiot, dolt, dunce, ass, ignoramus, imbecile, simpleton; informal chump, booby, nincompoop, ninny, dunderhead, blockhead, fathead, halfwit, cretin, dummy, numbskull, dimwit; Brit. informal twerp, clot, twit, nitwit; N. Amer. informal schmuck.

morsel n BITE, nibble, bit, crumb, grain, particle, fragment, piece, scrap, segment, soupçon, taste.

mortal adj ❶ TEMPORAL, transient, ephemeral, passing, impermanent, perishable, human, earthly, worldly, corporeal, fleshly. ❷ DEADLY, sworn, irreconcilable, bitter, implacable, unrelenting, remorseless.
– OPPOSITES immortal.

mortify v HUMILIATE, humble, bring low, disgrace, shame, abash, chasten, degrade, abase, deflate, crush, discomfit, embarrass.

mostly adv FOR THE MOST PART, on the whole, in the main, largely, mainly, chiefly, predominantly.

mother n FEMALE PARENT, materfamilias, matriarch; informal ma, mam, mammy, old lady, old woman; Brit. informal mum, mummy; N. Amer. informal mom, mommy; Brit. informal, dated mater.

motherly adj MATERNAL, protective, comforting, caring, loving, affectionate, fond, warm, tender.

motion n MOBILITY, locomotion, movement, moving, travel, travelling, progress, passing, passage, flow, action, activity.

motionless adj UNMOVING, stock-still, at a standstill, stationary, immobile, immovable, static, at rest, frozen, inert, lifeless.
– OPPOSITES mobile.

motivate v MOVE, cause, lead, persuade, prompt, actuate, drive, impel, spur, induce, provoke, incite, inspire.

motive n MOTIVATION, reason, rationale, grounds, cause, basis, occasion, incentive, inducement, incitement, influence, stimulus, spur, goad; informal what makes one tick.

motley adj ASSORTED, varied, miscellaneous, mixed, diverse, diversified, variegated.

mottled adj BLOTCHED, blotchy, speckled, spotted, streaked, marbled, flecked, freckled, dappled, stippled; informal splotchy.

motto n MAXIM, aphorism, adage, saying, saw, axiom, truism, precept, epigram, proverb.

mould v SHAPE, form, fashion, model, create, design, carve, sculpt, chisel, forge.

mouldy adj MILDEWED, blighted, musty, fusty, decaying, rotting, rotten, bad, spoiled.

mound n HILLOCK, knoll, rise, hummock, tump, embankment, bank, dune.

mount v ❶ ASCEND, go up, climb up, clamber up, make one's way up, scale. ❷ INCREASE, grow, escalate, intensify. ❸ STAGE, put on, install, prepare, organize, arrange, set in motion, get up.
– OPPOSITES descend.

mountain n PEAK, mount, height, elevation, eminence, pinnacle, fell, alp; Scottish ben.

mountainous adj HILLY, high, highland, steep, lofty, towering, soaring, alpine, rocky.

mourn v GRIEVE, sorrow, keen, lament, bewail, bemoan.

mournful adj SAD, sorrowful, doleful, gloomy, sombre, melancholy, lugubrious, funereal, dejected, depressed, downcast, miserable, woeful, unhappy.
– OPPOSITES cheerful.

mouth n ❶ LIPS, jaws, maw, muzzle; *informal* trap, chops, kisser; *Brit. informal* gob. ❷ OPENING, entrance, entry, inlet, door, doorway, gateway, hatch, aperture, orifice.

mouthful n BITE, swallow, nibble, sip, sup, taste, drop, bit, piece, morsel, sample.

mouthpiece n SPOKESMAN, spokeswoman, spokesperson, negotiator, intermediary, mediator, agent, representative.

move v ❶ GO, walk, march, proceed, progress, advance. ❷ CARRY, transport, transfer, transpose, change over, shift, switch. ❸ TAKE ACTION, act, do something, get moving. ❹ MOVE HOUSE, relocate, move away, leave, go away. ❺ AFFECT, touch, impress, upset, disturb, disquiet, agitate, make an impression on, have an impact on. ❻ PROVOKE, incite, actuate, rouse, excite, urge, incline, stimulate, motivate, influence, persuade, lead, prompt, cause, impel, induce. ❼ PROPOSE, put forward, advocate, recommend, urge, suggest.
▶n ❶ MOVEMENT, motion,

moving, action, activity, gesture, gesticulation. ❷ ACTION, act, deed, measure, step, tack, manoeuvre, tactic, stratagem, ploy, ruse, trick. ❸ TURN, go.
■ **get a move on** HURRY UP, make haste, speed up, move faster, get moving; *informal* get cracking, make it snappy, step on it, shake a leg.

movement n ❶ MOVING, carrying, transportation, transferral, shifting. ❷ MOVE, motion, action, activity, gesture, gesticulation. ❸ MECHANISM, machinery, works, workings, action. ❹ CAMPAIGN, crusade, drive, group, party, organization, coalition, front.

moving adj ❶ AFFECTING, touching, emotive, emotional, poignant, stirring, arousing, upsetting, disturbing. ❷ MOVABLE, mobile, motile, unfixed. ❸ DRIVING, dynamic, impelling, motivating, stimulating, inspirational.

mow v CUT, trim, crop, clip, scythe, shear.

muck n ❶ DIRT, grime, filth, mud, slime, sludge, scum, mire; *informal* gunk; *Brit. informal* gunge. ❷ DUNG, manure, ordure, excrement, guano, droppings, faeces.
■ **muck up** BUNGLE, muff, make a mess of, mess up, mar, spoil, ruin, foul up; *informal* botch, screw up.

muddle v ❶ MIX UP, get confused, confuse, jumble, scramble, throw into disorder, get into a tangle, make a mess of, mess up. **②** BEWILDER, disorientate, confuse, befuddle, daze, perplex, puzzle, baffle, nonplus, confound.

muddy v **①** DIRTY, begrime, soil. **②** MAKE UNCLEAR, cloud, confuse, mix up, jumble, scramble, get into a tangle.

muffle v **①** WRAP UP, cover up, swathe, swaddle, envelop, cloak. **②** DEADEN, dull, dampen, stifle, smother, suppress, soften, quieten, mute.

mug v ASSAULT, attack, beat up, knock down, rob; *informal* rough up, do over.

muggy adj CLOSE, stuffy, sultry, oppressive, airless, humid, clammy, sticky.
– OPPOSITES fresh.

multiple adj SEVERAL, many, numerous, various, collective, manifold.
– OPPOSITES single.

multiply v **①** BREED, reproduce. **②** INCREASE, grow, accumulate, augment, proliferate, spread.

multitude n CROWD, assembly, throng, host, horde, mass, mob, legion, army.

munch v CHEW, champ, chomp, masticate, eat.

mundane adj COMMON, ordinary, everyday, workaday, usual, prosaic, pedestrian, routine, customary, regular, normal, typical, commonplace, banal, hackneyed, trite, stale, platitudinous.
– OPPOSITES extraordinary.

municipal adj CIVIC, civil, city, metropolitan, urban, town, borough.

murder n KILLING, manslaughter, homicide, slaughter, assassination, butchery, carnage, massacre; *poetic/literary* slaying.
▶ v *see* KILL (1).

murderer n KILLER, slaughterer, cut-throat, assassin, butcher; *poetic/literary* slayer.

murderous adj FATAL, lethal, deadly, mortal, homicidal, savage, barbarous, brutal, bloodthirsty.

murky adj DARK, dim, gloomy, dirty, muddy, dingy, dull, cloudy, turbid, opaque.
– OPPOSITES clear.

murmur n **①** WHISPER, undertone, mutter, mumble. **②** BABBLE, burble, whisper, purl, rustle, buzzing, drone.
▶ v **①** WHISPER, speak in an undertone, speak sotto voce, mutter, mumble. **②** BABBLE, burble, whisper, purl, rustle, buzz, drone.

muscular adj BRAWNY, strapping, powerfully built, solidly built, hefty, sturdy, rugged, burly; *informal* beefy.
– OPPOSITES weak, puny.

muse v THINK, meditate, ruminate, contemplate, reflect, deliberate, day dream, be in a reverie.

musical adj TUNEFUL, melodic, melodious, harmonious, mellifluous, dulcet, euphonious.

muster v ASSEMBLE, bring together, call/gather together, call up, summon, rally, mobilize, round up, marshal, collect; *formal* convoke.

musty adj MOULDY, mildewed, fusty, decaying, stale, stuffy, airless, damp, dank.

mutation n CHANGE, variation, alteration, modification, transformation, metamorphosis, evolution, transmutation, transfiguration.

mute adj SILENT, speechless, wordless, unspeaking, taciturn, uncommunicative; *informal* mum.

▶ v *see* MUFFLE (2).

muted adj SOFT, softened, subdued, subtle, discreet, toned down, quiet, understated.

mutinous adj REBELLIOUS, insurgent, insurrectionary, revolutionary, subversive, seditious, traitorous, insubordinate, disobedient, riotous, unruly, restive, contumacious, refractory; *Brit. informal* bolshie.

mutiny n REBELLION, revolt, insurrection, insurgence, insurgency, uprising, rising, revolution, disobedience, defiance, insubordination.

mysterious adj ENIGMATIC, impenetrable, inscrutable, incomprehensible, inexplicable, unexplainable, unfathomable, unaccountable, dark,

obscure, arcane, abstruse, cryptic, unknown, recondite, secret, preternatural, supernatural, uncanny, mystical, peculiar, strange, weird, curious, bizarre, undisclosed, mystifying, baffling, puzzling, perplexing, bewildering.

mystery n ENIGMA, puzzle, secret, riddle, conundrum, question, question mark, closed book, unexplored ground, terra incognita.

mystic, mystical adj SPIRITUAL, paranormal, transcendental, other-worldly, supernatural, preternatural, occult, metaphysical.

mystify v CONFUSE, bewilder, confound, perplex, baffle, nonplus, puzzle, elude, escape; *informal* stump, beat, bamboozle.

myth n ❶ LEGEND, saga, tale, story, fable, folk tale, allegory, parable, fairy story/tale. ❷ FANTASY, delusion, invention, fabrication, untruth, lie.

mythical adj ❶ LEGENDARY, mythological, fabled, chimerical, fabulous, fantastical, fairytale, storybook, fictitious, allegorical. ❷ IMAGINED, imaginary, pretend, make-believe, unreal, fictitious, invented, fabricated, made up, untrue.
– OPPOSITES real.

Nn

nadir n THE LOWEST POINT, rock bottom, the depths, all-time low, as low as one can get; *informal* the pits.
– OPPOSITES zenith.

nag v SCOLD, carp, pick on, keep on at, harp on at, henpeck, bully, upbraid, berate, chivvy, criticize, find fault with, complain to, grumble to.
▶ n SHREW, scold, harpy, termagant, carper, caviller, complainer, grumbler.

naive adj INNOCENT, artless, childlike, simple, ingenuous, guileless, trusting, unsophisticated, unworldly, jejune, natural, unaffected, unpretentious, frank, open, candid.
– OPPOSITES worldly.

naked adj STARK NAKED, nude, in the nude, bare, stripped, unclothed, undressed, uncovered, undraped, disrobed, au naturel; *informal* in the buff, butt naked; *Brit. informal* starkers; *N. Amer. informal* buck naked.
– OPPOSITES clothed.

name n DESIGNATION, title, label, tag, cognomen, sobriquet, epithet, first name, given name, surname, family name, maiden name, nickname, pet name, stage name, pseudonym, alias; *informal* moniker, handle; *formal* denomination, appellation.
▶ v CHRISTEN, baptize, call, entitle, label, style, term, title, dub, denominate.

nameless adj UNNAMED, untitled, unlabelled, untagged, anonymous, unidentified, undesignated, unspecified.

nap n SHORT SLEEP, catnap, doze, light sleep, rest, lie-down; *informal* snooze, forty winks, shut-eye; *Brit. informal* kip.

narrate v TELL, relate, recount, recite, unfold, chronicle, describe, detail, portray, sketch out, rehearse, repeat.

narrator n REPORTER, describer, chronicler, annalist, storyteller, raconteur.

narrow adj ❶ SLENDER, thin, slim, slight, spare, attenuated, tapering. ❷ LIMITED, restricted, select, exclusive.
– OPPOSITES wide.

narrow-minded adj INTOLERANT, illiberal, reactionary, close-minded, unreasonable, prejudiced, bigoted, biased, discriminatory, jaundiced, parochial, provincial, insular, small-minded, petty-minded, petty, mean-spirited, prudish, strait-laced.
– OPPOSITES broad-minded.

nasty adj UNPLEASANT, disagreeable, distasteful, horrible, vile, foul, hateful, loathsome, revolting, disgusting, odious,

obnoxious, repellent, repugnant, ugly, offensive, objectionable, squalid, dirty, filthy, impure, polluted, tainted, unpalatable, unsavoury, unappetizing, evil-smelling, foulsmelling, stinking, rank, fetid, malodorous; *poetic/literary* mephitic; noisome.
– OPPOSITES pleasant.

nation n COUNTRY, land, state, kingdom, empire, realm, republic, commonwealth, people, race, tribe, society.

national adj NATIONWIDE, countrywide, state, coast-to-coast, widespread, comprehensive, general.
▶ n CITIZEN, subject, native.

native adj ❶ INBORN, inherent, innate, intrinsic, instinctive, intuitive, natural, congenital, hereditary. ❷ INDIGENOUS, homegrown, domestic, local.

natural adj ❶ ORGANIC, pure, unrefined, unmixed, whole, plain, real, chemical-free, additive-free. ❷ NATIVE, inborn, inherent, innate, intrinsic, instinctive, intuitive, congenital, hereditary, inherited, ingrained. ❸ GENUINE, real, authentic, simple, unaffected, unpretentious, spontaneous, artless, ingenuous, candid, open, frank, relaxed, unstudied.
– OPPOSITES unnatural.

nature n ❶ NATURAL FORCES, creation, the environment, the earth, mother earth, landscape, scenery. ❷ KIND, sort, type, variety, description, category,

class, classification.
❸ TEMPERAMENT, temper, personality, disposition, humour, mood, outlook.

naughty adj MISCHIEVOUS, badly behaved, misbehaving, disobedient, defiant, unruly, roguish, wayward, delinquent, undisciplined, unmanageable, ungovernable, fractious, refractory, perverse, errant.
– OPPOSITES well behaved.

nausea n SICKNESS, vomiting, retching, gagging, biliousness, queasiness, faintness.

nauseous adj ❶ SICK, queasy, unwell, indisposed; *Brit.* off colour; *informal* green about the gills. ❷ DISGUSTING, revolting, repulsive, repellent, repugnant, offensive, loathsome, abhorrent, odious.

nautical adj MARITIME, naval, marine, seagoing, seafaring.

navigable adj NEGOTIABLE, passable, traversable, clear, unobstructed.

near adj ❶ CLOSE, nearby, alongside, at close range/quarters, accessible, within reach, close/near at hand, at hand, neighbouring, adjacent, adjoining, bordering, contiguous, proximate. ❷ APPROACHING, coming, imminent, forthcoming, in the offing, impending, looming.
– OPPOSITES distant.

nearly adv ALMOST, virtually, next to, close to, well-nigh, about, just about, practically, roughly, approximately, not quite.

neat adj **❶** TIDY, orderly, well ordered, in good order, spick and span. **❷** SMART, spruce, trim, tidy, dapper, well groomed, well turned out. **❸** ADROIT, skilful, expert, practised, dexterous, deft, accurate, precise, nimble, agile.
– OPPOSITES untidy.

necessary adj NEEDED, needful, essential, required, requisite, vital, indispensable, imperative, mandatory, obligatory, compulsory, de rigueur.
– OPPOSITES unnecessary.

need v REQUIRE, necessitate, demand, call for, have occasion for, want, lack, be without.
▶ n REQUIREMENT, want, wish, demand, prerequisite, requisite, essential, desideratum.

needless adj UNNECESSARY, uncalled for, gratuitous, undesired, unwanted, pointless, useless, dispensable, expendable, inessential.
– OPPOSITES necessary.

negative adj PESSIMISTIC, defeatist, gloomy, gloom-laden, cynical, jaundiced, critical, fault-finding, complaining, unhelpful, uncooperative.
– OPPOSITES positive.

neglect v **❶** FAIL TO LOOK AFTER, fail to provide for, abandon, forsake, leave alone. **❷** LET SLIDE, skimp on, shirk, be remiss about, be lax about, not attend to, leave undone, procrastinate about.
▶ n NEGLIGENCE, neglectfulness, remissness, carelessness, heed-

lessness, slackness, laxity, laxness, dereliction.
– OPPOSITES care, attention.

negligent adj NEGLECTFUL, remiss, lax, careless, inattentive, heedless, thoughtless, unmindful, uncaring, forgetful, indifferent, offhand, cursory, slack, sloppy, slapdash, slipshod, procrastinating, dilatory.
– OPPOSITES attentive.

negligible adj TRIVIAL, trifling, insignificant, of no account, paltry, petty, tiny, minute, small, minor, inconsequential, inappreciable, imperceptible.
– OPPOSITES significant.

negotiate v BARGAIN, drive a bargain, hold talks, confer, debate, discuss, discuss terms, discuss a settlement, consult together, parley, haggle.

neighbourhood n DISTRICT, area, region, locality, part, quarter, precinct, community; *informal* neck of the woods, stamping ground.

neighbouring adj ADJACENT, adjoining, bordering, abutting, contiguous, nearby, near, very near, close/near at hand, not far away, in the vicinity.

nervous adj ON EDGE, edgy, tense, strained, anxious, nervy, agitated, worried, fretful, uneasy, disquieted, on tenterhooks, fidgety, ruffled, flustered, apprehensive, perturbed, fearful, frightened, scared, with one's heart in one's mouth, quaking, trembling, shaking, shaky; *informal* jittery,

nestle | nimble

twitchy, jumpy, in a state, uptight, wired.
– OPPOSITES calm.

nestle v SNUGGLE, curl up, huddle together, cuddle up, nuzzle.

net n NETTING, fishnet, mesh, latticework, lattice, openwork, webbing, tracery.
▶ v CATCH, trap, snare, ensnare, entangle, enmesh, bag.

nettle v IRRITATE, provoke, ruffle, annoy, incense, exasperate, irk, vex, plague, bother, pester, harass, torment, plague.

neurotic adj UNSTABLE, maladjusted, obsessive, phobic, fixated, compulsive, oversensitive, hysterical, irrational.
– OPPOSITES stable.

neuter adj ASEXUAL, sexless, unsexed.
▶ v CASTRATE, geld, emasculate, spay, dress; informal fix, doctor.

neutral adj IMPARTIAL, unbiased, unprejudiced, open-minded, non-partisan, without favouritism, even-handed, disinterested, non-aligned, dispassionate, objective, detached, uninvolved, uncommitted.

neutralize v COUNTERACT, cancel, nullify, negate, annul, undo, invalidate, frustrate, be an antidote to.

new adj MODERN, recent, advanced, state-of-the-art, present-day, contemporary, current, latest, up to date, up to the minute, new-fashioned, modish, brand new, newly arrived, modernist, ultra-modern, avant-garde, futuristic, newfangled.
– OPPOSITES old.

newcomer n ARRIVAL, incomer, immigrant, settler, stranger, outsider, foreigner, alien, intruder, interloper; informal johnny-come-lately.

news pl n INFORMATION, facts, data, report, story, news item, news flash, account, statement, announcement, press release, communiqué, message, bulletin, dispatch, disclosure, revelation, word, talk, the latest; informal gen, info.

newspaper n PAPER, gazette, journal, tabloid, broadsheet, weekly, scandal sheet; informal rag.

next adj ❶ FOLLOWING, succeeding, successive, subsequent, later, ensuing. ❷ NEIGHBOURING, adjacent, adjoining, bordering, contiguous.
– OPPOSITES previous.

nice adj ❶ GOOD, pleasant, enjoyable, pleasurable, agreeable, delightful, marvellous. ❷ FINE, ultra-fine, subtle, minute, precise, exact, accurate, strict, close.
– OPPOSITES unpleasant, rough.

nicety n FINER POINT, subtlety, nuance, detail.

niggardly adj MEAN, miserly, parsimonious, penny-pinching, cheese-paring; informal tight-fisted, stingy.
– OPPOSITES generous.

nimble adj AGILE, lithe,

sprightly, spry, graceful, skilful, deft.
- OPPOSITES clumsy.

nippy adj ICY, chilly, bitter, raw, piercing, stinging.
- OPPOSITES warm.

no adv ABSOLUTELY NOT, under no circumstances, by no means, never; informal not on your life, no way, nope.

noble adj ❶ ARISTOCRATIC, patrician, blue-blooded, titled, landed. ❷ NOBLE-MINDED, magnanimous, generous, self-sacrificing, honourable, virtuous, brave.
- OPPOSITES common, dishonourable.

nod v INCLINE, bob, bow, dip, duck.

noise n SOUND, din, hubbub, clamour, racket, row, uproar, tumult, commotion, rumpus, pandemonium.
- OPPOSITES silence.

noisy adj ❶ ROWDY, clamorous, boisterous, obstreperous, turbulent; informal rackety. ❷ LOUD, blaring, blasting, deafening, ear-splitting.
- OPPOSITES quiet.

nomad n ITINERANT, traveller, migrant, wanderer, transient, vagabond, vagrant, tramp.

nominal adj ❶ IN NAME ONLY, titular, formal, theoretical, self-styled, purported, supposed. ❷ TOKEN, symbolic, minimal, trivial, insignificant.

nominate v NAME, propose, put forward, submit, present, recommend; informal put up.

nonchalant adj SELF-POSSESSED, imperturbable, calm, cool, collected, cool as a cucumber, unconcerned, indifferent, blasé, casual, offhand, carefree, insouciant, easygoing, careless; informal laid-back.
- OPPOSITES anxious.

nonplus v TAKE ABACK, stun, dumbfound, confound, astound, astonish, amaze, surprise, disconcert, stump, confuse, bewilder, embarrass, fluster; informal faze, flummox, floor.

nonsense n RUBBISH, balderdash, drivel, gibberish, blather, trash, claptrap; informal twaddle, waffle, tripe, bilge, bull, tosh, bosh, gobbledegook, mumbo-jumbo, poppycock, stuff and nonsense; Brit. informal flannel; informal, dated bunkum, tommyrot.
- OPPOSITES sense.

nonsensical adj MEANINGLESS, incomprehensible, unintelligible, senseless, foolish, absurd, silly, inane, stupid, ridiculous, ludicrous, preposterous, hare-brained, irrational, idiotic, insane; informal crazy, crackpot, nutty, wacky.
- OPPOSITES sensible.

non-stop adj INCESSANT, unceasing, ceaseless, constant, continuous, continual, unbroken, unfaltering, steady, unremitting, relentless, persistent, endless, never-ending, unending, interminable.

nook n CORNER, cranny, recess,

alcove, niche, opening, cavity, crevice, gap.

normal adj ❶ USUAL, standard, average, common, ordinary, natural, general, commonplace, conventional, typical, regular, routine, run-of-the-mill, everyday, accustomed, habitual, prevailing, popular, accepted, acknowledged. ❷ WELL ADJUSTED, well balanced, rational, compos mentis, sane.
– OPPOSITES abnormal.

normally adv USUALLY, ordinarily, as a rule, as a general rule, generally, in general, mostly, commonly, habitually.

nose n PROBOSCIS, bill, beak, snout, muzzle; *informal* snoot, hooter; *Brit. informal* conk; *N. Amer. informal* schnozz.

nosy adj INQUISITIVE, curious, interfering, meddlesome, intrusive; *informal* snooping, snoopy.

notable adj ❶ NOTEWORTHY, remarkable, outstanding, important, significant, momentous, memorable, unforgettable, pronounced, marked, striking, impressive, uncommon, unusual, particular, special, extraordinary. ❷ NOTED, of note, distinguished, eminent, pre-eminent, well known, prominent, illustrious, great, famous, famed, renowned, celebrated, acclaimed.
– OPPOSITES insignificant.

note n ❶ RECORD, account, entry, item, notation, comment, jotting, inscription. ❷ LETTER, message, memorandum, memo, epistle, missive, communication. ❸ FOOTNOTE, annotation, commentary, gloss, marginalia, explanation, explication, exposition, exegesis. ❹ DISTINCTION, eminence, pre-eminence, illustriousness, greatness, prestige, fame, renown. ❺ TONE, intonation, inflection, sound, indication, hint, element.
▶ v ❶ WRITE DOWN, jot down, mark down, enter, mark, record, register. ❷ TAKE NOTE OF, take notice of, see, observe, perceive, behold, detect, take in.

noted adj NOTABLE, distinguished, eminent, pre-eminent, well known, prominent, illustrious, great, famous, famed, renowned, celebrated, acclaimed.
– OPPOSITES unknown.

notice n ❶ ATTENTION, attentiveness, heed, note, observation, cognizance, regard, consideration, watchfulness, vigilance. ❷ BULLETIN, poster, handbill, bill, circular, leaflet, pamphlet, advertisement.
▶ v SEE, note, take note of, observe, perceive, discern, detect, behold, spot, distinguish, make out, take heed of, heed, pay attention to, take notice of, mark, regard.
– OPPOSITES overlook.

noticeable adj OBSERVABLE, visible, discernible, perceptible, detectable,

distinguishable, distinct, evident, obvious, apparent, manifest, patent, plain, clear, conspicuous, unmistakable, pronounced, striking, blatant.
– OPPOSITES imperceptible.

notify v INFORM, tell, advise, acquaint, apprise, warn, alert, caution.

notion n IDEA, belief, opinion, thought, impression, view, conviction, concept, assumption, presumption, hypothesis, theory, postulation, apprehension, understanding.

notorious adj INFAMOUS, ill-famed, disreputable, dishonourable, of ill repute, well known, prominent, scandalous, opprobrious, legendary.

nourishing adj NUTRITIOUS, nutritive, wholesome, healthy, health-giving, healthful, beneficial, good for one.
– OPPOSITES unhealthy.

nourishment n FOOD, nutriment, nutrition, sustenance, subsistence, provisions; *informal* grub, chow; *Brit. informal* scoff; *dated* victuals.

novel adj NEW, fresh, different, original, unusual, rare, unique, imaginative, unconventional, innovative, ground-breaking, trailblazing, modern, advanced.

novice n BEGINNER, newcomer, apprentice, trainee, learner, probationer, student, pupil, recruit, tyro, initiate, neophyte; *informal* rookie; *N. Amer. informal* greenhorn.

now adv AT PRESENT, at the present time, at this time, at the moment, for the time being, currently.

noxious adj UNWHOLESOME, unhealthy, poisonous, toxic, harmful, injurious, malignant, detrimental, deleterious.
– OPPOSITES innocuous.

nuance n SHADE, shading, gradation, subtlety, nicety, refinement, degree.

nucleus n CORE, kernel, centre, heart, nub.

nude adj *see* NAKED.

nudge v POKE, jab, prod, dig, jog, elbow, touch, push, shove.

nuisance n PEST, bother, plague, irritant, annoyance, trouble, burden, problem, difficulty, worry; *informal* drag.
– OPPOSITES blessing.

numb adj WITHOUT FEELING, deadened, benumbed, insensible, insensate, dull, anaesthetized, dazed, stunned, stupefied, paralysed, immobilized, frozen.
– OPPOSITES sensitive.
▶ v DEADEN, dull, anaesthetize, benumb, daze, stun, stupefy, paralyse, immobilize, freeze.

number n ❶ FIGURE, digit, numeral, cipher, character, symbol, unit, integer. ❷ TOTAL, aggregate, score, tally, count, sum.
▶ v COUNT, add up, enumerate, total, calculate, compute, reckon, tell, estimate, assess.

numerous adj MANY, a lot,

lots, innumerable, myriad, multitudinous, several, quite a few, various, diverse.
– OPPOSITES few.

nurse v ❶ TAKE CARE OF, care for, look after, tend, attend to, minister to. ❷ SUCKLE, breast-feed, feed, wet-nurse.

nurture v FEED, nourish, provide for, care for, take care of, tend, attend to, bring up, rear.

nutritious adj see NOURISHING.

nuzzle v NOSE, nudge, prod, push.

Oo

oaf n LOUT, blunderer, bungler, boor, churl, bumpkin, yokel, brute, galoot; informal clodhopper; N. Amer. informal lummox.

oath n ❶ VOW, promise, pledge, avowal, affirmation, attestation, bond, word of honour, word. ❷ CURSE, swear word, expletive, blasphemy, profanity, imprecation, malediction, obscenity, epithet, four-letter word, dirty word.

obedient adj COMPLIANT, acquiescent, biddable, dutiful, deferential, respectful, tractable, amenable, malleable, governable, well trained, submissive, docile, meek, subservient, obsequious, servile.
– OPPOSITES disobedient.

obese adj see FAT (1).

obey v ❶ ABIDE BY, comply with, adhere to, observe, conform to, respect, acquiesce in, consent to, agree to, follow. ❷ PERFORM, carry out, execute, put into effect, fulfil, act upon.
– OPPOSITES disobey.

object n ❶ THING, article, body, entity, item, device, gadget; informal thingamajig, thingamabob, thingummy, whatchamacallit, whatsit. ❷ OBJECTIVE, aim, goal, target, end, ambition, purpose, design, intent, intention, idea, point.
▶ v PROTEST, demur, beg to differ, remonstrate, expostulate, take exception, argue against, oppose, be in opposition to, complain about.

objection n PROTEST, protestation, complaint, demurral, opposition, remonstration, remonstrance, expostulation, dissatisfaction, disapproval, grievance, scruple, qualm; informal niggle.
– OPPOSITES approval.

objectionable adj OFFENSIVE, obnoxious, unpleasant, disagreeable, unacceptable, nasty, disgusting, repulsive, repellent, abhorrent, repugnant, revolting, loathsome, hateful, detestable,

reprehensible, deplorable, insufferable, intolerable, despicable, contemptible, odious, vile, obscene, foul, horrible, horrid, noxious.
– OPPOSITES agreeable.

objective adj UNBIASED, unprejudiced, impartial, neutral, uninvolved, non-partisan, disinterested, detached, dispassionate, even-handed, equitable, fair, just, open-minded.
– OPPOSITES subjective.
▶ n OBJECT, aim, goal, target, end, ambition, aspiration, intent, intention, purpose, design, plan, scheme, plot.

obligatory adj COMPULSORY, mandatory, enforced, necessary, essential, required, requisite, imperative, de rigueur, unavoidable, inescapable.
– OPPOSITES voluntary.

oblige v ❶ COMPEL, require, necessitate, obligate, impel, force, constrain, press, pressure, pressurize. ❷ DO SOMEONE A FAVOUR, do someone a kindness, do someone a service, help, accommodate, meet someone's wants/needs, put oneself out for, indulge, assist.

obliging adj see HELPFUL (2).

oblique adj ❶ SLANTING, slanted, sloping, italic, sloped, inclined, at an angle, angled, tilted, listing, diagonal. ❷ INDIRECT, implied, roundabout, circuitous, circumlocutory, ambiguous, evasive, backhanded.
– OPPOSITES direct.

obliterate v ERASE, eradicate, efface, blot out, rub out, wipe out, expunge, delete, destroy, annihilate, eliminate, extirpate, decimate, liquidate, demolish.

oblivious adj HEEDLESS OF, unmindful of, unaware of, unconscious of, insensible of, ignorant of, blind to, unobservant of, deaf to, inattentive to, neglectful of, forgetful of, absent-minded, careless of, unconcerned with, abstracted, preoccupied, absorbed, far away.
– OPPOSITES conscious.

obscene adj INDECENT, pornographic, off colour, risqué, lewd, salacious, smutty, lecherous, lascivious, licentious, prurient, lubricious, ribald, scatological, scabrous, bawdy, suggestive, vulgar, dirty, filthy, foul, coarse, gross, vile, nasty, offensive, immoral, impure, immodest, shameless, unchaste, improper, unwholesome, erotic, carnal, sexy; *informal* raunchy, blue.
– OPPOSITES decent.

obscenity n ❶ INDECENCY, lewdness, salaciousness, lasciviousness, licentiousness, prurience, lubricity, ribaldry, scabrousness, bawdiness, suggestiveness, vulgarity, dirtiness. ❷ CURSE, oath, swear word, expletive, imprecation, blasphemy, epithet, profanity, four-letter word, dirty word.

obscure adj ❶ UNCLEAR, indeterminate, opaque, abstruse,

recondite, unexplained, concealed, hidden, arcane, enigmatic, deep, cryptic, mysterious, puzzling, perplexing, confusing, involved, unfathomable, incomprehensible, impenetrable, vague, indefinite, hazy, uncertain, doubtful, dubious, ambiguous, equivocal. **②** INDISTINCT, vague, shadowy, hazy, blurred, fuzzy, cloudy. **③** LITTLE KNOWN, unknown, unheard of, undistinguished, insignificant, inconspicuous, minor, unimportant, unrecognized, unsung.
– OPPOSITES clear, famous.

obsequious adj SERVILE, subservient, submissive, slavish, menial, abject, fawning, grovelling, cringing, toadying, truckling, sycophantic, ingratiating, unctuous, oily, Uriah Heepish; *informal* bootlicking.

observant adj ALERT, sharp-eyed, sharp, eagle-eyed, attentive, vigilant, wide awake, watchful, heedful, on the lookout, on guard, mindful, intent, aware, conscious; *informal* not missing a thing/trick, on the ball.
– OPPOSITES inattentive.

observation n **①** SCRUTINY, scrutinization, watch, monitoring, surveillance, inspection, attention, consideration, study, review, examination. **②** REMARK, comment, statement, utterance, pronouncement, declaration.

observe v **①** SEE, catch sight of, notice, note, perceive, discern, detect, espy, behold, watch, view, spot, witness; *informal* get a load of. **②** KEEP, obey, adhere to, abide by, heed, follow, comply with, conform to, acquiesce in, consent to, accept, respect, defer to. **③** CARRY OUT, perform, execute, discharge, fulfil. **④** CELEBRATE, keep, recognize, commemorate, mark, remember, solemnize.

observer n WATCHER, looker-on, onlooker, witness, eyewitness, spectator, bystander, beholder, viewer, spotter.

obsess v PREOCCUPY, haunt, have a hold on, possess, consume, engross, have a grip on, grip, dominate, rule, control, be on someone's mind, prey on, plague, torment, hound, bedevil.

obsession n PREOCCUPATION, fixation, consuming passion, mania, enthusiasm, infatuation, compulsion, phobia, complex, fetish, craze; *informal* bee in one's bonnet, hang-up.

obsessive adj EXCESSIVE, overdone, consuming, compulsive, besetting, gripping, haunting.

obsolete adj OUTWORN, discarded, discontinued, extinct, bygone, outmoded, antiquated, out of date, superannuated, old-fashioned, behind the times, old, dated, antique, archaic, ancient, antediluvian, time-worn, past its prime.
– OPPOSITES current.

obstacle n BAR, barrier, obstruction, impediment, hindrance, hurdle, barricade, blockade, stumbling block, blockage, curb, check, snag, difficulty, catch, drawback.
– OPPOSITES advantage, aid.

obstinate adj STUBBORN, mulish, pig-headed, wilful, self-willed, strong-minded, perverse, refractory, recalcitrant, contumacious, unmanageable, firm, steadfast, unyielding, inflexible, unbending, immovable, intransigent, intractable, uncompromising, persistent, tenacious, dogged, single-minded.
– OPPOSITES amenable, tractable.

obstruct v BLOCK, barricade, bar, cut off, shut off, choke, clog, hold up, bring to a standstill, stop, halt, hinder, impede, hamper, interfere with, frustrate, thwart, baulk, inhibit, curb, hamstring, encumber.
– OPPOSITES clear, facilitate.

obtain v ❶ GET, get hold of, acquire, come by, procure, secure, gain, earn, achieve, attain, get one's hands on, seize, grab, pick up. ❷ BE IN FORCE, be effective, exist, stand, prevail, hold, be the case, reign, rule, hold sway.

obtrusive adj NOTICEABLE, conspicuous, obvious, unmistakable, blatant, flagrant, bold, audacious, intrusive.
– OPPOSITES unobtrusive.

obtuse adj see STUPID (1).

obvious adj CLEAR, plain, visible, noticeable, perceptible, discernible, detectable, recognizable, evident, apparent, manifest, palpable, patent, conspicuous, unconcealed, overt, pronounced, transparent, prominent, unmistakable, indisputable, undeniable; informal sticking out like a sore thumb, sticking out a mile.
– OPPOSITES imperceptible, inconspicuous.

occasion n ❶ TIME, juncture, point, situation, instance, case, circumstance. ❷ EVENT, incident, occurrence, happening, episode, affair, experience.
▶ v CAUSE, give rise to, bring about, result in, lead to, prompt, provoke, produce, create, generate, engender.

occasional adj INFREQUENT, intermittent, irregular, sporadic, odd, rare, casual, incidental.
– OPPOSITES regular, habitual.

occasionally adv NOW AND THEN, now and again, from time to time, sometimes, at times, every so often, once in a while, on occasion, periodically, at intervals, irregularly, sporadically, infrequently, intermittently, off and on.

occupation n ❶ JOB, profession, business, employment, employ, career, calling, vocation, trade, craft, line, field, province, area. ❷ OCCUPANCY, tenancy, tenure, residence, inhabitancy, habitation, possession, holding. ❸ INVASION, seizure, takeover, conquest, capture, overthrow, subjugation, subjection.

occupy v ❶ LIVE IN, inhabit, reside in, dwell in, tenant, have one's residence/abode in, make one's home in. ❷ FILL UP, fill up, take up, use up, utilize, cover. ❸ INVADE, overrun, seize, take over.

occur v ❶ HAPPEN, take place, come about, materialize, transpire, arise, crop up, turn up, eventuate; *poetic/literary* come to pass, befall. ❷ BE FOUND, be met with, be present, exist, obtain, appear, present itself, show itself, manifest itself.

occurrence n ❶ HAPPENING, event, incident, circumstance, affair, episode, proceedings, adventure. ❷ EXISTENCE, appearance, manifestation, materialization.

odd adj ❶ STRANGE, eccentric, queer, peculiar, idiosyncratic, unconventional, outlandish, weird, bizarre, freakish; *informal* offbeat, wacky, freaky. ❷ OCCASIONAL, casual, temporary, part-time, seasonal, periodic, irregular, miscellaneous. ❸ RANDOM, irregular, periodic, haphazard, chance, fortuitous. ❹ UNMATCHED, unpaired, left over, spare, remaining, surplus, superfluous, lone, single, solitary, sole.
– OPPOSITES ordinary.

odious adj ABHORRENT, offensive, repugnant, disgusting, repulsive, repellent, revolting, foul, vile, unpleasant, disagreeable, loathsome, detestable,

hateful, despicable, contemptible.
– OPPOSITES delightful.

odour n AROMA, smell, scent, perfume, fragrance, bouquet, essence, stench, stink; *Brit. informal* niff, pong; *poetic/literary* redolence.

offence n ❶ CRIME, illegal act, wrongdoing, wrong, misdemeanour, misdeed, peccadillo, sin, transgression, shortcoming, fault, lapse; *Law* malfeasance. ❷ ANNOYANCE, anger, indignation, exasperation, wrath, displeasure, disapproval, dislike, animosity, resentment; *poetic/literary* ire.

offend v ❶ GIVE OFFENCE TO, affront, upset, displease, annoy, anger, incense, exasperate, vex, pique, put out, gall, irritate, provoke, ruffle, disgruntle, rankle with, outrage, insult, slight, humiliate; *informal* put someone's back up. ❷ COMMIT A CRIME, break the law, do wrong, sin, go astray, fall from grace, err, transgress.

offender n WRONGDOER, culprit, criminal, lawbreaker, miscreant, delinquent, sinner, transgressor, malefactor.

offensive adj ❶ HURTFUL, wounding, abusive, affronting, displeasing, annoying, exasperating, vexing, galling, irritating, provocative, objectionable, outrageous, insulting, rude, discourteous, uncivil, impolite. ❷ DISAGREEABLE, unpleasant, nasty, foul, vile, objectionable, odious, abominable, detestable,

loathsome, repugnant, disgusting, obnoxious, repulsive, repellent.
– OPPOSITES complimentary.

offer v ❶ PUT FORWARD, propose, advance, submit, propound, suggest, recommend. ❷ VOLUNTEER ONE'S SERVICES, volunteer, offer one's service, offer assistance/help, make oneself available.

offering n CONTRIBUTION, donation, subscription, gift, present, handout.

offhand adj CASUAL, unceremonious, cavalier, careless, indifferent, perfunctory, cursory, abrupt, brusque, discourteous, uncivil, impolite, rude.

office n ❶ PLACE OF BUSINESS, base, workplace. ❷ POST, position, role, place, situation, station, function, responsibility, obligation, charge, tenure.

official adj AUTHORIZED, accredited, approved, validated, authenticated, certified, endorsed, sanctioned, licensed, recognized, accepted, legitimate, legal, lawful, bona fide, proper, ex cathedra; informal kosher.
– OPPOSITES unofficial.

officiate v TAKE CHARGE, be in charge, preside, oversee, superintend, conduct, run, take the chair.

officious adj OVERZEALOUS, interfering, intrusive, meddlesome, importunate, forward, obtrusive, self-important, opinionated, dictatorial,

domineering, pushy; informal nosy.
– OPPOSITES self-effacing.

offset v COUNTERBALANCE, counteract, countervail, balance, balance out, cancel out, neutralize, compensate for, make up for, make good.

offshoot n BRANCH, subsidiary, adjunct, appendage.

offspring n CHILDREN, family, progeny, young, descendants, heirs, successors, spawn; informal kids; Law issue.

often adv FREQUENTLY, a lot, many a time, repeatedly, again and again, time and again, time after time, over and over, over and over again, {day in, day out}; poetic/literary oft, ofttimes.
– OPPOSITES seldom, never.

oily adj ❶ GREASY, fatty, buttery. ❷ SMOOTH, smooth-talking, flattering, fulsome, glib, unctuous, subservient, servile, oleaginous.

ointment n CREAM, lotion, emollient, salve, balm, liniment, embrocation, unguent, gel.

old adj ❶ OLDER, elderly, aged, advanced in years, long in the tooth, mature, grey-haired, grizzled, hoary, past one's prime, ancient, decrepit, senile, venerable, senior; Biology senescent; informal getting on, past it, over the hill. ❷ OUT OF DATE, outdated, old-fashioned, outmoded, passé, archaic, obsolete, extinct, antiquated, antediluvian, superannuated;

informal old hat. ❸ BYGONE, past, early, earlier, primeval, primordial, prehistoric. ❹ AGE-OLD, long-standing, long-lived, long-established, time-honoured, enduring, lasting. ❺ EX-, former, previous, one-time, sometime, erstwhile; *formal* quondam.
– OPPOSITES young.

old age n OLDNESS, elderliness, age, declining years, advanced years, winter/autumn of one's life, twilight years, senility, dotage; *Biology* senescence.

old-fashioned adj OUT OF FASHION, outmoded, unfashionable, out of style, out of date, outdated, dated, out, dead, old-time, behind the times, past, bygone, passé, archaic, obsolescent, obsolete, ancient, antiquated, superannuated, antediluvian, old-fangled; *informal* old hat, not with it.
– OPPOSITES up to date, fashionable.

omen n PORTENT, sign, token, foretoken, harbinger, premonition, forewarning, warning, prediction, forecast, prophecy, augury.

ominous adj THREATENING, menacing, minatory, black, dark, gloomy, heavy, sinister, bad, unpromising, unpropitious, pessimistic, inauspicious, unfavourable, unlucky.
– OPPOSITES auspicious.

omission n ❶ EXCLUSION, exception, deletion, erasure, elimination, expunction. ❷ NEGLECT, negligence, derelic-

tion, forgetfulness, oversight, disregard, default, failure.

omit v ❶ LEAVE OUT, exclude, except, miss out, miss, fail to mention, pass over, drop; *informal* give something a miss. ❷ FORGET TO, neglect to, fail to, leave undone, overlook, skip.

omnipotent adj ALL-POWERFUL, almighty, supreme, pre-eminent, invincible.

onerous adj ARDUOUS, strenuous, difficult, hard, burdensome, crushing, back-breaking, taxing, demanding, exacting, wearing, wearisome, fatiguing.
– OPPOSITES easy.

ongoing adj IN PROGRESS, current, progressing, advancing, successful, developing, evolving, growing, extant.

onset n START, beginning, commencement, inception, outbreak; *informal* kick-off.
– OPPOSITES end.

onslaught n ASSAULT, attack, charge, storming, sortie, sally, raid, foray, push, thrust, drive, blitz.

onus n BURDEN, weight, load, responsibility, liability, obligation, duty, charge, encumbrance.

open adj ❶ NOT SHUT, not closed, unlocked, unbolted, unlatched, unbarred, unfastened, unsecured, ajar, wide open, agape, gaping, yawning. ❷ UNCOVERED, topless, unsealed. ❸ EXPOSED, unsheltered, wide, wide open, extensive, broad, spacious, sweeping, airy,

uncrowded, uncluttered, un-developed. **❹** FRANK, candid, honest, forthright, direct, blunt, plain-spoken, down-right. **❺** OBVIOUS, clear, notice-able, visible, apparent, evident, manifest, overt, conspicuous, patent, unconcealed, unhid-den, undisguised, blatant, fla-grant. **❻** WIDE OPEN TO, allowing of, permitting, vulnerable to, exposed to, susceptible to, liable to, at the mercy of, an easy target for. **❼** UNBIASED, unprejudiced, non-partisan, impartial, objective, disinterested, dispassionate, detached.
▶ v **❶** THROW OPEN, unlock, unbolt, unlatch, unbar, unfas-ten. **❷** UNWRAP, undo, untie, unseal.
– OPPOSITES close.

opening n **❶** GAP, aperture, space, hole, orifice, vent, slot, breach, crack, split, fissure, cleft, crevice, chink, interstice, rent, rupture. **❷** VACANCY, position, job, opportunity, chance; *informal* break, lucky break.

operate v **❶** FUNCTION, work, go, run, perform, act. **❷** MANAGE, run, work, use, utilize, employ, handle, be in charge of. **❸** PERFORM AN OPERATION, perform surgery; *informal* put under the knife.

operational adj OPERATIVE, workable, in operation, working, in working order, functioning, functional, going, in use, usable, in action, ready for action.

operative adj **❶** IN OPERATION, in force, effective, valid. **❷** OPERATIONAL, workable, working, functioning, func-tional, usable.
– OPPOSITES inoperative.
▶ n WORKER, workman, machin-ist, operator, mechanic, factory hand/employee.

opinion n POINT OF VIEW, view, viewpoint, belief, thought, thinking, way of thinking, standpoint, theory, judgement, estimation, feeling, sentiment, impression, notion, assump-tion, conception, conviction, persuasion, creed, dogma.

opponent n OPPOSITION, rival, adversary, opposer, contestant, competitor, enemy, foe, antag-onist, contender, dissenter, dis-putant.
– OPPOSITES ally.

opportune adj ADVANTAGEOUS, favourable, auspicious, propi-tious, good, lucky, happy, timely, well timed, fortunate, providential, felicitous, convenient, expedient, suitable, apt, fitting, relevant, pertinent.
– OPPOSITES unfavourable.

opportunity n CHANCE, good time, golden opportunity, favourable time/occasion/moment, right set of circum-stances, appropriate time; *informal* break.

oppose v BE HOSTILE TO, take a stand against, stand up to, take issue with, take on, contradict, counter, argue against, coun-ter-attack, confront, resist,

withstand, defy, fight, put up a fight against, combat, fly in the face of.
– OPPOSITES support.

opposite adj ❶ FACING, face to face with; *informal* eyeball to eyeball with. ❷ OPPOSING, differing, different, unlike, contrary, reverse, contradictory, conflicting, clashing, discordant, dissident, at variance, incompatible, irreconcilable, antipathetic, poles apart.

opposition n ❶ HOSTILITY, dislike, disapproval, resistance, defiance. ❷ OPPONENT, opposing side, other side/team, rival, adversary, competition, antagonist, enemy, foe.

oppress v SUBJUGATE, enslave, suppress, crush, subdue, quash, quell, bring someone to their knees, tyrannize, repress, abuse, maltreat, persecute, rule with a rod of iron, trample on, trample underfoot, ride roughshod over.

oppressed adj ENSLAVED, crushed, subdued, repressed, persecuted, abused, maltreated, misused, browbeaten, downtrodden, disadvantaged, underprivileged.

oppression n SUBJUGATION, subduing, tyranny, suppression, persecution, abuse, maltreatment, cruelty, brutality, injustice, ruthlessness, harshness.

oppressive adj ❶ TYRANNICAL, despotic, Draconian, iron-fisted, high-handed, repressive, domineering, harsh, crushing, cruel, brutal, ruthless, merciless, pitiless, unjust. ❷ MUGGY, close, airless, stuffy, stifling, suffocating, sultry, torrid.
– OPPOSITES lenient.

oppressor n TYRANT, despot, autocrat, persecutor, bully, iron hand, slave-driver, hard taskmaster, scourge, dictator.

optimistic adj POSITIVE, sanguine, hopeful, confident, bullish, cheerful, buoyant; *informal* upbeat.
– OPPOSITES pessimistic.

optimum adj ❶ MOST FAVOURABLE, best, most advantageous, most appropriate, ideal, perfect. ❷ PEAK, top, best, perfect, ideal, flawless, superlative, optimal.

option n CHOICE, freedom of choice, alternative, other possibility, preference.

optional adj NON-COMPULSORY, not required, voluntary, discretionary, at one's discretion, elective.
– OPPOSITES compulsory.

opulent adj ❶ LUXURIOUS, sumptuous, lavishly appointed; *informal* plush, plushy, ritzy. ❷ AFFLUENT, wealthy, rich, well off, well-to-do, moneyed, prosperous; *informal* well heeled, rolling in it.
– OPPOSITES spartan, poor.

orbit n ❶ REVOLUTION, circle, circuit, cycle, rotation. ❷ SPHERE, sphere of influence, range, reach, scope, ambit, sweep, domain.

ordeal n TRIAL, test, tribulation, suffering, affliction, distress, agony, anguish, torture, torment, calamity, trouble, nightmare.

order n ❶ ORDERLINESS, neatness, tidiness, trimness, harmony. ❷ METHOD, organization, system, plan, uniformity, regularity, symmetry, pattern. ❸ CONDITION, state, shape, situation. ❹ ARRANGEMENT, grouping, system, organization, form, structure, disposition, classification, categorization, codification, series, sequence, progression, succession, layout, set-up. ❺ COMMAND, direction, directive, instruction, decree, edict, injunction, law, rule, regulation, ordinance, stipulation, dictate. ❻ REQUEST, call, requirement, requisition, demand, booking, reservation, commission. ❼ BROTHERHOOD, sisterhood, community.
▶ v ❶ GIVE THE ORDER TO, command, instruct, direct, bid, enjoin. ❷ PUT IN / PLACE AN ORDER FOR, request, call for, requisition, book, reserve, contract for, apply for, send away for.

orderly adj ❶ IN ORDER, neat, tidy, trim, shipshape, shipshape and Bristol fashion, in apple-pie order. ❷ ORGANIZED, well organized, methodical, systematic, efficient, businesslike. ❸ WELL BEHAVED, disciplined, quiet, peaceful, controlled, restrained.
– OPPOSITES disorderly.

ordinary adj ❶ USUAL, normal, standard, typical, stock, common, customary, habitual, accustomed, everyday, quotidian, regular, routine, established, settled, fixed, prevailing, humdrum; *poetic/literary* wonted. ❷ RUN-OF-THE-MILL, common, conventional, standard, typical, average, commonplace, workaday, humdrum, unremarkable, unexceptional, undistinguished, unmemorable, pedestrian, prosaic, unpretentious, modest, plain, simple.
– OPPOSITES unusual.

organization n ❶ ARRANGEMENT, regulation, coordination, systematization, categorization, administration, running, management. ❷ COMPANY, firm, concern, operation, corporation, institution, group, consortium, conglomerate, combine, syndicate, federation, confederation, association, body.

organize v ❶ ARRANGE, dispose, regulate, marshal, put in order, put straight, coordinate, systematize, methodize, standardize, collocate, group, sort, sort out, classify, categorize, catalogue, codify, tabulate. ❷ BE RESPONSIBLE FOR, be in charge of, take care of, administrate, run, manage, lick/ knock into shape, see to.
– OPPOSITES inefficient.

orientate v ❶ FIND ONE'S BEARINGS, get the lie of the land, establish one's location. ❷ ADAPT, adjust, accommodate, familiarize, acclimatize, find one's feet. ❸ DIRECT, guide, lead, point someone in the direction of, turn.

orifice n OPENING, hole, vent,

aperture, gap, space, breach, break, rent, slot, slit, cleft, cranny, fissure, crevice, rift, crack, chink.

origin n **1** SOURCE, basis, base, derivation, root, roots, provenance, etymology, genesis, spring, wellspring, fountain, fountainhead, aetiology. **2** DESCENT, ancestry, pedigree, lineage, heritage, parentage, extraction, beginnings.

original adj **1** ABORIGINAL, indigenous, early, earliest, first, primary, primordial, primal, primeval, primitive, autochthonous. **2** INNOVATIVE, innovatory, inventive, new, novel, fresh, creative, imaginative, individual, ingenious, unusual, unconventional, unorthodox, unprecedented, ground-breaking.
– OPPOSITES unoriginal, derivative.

originate v **1** ARISE, stem, spring, result, derive, start, begin, commence. **2** GIVE BIRTH TO, set in motion, set up, invent, dream up, conceive, discover, initiate, create, formulate, inaugurate, pioneer, introduce, establish, found, evolve, develop, generate.

ornament n **1** KNICK-KNACK, trinket, bauble, gewgaw, accessory, decoration, frill, whatnot, doodah. **2** DECORATION, adornment, embellishment, trimming, garnish, garnishing.

ornamental adj DECORATIVE, attractive, showy, embellishing, ornamenting.

ornate adj ELABORATE, over-elaborate, decorated, embellished, adorned, ornamented, fancy, fussy, busy, ostentatious, showy, baroque, rococo; informal flash.
– OPPOSITES plain.

orthodox adj **1** DOCTRINAL, of the faith, of the true faith, sound, conservative, correct, faithful, true, devoted, strict, devout. **2** CONVENTIONAL, accepted, approved, correct, proper, conformist, established, traditional, usual, regular.
– OPPOSITES unconventional.

ostensible adj APPARENT, seeming, professed, outward, alleged, claimed, purported, pretended, feigned, supposed.
– OPPOSITES genuine.

ostentation n SHOWINESS, show, conspicuousness, obtrusiveness, loudness, extravagance, flamboyance, gaudiness, flashiness, pretentiousness, affectation, exhibitionism; informal swank.

ostentatious adj SHOWY, conspicuous, obtrusive, loud, extravagant, flamboyant, gaudy, flashy, pretentious, affected, overdone; informal flash, swanky.
– OPPOSITES unobtrusive.

ostracize v COLD-SHOULDER, give someone the cold shoulder, send to Coventry, exclude, shut out, shun, spurn, avoid, boycott, repudiate, cast out, reject, blackball, blacklist.
– OPPOSITES welcome.

other adj **1** DIFFERENT, unlike,

variant, dissimilar, distinct, separate, alternative. ❷ MORE, additional, further, extra.

outbreak n ERUPTION, flare-up, upsurge, outburst, start, rash.

outburst n BURST, explosion, eruption, outbreak, flare-up, attack, fit, spasm, paroxysm.

outcome n RESULT, upshot, issue, product, conclusion, after-effect, aftermath, wake; *informal* pay-off.

outdated adj OUT OF DATE, out of fashion, old-fashioned, unfashionable, outmoded, dated, passé, behind the times, antiquated, archaic.
– OPPOSITES modern.

outdo v SURPASS, top, exceed, excel, get the better of, outstrip, outshine, eclipse, overshadow, outclass, overcome, beat, defeat.

outer adj ❶ OUTSIDE, outermost, outward, exterior, external, surface, superficial. ❷ OUTLYING, distant, remote, faraway, peripheral, fringe, perimeter.
– OPPOSITES inner.

outgoing adj ❶ EXTROVERT, demonstrative, affectionate, warm, friendly, genial, cordial, affable, sociable, communicative, open, expansive, talkative, gregarious, approachable. ❷ RETIRING, departing, leaving, withdrawing, ex-, former.
– OPPOSITES reserved, incoming.

outlandish adj STRANGE, unfamiliar, unknown, unheard of, odd, unusual, extraordinary,

peculiar, queer, curious, singular, eccentric, quaint, bizarre, grotesque, preposterous, weird; *informal* freaky, wacky, far out, off-the-wall.
– OPPOSITES ordinary.

outline n ❶ THUMBNAIL SKETCH, rough idea, quick rundown, abbreviated version, summary, synopsis, main points, bones, bare bones. ❷ CONTOUR, silhouette, profile, lineaments, delineation, configuration, perimeter, circumference.

outlook n ❶ POINT OF VIEW, viewpoint, view, perspective, attitude, frame of mind, standpoint, slant, angle, interpretation, opinion. ❷ VISTA, view, prospect, panorama, aspect.

outlying adj OUTER, outermost, out of the way, remote, distant, far-flung, peripheral, isolated, inaccessible, off the beaten track.

output n PRODUCTION, product, productivity, yield, harvest, crop.

outrage n ❶ ATROCITY, crime, horror, enormity, brutality. ❷ OFFENCE, affront, insult, injury, abuse, scandal, desecration, violation. ❸ ANGER, fury, rage, indignation, wrath, annoyance, shock, resentment, horror.

outrageous adj ❶ INTOLERABLE, insufferable, insupportable, unendurable, unbearable, impossible, exasperating, offensive, provocative, maddening, distressing. ❷ ATROCIOUS, heinous, abominable, wicked, vile, foul, monstrous, horrible, horrid, dreadful, terrible, horrendous, hideous, ghastly, unspeakable, gruesome.

outside n adj ❶ OUTER, outermost, outward, exterior, external. ❷ OUTDOOR, out of doors. ❸ UNLIKELY, improbable, slight, slender, slim, small, faint, negligible, marginal, remote, distant, vague.
– OPPOSITES inside.

outsider n ALIEN, stranger, foreigner, outlander, immigrant, incomer, newcomer, parvenu/parvenue, arriviste, interloper, intruder, gatecrasher, outcast, misfit.

outskirts pl n VICINITY, neighbourhood, environs, outlying districts, fringes, margin, periphery, borders, boundary, suburbs.

outspoken adj CANDID, frank, forthright, direct, straightforward, plain-spoken, explicit, blunt.
– OPPOSITES diplomatic.

outstanding adj ❶ EXCELLENT, remarkable, exceptional, superlative, pre-eminent, eminent, well known, notable, noteworthy, distinguished, important, famous, famed, renowned, celebrated, great. ❷ UNPAID, unsettled, owing, due.
– OPPOSITES unexceptional.

outwardly adv ❶ EXTERNALLY, on the outside. ❷ ON THE SURFACE, superficially, on the face of it, to all appearances, as far as one can see, to all intents and purposes, apparently, evidently.

outwit v GET THE BETTER OF, be cleverer than, outsmart, outmanoeuvre, steal a march on, trick, dupe, make a fool of; *informal* put one over on, pull a fast one on.

overall adj COMPREHENSIVE, universal, all-embracing, inclusive, all-inclusive, general, sweeping, complete, blanket, umbrella, global.
▶ adv ON THE WHOLE, in general, generally speaking.

overawe v INTIMIDATE, daunt, disconcert, abash, dismay, frighten, alarm, scare, terrify, terrorize.

overcome v CONQUER, defeat, vanquish, beat, prevail over, get the better of, triumph over, best, worst, trounce, rout, master, overpower, overwhelm, overthrow, subdue, subjugate, quell, quash, crush; *informal* thrash, lick, clobber, whip.
▶ adj OVERWHELMED, emotional, moved, affected, speechless, at a loss for words; *informal* bowled over.

overdue adj ❶ LATE, behind schedule, delayed, belated, tardy, unpunctual. ❷ UNPAID, owed, owing, outstanding, unsettled, in arrears.

overflow v FLOW OVER, run over, spill over, brim over, well over, pour forth, stream forth, discharge, surge, debouch.

overhead adv ABOVE, up

above, high up, up in the sky, on high, aloft.

overlook v ❶ FAIL TO NOTICE, miss, leave, neglect; *informal* slip up on. ❷ LEAVE UNDONE, ignore, disregard, omit, neglect, forget. ❸ LOOK OVER, look on to, front on to, have/afford a view of, command a view of.

overpowering adj OVERWHELMING, burdensome, weighty, unbearable, unendurable, intolerable, shattering; *informal* mind-blowing.

overriding adj MOST IMPORTANT, predominant, principal, primary, paramount, chief, main, major, foremost, central.

oversight n ❶ CARELESSNESS, inattention, neglect, inadvertence, laxity, dereliction, omission. ❷ MISTAKE, error, blunder, gaffe, fault, omission, slip, lapse.

overt adj OBVIOUS, noticeable, undisguised, unconcealed, apparent, plain, manifest, patent, open, public, blatant, conspicuous.
– OPPOSITES covert.

overtake v PASS, get past, go past, go by, overhaul, leave behind, outstrip, go faster than.

overthrow v *see* OVERCOME.

overtone n IMPLICATION, innuendo, hint, suggestion, insinuation, association, connotation, undercurrent, nuance.

overwhelm v ❶ OVERCOME, move, make emotional, daze, dumbfound, shake, take aback, leave speechless, stagger. ❷ INUNDATE, flood, deluge, engulf, submerge, swamp, bury, overload, overburden, snow under.

overwhelming adj
❶ UNCONTROLLABLE, irrepressible, irresistible, overpowering.
❷ VAST, massive, great, large.

owe v BE IN DEBT, be indebted, be under an obligation, be obligated, be beholden.

own v POSSESS, have in one's possession, have, keep, retain, maintain, hold, enjoy.
■ **own up** *see* CONFESS.

Pp

pace n ❶ STEP, stride. ❷ GAIT, walk, tread. ❸ SPEED, swiftness, fastness, quickness, rapidity, velocity.

pacify v CALM DOWN, placate, conciliate, propitiate, appease, mollify, soothe, tranquillize, quieten.
– OPPOSITES enrage.

pack n ❶ PACKET, container,

package, carton. ❷ BACKPACK, rucksack, knapsack, kitbag, satchel.

▶ v ❶ FILL, store, stow, load, bundle, stuff, cram. ❷ FILL, crowd, throng, mob, cram, jam, press into, squeeze into.

packed adj FULL, filled to capacity, crowded, thronged, mobbed, crammed, jammed, brimful, chock-full, chock-a-block, jam-packed.

pact n AGREEMENT, treaty, deal, contract, settlement, bargain, compact, covenant, bond, concordat, entente.

pad n ❶ PADDING, wadding, stuffing, buffer. ❷ CUSHION, pillow, bolster. ❸ NOTEPAD, writing pad, notebook; *Brit.* jotter; *informal* memo pad.

▶ v PACK, stuff, line, cushion, protect.

paddle v ROW, pull, oar, scull, pole, punt.

paddock n FIELD, meadow, enclosure, yard, pen, pound, corral.

pagan n UNBELIEVER, heathen, infidel, idolater, pantheist, polytheist.

▶ adj HEATHEN, infidel, idolatrous, pantheistic, polytheistic.

pageantry n SPECTACLE, magnificence, pomp, splendour, grandeur, glamour, theatricality, show, showiness; *informal* pizzazz.

pain n ❶ SORENESS, hurt, ache, aching, agony, throb, throbbing, smarting, twinge, pang, spasm, cramp, discomfort, irri-

tation, tenderness. ❷ SUFFERING, hurt, sorrow, grief, heartache, sadness, unhappiness, distress, misery, wretchedness, anguish, affliction, woe.

pained adj HURT, aggrieved, reproachful, offended, insulted, upset, unhappy, distressed; *informal* miffed.

painful adj ❶ SORE, hurting, aching, throbbing, smarting, tender, inflamed, agonizing, excruciating. ❷ DISAGREEABLE, unpleasant, nasty, distressing, disquieting, disturbing, miserable, wretched, agonizing, harrowing.

painless adj ❶ PAIN-FREE, without pain. ❷ EASY, simple, trouble-free, effortless, plain sailing; *informal* as easy as pie, as easy as falling off a log, child's play, a cinch.
– OPPOSITES painful, difficult.

painstaking adj CAREFUL, thorough, assiduous, conscientious, meticulous, punctilious, sedulous, scrupulous.
– OPPOSITES careless.

painting n PICTURE, illustration, portrayal, depiction, delineation, representation, likeness.

pair n COUPLE, duo, brace, two, twosome, matched set, matching set.

■ **pair off** ARRANGE / GROUP IN PAIRS, pair up, put together, get together, join up, link up, team up.

palatable adj ❶ TASTY, appetizing, pleasant-tasting,

flavoursome, delicious, mouth-watering, savoury; *informal* scrumptious, yummy. ❷ AGREE-ABLE, pleasant, pleasing, pleasurable, nice, attractive, acceptable, satisfactory.
– OPPOSITES unpalatable.

palatial adj LUXURIOUS, imposing, splendid, grand, magnificent, stately, majestic, opulent, sumptuous, plush.
– OPPOSITES humble.

pale adj ❶ WHITE, white-faced, colourless, anaemic, wan, drained, pallid, pasty, peaky, ashen, waxen, as white as a sheet/ghost, deathly pale. ❷ LIGHT, pastel, muted, low-key, restrained, faded, bleached, washed out, etiolated. ❸ DIM, faint, weak, feeble, thin.
– OPPOSITES dark.
▶ V GROW / BECOME PALE, go/turn white, blanch, lose colour.

pallid adj *see* PALE adj (1).

palpable adj TANGIBLE, feelable, touchable, solid, concrete.
– OPPOSITES intangible.

paltry adj ❶ SMALL, meagre, trifling, minor, insignificant, trivial, derisory; *informal* piddling. ❷ WORTHLESS, despicable, contemptible, miserable, wretched, sorry, puny.
– OPPOSITES considerable.

pamper v SPOIL, cosset, indulge, overindulge, humour, coddle, mollycoddle.

pamphlet n LEAFLET, booklet, brochure, circular.

panache n STYLE, verve, flamboyance, zest, dash, flourish, brio, elan; *informal* pizzazz.

pander v GRATIFY, indulge, humour, give in to, please, satisfy, cater for.

panic n ALARM, fright, fear, terror, horror, agitation, hysteria.
– OPPOSITES calm.
▶ V BE ALARMED, take fright, be terrified/horrified, be agitated, be hysterical, lose one's nerve, overreact.

panoramic adj WIDE, extensive, sweeping, bird's-eye, comprehensive.

pant v PUFF, huff and puff, blow, gasp, wheeze.

paper n ❶ NEWSPAPER, magazine, journal, gazette, broadsheet, tabloid; *informal* rag. ❷ ESSAY, article, work, dissertation, treatise, thesis, monograph, study, report.

parade n PROCESSION, progression, cavalcade, spectacle, pageant, array.
▶ V ❶ MARCH, go in columns, file by. ❷ DISPLAY, show off, exhibit, show, demonstrate, make a show of, flaunt.

paradox n CONTRADICTION, inconsistency, incongruity, anomaly, enigma, puzzle, absurdity, oxymoron.

paradoxical adj SELF-CONTRADICTORY, inconsistent, incongruous, anomalous, enigmatic, puzzling, absurd.

parallel adj ❶ SIDE BY SIDE, equidistant, collateral. ❷ SIMILAR, like, resembling, analogous, comparable, equivalent, corresponding, matching.
▶ n COUNTERPART, equivalent,

analogue, match, duplicate, equal.
▶ v BE SIMILAR TO, be like, resemble, be analogous to, correspond to, compare with, be comparable/equivalent to.

paralyse v IMMOBILIZE, numb, deaden, dull, incapacitate, debilitate, disable, cripple.

paralysis n IMMOBILITY, powerlessness, lack of feeling, numbness, palsy, incapacity, debilitation; *Medicine* paresis.

parameter n LIMIT, limitation, limiting factor, restriction, specification, guidelines, framework.

parched adj DRIED UP / OUT, dry, baked, burned, scorched, seared, desiccated, dehydrated, withered, shrivelled.

pardon n ❶ FORGIVENESS, forbearance, indulgence, clemency, lenience, leniency, mercy. ❷ FREE PARDON, reprieve, release, acquittal, absolution, amnesty, exoneration, exculpation.
▶ v ❶ EXCUSE, condone, let off. ❷ REPRIEVE, release, acquit, absolve, exonerate, exculpate.

pardonable adj FORGIVABLE, excusable, allowable, condonable, understandable, minor, slight, venial.
– OPPOSITES inexcusable.

parentage n FAMILY, birth, origins, extraction, ancestry, lineage, descent, heritage, pedigree.

parliament n LEGISLATIVE ASSEMBLY, congress, senate, chamber, house, convocation, diet.

parody n LAMPOON, spoof, send-up, satire, pastiche, caricature, mimicry, take-off, burlesque.
▶ v LAMPOON, satirize, caricature, mimic, take off, send up, burlesque.

parry v WARD OFF, fend off, stave off, turn aside, avert, deflect, block, rebuff, repel, repulse, hold at bay.

part n ❶ PORTION, division, section, segment, bit, piece, fragment, scrap, slice, fraction, chunk. ❷ SECTION, area, region, sector, quarter, territory, neighbourhood. ❸ FUNCTION, role, job, task, work, responsibility, capacity, participation. ❹ ROLE, character.
▶ v ❶ DIVIDE, separate, split, break up, sever, disjoin. ❷ LEAVE, go away, say goodbye, say one's goodbyes, separate; *informal* split, push off, hit the road.

partial adj ❶ PART, in part, limited, incomplete, imperfect, fragmentary. ❷ BIASED, prejudiced, partisan, one-sided, discriminatory, preferential, unjust, unfair.
– OPPOSITES complete, impartial.
■ **be partial to** *see* LIKE[1] (2).

participate v TAKE PART IN, join in, engage in, play a part in, contribute to, be involved in, share in, have a hand in.

participation n PART, contribution, association, involvement, partaking.

particle n ❶ BIT, piece, speck,

spot, atom, molecule. ❷ IOTA, jot, whit, grain, bit, scrap, shred, morsel, atom, hint, touch, trace, suggestion.

particular adj ❶ SPECIFIC, individual, single, distinct, precise. ❷ SPECIAL, especial, singular, peculiar, exceptional, unusual, uncommon, notable, noteworthy, remarkable. ❸ FASTIDIOUS, discriminating, selective, fussy, painstaking, meticulous, punctilious, demanding, critical, finicky; informal pernickety, choosy, picky.
– OPPOSITES general, careless.

particularly adv ❶ ESPECIALLY, specially, singularly, peculiarly, distinctly, markedly, exceptionally, unusually, uncommonly. ❷ IN PARTICULAR, specifically, explicitly, expressly, specially, especially.

partisan n ❶ GUERRILLA, resistance fighter, underground fighter. ❷ SUPPORTER, adherent, devotee, backer, follower, disciple.
▶ adj see PARTIAL (2).

partition v DIVIDE, divide up, subdivide, separate, separate off, screen off, wall off, fence off.

partly adv IN PART, partially, not wholly, not fully, half, somewhat, to some extent/degree, in some measure, fractionally, slightly.
– OPPOSITES completely.

partnership n ❶ ASSOCIATION, cooperation, collaboration, alliance, union, fellowship, companionship.

❷ COLLABORATION, collusion, connivance, conspiracy.

party n ❶ GATHERING, function, reception, celebration, festivity, at-home, soirée, bacchanal; informal do, bash, shindig; Brit. informal rave-up. ❷ POLITICAL PARTY, alliance, association, grouping, faction, camp, set, caucus.

pass v ❶ GO, move, proceed, progress, drive, run, travel, roll, flow, course. ❷ GO PAST, move past, go/get ahead of, go by, overtake, outstrip. ❸ HAND OVER, reach, let someone have, give, transfer. ❹ ELAPSE, go by, proceed, progress, advance. ❺ SPEND, occupy, fill, take up, use, employ, while away. ❻ GAIN A PASS IN, get through, be successful in, succeed in, pass muster in. ❼ VOTE FOR, accept, approve, adopt, authorize, ratify.
▶ n PERMIT, warrant, authorization, licence, passport, visa, safe conduct, exeat.
■ **pass for** BE TAKEN FOR, be accepted as, be mistaken for.
pass out FAINT, collapse, black out, keel over, swoon.

passable adj ❶ ADEQUATE, all right, tolerable, fair, acceptable, satisfactory, mediocre, middling, ordinary, average, run-of-the-mill, not too bad, unexceptional, indifferent. ❷ OPEN, clear, crossable, traversable, navigable, unblocked, unobstructed.

passage n ❶ PASSING, progress, advance, process,

flow, course. ❷ JOURNEY, voyage, transit, trek, crossing, trip, tour. ❸ PASSAGEWAY, corridor, hall, hallway, entrance hall, entrance, vestibule, lobby. ❹ EXTRACT, excerpt, quotation, citation, section, verse.

passer-by n BYSTANDER, onlooker, witness, spectator.

passion n ❶ INTENSITY, fervour, ardour, zeal, vehemence, fire, emotion, feeling, zest, eagerness, excitement, animation. ❷ FASCINATION, keen interest, obsession, fixation, craze, mania.

passionate adj ❶ IMPASSIONED, intense, fervent, fervid, ardent, zealous, vehement, fiery, emotional, heartfelt, animated. ❷ ARDENT, aroused, desirous, hot, sexy, amorous, sensual, erotic, lustful.
– OPPOSITES apathetic, frigid.

passive adj ❶ INACTIVE, unassertive, uninvolved, unresisting, yielding, submissive, compliant, pliant, acquiescent, quiescent, resigned, obedient, tractable, malleable. ❷ IMPASSIVE, emotionless, unmoved, unresponsive, undemonstrative, dispassionate, detached, distant, remote, aloof, indifferent.
– OPPOSITES active.

past adj ❶ GONE BY, gone, bygone, elapsed, over, ended, former, long ago. ❷ FORMER, previous, prior, erstwhile, one-time, sometime.
– OPPOSITES present.

pastel adj PALE, soft, delicate, muted, subdued, faint, low-key.
– OPPOSITES vivid.

pastime n HOBBY, leisure activity, sport, game, recreation, diversion, amusement, entertainment, distraction, relaxation.

pastoral adj RURAL, country, rustic, simple, idyllic, innocent, Arcadian, agricultural, bucolic, georgic.

pasture n PASTURAGE, grazing, grassland, grass, field, meadow.

patch n ❶ COVER, covering, pad, shield. ❷ PLOT, area, piece, tract, parcel.
▶ v COVER, mend, repair, fix, sew up, stitch.

patent adj OBVIOUS, clear, plain, evident, apparent, manifest, transparent, conspicuous, blatant, unmistakable.

path n ❶ PATHWAY, footpath, footway, track, trail, towpath, walk. ❷ COURSE, route, circuit, track, orbit, trajectory.

pathetic adj ❶ PITEOUS, pitiful, moving, touching, poignant, affecting, heartbreaking, heart-rending, sad, wretched, mournful, woeful. ❷ LAMENTABLE, deplorable, miserable, wretched, feeble, pitiful, woeful, poor, contemptible, inadequate, unsatisfactory, worthless.

pathological adj COMPULSIVE, obsessive, irrational, unreasonable, illogical.

patience n ❶ CALMNESS, composure, even-temperedness,

equanimity, serenity, tranquillity, restraint, imperturbability, tolerance, indulgence, forbearance, endurance, resignation, stoicism, fortitude. ❷ PERSEVERANCE, persistence, endurance, tenacity, assiduity, diligence, staying power, indefatigability, doggedness, singleness of purpose.
– OPPOSITES impatience.

patient adj UNCOMPLAINING, serene, calm, composed, even-tempered, tranquil, restrained, imperturbable, tolerant, accommodating, long-suffering, forbearing, indulgent, resigned, stoical, unflappable; *informal* cool.
– OPPOSITES impatient.

patriotic adj NATIONALIST, nationalistic, chauvinistic, flag-waving, jingoistic.

patrol v MAKE THE ROUNDS OF, range, police, keep watch on, guard, keep guard on, monitor.
▶ n ❶ PATROLLING, round, policing, watch, guard, monitoring. ❷ SENTRY, guard, watchman, watch, nightwatchman, policeman/policewoman.

patron n ❶ SPONSOR, backer, benefactor/benefactress, promoter, friend; *informal* angel. ❷ CUSTOMER, client, shopper, regular, frequenter.

patronize v ❶ LOOK DOWN ON, talk down to, condescend to, treat condescendingly, treat scornfully/contemptuously, be snobbish to. ❷ BE A CUSTOMER OF, be a client of, frequent, shop at,

buy from, do business with, deal with, trade with.

patronizing adj CONDESCENDING, supercilious, superior, haughty, lofty, lordly, snobbish; *informal* snooty, toffee-nosed.

pattern n ❶ DECORATION, design, motif, ornamentation, device, figure. ❷ PLAN, guide, blueprint, model, design, template, instructions.

pause v STOP, halt, cease, discontinue, take a break, desist, rest, hold back, delay, hesitate, waver; *informal* take a breather.
▶ n BREAK, halt, stoppage, cessation, interruption, lull, respite, stay, discontinuation, gap, interlude, intermission, interval, rest, delay, hesitation.

pay v ❶ SETTLE UP WITH, remunerate, reimburse, recompense. ❷ PAY OUT, spend, expend, lay out, part with, disburse, hand over, remit, render; *informal* shell out, fork out, cough up. ❸ MAKE MONEY, be profitable, make a profit, be remunerative, make a return. ❹ REPAY, be advantageous to, be of advantage to, be of benefit to, be beneficial to, be profitable to, be worthwhile to.
▶ n PAYMENT, salary, wages, earnings, fee, remuneration, recompense, reimbursement, reward, stipend, emoluments.

payment n ❶ SETTLEMENT, discharge, clearance, squaring, liquidation. ❷ See PAY n. ❸ INSTALMENT, premium, amount, remittance.

peace n ❶ TRANQUILLITY, peace-

fulness, serenity, calm, calmness, composure, placidity, rest, repose, contentment. ❷ HARMONY, peaceableness, peacefulness, accord, amity, amicableness, goodwill, friendship, cordiality; *formal* concord. ❸ TREATY, truce, agreement, armistice, cessation of hostilities, non-aggression, ceasefire.
– OPPOSITES anxiety, war.

peaceable adj PEACE-LOVING, non-violent, easy-going, placid, gentle, mild, good-natured, even-tempered, amiable, amicable, pacific, pacifist, dovelike, dovish.
– OPPOSITES aggressive.

peaceful adj TRANQUIL, restful, quiet, calm, still, serene, composed, placid, reposeful, undisturbed, untroubled, unworried, anxiety-free.
– OPPOSITES noisy, agitated.

peacemaker n CONCILIATOR, mediator, arbitrator, pacifier, appeaser, peace-monger.

peak n ❶ TOP, summit, crest, pinnacle, mountain, hill, height, alp. ❷ HEIGHT, high point, climax, culmination, zenith, acme, meridian, apogee, prime, heyday.
– OPPOSITES nadir.

peculiar adj ❶ STRANGE, odd, queer, funny, curious, unusual, abnormal, eccentric, unconventional, bizarre, weird, quaint, outlandish, out of the way, grotesque, freakish, offbeat, droll, comical; *informal* far out, way-out. ❷ CHARACTERISTIC, distinctive, distinct, individual, distinguishing, special, unique, idiosyncratic.
– OPPOSITES ordinary.

peculiarity n ❶ STRANGENESS, oddness, queerness, abnormality, eccentricity, unconventionality, bizarreness, weirdness, outlandishness, grotesqueness, freakishness. ❷ CHARACTERISTIC, feature, quality, property, trait, attribute, mark, stamp, hallmark.

pedantic adj PRECISE, exact, scrupulous, over-scrupulous, punctilious, meticulous, over-nice, perfectionist, formalist, dogmatic, literalist, literalistic, quibbling, hair-splitting, casuistic, casuistical, pettifogging; *informal* nit-picking.

pedestal n BASE, support, stand, foundation, pillar, column, plinth.

pedestrian n WALKER, person on foot, hiker, footslogger.
▶ adj ❶ PEDESTRIANIZED, for pedestrians. ❷ PLODDING, unimaginative, uninspired, unexciting, dull, flat, prosaic, turgid, stodgy, mundane, humdrum, banal, run-of-the-mill, commonplace, ordinary, mediocre.
– OPPOSITES inspired.

peek v PEEP, glance, sneak a look, cast a brief look, look hurriedly, look; *informal* take a gander, have a look-see.

peephole n APERTURE, opening, spyhole, judas, slit, crack, chink, crevice, fissure.

peer v LOOK CLOSELY, try to see, narrow one's eyes, screw up one's eyes, squint.

peer² n ❶ NOBLE, nobleman, aristocrat, lord, patrician. ❷ COMPEER, fellow, equal, match, like, co-equal.

peeve v IRRITATE, annoy, anger, vex, provoke, upset, exasperate, irk, pique, nettle, get on someone's nerves; Brit. rub up the wrong way; informal aggravate, miff; Brit. informal nark.

penalize v PUNISH, discipline, fine, correct; formal castigate. – OPPOSITES reward.

penalty n PENANCE, fine, forfeit, sentence, mulct.

penance n ATONEMENT, reparation, amends, mortification.

penchant n LIKING, fondness, preference, taste, partiality, inclination, bent, proclivity, predilection.

pending adj IMMINENT, impending, on the way, coming, approaching, forthcoming, near, nearing, close, close at hand, in the offing.

penetrate v ❶ PIERCE, bore, perforate, stab, prick, gore, spike. ❷ PERMEATE, pervade, fill, imbue, suffuse, seep through, saturate.

penitent adj REPENTANT, contrite, regretful, remorseful, sorry, apologetic, rueful, ashamed, abject, sorrowful. – OPPOSITES unrepentant.

penniless adj IMPECUNIOUS, penurious, impoverished, indigent, poor, poverty-stricken, destitute, bankrupt, hard up; informal broke; Brit. informal skint. – OPPOSITES wealthy.

pensive adj THOUGHTFUL, reflective, lost in thought, contemplative, meditative, cogitative, ruminative, absorbed, preoccupied.

people n ❶ PERSONS, individuals, human beings, humans, mortals, living souls, {men, women, and children}. ❷ RACE, tribe, clan, nation, country, population, populace. ❸ THE GENERAL PUBLIC, the public, the masses, the rank and file, commonalty, the mob, the multitude, the hoi polloi.

perceive v ❶ SEE, catch sight of, spot, observe, glimpse, notice, make out, discern, behold, espy, detect, witness, remark. ❷ DISCERN, appreciate, recognize, be aware of, be conscious of, know, grasp, understand, comprehend, apprehend, see, sense.

perceptible adj PERCEIVABLE, discernible, noticeable, detectable, distinguishable, appreciable, visible, observable, distinct, palpable, tangible. – OPPOSITES imperceptible.

perception n ❶ DISCERNMENT, appreciation, recognition, awareness, consciousness, knowledge, grasp, understanding, comprehension, apprehension, notion, conception, idea, sense. ❷ PERSPICACITY, discernment, perceptiveness, understanding, discrimination, insight, intuition, feeling, sensitivity.

perceptive adj PENETRATING, astute, shrewd, discerning,

perspicacious, percipient, understanding, discriminating, intuitive, responsive, sensitive.
– OPPOSITES obtuse.

perch n POLE, rod, branch, roost, rest.
▶ v SIT, rest, roost, settle, alight, land.

peremptory adj IMPERIOUS, high-handed, overbearing, dogmatic, autocratic, dictatorial, domineering, arbitrary, tyrannical, despotic, arrogant.

perfect adj ❶ FLAWLESS, faultless, unmarred, ideal, impeccable, consummate, immaculate, exemplary, superb, superlative, supreme, excellent, complete, full, whole, entire. ❷ EXACT, precise, accurate, faithful, strict; Brit. informal spot on. ❸ ABSOLUTE, complete, out-and-out, thorough, thoroughgoing, downright, utter, sheer, consummate, unmitigated, unqualified.
▶ V MAKE PERFECT, render faultless/flawless, polish, refine, complete, consummate, put the finishing touches to.

perfection n ❶ PERFECTING, polishing, refinement, completion, consummation. ❷ FLAWLESSNESS, faultlessness, impeccability, immaculateness, exemplariness, superbness.

perfidious adj TREACHEROUS, traitorous, treasonous, false, untrue, disloyal, faithless, unfaithful, deceitful.
– OPPOSITES faithful.

perform v ❶ DO, carry out, execute, discharge, conduct, effect, bring about, bring off, accomplish, achieve, fulfil, complete. ❷ ACT, play, appear. ❸ FUNCTION, work, operate, run, go.

performance n ❶ EXECUTION, discharge, accomplishment, achievement, fulfilment. ❷ SHOW, production, entertainment, act, presentation; informal gig.

performer n ACTOR / ACTRESS, player, entertainer, artist, artiste, Thespian, musician, singer, dancer.

perfume n ❶ SMELL, fragrance, aroma, scent, bouquet; poetic/literary redolence. ❷ FRAGRANCE, scent, eau de Cologne, cologne.

perfunctory adj CURSORY, superficial, desultory, mechanical, automatic, routine, sketchy, brief, hasty, hurried, rapid, fleeting, quick, fast, offhand, casual, indifferent, careless, inattentive, negligent.
– OPPOSITES careful, thorough.

perhaps adv MAYBE, possibly, it is possible that, conceivably, feasibly, for all one knows; poetic/literary peradventure.

peril n DANGER, jeopardy, risk, hazard, menace, threat.
– OPPOSITES safety.

perilous adj DANGEROUS, risky, precarious, hazardous, chancy, threatening, unsafe.
– OPPOSITES safe.

perimeter n BOUNDARY, border, frontier, limits, outer

limits, confines, edge, margin, fringe, periphery.

period n SPACE, spell, interval, term, stretch, span, age, era, epoch, aeon.

periodic adj PERIODICAL, recurrent, recurring, repeated, cyclical, cyclic, regular, intermittent, occasional, infrequent, sporadic.

peripheral adj ❶ OUTER, on the edge/outskirts, surrounding, neighbouring. ❷ MINOR, lesser, secondary, subsidiary, ancillary, unimportant, superficial, irrelevant.
– OPPOSITES central.

perish v ❶ DIE, lose one's life, be killed, lay down one's life, meet one's death, breathe one's last, draw one's last breath; *informal* bite the dust, kick the bucket. ❷ GO BAD, go off, go sour, rot, decay, decompose.

perk
■ **perk up** CHEER UP, brighten up, take heart; *informal* buck up, pep up.

permanent adj LASTING, long-lasting, stable, fixed, established, everlasting, perpetual, eternal, enduring, perennial, abiding, constant, persistent, unending, endless, never-ending, immutable, unchangeable, unalterable, invariable.
– OPPOSITES impermanent.

permeate v SPREAD THROUGH, pass through, pervade, saturate, fill, diffuse through, extend throughout, imbue, penetrate, infiltrate, percolate through.

permissible adj PERMITTED, allowable, admissible, acceptable, tolerated, authorized, sanctioned, legal, lawful, legitimate, licit, within bounds; *informal* legit.
– OPPOSITES forbidden.

permission n AUTHORIZATION, sanction, leave, licence, dispensation, empowerment, allowance, consent, assent, acquiescence, agreement, approval, approbation, tolerance, sufferance; *informal* green light, go-ahead, thumbs up.

permissive adj LIBERAL, tolerant, broad-minded, open-minded, easy-going, indulgent, lenient, overindulgent, lax, unprescriptive.
– OPPOSITES intolerant, strict.

permit v GIVE PERMISSION, allow, let, authorize, give leave, sanction, grant, license, consent to, assent to, acquiesce in, agree to, approve of, tolerate, countenance, suffer; *informal* give the green light to, give the go-ahead to, give the thumbs up to; *formal* brook.
– OPPOSITES forbid.
▶ n LICENCE, authorization, warrant, sanction, pass, passport.

perpetual adj ❶ EVERLASTING, eternal, never-ending, unending, endless, undying, perennial, permanent, lasting, enduring, constant, unfailing, unchanging, unvarying, invariable; *poetic/literary* perdurable. ❷ INCESSANT, unceasing, ceaseless, unending, endless, non-stop, continuous, un-interrupted, unbroken, unremitting. ❸ INTERMINABLE, persistent, frequent, continual, recurrent, repeated; *informal* eternal.

perpetuate v KEEP ALIVE, keep going, keep up, preserve, conserve, sustain, maintain, continue.

perplex v PUZZLE, baffle, mystify, stump, bewilder, confound, confuse, nonplus, disconcert, dismay, dumbfound; *informal* bamboozle.

perk n BENEFIT, advantage, bonus, dividend, extra, plus; *informal* freebie; *formal* perquisite.

persecute v OPPRESS, tyrannize, abuse, mistreat, maltreat, ill-treat, molest, afflict, torment, torture, victimize, martyr.

persevere v PERSIST, go on, keep on, keep at, keep going, continue, carry on, struggle, work, hammer away, be tenacious, be persistent, be pertinacious, be resolute, be purposeful, be obstinate, be insistent, be intransigent, be patient, be diligent; *informal* plug away.
– OPPOSITES give up.

persist v *see* PERSEVERE.

persistent adj ❶ PERSEVERING, tenacious, pertinacious, determined, resolute, purposeful, obstinate, stubborn, insistent, intransigent, obdurate, intractable, patient, diligent. ❷ CONSTANT, continual, continuous, continuing, interminable, in-

cessant, unceasing, endless, unremitting, unrelenting, relentless.
– OPPOSITES irresolute, intermittent.

person n INDIVIDUAL, human being, human, creature, living soul, soul, mortal.

personable adj PLEASANT, agreeable, amiable, affable, likeable, charming, nice, attractive, presentable, good-looking.
– OPPOSITES disagreeable.

personal adj ❶ INDIVIDUAL, private, confidential, secret, one's own business. ❷ PERSONALIZED, individual, idiosyncratic, characteristic, unique, peculiar. ❸ INSULTING, slighting, derogatory, disparaging, pejorative, offensive.
– OPPOSITES public, general.

personality n ❶ NATURE, disposition, character, temperament, temper, make-up, psyche. ❷ FORCE OF PERSONALITY, character, charisma, magnetism, powers of attraction, charm. ❸ CELEBRITY, VIP, household name, dignitary, notable, personage, luminary, worthy.

personally adv FOR MY PART, for myself, from my own point of view, as far as I am concerned.

personification n EMBODIMENT, incarnation, epitome, quintessence, essence, symbol, representation, image.

personnel n STAFF, employees, workers, workforce, labour force, manpower, human resources, liveware.

perspective n ❶ OUTLOOK, view, viewpoint, point of view, standpoint, stance, angle, slant, attitude. ❷ VIEW, vista, bird's-eye view, prospect, scene, outlook, panorama, aspect, sweep.

persuade v PREVAIL UPON, induce, convince, win over, talk into, bring round, influence, sway, prompt, coerce, inveigle, cajole, wheedle; informal sweet-talk, soft-soap.
– OPPOSITES discourage.

persuasive adj EFFECTIVE, effectual, convincing, cogent, plausible, compelling, forceful, eloquent, weighty, influential, telling.
– OPPOSITES ineffective.

pertain v BE CONNECTED, relate, be relevant, have relevance, concern, apply to, be pertinent to, have reference to, have a bearing upon.

pertinent adj RELEVANT, appropriate, suitable, fitting, fit, apt, apposite, to the point, applicable, material, germane to the purpose, apropos.
– OPPOSITES irrelevant.

perturb v DISTURB, make anxious, worry, alarm, trouble, upset, disquiet, discompose, disconcert, vex, bother, agitate, unsettle, fluster, ruffle, harass.
– OPPOSITES reassure.

pervade v SPREAD THROUGH, permeate, fill, pass through, suffuse, diffuse through, imbue, infuse, penetrate, infiltrate, percolate.

pervasive adj PERVADING, permeating, prevalent, extensive, ubiquitous, omnipresent, rife, widespread, universal, suffusive.

perverse adj CONTRARY, wayward, troublesome, difficult, awkward, unreasonable, disobedient, unmanageable, uncontrollable, rebellious, wilful, headstrong, capricious, stubborn, obstinate, obdurate, pertinacious, mulish, pig-headed, wrong-headed, querulous, fractious, intractable, refractory, intransigent, contumacious; Brit. informal bolshie, stroppy.

perversion n ❶ DISTORTION, misuse, misrepresentation, falsification, misinterpretation, misconstruction. ❷ DEVIATION, aberration, abnormality, irregularity, unnaturalness, corruption, debauchery, depravity, vice; informal kinkiness.

pervert v ❶ MISAPPLY, misuse, distort, garble, warp, twist, misinterpret, misconstrue. ❷ LEAD ASTRAY, corrupt, warp, deprave, debauch, debase, degrade.
▶ n DEVIANT, deviate, degenerate, debauchee; informal perv.

perverted adj DEPRAVED, debauched, debased, corrupt, deviant, abnormal, aberrant, warped, distorted, twisted, sick, unhealthy, immoral, evil, vile; informal kinky.

pessimist n PROPHET OF DOOM, cynic, defeatist, fatalist, alarmist, doubter, doubting Thomas;

informal doom merchant, gloom merchant.
- OPPOSITES optimist.

pessimistic adj GLOOMY, gloom-ridden, cynical, defeatist, fatalistic, hopeless, distrustful, alarmist, doubting, suspicious, bleak, resigned, depressed, dejected, despairing.
- OPPOSITES optimistic.

pest n NUISANCE, bother, irritant, thorn in the flesh, problem, trouble, worry, inconvenience, trial, tribulation, the bane of one's life; *informal* pain, pain in the neck.

pester v BADGER, hound, irritate, annoy, bother, irk, nag, harass, chivvy, torment, plague, bedevil, harry; *informal* bug, hassle.

pet n FAVOURITE, darling, idol, apple of one's eye; *Brit. informal* blue-eyed boy/girl; *N. Amer. informal* fair-haired boy/girl.
▶ v STROKE, caress, fondle, pat.

peter
■ **peter out** FADE, wane, ebb, diminish, taper off, come to nothing, die out, fail, fall through, come to a halt, come to an end.

petition n APPEAL, request, entreaty, supplication, plea, prayer, application, suit.
▶ v APPEAL TO, request, ask, apply to, entreat, beg, plead with, make a plea to; *poetic/literary* beseech.

petrify v ❶ TERRIFY, frighten, horrify, fill with fear, panic, alarm, scare someone out of their wits, paralyse, stun, stu-pefy, transfix. ❷ TURN TO STONE, fossilize, calcify, ossify.

petulant adj QUERULOUS, complaining, peevish, fretful, impatient, cross, irritable, moody, crabbed, crabby, crotchety, touchy, bad-tempered, irascible, sulky; *informal* snappish; *Brit. informal* ratty.

phantom n GHOST, apparition, spectre, shade, spirit, revenant, wraith, shadow; *informal* spook; *poetic/literary* phantasm.

phenomenal adj EXTRAORDINARY, remarkable, exceptional, singular, uncommon, unheard of, unique, unparalleled, unprecedented, amazing, astonishing, astounding, unusual, marvellous, prodigious, sensational, miraculous; *informal* mind-blowing.

phenomenon n ❶ FACT, experience, occurrence, happening, event, incident, episode. ❷ MARVEL, prodigy, rarity, wonder, sensation, miracle, nonpareil.

philanthropic adj BENEVOLENT, beneficent, benignant, charitable, almsgiving, generous, kind, munificent, bountiful, liberal, open-handed, giving, helping; *poetic/literary* bounteous.
- OPPOSITES selfish.

philistine adj UNCULTURED, uncultivated, uneducated, unenlightened, unread, ignorant, boorish, barbaric.

philosophical adj
❶ THOUGHTFUL, reflective, pensive, meditative,

contemplative. **2** CALM,
composed, cool, collected,
self-possessed, serene, tranquil,
stoical, impassive, phlegmatic,
unperturbed, imperturbable,
dispassionate, unruffled,
patient, resigned, rational,
logical, realistic, practical.

philosophy n **1** THOUGHT,
thinking, reasoning, logic,
wisdom. **2** BELIEFS, convictions,
ideology, ideas, doctrine,
tenets, values, principles, attitude, view, viewpoint, outlook.

phlegmatic adj CALM, COOL,
composed, collected, serene,
tranquil, placid, impassive,
imperturbable, dispassionate,
philosophical.
– OPPOSITES excitable.

phobia n AVERSION, fear, dread,
horror, terror, dislike, hatred,
loathing, detestation, distaste,
antipathy, revulsion, repulsion;
informal thing, hang-up.

phone v TELEPHONE, call, give
someone a call; Brit. ring, ring
up; informal buzz, get on the
blower to.

phoney adj BOGUS, sham,
counterfeit, imitation, spurious, mock, ersatz, fake, forged,
feigned, simulated, make-believe, false, fraudulent.
– OPPOSITES genuine.

photograph n PHOTO, snap,
snapshot, picture, likeness,
shot, print, slide, transparency.

photographic adj **1** PICTOR-
IAL, in photographs. **2** DETAILED,
graphic, exact, accurate, precise.

phrase n EXPRESSION, idiom,
remark, saying, utterance,
witticism, tag.
▶ v PUT INTO WORDS, put, word,
express, formulate, couch,
frame.

phraseology n PHRASING,
wording, words, choice of
words, language, vocabulary,
terminology.

physical adj MATERIAL, substantial, solid, concrete,
tangible, palpable, visible, real,
bodily, non-mental, corporeal,
corporal.
– OPPOSITES mental, spiritual.

physician n DOCTOR, medical
practitioner, general practitioner, GP, specialist, consultant; informal doc, medic, medico;
Brit. informal quack.

physique n BODY, build,
shape, frame, form, figure.

pick v **1** CHOOSE, select, opt for,
plump for, single out, hand-
pick, decide upon, settle upon,
fix upon, prefer, favour, elect.
2 HARVEST, gather, collect, take
in, pluck, pull, cull.
▶ n **1** CHOICE, selection, option,
preference. **2** BEST, choicest,
prime, cream, flower, prize.
■ **pick on** BULLY, victimize, tyrannize, torment, persecute,
harass, hound, taunt, badger.

pick up IMPROVE, get better,
recover, rally, perk up, be on
the mend, make headway,
make progress, take a turn for
the better.

picture n **1** PAINTING, drawing,
sketch, oil painting, watercol-
our, print, canvas, delineation,
portrait, portrayal, illustration,

likeness, representation, similitude, semblance. ❷ See PHOTOGRAPH.

▶ v ❶ SEE IN ONE'S MIND / MIND'S EYE, imagine, call to mind, visualize, see, evoke. ❷ PAINT, draw, sketch, depict, delineate, portray, illustrate, reproduce, represent.

picturesque adj ❶ BEAUTIFUL, pretty, lovely, attractive, scenic, charming, quaint, pleasing, delightful. ❷ VIVID, graphic, colourful, impressive, striking.
– OPPOSITES ugly.

pie n PASTRY, tart, tartlet, pasty, quiche.

piece n ❶ PART, bit, section, segment, length, quantity, unit, slice, chunk, lump, hunk, wedge, remnant, scrap, snippet. ❷ FRAGMENT, smithereens, shard, shred, tatter. ❸ SHARE, slice, portion, allotment, allocation, quota, percentage, fraction.
■ **piece together** PUT TOGETHER, assemble, join up, fit together, unite.

piecemeal adv PIECE BY PIECE, bit by bit, gradually, in stages, in steps, little by little, by degrees, in fits and starts.

pier n ❶ JETTY, quay, wharf, dock, landing, landing place, promenade. ❷ SUPPORT, upright, pillar, post, column, pile, piling, buttress.

pierce v PENETRATE, puncture, perforate, prick, stab, spike, enter, pass through, transfix, bore, drill.

piercing adj ❶ SHREWD, sharp, keen, searching, alert, penetrating, perceptive, probing. ❷ SHRILL, penetrating, ear-splitting, high-pitched, loud. ❸ SEVERE, sharp, stabbing, shooting, penetrating, intense, fierce, excruciating, agonizing, exquisite.

piety n PIOUSNESS, religiousness, holiness, godliness, devoutness, devotion, veneration, reverence, religious duty, spirituality, sanctity, religious zeal.
– OPPOSITES impiety.

pile n ❶ HEAP, bundle, stack, mound, mass, accumulation, collection, assemblage, store, stockpile, hoard, load, mountain. ❷ GREAT DEAL, a lot, lots, quantity, abundance, mountain; *informal* heap, ocean, stacks, oodles, scuds.
▶ v ❶ HEAP, stack. ❷ ACCUMULATE, amass, collect, gather, stockpile, hoard, store up, assemble, lay by/in. ❸ FORM PILES, form heaps, heap up, amass, accumulate.

pile-up n CRASH, collision, smash, smash-up, accident, road accident.

pill n TABLET, capsule, pellet, lozenge, bolus.

pillage v PLUNDER, rob, raid, loot, maraud, sack, ransack, ravage, lay waste, despoil.
▶ n PLUNDER, robbery, raiding, looting, marauding, sacking, ransacking, ravaging, rapine, despoiling, laying waste, spoliation, depredation.

pillory v STIGMATIZE, cast a slur

on, denounce, hold up to
shame, hold up to ridicule,
ridicule, heap scorn on; *informal*
show up.

pilot n ❶ AIRMAN / AIRWOMAN, avi-
ator, flier, captain, commander, co-pilot. ❷ NAVIGATOR,
guide, steersman, helmsman.
▶ v FLY, drive, operate, navigate,
guide, steer, control, handle,
manoeuvre.

pimple n SPOT, pustule, boil,
swelling, papule; *informal* zit.

pin n ❶ ATTACH, fasten, affix, fix,
stick, tack, nail. ❷ PINION, hold,
press, restrain, constrain, hold
fast, immobilize, pin down.

pinch v ❶ NIP, tweak, squeeze,
compress. ❷ *See* STEAL (1, 2).
❸ *See* ARREST.

pinched adj DRAWN, haggard,
worn, peaky, pale, wan,
strained, stressed, drained.
– OPPOSITES healthy.

pinnacle n PEAK, height, culmination, high point, acme,
zenith, climax, crowning point,
summit, apex, vertex, apogee.
– OPPOSITES nadir.

pinpoint v IDENTIFY, discover,
distinguish, locate, spot, home
in on, put one's finger on.

pioneer n ❶ SETTLER, colonist,
colonizer, explorer. ❷ DEVEL-
OPER, innovator, ground-
breaker, trailblazer, founder,
founding father, architect.
▶ v DEVELOP, introduce, launch,
instigate, initiate, institute, originate, create, open up, blaze a
trail, break new ground.

pious adj ❶ RELIGIOUS, holy,

godly, spiritual, devout, devoted, dedicated, reverent,
God-fearing, righteous, faithful. ❷ SANCTIMONIOUS, hypocritical, self-righteous, unctuous,
pietistic, holier-than-thou,
goody-goody.
– OPPOSITES impious.

pipe n TUBE, cylinder, conduit,
main, duct, channel, pipeline,
drainpipe.
▶ v CONVEY, duct, channel,
transmit, bring in, siphon.

piquant adj ❶ SPICY, flavoursome, peppery, tangy, pungent,
sharp, tart, zesty, biting, stinging. ❷ STIMULATING, intriguing,
interesting, fascinating, alluring, racy, salty, provocative.
– OPPOSITES insipid.

pirate n FREEBOOTER, marauder, raider; *historical* privat-
eer; *archaic* buccaneer, corsair.

pit n ABYSS, chasm, crater, hole,
cavity, excavation, quarry, coal
mine, mine, diggings, working.

pitch v ❶ THROW, cast, fling,
hurl, toss, lob, launch; *informal*
chuck, heave, bung. ❷ PUT UP,
set up, erect, raise. ❸ FALL HEAD-
LONG, fall, tumble, topple,
plunge, dive.
▶ n ❶ FIELD, ground, park,
stadium, arena, playing field.
❷ LEVEL, point, degree, height,
extent, intensity.
■ **pitch in** HELP, assist, lend a
hand, join in, participate, play
a part, do one's bit, cooperate,
collaborate.

piteous adj PITIFUL, pitiable,
pathetic, distressing, affecting,
moving, sad, heart-rending,

heartbreaking, poignant, emotional, emotive.

pitfall n TRAP, snare, catch, stumbling block, hazard, peril, danger, difficulty.

pitiful adj ❶ See PITEOUS. ❷ CONTEMPTIBLE, despicable, poor, sorry, miserable, inadequate, worthless, base, shabby, pathetic.

pitiless adj MERCILESS, ruthless, relentless, cruel, severe, harsh, heartless, callous, brutal, inhuman, inhumane, cold-hearted, hard-hearted, unfeeling, uncaring, unsympathetic.
– OPPOSITES merciful.

pity n ❶ COMMISERATION, condolence, sympathy, compassion, fellow feeling, understanding, forbearance, distress, sadness, emotion, mercy, clemency, kindness. ❷ SHAME, crying shame, misfortune, sad thing, sin.
– OPPOSITES indifference.
▶ v FEEL SORRY FOR, commiserate with, feel sympathy for, sympathize with, feel for.

pivot n AXIS, fulcrum, axle, swivel, spindle, central shaft.

placate v CALM, pacify, soothe, appease, conciliate, propitiate, mollify.

place n ❶ LOCATION, spot, scene, setting, position, site, situation, venue, area, region, whereabouts; technical locus. ❷ POSITION, status, grade, rank, station, standing, footing, role, niche.
▶ v ❶ PUT, position, set/lay down, deposit, rest, settle, sta-

tion, situate. ❷ ORDER, rank, grade, group, arrange, sort, class, classify, categorize, bracket.

placid adj ❶ STILL, calm, peaceful, at peace, pacific, tranquil, motionless, smooth, unruffled, undisturbed. ❷ CALM, cool, composed, self-possessed, serene, tranquil, equable, even-tempered, peaceable, easy-going, unmoved, undisturbed, unperturbed, imperturbable, unexcited, unexcitable, unruffled, unemotional.
– OPPOSITES excitable, bustling.

plagiarize v COPY, pirate, poach, borrow, reproduce, appropriate; informal rip off, crib.

plague n ❶ CONTAGION, disease, pestilence, sickness, epidemic, pandemic. ❷ MULTITUDE, host, swarm, influx, infestation.
▶ v AFFLICT, cause suffering to, torture, torment, bedevil, trouble.

plain adj ❶ CLEAR, crystal-clear, obvious, evident, apparent, manifest, transparent, patent, unmistakable. ❷ CLEAR-CUT, simple, straightforward, uncomplicated, comprehensible, intelligible, understandable, lucid, unambiguous. ❸ SIMPLE, austere, stark, severe, basic, ordinary, unsophisticated, spartan. ❹ UNATTRACTIVE, ugly, unprepossessing, unlovely, homely.
– OPPOSITES obscure, fancy, attractive.

plaintive adj MOURNFUL, doleful, melancholy, sad, sorrowful, unhappy, disconsolate.

plan n ❶ PLAN OF ACTION, scheme, system, procedure, method, programme, schedule, project, way, means, strategy, tactics, formula. ❷ SCALE DRAWING, blueprint, layout, sketch, diagram, chart, map, illustration, representation, delineation.
▶ v ❶ ARRANGE, organize, line up, schedule, programme. ❷ MAKE PLANS, intend, aim, propose, mean, purpose, contemplate, envisage, foresee.

plane adj FLAT, level, horizontal, even, flush, smooth, regular, uniform.

plant n ❶ FLOWER, vegetable, herb, shrub, weed. ❷ MACHINERY, equipment, apparatus; informal gear. ❸ FACTORY, works, foundry, mill, workshop, shop, yard.
▶ v ❶ IMPLANT, set out, sow, scatter. ❷ PLACE, position, set, situate.

plaster v COVER THICKLY, spread, coat, smear, overlay, bedaub.

plastic adj ❶ MOULDABLE, malleable, workable, ductile, pliant, pliable, supple, flexible, soft. ❷ FALSE, artificial, synthetic, spurious, sham, bogus; informal phoney.

plate n ❶ DISH, platter, dinner plate, side plate. ❷ PLAQUE,

tablet, sign; Brit. brass. ❸ ILLUSTRATION, picture, photograph, print, lithograph. ❹ SHEET, panel, slab.

platform n ❶ DAIS, rostrum, podium, stage, stand. ❷ PROGRAMME, policy, manifesto, plan, objectives, principles, tenets.

platitude n TRUISM, hackneyed expression, commonplace, stock expression, trite phrase, banality, bromide, inanity.

platter n SERVING PLATE, salver, plate, dish, tray.

plausible adj BELIEVABLE, credible, convincing, persuasive, likely, probable, conceivable, imaginable, tenable, cogent, reasonable.
– OPPOSITES implausible.

play v ❶ AMUSE ONESELF, entertain oneself, enjoy oneself, have fun, play games, frolic, frisk, gambol, romp, cavort. ❷ PLAY THE PART OF, act, act the part of, perform, portray, represent, execute. ❸ PERFORM, carry out, execute, do, accomplish. ❹ TAKE PART IN, participate in, engage in, be involved in. ❺ COMPETE AGAINST, contend against, oppose, take on, challenge, vie with, rival.
▶ n ❶ AMUSEMENT, entertainment, recreation, diversion, leisure, enjoyment, fun, merrymaking, revelry. ❷ MOVEMENT, freedom of movement, free motion, slack, give.
■ **play at** PRETEND TO BE, give the appearance of, assume/affect

the role of; *informal* make like.

play down MAKE LIGHT OF, make little of, gloss over, minimize, diminish, set little store by, underrate, underestimate, undervalue, think little of; *informal* soft-pedal.

player n ❶ COMPETITOR, contestant, participant, team member, sportsman/sportswoman. ❷ ACTOR / ACTRESS, performer, entertainer, artist, artiste, trouper, Thespian. ❸ PERFORMER, musician, instrumentalist, artist, artiste, virtuoso.

playful adj ❶ FUN-LOVING, full of fun, high-spirited, frisky, skittish, coltish, sportive, mischievous, impish, puckish; *poetic/literary* frolicsome. ❷ IN FUN, joking, jesting, humorous, facetious, waggish, tongue-in-cheek, arch, roguish.
– OPPOSITES serious.

plea n ❶ APPEAL, entreaty, supplication, petition, prayer, request, solicitation, suit, invocation. ❷ EXCUSE, pretext, claim, vindication.

plead v ❶ APPEAL TO, beg, entreat, implore, petition, supplicate, importune, pray to, solicit, request, ask earnestly; *poetic/literary* beseech. ❷ PUT FORWARD, state, assert, argue, claim, allege.

pleasant adj ❶ PLEASING, pleasurable, agreeable, enjoyable, entertaining, amusing, delightful, satisfying, gratifying, nice, good, fine. ❷ AGREEABLE, friendly, amiable, affable, genial, likeable, nice, good-humoured, charming, engaging, winning, delightful.
– OPPOSITES unpleasant.

please v ❶ GIVE PLEASURE TO, be agreeable to, make pleased/happy/glad etc., gladden, delight, cheer up, charm, divert, entertain, amuse. ❷ WANT, wish, see fit, will, like, desire, be inclined, prefer.
– OPPOSITES displease.

pleased adj HAPPY, glad, cheerful, delighted, thrilled, elated, contented, satisfied, gratified, fulfilled; *informal* over the moon; *Brit. informal* chuffed.

pleasure n ❶ HAPPINESS, gladness, delight, joy, enjoyment, entertainment, amusement, diversion, satisfaction, gratification, fulfilment, contentment.

pledge n ❶ PROMISE, word, word of honour, vow, assurance, undertaking, oath, covenant, warrant. ❷ SECURITY, surety, guarantee, collateral.
▶ v ❶ PROMISE, give one's word, vow, give an undertaking, undertake, take an oath, swear, vouch, engage, contract. ❷ MORTGAGE, put up as collateral, guarantee, plight, pawn.

plentiful adj ABUNDANT, copious, ample, profuse, lavish, liberal, generous, large, huge, bumper, infinite.
– OPPOSITES scanty.

plenty n PLENTIFULNESS, affluence, prosperity, wealth, opulence, luxury, abundance, copiousness, fruitfulness, profusion; *poetic/literary* plenteousness.

■ **plenty of** ENOUGH, sufficient, a good deal of, a great deal of, masses of; *informal* lots of, heaps of, stacks of, piles of.

plethora n OVER-ABUNDANCE, superabundance, excess, superfluity, surplus, surfeit, glut.
– OPPOSITES dearth.

pliable adj ❶ FLEXIBLE, bendable, bendy, pliant, elastic, supple, stretchable, ductile, plastic. ❷ MALLEABLE, compliant, docile, biddable, tractable, manageable, governable, controllable, amenable.
– OPPOSITES rigid, obdurate.

plot n ❶ PIECE OF GROUND, parcel, patch; *Brit.* allotment; *N. Amer.* lot. ❷ CONSPIRACY, intrigue, stratagem. ❸ ACTION, theme, subject, story line, story, scenario, thread.
▶ v ❶ MAP OUT, draw, draw a diagram of, draw the layout of, make a blueprint/chart of, sketch out, outline. ❷ TAKE PART IN A PLOT, scheme, conspire, participate in a conspiracy, intrigue, form an intrigue.

plough v TILL, work, cultivate, break up, turn up.

ploy n DODGE, ruse, scheme, trick, stratagem, manoeuvre, move.

plummet v FALL, fall headlong, plunge, hurtle, nosedive, dive, drop.

plump adj CHUBBY, well rounded, of ample proportions, rotund, buxom, stout, fat, obese, corpulent, fleshy, portly, tubby, dumpy, roly-poly, well covered; *Brit. informal* podgy.
– OPPOSITES slim, skinny.

plunder v ROB, pillage, loot, raid, ransack, strip, fleece, lay waste, despoil, maraud, sack, rape.
▶ n LOOT, booty, spoils, prize, pillage, ill-gotten gains; *informal* swag.

plunge v ❶ THRUST, stick, jab, push, drive. ❷ DIVE, dip, swoop, jump, plummet, drop, fall, descend.

plush adj LUXURIOUS, luxury, sumptuous, lavish, gorgeous, opulent, rich, costly; *informal* ritzy, classy.
– OPPOSITES plain.

pocket n POUCH, compartment, receptacle.
▶ adj SMALL, little, miniature, compact, concise, abridged, potted.
▶ v MISAPPROPRIATE, steal, thieve, purloin; *informal* lift, filch, swipe, snaffle; *Brit. informal* pinch, nick.

poet n VERSIFIER, rhymester, sonneteer, balladeer, lyricist, bard, minstrel.

poetic adj IMAGINATIVE, creative, figurative, symbolic, flowery.

poignant adj MOVING, affecting, touching, tender, emotional, sentimental, heartfelt, sad, sorrowful, tearful, evocative.

point n ❶ TIP, top, extremity, prong, spike, tine. ❷ PROMONTORY, headland, head, foreland, cape, bluff. ❸ PLACE, position, location, situation, site, spot, area, locality. ❹ TIME, juncture,

stage, period, moment, instant. **⑤** MAIN POINT, central point, essential point, focal point, salient point, keynote, heart of the matter, essence, nub, core, pith, marrow, meat, crux. **⑥** MEANING, significance, signification, import, essence, gist, substance, drift, thrust, burden, theme, tenor, vein. **⑦** AIM, purpose, object, objective, goal, intention, reason for, use, utility. **⑧** CHARACTERISTIC, trait, attribute, quality, feature, property, predisposition, streak, peculiarity, idiosyncrasy.
▶ V DIRECT, aim, level, train.
■ point out CALL ATTENTION TO, draw attention to, indicate, show, specify, designate, identify, mention, allude to.

pointed adj **①** SHARP, sharp-edged, edged; formal cuspidate, acicular. **②** CUTTING, trenchant, biting, incisive, penetrating, forceful, telling, significant.

pointless adj FUTILE, useless, in vain, unavailing, to no purpose, valueless, unproductive, senseless, absurd, foolish, nonsensical, stupid, silly.
– OPPOSITES useful.

poise n COMPOSURE, equanimity, self-possession, aplomb, self-assurance, calmness, coolness, serenity, dignity, imperturbability, suaveness, urbanity; informal cool.
▶ V BALANCE, steady, position, support.

poised adj **①** COMPOSED, serene, self-possessed, self-as-sured, calm, cool, imperturbable, unruffled, unflappable. **②** READY, prepared, all set, standing by, waiting.
– OPPOSITES flustered.

poison n **①** VENOM, toxin. **②** BLIGHT, contagion, cancer, canker, malignancy, corruption, pollution.
▶ V **①** CONTAMINATE, pollute, blight, spoil. **②** CORRUPT, warp, pervert, deprave, defile, debauch.

poisonous adj VENOMOUS, deadly, fatal, lethal, noxious.
– OPPOSITES non-toxic.

poke V JAB, prod, dig, elbow, nudge, push, thrust, shove, stick.

poky adj CONFINED, cramped, narrow, cell-like, small, little, tiny.
– OPPOSITES spacious.

pole n POST, upright, pillar, stanchion, standard, support, prop, rod, shaft, mast.

police n POLICE FORCE, police officers; Brit. constabulary; informal the cops, the fuzz, the law, the boys in blue; Brit. informal the (Old) Bill, the rozzers, the force, the pigs, the filth.
▶ V GUARD, keep guard over, keep watch on, protect, keep in order, control, keep under control, regulate.

police officer n POLICEMAN, POLICEWOMAN; Brit. constable, PC, WPC; N. Amer. patrolman, trooper; informal cop; Brit. informal bobby, copper, rozzer.

policy n PLAN, scheme, programme, schedule, code,

system, approach, procedure, guideline, theory.

polish v ❶ WAX, buff, rub up, burnish, shine. ❷ PERFECT, refine, improve, brush up, touch up, finish off.

polished adj ❶ WAXED, buffed, burnished, shining, shiny, glossy, gleaming, lustrous, glassy, slippery. ❷ REFINED, cultivated, civilized, well bred, polite, well mannered, genteel, courtly, urbane, suave, sophisticated. ❸ EXPERT, accomplished, masterly, skilful, proficient, adept, impeccable, flawless, faultless, perfect, consummate, outstanding, remarkable.
– OPPOSITES dull, gauche, inexpert.

polite adj ❶ WELL MANNERED, mannerly, courteous, civil, respectful, deferential, well behaved, well bred, genteel, polished, tactful, diplomatic. ❷ WELL BRED, civilized, cultured, refined, polished, genteel, urbane, sophisticated, elegant, courtly.
– OPPOSITES rude.

politic adj WISE, prudent, sensible, advisable, judicious, well judged, sagacious, expedient, shrewd, astute, discreet, tactful, diplomatic.
– OPPOSITES unwise.

political adj ❶ GOVERNMENTAL, ministerial, public, civic, administrative, bureaucratic. ❷ FACTIONAL, partisan, bipartisan, power, status.

poll n ❶ VOTE, ballot, canvass,

headcount. ❷ RETURNS, count, tally.
▶ v ❶ REGISTER, record, return, get, gain. ❷ BALLOT, canvass, question, interview, survey, sample.

pollute v CONTAMINATE, adulterate, infect, taint, poison, befoul, foul.
– OPPOSITES purify.

pomp n CEREMONY, ritual, display, pageantry, show, spectacle, splendour, grandeur, magnificence, majesty.

pompous adj SELF-IMPORTANT, presumptuous, imperious, overbearing, grandiose, affected, pretentious, arrogant, vain, haughty, proud, conceited, egotistic, supercilious, condescending, patronizing; informal uppity, uppish.
– OPPOSITES humble.

ponder v THINK ABOUT, give thought to, consider, reflect on, mull over, contemplate, meditate on, deliberate about/on, dwell on, brood on/over, ruminate about/on/over, puzzle over, cogitate about/on, weigh up, review.

pontificate v HOLD FORTH, expound, declaim, preach, lay down the law, sound off, dogmatize, sermonize; informal preachify.

poor adj ❶ PENNILESS, hard up, badly off, poverty-stricken, needy, deprived, in need, needful, in want, indigent, impoverished, impecunious, destitute, penurious, beggared, in straitened circumstances, in

the red, on one's beam-ends; *informal* broke, flat broke, on one's uppers; *Brit. informal* skint, stony broke. ❷ INFERIOR, unsatisfactory, below standard, below par, imperfect, bad, low-grade, inadequate, deficient, insufficient, sparse, scanty, meagre, scarce, skimpy, paltry, miserable. ❸ UNFORTUNATE, wretched, pitiable, pitiful, unlucky, luckless, unhappy, hapless, ill-fated, ill-starred.
– OPPOSITES rich.

populace n THE GENERAL PUBLIC, the public, the people, the population, the common people, the masses.

popular adj ❶ WELL LIKED, liked, favoured, in favour, favourite, well received, approved, admired, accepted. ❷ PUBLIC, general, civic. ❸ CURRENT, prevalent, prevailing, accepted, recognized, widespread, universal, general, common, customary, usual, standard, stock, conventional.
– OPPOSITES unpopular.

popularity n ❶ FAVOUR, approval, approbation, admiration, acceptance. ❷ DEMAND, fashionableness, vogue.

populate v ❶ INHABIT, dwell in, occupy, people. ❷ SETTLE, colonize, people.

population n INHABITANTS, residents, community, people, citizenry, populace, society.

populous adj DENSELY POPULATED, heavily populated, thickly populated, overpopulated, crowded.
– OPPOSITES deserted.

pore n OPENING, orifice, hole, outlet.

pornographic adj OBSCENE, indecent, erotic, dirty, smutty, filthy, salacious, lewd, prurient; *informal* porno, blue.

porous adj ABSORBENT, permeable, penetrable, pervious, spongy, sponge-like.
– OPPOSITES impermeable.

port n HARBOUR, harbourage, haven, anchorage, dock, mooring, marina.

portable adj TRANSPORTABLE, movable, conveyable, easily carried, lightweight, compact, handy, manageable.

portend v BE A SIGN OF, be a warning of, point to, be an omen of, herald, bode, augur, presage, forebode, foreshadow, foretell.

portion n ❶ HELPING, serving, piece, quantity. ❷ SHARE, division, quota, part, bit, allocation, allotment, piece; *informal* cut; *Brit. informal* whack.

portly adj STOUT, plump, fat, corpulent, obese, tubby, stocky.
– OPPOSITES slim.

portrait n PORTRAYAL, representation, likeness, image, study, depiction.

portray v ❶ PAINT, draw a picture of, draw, sketch, depict, represent, delineate. ❷ DESCRIBE, depict, characterize, put into words.

pose v ❶ SIT, model, take up a position. ❷ ARRANGE, position, lay out, set out, dispose, place, put, locate, situate. ❸ STRIKE AN ATTITUDE, posture, put on an act, play-act, attitudinize, put on airs, show off. ❹ PRESENT, set, create, cause, give rise to.
▸ n ❶ POSTURE, stance, position, attitude. ❷ ACT, pretence, facade, front, masquerade, attitudinizing, affectation, airs.

poser[1] n VEXED QUESTION, enigma, dilemma, puzzle, mystery, conundrum.

poser[2] n POSEUR, attitudinizer, posturer, play-actor, impostor, exhibitionist, show-off; informal phoney.

posh adj ❶ LUXURIOUS, luxury, sumptuous, opulent, lavish, rich, fancy; informal plushy, ritzy, swanky. ❷ UPPER-CLASS, aristocratic, upmarket, fancy; informal upper-crust.

position n ❶ SITUATION, location, site, place, spot, area, locality, locale, scene, setting. ❷ POSTURE, stance, attitude, pose, bearing. ❸ STATE, condition, situation, circumstance, predicament, plight, pass. ❹ POINT OF VIEW, viewpoint, opinion, way of thinking, outlook, attitude, stand, standpoint, stance. ❺ POST, job, situation, appointment, role, office, place, capacity, duty. ❻ PLACE, level, grade, grading, rank, status, standing.
▸ v PLACE, locate, situate, put, arrange, set, settle, dispose, array.

positive adj ❶ CONFIDENT, optimistic, assured, assertive, firm, forceful, determined, resolute, emphatic, dogmatic. ❷ GOOD, favourable, effective, promising, encouraging, heartening. ❸ CONSTRUCTIVE, productive, helpful, practical, useful, beneficial.
– OPPOSITES negative.

possess v ❶ OWN, be the owner of, have, be the possessor of, count among one's possessions, have to one's name, hold, be blessed with, enjoy, be endowed with, be gifted with. ❷ INFLUENCE, control, dominate, have mastery over, bewitch, enchant, put under a spell, obsess.

possessions pl n BELONGINGS, things, property, assets, luggage, baggage, personal effects, goods and chattels, accoutrements, paraphernalia, appendages, impedimenta.

possessive adj ❶ ACQUISITIVE, greedy, grasping, covetous, selfish. ❷ OVERPROTECTIVE, clinging, controlling, dominating, jealous.

possibility n FEASIBILITY, practicability, attainability, likelihood, potentiality, conceivability, probability.

possible adj ❶ FEASIBLE, able to be done, practicable, doable, attainable, achievable, realizable, within reach; informal on. ❷ LIKELY, potential, conceivable, imaginable, probable, credible, tenable.
– OPPOSITES impossible.

possibly adv ❶ PERHAPS,

maybe, for all one knows, very likely. ❷ CONCEIVABLY, by any means, by any chance, at all.

post n STAKE, upright, pole, shaft, prop, support, column, stanchion, standard, stock, picket, pillar, palisade, baluster, newel.

▶ v PUT UP, stick, stick up, pin, pin up, tack, tack up, attach, affix, hang, display. ❷ ANNOUNCE, make known, advertise, publish, publicize, circulate, broadcast.

poster n PLACARD, bill, notice, public notice, sticker, advertisement, announcement, bulletin; Brit. informal advert.

postpone v DEFER, put off, put back, delay, hold over, adjourn, shelve, table, pigeonhole; informal put on ice, put on the back burner.
– OPPOSITES advance.

postscript n PS, subscript, afterthought, afterword, addendum, appendix, codicil, supplement.

posture n ❶ POSITION, pose, attitude, carriage, bearing, stance. ❷ ATTITUDE, position, point of view, viewpoint, opinion, outlook, stand, standpoint, stance, angle, slant.
▶ v POSE, strike an attitude, put on an act, act, play-act, attitudinize, show off.

potent adj POWERFUL, forceful, strong, vigorous, mighty, influential, authoritative, commanding, compelling, dominant, energetic, dynamic, convincing, cogent, effective,

persuasive, eloquent; poetic/literary puissant.
– OPPOSITES impotent.

potential adj ❶ BUDDING, embryonic, developing, promising, prospective, likely, possible, probable. ❷ LIKELY, possible, probable.
▶ n PROMISE, possibilities, capability, capacity, ability, aptitude.

potion n DRINK, beverage, brew, concoction, mixture, draught, elixir, philtre.

potter v DAWDLE, loiter, dally, dilly-dally; informal mess about/around.

pouch n BAG, purse, wallet, container.

pounce v SWOOP ON, spring on, lunge at, leap at, jump at/on, ambush, take by surprise, take unawares, attack suddenly.

pound¹ v ❶ CRUSH, beat, pulverize, powder, smash, mash, grind; technical comminute, triturate. ❷ BEAT, pulsate, pulse, throb, thump, pump, palpitate.

pound² n COMPOUND, enclosure, pen, yard.

pour v ❶ GUSH, rush, stream, flow, course, spout, jet, spurt. ❷ LET FLOW, decant, splash, spill.

poverty n ❶ PENNILESSNESS, neediness, need, want, hardship, deprivation, indigence, impoverishment, impecuniousness, destitution, penury, privation, beggary.

❷ DEFICIENCY, dearth, shortage, scarcity, paucity, insufficiency, lack, want, meagreness.
– OPPOSITES wealth.

powder v **❶** DUST, sprinkle, scatter, strew. **❷** See POUND¹ (1).

powdery adj POWDER-LIKE, fine, dusty, chalky, floury, friable, granulated, ground, crushed, pulverized.

power n **❶** ABILITY, capability, capacity, faculty, potential, potentiality. **❷** STRENGTH, force, might, weight. **❸** CONTROL, authority, mastery, domination, dominance, rule, command, ascendancy, supremacy, dominion, sway.

powerful adj **❶** STRONG, sturdy, strapping, stout, robust, vigorous, tough. **❷** INFLUENTIAL, dominant, authoritative, commanding, forceful, strong, vigorous, potent. **❸** FORCEFUL, strong, effective, cogent, compelling, convincing, persuasive, eloquent, impressive.
– OPPOSITES weak.

powerless adj WEAK, feeble, impotent, helpless, unfit, ineffectual, inadequate, paralysed, disabled, incapacitated, debilitated.
– OPPOSITES powerful, strong.

practicable adj FEASIBLE, possible, viable, workable, doable, achievable, attainable, accomplishable.
– OPPOSITES theoretical.

practical adj **❶** APPLIED, empirical, pragmatic, workaday, hands-on. **❷** FUNCTIONAL, useful, utilitarian, sensible. **❸** BUSI-

nesslike, sensible, down-to-earth, pragmatic, realistic, hard-headed; informal hard-nosed.
– OPPOSITES impractical.

practically adv ALMOST, nearly, virtually, all but, in effect; informal pretty nearly/well.

practice n **❶** ACTION, operation, application, effect, exercise, use. **❷** TRAINING, preparation, study, exercise, drill, workout, rehearsal. **❸** PROCEDURE, method, system, usage, tradition, convention.

practise v **❶** PERFORM, carry out, do, execute, follow, pursue, observe. **❷** REHEARSE, go through, run through, go over, work at, polish, refine. **❸** WORK IN, have a career in, pursue a career in, engage in.

praise v **❶** EXPRESS ADMIRATION FOR, applaud, acclaim, express approval of, cheer, compliment, congratulate, commend, pay tribute to, extol, sing the praises of, eulogize; formal laud. **❷** WORSHIP, glorify, honour, exalt, adore, pay tribute to, give thanks to; formal laud.
– OPPOSITES condemn.
▶ n **❶** APPROBATION, applause, acclaim, approval, acclamation, compliments, congratulations, commendation, tributes, accolades, plaudits, eulogy, panegyric, encomium, extolment; formal laudation. **❷** WORSHIP, glory, honour, devotion, exaltation, adoration.

praiseworthy adj COMMEND-ABLE, laudable, admirable, estimable, creditable, deserving, meritorious, worthy, excellent, exemplary, sterling, fine.

prance v ❶ LEAP, spring, jump, skip, cavort, caper, frisk, gambol. ❷ PARADE, cavort, strut, swagger; *informal* swank.

prank n TRICK, practical joke, joke, hoax, caper, stunt; *informal* lark.

pray v ❶ OFFER PRAYERS TO, say prayers to. ❷ APPEAL FOR, beg for, petition for, solicit, plead for.

prayer n DEVOTION, communion, litany, collect.

preach v ❶ GIVE / DELIVER A SERMON, sermonize, spread the gospel, evangelize.
■ **preach at** LECTURE, moralize at, admonish, harangue, sermonize.

preacher n MINISTER, parson, clergyman, churchman, cleric, missionary, revivalist, evangelist, televangelist.

precarious adj RISKY, hazardous, insecure, unstable, shaky, tricky, perilous, dangerous, touch-and-go; *informal* dicey, hairy.
– OPPOSITES safe.

precaution n ❶ PREVENTIVE MEASURE, preventative measure, safety measure, safeguard, provision. ❷ FORESIGHT, foresightedness, forethought, farsightedness, anticipation, prudence, circumspection, caution, care, attentiveness, chariness, wariness.

precede v ❶ GO BEFORE, come before, go/come ahead of, lead, usher in. ❷ LEAD TO, lead up to, antedate, antecede, usher in, herald, pave the way for.
– OPPOSITES follow.

precedence n RANK, seniority, superiority, pre-eminence, eminence, supremacy, primacy, ascendancy.

precedent n PREVIOUS CASE, prior case, previous instance, prior instance, pattern, model, example, exemplar, paradigm, criterion, yardstick, standard.

precious adj ❶ VALUABLE, costly, expensive, dear, priceless, rare, choice. ❷ VALUED, cherished, prized, treasured, favourite, dear, beloved, adored, revered, venerated.

precipitate v HASTEN, accelerate, expedite, speed up, push forward, bring on, trigger.
▶ adj HURRIED, rapid, swift, speedy, headlong, abrupt, sudden, unexpected, breakneck, precipitous.

precipitous adj ❶ STEEP, sheer, perpendicular, abrupt, high. ❷ See PRECIPITATE adj.

precise adj ❶ EXACT, literal, actual, close, faithful, strict, express, minute, accurate, correct. ❷ EXACT, very, actual, particular, specific, distinct.
– OPPOSITES imprecise.

preclude v PREVENT, prohibit, make impossible, rule out, eliminate, debar, interdict, block, bar, hinder, impede.

precocious adj ADVANCED, ahead, forward, gifted, brilliant, quick, smart.
– OPPOSITES backward.

preconception n PRECONCEIVED IDEA, assumption, presupposition, presumption, prejudgement, prejudice, bias.

predatory adj ❶ HUNTING, predacious, rapacious, raptorial. ❷ EXPLOITATIVE, greedy, acquisitive, rapacious, vulturine.

predecessor n PRECURSOR, forerunner, antecedent, ancestor, forefather, forebear, progenitor.
– OPPOSITES successor.

predestine v FATE, predetermine, destine, foreordain, predestinate.

predicament n DIFFICULT SITUATION, plight, tight corner, mess, emergency, crisis, dilemma, quandary, trouble; *informal* jam, hole, fix, pickle, scrape, tight spot.

predict v FORECAST, foretell, prophesy, foresee, divine, prognosticate, forewarn, forebode, portend, presage, augur.

predictable adj FORESEEABLE, expected, anticipated, probable, likely, certain, sure; *informal* on the cards.

predilection n LIKING, fondness, preference, love, partiality, taste, weakness, penchant, fancy, inclination, leaning.
– OPPOSITES dislike.

predominate v BE DOMINANT, be in control, rule, hold ascendancy, hold sway, have the upper hand, carry most weight.

pre-eminent adj OUTSTANDING, leading, foremost, chief, excellent, distinguished, prominent, eminent, important, superior, unrivalled, unsurpassed.
– OPPOSITES undistinguished.

preface n INTRODUCTION, foreword, preamble, prologue, prelude, front matter, proem, exordium, prolegomenon; *informal* prelims, intro.
▶ v PRECEDE, prefix, introduce, begin, open, launch.

prefer v LIKE BETTER, favour, fancy, be more partial to, incline towards, choose, select, pick, opt for, go for, plump for, single out.

preferable adj BETTER, superior, more desirable, more suitable.

preference n ❶ CHOICE, first choice, first option, liking, fancy, desire, wish, inclination, partiality, predilection, leaning, bias, bent. ❷ PREFERENTIAL TREATMENT, favour, precedence, priority, advantage.

preferential adj SPECIAL, better, advantageous, favoured, privileged, partial, partisan.

pregnant adj ❶ HAVING A BABY / CHILD, expectant, expecting, in the family way, with child, enceinte; *informal* preggers, with a bun in the oven; *Brit. informal* in the club; *technical* gravid.
❷ MEANINGFUL, significant, eloquent, expressive, suggestive, pointed, telling.

prejudice n BIAS, discrimination, partisanship, partiality, preference, one-sidedness, chauvinism, bigotry, narrow-mindedness, intolerance, unfairness, unjustness, racism, sexism, ageism, heterosexism.
▶ v BE PREJUDICIAL TO, be disadvantageous to, damage, injure, harm, hurt, mar, spoil, impair, undermine.

prejudiced adj BIASED, discriminatory, partisan, partial, one-sided, jaundiced, chauvinistic, bigoted, intolerant, narrow-minded, unfair, unjust, racist, sexist, ageist.
– OPPOSITES impartial.

prejudicial adj DETRIMENTAL, deleterious, unfavourable, damaging, injurious, harmful, hurtful, inimical.
– OPPOSITES beneficial.

preliminary adj INTRODUCTORY, prefatory, prior, precursory, opening, initial, beginning, preparatory, initiatory.
– OPPOSITES final.

prelude n ❶ PRECURSOR, forerunner, curtain-raiser, harbinger, herald, preliminary, introduction, start, beginning. ❷ INTRODUCTION, preface, prologue, preamble, proem, exordium, prolegomenon; informal intro.

premature adj TOO SOON, too early, early, untimely, overhasty, precipitate, impulsive, impetuous, rash.
– OPPOSITES overdue.

premeditated adj PLANNED, pre-planned, pre-arranged, intentional, intended, deliberate, calculated, wilful.
– OPPOSITES spontaneous.

premier n HEAD OF GOVERNMENT, president, prime minister, PM.
▶ adj LEADING, foremost, chief, principal, head, top, first, highest, main.

premonition n FOREBODING, presentiment, intuition, feeling, hunch, suspicion, sneaking suspicion, misgiving, apprehension, fear, feeling in one's bones, funny feeling.

preoccupied adj LOST IN THOUGHT, deep in thought, in a brown study, absorbed, engrossed, pensive, absent-minded, distracted, abstracted, distrait, oblivious, faraway, rapt.

preparation n ❶ ARRANGEMENT, provision, preparatory measure, necessary step, groundwork, spadework. ❷ COACHING, training, grooming, priming. ❸ MIXTURE, compound, concoction, composition, tincture.

prepare v ❶ GET READY, make ready, arrange, develop, put together, assemble, draw up, produce, construct, compose, concoct, fashion, work up. ❷ REVISE, study, cram, do homework; Brit. informal swot. ❸ COACH, train, groom, prime.

preposterous adj ABSURD, ridiculous, foolish, ludicrous, farcical, asinine, senseless, unreasonable, crazy, insane, outrageous, unbelievable, incredible, unthinkable.
– OPPOSITES sensible.

prerequisite adj NECESSARY, needed, required, called for, essential, requisite, vital, indispensable, imperative, obligatory, mandatory.
– OPPOSITES unnecessary.
▶ n REQUIREMENT, necessity, essential, requisite, precondition, condition, sine qua non; *informal* must.

prescribe v ❶ ADVISE, recommend, commend, suggest. ❷ LAY DOWN, require, stipulate, specify, decree, order, command, ordain, enjoin.

presence n ❶ EXISTENCE, being. ❷ COMPANY, proximity, neighbourhood, vicinity, closeness, nearness. ❸ MAGNETISM, aura, charisma, personality, attraction, poise.
– OPPOSITES absence.

present[1] adj ❶ EXISTING, existent, extant. ❷ PRESENT-DAY, existing, current, contemporary. ❸ IN ATTENDANCE, near, nearby, available, at hand, ready.
– OPPOSITES absent.
▶ n TODAY, now, here and now, the present moment, the time being.

present[2] v ❶ GIVE, hand over, confer, bestow, donate, award, grant, accord. ❷ INTRODUCE, make known, announce. ❸ PUT ON, produce, perform, stage, mount.

present[3] n GIFT, donation, offering, contribution, gratuity, handout, presentation, award, bounty, benefaction; *informal* freebie; *Brit. informal* pressie.

presentable adj WELL GROOMED, smartly dressed, tidily dressed, tidy, spruce, of smart appearance, fit to be seen.

preserve v CONSERVE, protect, care for, safeguard, guard, defend, shield, save, keep, maintain, perpetuate, uphold.
– OPPOSITES neglect.

preside v BE IN CHARGE OF, control, direct, run, conduct, supervise, govern, rule.

press v ❶ DEPRESS, push down, force down, bear down on. ❷ CRUSH, squeeze, compress, mash, reduce. ❸ SMOOTH OUT, flatten, iron. ❹ URGE, entreat, exhort, implore, put pressure on, pressurize, force, compel, coerce.
▶ n NEWSPAPERS, the media, journalists, reporters; *Brit.* Fleet Street.

pressing adj see URGENT (1).

pressure n ❶ FORCE, weight, heaviness, compression. ❷ COERCION, compulsion, force, constraint, duress. ❸ STRAIN, stress, tension, burden, load, weight, trouble; *informal* hassle.
▶ v PUT PRESSURE ON, pressurize, press, force, compel, coerce, constrain, bulldoze, dragoon.

prestige n STATUS, kudos, standing, stature, importance, reputation, fame, renown, esteem, influence, authority, supremacy, eminence, superiority, predominance.

prestigious adj IMPORTANT, prominent, impressive, high-ranking, reputable, respected, esteemed, eminent, distinguished, of high standing, well known, celebrated, illustrious, renowned, famous.

presume v ❶ ASSUME, take for granted, take it, take as read, suppose, presuppose, believe, think, imagine, judge, guess, surmise, conjecture, hypothesize, infer, deduce. ❷ HAVE THE TEMERITY, have the audacity, be so bold as, have the effrontery, go so far as, dare, venture.

presumptuous adj OVER-CONFIDENT, cocksure, arrogant, egotistical, conceited, bold, audacious, forward, pushy, insolent, impudent, bumptious; *informal* too big for one's boots.

pretence n ❶ FALSE SHOW, show, semblance, appearance, false front, guise, facade, masquerade, mask, veneer, cover, charade. ❷ PRETEXT, false excuse, guise, sham, ruse, wile, trickery, lie, falsehood. ❸ PRETENTIOUSNESS, display, ostentation, affectation, showiness, flaunting, posturing.

pretend v ❶ PUT ON AN ACT, act, play-act, put it on, dissemble, sham, feign, fake, dissimulate, make believe, put on a false front, posture, go through the motions. ❷ CLAIM, make believe, purport, affect, profess, make out, fabricate.

pretender n CLAIMANT, claimer, aspirant.

pretentious adj AFFECTED, ostentatious, showy, pompous, artificial, mannered, high-flown, high-sounding, flowery, grandiose, elaborate, extrava-gant, flamboyant, grandiloquent, bombastic, orotund; *informal* highfalutin.
– OPPOSITES plain, simple.

pretty adj LOVELY, attractive, good-looking, nice-looking, personable, prepossessing, appealing, charming, delightful, nice, engaging, pleasing, winning, winsome, as pretty as a picture; *Scottish & N. English* bonny; *N. Amer. informal* cute; *archaic* fair, comely.
– OPPOSITES ugly.
▶ adv QUITE, rather, fairly, somewhat, moderately, reasonably; *informal* kind of.

prevail v WIN, triumph, be victorious, carry the day, conquer, overcome, gain mastery.

prevalent adj ❶ PREVAILING, current, frequent, usual, common, general, widespread, pervasive, universal, set, established, accepted, popular, fashionable, in fashion, in style, in vogue. ❷ WIDESPREAD, extensive, frequent, usual, endemic, universal, ubiquitous, rampant, rife.
– OPPOSITES uncommon.

prevaricate v BE EVASIVE, shilly-shally, dodge the issue, hedge, beat about the bush, equivocate, quibble; *Brit.* hum and haw.

prevent v PUT A STOP TO, halt, arrest, avert, nip in the bud, fend off, turn aside, stave off, ward off, block, check, hinder, impede, hamper, obstruct, baulk, foil, thwart, frustrate, forestall, inhibit,

hold back, restrain, prohibit, bar, deter.
– OPPOSITES encourage.

preventative, preventive adj PRECAUTION-ARY, protective, deterrent, prophylactic.

previous adj ❶ FORMER, ex-, past, sometime, one-time, erst-while; *formal* quondam. ❷ PRE-CEDING, foregoing, earlier, prior, above, precursory, antecedent, anterior.
– OPPOSITES following.

previously adv FORMERLY, earlier on, before, until now, hitherto, heretofore, once, at one time, in the past, in years gone by.

price n ❶ COST, asking price, charge, fee, payment, rate, amount, figure, value, valu-ation, bill. ❷ RESULT, cost, pen-alty, sacrifice, forfeit, forfeiture, punishment.
▶ FIX / SET THE PRICE OF, cost, value, rate, evaluate, assess, es-timate, appraise, assay.

priceless adj ❶ INVALUABLE, precious, rare, incomparable, expensive, costly, rich, dear, ir-replaceable, treasured, prized. ❷ See HILARIOUS.
– OPPOSITES worthless.

prick v PIERCE, puncture, per-forate, stab, nick, gash, slit, bore, spike.

prickle n ❶ THORN, needle, barb, spike, spine, spur. ❷ TINGLE, tingling, sting, sting-ing, smarting, itching.
▶ v TINGLE, sting, smart, itch.

pride n ❶ SELF-ESTEEM, self-respect, ego, amour propre, self-worth, self-image, feelings, sensibilities. ❷ CONCEIT, vanity, arrogance, haughtiness, self-importance, self-love, egotism, presumption, hauteur, super-ciliousness, disdain; *informal* big-headedness. ❸ SATISFACTION, gratification, pleasure, joy, delight.
– OPPOSITES humility.
▶ BE PROUD OF, take pride in, take satisfaction in, congratu-late oneself on, revel in, glory in, exult in, boast about, brag about, crow about.

priest n CLERGYMAN, cleric, man/woman of the cloth, man/woman of God, father, padre.

prim adj PROPER, demure, for-mal, precise, stuffy, starchy, strait-laced, prudish, prissy, old-maidish, priggish, puritanical.

primarily adv BASICALLY, es-sentially, in essence, funda-mentally, in the first place, first and foremost, chiefly, mainly, in the main, principally, mostly, for the most part, on the whole, predominantly, pre-dominately.

primary adj ❶ PRIME, chief, main, principal, leading, pre-dominant, most important, paramount, basic, fundamen-tal, elemental, rudimentary, essential. ❷ EARLIEST, original, initial, beginning, first, opening.
– OPPOSITES secondary.

prime adj ❶ See PRIMARY (1). ❷ TOP-QUALITY, highest, top, best,

first-class, high-grade, grade A, superior, choice, select.
– OPPOSITES inferior.
▶ n BEST PART, peak, pinnacle, best days, height, zenith, acme, culmination, apex, heyday, full flowering.

primitive adj ❶ ANCIENT, earliest, primeval, primordial, primal, pristine. ❷ CRUDE, simple, rudimentary, undeveloped, unrefined, rough, unsophisticated, rude.
❸ UNCIVILIZED, barbarian, barbaric, savage, wild.
– OPPOSITES advanced.

principal adj ❶ FOREMOST, chief, leading, pre-eminent, most important, most influential, dominant, controlling, ruling, in charge. ❷ MAJOR, main, chief, leading, key, primary, prime, paramount.
– OPPOSITES subsidiary.
▶ n ❶ HEAD TEACHER, headmaster, headmistress, head, rector, master, dean. ❷ LEADING PLAYER / PERFORMER, leading man/lady, lead, star.

principle n ❶ THEORY, basis, fundamental, essence, assumption, rule, law, canon, tenet, code, maxim, axiom, dictum, postulate. ❷ MORALS, ethics, integrity, uprightness, righteousness, probity, rectitude, honour, conscience, scruples.

print v ❶ SET IN PRINT, send to press, publish, issue, run off, put to bed. ❷ IMPRINT, stamp, mark.
▶ n ❶ TYPE, letters, lettering, typeface, newsprint. ❷ COPY, reproduction, replica.

prior adj EARLIER, previous, anterior.
– OPPOSITES subsequent.
■ **prior to** BEFORE, until, up to, earlier than, preceding.

priority n ❶ FIRST / PRIME CONCERN, most important thing. ❷ PRECEDENCE, preference, urgency.

prison n JAIL, lock-up, penal institution, place of detention, place of confinement, dungeon; N. Amer. penitentiary, correctional facility; informal clink, cooler, slammer, stir, jug; Brit. informal nick; N. Amer. informal can, pen; Brit. informal, dated chokey.

prisoner n CONVICT, captive, detainee, internee hostage; informal con, lag, lifer, jailbird.

pristine adj UNMARKED, unblemished, unspoilt, spotless, immaculate, clean, in mint/perfect condition.
– OPPOSITES dirty, spoilt.

private adj ❶ CONFIDENTIAL, secret, unofficial, off-the-record, in camera, closet, privileged; informal hush-hush. ❷ PERSONAL, intimate, secret. ❸ SECLUDED, secret, remote, out of the way, quiet. ❹ RESERVED, retiring, self-contained, uncommunicative, diffident, secretive.
– OPPOSITES public, open, extrovert.

privileged adj ❶ ADVANTAGED, socially advantaged, favoured, elite, indulgent, spoilt. ❷ CONFIDENTIAL, private, off-the-record,

secret, top secret; *informal* hush-hush.
– OPPOSITES disadvantaged, public.

prize n TROPHY, medal, award, accolade, reward, premium, honour, laurels, palm, bays.
▶ adj PRIZEWINNING, award-winning, winning, champion.
▶ v VALUE, treasure, cherish, hold dear, esteem, hold in high regard.

probable adj LIKELY, most likely, odds-on, expected, anticipated, predictable, foreseeable, on the cards, credible, quite possible, possible.
– OPPOSITES improbable.

probably adv IN ALL PROBABILITY, in all likelihood, as likely as not, it is to be expected that, perhaps.

probe n INVESTIGATION, scrutiny, inquest, exploration, examination, study.
▶ v ❶ FEEL, feel around, prod, poke, explore. ❷ INVESTIGATE, scrutinize, inquire into, examine, study, research, analyse.

problem n ❶ DIFFICULTY, complication, trouble, mess, predicament, plight, dilemma, quandary; *informal* pickle, can of worms. ❷ PUZZLE, poser, enigma, riddle, conundrum; *informal* teaser, brain-teaser.

problematic adj ❶ PROBLEMATICAL, difficult, troublesome, complicated, puzzling, knotty, thorny, ticklish, tricky; *Brit. informal* dodgy. ❷ DOUBTFUL, uncertain, unsettled, question-

able, open to question, debatable, arguable.
– OPPOSITES straightforward.

procedure n ❶ COURSE OF ACTION, plan of action, policy, system, method, methodology, modus operandi, technique, means, practice, operation, strategy. ❷ STEP, process, measure, move, operation, transaction.

proceed v ❶ MAKE ONE'S WAY, go, advance, carry on, move on, press on, progress. ❷ ARISE, originate, spring, stem, come, derive, result, follow, ensue, emanate, issue, flow.

proceedings pl n ❶ ACTIVITIES, events, action, process, affairs, doings, happenings. ❷ CASE, lawsuit, litigation, trial. ❸ MINUTES, report, account, record, transactions.

proceeds pl n TAKINGS, profits, returns, receipts, income, earnings.

process n ❶ METHOD, system, technique, means, practice, way, procedure. ❷ DEVELOPMENT, evolution, changes, stages, steps.

procession n ❶ PARADE, march, column, file, train, cortège, cavalcade, motorcade. ❷ STREAM, steady stream, succession, series, sequence, run.

proclaim v ❶ ANNOUNCE, declare, make known, give out, notify, circulate, advertise, publish, broadcast, promulgate. ❷ PRONOUNCE, announce, declare to be.

procrastinate v DELAY, postpone action, defer action, be dilatory, use delaying tactics, stall, temporize, play for time, play a waiting game, dally, dilly-daily, drag one's feet/heels.

prod v ❶ POKE, jab, dig, nudge, elbow, butt, push, shove, thrust. ❷ *See* URGE v (1).

prodigious adj IMPRESSIVE, striking, startling, extraordinary, remarkable, exceptional, amazing, staggering, stupendous, phenomenal, miraculous.
– OPPOSITES small, unexceptional.

prodigy n CHILD GENIUS, wonder child, wunderkind, gifted child, wonder, marvel, phenomenon, sensation.

produce v ❶ MAKE, manufacture, create, construct, build, fabricate, put together, assemble, turn out, compose, originate, prepare, develop, fashion. ❷ PRESENT, offer, set forth, proffer, advance, show, exhibit, demonstrate, disclose, reveal. ❸ YIELD, bear, give, bring forth, supply, provide, furnish. ❹ GIVE BIRTH TO, bring forth, bear, breed, give life to, bring into the world, procreate. ❺ MOUNT, stage, put on, present.
▶ n YIELD, crops, harvest, output.

product n ❶ COMMODITY, artefact, goods, wares, merchandise. ❷ RESULT, outcome, effect, consequence, upshot, fruit, spin-off, legacy.

productive adj ❶ FERTILE, fruitful, fecund, rich, high-yielding. ❷ PROLIFIC, energetic, vigorous, efficient, effective, valuable.
– OPPOSITES sterile, unproductive.

profess v DECLARE, announce, proclaim, assert, state, utter, affirm, avow; *formal* aver.

profession n ❶ CAREER, job, calling, business, vocation, occupation, line of work, métier, position, situation. ❷ DECLARATION, announcement, proclamation, assertion, statement, affirmation, avowal; *formal* averment.

professional adj ❶ SKILLED, skilful, proficient, expert, adept, competent, efficient, experienced. ❷ SKILFUL, expert, adept, masterly, excellent, fine, polished, finished. ❸ NON-AMATEUR, paid.
– OPPOSITES amateurish, amateur.

proffer v OFFER, tender, present, extend, give, submit, volunteer, suggest.
– OPPOSITES withdraw.

profile n ❶ OUTLINE, silhouette, contour, lines, shape, form, figure. ❷ SHORT BIOGRAPHY, sketch, thumbnail sketch, portrait, vignette.

profit n ❶ TAKINGS, proceeds, gain, yield, return, receipts, income, earnings, winnings. ❷ GAIN, benefit, advantage, good, value, use, avail.
– OPPOSITES loss.
▶ v BENEFIT, be of benefit to, be of advantage to, be of use/value to, serve, help, be helpful

to, assist, aid, stand in good stead.

profitable adj ❶ MONEY-MAKING, commercial, gainful, remunerative, paying, lucrative. ❷ BENEFICIAL, advantageous, rewarding, helpful, productive, useful, worthwhile, valuable.
– OPPOSITES unprofitable.

profound adj ❶ SERIOUS, weighty, deep, learned, discerning, penetrating, thoughtful, philosophical, erudite, wise, sagacious. ❷ SINCERE, intense, keen, great, extreme, deep, heartfelt. ❸ FAR-REACHING, radical, extensive, exhaustive, thoroughgoing.
– OPPOSITES shallow, superficial.

profuse adj ❶ COPIOUS, prolific, abundant, liberal, effusive, lavish, extravagant, inordinate. ❷ LUXURIANT, plentiful, lush, rich, exuberant, riotous, rank, rampant.
– OPPOSITES meagre.

programme n ❶ AGENDA, calendar, schedule, syllabus, list of events, order of the day. ❷ PRODUCTION, presentation, show, performance, broadcast. ❸ SYLLABUS, prospectus, schedule, list, curriculum, literature.

progress n ❶ FORWARD MOVE-MENT, headway, advance, going, passage, advancement, progression. ❷ PROGRESSION, improvement, betterment, upgrading, development, growth.
▶ v ❶ GO FORWARD, move forward/on, make one's way, advance, go on, continue, proceed,

push forward, forge ahead. ❷ MAKE PROGRESS, get better, improve, recover, recuperate.
– OPPOSITES regress.

progressive adj ❶ INCREAS-ING, growing, intensifying, accelerating, escalating. ❷ MODERN, advanced, radical, reforming, innovative, revolutionary, forward-looking, enlightened, avant-garde; *informal* go-ahead.
– OPPOSITES conservative.

prohibit v ❶ FORBID, ban, bar, disallow, proscribe, veto, interdict, outlaw. ❷ PREVENT, stop, rule out, preclude, make impossible, hinder, impede, hamper, obstruct, restrict, constrain.
– OPPOSITES allow.

prohibitive adj EXORBITANT, steep, extortionate, excessive, preposterous, high-priced, high-cost, sky-high.

project n SCHEME, plan, programme, enterprise, undertaking, venture, activity, operation, campaign.
▶ v ❶ PLAN, propose, map out, devise, design, outline. ❷ LAUNCH, discharge, propel, hurl, throw, cast, fling, shoot. ❸ JUT OUT, protrude, extend, stick out, stand out, hang over, obtrude.

proliferate v INCREASE, multiply, extend, expand, burgeon, accelerate, escalate, rocket, snowball, mushroom.
– OPPOSITES decrease.

prolong v LENGTHEN, make longer, elongate, extend,

stretch out, draw out, drag out, protract, spin out.

prominent adj ❶ PROTRUDING, protuberant, jutting, projecting, standing out, bulging. ❷ CONSPICUOUS, noticeable, obvious, unmistakable, obtrusive, eye-catching, striking. ❸ EMINENT, important, pre-eminent, distinguished, notable, noted, illustrious, celebrated, well known, famous, renowned, leading.
– OPPOSITES inconspicuous.

promiscuous adj DISSOLUTE, dissipated, fast, licentious, loose, profligate, abandoned, immoral, debauched, wanton, of easy virtue, unchaste.
– OPPOSITES chaste.

promise v ❶ GIVE ONE'S WORD, give an undertaking, give one's assurance, swear, vow, pledge, contract. ❷ AUGUR, indicate, denote, signify, be a sign of, show signs of, suggest, betoken, presage.
▶ n ❶ WORD, undertaking, assurance, guarantee, commitment, vow, oath, pledge, bond, contract, covenant. ❷ POTENTIAL, flair, talent, ability, aptitude, capability, capacity.

promising adj ENCOURAGING, hopeful, favourable, auspicious, propitious, optimistic, bright.
– OPPOSITES unfavourable, hopeless.

promontory n HEADLAND, point, cape, foreland, bluff, cliff, precipice, overhang, height, projection, prominence.

promote v ❶ ELEVATE, advance, move up, upgrade, prefer, aggrandize. ❷ ADVANCE, further, assist, aid, help, contribute to, foster, boost. ❸ ADVERTISE, publicize, push, puff, beat the drum for; *informal* plug, give a plug to, hype.
– OPPOSITES demote, obstruct.

promotion n ❶ UPGRADING, elevation, advancement, preferment, aggrandizement. ❷ ADVANCEMENT, furtherance, furthering, assistance, aid, help, contribution to, fostering, boosting. ❸ ADVERTISING, publicity, hard sell, puff; *informal* plug, hype, hyping.

prompt adj ❶ IMMEDIATE, instant, instantaneous, swift, rapid, speedy, quick, fast, expeditious, early, punctual, in good time, timely. ❷ SWIFT, rapid, speedy, quick, fast, ready, willing, eager.
– OPPOSITES slow.
▶ v ❶ CAUSE, make, encourage, move, induce, urge, incite, impel, spur on, motivate, stimulate, inspire, provoke. ❷ REMIND, jog someone's memory, refresh someone's memory, cue, help out.

pronounce v ❶ ENUNCIATE, articulate, say, utter, sound, voice, vocalize. ❷ ANNOUNCE, declare, proclaim, assert, affirm, rule, decree.

pronounced adj ❶ MARKED, noticeable, obvious, evident, conspicuous, striking, distinct, unmistakable. ❷ DECIDED,

definite, clear, strong, positive, distinct.
– OPPOSITES slight.

pronunciation n ENUNCI-ATION, articulation, accent, saying, uttering, utterance, sounding, voicing, vocalization.

proof n EVIDENCE, demonstration, substantiation, corroboration, confirmation, attestation, testimony, certification, verification, authentication, validation.
▶ adj IMPERVIOUS, impenetrable, resistant, repellent.

prop n SUPPORT, upright, brace, buttress, stay, bolster, stanchion, truss, column, post, rod, pole, shaft.
▶ v LEAN, rest, set, lay, stand, balance, steady.
■ **prop up** HOLD UP, shore up, bolster up, buttress, support, brace, underpin, reinforce, strengthen.

propaganda n PUBLICITY MA-TERIAL, publicity, promotion, advertising, advertisement, information, agitprop.

propagate v ① GROW, breed, multiply, reproduce. ② SPREAD, communicate, circulate, disseminate, transmit, distribute, broadcast, publish, publicize, proclaim, promulgate.

propel v MOVE, set in motion, push forward, drive, thrust forward, force, impel.

propensity n see TENDENCY.

proper adj ① SUITABLE, fitting, appropriate, apt. ② CORRECT, right, precise, accepted, established, orthodox, conventional,

formal. ③ SEEMLY, decorous, respectable, decent, refined, genteel, formal, conventional, orthodox, strict, punctilious.
– OPPOSITES improper.

property n ① POSSESSIONS, belongings, things, goods, effects, chattels, assets, resources. ② REAL ESTATE, buildings, land. ③ QUALITY, attribute, characteristic, feature, power, peculiarity, idiosyncrasy, quirk.

prophecy n PREDICTION, forecast, prognostication, divination, augury.

prophesy v PREDICT, foretell, forecast, foresee, forewarn of, presage, prognosticate, divine, augur.

prophet n SEER, soothsayer, diviner, clairvoyant, prophesier, oracle, augur, sibyl, Cassandra.

proportion n ① RATIO, distribution, relative amount/number, relationship. ② POR-TION, part, segment, share, quota, division, percentage, fraction, measure; *informal* cut. ③ BALANCE, symmetry, harmony, correspondence, congruity, agreement.

proportional adj PROPORTION-ATE, corresponding, commensurate, equivalent, comparable.
– OPPOSITES disproportionate.

proposal n SCHEME, plan, project, programme, motion, bid, proposition, presentation, suggestion, recommendation, tender, terms.

propose v ① PUT FORWARD, advance, offer, proffer, present, submit, tender, propound, suggest, recommend, advocate. ❷ INTEND, mean, plan, have in mind, aim, purpose. ❸ NOMINATE, name, put forward, put up, suggest, recommend.

proprieties pl n ETIQUETTE, social niceties, protocol, civilities, formalities, rules of conduct, accepted behaviour, good manners, good form, the done thing, punctilio.

proprietor n OWNER, possessor, title-holder, deed-holder, landowner, landlord/landlady.

prosaic adj UNIMAGINATIVE, ordinary, uninspired, commonplace, dull, tedious, boring, dry, humdrum, mundane, pedestrian, lifeless, spiritless, stale, bland, vapid, banal, hackneyed, trite, insipid, monotonous, flat.
– OPPOSITES imaginative.

prosecute v ❶ CHARGE, prefer charges against, bring an action against, try, bring to trial, put on trial, sue, bring a suit against, interdict, arraign. ❷ CARRY ON, conduct, direct, engage in, work at, proceed with, continue with.

prospect n ❶ LIKELIHOOD, likeliness, hope, expectation, anticipation, chance, chances, odds, probability, possibility. ❷ VIEW, vista, outlook, perspective, panorama, scene, spectacle.
▶ v EXPLORE, search, inspect, survey, examine, check out.

prospective adj FUTURE, to-be, soon-to-be, intended, expected, would-be, potential,

possible, likely, hoped for, looked for, awaited, anticipated.

prospects pl n POTENTIAL, promise, possibilities, expectations, scope.

prosper v DO WELL, get on well, thrive, flourish, be successful, succeed, get ahead, progress, advance, get on in the world, make headway, make good, become rich, be in clover.
– OPPOSITES fail.

prosperity n AFFLUENCE, wealth, riches, prosperousness, success, good fortune, ease, plenty, the good life, luxury.
– OPPOSITES hardship.

prosperous adj WELL OFF, well-to-do, affluent, wealthy, rich, successful, moneyed, opulent, in clover; *informal* well heeled, in the money, on Easy Street.
– OPPOSITES poor.

prostitute n CALL GIRL, whore; *informal* tart, pro, working girl, member of the oldest profession; *Brit. informal* tom; *N. Amer. informal* hooker, hustler; *dated* loose woman, woman of ill repute, streetwalker, woman of the streets, fallen woman; *archaic* courtesan, strumpet, harlot, trollop, wench.

prostrate adj PRONE, lying down, flat, stretched out, horizontal, procumbent.
▶ v KNOCK FLAT, flatten, knock down, floor, level.

protect v ❶ KEEP SAFE, save, safeguard, shield, preserve, defend, shelter, secure.

❷ GUARD, mount/stand guard on, defend, secure, watch over, look after, take care of.
– OPPOSITES endanger.

protection n **❶** SAFE KEEPING, safety, care, charge, keeping, preservation, defence, security. **❷** SAFEGUARD, shield, barrier, buffer, screen, cover.

protective adj **❶** PROTECTING, safeguarding, shielding, covering. **❷** CAREFUL, watchful, vigilant, paternal/maternal, fatherly/motherly, overprotective, possessive, clinging.

protector n DEFENDER, champion, bodyguard, guardian, guardian angel.

protest v **❶** OBJECT, raise objections, take issue, make/take a stand, put up a fight, take exception, complain, demur, remonstrate, make a fuss, demonstrate; *informal* kick up a fuss, beef, bitch. **❷** DECLARE, announce, profess, proclaim, assert, affirm, argue, attest, maintain, insist on, avow; *formal* aver.
▶ n OBJECTION, opposition, exception, complaint, disapproval, disagreement, dissent, demurral, remonstration, fuss, outcry, demonstration, protestation.

protocol n ETIQUETTE, rules of conduct, code of behaviour, conventions, formalities, customs, propriety, proprieties, decorum, manners, courtesies, civilities, good form, politesse.

protract v PROLONG, extend, stretch out, draw out, lengthen,

make longer, drag out, spin out, keep going, continue.
– OPPOSITES curtail, shorten.

proud adj **❶** PLEASED, glad, happy, satisfied, gratified, content, appreciative. **❷** ARROGANT, conceited, vain, self-important, egotistical, boastful, haughty, disdainful, scornful, supercilious, snobbish, imperious, overbearing, overweening, highhanded; *informal* high and mighty, stuck up, snooty, toffee-nosed. **❸** GRATIFYING, satisfying, happy, memorable, notable, red-letter, glorious, marvellous.
– OPPOSITES ashamed, humble.

prove v ESTABLISH, determine, demonstrate, show beyond doubt, substantiate, corroborate, verify, validate, authenticate, confirm.
– OPPOSITES disprove.

proverb n SAYING, adage, maxim, saw, axiom, aphorism, dictum, apophthegm.

proverbial adj LEGENDARY, notorious, infamous, famous, famed, renowned, well known, acknowledged, accepted, traditional, time-honoured.

provide v **❶** SUPPLY, furnish, equip, accommodate, provision, outfit. **❷** GIVE, bring, afford, present, offer, accord, yield, impart, lend.
■ **provide for** SUPPORT, maintain, keep, sustain, take care of, care for, look after.

provided conjunction PROVIDING THAT, on condition that, if, as long as, given, with the provision/proviso that, contingent upon, on the assumption that.

provident adj FAR-SIGHTED, prudent, judicious, shrewd, cautious, careful, thrifty, canny, economical, frugal.

provincial adj ❶ LOCAL, small-town, rural, country. ❷ UNSOPHISTICATED, parochial, limited, small-minded, insular, inward-looking, illiberal, narrow, narrow-minded, inflexible, bigoted, prejudiced, intolerant.
– OPPOSITES metropolitan, sophisticated.

provisional adj PROVISORY, temporary, interim, stopgap, transitional, to be confirmed, conditional, tentative, contingent, pro tem.
– OPPOSITES permanent.

provisions pl n SUPPLIES, stores, groceries, food and drink, foodstuffs, staples, rations, provender, eatables, edibles, comestibles; poetic/literary viands; dated victuals.

proviso n CONDITION, stipulation, provision, clause, rider, qualification, restriction, reservation, limitation.

provocative adj ❶ PROVOKING, annoying, irritating, exasperating, infuriating, maddening, vexing, galling, affronting, insulting, inflaming, goading; informal aggravating. ❷ SEDUCTIVE, sexy, tempting, suggestive, arousing, exciting, alluring, erotic, titillating.

provoke v ❶ ANNOY, anger, incense, enrage, irritate, exasperate, infuriate, madden, pique, nettle, vex, harass, irk, gall, affront, insult; informal make someone's blood boil, aggravate. ❷ INCITE, rouse, stir, move, stimulate, motivate, excite, inflame, prompt, induce, spur, goad, prod, egg on.
– OPPOSITES allay, pacify.

prowess n SKILL, skilfulness, expertise, facility, ability, capability, talent, genius, adroitness, adeptness, aptitude, competence, proficiency; informal know-how.

prowl v ROAM, range, move stealthily, slink, skulk, steal, sneak, stalk.

proxy n REPRESENTATIVE, deputy, substitute, agent, delegate, surrogate.

prudent adj ❶ WISE, well judged, judicious, sagacious, sage, shrewd, sensible, circumspect, far-sighted, politic. ❷ CAUTIOUS, careful, discreet, wary, vigilant, heedful, thrifty, economical, canny, sparing, frugal, provident.
– OPPOSITES imprudent.

prudish adj PRIGGISH, prim, strait-laced, prissy, puritan, puritanical, stuffy, starchy, Victorian, Grundyish, old-maid, old-maidish, schoolmarmish; informal goody-goody.
– OPPOSITES permissive.

prune v CUT, lop, chop, clip, snip, remove.

pry v BE INQUISITIVE, interfere, meddle, intrude, be nosy, be a busybody; *informal* stick/poke one's nose in, stick one's oar in, snoop; *Austral./NZ informal* sticky-beak.

pseudonym n ASSUMED NAME, alias, false name, nom de plume, pen-name, stage name, professional name, sobriquet, nickname, nom de guerre.

psychological adj MENTAL, of the mind, cerebral, psychic, psychical.

pub n BAR, tavern, inn; *Brit.* public house; *Brit. informal* local, boozer.

puberty n PUBESCENCE, adolescence, young adulthood, teenage years, teens.

public adj ❶ POPULAR, general, common, universal, widespread. ❷ KNOWN, widely known, acknowledged, overt, in circulation, published, publicized, plain, obvious. ❸ PROMINENT, well known, important, eminent, respected, influential, prestigious, famous.
– OPPOSITES private.
▶ n PEOPLE, population, country, nation, community, citizens, populace, the masses, the multitude, the mob, the hoi polloi.

publication n ❶ PUBLISHING, production, issuing, issuance. ❷ BOOK, newspaper, magazine, periodical, journal, daily, weekly, monthly, quarterly, booklet, brochure, leaflet, pamphlet, handbill.

publicize v ❶ MAKE PUBLIC, make known, announce, publish, broadcast, distribute, disseminate, promulgate. ❷ GIVE PUBLICITY TO, promote, advertise, puff, puff up, push, beat the drum for; *informal* hype, plug.
– OPPOSITES conceal.

publish v ❶ PRODUCE, issue, print, bring out. ❷ See PUBLICIZE (1).

pucker v SCREW UP, wrinkle, crease, furrow, knit, crinkle, corrugate.

puerile adj CHILDISH, immature, infantile, juvenile, adolescent, foolish, silly, inane, asinine.
– OPPOSITES mature.

puff n GUST, blast, whiff, breath, flurry, draught.
▶ v ❶ PANT, blow, gasp, gulp. ❷ SWELL, distend, inflate, dilate, bloat. ❸ See PUBLICIZE (2).

pugnacious adj BELLIGERENT, bellicose, combative, aggressive, antagonistic, disputatious, hostile, irascible, threatening, ill-tempered, bad-tempered.
– OPPOSITES peaceable.

pull v ❶ HAUL, drag, draw, trail, tow, tug. ❷ STRAIN, sprain, wrench, stretch, tear, dislocate, damage.
– OPPOSITES push.
■ **pull back** WITHDRAW, retreat, draw back, fall back. **pull down** KNOCK DOWN, demolish, raze, level, destroy, bulldoze. **pull oneself together** REGAIN ONE'S COMPOSURE / CALM, get a grip on oneself; *informal* snap out of it. **pull out** WITHDRAW, retreat from, leave, abandon, give up, quit.

pulp n PURÉE, mush, mash, pap, triturate.

▶ v CRUSH, squash, mash, purée, pulverize, triturate.

pulsate v BEAT, throb, vibrate, pulse, palpitate, pound, thud, thump, drum.

pulse n BEAT, rhythm, throb, throbbing, vibration, pulsation, pounding, thud, thumping, thump, drumming.

▶ v *see* PULSATE.

pump v ❶ DRIVE, force, push, send. ❷ QUESTION, quiz, interrogate, cross-examine; *informal* grill.

punch v STRIKE, hit, knock, thump, thwack, box, jab, cuff, slug, smash, slap, batter, pound, pummel; *informal* sock, biff, bash, bop, wallop, whack, clout.

punctilious adj CAREFUL, scrupulous, meticulous, conscientious, exact, precise, particular, strict, nice, finicky, fussy.
– OPPOSITES careless.

punctual adj ON TIME, on the dot, prompt, in good time, when expected, timely, well timed.

puncture n HOLE, perforation, flat, prick, rupture, cut, nick, slit, leak.

▶ v MAKE A HOLE IN, hole, perforate, pierce, bore, prick, penetrate, rupture, cut, nick, slit.

pungent adj ❶ SHARP, acrid, acid, sour, biting, stinging, burning, bitter, tart, tangy, spicy, highly flavoured, aromatic, piquant, peppery, hot, fiery. ❷ CAUSTIC, acid, biting,

cutting, sharp, incisive, scathing, pointed, acrimonious, trenchant, mordant.
– OPPOSITES bland, mild.

punish v ❶ DISCIPLINE, teach someone a lesson, penalize, chastise, smack, slap, beat, cane, whip, flog, lash, scourge; *formal* castigate. ❷ MALTREAT, mistreat, abuse, manhandle, damage, harm.

punishing adj ARDUOUS, demanding, taxing, strenuous, hard, exhausting, fatiguing, wearing, tiring, gruelling, uphill, back-breaking.

punitive adj ❶ PENAL, disciplinary, corrective, correctional. ❷ HARSH, severe, stiff, cruel, savage.

puny adj WEAK, weakly, frail, feeble, undersized, underdeveloped, stunted, small, slight, little.
– OPPOSITES strong.

pupil n SCHOOLBOY / GIRL, schoolchild, scholar, student.

puppet n ❶ MARIONETTE, string puppet, glove puppet, finger puppet. ❷ TOOL, instrument, cat's-paw, pawn, creature, dupe, mouthpiece; *Brit. informal* poodle.

purchase v *see* BUY.

▶ n ❶ ACQUISITION, order, investment; *informal* buy. ❷ GRIP, hold, foothold, footing, toehold, support, grasp, leverage.

pure adj ❶ UNALLOYED, unmixed, unadulterated, uncontaminated, flawless, perfect, genuine, real, true. ❷ CLEAN, clear, fresh, unpolluted,

untainted, unadulterated, uncontaminated, uninfected, wholesome, natural. ❸ VIRGINAL, chaste, maidenly, virtuous, undefiled, unsullied. ❹ STAINLESS, spotless, unsullied, unblemished, impeccable, immaculate, blameless, sinless. ❺ SHEER, utter, absolute, downright, out-and-out, complete, total, perfect, unmitigated, unqualified.
– OPPOSITES adulterated, polluted, immoral.

purely adv ENTIRELY, completely, totally, wholly, solely, only, simply, just, merely.

purge v ❶ CLEANSE, clear, purify, make pure. ❷ REMOVE, clear out, expel, eject, dismiss, oust, depose, eradicate, root out, weed out.

purify v MAKE PURE, clean, cleanse, decontaminate, filter, refine, disinfect, sterilize, sanitize, fumigate.
– OPPOSITES contaminate.

puritanical adj PRUDISH, prim, priggish, prissy, puritan, ascetic, austere, strait-laced, narrow-minded, rigid, stiff.
– OPPOSITES broad-minded.

purpose n ❶ REASON, point, basis, motivation, cause, justification. ❷ AIM, intention, object, objective, goal, end, target, ambition, aspiration, desire, wish, hope. ❸ DETERMINATION, resolution, resolve, firmness, steadfastness, single-mindedness, persistence, perseverance, tenacity, doggedness.
▸ v see INTEND (1).

purposeful adj DETERMINED, resolute, resolved, firm, steadfast, single-minded, persistent, tenacious, dogged, unfaltering, unwavering.
– OPPOSITES aimless.

purposely adv ON PURPOSE, intentionally, deliberately, by design, wilfully, wittingly, knowingly, consciously.

pursue v ❶ GO AFTER, run after, follow, chase, hunt, stalk, track, trail, shadow; informal tail. ❷ PROCEED WITH, go on with, follow, keep/carry on with, continue with, continue, persist in. ❸ WORK AT, engage in, follow, practise, prosecute, apply oneself to.

push v ❶ SHOVE, thrust, propel, drive, ram, butt, jostle. ❷ URGE, press, egg on, spur on, prod, goad, incite, impel, dragoon, force, coerce, constrain, browbeat, strong-arm. ❸ PROMOTE, advertise, publicize, puff, puff up, boost, beat the drum for; informal plug, hype.
■ **push around** BULLY, ride roughshod over, browbeat, tyrannize, intimidate, domineer.

pushy adj ASSERTIVE, self-assertive, aggressive, forceful, forward, bold, brash, bumptious, presumptuous, cocksure, loud, obnoxious.
– OPPOSITES submissive.

put v ❶ PLACE, lay, set down, deposit, position, rest, stand, locate, situate, settle, install. ❷ LAY, present, bring forward, forward, submit, tender, offer, proffer, put forward, set forth, advance. ■ **put about** SPREAD, bandy about, circulate, disseminate, make public, make known, give out, publicize, broadcast, propagate, announce, bruit. **put away** IMPRISON, confine, lock up, shut away/up. **put down ❶** PUT TO SLEEP, put out of its misery, destroy, do away with, kill; *N. Amer.* euthanize. **❷** SNUB, disparage, deprecate, belittle, denigrate, deflate, slight, humiliate, crush, mortify. **put out ❶** INCONVENIENCE, trouble, bother, impose upon,

discommode, incommode. **❷** EXTINGUISH, quench, douse, stamp out.

puzzle V PERPLEX, baffle, stump, beat, mystify, confuse, bewilder, nonplus, stagger, dumbfound, daze, confound; *informal* flummox.

puzzling adj DIFFICULT, hard, unclear, perplexing, knotty, baffling, enigmatic, abstruse, mystifying, bewildering, unfathomable, inexplicable, incomprehensible, beyond one, above one's head.
– OPPOSITES clear.

Qq

quail V FLINCH, shrink, recoil, shy away, pull back, draw back, cower, cringe, shudder, shiver, tremble, shake, quake, blench, blanch.

quake V SHAKE, tremble, quiver, shiver, shudder, rock, vibrate, pulsate, throb.

qualification n **❶** CERTIFICATION, training, competence, competency, accomplishment, eligibility, acceptability, suitableness, preparedness, fitness, proficiency, skilfulness, adeptness, capability, aptitude, skill, ability, attribute, endowment. **❷** MODIFICATION, limitation, restriction, reservation, stipulation, allowance, adaptation,

adjustment, condition, proviso, provision, caveat.

qualified adj **❶** TRAINED, certificated, equipped, prepared, competent, accomplished, proficient, skilled, skilful, adept, practised, experienced, expert, capable, able. **❷** MODIFIED, limited, conditional, restricted, bounded, contingent, confined, circumscribed, reserved, guarded, equivocal.

qualify V **❶** CERTIFY, license, empower, authorize, allow, permit, sanction, warrant, fit, equip. **❷** COUNT, be considered, be designated, be eligible, meet the requirements of. **❸** MODIFY, limit, make conditional, restrict.

quality n ❶ DEGREE OF EXCEL-
LENCE, standard, grade, level,
sort, type, kind, variety. ❷ FEA-
TURE, trait, attribute, characteristic, aspect, property,
peculiarity.

qualm n DOUBT, misgiving,
scruple, hesitation, hesitancy,
reluctance, anxiety, apprehension, disquiet, uneasiness, concern.

quantity n NUMBER, amount,
total, aggregate, sum, quota,
weight, capacity, mass, volume, bulk, extent, length, area.

quarrel n ARGUMENT, fight, disagreement, difference of opinion, dispute, disputation,
squabble, altercation, wrangle,
misunderstanding, feud, vendetta; *informal* row, spat, scrap,
tiff.
▶ v ARGUE, have a fight, fight,
dispute, squabble, bicker, spar,
wrangle, have a misunder-
standing, fall out; *informal* row,
have a row.
– OPPOSITES agree.

quarrelsome adj ARGUMENTA-
TIVE, belligerent, disputatious,
contentious, pugnacious, combative, ready for a fight, bellicose, litigious, hot-tempered,
irascible, choleric, irritable.
– OPPOSITES peaceable.

quarry n PREY, victim, prize.

quarter n ❶ DISTRICT, area,
region, part, side, neighbourhood, locality, zone. ❷ MERCY,
leniency, clemency, compassion, pity.
▶ v PUT UP, house, board, billet,
accommodate, lodge, install.

quarters pl n ACCOMMODATION,
billet, residence, habitation,
lodgings, rooms, barracks;
informal digs, pad; *formal* dwelling,
abode, domicile.

quash v ❶ ANNUL, declare null
and void, nullify, invalidate,
void, cancel, overrule, override,
overthrow, reject, set aside, reverse, revoke, rescind, repeal.
❷ CRUSH, put down, squash,
quell, subdue, suppress, repress, quench, extinguish,
stamp out, put a stop to, end,
terminate, defeat, destroy.
– OPPOSITES validate.

quaver v QUIVER, vibrate,
tremble, shake, waver.

queasy adj SICK, nauseated, ill,
indisposed, dizzy, sick to one's
stomach.

queer adj ❶ ODD, strange, unusual, extraordinary, funny,
curious, peculiar, weird, outlandish, singular, eccentric,
unconventional, unorthodox,
atypical, abnormal, irregular,
anomalous, deviant, offbeat;
informal off-the-wall. ❷ SUSPI-
CIOUS, suspect, irregular, questionable, dubious, doubtful;
informal fishy, shady.

quell v ❶ ALLAY, lull, quiet, silence, calm, soothe, appease,
assuage, abate, deaden, dull,
pacify. ❷ *See* QUASH (2).

quench v ❶ SATISFY, slake,
sate, satiate. ❷ EXTINGUISH, put
out, snuff out, blow out, douse.

quest n ❶ SEARCH, seeking,
pursuit, chase, hunt. ❷ ADVEN-
TURE, expedition, journey,
voyage, exploration, crusade.

question n ❶ QUERY, enquiry, interrogation. ❷ ISSUE, problem, matter, point, subject, topic, theme, bone of contention.
– OPPOSITES answer.
▶ v ❶ ASK QUESTIONS OF, interrogate, cross-examine, quiz, interview, sound out, examine; *informal* grill, pump. ❷ CALL INTO QUESTION, query, raise doubts about, throw doubt on, have suspicions about, challenge.

questionable adj OPEN TO QUESTION / DOUBT, doubtful, dubious, uncertain, debatable, in dispute, arguable, controversial, controvertible.
– OPPOSITES indisputable.

queue n LINE, row, column, file, chain, string, train, succession, sequence, series, concatenation.

quibble n CRITICISM, complaint, protest, objection, niggle, cavil, nicety.
▶ v CAVIL, carp, pettifog, split hairs, chop logic; *informal* nitpick.

quick adj ❶ FAST, rapid, speedy, swift, fleet, express. ❷ PROMPT, without delay, immediate, instantaneous, expeditious. ❸ BRIEF, brisk, fleeting, momentary, hasty, hurried, cursory, perfunctory. ❹ QUICK-WITTED, sharp-witted, alert, intelligent.
– OPPOSITES slow, long.

quicken v ❶ BECOME / GROW FASTER, speed up, accelerate, hurry, hasten. ❷ *see* AROUSE.

quiet adj ❶ SILENT, hushed, noiseless, soundless, peaceful. ❷ SOFT, low, inaudible. ❸ PEACEFUL, sleepy, undisturbed, unfrequented, secluded, isolated, out of the way, off the beaten track.
– OPPOSITES noisy.

quieten v ❶ SILENCE, hush, shush, quiet, still; *informal* shut up. ❷ ALLAY, soothe, calm, appease, lull, pacify, mollify, palliate.

quit v ❶ GIVE UP, stop, cease, leave off, abandon, abstain from, desist from. ❷ LEAVE, depart from, vacate, walk out on.

quite adv ❶ COMPLETELY, fully, entirely, totally, wholly, absolutely, in all respects. ❷ FAIRLY, relatively, moderately, reasonably, to some extent/degree, rather, somewhat.

quiver v TREMBLE, shiver, vibrate, quaver, quake, shudder, pulsate, convulse, palpitate.

quota n SHARE, allowance, allocation, portion, ration, part, slice, measure, proportion; *informal* cut; *Brit. informal* whack.

quotation n ❶ CITATION, reference, quote, allusion, excerpt, extract, selection, passage, line. ❷ ESTIMATE, estimated price, quote, cost, charge, figure.

quote v ❶ REPEAT, iterate, recite, reproduce. ❷ CITE, give, name, instance, mention, refer to, make reference to, allude to. ❸ ESTIMATE FOR, price, set a price for.

Rr

rabble n MOB, horde, swarm, crowd, throng.

race¹ n ❶ CONTEST, competition, competition, chase, pursuit, relay. ❷ CHANNEL, waterway, watercourse, sluice, spillway.
▶ v ❶ RUN AGAINST, compete against, be pitted against. ❷ RUN, sprint, dash, dart, bolt, speed, hare, fly, tear, zoom, accelerate, career.

race² n ETHNIC GROUP, people, bloodline, stock, line, lineage, breed, strain.

racial adj RACE-RELATED, ethnic, ethnological.

racism n RACIALISM, racial discrimination, racial prejudice/bigotry, chauvinism, xenophobia.

racist n RACIALIST, bigot.
▶ adj RACIALIST, discriminatory, prejudiced, bigoted, intolerant, illiberal.

rack n FRAME, framework, stand, form, trestle, structure, holder, shelf.

racket n NOISE, din, row, commotion, disturbance, uproar, hubbub, hullabaloo, clamour, pandemonium, tumult.

radiant adj ❶ SHINING, bright, illuminated, brilliant, luminous, luminescent, lustrous. ❷ JOYFUL, happy, elated,

ecstatic, delighted, pleased. See also HAPPY (1).
– OPPOSITES dark, gloomy.

radiate v SEND OUT / FORTH, give off/out, emit, emanate, scatter, disperse, diffuse, spread, shed.

radical adj ❶ FUNDAMENTAL, basic, rudimentary, elementary, elemental, constitutional. ❷ THOROUGH, complete, total, entire, absolute, utter, comprehensive, exhaustive, sweeping, far-reaching, profound, drastic. ❸ EXTREMIST, extreme, immoderate, revolutionary, rebel, rebellious, militant.
– OPPOSITES superficial, moderate.

raffle n LOTTERY, draw, sweepstake, tombola.

rage n FURY, anger, wrath, high dudgeon, frenzy, madness; poetic/literary ire.
▶ v BE FURIOUS, be infuriated, be angry, seethe, be beside oneself, lose one's temper, boil over, rant, rave, storm, fume, fulminate; informal blow one's top, flip one's lid, freak out.

ragged adj ❶ TATTERED, threadbare, frayed, the worse for wear, torn, rent, in holes, worn to shreds, falling to pieces. ❷ JAGGED, uneven, irregular, notched, serrated, saw-toothed, craggy.
– OPPOSITES smart.

raid | range

raid n SURPRISE ATTACK, assault, onslaught, invasion, incursion, thrust, sortie, sally.
▶ v ❶ ATTACK, assault, invade, assail, storm, rush, set upon, descend upon, swoop upon. ❷ PLUNDER, pillage, loot, rifle, forage, ransack, steal from.

rain n RAINFALL, precipitation, raindrops, drizzle, shower, rainstorm, cloudburst, torrent, downpour, deluge.
▶ v POUR, pour/come down, precipitate; informal rain cats and dogs, come down in buckets.

rainy adj WET, showery, drizzly, damp.

raise v ❶ LIFT, lift up, raise aloft, elevate, uplift, hoist, heave up. ❷ INCREASE, put up, escalate, inflate, heighten, augment, amplify, intensify; informal step up, hike, jack up. ❸ BRING UP, rear, nurture, educate.
– OPPOSITES lower.

rally v ❶ COME / GET TOGETHER, assemble, group, band together, convene, unite. ❷ CALL / BRING TOGETHER, assemble, summon, round up, muster, marshall, mobilize. ❸ RECOVER, recuperate, revive, get better/well, improve, perk up.
▶ n MEETING, gathering, assembly, convention, convocation.

ram v ❶ FORCE, cram, stuff, compress, jam, squeeze, thrust, tamp. ❷ STRIKE, hit, run into, crash into, collide with, bump, slam.

ramble v ❶ WALK, hike, wander, stroll, amble, roam, range, rove, traipse. ❷ DIGRESS, wander, gabble; informal rattle on; Brit. informal rabbit on, witter on.

rambling adj ❶ DIGRESSIVE, wandering, roundabout, circuitous, periphrastic, disconnected, disjointed, maundering, long-winded, verbose, wordy, prolix. ❷ SPRAWLING, spreading, unsystematic, straggling.
– OPPOSITES concise.

ramification n CONSEQUENCE, aftermath, outcome, result, upshot, issue, sequel, complication, implication.

ramp n SLOPE, incline, gradient, acclivity, rise.

rampage v RUN RIOT, run amok, charge, tear, storm, go berserk.
▶ n UPROAR, furore, mayhem, turmoil.

rampant adj OUT OF CONTROL / HAND, unrestrained, unchecked, unbridled, widespread, pandemic, epidemic.
– OPPOSITES controlled.

random adj HAPHAZARD, chance, accidental, fortuitous, serendipitous, adventitious, arbitrary, hit-or-miss, indiscriminate, sporadic, stray, spot, casual, unsystematic, unmethodical, disorganized, unplanned.
– OPPOSITES systematic.

range n ❶ SCOPE, compass, limits, bounds, confines, radius, span, scale, gamut, reach, sweep, extent, area, field, orbit, province, domain, latitude. ❷ ASSORTMENT, variety, kind, sort, type, class, rank, order, genus, species.

▶ v ❶ EXTEND, stretch, reach, cover, go, run, pass, fluctuate between, vary between. ❷ ROAM, rove, ramble, traverse, travel over, wander, meander, amble, stroll, stray, drift.

rank[1] n ❶ GRADE, level, echelon, stratum, class, status, position, station. ❷ NOBILITY, aristocracy, eminence, distinction.

▶ v ❶ CLASSIFY, class, categorize, grade. ❷ HAVE A RANK, be graded, be placed, be positioned.

rank[2] adj ❶ see LUSH (1). ❷ see FOUL adj (2).

rankle v FESTER, annoy, anger, irk, vex, irritate, rile, chafe, gall, embitter; informal get someone's goat.

ransack v ❶ See PLUNDER v. ❷ See SEARCH v (1).

rapid adj QUICK, fast, swift, speedy, fleet, hurried, hasty, expeditious, express, brisk, lively, prompt, precipitate.
– OPPOSITES slow.

rapport n AFFINITY, bond, empathy, sympathy, understanding.

rapture n JOY, ecstasy, elation, exaltation, exhilaration, bliss, euphoria, rhapsody, enchantment, delight.

rare adj ❶ UNUSUAL, uncommon, out of the ordinary, exceptional, atypical, singular, remarkable, unique. ❷ INFREQUENT, few and far between, scarce, sparse, sporadic, scattered.
– OPPOSITES common.

rascal n ❶ IMP, scamp, scallywag, mischief-maker, little devil. ❷ SCOUNDREL, rogue, ne'er-do-well, good-for-nothing, wastrel, reprobate; dated cad; informal creep, rat; informal, dated rotter; archaic blackguard.

rash adj RECKLESS, impetuous, hasty, impulsive, bold, madcap, audacious, brash, daredevil, foolhardy, foolish, harumscarum, devil-may-care, headstrong, hot-headed, incautious, careless, heedless, thoughtless, unthinking, imprudent, injudicious.
– OPPOSITES prudent.

rate n ❶ PERCENTAGE, ratio, proportion, scale, degree, standard. ❷ PACE, stride, gait, motion, speed, tempo, velocity, measure.

▶ v ❶ JUDGE, assess, appraise, evaluate, value, measure, weigh up, grade, rank, adjudge. ❷ REGARD AS, consider, deem, reckon, account.

rather adv ❶ SOONER, preferably, more readily. ❷ QUITE, fairly, a bit, a little, slightly, somewhat; informal sort of, kind of, pretty.

ratify v CONFIRM, endorse, sign, sanction, warrant, approve, authorize, validate.
– OPPOSITES revoke.

ratio n PROPORTION, comparative size/extent, correlation, correspondence, percentage, fraction, quotient.

ration n ALLOWANCE, quota, allotment, portion, share, measure, part, lot, amount, helping, proportion, percentage.
▶ v LIMIT, restrict, control, conserve, budget.

rational adj SENSIBLE, reasonable, logical, sound, intelligent, wise, judicious, sagacious, prudent, circumspect, politic, astute, shrewd, perceptive, well advised, well grounded.
– OPPOSITES irrational.

rationalize v ❶ EXPLAIN AWAY, account for, make excuses, make plausible, try to vindicate/justify. ❷ STREAMLINE, trim, make cuts in, cut back on, retrench on.

rattle v ❶ BANG, knock, rap, clatter, clang, clank, jangle, clink. ❷ DISCONCERT, disturb, fluster, upset, shake, perturb, faze, discompose, discomfit.

raucous adj STRIDENT, piercing, ear-splitting, shrill, screeching, harsh, sharp, grating, rasping, discordant, dissonant, jarring.
– OPPOSITES soft, quiet.

ravage v DEVASTATE, lay waste, ruin, wreak havoc on, destroy, level, raze, demolish.

rave v ❶ RANT AND RAVE, rage, storm, fulminate, explode in anger; *informal* fly off the handle, flip one's lid. ❷ RHAPSODIZE OVER, enthuse about, praise to the skies, gush over.

ravenous adj STARVING, starved, famished, ravening, wolfish, voracious, insatiable, insatiate.

ravishing adj BEAUTIFUL, lovely, stunning, gorgeous, dazzling, radiant, enchanting, bewitching, charming.
– OPPOSITES hideous.

raw adj ❶ UNCOOKED, fresh. ❷ UNREFINED, crude, green, coarse, unprocessed, unprepared, untreated. ❸ INEXPERIENCED, untrained, unskilled, untutored, new, callow, immature, green; *informal* wet behind the ears. ❹ COLD, chilly, freezing, bitter, biting, nippy, piercing, penetrating.
– OPPOSITES cooked, processed.

ray n BEAM, shaft, streak, stream, gleam, glint, flash, glimmer.

raze v TEAR / PULL DOWN, knock down, level, bulldoze, flatten, demolish, ruin, wreck.

reach v ❶ STRETCH, extend, hold out, thrust out, stick out. ❷ GET AS FAR AS, get to, arrive at, come to. ❸ CONTACT, get in touch with, get hold of, get through to, communicate with.
▶ n SCOPE, range, compass, latitude, ambit, orbit, sphere, area.

react v ❶ HAVE A REACTION / RESPONSE TO, respond. ❷ BEHAVE, act, conduct oneself, proceed, operate, function, cope.

reactionary adj ULTRA-CONSERVATIVE, conservative, obscurantist, diehard, rightist, rightwing; *Brit.* Colonel Blimp.
– OPPOSITES progressive.

read v ❶ PERUSE, study, scan, pore over, scrutinize; *informal* wade through, dip into.

❷ INTERPRET, construe, decipher, deduce, understand, comprehend. ❸ REGISTER, record, display, show, indicate.

readable adj ❶ LEGIBLE, easy to read, decipherable, clear, intelligible, understandable, comprehensible. ❷ ENJOYABLE, entertaining, interesting, gripping, enthralling, stimulating.
– OPPOSITES unreadable.

readily adv ❶ WILLINGLY, gladly, happily, cheerfully, eagerly. ❷ EASILY, without difficulty, effortlessly.
– OPPOSITES reluctantly.

ready adj ❶ FINISHED, completed, prepared, organized. ❷ PREPARED, equipped, organized, all set, in a fit state; *informal* fit. ❸ WITHIN REACH, available, on hand, present, near, near at hand, accessible, handy, convenient, on call, at one's fingertips; *informal* on tap. ❹ ABOUT TO, on the verge/brink of, in danger of, liable to, likely to. ❺ EAGER, prepared, enthusiastic, anxious, keen; *informal* psyched up, geared up.

real adj ❶ ACTUAL, existent, factual, non-fictitious. ❷ AUTHENTIC, genuine, bona fide. ❸ SINCERE, heartfelt, earnest, fervent, unfeigned, unaffected, honest, truthful.
– OPPOSITES imaginary, false.

realistic adj ❶ PRACTICAL, pragmatic, rational, down-to-earth, matter-of-fact, sensible, no-nonsense, commonsensical, level-headed, hard-headed, businesslike,

hard-boiled, sober, unromantic, unsentimental, with both feet on the ground. ❷ LIFELIKE, true-to-life, true, faithful, close, representational, graphic, naturalistic, authentic, genuine.
– OPPOSITES unrealistic.

reality n ❶ REAL WORLD, actuality, physical existence, corporeality, substantiality, materiality. ❷ FACT, actuality, truth.
– OPPOSITES fantasy.

realize v ❶ UNDERSTAND CLEARLY, grasp, take in, know, comprehend, apprehend, appreciate, recognize, perceive, discern, conceive; *informal* latch on; *Brit. informal* twig. ❷ FULFIL, achieve, accomplish, bring about, bring off, bring to fruition, consummate, effect, perform, execute, actualize, reify; *formal* effectuate. ❸ MAKE, clear, acquire, gain, bring in, obtain, earn.

realm n KINGDOM, country, land, state, province, empire, domain, monarchy, principality.

reap v ❶ CUT, crop, harvest, gather in, bring in, take in. ❷ REALIZE, receive, obtain, get, acquire, secure, procure.

rear¹ v ❶ BRING UP, raise, care for, nurture, parent, educate, train, instruct. ❷ RAISE, lift up, hold up, elevate, upraise.

rear² n BACK, back part, hind part, back end, tail, tail end.
– OPPOSITES front.

reason n ❶ GROUNDS, cause, basis, motive, motivation,

impetus. ❷ EXPLANATION, justification, argument, case, defence, vindication, apologia, rationalization, excuse, apology. ❸ REASONING, intellect, intelligence, intellectuality, mind, judgement, logic, rationality, thought, understanding, apprehension, comprehension, ratiocination. ❹ SANITY, mind, soundness of mind, senses.
▶ V ❶ THINK, think straight, use one's mind, use one's brain/head, analyse, cogitate, cerebrate, intellectualize, ratiocinate; *informal* put on one's thinking cap. ❷ USE LOGIC ON, argue with, debate with, dispute with, try to persuade, plead with.

reasonable adj ❶ LOGICAL, practical, rational, sensible, intelligent, wise, sound, judicious, advisable, well thought out, tenable, plausible. ❷ OPEN TO REASON, fair, just, equitable, impartial, dispassionate, unbiased, disinterested. ❸ MODERATE, low, modest, cheap, within one's means. ❹ TOLERABLE, passable, acceptable, average; *informal* OK.
– OPPOSITES unreasonable.

reasoned adj LOGICAL, rational, well thought out, clear, systematic, methodical, organized, well expressed, well presented.

reassure V PUT ONE'S MIND AT REST, put at ease, restore/give confidence to, encourage, hearten, buoy up, cheer up.

rebel n REVOLUTIONARY,

revolutionist, insurrectionist, insurgent, mutineer.
▶ V MUTINY, riot, revolt, rise up, rise up in arms, take to the streets.
– OPPOSITES conform.

rebellion n ❶ REVOLT, revolution, insurrection, uprising, rising, mutiny. ❷ DEFIANCE, disobedience, resistance, dissent, nonconformity, heresy, apostasy, schism, recusancy.

rebellious adj ❶ DEFIANT, disobedient, unruly, ungovernable, unmanageable, turbulent, disorderly, intractable, recalcitrant, incorrigible; *formal* contumacious. ❷ REVOLUTIONARY, insurrectionary, insurgent, mutinous.
– OPPOSITES obedient.

rebound V ❶ BOUNCE BACK, recoil, ricochet, boomerang. ❷ MISFIRE, backfire, come back on, redound on.

rebuff n REJECTION, repudiation, discouragement, snub, slight; *informal* brush-off, slap in the face.
▶ V REJECT, refuse, turn down, turn away, spurn, brush off, repudiate, snub, slight.

rebuke V REPRIMAND, tell off, scold, chide, admonish, reproach, reprove, remonstrate with, lecture, reprehend, berate, upbraid, take to task; *informal* bawl out; *Brit. informal* tick off, tear off a strip, carpet; *formal* castigate.
– OPPOSITES praise.

recalcitrant adj INTRACTABLE, refractory, unmanageable,

ungovernable, disobedient, insubordinate, defiant, contrary, wayward.
– OPPOSITES compliant.

recall V ❶ SUMMON BACK, call back, bring back. ❷ See REMEMBER (1).

receive V ❶ BE IN RECEIPT OF, accept delivery of, accept, take into one's possession. ❷ UNDERGO, experience, meet with, encounter, be subjected to, bear, suffer. ❸ WELCOME, greet, entertain, be at home to.
– OPPOSITES give, send.

recent adj ❶ NEW, fresh, novel, latest, late, modern, contemporary, latter-day, current, up to date. ❷ OCCURRING / APPEARING RECENTLY, not long past.

recently adv LATELY, of late, latterly, in recent times, not along ago.

receptacle n CONTAINER, holder, repository.

receptive adj OPEN, open to suggestions, flexible, willing, perceptive, sensitive, alert, bright, quick, keen.
– OPPOSITES unresponsive.

recess n ❶ ALCOVE, niche, nook, corner, cavity, bay, oriel. ❷ BREAK, respite, rest, interval, intermission, holiday, time off, vacation.

recession n DOWNTURN, depression, slump.
– OPPOSITES boom.

recipe n DIRECTIONS, instructions, guide, method, system, procedure.

reciprocal adj MUTUAL, shared, common, exchanged, give and take, complementary, corresponding, correlative.

reciprocate V RETURN, requite, repay, give back.

recital n ❶ PERFORMANCE, concert, show. ❷ ACCOUNT, report, telling, relation, description, detailing, rendering, record, chronicle.

recite V SAY, repeat, read aloud, deliver, declaim, speak, render.

reckless adj RASH, careless, thoughtless, incautious, heedless, unheeding, regardless, daredevil, devil-may-care, madcap, harum-scarum, wild, precipitate, headlong, hasty, irresponsible, hare-brained, foolhardy, imprudent, unwise, indiscreet, mindless, negligent.
– OPPOSITES cautious.

reckon V ❶ BE OF THE OPINION, think, believe, suppose, assume. ❷ COUNT, calculate, add up, compute, total, tally, put a figure on, give a figure to.

reclaim V HAVE RETURNED, get back, take back, regain, retrieve, recover.

recline V LIE DOWN, be recumbent, rest, repose, loll, lounge, sprawl, stretch out.

recluse n HERMIT, anchorite, eremite, solitary, lone wolf, loner.

recognize V ❶ KNOW, know again, identify, place, spot, recall, recollect, remember, call to mind. ❷ REALIZE, see, be aware of, be conscious of, perceive, discern, appreciate, understand, apprehend, acknowledge, accept, admit, concede, allow, grant, confess, own. ❸ ACKNOWLEDGE, accept, admit, concede, allow, grant, endorse, sanction, approve, validate, ratify, uphold.

recoil v DRAW BACK, jump back, pull back, shrink, shy away, flinch, start, wince, cower, quail.

recollect v REMEMBER, recall, call to mind, think of, summon up, place; *informal* put one's finger on.
– OPPOSITES forget.

recommend v ADVOCATE, commend, put in a good word for, speak favourably of, endorse, approve, vouch for, suggest, offer, put forward, propose, advance.

recommendation n COMMENDATION, endorsement, suggestion, tip, hint, proposal, good word, favourable mention, praise; *informal* plug.

reconcile v REUNITE, bring together, restore harmony between, make peace between, bring to terms, pacify, appease, placate, propitiate, mollify.
– OPPOSITES estrange, quarrel.

reconnaissance n SURVEY, exploration, scouting, probe, inspection, observation; *informal* recce.

reconnoitre v SURVEY, see how the land lies, spy out, take stock of, explore, scout, investigate, scrutinize, scan, inspect,

observe; *informal* recce, check out.

reconsider v RETHINK, review, re-examine, re-evaluate, reassess, think again, think twice, have second thoughts, change one's mind.

reconstruct v REBUILD, remake, reassemble, refashion, recreate, remodel, revamp, renovate, recondition.

record n ❶ DOCUMENT, register, log, logbook, file, official report/account, chronicle, documentation, minutes, notes, annals, archives. ❷ DISC, album, single, recording, release; *informal* platter.
▶ v ❶ PUT ON RECORD, set down, write down, put in writing, take down, put down, enter, make a note of, document. ❷ REGISTER, read, indicate, show, display.

recount v DESCRIBE, detail, enumerate, list, specify, itemize, cite, particularize, catalogue.

recover v ❶ GET BACK, win back, regain, recoup, retrieve, reclaim, repossess, redeem, recuperate, recapture. ❷ GET BETTER, get well, recuperate, convalesce, heal, get back on one's feet, feel oneself again, improve, mend, pick up, perk up, rally, revive, pull through, bounce back.
– OPPOSITES deteriorate.

recovery n ❶ RECOUPING, regaining, retrieval, reclamation, repossession, recapture.

❷ RECUPERATION, convalescence, healing, rallying, revival.

recreation n **❶** RELAXATION, leisure, refreshment, amusement, entertainment, distraction, diversion. **❷** ACTIVITY, pastime, hobby, diversion, distraction.

recrimination n COUNTER-ACCUSATION, countercharge, counter-attack, retaliation, reprisal.

recruit v ENLIST, enrol, sign up, draft, conscript, levy, engage, obtain, acquire, procure, take on, round up, muster.
▶ n **❶** DRAFTEE, conscript. **❷** NEWCOMER, initiate, beginner, learner, trainee, apprentice.

rectify v PUT / SET RIGHT, right, correct, amend, emend, remedy, repair, fix, make good.

rectitude n RIGHTEOUSNESS, virtue, honour, integrity, principle, probity, uprightness, good character, decency, honesty.

recuperate v see RECOVER.

recur v REOCCUR, happen/occur again, come back, return, reappear, be repeated, happen repeatedly.

recurrent adj RECURRING, repeated, repetitive, reiterative, periodic, cyclical, regular, habitual, continual, frequent, intermittent, chronic.

recycle v REUSE, reprocess, salvage, save.

redden v GO RED, blush, flush, colour, colour up, crimson.

redeem v **❶** EXCHANGE, cash in, convert, turn in, trade in. **❷** SAVE, deliver from sin, turn from sin, convert, purge/absolve of sin.

redolent adj **❶** EVOCATIVE, suggestive, reminiscent. **❷** SWEET-SMELLING, fragrant, scented, perfumed, aromatic.

reduce v **❶** MAKE SMALLER, lessen, lower, decrease, diminish, cut, curtail, contract, shorten, abbreviate, moderate, dilute, alleviate, abate. **❷** BRING TO, bring to the point of, force to, drive to. **❸** DEMOTE, downgrade, lower, lower in rank/ status, humble. **❹** LOWER / CUT IN PRICE, lower, make cheaper, cheapen, cut, mark down, slash, discount, put on sale.
– OPPOSITES increase.

reduction n **❶** LESSENING, lowering, decrease, diminution, cut, contraction, abbreviation, moderation, dilution, alleviation, abatement. **❷** DISCOUNT, deduction, cut, concession, allowance. **❸** DEMOTION, downgrading, lowering, humbling.

redundant adj SURPLUS TO REQUIREMENTS, not required, unnecessary, inessential, unwanted, surplus, supernumerary.

reel v **❶** STAGGER, lurch, sway, stumble, totter, wobble, falter, waver, pitch, roll. **❷** FEEL GIDDY / DIZZY, feel confused, be shaken, be in shock, be upset.

refer v **❶** CONSULT, turn to, look at, look up, have recourse to. **❷** PASS, hand on, send on, transfer, remit, direct. ❸ MENTION, make mention of, make reference to, allude to, touch on, speak of, cite, hint at; *formal* advert to. ❹ APPLY TO, be relevant to, have relevance to, concern, relate to, belong to.

referee n UMPIRE, judge, adjudicator, arbitrator, arbiter, mediator; *informal* ref.

reference n ❶ MENTION, allusion, citation, hint. ❷ REGARD, respect, relation, bearing, relevance, pertinence. ❸ SOURCE, citation, authority, bibliography. ❹ TESTIMONIAL, recommendation, good word, credentials.

refine v PURIFY, rarefy, clarify, clear, cleanse, strain, sift, filter, distil, process.

refined adj ❶ PURIFIED, pure, rarefied, clarified, clear, filtered, distilled, processed. ❷ CULTIVATED, cultured, polished, civilized, civil, gracious, stylish, elegant, sophisticated, urbane, courtly, well mannered, well bred, gentlemanly, ladylike, genteel.
– OPPOSITES crude.

refinement n ❶ PURIFICATION, processing, distillation, filtration. ❷ CULTIVATION, culture, taste, discrimination, polish, finish, civility, grace, graciousness, style, elegance, finesse, sophistication, urbanity, courtliness, good breeding, politeness, good manners, gentility. ❸ SUBTLETY, nicety, nuance, fine point.

reflect v ❶ THROW BACK, cast

back, send back, give back, scatter, diffuse. ❷ MIRROR, echo. ❸ THINK, consider, mull over, contemplate, deliberate, ponder, meditate, muse, ruminate, cogitate, brood.

reflection n ❶ IMAGE, mirror image, echo. ❷ THINKING, thought, consideration, contemplation, deliberation, meditation, rumination, cogitation. ❸ OPINION, thought, view, idea, impression, comment, findings.

reform v ❶ IMPROVE, make better, ameliorate, amend, mend, rectify, correct, rehabilitate, change, make over, revamp, renovate. ❷ MEND ONE'S WAYS, change for the better, turn over a new leaf, improve; *informal* go straight.

refrain v DESIST, abstain, hold back, forbear, forgo, do without, avoid, eschew, cease, stop, give up, leave off, renounce; *informal* quit.

refresh v ❶ FRESHEN, invigorate, revitalize, revive, brace, fortify, enliven, perk up, stimulate, energize, exhilarate, rejuvenate, regenerate, breathe new life into, inspirit. ❷ STIMULATE, prompt, prod, jog, activate, rouse, arouse.
– OPPOSITES weary.

refreshing adj FRESHENING, invigorating, revitalizing, reviving, bracing, stimulating, exhilarating, energizing.

refuge n ❶ SHELTER, safety, security, protection, asylum, sanctuary. ❷ PLACE OF SAFETY, shelter, haven, retreat, bolt-hole, sanctuary, harbour.

refund v GIVE BACK, return, repay, pay back, reimburse, make good, restore, replace.
▶ n REPAYMENT, reimbursement.

refuse[1] v ❶ TURN DOWN, decline, say no to, reject, spurn, rebuff, repudiate; *informal* pass up, knock back. ❷ DECLINE, be unwilling, baulk at, demur at, avoid, resist, protest at.
– OPPOSITES accept.

refuse[2] n RUBBISH, waste, debris, litter, dross, dregs, leavings, sweepings; *N. Amer.* garbage, trash; *informal* junk.

refute v PROVE WRONG, disprove, negate, invalidate, discredit.

regain v GET BACK, win back, recover, recoup, retrieve, reclaim, repossess, redeem, recuperate, take back, retake, recapture.

regal adj ROYAL, majestic, noble, proud, kingly, queenly, princely, fit for a king/queen/prince/princess.

regard v ❶ WATCH, look at, gaze at, keep an eye on, stare at, observe, view, study, scrutinize, eye, mark, behold. ❷ LOOK UPON, view, consider, contemplate, think of, weigh up, mull over, reflect on, deliberate on.
▶ n ❶ LOOK, gaze, stare, observation, scrutiny. ❷ HEED, attention, notice, consideration, thought, mind. ❸ RESPECT, esteem, admiration, approval, approbation, favour.

regarding prep WITH / IN REGARD TO, as regards, as to, with reference to, on the subject/matter of, apropos, concerning, about, respecting.

regardless
■ regardless of WITHOUT REGARD TO, disregarding, unmindful of, heedless of, without consideration of, indifferent to, negligent of.

regards pl n BEST / GOOD WISHES, greetings, salutations, respects, compliments.

regenerate v RENEW, breathe new life into, restore, invigorate, refresh, revitalize, revive, revivify, rejuvenate.

regiment v ORGANIZE, order, control, discipline, keep a tight rein on, bring into line, rule with a rod of iron.

region n AREA, province, territory, division, section, sector, zone, tract, part, quarter, locality.

register n LIST, listing, roll, roster, index, directory, catalogue.
▶ v ❶ RECORD, put on record, enter, set down, chronicle, write down, take down, note, minute, list, catalogue. ❷ READ, record, indicate, show, display. ❸ SHOW, express, display, exhibit, evince, betray, reveal, manifest, demonstrate, reflect. ❹ MAKE AN IMPRESSION, get through, sink in, penetrate, have an effect.

regret v ❶ FEEL SORRY / CONTRITE ABOUT, feel remorse about, wish undone, repent, rue. ❷ LAMENT,

bemoan, be upset/disappointed about, mourn, grieve over, weep over, fret about, pine over, deplore.
– OPPOSITES welcome.

▶ n ❶ SORROW, remorse, contrition, repentance, pangs of conscience, compunction, ruefulness, self-reproach, penitence. ❷ DISAPPOINTMENT, lamentation, grief, mourning, pining.
– OPPOSITES satisfaction.

regretful adj SORRY, apologetic, remorseful, contrite, repentant, conscience-stricken, rueful, penitent.
– OPPOSITES unrepentant.

regrettable adj DEPLORABLE, reprehensible, disgraceful, blameworthy, unfortunate, unwelcome, ill-advised.

regular adj ❶ USUAL, normal, customary, habitual, routine, typical, everyday, daily, unvarying, common, average, commonplace. ❷ RHYTHMIC, steady, even, uniform, constant, consistent, orderly. ❸ REAL, thorough, absolute, utter, complete.
– OPPOSITES occasional, erratic.

regulate v ❶ CONTROL, direct, guide, govern, rule, manage, order, organize, conduct, run, supervise, oversee, superintend, monitor. ❷ ADJUST, balance, set, synchronize, modulate.

regulation n ❶ CONTROL, direction, guidance, government, rule, management,

administration, organization, supervision. ❷ RULE, ruling, order, directive, act, law, decree, statute, edict, ordinance.

rehearsal n PRACTICE, preparation, trial performance, run-through, going-over.

rehearse v PRACTISE, try out, run through, go over.

reign v ❶ BE KING / QUEEN, sit on the throne, occupy the throne, wear the crown, wield the sceptre. ❷ BE IN POWER, govern, rule, be in charge/control, administer, hold sway.
▶ n ❶ MONARCHY, sovereignty. ❷ POWER, government, rule, command, control, administration, charge.

rein
■ **rein in** CHECK, curb, restrain, constrain, hold back, restrict, control, bridle.

reinforce v ❶ STRENGTHEN, fortify, bolster up, shore up, buttress, prop up, brace, support, back up, uphold, stress, underline, emphasize. ❷ AUGMENT, increase, add to, supplement.

reiterate v REPEAT, say again, go over again, belabour, dwell on, harp on, hammer away at.

reject v ❶ REFUSE, turn down, decline, say no to, spurn, rebuff, repudiate, veto, deny; *informal* pass up, knock back, give the thumbs down to. ❷ CAST OUT, cast aside, discard, jettison, renounce, abandon, forsake, scrap, exclude, eliminate.
– OPPOSITES accept.

▶ n ❶ SUBSTANDARD ARTICLE, discard, second. ❷ FAILURE, outcast, derelict; *informal* drop-out.

rejoice v BE JOYFUL, be happy, be pleased, be glad, be delighted, be elated, be overjoyed, be jubilant, be euphoric, exult.
– OPPOSITES mourn.

rejoinder n ANSWER, response, reply, riposte, retort; *informal* comeback.

relapse v LAPSE, regress, retrogress, revert, backslide, fall away, go backwards, slip back, degenerate.
– OPPOSITES improve.
▶ n LAPSE, regression, retrogression, reversion, backsliding, recidivism.

relate v ❶ RECOUNT, tell, narrate, describe, report, impart, communicate, recite, rehearse, present, detail, delineate, chronicle, set forth. ❷ CONNECT, associate, link, correlate, ally, couple, join. ❸ APPLY TO, be relevant to, have relevance to, concern, refer to, have reference to, pertain to, bear on.

related adj ❶ CONNECTED, interconnected, associated, linked, correlated, allied, affiliated, accompanying, concomitant, akin. ❷ OF THE SAME FAMILY, connected, akin, kindred, agnate, cognate, consanguineous.
– OPPOSITES unrelated.

relation n ❶ CONNECTION, association, link, tie-in, correlation, alliance, bond, relationship, interdependence. ❷ RELATIVE, family member, kinsman, kinswoman, connection, kin.

relationship n ❶ See RELATION (1). ❷ FRIENDSHIP, love affair, affair, liaison.

relative adj ❶ COMPARATIVE, comparable, respective, correlative, parallel, corresponding. ❷ PROPORTIONATE, in proportion/ratio, based.
▶ n *see* RELATION (2).

relax v ❶ LOOSEN, slacken, weaken, lessen, let up, reduce, diminish. ❷ BECOME LESS TENSE / STIFF / RIGID, loosen, slacken. ❸ MODERATE, make less strict/formal, soften, ease. ❹ LOOSEN UP, ease up/off; *informal* unwind, take it easy, let it all hang out, hang loose.
– OPPOSITES tense, tighten.

relaxation n ❶ LOOSENING, slackening, weakening, letting up. ❷ LESSENING, reduction, easing off, abatement. ❸ LEISURE, recreation, enjoyment, amusement, entertainment, pleasure, rest, refreshment.

relay v PASS ON, hand on, communicate, send, transmit, broadcast, spread, circulate.

release v ❶ SET FREE, free, let go, set/turn loose, let out, liberate, untie, undo, unloose, unbind, unchain, unfetter, unshackle, extricate, deliver, emancipate; *historical* manumit. ❷ MAKE PUBLIC, make known, issue, break, announce, reveal, divulge, unveil, present, disclose, publish, broadcast,

put out, circulate, disseminate, distribute, spread.
– OPPOSITES imprison, suppress.

relent v SOFTEN, become merciful/lenient, show mercy/pity, give quarter, capitulate, yield, give way, give in, unbend, come round, forbear, change one's mind.

relentless adj ❶ UNCEASING, unrelenting, unremitting, persistent, unswerving, persevering, unflagging, unfaltering, unstoppable, incessant. ❷ HARSH, ruthless, merciless, pitiless, remorseless, unforgiving, implacable, inexorable, cruel, grim, hard, cold-hearted, fierce, strict, obdurate, unyielding, inflexible, unbending.
– OPPOSITES lenient.

relevant adj APPLICABLE, pertinent, apposite, material, appurtenant, to the point/purpose, germane, admissible, appropriate, apt, fitting.
– OPPOSITES irrelevant.

reliable adj ❶ TRUSTWORTHY, dependable, trusty, true, faithful, devoted, steady, steadfast, constant, unfailing, certain, sure. ❷ WELL FOUNDED, well grounded, sound, trustworthy, dependable, credible, authentic, genuine.
– OPPOSITES unreliable.

relic n ❶ ANCIENT / HISTORICAL OBJECT, artefact, antique, heirloom. ❷ VESTIGE, trace, survivor, remnant.

relief n ❶ ALLEVIATION, mitigation, assuagement, palliation,

ease, appeasement, abatement. ❷ AID, help, assistance, succour. ❸ RESPITE, remission, interruption, break, variation, diversion; informal let-up.
– OPPOSITES intensification.

relieve v ❶ ALLEVIATE, mitigate, assuage, allay, soothe, soften, palliate, appease, ease, dull, abate, reduce, lessen, diminish. ❷ BRING AID TO, aid, help, assist, rescue, save, succour. ❸ BRING RESPITE TO, interrupt, break up, vary, lighten.
– OPPOSITES aggravate.

religious adj ❶ CHURCH, holy, divine, theological, doctrinal, spiritual, sectarian. ❷ CHURCHGOING, God-fearing, godly, pious, devout. ❸ SCRUPULOUS, conscientious, meticulous, zealous, strict, rigid, rigorous.
– OPPOSITES irreligious.

relinquish v GIVE UP, renounce, resign, abdicate, surrender, sign away.
– OPPOSITES retain.

relish n ENJOYMENT, delight, pleasure, satisfaction, gratification, appreciation, liking, zest, gusto.
▶ v ENJOY, delight in, like, love, adore, appreciate, revel in, luxuriate in.
– OPPOSITES dislike.

reluctant adj UNWILLING, disinclined, hesitant, unenthusiastic, grudging, loath, averse, slow, chary.
– OPPOSITES eager.

rely
■ rely on DEPEND ON, count on,

bank on, trust, lean on, be confident/sure of, swear by.

remain v ❶ BE LEFT, be left over, stay behind, survive, last, abide, endure, prevail. ❷ WAIT, stay, linger; *informal* stay put; *archaic* tarry. ❸ STAY, continue to be, persist in being.

remainder n REMNANT, residue, leavings, dregs, residuum, balance, surplus, excess, superfluity.

remains pl n ❶ REMNANTS, leftovers, leavings, scraps, residue, debris, detritus. ❷ RELICS, reliquiae, fragments, shards. ❸ CORPSE, dead body, body, carcass; *Medicine* cadaver; *informal* stiff.

remark v ❶ MENTION, say, state, declare, pronounce, assert, observe. ❷ NOTE, notice, observe, mark, perceive, discern.
▶ n COMMENT, statement, utterance, declaration, pronouncement, observation, reference, opinion.

remarkable adj OUT OF THE ORDINARY, extraordinary, unusual, uncommon, conspicuous, singular, notable, noteworthy, memorable, signal, rare, exceptional, outstanding, striking, impressive, considerable, pre-eminent, significant, important, momentous, phenomenal, wonderful.
– OPPOSITES ordinary, commonplace.

remedy n ❶ CURE, treatment, medicine, medication, medicament, therapy, antidote, restorative, nostrum, panacea.

❷ CORRECTIVE, solution, redress, panacea.
▶ v ❶ CURE, heal, treat, counteract, control. ❷ RECTIFY, solve, set to rights, put right, redress, fix, sort out.

remember v ❶ RECALL, call to mind, recollect, think of, keep/bear in mind, not forget. ❷ REMINISCE ABOUT, look/think back on, hark back to, summon up.
– OPPOSITES forget.

remind v CAUSE TO REMEMBER, jog/refresh someone's memory, prompt.

reminiscent adj EVOCATIVE, suggestive, redolent.

remiss adj NEGLIGENT, neglectful, lax, slack, slipshod, sloppy, careless, forgetful, inattentive, heedless, thoughtless, unthinking, culpable, delinquent.
– OPPOSITES careful, diligent.

remission n ❶ CANCELLATION, revocation, repeal, rescinding. ❷ EASING, moderation, abatement, lessening, decrease, dwindling, wane, waning, ebb, ebbing, subsidence.

remit v ❶ CANCEL, revoke, repeal, rescind, stop, halt. ❷ EASE, moderate, abate, lessen, decrease, dwindle, wane, ebb, subside. ❸ SEND, dispatch, forward, transmit, post, mail.

remnant n ❶ REMAINDER, residue, balance, remains, vestiges. ❷ PIECE, fragment, scrap.

remonstrate
■ **remonstrate with** TAKE ISSUE WITH, argue with, dispute with,

protest to, complain to, expostulate with.

remorse n REGRET, sorrow, contrition, penitence, repentance, guilty conscience, guilt, shame, self-reproach, ruefulness, pangs of conscience, compunction.

remorseful adj SORRY, regretful, contrite, apologetic, penitent, repentant, guilt-ridden, conscience-stricken, ashamed, chastened, rueful.
– OPPOSITES unrepentant.

remorseless adj see RELENTLESS.

remote adj ❶ DISTANT, far, far-off, faraway, out of the way, outlying, inaccessible, off the beaten track, isolated, secluded, lonely, godforsaken. ❷ UNLIKELY, improbable, implausible, negligible, insignificant, doubtful, dubious, slight, slender, slim, small, poor. ❸ ALOOF, distant, detached, withdrawn, reserved, uncommunicative, unapproachable, stand-offish, cool, haughty, uninvolved, indifferent, unconcerned.
– OPPOSITES near, likely, friendly.

removal n ❶ DISMISSAL, eviction, ejection, expulsion, ousting, dislodgement, deposition. ❷ TAKING AWAY, withdrawal, deprivation, abolition. ❸ DELETION, elimination, erasure, effacing, obliteration.

remove v ❶ TAKE AWAY, carry away, move, shift, convey, transfer, transport. ❷ DISMISS,

get rid of, eject, expel, cast out, oust, throw out, dislodge, relegate, unseat, depose, displace; *informal* sack, fire. ❸ TAKE OFF, pull off, strip off; *Brit. informal* peel off. ❹ DELETE, eliminate, erase, rub out, cross out, strike out, blue-pencil, efface, obliterate. ❺ TAKE OUT, pull out, uproot, eradicate, extirpate, destroy, exterminate, annihilate. ❻ CUT OFF, amputate, lop off, chop off, excise.

remunerative adj PROFITABLE, moneymaking, paying, lucrative, gainful, financially rewarding, rich.

render v ❶ MAKE, cause to be/become, leave. ❷ GIVE, contribute, make available, provide, supply, furnish. ❸ PRESENT, send in, submit, tender. ❹ ACT, perform, play, execute, interpret.

rendezvous n APPOINTMENT, date, engagement, meeting, assignation.

renegade n DEFECTOR, deserter, turncoat, traitor, apostate, revolutionary, rebel, mutineer.

renege v GO BACK ON ONE'S WORD, break one's promise, default, back out, welsh, pull out; *informal* cop out.
– OPPOSITES honour.

renounce v ❶ RELINQUISH, give up, resign, abdicate, surrender, sign away, waive, forego. ❷ DISOWN, repudiate, cast off, discard, reject, disinherit, wash one's hands of, spurn, shun. ❸ ABSTAIN FROM,

give up, desist from, swear off, eschew.
– OPPOSITES embrace.

renovate v MODERNIZE, recondition, refurbish, rehabilitate, overhaul, restore, revamp, remodel, repair, redecorate, refit; *informal* do up, fix up.

renown n FAME, repute, acclaim, celebrity, distinction, illustriousness, eminence, pre-eminence, prominence, mark, note, consequence, prestige.

renowned adj FAMOUS, famed, well known, of repute, acclaimed, celebrated, distinguished, illustrious, eminent, pre-eminent, prominent, noted, notable, of note, of consequence, prestigious.
– OPPOSITES obscure.

rent[1] n RENTAL, payment, hire fee.
▶ v ❶ LEASE, hire, charter. ❷ LET, lease, hire, hire/let out, farm out.

rent[2] n TEAR, rip, split, gash, slash, hole, perforation, break, crack, fracture, crevice, fissure, cleft.

repair[1] v ❶ MEND, fix, put right, restore, adjust, regulate, overhaul. ❷ PUT RIGHT, make good, rectify, correct, redress, compensate for.

repay v ❶ PAY BACK, refund, reimburse, recompense, remunerate, square accounts with, settle up with. ❷ GET BACK AT, hit back, retaliate against, get even with, settle the score with; *informal* get one's own back on.

repeal v REVOKE, rescind, abrogate, annul, nullify, make void, void, invalidate, quash, set aside, cancel, countermand, retract, overrule, override, reverse.

repeat v ❶ SAY AGAIN, restate, retell, reiterate, recapitulate, recap, echo, parrot, quote. ❷ DO AGAIN, redo, duplicate, replicate.

repeated adj RECURRENT, frequent, continual, incessant, constant, endless.

repel v ❶ REPULSE, drive back, push back, thrust back, force back, beat back, ward off, fend off, keep at bay, keep at arm's length. ❷ REVOLT, disgust, sicken, nauseate, make someone sick, turn someone's stomach, be repugnant to, make someone's flesh creep; *informal* give someone the creeps.
– OPPOSITES welcome, attract.

repellent adj REPULSIVE, revolting, disgusting, sickening, nauseating, distasteful, repugnant, abhorrent, offensive, obnoxious, loathsome, off-putting, hateful, vile, nasty, odious, abominable, horrible, horrid, foul, heinous, obscene.
– OPPOSITES attractive.

repent v BE SORRY, be contrite, be conscience-stricken, reproach oneself, be ashamed, regret, rue, be penitent.

repentant adj PENITENT, sorrowful, apologetic, regretful, contrite, remorseful, conscience-stricken, rueful, ashamed, guilt-ridden.
– OPPOSITES unashamed.

repercussion n EFFECT, result, consequence, reverberation, backlash.

repetitive adj RECURRENT, unchanging, unvaried, monotonous, humdrum, tedious, boring, mechanical, automatic; Brit. informal samey.

replace v ❶ PUT BACK, return, restore. ❷ TAKE THE PLACE OF, succeed, supersede, follow after, come after, supplant, substitute for, stand in for, act for, fill in for, cover for.

replacement n SUCCESSOR, substitute, stand-in, fill-in, locum, understudy, proxy, surrogate.

replenish v REFILL, top up, fill up, recharge, reload.

replica n COPY, carbon copy, duplicate, facsimile, model, reproduction, imitation.

reply v ANSWER, respond, write back, rejoin, retort, return, riposte, come back, counter.
▶ n ANSWER, response, acknowledgement, rejoinder, retort, return, riposte; informal comeback.

report n ❶ ACCOUNT, statement, record, exposition. ❷ ARTICLE, piece, story, write-up, communiqué, dispatch, bulletin. ❸ EXPLOSION, bang, boom, crack, crash.
▶ v ❶ ANNOUNCE, pass on, communicate, relay, relate, tell, recount, give an account of, set forth, document, narrate, describe, delineate, detail, divulge, disclose, circulate. ❷ TELL ON, inform on, accuse,

make a charge/complaint against; informal squeal on, rat on; Brit. informal grass on. ❸ PRESENT ONESELF, be present, appear, arrive, come, turn up, clock in; Brit. clock on; informal show up.

reporter n JOURNALIST, newsman, newswoman, pressman, correspondent, writer, broadcaster, announcer, presenter; informal newshound, hack.

reprehensible adj BLAMEWORTHY, culpable, bad, shameful, errant, wrong, bad, shameful, disgraceful, discreditable, dishonourable, objectionable, unpardonable, indefensible, unjustifiable, inexcusable.
– OPPOSITES praiseworthy.

represent v ❶ STAND FOR, symbolize, personify, epitomize, typify, embody, incorporate, exemplify. ❷ DEPICT, portray, delineate, illustrate, picture, denote, paint, draw, sketch, exhibit, show, display, evoke. ❸ ACT FOR, appear for, speak for, be the representative of.

representation n DEPICTION, portrayal, portrait, delineation, illustration, picture, painting, drawing, sketch, image, model.

representative adj ❶ TYPICAL, archetypal, exemplary, characteristic, indicative, illustrative. ❷ ELECTED, elective, chosen, delegated.
– OPPOSITES unrepresentative.
▶ n ❶ SPOKESMAN, spokeswoman, spokesperson, agent, deputy, proxy. ❷ MEMBER OF

PARLIAMENT, MP, Member, deputy, councillor.

repress v ❶ SUBJUGATE, conquer, vanquish, overpower, overcome, crush, master, dominate, domineer, bully, intimidate, oppress. ❷ HOLD / KEEP BACK, hold in, bite back, restrain, suppress, keep in check, check, inhibit, bottle up, silence, muffle, stifle, smother.

repressed adj ❶ SUBJUGATED, oppressed, tyrannized. ❷ RE-STRAINED, suppressed, muffled, smothered. ❸ INHIBITED, withdrawn, restrained.

repression n ❶ OPPRESSION, dictatorship, authoritarianism, tyranny, despotism, domination, coercion, suppression, subjugation. ❷ HOLDING BACK, biting back, restraint, suppression, smothering.

repressive adj TYRANNICAL, despotic, dictatorial, authoritarian, oppressive, coercive, suppressive, harsh, severe, strict, cruel.

reprieve v POSTPONE / CANCEL PUNISHMENT, grant a stay of execution to, let off, spare, pardon, let off the hook, show clemency to.

reprimand v REBUKE, scold, chide, reproach, reprove, lecture, admonish, berate, upbraid, correct, take to task, haul over the coals; *informal* tell off, give someone a dressing-down, bawl out; *Brit. informal* tick off; *formal* castigate.
– OPPOSITES praise
▶ n REBUKE, scolding, chiding,

reproach, reproof, admonition, berating, upbraiding, tongue-lashing; *informal* talking-to, telling-off, dressing-down, bawling-out; *Brit. informal* ticking-off, wigging; *formal* castigation.
– OPPOSITES commendation.

reprisal n RETALIATION, revenge, vengeance, retribution, redress, requital, recrimination, an eye for an eye; *informal* tit for tat.

reproach v & n *see* REPRIMAND.

reproachful adj DISAPPROV-ING, disappointed, critical, censorious, admonitory, condemnatory, disparaging, reproving; *formal* castigatory.
– OPPOSITES approving.

reproduce v ❶ COPY, duplicate, replicate, photocopy, recreate, redo, remake, imitate, follow, emulate, echo, mirror, parallel, match, mimic, ape. ❷ BREED, procreate, bear young, produce offspring, give birth, multiply, propagate, proliferate, spawn.

reproduction n ❶ COPY, duplicate, replica, facsimile, imitation, print. ❷ BREEDING, procreation, propagation, proliferation.

repudiate v DISOWN, reject, cast off, cut off, abandon, forsake, desert, discard, renounce, disavow, abjure, turn one's back on, have nothing to do with, wash one's hands of.
– OPPOSITES embrace.

repugnant adj ABHORRENT, revolting, repulsive, repellent,

disgusting, sickening, nauseating, disagreeable, distasteful, offensive, objectionable, obnoxious, loathsome, off-putting, hateful, despicable, reprehensible, contemptible, abominable, horrible, horrid, foul, nasty, vile, ugly, odious, heinous.
– OPPOSITES agreeable.

repulsive adj *see* REPUGNANT.

reputable adj RESPECTABLE, respected, well thought of, esteemed, estimable, of good repute, worthy, creditable, reliable, dependable, conscientious, trustworthy, above board, legitimate, upright, virtuous, good, excellent.
– OPPOSITES disreputable.

reputation n REPUTE, standing, name, character, position, status, station.

request n ENTREATY, appeal, petition, plea, application, demand, solicitation, call, suit.
▶ v ASK FOR, solicit, seek, apply for, put in for, call for, beg for, plead for, pray for, petition, implore, sue for, supplicate for, requisition, demand, desire; *poetic/literary* beseech.

require v ❶ NEED, have need of, lack, be short of, want, wish, desire, crave, miss. ❷ CALL FOR, demand, necessitate, involve, take.

required adj COMPULSORY, obligatory, mandatory, prescribed, recommended, requisite, set, essential, necessary, vital.
– OPPOSITES optional.

requirement n NEED, want, lack, must, necessity, demand, prerequisite, requisite, precondition, specification, qualification, sine qua non, stipulation.

requisite adj *see* REQUIRED.

requisition n ❶ APPLICATION, order, claim, request, call, demand. ❷ COMMANDEERING, appropriation, possession, occupation, seizure, confiscation.
▶ v ❶ APPLY FOR, order, put in a claim for, request, call for, demand. ❷ COMMANDEER, appropriate, take over, take possession of, occupy, seize, confiscate.

rescue v SAVE, come to someone's aid, free, set free, release, liberate, emancipate, get out, extricate, redeem, salvage, relieve.
▶ n DELIVERANCE, freeing, release, liberation, emancipation, extrication, redemption, salvage, relief.

research n EXPERIMENT, assessment, study, tests, investigation, experimentation, fact-finding, testing, exploration.
▶ v DO TESTS ON, investigate, inquire into, look into, probe, explore, analyse, study, examine.

resemblance n LIKENESS, similarity, semblance, sameness, uniformity, correspondence, comparability, affinity, closeness, nearness, agreement, congruity, concurrence, conformity.

resemble V BE LIKE, look like, bear a resemblance to, be similar to, remind one of, take after, echo, mirror, parallel, favour.

resent V TAKE OFFENCE / UMBRAGE AT, take exception to, take amiss, be annoyed/angry at, begrudge, feel bitter about, dislike.
– OPPOSITES welcome.

resentful adj AGGRIEVED, offended, indignant, irritated, displeased, annoyed, angry, irate, incensed, piqued, in high dudgeon, grudging, bitter, embittered, wounded; *informal* in a huff.

resentment n OFFENCE, indignation, irritation, displeasure, annoyance, anger, pique, grudgingness, bitterness, animosity, hostility, hard feelings; *poetic/literary* ire.

reservation n ❶ BOOKING, engagement, appointment. ❷ CONDITION, stipulation, qualification, proviso, provision, qualm, scruple, hesitancy, doubt.

reserve V ❶ PUT / SET / LAY ASIDE, put away, keep back, keep, withhold, conserve, save, retain, store, hoard, stockpile; *informal* hang on to. ❷ BOOK, engage, arrange for, charter, hire.
▶ n ❶ STORE, stock, supply, reservoir, pool, cache, fund, stockpile, accumulation, backlog, hoard. ❷ ALOOFNESS, detachment, distance, remoteness, formality, coolness, coldness, frigidity, reticence,

unapproachability, uncommunicativeness, shyness, diffidence, taciturnity. ❸ PRESERVE, reservation, sanctuary, park.

reserved adj ALOOF, detached, remote, formal, unemotional, undemonstrative, cool, cold, frigid, reticent, unapproachable, uncommunicative, unsociable, unfriendly, unresponsive, unforthcoming, shy, retiring, diffident, secret, secretive, taciturn, silent.
– OPPOSITES outgoing.

reside
■ **reside in** LIVE IN, dwell in, stay in, inhabit, occupy.

residence n HOUSE, home, habitation, quarters, lodgings; *formal* dwelling, domicile.

resident n REMAINDER, occupant, householder, denizen; *Brit.* occupier.

residue n REMAINDER, remnant, residuum, rest, surplus, extra, excess, remains, leftovers, dregs, lees.

resign V ❶ GIVE NOTICE, hand in one's notice, leave; *informal* quit. ❷ RENOUNCE, relinquish, give up, abdicate, surrender, cede.

resilient adj ❶ ELASTIC, springy, rubbery, whippy, flexible, pliant, supple, pliable, plastic. ❷ TOUGH, strong, hardy, quick to recover, difficult to keep down, irrepressible.

resist V ❶ WITHSTAND, be proof against, repel. ❷ STOP, halt, prevent, check stem, curb, obstruct, hinder, impede, block, thwart, frustrate, inhibit, restrain.

resistant adj PROOF AGAINST, impervious to, unaffected by, immune to.

resolute adj DETERMINED, resolved, decided, firm, fixed, set, intent, steadfast, constant, earnest, staunch, bold, courageous, serious, purposeful, deliberate, inflexible, unyielding, unwavering, unfaltering, unhesitating, unswerving, unflinching, obstinate, obdurate, strong-willed, dogged, persevering, persistent, tenacious, relentless, unshakeable, dedicated.
– OPPOSITES irresolute.

resolution n ❶ RESOLVE, determination, firmness, intentness, steadfastness, constancy, staunchness, boldness, courage, seriousness, purposefulness, obstinacy, obduracy, will power, doggedness, perseverance, persistence, tenacity, staying power, dedication. ❷ MOTION, declaration, decree, verdict, judgement. ❸ SOLVING, solution, answer, sorting out, working out, unravelling, disentanglement, cracking.

resolve v ❶ DECIDE, make up one's mind, determine, settle on, undertake. ❷ SOLVE, answer, sort out, work out, clear up, fathom, unravel, disentangle, crack.
▶ n see RESOLUTION (1).

resort v FALL BACK ON, turn to, have recourse to, look to, make use of, use, avail oneself of, bring into play/service, exercise.

▶ n ❶ HOLIDAY / TOURIST CENTRE, centre, spot, retreat. ❷ RECOURSE, source of help, expedient, alternative, choice, possibility, hope.

resound v REVERBERATE, resonate, echo, ring.

resource n ❶ ASSET, reserve, reservoir, store, stock, supply, pool, fund, stockpile. ❷ RESOURCEFULNESS, initiative, ingenuity, inventiveness, quick-wittedness, cleverness, native wit, talent, ability, capability.

respect n ❶ ESTEEM, high regard, regard, high opinion, admiration, approval, appreciation, veneration, reverence, deference, honour, praise, homage. ❷ ASPECT, facet, feature, way, sense, characteristic, particular, point, detail.
– OPPOSITES contempt.
▶ v ESTEEM, have a high opinion of, think highly of, admire, approve of, appreciate, venerate, revere, honour, praise.
– OPPOSITES despise.

respectable adj ❶ REPUTABLE, of good repute, upright, honest, honourable, trustworthy, above board, worthy, decent, good, virtuous, admirable, well bred, proper, decorous. ❷ REASONABLE, fairly good, fair, considerable, ample, sizable, substantial; informal not to be sneezed at.
– OPPOSITES disreputable, paltry.

respective adj INDIVIDUAL, separate, personal, own, particular, specific.

respects pl n IN REGARDS, best wishes, greetings, compliments, remembrances.

respite n IN REST, break, interval, intermission, recess, lull, pause, hiatus, halt, relief, relaxation; *informal* breather, let-up.

respond v ❶ ANSWER, reply to, say in response to, acknowledge. ❷ SAY IN RESPONSE, answer, reply, rejoin, retort, return, riposte, come back, counter.

response n ANSWER, reply, acknowledgement, rejoinder, retort, return, riposte; *informal* comeback.
– OPPOSITES question.

responsibility n ❶ DUTY, charge, onus, task, role, liability, accountability, answerability. ❷ BLAME, fault, guilt, culpability.

responsible adj ❶ IN CHARGE / CONTROL OF, at the helm of, accountable for, liable for. ❷ ACCOUNTABLE, answerable, to blame, blameworthy, at fault, guilty, culpable. ❸ SENSIBLE, level-headed, rational, reasonable, sound, stable, reliable, dependable, trustworthy, competent, conscientious, hard-working, industrious.
– OPPOSITES irresponsible.

responsive adj QUICK TO REACT, reactive, receptive, forthcoming, sensitive, perceptive, sympathetic, susceptible, impressionable, open, alive, awake, aware, sharp.

rest n ❶ REPOSE, relaxation, leisure, ease, inactivity, respite, time off, breathing space, sleep, slumber. ❷ BREAK, interval, interlude, intermission, lull, pause, time off. ❸ STAND, base, holder, support, prop, shelf.
▶ v ❶ TAKE A REST, relax, sit down, lie down, go to bed, sleep, take a nap, nap, catnap, doze, slumber; *informal* take it easy. ❷ BE SUPPORTED BY, be propped up by, lie on, be laid on, recline on, stand on, sit on. ❸ DEPEND, rely, hang, hinge, be based, be founded.

restful adj ❶ QUIET, calm, tranquil, relaxed, peaceful, placid, still, languid, undisturbed, unhurried, sleepy.
– OPPOSITES hectic.

restless adj ❶ SLEEPLESS, wakeful, tossing and turning, fitful. ❷ UNEASY, ill at ease, on edge, agitated. ❸ UNSETTLED, roaming, roving, wandering, itinerant, travelling, nomadic, peripatetic.

restore v ❶ RENOVATE, repair, fix, mend, set to rights, recondition, rehabilitate, refurbish, rebuild, reconstruct, remodel, revamp, redecorate, touch up; *informal* do up, fix up. ❷ RETURN, give back, hand back, send back. ❸ RE-ESTABLISH, reinstitute, reinstate, reinstall, reimpose.

restrain v CONTROL, keep under control, check, hold in check, curb, keep within bounds, subdue, suppress, repress, contain, smother, stifle, bottle up, rein in; *informal* keep the lid on.

restraint n ❶ CONSTRAINT, check, curb, block, hindrance, impediment, deterrent, inhibition. ❷ SELF-RESTRAINT, self-control, self-discipline, moderation, temperateness, prudence, judiciousness.

restrict v ❶ HINDER, impede, hamper, retard, handicap, cramp. ❷ LIMIT, set/impose limits on, keep under control, regulate, control, moderate.

restriction n CONSTRAINT, limitation, control, check, curb, regulation, condition, provision, proviso, stipulation, qualification, demarcation.

result n ❶ OUTCOME, consequence, issue, upshot, sequel, effect, repercussion, end, conclusion, termination, aftermath, product, by-product, fruits. ❷ ANSWER, solution.
– OPPOSITES cause.
▶ v FOLLOW, ensue, issue, develop, stem, evolve, emerge, emanate, occur, happen, come about, eventuate.
■ **result in** END IN, culminate in, finish in, terminate in.

resume v CARRY ON, continue, recommence, begin again, reopen, reinstitute.

resurrect v RAISE FROM THE DEAD, restore to life, bring back to life, revive, breathe new life into, give new life to.

retain v ❶ KEEP, keep possession/hold of, hold on to, hang

on to, preserve, maintain. ❷ HIRE, employ, engage, commission.

retaliate v TAKE / EXACT / WREAK REVENGE, avenge oneself, exact retribution, give as good as one gets, get one's own back, get back at, make reprisals, get even with, even the scores, settle a score.

retard v SLOW DOWN, slow up, hold back, set back, hold up, delay, hinder, hamper, obstruct, impede, decelerate, put a brake on, check, arrest, interfere with, interrupt, thwart, frustrate.
– OPPOSITES expedite.

reticent adj *see* RESERVED.

retire v ❶ GIVE UP WORK, stop working, be pensioned off; *informal* be put out to grass. ❷ WITHDRAW, go out, depart, exit, leave, absent oneself. ❸ GO TO BED, go to sleep, turn in, call it a day; *informal* hit the sack.

retiring adj SHY, diffident, bashful, self-effacing, shrinking, unassuming, reserved, reticent, timid, timorous, nervous, modest, demure.
– OPPOSITES brash.

retract v ❶ DRAW IN, pull in, pull back. ❷ TAKE BACK, withdraw, revoke, repeal, rescind, annul, cancel, abrogate, disavow, abjure, renounce, recant, disclaim, backtrack on, renege on.

retreat v ❶ WITHDRAW, pull back, fall back, back off, give way/ground, decamp, depart, leave, flee, take flight, turn tail,

beat a retreat, beat a hasty retreat. ❷ GO BACK, recede, ebb.
▶ n ❶ WITHDRAWAL, pulling back, departure, flight, evacuation.
❷ REFUGE, haven, shelter, sanctuary, sanctum sanctorum, hideaway, resort, asylum.

retribution n REPRISAL, retaliation, revenge, vengeance, punishment, justice, nemesis, reckoning, requital, an eye for an eye, tit for tat.

retrieve v GET BACK, recover, regain, win back, recoup, redeem, reclaim, repossess, recapture, salvage, rescue.

retrograde adj RETROGRESSIVE, backwards, deteriorating, declining, on the wane.

retrospect
■ in retrospect ON REFLECTION, on looking/thinking back, with hindsight.

return v ❶ GO BACK, come back, reappear, reoccur, come again, come round again. ❷ GIVE BACK, send back, take back, carry back, put back, restore, reinstate, reinstall. ❸ RECIPROCATE, repay, requite, send/give in response to.
– OPPOSITES depart.
▶ n ❶ HOMECOMING, reappearance, reoccurrence. ❷ REPLACEMENT, restoration, reinstatement, reinstallation.
❸ PROFIT, yield, gain, income, revenue, interest.
– OPPOSITES departure.

reveal v ❶ SHOW, display, exhibit, expose to view. ❷ BRING TO LIGHT, uncover, expose to view, lay bare, unearth, unveil,

unmask. ❸ DISCLOSE, divulge, tell, let out, let on, let slip, give away, give out, leak, betray, make known/public, broadcast, publicize, publish, proclaim.
– OPPOSITES conceal, hide.

revel v CELEBRATE, make merry, have a party, party, carouse, roister.
■ revel in DELIGHT IN, take pleasure in, bask in, rejoice in, relish, savour, gloat over, luxuriate in, wallow in.

revelation n DISCLOSURE, divulgence, telling, leak, betrayal, broadcasting, publicizing, communication, publishing, proclamation.

revelry n CELEBRATIONS, festivities, jollification, merrymaking, carousal.

revenge n VENGEANCE, retaliation, retribution, reprisal, redress.
▶ v TAKE REVENGE FOR, avenge, retaliate, exact retribution for, take reprisals for, requite.

revenue n INCOME, return, yield, interest, profits, returns, receipts, proceeds, takings, rewards.
– OPPOSITES expenditure.

reverberate v RESOUND, echo, ring, vibrate.

revere v LOOK UP TO, think highly of, admire, respect, esteem, defer to, honour, venerate, exalt, put on a pedestal, idolize.
– OPPOSITES despise.

reverence n ESTEEM, admiration, respect, deference, honour, veneration, worship,

homage, adoration, devotion, awe, exaltation.
– OPPOSITES scorn.

reverent adj REVERENTIAL, admiring, respectful, deferential, adoring, loving, devoted, awed, submissive, humble, meek.

reversal n ❶ TURNAROUND, turnabout, about-face, volte-face, U-turn, change of heart; Brit. about-turn. ❷ CHANGE, exchange, trading, trade-off, swapping. ❸ OVERTURN, overthrow, revocation, repeal, rescinding, annulment, invalidation.

reverse v ❶ TURN ROUND, put back to front, turn upside down, upend, invert. ❷ MOVE / DIRECT BACKWARDS, back. ❸ CHANGE, exchange, trade, swap. ❹ SET ASIDE, overturn, overthrow, revoke, repeal, rescind, annul, nullify, declare null and void, void, invalidate, quash.
▶ adj REVERSED, backwards, inverted, transposed, turned round.
▶ n ❶ OPPOSITE, contrary, converse, antithesis. ❷ OTHER SIDE, back, rear, underside, flip side. ❸ REVERSAL, upset, setback, failure, misfortune, mishap, blow, disappointment.

review n ❶ STUDY, analysis, survey, examination, scrutiny, assessment, appraisal. ❷ CRITICISM, critique, notice, assessment, evaluation, rating.
▶ v ❶ ANALYSE, examine, study, survey, scrutinize, assess, appraise. ❷ CRITICIZE, evaluate,

assess, appraise, judge, weigh up, discuss.

revise v ❶ AMEND, emend, correct, alter, change, edit, rewrite, redraft, rework, update, revamp. ❷ GO OVER, reread, run through, study; informal bone up on; Brit. informal swot up on.

revival n RESUSCITATION, resurrection, rebirth, renaissance, comeback, restoration, reintroduction.

revive v ❶ BRING ROUND, resuscitate, give artificial respiration to, save, restore to health; informal give the kiss of life to. ❷ REFRESH, restore, cheer up, comfort, enliven, revitalize.

revoke v REPEAL, rescind, abrogate, countermand, annul, nullify, declare null and void, void, invalidate, quash.
– OPPOSITES enact.

revolt v ❶ RISE UP, take to the streets, take up arms, rebel, mutiny. ❷ DISGUST, repel, sicken, nauseate, turn someone's stomach, be repugnant to, make someone's flesh creep, put off, offend, shock.

revolting adj see REPELLENT.

revolution n ❶ REBELLION, revolt, insurrection, uprising, rising, insurgence, coup, putsch. ❷ DRASTIC CHANGE, metamorphosis, sea change, upheaval, upset, transformation. ❸ ROTATION, single turn, whirl, round, spin, wheel.

revolutionary adj ❶ REBELLIOUS, insurrectionary, mutinous, seditious, subversive,

extremist. ❷ PROGRESSIVE, radical, innovative, new, novel, avant-garde, experimental, different, drastic.
▶ n REBEL, insurgent, insurrectionist.

revolve v GO ROUND, turn round, rotate, spin, circle, orbit, gyrate, whirl.

revulsion n REPULSION, disgust, nausea, distaste, aversion, repugnance, abhorrence, loathing.
– OPPOSITES delight.

reward n RECOMPENSE, payment, remuneration, bonus, bounty, present, gift, tip, gratuity, prize.
– OPPOSITES punishment.
▶ v RECOMPENSE, pay, remunerate, give a present to, tip.

rewarding adj SATISFYING, fulfilling, enriching, edifying, beneficial, profitable, advantageous, productive, valuable.

rhetoric n BOMBAST, grandiloquence, magniloquence, hyperbole, pomposity, verbosity, prolixity, turgidity.

rhetorical adj POMPOUS, high-flown, flamboyant, showy, flowery, florid, oratorical, declamatory, bombastic, grandiloquent, magniloquent, hyperbolical, verbose, longwinded, prolix, turgid, periphrastic.

rhythm n BEAT, cadence, tempo, pulse, metre, pattern.

ribald adj BAWDY, risqué, smutty, vulgar, coarse, earthy, off colour, rude, naughty, racy,

suggestive, indecent, indelicate. See also OBSCENE.

rich adj ❶ WEALTHY, affluent, well off, well-to-do, prosperous, moneyed, propertied; informal well heeled, filthy rich, loaded, made of money, rolling in it/money, flush, worth a packet/bundle, on Easy Street.
❷ OPULENT, expensive, costly, precious, valuable, priceless, beyond price, lavish, luxurious, lush, sumptuous, palatial, splendid, superb, resplendent, elegant, fine, exquisite, magnificent, grand, gorgeous.
❸ WELL PROVIDED, well supplied, well stocked, abounding, overflowing, replete, rife. ❹ FERTILE, productive, fecund, fruitful, lush. ❺ CREAMY, fatty, heavy.
– OPPOSITES poor, plain, barren.

riches pl n WEALTH, affluence, prosperity, money, capital, property, treasure, assets, resources.

richly adv ❶ EXPENSIVELY, lavishly, luxuriously, sumptuously, palatially, splendidly, superbly, magnificently.
❷ FULLY, in full measure, well, thoroughly, completely, amply, utterly.
– OPPOSITES meanly.

rid v DO AWAY WITH, remove, get rid of, dispense with, eliminate, dump, dispose of, unload, expel, eject, weed out, clear, cleanse, purge, purify.

riddle n PUZZLE, poser, conundrum, brain-teaser, problem, enigma, mystery.

ride v ❶ SIT ON, mount, be mounted on, bestride, manage, control. ❷ TRAVEL, go, move, progress.
▶ n TRIP, outing, journey, jaunt; *informal* spin.

ridicule n DERISION, mockery, laughter, scorn, jeering, gibing, teasing, taunting, chaff, banter, badinage, raillery, satire, sarcasm, irony; *informal* kidding, ribbing, ragging.
– OPPOSITES respect.
▶ v DERIDE, mock, laugh at, scoff at, scorn, jeer at, gibe at, make fun of, poke fun at, make a fool of, tease, taunt, chaff; *informal* kid, rib, rag, take the mickey out of, send up.

ridiculous adj ❶ ABSURD, comical, funny, laughable, hilarious, humorous, droll, farcical, facetious, ludicrous, risible, derisory. ❷ POINTLESS, senseless, foolish, inane, fatuous, nonsensical, mindless. ❸ UNBELIEVABLE, incredible, outrageous, preposterous, shocking, monstrous.
– OPPOSITES sensible.

rife adj WIDESPREAD, common, prevalent, predominant, general, extensive, ubiquitous, universal, global, rampant.

rifle
■ **rifle through** RANSACK, rummage through, go through, rake through, search.

rift n ❶ SPLIT, break, breach, fissure, cleft, crevice, gap, crack, cranny, slit. ❷ DISAGREE-MENT, fight, falling-out, breach, division, estrangement, schism, split, alienation, quarrel, altercation, conflict, feud; *informal* row.

rig[1]
■ **rig out** CLOTHE, dress, attire, accoutre, array, deck, bedeck, drape. **rig up** PUT TOGETHER, erect, assemble, throw together, cobble together.

rig[2] v FALSIFY, fake, tamper with, doctor, engineer, manipulate.

right adj ❶ JUST, fair, equitable, impartial, good, upright, right-eous, virtuous, proper, moral, ethical, honourable, honest, principled, lawful, legal. ❷ COR-RECT, accurate, unerring, exact, precise, valid; *informal* on the mark; *informal* spot on, bang on. ❸ SUITABLE, appropriate, fit, proper, desirable, ideal, opportune, favourable, convenient, propitious. ❹ RIGHT-HAND, dextral; *Nautical* starboard; *Heraldry* dexter. ❺ CONSERVATIVE, right-wing, Tory, reactionary.
– OPPOSITES wrong, left.
▶ n ❶ LAWFULNESS, legality, goodness, righteousness, virtue, virtuousness, integrity, rectitude, propriety, justice, justness, fairness, equity, equitableness. ❷ PREROGATIVE, privilege, authority, power, licence, permission, entitlement.
▶ v PUT TO RIGHTS, sort out, straighten out, rectify, fix, put in order, repair.

righteous adj GOOD, virtuous, upright, moral, ethical, law-abiding, honest, honourable, pure, noble, God-fearing.
– OPPOSITES sinful.

rigid adj ❶ STIFF, hard, taut, inflexible, unbendable, unbending, unyielding, inelastic, non-pliant. ❷ STRICT, severe, stern, stringent, rigorous, austere, spartan, harsh, inflexible, intransigent, uncompromising.
– OPPOSITES flexible.

rigorous adj ❶ METICULOUS, painstaking, thorough, laborious, scrupulous, conscientious, nice, exact, precise, accurate. ❷ HARSH, severe, bad, bleak, extreme, inclement.
– OPPOSITES slapdash, mild.

rim n BRIM, edge, lip, circumference, border, verge, margin, brink.

rind n OUTER LAYER, peel, skin, husk, crust.

ring¹ n ❶ BAND, circle, loop, circuit, halo, disc, round. ❷ ARENA, enclosure, area. ❸ GANG, syndicate, cartel, association, league.
▶ v CIRCLE, encircle, circumscribe, encompass, loop, gird, enclose, surround, hem in, fence in, seal off.

ring² n ❶ RINGING, tolling, peal, pealing, knell, chime, clang, tinkle. ❷ CALL, telephone call, phone call; informal phone, buzz.
▶ v ❶ TOLL, peal, sound, chime, ding, ding-dong, clang, tinkle. ❷ CALL, telephone, phone; informal buzz.

rinse v WASH, wash out, clean, sluice, flush, drench.

riot n STREET FIGHT, commotion, disturbance, uproar, tumult, melee, scuffle, fracas, fray, brawl, free-for-all, uprising, insurrection.
▶ v RUN RIOT, rampage, go on the rampage, run wild/amok, go berserk, fight, brawl, take to the streets.

riotous adj ❶ DISORDERLY, uncontrollable, ungovernable, unmanageable, rowdy, wild, violent, brawling, lawless, anarchic, rebellious, mutinous. ❷ LOUD, noisy, boisterous, uproarious, rollicking, orgiastic. ❸ HILARIOUS, funny, uproarious, side-splitting.
– OPPOSITES peaceable.

ripe adj ❶ MATURE, developed, full grown, ready to eat, ready, mellow, seasoned, tempered. ❷ READY, fit, suitable, right.
– OPPOSITES immature.

ripen v MATURE, come to maturity, develop, mellow.

riposte n RETORT, rejoinder, reply, response, sally; informal comeback.

rise v ❶ ARISE, come/go up, move up, ascend, climb up. ❷ RISE UP, tower, soar, loom, rear up. ❸ GO UP, get higher, increase, soar, rocket, escalate. ❹ STAND UP, get to one's feet, get up, jump up. ❺ GET UP, get out of bed, wake up, surface.
– OPPOSITES fall.
▶ n ❶ INCLINE, elevation, slope, acclivity, rising ground, hillock, hill. ❷ INCREASE, escalation, upsurge, upswing.

risk n ❶ CHANCE, possibility. ❷ DANGER, peril, jeopardy.
– OPPOSITES impossibility, safety.

▶ v **①** PUT AT RISK, endanger, imperil, jeopardize. **②** TAKE THE RISK OF, chance, venture. **③** BET, gamble, hazard, chance, venture.

risky adj DANGEROUS, hazardous, perilous, unsafe, precarious, touch-and-go, tricky, uncertain; *informal* chancy, dicey; *Brit. informal* dodgy.

rite n RITUAL, ceremony, ceremonial, observance, service, sacrament, celebration, performance, act, practice, tradition, convention, formality, procedure, usage.

rival n OPPONENT, opposition, adversary, antagonist, contestant, competitor, challenger, contender.
– OPPOSITES ally.
▶ v COMPETE WITH, vie with, match, equal, emulate, measure up to, compare with, parallel.
▶ adj OPPOSING, competing, in competition, contending, in conflict, conflicting.

rivalry n OPPOSITION, competition, competitiveness, vying, contention, conflict.

road n STREET, thoroughfare, highway.

roam v WANDER, rove, ramble, meander, drift, range, travel, walk, tramp, traverse, trek, peregrinate.

roar v BELLOW, yell, bawl, shout, howl, thunder, shriek, scream, cry, bay.

rob v STEAL FROM, burgle, burglarize, hold up, break into, mug, defraud, swindle, cheat,

mulct; *informal* rip off, diddle, bilk, do out of.

robber n BURGLAR, thief, mugger, pilferer, housebreaker, looter, raider, bandit, brigand, pirate, highwayman.

robbery n THEFT, burglary, stealing, housebreaking, larceny, pilfering, embezzlement, misappropriation, swindling, fraud, mugging, hold-up, break-in, raid; *informal* filching.

robe n **①** VESTMENT, habit, costume, gown. **②** DRESSING GOWN, housecoat, wrapper, peignoir.

robust adj STURDY, tough, rugged, strong, healthy, vigorous, hale and hearty, muscular, powerful, strapping, burly.
– OPPOSITES weak.

rock¹ v **①** MOVE TO AND FRO, swing, sway, roll, lurch, pitch. **②** STUN, shock, stagger, astound, astonish, dumbfound, shake, take aback.

rock² n BOULDER, stone.

rocky¹ adj ROCK-STREWN, stony, pebbly, rough.

rocky² adj UNSTEADY, unstable, shaky, tottering, teetering, wobbly.
– OPPOSITES steady, stable.

rod n BAR, stick, pole, baton, staff.

rogue n VILLAIN, scoundrel, rascal, reprobate, swindler, fraudster, cheat, deceiver, confidence trickster, charlatan, mountebank, sharper, wretch, ne'er-do-well, wastrel, good-for-nothing, crook; *informal, dated* rotter, bounder; *dated* cad; *archaic* blackguard.

role n ❶ PART, character, representation, portrayal. ❷ CAPACITY, function, position, place, situation, job, post, task.

roll v ❶ GO ROUND, turn, turn round, rotate, revolve, spin, whirl, wheel. ❷ FURL, coil, fold. ❸ PASS, go, flow, travel. ❹ FLATTEN, level, smooth, even, press down, crush.
▶ n ❶ TURN, rotation, revolution, spin, whirl. ❷ SPOOL, reel, bobbin, cylinder. ❸ REGISTER, list, file, index, roster, directory, catalogue.

romance n ❶ FANTASY, fancy, whimsy, fabrication, glamour, mystery, legend, fairy tale, idyll. ❷ LOVE AFFAIR, affair, liaison, attachment, intrigue, courtship, amour.

romantic adj ❶ LOVING, amorous, passionate, fond, tender, sentimental, sloppy; *informal* mushy; *Brit. informal* soppy. ❷ UNREALISTIC, idealistic, visionary, utopian, starry-eyed, optimistic, hopeful. ❸ FASCINATING, mysterious, glamorous, exotic, exciting.
– OPPOSITES unsentimental.
▶ n DREAMER, visionary, idealist, utopian.
– OPPOSITES realist.

room n ❶ SPACE, area, territory, expanse, extent, volume, elbow room. ❷ SCOPE, capacity, margin, leeway, latitude, occasion, opportunity.

roomy adj SPACIOUS, commodious, capacious, voluminous,

ample, generous, sizeable, large, broad, wide, extensive.
– OPPOSITES cramped.

root n ❶ ROOTSTOCK, tuber, tap root; *Botany* rhizome, radicle. ❷ SOURCE, origin, starting point, basis, foundation, beginnings, seat, cause, reason, rationale, occasion; *formal* radix.
▶ v TAKE ROOT, grow roots, become established, set.

rope n CORD, cable, line, strand, hawser.

roster n LIST, listing, rota, roll, register, schedule, agenda, calendar, directory, index, table.

rot v ❶ DECOMPOSE, decay, crumble, disintegrate, corrode, perish. ❷ GO BAD, spoil, go sour, putrefy, fester; *informal* go off.
▶ n ❶ DECOMPOSITION, decay, disintegration, corrosion, putrefaction, mould, blight. ❷ RUBBISH, nonsense, claptrap, drivel; *informal* bosh, twaddle, poppycock, guff, tosh; *Brit. informal* codswallop; *informal, dated* bunkum, bunk.

rotary adj ROTATING, rotational, revolving, turning, gyrating, gyratory, spinning, whirling.

rotate v ❶ GO ROUND, move round, turn, revolve, spin, whirl, swivel, reel, wheel, gyrate. ❷ ALTERNATE, take turns, take in turn.

rotten adj ❶ BAD, off, mouldy, mouldering, spoiled, tainted, sour, rancid, rank, decaying, decomposed, putrid, putrescent, festering, fetid, stinking. ❷ NASTY, foul, mean, bad, dirty,

filthy, contemptible, despicable.
– OPPOSITES fresh, kind.

rough adj ❶ UNEVEN, irregular, bumpy, broken, stony, rugged, craggy, lumpy, nodulous. ❷ BOISTEROUS, rowdy, disorderly, wild, violent, savage. ❸ TURBULENT, tumultuous, choppy. ❹ STORMY, squally, wild, tempestuous, wintry. ❺ COARSE, crude, uncouth, vulgar, unrefined, loutish, boorish, churlish, brutish, ill-mannered, unmannerly, impolite, discourteous, uncivil. ❻ HARSH, severe, hard, tough, difficult, unpleasant, disagreeable, nasty, cruel. ❼ ROUGH AND READY, hasty, quick, cursory, crude, incomplete, rudimentary, basic. ❽ APPROXIMATE, inexact, imprecise, vague, hazy. ❾ ILL, sick, unwell, unhealthy, below par; *Brit.* off colour.
– OPPOSITES smooth, exact.

round adj ❶ CIRCULAR, ring-shaped, cycloid, discoid, disklike, cylindrical, spherical, spheroid, ball-shaped, globelike, convex, curved. ❷ WELL ROUNDED, ample, rotund, chubby, buxom, roly-poly, tubby, portly, stout, corpulent, fat, obese; *Brit. informal* podgy.
▶ n ❶ SUCCESSION, sequence, series, cycle. ❷ CIRCUIT, course, beat, routine, schedule. ❸ STAGE, level, division, lap, heat.
▶ v GO ROUND, travel round, sail round, circumnavigate.

roundabout adj INDIRECT,

circuitous, meandering, winding, tortuous, discursive, oblique, circumlocutory, periphrastic.
– OPPOSITES direct.

rouse v ❶ WAKE, wake up, rise, call, get up. ❷ STIR UP, excite, incite, egg on, induce, impel, inflame, agitate, whip up, galvanize, stimulate.
– OPPOSITES calm, pacify.

rout v DEFEAT, trounce, worst, conquer, subjugate, overthrow, crush, beat; *informal* lick, thrash, give someone a pasting.
– OPPOSITES victory.

route n COURSE, way, itinerary, road, path.

routine n ❶ PATTERN, procedure, practice, custom, habit, programme, schedule, formula, method, system, order. ❷ ACT, performance, piece; *informal* spiel.
▶ adj USUAL, normal, everyday, workaday, common, ordinary, typical, customary, habitual, scheduled, conventional, standard.
– OPPOSITES unusual.

row[1] n LINE, column, queue, procession, chain, string; *Brit. informal* crocodile.

row[2] n ❶ ARGUMENT, dispute, disagreement, falling-out, controversy, quarrel, squabble, fight, conflict, altercation, wrangle; *informal* set-to, tiff. ❷ NOISE, din, clamour, commotion, rumpus, uproar, tumult, hubbub, pandemonium.

rowdy adj UNRULY, disorderly, noisy, boisterous, loud,

obstreperous, wild, rough, unrestrained, lawless.
– OPPOSITES quiet.

royal adj KINGLY, queenly, kinglike, queenlike, princely, regal, monarchical, sovereign.

rub v ❶ MASSAGE, knead, stroke, caress, fondle. ❷ SCRUB, scour, wipe, clean.
■ **rub out** ERASE, wipe off, efface, obliterate, expunge, remove.

rubbish n ❶ WASTE, refuse, litter, lumber, junk, debris, detritus, dross, rubble, sweepings, leavings, dregs, offscourings; *N. Amer.* garbage, trash. ❷ *See* NONSENSE.

rude adj ❶ ILL-MANNERED, bad-mannered, mannerless, impolite, discourteous, impertinent, insolent, impudent, cheeky, uncivil, disrespectful, churlish, curt, brusque, blunt, offhand, short, offensive. ❷ VULGAR, coarse, indelicate, smutty, dirty, naughty, risqué, ribald, bawdy, licentious; *informal* blue. ❸ PRIMITIVE, crude, rudimentary, rough, rough-hewn, simple.
– OPPOSITES polite.

rudimentary adj ❶ ELEMENTARY, basic, fundamental, introductory, early, primitive, crude, rough, simple. ❷ UNDEVELOPED, immature, incomplete, vestigial.

rudiments pl n BASICS, fundamentals, beginnings, elements, essentials, foundation; *informal* nuts and bolts.

rueful adj REGRETFUL,

apologetic, sorry, remorseful, contrite, repentant, penitent, woebegone, woeful, plaintive.

ruffle v ❶ RUMPLE, dishevel, tousle, disarrange, discompose, disorder, derange, tangle, mess up; *informal* muss up. ❷ FLUSTER, agitate, harass, upset, disturb, discompose, perturb, unsettle, disconcert, worry, alarm, trouble, confuse, rattle, shake up.
– OPPOSITES smooth, soothe.

rugged adj ❶ ROUGH, uneven, irregular, bumpy, rocky, stony, broken up, jagged, craggy. ❷ WRINKLED, furrowed, lined, gnarled, weather-beaten, leathery. ❸ TOUGH, hardy, robust, sturdy, strong, vigorous, stalwart, hale and hearty, muscular, brawny.
– OPPOSITES smooth, flimsy.

ruin n ❶ DESTRUCTION, devastation, wreckage, demolition, disintegration, decay, disrepair. ❷ RUINATION, loss, failure, bankruptcy, insolvency, penury, impoverishment, indigence, destitution, calamity, disaster.
▶ v ❶ DESTROY, devastate, lay waste, raze, demolish, damage, spoil, wreak havoc on. ❷ BANKRUPT, make insolvent, impoverish, pauperize.
– OPPOSITES save.

ruined adj IN RUINS, ruinous, dilapidated, decaying, in disrepair, derelict, ramshackle, decrepit.

ruinous adj ❶ DISASTROUS, devastating, calamitous, catastrophic, cataclysmic, dire, injurious, damaging, crippling. **2** see RUINED.

rule n **1** RULING, law, regulation, statute, ordinance, tenet, order, decree, commandment, directive. **2** PRINCIPLE, precept, standard, axiom, maxim. **3** GOVERNMENT, administration, jurisdiction, reign, authority, control, direction, mastery, leadership, command.
▶ v **1** PRESIDE OVER, govern, control, dominate, direct, administer, manage, regulate. **2** ORDER, decree, direct, pronounce, make a judgement, judge, adjudge, adjudicate, lay down, decide, determine, resolve, settle, establish.
■ **rule out** see EXCLUDE (2).

ruling n JUDGEMENT, adjudication, finding, verdict, resolution, decree, pronouncement.

rumour n REPORT, story, whisper, word, news, tidings, gossip, hearsay, talk.
▶ v SAY, report.

run v **1** RACE, rush, hasten, hurry, dash, sprint, bolt, dart, gallop, career along, tear along, charge along, speed along, jog along; informal scoot, hare, step on it, hotfoot it. **2** MOVE, go, get along, travel. **3** GLIDE, course, roll, slide. **4** OPERATE, be in operation, be valid, be current, continue. **5** GO, continue, proceed, extend, stretch. **6** FLOW, issue, stream, pour, gush, cascade, spurt, jet, trickle, leak. **7** OWN, operate, conduct, carry on, direct, manage,

administer, be in charge of, control, head, lead, look after, organize, coordinate, supervise, superintend, oversee.
▶ n **1** JOG, sprint, dash, gallop, canter, headlong rush, scamper. **2** DRIVE, ride, trip, outing, excursion, jaunt, short journey; informal spin. **3** SPELL, stretch, streak, chain, string, round, cycle, sequence, series, succession.
■ **run after** see PURSUE (1). **run into** see MEET (1).

runner n **1** RACER, sprinter, hurdler, harrier, jogger, athlete. **2** BRANCH, shoot, offshoot, tendril.

rupture n BREAK, fracture, crack, split, burst, rent, tear, rift, fissure.
▶ v **1** BREAK, fracture, crack, split, breach, burst, rend, tear, puncture. **2** SEVER, cut off, break off, disrupt, breach.

rural adj COUNTRY, rustic, bucolic, pastoral, agricultural, agrarian, Arcadian.
– OPPOSITES urban.

rush v HURRY, hasten, run, race, dash, sprint, bolt, dart, gallop, career, tear, charge, speed, scurry, scamper; informal step on it, save a move on, hotfoot it.
– OPPOSITES dawdle.
▶ n **1** ONSLAUGHT, attack, assault, charge. **2** SURGE, flow, gush, stream, flood. **3** HURRY, haste, speed, swiftness, rapidity, dispatch.

rushed adj HURRIED, hasty, speedy, quick, fast, swift, rapid, expeditious, prompt.

rustle v ❶ SWISH, whisper, whoosh. ❷ STEAL, purloin, plunder, abduct, kidnap; *informal* filch.

rusty adj ❶ RUSTED, corroded, oxidized. ❷ WEAK, below par, unpractised, out of practice, neglected, not what it was.

rut n ❶ FURROW, groove, track, crack, hollow, hole, pothole. ❷ HUMDRUM EXISTENCE, routine job, boring routine, treadmill, dead end.

ruthless adj MERCILESS, pitiless, relentless, unrelenting, remorseless, unforgiving, unsparing, inexorable, implacable, heartless, unfeeling, hard, harsh, severe, grim, cruel, vicious, brutal, barbarous, callous, savage, fierce, ferocious.
– OPPOSITES compassionate.

Ss

sabotage n DAMAGE, destruction, vandalism, disruption, ruining, wrecking.
▶ v DAMAGE, destroy, wreck, ruin, impair, incapacitate, cripple, vandalize, disrupt; *Brit.* throw a spanner in the works; *informal* foul up.

sack n ❶ BAG, pack. ❷ DISMISSAL, discharge, redundancy; *informal* the boot, the chop, the axe; *Brit. informal* the push.
▶ v ❶ DISCHARGE, dismiss, declare redundant; *informal* kick out, give someone their marching orders, boot out, give someone the sack/boot/chop/axe, give someone the old heave-ho; *Brit. informal* give someone their cards. ❷ See PLUNDER v.

sacred adj ❶ HOLY, blessed, blest, hallowed, consecrated, sanctified. ❷ RELIGIOUS, spiritual, devotional, church, churchly, ecclesiastical.
– OPPOSITES profane.

sacrifice n ❶ GIVING UP, renunciation, abandonment, surrender, relinquishment, yielding, ceding, forfeiture. ❷ OFFERING, gifts, oblation.
▶ v ❶ GIVE UP, forgo, renounce, abandon, surrender, relinquish, yield, cede, forfeit. ❷ OFFER UP, offer, immolate.

sacrilege n DESECRATION, profanity, blasphemy, impiety, irreverence, irreligion, godlessness, disrespect.
– OPPOSITES piety.

sad adj ❶ UNHAPPY, miserable, sorrowful, gloomy, melancholy, blue, mournful, woebegone, wretched, dejected, downcast, despondent, in low spirits, low-spirited, low, downhearted, depressed, doleful, glum, cheerless, dispirited,

disconsolate, heartbroken, broken-hearted, sick at heart, grief-stricken, grieving; *informal* down, down in the dumps, down in the mouth, in the pits. ❷ UNFORTUNATE, unhappy, sorrowful, miserable, sorry, depressing, upsetting, distressing, dispiriting, heartbreaking, heart-rending, pitiful, pitiable, grievous, tragic, disastrous, calamitous. ❸ SORRY, wretched, deplorable, lamentable, regrettable, unfortunate, pitiful, pitiable, pathetic, shameful, disgraceful.
– OPPOSITES happy.

sadden v CAST DOWN, deject, depress, dishearten, dispirit, dampen someone's spirits, cast a gloom upon, desolate, upset, distress, grieve, break someone's heart, make someone's heart bleed.
– OPPOSITES cheer.

sadness n UNHAPPINESS, misery, sorrow, gloom, melancholy, wretchedness, dejection, despondency, low spirits, depression, dolefulness, glumness, cheerlessness, disconsolateness, broken-heartedness, heartache, grief.
– OPPOSITES happiness.

safe adj ❶ SAFE AND SOUND, secure, protected, sheltered, guarded, defended, free from harm/danger, out of harm's way. ❷ UNHARMED, all right, alive and well, well, unhurt, uninjured, unscathed, undamaged, out of danger; *informal* OK, out of the woods. ❸ CAUTIOUS, circumspect, prudent, unadventurous,

conservative, timid, unenterprising. ❹ HARMLESS, innocuous, non-toxic, non-poisonous, wholesome.
– OPPOSITES dangerous.
▶ n STRONGBOX, safety-deposit box, safe-deposit box, cash box, repository, depository, locker, vault, crypt.

safeguard n PROTECTION, defence, preventive, precaution, security, surety.
▶ v PROTECT, look after, defend, guard, preserve, secure.
– OPPOSITES endanger.

safety n ❶ SAFENESS, security, secureness, soundness, impregnability. ❷ RELIABILITY, dependability, responsibility, trustworthiness. ❸ SHELTER, sanctuary, refuge.

sag v SINK, subside, slump, curve down.

saga n EPIC, chronicle, legend, history, romance.

sail v ❶ CRUISE, ride the waves, go by water, go on a sea voyage, voyage. ❷ SET SAIL, embark, put to sea, leave port/dock, raise sail, put off, shove off. ❸ STEER, captain, pilot, navigate.

sailor n SEAMAN, seafarer, mariner, salt, sea dog, boatman, yachtsman/woman; *Brit. informal* matelot; *informal, dated* tar, Jack Tar.

saintly adj SAINTLIKE, sainted, holy, godly, pious, God-fearing, religious, devout, blessed, virtuous, righteous, good, innocent, sinless, blameless, pure, angelic.
– OPPOSITES ungodly.

sake n WELL-BEING, welfare, behalf, benefit, advantage, interest, gain, profit, consideration, fee, emolument, regard, concern, account, respect.

salary n PAY, wages, earnings, remuneration, fee, emolument, stipend, honorarium.

sale n SELLING, marketing, trade, traffic, vending, bargaining.
■ **on sale** FOR SALE, in stock, on the market, purchasable, available, obtainable.

salubrious adj HEALTHY, health-giving, beneficial, good for one's health, wholesome, salutary, refreshing, invigorating, bracing.
– OPPOSITES unhealthy.

salute n ❶ GREETING, salutation, address, welcome. ❷ TRIBUTE, testimonial, honour, homage, recognition, acknowledgement.
▶ v ❶ GREET, address, hail, acknowledge, pay one's respects to. ❷ PAY TRIBUTE TO, pay homage to, honour, recognize, acknowledge; informal take one's hat off to.

salvage n ❶ RESCUE, saving, recovery, reclamation, salvation. ❷ WASTE MATERIAL, scrap, remains.
▶ v RESCUE, save, recover, retrieve, reclaim, get back.

salvation n REDEMPTION, deliverance, saving, rescue.
– OPPOSITES damnation, destruction.

same adj ❶ IDENTICAL, the very same, selfsame, one and the same, the very. ❷ EXACTLY SIMILAR, identical, alike, duplicate, twin, indistinguishable, interchangeable, corresponding, equivalent. ❸ UNCHANGING, unchanged, unvarying, unvaried, invariable, constant, consistent, uniform.
– OPPOSITES different.

sample n ❶ SPECIMEN, example, instance, illustration, exemplification, representative type, model, pattern. ❷ CROSS-SECTION, sampling, test.
▶ v TRY, try out, test, examine, inspect, taste.

sanctify v CONSECRATE, make holy/sacred, bless, hallow, set apart, dedicate.

sanctimonious adj SELF-RIGHTEOUS, holier-than-thou, pietistic, unctuous, smug, mealy-mouthed, hypocritical, Pharisaic, Tartuffian; informal goody-goody.

sanction n ❶ AUTHORIZATION, warrant, accreditation, licence, endorsement, permission, consent, approval, backing, support, seal/stamp of approval, approbation, acceptance; informal thumbs up, go-ahead, the green light, OK. ❷ PENALTY, punishment, penalization, penance, sentence.
▶ v AUTHORIZE, warrant, accredit, license, endorse, permit, allow, consent to, back, support, approve, accept; informal give the thumbs up to, give the green light to, OK.
– OPPOSITES reject.

sanctity n ❶ SACREDNESS,

holiness, inviolability.
2 HOLINESS, godliness, saintliness, spirituality, religiosity, piety, devoutness, devotion, righteousness, goodness, virtue, purity.

sanctuary n **1** REFUGE, haven, shelter, retreat, hideout, hiding place. **2** HOLY PLACE, church, temple, shrine, altar, sanctum. **3** PRESERVE, reserve, wildlife reserve, reservation. **4** SAFETY, safe keeping, protection, shelter, security, immunity.

sane adj **1** OF SOUND MIND, in one's right mind, compos mentis, rational, lucid, in possession of one's faculties; informal all there. **2** SENSIBLE, reasonable, balanced, judicious, responsible, prudent, wise, advisable.
− OPPOSITES insane.

sanguine adj OPTIMISTIC, confident, assured, hopeful, buoyant, cheerful, spirited.
− OPPOSITES gloomy.

sanitary adj HYGIENIC, clean, germ-free, antiseptic, aseptic, sterile, unpolluted, salubrious, healthy.

sanity n **1** SANENESS, soundness of mind, mental health, reason, rationality, lucidity. **2** SENSE, sensibleness, common sense, good sense, reasonableness, rationality, soundness, judiciousness, prudence, wisdom, advisability.

sap n **1** FLUID, moisture, juice, secretion. **2** VIGOUR, energy,

vitality, vivacity, enthusiasm, spirit; informal pep, zip, oomph.
▶ v DRAIN, enervate, exhaust, weaken, enfeeble, debilitate, devitalize. See also EXHAUST (1).

sarcasm n DERISION, scorn, mockery, ridicule, irony, satire, trenchancy, acerbity, asperity, mordancy, bitterness, spitefulness.

sarcastic adj DERISIVE, derisory, scornful, mocking, sneering, jeering, scoffing, taunting, ironic, sardonic, satirical, caustic, trenchant, acerbic, acrimonious, mordant, bitter, spiteful; Brit. informal sarky.

sardonic adj DRY, wry, derisory, cynical, ironic, sarcastic, caustic, trenchant, acerbic, mordant, bitter.

satanic adj DIABOLICAL, fiendish, devilish, demonic, demoniac, demoniacal, hellish, infernal, accursed, wicked, evil, sinful, iniquitous, malevolent, vile, foul.

satire n **1** TAKE-OFF, spoof, send-up, burlesque, parody, travesty, caricature, lampoon, pasquinade. **2** MOCKERY, ridicule, irony, sarcasm.

satirical adj MOCKING, ridiculing, taunting, ironic, sarcastic, sardonic, caustic, biting, cutting.

satirize v MOCK, ridicule, hold up to ridicule, take off, send up, deride, make fun of, poke fun at, parody, lampoon, burlesque, travesty, criticize, censure.

satisfaction n FULFILMENT, gratification, pleasure, enjoyment, delight, happiness, pride, comfort, content, contentment, smugness.
– OPPOSITES dissatisfaction.

satisfactory adj ADEQUATE, all right, acceptable, fine, good enough, sufficient, competent, up to standard, up to the mark, up to par, up to scratch, passable, average; *informal* OK, okay.
– OPPOSITES unsatisfactory.

satisfy v ❶ SATIATE, sate, slake, quench. ❷ FULFIL, gratify, appease, assuage, meet, indulge, content. ❸ CONVINCE, persuade, assure, reassure, remove/dispel doubts, put someone's mind at rest.
– OPPOSITES frustrate.

saturate v WET THROUGH, wet, soak, drench, souse, steep, douse, permeate, imbue, pervade, suffuse.

sauce n ❶ RELISH, dressing, condiment, flavouring. ❷ *See* INSOLENCE.

saucy adj IMPUDENT, cheeky, impertinent, insolent, rude, disrespectful, audacious, presumptuous, bold, brash; *informal* fresh.
– OPPOSITES demure, polite.

saunter v STROLL, amble, wander, meander, walk, promenade; *informal* mosey.

savage adj ❶ VICIOUS, ferocious, fierce, brutal, cruel, bloody, murderous, bloodthirsty, inhuman, harsh, grim, terrible, merciless, ruthless, pitiless, sadistic, barbarous. ❷ UNTAMED, wild, undomesticated, feral. ❸ UNCIVILIZED, uncultivated, barbarous, barbaric, wild, primitive.
– OPPOSITES mild, tame.
▶ n BARBARIAN, wild man/woman, primitive, heathen.
▶ v MAUL, lacerate, mangle, tear to pieces, attack.

save v ❶ RESCUE, free, set free, liberate, deliver, snatch, bail out, salvage, redeem. ❷ PROTECT, safeguard, guard, keep, keep safe, shield, screen, preserve, conserve. ❸ PREVENT, obviate, forestall, spare, make unnecessary, rule out. ❹ PUT ASIDE, set aside, put by, put away, lay by, keep, reserve, conserve, salt away, stockpile, store, hoard.

savings pl n CAPITAL, assets, resources, reserves, funds, nest egg.

saviour n RESCUER, liberator, deliverer, emancipator, champion, knight in shining armour, Good Samaritan, friend in need.

savour n TASTE, flavour, tang, relish, smack, smell, aroma, fragrance.
▶ v TASTE, enjoy, appreciate, delight in, take pleasure in, relish, revel in.

savoury adj ❶ APPETIZING, mouth-watering, fragrant, flavoursome, palatable, tasty, delicious, delectable, luscious, toothsome; *informal* scrumptious. ❷ SALTY, piquant, tangy.
– OPPOSITES unpalatable, sweet.

say v ❶ MENTION, voice, pronounce, put into words, give utterance to, give voice to, vocalize. ❷ STATE, remark, announce, affirm, assert, maintain, declare, allege, profess, avow, opine; *informal* come out with; *formal* aver. ❸ ESTIMATE, judge, guess, hazard a guess, predict, speculate, conjecture, surmise, imagine, assume, suppose, presume. ❹ PROPOSE, advance, bring forward, offer, introduce, adduce, plead.

saying n PROVERB, maxim, aphorism, axiom, adage, saw, epigram, dictum, gnome, apothegm, platitude, cliché.

scaffold n ❶ SCAFFOLDING, frame, framework, gantry. ❷ GALLOWS, gibbet.

scale[1] n ❶ PLATE, flake; *technical* lamella, lamina, squama. ❷ COATING, coat, crust, encrustation, limescale; *Brit.* fur.

scale[2] n ❶ PROGRESSION, succession, sequence, series, ranking, register, ladder, hierarchy; *informal* pecking order. ❷ EXTENT, scope, range, degree, reach.
▶ v CLIMB, ascend, go up, clamber, mount, clamber up.
■ **scale down** REDUCE, cut down, cut back on, decrease, lessen, lower.

scaly adj FLAKY, scurfy, rough, scabrous.

scamp n RASCAL, rogue, imp, devil, monkey, scallywag, mischief-maker, troublemaker, prankster, tyke.

scan v ❶ STUDY, examine, scrutinize, survey, inspect, take stock of, search, scour, sweep. ❷ SKIM, look over, glance over, run one's eye over, read through, leaf through, thumb through.

scandal n ❶ DISGRACE, shame, dishonour, disrepute, discredit, odium, opprobrium, censure, obloquy. ❷ SLANDER, libel, calumny, defamation, aspersion, gossip, malicious rumours, dirt, muckraking, smear campaign.

scandalous adj ❶ DISGRACEFUL, shameful, dishonourable, outrageous, shocking, monstrous, disreputable, improper, unseemly, discreditable, infamous, opprobrious. ❷ SLANDEROUS, libellous, defamatory, scurrilous, malicious, gossiping.

scant adj LITTLE, minimal, limited, insufficient, inadequate, deficient.
– OPPOSITES abundant.

scanty adj MEAGRE, scant, sparse, small, paltry, slender, negligible, skimpy, thin, poor, insufficient, inadequate, deficient, limited, restricted, exiguous.
– OPPOSITES ample, copious.

scapegoat n WHIPPING BOY, Aunt Sally; *informal* fall guy; *N. Amer. informal* patsy.

scar n ❶ MARK, blemish, blotch, discoloration, cicatrix, disfigurement, defacement. ❷ DAMAGE, trauma, shock, injury, suffering, upset.

▶ v ❶ MARK, blemish, blotch, discolour, disfigure, deface. ❷ DAMAGE, traumatize, shock, injure, upset.

scarce adj ❶ IN SHORT SUPPLY, short, meagre, scant, scanty, sparse, paltry, not enough, too little, insufficient, deficient, inadequate, lacking, at a premium, exiguous. ❷ RARE, infrequent, few and far between, seldom seen/found, sparse, uncommon, unusual.
– OPPOSITES plentiful, abundant.

scarcely adv HARDLY, barely, only just.

scarcity n ❶ DEARTH, shortage, undersupply, paucity, meagreness, sparseness, insufficiency, deficiency, inadequacy, lack, exiguity. ❷ RARITY, rareness, infrequency, sparseness, uncommonness.

scare v FRIGHTEN, alarm, startle, make fearful, make nervous, terrify, terrorize, petrify, horrify, appal, shock, intimidate, daunt, awe, cow, panic, put the fear of God into, scare stiff, make someone's blood run cold, make someone's flesh creep, make someone's hair stand on end; informal scare the pants off; Brit. informal put the wind up.
▶ n FRIGHT, alarm, start, fearfulness, nervousness, terror, horror, shock, panic.

scathing adj VIRULENT, savage, fierce, ferocious, brutal, stinging, biting, mordant, trenchant, caustic, vitriolic, withering, scornful, harsh, severe, stern.
– OPPOSITES mild.

scatter v ❶ DISSEMINATE, diffuse, spread, sow, sprinkle, strew, broadcast, fling, toss, throw. ❷ BREAK UP, disperse, disband, separate, dissolve.
– OPPOSITES gather, assemble.

scavenge v SEARCH, look for, hunt, forage for, rummage for.

scenario n PLOT, outline, synopsis, summary, precis, rundown, storyline, structure, scheme, plan, sequence of events.

scene n ❶ PLACE, location, site, position, spot, setting, locale, whereabouts, arena, stage. ❷ EVENT, incident, happening, situation, episode, affair, moment, proceeding. ❸ FUSS, exhibition, outburst, commotion, to-do, row, upset, tantrum, furore, brouhaha.

scenery n ❶ VIEW, outlook, landscape, vista, panorama, prospect. ❷ SET, stage set, setting, background, backdrop.

scenic adj PICTURESQUE, pretty, beautiful, pleasing.

scent n ❶ AROMA, perfume, fragrance, smell, bouquet, odour; poetic/literary redolence. ❷ TRACK, trail, spoor.

sceptic n QUESTIONER, doubter, agnostic, unbeliever, doubting Thomas, disbeliever, dissenter, scoffer, cynic.

sceptical adj DOUBTING,

doubtful, dubious, questioning, distrustful, mistrustful, suspicious, hesitant, disbelieving, misbelieving, incredulous, unconvinced, scoffing, cynical.
– OPPOSITES certain, convinced.

scepticism n DOUBT, doubtfulness, dubiety, agnosticism, distrust, mistrust, suspicion, hesitancy, disbelief, misbelief, incredulity, cynicism.

schedule n PLAN, scheme, timetable, programme, diary, calendar, itinerary, agenda.
▶ v ARRANGE, timetable, organize, plan, programme, book.

scheme n ➊ PLAN, programme, project, course of action, system, procedure, strategy, design, tactics, contrivance. ➋ ARRANGEMENT, system, organization, disposition, schema. ➌ PLOT, ruse, ploy, stratagem, manoeuvre, machinations, intrigue, conspiracy; informal game, racket.
▶ v PLOT, conspire, intrigue, manoeuvre, plan, lay plans.

scheming adj CALCULATING, designing, conniving, wily, crafty, cunning, sly, artful, slippery, underhand, duplicitous, devious, Machiavellian; informal tricky.
– OPPOSITES ingenuous, honest.

schism n DIVISION, breach, split, rift, break, rupture, separation, severance, detachment, discord, disagreement.

scholar n MAN / WOMAN OF LETTERS, learned person, academic, highbrow, intellectual, pundit, savant; informal bookworm, egghead.

scholarly adj LEARNED, erudite, academic, well read, intellectual, highbrow, scholastic, literary, studious, bookish, lettered.
– OPPOSITES ignorant.

scholarship n ➊ LEARNING, knowledge, education, erudition, letters. ➋ GRANT, fellowship; Brit. bursary.

school n ➊ EDUCATIONAL INSTITUTION, academy. ➋ SCHOOL OF THOUGHT, outlook, persuasion, opinion, point of view, belief, faith, creed.
▶ v EDUCATE, teach, instruct, train, coach, drill, discipline, direct, guide, prepare, prime, verse.

scientific adj SYSTEMATIC, methodical, orderly, regulated, controlled, exact, precise, mathematical.

scintillating adj SPARKLING, dazzling, vivacious, effervescent, lively, animated, ebullient, bright, brilliant, witty, exciting, stimulating, invigorating.
– OPPOSITES dull, boring.

scoff v JEER AT, mock at, sneer at, gibe at, taunt, laugh at, ridicule, poke fun at, make a fool of, make sport of, rag, revile, deride, belittle, scorn, knock; informal pooh-pooh.

scold v see REPRIMAND V.

scoop n ➊ LADLE, spoon, dipper. ➋ EXCLUSIVE STORY, revelation, exposé.

■ **scoop out** HOLLOW OUT, gouge out, dig, excavate. **scoop up** GATHER UP, pick up, lift.

scope n ❶ EXTENT, range, sphere, area, field, realm, compass, orbit, reach, span, sweep, confine, limit. ❷ OPPORTUNITY, freedom, latitude, capacity.

scorch v BURN, singe, char, sear, discolour, blacken.

score n ❶ NUMBER OF POINTS / GOALS, total, result, outcome. ❷ NOTCH, mark scratch, scrape, groove, cut, nick, chip, gouge.
▶ v ❶ WIN, gain, achieve, chalk up, notch up. ❷ MAKE A NOTCH IN, mark, scratch, scrape, groove, cut, nick, chip, gouge.

scorn n CONTEMPT, contemptuousness, disdain, haughtiness, disparagement, derision, mockery, contumely.
– OPPOSITES praise.
▶ v ❶ BE CONTEMPTUOUS, hold in contempt, look down on, disdain, disparage, slight, deride, mock, scoff at, sneer at. ❷ REBUFF, spurn, shun, refuse, reject, turn down.

scornful adj CONTEMPTUOUS, disdainful, haughty, supercilious, disparaging, slighting, scathing, derisive, mocking, scoffing, sneering, contumelious.
– OPPOSITES respectful.

scoundrel n VILLAIN, rogue, rascal, miscreant, reprobate, scapegrace, good-for-nothing, ne'er-do-well, wastrel; *dated* cad; *informal, dated* rotter, bounder.

scour¹ v SCRUB, rub, clean, cleanse, abrade, wash, wipe, polish, buff, burnish.

scour² v SEARCH, comb, go over, look all over, ransack, hunt through, rake through, rummage through, leave no stone unturned.

scourge n BANE, curse, affliction, plague, trial, torment, torture, suffering, burden, cross to bear, thorn in one's flesh/side, nuisance, pest, punishment, penalty.

scout n LOOKOUT, outrider, spy.
▶ v RECONNOITRE, make a reconnaissance of, spy out, survey, inspect, investigate, examine, scan.

scowl v FROWN, glower, glare, lower, look daggers.
– OPPOSITES smile.
▶ n FROWN, glower, glare, black look, dirty look.

scraggy adj see SCRAWNY.

scramble v ❶ CLAMBER, climb, crawl. ❷ HURRY, hasten, rush, race, scurry. ❸ MIX UP, jumble, tangle, throw into confusion, disorganize.
▶ n ❶ CLAMBER, climb, trek. ❷ HURRY, rush, race, scurry.

scrap n ❶ FRAGMENT, piece, bit, snippet, remnant, leftover, tatter, morsel, particle, sliver. ❷ WASTE, junk, rubbish.
▶ v THROW AWAY, get rid of, discard, toss out, abandon, jettison, dispense with, shed; *informal* ditch, junk.
– OPPOSITES keep, preserve.

scrape v SCOUR, rub, scrub, abrade, remove, erase, grate, rasp, grind, file, sandpaper.

❷ GRAZE, scratch, skin, cut, lacerate, bark.
▶ n GRAZE, scratch, abrasion, cut, laceration, wound.

scratch v SCRAPE, abrade, graze, score, cut, lacerate.
▶ n SCRAPE, abrasion, graze, cut, laceration, wound, mark, line.

scream v SHRIEK, howl, shout, cry out, call out, yell, screech, wail, squawk, bawl; *informal* holler.
▶ n SHRIEK, howl, shout, yell, cry, screech, wail, squawk.

screen n ❶ SHIELD, protection, shelter, guard, safeguard, buffer. ❷ COVER, cloak, veil, mask, camouflage, disguise, facade, front, blind. ❸ SIEVE, riddle, strainer, colander, filter.
▶ v ❶ PARTITION OFF, divide off, conceal, hide. ❷ SHELTER, shield, protect, guard, safeguard. ❸ VET, check, test, examine, investigate, scan.

scribble v DASH OFF, jot down, scrawl.

scrimp v SKIMP, economize, be frugal, be thrifty, husband one's resources, tighten one's belt, draw in one's horns.

script n ❶ HANDWRITING, writing, hand, pen, calligraphy. ❷ TEXT, book, libretto, score, lines, words, manuscript.

scrounge v BEG, borrow; *informal* sponge, cadge, bum; *N. Amer. informal* mooch.

scrounger n BEGGAR, borrower, parasite; *informal* sponger, cadger, freeloader.

scrub v RUB, scour, clean, cleanse, wash, wipe.

scruffy adj UNTIDY, unkempt, dishevelled, ungroomed, ill-groomed, shabby, down at heel, ragged, tattered, slovenly, messy, slatternly, sluttish.
– OPPOSITES smart.

scruple v HAVE QUALMS ABOUT, hesitate to, think twice about, balk at, demur about, be reluctant to, recoil from, shrink from, waver about, vacillate about.

scruples pl n QUALMS, compunction, hesitation, second thoughts, doubt, misgivings, uneasiness, reluctance, restraint, wavering, vacillation.

scrupulous adj ❶ METICULOUS, careful, painstaking, thorough, rigorous, strict, conscientious, punctilious, exact, precise, fastidious. ❷ HONEST, honourable, upright, righteous, right-minded, moral, ethical.
– OPPOSITES careless, unscrupulous.

scrutinize v EXAMINE, study, inspect, survey, scan, look over, investigate, go over, peruse, probe, inquire into, sift, analyse, dissect.

scrutiny n EXAMINATION, study, inspection, perusal, investigation, exploration, probe, inquiry, analysis, dissection.

sculpture n STATUE, statuette, bust, figure, figurine.
▶ v SCULPT, chisel, model, fashion, shape, cast, carve, cut, hew.

scum n ❶ FILM, crust, algae, filth, dirt. ❷ LOWEST OF THE LOW, dregs of society, riff-raff, rabble.

scupper v ❶ SINK, submerge. ❷ RUIN, defeat, demolish, wreck, smash.

scurrilous adj ABUSIVE, insulting, offensive, disparaging, defamatory, slanderous, gross, foul, scandalous.

scurry v HURRY, hasten, make haste, rush, race, dash, run, sprint, scuttle, scamper, scramble.

seal n ❶ EMBLEM, symbol, insignia, badge, crest, token, mark, monogram. ❷ SEALANT, sealer, adhesive.
▶ v ❶ FASTEN, secure, shut, close up. ❷ MAKE AIRTIGHT, make watertight, close, shut, cork, stopper. ❸ SECURE, clinch, settle, decide, complete.
■ **seal off** CLOSE OFF, shut off, cordon off, fence off.

seam n ❶ JOINT, join, junction. ❷ LAYER, stratum, vein, lode.

sear v BURN, singe, scorch, char, dry up, wither, discolour, brown.

search v ❶ GO THROUGH, look through, hunt through, rummage through, forage through, rifle through, scour, ransack, comb, go through with a fine-tooth comb, sift through, turn upside down, turn inside out, leave no stone unturned in. ❷ LOOK FOR, seek, hunt for, look high and low for, cast around for, ferret about for, scout out. ❸ EXAMINE, inspect, check; informal frisk.
▶ n ❶ HUNT, rummage, forage, ransacking. ❷ EXPLORATION, quest, probe.

season n PERIOD, time, time of year, spell, term.
▶ v ❶ FLAVOUR, add flavouring to, spice, add spices to; informal pep up, add zing to. ❷ MATURE, age, mellow, prime, prepare.

seasonable adj OPPORTUNE, timely, well timed, appropriate, suitable, apt.

seasoned adj EXPERIENCED, practised, well versed, established, long-serving, veteran, hardened, battle-scarred.
– OPPOSITES inexperienced.

seat n ❶ CHAIR, bench, settle, stool, stall. ❷ HEADQUARTERS, location, site, base, centre, hub, heart. ❸ BUTTOCKS, rump, hindquarters; Brit. bottom; informal behind, backside; Brit. informal bum; N. Amer. informal butt, tail, fanny; humorous posterior.
▶ v ❶ PLACE, position, put, situate, deposit. ❷ HOLD, take, have room for, accommodate.

secluded adj SHELTERED, concealed, hidden, private, solitary, lonely, sequestered, retired, out of the way, remote, isolated, off the beaten track, tucked away, cut-off.
– OPPOSITES accessible.

seclusion n PRIVACY, solitude, retreat, retirement, withdrawal, sequestration, isolation, concealment, hiding, secrecy.

second¹ adj ❶ SECONDARY, lower, subordinate, lesser.

lower-grade, inferior. ❷ ADD-ITIONAL, extra, further.

▶ n ASSISTANT, attendant, helper, supporter, backer, right-hand man/woman.

▶ v SUPPORT, give one's support to, back, approve, give one's approval to, endorse, promote.

second[2] n MOMENT, instant, trice, twinkling, twinkling of an eye; *informal* sec, jiffy, tick, two shakes of a lamb's tail, two shakes.

secondary adj ❶ LESSER, subordinate, minor, ancillary, subsidiary, non-essential, unimportant. ❷ NON-PRIMARY, derived, derivative, indirect, resulting, resultant. ❸ RESERVE, back-up, relief, auxiliary, extra, alternative, subsidiary.
– OPPOSITES primary.

second-hand adj USED, pre-owned, worn, nearly new, handed down, hand-me-down; *Brit. informal, dated* reach-me-down.
– OPPOSITES new.

▶ adv AT SECOND HAND, indirectly.
– OPPOSITES directly.

second-rate adj SECOND-CLASS, low-class, inferior, lesser, substandard, poor-quality, low-quality, low-grade, shoddy, rubbishy, tawdry.
– OPPOSITES first-rate, excellent.

secret adj ❶ CONFIDENTIAL, private, unrevealed, undisclosed, under wraps, unpublished, untold, unknown; *informal* hush-hush. ❷ HIDDEN, concealed, camouflaged, dis-

guised, clandestine, furtive, conspiratorial, undercover, surreptitious, stealthy, cloak-and-dagger, covert.
– OPPOSITES open, obvious.

secrete[1] v DISCHARGE, emit, excrete, exude, ooze, leak, give off, send out.
– OPPOSITES absorb.

secrete[2] v HIDE, conceal, cover up, stow away, sequester, cache; *informal* stash away.
– OPPOSITES reveal.

secretive adj SECRET, reticent, uncommunicative, unforthcoming, reserved, taciturn, silent, quiet, tight-lipped, close-mouthed, close, playing one's cards close to one's chest; *informal* cagey.
– OPPOSITES open.

secretly adv IN SECRET, confidentially, privately, behind closed doors, in camera, sub rosa.

sectarian adj BIGOTED, prejudiced, doctrinaire, partisan, narrow-minded, insular, hidebound, extreme, fanatic, fanatical.
– OPPOSITES tolerant.

section n PART, segment, division, department, component, piece, portion, bit, slice, fraction, fragment.

sector n ❶ PART, division, area, branch, department, category, field. ❷ ZONE, quarter, district, area, region.

secular adj LAY, non-religious, non-spiritual, non-church, laical, temporal, worldly, earthly.
– OPPOSITES religious.

secure adj ❶ SAFE, free from danger, out of harm's way, invulnerable, unharmed, undamaged, protected, sheltered, shielded. ❷ FASTENED, closed, shut, locked, sealed. ❸ STABLE, fixed, steady, strong, sturdy, solid. ❹ UNWORRIED, at ease, comfortable, confident, assured.
– OPPOSITES insecure.
▶ v ❶ MAKE SAFE, make sound, fortify, strengthen, protect. ❷ FASTEN, close, shut, lock, bolt, chain, seal. ❸ ACQUIRE, obtain, gain, get, get hold of, procure, get possession of, come by; *informal* get one's hands on, land.

sedate[1] v GIVE A SEDATIVE TO, put under sedation, tranquillize.

sedate[2] adj ❶ CALM, tranquil, placid, dignified, formal, decorous, proper, demure, sober, earnest, staid, stiff. ❷ SLOW, slow-moving, leisurely, measured, deliberate, dignified.
– OPPOSITES exciting, fast.

sedative n TRANQUILLIZER, calmative, depressant, sleeping pill, narcotic, opiate; *informal* downer.
▶ adj CALMING, tranquillizing, soothing, relaxing, assuaging, lenitive, soporific, narcotic.

sedentary adj SITTING, seated, desk-bound, desk, inactive.
– OPPOSITES active.

sediment n DREGS, lees, grounds, deposit, residue, precipitate, settlings.

seduce v ❶ PERSUADE TO HAVE SEX; *informal* have one's (wicked) way with, take advantage of; *dated* debauch. ❷ ATTRACT, lure, tempt, entice, beguile, ensnare.

seductive adj ATTRACTIVE, alluring, appealing, inviting, tempting, enticing, beguiling, provocative, exciting, arousing, sexy.

see v ❶ MAKE OUT, catch sight of, glimpse, spot, notice, observe, view, perceive, discern, espy, descry, distinguish, identify, recognize. ❷ WATCH, look at, view. ❸ UNDERSTAND, grasp, get, comprehend, follow, take in, know, realize, get the drift of, make out, fathom. ❹ FIND OUT, discover, learn, ascertain, determine, ask, enquire, make enquiries, investigate. ❺ FORESEE, predict, forecast, anticipate, envisage, picture, visualize.
■ **see about** SEE TO, deal with, attend to, cope with, look after, take care of. **see through** NOT BE TAKEN IN BY, be wise to, get the measure of, penetrate; *informal* have someone's number.

seed n ❶ OVULE, pip, kernel, stone, germ. ❷ SOURCE, origin, root, cause, reason.

seek v ❶ SEARCH FOR, look for, be on the lookout for, be after, hunt for, be in quest of, be in pursuit of. ❷ ASK FOR, request, solicit, entreat, beg for.

seem v APPEAR, appear to be, have the appearance of being, give the impression of being, look, look like, look to be, have the look of.

seep | self-indulgence

seep v OOZE, leak, exude, drip, drain, percolate.

see-saw v FLUCTUATE, go from one extreme to the other, swing, oscillate.

seethe v ❶ BOIL, bubble, fizz, foam, froth, ferment, churn. ❷ BE FURIOUS, be livid, be incensed, storm, fume.

segment n SECTION, part, division, component, piece, portion, slice, wedge.

segregate v SEPARATE, set apart, isolate, cut off, sequester, ostracize, discriminate against.
– OPPOSITES amalgamate.

segregation n SEPARATION, setting apart, isolation, dissociation, sequestration, discrimination, apartheid, partition.

seize v ❶ GRAB, grab hold of, take hold of, grasp, take a grip of, grip, clutch at. ❷ CONFISCATE, impound, commandeer, appropriate, sequester, sequestrate. ❸ SNATCH, abduct, take captive, kidnap, hijack.

seizure n ❶ CONFISCATION, commandeering, appropriation, sequestration. ❷ SNATCHING, abduction, kidnapping, hijacking.

seldom adv RARELY, hardly ever, scarcely ever, infrequently, only occasionally; *informal* once in a blue moon.
– OPPOSITES frequently.

select v CHOOSE, pick, handpick, single out, opt for, decide on, settle on, prefer, favour.
▶ adj ❶ CHOICE, hand-picked,

prime, first-rate, first-class, finest, best, high-quality, top-quality. ❷ EXCLUSIVE, elite, limited, privileged, cliquey, cliquish; *Brit. informal* posh.
– OPPOSITES inferior.

selection n ❶ CHOICE, pick, option. ❷ VARIETY, assortment, anthology, miscellany, collection, range.

selective adj PARTICULAR, discriminating, discriminatory, discerning, fussy, careful, cautious; *informal* choosy, picky.

self-centred adj EGOCENTRIC, egotistical, self-absorbed, self-seeking, wrapped up in oneself, selfish, narcissistic.

self-confidence n SELF-ASSURANCE, confidence, self-reliance, self-dependence, self-possession, poise, aplomb, composure, sangfroid.

self-conscious adj AWKWARD, shy, diffident, bashful, blushing, timorous, nervous, timid, retiring, shrinking, ill at ease, embarrassed, uncomfortable.
– OPPOSITES confident.

self-control n SELF-RESTRAINT, restraint, self-discipline, will power, strength of will.

self-important adj POMPOUS, vain, conceited, arrogant, swollen-headed, egotistical, presumptuous, overbearing, overweening, haughty, swaggering, strutting.
– OPPOSITES humble.

self-indulgence n SELF-GRATIFICATION, lack of self-restraint, intemperance,

immoderation, excess,
pleasure-seeking, sensualism,
dissipation.

selfish adj SELF-SEEKING, self-
centred, egocentric, egotistic,
egoistic, self-interested, self-
regarding, self-absorbed; *informal*
looking out for number one.
– OPPOSITES unselfish,
selfless.

selfless adj UNSELFISH, altruistic, generous, self-sacrificing,
self-denying, magnanimous,
liberal, ungrudging.
– OPPOSITES selfish.

self-respect n SELF-ESTEEM,
self-regard, pride in oneself,
pride in one's abilities, belief in
one's worth, faith in oneself,
amour propre.

self-righteous adj SANCTIMO-
NIOUS, pious, holier-than-thou,
pietistic, too good to be true,
Pharisaic, unctuous, mealy-
mouthed; *informal* goody-goody.
– OPPOSITES humble.

self-sacrifice n SELF-DENIAL,
selflessness, unselfishness,
altruism.

self-seeking adj SELF-
INTERESTED, opportunistic, ambitious, mercenary, out for what
one can get, fortune-hunting,
gold-digging; *informal* on the
make, looking out for number
one.
– OPPOSITES altruistic.

sell v ❶ PUT UP FOR SALE, put on
sale, dispose of, vend, auction
off, trade, barter, trade in, deal
in, traffic in, stock, market,
handle, peddle, hawk.
❷ BOUGHT, be purchased, go,

move, be in demand. ❸ RETAIL,
go for, be, be found for. ❹ GET
ACCEPTANCE FOR, win approval
for, get support for, get across,
promote.
– OPPOSITES buy.

seller n VENDOR, retailer,
salesman/woman/person, shopkeeper, trader, merchant,
dealer, agent, representative,
rep.

semblance n APPEARANCE,
show, air, guise, pretence,
facade, front, veneer, mask,
cloak, disguise, camouflage,
pretext.

send v ❶ DISPATCH, forward,
mail, post, remit. ❷ THROW,
fling, hurl, cast, let fly, propel,
project. ❸ DRIVE, make, cause
someone to be/become.
– OPPOSITES receive.
■ **send for** CALL FOR, summon,
request, order.

senile adj DODDERING, decrepit,
failing, in one's dotage, in one's
second childhood; *informal* past
it.

senior adj ❶ HIGH-RANKING,
higher-ranking, superior.
❷ OLDER, elder.
– OPPOSITES junior.

sensation n ❶ FEELING,
sense, awareness, consciousness, perception, impression.
❷ STIR, excitement, agitation,
commotion, furore, scandal.

sensational adj ❶ SPECTACU-
LAR, stirring, exciting, startling,
staggering, dramatic, amazing,
shocking, scandalous, lurid.
❷ MARVELLOUS, superb, excellent, exceptional, remarkable;

informal fabulous, fab, out of this world.

sense n ❶ FEELING, sensation, faculty, sensibility. ❷ APPRECIATION, awareness, understanding, comprehension. ❸ COMMON SENSE, practicality, wisdom, sagacity, sharpness, discernment, perception, wit, intelligence, cleverness, understanding, reason, logic, brains, nous. ❹ MEANING, definition, import, signification, significance, implication, nuance, drift, gist, purport, denotation.
▶ v FEEL, get the impression of, be aware of, be conscious of, observe, notice, perceive, discern, grasp, pick up, suspect, divine, intuit.

senseless adj ❶ NONSENSICAL, stupid, foolish, silly, inane, idiotic, mindless, unintelligent, unwise, irrational, illogical, meaningless, pointless, absurd, ludicrous, fatuous, asinine, moronic, imbecilic. ❷ UNCONSCIOUS, insensible, out cold, out, stunned, numb, numbed, insensate.
– OPPOSITES wise.

sensible adj PRACTICAL, realistic, down-to-earth, wise, prudent, judicious, sagacious, shrewd, discerning, perceptive, intelligent, clever, reasonable, rational, logical.
– OPPOSITES foolish.

sensitive adj ❶ DELICATE, fine, soft, fragile. ❷ RESPONSIVE, receptive, perceptive, discerning, discriminatory, sympathetic, understanding,

empathetic. ❸ PROBLEMATIC, difficult, delicate, ticklish.
– OPPOSITES resilient, impervious, uncontroversial.
■ **sensitive to** RESPONSIVE TO, easily affected by, susceptible to, reactive to, sentient of.

sensual adj ❶ PHYSICAL, carnal, bodily, fleshly, animal, voluptuous, epicurean, sybaritic. ❷ VOLUPTUOUS, sexual, sexy, erotic.
– OPPOSITES spiritual.

sensuous adj PLEASING, pleasurable, gratifying, aesthetic.

sentence n ❶ JUDGEMENT, verdict, ruling, decision, decree. ❷ PRISON SENTENCE, jail sentence, prison term; *informal* time; *Brit. informal* porridge.
▶ v IMPOSE A SENTENCE ON, pass judgement on, penalize, punish, condemn, doom.

sentiment n ❶ EMOTION, emotionalism, finer feelings, tender feelings, tenderness, softness. ❷ FEELINGS, attitude, belief, opinion, view, point of view.

sentimental adj ❶ ROMANTIC, emotional, mawkish, maudlin; *informal* mushy, slushy, schmaltzy, corny; *Brit. informal* soppy. ❷ NOSTALGIC, emotional, affectionate, loving, tender, warm.

sentiments pl n FEELING, attitude, belief, thoughts, way of thinking, opinion, view, point of view, idea, judgement.

sentry n GUARD, lookout, watch, watchman, sentinel.

separate adj ❶ INDIVIDUAL, distinct, different, particular,

autonomous, independent.
❷ UNCONNECTED, distinct, different, disconnected, unrelated, detached, divorced, divided, discrete.
▸ v ❶ DISCONNECT, detach, sever, uncouple, divide, sunder.
❷ DIVIDE, come between, stand between, keep apart, partition.
❸ PART, part company, go their/your/our separate ways, go different ways, diverge, split, divide. ❹ BREAK UP, split up, part, become estranged, divorce.
– OPPOSITES join, unite.

separately adv ❶ APART, individually, independently, autonomously. ❷ INDIVIDUALLY, one by one, one at a time, singly, severally, independently.

septic adj INFECTED, festering, poisoned, putrefying, putrefactive, putrid.

sequel n FOLLOW-UP, development, result, consequence, outcome, issue, upshot.

sequence n CHAIN, course, cycle, series, progression, succession, set, arrangement, order, pattern.

serene adj CALM, composed, tranquil, peaceful, placid, still, quiet, unperturbed, imperturbable, undisturbed, unruffled, unworried, unexcited, unexcitable, unflappable.
– OPPOSITES excitable.

series n SUCCESSION, progression, sequence, chain, course, string, train, run, cycle, set, row, arrangement, order.

serious adj ❶ SOLEMN, earnest, unsmiling, thoughtful, preoccupied, pensive, grave, sombre, sober, long-faced, dour, stern, grim, poker-faced.
❷ IMPORTANT, significant, consequential, of consequence, momentous, weighty, far-reaching, urgent, pressing, crucial, vital, life-and-death.
❸ ACUTE, grave, bad, critical, grievous, dangerous, perilous.
❹ EARNEST, in earnest, sincere, honest, genuine, firm, resolute, resolved, determined, fervent.
– OPPOSITES cheerful, minor, trivial.

sermon n HOMILY, address, oration, lecture, preaching, teaching.

servant n DOMESTIC, help, domestic help, maid, handyman, menial, drudge, scullion, retainer, attendant, lackey; Brit. informal char; Brit. dated charwoman.

serve v ❶ HAVE / HOLD A PLACE ON, be on, perform duties, carry out duties. ❷ ACT AS, do duty as, function as, do the work of, be suitable for. ❸ DISH UP, give out, distribute, set out, present, provide. ❹ ATTEND TO, look after, take care of, assist.

service n ❶ GOOD TURN, assistance, help, advantage, benefit. ❷ WORK, employment, labour, duty, business. ❸ CEREMONY, ritual, rite, sacrament. ❹ SERVICING, overhaul, check, maintenance, repair.
▸ v CHECK, go over, overhaul, maintain, repair.

serviceable adj
❶ FUNCTIONAL, utilitarian, practical, useful, durable, hard-wearing, tough, strong.
❷ USABLE, of use, functioning, operative, repairable.
– OPPOSITES impractical, unusable.

servile adj ❶ MENIAL, low, lowly, humble, mean, base.
❷ SUBSERVIENT, obsequious, sycophantic, fawning, toadying, grovelling, submissive; *informal* bootlicking.
– OPPOSITES assertive.

serving n HELPING, portion, plateful.

session n ❶ PERIOD, time, spell, stretch. ❷ MEETING, sitting, assembly, conference, discussion.

set¹ v ❶ PUT, place, lay, lay down, deposit, rest, locate, lodge, situate, station; *informal* stick, park, plonk. ❷ FIX, embed, insert, lodge, mount, arrange, install. ❸ ADJUST, regulate, synchronize, coordinate, harmonize, calibrate, rectify, set right. ❹ STYLE, fix, arrange, curl, wave. ❺ SOLIDIFY, stiffen, thicken, jell, harden, cake, congeal, coagulate.
❻ DECIDE ON, fix, fix on, agree on, appoint, name, specify, stipulate, determine, designate, select, choose, arrange, schedule.

set² n ❶ COLLECTION, group, assemblage, series, batch, array, assortment, selection.
❷ STAGE SET, setting, scenery, backdrop.

set³ adj ❶ FIXED, prescribed, scheduled, specified, determined, arranged, appointed, established, decided, agreed.
❷ READY, prepared, equipped, primed; *informal* fit.
– OPPOSITES variable, unprepared.

setback n REVERSAL, reverse, upset, check, hitch, hold-up, hindrance, impediment, obstruction, disappointment, misfortune, blow.
– OPPOSITES breakthrough.

setting n ❶ ENVIRONMENT, surroundings, milieu, background, location, place, site.
❷ STAGE SETTING, set, scene, stage, scenery, backdrop.
❸ MOUNT, frame.

settle v ❶ MAKE ONE'S HOME, set up home, take up residence, put down roots, establish oneself, go to live, move to, emigrate to. ❷ ESTABLISH / FOUND A COLONY, colonize, occupy, people, inhabit, populate.
❸ CALM DOWN, quieten down, be quiet, be still, relax. ❹ LIGHT, land, come down, descend, repose, rest. ❺ RESOLVE, clear up, patch up, reconcile, conclude, bring to an end. ❻ PUT IN ORDER, order, arrange, set to rights, straighten out, organize, regulate, adjust, clear up.
– OPPOSITES agitate, rise.
■ **settle for** COMPROMISE ON, accept, agree to, accede to, acquiesce in. **settle on** DECIDE ON, agree on, determine, confirm, arrange, fix, choose, appoint, select.

settlement n ❶ COMMUNITY, colony, village, hamlet, encampment, outpost. ❷ RESOLUTION, reconciliation, conclusion, agreement, contract, pact, compact.

settler n COLONIST, colonizer, pioneer, immigrant.

sever v ❶ CUT OFF, chop off, lop off, hack off, break off, tear off. ❷ DIVIDE, split, cleave, dissect, halve. ❸ BREAK OFF, discontinue, suspend, dissolve, end, terminate, stop, cease, conclude.
– OPPOSITES join, maintain.

several adj SOME, a number of, a few.

severe adj ❶ HARSH, hard, stringent, rigorous, unsparing, relentless, merciless, ruthless, painful, sharp, caustic, biting, cutting, scathing, serious, extreme. ❷ EXTREME, very bad, serious, grave, acute, critical, dire, dangerous, perilous. ❸ FIERCE, strong, violent, intense, powerful, forceful. ❹ STERN, grim, cold, chilly, austere, forbidding, dour, disapproving, unsmiling, sombre, grave, sober, serious. ❺ AUSTERE, stark, spartan, ascetic, plain, simple, modest, bare, unadorned, unembellished, restrained, functional, classic.
– OPPOSITES mild, friendly, ornate.

sew v STITCH, seam, embroider, mend, darn.

sex n ❶ SEXUALITY, sexual attraction, sexual chemistry, sexual desire, desire, sex drive, sexual appetite, libido. ❷ FACTS OF LIFE, sexual reproduction, reproduction; informal the birds and the bees. ❸ SEXUAL INTERCOURSE, making love, intimacy, coitus, coition, coupling, copulation, carnal knowledge, mating, fornication. ❹ GENDER.

sexuality n ❶ SEX, gender, sexual characteristics. ❷ SEXUAL DESIRE, sexual appetite, sexiness, carnality, physicalness, eroticism, lust, sensuality, voluptuousness. ❸ SEXUAL ORIENTATION, sexual preferences.

sexy adj ❶ EROTIC, titillating, suggestive, arousing, exciting, stimulating. ❷ AROUSING, provocative, seductive, sensuous, slinky. ❸ ATTRACTIVE, alluring, seductive, shapely.

shabby adj ❶ DILAPIDATED, broken-down, run down, tumbledown, ramshackle, in disrepair, scruffy, dingy, seedy, squalid, tatty; informal tacky. ❷ WORN, worn out, threadbare, ragged, frayed, tattered, faded, scruffy, tatty, the worse for wear. ❸ CONTEMPTIBLE, despicable, rotten, dishonourable, disreputable, mean, base, low, dirty, odious, shameful, ignoble, unworthy, cheap, shoddy.
– OPPOSITES smart.

shackle v CHAIN, fetter, put in irons, manacle, tie up, bind, tether, hobble, handcuff.

shade n ❶ SHADINESS, shadow, shadowiness, shadows, shelter, cover. ❷ COLOUR, hue, tone,

tint, tinge. ❸ NUANCE, degree, gradation, difference, variety.
– OPPOSITES light.
▶ v ❶ SHUT OUT THE LIGHT FROM, block off light to, cast a shadow over, screen, darken, dim.
❷ COVER, obscure, mute, hide, conceal, veil, curtain.

shadow n ❶ See SHADE n (1).
❷ SILHOUETTE, outline, shape.
❸ A TRACE, a hint, a suggestion, a suspicion, a ghost.

shadowy adj ❶ SHADY, shaded, dim, dark, gloomy, murky, crepuscular, tenebrous.
❷ INDISTINCT, indeterminate, indefinite, unclear, vague, nebulous, ill-defined.
– OPPOSITES bright, distinct.

shady adj ❶ See SHADOWY (1).
❷ DISREPUTABLE, suspicious, suspect, questionable, dishonest, dishonourable, untrustworthy, devious, shifty, slippery, underhand, unscrupulous; informal crooked, tricky, fishy.
– OPPOSITES honest.

shaft n ❶ POLE, stick, rod, staff, shank, stem, handle, upright. ❷ RAY, beam, gleam, streak, pencil. ❸ PASSAGE, duct, tunnel, well, flue.

shaggy adj ❶ HAIRY, hirsute, long-haired, rough, coarse, matted, tangled, unkempt, untidy.
– OPPOSITES sleek.

shake v ❶ ROCK, bump, jolt, bounce, roll, sway, judder, swing, jar, oscillate, wobble, rattle, vibrate, jerk, joggle, jounce. ❷ SHIVER, tremble, quiver, quake, shudder.

❸ JIGGLE, joggle, jolt, jerk, rattle, agitate, jounce.
❹ AGITATE, upset, distress, shock, alarm, disturb, perturb, fluster, unsettle, discompose, disquiet, disconcert, unnerve, ruffle; informal rattle.

shaky adj ❶ TREMBLING, tremulous, quivering, quivery, unsteady, wobbly, weak, tottering, teetering, doddering, staggering. ❷ INFIRM, unsound, unwell, ill, below par, indisposed; informal under the weather. ❸ QUESTIONABLE, dubious, tenuous, flimsy, weak, unsound, unreliable.
– OPPOSITES steady, sound.

shallow adj ❶ FRIVOLOUS, foolish, unintelligent, unthinking, trivial, insincere, superficial. ❷ SUPERFICIAL, unsubstantial, trifling, trivial, petty, empty, meaningless.
– OPPOSITES serious, deep.

sham v FAKE, pretend, feign, counterfeit, put on, simulate, affect, imitate.
▶ n ❶ COUNTERFEIT, fake, forgery, copy, imitation, hoax, pretence, simulation. ❷ IMPOSTOR, fake, fraud, pretender, masquerader, dissembler, charlatan; informal phoney.
▶ adj PRETEND, feigned, artificial, synthetic, ersatz, fake, pseudo, contrived, simulated, affected, put on, insincere, false, bogus, spurious; informal phoney.
– OPPOSITES genuine.

shamble v SHUFFLE, hobble, limp, falter, totter, dodder.

shambles pl n CHAOS,

muddle, mess, confusion, disorder, disarray, disorganization, anarchy; *informal* disaster area.

shame n ❶ HUMILIATION, ignominy, mortification, loss of face, remorse, guilt, compunction, embarrassment, discomfort, discomposure. ❷ DISGRACE, dishonour, scandal, discredit, degradation, ignominy, disrepute, infamy, odium, opprobrium. ❸ PITY, misfortune, bad luck, ill luck, source of regret.
– OPPOSITES pride, honour.

shamefaced adj ❶ ASHAMED, embarrassed, guilty, conscience-stricken, remorseful, contrite, penitent, regretful, humiliated, mortified, shamed. ❷ SHY, bashful, timid, timorous, shrinking, coy, sheepish.
– OPPOSITES unrepentant.

shameful adj ❶ DISGRACEFUL, base, mean, low, vile, outrageous, shocking, dishonourable, unbecoming, unworthy, discreditable, deplorable, despicable, contemptible, reprehensible, scandalous, atrocious, heinous. ❷ SHAMING, humiliating, mortifying, embarrassing; *informal* blush-making.
– OPPOSITES admirable.

shameless adj ❶ UNASHAMED, without shame, unabashed, uncontrite, impenitent. ❷ BRAZEN, impudent, bold, brash, forward, audacious, immodest, unseemly, improper, unbecoming,

indecorous, wanton, abandoned, indecent.
– OPPOSITES modest.

shape n ❶ FORM, figure, configuration, formation, conformation, contour, outline, silhouette, profile, outward form, external appearance. ❷ GUISE, form, appearance, likeness, look, semblance, image, aspect. ❸ CONDITION, state, health, trim, fettle.
▶ v FORM, fashion, make, mould, model, cast, frame, block, carve, sculpt.

shapeless adj ❶ AMORPHOUS, formless, unformed, unshaped, unfashioned, undeveloped, embryonic. ❷ FORMLESS, badly cut, sack-like, ill-proportioned, inelegant.

shapely adj WELL FORMED, well proportioned, elegant, curvaceous, curvy.

share n ALLOWANCE, ration, allocation, division, quota, allotment, portion, part, lot, measure, helping, serving; *informal* cut, rake-off, piece of the cake, piece of the action; *Brit. informal* whack.
▶ v ❶ DIVIDE, split, have in common, have halves in; *informal* go halves in, go fifty-fifty in, go Dutch. ❷ DISTRIBUTE, divide, apportion, parcel out, deal out, dole out, give out.

sharp adj ❶ EDGED, razor-edged, keen, cutting, serrated, knife-like, pointed, needle-like, barbed, spiky. ❷ STEEP, sheer, abrupt, precipitous, vertical.

❸ SUDDEN, abrupt, rapid, unexpected. ❹ INTENSE, acute, keen, piercing, cutting, extreme, severe, stabbing, shooting, stinging. ❺ PUNGENT, biting, bitter, acid, sour, tart, vinegary. ❻ HARSH, curt, brusque, bitter, hard, cutting, scathing, caustic, biting, barbed, acrimonious, trenchant, venomous, malicious, vitriolic, hurtful, unkind, cruel. ❼ INTELLIGENT, bright, clever, quick. ❽ KEEN, acute, quick, ready, knowing, shrewd, discerning, perceptive, penetrating; *informal* smart.
– OPPOSITES blunt.

sharpen v PUT AN EDGE ON, edge, whet, hone, strop, grind.

shatter v ❶ SMASH, break, break into pieces, splinter, fracture, pulverize, crush, crack; *informal* bust. ❷ DESTROY, demolish, wreck, ruin, dash, blight, wipe out, devastate; *informal* torpedo.

shave v ❶ CUT OFF, trim, snip off, crop. ❷ PARE, plane, shear. ❸ BRUSH, graze, touch, scrape, rub.

sheath n ❶ CASE, casing, cover, covering, envelope, wrapper. ❷ CONDOM, contraceptive; *Brit. informal* rubber johnny; *N. Amer. informal* rubber.

shed[1] n HUT, outhouse, lean-to, shack.

shed[2] v ❶ LET FALL, let drop, cast off, slough off. ❷ TAKE OFF, remove, strip off, doff. ❸ SEND FORTH, radiate, disperse, scatter.

sheen n SHINE, lustre, gleam, sparkle, gloss, burnish, polish, patina.

sheer adj ❶ UTTER, complete, thoroughgoing, total, absolute, veritable, downright, out-and-out, unqualified, unconditional, unmitigated, unalloyed, unadulterated. ❷ STEEP, abrupt, sharp, precipitous, vertical. ❸ DIAPHANOUS, transparent, see-through, translucent, fine, thin.
– OPPOSITES gradual, thick.

sheet n ❶ BEDSHEET, bedlinen. ❷ PIECE, pane, panel, plate, slab. ❸ PIECE OF PAPER, leaf, page, folio. ❹ EXPANSE, stretch, span, reach, sweep, covering, blanket, carpet.

shell n ❶ CARAPACE, case, casing, husk, pod, integument. ❷ BULLET, grenade, shot, shrapnel. ❸ FRAMEWORK, frame, structure, chassis, hull, skeleton.
▶ v BOMB, bombard, blitz, strafe, fire on.

shelter n ❶ PROTECTION, shield, cover, screen, safety, security, defence. ❷ REFUGE, sanctuary, retreat, haven, harbour.
– OPPOSITES exposure.
▶ v ❶ PROTECT, shield, screen, safeguard, provide refuge/sanctuary from, guard, harbour, conceal, hide. ❷ TAKE SHELTER, take refuge, take protection, seek refuge/sanctuary.
– OPPOSITES expose.

sheltered adj ❶ SHADY, shaded, protected, screened, shielded, secluded. ❷ QUIET, withdrawn, retired, isolated, protected, cloistered, reclusive.

shepherd v ESCORT, conduct, usher, convoy, guide, marshal, steer.

shift v MOVE, carry, transfer, switch, reposition, rearrange.
▶ n ❶ MOVE, movement, transference, switch, repositioning. ❷ STINT, spell/period of work.

shifty adj EVASIVE, slippery, devious, duplicitous, deceitful, underhand, untrustworthy, double-dealing, dishonest, wily, crafty, artful, sly, scheming, contriving.
– OPPOSITES honest.

shimmer v GLISTEN, glint, flicker, twinkle, sparkle, gleam, glow, scintillate, dance.

shine v ❶ GLEAM, glow, glint, sparkle, twinkle, flicker, glitter, glisten, shimmer, flash, dazzle, beam, radiate, illuminate, luminesce, incandesce. ❷ POLISH, burnish, buff, wax, gloss. ❸ EXCEL, be expert, be brilliant, be very good, be outstanding.
▶ n ❶ LIGHT, brightness, gleam, glow, glint, sparkle, twinkle, flicker, glitter, glisten, shimmer, flash, dazzle, glare, beam, radiance, illumination, luminescence, luminosity, lambency, effulgence. ❷ POLISH, burnish, gleam, gloss, lustre, sheen, patina.

shiny adj SHINING, polished, burnished, gleaming, glossy, satiny, lustrous.
– OPPOSITES dull.

shirk v AVOID, evade, dodge, sidestep, shrink from, shun, get out of, play truant from; informal funk; Brit. informal skive off.

shirker n SLACKER, truant, absentee, malingerer, layabout, loafer, idler; Brit. informal skiver.

shiver v TREMBLE, quiver, shake, shudder, quaver, quake, vibrate.
▶ n TREMBLE, quiver, shake, quaver, shudder.

shock n ❶ IMPACT, blow, collision, crash, dash, jolt, bump, jar, jerk. ❷ BLOW, upset, bombshell, bolt from the blue, disturbance, state of agitation/perturbation, source of distress, revelation; informal eye-opener.
▶ v APPAL, horrify, scandalize, outrage, repel, revolt, disgust, nauseate, sicken, offend, traumatize, make someone's blood run cold, distress, upset, perturb, disturb, disquiet, unsettle, astound, dumbfound, stagger, amaze, astonish, stun.

shoddy adj POOR-QUALITY, inferior, second-rate, tawdry, rubbishy, trashy, junky, gimcrack, cheapjack, jerrybuilt; informal tacky, tatty.
– OPPOSITES quality.

shoot v ❶ HIT, shoot down, bring down, pick off, bag, fell, kill; informal plug, zap; poetic/literary slay. ❷ FIRE, discharge, launch, let fly, send forth. ❸ RACE, dash, sprint, charge, dart, fly, hurtle, bolt, streak, flash, whisk, run, speed. ❹ BUD,

burgeon, sprout, germinate, appear, spring up.
▶ n BUD, offshoot, slip, scion, sucker, sprout, branch, twig, sprig, cutting, graft.

shop n STORE, retail outlet, retailer, establishment, emporium, trading post.

shore¹ n SEASHORE, seaside, beach, coast, seaboard, water-side, foreshore; *poetic/literary* strand.

shore²
■ **shore up** PROP UP, support, hold up, underpin, strengthen, brace, buttress.

short adj ❶ SMALL, little, slight, petite, tiny, squat, dwarfish, diminutive, dumpy, Lilliputian; *Scottish* wee; *informal* pint-sized, pocket-sized, knee-high to a grasshopper. ❷ BRIEF, concise, succinct, to the point, compact, terse, summary, crisp, pithy, epigrammatic, abridged, abbreviated, condensed, summarized, contracted, curtailed, truncated.
❸ SHORT-LIVED, momentary, temporary, brief, imperman-ent, short-term, cursory, fleeting, passing, transitory, transient, ephemeral, fugacious, evanescent.
❹ DEFICIENT, lacking, wanting, insufficient, inadequate, scarce, scanty, meagre, sparse, tight, low. ❺ CURT, sharp, abrupt, blunt, brusque, terse, gruff, surly, testy, tart, rude, discourteous, uncivil, impolite.
– OPPOSITES tall, long, plentiful.

shortage n DEARTH, scarcity, lack, deficiency, insufficiency, paucity, deficit, inadequacy, shortfall, want, poverty.
– OPPOSITES abundance.

shortcoming n DEFECT, fault, flaw, imperfection, failing, drawback, weakness, weak point, foible, frailty, infirmity.
– OPPOSITES strength.

shorten v ABBREVIATE, con-dense, abridge, cut, cut down, contract, compress, reduce, lessen, decrease, diminish, curtail, duck, trim, pare down.
– OPPOSITES extend.

shortly adv SOON, in a short while, in a little while, pres-ently, before long, directly; *informal* before you can say Jack Robinson.

short-sighted adj ❶ MYOPIC, near-sighted. ❷ IMPRUDENT, injudicious, unwise, ill-advised, thoughtless, unthinking, heedless, rash, incautious.

shot n ❶ CRACK, bang, report, blast, explosion, gunfire. ❷ PELLET, bullet, slug, project-ile, ammunition. ❸ PHOTOGRAPH, photo, snap, snapshot.

shout v CRY OUT, call out, yell, roar, howl, bellow, scream, bawl, call at the top of one's voice, raise one's voice; *informal* holler.
– OPPOSITES whisper.

shove v PUSH, thrust, drive, force, shoulder, elbow, jostle, jolt.

shovel n SPADE, scoop.

▶ v SCOOP UP, dig, excavate, spade.

show v ❶ BE VISIBLE, be seen, be in view, appear, put in an appearance. ❷ EXHIBIT, display, present, demonstrate, set forth, uncover, reveal. ❸ INDICATE, express, manifest, reveal, make known, make plain, make obvious, evince, evidence, disclose, betray, divulge. ❹ DEMONSTRATE, point out, explain, expound, teach, instruct in, give instructions in, tutor in, indoctrinate in. ❺ ESCORT, accompany, usher, conduct, attend, guide, lead, direct, steer. ❻ APPEAR, put in an appearance, make an appearance, turn up, come, arrive, be present.
– OPPOSITES conceal.
▶ n ❶ DISPLAY, array, arrangement, exhibition, presentation, exposition, spectacle. ❷ EXHIBITION, demonstration, display, exposition, presentation. ❸ PERFORMANCE, production; *informal* gig. ❹ APPEARANCE, outward appearance, air, guise, semblance, pretence, illusion, pose, affectation, profession.

shower n ❶ FALL, drizzle, flurry, sprinkling. ❷ ABUNDANCE, profusion, plethora, flood, deluge.
▶ v ❶ DELUGE, inundate, overwhelm. ❷ LAVISH, pour, load, heap.

show-off n EXHIBITIONIST, extrovert, bragger, braggart, boaster; *N. Amer. informal* blowhard.

showy adj OSTENTATIOUS, flamboyant, elaborate, fancy, pretentious, overdone, glittering.
– OPPOSITES restrained.

shred n ❶ SCRAP, fragment, wisp, sliver, bit, piece, remnant, snippet, tatter. ❷ TRACE, iota, whit, particle, atom, modicum, scrap, speck.
▶ v CUT UP, tear up, rip up, grate.

shrewd adj ASTUTE, sharp, clever, intelligent, alert, quick-witted, discerning, perspicacious, perceptive, discriminating, wise, sagacious, far-seeing, canny, cunning, artful, crafty, wily, calculating; *informal* smart.
– OPPOSITES stupid.

shriek v SCREAM, screech, squeal, yell, howl, shout, cry out, call out, whoop, wail; *informal* holler.

shrill adj HIGH-PITCHED, high, sharp, piercing, ear-piercing, penetrating, ear-splitting, screeching, shrieking.

shrine n ❶ HOLY PLACE, temple, church. ❷ MEMORIAL, monument, cenotaph. ❸ RELIQUARY, burial chamber, tomb, sepulchre.

shrink v GET / BECOME / GROW SMALLER, contract, diminish, lessen, reduce, dwindle, narrow, decline, fall off, drop off, shrivel.
– OPPOSITES expand, increase.
■ **shrink from** DRAW BACK, pull back, back away, shy away, recoil, retreat, withdraw, flinch, cringe, wince.

shrivel v DRY UP, wither, desiccate, dehydrate, wrinkle, pucker up.

shroud n COVER, covering, pall, cloak, mantle, blanket, cloud, veil, screen.
▶ v COVER, enshroud, swathe, envelop, cloak, blanket, cloud, veil, screen, conceal, hide.

shrug
■ **shrug off** DISREGARD, take no notice of, not trouble about, dismiss, gloss over, play down, make light of, minimize.

shuffle v ❶ SHAMBLE, hobble, limp, drag one's feet. ❷ MIX, intermix, shift about, rearrange, reorganize, jumble.

shun v AVOID, evade, eschew, steer clear of, shy away from, recoil from, keep away from, keep one's distance from, cold-shoulder, give a wide berth to.
– OPPOSITES seek.

shut v CLOSE, draw to, pull to, fasten, bar, lock, secure, seal.
– OPPOSITES open.
■ **shut in** see IMPRISON. **shut out** EXCLUDE, leave out, omit, keep out, bar, debar, ostracize, blackball, banish, exile, outlaw. **shut up** KEEP QUIET, be quiet, keep silent, hold one's tongue; informal keep mum, pipe down, keep one's trap shut.

shy adj BASHFUL, diffident, reserved, reticent, retiring, self-effacing, withdrawn, timid, timorous, fearful, nervous, hesitant, wary, suspicious, chary, unconfident, self-conscious, embarrassed, abashed, modest.
– OPPOSITES brash, confident.

sick adj ❶ UNWELL, ill, ailing, indisposed, poorly, below par, out of sorts, laid up, on the sick list; informal under the weather. ❷ NAUSEATED, queasy, bilious; informal green about the gills. ❸ TIRED, weary, bored, jaded, surfeited, satiated, glutted; informal fed up, have had something up to here. ❹ MORBID, macabre, ghoulish, gruesome, sadistic, perverted, cruel.
– OPPOSITES well.
■ **be sick** VOMIT, throw up; informal spew, puke.

sicken v ❶ MAKE SICK, nauseate, turn someone's stomach, make someone's gorge rise, revolt, disgust, repel, shock, appal. ❷ TAKE / FALL ILL, become ill, become infected, contract, be stricken.
– OPPOSITES recover.

sickening adj see REPELLENT, ANNOYING.

sickly adj ❶ UNHEALTHY, in poor health, ill, delicate, frail, weak, feeble, puny. ❷ SENTIMENTAL, cloying, mawkish, maudlin, slushy, mushy, syrupy; informal schmaltzy; Brit. informal soppy.
– OPPOSITES healthy.

sickness n ❶ ILLNESS, disease, disorder, ailment, complaint, affliction, malady, infirmity, indisposition; informal bug. ❷ NAUSEA, queasiness, biliousness.

side n ❶ EDGE, border, verge, boundary, margin, rim, fringe, skirt, flank, brink, brim, periphery. ❷ PART, quarter, section, sector, neighbourhood. ❸ ASPECT, angle, facet, point of view, viewpoint, view, opinion, standpoint, position, slant. **4** CAMP, faction, caucus, party, wing, splinter group, sect. ■ **side with** TAKE SOMEONE'S SIDE, be on someone's side, take someone's part, support, give one's support to, back, give one's backing to, join with, favour.

sidelong adj SIDE, sideways, oblique, indirect, covert.
– OPPOSITES overt.

sidetrack v DIVERT, deflect, distract, lead away from.

sideways adv **1** SIDE FIRST, edgeways, edgewise. **2** OBLIQUELY, indirectly, sidelong.

sieve n STRAINER, filter, colander, riddle, screen.

sift v **1** FILTER, strain, riddle, screen. **2** EXAMINE, scrutinize, study, investigate, analyse, review.

sigh v BREATHE OUT, exhale.
■ **sigh for** YEARN FOR, long for, weep for, mourn for.

sight n **1** EYESIGHT, vision, power of sight. **2** RANGE OF VISION, field of vision, view. **3** VIEW, glimpse, look.
▶ v CATCH SIGHT OF, see, behold, spot, make out, descry, espy, perceive, observe, discern.

sign n **1** INDICATION, symptom, hint, suggestion, trace, mark, clue, manifestation, token, evidence, proof. **2** SIGNPOST, notice, placard, board, marker. **3** GESTURE, signal, motion, movement, wave, gesticulation. **4** SYMBOL, mark, cipher, code, hieroglyph.

▶ v **1** WRITE, inscribe, autograph, initial. **2** See SIGNAL v (1).

signal v **1** SIGN, give a sign to, indicate, beckon, gesture, motion, gesticulate, nod. **2** BE A SIGN OF, mark signify, designate.
▶ n SIGN, indicator, cue, indication, token, evidence, hint.

significance n **1** MEANING, sense, import, signification, purport, point, gist, essence, implications. **2** IMPORTANCE, consequence, momentousness, magnitude, seriousness.

significant adj **1** MEANINGFUL, eloquent, expressive, pregnant, knowing. **2** IMPORTANT, of importance, of consequence, momentous, of moment, weighty, material, impressive, serious, vital, critical.
– OPPOSITES insignificant.

signify v **1** BE A SIGN OF, indicate, mean, denote, suggest, point to, portend. **2** MEAN, denote, represent, symbolize, stand for. **3** MATTER, be of importance, be of consequence, be important, be significant, be of significance, carry weight, count.

silence n **1** QUIET, quietness, hush, still, stillness, peace, peacefulness, tranquillity, noiselessness, soundlessness. **2** SPEECHLESSNESS, wordlessness, dumbness, muteness, taciturnity, reticence, uncommunicativeness.
– OPPOSITES noise.
▶ v **1** QUIET, quieten, hush, still, calm, pacify, subdue, quell.

❷ MUFFLE, deaden, abate, extinguish.

silent adj ❶ QUIET, hushed, still, peaceful, tranquil, noiseless, soundless.
❷ SPEECHLESS, unspeaking, voiceless, dumb, mute, taciturn, reticent, uncommunicative, mum, tight-lipped, tongue-tied; *informal* struck dumb.
❸ UNSPOKEN, wordless, unvoiced, unsaid, unexpressed, unpronounced, tacit, implicit, understood, implied.
– OPPOSITES noisy, loquacious.

silhouette n OUTLINE, contour, profile, delineation, form, shape.

silky adj SILKEN, smooth, sleek, velvety, diaphanous.

silly adj ❶ UNINTELLIGENT, stupid, foolish, idiotic, brainless, witless, unwise, imprudent, thoughtless, reckless, foolhardy, irresponsible, mad, erratic, unstable, scatter-brained, feather-brained, flighty, frivolous, giddy, fatuous, inane, immature, childish, shallow, naive; *informal* crazy, dotty, scatty, loopy, screwy; *Brit. informal* daft. ❷ SENSELESS, stupid, foolish, mindless, idiotic, unwise, imprudent, inadvisable, injudicious, misguided, unsound, impractical, pointless, meaningless, purposeless, inappropriate, illogical, irrational, unreasonable, thoughtless, reckless, foolhardy, irresponsible,

erratic, hare-brained, absurd, ridiculous, ludicrous, laughable, risible, farcical, preposterous, fatuous, asinine; *informal* half-baked, crazy, screwy; *Brit. informal* daft.
– OPPOSITES sensible.

similar adj LIKE, alike, resembling, close, much the same, comparable, corresponding, analogous, parallel, equivalent, kindred, approximate.
– OPPOSITES dissimilar, different.

similarity n RESEMBLANCE, likeness, sameness, similitude, comparability, correspondence, analogy, parallel, parallelism, equivalence, approximation, closeness, affinity, kinship.
– OPPOSITES dissimilarity, difference.

similarly adv LIKEWISE, in the same way, in like matter, correspondingly, by the same token.

simmer v BOIL, cook, bubble, stew, poach, seethe.

simple adj ❶ EASY, uncomplicated, straightforward, uninvolved, effortless, manageable, elementary, facile; *informal* like falling off a log, a piece of cake, a cinch, easy-peasy, no sweat. ❷ CLEAR, plain, intelligible, comprehensible, understandable, lucid, direct, straightforward, uncomplicated, uninvolved. ❸ PLAIN, classic, clean-cut, unelaborate, unadorned, undecorated. ❹ SIMPLE-MINDED, feeble-minded,

retarded, backward, slow-witted, slow, dull-witted.
– OPPOSITES difficult, complex, ornate.

simplify v MAKE SIMPLE / SIMPLER, make easy/easier, make plainer, clarify, decipher, disentangle, explain, paraphrase, translate.
– OPPOSITES complicate.

simplistic adj OVERSIMPLE, oversimplified, facile, shallow, superficial, naive.

simply adv ❶ CLEARLY, plainly, intelligibly, lucidly, directly, straightforwardly. ❷ PLAINLY, unfussily, without clutter, austerely, starkly, spartanly, with restraint, naturally, casually.

simultaneous adj CONCURRENT, contemporaneous, concomitant, coinciding, coincident, synchronous, coexistent, parallel.

sin n WRONG, wrongdoing, act of evil/wickedness, crime, offence, misdeed, misdemeanour, transgression, error, lapse, fall from grace; archaic trespass.
– OPPOSITES virtue.
▶ v COMMIT A SIN, do wrong, offend, commit an offence, transgress, misbehave, go astray, stray from the straight and narrow, go wrong, fall from grace.

sincere adj ❶ GENUINE, real, true, honest, unfeigned, unaffected, bona fide, wholehearted, heartfelt, serious, earnest, fervent. ❷ HONEST, above board, trustworthy, frank, candid, straightforward,

plain-dealing, no-nonsense, genuine, artless, guileless, ingenuous; informal upfront.
– OPPOSITES insincere.

sincerely adv ❶ WITH ALL SINCERITY, wholeheartedly, with all one's heart, earnestly, fervently. ❷ GENUINELY, really, truly, in truth, without pretence, honestly, in good faith.

sinful adj WRONG, evil, wicked, bad, iniquitous, criminal, immoral, corrupt, unrighteous, ungodly, irreligious, irreverent, profane, blasphemous, impious, sacrilegious.
– OPPOSITES virtuous.

sing v CAROL, trill, warble, pipe, quaver, croon, chant, yodel.

singe v SCORCH, burn, sear, char, blacken.

single adj ❶ ONE, sole, lone, solitary, unique, isolated, by itself, exclusive. ❷ INDIVIDUAL, particular, separate, distinct. ❸ UNMARRIED, unwed, unwedded, wifeless/husbandless, spouseless, partnerless, unattached, free.
■ **single out** SEPARATE OUT, set apart, put to one side, pick, choose, select, fix on, decide on.

single-handed adv BY ONESELF, alone, on one's own, solo, independently, unaided, unassisted, without help.

single-minded adj UNSWERVING, unwavering, undeviating, set, fixed, devoted, dedicated, committed, determined, dogged, tireless, purposeful, obsessive, monomaniacal.

singular adj ❶ EXTRAORDINARY, exceptional, rare, unusual, unique, remarkable, outstanding, notable, noteworthy, striking, conspicuous, distinctive. ❷ STRANGE, unusual, odd, peculiar, curious, queer, bizarre, weird, abnormal, atypical.
– OPPOSITES ordinary.

sinister adj ❶ EVIL-LOOKING, villainous, malevolent, menacing, threatening, frightening. ❷ EVIL, wicked, bad, criminal, base, vile, vicious, cruel, malicious, malign. ❸ OMINOUS, inauspicious, portentous.
– OPPOSITES innocent.

sink v ❶ GO UNDER, submerge, founder, capsize. ❷ FALL, drop, descend, go down, go lower, plunge, plummet, slump.
– OPPOSITES float, rise.

sinner n WRONGDOER, evil-doer, criminal, offender, miscreant, transgressor, reprobate; archaic trespasser.

sit v ❶ SIT DOWN, take a seat, settle down, be seated; informal take the load/weight of one's feet. ❷ BE PLACED, be positioned, be situated, rest, perch. ❸ BE CONVENED, meet, assemble, be in session.

site n LOCATION, situation, position, place, locality, setting, scene.
▶ v see SITUATE.

situate v PLACE, position, locate, site, put, install, station, establish, set up.

situation n ❶ PLACE, position, location, site, setting,

milieu, environment. ❷ CIRCUMSTANCES, affairs, state of affairs, condition, case, predicament, plight; informal kettle of fish, ball game. ❸ POST, position, place, job, employment.

size n DIMENSIONS, measurements, proportions, bigness, largeness, magnitude, vastness, bulk, area, expanse, extent.

sketch n ❶ DRAWING, outline, diagram, plan, representation, delineation. ❷ OUTLINE, summary, abstract, precis, skeleton, bones, bare bones, draft, plan. ❸ SKIT, act, scene.
▶ v DRAW, rough out, outline, represent, delineate, depict.

sketchy adj ❶ PRELIMINARY, provisional, unfinished, unrefined, unpolished, rough, crude. ❷ LIGHT, superficial, cursory, perfunctory, meagre, scrappy, skimpy, bitty, insufficient, inadequate, imperfect, incomplete.
– OPPOSITES detailed.

skilful adj SKILLED, able, good, accomplished, adept, competent, efficient, adroit, deft, dexterous, masterly, expert, first-rate, experienced, trained, practised, professional, talented, gifted, clever; informal smart.
– OPPOSITES incompetent.

skill n SKILFULNESS, ability, accomplishment, adeptness, competence, efficiency, adroitness, deftness, dexterity, aptitude, expertise, expertness, art, finesse, experience,

professionalism, talent, cleverness; *informal* smartness.
– OPPOSITES incompetence.

skilled adj *see* SKILFUL.

skim v GLIDE OVER, move lightly over, brush, graze.
■ skim through READ QUICKLY, glance at, scan, run one's eye over, flip through, leaf through, thumb through.

skimp v BE SPARING, be economical, economize, be frugal, be mean, be parsimonious, be niggardly, scrimp, cut corners; *informal* be stingy.
– OPPOSITES lavish.

skin n ❶ INTEGUMENT, epidermis, cuticle, corium, derma. ❷ HIDE, pelt, fleece, fell, integument, tegument. ❸ PEEL, rind, hull, husk. ❹ FILM, coating, coat, layer, crust.

skinny adj THIN, thin as a rake, scraggy, scrawny, emaciated, skeletal; *informal* skin and bone. *See also* THIN adj (1).

skip v ❶ BOUND, jump, leap, spring, hop, bounce, dance, caper, prance, trip, cavort, gambol, frisk, bob. ❷ OMIT, leave out, miss out, pass over, bypass, skim over.

skirmish n BATTLE, fight, clash, conflict, encounter, confrontation, engagement, tussle, scrimmage, fracas.

skirt v ❶ GO ROUND, move round, walk round, circle, circumnavigate. ❷ EVADE, avoid, dodge, steer clear of, sidestep, circumvent, bypass.

skittish adj PLAYFUL, lively,

frisky, sportive; *poetic/literary* frolicsome.

sky n ATMOSPHERE, air, airspace; *poetic/literary* the heavens, the firmament, the blue, the (wide) blue yonder, the welkin.

slab n HUNK, piece, chunk, lump, slice, wedge, portion.

slack adj ❶ LOOSE, baggy, bagging, easy, hanging, flapping. ❷ SLOW, quiet, inactive, sluggish. ❸ LAX, negligent, remiss, neglectful, careless, inattentive, offhand, slapdash, slipshod, sloppy, disorderly, disorganized, tardy.
– OPPOSITES tight.
▶ v IDLE, shirk be inactive, be lazy, be indolent, be neglectful.

slacker n IDLER, shirker, loafer, dawdler, layabout, malingerer, good-for-nothing, clock-watcher.

slam v BANG, thump, crash, smash, dash, hurt, fling, throw.

slander n DEFAMATION, misrepresentation, calumny, libel, aspersions, vilification, verbal abuse, muckraking, smear campaigning, backbiting, obloquy, disparagement, denigration.
▶ v DEFAME, blacken someone's name, libel, cast aspersions on, malign, vilify, verbally abuse, smear, slur, backbite, disparage, denigrate, decry, run down; *formal* calumniate.

slanderous adj DEFAMATORY, libellous, damaging, abusive, muckraking, malicious, backbiting, disparaging, denigrating; *formal* calumnious.
– OPPOSITES complimentary.

slang n ❶ COLLOQUIALISM, informal language, lingo. ❷ JARGON, cant, argot; *informal* gobbledegook, technospeak, mumbo-jumbo.

slant v ❶ SLOPE, tilt, be askew, lean, dip, shelve, list. ❷ GIVE A SLANT TO, give a bias to, bias, angle, distort, twist.
▶ n ❶ SLOPE, tilt, dip, leaning, inclination, shelving, listing. ❷ BIAS, leaning, one-sidedness, prejudice, angle, distortion, twist.

slanting adj SLANTED, aslant, at an angle, sloping, italic, oblique, tilting, tilted, askew, leaning, dipping, shelving, listing, diagonal.

slap v SMACK, strike, hit, cuff; *informal* wallop, clout, whack, biff, belt, sock.

slapdash adj see CARELESS (1, 2).

slaughter v KILL, butcher, massacre, murder, put to death, do to death, put to the sword; *poetic/literary* slay. See also KILL (1).
▶ n MASSACRE, murder, butchery, killing, bloodshed, carnage.

slave n *historical* serf, vassal; *archaic* bondsman/woman.
▶ v TOIL, drudge, slog, labour, grind, work one's fingers to the bone, work day and night, work like a Trojan.

slavery n ENSLAVEMENT, bondage, servitude, subjugation; *historical* serfdom, vassalage, thraldom.
– OPPOSITES freedom.

slavish adj ❶ SERVILE, subser-

vient, obsequious, sycophantic, deferential, grovelling, fawning, cringing, menial, abject. ❷ IMITATIVE, unoriginal, uninspired, unimaginative.

slay v BE ASLEEP, murder, slaughter, put to death, do to death, assassinate, do away with; *informal* rub out.

sleek adj SMOOTH, glossy, shiny, lustrous, silken, silky, satiny, burnished.

sleep v BE ASLEEP, slumber, doze, nap, drowse; *informal* snooze, crash, have forty winks, be in the land of Nod.
– OPPOSITES wake up.
▶ n SLUMBER, doze, nap, rest, siesta, drowse; *informal* snooze, forty winks, a bit of shut-eye.

sleepiness n DROWSINESS, tiredness, somnolence, somnolency, languor, languidness, lethargy, sluggishness, inactivity, lassitude, torpor, torpidity.

sleepless adj WITHOUT SLEEP, wakeful, insomniac, restless, disturbed.

sleepy adj ❶ DROWSY, tired, somnolent, languorous, lethargic, sluggish, inactive, heavy, torpid, comatose. ❷ INACTIVE, quiet, peaceful, slow-moving, slumberous.
– OPPOSITES alert.

slender adj ❶ SLIM, thin, slight, lean, svelte, willowy, sylphlike. ❷ SMALL, slight, slim, faint, remote, feeble, flimsy, tenuous, fragile.
– OPPOSITES fat.

sleuth n DETECTIVE, investigator, private investigator; *informal*

slice n PIECE, portion, segment, sliver, wedge, chunk, hunk; Brit. informal wodge.
> ▸ v CUT UP / THROUGH, carve, chop, divide, cleave, sever.

slick adj ❶ WELL ORGANIZED, streamlined, efficient, smooth, polished. ❷ GLIB, smooth, fluent, plausible, specious. ❸ SUAVE, urbane, sophisticated, polished, glib, smooth, efficient, professional, smart, sharp, shrewd.

slide v SLIP, skid, slither, skate, skim, glissade, glide.

slight adj ❶ SMALL, little, tiny, minute, inappreciable, imperceptible, subtle, modest. ❷ SLIM, slender, small, spare, delicate, frail.
– OPPOSITES large.
> ▸ v SNUB, insult, affront, rebuff, give the cold shoulder to, cold-shoulder, keep at arm's length, disregard, ignore, neglect, take no notice of, disdain, scorn.
> ▸ n SNUB, insult, affront, rebuff, inattention, scorn, disdain; informal slap in the face.

slightly adv A LITTLE, a bit, somewhat, rather, to some degree.
– OPPOSITES very.

slim adj ❶ SLENDER, thin, slight, lean, narrow, svelte, willowy, sylphlike. ❷ SLIGHT, small, slender, faint, remote, feeble, flimsy, tenuous, fragile.
– OPPOSITES fat, strong.
> ▸ v LOSE WEIGHT, shed weight, diet, go on a diet.

slime n SLUDGE, muck, ooze, mud; informal goo, gunk.

slimy adj ❶ SLUDGY, mucky, oozy, muddy, slippery, sticky, viscous, mucous. ❷ OILY, unctuous, obsequious, sycophantic, servile, grovelling.

sling v TOSS, fling, throw, cast, hurl, pitch, shy, lob; informal chuck, heave.

slink v SKULK, lurk, sneak, creep, steal, slip, slide.

slip v ❶ SKID, slither, lose one's footing, lose one's balance. ❷ FALL, slide, drop. ❸ STEAL, slide, creep, sneak, slink. ❹ GO DOWN, decline, decrease, lessen, depreciate, sink, slump, plummet.
> ▸ n ❶ SLIP-UP, mistake, error, blunder, miscalculation, oversight; informal boo-boo; Brit. informal boob; Brit. informal, dated bloomer. ❷ UNDERSKIRT, petticoat.
> ■ **slip up** MAKE A MISTAKE, blunder, make a blunder, miscalculate, err; informal make a boo-boo, screw up; Brit. informal boob; Brit. informal, dated make a bloomer.

slippery adj ❶ GREASY, oily, slimy, icy, glassy, smooth, soapy; informal slippy, skiddy. ❷ SHIFTY, devious, deceitful, duplicitous, crafty, cunning, sneaky, treacherous, perfidious, two-faced, dishonest, false, unreliable, untrustworthy; informal tricky, foxy.

slit v CUT, split open, slash, gash, rip, make an incision in, tear, rend, pierce.

private eye, dick; N. Amer. informal gumshoe.

▶ n CUT, split, slash, gash, rip, incision, tear, rent, fissure, opening.

slither v SLIDE, slip, skid.

sliver n CHIP, flake, splinter, shred, fragment, scrap.

slobber v SLAVER, drool, dribble, splutter.

slog
■ slog away WORK, labour, toil, slave, drudge, plough.

slogan n MOTTO, logo, catchword, jingle, rallying cry, shibboleth.

slop v SPILL, overflow, splash, slosh, splatter, spatter.

slope v DROP AWAY, fall away, slant, incline, lean, tilt, dip.
▶ n SLANT, inclination, angle, skew, dip, gradient.

sloping adj SLANTING, oblique, leaning, inclined, angled, italic, askew, tilting, dipping.
– OPPOSITES level.

sloppy adj ❶ WATERY, wet, soggy, splashy, slushy, sludgy. ❷ CARELESS, slapdash, slipshod, disorganized, unmethodical, untidy, messy, slovenly.
– OPPOSITES meticulous.

slot n ❶ SLIT, crack, opening, aperture, groove, notch. ❷ PLACE, position, niche, space, opening, time, period.

sloth n LAZINESS, indolence, idleness, sluggishness, inertia, inactivity, lethargy, langour, slothfulness, torpor.

slothful adj LAZY, indolent, idle, work-shy, sluggish, inert,

inactive, lethargic, languorous, torpid.
– OPPOSITES industrious.

slovenly adj SLATTERNLY, untidy, dirty, unclean, messy, unkempt, dishevelled, bedraggled, tousled, rumpled.
– OPPOSITES tidy.

slow adj ❶ SLOW-MOVING, unhurried, leisurely, measured, deliberate, ponderous, creeping, dawdling, loitering, lagging, laggard, sluggish, snail-like, tortoise-like. ❷ BACKWARD, retarded, slow-witted, dull-witted, dull, unintelligent, stupid, thick, dense; *informal* dumb, dopey. ❸ TIME-CONSUMING, protracted, drawn-out, prolonged, interminable.
– OPPOSITES quick, bright.
▶ v ❶ REDUCE SPEED, decelerate, put the brakes on. ❷ HOLD BACK, keep back, delay, detain, restrain.

slowly adv AT A SLOW PACE, without hurrying, unhurriedly, at a leisurely pace, steadily, ploddingly, taking one's time, in one's own good time, with heavy steps, at a snail's pace.

sluggish adj INACTIVE, inert, heavy, lifeless, apathetic, listless, lethargic, languid, languorous, torpid, phlegmatic, indolent, lazy, slothful, drowsy, sleepy.
– OPPOSITES energetic.

slump n PLUNGE, nosedive, collapse, fall, falling-off, drop, downturn, downswing, slide, decline, decrease, lowering, devaluation, depreciation, depression.

▶ **1** COLLAPSE, sink, fall, subside. **2** PLUMMET, plunge, nosedive, fall, drop, go down, slide, decline, decrease, devalue.

– OPPOSITES rise.

slur n INSULT, slight, aspersion, imputation, affront, defamation, slander, libel, misrepresentation, smear, stain, stigma.

sly adj **1** CUNNING, crafty, wily, artful, conniving, scheming, devious, underhand, shrewd, astute; *informal* tricky, foxy, smart. **2** ROGUISH, impish, mischievous, playful, arch, knowing.

smack n & v SLAP, blow, hit, whack, thump, cuff, punch, spank, buffet, rap, bang; *informal* wallop, clout, belt, sock.

small adj **1** LITTLE, tiny, petite, slight, minute, miniature, pocket-size, mini, minuscule, diminutive, undersized, puny; *informal* pint-sized, teeny, teeny-weeny, teensy-weensy; *Scottish* wee. **2** SLIGHT, minor, unimportant, trifling, trivial, insignificant, inconsequential, inappreciable. **3** HUMBLE, modest, lowly, simple, unpretentious, poor, inferior. **4** NARROW, narrow-minded, mean, petty.

– OPPOSITES big, large.

smart adj **1** WELL DRESSED, well turned out, fashionably dressed, fashionable, stylish, modish, elegant, chic, neat,

spruce, trim; *informal* natty, snappy, out of a bandbox. **2** CLEVER, bright, intelligent, gifted, sharp, quick-witted, nimble-witted, shrewd, ingenious. **3** BRISK, quick, fast, swift, lively, energetic, spirited, vigorous, jaunty; *informal* cracking, spanking.

– OPPOSITES scruffy.

▶ v STING, nip, burn, bite, pain.

smash v **1** BREAK, shatter, crash, shiver, pulverize, splinter, crack. **2** CRASH, collide, wreck. **3** DESTROY, ruin, shatter, devastate.

smattering n BIT, modicum, dash, rudiments, elements.

smear v **1** SPREAD, daub, slap, plaster. **2** SMUDGE, streak, blur. **3** SULLY, tarnish, blacken, taint, stain, slur, defame, defile, vilify, slander, libel; *formal* calumniate.

▶ n **1** DAUB, spot, patch; *informal* splotch. **2** SMUDGE, streak. **3** TAINT, stain, slur, blot.

smell v **1** SCENT, sniff, get a sniff of; *Brit. informal* get a whiff of. **2** HAVE A BAD SMELL, stink, be stinking, reek, be malodorous; *informal* stink to high heaven; *Brit. informal* pong, whiff, hum.

▶ n **1** ODOUR, scent, aroma, perfume, fragrance, bouquet; *poetic/literary* redolence. **2** STINK, stench, reek; *Brit. informal* pong, whiff, hum.

smelly adj SMELLING, evil-smelling, foul-smelling, stinking, high, malodorous, fetid; *Brit. informal* ponging, humming, whiffy; *poetic/literary* noisome, mephitic.

smirk v LEER, sneer, simper, grin.

smitten adj TAKEN WITH, infatuated with, enamoured of, attracted by, charmed by, captivated by, enchanted by, beguiled by; *informal* bowled over by.

smog n HAZE, fog, pollution.

smoke v ❶ SMOULDER, reek.
❷ CURE, dry, preserve.

smoky adj SMOKE-FILLED, hazy, foggy, smoggy, reeky, murky.

smooth adj ❶ EVEN, level, flat, plane, flush, unwrinkled.
❷ CALM, still, tranquil, flat, glassy, mirror-like. ❸ EASY, effortless, trouble-free, simple, plain sailing. ❹ STEADY, regular, rhythmic, uninterrupted, flowing, fluid. ❺ SMOOTH-TONGUED, suave, urbane, sophisticated, courteous, gracious, glib, persuasive, slick, oily, ingratiating, unctuous; *informal* smarmy.
– OPPOSITES rough.
▶ v ❶ LEVEL, even, flatten, plane, press down, steamroll.
❷ EASE, make easy/easier, facilitate, clear the way for, pave the way for, open the door for, expedite, assist, aid, help, help along.

smother v ❶ SUFFOCATE, stifle, asphyxiate, choke.
❷ OVERWHELM, shower, inundate, envelop, surround, cocoon.

smoulder v ❶ SMOKE, reek.

❷ SEETHE, fume, burn, boil, foam, rage.

smudge n MARK, spot, smear, streak, stain, blotch, blot, blur, smut; *informal* splotch.

smug adj SELF-SATISFIED, complacent, pleased with oneself, superior, proud of oneself, conceited.

snack n LIGHT MEAL, bite, nibbles, titbit, bite to eat, little something.

snag n ❶ CATCH, drawback, hitch, stumbling block, obstacle, disadvantage, inconvenience, problem, complication.
❷ RIP, tear, run, hole.
▶ v CATCH, rip, tear.

snap v ❶ BREAK, fracture, splinter, separate, come apart, crack. ❷ CRACK, click, crackle.
❸ BITE, gnash, nip. ❹ SPEAK SHARPLY / BRUSQUELY, bark, snarl, growl, lash out at; *informal* jump down someone's throat, fly off the handle at.

snappy adj ❶ IRRITABLE, irascible, cross, touchy, testy, crabbed, crotchety, grumpy, grouchy, peppery. ❷ SMART, fashionable, stylish, chic, modish, dapper; *informal* natty, trendy.
– OPPOSITES peaceable, slovenly.

snare v TRAP, ensnare, catch, get hold of, seize, capture.
▶ n TRAP, gin, springe, net, noose.

snatch v ❶ SEIZE, grab, take hold of, pluck. ❷ GRAB, steal, make off with, appropriate;

informal nab, swipe. ❸ KIDNAP, abduct, grab, take as hostage.

sneak v ❶ CREEP, skulk, lurk, prowl, steal, slip, slide, slink, sidle. ❷ TELL TALES ON, inform on, report; *informal* tell on, squeal on, peach on; *Brit. informal* grass on.

sneaking adj SECRET, private, hidden, concealed, unexpressed, unvoiced, undisclosed, undivulged, unconfessed, unavowed.

sneer v ❶ CURL ONE'S LIP, smirk, snicker, snigger. ❷ SCOFF AT, scorn, be contemptuous of, hold in contempt, disdain, mock, jeer at, gibe at, ridicule, deride, taunt, insult, slight.
▶ n ❶ SMIRK, snicker. ❷ JEER, jibe, taunt, insult, slight.

sniff v ❶ SNUFFLE, inhale, breathe in. ❷ SMELL, catch the scent of, scent; *Brit. informal* get a whiff of.

snigger v SNICKER, sneer, smirk, titter, giggle, chortle.

snip v ❶ CUT, cut into, nick, slit, notch, incise, snick.
▶ n ❶ CUT, nick, slit, notch, incision, snick. ❷ BARGAIN; *informal* good buy, cheap buy, giveaway, steal.

snippet n BIT, piece, scrap, fragment, particle, shred, snatch.

snivel v ❶ WEEP, cry, sob, whimper; *informal* blub, blubber. ❷ SNIFFLE, snuffle, run at the nose, have a runny/running nose.

snobbish adj SNOBBY,

arrogant, proud, condescending, haughty, disdainful, supercilious, patronizing; *informal* snooty, uppity, stuck up, hoity-toity, toffee-nosed.

snoop v PRY, spy, interfere, meddle; *informal* poke one's nose in.
▶ n BUSYBODY, interferer, meddler; *informal* snooper, nosy parker; *Austral. / NZ informal* stickybeak.

snooze v DOZE, nap, catnap, drowse, sleep, slumber; *informal* take forty winks; *Brit. informal* have a kip, kip.
▶ n DOZE, nap, catnap, siesta, sleep, slumber; *informal* forty winks; *Brit. informal* kip.

snub v IGNORE, disregard, take no notice of, shun, rebuff, repulse, spurn, slight, give the cold shoulder to, cold-shoulder, insult, affront; *informal* give the brush-off to, give the go-by, put down.

snug adj ❶ COSY, comfortable, warm, homelike, homely, sheltered; *informal* comfy. ❷ CLOSE-FITTING, tight, skin-tight.
– OPPOSITES bleak, loose.

snuggle v NESTLE, cuddle, curl up, nuzzle.

soak v ❶ DRENCH, wet through, saturate, make sopping. ❷ STEEP, immerse, souse.

soaking adj SOAKED, soaked to the skin, wet through, drenched, sodden, saturated, sopping wet, dripping wet, wringing wet, streaming wet.
– OPPOSITES parched.

soar v ❶ FLY, take flight, take

off, ascend, climb, rise. **2** RISE, go up, increase, climb, rapidly, spiral.
– OPPOSITES plummet.

sob v WEEP, cry, shed tears, blubber, snivel, howl, bawl; *Scottish* greet; *informal* boohoo.

sober adj **1** NOT DRUNK / INTOXI-CATED, abstemious, teetotal, abstinent, temperate; *informal* on the wagon, dry. **2** SERIOUS, solemn, thoughtful, grave, earnest, calm, composed, sedate, staid, dignified, steady, level-headed, self-controlled, strict, puritanical. **3** DISPASSION-ATE, objective, rational, logical, well considered, circumspect, lucid, clear. **4** DARK, sombre, quiet, restrained, drab, severe, austere.
– OPPOSITES drunk.

sociable adj FRIENDLY, affable, cordial, social, neighbourly, companionable, gregarious, convivial, communicative, genial, outgoing, approachable, accessible.
– OPPOSITES unsociable, unfriendly.

social adj **1** COMMUNITY, civil, civic, public, societal. **2** ENTER-TAINMENT, recreation, amuse-ment. **3** See SOCIABLE.
– OPPOSITES individual.

socialize v BE SOCIABLE / SOCIAL, mix, mingle, keep company, fraternize, consort, hobnob, get together, get out and about.

society n **1** MANKIND, human-ity, civilization, the public, the general public, the people, the population, the world at large,

the community. **2** COMMUNITY, group, culture, civilization. **3** HIGH SOCIETY, polite society, aristocracy, gentry, nobility, upper classes, the elite, the smart set, beau monde, haut monde; *informal* the upper crust, the top drawer, toffs, nobs, swells. **4** ASSOCIATION, club, group, band, circle, body, fraternity, brotherhood, sister-hood, league, union, alliance, federation.

sodden adj see SOAKING.

soft adj **1** PLIABLE, pliant, supple, elastic, flexible, ductile, malleable, plastic, mushy, squashy, pulpy, doughy, spongy; *informal* gooey. **2** SMOOTH, velvety, cushiony, fleecy, downy, furry, silky, silken, satin; *informal* like a baby's bottom. **3** LOW, dim, shaded, subdued, muted, mellow. **4** HUSHED, whispered, murmured, stifled, inaudible, low, quiet, mellow, melodious, mellifluous. **5** EASY-GOING, tolerant, forgiving, forbearing, lenient, indulgent, permissive, liberal, lax.
– OPPOSITES firm, hard.

soften v **1** EASE, cushion, temper, mitigate, assuage. **2** ABATE, moderate, lessen, diminish, calm down. **3** MODER-ATE, temper, tone down.

soggy adj SOAKING, saturated, sodden, sopping wet, soft, boggy, swampy, miry, water-logged, over-moist.

soil[1] n EARTH, ground, clay, dirt, land.

soil[2] v DIRTY, stain, muddy, spot, smear, splash, smudge, sully, taint, blot; *poetic/literary* besmirch.

soldier n FIGHTER, serviceman, servicewoman, warrior, trooper; *informal* cannon fodder.

solemn adj ❶ SERIOUS, grave, important, formal, profound. ❷ DIGNIFIED, ceremonious, stately, majestic, imposing, impressive, grand. ❸ SOMBRE, serious, unsmiling, pensive, thoughtful, gloomy, glum, grim. ❹ EARNEST, sincere, honest, genuine, committed, heartfelt.
– OPPOSITES frivolous.

solicit v ❶ ASK FOR, request, apply for, seek, beg, plead for, crave. ❷ WORK AS A PROSTITUTE, engage in prostitution, make sexual advances; *informal* hustle.

solicitous adj CONCERNED, caring, attentive, considerate, anxious, worried, nervous, uneasy, apprehensive.

solid adj ❶ FIRM, hard, thick, dense, concrete, compact, compressed, condensed. ❷ STURDY, substantial, strong, sound, stout, durable, well built, well constructed, stable. ❸ SOUND, well founded, well grounded, concrete, valid, reasonable, logical, cogent, weighty, authoritative, convincing, plausible, reliable. ❹ SENSIBLE, level-headed, down-to-earth, decent, law-abiding, upright, upstanding, worthy. ❺ STAID, worthy, sound, unexciting, unimaginative, uninspired. ❻ FINANCIALLY SOUND, solvent, creditworthy, in good standing, in the black, secure. ❼ CONTINUOUS, uninterrupted, unbroken, undivided.
– OPPOSITES liquid, flimsy, unreliable.

solidarity n UNITY, union, unanimity, singleness of purpose, like-mindedness, team spirit, camaraderie, harmony, esprit de corps.

solidify v HARDEN, go hard, set, jell, congeal, cake.
– OPPOSITES liquefy.

solitary adj ❶ LONELY, lonesome, companionless, friendless, antisocial, unsocial, unsociable, withdrawn, reclusive, cloistered, introverted, hermitic. ❷ REMOTE, out of the way, isolated, secluded, hidden, concealed, private, unfrequented, unvisited, desolate. ❸ LONE, single, sole, alone, by oneself/itself.
– OPPOSITES sociable, accessible.
▶ n LONER, lone wolf, recluse, hermit, eremite, anchorite, stylite, coenobite.

solitude n LONELINESS, remoteness, isolation, seclusion, privacy, retirement, desolation.

solution n ❶ ANSWER, result, key, resolution, solving, resolving, explanation, clarification, elucidation, unravelling, unfolding. ❷ SUSPENSION, emulsion, mixture, mix, blend, compound.

solve v FIND THE SOLUTION TO, answer, find the answer to, resolve, work out, figure out, fathom, find the key to, decipher, clear up, get to the bottom of, unravel, disentangle, unfold; *informal* crack.

solvent adj ● FINANCIALLY SOUND, debt-free, creditworthy, in the black, viable.
– OPPOSITES insolvent.

sombre adj ● DARK, dark-coloured, dull, dull-coloured, drab, dingy. ● GLOOMY, depressed, sad, melancholy, dismal, doleful, mournful, joyless, cheerless, lugubrious, funereal, sepulchral.
– OPPOSITES bright, cheerful.

somehow adv BY SOME MEANS, in some way, in one way or other, no matter how, come what may, by fair means or foul, by hook or by crook; *informal* come hell or high water.

sometimes adv OCCASIONALLY, on occasion, on occasions, now and then, now and again, from time to time, once in a while, every so often, off and on.

somnolent adj SLEEPY, drowsy, half asleep, heavy-eyed, dozy, groggy, comatose; *informal* dopey.

sonorous adj DEEP, rich, full, round, resonant, resounding, booming, ringing, reverberating, vibrating, pulsating.

soon adv SHORTLY, in a short time, in a little while, before long, in a minute, in a moment, any minute, in the near future, in a twinkling, in the twinkling of an eye; *informal* before you can

say Jack Robinson, pronto, in two shakes of a lamb's tail.

soothe v EASE, assuage, alleviate, allay, moderate, mitigate, temper, palliate, soften, lessen, reduce.
– OPPOSITES aggravate.

sophisticated adj
● WORLDLY-WISE, worldly, experienced, seasoned, suave, urbane, cultured, cultivated, polished, refined, elegant, stylish, cosmopolitan, blasé. ● ADVANCED, highly developed, ultramodern, complex, complicated, elaborate, intricate.
– OPPOSITES unsophisticated, crude.

soppy adj MAWKISH, maudlin, sentimental, overemotional, sloppy; *informal* slushy, mushy, schmaltzy, corny.

sorcerer n MAGICIAN, wizard, enchanter, warlock, necromancer, magus, thaumaturgist.

sorcery n MAGIC, witchcraft, witchery, wizardry, necromancy, black art, enchantment, thaumaturgy.

sordid adj ● FILTHY, dirty, foul, unclean, grimy, sooty, soiled, stained, mucky, squalid, shabby, seedy, seamy, slummy, sleazy. ● VILE, foul, base, low, debased, degenerate, dishonourable, disreputable, despicable, ignominious, ignoble, abhorrent, abominable.
● MEAN, greedy, avaricious, covetous, grasping, mercenary, miserly, niggardly; *informal* stingy.
– OPPOSITES clean.

sore adj ❶ PAINFUL, in pain, aching, hurting, tender, inflamed, raw, smarting, stinging, burning, irritated, bruised, wounded, injured. ❷ DISTRESSED, upset, resentful, aggrieved, offended, hurt, pained, annoyed, angry, irritated, irked, nettled; *informal* peeved.
▶ n WOUND, scrape, abrasion, cut, laceration, graze, boil, abscess, swelling.

sorrow n ❶ SADNESS, unhappiness, grief, misery, distress, heartache, heartbreak, anguish, suffering, pain, woe, affliction, wretchedness, dejection, heaviness of heart, desolation, depression, disconsolateness, mourning. ❷ TROUBLE, worry, woe, misfortune, affliction, trial, tribulation.
– OPPOSITES joy.
▶ v BE SAD, feel sad, be miserable, suffer, be wretched, be dejected, be heavy of, heart, pine, weep.

sorrowful adj UNHAPPY, heartbroken, wretched, woebegone, tearful, miserable, dejected, desolated, depressed, disconsolate, mournful, doleful, melancholy, lugubrious. *See also* SAD (1).
– OPPOSITES happy.

sorry adj ❶ REGRETFUL, apologetic, repentant, penitent, remorseful, contrite, ashamed, conscience-stricken, guilt-ridden, in sackcloth and ashes, compunctious. ❷ SYMPATHETIC, pitying, full of pity, compassionate, moved, commiserative, empathetic.
– OPPOSITES glad, unsympathetic, unrepentant.

sort n ❶ KIND, type, variety, class, category, style, group, set, genre, genus, family, order, breed, make, brand, stamp. ❷ PERSON, individual, soul; *informal* fellow, guy, character, customer; *Brit. informal* bloke, chap.
▶ v CLASSIFY, class, categorize, catalogue, grade, rank, group, divide, arrange, order, put in order, organize, assort, systematize, methodize.
■ **sort out** CLEAR UP, put straight, put right, solve, find a solution to.

sortie n SALLY, foray, charge, rush, onrush, raid, attack.

soul n ❶ SPIRIT, psyche, inner self, true being, vital force, animating principle. ❷ PERSON, human being, individual, creature.

sound¹ n ❶ NOISE, utterance, cry. ❷ HEARING, distance, earshot, range.
– OPPOSITES silence.
▶ v ❶ RESOUND, reverberate, resonate. ❷ PRONOUNCE, utter, voice, enunciate, articulate, vocalize. ❸ APPEAR, seem, give/create the impression that, strike someone that, give every indication that.

sound² adj ❶ HEALTHY, in good health, in good condition, physically fit, hale and hearty, undamaged, unimpaired, in good shape, in fine fettle. ❷ STURDY, substantial, solid, well constructed, intact, whole, undamaged, unimpaired. ❸ WELL FOUNDED, well grounded,

solid, valid, reasonable, logical, cogent, weighty, authoritative, convincing, plausible, reliable. **④** SOLVENT, creditworthy, in good financial standing, in the black, solid, secure. **⑤** THOROUGH, complete, without reserve, unqualified, out-and-out, drastic, severe.
– OPPOSITES unhealthy, flimsy, insolvent.

sound³ V PLUMB, fathom, probe.
■ **sound out** INVESTIGATE, conduct a survey of, research, explore, look into, examine, probe, canvass.

sour adj **①** ACID, acidy, acidlike, acetic, acidulous, tart, bitter, sharp, vinegary, pungent. **②** TURNED, curdled, fermented, rancid, bad. **③** EMBITTERED, nasty, unpleasant, disagreeable, bad-tempered, ill-tempered, ill-natured, sharp-tongued, irritable, crotchety, cross, crabbed, testy, touchy, peevish, churlish, grumpy; informal grouchy, snappish.
– OPPOSITES sweet, fresh, amiable.

source n **①** ORIGIN, derivation, commencement, beginning, start, rise, cause, wellspring, fountainhead, provenance, author, originator; poetic/literary begetter. **②** WELLSPRING, well head, headspring. **③** REFERENCE, authority.

sovereign n RULER, monarch, king, queen, emperor, empress, tsar, crowned head, potentate.

▶ adj **①** SUPREME, absolute, unlimited, chief, paramount, principal, dominant, predominant, ruling. **②** INDEPENDENT, self-ruling, self-governing, autonomous.

sow V SCATTER, spread, broadcast, disperse, strew, bestrew, disseminate, distribute.

space n **①** ROOM, expanse, extent, capacity, area, volume, spaciousness, scope, elbow room, latitude, margin, leeway. **②** GAP, interval, opening, interstice, break. **③** TIME, duration, period, span, stretch, interval. **④** OUTER SPACE, the universe, the galaxy, the solar system, infinity.

▶ V PLACE AT INTERVALS, arrange, line up, range, order, interspace, set apart.

spacious adj ROOMY, commodious, capacious, sizable, ample, large, big, extensive, broad, wide, expansive, vast.
– OPPOSITES small.

span n **①** LENGTH, extent, reach, stretch, spread, distance. **②** TIME, duration, period, space, stretch, interval.

▶ V EXTEND OVER, stretch across, cover, range over, bridge, cross, traverse, pass over, arch over, vault over.

spare adj **①** EXTRA, additional, reserve, supplementary, auxiliary, surplus, supernumerary. **②** FREE, leisure, unoccupied. **③** LEAN, thin, slim, slender, skinny, skin and bone, wiry, lank.

▶ V **①** AFFORD, part with, give,

provide, dispense with, do without, manage without, get along without. ❷ BE MERCIFUL TO, show mercy to, be lenient to, deal leniently with, pardon, leave unpunished; *informal* let off, go easy on.

sparing adj ECONOMICAL, frugal, thrifty, careful, prudent, parsimonious, niggardly; *informal* stingy, tight-fisted.
– OPPOSITES extravagant.

spark n FLICKER, flash, flare, glint.
▶ v SET OFF, spark off, start off, trigger off, touch off, precipitate, provoke, stir up, incite.

sparkle v ❶ TWINKLE, flicker, shimmer, flash, glitter, glint, shine, gleam, glow, coruscate. ❷ BE VIVACIOUS, be lively, be animated, be ebullient, be effervescent, be witty, be brilliant.
▶ n ❶ TWINKLE, flicker, shimmer, flash, glitter, glint, shining, gleam, glow, coruscation. ❷ VIVACITY, liveliness, life, animation, energy, vitality, spirit, enthusiasm, dash, dan, panache; *informal* pizzazz, vim, zip, zing.

sparse adj SCANTY, meagre, slight, light, sparing, inadequate; *informal* thin on the ground.
– OPPOSITES abundant.

spartan adj AUSTERE, harsh, frugal, stringent, rigorous, strict, severe, bleak, grim, ascetic, abstemious, self-denying.
– OPPOSITES luxurious.

spasm n ❶ CONTRACTION, convulsion, cramp, twitch. ❷ FIT, paroxysm, convulsion, attack, bout, seizure, outburst, access.

spasmodic adj INTERMITTENT, fitful, irregular, sporadic, erratic, periodic, recurring, recurrent.
– OPPOSITES regular.

spate n RUSH, flood, deluge, torrent, outpouring, outbreak, cluster.

spatter v SPLASH, spray, shower, bespatter, daub.

speak v ❶ UTTER, voice, express, say, pronounce, articulate, enunciate, state, discourse upon, tell. ❷ ADDRESS, talk to, converse with, communicate with, have a discussion with, chat with, have a chat with, have a word with, accost; *informal* have a chinwag with, chew the fat/rag with, pass the time of day with.
■ **speak for** ❶ REPRESENT, act for, act on behalf of, intercede for. ❷ SUPPORT, uphold, defend, stand up for, advocate. **speak out** SPEAK BOLDLY, speak frankly, speak openly, speak one's mind, sound off, stand up and be counted.

speaker n PUBLIC SPEAKER, lecturer, orator, declaimer, haranguer, demagogue; *informal* tub-thumper, spieler.

spearhead n VANGUARD, van, forefront, driving force.
▶ v LEAD, head, set in motion, initiate, launch, pioneer.

special adj ❶ EXCEPTIONAL, remarkable, unusual, rare, out

of the ordinary, extraordinary, singular, distinctive, notable, outstanding, unique. ❷ SPECIFIC, particular, individual, distinctive, exact, precise, definite. ❸ ESPECIAL, extra special, particular, exceptional, out of the ordinary. ❹ SIGNIFICANT, momentous, memorable, festive, gala, red-letter.
– OPPOSITES ordinary.

specialist n EXPERT, authority, professional, consultant, master.

speciality n ❶ SPECIALTY, area of specialization, field of study. ❷ DISTINCTIVE FEATURE, forte, métier, talent, gift, claim to fame.

species n SORT, kind, type, variety, class, category, group, genus, breed, genre.

specific adj ❶ WELL DEFINED, clear-cut, unambiguous, unequivocal, exact, precise, explicit, express, detailed. ❷ PARTICULAR, specified, fixed, set, determined, distinct, definite.
– OPPOSITES vague, general.

specify v STATE, mention, name, stipulate, define, set out, itemize, designate, detail, list, spell out, enumerate, particularize, catalogue, be specific about.

specimen n SAMPLE, representative, example, illustration, instance, type, exhibit.

specious adj MISLEADING, deceptive, fallacious, unsound, casuistic, sophistic.

speck n ❶ SPOT, fleck, dot, speckle, stain, mark, smudge, blemish. ❷ PARTICLE, bit, piece, atom, iota, grain, trace.

speckled adj MOTTLED, flecked, spotted, dotted, dappled, brindled, stippled.

spectacle n ❶ SIGHT, vision, scene, picture. ❷ DISPLAY, show, exhibition, pageant, parade, extravaganza.

spectacles n GLASSES, eyeglasses; informal specs.

spectacular adj IMPRESSIVE, magnificent, splendid, eye-catching, breathtaking, glorious, dazzling, sensational, stunning, dramatic, exceptional, remarkable, unusual, picturesque; informal out of this world.
– OPPOSITES unimpressive, dull.

spectator n VIEWER, observer, onlooker, looker-on, watcher, beholder, witness, eyewitness, bystander; informal rubberneck.
– OPPOSITES participant.

spectre n APPARITION, ghost, phantom, wraith, spirit, shade, vision, revenant, manes; informal spook.

speculate v ❶ CONJECTURE, theorize, hypothesize, guess, take a guess, surmise, muse, reflect, mediate, deliberate, cogitate, consider, think. ❷ GAMBLE, take a risk on, venture on; informal have a flutter on.

speculative adj ❶ CONJECTURAL, theoretical, hypothetical, suppositional, notional, academic, tentative, unproven, vague, indefinite. ❷ RISKY, hazardous, gambling; *informal* chancy, dicey.

speech n ❶ COMMUNICATION, talk, conversation, discussion, dialogue, colloquy. ❷ DICTION, articulation, enunciation, pronunciation. ❸ TALK, lecture, address, discourse, oration, sermon, harangue, tirade; *poetic/literary* philippic. ❹ LANGUAGE, tongue, idiom, dialect, parlance; *informal* lingo.

speechless adj ❶ STRUCK DUMB, dumbstruck, dumbfounded, astounded, thunderstruck. ❷ SILENT, unspoken, unexpressed, unsaid, unvoiced, tacit.

speed n RAPIDITY, swiftness, quickness, fastness, haste, hurry, hurriedness, expeditiousness, expedition, alacrity, promptness, fleetness, celerity, velocity.
▶ v ❶ HURRY, hasten, make haste, rush, race, dash, sprint, scurry, tear, scamper, charge; *informal* scoot. ❷ DRIVE TOO FAST, break the speed limit, exceed the speed limit; *informal* put one's foot down, step on it. ❸ EXPEDITE, hasten, accelerate, advance, further, forward, facilitate, promote, boost, aid, assist.
– OPPOSITES slow, hinder.
■ **speed up** See ACCELERATE.

speedy adj RAPID, swift, quick, fast, high-speed, expeditious, fleet, prompt, immediate, express.
– OPPOSITES slow, leisurely.

spell[1] v MEAN, signify, amount to, add up to, signal, denote, result in, cause, bespeak, portend, augur, presage.
■ **spell out** SPECIFY, set out, itemize, detail, enumerate, particularize, stipulate, make clear, make plain, elucidate, clarify.

spell[2] n ❶ INCANTATION, conjuration, charm, abracadabra. ❷ TRANCE, entrancement, enthralment, bewitchment.

spell[3] n ❶ PERIOD, interval, stretch, course, extent, span, patch. ❷ TURN, stint, term, stretch, shift.

spellbound adj RIVETED, entranced, enthralled, enraptured, transported, rapt, bewitched, fascinated, captivated, mesmerized, hypnotized; *informal* hooked.

spend v ❶ PAY OUT, lay out, expend, disburse, dish out; *informal* fork out, shell out, splash out, splurge. ❷ OCCUPY, fill, take up, use up, pass, while away.

spendthrift n SQUANDERER, prodigal, profligate, wastrel; *informal* big spender.
– OPPOSITES miser.

spent adj USED UP, consumed, exhausted, finished, depleted, drained, emptied; *informal* played out, burnt out.

sphere n ❶ GLOBE, ball, orb, globule. ❷ AREA, field, range, scope, extent, compass, jurisdiction. ❸ SOCIAL CLASS, station, rank, status, social circumstances, walk of life.

spherical adj GLOBE-SHAPED, globular, globoid, round, orb-like, orbicular.

spice n ❶ FLAVOURING, seasoning, herb, condiment, relish. ❷ EXCITEMENT, interest, colour, piquancy, zest, gusto, pep; informal zip, zing, zap.

spicy adj ❶ SPICED, seasoned, tangy, sharp, tart, hot, peppery, piquant, pungent. ❷ LIVELY, spirited, suggestive, racy, off colour, improper, indecent, offensive; informal raunchy.
– OPPOSITES bland, boring.

spill v ❶ POUR, pour out, flow, overflow, brim over, run over, slop over, well over. ❷ REVEAL, disclose, divulge, leak, make known; informal let out, blab.
▶ n FALL, tumble; informal header, nosedive.

spin v ❶ REVOLVE, rotate, turn, turn round, circle, whirl, gyrate. ❷ WHIRL, reel, swim, be giddy.
■ **spin out** see PROLONG.

spine n ❶ SPINAL COLUMN, vertebrae, vertebral column, backbone, dorsum. ❷ NEEDLE, spike, barb, quill.

spiral adj COILED, corkscrew, winding, twisting, whorled, helical, cochlear, cochleate, voluted.
▶ n COIL, twist, whorl, corkscrew, wreath, curlicue, helix, volute.
▶ v COIL, wind, twist, swirl, wreathe.

spirit n ❶ SOUL, psyche, inner self, ego. ❷ BREATH OF LIFE, vital spark, animating principle, life force. ❸ APPARITION, ghost, phantom, spectre, wraith, shade, revenant, manes; informal spook. ❹ COURAGE, bravery, braveness, valour, mettle, pluck, grit, pluckiness, will power, motivation, backbone, determination, firmness of purpose, resoluteness; informal guts. ❺ ATTITUDE, way, state of mind, mood, frame of mind, point of view, reaction, feeling, humour. ❻ PREVAILING TENDENCY, animating principle, dominating characteristic, ethos, essence, quintessence, embodiment, personification.
– OPPOSITES body, flesh.

spirited adj ❶ COURAGEOUS, brave, valiant, valorous, heroic, mettlesome, plucky, gritty, determined, resolute. ❷ ANIMATED, lively, vivacious, enthusiastic, fervent, fiery, passionate, energetic.
– OPPOSITES timid, lifeless.

spiritual adj ❶ NON-MATERIAL, incorporeal, ethereal, intangible, other-worldly, unworldly. ❷ RELIGIOUS, sacred, divine, holy, non-secular, churchly, ecclesiastic, devotional, devout.
– OPPOSITES physical, secular.

spit v EXPECTORATE, hawk.
▶ n SPITTLE, saliva, sputum.

spite n MALICE, maliciousness, ill will, malevolence, venom, malignance, hostility, resentment, resentfulness, snideness, rancour, envy, hate, hatred, vengeance, vengefulness, vindictiveness.
– OPPOSITES benevolence.

■ **in spite of** DESPITE, despite the fact, notwithstanding, regardless of.

spiteful adj MALICIOUS, ill-natured, malevolent, venomous, poisonous, malignant, malign, hostile, resentful, snide, rancorous, grudging, envious, vengeful, vindictive, splenetic; informal bitchy, catty.
– OPPOSITES benevolent.

splash v ❶ SPATTER, sprinkle, spray, shower, splatter, squirt, slosh, slop; Brit. informal splodge. ❷ PADDLE, wade, wallow, dabble. ❸ BLAZON, display, exhibit, plaster, publicize, broadcast, headline, flaunt, trumpet.

splendid adj ❶ MAGNIFICENT, imposing, superb, grand, sumptuous, resplendent, opulent, luxurious, plush, de luxe, rich, costly, lavish, ornate, gorgeous, glorious, dazzling, brilliant, showy, elegant, handsome. ❷ DISTINGUISHED, impressive, glorious, illustrious, brilliant, notable, noted, remarkable, outstanding, eminent, celebrated, renowned, noble, venerable. ❸ EXCELLENT, fine, first-class, first-rate; marvellous, wonderful, great; informal fantastic, terrific, fabulous, fab.
– OPPOSITES inferior, undistinguished.

splendour n ❶ MAGNIFICENCE, grandeur, sumptuousness, opulence, luxury, luxuriousness, richness, lavishness, gloriousness, elegance.
❷ ILLUSTRIOUSNESS, brilliance, notability, eminence, renown, venerableness. ❸ GLORIOUSNESS, brilliance, brightness, gleam, glow, lustre, radiance.

splice v INTERWEAVE, braid, plait, intertwine, interlace, join, unite, connect, bind.

splinter n SLIVER, fragment, shiver, shard, chip, shaving, shred, piece, bit.
▶ v SHATTER, fracture, split, disintegrate, crumble.

split v ❶ BREAK, chop, hew, lop, cleave, rend, rip, tear, slash, slit, splinter. ❷ DIVIDE, separate, set apart, disunite. ❸ SHARE, divide, halve, apportion, distribute, dole out, parcel out, allot, allocate; Brit. informal divvy. ❹ BREAK UP WITH / FROM, separate from, part from, part company with, reach the parting of the ways, dissociate oneself from.
– OPPOSITES mend, unite, pool, converge.
▶ n ❶ BREAK, cut, rent, rip, tear, slash, slit, crack, fissure, breach. ❷ DIVISION, rift, schism, rupture, separation, break-up, alienation, estrangement.
– OPPOSITES marriage.

spoil v ❶ DAMAGE, impair, mar, blemish, disfigure, deface, injure, harm, ruin, destroy, wreck. ❷ UPSET, mess up, disorganize, ruin, destroy, wreck. ❸ PAMPER, overindulge, mollycoddle, cosset, coddle, baby, spoon-feed, feather-bed, wait on hand and foot, kill with kindness. ❹ GO BAD, go off, turn, go sour, become rotten, rot,

become tainted, decompose, decay.
– OPPOSITES improve, further.

spoilsport n KILLJOY, damper, dog in the manger; *informal* wet blanket, party-pooper, misery.

spoken adj ORAL, verbal, uttered, voiced, expressed, by word of mouth, unwritten.
– OPPOSITES non-verbal, written.

sponge v CLEAN, wash, wipe, mop, rub, swab.

spongy adj SOFT, cushiony, squashy, springy, resilient, elastic, porous, absorbent.

sponsor n PATRON, backer, promoter, subsidizer, guarantor, supporter, angel.
▶ V BE A PATRON OF, back, put up the money for, fund, finance, promote, subsidize, support, lend one's name to.

spontaneous adj ❶ VOLUNTARY, unforced, unconstrained, unprompted. ❷ UNPLANNED, unpremeditated, unrehearsed, impromptu, extempore, spur-of-the-moment, extemporaneous; *informal* off-the-cuff. ❸ NATURAL, instinctive, involuntary, automatic, impulsive, impetuous.
– OPPOSITES conscious, voluntary.

sporadic adj IRREGULAR, intermittent, scattered, random, infrequent, occasional, on and off, isolated, spasmodic.
– OPPOSITES frequent, regular.

sport n ❶ PHYSICAL ACTIVITY, physical exercise, physical recreation, athletics, game, pastime. ❷ AMUSEMENT, entertainment, diversion, play, fun, pleasure, enjoyment.
▶ V ❶ PLAY, have fun, amuse oneself, entertain oneself, divert oneself, frolic, gambol, frisk, romp, cavort, caper, disport oneself. ❷ WEAR, exhibit, display, have on show, show off.

sporting adj SPORTSMANLIKE, fair, just, honourable, generous.

spot n ❶ MARK, dot, speck, fleck, smudge, stain, blotch, patch; *informal* splotch. ❷ PIMPLE, pustule, papule, boil, whitehead, blackhead, blemish. ❸ STAIN, taint, blemish, defect, flaw, brand, stigma. ❹ AREA, place, site, location, scene, setting, situation.
▶ V ❶ CATCH SIGHT OF, see, notice, observe, espy, discern, descry, detect, make out, pick out, recognize. ❷ MARK, stain, dirty, soil, spatter; *poetic/literary* besmirch.

spotless adj ❶ CLEAN, snowy-white, whiter-than-white, spick and span, immaculate, shining, gleaming. ❷ PURE, flawless, faultless, blameless, unstained, unsullied, untainted, unblemished, unimpeachable, above reproach.
– OPPOSITES dirty, impure.

spotlight n LIMELIGHT, public eye, glare of publicity, publicity, public attention, public city, public interest.

spotted adj DAPPLED, mottled, dotted, piebald, speckled.

spotty adj ❶ PIMPLY, acned. ❷ *See* SPOTTED. ❸ PATCHY, irregular, non-uniform.

spouse n HUSBAND / WIFE, partner, mate, companion, consort, helpmate; *informal* better half, old man/woman/lady, missis.

spout v ❶ SPURT, gush, spew, squirt, jet, spray, emit, erupt, disgorge, pour, stream, flow. ❷ DECLAIM, orate, hold forth, ramble, rant, harangue, speechify, sermonize; *informal* spiel.

sprawl v ❶ STRETCH OUT, lounge, lie around, repose, recline, slump, flop, loll, slouch. ❷ SPREAD, stretch, spill over, ramble, straggle, trail.

spray[1] n ❶ SHOWER, jet, mist, drizzle, spindrift, foam, froth. ❷ ATOMIZER, vaporizer, aerosol, sprinkler.
▶ v ❶ SPRINKLE, shower, disperse, disseminate. ❷ JET, spout, gush.

spray[2] n SPRIG, posy, bouquet, nosegay, corsage, wreath, garland.

spread v ❶ STRETCH, extend, open out, unfurl, unroll. ❷ ENLARGE, extend, stretch out, grow bigger, widen, broaden, grow, develop, branch out. ❸ COVER, coat, layer, lay on, put on, apply, smear on; *informal* plaster on. ❹ DISSEMINATE, circulate, transmit, make public, make known, broadcast, publicize, propagate, promulgate, bruit.
▶ n ❶ EXTENT, stretch, span, reach, compass, sweep. ❷ EXPANSION, advance, increase, mushrooming, proliferation, escalation, diffusion. ❸ BEDSPREAD, bedcover, cover, coverlet, counterpane, throw. ❹ FEAST, banquet, repast; *informal* blowout.

spree n OUTING, fling, revel, junket, orgy, debauch, bacchanal, bacchanalia; *informal* binge, bender, jag.

sprightly adj SPRY, lively, energetic, active, agile, nimble, supple, animated, vivacious, spirited, brisk, vital, lighthearted, cheerful, merry, jolly, jaunty, perky, frisky, playful, sportive; *poetic/literary* frolicsome, blithe.
– OPPOSITES inactive, lethargic.

spring v ❶ JUMP, leap, bound, vault, hop.
▶ n ❶ JUMP, leap, bound, vault, hop. ❷ BOUNCE, bounciness, liveliness, light-heartedness, merriment.
■ **spring from** ORIGINATE, have its origins in, derive from, stem from, arise in, emanate from, proceed from, start from.
spring up APPEAR, come into being, come into existence, shoot up, develop quickly, mushroom, burgeon.

springy adj BOUNCY, elastic, resilient, flexible, stretchy, tensile.
– OPPOSITES rigid.

sprinkle v SPRAY, shower, splash, trickle, spatter, scatter, strew, dust, powder.

sprinkling n ❶ SCATTERING, dusting. ❷ FEW, handful, trickle.

sprint v RUN, race, rush, dash, put on a turn/burst of speed; *informal* scoot, tear, hare, hot-foot it.

sprout v BUD, germinate, put forth shoots, shoot up, spring up, grow, develop, appear, mushroom, proliferate.

spruce adj NEAT, well groomed, well turned out, smart, trim, dapper, elegant, chic; *informal* natty.
– OPPOSITES dishevelled.

spur n GOAD, prod, stimulus, stimulant, incentive, induce-ment, encouragement, im-petus.
– OPPOSITES disincentive.
▶ v PROD, goad, stimulate, give the incentive to, induce, en-courage, motivate, prompt, urge, impel.
– OPPOSITES discourage.

spurious adj COUNTERFEIT, fraudulent, fake, bogus, sham, mock, feigned, pretended, pseudo, make-believe, imita-tion, contrived, fictitious, de-ceitful, specious; *informal* phoney.
– OPPOSITES authentic, genu-ine.

spurn v REJECT, turn away, re-pulse, rebuff, repudiate, snub, slight, cold-shoulder, disdain, look down one's nose at, scorn, despise, condemn; *informal* kick in the teeth, give the go-by.
– OPPOSITES welcome, accept.

spurt v GUSH, squirt, shoot, surge, well, jet, spring, pour, stream, flow, issue, emanate.
▶ n ❶ GUSH, surge, jet, spray,

outpouring. ❷ BURST, outburst, fit, surge, access.

spy n SECRET AGENT, foreign agent, secret agent, undercover agent, intelligence agent, double agent, fifth columnist; *informal* mole, spook.
▶ v CATCH SIGHT OF, spot, see, notice, observe, glimpse, make out, discern, descry, espy.
■ **spy on** KEEP UNDER SURVEIL-LANCE, watch, keep a watch on, keep an eye on, observe, keep under observation, follow, shadow, trail.

squabble n DISPUTE, argu-ment, wrangle, brawl; *informal* row, scrap, set-to, dust-up, run-in, spat; *Brit. informal* barney.
▶ v HAVE A DISPUTE, argue, bicker, have a difference of opinion, have words, wrangle, brawl; *informal* row, have a tiff.

squalid adj ❶ DIRTY, filthy, dingy, grubby, grimy, mucky, foul, vile, low, wretched, mean, nasty, seedy, sordid, sleazy, slovenly, repulsive, disgusting, ramshackle, broken-down, tumbledown; *informal* grungy; *Brit. informal* grotty. ❷ SORDID, vile, nasty, repulsive, horrible, dis-graceful, shameful, abomin-able, odious, filthy, indecent, depraved.
– OPPOSITES clean, decent.

squander v WASTE, misspend, dissipate, fritter away, run through, lavish, splurge, be prodigal with, spend like water, pour down the drain; *informal* blow.
– OPPOSITES save.

square n PIAZZA, plaza, market square, marketplace, quadrangle.
▶ adj ❶ EQUAL, even, level-pegging, drawn. ❷ FAIR, just, equitable, honest, straight, upright, above board, ethical; *informal* on the level.

squash v ❶ CRUSH, squeeze, flatten, compress, press, smash, pulp, mash, pulverize, macerate. ❷ CROWD, crush, cram, pack tight, jam, squeeze, wedge. ❸ PUT DOWN, quash, quell, crush, suppress, scotch.

squashy adj PULPY, mushy, spongy, squishy, oozy, pappy.
– OPPOSITES firm.

squat adj DUMPY, stubby, chunky, thickset, stocky, short.

squeak n & v SQUEAL, peep, pipe, yelp, whimper.

squeamish adj ❶ EASILY NAUSEATED, liable to be made to feel sick, easily put off, nervous, unable to stand the sight of. ❷ SCRUPULOUS, particular, punctilious, finicky, fussy, fastidious.

squeeze v ❶ COMPRESS, crush, squash, mash, pulp. ❷ GRIP, clutch, pinch, press, compress. ❸ CROWD, crush, cram, pack tight, jam, squash, wedge. ❹ PRESSURE, pressurize, strong-arm, blackmail; *informal* put the squeeze on, lean on, bleed, put the screws on, put the bite on.

squirm v WRIGGLE, wiggle, writhe, twist, turn, shift.

squirt v SPURT, spout, jet, stream, spray, gush, surge, pour, flow, issue, spew out.

stab v KNIFE, pierce, puncture, run through, stick, skewer, gash, slash, wound, injure.
▶ n ❶ PUNCTURE, gash, slash, incision, wound, injury. ❷ PANG, twinge, ache, throb, spasm. ❸ TRY, attempt, endeavour, essay, effort, venture; *informal* go, crack.

stability n FIRMNESS, solidity, steadiness, secureness, strength, fastness, stoutness, sturdiness, sureness, durability, constancy, permanence, reliability, dependability.
– OPPOSITES instability.

stable adj ❶ FIRM, solid, steady, secure, fixed, strong, fast, stout, sturdy, immovable. ❷ SECURE, solid, strong, steady, firm, sure, steadfast, unwavering, unfaltering, unswerving, long-lasting, deep-rooted, well founded, well grounded, abiding, durable, enduring, lasting, constant, permanent. ❸ WELL BALANCED, balanced, steady, reasonable, sensible, responsible, equable, self-controlled, sane.
– OPPOSITES unstable.

stack n ❶ HEAP, pile, mass, accumulation, collection, hoard, store, stock, stockpile, mound, mountain. ❷ ABUNDANCE, amplitude, a great deal, a lot; *informal* lots, bags, loads, heaps, tons, oodles, scads.
▶ v HEAP, pile, pile up, amass, accumulate, collect, hoard, store, stockpile.

staff n ❶ STICK, cane, crook,

rod, pole, baton, truncheon. ❷ MACE, sceptre. ❸ EMPLOYEES, workers, workforce, personnel. ▶ v MAN, people, provide with staff.

stage n ❶ POINT, period, step, juncture, time, division, level. ❷ LAP, leg, phase, step. ❸ PLATFORM, dais, rostrum, podium. ▶ v PUT ON, produce, direct, perform, mount, present.

stagger v ❶ REEL, sway, teeter, totter, wobble, lurch, pitch, roll. ❷ AMAZE, astound, dumbfound, astonish, shock, shake, confound, nonplus, take aback, take someone's breath away, stupefy, stun, strike dumb; *informal* flabbergast.

stagnant adj ❶ STILL, motionless, standing, foul, stale, dirty, filthy, brackish. ❷ SLUGGISH, slow-moving, quiet, inactive, dull, static.
− OPPOSITES fresh, active.

stagnate v DO NOTHING, be sluggish, lie dormant, be inert, vegetate, idle, be idle, laze, loaf, hang about, languish.

staid adj SEDATE, quiet, serious, grave, solemn, sombre, sober, proper, decorous, formal, demure, stiff, starchy; *informal* stuffy.
− OPPOSITES frivolous.

stain v ❶ SOIL, mark, discolour, dirty, spot, blotch, blemish, smudge, smear, begrime; *poetic/literary* besmirch. ❷ BLACKEN, tarnish, sully, blemish, damage, mar, injure, defame, denigrate, dishonour, besmirch, defile, taint, blot,

slur. ❸ VARNISH, dye, paint, colour.
▶ n ❶ MARK, spot, blotch, blemish, smudge, smear. ❷ BLEMISH, damage, injury, taint, blot, slur, stigma. ❸ VARNISH, dye, paint, colourant.

stake¹ n ❶ POST, pole, stick, upright, rod, spike, pale. ▶ v ❶ SUPPORT, prop up, hold up, brace, tether. ❷ ESTABLISH, declare, state, lay claim to.

stake² n ❶ WAGER, bet, ante. ❷ FINANCIAL INTEREST, interest, share, investment, involvement, concern.
▶ v WAGER, bet, put on, gamble, pledge, chance, venture, risk, hazard.

stale adj ❶ DRY, dried out, hard, hardened, mouldy, decayed. ❷ STUFFY, close, musty, fusty; *Brit.* fuggy. ❸ HACKNEYED, tired, worn out, threadbare, banal, trite, stock, stereotyped, run-of-the-mill, commonplace, unoriginal, unimaginative, uninspired, flat, insipid, vapid; *informal* old hat.
− OPPOSITES fresh.

stalemate n DEADLOCK, impasse, standstill, stand-off.

stalk¹ n STEM, branch, shoot, twig.

stalk² v ❶ PURSUE, chase, follow, shadow, trail, track down, creep up on, hunt; *informal* tail. ❷ STRIDE, march, flounce, strut, prance.

stall n BOOTH, stand, table, counter.
▶ v ❶ PLAY FOR TIME, use delaying tactics, delay, drag one's feet,

beat about the bush; *Brit.* hum and haw. ❷ HOLD OFF, stave off, keep at bay, keep at arm's length, evade, avoid.

stalwart adj BRAVE, courageous, valiant, valorous, intrepid, fearless, manly, heroic, indomitable, bold, daring, plucky, spirited, adventurous; *informal* gutsy. *See also* BRAVE.
− OPPOSITES timid.

stamina n ENDURANCE, staying power, indefatigability, resilience, fortitude, strength, vigour, energy, staunchness, robustness; *informal* grit, guts.

stammer v STUTTER, stumble, mumble, splutter, hesitate, falter, pause.

stamp v ❶ TRAMPLE, step on, tread on, trample on, crush. ❷ IMPRINT, inscribe, engrave, emboss, mark, sign.
▶ n MARK, hallmark, label, brand, tag, characteristics, quality.
■ **stamp out** QUASH, suppress, put down, quell, crush, extinguish, scotch, put an end to, eradicate, eliminate.

stampede n CHARGE, rush, flight, scattering.
▶ v CHARGE, rush, flee, take flight, dash, race, run.

stance n STAND, standpoint, position, line, policy, attitude, angle, slant, viewpoint, point of view, opinion.

stand v ❶ BE UPRIGHT, be erect, rise, rise/get to one's feet, get up. ❷ BE SITUATED, be located. ❸ REMAIN / BE IN FORCE, remain/be valid, remain/be effective, hold,

hold good, obtain, prevail, be the case. ❹ PUT UP WITH, tolerate, bear, take, endure, abide, countenance, stomach, cope with, handle; *informal* wear; *formal* brook; *archaic* suffer.
▶ n ❶ STANDSTILL, halt, stop, rest. ❷ *See* STANCE. ❸ PLATFORM, stage, staging, dais, rostrum.
■ **stand by/stand up for** *see* SUPPORT v (5). **stand out** BE NOTICEABLE, be noticed, be conspicuous, be striking, attract attention, catch the eye; *informal* stick out a mile, stick out like a sore thumb.

standard n ❶ YARDSTICK, benchmark, gauge, measure, criterion, guide, guideline, norm, touchstone, model, pattern, example, exemplar, paradigm, ideal, archetype, specification, requirement, rule, principle, law, canon. ❷ LEVEL, grade, quality, worth, merit. ❸ FLAG, banner, pennant, streamer, ensign, colours. ❹ SUPPORT, prop, pole, cane, upright.
▶ adj ❶ USUAL, ordinary, average, normal, habitual, common, regular, stock, set, fixed, conventional. ❷ DEFINITIVE, established, classic, recognized, approved, accepted, authoritative, official.
− OPPOSITES unusual.

standardize v MAKE UNIFORM, regulate, systematize, normalize, homogenize, regiment, bring into line.

standing n STATUS, rank, social position, station, footing, place, circumstances.

stand-off n DEADLOCK, impasse, stalemate.

standpoint n POINT OF VIEW, viewpoint, opinion, perspective, angle, slant, frame of reference.

standstill n HALT, stop, dead stop, stoppage, rest, pause, cessation, stand.

staple adj CHIEF, primary, main, principal, basic, fundamental, essential, indispensable.

star n ❶ HEAVENLY BODY, celestial body. ❷ HOROSCOPE, forecast, augury. ❸ SUPERSTAR, name, lead, celebrity, dignitary, notable, somebody, VIP; *informal* bigwig, big shot, big cheese, big wheel.

stare v GAZE, gape, goggle, look; *informal* gawp.

stark adj ❶ SHARP, sharply defined, obvious, evident, clear, clear-cut. ❷ DESOLATE, bare, barren, arid, vacant, empty, forsaken, bleak, dreary, depressing, grim, harsh; *poetic/literary* drear.
– OPPOSITES indistinct, ornate.

start v ❶ BEGIN, commence, make a start, get going, go ahead, set things moving, buckle to/down, turn to, put one's shoulder to the wheel, put one's hand to the plough; *informal* get moving, start the ball rolling, get down to it, get down to business, get one's finger out, get the show on the road, take the plunge, kick off, pitch in, get off one's backside.

❷ START OUT, set out, set off, depart, leave, make a start; *informal* hit the road, push off, get the show on the road. ❸ SET IN MOTION, set moving, turn on, activate. ❹ BEGIN WORKING, start functioning, start operating. ❺ JUMP, leap up, jerk, twitch, recoil, shrink, flinch, blench, wince, shy.
– OPPOSITES finish.
▶ n ❶ BEGINNING, commencement, opening, inception, inauguration, dawn, birth; *informal* kick-off. ❷ JUMP, leap, jerk, twitch, flinch, blench, wince, spasm, convulsion.
– OPPOSITES end.

startle v MAKE SOMEONE JUMP, disturb, agitate, perturb, unsettle, scare, frighten, alarm, surprise, astonish, shock; *informal* give someone a turn.

startling adj DISTURBING, unsettling, alarming, surprising, unexpected, unforeseen, astonishing, amazing, staggering, shocking, extraordinary, remarkable.
– OPPOSITES predictable, ordinary.

starvation n EXTREME HUNGER, lack of food, fasting, famine, undernourishment, malnourishment.

starving adj STARVED, famished, ravenous, very hungry, fasting; *informal* able to eat a horse.

state[1] n ❶ CONDITION, shape, situation, circumstances, state of affairs, position, predicament, plight. ❷ ANXIETY, nerves, panic, fluster; *informal* flap, tizzy. ❸ COUNTRY, nation, land, realm, kingdom, republic.

state² v EXPRESS, voice, utter, say, tell, declare, set out, lay down, affirm, assert, announce, make known, reveal, disclose, divulge, pronounce, articulate, proclaim; *formal* aver.

stately adj CEREMONIAL, dignified, solemn, majestic, royal, regal, magnificent, grand, glorious, splendid, elegant, imposing, impressive, august, lofty, pompous.

statement n DECLARATION, account, recitation, report, affirmation, assertion, announcement, revelation, disclosure, divulgence, pronouncement, articulation, proclamation, presentation, promulgation; *formal* averment.

static adj UNMOVING, unvarying, undeviating, changeless, constant, stable, steady, stationary, motionless, at a standstill, frozen.
– OPPOSITES mobile, variable.

station n ❶ STOP, stopping place, terminus, terminal, depot. ❷ DEPOT, base, office, headquarters, seat. ❸ POST, place, position, location, site. ❹ CLASS, level, rank, grade, standing, status, caste.

stationary adj ❶ UNMOVING, motionless, at a standstill, parked. ❷ CHANGELESS, unchanging, constant, unvarying, invariable, undeviating.
– OPPOSITES moving.

statue n STATUETTE, sculpture, effigy, figure, figurine, bust, head.

statuesque adj DIGNIFIED, stately, majestic, splendid, imposing, impressive, regal.

stature n ❶ HEIGHT, tallness, size. ❷ STATUS, importance, import, standing, eminence, prominence, note, renown.

status n STANDING, rank, level, grade, degree, position, importance, reputation, consequence.

staunch adj LOYAL, faithful, dependable, reliable, steady, constant, stable, firm, steadfast, unswerving, unwavering, unhesitating, unfaltering.
– OPPOSITES disloyal.

stay¹ v ❶ REMAIN, wait, stay put, continue, linger, pause, rest, delay; *archaic* tarry. ❷ LODGE, take a room, put up, be accommodated, sojourn, visit, reside, take up residence, dwell, live. ❸ CHECK, curb, arrest, stop, delay, hold, prevent, hinder, impede, obstruct.
– OPPOSITES leave.
▶ n ❶ VISIT, sojourn, stop, stopover, holiday, vacation. ❷ POSTPONEMENT, suspension, adjournment, deferment, delay.

stay² n PROP, support, brace, bolster, buttress.

steadfast adj ❶ *See* STAUNCH. ❷ FIRM, determined, resolute, unchanging, unwavering, unfaltering, unswerving, unyielding, inflexible, uncompromising, relentless, implacable.
– OPPOSITES irresolute.

steady adj ❶ FIRM, fixed, stable, secure, immovable. ❷ STILL, motionless, unmoving, sure. ❸ STEADFAST, fixed, immovable, unwavering, unfaltering. ❹ UNIFORM, even, regular, rhythmic, consistent. ❺ WELL BALANCED, balanced, sensible, level-headed, rational, settled, down-to-earth, calm, equable, imperturbable, reliable, dependable, serious-minded, serious.
– OPPOSITES unstable, shaky, fluctuating.
▶ v ❶ MAKE STEADY, hold steady, stabilize, secure, balance, support. ❷ CALM, calm down, settle, compose, tranquillize, control, get a grip on.

steal v ❶ THIEVE, take, appropriate, misappropriate, pilfer, purloin, walk off with, embezzle, pocket, abstract, shoplift; informal filch, snitch, swipe, lift, rip off; Brit. informal pinch, nick; formal peculate. ❷ PLAGIARIZE, copy, pirate, appropriate; informal lift. ❸ SLIP, slide, tiptoe, sneak, creep, slink, slither, flit, glide.

stealthy adj SECRET, furtive, surreptitious, sly, sneaky, clandestine, covert, underhand, undercover; informal shady.
– OPPOSITES above board, open.

steam n VAPOUR, fume, smoke, exhalation.

steamy adj ❶ HUMID, muggy, sticky, moist, damp, sweltering, boiling. ❷ EROTIC, sexy, passionate, tempestuous, sensuous, lustful, wanton.

steep adj ❶ SHEER, abrupt, precipitous, sudden, sharp, perpendicular, vertical, declivitous. ❷ SHARP, rapid, sudden, precipitate. ❸ See EXPENSIVE.
– OPPOSITES gentle, gradual.

steeple n SPIRE, tower, campanile, turret, minaret.

steer v ❶ DRIVE, navigate, pilot, be at the wheel of. ❷ GUIDE, lead, direct, conduct, usher.

stench n STINK, foul smell/odour, reek; Brit. informal pong, whiff.

step n ❶ STRIDE, pace, footstep, footfall, tread, tramp. ❷ WALK, gait, bearing, carriage. ❸ RUNG, tread. ❹ COURSE OF ACTION, move, act, action, deed, measure, manoeuvre, procedure, expedient, effort. ❺ STAGE, level, grade, rank, degree.
▶ v WALK, tread, stride, pace, move, advance, proceed; informal hoof it.

stereotype n RECEIVED IDEA, standardized image, hackneyed conception, cliché.
▶ v TYPECAST, pigeonhole, conventionalize, standardize, label, tag, categorize.

sterile adj ❶ INFERTILE, barren, infecund. ❷ UNFRUITFUL, unproductive, infertile, unyielding, arid, dry, barren. ❸ STERILIZED, germ-free, antiseptic, disinfected, aseptic, uncontaminated, unpolluted, pure, clean.
– OPPOSITES fertile, productive.

sterilize v ❶ DISINFECT, purify, fumigate. ❷ MAKE INFERTILE, make barren, castrate, vasectomize, geld, neuter, spay, emasculate.

stern adj ❶ STRICT, harsh, hard, severe, rigorous, stringent, rigid, exacting, demanding, cruel, relentless, unsparing, inflexible, unyielding, authoritarian, tyrannical, despotic, Draconian. ❷ SEVERE, forbidding, frowning, unsmiling, sombre, sober, austere.
– OPPOSITES lax, genial.

stew v SIMMER, boil, casserole, fricassee.
▶ n CASSEROLE, ragout, fricassee.

stick¹ n PIECE OF WOOD, branch, twig, switch.

stick² v ❶ PUSH, insert, jab, poke. ❷ GLUE, paste, gum, tape, sellotape, fasten, attach, fix, pin, tack. ❸ BECOME BOGGED DOWN, become embedded, become lodged, be unable to move.

sticky adj ❶ ADHESIVE, adherent, gummy, gluey, tacky. ❷ GLUEY, glutinous, viscous; informal gooey. ❸ CLOSE, humid, muggy, clammy, sultry, sweltering, oppressive. ❹ AWKWARD, difficult, tricky, ticklish, delicate, thorny.

stiff adj ❶ RIGID, inflexible, unyielding, inelastic, firm, hard, hardened, brittle. ❷ TIGHT, tense, taut, aching; informal creaky. ❸ DIFFICULT, hard, arduous, tough, laborious, exacting, demanding, formidable, challenging, tiring, fatiguing, exhausting, Herculean. ❹ SEVERE, harsh, hard, stringent, rigorous, drastic, strong, heavy, Draconian. ❺ STRONG, vigorous, determined, resolute, dogged, tenacious, unflagging, stubborn, obdurate. ❻ FORMAL, ceremonial, ceremonious, dignified, proper, decorous, pompous.
– OPPOSITES soft.

stiffen v ❶ BECOME STIFF, thicken, set, jell, solidify, harden, congeal, coagulate. ❷ STRENGTHEN, fortify, brace, steel, reinforce.
– OPPOSITES liquefy, weaken.

stifle v ❶ SMOTHER, check, restrain, keep back, hold back, hold in, withhold, choke back, muffle, suppress, curb. ❷ SUPPRESS, quash, quell, put an end to, put down, stop, extinguish, stamp out, crush, subdue, repress. ❸ SUFFOCATE, smother, asphyxiate, choke.

stigma n SHAME, disgrace, dishonour, slur, stain, taint.
– OPPOSITES honour.

still adj ❶ MOTIONLESS, unmoving, without moving, immobile, unstirring, inert, lifeless, stock-still, stationary, static. ❷ QUIET, silent, hushed, soundless, sound-free, noiseless, undisturbed.
– OPPOSITES moving, noisy.
▶ n QUIETNESS, quiet, silence, hush, soundlessness, noiselessness, calmness, calm, tranquility, peace, peacefulness, serenity.
▶ adv ❶ AT THIS TIME, yet, up to this time, even now, until now.

❷ NEVERTHELESS, however, in spite of that, notwithstanding, for all that.

stilted adj STIFF, unnatural, wooden, forced, laboured, constrained, unrelaxed, awkward.
– OPPOSITES natural.

stimulant n ❶ TONIC, restorative, reviver, energizer, excitant, analeptic; *informal* upper, pick-me-up, bracer. ❷ STIMULUS, incentive, impetus, fillip, spur.
– OPPOSITES sedative, deterrent.

stimulate v ACT AS A STIMULUS / INCENTIVE TO, encourage, prompt, spur on, activate, stir up, excite, whip up, kindle, incite, instigate, foment, fan.
– OPPOSITES discourage.

stimulating adj ❶ RESTORING, restorative, reviving, energizing, analeptic; *informal* pick-me-up. ❷ INTERESTING, exciting, stirring, thought-provoking, inspiring, exhilarating, intriguing, provoking, provocative.
– OPPOSITES sedative, boring.

stimulus n STIMULANT, incentive, fillip, spur, push, drive, encouragement, inducement, incitement, goad, jog, jolt; *informal* shot in the arm.

sting n IRRITATION, smarting, tingling, tingle, pain, hurt.
▶ v ❶ SMART, tingle, burn, be irritated. ❷ HURT, wound, distress, grieve, vex, pain, anguish, torture, torment, harrow.

stingy adj MEAN, miserly, parsimonious, niggardly, cheese-paring, penny-pinching; *informal* tight, tight-fisted; N. Amer. *informal* cheap.
– OPPOSITES generous.

stink v SMELL BAD, give off a bad smell, reek; *informal* smell to high heaven.
▶ n BAD SMELL, foul smell, stench, reek, malodour.

stint v SKIMP ON, limit, restrict, hold back on, be sparing with, be economical with, be frugal with, be mean with, be parsimonious with, be niggardly with.

stipulate v SPECIFY, set down, lay down, state clearly, demand, require, insist upon, make a condition of, make a point of.

stipulation n SPECIFICATION, demand, requirement, condition, precondition, provision, proviso, prerequisite.

stir v ❶ MIX, blend, beat, whip. ❷ DISTURB, move, agitate, rustle. ❸ GET UP, get out of bed, rise, rouse oneself, bestir oneself, move about, be up and about, be active; *informal* shake a leg, look lively. ❹ STIMULATE, excite, rouse, awaken, waken, kindle, quicken, inspire. ❺ ROUSE, incite, provoke, inflame, goad, spur, egg on, urge, encourage, motivate, drive, impel.
▶ n EXCITEMENT, commotion, disturbance, fuss, uproar, to-do, flurry, ferment, brouhaha.

stirring adj EXCITING, dramatic, thrilling, gripping, riveting, spirited, stimulating, moving, lively, animated, heady, passionate, impassioned.
– OPPOSITES dull, unexciting.

stitch v SEW, sew up, repair, mend, darn.

stock n ❶ STORE, supply, stockpile, reserve, reservoir, accumulation, pile, heap, load, hoard, cache. ❷ SUPPLIES, goods, merchandise, wares, articles for sale, commodities. ❸ FARM ANIMALS, livestock, cattle, beasts, herds, sheep, flocks. ❹ DESCENT, line of descent, lineage, ancestry, extraction, family, parentage, relatives, pedigree, genealogy, strain, breed, background.
▶ adj ❶ STANDARD, regular, average, readily available. ❷ USUAL, routine, run-of-the-mill, commonplace, conventional, traditional, stereotyped, clichéd, hackneyed, overused, worn out, banal, trite.
– OPPOSITES unusual, original.
▶ v ❶ SELL, trade in, deal in, market, handle, supply, keep. ❷ EQUIP, fit, outfit, kit out, furnish, accoutre, supply, provide.

stockpile v COLLECT, gather, accumulate, amass, store, lay in, put away, put down, deposit; informal squirrel away, salt away, stash.

stocky adj HEAVY-SET, thickset, dumpy, stubby, stumpy, squat, chunky, solid, sturdy, mesomorphic.
– OPPOSITES slender.

stodgy adj ❶ HEAVY, solid, substantial, filling, starchy, leaden, indigestible. ❷ DULL, uninteresting, boring, tedious, dry, wearisome, heavy-going, unimaginative, uninspired,

monotonous, laboured, wooden, turgid.
– OPPOSITES light, interesting.

stoical adj IMPASSIVE, dispassionate, unimpassioned, unemotional, self-controlled, self-disciplined, forbearing, patient, long-suffering, resigned, philosophical, fatalistic, imperturbable, calm, cool, unexcitable, unflappable, phlegmatic.
– OPPOSITES excitable.

stolid adj IMPASSIVE, unemotional, apathetic, uninterested, unimaginative, indifferent, dull, stupid, bovine, lumpish, wooden, doltish, thick, dense.
– OPPOSITES lively, imaginative.

stomach n ABDOMEN, belly, paunch, pot belly; informal tummy, gut, pot, breadbasket.
▶ v STAND, put up with, bear, take, tolerate, abide, endure, swallow, submit to; archaic suffer.

stone n ❶ PEBBLE, rock, boulder. ❷ PRECIOUS STONE, jewel, gem, brilliant; informal rock. ❸ TOMBSTONE, gravestone, headstone, memorial stone, monument. ❹ KERNEL, pit, nut, seed, pip.

stony adj ❶ ROCKY, pebbly, gravelly, shingly, gritty, rough, hard. ❷ COLD, chilly, frosty, icy, frigid, hard, stern, severe, rigid, fixed, expressionless, blank, poker-faced, deadpan. ❸ UNFEELING, uncaring, unsympathetic, insensitive, callous, heartless, unmoved, unemotional, dispassionate,

unresponsive, stern, severe, harsh, hard, cruel, cold-hearted, merciless, pitiless.
– OPPOSITES sympathetic.

stooge n UNDERLING, subordinate, assistant, deputy; *informal* sidekick; *Brit. informal* dogsbody.

stoop v ❶ BEND DOWN, lean over, lean down, crouch down, duck, bow. ❷ CONDESCEND, deign, lower oneself, humble oneself, demean oneself. ❸ SINK TO, descend to, lower oneself to, demean oneself to, resort to.

stop v ❶ BRING TO A STOP, halt, bring to a halt, end, bring to an end, put an end to, finish, bring to a close, terminate, bring to a standstill, wind up, discontinue, cut short, interrupt, nip in the bud. ❷ DISCONTINUE, cease from, refrain from, desist from, leave off, break off, forbear from, abandon; *informal* quit, knock off, pack in. ❸ COME TO A STOP, come to a halt, end, come to an end, finish, come to a close, be over, cease, conclude, terminate, come to a standstill, pause. ❹ PREVENT, hinder, obstruct, impede, block, check. ❺ PLUG, seal, block, bung, staunch, stem.
– OPPOSITES begin, start.
▸ n ❶ HALT, end, finish, close, cessation, conclusion, termination, standstill, stoppage, discontinuation, discontinuance. ❷ STOPPING PLACE, station, halt, stage, terminus, terminal, depot. ❸ BREAK, stop-off, stop-over, stay, sojourn, overnight, rest.

stopgap n TEMPORARY SUBSTITUTE, substitution, fill-in, makeshift, improvisation, expedient, last resort.

store n ❶ SUPPLY, stock, stockpile, reserve, accumulation, pile, heap, cache, deposit, reservoir. ❷ STOREROOM, storehouse, warehouse, repository, depository. ❸ SHOP, department store, supermarket, retail outlet, emporium.
▸ v STOCK UP WITH, get in supplies of, stockpile, collect, gather, accumulate, amass, lay in, put away, put down, deposit, hoard; *informal* squirrel away, salt away, stash.

storm n GALE, hurricane, cyclone, tempest, squall, cloudburst, downpour, torrent.
▸ v ATTACK, charge, rush, make a raid/foray/sortie on, take by storm.

stormy adj BLUSTERY, blustering, windy, gusty, squally, rainy, wild, tempestuous, turbulent.
– OPPOSITES calm.

story n ❶ TALE, fairy tale, fable, myth, legend, anecdote, novel, novella, romance, narrative, chronicle; *informal* yarn. ❷ NEWS ITEM, news report, article, feature, scoop.

stout adj ❶ FAT, fattish, plump, portly, tubby, obese, corpulent, rotund, big, heavy, thickset, overweight, bulky, burly, brawny, fleshy. ❷ STRONG, heavy, solid, substantial, sturdy. ❸ STOUT-HEARTED, brave, courageous, valiant, valorous,

gallant, fearless, unafraid, intrepid, bold, plucky, heroic, lion-hearted, daring, tough, doughty; *informal* gutsy, spunky.
– OPPOSITES cowardly.

stow v PLACE, deposit, put, put away, pack, store, load, bundle, stuff.
– OPPOSITES unload.

straggle v ❶ WANDER, ramble, stray, roam, meander, rove, range, spread out. ❷ TRAIL BEHIND, fall behind, lag, string out, linger, loiter. ❸ GROW UNTIDILY, be messy, be dishevelled, be unkempt.

straight adj ❶ DIRECT, undeviating, unswerving, straight as an arrow. ❷ SUCCESSIVE, consecutive, in a row, running, uninterrupted, solid, non-stop. ❸ IN ORDER, orderly, neat, tidy, spruce, in place, organized, arranged, sorted out. ❹ FORTHRIGHT, honest, faithful, sincere, frank, candid, direct, straightforward, plain-speaking, matter-of-fact, outspoken, straight from the shoulder, unequivocal, unambiguous, unqualified, unmodified.
– OPPOSITES crooked, evasive.

straighten v MAKE STRAIGHT, adjust, arrange, put in order, make tidy, tidy up, neaten, put to rights.
■ **straighten out** PUT IN ORDER, put right, sort out, clear up, settle, resolve, regulate, rectify, disentangle, unsnarl.

straightforward adj ❶ STRAIGHT, direct, honest, frank, candid, forthright, plain-speaking, unambiguous, straight from the shoulder. ❷ UNCOMPLICATED, easy, simple, elementary, effortless, undemanding, routine; *informal* easy as falling off a log, easy as pie.
– OPPOSITES complicated.

strain v ❶ DRAW TIGHT, tighten, make taut, tauten, stretch, extend, elongate, distend. ❷ TAX, overtax, exert to the limit, overwork, push to the limit, fatigue, tire. ❸ MAKE EVERY EFFORT, strive one's utmost, push/drive oneself to the limit, struggle, labour; *informal* pull out all the stops, go all out, give it one's all. ❹ SIEVE, silt, screen, riddle, separate.
▶ n ❶ TIGHTNESS, tautness, tension, distension. ❷ STRESS, pressure, tension, overwork, exhaustion, anxiety.

strained adj ❶ FORCED, artificial, unnatural, false, constrained, laboured, wooden, stiff, self-conscious. ❷ AWKWARD, embarrassed, uneasy, uncomfortable, tense, unrelaxed. ❸ UNDER STRAIN, tense, troubled, uneasy, hostile.
– OPPOSITES natural, relaxed.

strainer n SIEVE, colander, filter, screen, riddle.

strand n ❶ THREAD, fibre, filament, length. ❷ ELEMENT, component, theme.

stranded adj ❶ LEFT HELPLESS, left penniless, in dire straits, in difficulties, left in the lurch, left high and dry, abandoned, forsaken. ❷ GROUNDED, beached, shipwrecked, wrecked, marooned.

strange adj ❶ PECULIAR, odd, bizarre, unusual, atypical, abnormal, surprising, curious, weird, funny, unfamiliar. ❷ UNKNOWN, unfamiliar. ❸ INEXPLICABLE, anomalous, unexpected, extraordinary.
– OPPOSITES ordinary, familiar.

stranger n NEW PERSON, new arrival, newcomer, incomer, foreigner.
■ **a stranger to** UNFAMILIAR WITH, unacquainted with, unaccustomed to, new to, fresh to, unused to, inexperienced in, unpractised in, unversed in, unconversant with.

strangle v ❶ THROTTLE, choke, strangulate, garrotte. ❷ SUPPRESS, inhibit, repress, check, restrain, hold back, curb, stifle, gag.

strap n BAND, belt, thong, cord, tie.
▶ v ❶ FASTEN, secure, tie, bind, lash, truss, pinion. ❷ BIND, bandage. ❸ FLOG, lash, whip, scourge, beat; informal belt.

strategic adj ❶ CALCULATED, planned, plotted, tactical, diplomatic, politic, cunning, wily. ❷ CRUCIAL, key, vital, critical, essential, important.

strategy n POLICY, approach, programme, scheme, plan of action, master plan, schedule, blueprint, game plan.

stray v ❶ WANDER, roam, rove, go astray, ramble, meander, drift. ❷ DIGRESS, wander, deviate, get off the subject, get sidetracked, go off at a tangent, lose the thread.
▶ adj ❶ STRAYED, gone astray, lost, homeless, wandering, vagrant, abandoned, unclaimed. ❷ ODD, random, isolated, scattered, occasional, incidental, accidental, chance, freak.

streak n ❶ LINE, band, strip, dash, bar, score, striation, vein, slash, smear. ❷ STRAIN, vein, element, trace, touch, dash. ❸ SMEAR, smudge, mark. ❹ SPELL, period, course, stretch, series.
▶ v ❶ BAND, stripe, mark, slash, striate, fleck, daub, smear. ❷ SMEAR, smudge, mark. ❸ RACE, rush, speed, dash, sprint, hurtle, scurry, fly, flee, flash, whistle, zoom, zip; informal tear, whizz, go hell for leather.

stream n ❶ RIVER, brook, rivulet, rill, freshet; N. English beck; Scottish & N. English burn; N. Amer. & Austral. / NZ creek. ❷ FLOW, rush, gush, surge, jet, outpouring, current, cascade.
▶ v ❶ FLOW, run, pour, course, spill, gush, surge, flood, cascade, well. ❷ EMIT, issue, shed, spill. ❸ FLUTTER, flap, swing, float, flow. ❹ SURGE, pour, crowd.

streamlined adj ❶ SMOOTH, sleek, elegant. ❷ EFFICIENT, smooth-running, well run, modernized, rationalized, slick.

street n ROAD, thoroughfare,

terrace, avenue, drive, row, crescent.

strength n ❶ POWER, might, force, brawn, muscle, muscularity, sturdiness, robustness, vigour, toughness, stamina. ❷ FORTITUDE, courage, bravery, pluck, firmness, stamina, backbone; *informal* grit, guts. ❸ ADVANTAGE, asset, strong point, forte.
– OPPOSITES weakness.

strengthen v ❶ MAKE STRONG, make stronger, give strength to, nourish, build up. ❷ GROW STRONG, grow stronger, gain strength, intensify, heighten. ❸ REINFORCE, support, back up, bolster, authenticate, confirm, substantiate, corroborate.
– OPPOSITES weaken.

strenuous adj ❶ ARDUOUS, laborious, taxing, demanding, difficult, hard, tough, uphill, heavy, weighty, burdensome, exhausting, tiring, fatiguing. ❷ ENERGETIC, active, vigorous, forceful, strong, spirited, bold, determined, resolute, tenacious, earnest, keen, zealous.
– OPPOSITES easy, half-hearted.

stress n ❶ STRAIN, pressure, tension, worry, anxiety. ❷ EMPHASIS, priority, importance, weight, significance, value, worth, merit. ❸ ACCENT, accentuation, emphasis.
▶ v ❶ LAY STRESS ON, emphasize, place emphasis on, give emphasis to, accentuate, underline, underscore, point up, highlight, spotlight, press home, dwell on, harp on, belabour. ❷ LAY STRESS ON, place the accent on, accentuate, emphasize. ❸ SUBJECT TO STRESS / STRAIN / TENSION, tax, overtax, pressurize, overwork, overstretch, overburden, push to the limit, push too far.
– OPPOSITES play down.

stretch v ❶ BE STRETCHY, be elastic, be tensile. ❷ EXTEND, elongate, lengthen, expand, draw out, pull out, get larger, get bigger, enlarge, pull out of shape. ❸ SPREAD, extend, unfold, cover, range. ❹ BE A CHALLENGE TO, challenge, extend, tax, push to the limit. ❺ STRAIN, overstrain, exaggerate, overdraw, push too far.
– OPPOSITES contract.
▶ n ❶ EXPANSE, area, tract, extent, spread, sweep. ❷ PERIOD, time, spell, term, space, run, stint.

strict adj ❶ PRECISE, exact, close, faithful, true, accurate, scrupulous, meticulous, conscientious, punctilious. ❷ STRINGENT, rigorous, severe, harsh, hard, stern, authoritarian, rigid, narrow, austere, illiberal, inflexible, unyielding, uncompromising. ❸ ABSOLUTE, utter, complete, total, perfect.
– OPPOSITES flexible, easy-going.

stride v STEP, pace, walk, stalk.

strident adj HARSH, raucous, rough, grating, discordant

rasping, jarring, shrill, loud, screeching, unmelodious, unmusical.
– OPPOSITES soft.

strife n CONFLICT, friction, discord, disagreement, dissension, dispute, argument, quarrelling, wrangling, bickering, controversy, contention, ill feeling, hostility, animosity.
– OPPOSITES harmony.

strike v ❶ BANG, beat, hit, pound, batter. ❷ HIT, slap, smack, beat, batter, thrash, thump, thwack, punch, cuff, box, rap, buffet, smite, cane, lash, whip; *informal* wallop, belt, clout, whack, bash, clobber, bop, biff, sock, plug. ❸ RUN INTO, knock into, bang into, bump into, smash into, collide with, be in collision with, dash against. ❹ ATTACK, charge, make an assault on, assault, storm, set upon, fall upon. ❺ GO ON STRIKE, take industrial action, walk out; *Brit. informal* down tools.
▶ n ❶ HIT, slap, smack, thump, thwack, punch, cuff, box, knock; *informal* wallop, clout, whack, bop, buffet, plug. ❷ INDUSTRIAL ACTION, walkout.
■ **strike out** DELETE, cross out, erase, rub out, obliterate.

striking adj ❶ NOTICEABLE, obvious, conspicuous, evident, visible, distinct, prominent, clear-cut, unmistakable, remarkable, extraordinary, incredible, amazing. ❷ IMPRESSIVE, imposing, grand, splendid, magnificent, superb, marvellous, wonderful, dazzling; *Brit. informal* smashing.
– OPPOSITES unremarkable.

string n ❶ TWINE, cord, yarn, rope, cable, line. ❷ QUEUE, line, row, procession, file, column, stream, succession, sequence.
▶ v ❶ HANG, suspend, sling. ❷ STRETCH, sling, run, fasten, tie, secure together.

stringent adj STRICT, firm, rigid, rigorous, severe, harsh, tough, tight, exacting, demanding, inflexible, hard and fast, uncompromising.
– OPPOSITES easy.

stringy adj ❶ LANK, straggly, straggling. ❷ TOUGH, fibrous, gristly, leathery.

strip¹ v ❶ STRIP NAKED, undress, take one's clothes off, remove one's clothes, disrobe. ❷ PEEL, pare, skin, excoriate. ❸ TAKE AWAY, dispossess of, deprive of, confiscate. ❹ DISMANTLE, take to pieces, take to bits, take apart.

strip² n PIECE, bit, band, belt, ribbon, stripe, bar, swathe, slip, fillet.

stripe n STRIP, band, belt, bar.

striped adj STRIPY, banded, barred, striated, variegated.

stripling n YOUTH, adolescent, youngster, boy, lad, teenager, child, juvenile, minor, young man; *informal* kid, nipper, young 'un.

strive v TRY, attempt, endeavour, make an effort, make every effort, exert oneself, do one's best, do all one can, do one's utmost, labour, toil,

strain, struggle; *informal* go all
out, give it one's best shot.

stroke n ❶ BLOW, hit, slap,
smack, thump, thwack, punch,
cuff, box, knock, rap, buffet,
smite. ❷ MOVEMENT, action,
motion. ❸ THROMBOSIS, embol-
ism, cerebral vascular accident,
CVA, seizure, shock, apoplexy.
▶ v CARESS, fondle, pat, touch,
rub, massage, soothe.

stroll v SAUNTER, amble,
wander, meander, ramble,
dawdle, promenade, go for a
walk, take a walk, stretch one's
legs, take the air; *informal* mosey
along.

strong adj ❶ POWERFUL,
mighty, brawny, muscular,
well built, strapping, sturdy,
burly, robust, vigorous, tough,
hardy, lusty, Herculean, strong
as an ox/horse/lion. ❷ COURAGE-
OUS, brave, plucky, firm, resolute, strong-minded; *informal*
gutsy. ❸ DETERMINED, forceful,
high-powered, assertive, tough,
formidable, aggressive, redoubtable. ❹ SOLID, well built,
heavy, heavy-duty, hard-wearing, sturdy, durable, long-
lasting, tough, secure. ❺ KEEN,
eager, enthusiastic, deep,
acute, dedicated, passionate,
fierce, loyal, fervent, zealous.
❻ INTENSE, forceful, vehement,
passionate, fervent. ❼ COMPEL-
LING, powerful, cogent, potent,
weighty, convincing, plausible,
effective, efficacious, sound,
valid, well founded. ❽ DEEP, intense, vivid, graphic. ❾ BRIGHT,
brilliant, intense, radiant,
gleaming, dazzling, glaring,

❿ CONCENTRATED, undiluted,
highly flavoured.
– OPPOSITES weak.

structure n ❶ BUILDING,
edifice, construction, erection,
pile, complex. ❷ CONSTRUCTION,
form, configuration, conformation, shape, constitution,
composition, make-up, organization, system, arrangement,
design, frame, framework.
▶ v CONSTRUCT, build, form, put
together, assemble, shape, design, organize, arrange, order.

struggle v ❶ STRIVE, try hard,
endeavour, make every effort,
exert oneself, do one's best, do
all one can, do one's utmost,
battle, labour, toil, strain;
informal go all out. ❷ FIGHT,
grapple, wrestle, scuffle, brawl;
informal scrap.
▶ n ❶ STRIVING, battle, endeavour, effort, exertion, labour,
toiling, pains. ❷ FIGHT, scuffle,
brawl, tussle; *informal* scrap, set-
to, dust-up.

strut v SWAGGER, prance,
parade, flounce; *N. Amer.* sashay.

stubborn adj OBSTINATE, headstrong, wilful, strong-willed,
pig-headed, mulish, dogged,
persistent, adamant, inflexible,
uncompromising, unbending,
unyielding, unmalleable, obdurate, intractable, refractory,
recalcitrant, contumacious.
– OPPOSITES malleable.

stuck adj ❶ IMMOVABLE,
immobile, fast, fixed, rooted.
❷ BAFFLED, beaten, stumped, at
a loss, perplexed, nonplussed,

at one's wits' ends; *informal* up against a brick wall.

student n UNDERGRADUATE, pupil, schoolboy, schoolgirl, trainee, apprentice, probationer.

studied adj DELIBERATE, wilful, conscious, calculated, purposeful, contrived, affected, forced, feigned, artificial.
– OPPOSITES natural.

studious adj SCHOLARLY, academic, intellectual, bookish, book-loving, serious, earnest.

study v ❶ APPLY ONESELF, revise, burn the midnight oil; *informal* cram, mug up; *Brit. informal* swot. ❷ LEARN, read up on, read, work at; *informal* mug up on. ❸ INVESTIGATE, inquire into, research, look into, examine, analyse, review, survey, conduct a survey of, scrutinize.

stuff n ❶ MATERIAL, fabric, matter, substance. ❷ THINGS, objects, articles, items, luggage, baggage, belongings, possessions, goods, paraphernalia. ❸ FACTS, information, data, subject.
▶ v ❶ FILL, pack, pad. ❷ PACK, load, cram, squeeze, crowd, stow, press, force, compress, jam, wedge.

stuffy adj ❶ AIRLESS, close, muggy, stifling, suffocating, musty, stale; *Brit. informal* fuggy. ❷ DULL, boring, dreary, staid, sedate, stiff, formal, pompous, starchy, prim, priggish, strait-laced, conventional, conservative, stodgy; *informal* fuddy-duddy, square.
– OPPOSITES airy, exciting.

stumble v ❶ TRIP, slip, blunder, lumber, lurch, stagger, reel. ❷ STAMMER, stutter, hesitate, falter; *informal* fluff one's lines.

stump n END, stub, remnant, remains.
▶ v BAFFLE, be too much for, put at a loss, nonplus, mystify, foil, perplex, puzzle, confound, bewilder; *informal* flummox.

stun v ❶ DAZE, stupefy, knock senseless, knock out, lay out, knock stupid. ❷ SHOCK, astound, dumbfound, stupefy, overwhelm, overcome, overpower, devastate, stagger, amaze, astonish, bewilder, confuse; *informal* flabbergast, knock sideways; *Brit. informal* knock for six.

stunning adj SENSATIONAL, ravishing, dazzling, wonderful, marvellous, magnificent, glorious, exquisite, impressive, splendid, beautiful, lovely, gorgeous.
– OPPOSITES ordinary.

stupendous adj AMAZING, fantastic, astounding, astonishing, extraordinary, remarkable, wonderful, prodigious, phenomenal, staggering, breathtaking; *informal* mind-boggling, mind-blowing.
– OPPOSITES ordinary.

stupid adj ❶ UNINTELLIGENT, foolish, dense, brainless, mindless, obtuse, dull-witted, dull, slow-witted, slow, dunce-like, doltish, simple-minded,

half-witted, gullible, naive, moronic, imbecilic, cretinous; informal thick, dim, dumb, dopey; Brit. informal dozy. ❷ FOOL-ISH, silly, idiotic, brainless, mindless, crackbrained, non-sensical, senseless, irresponsible, unthinking, ill-advised, ill-considered, inept, unwise, injudicious, indiscreet, short-sighted, inane, absurd, ludicrous, ridiculous, laughable, fatuous, asinine, pointless, meaningless, futile, fruitless, mad, insane, lunatic; informal cock-eyed. ❸ DAZED, stupefied, unconscious.
– OPPOSITES intelligent, sensible.

stupidity n ❶ LACK OF INTELLIGENCE, foolishness, denseness, brainlessness, mindlessness, dull-wittedness, dullness, slow-wittedness, slowness, doltishness; informal thickness, dimness, dumbness, dopiness, doziness. ❷ FOOLISHNESS, folly, silliness, idiocy, brainlessness, senselessness, irresponsibility, injudiciousness, ineptitude, inaneness, inanity, absurdity, ludicrousness, ridiculousness, fatuousness, fatuity, asininity, pointlessness, meaninglessness, futility, fruitlessness, madness, insanity, lunacy.

sturdy adj ❶ WELL BUILT, well made, muscular, athletic, strong, strapping, brawny, powerfully built, powerful, solid, substantial, robust, vigorous, tough, hardy, stalwart, mighty, lusty. ❷ STRONG, vigorous, stalwart, firm, deter-

mined, resolute, tenacious, staunch, steadfast, unyielding, unwavering, uncompromising. ❸ See STRONG (4).
– OPPOSITES weak.

stutter v STAMMER, stumble, hesitate, falter, splutter.

style n ❶ KIND, type, variety, sort, design, pattern, genre. ❷ TECHNIQUE, method, methodology, approach, manner, way, mode, system. ❸ STYLISHNESS, smartness, elegance, polish, suavity, urbanity, chic, flair, dash, panache, elan; informal pizzazz, ritziness. ❹ FASHION, trend, vogue, mode.

stylish adj FASHIONABLE, smart, elegant, chic, modish, à la mode, voguish, modern, up to date; informal trendy, dressy, natty, classy, nifty, ritzy, snazzy, snappy, with it.
– OPPOSITES unfashionable.

subdue v ❶ CONQUER, defeat, vanquish, get the better of, overpower, overcome, overwhelm, subjugate, master, gain the upper hand at, triumph over, crush, quash, quell, tame, humble, bring someone to their knees, hold in check. ❷ CONTROL, curb, restrain, check, hold back, inhibit, rein in, repress, suppress, stifle.
– OPPOSITES arouse.

subdued adj ❶ DIM, muted, toned down, softened, soft, lowered, shaded, low-key, subtle, unobtrusive. ❷ LOW-SPIRITED, downcast, dejected, depressed, restrained, repressed, inactive, lifeless, dull,

passive, unexcited, unresponsive; *informal* down in the mouth.
– OPPOSITES bright, lively.

subject n ❶ TOPIC, theme, question, substance, gist, text, thesis. ❷ BRANCH OF KNOWLEDGE, course of study, course, discipline. ❸ CITIZEN, national.
▶ v SUBMIT, put through, expose, lay open, treat.
■ **subject to** ❶ CONDITIONAL UPON, contingent upon, dependent on. ❷ SUSCEPTIBLE TO, liable to, prone to, in danger of, vulnerable to.

subjective adj PERSONAL, personalized, individual, biased, prejudiced, bigoted.
– OPPOSITES objective.

subjugate v GAIN MASTERY OVER, gain control of, bring someone to their knees, bring to heel, bring under the yoke, conquer, vanquish, defeat, crush, quell, quash, overpower, overcome, subdue, tame, break, humble, tyrannize, oppress, enslave.
– OPPOSITES liberate.

submerge v ❶ GO UNDER WATER, dive, sink, plummet. ❷ IMMERSE, dip, plunge, duck dunk. ❸ FLOOD, inundate, deluge, engulf, swamp, overflow.

submission n ❶ SURRENDER, yielding, capitulation, agreement, acceptance, consent, accession, compliance. ❷ PRESENTATION, tender, proposal, suggestion. ❸ ARGUMENT, assertion, contention, statement, claim; *formal* averment.
– OPPOSITES defiance.

submissive adj YIELDING, compliant, malleable, acquiescent, accommodating, tractable, manageable, unassertive, passive, obedient, biddable, dutiful, docile, meek, patient, resigned, subdued, humble, self-effacing, deferential, obsequious, servile, self-abasing; *informal* bootlicking.
– OPPOSITES intractable.

submit v ❶ GIVE IN, yield, give way, capitulate, agree, accept, consent, accede, acquiesce, comply, conform. ❷ PUT FORWARD, present, proffer, tender, advance, propose, suggest, table, introduce, move.
– OPPOSITES resist, withdraw.

subordinate adj LOWER-RANKING, junior, lower, lesser, inferior, minor, secondary, subsidiary, ancillary, auxiliary.
– OPPOSITES senior.
▶ n JUNIOR, assistant, second, deputy, aide, subaltern, underling, inferior, second fiddle.
– OPPOSITES superior.

subscribe
■ **subscribe to** ❶ PAY A SUBSCRIPTION TO, buy regularly, take regularly. ❷ MAKE A DONATION TO, donate to, give to, give money to, make a contribution to, contribute towards; *informal* chip into. ❸ AGREE WITH, accede to, consent to, accept, believe in, endorse, back, support.

subscription n ❶ FEE, membership fee, dues, annual payment. ❷ DONATION, contribution, offering.

subsequent adj FOLLOWING,

ensuing, succeeding, later, future, next, consequent.
– OPPOSITES previous.

subservient adj SERVILE, submissive, deferential, obsequious, sycophantic, grovelling, fawning, ingratiating, toadying, unctuous, truckling; informal bootlicking.
– OPPOSITES domineering.

subside v ❶ ABATE, let up, moderate, quieten down, calm, slacken, die out, peter out, taper off, recede, lessen, diminish, dwindle. ❷ GO DOWN, get lower, sink, settle, fall back, recede.
– OPPOSITES strengthen, rise.

subsidize v PAY A SUBSIDY TO, contribute to, give money to, back, support, invest in, sponsor, finance, fund, underwrite, foot the bill for; informal pick up the tab for.

subsidy n GRANT, contribution, backing, support, investment, sponsorship, finance, funding, subvention.

subsist
■ **subsist on** LIVE ON, exist on, eke out an existence on, survive on.

substance n ❶ MATTER, material, stuff, medium, mass, fabric. ❷ SOLIDITY, body, corporeality, reality, actuality, materiality, concreteness, tangibility. ❸ MEANINGFULNESS, significance, weight, power, soundness, validity. ❹ WEALTH, affluence, prosperity, money, capital, means, resources, assets.

substantial adj ❶ REAL, material, weighty, sizeable, considerable, meaningful, significant, important, notable, major, marked, valuable, useful, worthwhile. ❷ SOLID, sturdy, stout, strong, well built, durable. ❸ ESSENTIAL, basic, fundamental.
– OPPOSITES insubstantial.

substitute n REPLACEMENT, deputy, relief, proxy, reserve, surrogate, fill-in, stand-in, standby, locum, stopgap.
▶ v ❶ USE AS A REPLACEMENT, replace with, use instead of, exchange, switch, swap. ❷ TAKE THE PLACE OF, replace, deputize for, act as deputy for, relieve, fill in for, act as stand-in for, cover for, take over from.

subterfuge n TRICK, ruse, wile, ploy, stratagem, artifice, dodge, manoeuvre, pretext, expedient, intrigue, scheme, deception.

subtle adj ❶ DELICATE, faint, understated, low-key, muted, toned down. ❷ FINE, fine-drawn, nice, slight, minute, tenuous, indistinct, indefinite.
– OPPOSITES crude.

subtract v TAKE AWAY, take from, deduct, remove, debit; informal knock off.
– OPPOSITES add.

suburb n OUTLYING DISTRICT, residential area, dormitory area, purlieus.

suburban adj PROVINCIAL, unsophisticated, parochial, insular.
– OPPOSITES cosmopolitan.

subversive adj UNDERMINING, discrediting, destructive, disruptive, trouble-making, inflammatory, seditious, revolutionary, insurrectionary, treasonous, treacherous.

subvert v OVERTHROW, overturn, wreak havoc on, sabotage, ruin, destroy, demolish, wreck, upset, disrupt, undermine, weaken.

subway n UNDERGROUND RAILWAY, underground, metro, tube.

succeed v ❶ TRIUMPH, achieve success, be successful, do well, flourish, thrive; informal make it, make the grade, make a name for oneself. ❷ BE SUCCESSFUL, turn out well, work, work out, come off; informal pan out, do the trick. ❸ COME AFTER, follow, replace, take the place of, supplant, supersede.
– OPPOSITES fail, precede.

success n ❶ ACCOMPLISHMENT, achievement, attainment, fulfilment, victory, triumph. ❷ PROSPERITY, affluence, wealth, fame, eminence. ❸ BEST-SELLER, winner, triumph; informal hit, smash hit, sensation.
– OPPOSITES failure.

successful adj ❶ VICTORIOUS, triumphant. ❷ PROSPEROUS, affluent, wealthy, well-to-do, famous, eminent, at the top, top. ❸ FLOURISHING, thriving, booming, profitable, profit-making, moneymaking, lucrative.
– OPPOSITES unsuccessful.

succession n SEQUENCE, series, progression, course, cycle, chain, train, run, continuation.

successor n HEIR, heir apparent, next-in-line, replacement, supplanter.
– OPPOSITES predecessor.

succinct adj SHORT, brief, concise, compact, condensed, crisp, terse, tight, to the point, pithy, summary, short and sweet.
– OPPOSITES lengthy.

succulent adj JUICY, moist, luscious, mouth-watering.
– OPPOSITES dry.

succumb v GIVE IN, give way, yield, submit, surrender, capitulate, be overcome/overwhelmed, fall victim.
– OPPOSITES resist.

suck v SUCK UP, draw up, absorb, soak up, blot up.

sudden adj ❶ IMMEDIATE, instantaneous, abrupt, unexpected, unforeseen, unanticipated, unlooked for, without warning. ❷ RAPID, swift, speedy, fast, quick, meteoric.
– OPPOSITES gradual.

suddenly adv ALL OF A SUDDEN, all at once, instantaneously, abruptly, unexpectedly, without warning; informal out of the blue.
– OPPOSITES gradually.

sue v TAKE TO COURT, bring an action against, prefer/bring charges against, charge, prosecute, bring to trial, summons, indict; informal have the law on.
■ **sue for** PETITION FOR, appeal for, solicit, request, ask for, beg for, plead for.

suffer v **①** BE IN PAIN, feel pain, be racked with pain, hurt, ache. **②** BE DISTRESSED, be in distress, be upset, be miserable, be wretched, be hurt, hurt. **③** EXPERIENCE, undergo, sustain, encounter, meet with, endure. ■ **suffer from** BE AFFECTED BY, be afflicted by, be troubled with.

suffice v BE ENOUGH, be sufficient, do, serve, fulfil/meet someone's needs; *informal* hit the spot.

sufficient adj ENOUGH, adequate, plenty of, ample, plenty.
– OPPOSITES insufficient.

suffocate v SMOTHER, stifle, asphyxiate.

suffuse v SPREAD OVER, cover, bathe, permeate, pervade, imbue.

suggest v **①** PROPOSE, put forward, move, submit, recommend, advocate; *informal* throw out. **②** INDICATE, lead to believe, give the impression, give the idea, insinuate, hint, imply, intimate.

suggestion n **①** PROPOSAL, proposition, plan, motion, submission, recommendation. **②** HINT, trace, touch, suspicion. **③** INSINUATION, hint, implication, intimation.

suggestive adj PROVOCATIVE, titillating, sexual, sexy, indecent, indelicate, improper, off colour, smutty, ribald, risqué, lewd, salacious; *informal* blue.

suit n **①** SET OF CLOTHES, outfit, costume, ensemble. **②** LAWSUIT, court case, action, proceedings, prosecution.
▶ v **①** BECOME, look attractive on, go well with, look right on. **②** BE SUITABLE FOR, be convenient for, be acceptable to, meet someone's requirements, satisfy someone's demands.

suitable adj **①** CONVENIENT, acceptable, satisfactory. **②** SUITED TO, befitting, appropriate to, relevant to, pertinent to, apposite to, in keeping with, in character with, tailor-made for. **③** RIGHT, appropriate, fitting, apt, well qualified, ideal.
– OPPOSITES unsuitable.

sulk v MOPE, pout, be sullen, be in a bad mood, be put out, be out of sorts, be grumpy; *informal* be in a huff.

sulky adj MOPING, pouting, moody, sullen, piqued, disgruntled, ill-humoured, out of humour, bad-tempered, grumpy, churlish, glowering.
– OPPOSITES cheerful.

sullen adj MOROSE, unresponsive, uncommunicative, unsociable, resentful, sulky, sour, glum, gloomy, dismal, cheerless, surly, cross, angry, frowning, glowering, grumpy.
– OPPOSITES cheerful.

sultry adj **①** CLOSE, airless, stuffy, stifling, suffocating, oppressive, muggy, humid, sticky, hot, sweltering. **②** SENSUAL, sexy, voluptuous, seductive, provocative, alluring, tempting, passionate, erotic.

sum n **①** SUM TOTAL, grand total, tally, aggregate, answer.

❷ ARITHMETICAL PROBLEM, problem, calculation, reckoning, tally.

■ **sum up** GIVE A SUMMARY OF, summarize, encapsulate, put in a nutshell.

summarize v GIVE / MAKE A SUMMARY OF, sum up, give a synopsis of, precis, give a precis of, give a résumé of, give an abstract of, abridge, condense, epitomize, outline, sketch, give the main points of, give a rundown of, review.

summary n SYNOPSIS, precis, résumé, abstract, abridgement, digest, epitome, outline, sketch, rundown, review, summing-up.
▶ adj IMMEDIATE, instant, instantaneous, direct, prompt, rapid, sudden, abrupt, peremptory.

summit n ❶ TOP, peak, crest, crown, apex, vertex, apogee. ❷ PEAK, height, pinnacle, culmination, climax, crowning point, zenith, acme.
– OPPOSITES base, nadir.

summon v ❶ SEND FOR, call for, bid, request someone's presence. ❷ ORDER, call, convene, assemble, muster, rally; formal convoke.

sumptuous adj LAVISH, luxurious, de luxe, opulent, magnificent.
– OPPOSITES plain.

sundry adj SEVERAL, various, varied, miscellaneous, assorted, diverse.

sunken adj ❶ AT A LOWER LEVEL, below ground level, lowered. ❷ HOLLOW, hollowed, concave, drawn, haggard.

sunlight n SUN, sunshine, light, daylight, light of day.

sunny adj ❶ SUNLIT, bright, clear, cloudless, unclouded, without a cloud in the sky. ❷ see CHEERFUL.
– OPPOSITES dull.

sunrise n DAWN, crack of dawn, daybreak, cockcrow; N. Amer. sun-up.

sunset n NIGHTFALL, close of day, twilight, dusk; N. Amer. sundown.

sunshine n see SUNLIGHT.

superb adj SUPERLATIVE, excellent, first-rate, first-class, outstanding, remarkable, dazzling, marvellous, magnificent, wonderful, splendid, exquisite; informal fantastic, fabulous; Brit. informal brilliant.
– OPPOSITES poor.

supercilious adj ARROGANT, haughty, conceited, proud, vain, disdainful, scornful, condescending, superior, patronizing, imperious, overbearing, lofty, lordly, snobbish, snobby; informal hoity-toity, uppity, snooty, stuck up.

superficial adj ❶ SURFACE, exterior, external, outer, outside, peripheral, slight. ❷ CURSORY, perfunctory, hasty, hurried, casual, sketchy, desultory, slapdash. ❸ SHALLOW, empty-headed, trivial, frivolous, silly, lightweight, insignificant.
– OPPOSITES thorough, deep.

superfluous adj SPARE, surplus, extra, unneeded, unrequired, excess, in excess,

unnecessary, needless, inessential, uncalled for, unwarranted, gratuitous.
– OPPOSITES necessary, essential.

superhuman adj ❶ HERCULEAN, phenomenal, prodigious, stupendous, heroic, extraordinary. ❷ DIVINE, god-like, holy, supernatural, preternatural, paranormal, other-worldly.
– OPPOSITES mundane.

superior adj ❶ BETTER, finer, higher-quality, higher-grade, greater, more expert, more skilful, more advanced, surpassing. ❷ HIGHER, higher-ranking, higher up. ❸ HAUGHTY, disdainful, condescending, supercilious, patronizing, lofty, lordly, snobbish, snobby; *informal* high and mighty, hoity-toity, uppity, snooty, stuck up, toffee-nosed.
– OPPOSITES inferior.

superlative adj BEST, greatest, supreme, consummate, first-rate, first-class, of the first water, of the first order, brilliant, excellent, magnificent, outstanding, unsurpassed, unparalleled, unrivalled, peerless, matchless, transcendent.
– OPPOSITES poor.

supernatural adj OTHERWORLDLY, unearthly, spectral, ghostly, phantom, magical, mystic, unreal, paranormal, supernormal, psychic, miraculous, extraordinary, uncanny.

supersede v ❶ TAKE THE PLACE OF, replace, take over from,

displace, succeed, supplant, usurp. ❷ DISCARD, cast aside, throw out, dispose of, abandon, jettison; *informal* chuck out.

supervise v SUPERINTEND, be in charge of, direct, administer, manage, run, oversee, keep an eye on, watch, observe, inspect, be responsible for, guide.

supervision n ADMINISTRATION, management, direction, control, charge, superintendence, observation, inspection, guidance.

supervisor n OVERSEER, superintendent, inspector, controller, manager, director, administrator, chief, guide, adviser; *informal* boss.

supplant v TAKE THE PLACE OF, take over from, replace, displace, supersede, oust, usurp, overthrow, remove, unseat.

supple adj ❶ LITHE, loose-limbed, limber. ❷ PLIANT, pliable, flexible, bendable, stretchable, elastic.
– OPPOSITES stiff.

supplement n ❶ ADDITION, supplementation, additive, extra, add-on. ❷ PULL-OUT, insert, special-feature section, magazine section.
▶ v ADD TO, augment, increase, top up, complement.

supplementary adj ❶ SUPPLEMENTAL, additional, extra, add-on, complementary. ❷ ADDED, appended, attached, extra.

suppliant n SUPPLICANT, petitioner, pleader, applicant, suitor, beggar, appellant.

supplicant n see SUPPLIANT.

supplication n PLEA, entreaty, begging, petition, appeal, solicitation, request, prayer, invocation; *poetic/literary* beseeching.

supplies n PROVISIONS, stores, rations, food, provender; *dated* victuals.

supply v ❶ PROVIDE, give, furnish, contribute, donate, grant, come up with; *informal* fork out, shell out. ❷ SATISFY, meet, fulfil.
▶ n ❶ SUPPLYING, providing, provision, furnishing. ❷ STOCK, store, reserve, reservoir, stockpile, heap, pile, mass, hoard, cache. See also STOCK n (2).

support v ❶ BEAR, carry, hold up, prop up, bolster up, brace, keep up, shore up, underpin, buttress. ❷ MAINTAIN, provide for, sustain, take care of, look after. ❸ GIVE MORAL SUPPORT TO, give strength to, comfort, help, sustain, encourage, buoy up, hearten, fortify; *informal* buck up. ❹ BACK UP, substantiate, give force to, bear out, corroborate, confirm, verify, validate, authenticate, endorse, ratify. ❺ BACK, champion, give help to, help, assist, aid, be on someone's side, side with, vote for, stand behind, stand up for, take up the cudgels for; *informal* stick up for. ❻ ADVOCATE, promote, further, champion, be on someone's side, espouse, be in favour of, recommend, defend.
– OPPOSITES neglect, contradict, oppose.

▶ n ❶ BASE, foundations, pillar, post, prop, underprop, underpinning, substructure, brace, buttress, abutment, bolster, stay. ❷ KEEP, maintenance, sustenance, food and accommodation, subsistence; *archaic* aliment. ❸ MORAL SUPPORT, friendship, strength, encouragement, buoying up, heartening, fortification; *informal* bucking up. ❹ BACKING, contribution, donation, money, subsidy, funding, funds, finance, capital. ❺ HELP, assistance, comfort, tower of strength, prop, backbone, mainstay.

supporter n ❶ SPONSOR, contributor, donor, backer, patron, friend, well-wisher. ❷ CHAMPION, advocate, promoter, backer, defender, apologist, helper. ❸ FAN, follower.

supportive adj HELPFUL, encouraging, caring, sympathetic, understanding, loyal, interested, positive, reassuring.
– OPPOSITES unsympathetic.

suppose v ❶ ASSUME, take for granted, dare say, take as read, presume, expect, imagine, believe, think, fancy, suspect, guess, surmise, reckon, conjecture, theorize, opine. ❷ TAKE AS A HYPOTHESIS, hypothesize, postulate, posit. ❸ PRESUPPOSE, require, imply.

supposed adj PRESUMED, assumed, believed, professed, so-called, alleged, putative, reputed.

supposition n ASSUMPTION, presumption, suspicion, guess, surmise, conjecture, speculation, theory, hypothesis, postulation.

suppress v ❶ VANQUISH, put an end to, crush, quell, conquer, squash, stamp out, extinguish, put out, crack down on, clamp down on. ❷ RESTRAIN, keep a rein on, hold back, control, keep under control, check, keep in check, curb, bottle up, choke back. ❸ KEEP SECRET, conceal, hide, keep hidden, keep silent about, withhold, cover up, smother, stifle, muzzle.
– OPPOSITES incite, reveal.

supremacy n ASCENDANCY, dominance, superiority, predominance, paramountcy, dominion, sway, authority, mastery, control, power, rule, sovereignty, lordship.

supreme adj ❶ HIGHEST-RANKING, highest, leading, chief, foremost, principal. ❷ EXTREME, greatest, utmost, uttermost, maximum, extraordinary, remarkable. ❸ FINAL, last, ultimate.
– OPPOSITES subordinate, minimal.

sure adj ❶ CERTAIN, definite, positive, convinced, confident, decided, assured, free from doubt, unhesitating, unwavering, unfaltering. ❷ ASSURED, certain, guaranteed, inevitable, irrevocable. ❸ RELIABLE, dependable, trustworthy, trusted, trusty, unfailing, infallible, never-failing, tested, true, fool-proof, effective, efficacious; informal sure-fire.
– OPPOSITES unsure, uncertain.

surface n ❶ OUTSIDE, exterior, top. ❷ OUTWARD APPEARANCE, superficial appearance, facade.
▶ adj SUPERFICIAL, external, exterior, outward.
▶ v ❶ COME TO THE SURFACE, come up, come to the top. ❷ REAPPEAR, appear, come to light, come up, emerge, crop up. ❸ GET UP, get out of bed, rise, wake, awaken.

surge n GUSH, rush, outpouring, stream, flow, sweep, efflux.
▶ v ❶ GUSH, rush, stream, flow. ❷ RISE, swell, heave, billow, roll, eddy, swirl.

surly adj BAD-TEMPERED, ill-natured, crabbed, grumpy, crotchety, grouchy, cantankerous, irascible, testy, crusty, gruff, abrupt, brusque, churlish, uncivil, morose, sullen, sulky.
– OPPOSITES good-natured, friendly.

surmise v GUESS, conjecture, suspect, deduce, assume, presume, gather, feel, be of the opinion, think, believe, imagine.

surmount v GET OVER, overcome, conquer, triumph over, prevail over, get the better of, beat.
– OPPOSITES descend.

surname n LAST NAME, family name, patronymic.

surpass v BE GREATER THAN, be

better than, beat, exceed, excel, transcend, outdo, outshine, outstrip, overshadow, eclipse.

surplus n EXCESS, remainder, residue, surfeit.
– OPPOSITES dearth, shortage.
▶ adj EXCESS, in excess, superfluous, leftover, unused, remaining, extra, spare.

surprise v ❶ ASTONISH, amaze, nonplus, take aback, startle, astound, stun, stagger, leave open-mouthed, take someone's breath away; *informal* flabbergast, bowl over, blow someone's mind. ❷ TAKE BY SURPRISE, catch unawares, catch off guard, catch red-handed, catch in the act, catch out, burst in on, spring upon, catch someone with their trousers down; *Brit. informal* catch on the hop.
▶ n ❶ ASTONISHMENT, amazement, incredulity, wonder. ❷ SHOCK, bolt from the blue, bombshell, revelation.

surprised adj ASTONISHED, amazed, nonplussed, startled, astounded, stunned, staggered, open-mouthed, speechless, thunderstruck; *informal* flabbergasted.

surprising adj ASTONISHING, amazing, startling, astounding, staggering, incredible, extraordinary, remarkable; *informal* mind-blowing.
– OPPOSITES predictable.

surrender v ❶ GIVE IN, give oneself up, yield, submit, capitulate, lay down one's arms, raise/show the white flag, throw in the towel/sponge.

❷ GIVE UP, relinquish, renounce, forgo, forsake, cede, abdicate, waive. ❸ HAND OVER, give up, deliver up, part with, let go of, relinquish.
– OPPOSITES resist.
▶ n ❶ YIELDING, capitulation, submission. ❷ RELINQUISHMENT, renunciation, forgoing, ceding, cession, abdication.

surreptitious adj STEALTHY, clandestine, secret, sneaky, sly, cunning, furtive, underhand, undercover, covert.
– OPPOSITES open, blatant.

surround v ENCIRCLE, enclose, go around, encompass, ring, gird, girdle, fence in, hem in, confine.

surrounding adj NEIGHBOURING, nearby, adjacent, adjoining, bordering.

surroundings pl n ENVIRONMENT, setting, location, neighbourhood, vicinity, milieu, element, background.

surveillance n OBSERVATION, watch, scrutiny, reconnaissance, spying, espionage.

survey v ❶ LOOK AT, look over, take a look at, observe, view, contemplate, regard, examine, inspect, scrutinize, scan, study, consider, review, take stock of; *informal* size up. ❷ MAKE A SURVEY OF, value, carry out a valuation of, estimate the value of, appraise, assess, prospect, triangulate.
▶ n ❶ STUDY, consideration, review, overview, examination, inspection, scrutinization, scrutiny. ❷ VALUATION,

appraisal. ❸ INVESTIGATION, inquiry, research, study, review, probe, questionnaire.

survive v ❶ REMAIN ALIVE, live, hold out, pull through, cling to life. ❷ LIVE ON, continue, remain, last, persist, endure, be extant, exist, be. ❸ OUTLIVE, outlast, live after, remain alive after.

susceptible adj IMPRESSIONABLE, credulous, gullible, innocent, defenceless, vulnerable, easily led, responsive, sensitive, thin-skinned.
– OPPOSITES immune, resistant.
■ **susceptible to** OPEN TO, responsive to, receptive to, vulnerable to, defenceless against.

suspect v ❶ FEEL, have a feeling, be inclined to think, fancy, surmise, guess, conjecture, have a suspicion that, speculate, have a hunch, suppose, believe, think, conclude. ❷ DOUBT, have doubts about, harbour suspicions about, have misgivings about, be sceptical about, distrust, mistrust.

suspend v ❶ HANG, put up, swing, dangle, sling. ❷ ADJOURN, interrupt, cut short, bring to an end, cease, discontinue, break off, arrest, put off, postpone, delay, defer, shelve, pigeonhole, table; informal put on ice. ❸ DEBAR, shut out, exclude, keep out, remove.

suspense n UNCERTAINTY, doubt, doubtfulness, anticipation, expectation, expectancy, excitement, tension, anxiety,

nervousness, apprehension, apprehensiveness.

suspicion n ❶ DOUBT, misgiving, qualm, wariness, chariness, scepticism, distrust, mistrust, funny feeling. ❷ FEELING, surmise, guess, conjecture, speculation, hunch, supposition, belief, notion, idea, conclusion; informal gut feeling. ❸ TRACE, touch, suggestion, hint, soupçon, tinge, shade.

suspicious adj ❶ DOUBTFUL, unsure, wary, chary, sceptical, distrustful, mistrustful, disbelieving. ❷ GUILTY-LOOKING, dishonest-looking, strange-looking, queer-looking, funny-looking; informal shifty, shady. ❸ QUESTIONABLE, doubtful, odd, strange, irregular, queer, funny; informal fishy, shady.
– OPPOSITES trusting, innocent.

sustain v ❶ BEAR, support, carry, keep up, prop up, shore up. ❷ SUPPORT, be a source of strength to, be a tower of strength to, comfort, help, assist, encourage, buoy up, cheer up, hearten; informal buck up. ❸ KEEP ALIVE, keep going, maintain, preserve, feed, nourish.

sustained adj CONTINUING, steady, continuous, constant, prolonged, perpetual, unremitting.
– OPPOSITES intermittent.

sustenance n FOOD, nourishment, provisions, rations, comestibles, provender; informal grub, chow; *Brit. informal* scoff; *dated* victuals; *archaic* aliment.

swagger v STRUT, parade, prance.

swallow v ❶ GULP DOWN, eat, drink, consume, devour, ingest; *informal* swig, swill; *Brit. informal* scoff. ❷ PUT UP WITH, tolerate, endure, stand, bear, abide, stomach, brook; *archaic* suffer. ❸ BELIEVE, accept; *informal* fall for, buy. ❹ REPRESS, restrain, hold back, control, rein in.

swamp n MARSH, bog, quagmire, mire, morass, fen, quag. ▶ v ❶ FLOOD, inundate, deluge, wash out, soak, drench, saturate. ❷ OVERWHELM, engulf, snow under, overload, overburden, weight down, besiege, beset.

swap v EXCHANGE, interchange, trade, barter, switch.

swarm n ❶ HIVE, flight. ❷ CROWD, multitude, horde, host, mob, throng, army, flock, herd, pack, drove. ▶ v FLOCK, crowd, throng, stream, surge.

swarthy adj DARK, dark-coloured, dark-skinned, dark-complexioned, dusky, tanned. – OPPOSITES pale, fair.

swashbuckling adj DASHING, daring, adventurous, bold, gallant, swaggering. – OPPOSITES timid.

swathe v WRAP, envelop, bind, swaddle, bandage, bundle up, cover, shroud, drape.

sway v ❶ SWING, shake, bend, lean, incline. ❷ WAVER, hesitate, fluctuate, vacillate, oscillate.

❸ INFLUENCE, affect, persuade, prevail on, bring round, win over, induce. ▶ n ❶ JURISDICTION, rule, government, sovereignty, dominion, control, command, power, authority, ascendancy, domination, mastery. ❷ CONTROL, domination, power, influence, guidance, direction.

swear v ❶ PROMISE, pledge, vow, give one's word, take an oath, swear on the Bible. ❷ VOW, insist, declare, assert, maintain, contend; *formal* aver. ❸ CURSE, blaspheme, utter profanities, be foul-mouthed, use bad language, swear like a trooper; *informal* cuss, turn the air blue, eff and blind.

sweat v PERSPIRE, exude perspiration, drip with sweat, break out in a sweat.

sweaty adj SWEATING, perspiring, clammy, sticky, moist, damp.

sweep v BRUSH, clean, clean up, clear up. ■ **sweep away / aside** CAST ASIDE, discard, disregard, ignore, take no notice of, dismiss.

sweet adj ❶ SWEETENED, sugary, sugared, honeyed, syrupy, saccharine. ❷ SWEET-SMELLING, fragrant, aromatic, perfumed, scented, balmy. ❸ SWEET-SOUNDING, musical, tuneful, dulcet, mellifluous, soft, harmonious, euphonious, silvery, silver-toned. ❹ GOOD-NATURED, amiable, pleasant, agreeable, friendly, kindly,

charming, likeable, appealing, engaging, winning, winsome, taking. ❺ DEAR, dearest, darling, beloved, loved, cherished, precious, treasured.
– OPPOSITES sour, savoury, harsh, disagreeable.
▶ n ❶ DESSERT, pudding; Brit. informal afters. ❷ BONBON, sweetmeat; N. Amer. candy; informal sweetie.

sweeten v ❶ MAKE SWEET, add sugar to, sugar. ❷ SOFTEN, soften up, mellow, pacify, appease, mollify.

sweetheart n GIRLFRIEND, boyfriend, lover, suitor, admirer, beau, inamorato, inamorata; poetic/literary swain; archaic paramour.

swell v ❶ EXPAND, bulge, distend, become distended, inflate, become inflated, dilate, become bloated, blow up, puff up, balloon, intumesce. ❷ INCREASE, grow larger, rise, mount, escalate, accelerate, step up, snowball, mushroom. ❸ GROW LOUD, grow louder, intensify, heighten.
– OPPOSITES contract.
▶ adj EXPENSIVE, luxurious, de luxe, fashionable, elegant, grand; informal plush, ritzy; Brit. informal posh.

swelling n BUMP, lump, bulge, blister, inflammation, protuberance, tumescence.

swerve v CHANGE DIRECTION, go off course, veer, turn aside, skew, deviate, sheer, twist.

swift adj FAST, rapid, quick, speedy, fleet-footed, fleet,

prompt, brisk, immediate, instantaneous; informal nippy.
– OPPOSITES slow.

swill v GULP DOWN, drink, quaff, swallow, down, drain, guzzle; informal swig.
■ **swill out** SLUICE, wash down, wash out, clean out, flush out, rinse out.

swim v GO SWIMMING, bathe, dive in; informal have a dip.
■ **be swimming in** BE SATURATED IN, be drenched in, be soaked in, be steeped in, be immersed in.

swindle v DEFRAUD, cheat, trick, fleece, dupe, deceive, rook, exploit; informal do, con, diddle, rip off, take for a ride, pull a fast one on, bilk.
▶ n FRAUD, trick, deception, exploitation, sharp practice; informal con trick, con, diddle, rip-off, fiddle.

swindler n FRAUDSTER, cheat, trickster, rogue, mountebank, exploiter; informal con man, con artist, shark, bilker.

swing v ❶ HANG, be suspended, dangle, be pendent. ❷ MOVE BACK AND FORTH, sway, oscillate, wag. ❸ CURVE, veer, turn, lean, incline, wind, twist. ❹ CHANGE, fluctuate, oscillate, waver, see-saw, yo-yo.
▶ n ❶ SWAYING, oscillation, wagging. ❷ MOVE, change, variation, turnaround.

swirl v WHIRL, eddy, circulate, revolve, spin, twist, churn, swish.

switch n ❶ CHANGE, change of direction, shift, reversal, turnaround, U-turn; *Brit.* about-turn. ❷ EXCHANGE, trade, swap. ▶ v ❶ CHANGE, shift, reverse. ❷ EXCHANGE, interchange, trade, barter, swap.

swollen adj EXPANDED, bulging, distended, inflated, dilated, bloated, blown up, puffed up, puffy, tumescent.

swoop v POUNCE, dive, descend, sweep down on, drop down on.

sycophant n TOADY, flatterer, truckler, Uriah Heep; *informal* bootlicker, yes-man.

sycophantic adj SERVILE, subservient, obsequious, toadying, flattering, ingratiating, unctuous, truckling, Uriah Heepish; *informal* bootlicking.

symbol n ❶ EMBLEM, token, sign, badge, representation, figure, image, type. ❷ SIGN, character, mark.

symbolic adj ❶ EMBLEMATIC, representative, typical. ❷ REPRESENTATIVE, illustrative, emblematic, figurative, allegorical.

symbolize v BE A SYMBOL OF, stand for, be a sign of, represent, personify, exemplify, typify, betoken, denote, epitomize, signify, mean.

symmetrical adj BALANCED, well proportioned, proportional, in proportion, regular, even, harmonious, uniform, consistent, in agreement.
– OPPOSITES asymmetrical.

sympathetic adj ❶ COMPASSIONATE, commiserating, commiserative, pitying, condoling, consoling, comforting, supportive, caring, concerned, solicitous, considerate, kindly, kind, kind-hearted, warm, warm-hearted, understanding, charitable, empathetic. ❷ PLEASANT, agreeable, likeable, congenial, friendly, sociable, companionable, neighbourly, easy to get along with; *informal* simpatico. ❸ IN SYMPATHY WITH, well disposed to, favourably disposed to, approving of, pro, on someone's side.
– OPPOSITES unsympathetic.

sympathize v SHOW / FEEL SYMPATHY FOR, be sympathetic towards, show compassion for, be compassionate towards, commiserate with, pity, offer condolences to, console, comfort, be supportive of, show understanding to, empathize with.

sympathy n COMPASSION, commiseration, pity, condolence, consolation, comfort, solace, support, caring, concern, solicitude, solicitousness, consideration, kindness, kind-heartedness, warmth, warm-heartedness, charity, charitableness, understanding, empathy.
– OPPOSITES indifference.

symptom n SIGN, indication, signal, warning, mark, characteristic, feature, token, evidence, demonstration, display.

symptomatic adj INDICATIVE of, signalling, characteristic of, suggesting, suggestive of.

synthesis n COMBINATION,

combining, union, unification, blend, merging, amalgamation, fusion, coalescence, integration.

synthetic adj MANUFACTURED, man-made, fake, artificial, mock, ersatz.
– OPPOSITES real, natural.

system n ❶ STRUCTURE, organization, order, arrangement, set-up. ❷ METHOD, methodology, technique, process, procedure, approach, practice, line, means, way, modus operandi. ❸ METHODICALNESS, systematization, orderliness, planning, logic, method, routine.

systematic adj STRUCTURED, organized, methodical, orderly, well ordered, planned, systematized, logical, efficient, businesslike.
– OPPOSITES unsystematic, chaotic.

Tt

table n ❶ COUNTER, bar, buffet, bench, stand. ❷ LIST, catalogue, tabulation, inventory, itemization, index.
▶ v SUBMIT, put forward, propose, suggest, move, enter.

tablet n ❶ SLAB, panel, stone. ❷ PILL, capsule, lozenge. ❸ BAR, cake.

taboo adj FORBIDDEN, prohibited, banned, proscribed, vetoed, ruled out, outlawed, not permitted, not acceptable, frowned on, beyond the pale.
– OPPOSITES acceptable.
▶ n PROHIBITION, proscription, veto, interdiction, interdict, ban.

tacit adj IMPLICIT, understood, implied, taken for granted, unstated, undeclared, unspoken, silent, wordless.
– OPPOSITES explicit.

taciturn adj UNFORTHCOMING, uncommunicative, reticent, untalkative, tight-lipped, close-mouthed, quiet, silent.
– OPPOSITES loquacious.

tack n ❶ DRAWING PIN, nail, pin, staple, rivet. ❷ COURSE / LINE OF ACTION, method, approach, process, way, policy.
▶ v NAIL, pin, staple, fix, fasten, affix, put up/down.

tackle n EQUIPMENT, apparatus, outfit, tools, implements, accoutrements, paraphernalia, things, trappings; *informal* gear, stuff.
▶ v ❶ UNDERTAKE, attempt, apply/address oneself to, get to grips with, set/go about, get to work at, embark on, set one's hand to, take on, engage in. ❷ GRAPPLE WITH, seize, take hold of, confront, face up to; *Brit. informal* have a go at.

tacky[1] adj STICKY, gluey, gummy; *informal* gooey.

tacky[2] adj TAWDRY, tasteless, kitsch, vulgar, crude, garish, gaudy, flashy; *informal* flash.
– OPPOSITES tasteful.

tact n DIPLOMACY, discretion, sensitivity, understanding, thoughtfulness, consideration, delicacy, subtlety, finesse, skill, perception, judgement, prudence, judiciousness.
– OPPOSITES tactlessness.

tactful adj DIPLOMATIC, politic, discreet, sensitive, understanding, thoughtful, considerate, delicate, subtle, perceptive, prudent, judicious.
– OPPOSITES tactless.

tactic n MANOEUVRE, expedient, device, stratagem, trick, scheme, plan, ploy, course/line of action, method, approach, tack, means.

tactical adj STRATEGIC, politic, planned, shrewd, skilful, adroit, clever, cunning, artful; *informal* smart.

tactless adj UNDIPLOMATIC, impolitic, indiscreet, insensitive, inconsiderate, indelicate, unsubtle, rough, crude, clumsy, awkward, inept, bungling, maladroit, gauche, undiscerning, imprudent, injudicious.
– OPPOSITES tactful.

tag n ❶ LABEL, ticket, sticker, docket. ❷ QUOTATION, stock phrase, platitude, cliché, epithet.
▶ v LABEL, put a ticket/sticker on, mark.

tail n BRUSH, scut, dock.

▶ v FOLLOW, shadow, stalk, trail, track, dog, keep under surveillance.

tailor n OUTFITTER, dressmaker, couturier, clothier, costumier.
▶ v FIT, suit, fashion, style, mould, shape, adapt, adjust, modify, convert, alter, accommodate.

take v ❶ GET / LAY HOLD OF, grasp, grip, clutch. ❷ OBTAIN, receive, get, gain, acquire, secure, procure, come by, win. ❸ SEIZE, catch, capture, arrest, carry off, abduct. ❹ REMOVE, appropriate, make off with, steal, pilfer, purloin, pocket; *informal* filch, swipe; *Brit. informal* pinch, nick. ❺ RESERVE, book, engage, rent, hire, lease. ❻ TRAVEL BY / ON, use, make use of, utilize. ❼ USE UP, require, call for, need, necessitate. ❽ CARRY, fetch, bring, bear, transport, convey, cart, ferry. ❾ ESCORT, accompany, conduct, guide, lead, usher, convoy.
– OPPOSITES give.
■ **take off** *see* IMITATE (2).

takings pl n PROCEEDS, returns, receipts, earnings, winnings, pickings, profit, gain, income, revenue.

tale n STORY, narrative, anecdote, legend, fable, myth, parable, allegory, epic, saga; *informal* yarn.

talent n GIFT, flair, aptitude, facility, knack, bent, ability, capacity, faculty, aptness, endowment, strong point, forte, genius.

talented adj GIFTED, accomplished, able, capable, apt, deft,

adept, proficient, brilliant, expert, artistic.
– OPPOSITES incapable, inept.

talk v ❶ SPEAK, give voice/utterance, discourse, chat, chatter, gossip, prattle, prate, gibber, jabber, babble, rattle on, gabble; *informal* natter, gab; *Brit. informal* natter, rabbit. ❷ COMMUNICATE, converse, speak to each other, discuss things, confer, consult each other, have negotiations, parley; *informal* chew the fat/rag, jaw, rap.
▶ n ❶ TALKING, speaking, chatter, chatting, gossiping, prattling; *Brit. informal* nattering. ❷ LECTURE, speech, address, discourse, oration, sermon, disquisition. ❸ GOSSIP, rumour, hearsay, tittle-tattle.

talkative adj LOQUACIOUS, garrulous, voluble, chatty, gossipy, conversational, long-winded, gushing, effusive; *informal* gabby, mouthy, big-mouthed.
– OPPOSITES taciturn.

tall adj ❶ BIG, colossal, gigantic, lanky, rangy, gangling. ❷ HIGH, lofty, towering, soaring, sky-high.
– OPPOSITES short.

tally n COUNT, record, total, reckoning, enumeration, register, roll, census, poll.
▶ v AGREE, accord, concur, coincide, conform, correspond, match, fit, harmonize.
– OPPOSITES disagree.

tame adj ❶ DOMESTICATED, gentle. ❷ UNEXCITING, uninteresting, uninspired, dull, bland, flat, insipid, vapid, prosaic,

humdrum, boring, tedious, wearisome.
– OPPOSITES wild.
▶ v ❶ DOMESTICATE, break, train. ❷ SUBDUE, discipline, curb, control, master, overcome, suppress, repress, humble.

tamper v MEDDLE, interfere, monkey around, mess about, tinker, fiddle.

tan v BECOME SUNTANNED, suntan, take a suntan/tan, brown, go/turn brown, darken.

tangible adj ❶ TOUCHABLE, palpable, tactile, visible. ❷ CONCRETE, real, actual, solid, substantial, hard, well documented, definite, clear.
– OPPOSITES abstract.

tangled adj ❶ ENTANGLED, twisted, snarled, ravelled, knotted, knotty, matted, tousled, messy. ❷ CONFUSED, jumbled, mixed up, messy, chaotic, complicated, involved, convoluted, complex.
– OPPOSITES neat, straight, simple.

tank n CONTAINER, receptacle, vat, cistern.

tantalize v TEASE, torment, torture, frustrate, disappoint, thwart, lead on, entice, titillate, allure, beguile.

tantamount
■ **tantamount to** EQUIVALENT TO, equal to, as good as, synonymous with.

tape n ❶ BAND, strip, string, ribbon. ❷ TAPE RECORDING, cassette, videotape, video cassette, video, audio tape, audio cassette.
▶ v ❶ BIND, tie, fasten, stick, seal.

❷ RECORD, tape-record, video-record, video.

taper v NARROW, thin, become narrow/thinner, come to a point.
– OPPOSITES thicken.
■ **taper off** *see* DECLINE v (2, 3).

target n ❶ OBJECTIVE, goal, object, aim, end, intention. ❷ BUTT, victim, scapegoat.

tariff n ❶ PRICE LIST / SCHEDULE, list of charges. ❷ TAX, duty, toll, excise, levy, impost.

tarnish v ❶ DULL, dim, discolour, rust. ❷ SULLY, besmirch, blacken, stain, blemish, blot, taint, befoul, drag through the mud.
– OPPOSITES polish, enhance.

tart[1] n PASTRY, flan, tartlet, quiche, pie.

tart[2] adj SHARP, sour, tangy, piquant, pungent, bitter, acid, acidulous, vinegary.
– OPPOSITES sweet.

task n JOB, duty, chore, charge, assignment, commission, mission, engagement, occupation, undertaking, exercise, errand, quest.

taste n ❶ FLAVOUR, savour, relish, tang. ❷ MORSEL, bite, mouthful, spoonful, sample, sip, drop, swallow, touch, soupçon. ❸ LIKING, love, fondness, fancy, desire, preference, penchant, predilection, inclination, partiality, leaning, bent, hankering, appetite, palate, thirst, hunger. ❹ DISCRIMINATION, discernment, judgement, refinement, polish, finesse, elegance, grace, stylishness.

▶ v ❶ SAMPLE, test, try, nibble, sip. ❷ MAKE OUT, perceive, discern, distinguish, differentiate.

tasteful adj IN GOOD TASTE, aesthetic, artistic, harmonious, pleasing, elegant, graceful, beautiful, pretty, charming, handsome, discriminating, refined, restrained.
– OPPOSITES tasteless.

tasteless adj ❶ FLAVOURLESS, bland, insipid, watery, watered down, weak, thin, unappetizing, uninteresting, vapid. ❷ VULGAR, crude, tawdry, garish, gaudy, loud, flashy, showy, cheap, gross, meretricious.
– OPPOSITES tasteful.

tasty adj FLAVOURSOME, full-flavoured, appetizing, palatable, toothsome, delectable, delicious, luscious, mouth-watering, piquant, pungent, spicy; *informal* scrumptious, yummy, finger-licking.
– OPPOSITES bland.

taunt v GIBE AT, jeer at, sneer at, insult, chaff, tease, torment, provoke, ridicule, deride, mock, poke fun at.

taut adj TIGHT, stretched, rigid, flexed, tensed.
– OPPOSITES slack.

tawdry adj SHOWY, gaudy, flashy, garish, loud, tasteless, cheap, cheapjack, shoddy, meretricious, Brummagem; *informal* flash, tatty, tacky, kitsch.
– OPPOSITES tasteful.

tax n LEVY, charge, duty, toll, excise, tariff, impost, tribute.
▶ v ❶ LEVY A TAX ON, impose a toll on, charge duty on. ❷ MAKE

DEMANDS ON, weigh heavily on, weigh down, burden, load, encumber, overload, push, stretch, strain, try, wear out, exhaust, sap, drain, enervate, fatigue, tire, weary, weaken.

teach v ❶ GIVE LESSONS TO, instruct, educate, school, tutor, coach, train, drill, ground, enlighten. ❷ GIVE LESSONS / INSTRUCTION IN, instil, inculcate, impart.

teacher n SCHOOLTEACHER, schoolmaster, schoolmistress, master, mistress, instructor, educator, tutor, coach, trainer, lecturer, professor, don, pedagogue, guide, mentor, guru.

team n GROUP, band, bunch, company, gang, crew, troupe, squad, side, line-up.

tear[1] n RIP, split, hole, rent, run, rupture.
▶ v RIP, split, rend, sever, rive, sunder, rupture.

tear[2] n TEARDROP, drop, droplet, globule, bead.

tearful adj IN TEARS, crying, weeping, weepy, sobbing, blubbering, snivelling, whimpering, wailing; informal blubbing.
– OPPOSITES cheerful.

tease v MOCK, ridicule, poke fun at, torment, provoke, badger, bait, goad, pest, bother, worry, vex, irritate, annoy, gibe; informal needle.

technical adj ❶ PRACTICAL, mechanical, scientific, technological. ❷ SPECIALIST, specialized, scientific.

technique n ❶ METHOD, system, procedure, style, manner, way, course of action, mode, fashion, means. ❷ EXECUTION, skill, skilfulness, proficiency, expertise, expertness, mastery, artistry, art, craftsmanship, craft, ability.

tedious adj WEARISOME, wearying, tiresome, tiring, fatiguing, soporific, overlong, long-winded, prolix, dull, deadly dull, boring, uninteresting, dry, dreary, drab, unexciting, lifeless, uninspired, flat, banal, vapid, insipid, monotonous, unvaried, prosaic, humdrum, run-of-the-mill, routine.
– OPPOSITES interesting.

teem v ABOUND, be abundant, be plentiful, be copious, swarm, crawl, bristle, seethe, brim.

teetotaller n ABSTAINER, non-drinker, Rechabite.

telephone n PHONE, handset, receiver; informal blower.
▶ v CALL, call up, phone; Brit. ring up, ring; informal get on the blower to, buzz.

telescope v CONCERTINA, crush, squash, squeeze, compress, compact.
– OPPOSITES elongate.

television n TV; informal small screen; Brit. informal telly, the box, goggle-box; N. Amer. informal the tube, idiot box.

tell v ❶ MAKE KNOWN, impart, communicate, announce, proclaim, broadcast, divulge, reveal, disclose, declare, state, mention, utter, voice, say, speak. ❷ INFORM, let know, make aware, apprise, notify. ❸ INSTRUCT, order, give orders, command, direct, bid, charge, enjoin, dictate to, call upon, require. **4** DISTINGUISH, differentiate, discriminate.

telling adj MARKED, significant, substantial, considerable, important, striking, impressive, potent, powerful, forceful, effective, influential, decisive.
– OPPOSITES insignificant.

temper n **1** TEMPERAMENT, disposition, nature, humour, mood, character, frame of mind, mind, attitude, stamp. **2** BAD MOOD, ill humour, fury, rage, passion, fit of temper/pique, tantrum; Brit. informal paddy.
▶ v **1** TOUGHEN, anneal, harden, strengthen, fortify. **2** MODERATE, soften, tone down, modify, mitigate, alleviate, allay, palliate, mollify, assuage, lessen, weaken.

temperament n DISPOSITION, nature, humour, mood, character, personality, make-up, constitution, complexion, temper, spirit, mettle, frame of mind, cast of mind, mind, attitude, outlook stamp, quality.

temperamental adj **1** CONSTITUTIONAL, inherent, innate, inborn, congenital, deep-rooted, ingrained. **2** EXCITABLE, emotional, volatile, mercurial, oversensitive, capricious, erratic, touchy, moody, hot-headed, explosive, impatient, petulant.
– OPPOSITES calm.

temperance n MODERATION, self-control, abstemiousness, continence, abstinence, self-denial.
– OPPOSITES alcoholism.

temperate adj MODERATE, mild, gentle, clement, balmy, pleasant, agreeable.
– OPPOSITES extreme.

tempestuous adj STORMY, turbulent, boisterous, violent, wild, uncontrolled, unrestrained, passionate, impassioned, emotional, intense, fierce.
– OPPOSITES calm.

temple n PLACE OF WORSHIP, holy place, shrine, sanctuary.

tempo n BEAT, rhythm, cadence, throb, pulse.

temporal adj SECULAR, non-spiritual, worldly, material, earthly, carnal.
– OPPOSITES spiritual.

temporary adj **1** SHORT-TERM, impermanent, interim, provisional, pro tem. **2** BRIEF, fleeting, passing, momentary, short-lived, transient, transitory, ephemeral, fugitive, evanescent.
– OPPOSITES permanent.

tempt v ENTICE, lure, attract, appeal to, seduce, tantalize, incite, persuade, induce, egg on, urge, goad, prompt, sway, influence, cajole, coax.
– OPPOSITES discourage, deter.

tempting adj ALLURING, enticing, attractive, captivating, appealing, beguiling, fascinating, tantalizing, appetizing, mouth-watering.
– OPPOSITES off-putting.

tenable adj JUSTIFIABLE, defensible, defendable, arguable, maintainable, supportable, plausible, credible, reasonable, rational, sound, viable.
– OPPOSITES untenable.

tenacious adj PERSISTENT, pertinacious, determined, dogged, resolute, firm, steadfast, purposeful, unshakeable, unswerving, relentless, inexorable, unyielding, inflexible, stubborn, obstinate, intransigent, obdurate, strong-willed.

tend[1] v HAVE / SHOW A TENDENCY TO, incline towards, be apt/disposed/liable to, be likely to.

tend[2] v LOOK AFTER, take care of, care for, attend to, minister to, see to, cater to, nurse, wait on, watch over, watch.
– OPPOSITES neglect.

tendency n INCLINATION, disposition, predisposition, proclivity, propensity, proneness, aptness, bent, leaning, penchant, susceptibility, liability.

tender adj ❶ EASILY DAMAGED, breakable, fragile, frail, delicate, sensitive. ❷ COMPASSIONATE, soft-hearted, kind, kindly, sympathetic, warm, caring, humane, gentle, solicitous, generous, benevolent, sentimental. ❸ LOVING, affectionate, warm, emotional, amorous. ❹ SORE, painful, aching, smarting, throbbing, inflamed, irritated, red, raw, bruised.
– OPPOSITES tough, hard-hearted.

tense adj ❶ TIGHT, taut, rigid, stretched, strained. ❷ ANXIOUS,

nervous, keyed up, worked up, overwrought, distraught, uneasy, worried, apprehensive, agitated, jumpy, edgy, on edge, restless, fidgety; informal uptight, wound up, jittery.
– OPPOSITES relaxed.

tension n ❶ TIGHTNESS, tautness, rigidity. ❷ ANXIETY, stress, stressfulness, suspense, pressure, strain, unease, disquiet, worry, apprehensiveness, agitation, jumpiness, edginess, restlessness.

tentative adj ❶ SPECULATIVE, conjectural, exploratory, trial, provisional, test, pilot, untried, unproven. ❷ HESITANT, hesitating, faltering, wavering, uncertain, unsure, doubtful, cautious, diffident, timid.
– OPPOSITES definite, confident.

tenuous adj SLIGHT, flimsy, weak, insubstantial, shaky, sketchy, doubtful, dubious, nebulous, hazy, vague, unspecific, indefinite.
– OPPOSITES definite.

term n ❶ WORD, expression, phrase, name, title, appellation, designation; formal denomination. ❷ PERIOD, time, spell, interval, stretch, span, duration.
▸ v CALL, name, entitle, style, dub, label, tag, designate, denominate.

terminal adj FATAL, deadly, mortal, lethal, killing, incurable.
▸ n ❶ TERMINUS, last stop, depot.

❷ WORKSTATION, visual display unit, VDU.

terminate v BRING TO A CLOSE / END / CONCLUSION, close, end, conclude, finish, stop, wind up, discontinue.
– OPPOSITES commence.

terminology n LANGUAGE, phraseology, vocabulary, nomenclature, jargon, terms, expressions, words; *informal* lingo.

terrible adj ❶ GREAT, extreme, incorrigible, outrageous, awful, dreadful, frightful, impossible. ❷ BAD, poor, incompetent, useless, talentless; *informal* rotten; *Brit. informal* duff. ❸ DREADFUL, terrifying, frightening, frightful, horrifying, horrible, horrific, horrendous, terrific, harrowing, hideous, grim, unspeakable, appalling, awful, gruesome.

terrific adj ❶ TREMENDOUS, great, very great, very big, huge, sizeable, considerable, intense, extreme, extraordinary, excessive. ❷ VERY GOOD, excellent, superb, remarkable, magnificent, wonderful, marvellous, great, sensational; *informal* super, fantastic, fabulous, fab, A1, ace, unreal, awesome.

terrify v FRIGHTEN, scare stiff, scare, petrify, make someone's hair stand on end, alarm, panic, intimidate.

territory n ❶ REGION, area, terrain, tract. ❷ AREA, province, field, sector, department.

terror n FRIGHT, dread, alarm, panic, intimidation, dismay, consternation, shock, horror; *informal* heebie-jeebies.

terrorize v STRIKE TERROR IN / INTO, terrify, scare stiff, petrify, horrify.

terse adj ❶ CONCISE, succinct, compact, brief, short, to the point, crisp, pithy, elliptical, epigrammatic. ❷ ABRUPT, curt, brusque, laconic, short, clipped, blunt.
– OPPOSITES long-winded.

test n EXAMINATION, check, assessment, evaluation, appraisal, investigation, inspection, analysis, scrutinization, scrutiny, study, probe, exploration.
▶ v PUT TO THE TEST, examine, check, assess, evaluate, appraise, investigate, scrutinize, study, probe.

testify v GIVE EVIDENCE, bear witness, attest, be a witness.

testimonial n REFERENCE, character reference, recommendation, commendation, credential, endorsement.

testimony n EVIDENCE, attestation, sworn statement, deposition, affidavit.

text n ❶ TEXTBOOK, book. ❷ THEME, subject matter, subject, matter, topic, issue. ❸ PASSAGE, verse, paragraph.

texture n FEEL, touch, appearance, surface, grain.

thank v OFFER / EXTEND THANKS TO, express/show gratitude to, show appreciation to.

thankful adj GRATEFUL, appreciative, pleased, indebted,

obliged, under an obligation, beholden.
– OPPOSITES ungrateful.

thankless adj UNAPPRECIATED, unrewarded, unrewarding, un-acknowledged, vain, in vain, fruitless, useless.
– OPPOSITES rewarding.

thanks pl n GRATITUDE, grate-fulness, appreciation, acknow-ledgement, recognition.

thaw v DEFROST, unfreeze, melt, soften, liquefy.
– OPPOSITES freeze.

theatre n ❶ DRAMA, drama-turgy, the stage, show business; *informal* show biz. ❷ AUDITORIUM, hall, playhouse.

theatrical adj ❶ DRAMATIC, stage, dramaturgical, thespian. ❷ OSTENTATIOUS, melodramatic, histrionic, emotional, exagger-ated, overdone, dramatic, showy, affected, mannered, stilted; *informal* hammy.

theft n STEALING, robbery, thieving, thievery, burglary, larceny, misappropriation, pilfering, purloining, shoplift-ing, embezzlement.

theme n ❶ TOPIC, subject, sub-ject matter, matter, thesis, text, argument. ❷ THEME SONG, melody, tune, air, leitmotif.

theoretical adj HYPOTHETICAL, conjectural, suppositional, speculative, notional, postula-tory, assumed, presumed.
– OPPOSITES proven.

theory n HYPOTHESIS, thesis, conjecture, supposition, guess, notion, speculation, surmise.

postulation, assumption, presumption, opinion, view.

therapy n ❶ TREATMENT, remedy, cure. ❷ PSYCHOTHERAPY, psychoanalysis.

thesis n ❶ THEORY, hypothesis, contention, argument, pro-posal, proposition, premise, postulation, idea. ❷ DISSERTA-TION, paper, treatise, disquisi-tion, essay, composition, monograph.

thick adj ❶ BROAD, wide, large, big, bulky, solid, substantial, fat; *informal* beefy. ❷ DENSE, close-packed, concentrated, crowded, condensed. ❸ OPAQUE, heavy, dense, soupy, murky, impenetrable.
– OPPOSITES thin.

thicken v SET, gel, solidify, congeal, clot, coagulate, cake.

thief n ROBBER, burglar, house-breaker, larcenist, pilferer, shoplifter, pickpocket, embez-zler, bandit, swindler, fraud-ster, mugger.

thieve v STEAL, rob, pilfer, purloin, embezzle, swindle; *informal* swipe, filch, rip off; *Brit.* *informal* nick, knock off.

thin adj ❶ SLIM, slender, lean, slight, svelte, light, skinny, spindly, scrawny, scraggy, bony, skeletal, wasted, emaci-ated, shrunken, anorexic, undernourished, underweight. ❷ FINE, light, delicate, flimsy, diaphanous, gossamer, sheer, transparent, see-through, gauzy, filmy, translucent. ❸ SPARSE, scarce, scanty, meagre, paltry, scattered.

❹ FLIMSY, insubstantial, weak, feeble, lame, poor, shallow, unconvincing, inadequate, insufficient.
– OPPOSITES fat.
▶ v ❶ DILUTE, water down, weaken. ❷ REDUCE IN NUMBER, lessen, decrease, diminish.

thing n ❶ OBJECT, article; *informal* whatchamacallit, what's-its-name, whatsit, thingummy, thingamabob, thingamajig. ❷ ACTION, act, deed, exploit, feat, undertaking, task, job, chore.

think v ❶ BELIEVE, suppose, expect, imagine, surmise, conjecture, guess, fancy. ❷ CONSIDER, deem, hold, reckon, regard as, assume, presume, estimate. ❸ PONDER, meditate, deliberate, contemplate, muse, cogitate, ruminate, concentrate, brood, rack one's brains, be lost in thought, be in a brown study.

thinker n PHILOSOPHER, scholar, sage, theorist, intellect; *informal* brain.

thirst n ❶ THIRSTINESS, dryness, dehydration. ❷ DESIRE, craving, longing, hankering, yearning, avidity, keenness, eagerness, hunger, lust, appetite, passion, covetousness; *informal* yen.
■ **thirst for/after** DESIRE, crave, long for, hanker after, yearn for, hunger after, lust after, covet.

thirsty adj ❶ PARCHED, dehydrated, dry. ❷ THIRSTING, avid, keen, eager, hungry, greedy, covetous.

thong n STRIP, belt, strap, cord, lash, rope, tie, tether.

thorny adj ❶ PRICKLY, spiky, barbed, spiny, spined, spinose, bristly, sharp, pointed. ❷ see DIFFICULT (2).

thorough adj ❶ IN-DEPTH, exhaustive, complete, comprehensive, intensive, extensive, widespread, sweeping, all-embracing, all-inclusive, detailed. ❷ METICULOUS, scrupulous, assiduous, conscientious, painstaking, punctilious, methodical, careful. ❸ THOROUGH-GOING, out-and-out, utter, downright, sheer, absolute, unmitigated, unqualified, complete, total, perfect.
– OPPOSITES cursory, careless.

thought n ❶ THINKING, reasoning, pondering, meditation, cogitation, rumination, musing, mulling, reflection, introspection, contemplation, consideration, cerebration. ❷ IDEA, notion, line of thinking, theory, opinion.

thoughtful adj ❶ PENSIVE, reflective, introspective, meditative, contemplative, ruminative, cogitative, absorbed, rapt/lost in thought, in a brown study. ❷ PROFOUND, deep, serious, pithy, meaty, weighty. ❸ CONSIDERATE, attentive, caring, solicitous, helpful, kind, kindly, compassionate, tender, charitable.
– OPPOSITES thoughtless.

thoughtless adj ❶ TACTLESS, undiplomatic, indiscreet, insensitive, inconsiderate,

thrash v BEAT, whip, horse-whip, flog, lash, birch, cane, flagellate, scourge, leather, spank, chastise, belt, wallop.

careless, selfish, impolite, rude. ❷ UNTHINKING, heedless, careless, unmindful, absent-minded, injudicious, ill-advised, ill-considered, imprudent, unwise, foolish, silly, stupid, reckless, rash, precipitate, negligent, remiss.
– OPPOSITES thoughtful.

thrash v BEAT, whip, horse-whip, flog, lash, birch, cane, flagellate, scourge, leather, spank, chastise, belt, wallop.

thread n ❶ YARN, cotton, filament, fibre. ❷ STRAND, line, streak, strip, seam.

threadbare adj WORN, frayed, tattered, ragged, holey, shabby.

threat n ❶ THREATENING REMARK, warning, ultimatum. ❷ DANGER, peril, hazard, menace, risk. ❸ POSSIBILITY, chance, probability, likelihood, risk.

threaten v ❶ MAKE THREATS, menace, intimidate, browbeat, bully, pressurize, lean on. ❷ BE IMMINENT, impend, hang over, loom, foreshadow.

threatening adj ❶ MENACING, warning, intimidating, bullying, minatory. ❷ OMINOUS, inauspicious, foreboding.

threshold n ❶ DOORWAY, doorstep, entrance. ❷ BEGINNING, commencement, start, outset, inception, opening, dawn, brink, verge, debut; informal kick-off.

thrifty adj ECONOMICAL, careful, frugal, sparing, scrimping, parsimonious, penny-pinching, miserly.
– OPPOSITES spendthrift.

thrill n ❶ EXCITEMENT, sensation of joy, wave of pleasure, glow, tingle; informal buzz, charge, kick. ❷ THROB, tremble, tremor, quiver, flutter, shudder, vibration.
▶ v EXCITE, stimulate, arouse, stir, electrify, move, give joy/pleasure to; informal give a buzz/charge/kick to.
– OPPOSITES bore.

thrilling adj EXCITING, stirring, electrifying, rousing, moving, gripping, riveting.
– OPPOSITES boring.

thrive v FLOURISH, prosper, do/go well, boom, burgeon, succeed, advance, get ahead, make progress.
– OPPOSITES decline.

throb v BEAT, pulse, pulsate, palpitate, pound, thump.

throng n CROWD, horde, mob, mass, host, multitude, swarm, flock, pack, herd, drove, press, assemblage, gathering, congregation.

throttle v CHOKE, strangle, strangulate, garrotte.

throw v ❶ HURL, toss, cast, sling, pitch, shy, lob, propel, launch, project, send; informal heave, chuck. ❷ CAST, project, send.

thrust v PUSH, shove, ram, drive, press, prod, propel.

thrusting adj FORCEFUL, pushing, forward, pushy, energetic, assertive, aggressive, insistent, ambitious.
– OPPOSITES meek.

thug n RUFFIAN, rough, hoodlum, bully boy, hooligan, villain, gangster; *informal* heavy, bovver boy, tough.

thunder n BOOM, booming, rumble, rumbling, outburst, roar, roaring.
▶ v BOOM, rumble, roar, blast, resound, reverberate.

thunderous adj BOOMING, rumbling, roaring, resounding, reverberating, deafening, ear-splitting, loud, noisy, tumultuous.

thwart v FRUSTRATE, foil, baulk, check, block, stop, prevent, defeat, impede, obstruct, hinder, hamper, stymie.
– OPPOSITES assist.

tic n TWITCH, spasm, jerk.

ticket n ❶ PASS, token, stub, coupon, card. ❷ LABEL, tag, tally.

tickle v ❶ STROKE, pet, touch. ❷ AMUSE, entertain, divert, cheer, gladden.

tide n TIDAL FLOW, tidewater, tide race, flow, ebb, current, stream.

tidy adj ❶ NEAT, trim, orderly, in order, in good order, well ordered, spruce, shipshape, well kept, clean, spick and span. ❷ ORDERLY, organized, methodical, systematic, businesslike.
– OPPOSITES untidy.
▶ v CLEAN, clean up, put to rights, put in order, straighten, make shipshape, spruce up, groom, smarten, neaten, brush down.

tie v ❶ TIE UP, fasten, attach, fix, bind, secure, tether, moor, lash, join, connect, link, couple, rope, chain. ❷ DRAW, be equal, be even, be neck and neck.

tier n ROW, rank, bank, line, layer, level, storey.

tight adj ❶ FAST, secure, fixed, clenched, clinched. ❷ TAUT, rigid, stiff, tense, strained. ❸ CRAMPED, restricted, limited, constricted. ❹ STRICT, rigorous, stringent, tough, rigid, uncompromising, exacting.
– OPPOSITES loose, slack.

tighten v ❶ TAUTEN, make tight/taut, stretch, make rigid, rigidify, stiffen, tense. ❷ INCREASE, make stricter, make rigorous/stringent/rigid.
– OPPOSITES slacken.

till v CULTIVATE, work, farm, plough, dig, turn over.

tilt v LEAN, list, slope, slant, incline, tip, cant.

time n ❶ AGE, era, epoch, period. ❷ WHILE, spell, stretch, span, period, term. ❸ OCCASION, point, juncture. ❹ MOMENT, point, instant, stage. ❺ RHYTHM, measure, tempo, beat, metre.
▶ v ❶ CLOCK, measure, calculate, regulate, count. ❷ SCHEDULE, arrange, fix, set, timetable, programme.

timeless adj AGELESS, enduring, lasting, permanent, abiding, unending, ceaseless, undying, deathless, eternal, everlasting, immortal, changeless.
– OPPOSITES ephemeral.

timely adj OPPORTUNE, well timed, convenient, appropriate, seasonable, felicitous.
– OPPOSITES ill-timed.

timetable n SCHEDULE, programme, calendar, list, agenda.
▶ v SCHEDULE, fix, set, programme.

timid adj ❶ FEARFUL, apprehensive, timorous, afraid, frightened, scared, faint-hearted, cowardly, pusillanimous; informal chicken, yellow, lily-livered. ❷ SHY, diffident, bashful, reticent, timorous, shrinking, retiring, coy, demure.
– OPPOSITES bold.

tingle v PRICKLE, prick, tickle, itch, sting, quiver, tremble.
▶ n TINGLING, prickling, pricking, tickle, itch, quiver, trembling, pins and needles.

tinker FIDDLE, play, toy, tamper, fool around, mess about.

tint n SHADE, colour, tone, tinge, cast, tincture.

tiny adj MINUTE, diminutive, miniature, mini, minuscule, infinitesimal, microscopic, dwarfish, midget, pocket-sized, Lilliputian, wee, small, little, insignificant, trifling, negligible, inconsequential; informal teeny, teeny-weeny, itsy-bitsy, pint-sized.
– OPPOSITES huge.

tip¹ n ❶ POINT, peak, top, summit, apex, crown. ❷ END, extremity, point.
▶ v CAP, top, crown.

tip² n RUBBISH DUMP, dump, refuse dump, rubbish heap, midden.
▶ v ❶ TILT, lean, list, cant, slant, topple, overturn, fall over, turn topsy-turvy, capsize. ❷ POUR, empty, unload, dump.

tirade n DIATRIBE, harangue, stream of abuse, verbal onslaught, lecture, upbraiding.

tire v ❶ FATIGUE, wear out, weary, exhaust, drain, enervate, debilitate, jade; informal take it out of, whack; Brit. informal fag out, knacker; N. Amer. informal poop; Austral./NZ informal bush. ❷ GET / GROW / BECOME TIRED, get fatigued, flag, droop.

tired adj FATIGUED, worn out, weary, wearied, exhausted, drained, enervated, debilitated, jaded; informal done, done in, all in, dead beat, dog-tired, whacked, dead on one's feet, ready to drop; Brit. informal fagged out, knackered; N. Amer. informal pooped; Austral./NZ informal bushed.
– OPPOSITES energetic, fresh.

tireless adj UNTIRING, unflagging, indefatigable, energetic, industrious, vigorous, determined, resolute, dogged.
– OPPOSITES lazy.

tiresome adj ❶ WEARISOME, laborious, wearing, tedious, boring, monotonous, dull, uninteresting, unexciting, humdrum, routine. ❷ TROUBLESOME, irksome, vexatious, irritating, annoying, exasperating, trying.
– OPPOSITES interesting, pleasant.

tiring adj WEARYING, wearing, fatiguing, exhausting,

draining, enervating, arduous, laborious, strenuous, exacting, taxing.

titillate v EXCITE, arouse, stimulate, provoke, thrill, interest, fascinate, tantalize, seduce; *informal* turn on.

title n ❶ NAME, designation, appellation, epithet, sobriquet; *informal* moniker, handle; *formal* denomination. ❷ ENTITLEMENT, right, claim, ownership, proprietorship, possession, holding.
▶ v ENTITLE, name, call, designate, label, tag, style, term.

titter n SNICKER, snigger, giggle, laugh, chuckle, chortle.

toast v ❶ BROWN, crisp, warm up, heat, heat up. ❷ DRINK THE HEALTH OF, drink to, pledge, salute.

toddle v TOTTER, teeter, wobble, falter, dodder.

together adv WITH EACH OTHER, in conjunction, jointly, in co-operation, as one, in unison, side by side, hand in hand, hand in glove, shoulder to shoulder, cheek by jowl.
– OPPOSITES separately.

toilet n LAVATORY, ladies' room, powder room, convenience, outhouse, urinal, latrine, privy; *Brit.* WC; *N. Amer.* washroom, bathroom; *informal* loo, bog; *N. Amer. informal* john, can.

token n ❶ SYMBOL, sign, emblem, badge, representation, indication, mark, manifestation. ❷ MEMENTO, souvenir, keepsake, remembrance, reminder, memorial.

▶ adj PERFUNCTORY, superficial, nominal, slight, hollow.

tolerable adj ❶ ENDURABLE, bearable, sufferable, supportable, acceptable. ❷ FAIRLY GOOD, fair, all right, passable, adequate, satisfactory, average, mediocre, ordinary, run-of-the-mill, indifferent, unexceptional; *informal* not bad, OK.
– OPPOSITES intolerable.

tolerance n ❶ TOLERATION, open-mindedness, lack of prejudice, broad-mindedness, liberalism, forbearance, patience, magnanimity, understanding, charity, lenience. ❷ ENDURANCE, sufferance, acceptance.

tolerant adj OPEN-MINDED, unprejudiced, unbiased, broad-minded, liberal, catholic, forbearing, long-suffering, magnanimous, sympathetic, understanding, charitable, lenient, indulgent, permissive, free and easy, easy-going.
– OPPOSITES intolerant.

tolerate v ❶ PERMIT, allow, sanction, accept, countenance; *formal* brook. ❷ ENDURE, bear, suffer, take, stand, put up with, abide, accept, stomach, submit to.

toll n ❶ CHARGE, fee, payment, levy, tariff. ❷ COST, damage, loss, inroads.

tomb n GRAVE, burial place/chamber, sepulchre, vault, crypt, catacomb, mausoleum.

tone n ❶ SOUND, sound quality, colour, pitch, timbre, tonality. ❷ TONE OF VOICE, expression, intonation, inflection, modulation, accentuation. ❸ MOOD, air, attitude, character, manner, spirit, temper, tenor, vein, drift.

tonic n RESTORATIVE, stimulant, analeptic; *informal* pick-me-up.

tool n IMPLEMENT, instrument, utensil, device, apparatus, gadget, appliance, machine, contrivance, contraption, aid.

top n ❶ HIGHEST POINT / PART, summit, peak, pinnacle, crest, crown, tip, apex, vertex, apogee. ❷ UPPER PART, upper surface, upper layer. ❸ CAP, lid, stopper, cork, cover.
– OPPOSITES bottom.
▶ adj ❶ TOPMOST, uppermost, highest. ❷ FOREMOST, leading, principal, pre-eminent, greatest, finest. ❸ MAXIMUM, maximal, greatest, utmost.
– OPPOSITES lowest, minimum.
▶ v ❶ CAP, cover, finish, garnish. ❷ HEAD, lead, be first in. ❸ SURPASS, exceed, go beyond, transcend, better, best, beat, excel, outstrip, outdo, outshine, eclipse.

topic n SUBJECT, theme, issue, matter, question, argument, thesis.

topical adj CURRENT, up to date, up to the minute, contemporary, popular.
– OPPOSITES out of date.

topple v ❶ FALL OVER, tip over, keel over, overturn, overbalance, capsize. ❷ OVERTHROW, oust, unseat, overturn, bring down, bring low.

torment n AGONY, suffering,

torture, pain, excruciation, anguish, hell, misery, distress, affliction, wretchedness.
▶ v CAUSE AGONY / SUFFERING / PAIN TO, afflict, harrow, plague, torture, distress, worry, trouble.

torn adj ❶ RIPPED, split, slit, cut, lacerated, rent. ❷ DIVIDED, wavering, vacillating, irresolute, uncertain, unsure, undecided.

torrent n FLOOD, deluge, inundation, spate, cascade, rush, stream, current, downpour, rainstorm.
– OPPOSITES trickle.

tortuous adj TWISTING, winding, curving, curvy, sinuous, undulating, coiling, serpentine, snaking, snaky, zigzag, convoluted, meandering.
– OPPOSITES straight.

torture n ❶ ABUSE, illtreatment, punishment, torment. ❷ AGONY, suffering, pain, excruciation, anguish, misery, distress.
▶ v ❶ INFLICT PAIN / SUFFERING ON, abuse, ill-treat, punish, torment; *informal* work over. ❷ TORMENT, afflict, harrow, plague, distress, worry, trouble.

toss v ❶ THROW, hurl, cast, sling, pitch, shy, lob, propel, launch, project; *informal* heave, chuck. ❷ ROLL, sway, undulate, pitch, lurch, heave.

total n SUM, sum total, aggregate, whole, entirety, totality.
▶ adj ❶ COMPLETE, entire, whole, full, comprehensive, combined, aggregate, composite, integral. ❷ THOROUGH, com-

plete, utter, absolute, downright, out-and-out, outright, unmitigated, unqualified.
▶ v ❶ ADD UP TO, come to, amount to. ❷ ADD UP, count, reckon, tot up.

totalitarian adj AUTOCRATIC, authoritarian, absolute, despotic, dictatorial, tyrannical, undemocratic, oppressive.
– OPPOSITES democratic.

totter v TEETER, wobble, stagger, stumble, reel, sway, roll, lurch.

touch v ❶ BE IN CONTACT, come into contact, come together, meet, converge, be contiguous, adjoin, abut. ❷ PRESS LIGHTLY, tap, brush, graze, feel, stroke, pat, fondle, caress. ❸ AFFECT, move, make an impression on, influence, upset, disturb, make sad, arouse sympathy; informal get to. ❹ REACH, attain, arrive at, come to.
▶ n ❶ FEEL, feeling, sense of touch, tactile sense, tactility. ❷ TEXTURE, feel, grain, finish, surface, coating. ❸ BIT, trace, dash, taste, spot, drop, pinch, speck, smack, suggestion, hint, soupçon, tinge, whiff, suspicion; informal smidgen.

touching adj MOVING, impressive, affecting, warming, heart-warming.

touchy adj SENSITIVE, oversensitive, hypersensitive, thin-skinned, tetchy, testy, irascible, irritable, grouchy, grumpy, peevish, querulous, bad-tempered, captious, crabbed, cross, surly.

tough adj ❶ STRONG, durable, resistant, resilient, sturdy, firm, solid, hard, rigid, stiff. ❷ CHEWY, leathery, gristly, stringy, fibrous, sinewy. ❸ HARDY, strong, fit, sturdy, rugged, stalwart, vigorous, strapping, robust, resilient. ❹ DIFFICULT, hard, arduous, onerous, laborious, strenuous, exacting, taxing, stressful. ❺ FIRM, strict, stern, severe, harsh, hard-hitting, adamant, inflexible. ❻ UNFORTUNATE, unlucky, hard, regrettable; informal too bad.
– OPPOSITES tender, easy, lax.

toughen v STRENGTHEN, fortify, reinforce, harden.

tour n TRIP, excursion, journey, expedition, jaunt, outing, peregrination.
▶ v TRAVEL ROUND / THROUGH, explore, holiday in, go round, visit.

tourist n VISITOR, sightseer, holidaymaker, tripper.

tournament n COMPETITION, contest, series, meeting, event.

tout
■ **tout for** ASK FOR, solicit, seek, petition for, appeal for, beg for.

tow v PULL, draw, drag, haul, tug, trail, lug.

towering adj ❶ HIGH, tall, lofty, elevated, sky-high. ❷ OUTSTANDING, extraordinary, pre-eminent, superior, great, incom parable, unrivalled, peerless.

toxic adj POISONOUS, venomous, virulent, noxious.
– OPPOSITES harmless.

trace n ❶ MARK, sign, vestige, indication, evidence, remains, remnant. ❷ BIT, hint, suggestion, suspicion, trifle, dash, tinge, jot, iota.
▶ v FIND, discover, detect, unearth, uncover, track down, turn up, ferret out, hunt down; *informal* dig up.

track n ❶ MARK, trace, impression, footprint, trail, spoor, scent. ❷ COURSE, line, path, orbit, route, trajectory. ❸ PATH, trail, route, way.
▶ v FOLLOW, pursue, trail, trace, tail, shadow, stalk, dog.

trade n ❶ COMMERCE, buying and selling, dealing, trafficking, business, merchandising. ❷ LINE OF WORK, line, occupation, job, career, profession, craft, vocation, calling, work, employment.
▶ v ❶ BUY AND SELL, deal, traffic, market, merchandise. ❷ SWAP, exchange, switch, barter.

trader n MERCHANT, dealer, buyer, seller, marketer, merchandiser, broker, tradesman, tradeswoman.

tradition n CUSTOM, belief, practice, convention, ritual, observance, habit, institution, usage, praxis.

traditional adj CUSTOMARY, accustomed, conventional, established, ritual, ritualistic, habitual, set, fixed, routine, usual, old, time-honoured, historic, folk; *poetic/literary* wonted.

tragedy n DISASTER, calamity, catastrophe, misfortune, misadventure, affliction, adversity.

tragic adj ❶ DISASTROUS, calamitous, catastrophic, fatal, terrible, dreadful, appalling, dire, awful, miserable, wretched, unfortunate. ❷ SAD, unhappy, pathetic, moving, distressing, pitiful, piteous, melancholy, doleful, mournful, dismal, gloomy.
– OPPOSITES fortunate, happy.

trail n ❶ TRACK, scent, spoor, traces, marks, signs, footprints. ❷ PATH, pathway, footpath, track, road, route.
▶ v ❶ DRAG, sweep, dangle, hang down, droop. ❷ FOLLOW, pursue, track, trace, tail, shadow, stalk, dog. ❸ LOSE, be down, be behind.

train n ❶ PROCESSION, line, file, column, convoy, caravan. ❷ RETINUE, entourage, following, staff, household, followers, attendants.
▶ v ❶ INSTRUCT, teach, coach, tutor, give lessons to, school, educate, drill, prepare, ground, guide. ❷ EXERCISE, do exercises, work out, practise, prepare. ❸ AIM, point, focus, direct, level, line up.

trait n CHARACTERISTIC, attribute, feature, quality, property, idiosyncrasy, peculiarity, quirk.

traitor n BETRAYER, turncoat, double-crosser, double-dealer, renegade, defector, deserter, apostate, Judas, quisling, fifth columnist.

trample v TRAMP ON, tread on, walk over, stamp on, squash, crush, flatten.

trance n DAZE, stupor,

tranquil | transport

hypnotic state, dream, reverie, brown study.

tranquil adj PEACEFUL, restful, reposeful, calm, quiet, still, serene, placid, undisturbed.

tranquillizer n SEDATIVE, opiate; *informal* downer.
– OPPOSITES stimulant.

transaction n BUSINESS, deal, undertaking, affair, bargain, negotiation.

transcend v GO BEYOND, exceed, overstep, rise above, surpass, excel, be superior to, outdo, outstrip.

transfer v ❶ CONVEY, move, shift, remove, take, carry, transport. ❷ MAKE OVER, turn over, sign over, hand on, hand down, pass on, transmit, assign, delegate.

transform v CHANGE, alter, convert, metamorphose, revolutionize, transfigure, transmogrify, remodel, redo, reconstruct, rebuild, reorganize, rearrange, renew, translate, transmute.

transformation n CHANGE, alteration, conversion, metamorphosis, sea change, revolution, transfiguration, transmogrification, remodelling, reconstruction, reorganization, renewal, transmutation.

transgress v GO BEYOND, overstep, exceed, infringe, breach, break, contravene, violate, defy, disobey.

transient adj TRANSITORY, short-lived, short-term, impermanent, temporary, brief,

short, ephemeral, evanescent, momentary, fleeting, flying, passing.
– OPPOSITES permanent.

transit n MOVEMENT, transport, transportation, conveyance, haulage, travel, journeying, passage.

transition n CHANGE, transformation, conversion, metamorphosis, shift, switch, jump, leap, progression, gradation, development, evolution, transmutation.

translate v RENDER, interpret, paraphrase, reword, convert, decipher, decode, explain, elucidate.

transmission n ❶ SENDING, conveyance, transport, dispatch, remission. ❷ BROADCASTING, relaying, sending out. ❸ BROADCAST, programme.

transmit v ❶ SEND, convey, transport, dispatch, forward, remit. ❷ TRANSFER, pass on, hand on, communicate, impart, disseminate, spread, carry, diffuse. ❸ BROADCAST, relay, send out, put on air.

transparent adj ❶ CLEAR, see-through, translucent, pellucid, crystal-clear, crystalline, limpid, glassy, transpicuous. ❷ *See* OBVIOUS.
– OPPOSITES opaque.

transpire v COME ABOUT, take place, happen, occur, turn up, arise, chance; *poetic/literary* befall.

transport v CONVEY, take, transfer, move, shift, bring, fetch, carry, bear, haul, cart, run, ship.

▶ n TRANSPORTATION, conveyance, transit, carriage, freight.

transpose v INTERCHANGE, exchange, switch, swap, transfer, reverse, invert, rearrange, reorder.

transverse adj CROSSWISE, crossways, cross, athwart.

trap n SNARE, net, mesh, gin, ambush, pitfall, booby trap.
▶ v ❶ SNARE, ensnare, enmesh, entrap, catch, corner. ❷ TRICK, dupe, deceive, lure, inveigle, beguile.

trappings pl n ACCOUTREMENTS, appurtenances, appointments, trimmings, paraphernalia, fittings, equipment, apparatus, gear, adornment, ornamentation, decoration, finery, frippery, panoply.

trash n ❶ RUBBISH, waste, refuse, litter, garbage. ❷ RIFF-RAFF, scum, rabble, vermin, good-for-nothings.

traumatic adj PAINFUL, agonizing, shocking, scarring, disturbing, distressing, damaging, injurious, harmful.

travel v JOURNEY, take a trip, tour, voyage, cross, traverse, cover, wander, ramble, roam, rove.
▶ n TRAVELLING, journeying, touring.

traveller n TRIPPER, tourer, tourist, explorer, passenger, voyager, holidaymaker, sightseer, globetrotter.

traverse v CROSS, go across, travel over, journey over, make one's way across, pass over, wander, roam, range.

treacherous adj ❶ See TRAITOROUS. ❷ HAZARDOUS, dangerous, unsafe, flooded, icy, ice-covered, slippery.

tread v WALK, step, go, pace, march, tramp.

treason n BETRAYAL, treachery, disloyalty, faithlessness, sedition, subversion, mutiny, rebellion, lese-majesty.

treasure n RICHES, valuables, wealth, fortune, hoard, jewels, gems, coins, gold.
▶ v VALUE, prize, set great store by, think highly of, hold dear.

treat n SURPRISE, celebration, entertainment, amusement, diversion.
▶ v ❶ ACT TOWARDS, behave towards, deal with, handle, cope with, contend with, manage, use. ❷ REGARD, consider, view, look upon, deal with. ❸ GIVE TREATMENT TO, medicate, doctor, nurse, care for, attend to, minister to, cure, heal. ❹ APPLY TO, put on, use on, ply with. ❺ PAY FOR, buy for, pay/foot the bill for, stand, finance, entertain, take out.

treatise n DISCOURSE, exposition, disquisition, dissertation, thesis, study, essay, paper, monograph, tract, pamphlet.

treatment n ❶ ACTION, behaviour, conduct, handling, management, use, dealings. ❷ MEDICAL CARE, medication, medicament, therapy, doctoring, nursing, first aid, care, ministration.

treaty n AGREEMENT, pact, deal, compact, covenant, bargain, pledge, contract, alliance, concordat, convention, entente.

trek v TRAMP, hike, trudge, march, slog, footslog, plod, walk, ramble, roam, range, rove, travel, journey; *Brit. informal* yomp.
▶ n EXPEDITION, trip, journey, trudge, tramp, hike, march, slog, walk, odyssey.

tremble v SHAKE, quiver, shudder, judder, teeter, totter, wobble, rock, vibrate, oscillate.

tremendous adj ❶ GREAT, huge, enormous, immense, massive, vast, colossal, prodigious, stupendous, gigantic, gargantuan, mammoth. ❷ EXCELLENT, very good, great, marvellous, remarkable, extraordinary, exceptional, wonderful, incredible; *informal* super, fabulous, terrific, fantastic.

tremor n TREMBLE, shake, shaking, shiver, quiver, twitch, judder, spasm, paroxysm.

trend n ❶ TENDENCY, drift, course, direction, bearing, current, inclination, bias, leaning, bent. ❷ FASHION, vogue, style, mode, look, craze; *informal* fad.

trendy adj *see* FASHIONABLE.

trespass v INTRUDE, encroach, infringe, invade, obtrude.

trial n ❶ COURT CASE, case, hearing, inquiry, tribunal, litigation. ❷ TEST, try-out, trial/test run, check, assay, experiment; *informal* dry run. ❸ NUISANCE, pest, bother, worry, vexation, annoyance, irritant, irritation,

bane, affliction, curse, burden, cross to bear; *informal* pain in the neck, hassle.

tribe n ETHNIC GROUP, family, dynasty, clan, sect.

tribute n ❶ ACCOLADE, commendation, testimonial, paean, eulogy, panegyric, encomium, applause, praise, homage, honour, exaltation, extolment, glorification, congratulations, compliments, bouquets; *formal* laudation.

trick n ❶ STRATAGEM, ploy, artifice, ruse, dodge, wile, device, manoeuvre, deceit, deception, subterfuge, swindle, fraud; *informal* con. ❷ KNACK, art, gift, talent, technique, ability, skill, expertise; *informal* know-how. ❸ HOAX, practical joke, joke, prank, jape, antic, caper, frolic, lark, gambol; *informal* leg-pull, gag, put-on.
▶ v DECEIVE, delude, mislead, take in, cheat, hoodwink, fool, outwit, dupe, hoax, gull, defraud, swindle; *informal* con, pull a fast one on, put one over on; *poetic/literary* cozen.

trickery n DECEIT, deception, cheating, subterfuge, guile, artifice, wiliness, craftiness, chicanery, dishonesty, fraud, swindling, imposture, double-dealing, duplicity; *informal* monkey/funny business, hanky-panky; *Brit. informal* jiggery-pokery.
– OPPOSITES honesty.

trickle v DRIP, dribble, leak, ooze, seep, exude, percolate.
– OPPOSITES pour, gush.

tricky adj ❶ DIFFICULT, problematic, awkward, delicate, sensitive, ticklish, thorny, knotty, touchy, risky. ❷ CUNNING, crafty, wily, artful, devious, scheming, sly, slippery, subtle, deceitful, deceptive; *informal* foxy.
– OPPOSITES straightforward, honest.

trim adj NEAT, tidy, neat and tidy, smart, spruce, well groomed, well dressed, well turned out, dapper, elegant; *informal* natty.
– OPPOSITES untidy.
▶ v CUT, clip, snip, shear, prune, pare, even up, neaten, tidy up.

trip n ❶ EXCURSION, tour, expedition, voyage, jaunt, outing, run. ❷ HALLUCINATION, drug experience, vision.
▶ v ❶ STUMBLE, lose one's footing/balance, stagger, slip, slide, misstep, fall, tumble. ❷ SKIP, dance, hop, prance, bound, spring, gambol, caper, frisk, cavort, waltz.

triumph n ❶ CONQUEST, victory, win, ascendancy, mastery, success; *informal* walkover. ❷ EXULTATION, jubilation, jubilance, elation, rejoicing, joy, joyfulness, pride.
– OPPOSITES failure, despair.
▶ v WIN, succeed, come first, be the victor, be victorious, gain a victory, carry the day, take the honours/prize/crown.

triumphant adj ❶ WINNING, victorious, successful, undefeated, unbeaten. ❷ EXULTANT, jubilant, elated, rejoicing,

joyful, joyous, proud, cock-a-hoop, gloating, boastful.
– OPPOSITES unsuccessful, despondent.

trivial adj UNIMPORTANT, insignificant, inconsequential, flimsy, insubstantial, petty, minor, of no account/matter, negligible, paltry, trifling, foolish, worthless; *informal* piddling.
– OPPOSITES significant.

troops pl n ARMED FORCES, army, military, services, soldiers, soldiery, fighting men/women.

trouble n ❶ PROBLEMS, worry, bother, anxiety, disquiet, unease, irritation, vexation, inconvenience, annoyance, agitation, harassment, difficulty, distress. ❷ DIFFICULTY, misfortune, adversity, hardship, bad luck, distress, pain, suffering, affliction, torment, woe, grief, unhappiness, sadness, heartache. ❸ BOTHER, inconvenience, disturbance, fuss, effort, exertion, work, labour, attention, care, thoughtfulness; *informal* hassle. ❹ DISORDER, disease, illness, dysfunction. ❺ DISTURBANCE, disorder, unrest, fighting, strife, conflict, tumult, commotion, turbulence, law-breaking.
▶ v ❶ WORRY, bother, disturb, annoy, irritate, vex, irk, fret, pester, torment, plague, inconvenience, upset, perturb, agitate, discompose, harass, distress; *informal* hassle. ❷ TAKE THE TROUBLE / TIME, bother, make the effort, exert/disturb oneself, go out of one's way.

troublemaker n MISCHIEF-

MAKER, agitator, instigator, rabble-rouser, demagogue.

troublesome adj ❶ WORRYING, worrisome, bothersome, tiresome, disturbing, annoying, irritating, irksome, upsetting, perturbing, harassing, distressing, difficult, problematic, demanding, taxing.

truancy n ABSENTEEISM, absence, French leave, shirking, malingering; informal bunking off; Brit. informal skiving.

truant n ABSENTEE, dodger, malingerer, shirker, deserter; Brit. informal skiver.
▶ v STAY AWAY FROM SCHOOL, play truant; Brit. informal skive (off), bunk off; N. Amer. informal play hookey, goof off.

truce n CEASE-FIRE, armistice, suspension/cessation of hostilities, peace, respite, moratorium.

true adj ❶ TRUTHFUL, accurate, correct, right, valid, factual, exact, precise, faithful, genuine, reliable, honest; formal veracious. ❷ REAL, genuine, authentic, actual, bona fide, valid, legitimate; informal honest-to-goodness. ❸ LOYAL, faithful, trustworthy, trusty, reliable, dependable, staunch, firm, fast, steady, constant, unswerving, unwavering, devoted, sincere, dedicated, supportive, dutiful.
– OPPOSITES untrue, false.

trump v SURPASS, outperform, outdo.
■ **trump up** INVENT, make up, fabricate, devise, concoct,

hatch, contrive, fake; informal cook up.

trust n ❶ FAITH, confidence, belief, conviction, credence, assurance, certainty, reliance, hope, expectation. ❷ RESPONSIBILITY, duty, obligation, commitment.
▶ v ❶ PUT / PLACE ONE'S TRUST IN, have faith/confidence in, be convinced of, pin one's hopes on. ❷ HOPE, assume, presume, expect, believe, suppose.
– OPPOSITES distrust.

trustful adj TRUSTING, unsuspicious, unguarded, unwary, unsuspecting, unquestioning, credulous, gullible, ingenuous, naive, innocent.
– OPPOSITES suspicious.

trustworthy adj RELIABLE, dependable, stable, staunch, loyal, faithful, trusty, responsible, sensible, level-headed, honest, honourable, upright, ethical, righteous, principled, virtuous.
– OPPOSITES untrustworthy.

truth n ❶ TRUTHFULNESS, accuracy, correctness, rightness, validity, fact, factualness, factuality, genuineness, veracity, verity, honesty. ❷ REALITY, actuality, factuality.
– OPPOSITES falsehood, fiction.

truthful adj ❶ HONEST, trustworthy, candid, frank, open, forthright, straight; formal veracious. ❷ TRUE, accurate, correct, right, valid, factual, exact, faithful, precise, genuine, reliable, honest; formal veracious.
– OPPOSITES untruthful, inaccurate.

try v ❶ ATTEMPT, aim, endeavour, make an effort, exert oneself, undertake, strive, assay, seek, struggle, do one's best; *informal* have a go/shot/crack/stab. ❷ TRY OUT, test, put to the test, experiment with, assay, investigate, examine, appraise, evaluate, assess, experience, sample; *informal* check out.

trying adj TROUBLESOME, bothersome, tiresome, irksome, vexatious, annoying, irritating, exasperating.

tuck v GATHER, push, ease, insert, stuff.

tug v PULL, jerk, yank, wrench, drag, draw.

tumble v FALL OVER, fall down, fall headlong, topple, fall head over heels, fall end over end, lose one's footing/balance, stumble, stagger, trip up.
– OPPOSITES rise.

tumbledown adj DILAPIDATED, ramshackle, crumbling, disintegrating, falling to pieces/bits, decrepit, ruined, in ruins, rickety, shaky, tottering, teetering.

tumour n LUMP, growth, cancer, cancerous growth, malignant growth, malignancy.

tumult n DIN, uproar, commotion, racket, hubbub, hullabaloo, clamour, shouting, yelling, pandemonium, babel, bedlam, noise.
– OPPOSITES tranquillity.

tumultuous adj LOUD, noisy, clamorous, ear-shattering, deafening, ear-piercing, blaring, uproarious, unrestrained, boisterous, rowdy, unruly, disorderly, fierce, obstreperous, wild, violent.

tune n MELODY, air, song, theme, strain, motif.

tunnel n UNDERGROUND / SUBTERRANEAN PASSAGE, underpass, subway, burrow.
▶ v DIG, excavate, burrow, mine, penetrate.

turbulent adj ❶ TEMPESTUOUS, stormy, raging, foaming, rough, choppy, agitated. ❷ DISTURBED, agitated, unsettled, unstable, troubled, distraught, in turmoil.
– OPPOSITES peaceful.

turgid adj BOMBASTIC, high-flown, high-sounding, rhetorical, oratorical, grandiloquent, magniloquent, extravagant, pretentious, pompous, flowery, fulsome, orotund, fustian.
– OPPOSITES simple.

turmoil n AGITATION, ferment, confusion, disorder, disarray, upheaval, chaos, pandemonium, bedlam, tumult.
– OPPOSITES peace.

turn v ❶ GO ROUND, rotate, revolve, circle, roll, spin, wheel, whirl, twirl, gyrate, swivel, pivot. ❷ TURN ROUND, change direction/course, go back, return, reverse direction, make a U-turn. ❸ TURN OVER, reverse, invert, flip over, turn topsyturvy. ❹ CHANGE, alter, transform, metamorphose, mutate. ❺ BECOME, come to be, get, go. ❻ GO / TURN SOUR, sour, curdle, become rancid, go bad, go off.
▶ n ❶ ROTATION, revolution,

circle, spin, whirl, twirl, gyration, swivel. ❷ TURNING, bend, curve, corner, twist, winding. ❸ TIME, opportunity, chance, stint, spell, move, try, attempt; *informal* go, shot, crack.

■ **turn down** *see* REJECT v (1).

turn up ❶ INCREASE, raise, amplify, make louder, intensify. ❷ ARRIVE, appear, put in an appearance, present oneself, be present; *informal* show up.

turnover n ❶ (GROSS) REVENUE, income, volume of business, business, financial flow. ❷ RATE OF REPLACEMENT, change, movement.

tutor v TEACH, instruct, coach, educate, school, train, drill, direct, guide.

twig n BRANCH, stick, offshoot, shoot, spray, stem.

twilight n DUSK, late afternoon, early evening, gloaming; *poetic/literary* crepuscule.

twin n DOUBLE, lookalike, image, duplicate, clone; *informal* spitting image, spit, dead spit, dead ringer.

▶ v JOIN, link, couple, pair, yoke.

twinge n STAB OF PAIN, spasm, pain, pang, ache, throb, tweak, tingle, cramp, stitch.

twist v ❶ BEND, warp, misshape, deform, contort, distort, wrench, wrest. ❷ WRENCH, turn, sprain, rick. ❸ WIND, curve, bend, twine, zigzag, meander, snake, worm. ❹ DISTORT, pervert, warp, garble, misrepre-

sent, falsify, misquote, misreport, change, alter.

▶ n ❶ BEND, warp, kink, deformity, contortion, distortion. ❷ WRENCH, turn, sprain, rick. ❸ DEVELOPMENT, turn, change, alteration, variation, slant.

twitch v JERK, jump, quiver, shiver, quaver.

▶ n SPASM, jerk, jump, quiver, tremor, shiver, quaver.

type n ❶ KIND, sort, variety, form, class, classification, category, group, order, set, genre, strain, species, genus, ilk. ❷ PRINT, fount, face, character.

typical adj ❶ REPRESENTATIVE, classic, standard, stock, orthodox, conventional, true to type, quintessential, archetypal. ❷ NORMAL, average, ordinary, regular, general, customary, habitual, routine. ❸ CHARACTERISTIC, in character, in keeping, to be expected.

– OPPOSITES atypical.

typify v EXEMPLIFY, characterize, personify, epitomize, symbolize, embody.

tyrannical adj DESPOTIC, autocratic, dictatorial, authoritarian, high-handed, imperious, oppressive, coercive, domineering, bullying, harsh, strict, severe, cruel, brutal, unjust.

tyrant n DESPOT, autocrat, dictator, absolute ruler, authoritarian, oppressor, martinet, slave-driver, bully.

Uu

ubiquitous adj EVERYWHERE, omnipresent, ever-present, all-over, pervasive, universal.
– OPPOSITES rare.

ugly adj ❶ UNATTRACTIVE, plain, homely, ill-favoured, unprepossessing, hideous, unlovely, unsightly, grotesque, horrible, horrid, frightful, vile, shocking, distasteful, disgusting, revolting; *informal* not much to look at. ❷ THREATENING, menacing, ominous, sinister, dangerous, nasty, unpleasant, disagreeable.
– OPPOSITES beautiful.

ulterior adj HIDDEN, concealed, unrevealed, undisclosed, secret, covert, unapparent.
– OPPOSITES overt.

ultimate adj LAST, final, eventual, concluding, conclusive, terminal, end, furthest.

umpire n ADJUDICATOR, arbitrator, arbiter, judge, moderator, referee; *informal* ref.

unable adj NOT ABLE, incapable, powerless, impotent, not up/equal to, inadequate, ineffectual, incompetent.
– OPPOSITES able.

unacceptable adj UNSATISFACTORY, inadmissible, unsuitable, insupportable, intolerable, objectionable, offensive, obnoxious, undesirable, disagreeable, distasteful, improper.
– OPPOSITES acceptable.

unaccompanied adj ALONE, on one's own, by oneself, solo, lone, solitary, single.

unaccustomed adj UNUSED, not used, new, unpractised, unfamiliar, inexperienced, unversed.

unanimous adj IN COMPLETE AGREEMENT / ACCORD, of one mind, like-minded, in harmony, at one, of a piece, with one voice, united, concordant.
– OPPOSITES divided.

unassailable adj IMPREGNABLE, invulnerable, invincible, secure, well defended.
– OPPOSITES defenceless.

unassuming adj see MODEST (1).

unattached adj UNMARRIED, unwed, unwedded, uncommitted, free, available, single, on one's own, by oneself, unescorted.
– OPPOSITES married.

unauthorized adj UNOFFICIAL, unsanctioned, uncertified, unaccredited, unlicensed, unwarranted, unapproved, disallowed, prohibited, forbidden, illegal.
– OPPOSITES official.

unavoidable adj INESCAP-

ABLE, inevitable, bound to happen, inexorable, ineluctable, certain, fated, predestined, necessary, compulsory, required, obligatory, mandatory.

unaware adj UNKNOWING, unconscious, ignorant, heedless, unmindful, oblivious, uninformed, unenlightened; *informal* in the dark.
– OPPOSITES conscious.

unbelievable adj BEYOND BELIEF, incredible, unconvincing, far-fetched, implausible, improbable, inconceivable, unthinkable, unimaginable, impossible, astonishing, astounding, staggering, preposterous.
– OPPOSITES credible.

unbending adj see INFLEXIBLE (3).

unbiased adj IMPARTIAL, unprejudiced, non-partisan, neutral, objective, disinterested, dispassionate, detached, even-handed, open-minded, equitable, fair, fair-minded, just.
– OPPOSITES prejudiced.

unbreakable adj see INDESTRUCTIBLE.

uncertain adj ❶ UNKNOWN, undetermined, unsettled, in the balance, up in the air. ❷ UNSURE, doubtful, dubious, undecided, unresolved, indecisive, irresolute, hesitant, wavering, vacillating, equivocating, vague, hazy, unclear, ambivalent, in two minds. ❸ HESITANT, hesitating, tentative, halting, unsure, unconfident.
– OPPOSITES predictable, sure, confident.

uncharted adj UNMAPPED, unsurveyed, unexplored, unplumbed, unfamiliar, unknown, strange.

uncivilized adj ❶ BARBARIAN, barbarous, barbaric, primitive, savage, wild. ❷ UNCOUTH, coarse, rough, boorish, vulgar, philistine, uneducated, uncultured, uncultivated, unsophisticated, unrefined, unpolished.

unclean adj see DIRTY adj (1).

uncomfortable adj UNEASY, ill at ease, nervous, tense, edgy, self-conscious, awkward, embarrassed, discomfited, disturbed, troubled, worried, anxious, apprehensive.
– OPPOSITES relaxed.

uncommon adj see UNUSUAL.

uncompromising adj INFLEXIBLE, unbending, unyielding, hard-line, tough, immovable, firm, determined, dogged, obstinate, obdurate, tenacious, relentless, implacable, inexorable, intransigent.
– OPPOSITES flexible.

unconcerned adj see INDIFFERENT (1).

unconditional adj COMPLETE, total, entire, full, absolute, downright, utter, all-out, thoroughgoing, unequivocal, conclusive, definite, positive, indubitable.

unconscious adj ❶ SENSELESS, insensible, comatose,

knocked out, stunned, dazed; *informal* out like a light, out cold, out. ❷ UNAWARE, heedless, ignorant, in ignorance, oblivious, insensible. ❸ UNINTENTIONAL, unintended, accidental, unthinking, unwitting, inadvertent, unpremeditated.
– OPPOSITES aware.

unconventional adj UNORTHODOX, irregular, unusual, uncommon, unwonted, rare, out of the ordinary, atypical, singular, individual, individualistic, different, original, idiosyncratic, nonconformist, bohemian, eccentric, odd.
– OPPOSITES orthodox.

uncouth adj ROUGH, coarse, uncivilized, uncultured, uncultivated, unrefined, unpolished, unsophisticated, crude, gross, loutish, boorish, oafish, rude, impolite, discourteous, unmannerly, bad-mannered, ill-bred, vulgar.
– OPPOSITES refined.

uncover v ❶ EXPOSE, lay bare, bare, reveal, unwrap. ❷ See DISCOVER (1).

undaunted adj UNAFRAID, unflinching, indomitable, resolute, intrepid, bold, valiant, brave, courageous.
– OPPOSITES fearful.

undemonstrative adj UNEMOTIONAL, impassive, restrained, self-contained, reserved, uncommunicative, unresponsive, stiff.

underestimate v ❶ MISCALCULATE, misjudge, set too low.

❷ UNDERRATE, rate too low, undervalue, set little store by, not do justice to.

undergo v GO THROUGH, experience, sustain, endure, bear, tolerate, stand, withstand, put up with, weather.

underground adj ❶ SUBTERRANEAN, below ground, buried, sunken. ❷ SECRET, clandestine, surreptitious, covert, undercover, concealed, hidden.

underhand adj DECEITFUL, devious, sneaky, furtive, surreptitious, covert, dishonest, dishonourable, unscrupulous, fraudulent.
– OPPOSITES honest.

undermine v ❶ WEAKEN, impair, damage, injure, sap, threaten, subvert, sabotage. ❷ TUNNEL UNDER, dig under, burrow under, excavate.
– OPPOSITES support.

underprivileged adj DISADVANTAGED, deprived, in need, needy, in want, destitute, poor, impoverished, impecunious.
– OPPOSITES wealthy.

understand v ❶ COMPREHEND, apprehend, grasp, see, take in, perceive, discern, make out, glean, recognize, appreciate, get to know, follow, fathom; *informal* get the hang/drift of, catch on, latch on to, tumble to, figure out; *Brit. informal* twig. ❷ APPRECIATE, accept, commiserate with, feel compassionate towards, sympathize with, empathize with. ❸ GATHER, hear,

be informed, learn, believe, think, conclude.
– OPPOSITES misunderstand.

understanding n ❶ COMPREHENSION, apprehension, grasp, perception, discernment, appreciation, interpretation. ❷ INTELLIGENCE, intellect, mind, brainpower, brains, powers of reasoning; *informal* grey matter. ❸ COMPASSION, sympathy, empathy, insight. ❹ AGREEMENT, gentleman's agreement, arrangement, bargain, pact, compact, contract.
▶ adj COMPASSIONATE, sympathetic, sensitive, considerate, kind, thoughtful, tolerant, patient, forbearing.

understate v DOWNPLAY, play down, make light of, minimize; *informal* soft-pedal.
– OPPOSITES exaggerate.

undertake v TAKE ON, set about, tackle, shoulder, assume, enter upon, begin, start, commence, embark on, venture upon, attempt, try.

undertone n ❶ LOW TONE / VOICE, murmur, whisper. ❷ UNDERCURRENT, hint, suggestion, intimation, insinuation, trace, tinge, touch, atmosphere, aura, tenor, flavour.

undervalue v *see* UNDERESTIMATE (2).

underwear n UNDERCLOTHES, undergarments, underclothing, lingerie; *informal* undies, unmentionables; *Brit. informal* smalls.

undesirable adj UNWANTED, unwished for, unpleasant, disagreeable, nasty, unacceptable.

undisciplined adj ❶ UNRULY, disorderly, disobedient, obstreperous, recalcitrant, refractory, uncontrolled, unrestrained, wild, wilful, wayward. ❷ UNSYSTEMATIC, unmethodical, disorganized, unorganized.

undisguised adj OPEN, obvious, evident, patent, manifest, transparent, overt, unconcealed, unmistakable.

undistinguished adj *see* ORDINARY (2).

undo v ❶ UNFASTEN, unhook, unbutton, untie, unlace, loosen, disentangle, release, free, open, unlock. ❷ DESTROY, ruin, wreck, smash, shatter, annihilate, obliterate, overturn.

undoubted adj UNDISPUTED, not in doubt, uncontested, unquestioned, not in question, certain, unquestionable, indubitable, incontrovertible, irrefutable.

undress v TAKE OFF ONE'S CLOTHES, remove one's clothes, strip, disrobe; *Brit. informal* peel off.

undue adj UNWARRANTED, unjustified, unreasonable, inappropriate, unsuitable, improper, ill-advised, excessive, immoderate.
– OPPOSITES appropriate.

undying adj *see* ETERNAL.

uneasy adj ILL AT EASE, troubled, worried, anxious, apprehensive, alarmed, disturbed, agitated, nervous, nervy, on edge, edgy, restive, restless, unsettled.

discomposed, discomfited, perturbed, upset; *informal* jittery.
– OPPOSITES calm.

unemotional adj UNDEMONSTRATIVE, passionless, cold, frigid, cool, reserved, restrained, unfeeling, unresponsive, unexcitable, unmoved, impassive, apathetic, indifferent, phlegmatic, detached.

unemployed adj JOBLESS, out of work, out of a job, workless, redundant, laid off, idle; *Brit. informal* on the dole.

unequal adj ❶ DIFFERENT, differing, dissimilar, unlike, unalike, disparate, varying, variable. ❷ UNEVEN, asymmetrical, unsymmetrical, unbalanced, lopsided, irregular, disproportionate. ❸ UNFAIR, unjust, inequitable, uneven, one-sided, ill-matched.
– OPPOSITES identical, fair.

unequivocal adj UNAMBIGUOUS, clear, clear-cut, plain, explicit, unqualified, categorical, direct, straightforward, blunt, point-blank, straight from the shoulder, positive, certain, decisive.
– OPPOSITES ambiguous.

unethical adj *see* IMMORAL.

uneven adj ❶ ROUGH, bumpy, lumpy. ❷ VARIABLE, varying, changeable, irregular, erratic, patchy. ❸ UNEQUAL, asymmetrical, unsymmetrical, unbalanced, lopsided, irregular, disproportionate.
– OPPOSITES flat, regular, equal.

uneventful adj UNEXCITING, uninteresting, monotonous, boring, dull, tedious, routine, ordinary, run-of-the-mill, pedestrian, commonplace, everyday, unexceptional, unremarkable.
– OPPOSITES exciting.

unexpected adj UNFORESEEN, unanticipated, unpredicted, not bargained for, sudden, abrupt, surprising, startling, astonishing, out of the blue, chance, fortuitous.
– OPPOSITES predictable.

unfair adj ❶ UNJUST, inequitable, partial, partisan, prejudiced, biased, one-sided. ❷ UNDESERVED, unmerited, uncalled for, unreasonable, unjustifiable, unwarrantable, out of proportion, disproportionate, excessive, extreme, immoderate.
– OPPOSITES just, justified.

unfaithful adj ❶ DISLOYAL, false-hearted, faithless, perfidious, treacherous, traitorous. ❷ ADULTEROUS, fickle, untrue, inconstant; *informal* two-timing.
– OPPOSITES loyal.

unfamiliar adj UNKNOWN, new, strange, alien, unaccustomed, uncommon.

unfashionable adj OUT OF FASHION / DATE, old-fashioned, outmoded, outdated, dated, behind the times, passé, archaic, obsolete, antiquated.

unfasten v *see* UNDO (1).

unfavourable adj ❶ ADVERSE, critical, hostile, inimical, unfriendly, negative,

discouraging, poor, bad. ❷ DISADVANTAGEOUS, adverse, unfortunate, unhappy, detrimental.
– OPPOSITES positive.

unfeeling adj *see* CALLOUS.

unfit adj ❶ UNSUITED, ill-suited, unsuitable, unqualified, ineligible, unequipped, unprepared, untrained, incapable, inadequate, incompetent, not up to, not equal to. ❷ OUT OF CONDITION, in poor condition/shape, flabby, unhealthy, debilitated, weak.
– OPPOSITES suitable.

unfold v OPEN OUT, spread out, stretch out, flatten, straighten out, unfurl, unroll, unravel.

unforgivable adj INEXCUSABLE, unpardonable, unjustifiable, indefensible, reprehensible, deplorable, despicable, contemptible, disgraceful, shameful.
– OPPOSITES venial.

unfortunate adj UNLUCKY, out of luck, luckless, ill-starred, star-crossed, hapless, wretched, miserable, unhappy, poor.

unfriendly adj UNCONGENIAL, unsociable, inhospitable, unneighbourly, unsympathetic, aloof, cold, cool, distant, disagreeable, unpleasant, surly, sour, hostile, inimical, antagonistic, aggressive, quarrelsome.

ungainly adj *see* AWKWARD.

ungrateful adj UNTHANKFUL, unappreciative, impolite, uncivil, rude.

unhappy adj ❶ SAD, miserable, sorrowful, dejected, despondent, disconsolate, broken-hearted, down, downcast, dispirited, crestfallen, depressed, melancholy, blue, gloomy, glum, mournful, woebegone. ❷ UNFORTUNATE, regrettable, inappropriate, unsuitable, inapt, tactless, ill-advised, injudicious.

unhealthy adj ❶ IN POOR HEALTH, unwell, ill, ailing, sick, sickly, poorly, indisposed, unsound, weak, feeble, frail, delicate, debilitated, infirm.
❷ UNWHOLESOME, unnourishing, detrimental, injurious, damaging, deleterious, noxious.

unheard of adj ❶ UNPRECEDENTED, exceptional, extraordinary, undreamed of, unbelievable, inconceivable, unimaginable, unthinkable. ❷ UNKNOWN, unfamiliar, new.
– OPPOSITES common, well known.

unhurried adj LEISURELY, leisured, easy, slow, slow-moving, deliberate, sedate.
– OPPOSITES hasty.

unidentified adj NAMELESS, unnamed, unknown, anonymous, incognito, obscure, unmarked, undesignated, unclassified.

uniform adj ❶ CONSTANT, consistent, invariable, unvarying, unvaried, unchanging, undeviating, stable, regular, even, equal. ❷ SAME, alike, like, selfsame, identical, similar, equal.
– OPPOSITES variable.

▶ n LIVERY, regalia, dress, regimentals.

unify v UNITE, bring together, merge, fuse, amalgamate, coalesce, combine, blend, mix, bind, link up, consolidate.
– OPPOSITES separate.

unimaginable adj UNTHINKABLE, inconceivable, incredible, unbelievable, unheard of, unthought of, implausible, improbable, unlikely, impossible, undreamed of, fantastic; *informal* mind-boggling, mind-blowing.

unimportant adj OF LITTLE / NO IMPORTANCE, insignificant, of no consequence, inconsequential, of no account, immaterial, irrelevant, not worth mentioning, minor, slight, trivial, petty, paltry, insubstantial, inferior, worthless, nugatory; *informal* no great shakes; *N. Amer. informal* dinky.

uninhabited adj VACANT, empty, unoccupied, unpopulated, unpeopled, unsettled, abandoned, deserted, forsaken, barren, desert, desolate.

uninhibited adj UNSELFCONSCIOUS, spontaneous, free and easy, relaxed, informal, open, candid, outspoken, unrestrained, unrepressed, unconstrained, uncontrolled, uncurbed, unchecked, unbridled.
– OPPOSITES repressed.

unintelligible adj *see* INCOMPREHENSIBLE.

unintentional adj UNINTENDED, accidental, inadvertent, unplanned, unpremeditated, uncalculated, chance, fortuitous, unconscious, involuntary, unwitting, unthinking.
– OPPOSITES deliberate.

uninterested adj INDIFFERENT, unconcerned, uninvolved, apathetic, unresponsive, impassive, dispassionate, aloof, detached, distant.

uninteresting adj UNEXCITING, dull, boring, tiresome, wearisome, tedious, dreary, flat, monotonous, humdrum, commonplace, pedestrian, prosaic, hackneyed, stale.
– OPPOSITES interesting.

uninterrupted adj UNBROKEN, undisturbed, continuous, continual, constant, steady, sustained, non-stop, unending, endless, incessant, interminable, unremitting.

union n ❶ JOINING, junction, merger, fusion, amalgamation, blend, mixture, coalition, combining, combination, consolidation, confederation. ❷ ASSOCIATION, alliance, league, coalition, consortium, syndicate, guild, confederation, federation, confederacy. ❸ MARRIAGE, wedding, wedlock.
– OPPOSITES separation.

unique adj ❶ ONLY, one and only, single, sole, lone, solitary, exclusive. ❷ UNEQUALLED, without equal, unparalleled, unmatched, matchless, peerless, unsurpassed, unexcelled, incomparable, inimitable, second to none.

unit n ❶ ENTITY, whole. ❷ COMPONENT, part, section, element, constituent, subdivision, portion, segment, module, item, member.

unite v ❶ JOIN, link, connect, combine, amalgamate, fuse, weld. ❷ COMBINE, mix, commix, blend, mingle, homogenize; *technical* admix. ❸ JOIN TOGETHER, join forces, combine, amalgamate, band/club together, cooperate, work/pull together, pool resources.
– OPPOSITES separate.

united adj ❶ COMBINED, amalgamated, allied, cooperative, concerted, collective, pooled. ❷ IN AGREEMENT, agreed, in unison, of the same opinion/mind, of like mind, like-minded, at one, in accord, unanimous.

unity n AGREEMENT, harmony, accord, concurrence, unanimity, consensus, concert, togetherness, solidarity; *formal* concord.
– OPPOSITES disunity.

universal adj GENERAL, all-embracing, all-inclusive, comprehensive, across the board, worldwide, global, widespread, common, predominant, preponderant, omnipresent, ubiquitous, catholic.
– OPPOSITES particular.

unjust adj ❶ UNFAIR, inequitable, prejudiced, biased, partisan, partial, one-sided. ❷ UNDESERVED, unmerited, unwarranted, uncalled for, unreasonable, unjustifiable.
– OPPOSITES fair.

unjustifiable adj INDEFENSIBLE, inexcusable, unforgivable,

unpardonable, uncalled for, unreasonable, blameworthy, culpable, unwarrantable.
– OPPOSITES justifiable.

unkempt adj UNTIDY, dishevelled, disordered, tousled, rumpled, windblown, scruffy, slovenly, sloppy.
– OPPOSITES neat.

unkind adj MEAN, cruel, vicious, spiteful, malicious, malevolent, harsh, pitiless, ruthless, unsympathetic, unfeeling, hard-hearted, heartless, cold-hearted, unfriendly, unkindly, unamiable, uncharitable, unchristian, inhospitable, ungenerous, nasty.
– OPPOSITES kind.

unknown adj ❶ UNREVEALED, undisclosed, undetermined, unsettled, unascertained, in the balance, up in the air. ❷ UNIDENTIFIED, unnamed, nameless, anonymous, incognito, unheard of, little known, obscure. ❸ UNFAMILIAR, unexplored, uncharted, untravelled, undiscovered.
– OPPOSITES familiar.

unlawful adj *see* ILLEGAL.

unlikely adj ❶ IMPROBABLE, doubtful, dubious, faint, slight, remote. ❷ IMPLAUSIBLE, questionable, improbable, unconvincing, incredible, unbelievable, inconceivable.
– OPPOSITES probable, believable.

unlimited adj ❶ UNRESTRICTED, unconstrained, uncontrolled, unrestrained, unchecked, unhindered, unhampered,

unimpeded, unfettered, untrammelled. **2** LIMITLESS, boundless, unbounded, immense, extensive, immeasurable, incalculable, untold, infinite.
– OPPOSITES restricted, finite.

unloved adj UNWANTED, unpopular, forsaken, rejected, jilted, disliked, hated, detested, loathed.

unlucky adj **1** LUCKLESS, out of luck, down on one's luck, unfortunate, hapless, ill-fated, ill-starred. **2** UNSUCCESSFUL, failed, ill-fated.
– OPPOSITES fortunate.

unmarried adj SINGLE, unwed, unwedded, divorced, unattached, bachelor, celibate, husbandless, wifeless.

unmistakable adj see OBVIOUS.

unmitigated adj see ABSOLUTE.

unnatural adj **1** UNUSUAL, uncommon, extraordinary, strange, queer, odd, bizarre, preternatural. **2** INHUMAN, heartless, uncaring, unconcerned, unfeeling, soulless, cold, hard, hard-hearted, callous, cruel, brutal, merciless, pitiless, remorseless, evil, wicked. **3** AFFECTED, artificial, feigned, false, self-conscious, contrived, forced, laboured, studied, strained, insincere, theatrical, stagy, mannered.
– OPPOSITES natural.

unnecessary adj NEEDLESS, unneeded, inessential, non-essential, uncalled for, unrequired, gratuitous, useless,

dispensable, expendable, redundant, superfluous.
– OPPOSITES necessary, essential.

unobtrusive adj see INCONSPICUOUS.

unofficial adj **1** INFORMAL, casual, unauthorized, unsanctioned, unaccredited. **2** UNCONFIRMED, unauthenticated, uncorroborated, unsubstantiated.

unorthodox adj **1** HETERODOX, uncanonical, heretical, nonconformist. **2** See UNCONVENTIONAL.
– OPPOSITES conventional.

unpalatable adj UNSAVOURY, unappetizing, uneatable, inedible, nasty, disgusting, repugnant, revolting, nauseating, sickening, distasteful, disagreeable, unpleasant.
– OPPOSITES tasty.

unparalleled adj WITHOUT PARALLEL, unequalled, without equal, matchless, unmatched, peerless, unrivalled, unprecedented.

unpleasant adj **1** DISGUSTING, unpalatable, unsavoury, unappetizing, repugnant, revolting, nauseating, sickening. **2** UNLIKEABLE, disagreeable, unlovable, unattractive, nasty, ill-natured, cross, bad-tempered. **3** DISAGREEABLE, irksome, troublesome, annoying, irritating, vexatious.
– OPPOSITES agreeable, likable.

unpopular adj DISLIKED, unliked, unloved, friendless,

unwanted, unwelcome, avoided, ignored, rejected, shunned, out in the cold, cold-shouldered, unattractive, undesirable, out of favour.

unpredictable adj ERRATIC, fickle, capricious, whimsical, mercurial, volatile, unstable, undependable, unreliable.

unpremeditated adj UNPLANNED, unintentional, extempore, impromptu, ad lib, spontaneous, spur of the moment, on the spot, impulsive, hasty; informal off the cuff.
– OPPOSITES planned.

unpretentious adj SIMPLE, plain, ordinary, humble, unostentatious, unassuming, modest, unaffected, natural, straightforward, honest.
– OPPOSITES pretentious.

unprofessional adj AMATEUR, amateurish, unskilled, inexpert, untrained, unqualified, inexperienced, incompetent.
– OPPOSITES professional.

unpromising adj UNFAVOURABLE, adverse, unpropitious, inauspicious, gloomy, black, discouraging, portentous, ominous.
– OPPOSITES auspicious.

unquestionable adj BEYOND QUESTION / DOUBT, indubitable, undoubted, indisputable, undeniable, irrefutable, incontestable, incontrovertible, certain, sure, definite, positive, conclusive, self-evident, obvious.

unravel v ❶ UNTANGLE, disentangle, unwind, straighten out,

separate out, unknot, undo. ❷ SOLVE, resolve, work out, clear up, puzzle out, get to the bottom of, fathom; informal figure out.
– OPPOSITES entangle.

unreal adj IMAGINARY, make-believe, fictitious, mythical, fanciful, fantastic, fabulous, hypothetical, non-existent, illusory, chimerical, phantasmagoric.

unrealistic adj IMPRACTICAL, impracticable, unworkable, unreasonable, irrational, illogical, improbable, foolish, wild, absurd, quixotic; informal half-baked.
– OPPOSITES pragmatic.

unreasonable adj ❶ EXCESSIVE, immoderate, undue, inordinate, outrageous, extravagant, preposterous. ❷ IRRATIONAL, illogical, blinkered, obstinate, obdurate, wilful, headstrong, temperamental, capricious. ❸ UNACCEPTABLE, outrageous, ludicrous, absurd, irrational, illogical.

unreliable adj ❶ UNDEPENDABLE, irresponsible, untrustworthy, erratic, fickle, inconstant. ❷ SUSPECT, questionable, open to question/doubt, doubtful, implausible, unconvincing, fallible, specious.

unrepentant adj IMPENITENT, unremorseful, shameless, unregenerate, abandoned.

unrest n DISSATISFACTION, discontent, unease, disquiet, dissent, discord, strife, protest, rebellion, agitation, turmoil, turbulence.

unrestricted adj UNLIMITED, open, free, unhindered, unchecked, unbounded; *informal* free-for-all, with no holds barred.

unsavoury adj UNPLEASANT, disagreeable, nasty, objectionable, offensive, obnoxious, repellent, repulsive, disreputable, degenerate, coarse, gross, vulgar, boorish, churlish, rude, uncouth.

unscrupulous adj UNPRINCIPLED, unethical, amoral, immoral, conscienceless, shameless, corrupt, dishonest, dishonourable, deceitful, devious, exploitative, wrongdoing, bad, evil, wicked; *informal* crooked.
– OPPOSITES honest.

unselfish adj ALTRUISTIC, self-sacrificing, selfless, kind, self-denying, open-handed, generous, liberal, unsparing, ungrudging, unstinting, charitable, philanthropic.
– OPPOSITES selfish.

unshakeable adj FIRM, steadfast, resolute, staunch, constant, unswerving, unwavering, unfaltering.

unsightly adj *see* UGLY (1).

unskilled adj UNTRAINED, unqualified, inexpert, inexperienced, amateurish, unprofessional.

unsophisticated adj ❶ UNWORLDLY, naive, simple, innocent, inexperienced, childlike, artless, guileless, ingenuous,

natural, unaffected, unpretentious, unrefined, unpolished, gauche, provincial. ❷ CRUDE, unrefined, basic, rudimentary, primitive.

unspeakable adj INDESCRIBABLE, unmentionable, appalling, shocking, horrible, frightful, terrible, dreadful, deplorable, despicable, contemptible, repellent, loathsome, odious, monstrous.

unspoilt adj PRESERVED, intact, perfect, unblemished, unimpaired, undamaged, untouched, unaffected, unchanged.

unstable adj ❶ UNSTEADY, infirm, rickety, shaky, wobbly, tottery, insecure, precarious. ❷ UNBALANCED, unhinged, irrational, deranged, mentally ill, insane, mad.
– OPPOSITES stable.

unsuccessful adj ❶ WITHOUT SUCCESS, failed, vain, unavailing, futile, useless, worthless, abortive, nugatory, ineffective, ineffectual, inefficacious, fruitless, unproductive, unprofitable, baulked, frustrated. ❷ FAILED, losing, unprosperous, unlucky, luckless, out of luck, unfortunate, ill-starred, ill-fated.

unsuitable adj INAPPROPRIATE, inapt, inapposite, unfitting, incompatible, incongruous, out of place/keeping, ineligible, unacceptable, unbecoming, unseemly, indecorous, improper.
– OPPOSITES appropriate.

unsure adj see UNCERTAIN (2).

unsuspecting adj UNSUSPI-CIOUS, unwary, off guard, trusting, gullible, credulous, ingenuous, naive, innocent.
– OPPOSITES wary.

unsympathetic adj UNCAR-ING, unfeeling, insensitive, un-concerned, indifferent, unkind, unpitying, pitiless, unrespon-sive, apathetic, unmoved, un-touched, heartless, cold, hard-hearted, stony-hearted, hard, harsh, callous.
– OPPOSITES sympathetic.

untangle v see UNRAVEL.

untenable adj INDEFENSIBLE, insupportable, unsustainable, unsound, weak, flawed, defect-ive, implausible, groundless, unfounded.

unthinkable adj see INCON-CEIVABLE.

unthinking adj see THOUGHT-LESS (2).

untidy adj DISORDERED, disor-derly, disarranged, disorgan-ized, chaotic, confused, muddled, jumbled, topsy-turvy, at sixes and sevens; informal hig-gledy-piggledy, every which way; Brit. informal like a dog's breakfast.
– OPPOSITES orderly.

untie v see UNDO (1).

untiring adj see TIRELESS.

untroubled adj UNWORRIED, unruffled, unbothered, uncon-cerned, calm, cool, collected, composed, serene.

untrue adj see FALSE (1).

unusual adj ❶ UNCOMMON, atypical, abnormal, rare, singu-lar, odd, strange, curious, queer, bizarre, surprising, unexpected, different, un-conventional, unwonted, unorthodox, irregular; informal weird. ❷ EXTRAORDINARY, excep-tional, singular, rare, remark-able, outstanding.
– OPPOSITES common.

unwarranted adj UNJUSTIFI-ABLE, unjustified, indefensible, inexcusable, unforgivable, unpardonable, uncalled for, gratuitous.
– OPPOSITES justified.

unwelcome adj ❶ UNWANTED, undesired, uninvited, unpopu-lar. ❷ UNPLEASANT, disagreeable, unpalatable, displeasing, distasteful, undesirable.

unwell adj see ILL adj (1).

unwieldy adj CUMBERSOME, unmanageable, awkward, clumsy, massive, hefty, bulky, ponderous; informal hulking.
– OPPOSITES manageable.

unwilling adj RELUCTANT, disinclined, unenthusiastic, grudging, involuntary, averse, loth, opposed, not in the mood.
– OPPOSITES willing.

unwind v ❶ See UNRAVEL (1). ❷ See RELAX (4).

unwitting adj UNKNOWING, un-conscious, unintentional, unintended, inadvertent.
– OPPOSITES deliberate.

unworthy adj ❶ NOT WORTHY, not good enough for, un-deserving, ineligible for,

unqualified for. ❷ DISREPUTABLE, dishonourable, base, contemptible, reprehensible.
– OPPOSITES deserving.

upgrade v IMPROVE, better, ameliorate, enhance, rehabilitate, refurbish.

upheaval n DISRUPTION, disturbance, disorder, confusion, turmoil, chaos.

uphill adj ARDUOUS, difficult, laborious, strenuous, hard, tough, burdensome, onerous, taxing, punishing.

uphold v SUPPORT, back up, back, stand by, champion, defend, maintain, sustain.

upkeep n MAINTENANCE, running, preservation, conservation, repairs.

upper adj ❶ HIGHER, further up, loftier. ❷ SUPERIOR, higher-ranking, elevated, greater.
– OPPOSITES lower.

upright adj ❶ ERECT, on end, vertical, perpendicular, standing up, rampant. ❷ HONEST, honourable, upstanding, decent, respectable, worthy, reputable, good, virtuous, righteous, law-abiding, ethical, moral.
– OPPOSITES horizontal, dishonourable.

uproar n TUMULT, turmoil, turbulence, disorder, confusion, commotion, mayhem, pandemonium, bedlam, din, noise, clamour, hubbub, racket.
– OPPOSITES calm.

upset v ❶ OVERTURN, knock over, push over, upend, tip over, topple, capsize. ❷ DISTURB, discompose, unsettle, disconcert, dismay, disquiet, trouble, worry, bother, agitate, fluster, ruffle, frighten, alarm, anger, annoy, distress, hurt, grieve. ❸ THROW INTO DISORDER / CONFUSION, disorganize, disarrange, mess up, mix up.

upshot n RESULT, outcome, conclusion, issue, end, end result, denouement, effect, repercussion, reaction; informal pay-off.
– OPPOSITES cause.

upstart n PARVENU / PARVENUE, social climber, nouveau riche, arriviste.

upward adj RISING, climbing, mounting, ascending, on the rise.
– OPPOSITES downward.

urbane adj SUAVE, debonair, sophisticated, smooth, worldly, cultivated, cultured, civilized, polished.
– OPPOSITES uncouth.

urge v ❶ PUSH, drive, propel, impel, force, hasten, hurry, spur, incite, stir up, stimulate, prod, goad, egg on, encourage, prompt, entreat, exhort, implore, appeal, beg, plead; poetic/ literary beseech. ❷ ADVISE, counsel, advocate, recommend, suggest, support, endorse, back, champion.
– OPPOSITES discourage.
▶ n DESIRE, need, compulsion, longing, yearning, wish, fancy, impulse.

urgent adj ❶ IMPERATIVE, vital, crucial, critical, essential, exigent, top-priority, high-priority, important, necessary, pressing, serious, grave. **❷** IMPORTANTE, insistent, clamorous, earnest, pleading, begging.

usable adj FOR USE, to be used, utilizable, available, ready/fit for use, in working order, functional.

use v **❶** MAKE USE OF, utilize, employ, work, operate, wield, ply, avail oneself of, put to use, put into service. **❷** CONSUME, get through, exhaust, deplete, expend, spend, waste, fritter away.
▶ n **❶** USEFULNESS, good, advantage, benefit, service, help, gain, profit, avail. **❷** NEED, necessity, call, demand, purpose.
■ **used to** ACCUSTOMED TO, familiar with, at home with, in the habit of, given to, prone to.

used adj SECOND-HAND, nearly new, pre-owned, cast-off, hand-me-down.
– OPPOSITES new.

useful adj **❶** OF USE, functional, utilitarian, of service, practical, convenient. **❷** BENEFICIAL, advantageous, of help, helpful, worthwhile, profitable, rewarding, productive, valuable.
– OPPOSITES useless.

useless adj **❶** VAIN, in vain, to no avail/purpose, unavailing, unsuccessful, futile, purposeless, fruitless, unprofitable, unproductive, abortive.

❷ WORTHLESS, ineffective, ineffectual, incompetent, incapable, inadequate; informal no good.
– OPPOSITES useful.

usual adj **❶** HABITUAL, customary, accustomed, normal, regular, routine, everyday, established, set, familiar; poetic/literary wonted. **❷** COMMON, typical, ordinary, average, run-of-the-mill, expected, standard, stock, regular.
– OPPOSITES unusual.

usually adv GENERALLY, as a rule, normally, by and large, in the main, mainly, mostly, for the most part, on the whole.

usurp v TAKE OVER, seize, expropriate, appropriate, commandeer, assume.

utilitarian adj PRACTICAL, functional, useful, to the purpose.

utter v VOICE, say, pronounce, express, put into words, enunciate, articulate, verbalize, vocalize.

utterance n **❶** VOICE, expression, articulation, enunciation, verbalization, vocalization. **❷** REMARK, word, comment, statement, opinion.

utterly adv ABSOLUTELY, completely, totally, entirely, thoroughly, positively, extremely, categorically, perfectly, consummately, to the core.

Vv

vacancy n ❶ OPENING, position, post, job, opportunity, slot. ❷ BLANKNESS, lack of expression, lack of emotion/interest, vacuousness.

vacant adj ❶ EMPTY, void, without contents. ❷ UNOCCUPIED, unfilled, free, empty, available, unengaged, uninhabited, untenanted, not in use, unused, abandoned, deserted; *informal* up for grabs. ❸ BLANK, expressionless, inexpressive, deadpan, poker-faced, emotionless, uninterested, vacuous, inane.
– OPPOSITES occupied.

vacate v LEAVE, quit, depart from, evacuate, abandon, desert.

vacillate v SHILLY-SHALLY, waver, dither, hesitate, equivocate, beat about the bush; *Brit.* hum and haw.

vacuous adj VACANT, blank, expressionless, deadpan, inane, unintelligent, brainless, stupid.
– OPPOSITES intelligent.

vagrant n TRAMP, beggar, person of no fixed address, itinerant, nomad, wanderer, vagabond; *N. Amer.* hobo; *N. Amer. informal* bum.

vague adj ❶ INDISTINCT, indeterminate, ill-defined, unclear, nebulous, amorphous, shadowy, hazy, fuzzy, blurry, bleary, out of focus. ❷ IMPRECISE, inexact, inexplicit, non-specific, loose, generalized, ambiguous, equivocal, hazy, woolly. ❸ ABSENT-MINDED, abstracted, dreamy, vacuous; *informal* with one's head in the clouds.
– OPPOSITES definite.

vaguely adv ❶ IN A GENERAL WAY, in a way, somehow, slightly, obscurely. ❷ ABSENT-MINDEDLY, abstractedly, vacantly, vacuously.

vain adj ❶ CONCEITED, self-loving, narcissistic, self-admiring, egotistical, proud, haughty, arrogant, boastful, swaggering, imperious, overweening, cocky, affected. ❷ UNSUCCESSFUL, futile, useless, unavailing, to no avail, ineffective, inefficacious, fruitless, unproductive, abortive, unprofitable, profitless.
– OPPOSITES modest, successful.

valiant adj BRAVE, courageous, valorous, heroic, intrepid, fearless, undaunted, bold, daring, audacious, staunch, stalwart, indomitable, resolute, determined.
– OPPOSITES cowardly.

valid adj ❶ SOUND, well founded, well grounded, substantial, reasonable, logical, justifiable,

defensible, vindicable, authentic, bona fide, effective, cogent, powerful, convincing, credible, forceful, weighty.
– OPPOSITES invalid.

validate V RATIFY, legalize, legitimize, authorize, sanction, warrant, license, approve, endorse, set one's seal to.
– OPPOSITES invalidate.

valley n DALE, dell, hollow, vale, depression; Brit. dene, combe; Scottish glen, strath.

valuable adj ❶ COSTLY, high-priced, expensive, priceless, precious. ❷ USEFUL, helpful, beneficial, advantageous, worthwhile, worthy, important.
– OPPOSITES worthless.

value n ❶ COST, face value, price, market price, worth. ❷ WORTH, merit, usefulness, advantage, benefit, gain, profit, good, avail, importance, significance.
▶ V ❶ SET A PRICE ON, price, evaluate, assess, appraise. ❷ RATE HIGHLY, appreciate, esteem, hold in high regard, think highly of, set store by, respect, admire, prize, cherish, treasure.

vanguard n ADVANCE GUARD, forefront, front, front line, front rank, leading position, van.
– OPPOSITES rear.

vanish V DISAPPEAR, be lost to sight/view, be/become invisible, evaporate, dissipate, disperse, fade, fade away, evanesce, melt away, recede from view, withdraw, depart, leave.
– OPPOSITES appear.

vanity n CONCEIT, conceitedness, narcissism, egotism, pride, haughtiness, arrogance, boastfulness, braggadocio, pretension, affectation, ostentation, show, airs.
– OPPOSITES modesty.

variable adj VARYING, variational, changeable, changing, mutable, protean, shifting, fluctuating, wavering, vacillating, inconstant, unsteady, unstable, fitful, capricious, fickle; informal blowing hot and cold.
– OPPOSITES constant.

variation n ❶ CHANGE, alteration, modification, diversification. ❷ VARIABILITY, changeability, fluctuation, vacillation, vicissitude. ❸ DIFFERENCE, dissimilarity.

varied adj DIVERSE, assorted, miscellaneous, mixed, motley, heterogeneous.

variety n ❶ VARIATION, diversification, diversity, multifariousness, many-sidedness, change, difference. ❷ ASSORTMENT, miscellany, range, mixture, medley, motley, collection, multiplicity. ❸ STRAIN, breed, kind, type, sort, class, category, classification, brand, make.
– OPPOSITES uniformity.

various adj ❶ VARYING, diverse, different, differing, dissimilar, disparate, assorted, mixed, miscellaneous, variegated, heterogeneous.

❷ NUMEROUS, many, several, varied, sundry; *poetic/literary* divers.

varnish v LACQUER, japan, shellac, enamel, glaze, veneer.

vary v **❶** DIFFER, be different, be dissimilar, be at variance, disagree, conflict, clash, be at odds. **❷** CHANGE, be transformed, alter, metamorphose, suffer a sea change, vacillate, fluctuate.

vast adj IMMENSE, huge, enormous, massive, bulky, tremendous, colossal, prodigious, gigantic, monumental, elephantine, Brobdingnagian, extensive, broad, wide, expansive, boundless, limitless, infinite; *informal* hulking.
– OPPOSITES tiny.

vault[1] n CELLAR, basement, underground chamber, tomb.

vault[2] v JUMP, leap, jump over, leap over, spring over, bound over.

veer v CHANGE COURSE / DIRECTION, turn, swerve, swing, sidestep, sheer, tack, be deflected.

vehemence n FORCE, passion, forcefulness, emphasis, vigour, intensity, violence, earnestness, keenness, enthusiasm, zeal.

vehement adj PASSIONATE, ardent, impassioned, fervent, fervid, strong, forceful, forcible, powerful, emphatic, vigorous, intense, earnest, keen, enthusiastic, zealous, spirited.
– OPPOSITES mild.

vehicle n **❶** MEANS OF TRANSPORT, transportation, convey-

ance, car, bus, lorry. **❷** CHANNEL, medium, means, agency, instrument, mechanism, organ, apparatus.

veil v HIDE, conceal, cover up, camouflage, disguise, mask, screen.

vein n **❶** BLOOD VESSEL, artery, capillary. **❷** LODE, seam, stratum. **❸** STREAK, stripe, line, thread, marking.

veneer n **❶** FACING, covering, coat, finish. **❷** FAÇADE, false front, show, outward display, appearance, semblance, guise, mask, pretence, camouflage.

venerable adj VENERATED, respected, revered, reverenced, worshipped, honoured, esteemed, hallowed.

veneration n RESPECT, reverence, worship, adoration, honour, esteem.

vengeance n REVENGE, retribution, requital, retaliation, reprisal, an eye for an eye, quid pro quo; *informal* tit for tat.

venomous adj **❶** POISONOUS, toxic, lethal, deadly, fatal, noxious. **❷** See SPITEFUL.

vent n **❶** OPENING, outlet, aperture, hole, gap, duct, flue.
▶ v GIVE VENT / EXPRESSION TO, express, air, utter, voice, verbalize, let out, come out with.

ventilate v AIR, aerate, oxygenate, freshen, cool, purify.

venture n ENTERPRISE, undertaking, project, speculation, fling, plunge, gamble.

▶ v DARE, take the liberty, make so bold as, presume to.

verbal adj ORAL, spoken, said, uttered, articulated.

verbatim adj WORD FOR WORD, literal, exact, faithful, precise.

verbose adj WORDY, loquacious, garrulous, long-winded, prolix, diffuse, pleonastic, circumlocutory, periphrastic, tautological.
– OPPOSITES succinct.

verdict n DECISION, judgement, adjudication, finding, conclusion, ruling, opinion.

verge n EDGE, border, margin, rim, limit, boundary, end, extremity.
■ **verge on** APPROACH, incline to/towards, tend towards, border on, come near.

verification n CONFIRMATION, evidence, proof, substantiation, corroboration, attestation, validation, authentication, endorsement, accreditation, ratification.

verify v CONFIRM, substantiate, prove, give credence to, corroborate, attest to, testify to, validate, authenticate, endorse, accredit, ratify.
– OPPOSITES refute.

vernacular n EVERYDAY / SPOKEN LANGUAGE, colloquial/ native speech, conversational language, common parlance, non-standard language, jargon, cant, patois; informal lingo, patter.

versatile adj ❶ RESOURCEFUL, flexible, all-round, multifa-

ceted, adaptable, ingenious, clever. ❷ MULTI-PURPOSE, all-purpose, adjustable, adaptable, handy.

verse n ❶ STANZA, canto, couplet. ❷ POEM, lyric, sonnet, ode, limerick, piece of doggerel, ditty, song, ballad.

version n ❶ ACCOUNT, report, story, rendering, interpretation, construction, understanding, reading, impression, side. ❷ ADAPTATION, interpretation, translation. ❸ VARIANT, variation, form, copy, reproduction.

vertical adj UPRIGHT, erect, on end, perpendicular.
– OPPOSITES horizontal.

vertigo n DIZZINESS, giddiness, light-headedness, loss of balance/equilibrium; informal wooziness.

verve n ENTHUSIASM, vigour, force, energy, vitality, vivacity, liveliness, animation, sparkle, spirit, life, dash, brio, fervour, gusto, passion, zeal, feeling, fire; informal zing, zip, vim, get-up-and-go, pizzazz.

very adv EXTREMELY, exceedingly, to a great extent, exceptionally, uncommonly, unusually, decidedly, particularly, eminently, remarkably, really, truly, terribly; informal awfully; Brit. informal jolly.
– OPPOSITES slightly.

vessel n ❶ SHIP, boat, yacht, craft; poetic/literary barque. ❷ CONTAINER, receptacle.

vet v CHECK, check out, investigate, examine, appraise, look over, review, scrutinize; *informal* give the once-over, size up.

veteran n OLD HAND, old-timer, old stager, past master; master; *informal* pro, old warhorse.
– OPPOSITES novice.
▶ adj LONG-SERVING, seasoned, old, adept, expert.

veto v REJECT, turn down, prohibit, forbid, interdict, proscribe, disallow, outlaw, embargo, ban, bar, preclude, rule out; *informal* give the thumbs down to, put the kibosh on.
– OPPOSITES approve.
▶ n REJECTION, prohibition, interdict, proscription, embargo, ban.

vex v ANGER, annoy, irritate, incense, irk, enrage, infuriate, exasperate, pique, provoke, nettle, disturb, upset, perturb, discompose, put out, try someone's patience, try; *informal* peeve, miff, bug, hassle, aggravate, drive up the wall.

viable adj WORKABLE, sound, feasible, practicable, applicable, usable.
– OPPOSITES impractical.

vibrant adj ❶ LIVELY, energetic, spirited, vigorous, animated, sparkling, vivacious, dynamic, electrifying. ❷ VIVID, bright, strong, striking.
– OPPOSITES lifeless, pale.

vibrate v SHAKE, oscillate, tremble, quiver, throb, pulsate, resonate, resound, reverberate, ring, echo.

vibration n SHAKING, oscillation, throb, pulsation,

resonance, reverberation, quivering, quiver.

vicarious adj INDIRECT, second-hand, surrogate, by proxy, at one remove.

vice n ❶ SIN, sinfulness, wrong, wrongdoing, wickedness, badness, immorality, iniquity, evil, evil-doing, venality, corruption, depravity, degeneracy. ❷ TRANSGRESSION, offence, misdeed, error, failing, flaw, defect, imperfection, weakness, foible, shortcoming.
– OPPOSITES virtue.

vicinity n SURROUNDING DISTRICT, neighbourhood, locality, area, district, environs, precincts, purlieus; *informal* neck of the woods.

vicious adj ❶ FIERCE, ferocious, savage, dangerous, ill-natured, bad-tempered, hostile. ❷ MALICIOUS, malevolent, malignant, spiteful, vindictive, venomous, backbiting, rancorous, caustic, mean, cruel; *informal* bitchy, catty. ❸ VIOLENT, savage, brutal, fierce, ferocious, inhuman, barbarous, fiendish, sadistic.
– OPPOSITES gentle.

vicissitude n CHANGE, alteration, transformation, inconstancy, instability, uncertainty, unpredictability, chanciness, fickleness, ups and downs.

victim n ❶ INJURED PARTY, casualty, sufferer. ❷ OFFERING, sacrifice, scapegoat.

victimize v PERSECUTE, pick on, discriminate against,

punish unfairly; *informal* have it in for, have a down on.

victor n WINNER, champion, prizewinner, conquering hero; *informal* champ, top dog, number one.
– OPPOSITES loser.

victorious adj CONQUERING, vanquishing, triumphant, winning, champion, successful, prizewinning, top, first.

vie v COMPETE, contend, contest, struggle, strive.

view n ❶ SIGHT, field/range of vision, vision, eyeshot. ❷ OUTLOOK, prospect, scene, spectacle, vista, panorama, landscape, seascape. ❸ POINT OF VIEW, viewpoint, opinion, belief, judgement, way of thinking, thinking, thought, notion, idea, conviction, persuasion, attitude, feeling, sentiment, impression.
▶ v LOOK AT, watch, observe, contemplate, regard, behold, scan, survey, examine, scrutinize, see over.

viewpoint n POINT OF VIEW, frame of reference, perspective, angle, slant, standpoint, position, stance, vantage point.

vigilant adj WATCHFUL, on the lookout, observant, sharp-eyed, eagle-eyed, attentive, alert, on the alert, awake, wide awake, on one's guard, careful, cautious, wary, circumspect, heedful.
– OPPOSITES inattentive.

vigorous adj ❶ ROBUST, healthy, in good health, hale and hearty, strong, sturdy, fit, in good condition/shape/kilter, tough. ❷ ENERGETIC, lively, active, spry, sprightly, vivacious, animated, dynamic, full of life, sparkling.
– OPPOSITES weak, feeble.

vigour n ENERGY, activity, liveliness, spryness, sprightliness, vitality, vivacity, verve, animation, dynamism, sparkle, zest, dash, gusto, pep; *informal* zip, zing, oomph, vim.
– OPPOSITES lethargy.

vile adj FOUL, nasty, unpleasant, disagreeable, horrid, horrible, offensive, obnoxious, odious, repulsive, repellent, revolting, repugnant, disgusting, distasteful, loathsome, hateful, nauseating, sickening, base, low, mean, wretched, dreadful, ugly, abominable, monstrous.
– OPPOSITES pleasant.

vilify v DEFAME, run down, impugn, revile, berate, denigrate, disparage, drag through the mud, speak ill of, cast aspersions at, criticize, decry, denounce, fulminate against, malign, slander, libel, traduce; *informal* bad-mouth, do a hatchet job on; *formal* calumniate.
– OPPOSITES commend.

villain n ROGUE, scoundrel, wretch, cad, reprobate, evildoer, wrongdoer, hoodlum, hooligan, miscreant; *informal* baddy, crook, rat, louse; *archaic* blackguard.

vindicate v ACQUIT, clear, absolve, free from blame, exonerate, exculpate.

vindictive adj VENGEFUL, revengeful, avenging, unforgiving, grudge-bearing, resentful, implacable, unrelenting, spiteful, rancorous, venomous, malicious, malevolent, malignant.
– OPPOSITES forgiving.

vintage adj CLASSIC, ageless, enduring, high-quality, quality, prime, choice, select, superior, best.

violate v ❶ BREAK, breach, infringe, contravene, infract, transgress, disobey, disregard, ignore. ❷ DESECRATE, profane, defile, blaspheme. ❸ DISTURB, disrupt, intrude on, interfere with, encroach on, invade.
– OPPOSITES respect.

violence n FORCE, brute force, roughness, ferocity, brutality, savagery; informal strong-arm tactics.

violent adj ❶ BRUTAL, vicious, destructive, savage, fierce, wild, intemperate, bloodthirsty, homicidal, murderous, maniacal. ❷ UNCONTROLLABLE, powerful, uncontrolled, unrestrained, unbridled, ungovernable, wild, strong, passionate. ❸ EXTREME, great, intense, strong, vehement, inordinate, excessive.
– OPPOSITES gentle, weak.

virile adj POTENT, manly, strong, vigorous, robust, muscular, rugged, strapping, sturdy, red-blooded; informal macho.
– OPPOSITES effeminate.

virtue n ❶ GOODNESS, righteousness, morality, uprightness, integrity, rectitude,

honesty, honourableness, honour, incorruptibility, probity, decency, respectability, worthiness, worth, trustworthiness. ❷ GOOD QUALITY / POINT, merit, asset, credit, attribute, advantage, plus, benefit, strength.
– OPPOSITES vice.

virtuoso adj SKILFUL, masterly, impressive, outstanding, dazzling, bravura.
– OPPOSITES incompetent.

virtuous adj ❶ GOOD, righteous, moral, ethical, upright, upstanding, honest, honourable, incorruptible, decent, respectable, worthy, trustworthy. ❷ VIRGINAL, celibate, pure, chaste, innocent, modest.
– OPPOSITES evil.

virulent adj ❶ POISONOUS, toxic, venomous, deadly, lethal, fatal, noxious, harmful. ❷ SEVERE, extreme, violent, rapidly spreading, highly infectious/contagious, harmful, lethal. ❸ HOSTILE, spiteful, venomous, vicious, vindictive, malicious, malevolent, malignant, bitter, rancorous, acrimonious, abusive, aggressive, violent.
– OPPOSITES harmless, amicable.

visible adj ❶ IN VIEW, perceptible, perceivable, discernible, detectable, seeable. ❷ APPARENT, evident, noticeable, observable, detectable, recognizable, manifest, plain, clear, obvious, patent, palpable, unmistakable, unconcealed,

undisguised, conspicuous, distinct, distinguishable.
– OPPOSITES invisible.

vision n ❶ EYESIGHT, sight, power of seeing. ❷ REVELATION, dream, hallucination, chimera, optical illusion, mirage, illusion, delusion, figment of the imagination. ❸ FORESIGHT, far-sightedness, prescience, breadth of view, discernment.

visionary adj ❶ IDEALISTIC, impractical, unrealistic, utopian, romantic, quixotic, dreamy, dreaming; informal starry-eyed. ❷ FAR-SIGHTED, discerning, wise. ❸ IMPRACTICAL, unrealistic, unworkable, unfeasible, theoretical, hypothetical, idealistic, utopian.
▶ n MYSTIC, seer, prophet, dreamer, daydreamer, idealist, romantic, romanticist, fantasist, theorist, utopian.

visit v PAY A VISIT TO, go/come to see, pay a call on, call on, call/look in on, stop by; informal pop/drop in on.
▶ n CALL, social call, stay, sojourn, stopover.

visitation n AFFLICTION, scourge, plague, pestilence, blight, disaster, tragedy, calamity, catastrophe, cataclysm.

visual adj ❶ SEEING, optical, ocular. ❷ TO BE SEEN, seeable, perceivable, discernible.

visualize v CONJURE UP, envisage, picture, envision, imagine, conceive.

vital adj ❶ ESSENTIAL, necessary, needed, indispensable, key, important, significant, imperative, urgent, critical, crucial, life-and-death. ❷ LIVELY, animated, spirited, vivacious, vibrant, zestful, dynamic, energetic, vigorous, forceful.
– OPPOSITES unimportant, apathetic.

vitality n LIFE, liveliness, animation, spirit, spiritedness, vivacity, vibrancy, zest, zestfulness, dynamism, energy, vigour; informal zing, zip, pep, get-up-and-go.

vitriolic adj CAUSTIC, mordant, acrimonious, bitter, acerbic, astringent, acid, acidulous, acrid, trenchant, virulent, spiteful, venomous, malicious, scathing, withering, sarcastic, sardonic; informal bitchy.

vivacious adj LIVELY, full of life, animated, effervescent, bubbly, ebullient, sparkling, scintillating, light-hearted, spirited, high-spirited, merry, jolly, vibrant, vivid, dynamic, vital; dated gay.
– OPPOSITES dull.

vivid adj ❶ STRONG, intense, colourful, rich, glowing, bright, brilliant, clear. ❷ GRAPHIC, clear, lively, stirring, striking, powerful, highly coloured, dramatic, memorable, realistic, lifelike, true to life.
– OPPOSITES dull.

vocal adj ❶ VOICED, vocalized, spoken, said, uttered, expressed, articulated, oral. ❷ VOCIFEROUS, outspoken, forthright, plain-spoken, clamorous, strident, loud, noisy.

vocation n PROFESSION,

calling, occupation, walk of life, career, life's work, métier, trade, craft, job, work, employment, business, line, speciality.

vogue n FASHION, mode, style, trend, taste, fad, craze, rage, latest thing.

voice n ❶ POWER OF SPEECH / ARTICULATION. ❷ EXPRESSION, utterance, verbalization, vocalization, airing.
▶ v PUT INTO WORDS, express, give utterance to, utter, articulate, enunciate, mention, talk of, communicate, declare, assert, divulge, air.

void adj ❶ EMPTY, emptied, vacant, bare, clear, free, unfilled, unoccupied, uninhabited, untenanted, tenantless. ❷ NULL AND VOID, nullified, invalid, cancelled, inoperative, ineffective, non-viable, useless, worthless, nugatory.
– OPPOSITES full, valid.

volatile adj ❶ MERCURIAL, changeable, variable, capricious, whimsical, fickle, flighty, giddy, inconstant, erratic, unstable. ❷ EXPLOSIVE, eruptive, charged, inflammatory, tense, strained.
– OPPOSITES stable.

voluble adj TALKATIVE, loquacious, garrulous, chatty, gossipy, chattering, articulate, eloquent, forthcoming, fluent, glib.
– OPPOSITES taciturn.

volume n ❶ BOOK, publication, tome. ❷ SPACE, bulk, capacity. ❸ LOUDNESS, sound, amplification.

voluminous adj CAPACIOUS, roomy, commodious, ample, full, big, vast, billowing.
– OPPOSITES small.

voluntary adj OF ONE'S OWN FREE WILL, volitional, of one's own accord, optional, discretionary, at one's discretion, elective, non-compulsory, non-mandatory.
– OPPOSITES compulsory.

volunteer v OFFER ONE'S SERVICES, present oneself, step forward.

voluptuous adj ❶ HEDONISTIC, sybaritic, epicurean, self-indulgent, sensual, carnal, licentious, lascivious. ❷ CURVY, shapely, full-figured, ample, buxom, seductive, curvaceous.
– OPPOSITES ascetic, scrawny.

vomit v ❶ THROW UP; Brit. be sick; informal spew, puke. ❷ BRING UP, regurgitate, spew up, spit up.

voracious adj ❶ GLUTTONOUS, greedy, ravenous, ravening, starving, hungry, insatiable. ❷ COMPULSIVE, enthusiastic, eager.

vote n BALLOT, poll, election, referendum, plebiscite.
▶ v CAST ONE'S VOTE, go to the polls, mark one's ballot paper.

vouch
■ vouch for ATTEST TO, bear witness to, give assurance of, answer for, be responsible for, guarantee, go/stand bail for.

voucher n CHIT, slip, ticket, token, document.

vow v SWEAR, state under oath,

pledge, promise, undertake, give one's word of honour.

voyage n JOURNEY, trip, expedition, crossing, cruise, passage.
▶ v TRAVEL, journey, take a trip, sail, cruise.

vulgar adj ❶ RUDE, indecent, indecorous, indelicate, crude, unseemly, offensive, distasteful, obnoxious, suggestive, off colour, ribald, bawdy, obscene, lewd, salacious, licentious, concupiscent, smutty, dirty, filthy, pornographic, scatological; informal raunchy, blue.
❷ TASTELESS, gross, crass, unrefined, tawdry, ostentatious, showy, flashy, gaudy.
– OPPOSITES tasteful.

vulnerable adj EXPOSED, unprotected, unguarded, open to attack, assailable, defenceless, easily hurt/wounded/damaged, powerless, helpless, weak, sensitive, thin-skinned.
– OPPOSITES invulnerable.

Ww

wad n ❶ LUMP, mass, chunk, hunk, bail, plug, block.
❷ BUNDLE, roll.

waddle v SWAY, wobble, totter, toddle, shuffle.

wade v FORD, CROSS, traverse, paddle.
■ **wade in** SET TO, set to work, pitch in, buckle down, go to it, put one's shoulder to the wheel; informal get cracking, get stuck in.

waffle n MEANINGLESS TALK / WRITING, padding, equivocation, prattle, jabbering, verbiage, logorrhoea; Brit. informal wittering.
▶ v RAMBLE, prattle, jabber, babble; Brit. informal rabbit, witter.

waft v ❶ FLOAT, glide, drift, be carried/borne/conveyed.
❷ CARRY, bear, convey, transport, transmit.

wag[1] v ❶ SWING, sway, vibrate, quiver, shake, rock, twitch.
❷ WAGGLE, wiggle, wobble, wave.

wag[2] n WIT, humorist, jester, joker, jokester, comic, comedian, comedienne, wisecracker, punner, punster.

wage n PAY, salary, earnings, payment, fee, remuneration, stipend, emolument.
▶ v CARRY ON, conduct, execute, engage in, pursue, undertake, devote oneself to, practise.

wager n BET, gamble, stake, pledge, hazard; Brit. informal flutter.
▶ v LAY A WAGER, bet, place/make/lay a bet, lay odds, put money on, speculate.

wail n CRY OF GRIEF / PAIN, lament, lamentation, weeping, sob, moan, groan, whine, complaint, howl, yowl, ululation.
▶ v CRY, lament, weep, sob, moan, groan, whine, howl, yowl, ululate.

wait v ❶ STAY, remain, rest, linger, abide; *archaic* tarry. ❷ BE PATIENT, hold back, stand by, bide one's time, hang fire, mark time; *informal* cool one's heels, sit tight, hold one's horses, sweat it out.
▶ n INTERVAL, stay, delay, hold-up.
■ **wait on** ACT AS A WAITER / WAITRESS TO, serve, attend to.

waiter, waitress n STEWARD, stewardess, server, attendant.

waive v RELINQUISH, renounce, give up, abandon, surrender, yield, cede, set aside, forgo, disregard, ignore.

wake v ❶ AWAKE, awaken, waken, wake up, waken up, rouse, stir, come to, get up, arise. ❷ ROUSE, stir up, activate, stimulate, spur, prod, galvanize, provoke.
– OPPOSITES sleep.
▶ n VIGIL, death watch, watch.

wakeful adj ❶ UNSLEEPING, restless, tossing and turning, insomniac. ❷ ALERT, on the alert, vigilant, on the lookout, on one's guard, on the qui vive, watchful, observant, attentive, heedful, wary.
– OPPOSITES asleep, inattentive.

walk v ❶ GO BY FOOT, travel on foot, foot it; *informal* hoof it. ❷ STROLL, saunter, amble, plod, trudge, hike, tramp, trek, march, stride, step out. ❸ ACCOMPANY, escort, convey.
▶ n ❶ STROLL, saunter, amble, promenade, ramble, hike, tramp, march, constitutional, airing. ❷ MANNER OF WALKING, gait, pace, step, stride. ❸ ROAD, avenue, drive, promenade, path, pathway, footpath, track, lane, alley.

walkover n EASY VICTORY; *informal* piece of cake, child's play, doddle, pushover.

wall n ❶ PARTITION, room divider. ❷ FORTIFICATION, rampart, barricade, parapet, bulwark, stockade, breastwork.

wallet n PURSE, pouch; *N. Amer.* billfold, pocketbook; *Brit. dated* notecase.

wallow v ❶ ROLL, tumble about, lie around, splash around. ❷ LUXURIATE IN, bask in, take pleasure/satisfaction in, indulge oneself in, delight in, revel in, glory in, enjoy.

wan adj PALE, pallid, ashen, white, white as a sheet/ghost, anaemic, colourless, bloodless, waxen, pasty, peaky, tired-looking, washed out, sickly.
– OPPOSITES ruddy.

wand n BATON, stick, staff, twig, sprig, withe, withy.

wander v ❶ RAMBLE, roam, meander, rove, range, prowl, saunter, stroll, amble, peregrinate, drift; *informal* traipse; *Brit. informal* mooch. ❷ STRAY, depart, diverge, veer, swerve, deviate. ❸ BE INCOHERENT, ramble, babble, talk nonsense, rave, be delirious.

▶ n RAMBLE, saunter, stroll, amble.

wanderer n RAMBLER, roamer, rover, drifter, traveller, itinerant, wayfarer, nomad, bird of passage, rolling stone, gypsy, vagabond, vagrant, tramp, derelict, beggar.

wane v DECREASE, decline, diminish, dwindle, shrink, contract, taper off, subside, sink, ebb, dim, fade away, vanish, die out, draw to a close, evanesce, peter out, wind down, be on the way out, abate, fail, become weak, deteriorate, degenerate.

– OPPOSITES strengthen.

want v ❶ WISH, wish for, desire, demand, call for, long for, hope for, yearn for, pine for, fancy, crave, hanker after, hunger for, thirst for, lust after, covet, need; *informal* have a yen for. ❷ NEED, be/stand in need of, require. ❸ LACK, be lacking, be without, be devoid of, be bereft of, be short of, be deficient in, have insufficient of.

▶ n ❶ LACK, absence, dearth, deficiency, inadequacy, insufficiency, shortness, paucity, shortage, scarcity, scarceness, scantiness. ❷ WISH, desire, demand, longing, yearning, fancy, craving, hankering, hunger, thirst, lust, covetousness. ❸ NEED, neediness, privation, poverty, destitution, penury, indigence.

wanting adj LACKING, deficient, inadequate, imperfect, not up to standard/par, not good enough, disappointing, not acceptable, not up to expectations, flawed, faulty, defective, unsound, substandard, inferior, second-rate.

– OPPOSITES sufficient.

wanton adj ❶ PROMISCUOUS, fast, immoral, loose, immodest, shameless, unchaste, unvirtuous, of easy virtue, impure, abandoned, lustful, lecherous, lascivious, libidinous, licentious, libertine, dissolute, dissipated, debauched, degenerate. ❷ WILFUL, malicious, malevolent, spiteful, wicked, evil, cruel, unmotivated, motiveless, arbitrary, groundless, unjustifiable, unjustified, needless, unnecessary, uncalled for, unprovoked, gratuitous, senseless, pointless, purposefulness.

war n WARFARE, conflict, hostilities, strife, combat, fighting, struggle, armed conflict, battle, fight, confrontation, skirmish.

– OPPOSITES peace.

ward n ❶ ROOM, compartment, cubicle. ❷ ADMINISTRATIVE DISTRICT, district, division, quarter, zone. ❸ CHARGE, dependant, protégé/protégée, pupil.

■ **ward off** FEND OFF, stave off, parry, avert, deflect, turn aside, drive back, repel, repulse, beat back, rout, put to flight, scatter, disperse.

warder n PRISON OFFICER,

guard, warden, jailer; *informal* screw.

warehouse n STORE, storehouse, depot, depository, stockroom.

wares pl n GOODS, products, commodities, lines, merchandise, produce, stuff, stock.

warily adv CAREFULLY, with care, cautiously, gingerly, circumspectly, guardedly, on one's guard, on the alert, watchfully, vigilantly, suspiciously, distrustfully, mistrustfully, charily.
– OPPOSITES trustingly.

warlike adj AGGRESSIVE, belligerent, bellicose, pugnacious, combative, militaristic, militant, martial.
– OPPOSITES peaceful, peaceable.

warm adj ❶ HEATED, tepid, lukewarm. ❷ SUNNY, balmy. ❸ KINDLY, friendly, affable, amiable, genial, cordial, sympathetic, affectionate, loving, tender, caring, charitable, sincere, genuine. ❹ HEARTY, cordial, genial, friendly, hospitable, enthusiastic, eager, sincere, heartfelt, ardent, vehement, passionate, intense, fervent, effusive.
– OPPOSITES cool, cold.
▶ v WARM UP, make warm, heat, heat up, reheat.

warn v ❶ INFORM, notify, give notice, give prior notice, tell, let know, acquaint, give fair warning, forewarn; *informal* tip off, put wise. ❷ ADVISE, exhort, urge, counsel, caution, fore-

warn, put on the alert, make aware. ❸ GIVE A WARNING TO, admonish, remonstrate with.

warning n ❶ INFORMATION, notification, notice, word, forewarning; *informal* tip-off. ❷ CAUTION, advice, exhortation, counselling. ❸ ADMONITION, remonstrance. ❹ OMEN, premonition, foretoken, token, augury, signal, sign, threat.

warrant n ❶ AUTHORIZATION, consent, sanction, permission, validation, licence, imprimatur, seal of approval. ❷ OFFICIAL DOCUMENT, written order, papers.
▶ v JUSTIFY, vindicate, excuse, be a defence of, explain away, account for, be a reason for, offer grounds for, support.

wary adj CAREFUL, cautious, circumspect, leery, chary, on one's guard, alert, wide awake, on one's toes, on the alert/lookout, on the qui vive, attentive, heedful, watchful, vigilant, observant.
– OPPOSITES unwary.

wash v ❶ WASH ONESELF, have a wash, bath, shower, have a bath/shower. ❷ CLEAN, cleanse, sponge, scrub, launder, shampoo. ❸ SPLASH AGAINST, dash against, break against, beat against. ❹ BE ACCEPTED, be plausible, be convincing, hold up, hold water, stand up, bear scrutiny.
▶ n CLEAN, cleaning, cleansing, bath, shower.

waste v SQUANDER, dissipate, fritter away, misspend, misuse,

spend recklessly, throw away, go through, run through; *informal* blow.
– OPPOSITES conserve.
▶ n ❶ SQUANDERING, dissipation, frittering away, misspending, misuse, prodigality, unthriftiness. ❷ RUBBISH, refuse, debris, dross, dregs, leavings, garbage, trash.
▶ adj ❶ LEFTOVER, unused, superfluous, supernumerary, unwanted, worthless, useless. ❷ DESERT, barren, uncultivated, unproductive, arid, bare, desolate, solitary, lonely, empty, void, uninhabited, unpopulated, wild, bleak, cheerless.
■ **waste away** GROW WEAK, wither, atrophy, become emaciated.

wasteful adj PRODIGAL, profligate, thriftless, spendthrift, extravagant, lavish.
– OPPOSITES thrifty.

watch v ❶ LOOK AT, observe, view, eye, gaze at, stare at, gape at, peer at, contemplate, behold, inspect, scrutinize, survey, scan, examine. ❷ KEEP WATCH ON, keep an eye on, keep in sight, follow, spy on; *informal* keep tabs on. ❸ MIND, take care of, look after, supervise, superintend, tend, guard, protect, keep an eye on.
▶ n ❶ WRISTWATCH, pocket watch, timepiece, chronometer. ❷ GUARD, vigil.

watchful adj OBSERVANT, alert, vigilant, attentive, heedful, sharp-eyed, eagle-eyed, wary, circumspect. *See also* WARY, ALERT adj (1).

watchman n SECURITY GUARD / MAN, guard, custodian, caretaker.

water n ❶ ADAM'S ALE, tap water, mineral water, bottled water. ❷ SEA, river, lake, loch, pool, reservoir.
▶ v ❶ SPRINKLE, moisten, dampen, wet, water down, douse, hose, spray, drench, saturate, flood. ❷ EXUDE WATER, moisten, leak.
■ **water down** ❶ ADD WATER TO, dilute, thin, weaken, adulterate. ❷ PLAY DOWN, downplay, tone down, soft-pedal, understate, underemphasize.

waterfall n FALLS, cascade, cataract.

watertight adj ❶ WATERPROOF, sound. ❷ SOUND, flawless, incontrovertible, indisputable, foolproof, unassailable, impregnable.
– OPPOSITES leaky, flawed.

watery adj ❶ AQUEOUS, liquid, liquefied, fluid, hydrous. ❷ WET, damp, moist, sodden, soggy, squelchy, saturated, waterlogged, marshy, boggy, swampy, miry. ❸ THIN, runny, weak, dilute, diluted, watered down, adulterated, tasteless, flavourless; *informal* wishy-washy.
– OPPOSITES dry, thick.

wave v ❶ UNDULATE, ripple, stir, flutter, flap, sway, swing, shake, quiver, oscillate. ❷ MOVE UP AND DOWN, move to and fro, wag, waggle, flutter. ❸ GESTURE, gesticulate, signal, sign, beckon, indicate.

▶ n ❶ BREAKER, roller, comber, ripple, billow, white horse, white cap, swell, surf. ❷ STREAM, flow, rush, surge, flood. ❸ UNDULATION, curl, kink. ❹ SURGE, upsurge, groundswell, welling up, rush, outbreak, rash.

■ **wave aside** SET ASIDE, dismiss, reject, disregard, ignore.

waver v ❶ BECOME UNSTEADY, falter, wobble, hesitate. ❷ BE IR-RESOLUTE / INDECISIVE, hesitate, dither, equivocate, vacillate, shilly-shally, blow hot and cold, pussyfoot around, beat about the bush; *Brit.* hum and haw. ❸ WEAVE, reel, totter, teeter, stagger, wobble.

wavy adj UNDULATING, curvy, curling, squiggly, rippled, curving, winding.
– OPPOSITES straight.

wax v GET BIGGER, increase in size, enlarge, grow, develop, extend, widen, broaden, spread, mushroom.
– OPPOSITES wane.

way n ❶ DIRECTION, route, course, road, roadway, street, thoroughfare, track, path, pathway, lane, avenue, drive. ❷ METHOD, means, course of action, process, procedure, technique, system, plan, scheme, manner, modus operandi. ❸ MANNER, style, fashion, mode. ❹ DISTANCE, length, stretch, journey.

wayfarer n TRAVELLER, walker, hiker, rambler, wanderer, roamer, rover, nomad, gypsy, vagabond, vagrant.

waylay v LIE IN WAIT FOR, ambush, hold up, attack, accost, intercept, pounce on, swoop down on.

wayward adj WILFUL, self-willed, headstrong, stubborn, obstinate, obdurate, perverse, contrary, uncooperative, refractory, recalcitrant, contumacious, unruly, ungovernable, unmanageable, incorrigible, intractable, difficult, fractious, disobedient, insubordinate.
– OPPOSITES docile.

weak adj ❶ FRAIL, fragile, delicate, feeble, infirm, shaky, debilitated, incapacitated, ailing, indisposed, decrepit, puny, faint, enervated, tired, fatigued, exhausted, spent, worn out. ❷ COWARDLY, pusillanimous, timorous, timid, spineless, ineffectual, useless, inept, effete, powerless, impotent, namby-pamby, soft; *informal* yellow, weak-kneed. ❸ DEFECTIVE, faulty, poor, inadequate, deficient, imperfect, substandard, lacking, wanting. ❹ UNSOUND, feeble, flimsy, lame, hollow, pathetic, unconvincing, untenable, implausible, unsatisfactory. ❺ FAINT, low, muffled, stifled, muted, scarcely audible. ❻ UNDER-STRENGTH, dilute, diluted, watery, thinned down, thin, adulterated, tasteless, flavourless, insipid; *informal* wishy-washy.
– OPPOSITES strong.

weaken v ❶ ENFEEBLE, debilitate, incapacitate, sap someone's strength, enervate, tire,

exhaust, wear out. ❷ LESSEN, reduce, decrease, diminish, moderate, temper, sap, emasculate. ❸ ABATE, lessen, decrease, dwindle, diminish, ease up, let up.
– OPPOSITES strengthen.

weakling n COWARD, mouse, milksop, namby-pamby; *informal* wimp, sissy, drip, wet, doormat, chicken, yellow-belly.

weakness n ❶ FRAILTY, fragility, delicateness, delicacy, feebleness, infirmity, debility, incapacity, indisposition, decrepitude, puniness, enervation, fatigue. ❷ COWARDLINESS, timidity, spinelessness, ineffectuality, ineptness, powerlessness, impotence. ❸ DEFECTIVENESS, faultiness, inadequacy, deficiency. ❹ UNSOUNDNESS, feebleness, flimsiness, lameness, untenability, implausibility. ❺ FAINTNESS, low intensity, muteness. ❻ THINNESS, wateriness, tastelessness; *informal* wishy-washiness. ❼ WEAK POINT, failing, foible, fault, flaw, defect, shortcoming, imperfection, blemish, Achilles' heel, chink in one's armour.
– OPPOSITES strength.

wealth n ❶ MONEY, cash, capital, affluence, means, fortune, finance, property, riches, assets, possessions, resources, goods, funds, bread. ❷ MASS, abundance, profusion, copiousness, plenitude, amplitude, bounty, cornucopia.
– OPPOSITES poverty, scarcity.

wealthy adj RICH, well off, well-to-do, moneyed, affluent, prosperous, of means, of substance; *informal* well heeled, rolling in it/money, in the money, made of money, filthy/stinking rich, loaded, flush, on easy street, quids in.
– OPPOSITES poor.

wear v ❶ BE DRESSED IN, dress in, be clothed in, clothe oneself in, have on, put on, don, sport. ❷ HAVE, assume, present, show, display, exhibit. ❸ ERODE, corrode, abrade, wash away, rub away, rub down, grind away, wear down. ❹ BECOME WORN, wear thin, fray, become threadbare, go into holes.
■ **wear off** LOSE EFFECTIVENESS / EFFECT, lose intensity/strength, fade, peter out, dwindle, decrease, diminish, disappear, subside, ebb, wane. **wear out** FATIGUE, tire, weary, exhaust, drain, strain, stress, weaken, enfeeble, prostrate, enervate; *Brit. informal* knacker; *N. Amer. informal* poop.

weariness n FATIGUE, tiredness, exhaustion, enervation, lassitude, languor, listlessness, lethargy.

wearisome adj FATIGUING, tiring, exhausting, draining, wearing, trying, irksome, boring, tedious, dull, uninteresting, monotonous, humdrum, routine.
– OPPOSITES refreshing.

weary adj ❶ FATIGUED, tired, exhausted, drained, worn, worn out, spent, careworn,

wearied; *informal* dead tired/beat, dead on one's feet, dog-tired, all in, done in, whacked; *Brit. informal* fagged out, knackered; *N. Amer. informal* pooped; *Austral./NZ informal* bush. ❷ BORED, discontented, jaded, uninterested, listless, lethargic; *informal* browned off, fed up, sick and tired; *Brit. informal* cheesed off.
– OPPOSITES fresh, keen.
▶ v ❶ FATIGUE, tire, exhaust, drain, wear out; *informal* wear to a frazzle; *Brit. informal* knacker. ❷ BORE, irk, make discontented/jaded; *informal* make fed up. ❸ GROW WEARY, tire, get bored, have enough, grow discontented/jaded.
– OPPOSITES refresh, interest.

weather v ❶ DRY, season, expose, expose to the elements. ❷ COME / GET THROUGH, survive, withstand, live/pull through, bear up against, stand, endure, ride out, rise above, surmount, overcome, resist; *informal* stick out.

weave¹ v ❶ INTERLACE, intertwine, interwork, twist together, entwine, braid, plait. ❷ MAKE UP, fabricate, put together, construct, invent, create, contrive.

weave² v ZIGZAG, wind, criss-cross.

web n LACEWORK, lattice, latticework, mesh, net, netting.

wed v GET MARRIED, marry, become man and wife; *informal* get hitched/spliced, tie the knot.
– OPPOSITES divorce, separate.

wedding n WEDDING / MARRIAGE CEREMONY, marriage, nuptials.

wedge v THRUST, stuff, pack, ram, force, cram, squeeze, jam.

weep v CRY, shed tears, sob, blubber, snivel, whimper, whine, moan, lament, grieve, mourn, keen, wail; *informal* boohoo, blub.

weigh v ❶ MEASURE / GAUGE THE WEIGHT OF, put on the scales. ❷ HAVE A WEIGHT OF; *informal* tip the scales at. ❸ BALANCE, compare with, evaluate.
■ weigh up CONSIDER, contemplate, think over, mull over, ponder, deliberate upon, meditate on, muse on, brood over, reflect on.

weight n ❶ HEAVINESS, load, quantity, poundage, tonnage, avoirdupois. ❷ BURDEN, load, onus, millstone, albatross, oppression, trouble, worry, strain. ❸ IMPORTANCE, significance, consequence, value, substance, force, influence; *informal* clout.

weird adj ❶ STRANGE, queer, uncanny, eerie, mysterious, mystifying, supernatural, preternatural, unnatural, unearthly, ghostly; *informal* spooky, creepy. ❷ ODD, eccentric, bizarre, outlandish, freakish, grotesque; *informal* offbeat, far out, way-out, out on a limb.
– OPPOSITES normal, conventional.

welcome n GREETING, salutation, reception, warm reception.
▶ v ❶ BID WELCOME, greet, receive, embrace, receive with

open arms, roll out the red carpet for, meet, usher in. ❷ BE PLEASED BY, take pleasure in, feel satisfaction at.

▶ adj ❶ WANTED, appreciated, popular, desirable. ❷ GLADLY RECEIVED, pleasant, pleasing, agreeable, cheering, to one's liking, to one's taste.
– OPPOSITES unwelcome.

welfare n ❶ WELL-BEING, health, good health, soundness, happiness, comfort, security, prosperity, success, fortune, good fortune. ❷ STATE AID / BENEFIT, public assistance, social security, income support.

well[1] adj ❶ HEALTHY, in good health, fit, strong, robust, hale and hearty, able-bodied, up to par. ❷ SATISFACTORY, all right, fine, good, thriving, flourishing; informal OK, fine and dandy.

well[2] n ❶ SPRING, fountain, waterhole, pool, borehole. ❷ SOURCE, wellspring, fount, reservoir, repository, mine.

well advised adj SENSIBLE, wise, prudent, judicious, circumspect, far-sighted, sagacious.

well balanced adj ❶ WELL ADJUSTED, sensible, reasonable, rational, level-headed, sound, practical, discerning, logical, sane, in one's right mind. ❷ BALANCED, well proportioned, well ordered.

well built adj STRONGLY BUILT, strong, muscular, brawny, sturdy, robust, strapping, husky, burly, big; informal hulking, hefty, beefy.
– OPPOSITES puny.

well known adj ❶ KNOWN, widely known, familiar, common, usual, everyday. ❷ FAMOUS, famed, renowned, celebrated, noted, notable, illustrious, eminent.
– OPPOSITES unknown.

well-nigh adv VIRTUALLY, next to, practically, all but, just about, almost, nearly, more or less.

well off adj WEALTHY, rich, well-to-do, moneyed, affluent, prosperous, of means, of substance; informal well heeled, rolling in it/money, in the money, made of money, filthy/stinking rich, loaded, flush, on easy street, quids in.
– OPPOSITES poor.

well spoken adj ARTICULATE, nicely spoken, educated, polite, refined; Brit. informal posh.

wet adj ❶ DAMP, moist, moistened, wet through, soaked, drenched, saturated, sopping/dripping/wringing wet, sopping, dripping, soggy, waterlogged. ❷ RAINY, raining, pouring, showery, drizzling, damp, humid, dank, misty. ❸ FEEBLE, weak, inept, ineffective, ineffectual, effete, timid, timorous, cowardly, spineless, soft; informal namby-pamby, weedy.

▶ n WETNESS, damp, dampness, moisture, moistness, condensation, humidity, water, liquid.

▶ v DAMPEN, damp, moisten,

sprinkle, spray, splash, water, irrigate, douse.
– OPPOSITES dry.

wharf n PIER, quay, jetty, dock, landing stage.

wheel v TURN, go round, circle, rotate, revolve, spin, swivel round, pivot, whirl/twirl round, make a U-turn.

wheeze v GASP, puff, pant, cough, whistle, hiss, rasp.

whereabouts n LOCATION, site, position, situation, place, vicinity.

whet v SHARPEN, put an edge on, edge, hone, strop, file, grind, rasp.
– OPPOSITES blunt.

whim n NOTION, fancy, idea, impulse, urge, caprice, vagary, craze, passion, inclination, bent.

whimper v WHINE, cry, sniffle, snivel, moan, wall, groan.

whimsical adj CAPRICIOUS, fanciful, fantastical, playful, mischievous, waggish, quaint, unusual, curious, droll, eccentric, peculiar, queer, bizarre, weird, freakish.

whine v ❶ WHIMPER, cry, wail, groan; informal grizzle. ❷ See COMPLAIN (2).

whip v ❶ LASH, flog, scourge, flagellate, birch, switch, strap, cane, thrash, beat, strike, leather; informal belt, tan, give someone a hiding. ❷ BEAT, whisk, mix.
▶ n LASH, scourge, horsewhip, bullwhip, cat-o'-nine-tails, knout, crop, riding crop.

whirl v TURN ROUND, circle, spin, rotate, revolve, wheel, twist, swirl, gyrate, reel, pirouette, pivot.

whirlpool n VORTEX, maelstrom, eddy, whirl.

whirlwind n TORNADO, hurricane, typhoon.
▶ adj SWIFT, rapid, quick, speedy, hasty, headlong.

whisk v WHIP, beat, mix, stir.
▶ n MIXER, beater.

whisper v MURMUR, mutter, speak softly, speak in muted/hushed tones.
– OPPOSITES roar.
▶ n ❶ MURMUR, mutter, low voice, hushed tone, undertone. ❷ RUMOUR, report, insinuation, suggestion, hint, gossip, word.

whit n PARTICLE, bit, jot, iota, mite, trifle.

white adj ❶ PALE, wan, pallid, ashen, anaemic, colourless, bloodless, waxen, pasty, peaky, whey-faced, grey. ❷ GREY, silver, hoary, snowy-white, grizzled.

whiten v MAKE WHITE, make pale, bleach, blanch, fade, wash out, etiolate.

whole adj ❶ ENTIRE, complete, full, total, solid, integral, unabridged, unreduced, undivided, uncut. ❷ INTACT, sound, flawless, in one piece, unimpaired, undamaged, unharmed, unhurt, uninjured, unmutilated.
– OPPOSITES incomplete.

wholehearted adj UNRESERVED, unqualified, unstinting,

complete, committed, hearty, emphatic, real, sincere, genuine.
– OPPOSITES half-hearted.

wholesale adj INDISCRIMINATE, mass, all-inclusive, total, comprehensive, extensive, wide-ranging, sweeping, broad.
– OPPOSITES partial.

wholesome adj ❶ NUTRITIOUS, nourishing, health-giving, healthful, good, strengthening. ❷ MORAL, ethical, uplifting, edifying, helpful, beneficial.

wholly adv COMPLETELY, fully, entirely, totally, utterly, thoroughly, altogether, comprehensively, in every respect, perfectly, enthusiastically, with total commitment, unreservedly, heart and soul.

wicked adj EVIL, sinful, bad, wrong, unrighteous, villainous, dastardly, black-hearted, iniquitous, heinous, monstrous, atrocious, abominable, base, gross, vile, foul, mean, vicious, hideous, dishonourable, unprincipled, nefarious, criminal, perverted, immoral, amoral, unethical, corrupt, dissolute, dissipated, degenerate, reprobate, debauched, depraved, unholy, impious, irreligious, ungodly, godless, devilish, demonic, diabolic; *archaic* blackguardly.
– OPPOSITES good, righteous.

wide adj ❶ BROAD, extensive, spacious. ❷ BROAD, large, outspread, spread out, ample. ❸ WIDE-RANGING, extensive, large, large-scale, vast, far-ranging, immense, broad, expansive, sweeping, encyclopedic, comprehensive, general, all-embracing, catholic, compendious.
– OPPOSITES narrow.

wide-eyed adj ❶ SURPRISED, amazed, astonished, astounded. ❷ NAIVE, impressionable, ingenuous, credulous, trusting, unsuspicious, innocent, simple, unsophisticated, inexperienced, green; *informal* wet behind the ears.

widen v ❶ MAKE WIDER, broaden, expand, extend, enlarge, increase, augment, add to, supplement. ❷ OPEN WIDE, dilate.

widespread adj UNIVERSAL, common, general, far-reaching, prevalent, rife, extensive, sweeping, pervasive, epidemic.
– OPPOSITES limited.

width n ❶ WIDENESS, breadth, broadness, span, diameter. ❷ RANGE, breadth, scope, span, extensiveness, vastness, immensity, expansiveness, comprehensiveness.
– OPPOSITES length, narrowness.

wield v ❶ BRANDISH, flourish, wave, swing, use, employ, handle, ply, manipulate. ❷ EXERCISE, exert, be possessed of, have, have at one's disposal, hold, maintain, command, control.

wild adj ❶ UNTAMED, undomesticated, unbroken, feral, savage, fierce, ferocious.

2 UNCULTIVATED, natural, native, indigenous. **3** UNCIVILIZED, primitive, ignorant, savage, barbaric, barbarous, brutish, ferocious, fierce. **4** STORMY, tempestuous, turbulent, blustery, howling, violent, raging, furious, rough. **5** UNDISCIPLINED, unrestrained, unconstrained, uncontrolled, out of control, unbridled, unchecked, chaotic, disorderly. **6** ROWDY, unruly, disorderly, turbulent, violent, lawless, riotous, out of control, unmanageable, ungovernable, unrestrained, excited, passionate, frantic. **7** CRAZY, beside oneself, berserk, frantic, frenzied, in a frenzy, hysterical, crazed, mad, distracted, distraught, irrational, deranged, demented, raving, maniacal, rabid. **8** EXTRAVAGANT, fantastical, impracticable, foolish, ill-advised, ill-considered, imprudent, unwise, madcap, impulsive, reckless, rash, outrageous, preposterous.
– OPPOSITES tame, cultivated, calm, disciplined.

wilderness n DESERT, wasteland, waste, the wilds, jungle, no-man's-land.

wiles pl n TRICKS, ruses, ploys, schemes, dodges, manoeuvres, subterfuges, artifices, guile, artfulness, cunning, craftiness.

wilful adj **1** DELIBERATE, intentional, intended, conscious, purposeful, premeditated, planned, calculated. **2** HEADSTRONG, strong-willed, obstinate, stubborn, mulish, pigheaded, obdurate, intransigent,

adamant, dogged, determined, persistent, unyielding, uncompromising, intractable, refractory, recalcitrant, disobedient, contrary, perverse, wayward, self-willed.
– OPPOSITES accidental.

will n **1** VOLITION, choice, option, decision, discretion, prerogative. **2** DESIRE, wish, preference, inclination, fancy, mind. **3** WILL POWER, determination, resolution, resolve, firmness of purpose, purposefulness, doggedness, single-mindedness, commitment, moral fibre, pluck, mettle, grit, nerve. **4** LAST WILL AND TESTAMENT, testament, last wishes.

willing adj PREPARED, ready, game, disposed, content, happy, so-minded, consenting, agreeable, amenable, in the mood, compliant.
– OPPOSITES unwilling.

willingly adv VOLUNTARILY, of one's own free will, of one's own accord, by choice, by volition, spontaneously, unforced.

wilt v **1** DROOP, wither, shrivel, lose freshness, sag. **2** DIMINISH, dwindle, lessen, grow less, flag, fade, melt away, ebb, wane, weaken, fail.
– OPPOSITES flourish.

wily adj CRAFTY, cunning, artful, sharp, astute, shrewd, scheming, intriguing, shifty, sly, guileful, deceitful, deceptive, fraudulent, cheating, underhand; informal crooked, foxy; Brit. informal fly.
– OPPOSITES naive.

win v ❶ ACHIEVE, attain, earn, gain, receive, obtain, acquire, procure, get, secure, collect, pick up, come away with, net, bag. ❷ BE VICTORIOUS, be the victor, gain the victory, overcome, achieve mastery, carry the day, carry all before one, finish first, come out ahead, come out on top, win out, succeed, triumph, prevail.
– OPPOSITES lose.

wind¹ n ❶ AIR CURRENT, breeze, gust, blast, gale, storm, hurricane; *poetic/literary* zephyr. ❷ BREATH, respiration; *informal* puff. ❸ FLATULENCE, gas; *formal* flatus.

wind² v TWIST, twist and turn, curve, bend, loop, zigzag, snake, spiral, meander, ramble. ■ **wind down** UNWIND, relax, become less tense, ease up, calm down, cool off. **wind up** BRING TO AN END / CONCLUSION, end, conclude, terminate, finish; *informal* wrap up.

windfall n PIECE / STROKE OF GOOD LUCK, unexpected gain, godsend, manna from heaven, bonanza, jackpot.

windy adj ❶ BREEZY, blowy, blustery, blustering, gusty, gusting, boisterous, squally, stormy, wild, tempestuous, turbulent. ❷ LONG-WINDED, loquacious, wordy, verbose, rambling, meandering, prolix, diffuse, turgid. ❸ NERVOUS, scared, frightened, alarmed, fearful, timid, timorous, cowardly.
– OPPOSITES still.

wink v ❶ BLINK, flutter, bat; *technical* nictate. ❷ FLASH, twinkle, sparkle, glitter, gleam.

winner n CHAMPION, victor, vanquisher, conqueror, prize-winner.
– OPPOSITES loser.

winning adj ❶ VICTORIOUS, successful, triumphant, vanquishing, conquering. ❷ CAPTIVATING, enchanting, bewitching, beguiling, disarming, taking, engaging, endearing, winsome, charming, attractive, fetching, alluring, sweet, lovely, delightful, darling, pleasing.

wintry adj COLD, chilly, icy, frosty, freezing, frozen, snowy, arctic, glacial, biting, piercing, nippy.
– OPPOSITES warm.

wipe v RUB, brush, dust, mop, sponge, swab, clean, dry.

wiry adj ❶ LEAN, spare, sinewy, tough, strong. ❷ BRISTLY, prickly, thorny, stiff, rigid.

wisdom n ❶ SAGENESS, sagacity, cleverness, intelligence, erudition, learning, education, knowledge, enlightenment, reason, discernment, perception, insight. ❷ SENSE, common sense, prudence, judiciousness, judgement, shrewdness, astuteness, circumspection, strategy, foresight, reasonableness, rationality, logic, soundness, saneness; *informal* smartness.
– OPPOSITES folly.

wise adj ❶ SAGE, sagacious, clever, intelligent, erudite, learned, educated, well read,

knowledgeable, informed, enlightened, philosophic, deep-thinking, discerning, perceptive, experienced; *formal* sapient. **2** SENSIBLE, prudent, well advised, judicious, politic, shrewd, astute, reasonable, rational, logical, sound, sane; *informal* smart.
– OPPOSITES unwise.

wish v WANT, desire, long for, hope for, yearn for, pine for, have a fancy for, fancy, crave, hunger for, thirst for, lust after, covet, sigh for, set one's heart on, hanker after, have a yen for. ▶ n DESIRE, liking, fondness, longing, hope, yearning, want, fancy, aspiration, inclination, urge, whim, craving, hunger, thirst, lust, hankering, yen.

wistful adj YEARNING, longing, forlorn, disconsolate, melancholy, sad, mournful, dreamy, in a reverie, pensive, reflective, musing, contemplative, meditative.

wit n **1** WITTINESS, humour, jocularity, funniness, facetiousness, drollery, waggishness, repartee, badinage, banter, raillery. **2** HUMORIST, wag, funny person, comic, jokester, banterer; *informal* card.

witch n SORCERESS, enchantress, magician, necromancer, hex.

witchcraft n WITCHERY, sorcery, black art/magic, magic, necromancy, wizardry, occultism, the occult, sortilege, thaumaturgy, wonder-working.

withdraw v **1** TAKE BACK, pull back, take away, extract, remove. **2** RETRACT, take back, recall, unsay. **3** REVOKE, annul, nullify, declare void, rescind, repeal, abrogate. **4** PULL BACK, fall back, retire, retreat, disengage, back down, depart, go, leave; *informal* make oneself scarce.
– OPPOSITES insert, enter.

withdrawn adj RETIRING, reserved, uncommunicative, unforthcoming, unsociable, taciturn, silent, quiet, introverted, detached, aloof, self-contained, distant, private, shrinking, timid, timorous, shy, bashful, diffident.
– OPPOSITES outgoing.

wither v **1** DRY UP / OUT, shrivel, go limp, wilt, die. **2** DECLINE, fade, ebb, wane, disintegrate, die, perish.
– OPPOSITES thrive.

withhold v **1** HOLD BACK, keep back, restrain, hold/keep in check, check, curb, repress, suppress. **2** REFUSE TO GIVE / GRANT / ALLOW, refuse, decline, keep back.

withstand v HOLD OUT AGAINST, stand up to, stand firm against, resist, fight, combat, oppose, endure, stand, tolerate, bear, put up with, take, cope with, weather, brave.

witness n EYEWITNESS, observer, spectator, onlooker, looker-on, viewer, watcher, beholder, bystander. ▶ v SEE, observe, view, watch, look on at, behold, perceive, be present at, attend.

witticism n WITTY REMARK, clever saying, flash of wit, bon mot, quip, sally, pleasantry, riposte, joke, jest, epigram; *informal* wisecrack, crack, one-liner.

witty adj CLEVER, original, ingenious, sparkling, scintillating, humorous, amusing, jocular, funny, facetious, droll, waggish, comic.

wizard n SORCERER, warlock, enchanter, witch, necromancer, magician, magus.

wizened adj WITHERED, shrivelled, dried up, shrunken, wasted, wrinkled, lined, gnarled, worn.

wobble v ① ROCK, sway, see-saw, teeter, shake, vibrate. ② TEETER, totter, stagger, waddle, waggle.

woe n ① MISERY, wretchedness, misfortune, disaster, grief, anguish, affliction, suffering, pain, agony, torment, sorrow, sadness, unhappiness, distress, heartache, heartbreak, despondency, desolation, dejection, depression, gloom, melancholy. ② TROUBLE, misfortune, adversity, trial, tribulation, ordeal, burden, affliction, suffering, disaster, calamity, catastrophe.
– OPPOSITES joy.

woebegone adj MISERABLE, sad, unhappy, sorrowful, disconsolate, mournful, downcast, dejected, troubled, desolate, depressed, despairing, tearful.
– OPPOSITES cheerful.

woeful adj ① SAD, saddening, unhappy, sorrowful, miserable, dismal, wretched, doleful, gloomy, tragic, pathetic, grievous, pitiful, plaintive, heart-rending, heartbreaking, distressing, anguished, agonizing, dreadful, terrible. ② POOR, bad, inadequate, substandard, lamentable, deplorable, disgraceful, wretched, disappointing, feeble; *informal* rotten, lousy, shocking; *Brit. informal* duff.
– OPPOSITES cheerful, excellent.

woman n ① FEMALE, lady, girl, member of the fair/gentle sex; *informal* chick; *Brit. informal* bird; *N. Amer. informal* dame, broad. ② GIRLFRIEND, lady-love, sweetheart, partner, lover, wife, spouse.

wonder n ① WONDERMENT, awe, surprise, astonishment, amazement, bewilderment, stupefaction, fascination, admiration. ② MARVEL, phenomenon, miracle, prodigy, curiosity, rarity, nonpareil, sight, spectacle.
▶ v ① THINK, speculate, conjecture, ponder, meditate, reflect, deliberate, muse, ask oneself, puzzle, be curious about, be inquisitive about. ② MARVEL, stand amazed, stand in awe, be dumbfounded, gape, stare, goggle, look agog; *informal* be flabbergasted, gawk, boggle.

wonderful adj MARVELLOUS, awe-inspiring, awesome, remarkable, extraordinary, phenomenal, prodigious, miraculous, amazing, astonishing, astounding,

surprising, incredible, unprecedented, unparalleled, unheard of; *poetic/literary* wondrous. *See also* EXCELLENT.
– OPPOSITES dreadful.

wonted adj CUSTOMARY, accustomed, habitual, usual, normal, routine, regular, common, frequent, familiar, conventional.

woo v ❶ PAY COURT TO, seek someone's hand, pursue, chase after; *dated* court, set one's cap at. ❷ IMPORTUNE, press, urge, entreat, beg, implore, supplicate, solicit, coax, wheedle.

wood n ❶ FOREST, woodland, copse, thicket, coppice, grove. ❷ TIMBER, firewood, kindling; *N. Amer.* lumber.

wooded adj WOODY, forested, tree-covered, tree-clad, timbered, sylvan.

wooden adj ❶ MADE OF WOOD, wood, woody, timber. ❷ STIFF, stolid, stodgy, expressionless, graceless, inelegant, ungainly, gauche, awkward, clumsy, maladroit. ❸ EXPRESSIONLESS, inexpressive, blank, deadpan, empty, vacant, vacuous, glassy, impassive, lifeless, spiritless, unanimated, emotionless, unemotional, unresponsive.

woolly adj ❶ WOOLLEN, made of wool, wool. ❷ FLEECY, fluffy, shaggy, hairy, furry. ❸ VAGUE, hazy, indefinite, muddled, confused, disorganized.

word n ❶ TERM, expression, name. ❷ WORD OF HONOUR, promise, pledge, assurance, guarantee, undertaking, vow, oath. ❸ NEWS, intimation, notice,

communication, information, intelligence, message, report, account.
▶ v EXPRESS, phrase, couch, put, say, utter, state.

wordy adj LONG-WINDED, verbose, loquacious, garrulous, voluble, prolix, protracted, discursive, diffuse, rambling, digressive, maundering, tautological, pleonastic.

work n ❶ EFFORT, exertion, labour, toil, slog, sweat, drudgery, trouble, industry; *informal* grind, elbow grease; *poetic/literary* travail. ❷ TASK, job, chore, undertaking, duty, charge, assignment, commission, mission. ❸ EMPLOYMENT, occupation, business, job, profession, career, trade, vocation, calling, craft, line, field, métier, pursuit.
– OPPOSITES leisure.
▶ v ❶ BE EMPLOYED, have a job, hold down a job, earn one's living, do business, follow/ply one's trade. ❷ EXERT ONESELF, put in effort, make efforts, labour, toil, slog, sweat, drudge, slave; *informal* grind, plug away, knock oneself out. ❸ OPERATE, control, drive, manage, direct, use, handle, manipulate, manoeuvre, ply, wield. ❹ GO, operate, function, perform, run. ❺ SUCCEED, be successful, have success, go well, be effective, be effectual.
– OPPOSITES rest, fail.

workable adj PRACTICABLE, practical, viable, doable, feasible, possible.
– OPPOSITES impracticable.

worker n EMPLOYEE, hand, workman, working man/ woman/person, blue-collar worker, white-collar worker, labourer, artisan, craftsman, craftswoman, wage-earner, proletarian.

working adj ❶ IN WORK, employed, in a job, waged. ❷ FUNCTIONING, operating, going, running, in working order.
– OPPOSITES unemployed, broken.

workmanship n CRAFTSMANSHIP, craft, artistry, art, handicraft, handiwork, expertise, skill, technique, work.

workshop n ❶ FACTORY, plant, mill, garage. ❷ WORKROOM, studio, atelier, shop. ❸ SEMINAR, study/discussion group, class.

world n ❶ EARTH, globe, sphere, planet. ❷ SOCIETY, sector, section, group, division.

worldly adj ❶ EARTHLY, secular, temporal, material, materialistic, human, carnal, fleshly, corporeal, physical. ❷ WORLDLYWISE, experienced, knowing, sophisticated, cosmopolitan, urbane.
– OPPOSITES spiritual, naive.

worldwide adj UNIVERSAL, global, international, pandemic, general, ubiquitous, extensive, widespread, far-reaching, wide-ranging.
– OPPOSITES local.

worn adj ❶ WORN OUT, threadbare, tattered, in tatters, ragged, frayed, shabby, shiny.

❷ HAGGARD, drawn, strained, careworn; *informal* done in, dog-tired, dead on one's feet, fit to drop, played out, bushed; *Brit. informal* knackered; *N. Amer. informal* pooped.

worried adj ANXIOUS, disturbed, perturbed, troubled, bothered, distressed, concerned, upset, distraught, uneasy, ill at ease, disquieted, fretful, agitated, nervous, edgy, on edge, tense, overwrought, worked up, distracted, apprehensive, fearful, afraid, frightened; *informal* uptight; *N. Amer. informal* antsy.
– OPPOSITES carefree.

worry v ❶ BE WORRIED, be anxious, fret, brood. ❷ MAKE ANXIOUS, disturb, trouble, bother, distress, upset, concern, disquiet, discompose, fret, agitate, unsettle.
▶ n ❶ ANXIETY, disturbance, perturbation, trouble, bother, distress, concern, care, uneasiness, unease, disquiet, disquietude, fretfulness, agitation, edginess, tenseness, apprehension, fearfulness. ❷ NUISANCE, pest, plague, trial, trouble, problem, irritation, irritant, vexation, thorn in one's flesh.

worsen v ❶ MAKE WORSE, aggravate, exacerbate, damage, intensify, increase, heighten. ❷ GET / GROW / BECOME WORSE, take a turn for the worse, deteriorate, degenerate, retrogress, decline, sink, slip, slide, go downhill.
– OPPOSITES improve.

worship n REVERENCE, veneration, homage, respect, honour, adoration, devotion, praise, prayer, glorification, exaltation, extolment; *formal* laudation.

▶ v ❶ REVERE, venerate, pay homage to, honour, adore, praise, pray to, glorify, exalt, extol; *formal* laud. ❷ ADORE, be devoted to, cherish, treasure, admire, adulate, idolize, hero-worship, lionize; *informal* be wild about.

worth n ❶ FINANCIAL VALUE, value, price, cost. ❷ VALUE, use, usefulness, advantage, benefit, service, gain, profit, avail, help, assistance, aid.

worthless adj ❶ VALUELESS, of little/no financial value; *informal* rubbishy, trashy. ❷ USE-LESS, of no use, of no benefit, to no avail, futile, ineffective, ineffectual, pointless, nugatory. ❸ GOOD-FOR-NOTHING, useless, despicable, contemptible, base, low, vile, corrupt, depraved; *informal* no-good, no-account.
– OPPOSITES valuable, useful, worthwhile.

worthwhile adj WORTH IT, worth the effort, valuable, of value, useful, of use, beneficial, advantageous, helpful, profitable, gainful, productive, constructive, justifiable.

worthy adj VIRTUOUS, good, moral, upright, righteous, honest, decent, honourable, respectable, reputable, trustworthy, reliable, irreproachable, blameless, unimpeach-able, admirable, praiseworthy, laudable, commendable, deserving, meritorious.
– OPPOSITES disreputable.
■ **worthy of** DESERVING, meriting.

wound n INJURY, lesion, cut, graze, scratch, gash, laceration, tear, puncture, slash, sore.
▶ v CUT, graze, scratch, gash, lacerate, tear, puncture, pierce, stab, slash, injure, hurt, damage, harm.

wrap v ❶ ENVELOP, enfold, encase, enclose, cover, swathe, bundle up, swaddle. ❷ WRAP UP, parcel up, package, do up, tie up, gift-wrap.
▶ n SHAWL, stole, cloak, cape, mantle.

wrath n ANGER, rage, fury, annoyance, exasperation, high dudgeon, bad temper, ill humour, irritation, crossness, displeasure, irascibility; *poetic/literary* ire.
– OPPOSITES happiness.

wreathe v ❶ COVER, envelop, festoon, garland, adorn, decorate. ❷ TWIST, wind, coil, twine, entwine, curl, spiral, wrap.

wreck n ❶ SHIPWRECK, sunken ship/vessel, derelict. ❷ WRECKING, wreckage, destruction, devastation, ruination, ruin, demolition, smashing, shattering, disruption, disintegration, undoing.
▶ v ❶ SMASH, demolish, ruin, damage; *informal* write off. ❷ DESTROY, devastate, ruin, demolish, smash, shatter, disrupt,

undo, spoil, mar, play havoc with. ❸ SHIPWRECK, sink, capsize, run aground.

wreckage n WRECK, debris, ruins, remains, remnants, fragments.

wrench v TWIST, pull, tug, yank, wrest, jerk, tear, force.

wrest v TWIST, wrench, pull, snatch, take away, remove.

wretch n ❶ POOR CREATURE / SOUL / THING, miserable creature, unfortunate, poor devil. ❷ SCOUNDREL, villain, ruffian, rogue, rascal, reprobate, criminal, delinquent, miscreant; *informal* creep, jerk, louse, rat, swine, skunk; *informal, dated* rotter; *archaic* blackguard.

wretched adj ❶ MISERABLE, unhappy, sad, broken-hearted, sorrowful, sorry, distressed, disconsolate, downcast, down, downhearted, dejected, crestfallen, cheerless, depressed, melancholy, gloomy, doleful, forlorn, woebegone, abject. ❷ POOR, bad, substandard, low-quality, inferior, pathetic, worthless.
– OPPOSITES cheerful, excellent.

wriggle v TWIST, squirm, writhe, jiggle, wiggle, snake, crawl, slink.

wring v ❶ TWIST, squeeze. ❷ EXTRACT, force, coerce, exact, extort, wrest, wrench, screw.

wrinkle n CREASE, fold, pucker, gather, furrow, ridge, line, corrugation, crinkle, crumple, rumple.
▶ v CREASE, pucker, gather,

furrow, line, corrugate, crumple, rumple.

write v ❶ WRITE DOWN, put in writing, put in black and white, commit to paper, jot down, note, set down, take down, record, register, list, inscribe, scribble, scrawl. ❷ COMPOSE, draft, create, pen, dash off.
■ **write off** ❶ FORGET ABOUT, disregard, give up for lost, cancel, annul, nullify, wipe out, cross out, score out. ❷ DAMAGE BEYOND REPAIR, wreck, smash, crash, destroy, demolish; *N. Amer. informal* total.

writer n AUTHOR, wordsmith, penman, novelist, essayist, biographer, journalist, columnist, scriptwriter; *informal* scribbler, pen-pusher.

writhe v TWIST ABOUT, twist and turn, roll about, squirm, wriggle, jerk, thrash, flail, toss, struggle.

writing n ❶ HANDWRITING, hand, penmanship, script, print, calligraphy, scribble, scrawl. ❷ WORK, opus, book, volume, publication, composition.

wrong adj ❶ INCORRECT, inaccurate, in error, erroneous, wide of the mark, mistaken, inexact, imprecise, unsound, faulty, false; *informal* off beam, barking up the wrong tree, off target. ❷ UNSUITABLE, inappropriate, inapt, inapposite, undesirable, infelicitous. ❸ IMMORAL, bad, wicked, evil, unlawful, illegal, illicit, lawless, criminal, delinquent,

felonious, dishonest, dishonourable, corrupt, unethical, sinful, iniquitous, blameworthy, culpable; *informal* crooked. ❹ AMISS, awry, out of order, not right, faulty, defective.
– OPPOSITES right.
▶ n ❶ BADNESS, immorality, sin, sinfulness, wickedness, evil, iniquity, unlawfulness, crime, dishonesty, dishonour, injustice, transgression, abuse; *informal* crookedness. ❷ MISDEED, offence, injury, crime, infringement, infraction, injustice, grievance, outrage, atrocity.
– OPPOSITES right.
▶ v ❶ ABUSE, mistreat, maltreat, harm, hurt, do injury to. ❷ MIS-REPRESENT, malign, dishonour, impugn, vilify, defame, slander, libel, denigrate, insult; *informal* bad-mouth.

wrongdoer n LAWBREAKER, criminal, delinquent, culprit, offender, felon, villain, miscreant, evil-doer, sinner, transgressor, malefactor; *informal* wrong 'un.

wrongful adj UNFAIR, unjust, improper, unjustified, unwarranted, unlawful, illegal, illegitimate, illicit.

wry adj ❶ TWISTED, distorted, contorted, crooked, lopsided, askew. ❷ IRONIC, sardonic, mocking, sarcastic, dry, droll, witty, humorous.

Yy

yank v PULL, tug, jerk, wrench.
▶ n PULL, jerk, wrench.

yardstick n MEASURE, standard, gauge, scale, guide, guideline, touchstone, criterion, benchmark, model, pattern.

yarn n ❶ THREAD, fibre, strand. ❷ STORY, tale, anecdote, fable, traveller's tale; *informal* tall tale/story, cock and bull story.

yawning adj WIDE, wide open, gaping, cavernous.

yearly adj ANNUAL, once a year, every year.

yearn v LONG, pine, have a longing, crave, desire, want, wish for, hanker after, covet, fancy, hunger for, thirst for; *informal* have a yen for.

yell v SHOUT, cry out, howl, scream, shriek, screech, squeal, roar, bawl, whoop; *informal* holler.

yes adv ALL RIGHT, of course, by all means, sure, certainly, in the affirmative; *informal* yeah, yah, yep, uh-huh; *Brit. informal* righto.
– OPPOSITES no.

yield v ❶ GIVE, return, bring in, fetch, earn, net, produce, supply, provide, generate, furnish. ❷ GIVE UP, surrender, relinquish, part with, deliver up, turn over, give over, remit, cede, renounce, resign, abdicate, forgo. ❸ ADMIT / CONCEDE DEFEAT, surrender, capitulate, submit, lay down one's arms, give in, give up the struggle, succumb, raise/show the white flag, throw in the towel/sponge, cave in.
– OPPOSITES withhold, resist.

yoke n ❶ HARNESS, collar, coupling. ❷ OPPRESSION, tyranny, enslavement, slavery, servitude, bondage, thrall.

yokel n RUSTIC, countryman, countrywoman, peasant, country bumpkin, provincial; N. Amer. informal hayseed, hillbilly.

young adj ❶ YOUTHFUL, juvenile, junior, adolescent, in the springtime of life, in one's salad days. ❷ NEW, recent, undeveloped, fledgling, in the making.
– OPPOSITES old.

youngster n YOUNG ADULT / PERSON, youth, juvenile, teenager, adolescent, lad, boy, young man/woman, girl; Scottish & N. English lass; informal kid, shaver, young 'un.

youth n ❶ YOUNG DAYS, early years, teens, early life, adolescence, boyhood, girlhood. ❷ BOY, young man, lad, youngster, juvenile, teenager, adolescent; informal kid.

youthful adj YOUNG, active, vigorous, spry, sprightly.
– OPPOSITES old.

Zz

zany adj ECCENTRIC, peculiar, odd, ridiculous, absurd, comic, clownish, madcap, funny, amusing, weird; informal screwy, wacky; Brit. informal daft; N. Amer. informal kooky.
– OPPOSITES conventional.

zeal n ❶ ARDOUR, fervour, fervency, passion, fire, devotion, vehemence, intensity, enthusiasm, eagerness, keenness, earnestness, vigour, energy, verve, gusto, zest, fanaticism; informal zing. ❷ ZEALOTRY, fanaticism, extremism.
– OPPOSITES apathy.

zealot n ENTHUSIAST, fanatic, extremist, radical, militant, bigot.

zealous adj ARDENT, fervent, fervid, passionate, impassioned, devoted, intense, enthusiastic, eager, keen, earnest, vigorous, energetic, zestful, fanatical.
– OPPOSITES apathetic.

zenith n HIGHEST / HIGH POINT, crowning point, height, top, acme, peak, pinnacle, climax, prime, meridian, apex, apogee, vertex.
– OPPOSITES nadir.

zero n ❶ NOUGHT, nothing, cipher. ❷ NOTHING, naught, nil; *informal* zilch, not a sausage.
■ **zero in on** FOCUS ON, centre on, concentrate on, home in on, pinpoint.

zest n ❶ RELISH, gusto, enthu-
siasm, eagerness, zeal, vigour, liveliness, energy, enjoyment, joy, delectation, appetite; *informal* zing, oomph.
❷ PIQUANCY, spice, pungency, flavour, relish, tang, savour, interest.

zone n AREA, sector, section, belt, district, region, province.

zoom v FLY, buzz, rush, dash, pelt, race, tear, shoot, scurry, speed, hurry, hasten, whizz, hare, zip, zap.

Supplement

Contents

....

Commonly confused pairs of words

word 1	meaning	word 2	meaning
adverse	unfavourable	averse	opposed
affect	cause a change in	effect	bring about; a result
alternate	one after another	alternative	available instead
ambiguous	having more than one meaning	ambivalent	having mixed feelings
amend	change	emend	alter a text
amoral	having no moral sense	immoral	not conforming to moral standards
appraise	assess the quality of	apprise	inform
avoid	keep away from	evade	avoid by guile
biannual	twice a year	biennial	every two years
bought	past of *buy*	brought	past of *bring*
censor	act as censor of	censure	criticize harshly
climactic	forming a climax	climatic	relating to climate
complement	add to in a way that improves	compliment	politely praise
compose	make up a whole	comprise	consist of
continual	happening constantly or repeatedly	continuous	going on without a break
credible	believable	credulous	too ready to believe
decided	unquestionable	decisive	conclusive, unfaltering
definite	clear and distinct	definitive	conclusive, authoritative
defuse	remove the fuse from; reduce tension in	diffuse	spread out; not clear or concise
deprecate	disapprove of	depreciate	decrease in value
desert	a waterless area; abandon	dessert	a sweet course
discreet	careful to avoid attention	discrete	separate
disinterested	impartial	uninterested	not interested
draw	make a picture of; pull; have an equal score	drawer	sliding storage compartment
enormity	extreme seriousness; a grave crime	enormousness	great size or scale

word 1	meaning	word 2	meaning
ensure	make sure	insure	take out insurance on
especially	in particular, above all	specially	for a special purpose
exceptionable	causing disapproval	exceptional	unusually good
faint	hard to see or hear; temporarily lose consciousness	feint	paper with faint lines; a movement in boxing or fencing
flair	natural ability	flare	a burst of flame or light; become angry
flaunt	display ostentatiously	flout	disregard a rule or custom
flounder	(of a person) struggle or be in confusion	founder	(of an undertaking) fail or come to nothing
forego	(*old use*) go before	forgo	go without
forever	continually	for ever	eternally
fortuitous	happening by chance	fortunate	happening by good chance, lucky
gourmand	a glutton	gourmet	a food connoisseur
grisly	causing revulsion	grizzly	as in *grizzly bear*
hoard	a store of valuables	horde	a large group of people
illegal	against the law	illicit	not allowed
imply	suggest strongly	infer	deduce or conclude
impracticable	not able to be done	impractical	not sensible or realistic
incredible	(of a thing) not believable	incredulous	(of a person) unable to believe
ingenious	well thought out	ingenuous	innocent, honest
intense	extreme in force or degree	intensive	thorough or concentrated
interment	burial	internment	confinement
its	belonging to it	it's	it is, or it has
lead	as in *to lead the army*; metal	led	past of *lead*
loath	reluctant, unwilling	loathe	dislike greatly
loose	not fixed; unfasten or relax	lose	be deprived of or no longer have
luxuriant	lush	luxurious	comfortable and rich

word 1	meaning	word 2	meaning
masterful	powerful, domineering	masterly	highly skilful
militate	(militate against) hinder	mitigate	make less severe
naught	(old use) nothing (as in come to naught)	nought	the digit 0, nothing
naval	relating to a navy	navel	umbilicus
observance	the keeping of a law or custom	observation	a perception or remark
occupant	a person in a vehicle, seat, etc.	occupier	the person living in a property
official	having authorized status	officious	aggressive in asserting authority
ordinance	an authoritative order	ordnance	mounted guns, military stores
palate	the roof of the mouth; the sense of taste	palette	an artist's mixing board
pedal	a foot-operated lever	peddle	sell goods
perquisite	a special right or privilege	prerequisite	something needed in advance
personal	private	personnel	staff in a business
perspicacious	having a ready understanding, perceptive	perspicuous	clearly expressed
pitiable	deserving pity	pitiful	causing pity; very small or poor
pore	(pore over) read closely	pour	flow, cause to flow
practicable	able to be done	practical	effective or realistic; (of a person) skilled at manual tasks
precipitate	hasty, headlong	precipitous	abruptly steep
prescribe	recommend with authority; issue a prescription	proscribe	forbid or condemn
prevaricate	avoid giving a direct answer	procrastinate	delay or postpone action
principal	main, most important; the chief person	principle	a basis of belief or action

Commonly confused pairs of words

word 1	meaning	word 2	meaning
purposely	intentionally	purposefully	resolutely
refute	prove to be wrong	repudiate	refuse to accept or support
regrettable	causing regret, undesirable	regretful	feeling regret
sensual	relating to or giving physical pleasure	sensuous	relating to the senses rather than the intellect
shear	cut wool off, cut	sheer	utter, complete (as in *sheer delight*); swerve
site	a place where something happens	sight	the ability to see
sociable	friendly and willing to mix with people	social	relating to society
stationary	not moving	stationery	materials for writing
storey	part of a building on one level	story	an account of imaginary events
straight	extending without a curve	strait	narrow passage of water
their	belonging to them	there	in or to that place
titillate	excite pleasantly	titivate	adorn or smarten
tortuous	twisting, devious	torturous	causing torture, tormenting
triumphal	done or made to celebrate a victory	triumphant	victorious, jubilant after a victory
turbid	(of a liquid) cloudy; not clear	turgid	swollen or full; (of language) tediously pompous
unsociable	not willing to mix with people	unsocial	socially inconvenient
venal	open to bribery, corrupt	venial	(of a sin) minor
who's	who is	whose	belonging to which person

Frequently misspelled words

word	comment	word	comment
abscess	-scess, not -sess	commitment	one t in the middle
abseil	-seil, not -sail	committee	two m's, two t's
accommodate	two c's, two m's	comparative	-rative, not -ritive
accumulate	two c's, one m	compatible	-tible, not -table
achieve	i before e	consensus	not -census
acquaint, acquiesce, acquire, acquit	acq-	contemporary	-porary, not -pory
address	two d's	correspondence	not -ance; e before i
ageing	preferred to aging	deceive	e before i
aggressive, aggression, etc.	two g's, two s's	definite	-ite, not -ate
amateur	-eur, not -uer	desperate	-per- not -par-
anaesthetic	-ae-; American anesthetic	detach	not -atch
anoint	only one n in the middle	disappear	one s, two p's
apartment	only one p	disappoint	one s, two p's
appal	two p's, one l; American appall	ecstasy	ends -asy
appalling	two p's, two l's	eighth	two h's
aqueduct	aque-, not aqua-	embarrass	two r's, two s's
archaeology	-ae-; arche- is American	enthral	one l; American enthrall
artefact	arte- preferred to arti-	exercise	not exc-
attach	not -atch	extraordinary	extraor-, nor extror-
barbecue	not -que	extrovert	extro-, not extra-
beautiful	not beat-	fluorescent	fluor-, not fluer-
belief, believe	i before e	fulfil	two single l's; American fulfill
besiege	i before e	gauge	-au-, not -ua-
biased	preferred to biassed	guarantee	-ua-, not -au-
blatant	not -ent	guard, guardian, etc.	-ua-, not -au-
cappuccino	two p's, two c's	hamster	ham-, not hamp-
Caribbean	one r, two b's	harass, harassment, etc.	one r, two s's
commemorate	two m's followed by one m	helpful	one l at the end
		humorous	-or-, not -our-
		hygienic	i before e
		idiosyncrasy	not -cracy
		independent	ends -ent (noun and adjective)
		inoculate	one n, one c
		instalment	one l; American installment

Frequently misspelled words

word	comment	word	comment
integrate	not *inter-*	pronunciation	*-nunc-*, not
introvert	*-tro-*, not *-tra-*		*-nounc-*
itinerary	ends *-erary*	questionnaire	two *n*'s
judgement	*-dge-* preferred to *-dg-*	receive	e before i
		recommend	one c, two *m*'s
label	*-el*, not *-le*	restaurateur	no n in the
liaison	two is: *-iai-*		middle: *-ateur*
lightning	*-tn-*, not *-ten-*	rhythm	begins *rh-*
manoeuvre	*-oeu-*; American maneuver	risotto	one s, two *t*'s
		sacrilege	*-rilege*, not *-relige*
medieval	*-ev-* preferred to *-aev-*	schedule	*sche-*, not *she-*
		seize	e before i
Mediterranean	one t, two *r*'s	separate	*-par-*, not *-per-*
memento	*mem-*, not *mom-*	siege	i before e
millennium	two *l*'s, two *n*'s	sieve	i before e
millionaire	two *l*'s, one n	skilful	single *l*'s; American skillful
miniature	*-ia-* in second syllable		
		successful	two c's, two s's, one l
minuscule	*minu-*, not *mini-*	supersede	not *-cede*
mischievous	*-vous*, not *-vious*	suppress	not *sur-*; two p's
misspell	two s's	surprise	begins *sur-*
necessary	one c, two s's	threshold	one h
niece	i before e	tomorrow	one m, two *r*'s
occasion	two c's, one s	until	one l
occurrence	two c's, two *r*'s	unwieldy	*-dy*, not *-dly*
omit	one m	vegetable	*vege-*, not *vega-*
parliament	*-ia-* in second syllable	veterinary	note the *-er* in the middle
peculiar	*-iar*, not *-ier*		
permanent	*-nent*, not *-nant*	weird	*-ei-*, not *-ie-*
persistent	*-tent*, not *-tant*	whinge	remember the h
pharaoh	*-aoh*, not *-oah*	wilful	single *l*'s; American willful
pigeon	no d: *-igeon*		
privilege	ends *-ilege*	withhold	two h's

Different spellings for different parts of speech

word 1	part of speech	word 2	part of speech
advice	noun	advise	verb
annexe	noun	annex	verb
breath	noun	breathe	verb
dependant	noun	dependent	adjective
envelope	noun	envelop	verb
licence	noun	license	verb
practice	noun	practise	verb
thief	noun	thieve	verb
wreath	noun	wreathe	verb

Wedding anniversaries

Year	Name	Year	Name	Year	Name
1st	Paper	9th	Pottery (China)	25th	Silver
2nd	Cotton	10th	Tin (Aluminium)	30th	Pearl
3rd	Leather	11th	Steel	35th	Coral (Jade)
4th	Linen (Silk)	12th	Silk	40th	Ruby
5th	Wood	13th	Lace	45th	Sapphire
6th	Iron	14th	Ivory	50th	Gold
7th	Wool (Copper)	15th	Crystal	55th	Emerald
8th	Bronze	20th	China	60th	Diamond

Symbols and punctuation marks

,	comma	"	ditto	$\neq$	is not equal to
.	full stop; point	&	ampersand	$\approx$	is approximately equal to
;	semicolon	&c.	et cetera	$\sqrt{}$	square root
:	colon	@	at or per	°	degree
'	apostrophe	§	section	∞	infinity
' '	single quotation marks	~	swung dash	'	prime; minute(s) of arc; foot/feet
" "	double quotation marks	...	ellipsis	"	double prime; second(s) of arc; inch(es)
!	exclamation mark	¶	paragraph		
?	question mark	+	plus; positive	£	pound sterling
( )	brackets; parentheses	−	minus; negative	$	dollar
[ ]	square brackets	×	multiplication sign; by (in measurements)	€	euro
{ }	braces	÷	division sign	©	copyright
/	solidus; oblique; slash	=	equals	♂	male
\	backslash	:	ratio	♀	female
#	hash; number (N. Amer.)	>	greater than	○	new moon
%	percent	<	less than	◗	moon, first quarter
∴	therefore	≥	greater than or equal to	●	full moon
∵	because	≤	less than or equal to	◖	moon, last quarter

Chemical elements and symbols

* = radioactive

actinium*	Ac	hafnium	Hf	promethium*	Pm
aluminium	Al	hassium*	Hs	protactinium*	Pa
americium*	Am	helium	He	radium*	Ra
antimony	Sb	holmium	Ho	radon*	Rn
argon	Ar	hydrogen	H	rhenium	Re
arsenic	As	indium	In	rhodium	Rh
astatine*	At	iodine	I	rubidium	Rb
barium	Ba	iridium	Ir	ruthenium	Ru
berkelium*	Bk	iron	Fe	rutherfordium	Rf
beryllium	Be	krypton	Kr	samarium	Sm
bismuth	Bi	lanthanum	La	scandium	Sc
bohrium*	Bh	lawrencium*	Lr	seaborgium	Sg
boron	B	lead	Pb	selenium	Se
bromine	Br	lithium	Li	silicon	Si
cadmium	Cd	lutetium	Lu	silver	Ag
caesium	Cs	magnesium	Mg	sodium	Na
calcium	Ca	manganese	Mn	strontium	Sr
californium*	Cf	meitnerium*	Mt	sulphur	S
carbon	C	mendelevium*	Md	tantalum	Ta
cerium	Ce	mercury	Hg	technetium*	Tc
chlorine	Cl	molybdenum	Mo	tellurium	Te
chromium	Cr	neodymium	Nd	terbium	Tb
cobalt	Co	neon	Ne	thallium	Tl
copper	Cu	neptunium*	Np	thorium*	Th
curium*	Cm	nickel	Ni	thulium	Tm
dubnium*	Db	niobium	Nb	tin	Sn
dysprosium	Dy	nitrogen	N	titanium	Ti
einsteinium*	Es	nobelium*	Nb	tungsten	W
erbium	Er	osmium	Os	uranium*	U
europium	Eu	oxygen	O	vanadium	V
fermium*	Fm	palladium	Pd	xenon	Xe
fluorine	F	phosphorus	P	ytterbium	Yb
francium*	Fr	platinum	Pt	yttrium	Y
gadolinium	Gd	plutonium*	Pu	zinc	Zn
gallium	Ga	polonium*	Po	zirconium	Zr
germanium	Ge	potassium	K		
gold	Au	praseodymium	Pr		

Male, female, and young animals

animal	male	female	young
antelope	buck	doe	fawn, kid
ass	jack, jackass	jenny	foal, colt (M), filly (F)
badger	boar	sow	cub
bear	boar	sow	cub
bird	cock	hen	chick, fledgling
buffalo	bull	cow	calf
camel	bull	cow	calf
caribou	stag	doe	fawn
cat	tom	queen	kitten
cattle	bull, ox (castrated)	cow	calf, bullock (M), heifer (F)
chicken	cock	hen	chick
coyote	dog	bitch	pup
deer	buck, stag, hart	doe, hind	fawn
dog	dog	bitch	pup, puppy, whelp
donkey	jack, jackass	jenny	foal, colt (M), filly (F)
duck	drake	duck	duckling
eagle	—	—	eaglet
eel	—	—	elver
elephant	bull	cow	calf
elk	bull	cow	calf
ferret	dog, hob	bitch, doe, gill	kit
fish	cock	hen	fry (pl.)
fox	fox	vixen	cub
frog	—	—	tadpole
giraffe	bull	cow	calf
goat	billygoat	nannygoat	kid
goose	gander	goose	gosling
hare	buck	doe	leveret
hartebeest	bull	cow	calf
hawk	—	—	eyas
horse	stallion	mare	foal, colt (M), filly (F)
impala	ram	ewe	fawn
kangaroo	buck	doe	joey
leopard	leopard	leopardess	cub
lion	lion	lioness	cub
moose	bull	cow	calf

Male, female, and young animals

animal	male	female	young
mule	horse mule	mare mule	foal, colt (M), filly (F)
otter	dog	bitch	cub
owl	—	—	owlet
peafowl	peacock	peahen	peachick
pheasant	cock	hen	chick
pigeon	—	—	squab
pike	—	—	pickerel
pig	boar, hog (castrated)	sow	piglet
polecat	hob	gill	kit
rabbit	buck	doe	kitten
rat	buck	doe	pup, ratling
rhinoceros	bull	cow	calf
salmon	—	—	parr
seal	bull	cow	pup, cub
sheep	ram, tup, wether (castrated)	ewe	lamb
swan	cob	pen	cygnet
tiger	tiger	tigress	cub
whale	bull	cow	calf
wolf	dog	bitch	cub, pup, whelp
zebra	stallion	mare	foal, colt (M), filly (F)